COL. JOHN SINGLETON
MOSBY
IN THE NEWS 1862-1916

Colonel John Singleton Mosby"

COL. JOHN SINGLETON MOSBY
IN THE NEWS 1862-1916

V. P. HUGHES

Col. John Singleton Mosby In The News 1862-1916
Copyright© 2016, 2022 V.P. Hughes

ALL RIGHTS RESERVED. No part of this publication may be reproduced, distributed, or transmitted in any form or by any means, including photocopying, recording, or other electronic or mechanical methods, or by any information storage and retrieval system without the prior written permission of the publisher, except in the case of very brief quotations embodied in critical reviews and certain other noncommercial uses permitted by copyright law.

Produced in the Republic of South Carolina by

SHOTWELL PUBLISHING LLC
Post Office Box 2592
Columbia, So. Carolina 29202

www.ShotwellPublishing.com

Cover Image: Public Domain. Courtesy of Library of Congress

ISBN: 978-1-947660-64-9

REVISED EDITION

Previously published as *A Thousand Points of Truth: The History and Humanity of Col. John Singleton Mosby in Newsprint*

10 9 8 7 6 5 4 3 2 1

Table of Contents

Dedication I
Preface III
Taking Up the Cudgels
Introduction V
Chapter 1 1
The Fourth Estate
Chapter 2 4
Preamble and 1862
Chapter 3 10
1863
Chapter 4 17
1864
Chapter 5 39
1865
Chapter 6 53
1866
Chapter 7 61
1867
Chapter 8 69
1868
Chapter 9 80
1869
Chapter 10 99
1870 and 1871

CHAPTER 11	103
1872	
CHAPTER 12	123
1873	
CHAPTER 13	134
1874	
CHAPTER 14	158
1875	
CHAPTER 15	161
1876	
CHAPTER 16	186
1877	
CHAPTER 17	195
1878	
CHAPTER 18	205
1879	
CHAPTER 19	234
1880	
CHAPTER 20	255
1881	
CHAPTER 21	259
1882	
CHAPTER 22	263
1883	
CHAPTER 23	271
1884	

Chapter 24..276
1885

Chapter 25..297
1886

Chapter 26..312
1887

Chapter 27..324
1888

Chapter 28..345
1889

Chapter 29..361
1890

Chapter 30..383
1891

Chapter 31..393
1892

Chapter 32..399
1893

Chapter 33..405
1894

Chapter 34..416
1895

Chapter 35..430
1896

Chapter 36..442
1897

CHAPTER 37 483
1898

CHAPTER 38 504
1899

CHAPTER 39 514
1900

CHAPTER 40 522
1901

CHAPTER 41 540
1902

CHAPTER 42 583
1903

CHAPTER 43 600
1904

CHAPTER 44 621
1905

CHAPTER 45 641
1906

CHAPTER 46 648
1907

CHAPTER 47 661
1908

CHAPTER 48 668
1909

CHAPTER 49 674
1910

Chapter 50 704
1911

Chapter 51 712
1912

Chapter 52 720
1913

Chapter 53 724
1914

Chapter 54 735
1915

Chapter 55 742
1916

Chapter 56 763
John S. Mosby the Man: Fact vs. Fiction

Chapter 57 776
Conclusion

About The Author 784

Dedication

THIS BOOK IS dedicated to Colonel John Singleton Mosby, a man I believe to be unique for many reasons, not the least, his moral fortitude and courage.

I also believe that Mosby has been gravely misunderstood and misrepresented by those who have studied and written about him and for that reason it is hoped that much of the error and resultant censure afflicting the man's reputation will be eliminated by this work. If that happy outcome does obtain, I believe that John Mosby will be universally recognized as more than a soldier, however brilliant and heroic, but, as a true champion of the truth and the right.

In his old age Mosby denied that he was a Christian though he had been baptized into the Methodist Church in his youth. Yet if he "worshipped" anything within the meaning of that word, John Mosby worshipped *truth*. Regarding that which guided his life, an article in the *Washington Times* of May 30, 1916, stated:

> "In faith, Colonel Mosby espoused no creed, but claimed to be a follower of Socrates, who was always his ideal of a man."

Mosby's choice of paths was in no way without danger. As he stood trial for his life in Athens, Socrates was asked to carefully consider the consequences of relying upon his philosophy of life in presenting his defense to the charges against him. To this, the great philosopher replied:

> "A man who is good for anything ought not to calculate the chance of living or dying; he ought only to consider whether in doing anything he is doing right or wrong— acting the part of a good man or a bad. The difficulty, my friends, is not in avoiding death, but in avoiding unrighteousness; for that runs faster than death. And when faced with disaster which he can escape through his actions, his only question is if by doing so, *'Shall I be doing right, or shall I be doing wrong?'* [emphasis vph] And if we find that I should be doing wrong, then we must not take any account of any evil consequence, but only of doing wrong."

According to the record of the time, "Socrates was filled with the most intense conviction of the supreme and overwhelming importance of truth and the paramount duty of doing right, because it *is* right on every occasion, *be the consequences what they may* [emphasis vph]." In the end, Socrates was condemned for maintaining the principles of his "well considered life," a choice that also exemplified the life of John Mosby. To Mosby, truth and honor were more important than life or death, fame or ignominy—and he always acted on that belief.

Yet, believing Christian or not, the God of The Bible is not unaware of any man who lives such a life as is seen in this benediction written by a young minister whose faith was compromised by human weakness and whose perceptive words define the "cross" John Mosby carried throughout his own "well considered life:"

"In the darkest hour through which a human soul can pass, whatever else is doubtful, this at least is certain. If there be no God and no future state, yet even then, it is better to be generous than selfish, better to be chaste than licentious, better to be true than false, better to be brave than a coward. Blessed beyond all earthly blessedness is the man who, in the tempestuous darkness of the soul, has dared to hold fast to these venerable landmarks. Thrice blessed is he, who, when all is drear and cheerless within and without, when his teachers terrify him, and his friends shrink from him, has obstinately clung to moral good. Thrice blessed, because *his* night shall pass into clear, bright day."

(Rev. Frederick William Robertson 1816–1853)

Preface

TAKING UP THE CUDGELS

Apologia ~ To speak in one's defense or in defense of another

"Defending the truth is not something one does out of a sense of duty or to allay guilt, but is a reward in itself."

~ Simone de Beauvoir

I WAS INTRODUCED TO John Singleton Mosby upon reading Ranger Mosby by Virgil Carrington Jones. All subsequent encounters, whether in biographies, essays, articles and even in the accounts of other figures of the time, appear to have been influenced by Jones' work or reflect the sources from which that author took his account. Yet I was always troubled by Jones' assessment of the value of Mosby's life—at least as it was lived after the war:

> "From the standpoint of fame, better would it have been for Corporal Kane's revolver to have cast its bullet a shade higher that night at the Lake home. Then, perhaps, Mosby's name would have stood with such heroes as his beloved Stuart, with Forrest, Morgan, the gallant Pelham and others.
>
> For there was no fleeing from the Scalawags, the radicals, the die-hards; no escaping the boys and young men he angered in his senility. Whether the test came in politics or in every day social contact, it was his nature to stand by his guns. And in standing by them, he tore away the veil of mystery that had made him famous. The reckless abandon with which he attacked and galloped away as a Partisan could not be repeated as a citizen." (Virgil Carrington Jones, *Ranger Mosby*)

I took (and continue to take) exception to that statement by the man who, it is widely claimed, brought John Mosby's name before the American public and made him famous. Yet even that claim is misleading unless modified by the word "modern," as in "modern American public." For John Mosby was famous long before Ranger Mosby was published in 1944! The over five thousand newspaper articles available for, and used in the writing of this book clearly illustrate that fact. Further, I believe that these contemporary views of (and by) Mosby also demonstrate that Mr. Jones had far less understanding of—and even respect for—the man upon whom he ostensibly "bestowed fame." Pat Jones' view of Mosby's post-war life demonstrated a strong taint of the revulsion found in the minds of many of the man's fellow Southerners, past and present. Neither can this contention be realistically challenged for what else can it mean when Jones rejects fifty-two years of Mosby's life—years filled with excellent and honorable service to his country, his family, his friends and his fellow man—as of little value in comparison to the worldly fame he might have achieved by dying at the hands of his enemies in 1864?

It is my hope that by the conclusion of this book, John Mosby's postwar life will be far better understood and I will have proved that the man's heroism did not begin and end on the Field of Mars. Finally, and of greatest importance, I hope to show that John Singleton Mosby was a true hero who struggled not just against the armed might of a potent enemy, but against the forces of political, moral, and ethical chaos that raged about him in the course of his "well-considered" life.

V. P. Hughes

Introduction

FROM THE BEGINNING of that form of communication called the newspaper, the printed word has been augmented by the printed image. However, until the 1870s, actual photographs could not be reproduced except in books. As a result, newspapers and other periodicals were reduced to using engravings based upon photographs. Photogravure, invented in the 1850s and improved in the 1870s, was used to create an intaglio print from photographs; but this process was not used in newspapers because the print had to be produced separately from the text.

In 1873, the first "halftone" image appeared in print. Halftone was a process in which a photograph was converted into points of varying sizes and densities by passing it through a mechanical screen. These points were then printed in different sizes, tints and densities which, when taken together, gave the illusion of different tones from white to black and all shades of gray in between; and thus, the photograph found its way into the newspapers. While all the newspaper articles herein presented suffer from some degree of error and inaccuracy, there still arises from them taken as a whole an embodiment of John Singleton Mosby not found in the most searching and detailed of biographies. There are points of truth that are very small and others that are very large indeed. Taken with all the rest, these "points" produce a far more accurate and nuanced portrait of the subject than can be created using the limited testimonies and official documents of the time. In these accounts are found the direct witnesses of friends and enemies, contemporaries and scholars and, of course, of Mosby himself. Yes, it requires effort for the reader to get past the fog of prejudice, the tides of political partisanship, the petty spite, and the almost limitless range of human failings—but in the end, a much more complex portrayal of this unique man emerges than has hitherto been presented for public consideration.

AUTHOR'S NOTE: This work contains only a small percentage of the thousands of newspaper articles that reported on Colonel John Singleton Mosby beginning in 1862 and ending in 1916, the year of Mosby's death. For considerations of length, none of the postwar recounts of Mosby's wartime operations are included neither are the articles devoted to the accounts of alleged atrocities while only brief mention is made of the frequent reviews of his life and career and the reunions and other post-war accounts of his command. It was even necessary to severely limit the number of stories on important issues, though this resulted in a certain loss of information. As well, many esoteric accounts of great interest also had to be eliminated. To further limit the length of the book, frequently the contents of various articles are described in the narrative but only the name and date of the publication(s) together with the headlines and sub-headlines appear. Unlike those articles that contain the text—most of which are edited for length—these inclusions merely illustrate the amount and general content of the matter being covered and the newspapers involved. For the purposes of this book, with a few exceptions, only those articles appear that address the events influencing Mosby's life and illustrating that influence through the press.

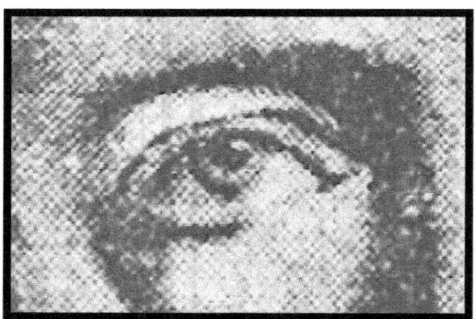

Example of the half-tone process

The Motto Of Mosby's Men

*Anywhere with Mosby—gladly, joyously,
in darkness, in light, in safety or in peril,
with no good reason or bad or no reason at all,
anywhere with Mosby!*

Chapter 1

THE FOURTH ESTATE

Inter caecos regnat strabo.~
Among the blind, the squinting one rules.

"There is a tide in the affairs of men, which taken at the flood, leads on to fortune. Omitted, all the voyage of their life is bound in shallows and in miseries." ~ William Shakespeare

FEW ALIVE TODAY remember a time when all news and information was distributed in print through newspapers, periodicals, journals, and books. There was no radio or television, much less the ubiquitous internet and if people wanted to know what was happening, they had to obtain a printed record or be restricted, like the ancients, to word of mouth.

Also, as with today's news sources, publications "shared" stories even when they did not share the same editorial viewpoint. But when there was a wide divergence between the two, the newspaper publishing the other's piece would provide some comment to keep the reader from straying too far from the desired interpretation. An excellent example of this journalistic "correction" is seen when The *Daily National Republican* of January 16, 1866, provided a story from the *Richmond Examiner* and printed its own conclusion in the closing paragraph:

> ***Daily National Republican* - January 16, 1866**
>
> Arrest of Colonel Mosby.
>
> We learn that Col. John S. Mosby was arrested, at his home in Fauquier, a few days since, by military authority, and taken to Washington and imprisoned. He is charged, we understand, with having hanged two Federal soldiers in the Valley, during the war, in retaliation for the murder of some of his men.
>
> When we remember that Colonel Mosby, though of that class known as partisan rangers, was a regularly commissioned officer in the service of the Confederate States, and, as such, received the parole awarded the other officers of General Lee's army, his arrest seems most extraordinary, and flatly in violation of the terms of parole.
>
> For some months Colonel Mosby has been quietly practicing law in Warrenton, demeaning himself as a good and loyal citizen of his section. - *Richmond Examiner.*
>
> *And when we remember that whether "commissioned" or not Mosby was the very worst of the gang of banditti who have desolated Virginia these four years past, we are astonished that he has been permitted to practice law otherwise than as his own counsel; and we are rejoiced to learn—and every loyal citizen will rejoice to learn — that at last there is a prospect of his being whipped of justice, and the blows we trust will be well laid on that he may get a punishment something like the measure of his desserts* [**emphasis vph**].

This book will present many such stories written about, and sometimes by John Singleton Mosby. Mosby was a man who received very wide attention from the press beginning early in the Civil War and continuing down to the present. One of the most interesting things about Mosby's press coverage is the widely differing assessments of the man presented by the fourth estate. Not only did he go from hero to villain (and back again), but these appraisals were not limited to any particular side of the many issues in which Mosby was involved throughout his life. Even individual publications over time found their judgment careening from one side to the other, depending upon the issue and Mosby's position on it. Indeed, the journalistic depiction of John Mosby is incredibly varied and intricate.

Also amazing were the thousands of determined conclusions about the man put forth during his life and even after his death. But most astonishing of all is the fact that *none* of this attention appeared to influence either Mosby's opinions or his behavior! He was an adamantine figure upon whom the oceans of acclaim and abuse beat endlessly while failing in any way to influence or affect their object. One of Mosby's biographers declared this to be the result of the man's personal indifference to the opinions of others. According to this author, such indifference resulted in a failure to respond to criticism, however virulent, or acclaim, however generous.

Yet John Mosby was anything but "indifferent" to public opinion, though he never permitted it to dissuade him from his determined course. But, in fact, all of his beliefs and actions were founded upon his own moral and intellectual compass and so both criticism and praise were simply irrelevant. However, Mosby was honest enough to admit that he was not averse to praise. After the capture of Edwin Stoughton, he had been dismissed out of hand by Col. Fitzhugh Lee while that Confederate officer embraced his old friend from West Point. Mosby was angered by this treatment and said so. However, he later declared that though he did not seek "official" praise, he was somewhat mollified by the praise he received from his friend General J.E.B. Stuart. He then made a very telling point regarding this issue: of those who did not seek or need the praise of their fellow man, John Mosby said that they were "either too good or too bad for the world." Mosby considered himself neither and as seen in these reports, he constantly made efforts to explain his actions when he believed them misunderstood and defend them when he was criticized anyway. But never did these reproaches or accolades result in a change of heart or course of action unless John Mosby became convinced that circumstances had changed or that he was in error. For unlike so many great men, John Mosby seemed willing enough to acknowledge when he was in the wrong. Indeed, early on in his political course after the war when he had been charged with and criticized for being "inconsistent" in his position on the adoption of the reconstruction constitution in Virginia, Mosby stated simply, *"I'd rather be right than consistent."*

As noted, while these articles are never one hundred percent accurate, when taken as a whole, they produce—as do the "dots" in the halftone process—a nuanced and sophisticated "image" of Mosby not to be found in simple recitations of the facts of his life or in "official records" and other historical documents. In these reports, one meets the man either in his own words or through the testimony of those around him, both friends and foes. And of course, as with the halftone process, the more "dots" (that is, the more information), the more detailed the image created. As it is my intention to prove that much of what is believed about John Mosby is erroneous, I cannot pretend complete disinterest in these matters; only machines are totally objective. However, when one ignores and/or falsifies the facts, empathy and support become dishonesty and fraud. John Mosby would have rejected any such actions even when taken in his defense.

At the same time, however, this will not be a *hagiography*. Mosby was no saint as that term is understood. It will be acknowledged when he was wrong or his actions did not meet his usual elevated ethical standards, or he was foolish and naïve—one of his very real failings! Yes, John Mosby had his faults but they tended, as he said of his friend Ulysses Grant, toward the virtues rather than the vices.

CHAPTER 2

PREAMBLE AND 1862

Ab initio ~ From the beginning

"It had long since come to my attention that people of accomplishment rarely sat back and let things happen to them. They went out and happened to things." ~ Leonardo da Vinci

Romance: Love affair; fascination with something

IN ORDER TO understand the relationship between the American press and John Mosby, it is necessary to realize that, first and foremost, it was a *romance* as that word is defined. Of course, one must not equate "romance" with "affection." After all, there are those whom we "love to hate." This "romance" began during the Civil War and continued throughout Mosby's life, persisting even after his death. The press response to Mosby *during* the war—positive and negative—remained the same in both method and intent *after* the war, a fact that led to a certain inevitability that can be recognized in the thousands of articles about him no matter how different the issues that appear therein.

When John Mosby began his career as a partisan (or guerrilla), newspaper coverage changed dramatically; and as his fame (or infamy, depending) escalated, the response of at least the Northern press was deeply affected by his continuing success. Indeed, the Northern press was very much conflicted regarding its coverage of the man. Most important, the newspapers needed to insist that his triumphs were "over-rated," lest they create a foe whose very name gave advantage to the enemy. To address these concerns, there was much reportage containing pronouncements that he was wounded or dead, or that his command had been "cut up" or that what he had captured had been recaptured or his attack (or attacks) had been repulsed or the Union cavalry was in pursuit and he could not long escape capture or destruction. Two examples of this *type* of coverage are seen here:

New York Tribune – April 20, 1863

Reported Cavalry Expedition under Gen. Stahel.

It is reported in the City today that the Rebel cavalry force which has been hovering around the Bull Run Mountains and Culpepper has been surrounded by an expedition sent out by Gen. Stahel and is or will be captured.

Daily National Republican – May 5, 1863

Moseby, the Rebel Captain, Certainly Wounded.

Moseby is certainly wounded in the shoulder. Moseby and the rebels all agree that their command is completely cut up.

Only when the matter was so serious that it could not be explained away did the reporting become more honest. Such coverage was more likely to occur when the publications involved were local to the Federal command that had suffered at Mosby's hands. For instance, there was a great deal of fairly accurate coverage from Vermont newspapers after the Miskel Farm skirmish in which the Vermont cavalry was severely manhandled by a force a quarter of its size:

Lamoille Newsdealer – **April 9, 1863**

Burlington Free Press – **April 10, 1863**

New York, April 3.

The Tribune's Washington dispatch says a skirmish occurred Wednesday morning near Drainsville between 150 of the 1st Vt. Cavalry under Capt. Flint and about an equal number of rebels under Capt. Mosby. Our side got the worst of it, Flint was killed and several prisoners taken. The rebel Capt. was seriously wounded… Mosby was in the house upon the plantation when he was surprised; but we learn that he rallied his men with lighting like celerity, and when our squadron broke he pursued and hack[ed] them severely. The guerrilla chief received a sabre cut on the forehead.

One of the charges most often made against Mosby was that he did not "fight fair." Mosby himself admitted as much, stating that his view of war was infinitely practical. He fought to win and took whatever advantage was available. The Yankee complaint regarding Mosby's refusal to "fight fair" simply meant that he didn't ride out and stand in serried ranks and either charge into or wait for a charge from a much larger force that was prepared for the fight. Now Mosby did fight in the field. He fought that way at Miskel Farm and Mt. Zion Church and a host of other skirmishes and operations. He also lured the Yankees into ambuscades and hit them in the rear as they were moving away. He hit them whenever and wherever he believed that he could prevail—and he made no apology for doing so. He did not feel obligated to stand and be slaughtered. Indeed, he stated flatly that he never stood to receive a charge; but instead, he charged the enemy, a maneuver that often led to them retreating despite their superior numbers. In fact, Mosby's military creed was that it was better to make a good run than a bad stand.

The problem with Mosby's tactics was not that they were "unfair," but that they were *successful!* Had he lost more than he won, there would have been no outcry from the Federal military. His most efficient operations frequently involved quick strikes in many places followed by the rousing of the whole Yankee camp and a long, hard ride after the miscreants generally ending in frustration and failure. It got to the point at which the very mention of Mosby's name and the belief that he was lurking somewhere in the dark outside the lights of Federal campfires destroyed the morale of the enemy. In fact, Mosby often said that he thought he was hated by Yankee soldiers more because of the sleep he made them lose than the number he captured and killed. The comment was made "tongue-in-cheek," but that did not make it wrong. The ordinary soldier hated Mosby because he filled his life with terror, foreboding, and uncertainty while officers hated him because he made them look impotent and foolish. Both situations, together with his victories, produced such a powerful hatred that it was still manifested in an interview with a Union general almost twenty years after the war:

Daily National Republican – **March 12, 1883 (Edited)**

A contributor to the Critic of Saturday …took issue with that portion of The Republican's interview with Gen. Whitaker, in which that gentleman stated he had captured Mosby at Beaver Dam station in 1862.

"'Ex-Rebel' is wrong...The reason that I did not wish Gilmor to be exchanged was on account of the havoc Mosby played after he was exchanged." "If you had caught him in 1865 he would not have been exchanged, would he?" inquired the reporter. [of General Whitaker].

"He would never have been taken to Fredericksburg alive," answered the general [emphasis vph].

Although the Northern press did what it could to minimize the effect Mosby was having on the Federal forces in their reports, they also recognized that he was, in fact, larger than life and of great interest to their readers. As a result, they provided him with coverage that the average military figure on either side—however exalted in rank— seldom received. He was a fabulous, almost mythical being. More important, he provided fascinating copy when the major armies were inactive. Indeed, the time arrived—not long after Mosby himself!—at which the press reported on him almost constantly because John Mosby operated almost constantly. But this too was problematic. On the one hand, they wanted to relegate him to a mere nuisance so that the public believed his victories were as the bite of a mosquito—which, indeed, he was called at one point. On the other hand, he was far better copy as a bestial villain! Therefore, to create the more interesting figure (that is, Mosby the Monster), the Northern press had to portray him as a fiend incarnate who perpetrated the most foul and inhuman crimes against Federal prisoners, the wounded, and innocent "loyal" civilians.

As might be imagined, such an extreme dichotomy was not easily maintained. Yet the Northern press did its best to move the public perception of Mosby and his men alternately from Mosby the ubiquitous, ruinous, almost-mythical monster to Mosby the sneak thief, an irksome pest hanging impotently on the rear of the glorious Federal army.

Below is a sample of the sort of report on Mosby as monster that appeared frequently in the Federal press, especially the *Daily National Republican*:

Daily National Republican – **November 1, 1864 (Edited)**
REBEL BARBARITY.—We have just learned of a fresh instance of rebel barbarism, which comes near home. Mr. W. L. Babbitt, a brother of A. S. Babbitt of this place, enlisted last winter into the 4th New York cavalry He was captured by Mosby's guerrillas, and a few days after was found bayoneted, with arms and legs cut off. We can only say we trust the time for showing quarter to these miscreants has gone by.—E—z County (Vt.) Republican.

Another format followed by the newspapers during the war involved recitations of Mosby's life. Usually, the publication of such "biographies" occurred in the Southern press after a Mosby triumph and in the Northern press when he had been declared dead or dying or had suffered a defeat. At the beginning of his partisan career, when the interest of the reading public (North and South) was being aroused by this young unknown, such "histories" were fairly common. Below is one that presents at least some recognition of the man's military talents, but despite a rather grudging admission of Mosby's abilities, ends in typical Yankee fashion—spiteful and inaccurate:

New York Tribune – **September 1, 1863 (Edited)**

JOHN S. MOSBY.

John S. Mosby, the noted guerrilla chief whose activity and daring have long rendered him a prominent object among the Rebels operating in Virginia is reported to have died at or near Dranesville on Friday of wounds received in a skirmish at Rector's Cross Roads on the 24th of last month. He was known to the soldiers of the Potomac army as the most successful perhaps, of the class of raiders to which he belonged. Many a story is told by sutlers whom he victimized of the manner in which he contrived to inform himself of where a rich haul of stores and provisions was to be made, the suddenness with which he pounced upon his victims, and the mysterious way in which his little band, their work done, would scatter and disappear He died in his native State, Virginia. Mosby was a man of medium height and not disagreeable appearance, and was 32 years old. He possessed qualities which, used in a good cause, might have won for him honor and fortune – as it is, he was simply Mosby the traitor guerrilla and he will soon be forgotten.

As Mosby was wounded a number of times during the war, reports of his death were not only frequent but (with the Northern press at least) continued on sometimes even after he had returned to his command. Such reports appeared in Southern papers, but minus the drumbeat of claims that he was dead or dying or would die and when he refused to do so, that he had been rendered *hors de combat* and his command had devolved upon fellow partisan Elijah White.

A Prelude to Greatness: John Mosby in 1862

In the beginning of the war, the name John Mosby found its way into the newspapers because of military operations. Very soon, however, military operations found their way into the newspapers because of the name John Mosby. In June of 1862, Southern papers celebrated General James Ewell Brown "Jeb" Stuart's great scout christened the "Ride Around McClellan." Stuart had taken his cavalry, ridden through the Federal lines and around McClellan's army, returning safely to Richmond after doing a fair amount of damage to the embarrassed foe. Of course, the Federals claimed that the matter was of little import, but there was no doubt that it "made the papers," North *and* South. In the *Dispatch* article, for the first time, mention was made of a young scout, John S. Mosby, who had devised the plan that Stuart had followed in triumph:

The (Richmond) Daily Dispatch, – **June 17, 1862 (Edited)**

(Part of a report on Stuart's "Ride Around McClellan.)

Among other interesting incidents occurring during this successful and brilliant adventure, we would not forget that in which Lieut. John S. Mosby was chief actor. Being of General Stuart's staff, and acting, we believe, as scout on the occasion, the gallant Lieutenant was far in advance of the column — our troops, in truth, not being then in sight — and espying a heavily laden wagon some distance ahead, and riding forward, discovered it to be freighted with pistols and other valuable stores, in charge of a Quartermaster. On being summoned to surrender, the Quartermaster refused — for he saw the cavalry camps were not more than 300 yards distant, and Federal cavalry drawn up in line of battle. Threatening to blow his brains out on the instant, the Quartermaster and teamster immediately surrendered, and the wagon was immediately faced about. The Federal, however, saw the state of things; their bugle blew the "charge," when Lieut. Mosby, turning in his saddle, waved his sabre to an imaginary force in his rear, shouting out lustily, "Come on, boys! come on!" Hearing which, the Federal wheeled to the right-about, leaving the Lieutenant, his prize, and prisoners, unmolested. Through force of circumstances the wagon and valuables were subsequently burned.

However, Mosby did not make the papers in triumph alone. One Yankee and one Southern paper mentioned him in articles about the Kilpatrick raid on the Virginia Central railroad in which the young scout was captured while waiting for a train at Beaver Dam station:

Columbia Spy – July 26, 1862 (Edited)

Brilliant Cavalry Exploit

Washington, July 21.

We have conversed with an officer who took part in the brilliant movement upon the Virginia Central Railroad at Beaver Dam, of which Gen. Pope gives the official report. It was executed by Col. Mansfield Davies, of the Harris Light Cavalry, with 370 men of his command. They left Fredericksburg at seven o'clock on Saturday night, and at eight o'clock were at Beaver Dam Station which is forty miles from Richmond, on the Virginia Central. Only about 140 men under Col. Davies reached the railroad station, where they were entirely unexpected. They captured Capt. J. L. Mosley of Virginia, an aide of Gen. Stewart's who was waiting for the cars. He had upon his person a letter from Gen. Johnson recommending him to that officer, and recommending that officer to study Napoleon's maxims. …

Captain Moseley was bearer of dispatches from Gen. Stewart to Gen. Jackson. Col. Davies destroyed the railroad and telegraph lines for four or five miles, and the station containing ammunition, flour and other valuable property, the water tanks and a large quantity of cordwood in the course of the hour which remained before the train from Richmond, which Captain Moseley had expected to take, and which had on board a brigade of troops going to reinforce Jackson, was due.

The next time Mosby was mentioned in 1862 was during his exchange. He was one of the first to be included in the exchange procedure set up by both sides. There was no end of lamentations both during and after the war about the fact that John Mosby had been exchanged—and no end of speculations concerning how easy life would have been for the Federals in northern Virginia had he remained their prisoner. As a matter of curiosity, it was determined that he had been exchanged for a Federal lieutenant, about whom, it was said, nothing further was ever heard:

The Press - August 2nd, 1862 (Edited)

Fortress Monroe, July 31, 1862

The steamer Georgia arrived here this morning, with 130 exchanged rebel prisoners … The officers' names are … Lieut. Mosby, Virginia Cavalry. …

The last mention of Mosby in 1862 involved another "expedition" of Stuart's cavalry behind enemy lines. He was mentioned here as one of a "few picked men," and his name was spelled incorrectly, a matter that was to become almost habitual on and off for the rest of his life:

> ***Daily (Richmond) Dispatch* – August 12, 1862 (Edited)**
>
> Report of Gen. Stuart of his expedition in rear of enemy's lines. – June 17th, 1862 A few picked men, including my Aides, Burke, Farley, and Mosley, were pushed forward rapidly to Tunstall's to cut the wires and secure the depot. …

Thus the second year of the war came to a close. For the first time, however, John Mosby—an "indifferent soldier"—had actually appeared in the newspapers, something he would never have predicted when he left Bristol in the Spring of 1861. Furthermore, he had made a "difference" and been chosen as a man of use and interest by a soldier who had been called "the greatest cavalryman ever foaled in America." And perhaps for the first time, John Mosby believed that he might contribute more to the war effort than he had ever thought possible as a homesick, shy, and taciturn private soldier. He was starting to dream larger dreams than just being a "good scout," and he had tried to fulfill those dreams when Stuart sent him to Jackson. That he did not reach that officer was a setback, no doubt; but whatever the case, John Mosby was ready to try more. In fact, John Mosby was ready to *do* more, and the press—North and South—was ready to report on those doings.

Chapter 3

1863

Hoc natura est insitum, ut quem timueris, hunc semper oderis.
~ It's an innate thing to always hate the one we've learnt to fear.

"Never was anything great achieved without danger."

~ Niccolò Machiavelli

MOSBY'S NEXT APPEARANCE in the newspapers was in March. A lot had happened between August of 1862 and March of 1863, all stemming from the fact that after Stuart's "Dumfries raid" in December of 1862, as the First Virginia Cavalry made to go into winter quarters, Stuart granted his favorite scout his dearest wish to remain behind in northern Virginia "with a few men" because Mosby thought that he could "do a little good." Never had there been such an understatement since Noah's neighbor looked at the sky and told his wife, "I think it's going to rain."

The first Yankee reference to Mosby insisted that he had met defeat at the hands of one "Captain Schultz." However, it is to be noted that he was already referred to as "notorious," indicating that in just three months, "Mosely" has caused considerable consternation among the invaders:

Janesville Daily Gazette - March 5, 1863 (Edited)

STAFFORD C. H., Va., March 2.

Captain Schultz, formerly a resident near Aldie, recently headed a body of Union cavalry to that neighborhood, to surprise some guerrillas commanded by the notorious Captain Mosely, of White's command…

The next appearance of so-called *Captain* Mosby (he was no such thing!) was carried in, of all places, the *New York Tribune!* In a short story dated March 10, the paper initiated coverage of a Mosby operation virtually unheard of in any war to that time! That operation never left the headlines throughout the rest of Mosby's life and down to today:

New York Tribune – March 10, 1863

News of The Day The War

We learn from Washington that the Rebel Capt. Moseley, with his command, entered Fairfax Court-House yesterday morning, and captured Provost-Marshal O'Scanner's [sic] patrols, horses &c., together with Gen. Stoughton and all men detached from his brigade. They also took every horse which could be found, public and private. The commanding officer of the post, Col. Johnston of the 5th New York cavalry made his escape.

And then the floodgates of news coverage opened, and as far as coverage of John Mosby was concerned, it never closed:

*Daily Globe** – March 10, 1863
(*Newspaper of the United States Congress)

News of the Day

About two o'clock yesterday morning, about a hundred rebel guerrillas, under Captain Mosely, entered Fairfax Court-House by way of the Vienna road, and captured Brigadier General Stoughton, of the Vermont brigade, all the pickets and patrols, and one hundred and ten fine horses. Captain Oscanner (O'Connor-vph), provost marshal of the town, was absent visiting and thus escaped. Colonel Johnston, commander of the post, escaped in his night-clothes.

Alexandria Gazette – March 10, 1863
RAID UPON FAIRFAX COURTHOUSE

The Abingdon Virginian – March 13, 1863
The following dispatch was received by Mrs. Mosby, at Bristol, on Wednesday: Culpeper C.H., March 11. I have just returned from a raid on the Yankees, captured Brig. Gen. Stoughton, two Captains, thirty men and fifty horses. I had only 29 men—no loss. JNO. S. MOSBY.

The Columbia Spy – March 14, 1863
Daring Rebel Raid into Fairfax Courthouse

Information has been received here that Captain Mosely, with his command, stealthily entering Fairfax Court House this morning at 2 o'clock, captured the Provost Marshal, O'Conner, his patrol, a number of horses, &c, together with General Stoughton, and all the men detached from his brigade. They also took every horse which could be found, public or private.

The commanding officer of the post was also taken prisoner. Colonel Johnston, of the 5th New York Cavalry, made his escape.

The rebels searched for men in every direction.

All our available cavalry forces were, at the latest accounts, in pursuit of the rebels.

The enemy made their appearance suddenly, during a rain storm. General Stoughton had established his headquarters at some distance from the brigade.

The rebels captured a hundred and ten horses. They went in search of Gen. Wyndham, but that gentleman happened to be in Washington. They, however, searched his trunk and took his papers. A telegraph operator was also taken prisoner.

But no sooner had Mosby amplified his reputation by his raid into Fairfax Court House than he rather "backed into" what turned out to be a glorious victory. It should not have been any kind of a victory! Indeed, it should have ended his days as an annoyance to the Yankees! However, his natural abilities together with his own courage and the courage of the men with him at the time—most of whom were strangers to him—turned sure defeat into triumph. This particular "operation," though it cannot be considered one such in truth, was the moment in which John Singleton Mosby went from a clever man with a good idea to a great military leader:

Daily National Republican – April 3, 1863

Union County Star and Lewisburg Chronicle – April 7, 1863

Cavalry Fight with Moseby's Guerillas.

A Captain, Lieutenant, and Seven Men Killed.

We learn that on Tuesday last Capt. Moseby visited Centreville with his notorious guerilla band, numbering about sixty, dressed in Federal uniform. They left for Dranesville or its neighborhood, and on Wednesday morning a squadron of the 1st Vermont cavalry came upon them at a plantation where they were bivouacked.

Moseby's men were dismounted and received our cavalry with a fire from behind fences, which stampeded some of the raw soldiers. The fight soon became desperate. Moseby threatened his men with death if they flinched, and himself wounded Capt. Flint five times with his revolver, killing him. Lieut. Grout, of the Vermont cavalry, and seven men were also killed. Our loss was about sixty in killed, wounded and prisoners.

Moseby was in the house upon the plantation when he was surprised, but we learn that he rallied his men with lightning-like celerity, and, when our squadron broke, he pursued and hacked them severely. He captured over fifty thousand equipments. The guerilla chief received a severe sabre cut on the forehead.

We learn that the Vermont carbine companies delivered their fire upon the enemy with good effect, and then opened to the right and left to allow the sabre companies to charge, but they did not come up to the work.

The bodies of Capt. Flint and Lieut. Grout, both remarkably fine looking men, were embalmed to-day by Messrs. Brown and Alexander, to be forwarded home.

There were many reports on this matter, only a few of which are included here. The press coverage of Mosby during the war was overwhelming, but while it differed in *content* (depending upon the operation obviously!) it did not differ very much in *intent!* Here is Mosby's next triumph after Miskel's Farm:

Staunton Spectator – April 7, 1863 (Edited)

Raids into the Enemy's Lines

Captain Mosby has been lately stirring up the Yankees with a sharp stick, and the newspapers have given some few straggling particulars of his exploits in this way, but for the first reliable account of the "raids" recently made by him on the enemy's lines, we are indebted, says the Examiner, to the courtesy of Mr. William E. Frankland, who is a member of his company, and was an active participant in the same.

On last Monday, Capt. Mosby, with sixty five men, attacked the enemy's picket post between Centreville and Little Run Turnpike, about two or three miles from Chantilly, driving in the pickets and capturing some eight or ten of the party. On Capt. Mosby turning about to bring back the men he had captured, the enemy, about two hundred and fifty strong, according to their own accounts, started in pursuit, which was kept up for about a mile and a half. Seeing that he was pursued, Captain Mosby started his prisoners to the rear under guard, leaving him with about fifty men. As soon as the prisoners were stared off Captain Mosby in an instant formed his men in line across the turnpike and waited the coming up of the Yankees. In a very little while the Yankees came dashing on at a furious speed, but on seeing our men drawn up they halted about a hundred yards off, and commenced a rapid fire. They refused to come to close quarters with our men, although ordered to advance by their commanding officer. Capt. Mosby here ordered his men to draw sabres and charge on them. The Yankees continued their fire until our men were within some twenty or thirty yards of the, when, at the sight of uplifted sabre, they turned about, put to their heels, our men keep closely on them for over two miles, killing and capturing them all along the way and completely routing them. Seven were left dead on the wayside, and some five or six wounded. Overtaking them Captain Mosby fell upon them and bagged some thirty-five of the number, among them a Lieutenant, capturing with them all their horses, arms and equipments. They all belonged to the Fifth New York cavalry. The best thing of the affair was that Capt. Mosby lost not a men – nor a man hurt...

We hope Captain Mosby will soon pay his respects again to the Yankees, and that in his next visit to them he may meet with the same good fortune.

Among accounts of actual clashes between Mosby and the Federals, articles began to appear claiming that he and his command were not soldiers but criminals and therefore unworthy to be treated as prisoners of war if captured. This type of reporting went on throughout—and after—the war. Sometimes such stories were also carried in the Southern press as seen here:

Daily Dispatch - **April 24, 1863**

Reports from Washington City.

The Washington dispatches, of the 10th, contain some matters of interest— among them the following:

Yesterday morning at daylight, the rebel cavalry — some of Mosby's forces took Mr. Sherman from his house, near Dranesville, and securing him of giving information to the Federals, hung him.—It is thought that the Government will retaliate for the hanging of Detective Sherman by summarily executing Captain Powers and a civilian in the old Capitol prison, against whom evidence is said to be conclusive of their being spies.

But Mosby had achieved what he desired; that is, he had become a "haunt" in the minds of his enemies, as he remained for the rest of the war. Soon, pieces such as this appeared in the press, North and South. Despite such "biographies" appearing earlier in his career, people still wanted to know more about the man; this was the true beginning of the romance. Of course, the nature of the description depended entirely upon the loyalties of the publication in which it appeared:

Richmond Dispatch - April 28, 1863

Mosby, the Raid maker.

It is often asked, who is Capt. John S. Mosby? The family is a very numerous one and many of his name are in our army. Capt. Mosby is the son of Mr. Alfred D. Mosby, formerly of Albemarle county, but at present residing in Amherst, in the vicinity of Lynchburg. Capt. M. is a very young man. He was educated at the University of Virginia; is by profession a lawyer, and had located himself in Washington county, where he is highly regarded and was rapidly advancing in his profession. He married the daughter of the Hon. Beverly L. Clark, of Kentucky, and late Minister to Central America – Capt. Mosby entered the service as a private in the Washington county cavalry.

All through 1863, Mosby's incessant raids received a great deal of publicity. Often, the Southern papers reprinted Northern accounts and vice versa. Of course, at this point, Mosby still did not have an actual command but rather what he called his "conglomerates," groups of various men from various places who met and went upon a raid and then often simply disappeared. He also had no command structure. He was the only "officer," and that lack of strategic help during an operation led to problems when something unexpected occurred, as with the Warrenton Junction skirmish.

While there are far more Union accounts than Confederate of Mosby's operations, these latter also appeared from time to time, especially in the *Abingdon Virginian*, the newspaper from the town that had raised the command Mosby originally joined, the Washington Mounted Rifles. The second article makes mention of a real coup—that is, Mosby's capture of General Hooker's aides with dispatches; intelligence gathering was one of his most important functions as a partisan and one in which he was exceptionally effective:

Lynchburg Virginian – June 30, 1863

Abingdon Virginia – July 3, 1863

Mosby, too, has not been idle. He has had several sharp skirmishes, but the most important thing effected by him, was the capture of one of Hooker's aids, who had in his possession a letter of instructions from Hooker to his cavalry commander. This letter was of incalculable service to us, disclosing, as it did, the plans of the enemy. It is said to have shown that Hooker was terribly puzzled to know where Lee was, and what he was going to do.

And so the coverage went on through 1863. However, every once in a while, an article appeared in a paper that was far more "intuitive;" that is, it recognized a situation, made a comparison and then a point arising from that comparison. This story appeared in the *Cleveland Morning Leader*—obviously a Union paper and paid a higher tribute to John Mosby than had any paper, North or South, to that point in time. The article doubtless received little attention, but had Mosby seen it, he would have understood the high compliment he had been paid by a member of the enemy's press:

Cleveland Morning Leader – July 31, 1863

"The people are asking, and the world will ask, where was General Johnston, and what part did he perform in this grand tragedy. In answer it will be said that, with an army larger than won the first battle of Manassas, he made not a motion, struck not a blow, for the relief of Vicksburg. For nearly seven weeks he sat down in sound of the conflict, and he fired not a gun. He heard the confident declarations with which the besieged animated their courage—'Never mind!—Johnston is coming!'—but Johnston never came. He did not so much as harass the enemy, but left Grant to pursue his work without interruption. *If Mosby and his little band had been there, instead of Johnston and his army, Grant would not have enjoyed such impunity* [emphasis vph].

But the Northern press did not just cover Mosby's military operations. The man personally intrigued them. He tempted them and made them desire more because their readers demanded more. He was more interesting than the tens of thousands of uniformed nonentities who, save for a few individuals—mostly of high rank—were a part of a nameless, faceless military behemoth both blue and gray. John Mosby was Robin Hood and the Swamp Fox to the South! To the North, he was a combination of Blackbeard and Captain Kidd! Sometimes the articles appearing in Northern papers grudgingly painted Mosby as a man of courage and daring, but whose inevitable end would be an unhallowed grave or the gallows—and *then* an unhallowed grave:

The Philadelphia Press – August 5, 1863 (Edited)

Personal

An Army correspondent writes of the guerilla Mosby: At a town, which shall be nameless, that we passed through, I was told the following circumstances about Mosby, which as it has never found it way into print, I think worth giving, as illustrative of the bold and reckless audacity of the man. A squad of Northern cavalry got on the track of him and his men, pursued him into the village, captured some of his men, and hoped to take him captive. Guards were placed at every street entrance, and the search for Mosby began – a search up stairs, down stairs, in garret, in cellar, in beds, under beds, in closets, wardrobes, and every imaginable cubby-hole capable of hiding a man. Mosby was not to be found. In quick time he had exchanged his military dress for the coarse spun habiliments of a non-combatant, and while the search was progressing passed for one of the curious throng of street lookers-on. He took ninety-nine chances out of a hundred of being captured, and fortune favored him, as it always does the brave. It is this bravery and this good fortune that make him and his exploits the theme of every tongue, and particularly tongues feminine …

Southern papers, of course, were more than willing to trumpet the triumphs of John Mosby:

The Southern Illustrated News – August 8, 1863 (Edited)

With such great terror do the Yankees regard this gallant young partisan, that during the early part of the Spring, upon a rumor being put in circulation that he was on his way to Washington, they went to work and tore up all the planks of the Chain Bridge.

In speaking of Captain Mosby, our talented and valued correspondent, "Tristan Joyeuse," says: "His figure is slight, muscular, supple and vigorous; his eye is keen, penetrating, ever on the alert; he wears his sabre and pistol with the air of a man who sleeps with them buckled around his waist, and handles them habitually, almost unconsciously. The Captain is a determined man in a charge—dangerous on a scout— hard to outwit, and prone to 'turn up' suddenly where he is least expected, and bang away with pistol and carbine."

In a skirmish at Gooding's Tavern, for the first time, Mosby was seriously wounded. He was shot through the left thigh and the left side at the waist, the latter wound, though superficial, was painful and bled profusely. The leg wound, however, was far more serious as Mosby himself later admitted, not only because of the bleeding but because of the possibility of infection and subsequent amputation of the limb close to the hip. In the Northern press, such news created an oft-repeated narrative: He was dead. No, he was dying. No, he was neither dead nor dying but would not be able to return to his command. And finally, he *had* returned to his command:

Daily Green Mountain Freeman - August 27, 1863 (Edited)

The Times' special Washington dispatch says that Mosby's operations in our immediate front are assuming rather gigantic proportions. From a gang of 60 desperadoes his force has grown to 800 guerrillas who prey upon everything which passes between Fairfax and Warrenton. A Washington dispatch to the Herald states that is generally believed that Mosby was fatally wounded on Monday. It says on Monday a large drove of cattle and horses had been sent out to the front from Alexandria, and the horses falling behind the cattle, and having a small escort, were attacked near Annandale by Mosby, who succeeded in capturing a number of animals and escaping without loss The guerrillas fled as far as Mills' cross roads, where the collected and sent back a wagon for a wounded officer who had been left near the scene of the engagement. Securing the man, the rebels passed through Drainsville, to which point they were pursued without success.

All the inhabitants along the route taken by the guerrillas state that the wounded man was Mosby, and that is injuries are regarded by his men as being of a dangerous character, the ball entering his back. The wound bled profusely.

Of course, Mosby didn't die but recovered and returned. However, now the war that both sides believed would be over in a few months headed into its fourth year with little hope for the triumph of the Confederacy. But John Mosby had enough to do in his own small sphere of action, and he intended to do it to the best of his considerable ability. As that was the case, there was no question that the press would be there to report on what he did when he did it.

Chapter 4

1864

Dulce bellum inexpertis. ~
War is sweet for those who haven't experienced it.

"Nothing in the world is worth having or worth doing unless it means effort, pain [and] difficulty." ~ Theodore Roosevelt

1864 BEGAN WITH a situation the reverse of the Miskel Farm skirmish. Whereas that operation should have been a disaster but turned into a great triumph, Loudoun Heights should have been a great triumph but became if not a disaster, then certainly a sharp setback for Mosby. The *National Republican* was glad enough to report the matter, though it was wrong in saying that Cole was ready for the attack. Indeed, the entire camp was caught fast asleep in their tents and that is why it should have been a Mosby triumph:

> ***National Republican* – January 11, 1864**
>
> Battle with Moseby's Guerrillas SEVERE FIGHT
>
> Mosby is Repulsed, Leaving His Dead and Wounded on the Field Our Loss Two Killed and Eleven Wounded.

A better face was put upon the matter in Southern papers:

> ***Western Democrat* – January 19, 1864**
>
> FROM VIRGINIA
>
> It has been stated that our troops under Mosby had attacked Harper's Ferry and were repulsed, but the following is the true version of the affair: Mosby did not attack the garrison at Harper's Ferry, but the yankee camp on Loudoun Heights, 1-1/2 miles from the Ferry, occupied by a battalion of cavalry. The enemy's camp was completely surprised and thrown into considerable confusion. Owing to the proximity of the enemy's infantry, Mosby was compelled to act hurriedly. Six prisoners and 40 horses were captured. The enemy's loss in killed and wounded was not ascertained. Our casualties amount to 15.

Obviously, 1864 was going to be a busy year for John Mosby. The *Daily Intelligencer* made note of the fact that the folks of West Virginia should complain less about their lot and consider what happened wherever Mosby and his command held sway:

> ***Daily Intelligencer* – February 10, 1864**
>
> When the people of West Virginia are impatient of raids, and inclined to charge them to the incapacity or inefficiency of those in command, they should remember that raids are made elsewhere and with more frequency than they are into our territory. Look over about Washington city—especially to the vicinity of Alexandria—immediately in the rear of the great Potomac army. How many times have Mosby's men been reported

within sight of the very capitol—within range of the Arlington forts—almost within the corporate limits of Alexandria? This has not happened once, or twice, or thrice, but a dozen times. Mosby has held sway, we may say, over the country between Washington and Manassas. He has captured trains, torn up the railroads, and carried off important officers.

And Mosby also figured in other debates that were taking place in the North. This little piece in the *Press* of February 17 makes a very interesting point regarding the inability of Federal forces to secure the persons of at least two pesky Confederates:

The Press – February 17, 1864
WHY DO WE NOT CATCH THE ALABAMA?

But, Mr. President, it is asked why we do not catch the Alabama, if our vessels are so fast. I might ask why do you not catch Moseby? Moseby, for eighteen months, or nearly that time, has been living within the lines of the American army, and has destroyed three times as much property as the Alabama has. Do you condemn the army or the War Department because he is not caught?

Mosby's very successful encounter with the "California 100," the skirmish in which Baron Robert von Massow was so foully wounded, first appeared in late February. The matter was presented as an "ambush," but it was an open battle between forces that were relatively equal in experience and strength, although Mosby's numbers were greatly exaggerated in one press account. Therefore, the defeat of the Californians could not be charged to Mosby's "unfair" tactics *or* numerical superiority:

Daily National Republican – February 24, 1864
FROM MOSBY'S DEPARTMENT.

Scouting Party Ambushed by Guerrillas.

A scouting party, consisting of a detachment of 150 men, Second Massachusetts cavalry, commanded by Captain J. Sewall Reed, fell into an ambush on the Drainesville pike between that place and Vienna, Monday forenoon. They were fired upon in flank from the dense woods by a force of Mosby's guerrillas, said to be larger than their own, and eight men were killed, seven wounded and about sixty missing.

Captain Reed was shot through the chest, the ball entering the left side. He died almost instantly. The body was brought to this city and embalmed by Drs. Brown and Alexander. Captain Reed commanded the first company of the battalion of cavalry furnished from California for Massachusetts. Among the prisoners is Captain Manning, of Maine, who also belonged to the California battalion.

There were also press reports of the recognition Mosby was receiving from his government:

Yorkville Enquirer – February 24, 1864

—The efficient and untiring services of the gallant partizan Mosby, have been complimented by promotion; so that he is to be known hereafter not as Major, but as Lieutenant-Colonel Mosby.

By this time, the Yankees, and especially their press, were getting tired of Mosby's ubiquity and his ability to move and act at will despite the fact that he was virtually in the middle of the largest Federal army extant and within only a few miles of the Federal capital itself. Frustration about this state of affairs was clearly seen in this article in the *Daily National Republican*. Two things are of particular interest: First, the matter was considered "discreditable"—meaning that it evidenced a lack of ability and/or will on the part of the Army of the Potomac to stop Mosby. Second, mention was made that in one operation, "Moseby was along in person," indicating that his appearance made the situation even more dangerous than it would have been otherwise! In other words, Mosby's actual presence was, as they say in the military, a force multiplier:

> ***Daily National Republican* - March 2, 1864**
>
> Alexandria Affairs.—Moseby's Guerrillas.—We would not be surprised, within a day or two to hear of a raid on the wagon trains on the Orange and Alexandria road, as well as in the neighborhood of Vienna, as a force of Moseby's guerrillas were seen yesterday within two miles and a half of Fall's Church, watching the movements of our trains. We hope this discreditable state of affairs will soon end. Moseby was along in person.

But other articles of interest also continued in the North. One such acknowledged that the atrocities being charged to Mosby and his command were in fact false. Actually, it is probable that no such atrocities ever happened at all:

> ***Daily Evening Bulletin* – March 22, 1864**
>
> From rebel prisoners and deserters we learn that Mosby has been wearing the laurels properly belonging to other officers, and that a great number of the depredations committed within our lines have been by squads of rebel cavalry with whom Mosby has no connection. It is known that two regiments of rebel cavalry were some times since detailed for such duties, and that their officers represent themselves [as] Mosby upon all occasions when riding through the country in the vicinity of our lines.

Meanwhile, the ever-active partisan chief was back operating against the railroads, with Northern accounts again greatly overstating his numbers:

> ***Nashville Daily Union* – April 17, 1864**
>
> Guerrillas on the Potomac.
>
> Alexandria, Va., April 16.—Mosby with 500 rebel cavalry, took by surprise the Patrol guarding the road between Bristow Station and Manassas. From 25 to 30 of our soldiers were captured. The rebels went away in the direction of Fredericksburg.

At the end of April, the United States government responded to Confederate "guerrillas" by passing a bill. General Order 100—the so-called Lieber Code— recognized the legitimacy of partisan commands if and when they fulfilled certain criteria. According to Lieber, those who fought in uniform as soldiers and had some association with the regular military—both criteria Mosby fulfilled—were to be treated as prisoners of war rather than outlaws. But as with so much else in Lincoln's "code of war," when it was considered a matter of "military necessity," the "code" was abandoned:

New York Tribune – April 28, 1864

EXECUTION OF GUERRILLAS

It is understood that a House Military Committee will report a bill authorizing commanders in the field to execute convicted guerrillas without the President's approval.

Naturally, Mosby—who kept abreast of the doings in Washington—would not have found such a determination comforting.

Another little article appeared in the *Daily National Republican* in response to Mosby's "gift" of a lock of his hair to Abraham Lincoln along with the promise that he would come and see that gentleman in Washington to obtain a lock of his in return. It was another of Mosby's "psychological" strikes. Apparently (at least as was reported years later), Lincoln was amused. But the paper was not—and in this waspish retort is found all the frustration extant in the North concerning this irresistible and roguish foe:

Daily National Republican – April 30, 1864

It is reported that Moseby, the guerrilla, sent a lock of his hair to the President a few days ago. It wouldn't be a bad idea to send "Hole-in-the-Day," or some other of the Indian chiefs lying around here loose, to bring in the balance of Moseby's hair, scalp and all.

Meanwhile, as they say, reports of Mosby's operations continued in the press, North and South, and such reports occasionally included the odd bit of wishful thinking:

Vermont Watchman and State Journal – May 27, 1864

Gen. Stevenson of our corps is killed; and by a contraband. I learn that Longstreet is wounded. It is reported that Mosby is wounded and a prisoner. J.B.L.

Mosby's war against Northern railroads continued; and in this article in the *Daily National Republican*, as well as the report on his raid, we again see the cry of frustration regarding the failure of the Federal military to exterminate the man and his followers:

Daily National Republican – June 30, 1864

A Rebel Raid on the Baltimore and Ohio Railroad.

THIRTY MEN CAPTURED BY THE REBELS.

We learn that some time last night, between five and six hundred mounted guerrillas, with two or three pieces of artillery, made a dash into "Duffield Station," on the Baltimore and Ohio railroad, about five miles above Harper's ferry, and, without any fight, gobbled up about thirty of our soldiers who were guarding the road at that point. We do not learn what damage, if any, the raiders did to the railroad, but they cut and damaged the telegraph line considerably. Where is General Sigel?

No sooner had the *Republican* complained loudly about Mosby's depredations against the railroads than it had to acknowledge an attack on a canal boat near Nolan's Ferry:

Daily National Republican – July 7, 1864

MOSBY MAKES A RAID ON THE CANAL.

The Steamer Flying Cloud Captured—Capt. Herbert, of the Treasury Department, Killed.

But as usual, John Mosby did not sit on his laurels. In a superb operation, he met and defeated "Fighting Major" William H. Forbes who had gone out looking for the Rangers while Mosby was looking for Forbes. As had happened so often in the past (and continued to happen), Major Forbes and his contingent of Second Massachusetts and Thirteenth New York found their prey but soon had reason to regret their apparent good fortune. However, it was the wording in the headline of this article in the *Evening Star*, a Washington paper, that is of interest: "Another Exploit of Moseby." The fact that this Northern paper spoke of Mosby's victory as an "exploit" is pivotal; for that word is defined as an "exciting act," "adventure," or "feat." There is nothing negative in its definition, and therefore, it seems odd that a Northern paper would use it to describe Mosby's triumph over a Federal force. There can be no doubt that by this time there was a certain amount of grudging admiration for the man by at least *some* in the Yankee press corps:

Evening Star – July 9, 1864

ANOTHER EXPLOIT OF MOSEBY

He Captures a Cavalry Force near Aldie, with Horses and Accouterments—Rebel Raiders at Fairfax Court House.

Mosby's activities were such that the press on both sides were filled with accounts of his various operations. Two Southern papers made mention of the prisoners sent to Richmond from these campaigns with a further report on his raid on Duffield's Station. It was in this raid that Mosby was approached under a white flag by the Federal officer in command and asked his conditions for surrender, to which he replied, "unconditionally, and that very quickly." John Mosby was not a patient man.

As time went on, Mosby had become ever more mythical in the eyes of the fourth estate as this little article makes obvious:

Daily Ohio Statesman – July 18, 1964

Mosby's Guerrillas Steal 10,000 Head of Cattle

Philadelphia, July 16.—The Inquirer has the following special from Washington: A portion of Mosby's command—about two hundred—passed near Leesburg at an early hour Tuesday night. Each rider led a horse, and they were driving before them ten thousand head of cattle. When last heard from they were making for Ashby's Gap.

By now, there was an almost-familial tone in some Northern coverage. The Northern press had become a sort of "Dutch uncle," admonishing a naughty nephew with dire threats of a painful visit to the woodshed if he did not behave himself. One such article appeared in the *Daily National Republican*, warning Mosby that he had "best remain within the limits of his own department," the natural assumption being that if he failed to do so, he would certainly make that promised trip:

Daily National Republican – July 30, 1864

Mosby.—A small force of rebel cavalry, supposed to be Mosby's guerrillas, crossed the Potomac, a little below Edward's Ferry, on Thursday, and returned, after reconnoitering the country for wagon trains. Mosby had best remain within the limits of his own department, foraging upon his Virginia friends.

It would seem that these continuous reports in the press were beginning to annoy some Northern publications fortunate enough to be separated from Mosby's ubiquity by distance. These papers were impatient with the coverage of the man by those who experienced him far more intimately. This apparently was the case with the *Janesville Weekly Gazette*:

Janesville Weekly Gazette – August 12, 1864

Letter from Washington Washington, D. C. July 31st:

Well, the raiders are upon us again! The inevitable Moseby, the dashing Moseby, the chivalrous highway robber Moseby, Moseby the "audacious cuss," Moseby the rebel, scare crow, is again advancing constituting as usual, the advance guard, the forlorn hope of an immense army of invasion, numbering all the way from five thousand to a million, be the same more or less, according to the imagination of the reporter.

On the other hand, the *National Republican* knew how Mosby worked and what he accomplished. In this article of August 15, it even bemoaned the capture of one of their own but admitted that Mr. Shelby, after being robbed, had been given a parole and released:

Daily National Republican, – August 15, 1864 (Edited)

Mosby's guerrillas are hanging on the rear of our columns, and captured, yesterday, Mr. Shelby, of the *New York Tribune*, going to the front, and robbed him in a most approved style, and, giving him what they called a parole, let him go.

The previous year, Mosby had captured two journalists who were not so fortunate, having been conveyed to Richmond as prisoners. However, the treatment they received at his hands was graciously described in an article of the time:

Abingdon Virginian – December 11, 1863 (Edited)

A Yankee Correspondent.

A Mr. George Hart, a correspondent of the "'Herald," was lately captured by Major Mosby. He seems surprised at being treated with common courtesy, and does Major Mosby the honor to say that he felt himself not his prisoner, but his companion:

Headquarters in the Saddle, En Route to Richmond under Mosby's Escort, White Plains, Va., Nov. 1, 1863.

Early this morning Major Mosby, accompanied by several of his men, suddenly made his appearance at the home of Mr. McCormick, in the town of Auburn... We rode along leisurely, Major Mosby opening a conversation which soon became highly interesting. We soon discovered that the Major was a very different personage from what he is described... In his address and demeanor he is a perfect gentleman, and in his relations with ourselves was highly courteous. He is about twenty eight years of age, of prepossessing appearance, and certainly the reverse of the picture drawn of him in newspapers generally. He wears the uniform of a Major in the regular rebel service ... In his movements he displays great energy, and, as an evidence of his powers of endurance, accompanies his men on all their expeditions. On this occasion the object of his visit to Auburn was to make a reconnoissance, as he frequently does prior to the period he contemplates making a strike and, through the further courtesy of Major Mosby, I nowwrite these particulars, and forward them by his special express.

For his very marked attention, if we do not feel grateful, we feel at least complimented and bid him here accept our thanks for many kind courtesies which have so far succeeded in their intent as to make us feel his companions, not his prisoners.

But Mosby was now engaged in the greatest work laid upon his capable if somewhat stooped shoulders by General Robert E. Lee himself after his dear friend and immediate superior, General "Jeb" Stuart had been killed at Yellow Tavern in May. With Stuart's death, Mosby now reported directly to Lee, the only officer under corps rank to do so. That General was being pressed by the new leader of the Army of the Potomac, General Ulysses S. Grant who had put General Philip Sheridan in charge of his cavalry.

Whether either Federal officer was concerned with Mosby at that time is questionable. Most of what Grant knew about "guerrillas" stemmed from his experience in the Western theater, but the comparison between East and West in this matter was neither militarily useful nor valid. In any event, Sheridan was about to meet John Mosby when the pesky partisan attacked his very large train of supply wagons moving through Berryville. It was one of Mosby's greatest achievements, and in fact, it was the operation in which he used the largest number of men he had used to that point in time—some three hundred:

Daily Dispatch -**August 16, 1864**

FROM THE VALLEY—MOSBY AT WORK.

A few days ago Mosby attacked one of the enemy's wagon trains at Berryville, in Clarke county, destroyed it, and captured a quartermaster's wagon with a large amount of greenbacks. He also took some two hundred or three hundred prisoners, who were at Gordonsville yesterday on their way South. Good for Mosby.

Then of all publications, the *Army-Navy Journal* paid John Singleton Mosby perhaps the greatest compliment that had been paid to him to that date in this article frankly admitting that Sheridan—with an army of ninety-four thousand men—was "compelled ... to act upon the defensive, *not having sufficient strength* [emphasis vph] to advance in the face of the force opposing him ..." The "force" here mentioned was Jubal Early's army of fifteen thousand men, but the reason that Early's small army could not be assailed was because of the operations of John Mosby, who commanded a force in his various operations that was about the same size as Sheridan's personal guard! Mosby wrote many years later that Sheridan considered his huge army to be the equal of Early's small force *because of the guerrillas operating in his rear*! Thus, Mosby stated, Sheridan made of him a greater general than Napoleon or Grant. Apparently, the *Army-Navy Journal* agreed:

> ### *Army-Navy Journal* - August 27, 1864
>
> The reports from the Shenandoah Valley show that General Sheridan is compelled for the present to act strictly upon the defensive, not having the strength sufficient to advance in the face of the force opposing him, exposed as he would be to flank movements through the passes of the Blue Ridge and attacks upon his communications by the guerrilla bands of the ever-active Moseby.

Warfare in northern Virginia and especially in the Shenandoah Valley had become very ugly, and at one point, Ranger Lt. Colonel William Chapman came across a troop of Federal soldiers burning homes and stealing the belongings of civilians. With a cry of "No quarter," Chapman and his men attacked the home burners, and those who did not manage to escape were executed. For the first time, there was the real threat of "black flag" warfare [*] in Virginia:

> ### *Cleveland Morning Leader* – August 30, 1864
>
> Mosby has hanged thirty of our men in Clark county, Va., for burning guerrillas' houses.
>
> ### *The Press* – August 30, 1864
>
> ### *New York Times* - August 31, 1864
>
> Rebel News
>
> MOSBY HANGING UNION MEN
>
> ### *Burlington Weekly Hawk Eye* - September 3, 1864
>
> Mosby has hanged thirty of our men in Virginia for burning guerrillas' houses.

[*] Black flag warfare meant that no quarter was given or expected in a battle. Prisoners taken were put to death. Mosby had never fought this kind of war until the incident in the Valley. However, as those prisoners executed had committed what were considered "war crimes," neither Mosby nor his men were charged with any violation of the rules of war. The response of Chapman in the Valley was not the same as Mosby's response to the hanging and shooting of his men at Front Royal and Flint Hill; that was *retaliation*, an accepted military response.

As happened every once in a while in the Yankee press, another little bit of wishful thinking made the papers:

> ### *The Press* – September 10, 1864
>
> They have nothing important from the Valley. Only an unauthentic report of the capture of Moseby, "the prince of guerilas," is given.

Apparently, the above article roused in some Southern organs concern about its possible truth, a concern that resulted in a story regarding the earlier story. This "feeding cycle" of the press had been—and would continue to be—an ongoing manifestation of the journalism of that time. In this instance, a Northern newspaper questioned the accuracy of a Southern report that had been taken from a Northern newspaper:

Evening Telegraph – September 10, 1864

Reported Capture of Moseby.

We have received files of Richmond papers to the 7th inst., which contain the following interesting news:

The Reported Capture of Moseby.

From the Richmond Examiner, September 7.

For several days a report has been going about to the effect that Moseby, our prince of guerillas, had been captured by the enemy. We have been unable to discover any foundation for the story, and think if it had been true, we should have heard it through the Northern papers, if not through other sources.

As September opened in the Valley, the *Army-Navy Journal* once again reported on the Berryville wagon train raid of August 13 under the heading of "The Retreat." The Journal did not mince words but called the operation a "disaster" for Sheridan and the Union war effort. Because it is one of the more accurate reports on this seminal operation, the article (with very little editing) is presented here:

Army-Navy Journal - September 10, 1864 (Edited)

The Retreat

Our plans for repossessing the Valley were now suddenly reversed by a rapid and skillful move of the enemy, and once more the 'same old tune' of retreat, so often heard in the Valley, was sounded. A glance at the map will show that our forces, in their forward march, had passed across several gaps in the mountain range which lay on their left flank. The most important of them are Snicker's Gap and Island Ford, - old and established guerrilla routes to and from the Valley, known as such from the outbreak of the war. Common prudence would have dictated the guarding of these gaps in our rear. But it seems that not even cavalry vidette was posted at either point. Through Snicker's Gap, accordingly, Mosby rode with his few light troops, on Saturday, the 13th, and completely surprised our supply train, which was at that time dragging its slow length along the road at Berryville, four miles from the Gap. It was on the way to Winchester. The attack was well managed, the head of the train being suffered to go by, and the enemy coming upon the rear. The train was guarded by Kenley's brigade of 100 days men, who were posted along the train in the customary disposition. At Mosby's charge, a part of the guard were panic-stricken. A few brave men fought as long as possible, while the rest took to their heels. The teams were unhitched, the wagons fired, and all the plunder possible was taken off to the Ferry. The chief loss was in the cavalry baggage. Mosby captured and destroyed 75 wagons, secured over 200 prisoners, 500 or

600 horses and mules, 200 beef cattle, and a few valuable stores. His loss was two killed and three wounded. Ours was a little greater, besides the prisoners.

This disaster in our rear caused great commotion.... The rest of the Army now came up and went into position near Berryville, and there for the present they remain. An ambulance train of 35 wagons which left the battlefield was captured by the ubiquitous Mosby.

At this point, Mosby was about to undertake his most important operation to date. He was ordered to stop the attempt by the Federals to rebuild the Manassas Gap Railroad. In late September, Grant had ordered Sheridan to take Charlottesville in order to cut the Virginia Central Railroad supplying Lee's army. Historian A. Wilson Green noted, "Once this was accomplished, Lee's supply routes would confront near-fatal constriction." But for Sheridan to obey, the Manassas Gap Railroad had to be reopened. Supplies for Sheridan's men and horses would then flow along two connecting railroads, greatly easing the supply situation and inhibiting Mosby's attacks on Federal supply lines as steam trains were more difficult to obstruct than wagon trains. But General Halleck warned on October 4 that to rebuild and keep the line open, they would have to clean out, in Halleck's words, "Mosby's gang of robbers who have so long infested that district of the country." And so in September 1864, John Mosby prepared to fulfill the order received from General Robert E. Lee: *"Do all in your power to prevent construction of the road."*

Though great events were soon to transpire, there seemed always to be time for another silly story or two about John Mosby, especially if his death could be "accurately reported":

West-Jersey Pioneer – September 17, 1864

Moseby's Death

The Richmond reports that this notorious guerrilla has been killed, seems to be true. He was captured in a skirmish, on the 2d of September, and in attempting to make his escape was shot by the sentinel. When captured he had no passants, stripes, stars, or insignia to designate his rank, but was recognized by a rebel deserter who viewed his remains. Nothing was found on his person which might not have belonged to a private in the rebel ranks, and doubts were expressed about his being Moseby, until his capture was reported in the Richmond papers a day or two since.

Burlington Free Press – September 23, 1864

It was currently reported in Washington, that Mosby was killed in a duel with one of his officers on Friday last.

If anyone doubts the spell that Mosby cast upon the newspapers, and especially those in the North, such articles as the above make clear that any little thing of interest about the man, true or false, found its way into print somewhere. The *Army-Navy Journal* then, supposedly, "set the record straight about the goings on in the Shenandoah Valley." Of course, not all was as the Journal *said* it was:

***Army-Navy Journal* - September 17, 1864 (Edited)**

The Shenandoah Valley

In order to comprehend the present position in the Valley, it will be necessary to review a little. The first advance of Sheridan to Strasburg was checked by the raid of Mosby on his rear on Saturday, the 13th of August, Preparations were made to retreat on the Monday following. The affair of Saturday had been represented by our papers rather contemptuously as a raid by "Mosby's gang." But, at all events, the "gang" accelerated the retreat of three Army corps, and the numerous cavalry brigades and artillery batteries which make up the Army of the Middle Department. Our Army in the Valley has acquired the humorous sobriquet of Harper's Weekly, from certain characteristics in its history which do not require the joke to be explained. On Monday night, the 15th, it being the familiar 'masterly retreat' to Harper's Ferry, the Nineteenth corps taking the lead towards Winchester. The reason of the retreat was the raid of Mosby's gang (otherwise known as 'Longstreet's entire corps') on the cavalry baggage wagons, the alleged arrival of those 'heavy reinforcements' which have so often 'just reached' Early, according to the reports, and which were pressing across the Shenandoah River, at Front Royal. ... The same night, our cavalry bivouacked at Berryville, and the next day, took up its retreat towards Harper's Ferry. 'Mosby's gang,' meanwhile, had been busy, as usual, on our flanks. On Monday night, he had boldly surprised and attacked the Fifth New York cavalry, just as it went into camp near Berryville, and killed two men, wounded several more, and captured about 20 horses. All the week Mosby's guerrillas – for whatever is done near the Potomac is at once laid to Mosby – were very active. On Tuesday and Wednesday, Lieutenant Walker and two men of the First cavalry were killed, and Lieutenant Gwyer of the Fifth, with several others were wounded by guerrillas between Charlestown and Berryville. On Thursday, some guerrillas in citizen's dress accosted an advanced post of the Fifth Michigan cavalry, picketing at Snicker's Gap, and while conversing, suddenly fired, killed the corporal captured two men, and hastily escaped. Several other soldiers were wounded or taken prisoners under like circumstances, the same day and next. On Friday, General Custer ordered a detachment of the Fifth Michigan to destroy some houses of disloyal citizens in retaliation. While so engaged, the squad was charged upon by Mosby's men in equal or superior numbers, and broke and fled in confusion. Many were overtaken, and, surrendering, were shot and either killed or left for dead. Ten men were instantly murdered after surrendering.

The claim of surrendered men being murdered was a reference to the home burners mentioned earlier. These men were not murdered but executed for a war crime. The idea that Mosby murdered Federal prisoners had started early on and continued as long as there were newspaper articles about John Mosby. But had this been true, he would not have survived the end of the war or found himself shielded by Grant.

Mosby's much-lauded luck ran out yet again when he was wounded in an encounter between himself, two Rangers, and five Federal soldiers sent by Colonel H. S. Gansevoort, who had heard that the guerrilla leader was at Piedmont. The five men met on the road, and in an exchange of gunfire, Mosby was wounded by a bullet that ricocheted into his left groin. His men supported him in the saddle until they reached a house where the wound could be treated, after which he returned to Lynchburg to recuperate. Needless to say, as had been the case with every Mosby wound to that point, it was well covered in the press with the usual caveats—that is, the Southern papers dismissed it as slight, while the Northern press had him dead or dying or permanently disabled:

Cleveland Morning Leader – September 21, 1864

The Alexandria, (Va.,) Journal says:

We learn through sources which cannot be discredited that Mosby has received a severe wound in the groin during a recent engagement between our forces and a small portion of his guerrilla band, in the vicinity of Centreville.

General Lee continued to shower praise on Mosby as can be seen in the *Richmond Dispatch* of September 27:

The Richmond Dispatch - September 27, 1864

Mosby's operations.

The following is a copy of General Lee's endorsement on Lieutenant-Colonel Mosby's report of his operations from the 1st of March to the 11th of September, 1864

"Headquarters army Northern Virginia," September 19, 1864.

—"Respectfully forwarded to the Adjutant and Inspector-General for the information of the department. Attention is invited to the activity and skill of Colonel Mosby, and the intelligence and courage of the officers and men of his command, as displayed in this report.

"With the loss of little more than twenty men, he has killed, wounded and captured, during the period embraced in this report, about twelve hundred of the enemy, and taken more than sixteen hundred horses and mules, two hundred and thirty beef cattle, and eighty-five wagons and ambulances, without counting many smaller operations. The services rendered by Colonel Mosby and his command in watching and reporting the enemy's movements have also been of great value. His operations have been highly creditable to himself and his command"

[Signed] R. E. Lee, General. "Official
John Blair Hoge,
"Major and Assistant Adjutant-General."

We hope that this high endorsement of Mosby's efficient action will not go unnoticed by the authorities. If any officer merits promotion, surely Colonel John S. Mosby is entitled to it.

Finally, the Yankee press decided it was time to put the story of Mosby's wound "to bed"; and if they could not kill him off, then they would "honorably retire" him whether he wished to retire or not. As usual, Elijah White was chosen by Northern pundits as his replacement:

Daily National Republican – October 3, 1864

Exit Mosby.—Mosby is so badly wounded that he has sent word to his villains that he never expects to lead them again. His command has devolved on Major White.

However, spurred by discord among his officers, John Mosby was forced to return to his command earlier than anticipated and was still so physically compromised by his groin wound that he had to be lifted into and out of the saddle. If that situation annoyed Mosby, it absolutely enraged the Yankee press:

Daily National Republican – October 7, 1864

Mosby Again in the Field.—We have positive information to-day that Mosby has so far recovered from his recent wound as to be able to again take to the saddle. The wound he received was only a flesh wound, and not near so serious as we had been led to believe. Certain it is he is again in command, and it will not be many days, we apprehend, before a reoccurrence of guerrilla depredations in the adjoining counties.

Mosby had now returned to his work against Sheridan. After a raid into Maryland with what the press assured its readers was "five hundred men" and a report that Mosby was riding in a carriage because of his recent wound, the paper then went on to assure the faithful that the guerrilla chief would not succeed because General Tyler was "already after him with sufficient force of artillery and cavalry." As such "sufficient force" had been sent after John Mosby many times without success, one wonders what the press hoped to prove by this contention.

Then work began in earnest by both sides on the Manassas Gap Railroad as the *Daily National Republican* reported:

Daily National Republican – October 11, 1864 (Edited)

GUERRILLA OUTRAGES ON THE MANASSAS GAP RAILROAD

Murder of Assistant Superintendent McCrickett

The Manassas Gap railroad has been repaired as far as Rectortown, and trains have recently run between Washington and Alexandria and at that point a much more serious guerrilla operation took place yesterday morning. The superintendent of the Manassas road had started on the way to Piedmont, or beyond that point, with two trains containing material for building the road. When a mile and a half the other side of White Plains, which is about fifty-eight miles from Washington, it was discovered that the track had been torn up and a party of guerrillas at once fired into the trains, killing Mr. J. McCrickett, the assistant superintendent, Edward J. Belt, the conductor, and ex-Lieut. Col. Fuller, formerly of the 16th Michigan, who had gone out on the train to acquire experience as a conductor. An engineer is also reported killed. Mr. Glascott, the agent, and a number of others are wounded. After executing their murderous work, the guerrillas fled.

Is it not time that our policy towards the murders who infest the region known as "Mosby's Department" was changed? It seems to us that a dose like that administered by Sheridan in the Valley would have a beneficial effect upon the guerrilla population that has been allowed to live within our lines diversifying their ostensible employment as farmers with raids, robberies and murders. It would have cost the Government infinitely less in blood and treasure to have removed every family and destroyed every habitation in that region, even if we had been compelled to support those families at the North, that it has to allow them to remain upon the soil.

It is interesting to note that Mosby's attacks on a *military* line were called atrocities while use of noncombatants by Federal forces to shield their military trains, a crime according to their own Code of War, went without comment.

Cleveland Morning Leader – October 12, 1864

The Richmond Whig, of yesterday morning, says official a dispatch received yesterday at the War Department states that a body of about a thousand of the enemy advanced upon the Manassas Gap Railroad on the fourth, with trains of cars loaded with rail road material and occupied Salem and Rectortown. Col. Mosby attacked them at Salem, defeating them, capturing fifty prisoners, all their baggage, camp equipage, stores &c., and killed and wounded a considerable number. His loss was only two wounded.

While the other newspapers focused on the derailing and the death of those on board the train, the *Cleveland Leader* covered the *real* story, and that was Mosby's attack on the men that had come to rebuild the railroad at Salem. On October 3rd, Mosby's scouts discovered two thousand Federal troops under Colonel George S. Gallupe rebuilding the roadbed, and Mosby began a systematic campaign against this effort. On October 5th, he attacked at Salem midway between the Plains and Rectortown, placing two cannons on a hill south of the town. The assault opened with a terrific outburst of both large and small arms fire, followed by a mounted attack. Federal guards and workmen incontinently fled toward Rectortown in panic and confusion, littering their route with weapons, tools, and clothing. Lee promptly commended Mosby: "Your success at Salem gives great satisfaction." His victory in this operation was absolute and roused the Federals to fury, but, surprisingly, the matter received very little press coverage. The report of the derailing of the train that came a few days later was a matter of salt in an already open wound.

Yorkville Enquirer – October 13, 1864

Mosby at Work Again

Richmond, October 9.—An official dispatch to the War Department states that the enemy, one thousand strong, advanced up the Manassas Gap Road, on the 4th, with trains of cars loaded with railroad material, and occupied Salem and Rectortown.

Mosby attacked them at Salem, capturing fifty prisoners, all their camp equipage, baggage, stores, and he killed and wounded a considerable number. His loss was two wounded.

But Mosby was about to pull one of his greatest coups against Sheridan. That general had claimed that a main Union rail line, the Baltimore and Ohio, was safe from Mosby's depredations. Whether that was the goad that caused the partisan to consider an attack on the B&O is not known. Mosby stated much later that he wanted to reward those men with him on a skirmish in which he had been thrown from his horse and his foot trod upon. The outcome of the contest was in doubt, but when the Rangers saw their beloved commander in danger, they rallied and not only saved him but also won the day. Mosby sent one of his men into Baltimore for a railroad time-table and picked the desired target, a midnight express. It is probable that he knew that some of Sheridan's paymasters would be making the trip. The end result was what became known as "The Greenback Raid:"

The Press – October 15, 1864 (Edited)
MOSEBY'S GUERRILLAS

Rebel Guerilla Raid on the Baltimore and Ohio Railroad.

Baltimore, Oct. 14.—A party of guerillas captured the Western-bound train last night, on the Baltimore and Ohio Railroad, robbed the passengers, and burned the cars. No other particulars have been received

THE ATTACK ON THE BALTIMORE AND OHIO RAILROAD.

Baltimore, Oct. 14.—On Thursday night the express passenger train for Wheeling, left the Camden station at 9:15, with the U.S. mails, Adams & Co.'s express car, and 200 passengers, under the charge of Conductor Shutt The passengers were considerably alarmed, and were soon informed of the real state of affairs, for the rebel Moseby appeared, accompanied by a mounted force estimated at from 100 to 200, who commenced robbing the passengers, among whom was Mr. Louis M. Cole, general ticket agent of the company, who was proceeding West on important business. From him they took all he had—namely, $19 and a gold watch. After the thieves had completed their depredations they ordered all the passengers out of the train, and after burning the train, remounted and dashed off. The burned cars contained the body of a soldier's remains on their way to his relatives. The contents of the mail are not known. None of the employees of the company were injured except the engineer and fireman, who are reported to be badly scalded.Detachments of cavalry are in pursuit of the guerillas, but no tidings have yet been heard from them.

After Sheridan's boast that the B&O was "safe" from Mosby, the press—North and South—was happy to carry the story of Little Phil's humiliation. Sheridan was not liked by the press:

Evening Star – October 15, 1864

Daily National Republican – October 15, 1864
Raid on the Baltimore and Ohio Railroad—Train of Cars Destroyed.

The Press – October 17, 1864
Moseby's Raid on the Baltimore and Ohio Road – Description of the Captured Train – All the Cars but Three Burned by the Rebels – The Trains Now Running As usual.

Daily Dispatch, – October 18, 1864
BRILLIANT DASH OF MOSBY—A TRAIN CAPTURED WITH TWO HUNDRED THOUSAND DOLLARS IN GREENBACKS—OTHER MOVEMENTS.

These were only a few of the stories about this raid; and in fact, it became another of Mosby's operations, as with his Fairfax Court House raid and the unfortunate "Death Lottery," which received press coverage from then until now.

On October 9th, the first report was found in the papers in both sections on the execution of Mosby's men at Front Royal:

Camden Daily Journal – October 19, 1864 (Edited)

Murder of Confederate Soldiers and Citizens at Front Royal.

The Richmond Sentinel has received from a gentleman, who was an eye-witness of the atrocious acts of the Federal troops at Front Royal, the following particulars of the affair . . A party of Mosby's men under the command of Capt. Chapman, annoyed the enemy very much on their return to Front Royal, which with the mortification of their defeat by Wickham, excited in them such savage feelings as to prompt them to murder six of our men who fell into their hands. Anderson, Overby, Love and Rhodes were shot, and Carter and one other, whose name our informant did not recollect, were hung to the limb of a tree at the entrance of the village, with a card attached to the bodies, threatening with hanging on the same limb any one who should remove the corpses from the tree. Henry Rhodes was a quiet youth, living with is widowed mother, and supporting her by his labor. He did not belong to Mosby's command. His mother entreated them to spare the life of her son, and treat him as a prisoner of war, but the demons answered by whetting their sabres on stones, and declaring they would cut off his head and hers if she came near.—They ended by shooting him in her very presence.

The murders were committed on the 22d of Sept., Gens. Torbert, Merritt and Custer being present. It is said that Torbert and Merritt turned the prisoners over to Custer for their fate, who ordered the execution.

Carter, one of the two that were hung, died the death of a brave man, defying his executioners, and threatening them with tenfold vengeance of his comrades. If either of the three generals in command on that day, who are responsible for these brutal massacres should be captured, his immediate execution by hanging would meet the demand of justice and the approval of the people.

The *Richmond Dispatch* made note of the demands by various captains on the Chesapeake and Ohio Canal for protection by the Federal military from Mosby, who apparently was not averse to adding naval engagements to his stock-in-trade:

The Richmond Dispatch - October 22, 1864

The superintendent of the Chesapeake and Ohio canal, in a letter dated at Point of Rocks, Maryland, says Mosby made a raid on the boats on Saturday, capturing and burning four or five and carrying away many mules and horses and some prisoners.—Many boats are there, but will not move until something be done by the military authorities for their protection.

Mention was made once again of the murder of Mosby's men at Front Royal along with some other matters of the time. It is interesting to note that this subject appeared not in a Southern paper, but in the *New York Herald*:

New York Herald - October 25, 1864 (Edited)

The Terrible Mosby – The Hanging of His Men at Front Royal. [Correspondence of the Richmond Enquirer, October 22]

Edge Hill Near Upperville Fauquier County, Oct. 11, 1864

Since my last, the Yankees having gallantly marched in and disputed Mosby's right to rule his confederacy, your correspondent has been so continuously and closely engaged as to have little time for indicting epistolary communications. At the time of the invasion Colonel Mosby was somewhere in your confederacy having his wound attended to, and, though hardly able to walk or ride, he hurried to his command and at once informed Gen. Gallop [sic] (the Yankee General in command) that he had fought and bled for that portion of Virginia, and could not think of disposing of it on such reasonable terms, which assurance you will hereafter learn he has fully supported. During his short absence the battalion has been under the command of Captain W. H. Chapman, who, with a portion of his force, attacked a cavalry camp of the enemy near Front Royal and succeeded in routing them completely, capturing their entire camp, when the Yankees being suddenly and heavily reinforced, he was compelled to withdraw, not, however, without leaving the ground strewn with their dead and wounded, but, up to this time, without the loss of a man; but, unfortunately, several of his men having had their horses killed, fell into the hands of the enemy who cowardly beat them with sabers and tortured them in every possible way for hours and finally hung them in the streets of Front Royal, with orders to the citizens that if they should be taken down within three days, the whole community would be hung, and the village burnt. Very fortunately the battalion were able to chalk the command who treated their comrades with such brutal inhumanity and will take occasion to return the same with interest at the earliest opportunity, having long since ceased to look to their government for protection.

On the night of the 6th of October, Mosby attacked General Gallop in camp near Rectortown, and after a desperate fight succeeded in routing him completely, capturing his entire camp together with a train of cars heavily laden with commissary stores, also all of the utensils with which he was rebuilding the railroad, tore up the railroad for six miles, and brought off seventy prisoners…From the 1st of January to the 1st of October, by a minute calculation, Mosby had killed and captured sixty-nine Yankees for every man he had lost.

The most important point made by this article was in the last paragraph. If, in fact, the war devolved into "black flag" combat, Mosby would win simply because far more Yankees came under his hand than his men under Sheridan's.

And still, more about Mosby was appearing in the papers as the war being waged by and against him became more furious. Mention was made of the capture of Union General Alfred N. Duffie. Duffie had volunteered to capture Mosby and became his prisoner instead. Because the man had used somewhat "intemperate" language regarding the partisan chief's fate when he "inevitably fell into his (Duffie's) hands," that general was most concerned about his *own* fate when the matter was reversed. But Mosby, as was his way, simply sent the man on to Richmond as a prisoner of war:

> ***Daily Dispatch* – October 28, 1864**
> MOSBY AT WORK
>
> Mosby, on Wednesday, attacked a federal supply train at Bunker Hill, on the turnpike leading from Martinsburg to Winchester. He found it guarded by a strong party of Federals on whom he made a sudden attack, dismounting them and killing a number. Among the slain is said to be one Brigadier General Duffie. The Yankees outnumbering our men very largely, Mosby was unable to destroy the train, and finally withdrew his troops.

A decision had been made by the Federals in the Valley to put Southern civilians on the trains to discourage attacks by Mosby, but they soon discovered that such barbaric usage of non-combatants would not dissuade the guerrilla chief from the performance of his duty as was pointed out here:

> ***The Richmond Dispatch* - October 31, 1864**
>
> From the vicinity of Manassas Gap railroad.
>
> Additional accounts from this section describe the enemy as reiterating the scenes of the Valley of Virginia — burning both houses and barns, capturing the citizens and forcing them to ride on the railroad cars to prevent Mosby's firing into the trains.
>
> They need not, however, lay this flattering unction to their souls, for Mosby knows very well how to foil them; and, indeed, any one who knows the ways of this uncompromising partisan, will vouch for it, that if Colonel Mosby knew that all who were dear to him were on a train, he would not, on that account, hesitate to attack it, provided he were assured that the good of his country demanded the sacrifice.

Of course, the spate of atrocity tales now began in earnest, including a claim that Duffie had been murdered based upon an erroneous report in the *Dispatch*. Of course, most of these horror stories were believed by Northern readers, who had made of John Singleton Mosby the most hated Southerner in the war, bar none. Not even Davis or Wirz of Andersonville was as hated as John Mosby, a matter that did not bode well for him as the future of the Confederacy became more and more dire:

> ***Cleveland Morning Leader* – November 1, 1864**
>
> ***Janesville Weekly Gazette* – November 4, 1864**
> SOUTHERN NEWS
>
> New York, Oct. 31.
>
> The Richmond Enquirer of Friday contains the following:
>
> Official news comes to hand of an attack by Mosby upon a heavily guarded wagon train of the enemy near Bunker Hill, in which, although unable to

bring off any booty on account of the heavy guard which attended it, killed one General, captured and killed several others, and made good his retreat.

Our readers will remember that Gen. Duffie was captured and seen alive and well afterward by a prisoner who escaped. If dead, as the above rebel dispatch asserts, he was murdered in cold blood.

The Richmond papers gave notice a few days since, that Mosby would stretch to trees any Yankee prisoners whom he might take, in retaliation for the murder of several of his men. General Duffie was the son of the Rev. Dr. Duffield, the Presbyterian divine of Detroit, and entered the service at the first outbreak of the rebellion.

Camden Daily Journal – **November 11, 1864**

The Black Flag.—The Richmond correspondent of The Appeal says:

The black flag has at last been raised openly in the lower Valley, where Mosby ranges. War in the knife has been declared against him by Auger and Sheridan, and he gives them as good as they send. You will hear ere long of men being flayed alive and burnt at the stake, or I am much mistaken.

And so the effort to rebuild the Manassas Gap Railroad, begun with a "bang," ended with a "whimper"; and there can be no doubt who was responsible for Grant's grand strategy failing miserably:

Richmond Dispatch - **November 15, 1864**

The Yankees on the Manassas Gap railroad—Mosby's operations.

An official dispatch, received at the War Department yesterday, states that the enemy are removing the rails from the Manassas Gap to the Winchester railroad, and that since the enemy occupied the Manassas road he (Mosby) had killed, wounded and captured over six hundred of their men, and captured an equal number of their horses.

This short announcement of the end of the effort to rebuild the road should have been given *much* greater coverage by the Southern press. Alone against the entire might of the Army of the Potomac, Mosby and his small command had prevented the road's reconstruction and, as a result, prevented the defeat of Lee and the fall of Richmond in the fall of 1864. No other Confederate forces, including other partisan commands, were engaged.

The next story of interest in late 1864 was the defeat of Captain Richard Blazer's guerrilla hunters. Sheridan had created the command to get Mosby, but Mosby got Blazer. Blazer knew that Mosby's men were in the area, but he thought that they were attempting to flee and so pressed his advantage—*and* his luck. The coverage was fairly heavy, but really, about all that had to be said was contained in a dispatch dated November 19 sent from General Stevenson to General Forsythe:

"Two of Captain Blazer's men came in this morning, privates Harris and Johnson. They report that Mosby attacked Blazer near Kabletown yesterday about eleven o'clock. They say the entire Command with the exception of themselves was either captured or killed."

November ended, and December passed with the usual articles about Mosby's activities, praised in the Southern papers and damned in the Northern. The Blazer matter was rehashed, and there was even a "first person" account of being captured by Mosby, leading to a "first person" account of the Death Lottery by one Captain Brewster. Indeed, the good captain made a cottage industry out of recounting the affair for years until his death as an old man, at which time his good widow swore that her dear husband never talked about the sad event.

On December 21, the *Daily National Republican* reported another raid into Mosby's department. Little did the paper know at the time that this was rather a momentous announcement, for on December 24, the first report came of another wounding of John Mosby:

Cleveland Morning Leader – December 24, 1864

The Herald's Washington special says:

Mosby was wounded a few days since in a reconnaissance towards Aldie. He received a pistol ball in his mouth, which passed through the back part of the jaw, and another in the abdomen inflicting a severe wound.

The Richmond Examiner says he was only wounded in the thigh, and would soon be in the saddle again.

But the originally dismissive attitude could not last, and within days both the *Dispatch* in Richmond and the *Evening Star* in Washington reported a story that horrified the South and thrilled the North:

Richmond Dispatch - December 27, 1864
Evening Star – December 30, 1864

Colonel Mosby reported killed.

It was reported on the streets yesterday that the daring and distinguished guerrilla chief, Colonel John S. Mosby, had been killed by the enemy. The story was that he had been surrounded while dining at the house of a friend in Culpeper and ordered to surrender; that he drew his pistol and fired upon the enemy, when he was shot dead. But a telegram from Fredericksburg, dated the 25th, was received yesterday morning, which contradicted the report of his death, stating that he had been shot, but not mortally wounded, and was in the hands of his friends. The question of his condition is, however, not yet definitely ascertained.

A gentleman who reached here yesterday from Fredericksburg, learned there, from two of Colonel Mosby's men, that their chief was shot through the abdomen while scouting in Prince William county. They further stated that the surgeon did not consider the wound mortal, though they themselves thought differently. This, we are disposed to believe, is the correct rumor of the lamentable casualty; but it will be observed that the *New York Tribune*, quoted elsewhere, locates the shooting in the neighborhood of Piedmont, on the Baltimore and Ohio railroad.

We heard last night that Colonel Mosby had been carried to Charlottesville.

A dispatch from Washington, under the heading of "Mosby killed once more," says: The pleasant intelligence that the pest Mosby was shot yesterday morning near Piedmont and killed was brought here to-night by a soldier.

In the *Evening Star* alone:

The Wounding of Mosby.

It was reported last evening that Colonel Mosby had been very seriously wounded in an encounter with the enemy in Prince William county. He is said to have been shot through the body.

We could obtain no particulars of the affair; but as a raiding party of the enemy, composed of whites and negroes, were in Dumfries on Wednesday, it is probable that Mosby encountered them on their return to Alexandria.

And thus began weeks of reports, speculations, declarations, and perturbations across the newspapers of both sections. Indeed, it wasn't very different from past coverage of a Mosby wounding save that, in this case, the wound was every bit as serious and his condition and situation every bit as dangerous and dire as the worst of the reports except for those declaring him dead. The *Camden Daily Journal* was the first to report that he had been wounded "dangerously but not fatally" and that he was "in our hands and well cared for." And then came the deluge:

Camden Daily Journal – December 28, 1864

New York Herald – December 30, 1864

THE FATE OF MOSBY

Death of the Notorious Pirate of the Valley

The Rebel papers Acknowledge His Mortal Wounding

Daily National Republican - December 30, 1864

MOSBY DEAD

THE REBEL PAPERS ACKNOWLEDGE IT.

Richmond Dispatch - December 31, 1864

The wounding of Colonel Mosby.

—The Lynchburg Republican gives the following particulars of the wounding of Colonel Mosby:

"The gallant partizan chief, Colonel John S. Mosby, was severely, though not dangerously, wounded on Thursday night last in Prince William county. He had started on one of his daring expeditions, and stopped at the house of a friend, with three or four of his men, to get supper. While engaged at his meal, a party of the enemy came up and fired through the windows, one of the balls striking Mosby in the abdomen, but, fortunately, without penetrating, ranged around and came out just above and back of the hip. The enemy then rushed into the house, but the lady whose guest he was, with ready presence of mind, cut off the stars from his coat collar, which indicated his rank, before they got in the room, and upon inquiring who it was they had shot, were told that it was 'one of Mosby's lieutenants.' They examined his wound, and thinking from the direction of the ball that it was mortal, left him where he was, remarking that the 'd — d thief would do his master no more service.' They then decamped, and as soon as they were out of reach, Mosby was removed to a place of safety, where he is kindly cared for, and we hope sincerely will rapidly recover."

John Mosby had survived his most serious wound. There are those who have suggested that perhaps it would have been better for him had he not done so but such a supposition is wrong. First, his enemies would have "conquered" him personally by bringing him down to the grave as they did Stuart, Pelham, Morgan, and Jones. What is even more important, however, is that John Mosby as a man was so much more than just a soldier—even a *great* soldier—something to which the rest of his life attested.

Chapter 5

1865

Unaquaeque optio exitum habet. ~ Every choice has consequences.

"The oak fought the wind and was broken, the willow bent when it must and survived." ~ Robert Jordan

JOHN MOSBY HAD been seriously wounded on December 21, 1864. He had survived the wound and been conveyed in an open oxcart a distance of two miles over rutted, iron-hard ground to the home of Quilly Glasscock. Mrs. Glasscock had a son in the Rangers, and another Ranger boarded with her, so it was deemed that Mosby would be safe—for a short time at least. The night had been horrendous—a high wind with freezing sleet punished the badly injured man as he lay, suffering, in a mean cart clothed only in a shirt, socks, and drawers and covered by a thin quilt for protection against the tempest. Mosby later recalled that by the time he reached "safety," his beard and hair were clotted with ice. It was in this frigid weather that, after the removal of the bullet on the next day, he was eventually conveyed in short stages back across Confederate lines. Though little has been written of this ordeal, nor is it actually known how long it took Mosby to reach the Confederate lines during which time he was fiercely hunted by every Yankee—military and civilian—in the area. But as 1865 dawned, the weather in Virginia only got worse, presaging a state of affairs in the South that encompassed far more than the elements.

Meanwhile, the newspapers, of course, continued to speculate upon Mosby's situation. Southern papers assured their readerships that he indeed lived and would return to the saddle once more. Whether they actually believed at least the latter claim is not known. The Northern papers, on the other hand, tended to take a much more optimistic view of the matter at least in their opinion:

> *Daily Dispatch* – **January 3, 1865**
>
> RECOVERING.—We are highly gratified to learn from an authentic source that Colonel Mosby is rapidly recovering from his wound, and in a short time will be in the saddle again.—Lynchburg (Va.) Republican.
>
> *New York Times* - **January 1, 1865**
>
> From Sheridan's Army - Rumored Death of Mosby
>
> Several of Mosby's men captured on this expedition, assert that Mosby was shot and mortally wounded a few days ago at Rector's Cross-roads, by a trooper from the Department of Washington. He was eating dinner at the time the shot was fired, the ball passing through his heart. Running into the yard he was shot again through the bowels; and the man who fired this shot pulled off Mosby's boots—he wore a very nice pair—but the man did not know who he was at the time. This report is confirmed by citizens and negroes, so the officers say, in the vicinity of where the transaction occurred, and simultaneously comes a published report from Washington, that the notorious guerrilla chief has at last met the fate he so richly deserved. I state the facts and circumstances as reported to me,

without giving any opinion in relation to the matter, only that the officers of the different brigades make the same reports, and they believe that Mosby is really dead.

As was the usual manner of such things, the Northern press began its expositions on the "dead" guerrilla. Although Mosby was a man that the people of the North hated, the simple fact is that he fascinated them as well. There is an old adage in the entertainment industry that any publicity is good, even when it is bad. The same thing applied to Mosby. The more people hated him, the more they wanted to know about him, to read about him, and to learn all that they could about him. If all of this included the belief that he had been killed, so much the better:

Evening Star – **January 4, 1865**

A Sketch of Mosby, the Rebel Guerrilla Chief.

Soon, however, articles began to appear even in the Northern press—short in length and disappointed in tone—admitting John Mosby wasn't so very dead after all:

Gallipolis Journal – **January 5th, 1865**

Village Record – **January 6, 1865**

Daily Intelligencer – **January 6, 1865**

Perhaps the best example of this sort of exasperation appeared in a very long article carried by the New York Herald on the last day of December 1864 and the Evening Star on January 4, 1865. The article began with comments about the man that were more than ordinarily nasty:

New York Herald – **December 31, 1864 (Edited)**

Evening Star – **January 4, 1865**

Sketch of the Rebel Guerrilla Mosby

It will be seen from the rebel extracts which we give that the rumor of the wounding of Mosby which we published yesterday morning, proves to be true. Like Morgan, Anderson and other guerillas of like character, Mosby has met with a dog's death. His career, like theirs, has been short and inglorious. He added nothing to the cause of the rebellion by his conquests. He has only served to disgrace the country and degrade the profession of arms...

It then went on in depth on various matters already covered in earlier articles except to claim that he was "an Irishman by birth" and that he "swears a great deal and does not ... treat his men kindly." The article then described Mosby's wife, Pauline (whom they did not mention by name), as a "middle-aged woman, and rather handsome," followed by the comment that "Mosby is with her often." This glorious recitation of "error elevated to legendary proportions" ended with the following: "if we are to believe the rebel stories, Mosby is not yet dead. He may possibly recover; *'the devil takes care of his own.'* [emphasis vph]"

But for all of the vitriol directed at Mosby by the Northern press, the *Army-Navy Journal*, an obviously *military* publication, opined in a much different manner about the man, naming him "the great guerrilla leader." It is evident that Mosby's genius was not lost on those who understood the subject no matter on which side they fought:

Army-Navy Journal - **January 7, 1865**

The principal news from the Shenandoah Valley is the wounding of the great guerrilla leader Mosby. An expedition consisting of the Thirteenth and Sixteenth New York and the Eighth Illinois cavalry started on the 17th, to scout the east side of the Blue Ridge. Next day, Captain Taylor's company of the Thirteenth New York surrounded a house near Middleburgh when a man fired through the window at Corporal Kane. The latter returned it, and dangerously wounded the other. It was Mosby, who had supposed himself discovered. Our men left the wounded man, without learning that it was Mosby. At last accounts, he was alive, though in a dangerous condition at Fredericksburg. ...

In the midst of news' speculations regarding Mosby's health, a very problematic story appeared in the *New York Herald*, a story that held significant danger for Mosby as the war progressed toward its inevitable close:

New York Herald – **January 8, 1865 (Edited)**
SHENANDOAH

The New Guerrilla Programme in the Valley, &c., &c., &c.

Systemizing Guerrilla Warfare.

On my late trip with or cavalry raid to Gordonsville, I made special inquiry in regard to the movements of the guerrilla bands which now infest the counties we passed through. It appears that Mosby's late visit to Richmond was at the suggestion of Jeff. Davis, to confer with his "Excellency" on the reorganization of the guerrilla bands of Eastern Virginia. The conference was had, Mosby was to receive the rank of brigadier general at the proper time. Fauquier county was to be the great rendezvous of the rebel bandits. Mosby's command was to be raised to the maximum of eight battalions of four companies, and then divided, as to the necessities of the service required, into smaller detachments. A system of mountain signal stations was to be arranged, and the headquarters of the bands to be located in mountain fastnesses, secure from surprise or easy attack from our troops. The watchword of this organization was to be "No quarter to the Yankees" —no quarter under any pretense—no prisoners to be captured—"murder! murder!" was to be the cry.

It was on his mission to execute this bloody programme that Mosby was going when the avenging hand of Providence, through the medium of a Yankee bullet, by the instrumentality of Corporal Kane, of the Thirteenth New York cavalry, brought him down to the verge of the grave. Whether he recovers or dies, the facts I have briefly related should command the attention of the military authorities. Certain it is the men and women of at least one county (Fauquier) have endorsed the new system. There is but one remedy where people have determined upon such diabolism, and that is to smoke them out and drive them with fire and sword until not a vestige of them or their places remain to blot the fair face of the earth. It would be a righteous judgment to people so confessedly abandoned to all the instincts of humanity and civilization.

As the accounts of Mosby's health were confused and confusing, the press started to address efforts put forth by the Federal army to recapture him or at least retrieve his body and put an end to the speculation. And finally, there were countless reiterations of his wounding—none of which were accurate. In a Southern publication, there appeared an account of the brutal treatment afforded the wounded and helpless man at the hands of his fiendish captors. This account was no more accurate than those of Mosby's treatment of his prisoners appearing in Northern newspapers:

Daily Dispatch – January 10, 1865
LOOKING FOR MOSBY.

A dispatch from Washington, dated the 5th instant, announces the failure of a scout for Mosby. It says:

A scout set out, last week, to look for Mosby, under command of Major Frazer. They proceeded to Mr. Lake's house, where Mosby was wounded, near Rector's cross-roads, and learned that he was moved, within half an hour after he was wounded, to Mr. Glasscock's, about one and a half miles distant, where he remained three days. The ball was there extracted, having passed round, or perhaps, through his bowels, coming out behind the right thigh. The Major conversed with persons who saw him. He was reported very low the first two days, but better the third. He was then tracked to Piedmont, and from thence to Salem, and out of Salem towards the Warrenton pike.

Several persons who saw him in the ambulance report his spitting blood, and the belief that he cannot live seems to be general. He is probably concealed in the country, seriously if not fatally, injured. A farmer who saw him last Sunday said he was not expected to live.

New York Herald – January 11, 1865 (Edited)
MOSBY STILL ALIVE

Mosby Redivivus

CIRCUMSTANCES OF HIS WOUNDING AND ESCAPE.

(From the Richmond Sentinel, Jan. 7)

Several premature reports have gained currency of the escape of Colonel Mosby from the vicinity of the enemy, after receiving his wound on the 21st December. Some of them were put out through policy, others through mistake. We have the gratification of announcing now, on the authority of one who attended him in his journey, that the gallant Colonel has, within the last three days, reached a place of safety and repose. His situation on the lines has been very hazardous, from the slow movement and the care which his wound required and from the diligent search made for him by the enemy – no less than three hunting parties having endeavored to find him. At one time, they were nearly upon him, and his escape seemed very improbable. It would be indiscreet to describe, as we should like to do, and have the means of doing, the adventures of those critical days The ball entered just under the ends of the ribs, on the left side, and passed out at a similar point on the right side, without wounding the bowels. He walked into a room and lay down. The Yankees rolled him over and examined his wound, declaring that it was mortal, in which opinion Colonel Mosby expressed his concurrence. They robbed him of his hat, his trousers, his overcoat, and his boots. Officers of a rank as high as Major were engaged in this stripping of a dying man. A Yankee letter writer coolly says: "Some of the men proposed finishing the rebel, but Captain Taylor, having examined the nature of his wound, pronounced it mortal. Major Frazer, Thirteenth New York cavalry, also examined the wound, and declared that the man would die."

According to this confession, nothing prevented the murder of a prisoner but the conviction that it was unnecessary. They did not know who Colonel M. was, but accepted his statement that he was an officer of the Sixth cavalry.

Shortly thereafter, articles began emerging in especially the *Army-Navy Journal* containing official reports regarding the events of December 21:

Army-Navy Journal - January 14, 1865 (Edited)

The Wounding of Mosby

The Union Version.

Colonel W. Gamble, commanding cavalry brigade: -

Colonel – In obedience to your command, I have the honor herewith to report what I know concerning the wounding of Colonel Mosby. [The matter was then presented at considerable length and appeared under the signature below:-vph]

Very respectfully, your obedient servant
Douglas Fraser
Major Thirteenth New York cavalry
Fairfax Court House December 31, 1864

Aside from an article in the *Illustrated London News* containing an etching of Mosby meeting with his men in the mountain passes above the Shenandoah River, news coverage continued on his wounding along with brief reviews of the engagements of his command. Such coverage of actual attacks by the Forty-third always ended with speculations on Mosby's recovery or lack thereof until the *Daily Dispatch* printed a short article on the guerrilla chief's reception in Richmond and an even shorter article in the *Cleveland Morning Leader* and the *Vermont Transcript* announcing that Mosby would be returning to his command by the first of February:

Cleveland Morning Leader – February 1, 1865

GEN. MOSBY'S WOUND NEARLY HEALED.

The Lynchburg Virginian says: Mosby will be in the saddle again by the first of February, his wound being nearly healed.

Vermont Transcript – February 10, 1865

—The only item of interest from the Shenandoah valley is the announcement that the guerilla Mosby, who has been killed any number of times, but is not dead yet, is nearly well of his wounds, and will soon be ready for the saddle again.

March saw another victory by Mosby's men, now led by their commander who had in fact returned. But more important was the mention of the possibility of the war being continued after the collapse of the Confederate regular military. Few in the South believed that they could hold out much longer against the might of the Federal behemoth. Indeed, it was Lee's intention to slip away from Petersburg and join Johnston, but when that option was eliminated, he contacted General Ulysses Grant to arrange for the surrender of his army. Meanwhile, the idea of a protracted guerrilla war was being considered by many on both sides, including Mosby. Given that after Appomattox, Mosby sent Channing Smith to speak with Lee (then in Richmond) to ask if he, Mosby, should fight on, it is probable that had Lee said yes, Mosby would have done so:

Wyandot Pioneer – March 1, 1865

The Herald's correspondent say a party of Sheridan's cavalry, consisting of 125 men, of the 14th Pennsylvania, went up the valley of the Shenandoah the other day, on a scouting expedition, and while on their return fell into an ambuscade prepared by Mosby's men, and a terrible fight ensued; but the guerrillas were so numerous and so strongly fortified that our cavalry were roughly handled, and only made good their retreat after losing a number of killed and wounded and some sixty taken prisoners.—Captain Coffinger, of General Torbett's staff was captured.

In the same paper:

The Richmond Sentinel, of the 15th, has an article in which it says submission will not bring peace nor inaugurate a truce; the rebels will take to the bush, and carry on a guerrilla warfare. It is very severe on submissionists, who appear to still exist, notwithstanding the late firing of the Southern heart.

And then it was over—and John Mosby found himself in the most unenviable position of any Southern soldier with the possible exception of Captain Henry Wirz. Wirz, the commandant of Andersonville, was doomed—as, in fact, was John Mosby. There had been a glimmer of hope for him when Ulysses Grant paroled all the soldiers of the Army of Northern Virginia, *including* Mosby and the men of the Forty-third. However, that hope was dashed when Secretary of War Edwin Stanton revoked Grant's parole to Mosby alone and declared him an outlaw. This situation was made public in federal dispatches carried in the Northern press. Of course, it is necessary to remember that upon the surrender of Lee and the fall of the Confederate government, there no longer was, for all intents and purposes, a "Southern press":

Evening Star – April 12, 1865 (Edited)

Daily National Republican – April 14, 1865

Gen. Hancock's Notification to Stragglers in the Valley

Major General Hancock announces the surrender of Lee and his army to the people living in his Department, and says that all stragglers from the Army of Northern Virginia who comply with the terms of Lee's surrender will be permitted to return to their homes, and those who do not surrender will be considered as prisoners of war. He does not include the notorious Mosby in this parole. The following is General Hancock's order: HEADQUARTERS MIDDLE MILITARY. DIVISON,

WINCHESTER, VA., APRIL 10, 1865.

The Major General Commanding announces to the citizens in the vicinity of his lines that General Robert E. Lee surrendered with the Army of Northern Virginia yesterday to Lieutenant General Grant near Appomattox Court-House The Major General Commancing trusts that the people to whom this is sent will regard the surrender of General Lee with his army as Lee himself regards it, as the first great step to peace, and will adapt their conduct to the new condition of affairs and make it practicable for him to exhibit towards them every leniency the situation will admit of. Every military restraint shall be removed that is not absolutely essential, and your sons, your husbands and your brothers shall remain with you unmolested.

It is for you to determine the amount of freedom you are to enjoy. The marauding bands which have so long infested this section, subsisting on the plunder of the defenseless, effecting no great military purpose, and bringing upon you the devastation of your homes, must no longer find shelter and concealment among you. Every outrage committed by them will be followed by the severest infliction, and it is the purpose of the Major General Commanding to destroy entirely the haunts of these bands, if their depredations are continued.

W. S. Hancock

Maj. Gen. U. S. Vol.

Official: Geo. Lee, Asst. Adj't Gen.

The Virginia Guerrillas—What Shall be Done With Them?

Now, that the largest part of Virginia, if not the whole, is within the lines of our armies, it behooves the Government to clear the country between Washington and Richmond and on the Peninsula of guerrillas. A scoundrelly set of robbers and thieves infest this region, and prompt measures should be taken to put a stop to their raids upon farmers who desire to cultivate the country in peace. Some good squadrons of cavalry, well provided with hemp, ought to scour the country and decorate the trees with Mosby's men until the murderers and robbers are driven off or extirpated. A few examples would probably be sufficient to give peace and order to the agricultural districts where these cowardly scoundrels are now the terror of peaceable citizens.

Mosby, devastated upon learning of Lee's surrender, was at first not willing to quit the field. He did indeed say at that time that he would fight as long as he had a man with him; but as with so many other Southerners, when the first pain of defeat passed, he realized that he could not continue to fight at least in Virginia and determined to join General Joe Johnston if he still soldiered on. Mosby's passionate outburst, however, was reported in the *New York Times*:

New York Times - April 14, 1865

Mosby Does Not Recognize Lee's Surrender

Col. Gambel, commanding the Union forces at Fairfax Station, has received a message from Mosby in which the latter says he does not care about Lee's surrender, and that he is determined to fight so long as he has a man left.

The story of the Federal military dealings with John Mosby is well-known. He was sent a dispatch from General Winfield Hancock demanding his surrender upon the terms offered to Lee and the rest of the Army of Northern Virginia—though, of course, the dispatch made clear that he was not included in those terms. Mosby sent back a reply that he had no reason to surrender his command as the only information he had came from the enemy, and he needed time to determine what his government wanted him to do; he then asked for a period of truce. It is this truce that was misidentified as an offer to surrender and it continued to be so mis-identified even well after the war. It was no such thing:

Evening Star – April 17, 1865

MOSBY OFFERS TO SURRENDER.

Daily National Republican – April 17, 1865

EXTRA

Surrender of Mosby.

New York Herald – April 17, 1865

MOSBY VOLUNTEERS TO SURRENDER

The Press – April 18, 1865

MOSEBY OFFERS TO SURRENDER HIMSELF

The next story in the *Cleveland Morning Leader* presented Mosby's situation as it existed, especially after the assassination of Abraham Lincoln. Indeed, it was that act that prevented the Federal military from sending forty thousand troops to burn "Mosby's Confederacy" as they had burned the Shenandoah Valley! Mosby learned of that in his second meeting with General Chapman at Millwood and returned to Salem to disband rather than cause further harm to those who had succored him during the war:

Cleveland Morning Leader – April 21, 1865

The Surrender of Mosby.

A special to the New York Herald reports that the guerrilla leader Mosby has surrendered to our forces at Berryville, a small town in the Shenandoah Valley, ten miles east of Winchester. The term accorded to this notorious murderer and robber are said to be the same as those granted to Lee. If this be true the whole North will be stirred rather by indignation than by joy at the news. That this notorious gang of villains and cut-throats, whose deeds of violence and murder have filled the land with horror and made the name of Mosby infamous, should be left unwhipped of justice, should be permitted to return to the protection of the Union, and go back and settle among villages that they have burned, and by the side of homesteads which they have left in mourning is an outrage.

We do not now mean to discuss here the propriety of Grant's terms for the surrender of Lee's army. Everyone can see how great is the difference between the deluded soldiers of Lee's army and the plunderers and assassins that make up Mosby's band. Lee's soldiers fought honestly enough for what they believed their government—the sole object of Mosby's men was plunder. Lee's soldiers observed the rules of warfare—Mosby's men knew no restraint. Lee's soldiers could be chargeable only with armed resistance to the Union— Mosby's men added to that crime murder of defenseless women, children, and old men, the burning of unprotected homesteads, and indiscriminate robbery and pillage. In behalf of the Union refugees whom Mosby's gang have made homeless, in behalf of women whom they have ravished, and men whom they have murdered, we protest against amnesty to these traitors, thieves, incendiaries and assassins.

Another point of interest in the *Leader* article is the beginning of a theme that ran through the Yankee response to Mosby for pretty much the rest of his life; that is, Lee and *regular* Confederates, (though "deluded,") were worthy of at least respect, whereas Mosby was a plunderer and an assassin. That theme never changed. It is interesting to note, however, if the article ran on long enough, the writer would admit that he hated "regular Confederates" deluded or otherwise, only slightly less than he hated John Mosby.

After the disbanding, Mosby went off with some of his men—the number of whom has been debated—to seek and, if possible, join Joe Johnston. Upon learning that that general had also surrendered and that the war was indeed over, Mosby dismissed the men with him and went to seek his fate. He wrote very little about his actions or intentions of that period other than his belief that he had done nothing that would prevent him being offered the same parole as every other Confederate soldier.

During his period of outlawry, Mosby was hunted for a reward. There was even a claim that his own men were willing to bring him in alive, but not for the paltry sum of $2,000 offered by the government. This was probably the reward that had been fixed on Mosby during the war, though no actual date is mentioned as to when that occurred. After the disbanding, there were many articles in the Yankee press—now the *only* news accounts—that took especial delight in Mosby's situation, for by now, it was obvious that there was no safety for him anywhere. With the close of the war, all the ferocity and hatred of the North that had been directed at him could now be pursued unfettered by other military concerns while he, as an outlaw, had no relief in law or custom. This fact becomes very clear in an article in the *Franklin* (Pennsylvania) *Repository*, which presents a good gauge of the reaction of the Northern press to Mosby's plight:

Franklin Repository - May 10, 1865 (Edited)

Exit Mosby

John S. Mosby, who boasted the title of Confederate Colonel when convenient, and made all free-booters of the past respectable by his robberies of all classes and conditions of men and things, has faded out as a brigand chief and employed his heels to save his neck. For two years past he has been the pest of the border. He has committed more robberies, vacated more hen- roosts, emptied more stables and charged upon more larders than any other guerrilla commander in this war. If, as Gov. Brownlow suggested, every stable door should have been draped in mourning when Morgan was killed, the exit of Mosby for more genial climes should be signalized by an effusion of crape that would soften the shrill song of the early rooster, and make Virginia stables hideous with the habiliments of woe.

Mosby has been emphatically an institution on the border. One day he would sweep into Fairfax and capture a Brigadier and a score of fresh horses. Another he would whirl across Gen. Meade's communications, capture a train, steal what he wanted from the cars and pockets of the luckless persons on board, and end the scene by a bon-fire. Next he would swoop around the chain bridge in the very fortifications of Washington to capture some one or ones for whom he had a military attachment, and battalions would hurry after him in vain. Once in a while he amused himself by stopping trains on the Baltimore and Ohio Railroad, especially when Pay Masters happened to be on board, and pocket one or two hundred thousand greenbacks to reward him for his trouble; and woe to the hapless command that guarded important trains to Winchester when he was about. He would await a favorable opportunity and between liberal appropriations to himself and men and the torch, the destruction would be complete. Sometimes, he would amuse himself by hanging a score or so of captured Union soldiers for some imaginary offense of our commanders, and he would formally communicate his intentions to our officers by placards on the swinging bodies of his victims. Occasionally, he would play the magnanimous, and was the mildest mannered man that ever scuttled ship or cut a throat. His haunts by day were invisible and beyond comprehension. He would sally out at night with from three to five hundred men, and by early dawn his well trained thieves would be the meekest of farmers or laborers in pursuance of their daily vocations at their homes, and their leader would be secreted in some fastness.

Thus for more than two years, this guerrilla robbery and murder have been practiced within a few miles of the border of Pennsylvania. But if 'the mills of the gods grind slowly, they grind exceeding fine,' and the day has come at last when the petted and honored guerrilla must fly even from the places which ever afforded him a welcome refuge. By the surrender of Lee and the flight of Davis and his companions in crime, the war was practically ended, and the border robbery ceased to be protected by the flimsy pretext of a rebel commission and the concession of belligerent rights. The soldier and hero of yesterday became the thief and outlaw of today, and the same perfidious wretches who were his aiders and abettors before became hounds upon his track. They wanted safety for themselves and more than all wanted the price that was upon his guilty head. He thereupon became friendless. His own trained thieves became forgetful of the old adage that there must be honor in their profession. There was none to trust – none to succor; and the guerrilla summoned his stragglers for his final command. It was not to capture some corral, demolish a hen-roost, rob women and children on a train, or hang a few of his prisoners by way of a morning's amusement. It was to say farewell – to say that he was about to leave his country for his country's good, and bid them look out for their own necks and escape justice if possible. He delivered his final order – his command dispersed, and the redoubtable robber Mosby left for parts unknown. [The article ends with Mosby's farewell address to his command.-vph]

This was John Mosby's situation after the surrender of the Army of Northern Virginia. He found himself faced with a future in which, at best, he could expect incarceration and, at worst, execution. And although he spoke and wrote later of being "driven into exile," his refusal to leave northern Virginia to avoid the appearance of guilt, prevented him from following Early and other Confederate leaders out of the country. For John Singleton Mosby, the future was both simple and grim: parole, prison, or death. The matter was given wide coverage in the press:

Harper's Weekly – **May 13, 1865**

THE SITUATION.

General Grant reached Raleigh early on Monday. Even the irregular forces of the rebellion, from whom much trouble was expected, are giving up their arms. Mosby's men have nearly all surrendered; and though their commander is still at large his whereabouts are known and his capture is assured. Morgan's command in the west is taking the same course.

Englefield Advertiser, – **May 24, 1865**

Mosby, the Guerilla Chief.

Mosby was at Salem, near Warrenton, last Friday, and is still harbored in that neighborhood by the rebel inhabitants. His command has deserted him entirely, four hundred having been paroled at Winchester. Some of them offer to bring in Mosby alive for five thousand dollars. Two thousand dollars is now offered, but as the capture would require several men in its performance, the sum each might receive is regarded as being too small to justify the attempt.

Official United States records show that General Halleck added an additional $5,000 to the reward when Mosby remained at large by June of 1865, thus raising the total amount of the reward to $10,000, a not-inconsiderable sum at the time. But it made no difference. For whatever reason, the Union was no more successful in apprehending Mosby directly after the war than they had been during the conflict. Yet this was a very dangerous time. Had John Mosby defended himself, even against bounty hunters, any hope of a parole would have vanished; he would have become a genuine felon by virtue of that act alone whatever had happened in the war. The hunted man spent some time with his namesake uncle in Nelson County while his family worked through General Robert E. Lee to gain his parole. Originally, Grant refused that request; but after Lee signed President Johnson's Amnesty agreement, Grant determined that Mosby's parole was little enough to recompense Lee for that unpopular action. Though Mosby's first effort to gain the promised parole was unsuccessful, on the second attempt, he was in fact paroled and returned to his family to begin his postwar life. However, his troubles with the Yankees had just begun.

Almost immediately, the harassment started, and neither was it limited to being arrested every time he left Fauquier County. Indeed, there were numerous published speculations of far worse to come:

Village Record – August 4, 1865

A New York paper, of this morning, contains a rumor that Moseby, the guerilla chieftain has been arrested; and is now confined in Fort Lafayette. This man was for a long time a terror to the people living along the border, who will no doubt be greatly pleased should the rumor be verified that he has at last come to grief. The announcement a week or two ago that he had been paroled, and permitted to return to the practice of law in Culpepper, Va., caused considerable indignation to be around here, as it was feared that the infamous transgressor would escape justice altogether. The crimes of this man Moseby are numberless. He never made an assault in the open field where all are equal, but it was always in the night, when some wounded and weary soldier lay asleep that this type of 'southern chivalry' was revenged upon his foes. He was the assassin of hundreds of defenseless men, and the murderer of scores of honorable soldiers. The sick were his victims, and his only triumphs were over the harmless. Let the authorities see to it that John S. Moseby meets with the punishment he deserves.

Village Record – August 11, 1865

It appears that the rumored arrest of the 'chivalric' Moseby was a mistake. So this man, the murderer of hundreds of Union men and the destroyer of millions of property belonging to the Government and to loyalists, is permitted to practice his profession and live at ease undisturbed in Virginia.

Franklin Repository, – August 16, 1865

Moseby was a few days since arrested in Alexandria for violating his parole. He came down from Culpepper to Alexandria to be admitted as an attorney. Wherever he went in Alexandria he was followed by an immense crowd of sympathizers. His headquarters (Harper's Store) was sometimes so blockaded with people as to interrupt travel in the street. Hundreds of people went down from this city to have a shake of the great guerrilla and cut-throat's hand. His friends were always so numerous as to prevent any interference with 'free speech' by outsiders. One negro said something defamatory to Moseby and the proceedings of his sympathizers, when he was at once slapped on the mouth by a Jew who said that 'nothing should be said against Col. Moseby, who was a gentleman.' This proved too much for loyal men, and the Jew was arrested and confined for twenty-four hours in the old slave pen. Moseby was also arrested, but afterwards discharged by the military when he took the cars for his home at Culpepper. As has been stated before, he intends running for Congress in the Culpepper district, and, under the present mode of voting in Virginia, will be elected easily. Of course, such a loose manner of electing such scamps and notorieties to Congress will be the means of throwing out the entire delegation likely to be elected throughout the seceded States the coming fall.

Daily Index – August 18, 1865

General Welles told Mosby that he was arrested to prevent violence being done to him on the one hand or honor shown him on the other. The guerilla chief said he had taken the oath of allegiance and claimed the privilege of going where he pleased. He was sent home with the understanding that if he ever came into this department again he would be placed in the Old Capitol Prison.

Coshocton Democrat - October 31, 1865

Efforts Being Made to Have Mosby Arrested

New York, Oct. 24 – The Herald's special says: Since the execution of Champ Ferguson at Nashville, certain parties here who are familiar with Col. Mosby's war history are interesting themselves with a view to bringing the latter to what they call justice. They allege that Mosby, although a rose-colored gentlemanly sort of villain, was guilty of guerrilla atrocities which would have made Champ Ferguson blush. They claim they have the names of ex-rebel officers among the list of witnesses to prove inhuman crimes upon the Virginia partisan.

Franklin Repository – November 1, 1865

Efforts are being made by parties in Washington to bring Colonel Moseby to trial before a military court.

The matter was considered of such moment that it was even reported upon overseas. The *London Times*, hardly a journalistic nonentity, had this to say:

London Times – November 10, 1865

Efforts are being made in Washington to prevail on the President to order the arrest and try for murder Colonel John S. Mosbey, the guerrilla chief, who now resides at Culpepper, Virginia. The President has not yet yielded to the pressure, however.

Of special importance was the report by the *Coshocton Democrat* that "ex-rebel officers" were among the list of witnesses willing "to prove inhuman crimes upon the Virginia partisan." Although one of Mosby's most virulent enemies, General Jubal Early had fled the country, there were certainly others—Generals Rosser and Fitzhugh Lee among them—who would not have minded at all helping their former enemies send John Mosby to prison or the gallows. As he himself noted during the war, he had as much fire in his rear as in his front.

The drumbeat demand for Mosby's arrest, trial, and immediate—and severe—punishment continued through the rest of 1865 and on into the following year. But surprisingly enough, there were those publications that did dare to defend him. The *Dallas Herald* reprinted an item that originated in, of all places, the *New York World*. It was written by Colonel John Esten Cooke of Stuart's command and stands as a fine tribute to a much maligned and misjudged man whose life still hung by a very tenuous thread:

Dallas Herald – October 28, 1865 (Edited) From the *New York World*

MOSBY BY ONE WHO KNEW HIM.

Without further preface, it may surprise some of our Northern readers to hear that this man, figuring in the popular eye as a ruffian and low adventurer, was born and bred, and is, in character and manners, a gentleman. His family is one of high standing and intelligence in Virginia, where he studied the law... Col. Mosby can afford to wait to have justice done him. He was respected by Jackson, Stuart and Lee, and the world will not willingly believe him to have been a bandit. The works of "Lieutenant-Colonel —" and kindred penny-a-liners will make a popular monster, for the moment, of the popular partisan;

but the writings of this class do not last long. It is to counteract their position at the moment, and dissipate the vapid mist of false accusation, that this page is written. The brigand outline of the yellow-covered trash has been alluded to and the "bloody baron" character attributed to Mosby mentioned. What was the appearance and character of the actual individual? ... If the reader will accompany me, I ... will introduce him—remember the date is 1864—to a plain and unassuming personage, clad in gray with three stars upon his coat collar, and two pistols in his belt. He is slender, gaunt and active in figure; his feet are small and cased in cavalry boots, with brass spurs, and the revolvers in his belt, are worn with an air of "business" which is unmistakable. The face of this person is tanned, beardless, youthful-looking and pleasant. He has white and regular teeth which his habitual smile reveals. His piercing eyes flash out from beneath his brown hat, with its golden cord, and he reins in his horse with the ease of a practiced rider.

A plain soldier, low and plain of stature, ready to talk, to laugh, to ride, to oblige you in any way—such was Mosby, in outward appearance. Nature had given no sign but the restless, roving, flashing eyes, that there was much worth considering beneath. The eye did not convey a false expression. The commonplace exterior of the partisan concealed one of the most active, daring and penetrating minds of an epoch fruitful in such. Mosby was born to be a partisan leader, and as such was probably greater than any other who took part in the late war. He had by nature all the qualities which make the accomplished ranger; nothing could daunt him; his activity of mind and body—call it, if you choose, a restless, eternal love of movement, was something wonderful; and that untiring energy which is the secret of half the great successes of history, drove him incessantly to plan, to scheme, to conceive, and to execute. He could not rest when there was anything to do, and scouted for his amusement, charging pickets solus by way of sport.

The burly ruffian view of him will not bear inspection; and if there are any who cannot erase from their minds this fanciful figure of a cold, coarse, heartless adventurer, I would beg them to dwell for a moment upon the picture which the Richmond correspondent of a Northern Journal drew the other day. On a summer morning a military man was seen beside the grave of Stuart, in the Hollywood cemetery, near Richmond. The dew was on the grass, the birds sang overhead, the green hillock at the man's feet was all that remained of the daring leader of the Southern cavalry, who, after all his toils, his battles, and the shocks of desperate encounters, had come here to rest in peace. Beside this unmarked grave the solitary mourner remained long, pondering. Finally, he plucked a wild flower, dropped it upon the grave, and with tears in his eyes, left the place.

Such was the picture which I hope history will not omit, of Mosby at the grave of Stuart.

J. E. C.

And so 1865 ended in the fog of defeat and despair for many in the South, but not for John Mosby. Mosby had never despaired. He was confident that he would be able to overcome whatever fortune had in store for him, but sadly, he had no idea how costly that "victory" would be.

Chapter 6

1866

De fumo in flammam ~ Out of the smoke into the flame

"These are *The Times* that try men's souls." ~ Thomas Paine

JOHN MOSBY HAD survived 1865 in the face of every obstacle and every effort to bring him to the gallows or at least to a federal penitentiary. He had moved to Warrenton—that beautiful little town in Mosby's Confederacy through which he had passed on his way from Stuart to begin his partisan career and had determined to pick up the threads of his life, putting the war behind him. It was a most unusual mindset that found little sympathy in the South except, perhaps, among those who had actually fought, bled, and suffered in the defense of the Confederacy. Of course, few Southerners suffered the yoke of occupation with either ease or indifference. It had been, after all, an ugly war. In Mosby's case, the war had been a lot nastier for him than for most—and its aftermath promised a continuation of the same. In January, the *Daily National Republican* reported Mosby's first arrest of the new year.

> *Daily National Republican* –- **January 16, 1866**
>
> Arrest of Colonel Mosby.
>
> We learn that Col. John S. Mosby was arrested, at his home in Fauquier, a few days since, by military authority, and taken to Washington and imprisoned. He is charged, we understand, with having hanged two Federal soldiers in the Valley, during the war, in retaliation for the murder of some of his men.
>
> When we remember that Colonel Mosby, though of that class known as partisan rangers, was a regularly commissioned officer in the service of the Confederate States, and, as such, received the parole awarded the other officers of General Lee's army, his arrest seems most extraordinary, and flatly in violation of the terms of parole.
>
> For some months Colonel Mosby has been quietly practicing law in Warrenton, demeaning himself as a good and loyal citizen of his section. -Richmond Examiner.
>
> And when we remember that whether "commissioned" or not Mosby was the very worst of the gang of banditti who have desolated Virginia these four years past, we are astonished that he has been permitted to practice law otherwise than as his own counsel; and we are rejoiced to learn - and every loyal citizen will be rejoiced to learn - that at last there is a prospect of his being whipped of justice,* and the blows we trust will be well laid on that he may get a punishment something like the measure of his desserts.

*The term "whipped of justice" as used at the time referred to corporal punishment then widely in use in the American penal system. When the *Republican* spoke of "the blows" it advocated be "well laid on," the paper was referring to actual strokes of a whip or strap. Such vehement language reflected the severe frustration engendered by the general belief that there was little chance of John Mosby actually being hanged at that point. Where such draconian punishments had been implemented, they had been carried out soon after the close of the war as seen in the fates of Captain Henry Wirz, guerrillas Champ Ferguson and Jerome Clarke, and the Lincoln assassins.

But the possibility of Mosby being *tried and imprisoned* was not unreasonable (see the articles following), and the paper spoke for most in the North—and even some in the South—who wanted him severely punished for his "crimes." Furthermore, it is important when considering this time in Mosby's life to recognize that imprisonment would have been a sentence of death differing from the gallows only in its excruciating duration. Even a relatively short sentence—something very unlikely under the circumstances—would not have spared him especially if he found himself in a Northern prison. And finally, even if he had survived, as a convicted felon John Mosby would have been precluded from practicing law! So the matter was very serious indeed and should be recognized as such, but it never is:

Cleveland Daily Leader – January 17, 1866

The guerrilla colonel Mosby was arrested in Leesburg a few days ago, and is held subject to the orders of General Ayre, military commandant at Winchester. The cause of the arrest has not transpired.

Cleveland Daily Leader – January 22, 1866

Mosby the Partisan

All loyal persons will be glad to know that the Government is evincing a disposition to bring to trial and punishment those guerrilla chiefs who, during the rebellion, were the scourge of regions adjacent to the theatre of war. The fact that such men generally confined their operations to points within supporting distance of the rebel army, proved the responsibility of the rebel authorities for the system of guerrilla warfare; but does not entitle guerrillas to the treatment due regular soldiers, for they were not in the actual employ of even a rebel government. Mosby, the famous "partisan," as his admirers term him—who made himself a terror to loyal men in Virginia— having recently been arrested by order of the Government, both the Northern and Southern rebel press have raised a plaintive wail in his behalf. Could these self-appointed patriots be believed, Mosby was a soldier of honor and an authorized officer of the "Confederate States." The New York News, in commenting upon the specification against Mosby—which is nothing less than the killing of two Federal soldiers in retaliation for the execution of two of his marauders—says, in justification of the crime, there were "many similar instances of retaliation on "the part of Federal commanders." This logic would place the Government of the United States on a par with the authority of any free-booter who could surround himself by a half-dozen followers—would make a clan of guerrillas as respectable as the authorized army of a nation. Mosby evidenced his independence of the rebel authorities when he refused to surrender after the whole of the rebel troops east of the Mississippi had submitted themselves to the authority of the Federal Government. Instead of acquiescing in the surrender of General Lee, he acted upon his own responsibility, maintaining his organization until the dispersion of

Johnston's forces rendered such a course longer impracticable, when he said he would not surrender, but would disband his battalion, which he proceeded to do. By this act he avowed his absolute authority over the men under his command; and now he cannot put in the poor plea made by Wirz and other rebel murders, that he is protected by the terms of surrender agreed upon by Lee and Grant or Johnston and Sherman. Mosby essayed to act for himself. He refused to be governed by the rules of war. He would not surrender and accept a parole. He disbanded his followers only when to retain them longer would have put his life in serious jeopardy. Now let him reap the reward of his savage warfare.

This tense situation went on for quite some time, and there was always the threat of the matter going beyond simple harassment and into the more dangerous situations inferred by these articles, for the legend of "Mosby the monster" cultivated during the war by the Northern press continued to cast a sinister influence over the man's future. Occasionally, however, a Northern newspaper astonished many by coming to Mosby's defense. This article appeared in the *Anderson Intelligencer*, but it is a reprint from the *New York News*:

Anderson Intelligencer – January 25, 1866

ARREST OF MOSBY.—Col. John S. Mosby, whose dash and daring during the war rendered him conspicuous among the partisan leaders of the South, has been singled out by the War Department for persecution under the still arbitrary system of military rule. Col. Mosby, after having been paroled with the other officers of Gen. Lee's Army, retired to his home in Fauquier, and engaged in the practice of law. Accepting the defeat of the cause to which he had been devoted, he asked only the privilege of pursuing an honorable vocation as a quiet and law abiding citizen. This has been denied him. We learn that he has been arrested by military authority, conveyed to Washington, and thrown into prison, in violation of the terms of his parole. It is alleged that the charge against him is that he caused the execution of two Federal soldiers during the war, in retaliation for the murder of some of his own men. What if the charge be true—were there not many similar instances of retaliation on the part of Federal Commanders? Is it possible that the War Department proposes to search the gloomy record of civil strife to drag every case of Confederate retaliation before a military tribunal? Col. Mosby did not shed blood for pastime, or to gratify a savage nature. He was a soldier and subject to the stern discipline of war. If, in his judgment or that of his superiors, the exigencies of the strife, under the martial code, demanded a military execution, he but fulfilled a soldier's duty in carrying the harsh sentence into effect. The gentle eyes of Peace should not dwell with severe scrutiny upon the terrible routine of war, for it is impossible, in such retrospection, to appreciate the necessities or the sense of justice that provoked retaliation. Blood enough has been shed to satisfy even vengeance; justice demands no further suffering, and policy forbids its infliction upon men who are beloved and honored by the Southern people. If we would be friends with them, we must not brand and persecute their heroes.—N. Y. News

And there the matter continued with each arrest and incarceration, promising "this time" to go beyond the whim of the local provost marshal. And then Pauline Mosby stepped in and secured the protection of Union General Ulysses S. Grant for her beleaguered husband. The story of Pauline's mission does not need to be recounted here; but of course, when her mission and its result were made public, it became of great interest to the press:

***Nashville Daily Union* – February 17, 1866**

***New Orleans Daily Crescent* – February 23, 1866**

Mosby Gets a Pass.

It will be gratifying to the family, friends and relatives of Colonel John Singleton Mosby to hear that he has at length succeeded in flanking his tormentors, and can now, on condition of his good behavior, enjoy peace and quiet, fortified with the following impregnable document:

Headq'rs Army of the U. S., Washington, D. C. Feb. 2, 1866

John S. Mosby, lately of the Southern army, will hereafter be exempt from arrest by the military authorities, except for violation of his parole, unless directed by the President of the United States, Secretary of War, or from these headquarters.

His parole will authorize him to travel freely with the State of Virginia, and as no obstacle has been thrown in the way of paroled officers, and men from pursuing their civil pursuits, or traveling out of this State, the same privileges will be extended to J. S. Mosby, unless otherwise directed by competent authority.

U. S. Grant Lieutenant General

But Pauline wasn't only in the news regarding her visit with General Grant! She had also put in a claim for her husband in the matter of some tobacco the couple owned, which had been "confiscated" by Federal soldiers without due compensation after the end of the war. Frankly, the press thought the whole affair was a matter of "cheek" and said so:

***Daily National Republican* – February 5, 1866**

CHEEK.

One of the most alarming exhibitions imaginable of faith in human forgiveness and Governmental forbearance was presented on Friday last in the appearance at the Treasury Department of the wife of the notorious guerrilla, John S. Mosby, asking for the payment of the value of certain tobacco, of which, it is alleged, her chivalrous husband was unjustly deprived by the "Yankee Government" in the capture of Richmond. It is understood the money was not paid, but the willingness of the freebooter to resume his "old relations with the Government" is none the less to be admired.

When it is decided to favorably consider the claim, we think public notice of the fact ought to be given, as it is not unlikely that a large number of Union soldiers and civilians, who have been relieved of greenbacks, watches, pocket-knives, tooth-brushes, etc. by the gallant John, might desire to file counter claims.

White Cloud Kansas Chief – February 22, 1866

The wife of the rebel General Mosby has applied for compensation for damage done her husband's property during the war. She has cheek, and pretty cheeks too, it is said.

In the midst of newspaper reports alternately castigating and celebrating Mosby, these very odd little items appeared virtually out of nowhere. As happened so often in newspaper coverage, some little story came along that provided a blinding light on the state of things, but was unfortunately not considered important enough to receive any follow-up coverage. These little stories heralded the John Mosby that would, over time, become known to his fellow countrymen, North *and* South. The problem was, alas, that this "new" Mosby would be disregarded by the North and rejected by the South:

Cleveland Daily Leader – March 1, 1866

An agent of the American Missionary Society, laboring in Virginia, recently called on a Presbyterian Doctor of Divinity, to interest him for the education of freedmen, and the doctor coldly informed him that the Northern people had undertaken that job, and it would be left to them; when they got tired of it, as they soon would, then the Southern Christians would take it up. The missionary afterwards called upon Mosby, the guerrilla chief, who treated him in a very gentlemanly way, said the blacks ought to be educated, and there could be no reasonable objection to it, and gave him assistance in finding citizens likely to assist him in his work.

Daily Phoenix – March 28, 1866

SPOKEN LIKE A HERO.—A literary gentleman, who is engaged in writing a book on some events in the war, in which Mosby was concerned, has recently had some correspondence with that noted personage, and a short time ago inquired of him if it would be safe for "a Black Republican—one dyed in the wool"—so he described himself—to make at the present time a horseback journey through Virginia. In reply that famous rough-rider writes the gentleman as follows:

"If you have any desire to visit the historic scenes of Virginia, I hope you will not be deterred by any apprehension for your personal safety. You will be just as safe from molestation here as in the streets of Boston. Should you determine to visit Northern Virginia, I would be glad to see you at my home; and I can at least promise that you will not find me the monstrum horrendum of the Northern imagination. By-the-by, one of the regiments most frequently encountered was from Boston—the 2d Massachusetts, Col. Lowell. I once met a detachment of it under the command of Maj. Forbes, of Boston; and although our encounter resulted in his overthrow, he bore himself with conspicuous gallantry, and I saw him wound one of my best men with his sabre. I also had an interview with a Capt. Barton, of Massachusetts, who served on Gen. Eustace's staff, and interested myself to procure his exchange. In the event of your visiting Virginia, I shall be most happy to extend to you any facility in my power for seeing places of interest, &c."

But Mosby had not yet managed to entirely escape the desire of the Yankee occupiers to cause him grief, and from the following incident, the story we have today of him going to Leesburg "in full Confederate uniform" and challenging the garrison there to "do something about it" arises. It was covered in the newspapers in *both* versions, but as the latter includes a quote from Mosby, we must accept it as the truth:

Cleveland Daily Leader – April 17, 1866

Nashville Daily Union – April 17, 1866

An Attempt to Arrest Mosby.

New York, April 16.—The Tribune's Washington special says that an attempt was made last week by the Federal troops, at Leesburg, Virginia, to arrest the ex-guerrilla John J. Mosby, for appearing in the streets in Confederate uniform. Mosby took to the woods and thus avoided the guards, who fired several shots at him.

The *Anderson Intelligencer* – May 17, 1866

The Last Volley.—Colonel John S. Mosby visited Leesburg last Monday on professional business. Because he happened to wear a cape in these piping times of peace which had on it several brass buttons with the coat of arms of Massachusetts on them, the Federal Captain in command there declared his purpose to arrest him and cut them off.—Being unwilling to submit to this treatment but disposed to do anything to avoid a breach of the peace, the Colonel at the suggestion of a friend, consented to leave the burg. The Captain with four troopers and sixty infantry, endeavored to intercept his retreat, but was too late by several moments to effect this object. When the Colonel rode upon the crest of a hill, he looked back and saw the doughty warriors make a furious charge upon a haystack which had served to conceal him from their view when he had made his exit. The spectacle was so ludicrous he could not repress an inclination to whoop. He did so, and at the same time raising his hat, he waived a parting adieu. The irate Captain acknowledged the compliment by ordering a leaden volley from sixty guns to be fired at the Colonel.—The bullets whistled closely but harmlessly past him and made music which reminded him of by-gone years of strife.

We believe the Massachusetts button is the symbol of treason, and are somewhat surprised that the Colonel was so disloyal as to retain one on his cape at the risk of liberty and life.—Warrenton Index.

Shreveport Semi-Weekly News - June 2, 1866

Mosby, the guerrilla, is making very merry over the attempt of a Union Captain at Leesburg to arrest him and cut the uniform brass buttons from his cape. Mosby says that the buttons were the Massachusetts coat of arms, and he did not know that they were symbols of disloyalty.

It is probable that Mosby received the notorious cloak with the offending brass buttons from his sisters' former tutor, New England spinster Abby Southwick. Miss Southwick had gone through the war very anxious about the fate of the studious young man whom she had known as an adolescent. Her concern for the Mosby family was such that she sent clothing and other necessities to them at the close of the war, and doubtless, John's mother sent the cloak on to him. Still, one cannot doubt that Mosby took considerable glee in seeing the self-righteous Yankees charging a haystack in the attempt to apprehend him only to find out that their actions were as futile as they had been during the course of the war.

The *Wilmington Journal* put out this little bit of historical interest. It appeared that a Yankee entrepreneur desired to engage some of Mosby's men for "tournaments" in the North. The gentleman also attempted to hire Mosby himself, but without success. However, no mention was made that Mosby treated the man in any but a civilized manner as surely would have been the case had he done otherwise:

Wilmington Journal – August 30, 1866

TOURNAMENT RIDERS.—An enterprising Yankee visited the county of Fauquier recently, and succeeded in engaging twelve or fourteen of 'Mosby's men," to go North and ride tournaments. He is to foot all expenses, furnish them with fine horses, and pay them three dollars a day. He boldly approached Mosby himself with a proposition, offering him first fifty dollars a day, and gradually increasing the offer to one hundred and twenty-five, which, of course, was declined. By way of friendly warning to this original caterer to the public enjoyment, the *Alexandria Gazette* advises him to deal fairly with "the boys," for if he does not they won't leave a whole bone in his body. Petersburg Express.

It is quite possible that such a thing took place. Mosby's command had achieved an almost-mythological status in the North, and as they were now "surrendered," the fear that was part of that fixation was no more. Undoubtedly, people would pay to see "Mosby's men" and, had Mosby gone, the "tournament" would have been unprecedented as a "public entertainment!" Somehow the idea of Mosby's intercourse with this Yankee entrepreneur as that gentleman continued to "up the ante" is amusing indeed!

However, there is something here that manifested itself later in Mosby's life, and that was his horror of being "exhibited" as some sort of sideshow freak. Years later, he wrote to son Beverly: "It is a crucifixion for me to undergo any kind of ceremonial." In a very startling episode that took place in 1897, during what was supposed to be a genial gathering, Mosby refused to enter the room in which this gathering took place and, upon his refusal, was actually physically carried into it! He was so upset that he fought with considerable violence to escape from his captors. Later, he referred to the matter by roundly declaring that he resented being "exhibited." He stated, "I just told them that I wouldn't go into that room; that I was neither a lion nor a hippopotamus to be put on exhibition." At the time, the matter was carried in the press as being the result of "stage fright."

In October, the *Staunton Spectator* and the *Daily Evening Telegraph* printed a very lengthy article that they identified as an excerpt on the Miskel Farm fight, which would appear in the soon-to-be released work by Major John Scott on Mosby's command, *Partisan Life with Col. John S. Mosby*. Mosby had approached Scott to write the book and had fully collaborated with him on it. But why Mosby's name was misspelled is anyone's guess:

Staunton Spectator and Vindicator – October 9, 1866

Daily Evening Telegraph – November 11, 1866

PARTISAN LIFE IN THE SOUTH.

Incident from Scott's Forthcoming Narrative of Moseby and His Men
From the Letters of an Englishman

The First Dranesville, or the Fight at Miskel's House.

But October also brought the first family tragedy, the death of one of Mosby's younger sisters, Victoria:

Spirit of Jefferson – October 23, 1866

—The Richmond Whig announces the death of Miss Victoria C. Mosby, a sister of Col. John S. Mosby, in Amherst county, Virginia, on the 7th, inst.

It would seem that John Mosby, as they say, "dodged a bullet" in 1866. His safety was in doubt for a considerable time. Even the much-vaunted pass obtained from General Grant was hardly a *carte blanche* as it could be revoked upon the order of "any competent authority." But Mosby had also been careful. Despite his frequent arrests, he never lost his temper and was termed "respectful" in his dealings with his tormentors. In everything else, he lived quietly and did not "kick against the goads" as so many of his biographers take so much satisfaction in declaring that, in fact, he did. Even the ridiculous claim that he rode into Leesburg in full Confederate uniform—an actual crime!— challenging the Federal authorities is irrational. But finally, what has become the "accepted version" of the story was refuted in the articles in which Mosby admitted to the "brass buttons of Massachusetts" as the *cause celeb* of the whole affair.

As 1867 dawned, matters for the South in general—and John Mosby in particular— had not yet reached the point at which all was entirely "settled." The war had ended only less than two years earlier; and certainly in Mosby's case, always in the background there lurked the very real threat of serious consequences that still might arise, pass or no pass.

Chapter 7

1867

Bono malum superate. ~ Overcome evil with good.

"What is past is prologue." ~ William Shakespeare

JOHN MOSBY CONTINUED to be of interest to the press as the year began, but no longer were their articles pronouncements of doom. Often, they were innocuous and a little "gossipy" and were either about Mosby directly or as a consequence of something in which he took part. The next articles are examples of this type of coverage and seemed to be nothing but a means of keeping his name in print:

> ***Charleston Daily News* – April 11, 1867**
>
> The Index, published at Warrenton, Va., Col. Mosby's present home, has the following paragraph in relation to the work entitled "Mosby and his Men": 'We are requested by Col. J. S. Mosby to state for public information, that a book purported to contain a history of his campaigns of the war, lately published by J. Marshall Crawford, is unworthy of credit and contains about as much truth as the Arabian Nights' entertainments, or Gulliver's Travels."

Mosby was not at all happy with Crawford's book. He dismissed it as "unworthy of credit," but the book was no more inaccurate than all the other versions of the history of the Forty-third that followed, including Scott's. Certainly, Crawford was effusive in his praise of Mosby personally, so it is not known as to why his commander was so churlish about the matter. It could be that as Crawford did not seek either Mosby's permission or his help, he took umbrage at his making so free of the story. But whatever the case, Crawford's book was the first on the command whether John Mosby liked it or not.

Another article appeared in June, part of which contained a report on an encounter between a correspondent with the *Cincinnati Commercial* and John Mosby on the Bull Run battlefield. It was another of those small incidents demonstrating Mosby's behavior toward his former enemies—that is, that he carried no grudge and was more than willing to be "fraternal" in his dealings with them:

> ***Public Ledger* – June 11, 1867 (Part of a larger article)**
>
> BATTLEFIELD OF BULL RUN.
>
> Interesting Account.
>
> A correspondent of the Cincinnati Commercial, who recently visited the famous battlefield of Bull Run, has this account of it:
>
> As I was standing at the foot of the hill on which the Henry House once stood—a high reach of rolling land, where the hottest contest of the day was fought—a solitary horseman came riding by, from the lower fords of Bull Run. He drew rein as he approached, and with a courteous salute, he asked if I came to see the battlefield. Assenting, I inquired whether the second battle of Bull Run had not been, in part, fought on this very ground. He turned in the saddle, and pointed me to another ridge within

a quarter of a mile, where, said he, "Jackson got Pope between two fires, enfilading his column in the shape of a V and mowed 'em down as thick as grasshoppers. I was in both battles," he said, "I'm a Confederate of course. My name is Mosby (pronounced Moseby)."

"Are you Col. John Mosby?" I inquired.

"That's my name," he replied. I told him I found a good many of his men around, and he assented with evident satisfaction. He was a private in both battles—in the second one attached to Stuart's cavalry—and his development into the dashing and formidable guerrilla captain came at a later day.

In person, Mosby is a tall wiry, active man of thirty-five, with a clear, good-humored eye, and an off-hand readiness of speech. He is now a practicing lawyer in Warrenton, the county east of Fauquier. He had been to Ball's Ford, he said to cross Bull Run, but the stream was too high. He had tried all the fords below Stone Bridge, except Blackburn's, with the same result. (There is not a solitary bridge of any kind over Bull Run, as they have been repeatedly destroyed by both armies.) He was now "going round by Sudley's Ford," and telling me that I could not cross over there with a carriage till the next day, and that he was "going to Fairfax to attend court," and was already late, he bade me a courteous "good morning," and rode on.

Perhaps the most interesting little detail in the above article was Mosby's statement: "I'm a Confederate of course." Notice that he did not say, "I *was* a Confederate" although later, Mosby did make rather much of having "surrendered" and therefore having abandoned that identity.

In July, the announcement came of the release of Major Scott's book, which was greeted with approval by Southern newspapers:

Staunton Spectator – July 23, 1867

PARTISAN LIFE WITH COL. JOHN S. MOSBY

We promise our readers a great deal of instruction and entertainment from the "Partisan Life." What is more, it contains an authentic history of the facts treated of, drawn from sources that admit of no dispute, having been for the most part furnished by Colonel Mosby himself... There are appearing from time to time various accounts of the thrilling scenes connected with the "Lost Cause," but we can assure our readers that not one conveys more valuable, because truthful information concerning one of the most exciting narratives of the war, than does this "Partisan Life with Mosby."

Galveston News – August 1, 1867

The New Orleans Bee says, "Partisan Life, with Col. John Mosby," by Major John Scott, of Fauquier, and published (strangely enough) by Harper & Brothers, stands unequalled by any book written on the war, either North or South."

The *Semi-Weekly Wisconsin*—hardly a local paper!—carried an interview with Mosby that was of interest as it included some incidents just prior to the war. A similar article was carried in the *New York Times*, a very influential publication. The real meaning of these stories seems to be that Mosby was considered objective and intelligent enough to provide credible testimony about matters that went far beyond the simple "waging of war." In fact, he was considered capable of expounding on the political, social, and cultural issues that had *precipitated* war. Of course, the *Wisconsin* could not resist identifying him as "the celebrated Virginian brigand":

The Semi-Weekly Wisconsin – August 3, 1867 (Edited)

Mosby's Interview with the Rebel Ex-Secretary of War Floyd –

A Prophecy.

Recently a biography of the celebrated Virginian brigand, John Singleton Mosby, has been written by Maj. John Scott, of the ex-rebel army. It is published in New York. It is an interesting book, as the adventures of Mosby will be regarded by the historian as scarcely less remarkable than those of any partisan brigand who ever harassed a country. The civil war of England from 1642 to 1649, produced no partisan trooper on either side who engaged in more raids upon his enemy, and ventured into more peril than this Virginia lawyer – for such was his original profession. Mosby was, no doubt, a remarkable man. He was of a higher stamp then either Champ Ferguson or John Morgan. In reading this book one of the most interesting chapters is that in which Mosby has an interview with John B. Floyd, at his home in southwestern Virginia. Mr. Floyd was the Secretary of War of President Buchanan . . Floyd died in the first year of the war, and thus he did not witness the horrible desolation which swept over Virginia, but his words were mournfully prophetic:

"As soon as Mosby had enrolled his name he visited the Honorable John B. Floyd, who had been but recently Secretary of War of the United States, to hear his views about the condition of the country. Amid the general excitement, that able statesman wore a grave and ominous brow. He said: 'The leaders of this movement in the South know not whither they are going. Some of them talk of a short war; some of them talk of no war; while other visionaries admit the possibility of war, yet say the battles of the south will be fought by the fleets of England and the bayonets of France. There are no reveries and conjectures that are too wild and improbable for the dreamers at Montgomery to indulge in. Instead,' he added, 'of there being no war, or a short war, or a war which will be fought for us by foreign powers, it will prove to be one of the longest and most sanguinary conflicts between the North and South that ever desolated the earth. The men who prevented the secession of Virginia three months ago, and those at Montgomery who have fooled away the season of preparation, will be responsible for the tears of every widow and orphan.'"

The *Edinburgh Evening Courant* next printed a fairly lengthy article on Scott's book, which the reviewer did not like. Yet it is a very interesting review in that it looked at the matter not simply from the point of view of the war itself, but also from the condition in which the South found itself after the war. The conclusions it drew sounded a warning, though faint and indirect, regarding the consequences that would eventually arise as a result of Mosby's desire for true reconciliation with the North; the recitation of various affairs of the command have been edited out for the sake of length:

Edinburgh Evening Courant – **August 31, 1867 (Edited)**
LITERATURE

With the Guerrillas In The South.

This is a poor book on a good subject. All the world has heard of the daring and doings of the great Confederate guerrilla leader, Mosby, and we would hardly conceive a better or a more interesting topic to engage the attention and exercise the ability of a really skillful literary artist. …

Most people know enough of Mosby to desire to know a little more, and a spirited record of his numerous fierce fights with the Yankees, at long odds against him, and his clever and generally successful attacks upon pickets and outposts would have been fraught with interest to the general reader, and specially acceptable to those who have sympathized with the gallant efforts of the Southern States to win their independence, but who now mourn the disappointment of their hopes, and the broken and crushed condition in which they lie under the harassing and vexatious tyranny of Yankee military commanders, such as Sheridan; or, worse still, under the oppressive and repulsive regime of a Parson Brownlow.

It were needless, however, to remove the lament over the irreparable defeat of General Lee. The South has met its doom and must face it: and although it is impossible that eight million brave Southern whites will be content to be ruled in perpetuity by four million emancipated black slaves, even although backed by a Radical Congress, there is nothing for it now but that they should possess their souls in patience, and feed their hearts with the memories of the brave deeds performed by their defenders during the four years' unequal struggle with the North.

The mode of warfare waged by Mosby was novel. It was of such a nature as to be eminently suited to a nation defending itself against invaders who vastly outnumbered its effective forces The following description of Mosby's Partisan warfare, from the preface to the volume before us, will explain its nature:—

"Partisan warfare, until it was systematized and its capabilities displayed by the genius and energy of Mosby, had no place among the military arrangements of any nation. It was indeed as unknown as, at the time of their introduction, were any of the inventions of modern science. The weapon which he fashioned and wielded with such dexterity and effect has found a place in the armoury of the United States, and Partisan warfare, as developed by him, must hereafter constitute a part of defence whenever one nation is invaded by another nation. Mosby deliberately planted himself in a district abandoned by the Confederate armies to the occupation of the enemy, and, though environed by hostile camps, and in that distant and isolated position, maintained an aggressive attitude for more than two years, his command during this period growing and spreading out under his nourishing hand, notwithstanding the most persistent and vindictive attempts to destroy or drive it away. But this was not all. In the course of this career he more than once compelled Generals to relinquish actual and projected lines of communication, to fall back from advanced positions, and, if we may give credit to the assertion of a Federal Secretary of War, occasioned the loss by the enemy of an important battle. Such deeds are worthy of the pen of history, and Europe as well as America may listen to the tale of his exploits." The writer of the work before us quotes the words of a Federal general of high rank and merit, who said that Mosby was the only perfect success in the Southern army, but that he was not appreciated at home. And the same General added that if, with his Partisans, Mosby had been thrown on Sherman's rear on his long and toilsome march towards Atlanta, Johnston would have driven him back to the mountains or have destroyed his army. As it was, Sherman's communications were never molested, and he did not lose even so much as a tar bucket.

There is much truth in this. We believe from what Mosby actually did accomplish against Sheridan and other Northern officers that if had been brought to operate against Sherman, the latter would never have been able, as he did, to cut through the Southern Confederacy and make his way to the coast, leaving fire and destruction all along his path. The actual achievements of Mosby seem almost incredible. He often attacked with his Partisan Rangers bodies of Federals outnumbering him more than three to one, and routed them. He was constantly on the alert, and almost constantly successful. Of course, he was often subject to great perils, and ran many risks of his life. But he always contrived to escape, and was able to reward his men with the spoils he took from the Yankees. ...[Hereinafter follows an account of the Miskel Farm engagement as well as a very long recitation of other facts about the command.-vph]

But Scott's book received its finest tribute from across the sea. Of especial interest is the claim by the reports that Mosby was credited with a "newly developed system of warfare," though John Mosby would have respectfully—and modestly—disagreed:

Daily Phoenix – October 11, 1867

Lexington Caucasian and Express – October 10, 1867

Republican Compiler – November 8, 1867

Royal Compliments to Colonel Mosby.—Major John Scott of Fauquier, now in Europe, has just written informing his friend here that the Prussian War Minister, Count Bismarck, has ordered a government translation of his late work, "Partizan Life with Mosby," for the purpose of adopting in the Prussian service, the system developed by Col. Mosby during the war, regarding it as entirely original and effective. Also, that the Russian War Minister and his royal highness Crown Prince of Russia, have written him letters in high commendation of Colonel Mosby's newly developed system of warfare.—Warrenton Sentinel.

And still, wherever he appeared, Mosby was recognized and acknowledged—if not always in a positive way. The *Keowee* (South Carolina) *Courier* mentioned Mosby attending a railroad meeting in Leesburg. He did not announce his presence—he didn't have to:

Keowee Courier - **November 9, 1867**

Mosby.—While the rail road meeting was in progress yesterday at Leesburg, a turning of heads in the direction of an individual at the rear of the hall indicated that he was a personage of more note than his outward appearance indicated; and presently the word "Mosby" buzzed about the room told the story. The famous partisan chieftain practices law in Warrenton, and is now attending the court in session at Leesburg. He knows everybody in that part of Virginia, and has a very good practice, It will be remembered that he abandoned law to enter upon his wild military career. In personal appearance he looks the lawyer even less than the warrior. Dressed in a careless, easy Virginia country style, with white slouch hat, a dust stained bob-tail coat, milk and molasses colored pants and vest, (the latter minus two or three buttons) a badly adjusted false front tooth, a figure of medium size, close-shaven, sun-burnt youthful face, slouched shoulders, quiet, taciturn undemonstrative in manner, it was not quite easy to believe that he was the individual whose name and dare-devil achievements figured in the papers almost daily during the war.

But perhaps the most "fuss" Mosby created was his visit to the Gold Room in New York City. He was there by invitation. He did not simply "intrude" as that was not his way. But invited or not, he caused quite a stir as these reports indicated:

New York Evening Post – **November 19, 1867**

Public Ledger – **November 26, 1867**

Yorkville Enquirer – **November 28, 1867**

A Scene in the New York Gold Room—Colonel Mosby Among the New York Bears

The New York Evening Post of the 19th says:

Considerable excitement was caused at the Gold Board this afternoon by the appearance at the Vice President's desk of the rebel General John S. Mosby.—Mosby appeared at the door and sent his card to Mr. Hoyt, the Vice President, and a reply was sent to admit Mosby, which was complied with by the doorkeeper. Mosby entered the door and took his seat beside Mr. Hoyt. As soon as it became known who the stranger was, a note was sent to Mr. Hoyt asking for the withdrawal of Mosby and also denouncing him. This note was read aloud, when Mosby took his hat in his hand, and was preparing to leave, when he was shaken by the hand by some of the members, and denounced in a loud tone as a traitor by others. He was also loudly hissed.—The affair caused considerable excitement, which did not subside until long after the adjournment of the Board.

Spirit of Jefferson – **November 26, 1867**

MOSBY'S LAST RAID.

The inimitable cavalier, Mosby, has made another raid, and this time he has shattered the nerves, confused the ideas, and upset the manners of the bulls and bears of Gotham.

Being in New York last week, by invitation he visited the Gold Board to witness the operations of the money changers, where he was identified as the dashing raider, when, in an instant the house was thrown into "confusion worse confounded." A member named Colgate—perhaps the celebrated soap man—who may have suffered the loss of a few packages of Yankee soap by Mosby's raids during the rebellion, sent a note to the Vice President of the Board enquiring, "is that the traitor, Mosby? If so, he has no business in the desk."

The Vice-President became very indignant at the insult to himself, as well as to Colonel Mosby, arose, called the board to order, read the note, and stated that it was an insult to which he would not submit; that the gentleman by his side was Colonel John S. Mosby, and he had a right to have him in the desk. Amid great applause, Mr. Colgate tried to justify himself, but the board would not listen to him, and as Colonel Mosby arose to leave the room, the members crowded around him, of all political opinions, shook him by the hand, and welcomed him to the room. Soon after Col. Mosby had left, the Vice-President ordered the room cleared of all except members, and had a special meeting of the board, who endorsed and applauded his course to the echo, only six votes being given in support of Mr. Colgate's action, and three of them qualified their votes by an explanation.

Fairfield Herald – December 4, 1867

The Episode in the Gold Room

The littleness by which "patriotism" sometimes undertakes to vaunt itself, is well illustrated by the late incident in connection with the momentary presence of Colonel John S. Mosby, in the New York gold room, of which a correspondent who knows has given the following account:

"We had a great excitement in the yesterday, 19th instant, as you will see by the paper, but as you will wish a correct account, I give you the facts as they occurred. Colonel Mosby was brought to the board by a broker, who applied to Mr. Hoyt, the presiding officer of the board, for permission to bring him in to see its operations. Mr. Hoyt, being alone authorized to give permits for strangers to visit the board, and to admit anyone he pleases, promptly consented to Colonel Mosby's admission, and he was taken to the desk and introduced to Mr. Hoyt, and invited to take a seat by him. His presence being known, considerable desire was manifested by the liberal and real reconstruction members to see him, and by many to be introduced. Seeing so much attention shown the Colonel by the most influential members of the board, Mr. Colgate (of Trevor & Colgate) wrote a note and sent it [to] Mr. Hoyt, as follows: "Is that the traitor Mosby? If so, he has no business in the desk," signed, "Colgate and others." Mr. Hoyt became very indignant at the insult to himself, as well as to Colonel Mosby, arose called the board to order, read the note, and stated it was an insult to which he would not submit; that the gentleman by his side was Colonel John S. Mosby, and he had a right to have him in the desk. Amid great applause, Mr. Colgate tried to justify himself; but the board would not listen to him, and as Colonel Mosby arose to leave [the] room, the members crowded around him, of all political opinions, shook him by the hand, and welcomed him to the room. Soon after Colonel Mosby had left Mr. Hoyt ordered the room cleared of all except members, and had a special meeting of the board, who endorsed and applauded his course to echo, only six votes being given in support of Mr. Colgate's action, and three of them qualified their votes by an explanation.

Again, we see John Mosby willing to *leave* when the controversy occasioned by his presence arose. Far from being a man who pushed himself forward, he was extremely self-effacing. Apparently, most of those in the Gold Room had no problem with his presence, and the "patriotism" whose "littleness" the paper holds up to ridicule was that of Mr. Colgate and those who rejected Mosby even when he had been invited by their own presiding officer.

And so it would seem that John Mosby was able to appear around the country, even in the North; and though he still had his problems (he was arrested at a racetrack in New York City after he was recognized!), in general, he found not a few Northern people who offered him their hands open in friendship rather than as a closed fist. But it is more than probable that these gracious souls were Democrats, many of whom had deep sympathies for the people of the South. The time would come when John Mosby would lose their affection without gaining much support from those who currently despised him.

Chapter 8

1868

Ducunt volentem fata. ~ The fates lead the willing
and drag the unwilling.

**"Suspicion always haunts the guilty mind."
~ William Shakespeare**

NEWSPAPER COVERAGE OF Mosby in 1868 began with perhaps the oddest matter that ever arose in all of his life in or out of the press—that is, reports of the fixation of the powerful Secretary of War, Edwin Stanton with John Mosby, his purported fear of the man and his rather astonishing efforts to protect himself from a danger that none of Stanton's colleagues believed existed! The matter received wide press coverage at the time—none of it favorable to Stanton. No mention was ever made that Mosby was advised of the situation except with regard to a related incident that coaxed from his pen a remarkable telegram to an old friend in Boston, illustrative of the man's roguish sense of humor. Of course, this too also found its way into print:

Paper unknown – Date: sometime after March 13, 1868

A Washington Dispatch from the New York Herald of yesterday says:

Although the greatest care has been taken to smother the matter, the real cause of locking the back door of the War Department has leaked out. A detective employed by Mr. Stanton to bring him early intelligence on any danger that might threaten the safety of his official sanctuary appeared before him one day last week and imparted the startling intelligence that Mosby, the famous rebel guerrilla of Virginia during the war, had organized a force in the country adjacent to the Potomac river, and was prepared to enter Washington, surround the War Department and seize the Secretary of War.

What disposition was then to have been made of the illustrious prisoner was not clearly known, but he at once ordered out a force of seventy-five men. This force was held under orders to move to the scene of action at a moment's notice.

At night while the weather was quite cold a strong guard was sent to the Long Bridge across the Potomac to look for the approach of the enemy and contest the passage of the river. The guard, much to their disgust, bivouacked in the cold night air on the Long Bridge for two nights, but were doomed to disappointment, for no Mosby made his appearance.

Gazette and Comet – **March 19, 1868**

A "Big Scare."—Cito, the special correspondent at Washington of the New Orleans Times, telegraphs to that journal, from the former place, under date the 16th inst., as follows:

A "big scare" seems to have taken possession of certain officials here, and upon the suggestion of Stanton and others, who apprehend some mysterious combination of Mosby and other ex-Confederates to attack and take possession of the capital, an additional military force has been ordered here, and for three days past have been "sleeping upon their arms." Four artillery companies are among the most recent acquisitions to the troops stationed here. All this military movement seems to be based upon the curb-stone gossip of the revolutionary purposes of somebody who wants to get rid of Congress. The "scare" excites the merriest ridicule among law abiding people.

Vermont Transcript **March 20, 1868**

A Virginia Union man, who was at Leesburg that State on Sunday, says that John S. Mosby who resides there, was visited by nearly a thousand of his guerilla command. They were all well mounted, and many of them were armed. After riding through the streets of Leesburg in column, they were exercised in battalion movements and then formed into a square to hear a speech from Mosby. What he said my informant could not hear, but some of the men afterward declared that they might at any day be called upon to oust Stanton from the War Office.

Union and Dispatch **– March 20, 1868**

Daily Phoenix – March 20, 1868

"SHADOWS, MY LORD"

"Secretary Stanton has issued orders requiring troops in Washington to be in readiness to move at a moment's notice, while forty army wagons, to transport supplies, are ordered to be kept available. This redoubtable array is supposed to be intended for the defense of the War office against Mosby's mythic guerrillas from Virginia."

During the late war, says the New York Express, Stanton's entire mind was devoted to Mosby. The predominant hallucination of the Secretary of War was that, whenever Mosby wanted to capture the national capital, he could do it, if not opposed by the flower of the Federal army; and between the harassing anticipations of being "gobbled up" by Mosby and his dreadful guerrillas, and the dread of being tied to the tail of a cart and driven off to some remote Southern plantation by Stonewall Jackson and his followers, (who were forever threatening to dine under the dome of the capitol, and stable their horses in the White House,) poor Stanton obtained but little rest. He believes that Mosby is still a guerrilla chieftain, and forgets that Stonewall Jackson is dead. Why should he tremble when that brick edifice near the Treasury, of which the Boston Traveler lately made such particular mention, from which a sharpshooter could put a bullet through the brain of a "traitor" standing on the steps of the White House, is still standing, and in possession of the terrible office-seeking Grand Army of the Republic?

This was one of several references regarding Stanton's fear of Mosby even well after the war. Notice, however, that Stanton feared being *kidnapped*—"gobbled up"—rather than being assassinated, though, of course, it was Stanton who first blamed Mosby for leading the conspiracy to assassinate President Lincoln.

Native Virginian – March 20, 1868
STANTON AFRAID OF MOSBY.

A more absurd story never emanated from the intelligent contraband of the rebellion than the report which caused such consternation in the War Department on Friday last.

That it was:—A detective employed by Mr. Stanton to bring him early intelligence of any danger that might threaten the safety of his official sanctuary, appeared before him on that day and imparted the startling intelligence that Mosby had organized a force in the country adjacent to the Potomac river and was prepared to enter Washington, surround the War Department and seize the refractory Secretary of War, so called. What disposition was then to have been made of the illustrious prisoner was not clearly known, but uncomfortable visions of a midnight ride on a Virginia fence rail, exposed to the biting blasts of wintry air, with no other covering than a liberal coat of tar and feathers, or, perhaps, a sudden dissolution of all that is mortal of the great War Secretary and his remains thrust into some one of the half filled holes that cover the Bull Run battlefield, filled the mind of the nervous Stanton and he at once ordered out a force of seventy-five men. This force was held under marching orders to move to the scene of action at a moment's notice. At night while the weather was quite cold a strong guard was sent to the Long Bridge across the Potomac to look out for the approach of the enemy and contest the passage of the river. The guard, much to their disgust, bivouacked in the cold night air on the Long Bridge for two nights, but were doomed to disappointment, for no Mosby made his appearance.

Republican Compiler - March 20, 1868

A Washington correspondent of The Age under date of Tuesday, says: According to the current report, the valiant Stanton and his equally valiant followers hereabouts are still apprehensive that they may be suddenly forced to leave their comfortable quarters and 'carried away captive' by a band of Virginians, headed by Colonel Mosby. The long bridge has been strongly guarded at each end for some time, and the War Department still bristles with bayonets, although no armed foe has been seen within cannon's shot of the Federal capital since Early's raid in 1864. The truth is that Stanton is a natural coward, besides a very artful politician and he imagines that by creating an impression on the public mind that the city is about to be invaded by ex-rebels, as they are called, he can hide some of his own rapscality and expedite the removal of President Johnson. That's about what he is after.

Fairfield Herald – March 25, 1868
Washington News STANTON'S FEARS

Although the greatest care has been taken to smother the matter, the real cause for locking the back door of the War Department has leaked out most probably through a discontented soldier. Cut into the mildest form possible, it cannot be concealed that the high-minded occupant of the War Department was overtaken last week with so great a panic that it almost resulted in stampeding him. When the terrors of the nitroglycerine burst upon him he resorted to the military for protection, and while even the most nervous people regarding the story as a very weak hoax, Mr. Stanton saw danger enough in it to surround the Department with a strong skirmish line, having a heavy reserve for support located within the building and camping out on the hard brick floor. A more absurd story never emanated from the intelligent contraband of the rebellion than the report that caused such consternation in the War Department on Friday last.

This it was: A detective employed by Mr. Stanton to bring him early intelligence of any danger that might threaten the safety of his official sanctuary appeared before him on that day and imparted the startling intelligence that Mosby had organized a force in the country adjacent to the Potomac River and was prepared to enter Washington, surround the War Department and seize the refractory Secretary of War, so-called. What disposition was then to have been made of the illustrious prisoner was not clearly known, but uncomfortable visions of a midnight ride on a Virginia fence rail, exposed to the biting blasts of Wintry air, with no other covering than a liberal coat of tar and feathers, or perhaps, a sudden dissolution of all that is mortal of the great War Secretary and his remains thrust into some one of the half filed holes that cover the Bull Run battlefield, filled the mind of the nervous Stanton and he at once ordered out a force of seventy-five men. This force was held under marching orders to move to the scene of action at a moment's notice. At night while the weather was quite cold a strong guard was sent to the Long Bridge across the Potomac to look out for the approach of the enemy and contest the passage of the river. The guard, much to their disgust, bivouacked in the cold night air on the Long Bridge for two nights, but were doomed to disappointment, for no Mosby made his appearance. Then it was resolved to lock the rear of the War Department in order that there should be but one entrance, which was thought the Forty-fourth regiment, assisted by the Twelfth regiment of infantry and the Fifth cavalry, would be able to hold against any force that could be brought upon it.—Wash. Cor. N.Y., Herald, March 12.

In the same paper:

MOSBY STILL A BUGBEAR.

The War Office has not recovered from the terrible fright of last week. The invincible Secretary had an attack of nightmare. He was visited by the pale spectres from Andersonville and Salisbury, who shook their wan fingers at him, and glared with famine-fevered eyes at the man who cared not what became of the imprisoned boys in blue, so that he kept the captured Confederate prisoners out of the rebel ranks. His nerves were unsettled all the next day, and when evening came, and one of his "reliable detectives" assured him that Mosby was gathering his clan, preparatory to making a raid on the War Department, and bearing off the great Carnot on a sharpened rail, great drops of perspiration rolled off the invincible brow.

A guard was dispatched to the Long Bridge with instructions to hold it in case Mosby appeared at the head of his expected five hundred, at all hazards, till all the military were aroused. They shivered in the midnight air—it was one of those cold nights—to see nothing more dangers than a cow or a market wagon, and wished aught but blessing on the head of those who assigned them such a fool's errand. Today cavalry men have been riding around like mad; whether in pursuit of Mosby's secreted band or not, we have not learned.

All this sounds ridiculous and perfectly incredible; but it is an absolute fact, that while Mosby has been quietly pursuing his profession by day, and sleeping cozily at home of nights, "the great Carnot* of rebellion" has been frightened out of his wits, and giving his subordinates any quantity of annoyance over an expected grand invasion of the War Department, with details of which he has been victimized by one of his honest detectives.— Washington Express.[*A French nobleman involved in the Irish rebellion of the eighteenth century.-vph]

The real question that was never asked is this: if Stanton had sufficient reason to believe that Mosby was going to launch such an assault, why did he not have the man arrested? Surely, even suspicion of such an act would constitute a violation of Mosby's parole and been more than adequate for his detention and interrogation. But not only didn't that happen, but it appears that Mosby was ignorant of the entire matter. Certainly there is no evidence that he ever responded to it either in personal letters or letters to the newspapers.

Cambria Freeman – **April 2, 1868**

[From the Metropolitan Record, March 1] MOSBY'S LAST RAID

It is not necessary to tell some of our readers, we suppose, that Stanton was the victim of a great hoax last week. Some practical joker started a report that Mosby, the one-time ubiquitous, had organized a force of trusty spirits to seize Stanton and bear him off to some secluded spot in the Blue Ridge, and was then lying in wait on the Virginia side of the Potomac, ready to pounce upon Edwin at the first favorable opportunity. The story goes that Stanton was so much scared by the prospect of falling into the hands of the great raider, that he had double guards stationed around the War Department, and then dispatched troops to guard the Potomac bridges, so that Mosby could not get at him without fighting his way, at least. The troops, we are told, watched the bridges one whole night, and then returned to their quarters, for Mosby had failed to put in an appearance, and they came to the conclusion that the story was a grand hoax. And so it was, for the gallant raider of the Blue Ridge was quietly attending to his business in Warrenton when Stanton thought he was getting ready to pounce upon Washington.

Our friend, Timothy Tripp, comes in just when we are wishing for some one to dress up the Stanton scare in the right way for the Portfolio, and hands us the following capital version of it:

STANTON'S LAST SCARE.

The night was dark, the night was chill,
All nature was a peace and still,
The hurly-burly of the day,
The sounds of pleasure or of fray;
The jester's laugh, the mourner's sigh,
Were heard no more. The starless sky
Gave not a ray to light the gloom,
Opaque, impervious as the tomb;
Impeachers and impeachee slept,
And rich and poor forgot a space
The cares that hide in rags and lace,
By all of which I would convey,
Though in a periphrastic way.
The fact, with wordy trimmings dight,
That day had yielded unto night,
And lamps, man's substitute for sun,
Lit up the streets of Washington.
What though 'tis locked with jealous care!
What though 'tis locked with jealous care!
What though no strangers enter there—
What though a "trooly loil" guard
Its sacred precincts watch and ward
With vigilant, unsleeping care—
I and Asmodeus, enter there.

But Hark! What sounds are those that strike?
Upon the ear and heart alike?
What means that measured, steady tramp?
Is Washington once more a camp?
Does Stuart still our pickets drive?
Is Stonewall Jackson yet alive?
See where a light in yonder room
Strikes like a lancehead through the gloom!
Surely there's something going on there—
Ah, Friend Asmodeus! Through the air
Convey me quick, that I may know,
And tell't to the Portfolio.

"Up with the roof," Asmodeus cries,
And up it goes. Before my eyes
The War Office lay open all,
From attic down to basement hall;

Good Lord, what sight affronts my gaze?
A quaking, shivering wretch displays
His coward fears without a blush—
Is it a man or what?— "Hush, hush,"
Asmodeus whispers, "he will speak,
List the half-bully and half-sneak."

Stanton (loquitor)—
"Oh! Are you sure the news is true,
And are you sure he's come;
This is not time to think of rest,
I wish he'd stayed tu hum,
This is no time to think of rest,
When Mosby's at the gate;
See that each door is double locked,
I—I think I'll—make him wait."
[Enter a messenger in a flurry.

"Your Excellency, there's great noise without, and much we wonder what it is about. A man's just come with terror almost dumb, who through white lips hisses, 'Mosby's come.' It can't be true, I'll not believe such stories; they're set afloat by Copperheads and Tories. And oh! your Excellency, he says that you had best be on your guard, or you will rue"—

Stanton—
"Away, away; rouse up the guard—
Let each see to his gun;
Put ammunition in the pouch
Of every mother's son,

Can it be true the rebs are here?
Will I and Mosby meet?
Not while there's reason in this brain
Or swiftness in these feet."
[Enter Sumner, Stevens and others.

Stevens—
"This is a bad business, Stanton; you'll have but little left to vaunt on, I fear, but still I knew, like Danton, you can rave and rage and rant for any length of time, Stanton, I came to you to-night, though sick, to say to you but one word."

Sumner (interrupting)—
"Stick!"

Stevens—
"Stanton, look out; there is a plot on foot to fright, assault and capture you to boot. The rebel rascals, driven on by Andy, would stop at nothing, and they're here quite handy. Therefore I come to you at double quick, to say the best thing you can do is:—

Sumner—
"Stick!"

Stanton—
"Oh! of all the plots agoing
There's but one I car for knowing,
The one that's terror throwing
Round all in my employ."

Stevens—
"The plot, no doubt of it's to get possession of the War Office, and secure the secession."
[A crowd of lackeys rush in, pale with terror and screaming in unison:

"John Mosby is coming, ohone!
Ohone!
And you bet he's not coming alone!
Ohone!
Pit-a-pat go all hearts
In these diggings and parts,
For Mosby is coming, 'tis known,
Ohone!
And you bet he's not coming alone!"

Stanton—
"Is there no peg wheron to hang a doubt?"

All—
"No, no, no, no, the rebs are all about!"

Stanton—
"What shall I do? We must take measures quick.
Come, friends, advise, advise."

All—   "Cut stick!"

Sumner—   "Ay, Stick!"

               You've seen enough, Asmodeus cries,
                 We must begone, for lo! times flies,
                 And very soon the morn will break.
                  Perhaps some other time I'll take
                 You on my rounds, and you shall see
                    More matter to Record, as we
                  Go roundabout here, Tripp & Co.,
                              Tripp—
                   And write for the Portfolio.
                    I wanted, oh! so bad, to stay.
                  But who could say Asmodeus nay;
                 So what they did and what they said,
               What means they too, what way they fled,
                   I knew not, yet, although so near
                    To everything I wished to hear—
                  Another proof, there's many a slip—
                       You know the proverb,

                                              Yours,
                                              Tim Tripp.

[*Asmodeus first appears in the Book of Tobit. According to Tobit iii. 8, vi. 14, the evil spirit Asmodeus—"king of the demons,"-vph]

Clarksville Chronicle – **April 10, 1868**

Mosby at the Head of an Army!

Colonel Mosby has just received a letter from a Boston lady friend, enclosing the following dispatch from the Boston Journal (Radical) She contemplated visiting Virginia and wrote to the Colonel to ascertain the truth of the startling news before she ventured on. The dispatch is headed in large capitals, "Mosby Gathering his Clans," "A Thousand Men Reviewed at Leesburg yesterday, "Serious Fears of an attack from the Virginia Shore," and is as follows:

Washington, March 16, 1868. A Virginia Union man, who was at Leesburg in that State yesterday (Sunday), says that John S. Mosby, who resides there, was visited by nearly a thousand of his old guerrilla command. They were all well mounted, many of them were armed.

After riding through the streets of Leesburg in columns they were exercised in battalion movements and then formed into a square to hear a speech from Mosby. What he said my informant could not hear, but some of the men afterward declared that they might at any day be called on to oust Stanton from the War Office.

                                              PENLEY.

Colonel Mosby telegraphed to the lady at once in accordance with the facts, that he was at the head of 15,000 veterans of the late war, armed and equipped according to law, and was about to invest Washington, proclaim Andy Johnson king, hang Stanton, wipe out Congress and blow up the Capitol with glycerin. Only one thing delayed him—the hourly expectation of some Northern friends on their way South of the Potomac for security. He advised her to come on instanter, nor "stand upon the order of her coming" as he intended to sweep the whole North and inaugurate the Devil in person as the Mayor of Boston.—Warrenton True Index, 21st.

The essence of Mosby's telegraph to the concerned lady, probably Miss Southwick of brass-buttoned cloak fame, was a beautiful admixture of sarcasm and deviltry of which Mosby was a past master. Knowing the man as she did, Miss Southwick may have had a chortle or two herself, especially upon considering Mosby's choice to be mayor of Boston!

Spirit of Jefferson – **April 21, 1868**

An Attempt to Procure Evidence for Impeachment.—The Warrenton Index publishes the following letter, just received by Colonel Mosby, which he intends to indorse, and refer to E. M. Stanton through Grant. If detective Forrester ought not to be bow-strung for his shallow artifice, he certainly should be cashiered. Here is his letter:

Lincoln Barracks
Washington, D. C. March 26, 1868

Col. John S. Mosby—Sir: The rumor is afloat that you are raising men to march on this city with the intention of putting things in shape to suit yourself. If so, I glory in your undertaking. I think it a Christian act.

I wish you to inform me at once if such is the case, and I will assist you in your undertaking.

I was once a Colonel in the Federal army, but only now a Sergeant. I have been misused, and will be avenged. Write in confidence to me; all will be right. No danger of betrayal. I will keep you posted in regard to Congress, military movements, &c.

Respectfully, your obedient serv't

Frank Forrester,
Co. H. 29th,
U. S. Infantry Washington, D. C.

The Stanton matter was still extant when another party was heard from. This time, it was a Federal soldier who supposedly played a practical joke. This "joke" was no laughing matter, at least for John Mosby. There were more than enough people in the North who would certainly believe that he was considering such a plan as seen by earlier reports in the papers. Interestingly enough, the government and the Federal military determined to treat the matter as a "practical joke" as seen in the following article:

National Republican, – May 12, 1868

Yorkville Enquirer, – May 21, 1868

A SOLDIER PUNISHED FOR A PRACTICAL JOKE.—

It will be remembered that shortly after the beginning of the War Department difficulty, it was reported that Mosby was coming to this city with an armed force, and a letter received by him from this city was published in most of the southern journals, who charged that it was from a Government detective here to trap Mosby, but the facts in the case are contained in an order just issued from headquarters department of Washington, which sets forth that before court-martial in session in this city, of which General John B. Ricketts is president, Sergeant Frank Forrester, company H, 29th infantry, was tried upon a charge of conduct to the prejudice of good order and military discipline.

The specification charges that he did with intent to incite insurrection and resistance of the laws of the United States, write, and cause to be sent to one John S. Mosby, formerly an officer in the confederate army, a letter, of which copy is appended, in which the writer says:

"The rumor is afloat that you are raising men to march on this city, with the intention of putting things in shape to suit yourself. If so, I glory in your undertaking. I think it a Christian act. I wish you to inform me at once if such is the case, and I will assist you in your undertaking. I was once a colonel in the Federal army, but now only a sergeant. I have been misused, and will be avenged. Write in confidence to me, all will be right; no danger of betrayal. I will keep you posted in regard to Congress, military movements, &c."

The court found the accused guilty, and sentenced him to be reduced to the ranks, and to forfeit to the United States ten dollars per month of his monthly pay. Gen. Emory has approved the sentence and says:

"The sentence awarded is evidently founded upon the belief that the accused had no malicious intent in writing the letter contained in the charge against him, of which he has been found guilty, and that he merely intended a practical joke. Concurring in this view the sentence is approved, and will be duly executed; and it is hoped it will serve as a warning that "jokes" upon matters of that kind, calculated to disturb the public peace, may not be again attempted."

As was often the case, small articles on Mosby appeared out of nowhere and apparently without reason:

Evening Telegraph – August 20, 1868

The correspondent adds the following in regard to Moseby—"At Warrenton I saw Moseby, the partisan chief, a lawyer of fair village ability, with a sad jawed face, a dull, stubborn eye, a grittiness, lankness, and bronzeness all over him, and a saucy ease of speech that became his record well. He fits in prettily with the new Democratic prospects, has a hopeful talk, and is, I think, by no means the best of the transformed Rebels. It is the miserable tradesmen's spirit that revives forever the lost issues of the war and carps upon them."

And then Stanton was back in the news, but involved in a slightly different matter. It appeared that papers and records were missing from the War Department. This Democratic publication speculated that they dealt with illegal arrests but so many such arrests happened during the war that a great deal more than the destruction of a wagonload of papers would have been necessary to cover them up—if that were indeed even possible:

Bloomsburg Democrat – **September 9, 1868**

WHO STOLE THE PAPERS, OR BURNED THE RECORDS.—

It will be remembered that when Stanton held the War Department last spring by force and the aid of the Radical Congress, it was given out that in consequence of an apprehended raid from Mosby, twenty wagon loads of arms and ammunition were sent one night from the War Department, to Virginia across the Long Bridge, so as to be ready for Mosby. But Mosby never appeared, and the arms and ammunition never were heard of.

It turns out now that all this was a trick to enable the Radicals to get away from the War Department some twenty loads of papers and records which it was necessary to hide before Stanton gave up the Department to a Johnson man.

What these records and papers contained, it is easy to guess. They were the files of the illegal arrests and imprisonments, caused by the usurping Stanton, and also evidence showing where, about one hundred million dollars had been wasted and lost without authority of law. Such is the Radical rule.—Digest.

Little further mention of Mosby appeared in 1868, and that which did appear was fairly innocuous and, as in the Stanton matter, even somewhat supportive. Of course, there were a few nasty items that manifested continuing deep-seated hostility; but often in these articles, Mosby was, individually, merely a means of identifying the people of the South as a whole. As he seemed to no longer be the focus of hostility, John Mosby probably believed that the next year was bound to be better.

Chapter 9

1869

Pro opportunitate ~ As circumstances allow

"There is no darkness but ignorance." ~ William Shakespeare

1869 BEGAN SOMEWHAT ominously as Congress considered the proposed Fourteenth Amendment to the Constitution. Mention was made of both Mosby and the amendment in this article:

Nashville Union and American – February 26, 1869

Col. Mosby, the noted guerrilla, was in the reporters' gallery of the United States Senate Tuesday. He listened to Trumbull and others, who were advocating the punishment of Rebels who held office under the fourteenth amendment.

However, if anyone believed that the hatred of John Mosby in the North or elsewhere had faded away, this article in the *Orleans Independent Standard* (Irasburg, Vermont) proved otherwise:

Orleans Independent Standard – April 27, 1869

Bushwhacker Mosby.

Yesterday, while riding in the Pennsylvania Avenue cars, who should enter but Col. Mosby, late C.S.A.?—From the fact that he carried in his hand a small black valise, on which was printed in large, white letters, "Col. John S. Mosby," everybody in the cars was perforce made acquainted with the countenance of this notorious bushwhacker and cowardly murderer. He comes to Washington very frequently, puts up at Willard's and attracts great attention. He seldom hears any good of himself from the conversing groups at the hotel, for some of his victims are generally about to make a few comments on his character as a "soldier." How soon the human heart forgives! The men murdered in cold blood by this wretch are legion, and yet he visits Washington, Philadelphia and New York and his democratic brethren receive him with distinguished honors!

One of his dastardly acts alone, which I never call to mind without a shudder, should bring him to the gallows and an ignominious death. In the fall of '64, when in the valley of the Shenandoah, with the prince of soldiers, Gen. Sheridan, a number brutal acts, perpetrated by this fiend, came under my personal observation. The one, however, to which I particularly refer, was the hanging of seven Union prisoners near Berryville. Gen. Custer had a few days previous executed a rebel spy near Middletown. This so exasperated Mosby that he determined to be avenged, and calling out his prisoners, he made them cast lots for death by hanging. Capt. Brewster of Sheridan's staff, as among the number, and was one of the lucky fellows drawing a blank—which, in that particular lottery, although not a winning card, was a very desirable one.

I shall never forget his narration of the terrible affair; the pathetic appeals for mercy; the brutal oaths of the captors as they tightened the fatal ropes about the necks of prisoners, and the frightful death struggle. One hour after this act was perpetrated, I saw the bodies as they hung by the roadside, the faces black from suffocation, and the tongues protruding from the bloody mouths. It was a sign to rouse the blackest demon of vengeance, and as Sheridan's dusky columns passed, many an eye kindled with wrath, and many a vow was taken to avenge that horrible atrocity.

"Vengeance is mine, saith the Lord of hosts," but Mosby, the rebel butcher, seems to fear neither the vengeance of God or man as he swaggers into Washington, ostentatiously parading to the public gaze in full name and former title and rank in the army of the rebellion.—Washington Co. St. Albans Messenger.

Before anyone can begin to understand John Mosby's political activity after the war, one must understand the situation extant in the South. Reconstruction—that period of military occupation—did not begin immediately after Appomattox. The Southern states returned to the Union as full states, a fact proved by their voting for the Thirteenth Amendment ending slavery. It was not until the attempt to pass the Fourteenth and Fifteenth Amendments—the latter granting suffrage to the Negro— that the states of the South became occupied military districts because they, with some states *outside* that section, refused to vote for the amendments. In the following article, John Mosby referenced the situation in speaking about his "change of mind" regarding the "expurgated" Virginia constitution, the passage of which was demanded in order to return that state to the Union:

National Republican – June 19, 1869

Fairfield Herald* - June 30, 1869

John S. Mosby on Virginia Politics.

A correspondent of the Richmond Dispatch, writing from Leesburg, gives the following as the result of an interview with John S. Mosby, the Virginia guerrilla chieftain:

I was gratified to notice Col. J. S. Mosby moving from group to group on the court green and urging the people to vote for Walker and the expurgated constitution as the only means of escaping the evils which now threaten us. A gentleman remarked,

"Why Colonel, a year ago you talked differently.

Mosby: *"Yes; I swore I wouldn't register, but think differently, and had rather be right than consistent. Then we had our own judges, our own county officers, and no one of them was required to take the iron-clad oath!"* [emphasis vph] [See "Addendum" at the end of the chapter.-vph]

Citizen: "You think we ought to vote for the expurgated constitution with negro suffrage and the county organization clause?"

Mosby: *"Certainly negro suffrage cannot possibly impose upon us a worse man than Wells, and by voting down the constitution you vote to disfranchise yourselves, and to keep the State under the rule of carpet-baggers* [emphasis vph]."

Citizen: "How is that?"

Mosby: "Why, the concurrent resolutions passed by the two Houses of Congress last winter prohibits anybody from holding even the most trivial office who cannot swallow the iron-clad oath. This gives all the offices to carpet-baggers, and how can you get them out of their clutches, and have them filled by capable and honest citizens until the State is reconstructed; and how can you reconstruct it except by the adoption of the expurgated constitution, which I admit, deserves all the abuse it has received? For my own part, I cannot see any sense in voting for Walker and against the expurgated constitution, because if you defeat the latter, you keep Wells and his party in office. A vote against the amended constitution is a vote for Wells."

Your Reporter: "Colonel, I am pleased to see that the—newspaper has at last come out for Walker."

Mosby: "Yes, and he heads his article 'We Surrender.' Rather late to be surrendering. For myself, I surrendered four years ago, and thought I (had) done it in good faith in April, '65.

Wells won his brevet by gallant services in capturing me in Alexandria the August following while I was paying a visit to some ladies of that city."
Reporter: "It is rather difficult to have to change from front to rear in this constitution."

Mosby: "Yes, I found no difficulty in bringing my judgment to the conclusion that it was the true policy to adopt the course I now advise, but my pride held out some time after my judgment was convinced. It now seems strange that any reasonable man can entertain a doubt as to his plain duty."

Reporter: "You ought to take the stump; your advice would have great weight with the young men of the State."

Mosby: "I have to go to Richmond soon, but on my return from there to Fauquier, I mean to do so, as I think it the duty of every man in a crisis like this to use whatever influence he possesses for the good of his State."

Mosby's position changed *as the circumstances changed!* In a way, this ability to respond to changing conditions was a large part of the success of his method of warfare— and he survived and was successful *because* he was able to adapt his actions to changing circumstances. This is what had happened, and continued to happen, in Virginia and the South. Before Reconstruction, Virginia had its own government; now it did not, and so it required a different strategy to deal with these new circumstances. *"Then we had our own judges, our own county officers, and no one of them was required to take the iron-clad oath!"*

This was John Mosby's response to the political scene pretty much for the rest of his life; he was willing to "change" as circumstances changed in order to achieve his desired ends. Of course, it helped that Mosby was not a *religious* man. Religion remains the same though circumstances change. But for many people (and not just in the South), their politics *was* "religious" in just that way. They were not able to adjust because they saw such "adjustments" as apostasy, the abandonment of principle. Mosby, not being hampered by strong religious sentiments, was able to look at matters objectively and determine the best course to take in order to obtain the desired end. And though he later became a staunch Republican—having been a staunch Whig—he had no more qualms about criticizing Republicans than Democrats. In other words, he did not worship at the "Altar of Party," something that can be seen in his refusal to vote for his cousin Benjamin Harrison when he ran a second time on the Republican ticket. Cousin Ben had proven to John Mosby that he was a sectional bigot and not worthy of his support. If Mosby had been "religious" in his politics, Harrison's shortcomings would have been overlooked because of his party affiliation. Mosby also spoke about the Virginia elections in which Walker replaced Wells. As can be seen, Mosby had little use for the latter:

> *Weekly Panola Star* – July 24, 1869
>
> Mosby spoke at a political meeting in Warrenton, Va., on the 23rd ult., and in the course of his remarks said: "Now I happen to know something about Wells. He was Provost Marshal of Alexandria during the time I was conducting military operations in the county. And I tell you that he never once showed his face outside of the stockade. If he had, I would have saved our people all the trouble they have had with him as Governor of Virginia."

The next difficulty in which John Mosby found himself was a "run in" with the federally appointed sheriff of Fauquier County, William Boyd, a former colonel in the Union cavalry. This was the same Colonel Boyd who had closely interrogated Pauline as she lay in bed while her husband spent a few very uncomfortable hours on a tree limb outside of their second-story bedroom window. Boyd obviously did nothing "ungentlemanly" in his conduct with Pauline, so that was not the basis of the quarrel. Rather, Mosby believed that Boyd was a thief—he had been hired by the man's former Washington landlady who charged that Boyd left owing her a considerable sum of money. Furthermore, Mosby knew that Boyd's bond as sheriff was worthless. Under military control, the Southern states were being robbed blind by such "officials"; and Mosby, with the other attorneys in Fauquier County, had gone to General Canby and demanded that Boyd be removed and replaced by someone who could provide a legitimate bond.

The matter between the two men, however, began with what Mosby believed was a challenge to him by Boyd when they met one day on the road. The code duello was the old-fashioned, time honored Southern way of settling important social disputes. But when Boyd backed off, Mosby challenged him in response to the insult Boyd had rendered to Mosby. And there the matter stood. Of course, dueling had been illegal in Virginia for many years and to be involved in a duel, even as a "second," was to be charged with a felony and disfranchised. To Mosby, however, that didn't matter; and as a result of what was a very spicy subject, the whole issue wound up in the papers. In the end, Boyd said that he was not permitted by law to duel; and besides, Mosby was "scum" and unworthy of his attention. But the judgment of Virginians was that Boyd had proven a coward, and to avoid his detractors, he sold his office and left the state. So Mosby prevailed *without* a duel. But for some little time, the matter provided considerable interest and gossip in more places than Warrenton as can be seen by the names of the newspapers that covered the matter:

New York Herald - October 7, 1869

Daily Phoenix – October 12, 1869

A Duel on the Table –

Mosby, the Raider, Challenges Colonel Boyd, of the Pennsylvania Cavalry.

Bristol News – October 15, 1869

The Mosby Duel.—Col. Boyd who was challenged by Col. John Mosby backed down and refused to fight. Boyd had said Mosby was a highway robber.

But the most detailed and complete coverage was found in, of all places, the *New York Herald*. As the *Herald* was one of the *premier* papers in the country, it is obvious that the incident held a great deal of interest for a lot of folks outside of Warrenton *and* Virginia. The reason for this unusual interest can only be attributed to the identity of one of the participants—John S. Mosby:

New York Herald – October 15, 1869 (Edited)

Mosby and Boyd.

Interview with the Ex-Rebel Leader – His Account of the Recent Trouble with a Carpet-Bagger – How General Canby Appointed Sheriffs – the Duello Not Acceptable to Boyd – Mosby's Opinion of Reconstruction – Boyd's Story – Why He Did Not Fight – The General Feeling and Impression of the People.

Washington, Oct. 13, 1869.

The quiet, sleepy little village of Warrenton, Va., is the last place in the world where you would expect to find duelists and dueling … There is so little to contribute to excitement, and everybody you meet is so civil withal, that it must require considerable effort to make the "angry passions rise." But even Warrenton has had its sensation… In a village like Warrenton, which, in respect to gossip, is like every other village, anything like a duel, even between two ordinary individuals, would naturally excite interest. But when Colonel Jack Mosby happens to be one of the principals and an ex-federal colonel named Boyd the other, the affair grows in interest far beyond the limits of Warrenton, or even of Fauquier county.

With a view to ascertain the origin of the difficulty I stepped into Colonel Mosby's law office to-day, and after introducing myself and making known my business I was cordially received by the celebrated partisan leader. I found him sitting in a small room in a building opposite the principal hotel of the village, looking more like a young country parson than a dashing cavalry colonel or a hot-headed duelist. His pantaloons were tucked inside his boots, but otherwise, his dress indicated taste and neatness. His hair was cut short, and his beardless face and genial, lively manner, make him look much younger than he really is. [Mosby was thirty-two at that time-vph.] On the table before him a number of papers, pamphlets and books were scattered; but the most prominent object was a six-barreled Colt's army revolver, loaded and ready for instant use. In a couple of bookcases around the room were enough books to constitute a decent law library for a country lawyer… The other furniture of the room was scanty, that is for a lawyer's office; but I presume Mosby has had worse quarters… I said: -

"Colonel Mosby, what was the origin of the difficulty between Colonel Boyd and yourself?"

Mosby – Well, I will tell you; and I am glad to do, because I suppose people outside will think that it arose out of political differences, which it did not. I had and have nothing personal against Colonel Boyd. He was sent here last April by General Canby to act as sheriff of Fauquier county. It was soon discovered that his bond was worthless, those who had agreed it not being worth anything. There was a meeting of the members of the bar here relative to the subject. At this meeting a memorial addressed to General Canby was drawn up and adopted. It set forth the fact that Colonel Boyd had failed to give a satisfactory bond, and that the members of the bar felt it to be their duty in the interest of their clients to protest against Colonel Boyd's performing the duties of sheriff without giving bond. I was selected to carry the memorial to General Canby, which I did.

Correspondent – What did General Canby say to you?

Mosby – He said he would look into the matter; but instead of doing so he sent Colonel Boyd here to institute an investigation into alleged conspiracy among the members of the bar of this place to defeat the reconstruction laws.

Correspondent – Was there a conspiracy for that purpose?

Mosby – Not a bit of it. We had no more notion of interfering with the reconstruction laws than you have. We wanted a man for sheriff who would not run away with the revenues of the county, or if he did run away we wanted to have some bondsmen that had something to take hold of.

Correspondent – Were Colonel Boyd's bondsmen persons of property?

Mosby – No; they had nothing. I believe that altogether they did not pay more than twenty cents Internal Revenue Tax. So you can judge how much property they had. One of them named Cannon appeared to be released from the bond shortly after Boyd qualified.

Correspondent – Why did he do that?

Mosby – Well, Cannon is the editor of a little paper here called the Southerner. Colonel Boyd went to him and said: - "Cannon, if you go on my bond I'll give you the advertising patronage of the sheriff's office." Cannon agreed to this and became one of Boyd's secretaries. Cannon soon discovered, however, that Boyd had no advertising, and no patronage of any sort, and so he petitioned to be released.

Correspondent – Then it was a sort of bargain between Boyd and Cannon for their mutual benefit.

Mosby – Precisely. The matter came up in court before Judge Hill. He decided that the bond was worthless and Cannon was released. What do you think Canby did? He appointed Colonel Boyd over again without any bond at all, although we told him he would be satisfied if he would detail General McKibbon or any other regular army officer to act as sheriff, because their commission would be some security.

Correspondent – Did General Canby assign any reason for appointing Boyd over again?

Mosby – No, he did not. I don't like to question a man's motives, but it was a little singular that Canby should hang on to this man Boyd when he knew he had no bond and was insolvent besides.

Correspondent – You don't mean to intimate that there was any corrupt purpose on the part of General Canby?

Mosby – Well, it looks as if there was something wrong. I think Canby is the Fagin of the business and Boyd is the Artful Dodger.

Here Colonel Mosby laughed, whether at the idea of his being well up in Dickens "Oliver Twist" or at the respective roles of General Canby and Colonel Boyd was not apparent.

Correspondent – Well, how does the case stand now?

Mosby – Colonel Boyd is still sheriff, but he has given no bond. He has, however, "farmed out" the office to Mr. Hume, who was sheriff before the war.

Correspondent – What do you mean by "farming out the office?"

Mosby – Mr. Hume can't take the "iron-clad", but Boyd can. Hume gives Boyd $500 for the privilege of acting as sheriff. Boyd signs the writs, but Hume does the work, and gets the perquisites or fees. That's what we call "farming out".

Correspondent – Is that a common thing here?

Mosby – Yes; it's done with nearly every office. It's the effect of the "iron-clad." Here's one of my boys, Chilton, who is Commonwealth attorney for this county. He gave some fellow a couple of hundred dollars to take the "iron-clad" for him, and he fills the office.

Correspondent – Is General Canby aware of this "farming out" business?

Mosby – Of course he is. I tell you it's done all over Virginia by the men whom Canby appoints to fill the offices.

Correspondent – How did all this difficulty about Colonel Boyd's bond lead to the correspondence about the duel?

Mosby – I took a very active part in having Colonel Boyd's bond broken, and when the matter was up in court I pronounced it a Peter Funk* affair [*a contemporary definition of a swindle-vph], and gave it as my opinion that Boyd came here to swindle the county. I was also employed as counsel to collect a bill of over $400 which Colonel Boyd owed a lady in Washington named Miss Smith for board or rent. He said I was persecuting him. One day I was coming in from the country and happened to meet Colonel Boyd on the road. I spoke to him in a friendly way, for I had nothing personal against him, when he turned his horse around and said, "Colonel Mosby, if you don't stop interfering with my business I will make it a personal matter with you." I said, "You can do so as soon as you please, and in any manner or at any time." He then said, "Mosby, if you will go with me to Pennsylvania I will prove you to be a damned highway robber." I replied that I would hold him responsible for those words when he got to town.

Correspondent – Why didn't you fight it out on the road?

Mosby – Well, I don't' think that it is quite the thing for two gentlemen who have served as colonels of cavalry to make bruisers of themselves. Besides, Colonel Boyd is a man of about 175 pounds and very athletic, while I don't weigh over 125 pounds. He could have crushed me in a fist fight like an egg shell.

Correspondent – On what terms did you agree to fight?

Mosby – At ten paces, with Colt's army revolver, the parties to advance as close as they pleased after the word was given to fire, and keep firing until all the barrels were emptied.

Correspondent – If the thing had come off somebody would have been hurt, I suppose?

Mosby – It would have settled the sheriff business, I think. I am a pretty good shot with an army pistol.

Correspondent – Do you keep that thing on the table all the time? (pointing to the Colt's revolver already alluded to).

Mosby – No. I carried that pistol all through the war with me. I brought it out when this trouble occurred because I expected to be assaulted in the street, and I wanted to be ready.

Correspondent – What's the general impression here about Colonel Boyd's conduct?

Mosby – Well, you have seen the correspondence. I wrote the last note and he replied to it. First I accepted what I presumed he meant as a challenge. He backed out of that, and then I challenged him for calling me a "highway robber." He has refused to accept my challenge, and there's where the matter stands. I saw in the Herald that there was some difficulty in Colonel Boyd getting a second. Now, the trouble with him was to get a principal. He could have got plenty of gentlemen to act as his second. Why, half a dozen of my friends volunteered to wait on him if he couldn't secure any of his own.

Correspondent – Then you think Boyd won't fight?

Mosby – Well, he had a chance, and he didn't accept it. You can draw your own inference. The truth is, this is the first time one of these carpet-baggers has been brought to that. They are accustomed to ride rough shod over our people and nobody calls them to account.

Correspondent – What do you think of reconstruction?

Mosby – Haven't we done all we were asked to do? I am in favor of doing anything to get back into the Union, so that we may get rid of these carpet-baggers.

Correspondent – What do you call a carpet-bagger?

Mosby – These adventurers that come her to prey on us, and roam through the State after offices under Canby. I don't want to be understood as objecting to Northern people coming here to settle. On the contrary, I wish we had more of them; I mean people who come to settle down. I want to sell them land and marble quarries and treat them well; but these harpies are a scourge to us. They have no interest in the State.

Taking a farewell glance at the formidable weapon which lay upon the table, and which looked as if it might be able to settle the business of half a dozen sheriffs, I took leave of Mosby.

[The correspondent then interviews Colonel Boyd, some parts of which are included below:-vph]

Colonel Boyd hales from Pennsylvania, and served as a volunteer officer during the rebellion. He is a large, athletic man, about forty-five years of age, and looks as if he could whip half a dozen men like Mosby in a fisticuff engagement. After introducing himself, he stated "I want to tell you exactly how this thing occurred. I suppose you have Mosby's version of it."

Boyd – Well, three days after I qualified as sheriff of Fauquier county, Mr. Cannon, one of my bondsmen, petitioned to be released. I ascertained afterwards that he had advised with Mosby and that Mosby told him it was better for him to be released. He acted on that advice and there's where the trouble began. General Canby was informed of the matter and he issued an order to the effect that if it should appear that any two persons had conspired to break the bond, Mr. Cannon should not be released. When the matter came up to court Colonel Mosby was the only one who testified to having advised Cannon to withdraw, so there was no proof of a conspiracy.

Correspondent – Was Cannon an ex-Confederate?

Boyd – Yes, he was influenced by Mosby to withdraw from my bond. After I had been thrown out by the decision of the court I commenced to settle up my affairs as sheriff. One day a man was paying his license tax to one of my deputies, when Mosby came up and said: - "You ought not to pay that money. There is no longer a sheriff of Fauquier county."

Correspondent – How did the difficulty originate which led to the correspondence?

Boyd – I was coming from a place called Salem and met Mosby on the road. I said to him, "Colonel Mosby, why do you interfere with my business; I never injured you in any way?" Mosby mumbled something in reply, when I said, "Colonel Mosby, do you know my opinion of you? You are a d—d highway robber; and if you go with me to Pennsylvania I will prove it on you by men and women whom you robbed."

Mosby replied, "I'll see you when you get back to Warrenton." I said, "you can see me now or at any time you please." When I got back to Warrenton I received Mosby's first note, and the other correspondence followed.

With regard to the duel, Colonel Boyd's friends say he never intended to fight one, for the reason that by so doing he would have violated his oath of office. The sheriff of Fauquier county, it appears is required to swear, among other things, the he has never been engaged in dueling, nor will be in any way connected with a duel… Be that as it may, there is no disguising the fact the community of Warrenton regard Colonel Boyd as a coward. To live in Warrenton or anywhere else in Virginia and refuse to fight when challenged is to be called a coward, no matter what a man's courage may be.

Colonel Mosby's second was Colonel Thomas Smith, formerly of the Confederate army, and a son of "Extra Billy" Smith. Like Mosby, he too has the reputation of being a fighting man Colonel Smith, who was quite lavish in his admiration of Mosby, said "Boyd got hold of the wrong man when he undertook to frighten Mosby." Everybody at Warrenton believes in Mosby. I suppose a majority of Virginians do the same. I am told that during "the season" at Warrenton this summer the ambition of the men was to take Mosby by the hand, while the women thought it the highest honor to be permitted to promenade with him. And yet, Mosby is not ambitious for fame. He told me he never would have allowed the correspondence between himself and Colonel Boyd to have seen the light but for the fact that Boyd boasted around town that Mosby had backed down. He is not anxious for a fight.

The *Herald* printed a "letter" from Boyd about the subject that used language about Mosby that he, Boyd, would not have used had he not left Virginia before its appearance in the paper. In it, he reiterated his position on the bond matter and defended General Canby, ending his letter with a bitter attack on the man whom he could not bully into submission:

New York Herald - **October 20, 1869 (Edited)**

A NEWSPAPER DUEL - The Boyd and Mosby Fight

WARRENTON, VA., Oct. 16, 1869

To THE EDITOR OF THE HERALD:—

I have just read an article in your paper of yesterday, which contains certain statements made by Colonel Mosby to your correspondent that are utterly false Mosby denies being engaged in persecuting me. The fact is I had hardly entered the town before he commenced attempting to annoy, impede and thwart me, and this he has continued to do in many different ways until the present time. Had he attacked me personally, in an open, manly way, I should have known how to meet him, but he has resorted to everything that is petty and mean, even to the setting at enmity our children Mosby's sole object has been to have me removed from the office of sheriff and to get one of his own stripe in my place. This attempt to get me to fight a duel, had it succeeded, would have accomplished all he desired.

Had I accepted his challenge I should have been arrested at once, and under the code of Virginia, removed from my office, sentenced to a year's imprisonment and probably fined $1,000 besides. Mosby knew this, and therefore never expected to fight the duel. But apart from this, Mosby's character has been such as, in my opinion, (illegible) him to associate with respectable men, and according to his code I could not lower myself to meet him. He was notorious during the war as a marauder and plunderer, the scourge of the helpless and defenseless, never daring to meet his enemy in open, fair fight. Whether he was a highway robber or not I leave you to judge from his past acts (illegible) his Baltimore and Ohio Railroad raid; his present denial is of no weight.

I have necessarily, Mr. Editor, been brought into contact with this class of men a good deal since my official career here began and I know them pretty well. I deny that they desire Northern men here. They have no use for them. They would undoubtedly be glad to sell them lands and quarries, as Mosby says, but Mosby and the rest would do all they could to prevent their being worked by them. They have not yet learned wisdom from their punishment and losses and I fear never will. They are as full or the same absurd notion about chivalry and the like as before the war, and it requires the supervision and strong arm of the government to restrain them from their former practices of murdering on sight, lynching and dueling. I do not refer to the more sensible class of this county, but to the inferior element, of which this Colonel Mosby is a representative.

In regard to my own courage Mosby and his clique are incompetent to judge But this much I may say, that I did not sneak through the country, plundering and marauding among the innocent and noncombatants The assertion of Mosby that he never would have suffered the publication of the letters but that I boasted about town that he had backed down, is a base lie, and Mosby knows it. I defy any man to say I did so. I considered him too contemptibly small fry to talk about, and treated the subject with disgust. I had nothing to gain in associating my name with such scum.

I am, sir, with much respect, your obedient servant,

WILLIAM H. BOYD,

Sheriff Fauquier county, Va.,

late Colonel Twenty-first Pennsylvania cavalry.

Now something very unusual occurred. The *National Republican*, an old foe of Mosby's, printed without comment a rebuke of Boyd that appeared in the *Lynchburg News* on October 28. There seems no reason at all that the *Republican* would print a "pro-Mosby" story without at least commenting upon it, but the paper did:

National Republican – October 29, 1869

The Mosby-Boyd Difficulty.—We learn from undoubted authority that the scurrilous letter of Col. Boyd, late sheriff of Fauquier county, though purporting to have been written in Warrenton, was written in Washington city, to which place, with that "discretion which is the better part of valor," he deemed it prudent to withdraw ere giving publicity to his slanderous charges against Col. Mosby. We presume, therefore that this is the last we shall hear of the matter, as Col. Mosby will scarcely condescend to reply through the papers to scurrilous charges which the author had not the hardihood to prefer until after placing the broad Potomac between himself and danger. It is understood that the carpet-bagger sold his office to the old sheriff ere taking his departure from the county. Exit Boyd.—Lynchburg News, 28th.

The press next reports Mosby in New York City, of all places. Here presented unedited, Mosby opines on a number of issues, including Boyd:

The Sun **– November 4, 1869**

WHAT MOSBY IS DOING.

The Duel that was not Fought—The Curiosities of Office-holding in Virginia—Virginia in a State of Vassalage—Butler as an Angel of Light—Mosby's Business in New York.

Mosby of Confederate memory, is at the Fifth Avenue Hotel. He is supposed to have come to this city to escape William H. Boyd, the spurious Sheriff of Fauquier county, Va. The difficulty between the two men arose from the fact that Mosby insisted that Boyd, who has since sold out his office, should give ample security for the discharge of its duties. Mosby, moreover, maintained that, according to the laws of Virginia, Boyd had no right to his office, and was liable to imprisonment in the penitentiary for attempting to act as Sheriff without legal qualification. He moreover holds that Boyd, in declining his challenge, invoked the statutes of the State merely to shield his cowardice. In accepting his summons to the field of honor Boyd would not have disqualified himself from holding office under a military appointment, inasmuch as the only oath required by military law is the "iron-clad" obligation.

BOYD A DEFAULTER.

Mosby says that Boyd is a defaulter to the State of Virginia for a large amount of revenue collected and not accounted for, and that he has sold his office to Hume, the former Sheriff, whom Gen. Canby displaced because he could not take the iron-clad oath. The result of imposing the iron-clad oath, Mosby thinks, is the placing in office of rascals and incompetents. Native citizens, he says, of respectable character, are not eligible under that restriction, as all in some way were connected with the rebellion; but they frequently purchase the right to the proceeds of the office from the loyal incumbent, and perform its duties as deputies.

WHO ARE DISLOYAL.

Every Southern man, Mosby says, is considered disloyal by those in authority, no matter how consistently he accepts the results of the war, and the State is made a penal colony by the present Administration on account of the numbers of scamps that are sent there. A sufficient recommendation of a men to Gen. Canby is, that he is from the North, whether lately escaped from Sing Sing or not.

BUTLER AN ANGEL OF LIGHT.

Mosby thinks Gen. Butler is an angel of light in comparison with Canby, who among other acts, appointed one Morton, of Palmyra, N.Y., Judge of the Fredericksburg District, a man who had not lived six weeks in the State, and who last year was expelled from the bar of his district for defrauding widows and orphans.

WHY MOSBY IS HERE.

Mosby disclaims any imputation of being in New York on Boyd's account, and says that he is trying to raise money for the development of his marble quarries in Loudoun and Fauquier counties. He is desirous that Northern men of good character should settle in his State, and he adds that all Virginians have the same wish. He accepts the failure of the Confederate cause, and now seeks only the material prosperity of his State. He returns next week to Warrenton, Va., where he resides.

Thus, John Mosby disposed of William Boyd despite General Canby's attacks against the Fauquier lawyers. As noted in the *Sun* article, Mosby considered Canby as dishonest as Boyd. But Mosby's encounter with Boyd brought forth former Union soldiers to take up their pens against their old enemy employing all of the usual charges—charges that never changed throughout the years even though they had been totally refuted countless times:

The Sun – November 6, 1869

MOSBY'S MURDEROUS WAR RECORD.

Monstrous Butcheries now first made Known—Indignant Protest from a Union Soldier.

To the Editor of The Sun.

Sir: I see in your varied columns that the rebel outlaw Mosby is bragging of his affair with the brave Union Col. Boyd, formerly of my regiment. Boyd would have dishonored himself by accepting a challenge from an outlaw. He should, however, have shot the insulting rebel down on the spot, and meted out to the murderer of Union men and the stripper of Union women his just deserts. The following two exploits of the chivalric Mosby, not generally known, may serve your readers in forming an idea of the character of the man. In October, 1864, an express train between Harper's Ferry and Martinsburg was attacked by Mosby and his command, and Mrs. C. W. Tolles, wife of Col. Tolles, Chief Quartermaster on Gen. Sheridan's staff, her child and sister, and the other passengers were turned out destitute and unprotected, the train being robbed and burned. At the same time Col. Tolles himself, while on his way with two orderlies to Cedar Creek, where his command lay, was shot by the same outlaw, and died in Winchester, in the presence of his heart-broken and destitute wife, who had been stripped of all by the villain Mosby. This outlaw also hanged five stragglers at Berryville to my knowledge. I acknowledge that he is a daring man, but as an unreconstructed rebel and a murderous outlaw he deserves no sympathy. I remain, enclosing my card, yours respectfully,

A UNION SOLDIER.

P.S.—Mosby wants Northern men with capital to go South. No doubt to give him a chance to steal the capital, and have the settler bushwacked [sic] if he complains.

In November, a positive article appeared in the *Nashville Union and American* headlined, "A Talk with Mosby." In it, the matter of alleged "atrocities" was addressed:

***Nashville Union and American* – November 17, 1869 (Edited)**

A TALK WITH MOSBY

What the Ex-Confederate Cavalry Officer Thinks of Matters and Things in General—Jefferson Davis—Sheridan—Gen. Butler—the Union Cavalry—Facts about the War, etc., etc.

From the Philadelphia Post.

Ascertaining that so noted a personage as Col. John S. Mosby, the dashing Confederate cavalry chieftain, was in town, and stopping at the Continental Hotel, one of the reporters of the Post, yesterday called upon him for the purpose of learning his views on some points of general public interest. We found the ex-Rebel leader reclining upon a lounge, and, upon our introducing ourself, he greeted us warmly and pleasantly.

HIS PERSONAL APPEARANCE.

The Colonel is a man five feet eleven inches in stature, slim build, but of an apparently iron-like frame; has a clear, gray, searching eye, a broad forehead, smooth-shaven face, and iron-gray hair. He was dressed in a neat-fitting suit of black, and altogether bore a gentleman-like appearance. The Colonel is but thirty-five years of age, and is the picture of health. No insurance agent, we think, would run any immediate risk in issuing a policy upon his earthly life.

HIS HISTORY BEFORE THE WAR. …

WHAT HE ACHIEVED. …

HIS MODE OF FIGHTING …

THE REPORTED ATROCITIES

"Colonel, was there any foundation for the reports published of the atrocities committed by your men?"

"Well, of course, excesses are practiced in all armies; but that any man or officer in the Confederate States army countenanced any acts of violence, rapine, or cruelty to prisoners, either in the camp or the field, I deny; there is not a word of truth in it.

"Mark me," said the Colonel, "I do not wish to defend that actions of those in charge at Andersonville, Belle Isle, Salisbury, or Libby; whether the charges made against them are true or false, I do not know, not having been at any of those places; but I do know this, that nothing could have exceeded the sufferings of our men whilst lying inactive during the winters of 1863-4-5. Why, sir, our men lived those winters through with nothing for food but parched corn, and, of course, such being the case, our prisoners could not reasonably expect luxuries.

HIS OWN COMMAND.

"During the war the Northern press complained bitterly of the acts of the men of my own immediate command, but I'll deny any man to cite any one authenticated instance in which a prisoner captured by me or my men was ill-treated. There are hundreds of men in Philadelphia to-day that I had prisoners, and I have met a great many of them since I have been here, and the first word they spoke to me was to thank me for the kind manner in which I treated them.

A WORD ABOUT GENERAL LEE

"Gen. Lee," said the Colonel, "is, I believe, acknowledged by all men to have been a Christian soldier. Well, I was under his immediate command and I reported all my actions to him, and during the whole war I never received but one reproof, and that was once, when badly wounded, I hobbled up to his tent on crutches, when he greeted me with 'Colonel, I have but one fault to find with you, and that is, you will get wounded.'"

HIS OPINION OF THE CAVALRY FORCES. ...

THE FEELING OF THE SOUTH.

"Are there any bitter feelings cherished?"

"No, sir; none except those engendered since the war by the manner in which we have been treated. The class of men to whom the conduct of affairs has been entrusted by the United States government are obnoxious. The whole administration of affairs in Virginia is in the hands of a set of bounty-jumpers and jail-birds, and their only qualification is that they can take the 'iron-clad oath.' But," he added, "they generally take anything else they can lay their hands on. Last spring all persons holding office were obliged to take the 'iron-clad' or leave, and one many named Boyd, from Pennsylvania, was appointed sheriff of Fauquier county, an office in which he had passing through his hands over $100,000 in revenue, and otherwise, according to the laws of the State, he would be obliged to give bonds in the sum of $90,000, but Gen. Canby reduced this to $30,000. The man was insolvent, and his bond was as well worth five dollars as it was five millions. Boyd is a defaulter to the State of Virginia for a large amount of revenue collected and not accounted for, and he has sold his office to Hume, the former sheriff, whom Gen. Canby displaced because he could not take the iron-clad oath.

When Boyd was appointed the members of the bar drew up a politely toned protest against the appointment of the man, and it fell to my lot to carry it to Gen. Canby. He received me kindly, and assured me the matter would be attended to. I returned to Warrenton and told my colleagues that the whole thing would be fixed. A few days afterwards Canby sent down troops and had the whole bar of Warrenton tried for conspiracy to defeat the reconstruction laws."

SHERIDAN …

THE OBJECT OF HIS VISIT. …

BEN BUTLER

"What do you think of Butler?" we asked.

"I don't think anything of Butler, "he replied, "and our opinion is that of a great many Northerners, I find. We don't hate him as a Northern man or General, but because he was a brute. We don't hate him because he wore a Northern uniform, but because he was a disgrace to it. But we have a meaner man than Butler, his name is Canby."

The above paper and the *Spirit of Jefferson* did a follow-up interview in which, as the headline stated, [the] "Misrepresentation of 'A Union Soldier' [Is] Corrected":

Spirit of Jefferson – **November 30, 1869**

Nashville Union and American – **November 23, 1869**

COL. JOHN S. MOSBY

The Valley of Virginia During the War—Misrepresentation of "A Union Soldier" Corrected.

The New York Sun having lately published a communication from a Union soldier commenting on the conduct of Col. John S. Mosby in the Valley of Virginia during the war, that gentleman has replied through the same journal to the following effect:

Sir: I am really amused at the piece in your valuable paper from "A Union Soldier," for it shows how hard pressed my enemies are for something to say against me, when they can finding nothing worse than the stuff he has published. I will notice them in their order. First—The capture of the train in October, 1864, on the road between Harper's Ferry and Martinsburg, Va. This was on a military road, and used by the Federal army—which was then in the Shenandoah Valley — for transporting troops and supplies. I was in command of about 300 men, and was charged with the duty of impeding the advance of the Federal army by intercepting their communication.

If I opposed Sheridan in front, my small force would count for nothing; but by throwing it in his rear and on his communication, it became a tremendous power, because 300 men under a skillful commander, operating in the rear of an army, are equivalent to 10,000 in front. It was just as legitimate for me to attack Sheridan in his rear as for Early to attack him in front; and Sheridan, in his report to the committee on the conduct of the war, has testified to the efficiency of my command, for he says that after the defeat of Early he could have gone on to Richmond, but that he had to detail two-thirds of his force to guard his communication against my attack.

The train I captured was on the way to supply Sheridan's army. It had on it, besides a number of officers and soldiers, a considerable number of passengers. Among the officers were two paymasters with $175,000, going to pay off Sheridan's troops. Of course it was just as legitimate war to capture and destroy this train as to kill or capture Sheridan and his men. I penetrated far in [the] rear of the Federal army, and captured this train within a mile of a large camp, and burned it. The object of my command was not so much to capture trains as to compel Sheridan to detach heavily from his front to guard his rear. If Mrs. Tolles and the other passengers on this train 'were turned out destitute and unprotected,' as this Union soldier avers, it was Sheridan's fault, not mine, for he ought to have had it properly guarded.

Again: These female passengers only suffered a little inconvenience, (no violence was offered them,) and if they choose to subject themselves to the hazard of riding on a military railroad, they had nobody to blame but themselves; otherwise, Sheridan might have guarded all his trains by putting a few females on board. He might as well have put women in front of his line of battle, to keep us from shooting his men. I was myself present when the train was captured, and there is no incident of my military life to which I refer with more pride and pleasure. If it was right for Sheridan to capture railroad trains, why shouldn't I do it? Sherman justified the burning of the city of Atlanta, and, in reply to Hood's complaint, said that "war meant cruelty." Is there more wrong in burning a train of cars and subjecting a few passengers to a temporary inconvenience, then in the destruction of a whole city, and turning a whole population out of doors?

Second Charge—He says: "At the same time Col. Tolles, Gen. Sheridan's quartermaster, was shot by this same outlaw at Cedar Creek," etc. Now, a small detachment of my command met Col. Tolles, with a small detachment of cavalry, near Newtown, on the Valley turnpike. Tolles and his party retreated, and were pursued by my men; Tolles, while running, was shot in the back. All right; he took the chance of escape in preference to surrender. I suppose, if Col. Tolles could have had the opportunity, he would have shot me. That is what men go to war for, and I can't see how there is any greater crime in killing Col. Tolles in the rear of Sheridan than in his front.

Third Point—"This outlaw hanged five stragglers at Berryville." In September, 1864, Gen. Custer captured and hanged seven of my men in the streets of Front Royal, Va. Immediately on hearing of this, having a lot of thirty prisoners on hand, I made them draw lots for seven to be hanged, as a measure of retaliation to protect my men. These men were hanged on the Valley pike, along which Sheridan's troops traveled every day, as a warning of what they might expect if any more of my men were hanged. At the same time I wrote a letter to Gen. Sheridan (which was published in the newspapers of the time, and can be found in the memoir of my command by Scott), avowing my responsibility for the act, and stating my reasons for it. Sheridan acknowledged the justice of the deed by ordering my men to be treated with the humanities of war. I have never been called in question for this act, although I assumed all responsibility for it.

The Union soldier pretends that the "exploits of the chivalric Mosby have never been given to the world." If he will only consult the memoir of my command by Scott, he will see that the death of Col. Tolles, the capture of the train, and incidents connected with it, and the hanging of the prisoners are all spoken of. They were all legitimate acts of war. I think it high time for a people who glory in "Sherman's march from the mountains to the sea," in which he made a desert of the country that lay in his track, who received with huzzas Sheridan's triumphant dispatch "that he had burned 3,000 barns and mills, and made the valley of Virginia so desolate that a crow could not fly over it without carrying his rations," to cease objecting that anybody did not observe the rules of mitigated war. Very truly, John S. Mosby

Mosby made a most interesting point here: *"I think it high time for a people who glory in 'Sherman's march from the mountains to the sea,' in which he made a desert of the country that lay in his track, who received with huzzas Sheridan's triumphant dispatch 'that he had burned 3,000 barns and mills, and made the valley of Virginia so desolate that a crow could not fly over it without carrying his rations,' to cease objecting that anybody did not observe the rules of mitigated war."* This was the first time that John Mosby pointed out that the atrocities committed by the Federal army found no outcry in the Northern populace while his perfectly legitimate acts of war were labeled as "atrocities."

Given all of the fuss being made about Mosby's "war crimes" in the Northern press, the *Ouachita Telegraph* determined to add its voice in his defense by reprinting an article from the *Virginia Herald*:

Ouachita Telegraph - November 27, 1869

Mosby—Those who know Col. Mosby personally, will bear testimony to the fact that he is one of the most quiet, unobtrusive gentlemen they ever met. The soul of honor, and a very pink of chivalry. Those who served under him will also bear testimony to the fact that he uniformly refused to permit the share his men pressed him to receive, to be so awarded. His object was, as the Warrenton Index well says, not to enrich himself but to benefit his cause and country. We are told by the same authority that when he captured the two Paymasters of the Federal army with their $152,000 in greenbacks, on the train of the Baltimore and Railroad, he never fingered one single note. The whole went among the men and subordinate officers of his command. Is such a man a "highway robber?"—Virginia Herald.

And so another year had ended, and John Mosby was still practicing law and living quietly with his wife and children. He hadn't been arrested even though he had challenged a former Union officer to a duel. He hadn't been overly harassed by those Federal forces remaining in Virginia, and he maintained not only the support of the Southern press, but also even some papers in the North that refused to believe his purported war-time misbehavior. His legal practice was thriving, and despite the desperate situation that remained in the South, Mosby's *personal* future looked bright. The next year would see a brand-new decade, and the deadly sixties would be no more. It would have been quite understandable if John Mosby looked upon the dawning decade with hope and confidence.

ADDENDUM

The Ironclad Oath: This was a key device for the removal of ex-Confederates from the political arena during the Reconstruction era in the United States. The previous oath had simply required a pledge of allegiance to the United States and that the individual swear never to take up arms against the country in the future. The Ironclad, on the other hand, required every white male to swear they had never borne arms against the Union or supported the Confederacy. Specifically, they swore they "never voluntarily bore arms against the United States," had "voluntarily" given "no aid, countenance, counsel or encouragement" to persons in rebellion, and had exercised or attempted to exercise the functions of no office under the Confederacy. In fact, few, if any, Southern men could take that oath. Those who could were eligible for office but were hated and reviled because they were considered traitors to their state and section. When the Radical Republicans gained full control of Congress in 1866, they used the backward-looking Ironclad Oath to prevent former Confederates from voting or serving on juries or in government. In 1867, the US Supreme Court held that the Federal Ironclad Oath was unconstitutional because it violated prohibitions against bills of attainder and *ex-post- facto* laws. The Ironclad Oath was fiercely hated by Southern whites because it stripped most of the region's leaders of political power and violated the principles of republicanism and the consent of the governed. The oath was effectively ended in 1871 and finally repealed in 1884, but it left a lasting legacy of hatred and distrust that redounded directly to the Republican Party.

Chapter 10

1870 AND 1871

Tempora mutantur, et nos mutamur in illis. ~ Times are changing, and we are changing with them.

"If it be a sin to covet honour, I am the most offending soul alive." ~ William Shakespeare

A NEW DECADE HAD dawned, and the South still survived—by a thread, no doubt, but survive it did. The section and her people had not been brought to utter ruin despite a war of such ferocity and destruction that it still stands as the most sanguinary in U.S. history bar none. John Mosby had survived the end of the war, which was a surprise to a large number of Northern publications and their readers; and the new decade held out some hope that things would, however slowly, improve. The early newspaper accounts mentioning Mosby linked him with the Fenians and the Cuban uprising, but Mosby had no respect for "soldiers of fortune" and said so; he also had no lust for war despite the belief by many who declare that the man "lived for conflict." Still, the idea that he could sit "idly by" in Virginia and practice law was not an easy "sell" for the press after years of presenting him as a fiend incarnate who subsisted upon the blood and suffering of his victims:

Gallipolis Journal – June 16, 1870

Mosby has written over his own signature that he has no sort of connection or sympathy with Fenian raids or Cuban filibusters.

It seemed that the newspapers insisted on promoting Mosby from his rank as a mere colonel to that of general, something else he did not appreciate. The following article was somewhat inaccurate in its physical description, but correct with regard to Mosby's demeanor. The idea that he was rude, imperious, and personally difficult is contradicted by just about all such articles that described him as "quiet, unassuming, modest [and] a perfect gentleman." The only thing that is altogether wrong is the claim that before the war, Mosby was wealthy. Indeed, he was too young to have had the time to gain affluence through his vocation:

Yorkville Enquirer - June 9, 1870

PEN PICTURE OF MOSBY.

"Brick" Pomeroy, writing to his paper, the New York Democrat, from Richmond, Va., thus sketches the dashing Confederate cavalry officer, Mosby:

"That smooth-face gentleman, who resembles a minister or student of anatomy, is General Mosby, one of the most active and efficient cavalry officers the South produced. All over the plains of Manassas and about there he did some terrible fighting. We remember during the war of hearing those who coming back from the front tell of the Black-horse Cavalry. And what devils the horses and riders were! And they would tell of Mosby till the people of the Northwest were led to think him a man about eleven feet tall, with the eye, sir, and face of a brigand—with long, fearful-looking hair, moustache and whiskers, flying wild in the wind; able to hold a horse from his feet with one hand, and wring the necks of a dozen prisoners with the other.

But the real, genuine Mosby is a different looking man. We first met him on the train coming from Washington to Lynchburg—have met him here several times—find him always a quiet, unassuming, modest, perfect gentleman. At present he is engaged in the practice of the law at Culpepper, making a good living thereby, and endeavoring to regain some portion of his shattered fortunes. Previous to the war he was wealthy, but where his State needed his services he gave freely—and he gave not only his services, but his property. He was in earnest, and counted all he had as belonging to the State. At the end of the war he was a bankrupt.

As a brave, dashing officer he was a success. Kind to his men, quick to catch the idea, rapid in his movements, bold and striking, he did terrible execution.

He is about five feet seven inches in height, weighing, perhaps one hundred and thirty five pounds. His face is, wearing, except when lit up with a smile, a calm, kind, earnest, studious, thoughtful expression. But those who have seen him on battle-fields tell us that when there was trouble ahead, or work to do, he seemed like a dozen men. The fire of deviltry danced in his eyes till the entire appearance of the man was changed, and instead of the man of thought and study, he was the man of uncontrollable action, yet with perfect control over himself and others.

Newspapers had begun to opine on the Franco-Prussian War, and at least two publications sought Mosby's opinion regarding the transport by the Germans of their heavy siege guns using the railways between Paris and the Rhine. Mosby, of course, was more than happy to satisfy their inquisitiveness and demonstrate his military acumen:

Wilmington Journal – **October 21, 1870**

Spirit of Jefferson – **November 1, 1870**

MOSBY ON THE FRENCH AND PRUSSIAN WAR.—There could be no better commentary upon the utter imbecility of the French military management than the fact of the uninterrupted use which the Prussians are suffered to make of the railways between Paris and the Rhine. According to the last accounts it will be noticed that the heavy siege guns are being transported by rail—a work which without the aid of steam power would take weeks instead of hours. How long would these facilities be permitted to the Germans if France had within her ranks such bold raiders as Stuart, Wilson, Forrest, Grierson, Mosby or Fitzhugh Lee? Mosby, writing to a friend in this city, says:

"With a thousand picked cavalrymen, I could give employment to one-third of the Prussian army simply in watching their long lines of communication."

This sounds rather boastful, but we verily believe he could do it. To keep only lines extending three hundred and fifty miles into an enemy's country, with such dashing leaders as those we have mentioned to contend against, would give the Germans about all the business they wanted.—N.Y. Commercial.

It is interesting to note that the press questioned Mosby about such matters, yet he had not been trained for war. He didn't attend West Point or VMI and never commanded anything larger than a battalion and even that was in irregular service. Yet it was Mosby to whom the press oft went for his opinion on various military contests abroad.

And so the first year of the new decade ended absent tragedies, assaults, difficulties, or problems. In 1871, another "pen and ink" sketch of Mosby appeared in the *Lincoln County Herald*. It was an excellent little vignette—with the exception of a physical description of a man far too large to be Mosby!

Lincoln County Herald – **November 2, 1871**

Col. Mosby

A Northern paper contains the following pen and ink sketch of the famous Col. Mosby:

"At Culpepper, a man five feet ten high, broad shouldered, heavy limbed, with straight, light brown hair cut close, keen gray eyes, sharp, thin nose, firmly set mouth, protruding chin with dimple, florid complexion, thirty six years old, the father of five children, centered our car and was introduced to us by a land agent as Colonel Mosby.

The Colonel is a very blunt man in his conversation; has his likes and dislikes, which he does not attempt to conceal. He is rather proud of his exploits during the war, and relates some wondrous performances that "my men" did. And he tells it in a manner that, knowing the man, you are perfectly willing to believe all he says is true, and the mind guards itself against any doubts, particularly while in his presence.

Just before reaching Warrenton Junction, the Colonel was approached by a gentleman, who introduced himself as somebody from Philadelphia, and after a moment's conversation, said:

"Colonel, I had a near and dear friend, who was an officer in one of our Pennsylvania regiments, and he was lost one night while on picket duty near here—they say captured by your men. Nothing has been heard of him since that night, and I though I would make bold to introduce myself and ask if you knew anything of him. His name was D—, Lieutenant D—."

"Yes, I killed him myself; and he is the only man that I am positive I killed during the war. My men brought me some papers he had on his person, and we gave him a decent burial the next morning. I will be pleased to show you where he sleeps at any time, or render any other assistance in my power."

The cars stop, the brakesman cries "Warrenton," the Colonel shakes the hand of the Philadelphian in a peculiar manner, a brotherly smile of recognition passes between them, another peculiar "shake" and out marches the "Guerrilla Mosby," "Wolf of the Piedmont," "Fox of the Valley," with a slight "stoop in the shoulders," and in that loose shambling manner common to men whose lives have been spent in the saddle."

The end of the article has two interesting points. The second are the names given him during the war of which the famous Gray Ghost was not one. Wolf of the Piedmont and Fox of the Valley are interesting, especially the former, which had a greater "threat" capacity than that of "fox" which is more a matter of cleverness than predation. The other point strongly suggested that Mosby was a Mason and that he and the "Philadelphian" were brothers in that fraternal order. That was untrue. Mosby was never a Mason. First, he probably would not have taken to any such fraternal group; the initiation ceremony alone would have precluded it. Second, Pauline was a Roman Catholic and would not have been happy had her husband entered an association forbidden by her Church. In a way, however, it is too bad. Mosby would have found considerable protection when he departed from the status quo had he been a Mason.

After two peaceful and trouble-free years inaugurating the new decade, John Mosby may have thought that in 1872 he would continue along that same quiet path—but such was not to be. Indeed, 1872 became a measure from whence proceeded all that came after.

Chapter 11

1872

Parva scintilla saepe magnam flamam excitat. ~ A small spark often initiates a large flame.

"Boldness be my friend." ~ **William Shakespeare**

JOHN MOSBY'S FIRST appearance in the press in 1872 was in an article in the *Spirit of Jefferson*, defending him from the usual accusations of "atrocities":

Spirit of Jefferson – **April 2, 1872 (Edited)**

Colonel Mosby

[From the Warrenton Index]

We see in an issue of the Grand Army Journal, of the 16th inst., published in Washington, D. C., a defamatory attack upon our townsman, Col. Mosby.

It is an easy matter for reckless editors anonymous correspondents to state that Col. Mosby or any other officer of the Confederate army was a monster of cruelty, and to bolster up such assertions by reference to cases of assassination to which none but dead men can testify.

But it is quite another matter to sustain such statements by admissible evidence. No greater mistake could be made than to suppose that Mosby acted without reference to accountability, or that his command was a "gang of cut-throats." He was regularly commissioned by the Confederate States Secretary of War and subjected to orders of General Lee, with whom he was in constant communication, and to whom he rendered valuable service. His command was composed of veterans selected for courage and discipline, as being most easily controlled on outposts, and of boys under military age, reared in this and contiguous counties, too fresh from their fireside altars to harbor a criminal thought or to strike a merciless blow. Friend and foe alike admit Lee to have been a Christian soldier, and it ought to be a sufficient refutation of the slanders of the Journal to answer that the only reproof which he ever gave Mosby was couched in these words, when the latter on crutches approached him: "Colonel, I have but one fault to find with you, and that is that you will get wounded." If this were not enough, the safe conduct given to more than six thousand Union soldiers taken during the last two years of the war and sent to Richmond, ought surely to silence the groundless charge that "he violated every principle of humanity."

If six thousand prisoners were safely conducted over a hundred miles to a Confederate prison by escorts from Mosby's command, what becomes of the sweeping charge that they were "a gang of cut-throats" and he "was their worthy leader?" And if those escorts are allowed to have had no respect for the helpless enemy, it is reasonable to suppose that they would have shocked the modesty of friends of both sexes along their route by exposing the nakedness of any one under their charge?

It is true that Custer's lawless behavior at Front Royal compelled Col. Mosby to appeal to the bloody code of retaliation. But that was neither a cold-blood[ed] assassination nor secret midnight murder. Mosby's men had been gibbeted after surrender by order of Custer. A squad of Custer's command were subsequently captured, and in the face of day forced to draw tickets in the lottery of death. The man upon whom the fatal decision rested were sent under guard to Berryville, across the Shenandoah, almost in sight of the enemy's bivouac, and there hung as examples of military justice.

It is also true that incendiaries in blue who were caught in the act of firing dwellings belonging to non-combatants were not treated as prisoners of war. The laws of humanity forbace that they should be so treated; and if any Union soldier fell with torch in hand, their blood lies rather on the head of the officers who ordered them upon fiendish errands than on the head of Mosby and his men.

Col. Mosby who lives almost with the shadow of the nation['s] Capitol, notified the Federal commander of the commission of these acts at the time they occurred, and does not now deny them. They furnish foundation for all the wild stories of his cruelty.—If criminality attaches to him on their account, why has he not been tried by a court properly constituted?

The answer is, Mosby is guiltless of any crime. While scores of Union officers of unquestionable reputation have paid him even higher compliments than Democratic Congressmen, only skulkers and bummers, who fattened on contracts and plunder during the war, and hope to grow richer by keeping alive sectional animosities since the inauguration of peace, seem to refuse him his just need of praise.

As had happened before (and would happen again) great issues were introduced by small stories appearing in the press. The story on May 9th gives the gist, while subsequent press coverage reported the matter in lesser or greater detail. But whatever the detail, this was a seminal moment in John Mosby's life, a veritable "Rubicon," albeit the first of many:

Daily State Journal – May 9, 1872

COL. MOSBY VISITS THE PRESIDENT FROM WASHINGTON.

Gen. John S. Mosby, of Virginia, visited President Grant to-day.

—Senator Lewis yesterday introduced Colonel John S. Mosby to President Grant. Colonel Mosby took occasion to say to the President that even should the Democrats make a nomination and Greeley withdraw, he will support and vote for Grant if nominated.

Knoxville Daily Chronicle – May 14, 1872

Mosby not for Greeley.

The Philadelphia Press contains a dispatch from Forney about an interview at the White House between the President, Mosby and himself:

"Well," said Mosby, "what are you going to do about the Cincinnati Convention?"

To which Col. Forney replied: "I am going to stand by the old flag and follow the old leader, Gen. Grant. We shall settle our difficulties in Pennsylvania, if there is any wisdom in our party leaders, and so help to secure a good editor for the *New York Tribune* and a good President for the country."

"Then," said Mosby, turning to Grant, "I will never vote for Horace Greeley. I will stump Virginia against him. I will undoubtedly support a Democratic candidate, if my party nominates one, and if it don't I will vote for President Grant."

The story in the Daily State Journal of May 9th quotes Mosby as saying that he would support Grant even should Greeley withdraw. The article in the Knoxville Daily Chronicle on the 14th presents Mosby's true position, "I will never vote for Horace Greeley... I will undoubtedly support a Democratic candidate, if my party nominates one, and if it don't I will vote for President Grant." This was a far cry from choosing to vote for Republican Grant, especially because he *was* a Republican. Realistically, the only hope Grant had for Southern backing was that Greeley would be totally unacceptable in the South even running as a Democrat and that for those who could stomach *neither* candidate, their "non-vote" would redound to Grant's benefit. The *Bristol News*, possibly the same newspaper whose editor was Mosby's friend before the war, commented on the matter; but its comments did not favor Mosby. Indeed, they even contained—for the first, but alas, not the last time in a Southern paper—negative reference to his wartime service:

The *Bristol News* – May 17, 1872

Col. Jno. S. Mosby has declared to Grant, that if the democrats fail to make a nomination, he will vote for him against Greely. Mosby is evidently getting worse. This business is a good deal meaner, than the hanging of those federal spies in the Valley.

Also for the first time John Mosby then put pen to paper to explain his position:

New York Times – May 21, 1872

Col. Mosby.

What the Ex-Guerrilla Chief Thinks of Mr. Greeley's Nomination.

The wranglings respecting the position of Co. John S. Mosby on the Presidential question in which Virginia and other Democratic papers have engaged since his interview with Gen. Grant, will perhaps be quieted by the following explicit statement from him to a personal friend in Richmond:

Warrenton, May 13, 1872

My Dear Sir:

I have received your favor inquiring my position in the Presidential contest. Of course, if a Democrat is nominated, I shall support his election with all my heart; but if it is reduced to a question of choice between Gen.

Grant and Greeley, I shall support the former. My own views of policy were, after the failure of the Cincinnati Convention, to nominate a man acceptable to Democrats; that the South should hold from the contest and not commit itself to either until the Philadelphia Convention had nominated its candidate and declared a platform of principles. For if the whole South were committed in advance against the election of Gen. Grant, what motives could he or his party have to try to conciliate us? Now, why should the South array itself on the side of Greeley, her unrepentant, life-long enemy, against Gen. Grant? I am no apologist for the oppression we have endured from the Federal Government; but will the partisans of Greeley point to one act that was odious to us that he has not justified and approved? Nay, more. The tyrannical acts of Congressional legislation were an expression of a Northern sentiment of hostility to the South for which Horace Greeley, more than any other man, is responsible. Gen. Grant has been the instrument of executing many laws obnoxious to us, which were enacted under the pressure of a public opinion, created by Greeley, which no man could resist. The pen was mightier than the sword.

Now, what is offered to the Southern people by the nominee of the Cincinnati Convention as a consideration for their votes: Amnesty–which simply means the relief of a few thousand men from the disability imposed by the Fourteenth Amendment. But the President has no control over this—it requires two-thirds vote of Congress to effect it. If the Southern vote is to be bartered for such a paltry consideration as this, why not bargain directly with those who have the ability to pay what they promise? Does any man doubt that the party in power would gladly grant universal amnesty to secure the electoral votes of Virginia alone? If so, how is there less of dishonor in a coalition with Greeley on condition as this than with the party who can give you now all you ask? The only difference that I can see is that in the one case you bargain with a set of political bankrupts and adventurers whose pledges will be redeemed about as soon as the Confederate debt – and therefore they will be profuse in promises; in the other you may at least expect to receive the small pittance required. Tell me one single reason why a Southern man should prefer Greeley to Grant.

They say that Greeley is honest—then so much the worse if he is honestly opposed to all I hold dear. They say he has abused carpet-baggers—which by the bye are only the natural product of institutions which he planted among us; but as he is indebted to this class (who assumed at Cincinnati to represent the South) for his nomination, surely honest Horace won't, if elected, go back on his friends. They say, too, that he is the friend of amnesty, and yet he advocated the impeachment of Johnson for pardoning rebels. On his recent electioneering tour through the South, when he looked on the land where he "had made a solitude and called it peace," his heart was for a moment touched with a sentiment of pity for the Southern people, as well as a desire for Southern votes, and he was tempted to say a few kind words for which he was swift to make atonement, when on his return to New York he regaled to a gaping crowd of his admirers the fabulous stories of Kuklux horrors, and applauded the vigor of the Administration in suspending the habeas corpus in South Carolina and enforcing the Kuklux laws.

The men who, as old Isaiah tell us, cooked their breakfast with one end of a stick of wood and made an image of the other, which they worshiped, were not more unreasoning idolaters than those who are now prostrating themselves before Horace Greeley. In both cases the virtues of the idol exist only in the imagination of the worshipers. I don't choose to bow at such a shrine, and am not led captive by such enchantments; and if we are compelled to go through the ceremony of choosing a master, to me there is less of humiliation in accepting the soldier to whom Lee surrendered his sword than the fanatic whose teachings have been "the Iliad of all our woes."

I am, very truly yours, John S. Mosby

Capt. A. G. Babcock

The *Daily State Journal* mentioned a matter begun in the *Bristol News* that soon became rather universal for those who rejected Mosby's position—that is, the belittling of his military service to the Confederacy:

Daily State Journal – May 23, 1872

The Dispatch is engaged in a labor just now, which must be anything but gratifying to its pride and vanity as a Southern journal. We refer to its effort at belittling the military services of such men as Colonel Mosby, Colonel Ewell, General Beauregard, General Longstreet, and other Confederate officers, who happen to prefer Grant to Greeley as a Presidential candidate. Republicans are notoriously ungrateful, but the most ungrateful things in them are such splenetic journals as turn their backs, for the most trifling cause, on their friends.

The riotous press coverage continued apace. Some were perceptive, but one paper brought to the fore for the first time a "motive" for Mosby's "treason:" *self-interest*. That charge became a tradition in all further news coverage of the man's politics even when known fact and common sense disproved it out of hand:

Whig and Tribune – May 25, 1872

MOSBY

The Memphis Appeal, in speaking of this gentleman, says:

Colonel Mosby, of Virginia cavalry fame, told Grant he would support a Democrat if nominated at Baltimore. If no such nomination were made, he (Mosby) would support the Republican who bid highest, by proposing generous terms, for the Southern vote. Such is that statement of a private letter from Virginia. Mosby is no Radical.—As between Greeley and Grant, he conceives himself under no obligation to vote for either. He did not make himself "an accessory before the fact" to the Cincinnati Convention, and was not bound by its actions as we were.

Ouachita Telegraph – June 1, 1872 (Edited)

Two Letters

The first page of to-day's paper presents to our readers Horace Greeley's letter of acceptance of the Cincinnati nomination…

We conclude from this letter that Mr. Greeley has formally and finally cut loose from the Philadelphia Convention, and intends to run the race through, "if it takes all summer" to run it. This consummates the Republican split,—at least until after the election, which is a qualification always in order when we are considering splits in that party.

However earnest Mr. Greeley may be when he says he will be the President not of a party, but of the people, we taken it for granted that, like Grant, who made a similar declaration, Mr. Greeley will be driven from, if he does not entirely forget, the pledge he has made. A President without a party, is a President without power and without principles. He must have a party, if he has any well-defined ideas of how government should be administered. What kind of party will Mr. Greeley's be, if he be elected President?

On this page will be found another letter which has attracted no little attention. It is from the famous Virginia cavalryman, Col. John T. Mosby [sic], in answer to aspersions upon his Southern fealty, because he paid a visit to Gen. Grant and had said that in choosing between the two Republican candidates, he would choose Grant. It will be seen that Col. Mosby is, like Mr. Greeley, familiar with the use of the pen, and is able to present a strong case in behalf of his position, a fact every one recognizing the force of truth and logic will not gainsay...

If we cannot elect Mr. Greeley—if we march to inevitable defeat—why not march under our old banner and led by men of our own choosing and whose principles and antecedents we can approve without reservation? [Mosby's letter to Babcock was annexed here.-vph]

The *Spirit of Jefferson* was also greatly exercised by the coming election. Greeley wasn't going down at all well in the South, and John Mosby's refusal to back the man while openly supporting Grant was making some Democratic publications nervous. The public perception, at least early on, was that Mosby had performed great military service on behalf of the South and as a result, deserved a hearing. Some little time would pass before many Southern papers would turn on him and ferociously denigrate that same service:

Spirit of Jefferson – June 4, 1872 (Edited)

COL. JNO. S. MOSBY.Perhaps no man in either army, of equal grade, achieved so wide spread a reputation for gallantry and efficiency as an officer in our late war between the States, as the one whose name heads this article. ...

It was therefore with regret that we read in the Baltimore Gazette, of the 27th inst., an article in which a comparison, most unjust to Mosby, was instituted between him and Longstreet. And why? For no other reason than because he sincerely believed that Grant was a little more fool than knave, and Greeley a great deal more knave than fool. Whether that be true or not, may not a man entertain the opinion without being branded with the term traitor? Is there any thing in Mr. Greeley's record to which any Southern man should be so warmly attached that, upon the mere mention of the word "Greeley," he should throw up his hat and give three cheers? Did he not sanction—or rather clamor for the flagrantly unconstitutional Ku Klux laws? ...

Should the Democratic-Conservative Convention, which assembles in Baltimore in July, see proper to nominate this "honest" Horace Greeley as our standard bearer in the coming contest, we will feel in duty bound to support him because he is the nominee of the party to which we belong, because, as a bid for Southern votes, he has at least pledged himself to universal amnesty, and last, but by no means least, we understand he has but one brother-in-law upon whom to lavish the public money. But our support certainly will not be given because we have any great confidence in his political honesty; or that we believe that, by his election, the centralizing tendency of the Federal government, will be in the least checked… We intend to abide by the action of the Baltimore Convention, whatever it may be; but we sincerely hope it will not compel us to swallow so bitter a pill as the "honest old man."

The view of this newspaper was the very construct upon which Mosby built his case: supporters of Greeley had embraced a party rather than principles and the men advancing them—and they would support that party no matter how much damage was done. Soon, however, those in the South for whom Grant and the Republicans were simply unacceptable began to appear in print in (supposedly) vigorous support of Greeley. But Mosby also had his defenders, and as was the case in such matters, he always acknowledged their efforts on his behalf:

Spirit of Jefferson – **June 11, 1872 (Edited)**

STANDING TO PRINCIPLE

When a brave and true man has been set upon by a party of deserters anxious to show their "loyalty" to their newly adopted faith by vehemently denouncing those who stand firmly to their life long principles, we don't know a more pleasant feeling than the consciousness of having struck at least one honest blow in defence of true courage and manhood. Such a consciousness we experienced after writing our article in our least issue entitled "Col. Jno S. Mosby;" and we were pleased to learn by private letter from that gentleman, that we had taken the proper view of his position.—

Office of John S. Mosby

Attorney at Law Warrenton, Va., June 5, 1872

My Dear Sir:—I hasten to express to you my sincere thanks for your editorial defense of me which appears in the Spirit of Jefferson. The men who are now accusing me of treason to my faith are themselves deserters, who have abandoned for success in an election every principle they once professed. Because I do not choose to follow these political vagrants in their hunt after plunder, they "assume a virtue if they have it not" and falsely accuse me of the crime they are themselves committing. "The head and front of my offending hath this extent—no more." I can't recognize Horace Greeley as the apostle of Democracy, or his disciple John Brown as entitled to a place in the Calendar of Saints. Having spent the best years of my life in combatting the ideas of Horace Greeley, which found their expression in the clash of arms and tread of armies during the war, and in the infamies of reconstruction since, I am not willing even in defeat to admit that we were wrong all the time by voluntarily exalting the chief author of our woes. Nor can I see the force of the logic of those who argue that Radicalism would be extinguished by surrendering to the control of its high priest, the only organization that opposes it, or how the cause of Conservatism would triumph by the election of the Red-Republican defender of the Commune and the advocate of the theories of Fourier.* Now, when the Democratic party does this thing, it is dead, its life has gone, its soul has fled. I am sir, very truly yours,

JNO. S. MOSBY

This was a very important letter, for in it, Mosby said far more than he usually did in his defensive statements. To begin with, he never mentioned Grant in that part of his letter appearing in the paper. Further, he revealed the connection between the Radical Republicans, Greeley, and the communist-socialist movement in Europe. His mention of Fourier was especially enlightening (see "Addendum" at the end of the chapter). To Mosby, the fact that the Democratic Party would "settle" for Greeley meant that it had abandoned its philosophical and ethical principles and was willing to do anything to win an election.

The press also presented others who agreed with his position on the matter:

Knoxville Daily Chronicle – June 12, 1872

ANOTHER DISSENTER HEARD FROM.—Hon. James Lyons, a prominent Richmond (Va.) Democrat, has written a letter to Col. John S. Mosby, endorsing the latter's political views. He says he will not vote for Grant, unless forced to choose between Grant and Greeley ... He hopes that the Baltimore Convention will nominate a straight ticket, and invokes Mosby and others to call a mass meeting of Virginia Democrats to appoint delegates.

But of course, a lot of Democratic publications, once Greeley became their candidate, were ferociously for him and against Grant and therefore against Mosby who was (rightly) seen as one of Grant's most powerful advocates in the South:

Semi-Weekly Republican – June 18, 1872

Colonel John S. Mosby, late of the Provisional army Confederate States, told Grant that if the Democrats make no nominations, he would "stump the Valley of Virginia for him (Grant). We would suggest if Col. Mosby does not find a sufficient number of "stumps," he can use the pillars of the barns and the chimneys of the dwellings that were burned in the Valley by Phil Sheridan, upon Grant's infamous order during the war.

And still, the articles about who would vote for whom continued. By this time, Mosby could be claimed as a one-man boon to journalism. Doubtless, the presses would have run without him, but one wonders if there would have been half as much interest. However, as time went on and the nomination of Greeley as the Democratic candidate seemed ever more sure, the articles against both Grant and Mosby became decidedly more nasty:

Daily State Journal – July 12, 1872

Colonel John S. Mosby chooses to cast in his lot with the Grant Republicans, and he and his friends will not be merely passive consenters to the re-election of the President, but will make active exertions towards securing that result. In his language, "They will not support a man who has been less friendly to the south than Grant himself." Colonel Mosby is of the opinion that if General Lee were alive at this time he would favor Grant in preference to Greeley Certainly the casting of such votes from honest motives will be more effective in the interests of peace and reconciliation than the giving of them to Greeley in pursuance of the dickering bargains by which the Democratic party was sold out to him. Colonel Mosby and the other ex-Confederates who think with him are wise enough to see this, and the triumphant Republican party will appreciate it when the victory is won.—Baltimore American.

In July of 1872, Horace Greeley was nominated as the presidential candidate of the Democratic Party, and the die was cast. And so the champions were chosen and the board set. Soon, adherents of both sides would take to "the stump" to display their candidates in a manner oddly and unpleasantly reminiscent of a slave auction. Mosby had promised his choice—President Ulysses S. Grant—that he would not be a spectator in the contest, but a willing participant. He intended to honor that promise.

But this was a unique election. While both sides had advantages, it was the nature of their disadvantages that made the election of 1872 so very different from any campaign that had come before. One of Grant's great disadvantages in the North was the knowledge that his administration was afflicted with considerable corruption and nepotism. On the other hand, few believed that Grant himself was corrupt, and he continued to garner the goodwill of the Northern people as the victor over Lee and the Confederacy. But that which blessed him in the North damned him in the South.

However, Horace Greeley had, if anything, worse problems, especially in the South. He was perhaps the first candidate whose record could not be used to any advantage at least in the South. Mosby was right. Greeley's record was too well-known to be ignored, much less defended! When the campaigning began in earnest, Greeley's supporters found that they had to base their "stump speeches" entirely on Grant and avoid as much as possible any attempt to defend Greeley! But for those who believed that the South would never vote for Grant, when Greeley became the Democratic candidate, the matter was starting to be seen in a different light:

Daily State Journal – **July 22, 1872**

THE SENTIMENTS OF THOUSANDS.—

An enterprising young merchant in this city, who was a brave Confederate soldier under Mosby during the war, says he is still willing to trust and follow his old comrade and commander, and will vote for Grant, and that thousands of Virginia Confederates will do the same thing.

Meanwhile, Greeley adherents were finding that it was difficult, if not impossible, to make the man palatable to their audiences; and the best that they could hope to do was to make Grant less palatable. But the people of the South were looking for relief in their continuing political, social, and economic misery. A campaign based upon "who is worse" was hardly liable to turn out the vote—a matter that was bound to benefit Grant!

And while, Mosby was being castigated by Democratic papers, another publication asserted that the ex-Confederate was one of the "big guns" for Grant:

Emporia News – July 26, 1872 (Edited)

GEN. J. E. JOHNSTON FOR GRANT.

At Charlottesville resides Judge Wm. S. Robertson, a prominent Lawyer, formerly member of the Virginia Court of Appeals, and in olden times a politician of eminence. He was included in the last amnesty bill passed by Congress. He is the leader of the anti-Greeley movement in the Conservative party of the State. In his wake follow such men as Colonel Mosby, John W. Jackson, of Fluvanna, John Harmer Gilmore of Richmond, Ex-Gov. Henry A Wise, and others, to numerous to mention, but of equal prominence. Of these gentlemen, Messrs. Mosby, Jackson and Gilmer may be counted on as ardent and actual supporters of the Grant and Wilson ticket. They will not only vote for it, but work for it, but will doubtless carry a sufficient number of their friends with them to make a significant mark in the final result. Judge Robertson's policy, however, is of the passive character. I am not at liberty to tell you the details of the programme in its entirety, but when the bolters become organized, or rather after the Baltimore Convention, you will see that the Southern opposition to Greeley is as Mosby has characterized, "a small h—ll in a nutshell," but the explosion may not injure anyone…

Gen. Joseph E. Johnston of Confederate fame, with Col. Mosby and others, whose names we did not learn, had consultations with Judge Robertson last week, at which this proposal was submitted. It did not meet their approval, however, and during interviews which followed General Johnston disclosed the fact that he had been in correspondence with Montgomery Blair regarding Mr. Greeley. From his statements it seems that Blair wrote to Johnston, requesting him to be present at the Baltimore Convention, to urge the indorsement of the Cincinnati movement. In the course of the argument to induce Johnston to act in Greeley's behalf, Blair predicted that the Sage of Chappaqua would sweep the country as Harrison did in 1840. General Johnston's reply was curt and characteristic. He said that he was not a Greeley man, and announced his intention to vote for Grant. He promised Blair, however, that if Greeley would follow Harrison's example, and die within a month after his inauguration, he would advocate his election. The result of the conference was not satisfactory to any of the parties interested.

This was of course the same Judge Robertson who prosecuted John Mosby in the Turpin matter and then taught him law. Mosby considered Robertson his mentor and friend, but Robertson's plan was the strategy Mosby rejected. The judge believed that if the South stood apart, it would be in a position to "make the next President." Mosby thought that if the people of the South did such a thing, it would only prove their total political irrelevance and lose whatever hope they had of help in recovering from the war. Mosby believed that the best the South could do was to support the man who was actually going to win—whom Mosby believed was Grant. The sort of strategy that Judge Robertson hoped would serve the interests of the South was anathema to John Mosby, first because passivity was not part of his nature and, even more to the point, because he did not think it would work.

Mosby's campaign efforts on behalf of Grant continued to appear in the press:

New North-West – August 3, 1872 (Edited)

Why Mosby is for Grant.

A correspondent of the Cincinnati Commercial, who is traveling through Virginia called upon John Mosby the other day, and reviving and old acquaintance, told him what his townsfolk said about him. "I don't care," said Mosby, "what they say about me. I know that I am right, as when I voted for Douglas. The same people said then that I was crazy There were six hundred votes cast at the precinct, and I was one of the two men only out of that six hundred that voted for Douglas. I've always been in the minority, from principle, and now my principles have probably placed me where I am likely to be—with the majority, for I believe that Grant will be re-elected. The people round here underrate Grant's strength. There are hundreds of people that I know personally who will vote for him in preference to Greeley, and as many more who will not vote at all. I believe in Grant, and if we've got to surrender again, I'd rather surrender to a soldier than an old woman. To tell the truth, I hate the Greeley movement, and many of the men who are in it, as earnestly as I hated the North when the fiercest passions of war prevailed, and when the fight was the hardest. The present situation reminds me of the time when Virginia was dragged out of the Union. The people are all protesting that they don't like Greeley, as the protested against South Carolina and secession then; but are following the schemers as blindly as ever, and the politicians have got the reins in their hands as usual. There are not a dozen men in the State who belong to the Conservative party, who will vote for Greeley because they like him, or believe in him, or because they know him, but they will do it because the politicians tell them to do so. I have knocked around through this section considerably of late, and have yet to find a Conservative who takes to Greeley kindly. They swallow him as they swallowed secession. You may tell your people that if there was any other choice than Greeley, the Democrats of Virginia would take it. As it is, and as I said before, many of them will vote for Grant, while others will not vote at all."

And then John Mosby was actually on the stump, proving that he was just as good a speaker as he was a soldier. Indeed, he was still a soldier—only his weapons were now reason and rhetoric:

Daily National Republican – **August 5, 1872**

THE DISCUSSION AT SALEM.

In another column to-day we print a full report, made for the Republican by our special correspondent, of the joint discussion which occurred on Saturday at Salem, Fauquier county, Va., between Generals Mosby and Hunton, both formerly officers in the rebel armies. Mosby, with his plain, common-sense talk, seems to have completely overwhelmed his opponent, who, in the points he attempted to make, displays either a willful disregard for the facts in the case or a woeful ignorance of the subjects on which he spoke. The gathering, our correspondent states, was a large one, and the evident sympathy in favor of the administration of President Grant may well be taken as a reflex of the feeling existing among the mass of the people of Virginia.

The Knoxville Chronicle went to Salem and reported on Mosby's debate with Eppa Hunton while the Vermont—yes, Vermont!—Phoenix printed a small but complimentary article on Mosby's rhetorical skills:

Knoxville Chronicle – August 8, 1872 (Edited)
MOSBY ON THE STUMP FOR GRANT.

Why Southern Men Ought to Oppose Greeley.

At Salem, Virginia, on the 3rd, Col. Jno. S. Mosby and Gen. Eppa. Hunton had a discussion on the political issues of the day. Mosby for Grant, Hunton for Greeley. A large crowd was present and the New York Herald correspondent says in reference to Mosby:

His voice is peculiar, as is the man, being in higher notes sharp and decisive and in the lower ones soft and melodious. People may say what they will, if the gathering of yesterday was any index to the opinion of the stay-at-homes, then the ex-Confederate chief has far more strength than they have been willing to admit.

Vermont Phoenix – August 9, 1872

Mosby has gone into the campaign for Grant with his whole heart. He made a vigorous and graceful speech at Salem, Va., Saturday, as the preliminary to a grand stumping tour.

But the press was never entirely positive, and again, the partisan statement was always accompanied by the personal sting:

Columbia *Daily Phoenix* – August 10, 1872 (Edited)

Mosby on a Raid—Col. John S. Mosby has been making a Grant speech at a political meeting in Salem, Fauquier County, Va., "Mosby on a Raid" is the attractive heading which his new allies give to his attack on the Greeleyites. "Mosby on a Raid" was not wont to fill the truly loil with pleasurable sensations. No one disputes the qualities of Col. Mosby as a guerrilla. Though not as prominent a personage among the Confederate leaders as Gen. Longstreet, he was, for a mosquito partisan, most active, drew blood quickly and eluded capture skillfully. In his late speech, he essays the role of the stump speaker, but it is no discredit to him that he does not show much advantage in a line in which he has had so little practice. Very few soldiers are good speech-makers. He is no doubt more a man of actions than of words.

Col. Mosby glorifies the conduct of Gen. Grant at Appomattox, and refers to the creditable fact that he did not have a triumphal procession through Richmond at the close of the war. All our generals acted befittingly in that regard, we believe, and no one questions that Gen. Grant was true to his military training, and soldierly instincts at that time. But Col. Mosby seems to ignore the difference between the politician and soldier, and the change which necessarily has come over Gen. Grant since he has been manipulated by mere party men for the perpetuation of their own power. ...the President seems to have changed, or he has so given way to others who are illiberal and proscriptive, that the results are no longer what they would have been, had he continued to set upon his original impulse; whereas, on the other hand, Greeley has shown the spirit throughout, and still holds and stands pledged to it for the future, which Grant exhibited at first, and has since unfortunately, fallen away from. Col. Mosby, however, is not likely to bring much strength to Gen. Grant in Virginia—Baltimore Sun.

Mosby was a man of words as well as action. He was a lawyer and thus often spoke in court. He did not however like to speak extemporaneously and often suffered more than a bit of "stage fright" before "going on." But it can be seen by those who reported his performance "on the stump" that he was certainly an advantage to the Grant campaign in Virginia.

The matter of "Republican type" found its way into print in this article. As noted, the contestants in the election of '72 were both Republicans as that party had begun to break down into factions as noted in an article in which Republican Judge Henry A. Foster of New York stated that he could not vote for electors "who are in favor of the re-election of President Grant."

And so the coverage continued:

Daily State Journal **– August 21, 1872**

MOSBY ON GREELEY,

His Views on the Presidential Canvass—What He Thinks of Greeleyism—The Philosopher's Position Criticized.

The following letter from Col. John S. Mosby, written to a gentleman in New York city, we find published in the *New York Times* of the 20th. It contains some facts and statements that will be found interesting:

Warrenton, Va., August 18th, 1872 Dear Sir: Your favor of the 13th inst. has been received, inviting me to speak in the city of New York on the questions of the Presidential canvass. I cannot accept your invitation now, as all the time I can spare from my professional duties will be more efficiently employed in my own State in exposing the fraud and delusion of this last ism—Greeleyism. I can see in the election of Horace Greeley no relief from any of the evils from which the Southern people are suffering, but rather an aggravation of them all. It is true, we have been plundered by carpet-baggers, as you have by Tammany thieves; but as the intelligence of the South was made the footstool of ignorance, by the policies of which Greeley was the foremost advocate and defender, and which he proposes to perpetuate, how can his elevation to the Chief Magistracy of the Union relieve us? Carpet-baggers have attained power through local majorities. Does he, as President propose to overrule them? If so, what then becomes of his boasted "local self-government?"

I have just read his speech at Portland, in which, while justifying the Ku-klux law as necessary to repress violence and disorder, he says that there never would have arisen any occasion for such a law if amnesty had been granted to the South. Now, this is one of those plausible sophistries with which Greeley has succeeded in gulling both North and South. Amnesty means nothing more than relief from the disabilities proposed by the Fourteenth Amendment, (which Greeley advocated), which only excluded certain classes from holding office but not from voting. Do the Hamptons, the Pickens and the Prestons, who governed South Carolina in the days of her glory, stand any better chance now of being elected to office than before the passage of the Amnesty bill? The condition of South Carolina can never be changed until Greeley's policy is reversed—his denunciation of carpet-baggers is all brutum fulmen[*]—his promises are a cheat and a snare "That mock the woe that lurks beneath, Like roses o'er a supulchre."

Which of the lost rights of the South does he propose to restore? A Greeleyite will answer "trippingly on the tongue," local government and universal suffrage—which only means—negro supremacy. How will he get rid of carpet-baggers? Is he going to do as he says the ku-klux will do—spirit them away? Or with all his professed horror of military power, is he going to play the part of Caesar or Cromwell—expel them vi et armis[**] from places to which they have been elected? As all that he offers us is a "Greeley pill," from the effects of which we have too long been suffering, I beg to be permitted to decline it; for while it may be "sweet on the tongue" it will certainly be "bitter in the belly."

I am, Sir, very respectfully, your obedient servant,

JOHN S. MOSBY.

[* brutum fulmen: a noisy but harmless threatening; an innocuous thunderbolt-vph] [** vi et armis: with force of arms-vph]

Evening Star – August 25, 1872

The Petersburg (Virginia) Index (Greeleyite) admits that Colonel Mosby's avowed opposition to Greeley and championship of Grant is not without its effects, especially in the upper portion of the district, and it will be necessary to get before the people a number of good canvassers to overcome it. Mosby is greatly liked through this country, and many people share his natural indignation at having his motives in this matter misconstrued.

The "misconstruing" of John Mosby's motives was only just beginning! Indeed, before many more months had passed, he was no longer "greatly liked" in the upper portion of Virginia or in any portion of Virginia or the South.

Daily State Journal – August 26, 1872 (Edited)

MOSBY

His Speech at Bealton on Saturday—

He goes for the Liberals and Uncle Horace.

From the Washington Chronicle

Colonel John S. Mosby delivered the second of his course of independent campaign speeches at Bealton, Fauquier county, Va., on Saturday. An audience, respectable in size, numbers, and quality, gathered in the new township hall …Colonel Mosby disclaimed at the outset any motives of personal ambition in assuming to address his Conservative fellow citizens, and to show them why they could not as honest men and true Democrats, follow the lead of the Baltimore Convention, and proceeded to review at length the political situation and the causes which have produced the present state of affairs. The common argument that the Democrats could not afford to be beaten again, he said, as a new maxim in politics, meaning in effect, that as soon as a party is in the minority it must renounce its principles, and in this particular case, the Democratic party couldn't afford to be honest any longer. Governor Vance, of North Carolina, may be able to sing this new Greeley tune, but he couldn't, and there would be just as much sense in a Christian congregation singing "Old Grimes" [a popular secular fiddle tune-vph] as in the Democratic party's voting for old Horace Greeley. The Cincinnati Convention was captured and perverted by disaffected soreheads and Radicals. Liberal Republicans, Mosby said, were those who had been disappointed in getting into office, or kicked out of it when they were in, and suddenly they became "liberal"—liberal toward themselves—they were never suspected of liberality toward anyone else.

The Baltimore Convention represented constituencies, but no principles, and the Cincinnati Convention principles but no constituencies, and the efforts of the two were to secure the support of the remarkable coalition for Greeley. Among the "Liberals" who are now leading in this venal transaction are McNeill of Missouri, whom President Davis outlawed at the same time he outlawed Beast Butler; Kilpatrick, who led the "pitch, tar and turpentine" raid on Richmond, and afterward of unsavory Chilean notoriety, and Charles A. Dana, editor of the vilest most malignant sheet on earth, next to the *New York Tribune*, and who was sent by Stanton to Fortress Monroe to see the chains put on Jefferson Davis. These are the men who in this new dispensation are to prescribe my political duties and control my political acts. Mosby then reviewed Greeley's record, showing that whatever oppression the South had suffered from the present Administration, it had all sprung from Greeley's brain, and that he was responsible for the most severe and obnoxious measures of Radical legislation. Greeley, however, says that the old issues are dead, and then in his letter of acceptance declares that he hasn't changed, and in another place that if the Democrats didn't support him he would support Grant ... Then as to Greeley's record. None of the Greeley orators defend his record. And isn't this an admission that his record is indefensible? They say Greeley, like St. Paul, has repented; but St. Paul the moment he was converted, didn't assume to be a leader and chief man among the Christians, but remained an humble disciple for years. Having disposed of Greeley the Colonel next "went for" the platform upon which he was placed at Cincinnati and accepted at Baltimore.

He admitted that the South was beaten in the war, but he never would say that he thanked the North for it; neither would he acquiesce in the fourteenth and fifteenth amendments to the Constitution. He submitted to them simply because he hadn't the physical power to get rid of them, and had always hoped that the North, when calm reason returned, would repeal them. This, he maintained, had been until within the last few months the position of the Democracy, and cited the solid Democratic vote against Representative Peters' resolution at the last session in proof of that fact. The Cincinnati platform was manipulated by Fenton, who owns and runs Horace Greeley, as old uncle Jno Harper owns and runs Longfellow. All of Greeley's talk about "clasping hands across the bloody chasm," Mosby said meant nothing more than that he would shake hands with those who would vote for him, which most candidates are always willing to do. Greeley's share in the enactment of the ku-klux and election laws and the suspension of the habeas corpus was also fully examined and explained altogether to the disadvantage of Greeley's cause among the Democrats.

Mosby spoke precisely and clearly when he said:

> "The Baltimore Convention represented constituencies, but no principles, and the Cincinnati Convention principles but no constituencies, and the efforts of the two were to secure the support of the remarkable coalition for Greeley. Among the "Liberals" who are now leading in this venal transaction are McNeill of Missouri, whom President Davis outlawed at the same time he outlawed Beast Butler; Kilpatrick, who led the "pitch, tar and turpentine" raid on Richmond, and afterward of unsavory Chilean notoriety, and Charles A. Dana, editor of the vilest and most malignant sheet on earth, next to the New York Tribune, and who was sent by Stanton to Fortress Monroe to see the chains put on Jefferson Davis. These are the men who in this new dispensation are to prescribe my political duties and control my political acts."

The men to whom John Mosby referred were these: General John McNeil, who gained the sobriquet the Butcher of Palmyra after executing ten Confederate prisoners of war for a matter in which they had no involvement. The "Richmond" or Dahlgren-Kilpatrick raid was designed to break Federal prisoners out of captivity at Belle Isle and Libby Prisons. These were then supposed to burn Richmond and murder the Confederate government living in that city. This was a complete rejection of the existing rules of warfare even of the Union's own Lieber Code. Charles A. Dana was one of the communist party members in the Lincoln administration.

Daily and State Journal – **August 28, 1872**

The Blue and the Grey—Letter from Colonel Mosby.

On the 6th inst. the Union Soldiers' and Sailors' Grant and Wilson Campaign club of Baltimore passed the following resolution:

Resolved, That as soldiers and sailors who served in the army and navy of the Union, we are ready to extend the hand of political fellowship to those who fought against us, exacting no conditions except a cordial support of Grant and Wilson.

Resolved, That we commend the efforts now being made by Colonel John S. Mosby and other distinguished soldiers of the late Confederate army in Virginia and elsewhere, to complete the work of reconciliation by assisting in the re-election of President Grant.

A copy of the resolutions was transmitted to Colonel Mosby, of this State, who returned the following replay:

Warrenton, Va., Aug. 20th, '72

Dear Sir—Absence from home has prevented an earlier reply to your communication of the 7th inst., accompanying the resolutions of the "Soldiers' and Sailors' Grant Campaign Club." I desire to return through you my sincere thanks to the Society for the resolution in reference to myself. Nothing is more grateful to the pride of a soldier's heart than the respect of the foeman he has met "on the perilous edge of battle." Recognizing, as I do, in General Grant the chivalrous soldier who threw his shield over his prostrate foe when many of those who now affect to call themselves "Liberals" were crying for his blood, I have announced a preference for him over the fanatic of the Tribune, who ought now instead of being candidate asking for Southern votes to be suppliant, begging our forgiveness and doing penance for all the wrongs he has done us. In making this choice I am not reduced to the necessity of my former associates who have gone off after the ignus fatuus* of Greeleyism, of "turning my back upon my past."

I desire it, however, to be understood that I reserve the right of supporting the candidate of any party that may appear professing principles in accordance with my own political convictions.

I am, sir, very respectfully, your obedient servant,

(Signed) John S. Mosby

[*ignus fatuus - a deceptive goal or hope-vph]

This response to the Union soldiers and sailors who had complimented Mosby on his attempt to further the reconciliation of the sections was very telling. To begin with, he was defined in these resolutions as a "distinguished soldier," though that must be considered a minority opinion as many newspaper articles continued to make obvious. Mosby accepted their good opinion, but with a caveat: yes, he supported Grant, but his real problem was with Greeley. He also made it clear that his support of Grant would have changed if a candidate who supported his own convictions had run against the president. Mosby could have accepted their praise as Greeley had already been nominated, but he did not want to take the chance that if they were to learn of his declaration to support a "true Democrat," he would be judged a hypocrite.

An article in the *Daily State Journal* reported Mosby's defense against a nasty slander, which was then followed by his "coup" in a debate with old friend "Extra Billy" Smith:

Daily State Journal - October 7, 1872

A Card from Colonel Mosby. Warrenton, VA., Oct. 2, 1872.

To the Editor of the Washington Chronicle:

I observe in the Patriot of the 2d instant an editorial saying that "Col. Mosby is agent and proprietor of a marble quarry situated on the left bank of the Potomac, and in that capacity is about to put in a bid for furnishing headstones to the national cemeteries." This statement is a lie from beginning to end, and known to be such by the cowardly slanderer who wrote it. I have no sort of interest either as proprietor or agent, in any quarry of any sort on the face of the earth, and the idea has never entered my head of applying to the Government for any kind of a contract. Very respectfully,

Jno. S. Mosby.

As may be remembered however, from the contretemps with "Sheriff" Boyd in 1869, John Mosby did represent "the marble quarry business" as testified to by the reporter who interviewed him at the time. However, it is probable that five years later he was no longer engaged by those interests. Certainly, he would not have made the statement had he continued to be retained by the quarries' owners as it would have been very easy to disprove his denial of any such business arrangement. As well, there were more than enough newspapers that would have jumped at the chance to prove Mosby a liar! On the other hand, it is more than probable that whoever made the charge was aware of his previous involvement and used the matter to discredit him.

Daily State Journal – October 17, 1872 (Edited)
MOSBY AND EXTRA BILLY SMITH.

We have already given our readers an account of the ambuscade into which Colonel Mosby led ex-Governor Billy Smith a few days ago, but the affair is so significant that we are induced to publish the facts again. ...:

This chivalrous Confederate officer of Virginia is as undaunted on the stump as he was in the stirrups. He seems to be as little inclined to "shake hands" with Mr. Greeley "across the bloody chasm" he and his "illustrious compeers" have made in the Constitution since the war for the union was over, by their reconstruction usurpations, enforcement acts, and Ku-klux bill, as he was when the same champion of "peace and amnesty" came with his cry of "On to Richmond!"

We see the following account of a recent discussion between Colonel Mosby and ex-Governor William Smith, the most distinguished of all the living speakers on the hustings in the Old Dominion: "The governor, in his speech said they were mere fabrications to excuse the exercise of arbitrary power by General Grant in the South.

"In his reply Colonel Mosby read from an editorial of Greeley's written a few days before the passage of the law, in which he said there had been five thousand negroes killed in South Carolina by the Ku-klux during Grant's administration, and 'not a single white man had been punished for it.' 'Now,' said Mosby, 'Governor, tell me candidly, did Greeley tell a lie or the truth when he wrote that?'

"Smith, jumping up, foaming and raving, said 'he told a d—d lie!' "He saw that if he admitted the truth of what Greeley had told over and over, he would have justified Grant for executing the law; so he preferred to hold up his own candidate as a liar."

Ex-Governor Smith was, perhaps, never before so completely unhorsed! The signal triumph so achieved, over such a Knight, was certainly a most gallant feat, and adds no little to the laurels of the young Ivanhoe of the invincible Democracy clad with the armor of truth.

A.H.S.

Daily State Journal – **November 4, 1872**

[Part of a larger story]

The same writer in the Patriot recently charged Colonel Mosby with being interested in a stone contact in Washington, and insinuated that as a reason for his support of General Grant. But the gallant Colonel "lopped his head" for him in a very summary manner, and the poor fellow didn't so much as "peep" afterwards. The meanest of all liars in the world is your chronic liar—one who persists in telling a falsehood after it is thoroughly exploded, or one in whom an old lie breaks out, like a vile cutaneous disease, periodically, for the want of a new irritation. Such a liar tops Falstaff, in forty cups of "sack with lime in it."

And then the election was over, and Grant had won. The Columbian scoffed at Mosby's rather touching and naïve message of congratulations, an opinion based upon his actions during the war. Why actions that were legitimate and honorable should invalidate Mosby's wishes for peace and reconciliation is not made clear:

The Columbian – **November 15, 1872**

Valuable!

Washington, November 8.—

The following dispatch has just been received at the White House:

"Warrenton, Va., November 7.—President Grant: Virginia casts her vote for Grant, peace and reconciliation.

(Signed) John S. Mosby."

The John S. Mosby whose name is signed to the above telegram, is the same Mosby who as marauder and guerilla earned the reprobation of decent men during the war. For reasons of his own he has become a Grant supporter and is now a bright and shining light in that collection of Christians and statesmen to be found in the Republican party. Had he not become a howler for Grant, he would have been denounced, as of old, as a scoundrel by all the papers which now support his master. He is a valuable witness concerning "peace and reconciliation."

Home Journal – **November 28, 1872**

Col. Mosby, the notorious guerrilla chief of the war, is to be rewarded, it is said, with a fat government office for his services in behalf of General Grant and the Republicans in, which services are recognized and appreciated by the President, who gives Mosby credit for having done more than any other one man in carrying Virginia for the Grant party.

Mosby was offered "a fat government office" by President Grant, as his services were recognized and appreciated. But John Mosby had promised not to accept any office from Grant in order to avoid the appearance of the very self-interest of which this paper—and others—accused him.

Pulaski Citizen – **December 10, 1872 (Edited)**

[Part of a much longer article]

The President's Liberalism

Concurrent with hints of the Washington correspondents, that the President meditates a change of policy toward the Southern people, we have certain tokens, direct from the South, of an equally suggestive, though not of a surprising or discouraging sort.

General Grant's second administration will with the least tact and circumspection on his part, pluck many converts from the midst of those who have been the most determined enemies of himself and his party... Gentlemen of the Confederate line, it is time to shut the books; to fold up and lay away the bonnie, bonnie, bonnie blue flag of the lost cause! Different conditions exist in different States On the old line we cannot stand together except to hopeless internal dissensions and certain defeat. New connections are inevitable. You must save yourself; for we can make no further sacrifices to save you. Because, be assured of this, that the prosperity of the whole—the healthful growth of the system — is our sole chance of prospering. We declared during the canvass that if Grant should be re-elected necessity would raise up for him the most ardent supporters of this revolutionizing policy among the Southern people ... Already this is being verified by the result ... Mosby in the late campaign was true to his character of a guerrilla, preceding the cavalry and exploring the enemy's country. The Mosbys will be multiplied if the President has the wit, forecast and assurance to set up for a patriot and pacifier. If he does, the entire aspect of partisan affairs will be changed, and we are inclined to think, on the whole, for the better, since they could hardly be worse than they are. If he does not, we shall merely run along on the line of the Liberal movement, gathering strength as we go, lopping off weakness, and, if there is no foreign war, preparing for a great peace struggle in 1876.

This article manifested Mosby's position on the South after the war and what he had hoped to achieve by supporting President Grant. Of course, that didn't happen; and the problems with Grant and the Republicans led only to a decline in the popularity of both, bringing about—as prophesied above—the bitterly contested election of 1876.

But with John Mosby, the struggle was fated to continue in the new year and on the same battlefield: politics. But in this instance, Mosby found himself fighting on the other side!

ADDENDUM

*Charles Fourier (1772-1837) was a utopian socialist and a relatively isolated thinker. He was without formal academic training, was mocked and ridiculed by his critics having no meaningful contacts with any political organizations. In other words, those who followed Fourier were as inept and irrelevant as their leader.

Chapter 12

1873

Ad iudicium ~ To common sense

"The fashion of the world is to avoid cost, and you encounter it."
~ **William Shakespeare**

IN 1873 THE path John Mosby followed in 1872 came back to haunt him as political matters moved from the national to the state arena—and all that that entailed. Of course, his situation of the past year was still sufficiently prominent to permit his enemies to exult about whatever catastrophe might descend upon his miserable unregenerate head. Indeed, the earliest newspaper reports in 1873 involved the matter of Federal patronage both for Mosby personally—that is, the positions, real and imagined, offered to him by Grant and his efforts to gain Federal offices for Virginians through Grant. The coverage of these efforts were of course influenced by the partisanship of the reporting publication.

Daily State Journal – 26, 1873

Colonel Mosby has certainly vindicated himself from the unjust suspicions so freely expressed before the late election as to his motive in favoring the election of General Grant instead of Mr. Greeley. He went with his state once to its damage and his own, and he thought it right that his state should go with him in repairing the wrong. He regarded the rebellion as played out, and believed that the sooner Virginia identified herself with the loyal sentiment of the country the sooner the scars of the war could be effaced and the chasm closed. He received, in consequence of his action, from some of the still disloyal men of his state, the treatment usually accorded to Republicans in the south although he made no profession of Republicanism. In again declining public office at the hands of the President, as he did a few days since, he admitted that one motive was to vindicate himself from unjust suspicion at home. — Washington Chronicle.

Mosby's old enemy, the *Bristol News* not able to condemn him for taking an office, determined it would report as to why he did not, at least according to the Petersburg Appeal:

The *Bristol News*, – March 18, 1873

Mosby.

Apropos of office-seeking, a gentleman who was in Washington last week and had a talk with Col. John S. Mosby says that the ex-Guerilla Chief is almost worried to death by persons who are candidates for office,and want him to recommend them to the President. His endorsement is said to be worth as much as any Senator's; and it is will known that he is one of the welcome guests at the White House. Col. Mosby was offered the District-Attorneyship for the Eastern District of Virginia, as well as a place in a Western State, but declined both for fear that his motives in favoring the re-election of Grant might be misconstrued.—He may yet, however, be offered something that will feel it his duty to accept; as to his running for Attorney-General on the Radical ticket, that is folly. The office does not pay as much as any country lawyer in good practice makes with ease.—Cor. Petersburg Appeal.

Soon, one newspaper determined just why Grant and Mosby "loved" each other. In an article of some length, the paper demonstrated the true depths into which the fourth estate was capable of sinking when partisan politics was involved:

***Eaton Weekly Democrat* – May 8, 1873**

Grant and Mosby.

Grant, the Union saver—Mosby the Union smasher—par nobile fratrum [a noble pair of brothers (Horace)]. "Behold how good and pleasant it is for brethren to dwell together in unity." [Psalm 133] From travelers in the South, and from Southern newspapers, it appears that Col. John S. Mosby has been given the virtual control of Grant's offices, not only in Virginia but throughout the tier of States, South, bordering on the tide-waters. Mosby will be remembered by all soldiers as most cruel, relentless, devilish and inhuman monster created by the rebellion. His command was, in fact, a part of the regular force of the rebel army, but was a partisan organization, created for the express purpose of pillage, torture and barbarism. It was his command, that after taking nineteen of the 4th Michigan cavalry prisoners of war, placed them in a row and shot them to death—it was his command that at one time, in the Valley of Virginia, burned one hundred of our army wagons, killed nearly all the drivers and captured six hundred mules, destroying at that one time over a million of dollars belonging to the United States—it was his command that hunted our boys when endeavoring to escape from the hell holes at Belle Isle and Richmond, and capturing them, tied them to the bridle reins of his fellow fiends and dragged them back to a captivity more brutal and barbarous than the world has ever known. Of all the leaders of the rebel army, Mosby was recognized as the most cruel, and irresponsible. In fact, at one time our government proclaimed him an outlaw and not entitled to receive the treatment of a prisoner of war if captured.

With the full knowledge of all these things, the dictator Grant, has take this infamous scoundrel into his counsels—has sent for him, and had private interviews with him at Washington—has dined him in the house erected and maintained by the people, and has given him carte blanche in the selection of office-holders in a large portion of the South. The reason of this warm feeling of the Emperor for the Guerilla has finally cropped out. Mosby was, and is to-day, a great lover, and a good judge of fine, fast horses, and his advice, and experience have been valuable to the Emperor in the selection of race horses. Our economical Congress presented the Emperor, (at his own suggestion) with $25,000 per year of the people's money, and at the suggestion of Mosby the Emperor purchased the stud horse "Cyclops" for $14,000 and sends him to his farm at St. Louis, (which, by the way, was stolen from the people by the Dent family). Long live Ulysses and his henchman Mosby—let them select their stud horses and the people will pay for them. "As it was in the beginning, is now and ever shall be, world without end. Amen!"

There isn't much that can be said about such preposterous claims and allegations except that the rage of the Democratic press after Mosby's "treason" wiped away all those defenses of him made just after the war, and now, these journals were more than willing to allow every evil ever attributed to him by the Republicans.

And while the Democratic press was firing away at both men, soon, the Republican newspapers began to complain bitterly about those whom Mosby put forth for office because they were both former Confederates and often Democrats. This outcry would become even louder when Mosby refused to support the state Republican Party in the election of 1873:

Nashville Union and American – June 13, 1873

Chicago Tribune – June 11, 1873

Special Dispatch to The Chicago Tribune. Dissatisfaction with Virginia Appointments Virginia Politics.

Washington, June 10.—Leading Republicans of Virginia are complaining bitterly about some of Federal appointments recently made in that State. It is charged that many of the appointees are not only ex-Confederates, but that they have not, since the close of the rebellion, identified themselves with the Republican party. The negroes, who form the largest part of the Republican voters in the Old Dominion, assert that they have not been recognized in the distribution of Federal patronage, while their former masters, who went into the rebellion, have had favors showered upon them. It is charged that all this has been accomplished by John S. Mosby, of rebel guerrilla fame, who is known to have considerable influence with the President. Mosby, while steadily refusing office himself, has provided for a large number of his friends. Very recently, two of Mosby's cavalry were appointed mail agents at a salary of $1,200 each. A prominent Republican from Virginia says that on account of the appointment made there by the President, the party is much discouraged, and that it will have a bad effect upon the pending campaign.

But just as John Mosby had turned the South and both political parties upside down by his support of Republican Ulysses S. Grant in 1872, he was about to do the same thing again—only in the other direction. He had refused to support the Democrat "fusion candidate" Horace Greeley, whom he despised, and had gone with Grant. Indeed, he had more than "gone with Grant!" He had written letters about issues of the election and even gone to various places in the state and "stumped" for his former enemy. With Grant's victory, the Republican Party congratulated itself on gaining another famous Confederate along with men like Key and Longstreet to showcase to the rest of the nation. But John Mosby was not Longstreet or Key; he was as much an unknown quantity in 1873 as he had been ten years earlier. For 1873 saw another election—this time at the state level. Mosby had already advised Grant that he could not support the state Party because it was a party of Radicals, carpetbaggers, and Negroes. As this new political season got under way, there appeared a small article in the *Daily State Journal*—a Republican organ. Of course, that party's new "treasure," Colonel John Mosby, was soon trotted out:

Daily State Journal – May 17, 1873

Postmaster-General Creswell on Virginia Politics.

A reporter of the Washington Republican has interviewed Postmaster-General Creswell.

"How is Virginia going in the fall?" asked the reporter.

"Well, from what I hear, we shall carry it. My information is very full, and I have reason to believe very accurate. Our friends down there seem to be alive and active, and to be working with the utmost earnestness. I saw a letter from Mosby this morning, and he appeared to be very confident."

"I do not think we shall have Mosby with us this time."

"Why?"

"You remember his position in the November campaign. He took the ground that as between General Grant and Mr. Greeley, he was for General Grant. His argument upon the stump was, 'You propose to take office under Mr. Greeley—one Republican; I propose to take office under General Grant—another Republican. That is the only difference between us.'"

"Yes; I know that was his position then, but I am inclined to think that he will work with us now the state issues."

Cresswell was wrong. Mosby's position on the state Republican Party became known or, more to the point, better known because it had never been a secret though few paid any attention at the time. The first indication of the "dawning light" was a positive article in a Southern Journal that suddenly noticed all of the things that Mosby had said with regard to his support of Grant the year before and just as suddenly (apparently) understood them. This revelation was followed by a Republican article that also understood that Mosby's support for Grant did not extend to that party at the state level and condemned him accordingly. It is in the latter sentiment that the "religiosity" of politics is seen; that is, party allegiance is party allegiance without fear or favor. John Mosby didn't see it that way. To Mosby, principle was first, party a distant second:

Fairfield Herald – **no date, 1873 (Edited)**

Colonel Mosby

In a recent number of the Southern Home we mentioned that Hughes, the black-and-tan candidate for Governor of Virginia, was too low down to be supported by even the renegade Mosby. It appears from the following extract from a private letter from a distinguished Virginia Representative in Congress that we were misinformed concerning Colonel Mosby's political status. Our friend says, "Colonel Mosby has just shown me a copy of your paper in which he (Mosby) is called a renegade and it is supposed that you wrote the article. I was sorry to see such a piece from you and because I think the epithet is not deserved. Mosby was for Grant against Greeley but never went with the Radicals, and has rendered us important services in the campaign," &c. It is stated, also, that Mosby supported General Kemper, and "uniformly lent his influence with Grant in favor of Conservatives, particularly of those who suffered from Governmental persecution."

We are always pleased to find ourselves in error when we have unwittingly imputed to any respectable person the disgrace of entertaining Radical sentiments; therefore, relying on our correspondent's assurances, we cheerfully withdraw the obnoxious epithet, only regretting that so gallant a soldier as Colonel Mosby should by his quasi affiliation with the stolid oppressor of the South lay himself liable to the misconstruction of being considered a renegade and a traitor to our cause and our people… If we have done Colonel Mosby an injustice by attributing to him such conduct, we regret it; for, in common with the Southern people, we have ever felt a high degree of pride in the successful exploits of the dashing Virginia partisan. And if it shall appear that he, in his odd fashion, has only worked around in the enemy's rear to operate on his communications, we shall be well pleased to chronicle the result.—*Southern Herald*

Now the *National Republican* saw overtures of "cooperation" with the Grant administration put forth by Virginia Conservatives (Democrats) in their platform as false. However, Mosby was not blamed. Rather, he was thought to have been gulled into believing such "sham" pronouncements of mutual accord. But in fact, the overtures were there because John Mosby pushed for them to be included in that platform:

National Republican – August 16, 1873 (Edited)
Sham-Conservative Support of the Administration

We learn that the resolution in the of the Virginia Conservatives relating to the National Administration was the result of a conference between James S. Barber, of Culpeper and Colonel Mosby. This information confirms us in our belief that the complimentary allusion to President Grant contained therein was expressly intended to propitiate the Conservative supporters of the Administration. We regret that Colonel Mosby is satisfied with this unmeaning allusion to the President, but we fear that his position has been somewhat shaken by influences above which a man of his caliber should rise with prompt and decisive independence. These influences we believe to be the product of the cry of "Virginia for white Virginians!" and the prejudice of race against race, which has been so sedulously cultivated by the Conservative press of the State. We understand that he is one of those who make a distinction between the support of the Republican party as a national and a State organization. However flattering this may be to President Grant, it is a mistaken policy, and one that would ruin the prospects of the party in every respect if it should be adopted generally… We cannot afford to trust them now, after they have proven themselves to be cheats, and when they intimate or promise, publicly or otherwise, that they will elect an Administration man to be United States Senator if they carry the Legislature we know that they do not intend to do anything of the kind… They may be shrewd enough to deceive Col. Mosby, bright-witted and sharp-sighted as he is, but they will fail in their attempts to delude the President. They have made the issue themselves, and having earned a reputation for falsehood, having voluntarily allied themselves with the opposition, it is useless for them at this late hour to hoist any but their true colors.

The idea that soon became illustrative of Mosby's politics in publications on both sides of the aisle was that he "worked around the enemy's rear" as he did during the war to achieve his ends. John Mosby denied using deception, claiming that he always acted sincerely, honestly, and openly for the benefit of the Virginia people and the South:

Yorkville Enquirer – **June 26, 1873 (Edited)**

Colonel Mosby Interviewed

The famous Confederate cavalry officer, who so astonished the country by his support of Grant in the last Presidential canvass, has recently been interviewed by a reporter of the *Richmond Dispatch*. The Colonel evidently has influence with the administration, and has never yet failed to secure any appointment that he has asked… [h]e says: "I have recommended men who voted for General Grant last year, and now sustain his administration from the same standpoint that I do. I have also recommended men who voted for Greeley, but who now agree with me that it is for the interest of the people of Virginia to stop the war on Grant's administration and cultivate friendly relations with it. By the use of Federal patronage, I have made Gen. Grant more friends in Virginia than all the Radical politicians in the State would have made him in a hundred years. The fact is that the judicial use that has been made of the patronage has already produced a revolution in public sentiment toward the administration in my portion of the State. Nearly every man I meet now applies to me to get him an office from Gen. Grant."

The Colonel says he has never represented himself to the President as a Republican, nor in any way identified himself with the radical party in Virginia that profess to support the administration. The Republican party of the North is altogether a different thing from the radical party of Virginia. [*] He argues further—

"When our people last year made their motto in the campaign, I thought that if reconciliation had any significance, it must mean an alliance between the Republican party of the North and the white people of the South, by which the white people of the South could get the shelter and protection of the Federal Government. I have urged our people, and do now urge them, to form such an alliance. If they were to do that, they would be relieved of the crew of carpet-baggers now controlling the negroes of the South through the influence of Federal patronage. If reconciliation was a good thing last year, it is a good thing this year; and as they certainly failed to get reconciliation through Greeley, I think now they ought to try to get it through Grant. There will never be any real peace and repose for southern society until we take this course."

The Colonel, giving his reasons for opposition to the Conservative party of Virginia, assigns the following:

"I am opposed to the Conservative party in the State, because by its war upon the Administration, it throws all the Federal patronage and Federal influence against the true people of Virginia; and thus keeps alive and affords sustenance to the radical party of negroes and carpet-baggers. I think it is wrong, too, in its policy of arraying white men against the negroes, for it turns the negroes over to the control of the worst element in the State. In this way about one-third of the counties in the State of Virginia, where negroes have local majorities, are under their dominion, and will be kept so long as this policy prevails. But if the Conservative party would reverse its policy the Radical party would be disbanded."

As a reason for not accepting office himself, Colonel Mosby says it would impair the moral influence of his position; that he had been trying to act as a mediator between the Virginia people and the National government, which he could not successfully do, if holding an office. To the question of the probability of a third Presidential term for Grant, Colonel Mosby made the following significant reply:

"I have never had any conversation with General Grant with reference to his reelection for a third term, but am perfectly free to say that if he makes as good a President as I believe he will, and is a candidate for reelection, I have no doubt I shall support him. And I not only think that, but I think, too, that four years from now General Grant will be the candidate of the whole southern people for President. But whether he desires a reelection, I do not know."

Soon, the matter of Mosby's "appointments" began to obtain fire from both sides, fire that became more bitter from the Republican press as it became obvious that they would not have John Mosby on their "side" in the gubernatorial contest:

[*] In this sentiment, John Mosby was one hundred percent wrong! The Northern Republican party was as anti-Southern white as were the local Southern Radicals. Sadly, Mosby held to the belief of a dichotomy between the two for a long time until his own treatment at the hands of the Republican administrations that followed Grant finally convinced him that there was little difference between the Republicans, North or South. The matter soon became worse, however, as it was claimed that Mosby, while not accepting an office, had become an "office broker," making money from those for whom he had acquired an office. This would have been if not directly illegal, then certainly sufficiently ethically questionable to put him in a very dangerous position with both Grant and the government while validating the claims on both sides that he was corrupt and venal:

Chicago Tribune – September 7, 1873

Col. Mosby Alleged to Have Been an Office Broker

Special Dispatch to the Chicago Tribune

MOSBY AS AN OFFICE-BROKER

It will be recollected that over a year ago Mosby one day called at the White House, paid his respects to the President, and scattered assurances broadcast that he considered the war a thing of the past, and the day of the Democratic party much more so. Pleased with his observations of reconstruction, the President received him kindly, and, desiring to further conciliate the Southern element of which Mosby was a representative, he offered him an official position in Vienna. This Mosby declined on the ground that it might excite ungenerous sentiment. He was disinterested, and did not want an office. Soon afterward he recommended a friend for an office of some profit in the Eastern part of the State, and there appearing to be no objection, the commission was made out. This operation was repeated, and again, and again, and two months ago information reached the ears of the President that Mosby was engaged in office-brokerage, and was really making more money out of it than he would have made out of the position tendered him. A period was immediately put to his importunities.

How much money Mosby has made out of the brokerage business it is of course impossible to say, as his arrangements with his clients have been of a strictly confidential character, but it is said that for securing one appointment he received $100 cash and 10 per cent a month of the official's salary. Directly and indirectly, by means of Representatives in Congress, he has secured fifteen or twenty appointments. It is probable he has made it pay handsomely. Some of the appointments made upon his recommendation have already been revoked, and more will be if it can be ascertained that the appointees paid him money for his influence. If not, and they are good officials, there is no reason why they should be removed; but if all stories are true, there is proof presumptive in every case. The whole subject will be investigated.

Apparently, nothing further came of the matter or Mosby would certainly have found himself in the dock. But while the "brokerage" matter waned, the anger of the Republican press and the glee of the Democratic organs at Mosby's second "apostasy" continued apace:

Spirit of the Age – September 11, 1873

—Guerilla Mosby who has until quite recently been so thick with the Grantites has now it appears broke friendship with them. And this disaffection of Mosby from the Republican cause has drawn upon him the anathemas of the organs of the party with which he lately affiliated. The Radical papers in Washington city now characterize him as a marauding guerila, who did nothing in the war but rob chicken coops, capture sutlers' wagons and harass and rob straggling Union men and waylay unprotected trains of supplies. It does seem too bad for them to go back on their friends. Should they do so in earnest and tell of each other what they know, some important and startling revelations will undoubtedly be made.

The Grant party is really getting into a confused condition.

Atlanta Constitution – September 12, 1873

Mosby

A Rich Characterization of His Radical Episode

The ungrateful Bushwhacker

[From the Chicago Tribune]

When the Administration party came to reconstruct the South it found Mosby among the assets of the institution, and accepted him as a first class article, at first cost and without question. The Administration opened wide its paternal arms, and embraced the bushwhacker and saluted him on both cheeks. The fatted calf was killed, and the paternal mansion was brilliantly illuminated in honor of the return of the prodigal son. The ninety-and nine faithful ones who had not wandered away grumbled some, but it was of no avail. The bushwhacker had the best in the house, and unlimited permission to range at his own sweet will, without let or hindrances. Nothing could better suit a bushwhacker. Then the administration, having accepted its convert, vaunted itself upon him, and held him up as an example to the South, and made some plaintive appeals to the ex-Confederates to follow the example of this illustrious chieftain, and return to their allegiance to the stars and stripes. The new convert, like the Fiji woman, made a great show of zeal, and became a propagandist. He took to the stump, and preached the doctrines of the administration, and, upon one occasion, even advocated Caesarism. His devotion was so great, and led him to such extremes of zeal, that he was first to nominate Grant for a third term. At last, however, there came a time when the ruling passion returned.

Then Mosby began to bushwhack. Having unlimited permission to do as he pleased, he availed himself of it. He gathered all the offices he could find lying about the White House. He ravaged the Treasury and Interior and Revenue Departments, and loaded himself with patronage. He got appointed High Steward and Purveyor for Virginia, and Dictator for all the rest of the South. When he had got all the plunder he could carry, the ungrateful bushwhacker made off as fast as he could to his friends, the Virginia Conservatives, and now there is not only weeping and wailing, but cursing and gnashing of teeth, in the camp of the Administration, and "political guerrilla," and "ungrateful gorilla," [sic] and "unprincipled bushwhacker," now take the place of the endearing epithets which the party organs were wont to bestow upon Mosby.

We doubt whether there will be much sympathy wasted upon the administration. We doubt even whether the bushwhacker is to blame for his course. Having got inside the Republican camp and witnessed nothing but plunder and corruption going on all around him, we are not surprised that he should follow the prevailing fashion, take all he could carry and quit.

And so Mosby lost his "friends" in the Republican press while he had yet to win back any Democratic organs. Worse, his motives in supporting Kemper were seen—and reported—as a betrayal of Grant. As a result, the concern now became will he betray Kemper? The matter was made worse when Mosby, after Kemper's election, sought to initiate greater cooperation between Richmond and Washington. For a while, these well-intentioned, rational efforts seemed to be bearing fruit:

Anderson Intelligencer – **December 11, 1873**

Yorkville Enquirer – **December 11, 1873**

PRESIDENT GRANT AND THE EX-CONFEDERATES.—

TheWashington correspondent of the New York Herald relates the following:

Colonel John S. Mosby to-day called on the President, for the first time since the Virginia gubernatorial canvass. He was received most cordially by the President and several members of the Cabinet. He offered his services in case of a war with Spain, and the President promised him a command and said there was no immediate danger of war; but in case there should be, he had perfect confidence in the late Confederate soldiers, and intended to give the commissions equally to the soldiers of the Federal and Confederate armies. He spoke of Hon. Alexander H. Stephens most kindly, and was glad that he had been returned to Congress.

The President said that in his forthcoming Message he intended to recommend universal amnesty.

Colonel Mosby told the President that the Virginia election was not a condemnation of his (Grant's) administration, and that he was stronger than ever in that State. The President agreed with him, and was not at all dissatisfied with the result. He expressed himself gratified at the tone of General Kemper's speeches, and favored Mosby's policy of reconciliation between the administration and the white people of the South. The President said that as long as he was in office the holders of appointments made through Mosby's influence, should not be turned out, no matter who tried to oust them; that hereafter he intended to appoint to office from the South the best men for the positions, and that he was very much gratified at the good feeling manifested by Virginia conservatives towards his administration, and was ready to respond to it.

Weekly Clarion – December 11, 1873
RECONCILIATION

Report of an Interview between President Grant and Col. Mosby of Virginia.

Washington, November 29. Col. Mosby to-day called on the President for the first time since the Virginia canvass commenced, and was received most cordially both by Gen. Grant and the members of his Cabinet. Col. Mosby offered his services in case of a war with Spain. The President replied that there was no immediate danger of war; but in case there should be he had perfect confidence in the

CONFEDERATE SOLDIERS

And would distribute commissions equally among the officers of the Northern and Southern armies. He spoke most kindly of Stephens, and was glad that he was returned to Congress, and sad that in his message he intended to recommend

UNIVERSAL AMNESTY.

Col. Mosby told the President that the Virginia election was not a condemnation of his administration and that he was stronger than ever in the State.

The President agreed with him and was not at all dissatisfied with the result. He expressed himself gratified at the tone of Gov. Kemper's speeches and of reconciliation between the administration and the white people of the south.

FAVORED MOSBY'S POLICY

The President said that as long as he was President, the officers appointed through Mosby's recommendation should not be molested no matter who tried to roust them; that hereafter he intended to appoint to office from the South

THE BEST MEN

for the position, and that he was very much gratified at the good feeling manifested by the Virginia Conservatives towards his administration, and was ready to respond to it.

Mosby was most gratified to see Grant's response not only to the Confederate soldier, but also to the Virginia Conservatives and to his own involvement with the election of Governor Kemper. He had told Grant that he could not support the Radicals in Virginia, for to do so would end any value he had to the president and the national party in the South. He still believed earnestly that he could bring about at least a working relationship between the Democrats in Virginia and Grant's administration, one of the reasons he devoutly hoped for a third term for the president. But just when things seemed to be working toward that end, the lack of courage and character on the part of a Virginia politician brought all to naught and initiated the final annihilation of John Mosby's reputation in the South.

Chapter 13

1874

Occasio aegre offertur, facile amittitur. ~ Opportunity is offered with difficulty, lost with ease.

"No legacy is so rich as honesty." ~ **William Shakespeare**

1874 WAS A *VERY* LONG YEAR for John Mosby—and not just in the press. It was not only long, but decidedly painful, humiliating, and personally damaging. The matter had begun two years earlier when Mosby deserted his postwar association with the Virginia Conservatives to support Ulysses Grant in his second run for the presidency. However, he had also made it very clear at the time that he supported *Grant* and the *National* Republican Party and not the local Radicals. Grant won the election and, with Mosby's help, won Virginia as well, leading to Mosby's ability to use patronage to obtain positions for Virginians in the Federal government. Indeed, this had been his considered strategy: to show Southerners that Grant was willing to help them—if they allowed him to do so! But even the boon of Grant's patronage, while it helped many in Virginia, did not help John Mosby with his fellow Southerners.

When the gubernatorial election of 1873 rolled around, Mosby could not support the state Republican Party, and so he returned to the Conservatives and supported their candidate, General James Kemper. Those who had made assumptions based upon Mosby's support of Grant considered this a "betrayal." The Republicans—politicians and the press—howled like scalded cats while the Conservatives and the Democratic press were suspicious. They too believed that Mosby betrayed Grant after he had gotten the "patronage" he wanted—although he had personally gained nothing from it—and now wondered what he wanted from *Kemper*. Most of all, Conservatives feared Mosby might seduce Kemper into some sort of an "arrangement" with Grant, a not-altogether-incorrect assumption as Mosby did indeed work long and hard for some sort of "truce" between the *National Republicans* and the white Virginia Conservatives. By 1874, Mosby considered that he had gone far in achieving both aims as can be seen in this article:

Atlanta Constitution – February 14, 1874

Col. John S. Mosby to a reporter: "We are all for Grant in Virginia. Governor Kemper has come into my schemes. The platform of the Virginia Conservatives, the third resolution of which I had introduced, pledges us not to seek to prolong issues of the civil war. Governor Kemper and President Grant will probably confer with each other pretty soon. I have but one object and that is to have the white men of the South and the white men of the North co-operate for the general government of the country. You must clearly see that since the war no Southern white has been a ponderable quantity at the Federal seat of government. Until I broke through my prejudices and met the President, I led a small faction of Virginians in his favor as against Greeley. When the second election came off in our State, I had to say to the President: 'General, for me to expect to have any influence with the Virginia people and go for Hughes would be as fatal as if you had abandoned your army in the wilderness and tried to go to Richmond alone. The only availability I have is to keep in reasonable harmony with my people." Colonel Mosby adds that the Republican party of Virginia has almost disappeared since their last defeat, and with them the negro has lost all distinctiveness."

Obviously, Mosby thought that he could help the South by creating or helping to create cooperation between local Democrats and *National Republican*s. But Mosby was not alone. There were organs of the press that supported a more "statesmanlike" arrangement between Southern state and Federal leaders and decried what they called the "wild yell" from "men and [the] press of Bourbonistic tendencies," arising in response to a proposed meeting between Kemper and Grant:

Virginia State Journal **– January 24, 1874 (Edited)**

THAT VISIT

[From the Alexandria Sentinel]

If the jealous watchfulness of politicians and "political newspapers" were not humiliating, it would be amusing. But the earnestness with which they throw themselves into the breach to prevent any breaking through the solid walls of party prejudice by the leaders, is rather deplorable than ridiculous. A short time ago, Colonel John S. Mosby, during one of his visits of friendship to President Grant, discussed with him the message of Governor Kemper. Grant expressed himself as highly pleased with the manly and conciliatory tone of the message, and remarked that he would like to see General Kemper, and have a talk with him on the condition of affairs. Col. Mosby, with that watchfulness of circumstances tending to harmonize the best elements of our two sections which has marked him, and for which we most highly commend him, proffered to take an invitation for a visit, which offer the President as cordially accepted, and the message was sent and received by Governor Kemper with the candor which might have been expected.

"At once there rose so wild a yell" from men and press of Bourbonistic tendencies, as if all the degraded traits that ever illustrated the character of devils were about to be exemplified in the person of our Governor… One paper has anxiously inquired if Gov. Kemper was going to betray us. Others wish to know if he is going to humble himself by calling on Grant for instructions on how to conduct himself… We are utterly disgusted with such frivolous stuff. The man who insinuates a belief in Kemper's contemplated degradation or treason to his people we should at once set down to be shaky himself, unless we knew him to be non compos. And the men who are seeking to prevent an interchange of simple civilities between the executive of the General Government and this state, which may result in such cordial relations as will gratify and benefit our whole people, are but little better than traitors, unless they do it from obliquity of mental discernment.

We have used strong language because the occasion demands it. We are happy to know that Governor Kemper is a man not to be shaken by the clamor of the dying.

According to the paper, Mosby's great virtue of "watchfulness," which served him so well during the war, continued to exist but was now bent toward "harmonizing the best elements of [our] two sections."

Daily State Journal – January 28, 1874

Some of the Virginia journals are still discussing the question whether Governor Kemper ought to visit President Grant or not. Some contend that as the President has courteously extended the governor an invitation to do so, he ought to accept, since the visit would be merely a friendly one and devoid of political significance. Others affect to be greatly alarmed lest the governor should accept, and insist that the President has a political motive for desiring to see him. They go further, and hint that the governor cannot visit the President without sacrificing his self-respect as a Virginian and a Conservative. This seems great nonsense, and the smallest kind of puerility. It is understood that in a conversation with Colonel Mosby relative to Governor Kemper the President incidentally remarked that he would be glad to make the governor's acquaintance. Colonel Mosby thereupon offered to convey an invitation to Governor Kemper, and did so, and the governor has the invitation under consideration. It is difficult to see the impropriety of the governor of any state paying a friendly visit to the Chief Executive of the nation, and we do not believe Governor Kemper will be influenced by narrow-minded partisans in this matter.

There was another lurking problem involved, however. After Grant's reelection, there was talk of a possible third term for the president, who was still popular despite the undoubted corruption in his administration. Meanwhile, Mosby had risen to political prominence by helping both Grant and Kemper. In two years, he had contributed substantially to the political landscape in Virginia. He had also influenced the Conservative platform to include certain statesman-like overtures to the Federal administration. Obviously, these results made it appear that Mosby's efforts at establishing a functioning relationship between the Conservatives in Richmond and the Grant administration in Washington were working. Indeed, soon after Governor Kemper took office, Mosby had visited Grant—the two men enjoyed each other's company—and as an afterthought, the president mentioned that he would like to meet with Kemper "socially." Mosby was charmed by the thought of these two powerful men, for whom he had successfully labored, getting together if not in friendship, then at least with toleration and civility, and he carried Grant's unwritten invitation to Kemper. An unnamed publication carried a report of the meeting, being carefully neutral in its tone:

Publication unknown – February?, 1874 (Edited)

GOVERNOR KEMPER AND PRESIDENT GRANT.

Governor Kemper, of Virginia, being in Washington on business, made a call of courtesy upon President Grant, on the 12th inst., remaining at the Executive Mansion not more than fifteen or twenty minutes. It was some time ago stated that Colonel Mosby had pre-arranged an interview between these two gentlemen, but the Governor says there is no truth in the report, and that he called merely to pay his respects to the Chief Magistrate, the same as any other citizen of the United States, and with no political objective in view... As the interview was private, the subject of conversation cannot be explicitly stated, but can only be inferred by the Governor's own free utterances tonight, that he and his political friends in Virginia stand on a broad conservative platform, which, he says, gives all the States co-equal rights as members of the Union, that they may discharge their duties, to restore perfect peace and reconciliation to all parts of the country.

Some historians declare that Kemper never met with Grant, that he got "cold feet" and pulled out at the last minute, leaving Mosby embarrassed. But Kemper did have a short informal meeting with the President, in which ordinary pleasantries were exchanged, but nothing of any moment discussed. However, in referring to the matter, the *New York Tribune* acknowledged Mosby's influence with the president and, indirectly, with Kemper:

New York Tribune – February 9, 1874

In an interview with a representative of a Washington Sunday paper Col. John S. Mosby has given his views of the political situation in Virginia, the gist of which seems to be that in his opinion the last election put an end to the Republican party in that State, and that the Conservatives are favorably disposed toward President Grant. Col. Mosby desires a union of white men, North and South, in behalf of what was lately called a "white man's government," and he apparently thinks that in such a union, President Grant could be counted on. These opinions derive their only significance from the fact that Mosby is frequent and welcome visitor at the White House, and even seems to enjoy in a large degree the President's confidence.

Mosby believed that the safety of the South depended upon the return of a "white man's government" because of what that section had suffered during Reconstruction at the hands of Radical Republicans who used the newly freed slaves to loot, pillage, and destroy states that had already suffered terribly in the war. No white Southerner ever wanted power to fall into the hands of blacks with or without carpetbagger and scalawag influence. Most in the North claimed that this was an effort to restore slavery, but they did not have enough blacks in their own states to be concerned with their ascension to political power. On the other hand, the South could speak with bitter experience in the matter.

This was the situation extant when Mosby determined that he could now do some good for Virginia as a representative in Congress and though he was no politician, John Mosby decided to throw his hat into the ring:

New York Tribune – February 21, 1874

COL. MOSBY A CANDIDATE FOR CONGRESS.

Certainly, Mosby had great influence with Grant. Unfortunately, however, John Mosby apparently either did not see or did not understand that a growing cloud was gathering not about him—or at least just him—but about his hero, Ulysses S. Grant. This cloud was brought to the fore in an article that appeared in the Nashville Union & American:

Nashville Union & American – March 8, 1874 (Edited)

DISSENSION IN THE CAMP.

A Republican Senator's Opinion of Grant—the War for the Succession. The Washington correspondent of the New York Sun writes as follows: I was somewhat surprised a few evenings ago, while talking to a Republican Senator on the political prospect of 1876, to hear him declare that Grant was "a political abortion." My friend was not the only Republican member of Congress I have of late heard express sentiments very similar to this.

"You would not dare to make that declaration in public," said I, hoping still further to draw him out. "You are too much fettered by the chains of party."

"Party or no party," he resumed, "the fact is too transparent, and the sooner we acknowledge it the better. He is the worst political abortion the country has ever had in the Executive Mansion."

"To what do you attribute this signal failure?" I inquired. I was indeed anxious to know what had produced this change of opinion in a Senator who had heretofore earnestly supported all that Grant did.

"He seems to have no respect for public sentiment," was the answer. "The fact is his West Point training, and habits acquired in the army, have totally unfitted him for the proper administration of civil government. ...

Grant has two dangerous weaknesses. One is an intense love of money; they other I will not mention. These have led him to make associates of and be influenced in his public acts by men no President should take into his confidence. It is only too true that Mosby, the guerrilla, would have more influence over him to-day than I could expect to obtain."

I interrupted him here by asking: "What,, can Grant expect to gain by this strange friendship for Mosby? He certainly cannot expect much political strength from such men as Mosby and Butler in laying pipe for a third term?"

"Not at all," he quickly resumed. "The question of a third term I regard as definitely settled. It never had any consideration except among a few prominent officer holders. Grant understands that perfectly Many of the leaders of the Republican party have mistaken Gen. Grant's real character. There exists under that quiet exterior an intense ambition, love of power, and spirit of intrigue. He has also that fondness of display common to all parvenus [upstarts-vph]. This of itself has seriously injured him among thinking people. Public sentiment is undergoing a revolution at this time such as it has not undergone for many years."

"To what do you attribute that, Senator?" I inquired, interrupting him. "To the simple fact that the people understand Grant and his administration better to-day than they have ever understood him before. There is no disguising that," he replied, with emphasis.

This very Republican Senator, during the last campaign, supported Grant with all his strength and ability, because, to use his own words, he "was afraid of Greeley." Two years ago this very same Republican Senator insisted that Grant was stronger than his party—scouted the prediction that Grant would yet be found the heaviest load the Republican party had to carry. He also scouted the prediction, made to him by the writer, that the time was not far off when the Republican party would have to defend itself against the idol it had set up...

"Do I understand you to admit, Senator, that Grant's administration has been a failure?" I inquired.

"I regard it as a misfortune to the Republican party—decidedly. The very worst feature of it is that he has allowed himself to get involved in these venal rings, and to be used by corrupt men, who have no respect for the principle of any party, but attach themselves to the strongest for mercenary purposes. Instead of adding dignity to the executive office, and preserving it above reproach, he has dragged it down into the dirty pool of real estate speculation."

"Was not that the natural result of what you call his intense love for money?" I interrupted.

"I suppose it may be attributed to that," was the quiet reply. "That infirmity is what has given the independent press of the country such power over his administration. Grant's friends say he does not love politicians; and yet no one that knows him intimately will deny that he loves to dabble in politics. Why sir, here he is, not content to retire quietly and peacefully from the field at the end of his second term, attempting to dictate who his successor shall be."

"What object can he have for that, pray?"

"Well, he fancies there may be irregularities in his administration which a captious and unfriendly successor might be inclined to inquire too closely into, especially if backed up by an unfriendly Congress. I do not myself think he has anything to fear from that."

"Has he expressed any choice as to who shall succeed him?"

The Senator smiled and continued: "It is very well known that conferences on the subject have been held between him and a number of prominent office-holders. His candidates are Washburne and Roscoe Conkling. But, thinking Washburne hardly available, Conkling is his great card, and he intends to play it like a skillful general putting his forces properly in the field. The combinations now being made to this end are very well understood here. Conkling has bowed before his idol with such reckless adulation, and has flattered his vanity to such an extent, that Grant feels he can only pay the debt by working for his nomination. This is what has stimulated the Blaine men to action recently. They understand the President's movements, and are already concocting measures to defeat them. The old feud between Blaine and Conkling has never been healed, and never will be. Conkling never will forgive Blaine, and Blaine never will forgive Conkling. And now the Blaine men are already sounding the alarm, measuring the field, and marshaling their forces. They contend, and I think correctly, that if either Conkling or Washburne is put on the track as Grant's choice, there will be another split in the Republican party, which will be fatal to it.

In this exceptionally pithy article, Mosby was mentioned only in passing and, sadly, as an example of Grant's moral failures. But the fact was that Grant—who had once been, as the senator said, "bigger than his party"—had now become an embarrassment to that party and a great assistance to the Democrats. But whatever the issue had become by that time, John Mosby's belief in Grant as the man to finish the healing process between the sections had been dashed. Yet Mosby did not admit to the change of circumstance. Perhaps he did not recognize it, or perhaps he had put so much of his human capital into that future that he could not—not then, not in 1876 and not even when he was in China—accept that Grant's race had been run.

More mention was made of Mosby's run for Congress, but there seemed no enthusiasm for it, even among those papers that had supported his efforts for a relationship between Grant and Kemper:

Alexandria Gazette – March 13, 1874

We have been requested by a contemporary to copy an article recommending Col. John S. Mosby as a candidate for Congress from this district. While we claim to occupy an independent position, we do not care to meddle much with politics, more especially thus early in the autumn canvass. About the surest thing Col. Mosby's friends could do for his defeat would be to bring him prominently forward prematurely. Besides, we fear colonels, both military and civic, are so common Grant will have to promote the colonel to the rank of general before he can take command of this division.

Thus, when the Kemper-Grant matter became public, there was state and even section-wide pandemonium. Kemper and Mosby had exchanged some letters; and with the press on both sides frothing at the mouth, all was dragged out for public scrutiny, most of which was based upon political prejudice and ignorance, exacerbated by a fear on both sides of any involvement by Kemper in machinations regarding a third term for Grant. Finding himself in political jeopardy, Kemper then got "cold feet" and proceeded to spend weeks explaining away what should have been seen as a statesman-like attempt to normalize relations between his state and the President of the United States. At that point, the Democratic press threw Kemper a bone by which to save himself—the very unpopular John Mosby! Kemper was happy enough to redirect the public rage. As a result, Mosby found himself insulted, debased, and derided for the crime of acting in a more statesman-like manner than the man whom he had helped obtain the governorship.

But the most powerful issue that arose in the following letters was related to the growing concern about Grant's possible run for a third term. Perhaps Kemper's meeting with the president would not have resonated so badly if there had been no question of a third term, but by this time the matter was very well-known and being widely discussed—and not in a positive way by either side. Mosby was very much in favor of a third term for the president and never wavered from his view on the matter; neither did he mind making his opinion public. However, by 1874, few in the North—and none in the South—were in favor of a third term for Ulysses Grant; and the articles and letters made an especial point of that issue and Kemper's possible involvement in helping to bring it about:

Bristol News – June 23, 1874

The Kemper Letters.

In at least Virginia, the letters of Gov. Kemper seem destined to provoke as much discussion as the letters of Junius. The rumor that Kemper had recently written to Mr. Scott of Fauquier, a long letter disapproving of Mosby's course, seems to have offended Mosby, who has now sought, through the Washington Chronicle, to make certain exposures, which, it is alleged will forever destroy Kemper in Virginia. We will leave the Chronicle to tell the story, and will then await further light.—Here is the article:

"Col. Mosby's friends charge that he has indisputable evidence of the cooperation of Gov. Kemper in his scheme to bring the Virginia Conservatives over to the support of Grant's administration and that Kemper had pledged himself for Grant, not only for the third, but the seventh term, and had promised that fifty thousand Confederate braves would follow him (Kemper) to Grant's support; that Mosby, in good faith, and with written evidence to support it, looked upon Kemper as an effective coadjutor in behalf of Grant's administration; that Gov. Kemper submitted his first message to Colonel Mosby, and two days thereafter, in January last, got Colonel Mosby to visit Washington to ask him (Kemper) to pay him (Grant) a visit for the purpose of effecting a political alliance; and further, that Gov. Kemper sent a prominent citizen of Fauquier county to Grant last December on a special embassy to let Grant know that he was about to wheel into line, and inform him as to the contents of his message."

Knoxville Weekly Chronicle – **June 24, 1874 (Edited)**

A VIRGINIA SENSATION.

The "third term" discussion will take a new form after the startling disclosures made by one George C. Wedderburn, who is we believe the Washington correspondent of the Richmond Enquirer. He is a friend of Col. Mosby, who is a candidate for Congress in Virginia. Gov. Kemper has written a letter to a friend, stating that he is not favorable to Mosby's Congressional aspirations. Thereupon, Wedderburn, who is a friend of Mosby, discloses this awful plot which will give the New York Herald a new excuse for crying "Caesarism." Henry Watterson and Bob Toombs and all the other sensationalists of the South will go mad over the very prospect. Wedderburn in a letter to the Washington Chronicle says: [The rest of the article is the same as in the *Bristol News* above.-vph]

Daily National Republican – **June 26, 1874 (Edited)**

A PROPHECY FULFILLED.

When the "Gentlemen Party" in Virginia nominated James L. Kemper, whom they subsequently elected to be Governor of the State, a resolution was embodied in their platform announcing in specious terms that the high-toned sham-Conservatives had no hostility to President Grant, but, on the contrary, rather admired his administration. We announced at the time our opinion that it was a deceptive bait throw out to catch such Grant-Democrats as Colonel Mosby, and denounced it as a piece of political treachery. We prophesied that in the event of Conservative success the spirit of the resolution would be violated and its implied pledges ignored. We did this because we honestly believed the leaders of the party to be capable of any degradation in the way of political falsehood and villainy. How far our predictions have been realized may be learned from the fact that Colonel Mosby has already been placed under the ban of the Conservative Central Committee, and that his aspirations to become a candidate for Congress, regardless of party nominations, have been visited even with the disapprobation of Governor Kemper himself. Now, Mosby has not changed one jot or tittle since his false friends tickled him with their meaningless praise of the President. He is as much of a "Grant man," whatever that may be, as ever; but the necessity for his influence in the coming election is not as apparent as it was in the last State campaign. He has, consequently, been thrown aside, left to shift for himself, and suffers under the stigma of having failed "to bring the Conservative party to Grant."

It is said that he has in his possession, or under his control, certain letters or correspondence with Gov. Kemper, in which the latter pledges himself to sustain Grant, by "fifty thousand Confederate soldiers." Rumors regarding this fact have been in circulation for some time, and having reached the public through the columns of the Virginia press, the Richmond Whig feels called upon to denounce the statement as false. As the Whig is the "organ" of Gov. Kemper, it is fair to presume that its assertion was inspired by him. But the Whig adds in behalf of the Governor "that he has no aspiration to be associated with President Grant upon a Presidential ticket; that he is thoroughly in accord with the Conservative party that elected him, and that if at home he would take the stump against Colonel Mosby or any independent candidate that might oppose the regular nominee of the Conservative party," &c.

New York Daily Tribune – July 1, 1874 (Edited)

GENERAL POLITICAL NEWS

GRANT AND KEMPER.

Gov. Kemper Makes a Statement Regarding His Call on the President and the Charges that He Favors a Third Term—He Declares His Opposition to The Third Term Principle—Conditions under Which Gen. Grant Will Merit the Support of the Conservative Party.

Richmond, June 30.—For several months past, it has been insinuated by some of the Virginia papers, and freely charged by many persons, that Gov. Kemper, who was elected last Autumn by the Conservatives, had entered into an arrangement, implied or definite, with Gen. Grant, through his friend, Col. Mosby, the ex-Confederate guerilla, by which the Governor was to support Gen. Grant for a third term and carry with him a considerable body of the Conservative party in Virginia and such others in the South as might be influenced by their example. The charges were deemed so important that numerous calls have been made upon Gov. Kemper to explain his position. He will do so tomorrow in a long letter, to be published in the Richmond papers, and which will doubtless cause new complications in Southern politics. As to the third term, Gov. Kemper declares his opposition to it on general principles, but uses the following language:

I do not believe the country can remain in its present abnormal condition. We are going to have either popular self-government or central imperialism. I intend to stand for the liberty side as long as a fragment of it remains. I am opposed to a third term for the reason that notwithstanding the past, I have faith in the cause of constitutional free government; but I oppose some other evils still more. One of the cruelest calamities which could befall all classes and colors at the South, would be the social intermixing of the races, to result from the enforcement of the Civil Rights fanaticism and barbarism, and it is hard to conceive what greater evil than that could be involved in any possible revolution of the Government.

The Governor recites the circumstances of his call upon President Grant in Washington shortly after Gov. Kemper's inauguration, which occasioned much comment at the time. This visit, he says was one of courtesy, made in response to a courteous invitation from the President that the Governor should call and make his acquaintance, and in making the call he claims that he was only carrying out the Virginia Conservative platform, which pledge the party to judge every act of Gen. Grant's on its own merits. He remarks: I went, because under my convictions of duty and propriety, I made up my mind to go, and under circumstances to justify it again, I should go again. I went and had a manly, square talk with the President, and while I shall not so violate propriety as to allude to its particulars, yet I regret that every word of it could not have been taken down and published, for, although I say it, its publication would have done credit to him and to me, and no discredit and no harm to any part of the country or the people. As to the Federal Executive head, I shall render him, not factious hostility, but a fair and unpredjudiced judgment. For the sake of ourselves and the whole country, I shall rejoice if he so emulates the example of Washington; if he so aids in restoring the landmarks of the Constitution, lately overthrown by the violence of arms; if he so respects the right of the States and the people to self-Government, as to command our united and hearty support of the whole of his future administration. So far as his influence has saved us from the degradation of test-oaths and the Civil Rights law; so far has he abstained from exercising the centralizing and dangerous powers of the Enforcement act, he is entitled to our gratitude and support. But I emphatically do not indorse a great part of his policy in respect to a National currency, and if he adopts, as a rule of his administration, such intermeddling in local affairs as that just resorted to at Petersburg by the Attorney-General of the United States, then he will establish between us and himself a gulf as impassable as that which separates good from evil in [the] other life.

In conclusion, Gov. Kemper transmits copies of his letters to Col. Mosby, written during the Gubernatorial campaign last Autumn. The only noticeable passage in these is the following:

It were better to elect Grant the third and the seventh term than go under Hughes and his negroes. To us the defeat of negro rule here is to save society and decent existence, to save us from barbarism and ruin.

And so the vicious press coverage continued. Indeed, both "wings"—Democrat and Republican—made the matter sound as if it were a cabal and conspiracy worthy of the Gunpowder Plot coupled with Arnold's efforts to deliver Washington to the British. Governor Kemper, of course, wanted to be "cleared" of the distasteful label of traitor or, worse, of being John Mosby's dupe, while the Republican press was now beginning to desert Grant both in the matter of a possible third term and in any effort to "get cozy" with Virginia Democrats! But whether the paper was for or against Grant or Kemper, they were all against Mosby. Things were getting ugly as Kemper had yet to make his public mea culpas:

Weekly Statesman – July 2, 1874 (Edited)

GOV. KEMPER, COL. MOSBY AND PRESIDENT GRANT.

The Richmond Enquirer calls upon Gov. Kemper to state how far the report is true that he, through Col. Mosby, had sought an alliance with Grant, and would support him for not the third but the seventh term?

That paper says "there had long been mutterings of this threatened storm in our political horizon, and no one should have been caught unprepared." And further that "the Conservatives of Virginia who elected Gov. Kemper, thought it due to them that he should in some clear and emphatic manner vindicate himself and them from the suspicion that had been cast upon his political integrity by these rumors, and we have shared the surprise that his unaccountable silence has caused."

These charges are certainly very grave, and in no small degree compromise the political integrity of Governor Kemper.

It would be a very great political heresy for any man as the South to advocate Grant for another term, in view of the history of that individual. But for a man of Governor Kemper's known ability and prominence to do so would show such political corruption as would be most damaging to the fair name and honor of the Southern people. It will be remembered that Governor Kemper commenced his administration under the most flattering circumstances, such as were calculated to give renewed confidence in the soundness and incorruptibleness of Southern politicians. He refused a fine carriage and horses which were presented to him after his election. This was in such marked contrast to the character and antecedents of Grant as to cause the remark to be made that he was not one of the "gift takers." But the character and standing of Governor Kemper apart from any acts of his since he took the gubernatorial chair were so clear and good as to preclude the idea of his ever betraying the high trust reposed in him. When then it is announced that he is soliciting a political alliance with Grant through Mosby who is known to be a warm friend of his, and for such ignoble purpose, a feeling of scorn and indignation is created in the breast of every honest heart. It is so base, so lost to every sense of duty and principle as to cause us to look with loathing upon the man who could so far forget the constituents who had elevated him to place… In order that our readers may fully understand the case, we append the article from the Sentinel, which is based upon the letter of Mr. Wedderburn, published in the Chronicle, which is as follows:

GOVERNOR KEMPER ARRAIGNED.

George C. Wedderburn publishes a letter in this morning's Washington Chronicle, in which he states the report that Governor Kemper did certainly induce Col. Mosby to believe he agreed with him in his policy, and challenges its denial by Kemper's friends Mr. Wedderburn's letter contains in one paragraph an epitome of the case which Colonel Mosby will be able to prove, viz.: The co-operation of Governor Kemper in his scheme to bring the Virginia Conservatives over to the support of Grant's administration, and that Kemper signified his willingness to go for Grant, not only for the third but the seventh term, and had promised that fifty thousand Confederate braves would follow him to Grant's support; that Mosby, in good faith, and with written evidence to support it, looks upon Kemper as an effective coadjutor in behalf of Grant's administration; that Governor Kemper, in January last, got Colonel Mosby to visit Washington to ask Grant to invite him (Kemper) to pay him (Grant) a visit for the purpose of effecting a political alliance; and further, that Governor Kemper sent a prominent citizen of Fauquier county to Grant last December, on the special embassy to let Grant know that he was about to wheel into line, and inform him as to the contents of his message.

Again, we dare Governor Kemper's friends to publish his letter to Major Scott.

National Republican – July 3, 1874 (Edited)
KEMPER'S LETTER.

Mr. Kemper, the Governor of Virginia, has certainly written a most remarkable and mysterious letter in regard to his present position politically, and to his position a year ago. As an explanation it is vague, unsatisfactory and inconclusive. It bears upon the face of it the stamp in insincerity, and leaves the impression of deception and double-dealing. …Now, is it true, or it is not, that the President invited him? Who made the first overture? "A desire spontaneously expressed" by whom? When? And where? upon the same subject and after the spontaneous expression Mr. Kemper goes on to say that he consulted with some of his friends, and after that "I went because, under my convictions of duty and propriety, I made up my mind to go. Under circumstances to justify it, I shall go again." A reference to the files of the newspapers of this city and Richmond [several illegible words follow] for Mr. Kemper, will show that he then declared that his visit to the President was merely accidental; the he was in Washington and merely called as a matter of courtesy. Mr. Kemper's letter in June is in direct conflict upon this point with his inspired statement in December. Which are we to believe? If he told the truth in December, what are we to think of his utterances upon the last day of the last month, printed in our column yesterday?

In that portion of the letter in which he attempts to explain his action toward the President and the Administration he has placed himself in a truly pitiable position. In his second letter to Col. Mosby he writes: "It were better to elect Grant the third and the seventh term than go under Hughes and his negroes;" and further on, "Surely Gen. Grant and all Northern gentlemen know that our white men, including over fifty thousand ex-Confederate braves in Virginia are the real moral, intellectual, and political power of the State, if not of the whole South, are implicitly to be relied upon, and are invaluable as friends." What did Kemper mean when he wrote that letter? The two conventions had been held. Judge Hughes had been nominated at Lynchburg and Gen. Kemper himself had been nominated at Richmond. The issue was fairly made up between the two parties. What did the offer of fifty thousand braves mean except that Gen. Grant might count upon him and upon them for a third term, if he would only consent to throw his influence for Kemper against Hughes. General Kemper now denies that he entertained sentiments of this character at that time; and he endeavors to wriggle out of it in a couple of newspaper columns. He has printed his letters to Colonel Mosby. Where are Mosby's letters to him? It is impossible to understand correctly the one without the other. In December, 1873, he writes to Mosby: "I bear in mind all that you say, and am alive to it." What did Mosby say to which Kemper was so much "alive?" The whole thing as it now stands is, as we said, unsatisfactory. It settles nothing, and in the opinion of all impartial men will place Kemper in a worse position than before By all means let us have the Mosby letters.

The *Bristol News* – July 7, 1874

THE KEMPER-MOSBY LETTERS

Views of the Governor on the Third Term.

He Opposes it and Declares that it would violate the unwritten Laws which in a Free Country Constitute some of the Bulwarks of Liberty.

The Matter fully Investigated—

Civil Rights, and What Gov. Kemper says on that subject.

His Opinion of the President's Message

We publish this morning the letters written by Governor Kemper to Col. Mosby, which have been under discussion in the public print for some time past, together with an explanation from the Governor setting forth his views in detail and at considerable length. The letter is written in the bold and manly style for which Gov. Kemper is noted, and will be read with great interest:—Rich. Dis.

To the Editors of the Dispatch:

No little discussion having appeared in the newspapers over the supposed contents of certain private letters written by myself, I have gone to much trouble to procure the originals, and now place them at your disposal. [A very long article precedes Kemper's request to Mosby for his letters.-vph]

* * * * * * *

Richmond, Va.,- June 28, 1874.

Col. John S. Mosby: Dear Sir—I respectfully request that you deliver to my friend Mr. N. B. Meade, the bearer of this, all letters heretofore addressed by me to yourself, retaining copies if you choose Or, if you prefer to keep the originals, I request that at least Mr. Meade be allowed to take copies of them.

Very truly yours, J. L. KEMPER

* * * * * * *

Office of John S. Mosby, Attorney at Law

Warrenton, Va., June 29, 1874

Gov. James L. Kemper: Dear Sir—Your letter has just been received requesting me to furnish you with copies of all letters addressed by you to myself. I enclose the only two in my possession.

Very respectfully, JOHN S. MOSBY [Below are the contents of the Letters Requested.]

Madison, Va., August, 1873

Dear Colonel: — The Index is doing more and better than the combined city press. If they don't haul off from Federal politics they will deeply hurt us. I am trying hard to get them on the right track.

It were better to elect Grant the third and the seventh term than go under Hughes and his negroes. To us the defeat of negro rule here is to save society and decent existence, to save us from barbarism and ruin.— Surely General Grant and all northern gentlemen know that our white men, including over 50,000 ex-Confederate braves in Virginia, are the real moral, intellectual and political power of the State, if not the whole South, are implicitly to be relied upon, and are invaluable as friends. It cannot be that he will spurn a proffer of reconciliation from such men for the sake of Hughes and his hordes.

Don't tire in your labors.

Truly yours, J. L. KEMPER.

* * * * * * *

Madison, Va., Dec. 9, 1873

Dear Colonel: — Yours received. I bear in mind all you say, and am alive to it. Although I was somewhat disappointed in General Grant's message and regret very much the civil-rights paragraph, especially in view of the Supreme Court decision in the "Butcher's case," yet I am going to fight it out on the present line, at least as long as [illegible] one summer.

Very truly yours, J. L. KEMPER

The press coverage went on chewing up and spitting out the same charges and "facts" regarding a situation that should have been nothing more than a matter of passing interest among rational people. But it had become some sort of horrible treasonous attempt to violate the godly and pure Conservative party created and directed by that political "Faust" of Virginia, the man who had sold his soul to Ulysses Grant—John S. Mosby. Suddenly, a newspaper ostensibly came to Mosby's defense, presenting the comments of his "friends," and leaving him in a worse place than he was before:

Fairfield Herald – **July 8, 1874**

Virginia.

KEMPER CHARGED WITH GOING BACK ON HIS PROMISE—HE ABANDONS COLONEL MOSBY, AFTER PROMISING TO SUPPORT HIM FOR CONGRESS.

Washington, D.C. June 17, 1874.

To the Editor of the Washington Chronicle:

Virginia is just now excited over rumors involving one of the gravest political scandals of her history.

It will be remembered that a few months since, Gov. Kemper visited President Grant, and had an interview with him; that the intention to do so had before that time been made public through the press, and that it was then broadly intimated that the visit was the inception of a political alliance between President Grant and Gov. Kemper; it was also understood that Col. Mosby was instrumental in bringing the President and Gov. Kemper together, and statements were made through the press to that effect, all of which the friends of Gov. Kemper have constantly denied, and declare that he has always been hostile to Grant's administration.

Colonel Mosby was one of the most active and energetic of Mr. Kemper's friends, and his opposition to Judge Hughes, the candidate of the Radical party, he (Mosby) being a cordial supporter of President Grant, concentrated the entire support of his friends, political followers, and a large number of white Radical vote in favor of Kemper.

Colonel Mosby is now an Administration for Congress in the 8th Congressional district of Virginia. It is charged that General Kemper has written a letter to Mosby's district condemning the independent candidacy of Mosby, and expressing his disapproval of Mosby's erratic political course.

Colonel Mosby's friends charge that he has indisputable evidence of the co-operation of Governor Kemper in his scheme to bring the Virginia Conservatives over to the support of Grant's administration, and that Kemper had pledged himself for Grant's administration, and for Grant, not only for the third, but the seventh term, and had promised that fifty thousand Confederate braves would follow him (Kemper) to Grant's support; that Mosby in good faith, and with written evidence to support it, looked upon Kemper as an effective coadjutor in behalf of Grant's administration; that Governor Kemper submitted his first message to Col. Mosby, and two days thereafter, in January last, got Colonel Mosby to visit Washington to ask Grant to invite him (Kemper) to pay him (Grant) a visit for the purpose of effecting a political alliance; and further, that Governor Kemper sent a prominent citizen of Fauquier county to Grant last December on a special embassy to let Grant know that he was about to wheel into line, and inform him as to the contents of his message.

I have confidence in Col. Mosby's integrity of character, and believe that he was attempting to relieve the people of the South, for whom he fought so gallantly, from the oppressions that followed the war by attempting to place them on friendly relations with the Administration; but I also believe that he was wrong and mistaken. I cannot doubt, from the high authority from which the foregoing information in regard to the controversy reaches me that Gov. Kemper induced Mosby to believe that he would cooperate with him in his political scheme to bring the Virginia Conservatives to the support of Grant. I am authorized by my informant to challenge denial of the above; the charge, in substance, being that Gov. Kemper was thoroughly in accord with Colonel Mosby's political policy, and that the only difference between them was that Col. Mosby openly declared his adherence to Grant.

GEORGE C. WIDDERBURN

Ah, but now, the Democratic press determined that the governor had "vindicated" himself(!) by denouncing Mosby and he could now return to the coveted ranks of political statesmanship:

The Enquirer Southerner – July 10, 1874

> The Virginia papers agree that Governor Kemper has fully vindicated himself from the charges recently brought against him of co-operating with Mosby in selling out the Conservative Party of Virginia.

So it was seen that any effort by Kemper to establish a relationship with the administration, however benign, was "selling out the Conservative Party of Virginia." And of course, the charge brought against him of "co-operating with Mosby" was directly connected to that "selling out." Where did this leave John Mosby? Castigated by the Republicans for his refusal to support the Radicals in 1873 and castigated by the Conservatives for his support of Grant in 1872 and his efforts to foster a relationship between Kemper and Grant in 1874, John Mosby found himself a despised outcast on all sides. Further, the patronage issue itself had become problematic as the Republican press had made it clear that Grant was permitting far too many former Confederates and "non-Republicans" to gain positions because of, yes, John Mosby.

Mosby's situation was defined in this nasty little article in the Spirit of Jefferson. And now even those who once delighted in his military triumphs began to use those triumphs against him—inaccurately as Mosby had never made any such "vow", but what did accuracy or truth matter, after all?

Spirit of Jefferson – July 14, 1874

> Mr. Thomas N. Ashby, a cousin of the noted cavalry captain, showed me a black oak tree in his beautiful grounds, twenty inches across the stump, through which a shell, fired from a Federal battery two miles distant, had passed. The wound is healing up and the tree promises to stand as a witness for many years to come. He also pointed out to me a tree near where the battery was located, upon which Custer's cavalry hung three of Mosby's men, placing placards upon their backs forbidding any one to cut the bodies down.—While on the road from Berryville to Winchester I was shown a hickory upon which Mosby hung three Yankees in retaliation.— He also hung three more at another place, to make good his vow that he would hang two to Custer's one of his men.
>
> He ought to send a cane off of one of these trees to his friend Grant, with a gold head, bearing a suitable inscription. He need not fear that it would be refused if he put gold enough on the head.

The New York Sun then opined in a reprint from the Savannah News in which it was supposed that Mosby had brought up the bugbear of a third term in order to destroy the Republican Party and overthrow his "friend" Grant. Now he was not only a traitor to Virginia and the South, but a Judas to the man who had "raised his shield" over him, Ulysses Grant:

The Sun (NY) – July 21, 1874

> Has the Guerilla Mosby Flanked Gen. Grant?
>
> From the Savannah News

It would perhaps be going too far to say that the third term movement at the South was a deep-laid conspiracy against Gen. Grant and the unity of the radical party. Nevertheless it is a significant fact that while the leading radical organs to which we have alluded received the first whisperings in the North of a "third term" with complacent approval, intimating that such a departure from time honored usage would under certain circumstances be justifiable as a political necessity, they have, since the development of a "third term" movement at the South without an exception pronounced against the startling innovation.

While it was considered a purely Radical expedient, for the preservation of the "legitimate results of the war"—chief among them the political subjugation and social degradation of the South—there was nothing so alarming in a third term for Gen. Grant. But since the disclosure of the Mosby Kemper plot, justified as a means of relieving the South from the most obnoxious of the so-called "legitimate results of the war"—political oppression and social degradation—the idea of a third term has loomed up as an evil of the most alarming proportions, and Gen. Grant has in the same degree fallen into disfavor.

There is seeming method in all of this. And we repeat that though Mosby and his coadjutators may not have planned their third term scheme as a flank movement against Gen. Grant and the "Simon pure" Radical party, yet the results may justify them in claiming credit for accomplishing the disintegration of the party and the overthrow of its idol.

So John Mosby was charged with working to destroy both his friend Grant and the Republican Party and God knows how many believed that. Mosby had no Republican friends, except for Ulysses Grant. Of course, the Kemper-Grant issue was labeled "Grantism" which was enough to get it condemned out of hand:

Nashville Union and American – July 23, 1874 (Edited)
KEMPER'S TRADE WITH GRANT.

The New York Sun publishes some interesting points connected with the political situation in Virginia. It calls attention to the fact that, while Gov. Kemper's alleged conversion to Grantism is strenuously denied by his friends, they admit that negotiations have been carried on between the President and the Governor, in the course of which the latter intimated that under certain conditions he would be willing to support Grant not only for a third but for a seventh term. One of the most interesting contributions to the controversy which has grown out of this affair is an article in the Alexandria Sentinel, the reputed mouthpiece of Col. Mosby, in which the charge is made that President Grant has been very badly treated by the Conservative party, as there was a distinct understanding between Grant through Mosby on the one side, and Kemper on the other, that if the President would refrain from interfering in the contest between Kemper and Hughes at the last election for Governor, then Kemper would agree that the Conservative vote of Virginia should be given to Grant for his coveted third term. The Sentinel shows ...indignantly asks: "Shall the Virginia people who purchased Gen. Grant's neutrality by the professions of friendship, now repudiate their pledges?" In answer to this appeal the Richmond Enquirer says that whether Governor Kemper pledged himself to Mosby or to Grant is a matter for his own consideration, but if one Conservative in twenty thousand had had an inkling of the fact that any such pledge had been made, the present Governor would be practicing law at Madison Court House instead of occupying the office he does.

It is difficult to see who is entitled to the most discredit in this transaction, Kemper or Grant.

And on it went with regard to the (nonexistent) "relationship" between Kemper and Grant, now seen as a "discredit" to both men. John Mosby, the malevolent Svengali, had not only brought about that dishonor, but in so doing dishonored all good Southerners as well. All belief that any goodwill such as might have accompanied at least a tacit rapport between the two men was long gone. It was now all a matter of scheming and plotting while all involved—and especially the traitor Mosby—were, at best, stooges and, at worst, scoundrels. By now, Mosby must have wondered what had happened to all of his hopes and plans for the bright future of Virginia and the South. His life was coming apart as this little article regarding the death of his youngest son, George Prentiss, made clear. At least the newspapers refrained from any insults to the grieving father:

Bristol News – July 28, 1874
EVENT and COMMENT

The funeral of Col. Mosby's infant, in Warrenton, Va., last Sunday, week, is said to have been the most largely attended one ever known in that town. It is thus we court the living by paying honors to the dead.

However, just when it seemed that all was adverse, the Press and Banner (Abbeville, South Carolina) brought up a possible third term with a much more favorable opinion on the matter:

Press and Banner – July 29, 1874 (Edited)
The Third Term Principle.

Senator Fenton of New York, a politician of twenty years experience in public life, and a sagacious observer of men and measures, has been interviewed by a correspondent of the Cincinnati Commercial, and expresses himself freely as to Grant's aspirations and prospects for a Third Term. He thinks the President has his eye fixed in that direction, and that with characteristic pertinacity ... that there is not a man in America who could defeat him, and that if the election were to come off now, he would be sure of success—that to effect his defeat would require a concentration of all the elements of opposition, Democrats, Liberals and Anti-Third Term Radicals which cannot be brought about now, and which if not accomplished in the next two years, will give us Grant as President for a Third Term—and if for a third term, perhaps for a fourth or fifth-term, as there is no law against his re-election, but only the practice of his predecessors, which is equally opposed to a third as to a fifth term. The Senator thinks that President Grant is looking to the South to aid him in his purposes, and that this furnishes a key to his late conciliatory policy. He says:

"I think it likely he would prefer an election from the people, irrespective of any party. Just now he is arranging matters in the South. His hold is secure on the negroes of that section, eight hundred thousand votes in a lump, and he is showing a fair side to the whites—the ex-rebel military—elements like Gordon, Mosby and Kemper. The Southern people would gladly accept a third or a fourth term, or any number of terms, if they could have a friend in the Presidential chair, one whom they had helped to elect, and whom they could approach for favors. They cannot hope to elect a Democrat as a Democrat—that is impossible—and the notion is getting into their heads that the next best thing they can do is to take Grant for a third term. They care less down there about breaking over a custom than we do. What little patriotism and reverence they had for our time-honored institutions after the war has been seriously affected by the conduct of the carpet-baggers and thieves who have swarmed in among them. We need not look to the South for any serious protests against a third term."

The *National Republican* reported on Mosby's intentions to run for Congress as an independent. He certainly could not run as a Conservative. Governor Kemper and his factotums had made that abundantly clear, and he still would not associate with the state Republicans. The *National Republican* had bluntly declared that Mosby must embrace the entire Republican Party at all levels, or he should not be supported by Virginia Republicans. It was Mosby's position on the political use of blacks that was (rightly) seen as problematic. The second article quietly acknowledged that John Mosby had removed himself from the race and put forth his friend James Barbour in his place. Barbour lost to Democrat Eppa Hunton, which was hardly surprising:

National Republican – July 31, 1874

We have received a long report of a meeting held by the Republicans of Fauquier county, Virginia, at Foxville, which we would gladly print if the crowded condition of our columns would permit. It is sufficient, however, to state that a strong feeling was developed in favor of the regular nomination of a candidate for Congress, and in opposition to the proposition that the party shall support Col. Mosby as an independent candidate. This is right. If Mosby will pledge himself to Republican principles as they find practical demonstration in his own State as plainly as he does to the same principles as applied to national politics, his ambitious determination to become a great leader will be entitled to consideration, but until he does this there is no reason why Virginia Republicans should show him any favor whatever. His election would not serve to strengthen the party in Congress, because, if he is honest in the expressing of his opinions regarding the colored race, he would not go into caucus with the colored members of the House, and while he might vote with the party as a general rule, he would be more apt to bolt from its discipline.

In its assessment of Mosby's response to any attempt to place blacks above whites in Virginia, the *National Republican* was quite correct. He would "bolt from its—the party's—discipline." That doesn't mean that Mosby would have disfranchised Negroes or permitted them to be mistreated or misused, but he was very much against any arrangement where the freedman ruled, period. Furthermore, Mosby did not accept "party discipline" as a guide to his behavior or opinions. Again, he was not a "religious" man when it came to politics.

As 1874 stumbled painfully along, John Mosby soon found his name in the headlines regarding a proposed duel between himself and Captain A. D. Payne, former commander of the famous Black Horse Cavalry, a fellow resident of Warrenton and a political enemy. The news coverage was vicious, voracious and relentless. Payne was a great chivalric hero of the South, a "true soldier" and not a "bushwhacking renegade" like Mosby. It didn't hurt that Payne was also a Democrat and no lover of Grant. And that is pretty much how the matter was played out in the press—and elsewhere:

Chicago Tribune – August 21, 1874

A DUEL INTERFERED WITH.

Warrenton, Va., Aug. 20. On suspicion of an intention to fight a duel, Judge Keith to-day ordered the arrest of Gen. W. H. Payne, Capt. A. D. Payne, Judge Thomas Smith, James Barbour and Col. John S. Mosby. Gen. Payne, Barbour, and Smith were arrested. Capt. Payne and Col. Mosby were not in town, and it is believed that if they can effect a meeting without the interference of the police they will fight.

National Republican – August 22, 1874

POLICE COURT NEWS.

A Chronicle of Yesterday's Business Before Judge Dawson.

The fact that the celebrated Colonel Mosby was expected to be arraigned before the Police Court for a preliminary hearing brought a large number of curious visitors into the court who were anxious to catch a glimpse of the rebel chieftain and squad of notables who had him under tow. At eleven o'clock the party entered the court room, and after taking a general survey of the premises found that the business of taking the required bond could not be accomplished, owing to the fact that sundry chicken thieves and nuisance committees were at that time being arraigned and tried for their respective crimes.

After taking a few notes of the situation they departed, and after an absence of nearly an hour returned to finish the work of giving bonds in the sum of $5,000 to be levied of the goods and chattels of Colonel John S. Barbour, provided Mosby does not fulfill the letter and spirit of the bond. Colonel Mosby, as he appeared before the august presence of the honorable court, is a man every way fitted to make a hard single-handed fight at ten paces. Being about five feet seven and a half inches in height, he stands erect, with straight square shoulders and a broad chest, and while in conversation assumes a spirit of animation, which indicates a fervid nature, supported and equipped with the elements of pluck and determination that make him the fearless and apparently invincible man that he is. With little dark eyes, which squint and flash beneath projecting brows, crowned with the remnants of a once luxuriant growth of brown hair and a sharp Roman nose, which overhangs with an independent air a firm and expressive mouth, he appears like an early picture of David that we ever saw. Of course, we mean the David who went down by the brook side and filled his little shepherd's bag with beautiful pebbles, which made the head of that corpulent old bone-crusher, Goliath, ache as it never ached before—nor since, for that matter.

Mosby is quite a different man, however, from David in divers and sundry particulars. We can hardly bring ourselves to believe that Mosby intends to or would chop off the head of Payne after the coming duel and then take it back to his followers as a trophy. We can't believe that he would do this, we say, for the simple reason that a man of Mosby's caliber who has lived as long as he has in this wicked world of ours without chopping off anybody's head isn't very liable to do it at this late hour merely for political capital. And, besides, not half as much depends on the hacking off of Payne's upper story as did in the case of that venerable old bully of the Philistines, and consequently David is quite excusable for having got upon the breastworks of that sinful and brass-coated big lubber heels, who had nearly frightened the host of Israel out of their wits by crying, in a loud and boisterous way, "Am I not a Philistine and ye servants of Saul? Choose you a man for you, and let him come down to me." And yet Mosby looks like David, nevertheless, and if he don't astonish some of the pompous Philistines of that Congressional district before the campaign is over, it will be for the simple reason that they have waltzed into their little houses and taken the precaution to waltz their little holes in after them. That, we would say, judging from a Conservative standpoint, is the kind of man Colonel Mosby is.

One has to wonder just who the correspondent was looking at! Mosby's shoulders were decidedly stooped even when he was younger, and he was still fairly slender, which somewhat belies his having a "broad chest." He was indeed "animated" if all the descriptions of the man are to be believed, but his eyes were hardly "little and dark;" they were blue and large enough to be his most striking feature. His hair was still luxuriant, though he wore it short after the war, and his nose had been described as aquiline—that is, narrow. Pictures of Mosby even in his mid-fifties when he was much heavier, still show a very fine-featured face. Again, it would seem that any description of John Mosby, physical or otherwise, tended to depend upon the opinion of the "recorder" rather than the man's appearance.

Payne's seconds called Mosby a coward for not being "on the field" on the morning of the duel, but Mosby had been arrested and forced to post a bond to assure that he would not do so. Furthermore, John Mosby did not have sufficient funds to repay his friend who had put up the bond money to keep him out of jail. That having been the case, Mosby could not have continued with the duel whatever his wishes in the matter.

New York Tribune – August 22, 1874

THE MOSBY-PAYNE DUEL PREVENTED

Col. Mosby Arrested in Washington and Held Subject to the Virginia Authorities—Payne's Friends Indignant—Mosby Stigmatized as a Coward.

CAPT. PAYNE AND HIS SECOND ON THE GROUND AND READY TO FIGHT—THE AFFAIR TO BE PREVENTED FROM GOING FURTHER

THE CAUSE OF THE QUARREL—ALL ENGAGED IN THE AFFAIR TO BE PUT UNDER BONDS.

New York Daily Tribune – August 22, 1874

The ex-guerrilla Mosby "Grant Republican and Virginia Conservative" candidate for Congress, manifests his fitness for Congressional honors by challenging Capt. Payne, a political opponent to fight a duel. Challenger and challenged have been placed under arrest, but as the former was in Washington, and the latter on the field at the time fixed for the meeting, the verdict of chivalry is in favor of Payne, and Mosby is "stigmatized as a coward." This is the second dueling scrape in which Mosby has figured since the war. Is it not about time for the Virginia courts to see that the Virginia law against such murderous schemes is enforced?

Daily Tribune – **August 24, 1874**

Col. Jno. S. Mosby may or may not be a coward, as charged by the friends of the man whom he challenged to fight a duel; but, certainly, he is not lacking in disposition to kill his man. He proposes to fight Capt. Payne with pistols, each man firing as he advances, it being understood that this work is to go on until one of the would-be homicides is unable to hold his weapon. There is only one agreeable issue of this affair, and that is that both of the politicians involved in it have by planning a duel rendered themselves ineligible to office.

Virginia had anti-dueling legislation disfranchising anyone involved in a duel. The legislation was later amended, and those previously removed from the voting roles were reinstated. However, those involved with the bill on both sides of the aisle attempted to exclude only one man by name from the relief offered by the legislation—John Mosby!

New York Tribune – **August 26, 1874 (Edited)**

MOSBY.

Really we must beg our Southern brethren to pause and consider. We have every wish to see the Union made whole again—with a difference. We are willing to take in again and welcome even the old fire-eater who killed his man before breakfast, quoted Tom Jefferson as he pulled the trigger, and ate his hot corn pone and fried chicken afterward with good appetite and serene spirit. He was a genuine fellow in his way, and deserved a place in the republic as well as the Missouri Pike or Denver Rough, whose ways are the same. But there was a bad imitation of the old man who, we hoped, had died out during the war—the duelist—whose pistols never smelled of fire… Now this little farce, amusing enough at first, was played on Southern boards so steadily that it became beyond measure stale and wearisome. In the name of humanity, don't let us have it to endure again. Col. Mosby (of railroad-train and stolen-jewelry notoriety) has been essaying the miserable old joke again, and the Washington police authorities were gullible enough to help him out with it. We have the ancient telegrams of An Affair of Honor Anticipated, the inevitable sequel of how the Affair was stopped. We have had quite enough of this sort of thing. There are a certain number of Colonels and Majors of the Mosby pattern hanging about every Southern town like green carrion flies about an animal trying to work… The next time a pair of them run into an affair of honor before the police authorities, let them be clapped into jail right off and dressed in a striped uniform, and perhaps that will extinguish the whole honorable breed.

Once again, Mosby was used as an example of everything contemptuous about the South as seen by the North as if he were the only party involved. Of course, the people of the North considered the wholesale stealing and violence of the Northern armies—

officers and men—as perfectly normal, acceptable and understandable because they were fighting a people not worthy of civilized consideration.

This publication had the happy occasion to kill two hated "birds" with one story:

Nashville Union and American – September 5, 1874

The disfranchisement of Col. Mosby will be a sad misfortune to President Grant. There goes another vote for the third term gone glimmering.

By this time, John Mosby probably thought the coverage of the "non-duel" would go on forever. But not so. Soon, his relationship with Grant was back in the news—but it afforded no relief:

Nashville Union and American – October 1, 1874 (Edited)

Mosby's Influence with Grant.

The influence of Col. Mosby, the great champion of the third term, with the Administration, has just received a fresh illustration. The city press of to-day records an appointment in the Treasury Department secured by the Colonel last Saturday.

The Virginia Sentinel, a paper published in the Eighth Virginia district, where Gen. Eppa Hunton, late of the rebel army, and a Democrat is a candidate for re-election, has in a recent issue the following, suggested by a claim set up by Mr. Hunton to the possession of peculiar influence in Washington: "Mosby has really represented the district. Within the last three weeks we have seen six ladies and gentlemen appointed to office solely through his influence, beside the many before. This, too, not because Gen. Hunton has not tried. He has tried repeatedly, it is said, but invariably without success.

And yet another long article about Grant and Mosby appeared. Members of Grant's party were asking him to abandon his association with Mosby, which, Grant was told, "does not inspire respect among the soldier element of the Union army:"

Memphis Daily Appeal – November 11, 1874 (Edited)

[Part of a much longer article]

MOSBY, MORRILL, SETTLE AND CLINGMAN ON THE RESULT.

Washington, November 7, 1874.—Colonel Mosby met the President for the first time to-day since the election. Both being in favor of a third term, they sat down and discussed matters for an hour. The congressional candidate in Mosby's district, Mr. Barbour, who was to vindicate the third term policy, was beaten by General Hunton, a Democratic member of the present congress, who said the people of Virginia were unconditionally opposed to a third term... Both agreed that Caesarism had nothing to do with the result, and his excellency was more convinced than ever of the policy of keeping silent.

MOSBY'S PATRIOTIC ACHIEVEMENTS.

But to return to Mosby. There are those who think and say in the President's absence that his friendship for the notorious raider on sutler wagons and straggling soldiers, does not inspire respect among the soldier element of the Union army. The President replies by appointing additional friends of Mosby to office… More than that, the President intends visiting Colonel Mosby at his home in Warrenton in a few days. This shows how much President Grant cares for public opinion and the voice of the press.

The *Atlanta Constitution* put forth an article declaring Grant a "Brutus" to the soldier voters of the North because of his friendship for Mosby:

***Atlanta Constitution* – November 14, 1874**

GRANT AND MOSBY

The Conciliatory Change Toward the South—The Southern Chieftain's Influence—Ellsworth's Blood Forgotten—

A forewarning of Caesarism. [Correspondence New York Herald]

Washington, November 9, 1874.

It was stated in these dispatches of Friday last, that Colonel John S. Mosby had that day received substantial evidence of the President's friendship. The significance of this statement may not have been apparent at the time, but it must be remembered that Colonel Mosby is an original advocate of the third term, and does not conceal his zeal in promoting the movement at all times How the president and Mosby kept up each other's courage has already been published in the Herald, but the most important fact has yet to be related. By many it will be doubted that the president is really an aspirant for continued honors. His evasive and partial notice of the "nonsense," as he call it, displays diplomatic skill in disguising his true intent, but with Mosby he has no secrets. The president uses it in the sense that it would add unnecessary weight to the nomination, or plainly speaking, it would be MOSBY'S INFLUENCE, when a republican congress, by reducing the appropriations, had compelled the dismissal of hundreds of worthy clerks, who deserved better of their country for the wounds they had received that the wounded confederates who rejoice in the influence of the guerrilla chieftain. But the president is in earnest, "dead earnest," and cares nothing for the wiser counsels of his immediate advisers, who are not only members of the cabinet but personal friends of long acquaintance, who have warned him that there was such a thing as carrying his good will too far If the president could hear what strong republicans say of him here in Washington, he would not attempt to deceive a few by the statement that the Herald's joke, as he calls it, is all 'nonsense,' for this Caesar is another Brutus to the soldier voters of the north."

The last spate of articles in the year were of course on Grant and/or Grant and Mosby. One mentioned a speech to a Democratic meeting by Jubal Early, who had never been Mosby's friend. Indeed, Mosby considered Early "my malignant enemy." Of course, Early was presented as an "honorable gentleman," while Mosby was a "characterless bushwhacker and guerrilla." Alas, the year ended no better than it began—with worse in the offing.

Chapter 14

1875

Vulnerant omnes, ultima necat. ~ Every hour wounds, the last kills.

"Hell is empty, all the devils are here." ~ William Shakespeare

AFTER THE HORRORS of 1874, it is doubtful that John Mosby was at all sanguine about 1875. It was the third year in Grant's second term, but there was still a lot of speculation about him seeking yet a third—and John Mosby had not given up on it, although the issue was a scourge used to flay him in the press not only in the South but in the country as a whole. In March, a fairly long article on presidential politics appeared in the *Atlanta Constitution*. These articles were never positive. Indeed, the article strongly suggested that it was Southerners like Mosby who "talked Grant" into considering a third-term run.

An interesting article then appeared in which the question about the Civil Rights and Force bills was raised:

> ***Daily Phoenix* – April 7, 1875**
>
> GOOD FOR THE VICE-PRESIDENT.—Vice-President Wilson has recently expressed the opinion that President Grant, while coquetting with Mosby and a few others of that peculiar type, for the Southern Conservative vote, let it be understood that he was ready to veto the Civil Rights Bill. But he became satisfied that Mosby & Co., had no influence, and that the South had a settled distrust of him, and so he changed his coat and got at the Arkansas and Force Bills. The Vice-President condemns them and gives a formula of his faith on the Southern question, which is quite respectable, all things considered. He says:
>
> "Although a Massachusetts and a New England man, and a party man in every sense of fidelity to my public associates and the general policy we begin to introduce, I am positive in the belief that we must get white men, born or bred in the South to rule it, and that State Governments of negroes and a handful of white men who absorb the patronage, and are Republicans for the sake of it, will not stand up. Therefore, I oppose force bills, if their objects are suspected of being political and trifling with State Governments, according as they stand in the path of a certain ambition or out of it."

Mosby truly believed that if not a "union," then at least a working relationship between local Democratic parties in the South and the Republican national party would accomplish an end to carpetbagger/freedmen governments and the type of black political power that made a disaster of the states of the South during Reconstruction. He also wanted an end to the "force bills" and Civil Rights legislation, which could be used to compel the social mixing of the races in the South at the point of the Federal bayonet, a very real fear for Southern whites.

At that point, Mosby received an invitation to speak in, of all places, Boston:

Somerset Press – **July 16, 1875**

Colonel John S. Mosby has declined the invitation to deliver one of a series of addresses in Tremont Temple, Boston. He writes: "Although circumstances compel me to decline it, I assure you that I do so from no want of sympathy with the noble object you profess a desire to promote the restoration of fraternal relations between the people of the long-estranged sections of our country. For the soldiers of the Union I cherish no feeling of bitterness, but, on the contrary, sentiments of the highest respect, and I trust the day is not far distant when the soldiers of both armies will receive from the whole country the credit due to their valor and patriotic devotions in the big wars that made ambition virtue."

In reply to this Colonel Mosby received a second letter asking him to reconsider his declination, because his letter had so much "true soldierly ring." He has not yet decided whether he will accept or not.

This was an interesting article in that his would-be hosts pressed him to come because his response to them had a "true soldierly ring." It would seem that the people of Boston had a better understanding of Mosby than the people of Virginia. He must have thought long and hard about the matter. A man so beleaguered would find great solace in such sentiments.

Mosby had no choice but to open an office in Washington. He could no longer earn a living in Virginia, and even in Washington, his chances of attracting clients were small. When even officials of the courts treated him with ill-disguised contempt and rebuff, he could hardly expect to be successful in his profession no matter how skilled he was—and he knew it:

Wichita City Eagle – **September 30, 1875**

Mosby the guerrilla, proposes to open a law office in Washington.

But the year could not possibly end without one more shot at the third-term bugbear. This time, it came from a Democratic organ, but the location or the politics of the newspaper didn't much matter anymore. Mosby's was among the names of those few who apparently openly supported a third term—proving at least that he was not alone! But alone or in the company of two or three, the matter had reached the state of a scandal and was treated as such:

Louisiana Democrat – **December 8, 1875**

The third term movement is evidently gaining ground. With Postmaster Edmunds to collect subsidies from the poor women who are employed in the departments, Zach Chandler to control the Prohibitionists, Boss Shepherd to supply honesty, the National Republican, and Sam Bard, of Atlanta, the organizer of the only third term club in existence, to furnish intellect, Mosby to provide patriotism, and Boss Grant to look wise and hold his tongue, a combination may be effected which cannot fail to exert a powerful influence upon the minds of intelligent American voters.—[New York Sun.]

Undoubtedly, the paucity of serious—and therefore negative—news coverage of John Mosby in 1875 was perhaps his one bright point in the year. Unable to earn a living in Virginia (and soon to be driven physically from his beloved state), Mosby's social life—and that of his family—must have been horrendous. But worse, 1876 was a presidential election year, and John Mosby knew that he would finally have to make a fateful decision. One has to wonder what thoughts went through his mind on those dark December nights when everything for which he had hoped and worked so long and so hard had been laid waste; and very soon, he was going to have to take that final plunge into ignominy—cutting all ties, present and future—politically at least—with his beloved Virginia.

Chapter 15

1876

Damnant quodnon intelligunt ~
They condemn what they do not understand.

"When sorrows come, they come not as single spies, but in battalions."~ William Shakespeare

FEDERAL TROOPS STILL lingered in the South, but the period of Reconstruction and therefore the era of Radical-carpetbagger-freedman domination in the states of that section was coming to an end. John Mosby saw this as partially due, in Virginia at least, to that state's support of Ulysses Grant in 1872; and for this reason, he had hoped that Grant would seek a third term, thus giving him time to complete the reunification of the nation and end the hateful period of Reconstruction. But Grant's popularity had run out. The known corruption in his government rather than the policies of the Radicals lessened the support of Republicans in the North, and such support as he had in the South was negligible. Mosby's belief that a Democrat could not be elected president—a belief he still held in 1876—was faulty, and the Democrats saw for the first time since the election of James Buchanan the possibility of regaining the White House and conceivably the Congress as well.

Yet the nation was still very much conflicted. Many in the North saw in the Democrats the "hope" of the defeated South and rejected the Democracy for that reason. Meanwhile, the South, seeing the matter in the same light, had recommitted to that party. In his attempt to create a bond between white Southerners and what he believed to be the "non-radical" Republicans of the North (a belief that also proved to be faulty), Mosby had, for his efforts, become a pariah in both sections. The North castigated him for his type of warfare and the government patronage he provided to former Confederates, while the South remembered his support of Grant and what was seen as his attempt to "seduce" Virginia Conservatives into an alliance with the hated Republicans. Such approval as he found was limited to those Southerners who had worked with him in his efforts to defeat the local Radicals. Some of the former were mentioned in a letter written by author and civil servant Frank J. Bramhall dated March 11, 1877, the first year of the Hayes administration:

> "Comparatively few strangers are in the city, but it seems to me that Virginians and North Carolinians are here in some force. Of the latter, I saw Douglas and Ike Young yesterday. The Va. State Central Com. holds a meeting here Tuesday and will probably call on the President Wednesday. Lewis, Rives, Mosby, Smith and others have formed a coalition for war on the carpet-baggers and Brady insists that Mosby will have more influence with Hayes than with Grant. From other sources, however, I am assured that Mosby has been notified by Hayes' friends that he must take a back seat. Old Smith was here a few days ago but I cannot learn what he was up to. I presume, doing Rives' dirty work with the assistance of Dr. Grant. Rives has been working very busily but quietly, doing all the harm to carpet-baggers and others not of his ilk … without exposing himself too much …"

By the time 1876 rolled around, it was clear that there was no possibility for a third term for Ulysses Grant, and the man eventually chosen to be the party standard-bearer was Rutherford B. Hayes from the liberal wing of the party; Hayes had defeated fellow Republican and Grant supporter Roscoe Conkling running as a "Stalwart." Hayes ran as a "reformer" in hopes of keeping the party faithful sufficiently engaged even if they were no longer as animated as they had once been. It is hard to say where Mosby might have come down in the election if the Democrats had run a man whom he could have, in good conscience, supported. But even if Mosby had gone Republican no matter who the Democrats ran, the choice of New York Governor Samuel Tilden settled the matter. New York had been a hotbed of corruption best known for the infamous New York City Tammany Hall ring led by William M. "Boss" Tweed. Mosby had been approached by Tilden backers in hopes of securing his support for that candidate. It was not a wise move for either party. Below is an excerpt from an article printed in August, 1876 in at least two newspapers clearly illustrating Mosby's opinion of Tilden and the Democrats:

New Orleans Republican – **August 20, 1876 (Edited)**

Jackson Standard – **August 31, 1876**

Letter from Colonel Mosby.

The following letter has been written by Colonel Mosby to a former comrade, in reply to one urging him to support Tilden:

Warrenton, Va., August 6, 1876 My Dear Sir—I have just received our communication asking if it be true, as reported that I am supporting Hayes and Wheeler. It is true that I am a cordial and earnest advocate of the election of that ticket, notwithstanding you say that all the Southern people and especially the Confederate soldiers, are united in support of the Democratic. I hope, however, that in this you are mistaken, and that many men in the South of sound conservative and National sentiments will be found on the other side; however this may be, it will not divert me from my purpose. The ground upon which you urge me to support Tilden and Hendricks is that they are the candidates of the Southern people, and, if elected, will be under their control. Now, it is because this thing is apparent that the election of Tilden was an impossibility. In attempting to grasp too much the South will lose everything. The sectional unity of the Southern people has been the governing idea and bane of their politics. So far from its being a remedy for anything it has been the cause of most of the evils they have suffered. So long as it continues the war will be a controlling element of politics, for any cry in the South that unites Confederate re-echoes through the North and rekindles the war fires there. The reconstruction measures necessarily divided parties in the South on a color line, for the issue they presented was the political equality of the races. While the South was opposing it, the Republican party was on the side of the negro. But since the South has accepted it and incorporated it in the platform on which it has mounted its candidate, I see no reason for continuing to divide on an issue which has become extinct. Having adopted all the principles of a party and sanctioned its measures, I can see no objection to voting for its candidate All that the Republicans propose is to preserve what they have accomplished; the Democrats are pledged not to disturb what the Republicans have done. You cannot complain that the sincerity of the pledges of Governor Tilden to execute certain laws is distrusted when his supporters justify their opposition to Governor Hayes on the ground that his party has enacted these laws. To be consistent they should go for repealing them if they come into power. You say that no one in the South is supporting Hayes but negroes and carpet-baggers. I should be sorry to think this were so, but if it were I should still vote for the candidate of my choice, and would not let this class deprive me of it. It is better for some to go right than for all to go wrong.

If I think they are going wrong I could do no good by going with them. If they insist on breaking their necks, I don't intend to assist them. Besides, you say that if Tilden is elected he will be under the control of the Confederates. If that is so then you will have no need of me It was for these reasons that four years ago I urged the Southern people that if they really desired peace and reconciliation, to bury their passions and resentments and support the man who was not only the representative of an overwhelming majority of the North, but was the most powerful, as he had been the most generous of our foes, I have seen no cause to change my opinions, or regret my course. Many things have since occurred which no one deplores more than I do …The responsibility is with those who adopted the fatal policy "Anything to beat Grant." In the conflict they invited Grant to beat them.

Having predicted all sorts of evils to result from the election of Grant, they have done all in their power to make their predictions come true. If you wish to know, then, the ground of my support of Hayes, it is this: Any good which the Southern people might derive from the election of Tilden would equally result from their support of Hayes. But I am far from thinking that the election of a Democrat would be an unmixed blessing to the South. On the contrary, I fear it would open a Pandora's box of evils. The very remote prospect has already excited hopes and expectations that can never be realized. If such a thing should occur as the election of a President by a united South combining with a mere fragment of the North it would simply revive the old conflict of the sections. A transformation has taken place in the state of both parties. The Republican now represents the principles of Conservatism, while I can conceive no worse from of Radicalism than the reactionary movements that would fall on a Bourbon restoration I allude to this to show the tone of political morality of the party of which Governor Tilden has been the acknowledged head ever since the retirement of Tweed. He proposes to reform the civil service, but how? By a change in the system of appointments? Not at all; but by filling the offices with his partisans, who will flock to Washington "as fierce as famine and hungry as the grave." When the offices have thus been all filled, somebody will then have to reform the reformers. The character of such pretenders is well described in the language of Junius, as "resembling the termagant chastity of a prude, who while she prosecutes one lover for rape, invites the lewd embraces of another." That official trusts held under the administration have been abused no one denies; that the delinquents have not been screened by their party associates is equally true. Any observer can see that those who have been most forward in exposing corruption are the most earnest in supporting Hayes. But it is said that no party can reform abuses in its own ranks. I cannot accept such a theory of human depravity. I do not see why a party, like an individual, can't reform itself. If this were not so we would have to chronicle daily the rise and fall of a new party, It is claimed that the Democrats have done great good by their investigations. This may be so, and yet is no proof of capacity for the administration of affairs. The act of the detective may be very necessary and useful in the economy of government, but has never been considered an element of statesmanship.

JOHN S. MOSBY.

But of course, Mosby's letter did not reach the papers until August. At the beginning of 1876, the matter of Mosby and Grant was still being raised, foreshadowing a long and contentious election cycle made even more contentious—at least for Mosby—by the fact that he would cross the Rubicon and join the Republican party in his support of Hayes:

Louisiana Democrat – **April 12, 1876**

MOSBY SAYS ABOUT IT.

I have just seen Colonel Mosby, who is, as you know, one of Grant's right bowers*. He had just come from a conference with the President at the White House, and he says that Grant is still in the field as a candidate for re-election—that he considers the New Hampshire election an endorsement of his administration, and is determined, if possible, to secure a third term. If this is true, we may expect some lively times with Blaine, Morton and Co., who thought the Boss was out of the race. They may not be willing to take back seats now.

*The term "right bower" does not indicate servility to the individual and/or organization named—in this case, Grant—rather, it is a card term from the most popular card game of the day, euchre. The highest trump is the jack of the trump suit; this card is called the "right bower." So to say that one is a "right bower" means that one is the most powerful associate of the person or organization mentioned. Mosby was often called one of Grant's "right bowers," indicating his power over Grant or the power he provided to Grant—or possibly both.

But as heartrending as things had become for John Mosby in Virginia by 1876, Providence then dealt him a crushing blow. In the spring of that year, his beloved wife, Pauline, had given birth to the couple's last child, a son named for Mosby's father Alfred. Mosby's youngest son prior to Alfred's birth, George Prentiss, had died at the age of eleven months in July of 1874 and was buried at Warrenton. The inscription his sorrowing mother had placed on his stone was "Gone to Play with the Angels." But George was not the last heartbreaking death for the family. Pauline, who never recovered from her last pregnancy, also died; and a short time later, her infant son followed his mother into the grave. John Mosby was shattered. At this time in his life, perhaps, he might well have agreed with biographer Jones' assessment that it would have been better for him had he died in December of 1864.

It is somewhat comforting to see that the newspaper coverage—at least that which is available today—was decent. The *Bristol News*, never one to miss an opportunity to crucify Mosby, was particularly civil in its announcement of the tragedy. However, the last sentence—taken from the Alexandria Sentinel—mentioned the "sympathy" Pauline's death would gain for "her husband" and it is possible to deduce that both papers thought such sympathy, even under such heartbreaking circumstances was probably undeserved:

Bristol News – May 16, 1876

Death of Mrs. Col. Mosby—We record with great sorrow the death of Mrs. Pauline Mosby, wife of Colonel John S. Mosby, which occurred at her residence in Warrenton Thursday morning. Mrs. Mosby was a daughter of the Hon. Mr. Clarke, formerly member of Congress from Kentucky. She was a lady of eminent Christian and social virtues, and a member of the Catholic church. She had been for a long time a sufferer, and leaves seven children, all quite young, the youngest only about two months old, who sad affliction will gain for them and her husband the sympathy of all.— Alexandria Sentinel.

Milan Exchange – May 25, 1876

The Alexandria (Va.) Sentinel records the death of Mrs. Pauline Mosby, at Warrenton. She had long been a sufferer, and died leaving seven small children.

Morning Star and Catholic Messenger – May 28, 1876

Gen. Mosby's Wife.—The following obituary appeared in the last number of the Louisville Catholic Advocate:

The many friends and acquaintances of Mrs. Pauline Mosby will be shocked by the announcement of her death which occurred at her residence in Staunton, Va., in the 10th inst. she died of pulmonary consumption. Mrs. Mosby was the eldest daughter of the lamented Beverly L. Clarke, of Kentucky. She was educated at old St. Mary's Academy, in Nashville, Tenn., where she won the lasting love and admiration of the good Sisters and the entire school, and through life has ever been noted for her piety and intelligence. In 1856 she was married to John S. Mosby of Virginia, who afterwards distinguished himself as a Confederate officer in the rear of the Federal army. The marriage ceremony was performed in Nashville, Tenn. by Rev. Ivo Schacht, of happy memory. As an instance of Mrs. Mosby's perseverance, when the war ended in Virginia, she was unwilling for her husband to surrender until she could first see President Johnson, and obtain from him a guarantee of his safety. The President, although a warm personal friend of her father, gave her poor comfort; but a woman of such spirit was not to be baffled, and by her tact obtained for her a pass to Gen. Grant's headquarters. The General treated her with the utmost kindness and gave all the protection necessary for the safety of her husband. Hence the amicable relations between President Grant and Col. Mosby. She leaves a family of six children, all well instructed in the Catholic religion, besides she has been the instrument in the hands of God for converting a great many—including the sisters of Col. Mosby, two of whom have attached themselves to religious orders.

Mosby buried his grief in the election, though his personal life and the life of his grieving family continued to suffer in a combination of politics and personal tragedy. The last article below showcases the ongoing charge that Mosby had "sold out" his principles for money. The fact that he could no longer earn a living in Virginia seemed not to intrude into the mind of the journalist making the charge:

National Republican – June 23, 1876 (Edited)

Virginia and the Coming Election

It will be remembered that four years ago the Presidential campaign was opened in Virginia by a joint discussion between the ex-guerrilla chief, Colonel John S. Mosby, and General Eppa Hunton, candidate for Congress, the former espousing the cause of General Grant, and the latter that of Greeley. Since that time the influence of Col. Mosby in securing appointments under the National Government has been marked and commented upon. Yesterday, in a conversation between Colonel Mosby and a representative of the *National Republican* on the coming campaign, the Colonel expressed himself fully and decidedly. He said that without regard to the nominees of the St. Louis convention he would support the Cincinnati nominees on the stump throughout his State, and felt sure that Virginia would give the a larger majority that it gave Grant in 1872.

As an evidence of this he cited the fact that the Alexandria Sentinel, a paper of considerable influence, heretofore Democratic, and edited by an ex- Confederate, had hoisted the Hayes and Wheeler flag, and that Hon. Lewis McKenzie, an ex-Congressman, and during the last campaign a supporter of Greeley, had also declared that he would take the stump for Hayes. The indications are that the campaign in Virginia will be a lively one, as the Colonel says it makes no difference whether Hancock, Tilden, Bayard, Parker or any other man is nominated at St. Louis, he is sure the State of Virginia will go for Hayes and Wheeler. Col. Mosby leaves for his home at Warrenton, Fauquier county, to-day, and before he returns he will probably have arranged with his neighbors and friends for the opening of a vigorous campaign.

Interior Journal – June 30, 1876

Most pitiful must be the condition and circumstances of one Col. John S. Mosby, at one time an honored Chieftain in the Confederate Army, but who, for the sake of "filthy lucre" and a place under a Radical government, forsook his high position, abandoned the principles for which he fought, and made himself a reproach for all honorable men. After playing traitor to his cause, he sought and found a teat in the public crib under Grant. Now, we find him declaring himself as an advocate of Hayes and Wheeler, for whom he will take the stump. Poor Mosby!

The only truth in this poisonous little diatribe were the last two words: "Poor Mosby" indeed! Soon, he would have to farm out his motherless children for lack of the ability to provide for them and take an office from the government—the thing he had relentlessly rejected so as to avoid the very charges made here of his "selling his honor." Worse still was the fact that very few of his remaining friends appeared willing to defend him against such calumnies as can be seen by the dearth of their letters appearing in the press. But the *National Republican* continued to defend him—for the moment:

National Republican – July 15, 1876 (Edited)

VIRGINIA

Colonel Mosby and the Old-Line Whigs Going for Hayes and Wheeler

Fauquier County, Va., July 12, 1876

To the Editor of the National Republican:

Sir:

An impression seems to prevail with superficial observes of *The Times* that Virginia is so hopelessly wedded to the idols of bogus Conservatism and effete-Bourbon-secession Democracy that her electoral vote is set down certain for the St. Louis ticket. It is true that the old political mountebanks are so stupefied by prejudice that they cannot realize the fact that the world moves, and so blinded by their musty abstractions that they can read nothing but the revolutions of '98. But ... the people of Virginia, ... knowing that this ruin has been brought upon them by the old Democratic politicians... the State can be reckoned upon for Hayes and Wheeler.

In 1872 Gen. Grant carried the State, and all who voted for Grant then will vote for Hayes in November, Besides we know positively of A LARGE NUMBER OF GREELEY MEN

Who will support the Cincinnati nominees. It is true, in 1873 Kemper was elected Governor by a large majority, but if the same men were before the people to-day for the same office the majority would be reversed. Many of the leading Grant men actively supported Kemper. In fact his majority is mainly due to Col. Mosby's influence. Col. Mosby's object was to destroy sectional partisanship; to obliterate the bitter memories of the past; to "bridge the bloody chasm" and place Virginia in a favorable position in the Union and on amiable terms with the National Administration. Kemper started right, but he had not been in office long before the old Bourbons took him in charge, and the noble mission of Col. Mosby was defeated and the people deceived by Kemper.

We cannot believe they will be duped any longer by such men.

THE MALADMINISTRATION

of the State government by the so-called Conservative Democratic party, the heavy burdens of taxation imposed upon the people, the intolerant and proscriptive spirit pursued by the so-called Conservatives toward all who differ with them, the bitter and vindictive sectionalism of the Virginia Democracy, will nerve all true friends of the Union, of peace and prosperity, by every consideration of duty to repudiate this destructive Democratic party. With the aid of your valuable and influential paper we expect to place Virginia in the line of Republican States... The people of Virginia have been deceived too often by demagogues and old Democratic party tricksters and trimmers. Tilden and Hendricks are of that class. In such a man as Governor Hayes the people have confidence. He has the training, experience, ability, integrity and high moral character which eminently fit him to adorn the executive chair of the nation. The Old-Line Whigs will rally to his support. C.

Though the identity of "C" is unknown, we cannot rule out Mosby as the source of the letter. It could be that he had grown heartily tired of his motives and actions being deliberately misconstrued and misrepresented and decided to put the matter bluntly, something that he might not expect would be believed if it were printed under his own name.

National Republican – July 28, 1876 (Edited)
VIRGINIA RATIFIES.

A Meeting in Alexandria Addresses by Distinguished Men The Old Dominion Hopeful Years of Democratic Misrule Idleness, Destitution and Despondency Disorderly Proceedings of Democrats

Alexandria ratified the nominations of Hayes and Wheeler last evening with great enthusiasm. The meeting was the largest political meeting that has ever been held in Alexandria. Distinguished speakers were present, and made the opening of the campaign in Virginia a memorable occasion. It was anticipated that attempts would be made by the ruffian element of the community to create disorder, as was done at the last Republican ratification meeting four years ago, when it seemed that all the energies of the Democracy were bent toward breaking up the meeting and creating confusion. That element was comparatively on its good behavior last night. While the visiting speakers were talking there was little disorder... He instanced this to show how Virginia Democrats are careful to curse and punish Republican corruption, but yet passed by unnoticed a Democratic defalcation. He wanted the Democrats of Virginia to see what had been the action of their leaders. The gentlemen of Virginia, without looking abroad, should set their own house in order. There was an idea abroad that gentlemen of Virginia could not join the Republican party without losing cast, although they believed in their hearts that the principles of the Republican party were the principles of truth. [He mentioned the name of Colonel Mosby, and there were loud hisses.] I venture to say, he continued, that nine out of ten men who hiss John S. Mosby's name never served in the field.

He appealed to those who had fought under Lee and Longstreet and Mosby to maintain the same honor and courage that they had maintained on the field. He urged that they honor the flag for which Old Virginia had fought long ago, which threw its protecting folds over all people of all nationalities. ...

And so John Mosby was hissed at a Republican! gathering. When he learned of that (and his enemies would have made sure that he did!), what went through Mosby's mind? Of course, there were those in the audience of Democratic sympathies who had come to "stir things up," but even so it is probable that he wondered if there was anywhere he was not a pariah and if there were any of his fellow Virginians who did not despise him.

But despite such treatment, Mosby not only came out for Hayes and Wheeler, but decided that his efforts to straddle the political line had failed and as he could not in good conscience support Tilden and the Democrats, that he may as well be hanged for a wolf as a sheep, as hanged he certainly would be. Thus, John Mosby formally embraced the Republican Party. He knew what this meant for what was left of his life in Virginia as can be seen in the excerpt of his lengthy letter of August 20 to the New Orleans Republican:

"I know very well the measure of denunciation which the expression of these sentiments will receive from the people in whose cause I shed my blood and sacrificed the prime of my life. Be it so; I wait on time for my vindication. To those who now assail me I reply, in the language of Edmund Burke when charged with deserting his constituents in opposing the American war, "I do not obey your instructions. No, I conformed to the instructions of truth and nature, and maintained your interests against your opinions. I am indeed, to look to your opinions as you and I must have five years hence. I was not to look to the flash of the day."

Since he could no longer do any good for Virginia as a Democrat (and as he was never a true member of that party anyway), John Mosby returned to his political roots. Of course, this meant that, as bad as things had been for him before, this was his Rubicon; that is, a decision never to be recalled or repented of. That does not mean that he did not regret the consequences; he did at least to some extent for most of the rest of his life as it made him an outcast and hated among those for whom, as he put it, "I shed my blood and sacrificed the prime of my life." But Mosby waited "upon time for [his] vindication." Time, however, neither knows nor cares about human suffering.

National Republican – June 23, 1876(Edited)

Virginia and the Coming Election

It will be remembered that four years ago the Presidential campaign was opened in Virginia by a joint discussion between the ex-guerrilla chief, Colonel John S. Mosby, and General Eppa Hunton, candidate for Congress, the former espousing the cause of General Grant, and the latter that of Greeley. Since that time the influence of Col. Mosby in securing appointments under the National Government has been marked and commented upon. Yesterday, in a conversation between Colonel Mosby and a representative of the *National Republican* on the coming campaign, the Colonel expressed himself fully and decidedly. He said that without regard to the nominees of the St. Louis convention he would support the Cincinnati nominees on the stump throughout his State, and felt sure that Virginia would give the a larger majority that it gave Grant in 1872 As an evidence of this he cited the fact that the Alexandria Sentinel, a paper of considerable influence, heretofore Democratic, and edited by an ex-Confederate, had hoisted the Hayes and Wheeler flag, and that Hon. Lewis McKenzie, an ex-Congressman, and during the last campaign a supporter of Greeley, had also declared that he would take the stump for Hayes. The indications are that the campaign in Virginia will be a lively one, as the Colonel says it makes no difference whether Hancock, Tilden, Bayard, Parker or any other man is nominated at St. Louis, he is sure the State of Virginia will go for Hayes and Wheeler. Col. Mosby leaves for his home at Warrenton, Fauquier county, to-day, and before he returns he will probably have arranged with his neighbors and friends for the opening of a vigorous campaign.

Mosby's support of Kemper and the Conservatives had brought down upon his head the wrath of the Republican press, but his support of Hayes and Wheeler had restored him in their eyes—for the moment, at least. Hence, there began a period in which he was defended by those Republican organs once again:

Daily National Republican – August 17, 1876 (Edited)

The Ishmaelite of the New York Sun does not relish the following paragraph in a recent letter of Col. John S. Mosby to the New York Herald: "It was only about twelve months ago that Tweed was released from prison on habeas corpus by a decision of the New York Court of Appeals, composed of seven Democratic judges. Mr. Charles O'Conor, the Nestor of the New York bar, in a letter published at the time, charged that the decision was procured through the corrupt influence of Tweed's money. Here was a splendid case for investigation, far excelling in enormity the sale of a suttlership; yet these judges remain unimpeached, and are still wearing the ermine of justice. I allude to this fact to show the tone of political morality of the party of which Gov. Tilden has been the acknowledged head ever since the retirement of Tweed."

He cannot refute its assertions, so he falls to abusing Mosby for a rebel guerrilla. Well, we are doubtful whether such ex-Confederate Hayes and Wheeler Republicans as General Longstreet and Col. Mosby are not a great deal more credible than the Ishmaelite who edits *The Sun*, although the latter was Union Assistant Secretary of War for a time during the rebellion. He is now a Democrat … [and] has abused General Grant ever since he found that he could not use him, and it is fair to believe that he is supporting Tilden because he can use him if he should be elected. We much prefer a repentant rebel before such people.

The *Daily National Republican* had chastised Mosby in the past, but in the above article, the paper pointed out the difference between its rebuke and that of the Democratic press. The Republican did not condemn or underestimate Mosby's performance during the war as did the Democratic organs. In those papers, when they disagreed with him, Mosby was called a bushwhacker and a murderer though previously he had been lauded as a hero! The motive for this change of status was entirely political.

This letter is unedited because of the castigation John Mosby received—and continues to receive to this day!—for his becoming a Republican though it was his natural political affiliation. It needs to be seen and read again as a means of setting the record straight, so to speak, on the man's political viewpoint.

Rutland Daily Globe - August 18, 1876
COLONEL MOSBY'S LETTER.

There is a great deal of sound sense, as well as sound politics, in the reason assigned by Colonel Mosby, of rebel guerrilla fame, for supporting Hayes and Wheeler, instead of Tilden and Hendricks. He says, "I ceased to be a Confederate soldier eleven years ago and became a citizen of the United States," and as he did what he believed to be his duty as a soldier, so he shall, as far as he knows, do his duty as a citizen. Herein, in a nutshell, lives the difference between such men as Longstreet and Mosby, and such men as Jeff Davis and Wade Hampton. The former fought gallantly and did noble service for the southern Confederacy so long as there seemed a chance for its success, but when the "lost cause" was lost, when they laid down their arms, they honestly accepted the situation, and became citizens of the United States in fact as well as in name. The latter still hug the delusion of a southern Confederacy, and, although defeated in the field, they have transferred to contest to the forum, and now seek, though the ascendancy of the democratic party, that which they were unable to obtain by force of arms. Mosby had been urged to support Tilden and Hendricks, because—mark the language as quoted by him—"they are candidates of the Southern people and, if elected, will be under their control." This is the language, not of northern republicans, not of southern "carpet-baggers," "scalawags" or negroes, but of southern democrats, representative men of the lost cause, men who say, and apparently believe, that no one in the south "except negroes and 'carpet-baggers,'" is supporting Hayes… But this very idea, as Mosby tells them, will lead to the defeat of the democracy. He says that the sectional unity of the southern people has always been their governing idea and the bane of their politics.

"So far from its being a remedy for anything, it has been the cause of most of the evils they have suffered. So long as it continues the war will be a controlling element of politics, for any cry in the south that unites the Confederates re-echoes through the north and rekindles the war fires there. Thus, every presidential contest becomes a battle between the two sections, and the south being the weaker must be the losing party. To insist on keeping up this sectional fight may be very heroic—so was the charge at Balaklava—but, in my opinion, is just as reckless and just as unwise. The reconstruction measures necessarily divided parties in the south on a color line, for the issue they presented was the political equality of the races. While the south was opposing it the republican party was on the side of the negro. But since the south has accepted it and incorporated it in the platform on which it has mounted its candidate I see no reason for continuing to divide on an issue which has become extinct. Having adopted all the principles of a party, and sanctioned all its measures, I can see no objection to voting for its candidate. Do you not see, then, that as long as we keep up the fight on the old lines, with the same allies and the same battle cries, the north will be suspicious of our good faith, no matter in what form we protest it! All that the republicans propose is to preserve what they have accomplished; the democrats are pledged not to disturb what the republicans have done. You cannot complain that the sincerity of the pledges of Governor Tilden to execute certain laws is distrusted when his supporters justify their opposition to Governor Hayes on the ground that his party has enacted these laws. To be consistent they should go for repealing them if they come into power."

Actually, had Tilden been elected, he would hardly have been under the control of the South. The South was politically impotent before the war! Indeed, that political impotency and what it meant to that section economically was one of the causes of the war. Tilden would just have been another Democrat like Buchanan and Cleveland and no more a pawn of the South than was any Republican office holder. But Mosby was wrong to believe that a Democrat could not win the presidency. Indeed, Tilden won the popular vote but was robbed of the office by a suspicious recount in the electoral college. It would therefore appear that the country did not line up North vs. South, or Tilden would have been overwhelmed even if the entire South had gone for him. It is obvious that many in the rest of the country were far less concerned with sectional issues than with matters of economics and the corruption in the Grant administration.

However, Tilden was no stranger to corruption, having been very much involved with New York City's infamous Tammany Hall, as Mosby was quick to point out. Apparently, however, the electorate preferred a new set of crooks to the old set.

In the following article Mosby was declared odd because of his method of warfare and now his politics. Apparently, the paper—a Democratic publication—felt the need to "comfort" Mosby by declaring that there was no longer any need for him to be concerned about the "Solid South" if a Democrat were elected:

Daily Democrat – **August 21, 1876**

MOSBY'S VIEWS

Col. John S. Mosby is as decided a partisan in politics as he was in war. The prompting motives under which he acts are always eccentric and peculiar. He went over to Grant when Grant was every day becoming more and more pronounced in his enmity to the Southern people, and he announces himself in favor of the election of Hayes and Wheeler, because though he fought for the Confederacy, he is now seriously alarmed at the prospect of a "Bourbon restoration."

Col. Mosby declares the sectional unity of the Southern people to have been "the governing idea and bane of their politics." While the white people of the south held undisputed political control of their own destinies, and had a common interest in the maintenance of the peculiar institution, which found its sanction and guarantee in the solemn utterances of the Federal Constitution, the charge of section unity might have been applied to them with some degree of propriety. But since the war these conditions have been entirely changed. The late amendments to the Federal Constitution have given to the emancipated slaves of the South a full and unquestioned political equality with the white voters of their section, and have at the same time destroyed that peculiar community of interest which the white Southrons had in the maintenance of an institution, forced upon them by exterior cupidity, and guaranteed by constitutional pledges. Hence, there no longer exist such a solidarity of political and material interests as, under ordinary circumstances, is likely to make the vote of the South a unit. Sectional unity among the Southern people need, therefore, be no longer dreaded.

One must wonder in which part of the country the journalist lived—or indeed, even in which country he lived! With the end of the war, the South was more a single political block than it had been before the war when there were a large number of old-fashioned Whigs—like John Mosby—active in the political arena! Mosby feared the continuation of what he termed "the solid South," and he was correct to do so, at least with regard to the effect that the war continued to have on that section politically and culturally. But the idea that only slavery knit the South together into a political and cultural unit could not have been more incorrect. There were far more reasons that the South remained united than mere slavery, just as slavery was not the only cause of the war. Indeed, the war as it was waged and Reconstruction as it played out did more to unify the South than anything that existed in the antebellum period. Southerners who opposed each other's viewpoints on many issues, including slavery and politics, were united by their ill-treatment at the hands of the rest of the nation led by the "Federal government!" Most unfortunate, at least for John Mosby, was that this ill-treatment had a political identity: the Republican Party.

Meanwhile the attacks on Mosby—almost always prefaced by negative comments on his service during the war—continued:

Burlington Weekly Free Press – August 25, 1876

R. Barnwell Rhett, Jr., of South Carolina, and Colonel John S. Mosby, of Virginia, have written letters. The former supports Tilden because he regards the Democratic party as friendly to the South. His argument is practically in support of the old doctrine of State rights. Mosby supports Hayes and Wheeler because he deprecates the perpetuation of sectional issues. The South, he says, professes to accept the results achieved by the Republican party, and if it does so honestly it should sustain them by supporting that party. He thinks that a Democratic victory would produce reaction where there should be progress.

John Mosby did not neglect the "rights" of the states as put forth in the Constitution, but he saw in the Southern claim of "states' rights" a rejection of the ultimate outcome as instituted by force of arms. It didn't mean that that decision was correct; it simply meant that it was irrevocable; that is, the South could do nothing to change it. And therefore, all attempts to return to a prewar sectional position was not only counterproductive but deeply damaging to the section. Mosby wanted his fellow Southerners to support policies favorable to the good of the country, including the South if they were put forth by the Republican Party. In other words, he wanted the name of the party to mean less than its policies to the voters!

But what was even more important, support of that party for its policies showed the rest of the nation that the war need no longer be fought in perpetuity—a situation that redounded very badly to the South! John Mosby wanted an end to a purely sectional positioning on the issues confronting the nation if for no other reason than that the South was wasting its political capital in an effort to achieve an impossible objective! If Southerners were supporting Tilden because his policies were good and he was an honest and decent man, then John Mosby had no problem with those who chose to support him. But he knew that neither was the case with Tilden, who was involved with Tammany Hall! He also knew that corruption tended to expand as its opportunities expanded. Thus, a little crook in New York City became a bigger crook in Albany and eventually a major criminal in Washington.

Daily National Republican – August 28, 1876

While in what I think we may as well designate in advance as Mosby's Congressional district, I found the ex-guerrilla chief's letter creating a great deal of interest. To my surprise, the Quakers were quite in love with it. They will support him, if nominated, almost to a man. It was curious enough to have some of the same persons who spoke favorably of his letter point out to me the supposed tree on which Mosby's men hung three disarmed Union prisoners in retaliation for something Custer had done, as it was said. It is in the western suburbs of Berryville. They are buried on a farm opposite the gallows-tree, owned by one of the Baltimore Tysons, a Quaker family.

This was a very odd article in the *National Republican*, a paper that had been supportive of Mosby. True, the paper had censured him when he supported the Conservatives, but they did not condemn his military service. Now as it was supposed that Mosby would not run for Congress as a Republican, the paper opposed his candidacy. But this story raised the issue of why the "Unionist" Quakers would support Mosby given his actions during war! Actually, Mosby's actions during the war were the reason that they supported him! They knew him to be just and merciful and, most important, honest!

And here now is the article, part of which is found at the beginning of this chapter:

New Orleans Republican – **August 20, 1876**

Jackson Standard – **August 31, 1876**

Letter from Colonel Mosby.

The following letter has been written by Col. Mosby to a former comrade, in reply to one urging him to support Tilden:

Warrenton, Va., August 6, 1876

My Dear Sir—I have just received our communication asking if it be true, as reported that I am supporting Hayes and Wheeler. It is true that I am a cordial and earnest advocate of the election of that ticket, notwithstanding you say that all the Southern people and especially the Confederate soldiers, are united in support of the Democratic. I hope, however, that in this you are mistaken, and that many men in the South of sound conservative and National sentiments will be found on the other side; however this may be, it will not divert me from my purpose. I thought you knew that I ceased to be a Confederate soldier about eleven years ago, and became a citizen of the United States. As a soldier I did conscientiously what I thought was my duty as a citizen I shall do the same thing as far as I know how.

The ground upon which you urge me to support Tilden and Hendricks is that they are the candidates of the Southern people, and, if elected, will be under their control. Now, it is because this thing is apparent that the election of Tilden was an impossibility. In attempting to grasp too much the South will lose everything. The sectional unity of the Southern people has been the governing idea and bane of their politics. So far from its being a remedy for anything it has been the cause of most of the evils they have suffered. So long as it continues the war will be a controlling element of politics, for any cry in the South that unites Confederate re-echoes through the North and rekindles the war fires there. Thus every Presidential canvass becomes a battle between the two sections, and the South, being the weaker must be the losing party. To insist on keeping up this sectional fight may be very heroic—so was the charge at Balaklava— but, in my opinion, is just as reckless and unwise.

The reconstruction measures necessarily divided parties in the South on a color line, for the issue they presented was the political equality of the races. While the South was opposing it, the Republican party was on the side of the negro. But since the South has accepted it and incorporated it in the platform on which it has mounted its candidate, I see no reason for continuing to divide on an issue which has become extinct. Having adopted all the principles of a party and sanctioned its measures, I can see no objection to voting for its candidate. Do you not see, then, that as long as we keep up the fight on the old lines, with the same allies and the same battle cries, the north will be suspicious of our good faith, no matter in what from we protest it.

All that the Republicans propose is to preserve what they have accomplished; the Democrats are pledged not to disturb what the Republicans have done. You cannot complain that the sincerity of the pledges of Governor Tilden to execute certain laws is distrusted when his supporters justify their opposition to Governor Hayes on the ground that his party has enacted these laws. To be consistent they should go for repealing them if they come into power.

I concur with you in a desire for a change in the policy of the National Government toward the South, but that can only come from a change in the attitude of the Southern people toward the Administration. You say that no one in the South is supporting Hayes but negroes and carpet-baggers. I should be sorry to think this were so, but if it were I should still vote for the candidate of my choice, and would not let this class deprive me of it. I suppose they support Hayes because they think it is to their interests to do so I think it would be equally to the interest of all the Southern people to do the same thing. But you say that even admitted it would be better for them to do so, yet, as it is notorious they will not, that I ought to surrender my individual convictions to the will of the majority. I don't think so. It is better for some to go right than for all to go wrong. If I think they are going wrong I could do no good by going with them. If they insist on breaking their necks, I don't intend to assist them. Besides, you say that if Tilden is elected he will be under the control of the Confederates. If that is so then you will have no need of me.

But suppose Hayes is elected, with a solid South against him—what are you going to do then? You do not see now, but you will then see the force of my logic. It was for these reasons that four years ago I urged the Southern people that if they really desired peace and reconciliation, to bury their passions and resentments and support the man who was not only the representative of an overwhelming majority of the North, but was the most powerful, as he had been the most generous of our foes, I have seen no cause to change my opinions, or regret my course. Many things have since occurred which no one deplores more than I do But "you can never say I did it" The responsibility is with those who adopted the fatal policy, "Anything to beat Grant." In the conflict they invited Grant to beat them. Having predicted all sorts of evils to result from the election of Grant, they have done all in their power to make their predictions come true.

You speak of the bitter hostility of the North toward the South. Well, four years of hard fighting is not calculated to make men love each other, neither is an everlasting rehearsal of the wrongs which each side imagines it has suffered going to bring us any nearer to a better understanding. Peace can only come with oblivion of the past. I know as well as you what the Southern people have had to endure; but this has been the experience of every conquered people. The figure of Judea on the Roman coin—veiled and weeping among her palm trees—was the type of those who fought for a cause that failed. It will always remain so.

The wound of war time alone can heal, but many grievances springing from our administration could long ago have been corrected by ceasing to oppose the inevitable. In doing this the Southern people have played into the hands of their worst enemies. From a chronic habit of complaining they too often injure a good cause by mixing up real with imaginary wrongs. For instance, Mr. Lamar, in the very able speech he recently delivered in the House of Representatives, said that what the South wanted was local self-government. I thought the South had it. If it has not, how did he get into Congress? If Mississippi has not local self-government, what sort of government is it which controls Mississippi and has just elected him to the United States Senate?

If you wish to know, then, the ground of my support of Hayes, it is this: Any good which the Southern people might derive from the election of Tilden would equally result from their support of Hayes. They can vote for Hayes, but they can't elect Tilden. But I am far from thinking that the election of a Democrat, even if such a thing were possible, would be an unmixed blessing to the South On the contrary, I fear it would open a Pandora's box of evils. The very remote prospect has already excited hopes and expectations that can never be realized. If such a thing should occur as the election of a President by a united South combining with a mere fragment of the North it would simply revive the old conflict of the sections. A transformation has taken place in the state of both parties. The Republican now represents the principles of Conservatism, while I can conceive no worse from of Radicalism than the reactionary movements that would fall on a Bourbon restoration. No one desires more than I do that the South should get its full share of the benefits and exercise a just influence in the administration of the Government. But this cannot be done by voting for Tilden.

But the Democrats are going to rebuild everything if they get possession of the Government, they say. Have you ever known a party out of power that did not promise reform to get in? Has there been one single abuse exposed for which the Democrats have not established a precedent? Do you think that a higher standard of morality would prevail in public life by transferring the influence of Tammany Hall to Washington? Has that been a proper school to educate reformers? I know noting of Governor Tilden except that he has long been the leader of his party in New York, whose colossal robberies have been the opprobrium of American politics. When Governor Tilden has purified politics in his own State it will be time enough then to turn his attention to the National Administration. It was only about twelve months ago that Tweed was released on habeas corpus by a decision of the New York Court of Appeals, composed of seven Democratic Judges. Mr. Charles O'Conor, the Nestor of the New York bar, in a letter published at the time, charged that the decision was procured through the corrupt influence of Tweed's money. Here was a splendid case for an investigation, far excelling in enormity the sale of sutlerships, yet these judges remain unimpeached, and are still wearing the ermine of justice.

I allude to this to show the tone of political morality of the party of which Governor Tilden has been the acknowledged head ever since the retirement of Tweed. He proposes to reform the civil service, but how? By a change in the system of appointments? Not at all; but by filling the offices with his partisans, who will flock to Washington "as fierce as famine and hungry as the grave." When the offices have thus been all filled, somebody will then have to reform the reformers. The character of such pretenders is well described in the language of Junius, as "resembling the termagant chastity of a prude, who while she prosecutes one lover for rape, invites the lewd embraces of another." That official trusts held under the administration have been abused no one denies; that the delinquents have not been screened by their party associates is equally true. Any observer can see that those who have been most forward in exposing corruption are the most earnest in supporting Hayes. But it is said that no party can reform abuses in its own ranks. I cannot accept such a theory of human depravity. I do not see why a party, like an individual, can't reform itself. If this were not so we would have to chronicle daily the rise and fall of a new party, It is claimed that the Democrats have done great good by their investigations. This may be so, and yet is no proof of capacity for the administration of affairs. The act of the detective may be very necessary and useful in the economy of government, but has never been considered an element of statesmanship.

I know every well the measure of denunciation which the expression of these sentiments will receive from the people in whose cause I shed my blood and sacrificed the prime of my life. Be it so; I wait on time for my vindication. To those who now assail me I reply, in the language of Edmund Burke when charged with deserting his constituents in opposing the American war, "I do not obey your instructions. No, I conformed to the instructions of truth and nature, and maintained your interests against your opinions. I am indeed, to look to your opinions as you and I must have five years hence. I was not to look to the flash of the day."

I have thus given you, at more length than I intended, the reasons that impel my political conduct.

Very truly, JOHN S. MOSBY.

The time had come for John Mosby. He could no longer support Ulysses Grant, to whom he owed so much personally, but he could do as he did with Grant—that is, support the Republican candidate because he found the Democratic contender unacceptable. And that is what he did.

In another article, it was claimed that this letter was a fraud in that Mosby was not responding to a former comrade who requested his support of Tilden but used the "letter to the editor" ploy to get his position into print. But John Mosby was never shy of approaching any publication directly if he wanted something to appear in print. His name was enough to assure that it would be printed. Whether the publication would agree or not, one doubts that such was a consideration with him. In fact, Mosby might have approached a paper known not to be an organ of the Republican Party for that very reason. But John Mosby was perfectly correct in his predictions of what Tilden's election would have meant to the South—a continuation of sectional politics with its resultant deleterious affects to that section.

The Advertiser – August 31, 1876

On the outside of this issue we publish "Extracts from Col. Mosby's Letter." Mosby was a rebel—a Confederate officer. He was wrong then but he is right now. Those old Union soldiers who are now with the Confederates, for the Confederate candidates Tilden and Hendricks, were right then but wrong now. They and Mosby and Foote, of Tennessee, and Longstreet, have changed places; the latter were against their country then, the former are against their country now. The man who was wrong and turns to do right, deserves more credit than the man who was right and then retrogrades. The man who is with Confederates now but was against them then, is deserving of more censure than praise. But the old Confederate who steps boldly forward out of the ranks of the Confederates and assists now in saving the Union from Confederate destruction, is deserving of more praise for his act now than censure for his act of rebellion then. The difference is this: the one takes a step forward while the other takes a step backward.

The "sectional" problem with the election of 1876 was not a matter of Democrat vs. Republican, but rather that the Democrat—Tilden—was being openly identified with the South; that is, the campaign was doing just what Mosby had warned against, keeping the political question directly involved with the war that had been over for a decade. As the South was never going to have the power to regain sufficient influence within the central government to force the nation to address its grievances—real or imagined—Mosby knew that the old bond of section had to be removed. As long as the South held on to sectionalism, Southerners could not rationally complain if the rest of the country did so as well.

The Democrat – September 1, 1876

COL. MOSBY'S LETTER

Probably no military officer in the Confederacy, with a like command did so much for Jeff and his cause as Colonel Mosby. Without doubt he was the most gallant and successful raider in the Southern army, and there can be no doubt as to his devotion to the "Lost Cause." Read his letter published elsewhere in this paper concerning the campaign now before us. It expresses the views of a fighting Confederate—not those of Southern patriots who "legislated" at Richmond in safety, while Mosby and his men were fighting gallantly in the field.

And still, the coverage went on; and in most of it, the war did indeed intrude. Ten years after Appomattox and with the various especially economic ills being suffered, the fact that the war was still the main topic—at least in Mosby's case—illustrated its importance not only as a political issue, but as a scourge with which to chastise John Mosby:

Bristol News – September 5, 1876

Col. Mosby objects to the election of Tilden, because he would be under the influence of ex-rebels. Is that all? Why it is said Grant is under Mosby's influence just in proportion to the number of federal soldiers Mosby hanged and shot.

The Democrat – September 7, 1876

How politics affect the character of some men is specially illustrated in Mosby's case. In war times he was denounced as a horse thief, an assassin, a bushwhacker and a guerrilla. Now that he is a friend of Grant journals of the Republican party tenderly refer to his war career as simply that of a soldier. It depends not a little whose mirror you look into as to the reflection you make.

Actually, the article in the Democrat was correct. Mosby was condemned during the war by the Northern organs, including those supporting the Democratic Party. It wasn't "party" that condemned him, but section. And certainly, he was more kindly treated by the Democratic papers after the war than the Republican—until he came out for Grant in 1872. But of course, this was to be expected just as those political organs changed position again in 1873 when Mosby supported Virginia Conservative Kemper. Well, actually, the Republican papers condemned him; but the Democratic papers chose to remain rather noncommittal. Mosby's politics lost him support in the press on both sides. Given that he was a most intelligent man, this fact alone proves that he acted from principle; there can be no other rational explanation.

A West Virginia paper defended Mosby's positions on both the election and the sectional policies of the South:

Wheeling Daily Intelligencer – October 12, 1876

Mosby, who did some of the best fighting on the Confederate side, and who since the war has, without reservations, honorably observed the terms of his surrender and sensibly conformed to the situation, perceives the suicidal folly of the Solid South movement. He sees that the unification of the South is but a reassertion of the old sectionalism that culminated in the rebellion. He sees that no matter how earnestly the South protests that it accepts the amendments and the results of the war, so long as it unites on the color-line, it gives the lie to all its protestations, and necessarily unites the people of the loyal State against that section, whose acceptance of the amendments is simply for the purpose of getting rid of them.

Yet Mosby's refusal to support the local Radicals was exactly upon that ground— that is, that it was the party of the Negro. Therefore, for the first time, there was a hint that John Mosby was not being as forthcoming as was usual with him or that he saw his rejection of "negro rule" as different from the policies of Southern Democrats with regard to race. He refused to support the local Republicans because he perceived them to be run by the Radicals and manned by carpetbaggers and freedmen. On the other hand, he supported the national party because he saw the Northern white man being against a government run by crooks and blacks. But in this, Mosby was wrong. Certainly, the Northern white man—Republican and Democrat—did not want Negroes in his government! (Indeed, the Northerner didn't even want them in his state!) But Northern whites had no problem with the South being thus afflicted and, in fact, enjoyed the humiliation of Southern whites forced to live under the power of a race that had been but lately in servitude to them. Nonetheless, Mosby walked a very fine line here, chiding his fellow Southerners for rejecting the Republican Party on the basis of race when he had done that same thing with the party in Virginia in 1873!

Of course, it is possible— though it is only speculation—that Mosby believed that the end of Reconstruction meant the end of the Radical-freedman Republican party in the Southern states and that now that party was little different than the Democrats, at least with regard to race. If this indeed was Mosby's reasoning, then his support of the post-Reconstruction state Republican Party could not be considered hypocrisy.

Finally, John Mosby believed that Hayes would be carried into office as had Grant. But the times were changing. Actually, Tilden won the popular vote, South and North, and should have been president. Mosby could not see how a Democrat could be elected this soon after the war, given the ongoing sectionalism; but he lived in the South, where the war remained the focal point of every political, moral, and social argument. Things were changing in the North. The war had been over for a decade, and most people had moved on, at least to a greater degree than had the people of the South albeit, it was far easier for Northerners than for Southerners as the war was fought in the South.

Furthermore, the rise of Democrats in larger Northern cities was changing electoral demographics. As a result, whereas Mosby was right in 1872 about the South needing to vote for a "sure winner" in Grant, by 1876, the Republican Party was no longer a "sure winner."

Then there appeared in the *National Republican* what must be seen as a true witness to Mosby's sad and sorry situation in his own state. It was a letter from an office seeker whose position in his "home" was "uncomfortable" because of the help he had received from John Mosby:

> **National Republican – October 13, 1876**
>
> Southern Public Opinion.
>
> At the solicitation of a young man of this city, Colonel J. S. Mosby procured his appointment to a position in the Internal Revenue Collector's office. The following is the young man's reply:
>
> "Richmond, Va., Sept. 25, 1876. "Colonel John S. Mosby:
>
> "My Dear Sir:
>
> Yours of the 21st has been duly received, and I have waited, so as to have time to consider your very kind offer. I find, after mature deliberation, that 'public opinion' here will not let me take it. I am under many obligations to you for your kindness. If it were anywhere else than here I should take it at once. Although a poor man, and have to make my living by working very hard, still I am bound to be governed by policy to a great extent. If you can do anything for me away from this city I shall esteem it a great kindness.
>
> What kind of a white man is this that is afraid of "public opinion." Even the negroes exercise a higher standard of manhood than that. The "public opinion" that prevents a young man from accepting an honorable position in the service of the United States Government sadly needs reforming, and the young man who shows so little true manhood needs reforming too.— Richmond (Va.) Republican.

This young man's letter demonstrated the situation in which Mosby found himself for simply living the dictates of his conscience. If anything, it was even worse in its point of view than was the case with those who openly rejected the man. This individual wanted Mosby's help—he just didn't want anyone to know that he has asked for or received it! Of course, it is hard to blame a mere youth when men like Wade Hampton wanted Mosby's help; but when it was discovered that they had asked (and received) that help, they promptly abused him in the press, declaring that they had "no idea" that Mosby was such a contemptible person and would never have sought his assistance had they but known! This young man at least had the decency not to blame John Mosby for his situation, but the opinion of his neighbors and his own lack of character.

Then there were some thoughts by two partisan newspapers on the sorry situation of the Republican Party's Southern adherents:

National Republican - October 17, 1876

The fierce denunciation and ostracism of such men as Longstreet and Mosby, who rendered faithful and gallant service to the cause of the Confederacy, and who now see that the only hope of a restoration of fraternal feeling and consequent peace and prosperity for the Southern States is in a frank and unreserved acceptance of the issues of the war, has no doubt deterred thousands of Southern men from openly opposing the mad policy and aims of the Democratic party.

The Republican – October 19, 1876

MOSBY ON THE SITUATION

The name of Colonel Mosby revives keen recollections of the rebellion, especially along the Potomac region. He was the gayest of the partisan troopers the conflict produced, and paid the least possible respect to the accepted warfare. He had a little army of his own, entertained it with his booty, and made his name a terror on the line of the Baltimore and Ohio highway, in the camps of Federal scouting parties, and in all Union homes within the possible swoop of his apparently ubiquitous command. He was the last of all the rebellious forces in Virginia to surrender, and he would be on the war-path yet had not the armies of the insurgents wasted away into peace. When the war ended, Colonel Mosby sat down in the desolation of his beloved Virginia, as he would say—like the figure of Judea on the Roman coin, veiled, and weeping among her palm trees;" but weeping and wailing didn't feed the empty stomachs of discomfited Confederates or buy their children frocks. He saw only husks as the offering of his brethren, while there were favors and fatness in the temples of Republicanism. A brave warrior in war, he was no less brave in peace, and he crossed his nether limbs under the Presidential mahogany and became fraternal with Grant. His brave guerrillas were summoned one by one to Washington or to official duties in Virginia, until an assessment upon the administration employees would be answered by most of the unkempt but fearless troopers who answered Mosby's roll-call in the mountain fastness after a raid.

Col. Mosby is therefore for peace, and why shouldn't he be? He is for Grant and regrets that a third or even a fourth term wasn't possible, and in that he is wise as the ox that knoweth its owner. He is for Hayes, and it is meet that he should be so, for sad would be the songs of his children if Tilden should happen to be called to revise the list of Washington and Virginia officials about the 4th of March next. Whatever may be thought of Mosby, let it not be said that he is a fool, for it wouldn't be true. He is a straight-forward politician, deals squarely all the time, always hits above the belt, and goes in for close bargains and prompt delivery. Grant is his man, and Hayes is his hope.—Phila. Times.

John Mosby was certainly "straight-forward" and dealt squarely and hit above the belt in all of his encounters, but he was no politician. Had he been one, his condition might have been considerably better; for a politician is a man who senses the way the wind is blowing and goes with it. It wasn't that Mosby didn't know which way the wind blew, but to him, all that mattered was what he believed was the right thing to do. If that went with the wind, fine! If it did not, so be it.

Mosby then reiterated his position on the sectional nature of politics and the damage that it did to the South:

The *Leavenworth Weekly Times* – October 19, 1876

WHAT MOSBY SAYS.

Col. John S. Mosby says that he does not think the Democratic politicians of the North have accepted in good faith and with loyal sentiments the results of the war. He also says: "Elect Tilden, and a lawless element would arise in the South that Tilden couldn't control. It would be Andy Johnson's Administration over again. If Tilden is defeated this time, the Southern people will cut loose from the Northern Democracy, and will never attempt another sectional contest."

WHAT IT MEANS.

In an interview with a New York Herald man, a few days ago, Colonel Mosby declared strongly his conviction that so long as the sectional unity of the Southern States shall continue, the war will be a controlling element in politics. Moreover, in the devotion of the South to Tilden, he sees the blooming hope of the defeated secessionists that, by a Democratic victory, they may in part at least, realize the better part of their lost cause. If the South elects Tilden, the South will rule him, and however Northern Democrats might resist, they could effect little.

In this, Mosby was wrong. The South hadn't the strength to rule any national politician, especially the chief executive. Tilden would have used the South as Northern Democrats used it before the war to further their own ambition and power in the North! But whatever the antebellum situation, Mosby was right in saying that the South, in aligning itself uncritically with the Democrats on issues arising out of the war assured that it was always going to be in the minority whatever the state of that party. Mosby believed that if the South could get past the war, the parties would begin to identify themselves along different lines and with other issues. This was seen most clearly in the populist campaign of William Jennings Bryan in which the old Democratic Party virtually disappeared, swallowed up by Bryan's Populists.

But the questionable election of Hayes in 1876 only served to deepen the South's dislike and contempt for the Republican Party in general and John Mosby in particular.

Richland Beacon – October 23, 1876 (Edited)

[Part of an article-vph]

COL. MOSBY AS A LAWYER.

Col. John A. [sic] Mosby, styled by some the Francis Marion of the great rebellion, by others a murderous bushwhacker, who put out his shingle as a lawyer in this city several months since, has not yet especially distinguished himself before the District bar. The fact is, his clients as yet, are few; the impression seeming to exist among litigious people that the Colonel, while he may have been a successful bushwhacker, does not occupy a place in the front rank of the legal profession.

But the law practice seems to be a secondary consideration with him. He is thoroughly absorbed in politics, and can be found almost any day discussing the situation with Zach Chandler, Chairman of the *National Republican* Committee, Judge Edmunds, its Secretary, or some one else who is running the political machinery of the Republican party. Mosby is now a social and political nonentity in his native State, Virginia; and having cast his lot with the Republican party, he is endeavoring to make the best of the situation.

Notwithstanding the disfavor with which he is regarded in Virginia there are hundreds among the Conservatives (the word "Democrat" is not much used in that State) who, while diametrically opposed to him in politics, and in reality execrating his apostasy, are quite willing to humbly solicit his kind offices in obtaining for themselves or their friends positions under Grant's administration. It is due to Mosby to say that, while understanding the feeling with which he is regarded by those self same people, he makes no distinction between them and Republicans, and that many a Virginia Conservative holding office under the Administration to-day owes his good fortune to Mosby and Mosby alone. Mosby no longer wields any influence in Virginia. The conservative element could have forgiven him for his opposition, in 1872, to a life-long abolitionist like Horace Greeley; but they regard his present advocacy of Hayes in opposition to a straight-out Democrat like Sam Tilden, as wholly unpardonable.

For some reason, one of the usual charges against Mosby was that he was a poor lawyer. And this charge was validated here because he opened a law office in Washington. But he had no choice because he was—as this article makes quite clear—"dead" in Virginia and could not earn a living there. Mosby's lack of clients had nothing to do with his legal ability, which was considerable. Along with everything else, potential clients realized that he was not popular with jurists, a fact that placed their cases in an awkward position despite his talents.

Even more significant, Tilden strenuously opposed the South during the war. If Mosby's rejection of Greeley was acceptable because of Greeley's history against the South, then his rejection of Tilden should also have been acceptable as he was little better than Greeley or Hayes. And finally, Mosby was rejected by Virginia Conservatives long before the election of 1876. His efforts to foster a relationship between them and the Grant administration destroyed him in that party.

All things, good and bad, come to an end and so did the election of 1876. John Mosby was said to have "paid his respects" to the "winner" Hayes while the *Chicago Tribune* printed a letter of thanks he had written to one of his very few defenders:

Chicago Tribune - November 6, 1876
MOSBY

He Pays His Respects to Tilden. Special Dispatch to The Tribune.

Philadelphia, Nov. 4.—Democrats have been making, in the South particularly, constant and virulent attacks on Col. Mosby. They represent him as a hired agent of the Administration, and endeavor to excite hostility against him as a deserter from the Confederacy. He has written in reply to one of these charges the following letter, which needs no further explanation:

Warrenton, Va., Nov. 2.—

Col. James R. O'Neal—

Dear Sir: I have just received your letter of the 30th ult., informing me that a democratic orator in Philadelphia has stated that Gen. Grant had appointed me to some office. I am glad that you denounce the statement as a lie. It originated with the Tilden Bureau, and was pronounced by me to be false in a letter published several weeks ago. They still continue to circulate this and other lies about me. I have never received in any shape the slightest favor or benefit of any kind from Gen. Grant's Administration, although I was his cordial supporter. The few Confederates he has appointed to office in the South were as loyal to the Government during the War as Tilden, and are much more so now. I am unable to account for the ferocity with which I have been pursued by the Tilden organs unless it be that they think their candidate has a claim upon me for my support on account of the messages of sympathy and cheer I received from him during that unhappy period when I was fighting to overthrow the government of the Union. But for the advice of such men in the North as Tilden the South would never have plunged into a disastrous war, and

> Launched her fortunes on that perilous bark,
> Built in the eclipse and rigged with curses dark.

In haste, very truly. John S. Mosby.

The foregoing letter was received by a gentleman in this city today.

Mosby's willingness to acknowledge those who defended him against the calumnies of his enemies and his readiness to take the time to address those attacks himself when no one else stepped forward puts the lie to those of his biographers who state that he "did not care" what other people thought or said of him. He most assuredly did care unless his critic was beneath his contempt. On the other hand, even then, he would respond if the newspaper had a large circulation and was read by what he considered objective and intelligent people.

Finally, an interesting article on Mosby's legal skills appeared. His abilities as a lawyer had been roundly abused by his detractors, a matter that continued throughout his life. This little story told quite another tale:

Evening Star - November 25, 1876 (Edited)
ALEXANDRIA

The receivership of the Midland Railroad—Judge Keith Refuses to Remove Mr. Barbour.—The case involving the receivership of the Virginia Midland railroad was fully argued to-day in the circuit court of Alexandria city by the distinguished counsel present representing the various parties interested.

Much was said on both sides, but the gist of the matter was most squarely put by Colonel Mosby when he said he might consent to admit all the allegations of the petitioners and still they would make a case for the interposition of the court, inasmuch as it was perfectly right that the parties having the largest interest should confer together in the selection of a receiver. Judge Keith was only a few minutes in deciding the case, and refused to allow the prayer of the petitioners by which decision Mr. J. S. Barbour is retained as receiver.

The above article should be remembered in light of the rise in the Virginia Republican Party of General William Mahone. The railroad mentioned was run by Mahone, and there was a good deal of financial "hanky-panky" involved in its bankruptcy of which Mosby became aware.

One of the last articles about John Mosby in the year was very poignant indeed and illustrated the pathos of his forlorn domestic situation:

Evening Star – **November 28, 1876**

ALEXANDRIA

In the Wrong Church.—Yesterday morning Col. John S. Mosby with two ladies and his little child started out to attend St. Mary's church, the Colonel's family being Catholics. Seeing the large cross which surmounts the front of St. Paul's church (Episcopal) the party mistook it for a Catholic church, entered the building and were shown to the pew of Mr. R. M. Lawson, where they were courteously received and provided with seats. They were confirmed in their previously conceived idea that they were in a Catholic church by the newly erected altar lights which are made in imitation of candles. In a few minutes the rector, Rev. Dr. Norton, appeared and commenced the service; when the Colonel, discovering his error, retired with his party, and was shown the way to St. Mary's church.

Pauline would not have mistaken the Episcopal edifice for her beloved Catholic sanctuary, but her husband was all at sea in these matters.

For some little time after the much-disputed election, there was concern that a coup d' état might be attempted. John Mosby promised that he would lead troops to prevent any attack upon outgoing president Grant arising from an effort to prevent Hayes taking office; but he was not the only person to fear such an event:

Memphis Daily Appeal – **December 29, 1876**

Mosby Ready to Fight for Grant

The New York Herald publishes an interview with Colonel John S. Mosby, in which the following occurs: "If," said Colonel Mosby, "there shall be any fighting as a result of all this political business, I shall be on the side of General Grant and the administration. I have read what General Shelby said to one of the Herald correspondents in St. Louis, and I stand precisely where he stands. He promises to raise a regiment in Missouri to sustain General Grant if he shall inaugurate Governor Hayes (that is, if it be necessary to do so), and I will undertake to do the same thing in Virginia, in less than twenty-four hours."

And so a year of turmoil and fateful decisions passed. Perhaps John Mosby hoped for better things in the upcoming year now that the election was over. If he did, he was bound to be severely disappointed.

Chapter 16

1877

Fluctuat nec mergitur ~
It is tossed by the waves, but it does not sink

"In a false quarrel there is no true valor." ~ **William Shakespeare**

1877 BEGAN WITH two papers supporting Mosby's contention that Hayes and the Republicans were better for the South than Tilden and The Democrats. Indeed, the whole idea that The Democrats from the North supported the South was ludicrous as this account of that party's convention before the fatal election of 1860 makes quite plain:

> "Men in the Free Soil faction of New York Democrats were nicknamed "Barnburners," and compared to the farmer who burned down his barn ... to get rid of the rats. The conservatives were called "Hunkers," apparently a Dutch term meaning "conservative." undisputed boss of [one faction] and their delegation to Charleston, was Dean Richmond, a tough, portly, broad-shouldered Buffalo businessman. Although he never could write or speak with perfect grammar, the often profane, intimidation chieftain achieved great power in both business and politics. Richmond consolidated seven upstate railroads into the New York Central system, lobbying the legislature—by fair means and foul—into making it all legal. Against Dean Richmond's [faction was] arrayed the mayor of New York City, Fernando Wood, and his Mozart Hall boys, Tammany's rivals, and his mouthpiece, the New York Daily News. [De Alva Alexander said of Wood]: "As a politician he was as false as his capacity would allow him to be, having no hesitation, either from principle or fear, to do anything to serve his purpose."
>
> Wood arrived early [in Charleston] at the Syracuse hall, bringing along a gang of roughs, headed by John C. Heenan, "the Benecia Boy," the champion prizefighter. When [Richmond's faction] came in later, Peter Cagger mounted the platform and declared John Stryker temporary chairman. In the ensuing melee, Stryker was pushed off the platform and "an intimidating array of pistols" appeared. To make sure that his delegates won all the New York seats at Charleston, Dean Richmond played a double game. He agreed to vote with the [Stephen] Douglas force ... At the same time he made a solemn promise to [Louisiana] Senator [John] Slidell and the Southerners that he would go along with them in nominating an acceptable presidential candidate who would unite the party. By his double-dealing, he persuaded the Southerners to go along with seating all of his delegates instead of letting half of them go to the forces of Mayor Wood, who promised to vote with the South. Some credentials committee members proposed dividing the New York seats evenly between the Hards and the Softs. But in the end, Dean Richmond got them all. The Southerners, who went along with the decision, found too late that they had been tricked. Douglas would hold New York. Also working for Douglas, and speaking up for him in the hotels and barrooms of Charleston, were numerous friends eager to share in the spoils of the next Democratic

administration in Washington. A hostile South Carolinian, writing from Charleston, sniffed that the Douglas men "came here like a gang of wolves, or a flock of vultures, bent on spoil, without compromise or alternative; their howlings are for blood."

[The] premier orator…William Lowndes Yancey, took the stage amid a storm of applause, cheers, "hi-hi's and cock-crows." He appealed to the Northerners to understand why the Southerners must have a platform that recognized their rights. "Ours," he said, "is the property invaded; ours are the institutions which are at stake; ours is the peace that is to be destroyed; ours is the honor at stake—the honor of children, the honor of families, the lives, perhaps of all—all of which your course may ultimately make a great heaving volcano of passion and crime." By "the great heaving volcano of passion and crime," Yancey referred to the Southerners' nightmare that the abolition of slavery would mean turning loose four million blacks to roam about in idleness and crime, and to threaten white peoples' lives. The prospect of a social revolution, even a race war, was no idle fancy; it filled the Southerners' minds with horror."

Richmond favored *"a platform to suit the North so as to make a great Northern Democratic party and gain a majority of the representatives in Congress and let the South go to the devil." "What the hell do we care about the South?" Richmond shouted. "What we want, by God, is a Democratic party at the North. Damn the South! …"* [emphasis vph](*Lincoln: The Road to War*, Frank van der Linden, 1998, (excerpts), pp. 29-38)

As can be seen, when the South appealed to The Democratic party in 1860 seeking protection for the rights, lives, and property of its citizens, The Democrats cared for nothing but gaining power in the North! It was this attitude that eventually split the party and produced three candidates, thus assuring the election of Abraham Lincoln. It was perhaps this memory of the history of The Democratic party that brought about the judgments made here:

Bismarck Weekly Tribune – **January 3, 1877**

The New York Herald says: "We agree with Col. Mosby that four years fair and conservative treatment of the South under the Presidency of Gov. Hayes would leave that section in a better condition than four years under Gov. Tilden or any other Democratic administration."

Wichita City Eagle – **January 4, 1877**

The Great Democratic Paper Says Hayes Election is Best for the South.

The *New York Herald* agrees with Col. Mosby "that four years fair and conservative treatment of the South under the Presidency of Gov. Hayes, would leave that section in a better condition than four years under Gov. Tilden or any other Democratic administration.

It is ironic to note that those papers agreeing with Mosby usually put that sentiment in very few words, while those against him printed much longer diatribes. It is also interesting to note that the Herald was a New York paper, and Tilden had been governor of that state. Had it desired to do so, the Eagle could have made a great deal more of that thought-provoking fact.

Bristol News – **January 9, 1877**

The apologists of Gov. Wade Hampton's recent course may say what they choose, but we are sorry to see the letter he wrote to Hayes, and to hear of the one he wrote to Mosby. To say that we have greatly admired his moderation and firmness during the month of November, is to use very temperate language, and we shall not condemn him for the letters alluded to. It is just possible that the horrors which have poisoned the cup of all genteel and honest South Carolinians have been such that they should be pardoned for any apparent readiness to abandon their democratic friends of the whole union to a fall which they think inevitable; but it does seem to us that they should at least continue to make a show, however moderate, of common cause with those who have never yet deserted them, and who have been willing to bear all things for periods that seem endless, rather than take any near cuts to their exclusive success.

If Gov. Hampton's letter to Mosby does not mean that Grant's assumption of power must be regarded, then what does it mean? If his letter to Hayes does not mean a readiness to acquiesce in his inauguration by the means used to obtain it, then what does it mean? If it does not place his prospects and rights to the Presidency as high as Tilden's, then what could it have been written for? Certain it is that its effect is and has been to strengthen Hayes column.

We shall not believe in the disloyalty of Hampton and Gordon and Hill and Lamar until the belief shall be irresistible, but we are sorry to see so much written about a coalition between Hayes and leading Southern Democrats, and to see these assertions confirmed by such letters as those of Gov. Hampton to Hayes and Mosby, and to have them followed by a visit on the part of Judge Mackey, of Columbus. We shall not believe that Gov. Hampton, at least, means to pander to the Grant-Hayes influence, but we are compelled to believe that these things, however intended, have stiffened and aided our enemies.

The setting for this article was twofold; the first was Hampton's plea to Mosby for him to ask Grant not to send Federal troops into South Carolina after widespread racial disturbances. Hampton had been elected governor of that state in a very questionable election; but he promised Mosby that upon assuming office, he would restore order, something that obviously meant protecting the rights of the Negroes. Mosby, happy to show Grant's willingness to succor the Southern people, immediately went to the president. Grant promised not to send troops as long as order was maintained. So far, so good! But when it was discovered that Hampton had gone to the "odious" Mosby for help, he (Hampton) was castigated in the press. Rather than pointing out that Mosby's efforts had prevented the Federal government sending troops into the state to restore order, Hampton turned on Mosby, something that hurt the latter deeply—another obvious example of Mosby's gentle naïveté. In response to Hampton's assault, Mosby made the comment about the fellow who was asked to "bell the cat" but received no thanks for that useful but hazardous, effort.

The second circumstance was the contested election of 1876 in which Tilden received the majority of the popular vote and would have prevailed in the electoral college had it not been for some very shifty political maneuverings. In return for those maneuverings, Hayes promised to, and did indeed remove the remaining Federal troops from the South. Interestingly, Mosby's old adversary Eppa Hunton, as a Virginia elector, voted for Hayes! Yet, Hunton did not become a pariah for helping to put Hayes in the White House, while Mosby became one for voting for him.

The article then complained that Hampton was "acquiescing" to Hayes's inauguration—as if Hampton could have done anything to prevent it! Yes, Hayes's election was bitterly contested; but in the end, he became president. And just as John Mosby would have had to accept Tilden had he been elected, for the paper to suggest that Hampton should have withheld his recognition of Hayes as chief executive of South Carolina is preposterous. To begin with, Mosby was a mere citizen while Hampton was the elected governor of a state! What would Hampton or South Carolina have gained by such a stupid and meaningless act? It would have changed nothing, and it certainly would not have benefitted either that state or the South! The nation was moving on, and the South was being left behind to wallow in self-pity and rage! It was that very condition John Mosby feared and worked so tirelessly to prevent, destroying himself in the effort. There was also a question as to whether those who held this worldview were altogether sane. The "Grant-Hayes influence?" One had been the president of the United States for two terms, and the other was the newly elected president when all was said and done. What other, and greater, "influence" was there for any politician? And then the paper referred to "enemies." Now political parties look upon the members of other party as "adversaries." But the term "enemies"—especially under these circumstances (that is, after a terrible war and a bitterly contested election)—suggested a very different understanding of that relationship. These were not just political and doctrinal differences, but matters that once occasioned the shedding of much blood. Is it any wonder that those having such an attitude saw in Mosby and men like him an adversary and a traitor rather than a well-intentioned, honorable man on the other side of the issues of the day?

The *National Republican* then came to the fore and publicly proclaimed Mosby's martyrdom for his support of that paper's party:

National Republican - January 10, 1877

Col. J. S. Mosby

[From the Valley Virginian]

An illustration of the intolerant and proscriptive spirit of The Democratic party of Virginia may be found in the recent history of Col. John S. Mosby. Probably no officer in the Southern army from Virginia gained a more brilliant reputation as a dashing cavalryman than Mosby—none won more unfading laurels on account of daring courage and unbroken success in nearly all of his hazardous campaigns. A supporter of Douglas in 1860—a Union man from conviction, he exerted his influence to arrest the wild spirit of secession that was careering over his State and section, believing that there were remedies in the Union for all the ills of which the South felt aggrieved.

But his devotion to his native State was stronger than his attachment to the Union, and when her authorities decided, against his views of expediency, to link her fortunes with the Cotton States, in a combined effort to establish a separate government, Mosby was one of the first to offer his services as a partisan ranger. His daring and brilliant military services are a part of the history of that sanguinary struggle. He did his duty as he understood it at the time, and did it nobly and bravely.

In 1872, when the Conservative or Democratic party of Virginia took to its embrace Horace Greeley as the exponent of its principles and its candidate for the Presidency, Col. Mosby, like a great many other Confederates, refused to support him, and cast his vote for Gen. Grant. He believed then and believes now that the South had no truer friend than Gen. Grant as President, and this would have been more signally illustrated if a disposition had been manifested by the people of the State to give his administration a fair trial, and live up to the obligations of amnesty and the situation which they had promised to accept. Col. Mosby himself proved this. His support of the administration was honest, unselfish and from a sense of duty. It was recognized as such, and consequently many favors were extended to Virginians (former Confederates) through his influence. Never asking a position that he himself might be benefited, yet many appointments were given to his friends, simply upon his request and recommendation.

There was nothing in this that any fair-minded man could object to, and much in it that every one should approve. It was the basis of a policy which, if it had been general adopted, would have placed Virginia in a far different condition to that which now distinguishes her. Had the same national spirit—the same loyal adherence to the results of the war—been more generally exhibited and practiced, thousands and thousands of intelligent immigrants, with their skill and capital, would now be aiding in developing the rich resources of the State, instead of contributing their energies to the growth and prosperity of less prejudiced and more liberal communities. Colonel Mosby saw, as every impartial and unprejudiced man must see, that this was the true policy of the South, especially of Virginia. It was what our obligations required of us, and it was precisely what was necessary to build up the material interests of the old Commonwealth. Instead of the people, however, joining in this liberal, wise and commendable policy, they turned against Colonel Mosby. They pursued him with a vindictive hatred and insane prejudice such as had never before been directed against any man, except in the case of General Longstreet in Louisiana and General Orr in South Carolina. Although a resident in Virginia, with family and property located where he had lived before and during the war, with all his sympathies and affections for his native State still warm and active, yet because from a sense of duty he gave an ardent support to the national administration, he was proscribed socially, his business taken from him, and he (was) absolutely driven from Virginia to seek, through his profession of the law, the means to provide the comforts of life for his children. He had a large and lucrative practice, but it all left him, and for no other reason than that he chose to support the laws and Constitution of his country and the administration that upholds them.

The Republican was one of the few publications that defended Mosby. However, later on, when he uncovered corruption among Republican office holders in China, the paper's view became considerably less favorable. In the end it apparently depended upon whose ox was being gored. Then suddenly, the huge events of the day gave way to smaller matters. But small or great, the papers still "asked Mosby":

Stark County Democrat – January 18, 1877

A member of Congress asked Mosby the other day what all this war amounted to, and he answered that—"the fellows who are talking fight remind me of barnyard chickens cackling for corn."—[Radical Exchange.]

A hundred years and more ago the British lords and their satellites used to talk thus, and turn up their noses at the Americans. They hooted at the idea of American "rebels" amounting to anything. Mosby is a base follower of a drunken master, and consorts at Washington with the Grant-Babcock-Shepherd crew.

The "war" being spoken of was a possible war with Great Britain arising out of evolving interpretations of the Monroe Doctrine regarding a small piece of land in South America. Mosby rejected any need or cause for such a war and said so. Obviously, this Democratic organ was desirous of "mixing it up" with the British or Mosby—or both. Mention was made of Mosby's first "visit" to the Hayes White House. Very soon, he would find that he was not nearly so welcome there as when Grant occupied that dwelling:

Ouachita Telegraph - **March 23, 1877**

Among those who had interviews with Governor Hayes, yesterday, was Col. Mosby. Col. Mosby called merely to pay his respects. During the war Gov. Hayes was at one period engaged in the campaigns in the Valley of Virginia, and he and Col. Mosby exchanged some jocular remarks on the alternate games of hide and seek in which they and their respective commands had indulged. In conversing on the political situation Gov. Hayes remarked that the question presented to the country was whether to continue in a semi-state of war or to have peace, and said that he intended to go in for a vigorous prosecution of peace. Col. Mosby said to him that in his belief his policy would be heartily responded to by the Southern people, that the ice was beginning to crack, a big thaw was coming, and in the course of a few weeks under his beneficent policy, the "solid South" would dissolve and break up. Gov. Hayes, with much animation and feeling replied, "I hope so."—Baltimore Sun, 12th.

Mosby continued to believe that the "solid South" could be broken up, allowing the individual states of the section to choose the party and the programs that were of benefit to that state. But it did not happen, at least in his lifetime with the occasional exception. Another article blamed Mosby for all the ills suffered by the Republicans in Virginia. He was accused of starting the "third term project" and also with "a great deal more deviltry":

Weekly Register - **April 5, 1877**

"A Republican" writes to the New York Tribune from Richmond to complain that Mosby is doing the Republican party in Virginia irreparable injury. He says Mosby was the author of the "Third-term" project and the originator of a great deal more of the deviltry that has brought the Republican party into such much ill-repute For these reasons, and because he claims Mosby "is not entitled to the respect of any decent man in this country," he wants him sat upon.

He confesses, though, that they are evidences that Mosby's influence will be greater Hayes than it was with Grant, so that it would be interesting to learn what he is going to do about it.

The Republican Party in Virginia was in "ill-repute" long before John Mosby had anything to do with it. Indeed, Mosby, an old-line Whig, could only support the national party because he considered Republicans at the state level to be the kind of men one found in a penitentiary. And it is doubtful that the "third term" movement was Mosby's idea. Whatever John Mosby's personal relationship with Ulysses Grant, it did not begin until 1872! And certainly, he was absent the sort of power necessary to initiate any such movement.

Finally, the "Republican" mentioned in the Tribune sounded suspiciously like someone in the Hayes administration who wanted to see John Mosby removed from sight as a reminder of the Grant presidency. In an earlier chapter, part of a letter from civil servant Frank Bramhall indicated that Mosby was to be "eased out" of any Southern Republican influence in the administration, influence that was more than likely to occur now that Mosby had actually embraced that party. It is probable that when Grant asked Hayes to find a post for the little lawyer "far away," Hayes was more than glad to do so. Of course, lest the party be seen as "ungrateful," stories began appearing in the Republican press that Mosby's situation had not changed despite the change of occupants in the White House:

Democratic Press – May 17, 1877

Mosby Still in Favor

The Washington special of the Enquirer says, 'It may gratify the Western Reserve of Ohio to know that Col. John S. Mosby is a daily visitor at the White House, and is consulted with reference to the distribution of patronage in Virginia. Although Hayes was foot-sore and weary to-day, after his Philadelphia trip, he gave Mosby an extended audience.'

The next article, however, was one of those that had no reason to exist except to insult and defame. This is "newspaper coverage" at its worst:

New Orleans Democrat – May 31, 1877

COL. MOSBY.

His Appearance at Washington.

Col. Mosby, ex-guerrilla, is described by a correspondent of the Cincinnati Gazette as a man of medium height and thickness, with light gray, nervous eyes, and hair of a subdued mouse color, just beginning to shade down into gray.

"When he was young and ardent it was probably enraged rat color. He appears ever to be looking for somebody, and if your eye meets his you at once fancy you are the man he is looking for, or that he means to watch you. I should, perhaps, call it an inquiring look; but, whatever it is, I don't exactly like it, [even] if the war has been over twelve years."

Suddenly, under the circumstances, the press began to report that John Mosby was no longer welcome at the White House. Of course, both sides were quite gleeful about the matter:

Ottawa Free Trader - July 7, 1877

Poor Mosby, Grant's peculiar guerilla cut-throat friend from Virginia, finds that things "ain't as they used to was" about the White House at Washington. Hayes and his cabinet have shown him an emphatic cold shoulder, and when he applied recently to have one of his friends appointed to the Richmond collectorship, the president took special pains to have the man appointed whom Mosby had been making war upon.

Now it would appear that John Mosby was "on the outs" despite finally throwing in the towel on his delicate balancing act between the national and the state parties and becoming a bona fide Republican. Hayes had his complete support; but the new "questionable" chief executive had apparently determined to throw over his earnest supporter, probably more as a way of distancing himself and his party from Grant than from Mosby, the two men now being considered almost as one. The downward spiral of both men was well underway, and soon, Grant would find himself almost as vilified as Mosby. Only his death brought him back to hero status. John Mosby, on the other hand, had no such redeeming act to fall back upon. Of course, the press loved the fact that Mosby would now get his "comeuppance" from the man he loyally supported after paying such a high price in his personal life for so doing:

Stark County Democrat **- September 6, 1877**

PERSONAL JOTTINGS

Gen. Mosby is not so well pleased with Hayes as he was with Grant. He complains of the distribution of offices.

Mosby's use of the distribution of offices was his way of fighting against the local Radical Republican government and an attempt to help white Southerners see the national party in a different light. When Hayes no longer allowed him the means to fight the Radicals, it soon became obvious that his ability to aid Virginia politically—whatever it had cost him personally—was over.

News & Times **– September 15, 1877 (Edited)**

Is He Entitled to Respect?

Editor Orangeburg News and Times:

It is said a child is born innocent. I believe it. But is that any argument that the child is still innocent at forty years? Sacred history does not tell us of anything derogatory to the character of Judas until he betrayed our Lord. On the contrary his conduct was so exemplary up to the very night, that we find the other apostles asking "who is it Lord." So that up to that time Judas must have lived and acted (at least to natural vision) as well as the best of them. And yet, he sold his very salvation for thirty pieces of silver…

Col. Mosby also once shown in the Southern constellation as a very comet, leaving a tail of honor and fame brilliantly illuminating his passage, as he rapidly moved onward in his orbit. Even the Northern astronomers turned their telescopes upon him with astonished admiration and honored, while they feared.

But how does Mosby stand today? It is true his war history is still attractive, but when we look at it through subsequent events, Mosby appears despicable. Gone back on the principles for which he fought and fighting became renowned. And for what? Money—the thirty pieces of silver. Honor, principle—integrity gone, lost for the "root of all evil."

Now, Mr. Editor, these men were heroes. They have a war record. They lost crimson drops. SOLDIER

This was another of the endless articles that contained supposed questions by supposed "soldiers" about why some Southern men—many of whom were "heroes" of the war—did not choose to continue to fight that war albeit not on the battlefield. Alas, it would seem that the only motives people like SOLDIER could see were money and bad character—or a combination thereof.

And so another year of pain, humiliation, and disappointment had ended. It can be assumed that John Mosby still had friends, but by this time, they no longer spent their personal capital supporting him publicly. Mosby's world had shrunk from one in which he was well-known and had the praise, admiration and support of those who at least believed as he did—or thought well of him anyway—to one in which he had nothing: no social life, no means of earning a living, and pretty much no future.

ADDENDUM

Below is the telegram Wade Hampton sent to John Mosby:

Columbia, S. C. Personal July 1876

Received at Washington To Col. Jno S. Mosby

Present our case as it stands, and help us. Supreme Court recognizes our House, which has 63 members holding certificates. We only ask that the Constitution be obeyed. Peace and quiet will follow my inauguration, and this only will secure these. See Bradley Johnson and consult him.

(Signed) Wade Hampton

Chapter 17

1878

Animus facit nobilem. ~ The spirit makes a human noble.

"If friends he had, he bade adieu to none."

~ Lord Byron (*Childe Harold's Pilgrimage*)

AFTER THE VERY disputed "election" of Rutherford B. Hayes, John Mosby found himself, if possible, more hated than before. First, of course, he was proven wrong in his contention that a Democrat could not be elected president; and with Hayes "unfairly" taking up the reins of government, Democrats, North and South, turned their wrath upon any highly visible Republican. One of those targets, especially in the South, was John Mosby. But he was not alone. Sadly, Ulysses Grant soon found himself an object of scorn and derision by Democrats while being consigned to virtual oblivion by the party whose head and hero he had been. However, Grant had some protection from the rage of the mob and the wrath of *The Times*, but John Mosby had none.

Of course, the Southern papers once again raised the cry that Mosby's Republican credentials had absolved him of his "war crimes," actions that such papers had formerly considered heroic deeds in defense of the South:

Atlanta Constitution – February 15, 1878

Hypocrisy uncovered – Memphis Appeal

The Republicans pretend to fear that the confederate generals in congress will inaugurate a new rebellion. Because the president appointed half a dozen rebel democrats to office in the south, a general howl was set up. But a few days since, the president nominated Mosby, of Virginia for a foreign mission. Mosby is an ex-guerilla, ex-freebooter, ex-bushwhacker, but he is a republican, and like charity, that covers a multitude of sins. If a man once killed Union men for past time, he is transformed into a marvelous patriot—provided he is a republican.

Now began the press coverage of the Federal appointment Mosby was finally forced to accept in order to provide for his motherless children:

St. Paul Daily Globe – July 15, 1878

Guerrilla Moseby.

[Special telegram to the Globe]

Washington, July 14.—There is a rumor going the rounds here that a day or two ago the President sent for Col. Moseby, of Virginia fame, and tendered him an important federal appointment, and that Col. Moseby, who has not been regarded as a tender sympathizer with Mr. Hayes' administration, was taken greatly by surprise, and courteously declined the appointment. It also states that on the first of the present month a brother of Col. Moseby was tendered and declined an appointment as special agent of the treasury department. Moseby was the greatest hanger on and office-seeker Grant ever had about him. When Hayes came in Virginia's great Republican, who won so much notoriety in his guerilla warfare was given the cold shoulder. Now it is said Mr. Hayes is in a pacifying mood and will go a great way to help any and everybody who is likely to influence the next Congressional election. It is very significant to see the President so anxiously considering the complexion of the next House.

Hayes did offer Mosby a position at Grant's request after somebody took a shot at the little lawyer when he returned to Warrenton from his office in Washington. It was clear to Grant, at least, that Mosby was not safe; and he wanted him provided for. This was no longer merely a political debt, but an act of real friendship and affection. In an interview in a "safe" paper, Grant extolled his embattled friend:

National Republican - July 25, 1878

[Part of a very long interview with former President Grant; this part begins with a conversation Grant had after the war with President Johnson, at which, among others, Secretary of State William Seward— later mentioned— was present. This part is presented here because of its mention of Mosby and his relationship with Grant.-vph]

"... I made certain terms with Lee. If I had told him and his army that their liberty would be invaded; that they would be open to arrest, trial and execution for treason, Lee would never have surrendered, and we should have lost many lives in destroying him. Now, my terms of surrender were according to military law, to the instructions of Mr. Lincoln and Mr. Stanton, and so long as Lee was observing his parole, I would never consent to his arrest. Mr. Seward nodded approval. I should have resigned my command of the army rather than have carried out any order directing me to arrest Lee or any of his commanders who obeyed the laws. By the way, one reason why Mosby became such a friend of mine was because, as General, I gave him a safe conduct to allow him to practice law and earn a living. Our officers in Virginia used to arrest leading Confederates whenever they moved out of their homes.

"Mrs. Mosby went to Mr. Johnson and asked that her husband might be allowed to earn his living. But the President was in a furious mood, and told her treason must be made odious, and so on. She came to me in distress, and I gave the order to allow Mosby to pass and re-pass freely. I had no recollection of this until Mosby called it to my attention. By the way, Mosby deserves great credit for his sacrifices in the cause of the Union. He is an honest, brave, conscientious man, and has suffered severely for daring to vote as he pleased among people who hailed him as a hero, and in whose behalf he risked his life."

Grant proved himself very like Mosby in that he had forgotten his generous deed until reminded of it by Mosby, who had not forgotten it.

For the first time, a report came of the offer— and acceptance —of a Federal position for John Mosby—with all the furor that such an announcement created in the press and elsewhere:

Iola Register – August 3, 1878

Col. John S. Mosby has been tendered and has accepted the position of Consul to Canton, China.

Mosby had been offered Canton but was able to have the venue changed to Hong Kong. However, just as this matter was being made public, for some reason, the US district attorney for South Carolina requested his services as an attorney. The same news story also posted a small notice that Mosby had been invited to meetings of the GAR in New Jersey and Ohio! Nothing was said, however, of the reason for either invitation, though one suspects that the Democratic papers hoped it was to participate in a "neck-tie party" in which Mosby would be the "guest of honor:"

Evening Star – August 16, 1878

Col. Mosby.—The Alexandria Gazette says:

The U.S. district attorney for South Carolina has written to Washington requesting that Col. Mosby be retained as special counsel to represent the government in the internal revenue cases to be tried in the U. S. circuit court before Chief Justice Waite. Col. Mosby has also been invited to the meeting of the grand army of the republic at Tuckerstown, N. J., August 27, and to the soldiers' and sailors' reunion at Marietta, O., September 3.

Obviously, Mosby did not become special counsel in the internal revenue matter; neither is it stated anywhere that he attended either function mentioned. It seems odd that after being so hated in the North, he was suddenly receiving all of these requests for his presence while efforts to put a bullet into him in Warrenton had led to a consulship in China.

Atlanta Constitution – August 23, 1878

While it is true that Col. John S. Mosby has been tendered the appointment of consul at Canton, China, it is not certain that he will accept.

Mosby had turned down so many offers of a post with the government that the papers were unsure he would accept this one. But his situation had changed greatly since 1872, and it had now become a matter of actual survival, both financial and physical:

Evening Star – August 24, 1878

What Col. Mosby Wanted and What Was Offered To Him.—A special dispatch to the Baltimore Sun says: Col. Mosby made application to the President for the position of Assistant Attorney General. He presented numerous letters of recommendation from radical republicans, conservative republicans and democrats. Among those who gave letters of strong commendation were Judge Hugh L. Bond, of Maryland, Alexander H. Stephens, Judge Rives of Va., ex-Senator Lewis, of Va., Simon Cameron, and several Union officers who and been his prisoners during the war. Mr. E. W. Stoughton also gave him a warm letter. The General Stoughton that Mosby captured in bed at Fairfax Court House was the nephew of Mr. E. W. Stoughton, and the Stoughton family have always been very friendly towards Mosby, on account of his courteous treatment of his prisoner. The President for satisfactory reasons concluded to make no change in the Assistant Attorneys General, of whom there are four, two in the Department of Justice, one assigned to service in the Post Office department and one the Department of the Interior. It was then determined to offer Col. Mosby an appointment under the Department of State, as has been done.

There were two matters in this article: The first concerned the stories of wartime atrocities that continued to haunt Mosby over the years. These should have been put to rest by this time given the support and friendship manifested by the men who had come under his hand during the war. Second, there is no record that Mosby requested a position in the Department of Justice, although the story continued in the press. On the other hand, there was considerable "talk" that Hayes wanted Mosby gone from Washington given his outspoken "third-term" sentiments. Virginia Republicans also wanted him gone. As a result, Mosby was sent to China; and the Republicans, Federal and state, believed he would no longer be a problem. This was not the last time that John Mosby's enemies believed that he had been rendered irrelevant and therefor harmless:

Los Angeles Herald – August 28, 1878

Bridges the Chasm—Col. Mosby in Office

Washington, Aug. 24th.—Among the indorsers of Col. Mosby for the position of Assistant Attorney General were E. W. Stoughton, Simon Cameron and several Union officers who had been prisoners during the war. General Stoughton is the one whom Mosby captured in bed at Fairfax Court House, Virginia. He was a nephew of E. W. Stoughton, and the Stoughton family have always been very friendly towards Mosby on account of his courteous treatment of his prisoner. The President, for satisfactory reasons, has concluded to make no change in the Assistant Attorney Generals, of whom there are four, two in the Department of Justice, one assigned to service in the Post office Department and one to the Department of the Interior. It was then determined to offer Col. Mosby an appointment under the Department of State, which has been done.

New Orleans Democrat – August 29, 1878

Mosby has been tendered the Consulate at Canton, China, and it is understood that he has accepted it, thereby abdicating his lonesome position of being the only Virginian that ever lived who positively declined an office when offered to him.

The Observer presented a conundrum. First, it stated that Mosby was given the office because he had served Hayes, suggesting that he was corrupt. However, it then reversed itself by calling him "a man of character" and wondered why he should accept the office from a man like Hayes. Even the press was having problems understanding the situation extant in Mosby's case:

Fayettesville Observer - August 29, 1878

People generally were surprised at Colonel Mosby's acceptance of office from the Administration. But the announcement is made this morning. The Colonel makes no secret of his hope that Grant will succeed Hayes as President, but has been active in working up public sentiment in support of the latter's title. It is singular that a civil service reformer like Hayes puts in office only those who have been active in the work—fraudulent or otherwise—of giving him office and sustaining him in it. All disqualifications are overlooked if service of this kind can be shown.

In this case, the wonder is that Mosby, who is really a man of character, conviction and ability, should accept office under such circumstances.

The paper had no need to "wonder" at Mosby's acceptance of the offer by the Hayes administration given his situation in Virginia. Meanwhile, John Mosby continued to support the third term even after he knew that Grant had become a figure of contempt and disdain as reported by the press. One of John Mosby's most laudable traits that helped him to survive his persecution was his unfailing optimism. Mosby truly believed that Grant would be returned to favor because he truly believed that Grant was a great man. But Mosby's chosen "vindicator," Time, had yet to put in an appearance as can be seen in the "coverage" of both men by a newspaper that had once defended Mosby from such defamations:

Anderson Intelligencer – August 29, 1878

General Mosby, of Virginia has, it is announced, accepted the consulate at Canton from President Hayes. This will necessitate his leaving the country, and thus one of Grant's third term yelpers will be gotten rid of. We are sure after his departure the atmosphere in Southern politics in general, and the politics of Virginia in particular, will be purer, and therefore we hope his sojourn may be perpetual.

Virginia's Republicans had yet to meet General William Mahone, whose presence in that state's political milieu would elevate John Mosby to the status of a voice of light and reason in the minds of many who had formerly disparaged him. However, as usual, Mosby was not even given the courtesy of the recognition of his efforts on behalf of Virginia and the South. His enemies, and some of his supposed friends, had finally managed to drive him into exile. Yet the *National Republican* put in one last small testimony to the truth of the matter:

National Republican – September 3, 1878

The Staunton Valley Virginian says that few men have endured more for his political convictions than Colonel Mosby, and it predicts that the time will come when fair and just men everywhere will give him full credit for the high courage he has shown in this respect.

Sadly, even into the twenty-first century, John Mosby has been condemned by those who saw him as a political apostate. Perhaps there was no more sure testimony to that fact than Mosby's first modern biographer, Virgil Carrington Jones, suggesting that it would have been better—for his reputation at least—had he died during the war rather than become a hated Republican.

This article in the *Stark County Democrat* proved that though the war had been over for more than a dozen years, it didn't matter when the object of scorn was John Mosby:

Stark County Democrat – September 5, 1878

Col. Mosby, the famous ex-rebel guerrilla, has been appointed by President Hayes U.S. Consul at Canton, China. Mosby has been a good Republican for a long time, being thoroughly reconstructed. His conversion dates back to the days of Grant's administration, so that President Hayes can hardly be abused for appointing rebels to office. It is said Mosby has accepted the position. The radical leaders don't object to these bloody-handed rebel converts.

Mosby next appeared in the press, probably in the New York Herald, in an interview regarding his new position:

New York Herald[?] - September 16, 1878 (Edited)
AN INTERVIEW WITH MOSBY.

[From the Washington Post, September 13.]

The Post paid Colonel John S. Mosby a visit yesterday and found him perusing his commission as Consul to Hong Kong, which he had just received from the State Department. "Your original appointment was to Canton, wasn't it, Colonel?" inquired the Post.

"Yes, but I didn't like that place, and I got the department to change me to Hong Kong, which is worth five times as much as Canton. Hong Kong is on the east coast of China, at the mouth of the Canton River, and is really the Liverpool of the East. It was acquired by the British government in the opium war, in 1841, and is entirely under British jurisdiction. There is a governor general there, and it is governed just like Canada. A great many wealthy merchants reside there; it is the headquarters of the British Navy, and is, in fact, a most desirous place to live."

"When will you start, Colonel, for your new residence?"

"Early in December. Our Court of Appeals doesn't meet in Richmond until December, and I have seven important cases to argue before that Court. I will leave for Hong Kong as soon as I am through with those arguments."

Mosby noted that he was originally destined for Canton but was able to change his consulship to Hong Kong, which he considered offered of a better way of life, both socially and financially. Of course, Hong Kong was only lucrative if one were part of the China consulate ring, something that he did not know at the time. But even Mosby's destination was ridiculed in the press, with some papers taking a gleeful attitude when it was remembered that Ulysses Grant and his family had embarked on a world tour that would eventually include China, where, it was supposed, Mosby would be waiting to scrape and bow before his bearded god:

Weekly Clarion – October 2, 1878
BETWEEN DRINKS IN PEKIN.

Which the same may be true and may be a lie,

How Grant will meet Mosby in the sweet by and by, in Pekin.

But I say all the same,

And my statement is square,

That Mosby and Grant are fond of a tare.

Now this Mosby and Grant will meet in Pekin,

In the land of Johnny Wah Koo;

They will order their rum,

And they will call for cigars, And they'll call for a hot rat stew.

Then Mosby and Grant will join in a song,

Which the same I swear is not new;

For the song they will sing, between drinks in Pekin

(And mark you the drinks are not few).

Is you tickle me and I'll tickle you.

BostonPost.

Longfellow and Byron had nothing to fear from the jolly journalist, who wrote that nasty little rhyme. However, it does show that Grant had pretty much fallen as far from favor as had Mosby. The heroism of both men was forgotten, and they had become figures of malicious fun. Consider that this little perversion was printed not in Atlanta, but in Boston. It was sad, really; for it reflected badly not on Mosby and Grant, but on the country—or rather, countries—on whose behalf they had both spent their health, lives and fortunes. In the end, one has to wonder if those sacrifices were worthily given under the circumstances.

Then another newspaper criticized Mosby for not leaving for China immediately. The paper obviously felt no need to see why Mosby was delayed in his departure. Indeed, it did not have to—and probably it did not want to. This was John Mosby, after all, and so any slander was acceptable:

Weekly Register – October 16, 1878

Colonel Mosby has not yet gone to the scene of his duties in China, although appointed more than a month ago. He has drawn a quarter's salary and is enjoying himself about Washington. Civil service reform goes on apace.

And then there was more of the same, but with the perennial "wounded Union soldier" thrown in for good measure:

The Democratic Press – October 24, 1878

It is announced that Col. John S. Mosby, Hayes' loyal pet, for whom some wounded Union soldier had to stand aside, will not to go his post in China until December. Meanwhile the salary goes on and he draws it with commendable punctuality.

The *Daily National Republican* pointed out that one of Mosby's former prisoners during the war was attempting to help him in his new position, a matter that strongly testified against the slanderous charges so often appearing in the Democratic press:

Daily National Republican – November 6, 1878

Colonel Mosby, who leaves shortly for his post of Consul at Hong Kong, carries with him letters of introduction to a leading Hong Kong firm, written by Major Forbes, of Boston. During the war the Second Massachusetts Cavalry, of which Major Forbes was then field officer, had frequent encounters with Mosby's troopers. In a skirmish Forbes was taken prisoner by Mosby, and entertained in the latter's quarters until sent down to Richmond. Seeing Mosby's appointment as Consul to Hong Kong, and remembering the courtesy of old times, Major Forbes testifies his friendship by tendering a letter of introduction and the hope that it will facilitate the Colonel's mission in China.

The Intelligencer was back and angry with Mosby for his desire to see Grant reelected. Indeed, the paper was enraged that he should continue to hold on to what it saw as something totally unacceptable to anyone but Grant and Mosby:

The *Anderson Intelligencer* – November 21, 1878

Mosby, the ex-Confederate, who holds a foreign consulate but resides in the country and draws pay, has settled the political problem, so far as his dictum can accomplish the result, by announcing that the battle of 1880 is already fought and won, and Grant is the man. Perhaps he is the man who is going to be run over in that battle. The people may intend to perpetuate Radicalism, but the certainly don't contemplate a repetition of Grantism. Mosby has become notorious as one of Grant's most servile understrappers, and it is difficult to say whether the opposition to Grant or the disgust with his man Friday (Mosby) is stronger in the minds of the American people.

This was another example of Grant and Mosby in tandem condemnation and scorn. Mosby was not "servile"; he was devoted, not with an eye toward gain, but in recognition of Grant's services to both himself, personally, and the South after the war. His affection was manly and proper; and furthermore, it was returned by Grant, the man who had ordered him hanged without trial during the war. But as the matter stood, the two men's friendship simply presented the press with a larger target for vituperation and scorn.

Public Ledger – December 4, 1878

LOYALTY REWARDED

Among the notable nominations sent in to the senate by the President yesterday are those of the famous guerilla chieftain, John S. Mosby, of Virginia for the position of United States consul at Hong Kong, China, and Henry S. Foote, of Mississippi, original blatant secessionist, to be superintendent of the mint at New Orleans. "Verily, they all have their reward."

Mosby was a fighter, sure enough, but has escaped denunciation by resting in the bosom of the Republican party. He has hitherto declared that he wanted no office, and has been quite a toady at the White House, especially while Grant was there. After serving his friends it appears that he concluded to take a crumb for himself in the form of a fat consularship. The inspectors who visit consular posts on the other side of the globe are usually of the Parson Newman stripe who know so little of worldly affairs that they are easily satisfied that a loyal men is in the right place to save the government. The rebel Mosby will no doubt be found right, and after he lives a few years at the important commercial city of Hong Kong will, with luck, come homes a wiser man, like some of his predecessors.

Mosby offered such help to Grant to heal the wounds of the country as he could give, and Grant trusted his opinions regarding those seeking office because he knew Mosby to be honest to a fault. If this was "toadying," then Grant could have used a great deal more of it during his presidency! Indeed, if there had been other men of Mosby's character in his administration Ulysses Grant might have served ten terms. But then, there was only one John Mosby.

Furthermore, the "fat consularship" was only "fat" when the consul stole from the government. Mosby later said that the job was not worth the pay, and he had to fight for years to get back from the government those fees that did in fact belong to him and which he had turned into the Treasury to avoid "the appearance of impropriety." He eventually did come home "a wiser man," but in a very different way than the paper prescribed.

Small stories then began to appear involving Mosby's departure for China. One wonders if the press, realizing that he would no longer be in Washington and believing that he would be lost in the East, were beginning to fear his enforced obscurity. They needn't have worried:

Evening Star – December 3, 1878

PERSONAL.—Col. Mosby will sail from San Francisco for Hong Kong, in the steamer City of Peking, on the 4th of January next.

Chicago Tribune – December 28, 1878

Col. John S. Mosby, of Virginia, the noted guerrilla, passed through the city yesterday, registering at the Palmer. He is on his way to Hongkong, where he is Consul.

But never let it be said that John Mosby could retire quietly and without fanfare! No such comfort was left to him as all the old charges were dragged out once more as a sort of wretched "salute" to his departure:

Atlanta Constitution – December 15, 1878

Hypocrisy uncovered Memphis Appeal.

The Republicans pretend to fear that the confederate generals in congress will inaugurate a new rebellion. Because the president appointed half a dozen rebel democrats to office in the south, a general howl was set up. But a few days since the president nominated Mosby, of Virginia, for a foreign mission. Mosby is an ex-guerrilla, ex-freebooter, ex-bushwhacker, but he is a republican, and like charity, that covers a multitude of sins. If a man once killed Union men for (a) past time, he is transformed into a marvelous patriot—provided he is a republican.

This was always the cry when Mosby received anything from the Republicans: he was a monster and not a soldier and should have received nothing but prison or the rope. Though Confederates like Longstreet were defamed for their Republican allegiance in the Democratic press, their service to the cause was sacrosanct. But it was always different for Mosby, though there was ample evidence that the charges were baseless. It didn't matter. It was an opportunity to revile him and was always used for that purpose—even when those same papers had honored him during and immediately after the war for those same services. The *Atlanta Constitution* well understood hypocrisy; it was a practitioner of that iniquity.

And so John Mosby set sail as did the protagonist in his favorite poem, Childe Harold's Pilgrimage. For like the young man in that ode, he was leaving his native land to escape a situation that had become intolerable:

And now Childe Harold was sore sick at heart, ...

And from his native land resolved to go,

And visit scorching climes beyond the sea;

With pleasure drugged, he almost longed for woe,

And e'en for change of scene would seek the shades below.

Unlike Childe Harold, however, Mosby did not long for woe. He could have stayed at home had that been his desire. Neither would he have chosen hell as a destination for he would have found it little different than Virginia as he himself testified many years later.

Chapter 18

1879

Fiat justitia, ruat caelum!
~ Let justice be done though the heavens fall!

"This above all: to thine own self be true."
~ William Shakespeare

ACTUALLY, 1879 BEGAN somewhat auspiciously for Mosby in the newspapers. The drumbeat of insult against him from 1872 right through to the Hayes election suddenly seemed to fade into somewhat more favorable press. Of course, it could be that as he journeyed west toward the broad Pacific, he found less hostility in the newspapers of the vast American midsection. The following articles were downright benign, even the one that mentioned his third-term sentiments:

Leavenworth Weekly Times – **January 2, 1879**

A Live Guerrilla.

[Council Bluffs Nonpareil, 29.]

On board the incoming passenger over the Burlington road yesterday morning was the celebrated Guerrilla Chief, Col. John Mosby, who during the war was the terror of many northern soldiers. This quiet, aged and grey headed celebrity was on his way to Hong Kong, China, he being the new minister to China. Col. Mosby is a man of fine bearing, and is quite reserved in his manners. At this point he took the Union Pacific for San Francisco.

The Carbon Advocate – **January 11, 1879**

—Consul Moseby on leaving Washington for his post in China the other day told his friends that "he would return to Washington on the 4th of March, 1881, to be present at the inauguration of General Grant for the third term."

Never let it be said that John Mosby was easily discouraged. But certainly, he could have wished worse things upon his fellow Southerners than Ulysses Grant.

The *Holt County Sentinel* – **January 17, 1879**

GUERRILLA MOSBY.

He Leaves His Foreign Mission—Not as Bad as he is Painted.

From Washington Letter of 28th.

This morning we hear of one public man however, who was astir. It was the noted John S. Mosby. He spent the afternoon in bidding his friends good-bye, previous to taking the evening train for San Francisco and Hong Kong, whence he has been appointed consul by the President, at the earnest solicitation of some of the Union soldiers who were taken prisoner by him during the war. About Mosby there has been much written since the war, but little of which has been true, but on the contrary, the grossest misrepresentation. Before the war broke out he stood at the head of the bar in the little town of Warrenton, Va. So able and popular as attorney was he that his practice amounted in the year preceding the outbreak of the rebellion to nearly $10,000. In the war he went with his state, became a cavalry leader of so dashing a character that he got the name of being a guerrilla, and has been slandered as one ever since. 'Tis is all a mistake. His troop was a regularly enlisted command, a picked body of men, and kept near the person of Lee, who continually detailed it for the execution of delicate duty. Its movements were so rapid and so daring that it got to be regarded as an irregular force by Union troops. It, however, was simply light cavalry, and its doings as such was always within the established rules of warfare; in fact, Mosby's conduct toward his prisoners of which so many falsehoods were told, was dictated by the principles of humanity, and to-day it is a well-established fact by those who know him that they were treated with the greatest kindness.

After the war Mosby went back to his native place and immediately got all of his old law business back and a great deal more that came to him because of the fame he had won by his brilliant services. He opened a branch office in Baltimore, which soon became almost as crowded as that at Warrenton. Office was offered him, and everything was generally lovely for the brilliant ex-soldier. The Presidential election of 1868 came on. Mosby got into profound study of the situation, and finally came to the conclusion that the thing for the "very best people" in the South to do was to come out and squarely acknowledge by their acts as well as words that they had been whipped. He accordingly went to the polls in November and voted for Grant. Although he did not electioneer for the Republican ticket or do anything but cast a ballot, this was enough for the hide-bound secession element, and he was dropped like a hot potato. That year his business in the Baltimore office did not amount to $100, and he barely kept out of the poor house at home. The next year and the year after his business continued to leave him, old acquaintances cut him dead on the street, he was hounded by the press of the whole south, his soldiers whom he had led to brilliant victory and nursed like a father in sickness united in damning him. Nobody asked him to fight, however, as he was known to be a man who rather enjoyed that sort of thing. With the exception of this compliment the scarlet letter of shame was universally put upon him. He became embarrassed financially and he had the pleasure of seeing his home sold to Eppa Hunton, a men in every way his inferior, who has since been taken up and elected (to) Congress in that district. Thus Mosby was literally froze(n) out. Had he chosen he could have run for office on the Republican ticket and been elected, but he never did. In the time of his distress he came to Washington and succeeded in starting a law practice among the Republicans. Here he was brought to the notice of President Grant, who took him up and made him a confidential friend. Time and again he offered Mosby office, but he refused all favors from him except an appointment for his son to the West Point Military Academy. Of late, his health impaired by the hardships of the war, (he) has become much broken, and at the solicitation of many of the very men he is said to have treated so harshly, he has been given the Hong Kong consulate.

In manners he is pictured as a most refined gentleman; his voice they say, is as tender as that of a woman, and his bravery, morals and ability are untarnished. A man of the greatest judgment, whom I heard speak of him last night, said "John S. Mosby is the sweetest man I ever knew."

Though perhaps it was a stretch to call Mosby "sweet" yet he certainly could be a very kindly, empathetic, and generous man when not goaded into anger. And it is indeed possible that to the writer, he was in fact "sweet" in disposition and nature in their dealings. Mosby did not parade his good works for the world to see, but he certainly did them, that we know. However, many of the points made in the rest of the article are also incorrect. Mosby was not permitted to run for Congress on the Republican ticket because he refused obedience to the party's position on the blacks. Also, he was already known to Grant by that time and had refused any office at his hands as he had promised in 1872; neither did his sons receive an appointment to West Point — but these are small matters considered in relationship to the whole of the situation presented by the article. He did not just "vote" for Grant but campaigned for him. Neither did he have an office in Baltimore—at least that has been placed on record. Furthermore, only one of his men criticized him about his "apostasy." The rest, whatever their political affiliations, retained their affection for their old commander. But aside from these misstatements, what remains is fairly accurate. He was in fact cut dead in the street and brought to financial ruin for his conscientious beliefs and actions.

However, the next report condemns both Mosby and Grant as seemed to be the fashion in the press at the time:

News & Herald – January 18, 1879

The New York Herald publishes a good deal of stuff in a reported conversation of a number of ex-Confederates on Grant's candidacy. These ex-Confeds are going for him and say that thousands of their old comrades will do likewise. Grant's clemency as a general received high praise, and the escape of General Lee from hanging was attributed to him. The names of the Grant Confederates are not given, and as John Mosby is on his way to eat rice with chopsticks with Chinese Mandarins, we are at a loss to guess. The clemency of the general was long ago buried beneath the malignity of a partisan president, and the South wants no more of Grant.

The News & Herald article is another example of the idiocy of those "reporting" on the issues of the day. First, the paper admitted that "ex-Confederates supported Grant"; and according to that report, they were not alone. These ex-Confederate soldiers were grateful to Grant for his integrity and decency at the end the war, but according to the paper, that was all in the past because president Grant was "partisan." Yet Andrew Johnson, a Southerner and a Democrat, was far more "partisan"—if by that the paper meant anti-Southern—than Grant. Johnson would have hanged Lee, Mosby, and anyone else who came under his hand had Grant not protected them! But then, the support by former Confederate soldiers for Grant was dismissed by the paper because it could not identify those soldiers—and besides, Mosby was gone! The reasoning—if one wishes to call it that—was that Mosby was the only former Confederate who supported or who could obtain support for Grant in the South.

The following article in the *Chicago Tribune* provided an example of Mosby's former military enemies defending him. Sadly, such testimonials were far too few when they were most needed:

Chicago Tribune – **January 21, 1879**

Mosby and The Democrats

Washington Republican (Rep.).

"Bushwhacker Mosby" is what the Baltimore Gazette now calls Col. Mosby since he has left The Democratic party. It was "the gallant and intrepid Mosby" when he was menacing the National Capital with his guerrillas during the Rebellion. The only difference is he surrendered and accepted the situation while his assailants have not.

John Mosby had left Washington, but though a Republican administration was still in power, it would seem that all of that party's honor and intestinal fortitude left with him:

Keowee Courier – **February 13, 1879**

Shenandoah Herald – **February 26, 1879**

Miss Jackson, the daughter of the Alexandria hotel-keeper, who killed Col. Ellsworth, of the Zouaves, in 1862, was kept in the Treasury Department place at Washington by Col. Mosby until he left for Hong Kong. Since his departure Miss Jackson has lost her place.

This story illustrated not only the triumph of petty cruelty, but the moral cowardice of those involved. The poor woman's only "crime" was that her father stood against the Northern aggressor and lost his life in so doing. Mosby was able to keep her place when she was fired for the "crime" of being her father's daughter, but apparently, Hayes and his "reformers" had not the stomach to do the same.

Before Mosby reached China, another article appeared making the same points usually made—that a "loyal" Union man should have been appointed to his position rather than a "repentant rebel." The writer referred to Mosby if not harshly, then certainly with considerable contempt:

Burlington Weekly Free Press – **March 21, 1879**

CROSSING THE BROAD PACIFIC.

From California to Japan.

Extracts from Dr. Thayer's Journal Saturday, Jan. 11, 1879

(Dr. Thayer spends much time describing the ship and the weather as well as crossing the 180th meridian in the night and the affect that has on the calculation of time.)

The discussion among the passengers on the subject of dropping and taking up a day in crossing the 180th degree meridian has not only relieved the monotony of the day, but has excited much merriment.

Our fellow passenger, Col. J. S. Mosby, of guerilla fame, now on his way to the consulate of Hong-Kong, did not participate with much earnestness in the discussion. He is at all times inclined to retirement. He is far from being the kind of man I supposed him to be, when he used to cut up capers with the officers and soldiers of the Union army during the "late unpleasantness" between the North and the South. He is a man of moderate size, light complexion, light hair, blue eyes, with a face smoothly shaven and of a mild expression of countenance. He has received a collegiate education and was bred to the law before the war. He is a native of Virginia, possessing all the peculiarities in view and dialect characteristic of the F. F. V.'s. His whole life having been spent in and south of Washington city, he appears quite unsophisticated in "knowledge of the world," so much so that I cannot but entertain feelings of sympathy for him in his new field of labor, with its social requirements and official duties and perplexities. The course Col. Mosby has pursued since the close of the war has been such that it would be quite presumptuous of me, even if I felt so disposed, to question the Colonel's sincerity in accepting the situation of the South, or the depth and extent of his fidelity to the Republican cause. Many of us, from personal experience during the war, do know that he spared neither the life nor property of Union soldiers, who sacrificed both in their support of the government he was trying to overthrow, and that he and his associates, if not the mediate were the immediate cause of mourning around many a fireside; and of empty coat sleeves and wooden legs of many men who now barely subsist upon a pittance from the government, though qualified to fill with honor to themselves and to the government any consulate in the world. It may be political policy, it is certainly a Christian virtue, to receive the eleventh hour servants to remunerative places.

Then a small article appeared in a paper that had defended Mosby in the past. It is very sad indeed that the "highly complimentary account" of Mosby written by the United States officer has not come down to us. It would have been worth the reading. However, it is equally sad that the paper's positive report was so limited. It seemed that when papers said something positive about John Mosby, the matter was handled in as few words as possible. On the other hand, attacks on him consumed lines of type:

Spirit of Jefferson – **March 25, 1879**

The China Mail, of Hong Kong, of the 3 ult., notices the arrival in that city of United States Consul J. S. Mosby, and contains a highly complimentary account of the Colonel, written by an officer in the United States army.

But if John Mosby thought that he was going to find a surcease of hostility and harassment in the East, he was very much mistaken as can be seen by the host of complaints and nasty gossip that erupted virtually as he landed in Hong Kong:

South Kentuckian – **April 15, 1879**

And next comes a complaint from Hong Kong, a most grievous complaint indeed; something must be done or else the American flag will be hereafter used as a dish rag or a nose wiper. The new United States minister to that port, the black-legged, fraud, John S. Moseby, of Virginia, has been recently requested by the Hong Kongoans to cease his disregard of their usual royal formalities and ceremonies to which the turn-coat politician pays no earthly attention. On a recent occasion of an entertainment of ceremony at the gubernatorial residence in Hong K—-he was requested to appear in the right costume of polite society. He replied that he would be d—d before he would wear anything except another American citizen would wear; that he represented the United States, and he proposed to introduce American manners and American customs.

The United States would be disgraced, in fact her name would go down in fable as connected with some pent up Utica, if Mr. Moseby had sacrificed her individuality by draping himself in the habiliments of a gentleman. It would never have done for Mr. Mosby to have lost the goodly opportunity of disclosing the length and depth and height of an American's capacity to swear; and then too, he is in that far off county to teach American religion and doctrine as much as possible, and may be despaired of ever finding another suitably opportunity of taking his text.

Bristol News – **April 15, 1879**

Col. Mosby is playing guerilla again; this time among the heathen Chinee.—He refused to appear at court in court costume. Well, well Mosby never did do business like other folks.

The Standard – **April 17, 1879**

Alarming news come from Hong Kong, China, with regard to the conduct of Col. Mosby, American Consul. A distinguished British officer gave a grand reception, and expected the American to appear in a garb suitable to the occasion. The Colonel is credited with the remark that he would only appear dressed as another American would dress, whereat there was great indignation in the city. The Chinese authorities should lose no time in informing Col. Mosby that he "must go."

The Comet – **April 19, 1879**

Anderson Intelligencer – **May 1, 1879**

Mosby Raising a Breeze in Hong Kong.

Washington, April 7.—A private letter, just received from a distinguished American merchant at Hong Kong, conveys some interesting particulars in a semi-official way, of the performances of the new Consul of the United States to that port—the ex-guerrilla Col. John S. Mosby, of Virginia. Hong Kong, as it is known, is the seat of British power in the waters of China and Japan, and ruled by an officer of the crown entitled Governor General. All the pomp and pageantry of a miniature court is maintained. Under these circumstances the proprieties of etiquette are closely observed, and the regimen of manners is dictated by the Governor General's official household. It appears on the occasion of Col. Mosby's appearance at his post, he disregarded the usual formalities towards the authorities and subsequently on the occasion of an entertainment of ceremony at the gubernatorial residence, he was requested to appear in the proper costume of polite society. He replied that he would be d—d before he would wear anything except what another American would wear; that he represented the United States, and he proposed to introduce American manners and American customs. His conduct in Hong Kong, since his arrival there has to only been unsatisfactory to the American residents, but has been exceedingly objectionable to the English, and residents of other nationalities.

This information has caused much comment here, and a prominent official observed to-day that it was a remarkable fact to him that a person of his character and political relations had been able to so successfully deceive

President Grant, and continue with the same success his operations on the present administration; that his manipulation of patronage has not been confined to the appointment of a brother in the Treasury department, but extends to "his sisters, and cousins and aunts." His success is mainly attributable to his assumption that he controls the Republican party of the Old Dominion, and in this way has practiced upon the credulity of two Presidents without ever showing the slightest evidence of practical results. It is not improbable that the Government will inquire into this matter, and if Col. Mosby has been guilty of what is alleged, action will be taken in the premises.

Daily National Republican – **April 21, 1879**

CURRENT CAPITAL TOPICS.

Colonel Mosby's Non-Compliance with Court Etiquette.

A Large Story Out of a Small Piece of Cloth—In Fact, out of the Want of Cloth

Colonel Mosby and his "Swallow-Tail."

Recently published reports of certain alleged cantankerous social proceedings by Colonel Mosby, United States Consul at Hong Kong, prove to be grossly exaggerated and to have very little foundation in fact. They are to the effect that he had created some scandal among the American and other foreign residents at Hong Kong by rudely refusing to comply with the rules of social etiquette, which require that the guests of the Governor-General and all of the English officials stationed there shall appear in full dress at formal receptions; and further that Mosby had declared his intention to wear North American clothes or none at all. The truth of the matter is that immediately on his arrival at Hong Kong he was invited to dine with several of the leading English officials and was compelled, as he writes to a friend in Alexandria, to decline the invitation for the reason that he "had no swallow-tail" with him.

As the letter containing this explanation was written directly after he had declined the invitation, and before the reports referred to were made public, it is evident that instead of refusing to comply with the august social requirements of the occasion he was simply a victim of unfortunate circumstances. Subsequent letters from him, also written before these reports were printed, contain the further information that the Colonel had succeeded in getting a swallow-tail built on short notice, and that he had worn it at a dinner given by the admiral of the English fleet in the harbor, and on one or two other occasions.

It is believed by some of Colonel Mosby's friends here that these reports were created and circulated by ex-Vice-Consul Loring, who was removed by him, and who, it is known, does not entertain the most kindly feelings to him on that account. And this is the true story of "Mosby and his swallow-tail."

Despite the fact that the entire matter had been thoroughly explained in the *Daily National Republican* back on the twelfth of April, the calumnies continued, probably because they were too good to be let go; and besides, so many people wanted to believe them:

Stark County Democrat – **April 24, 1879**

Mosby, the famous "Confedrit brigadier," now Hayes's consul at Hong Kong, China, the British post there, is showing his cussedness. He won't dress in court style as required by the British Governor in those calling upon his highness on court days. Mosby says he will see the Governor General d—d before he will do anything of the sort. He would rather put on the gray, probably.

Free Press – **April 25, 1879**

Col. Mosby, now United States Consul at Hong Kong, has given offense to the British officials there by refusing to appear in a court dress. It is suggested that as diplomats and consuls who served in the army are permitted to wear their uniforms, Mosby might as well wear his old Confederate gray uniform with slouch hat and high boots.

But the pettiness of the charges and complaints that the newspapers saw fit to print tended to validate the belief that all that was needed to make these matters newsworthy was the name "Mosby:"

Chicago Tribune – **May 6, 1879**

Col. Mosby is accused by a lady, who writes from Hong Kong to a friend in Norristown, of sitting with his feet on the table when American gentlemen called to pay their respects.

Spirit of Jefferson – **May 6, 1879**

Col. Mosby is accused by a lady, who writes from Hong Kong to a friend in Norristown, Pa., of sitting with his feet on the table when American gentlemen call to pay their respects. "At the table," continues the letter, an extract of which is printed in the Norristown Herald, "he does the most dreadful things, among the rest uses his napkin instead of a pocket handkerchief."

If he ever saw any of these press releases, John Mosby discovered that distance could not save him from attack, especially when it was useful for a Democratic paper to blast Hayes—and it was always useful for a Democratic paper to blast Hayes:

The Democrat – **May 29, 1879**

SEEKING INFORMATION

Ed. [Editor-vph] of the Democrat:

The attacks of the Eaton Register and Camden Herald, have awakened a determination among the "veteran boys in blue" to get at the truth of the charges you make at the present administration. Is it a fact that the present administration has appointed rebel officers to government positions. We cannot believe it—many of us are poor hard working men, who do not read much, but want the truth. For parties, as such, we do not care a straw—we love our government and have faced death in its defense. We shall read your answer carefully, and am bound to know whether you give us truth or falsehood. If the charge you make is true we think reform, like charity, should begin at home. Give us an answer. Yours, VETERAN.

We would say in regard to "Veteran," that the guerrilla Mosby who shot down the boys in blue, and whose name was a stench in the nostrils of all patriots, is to-day United States Consult to Hong Kong, was appointed by Mr. Hayes to the high office, and his appointment confirmed by a Republican Senate! A more sneaking and contemptible guerrilla and bushwhacker than Mosby, never assassinated a Union soldier under the flag of our country. We ask the valiant Col. Williams of the Register, or the blatant idiot of the Camden dish rag, to deny this to the veteran soldiers of our country. They who prate about a "red hot" campaign, would better be answering some of the modern ugly questions, lest they find the red hot end of the poker in their own hand.

Press these hard questions home and compel direct, square and unequivocal answers. Let not the shriek of these editors that The Democratic party is the Confederate party, deter you from forcing from their lips the humiliating confession that their own shameless and heartless administration has given its golden rewards to these red-handed murderers of your companions in arms Send such questions as you have sent us to these howlers and ask them to answer through their columns as squarely as we do. We would like to see them squirm over Mosby the guerrilla. Next.

In the same paper:

The guerrilla Mosby still holds the Consulship of Hong Kong, but no Republican editor utters a howl against the outrage. Why is it Mr. Williams?

We heard a Union soldier remark the other day, that when he shouldered his musket again it would be to put out of existence a party that keeps the guerrilla Mosby at Hong Kong. Such infernal hypocrisy won't fool sensible men. He wasn't a Democrat either!

This is one of those interminable articles appearing usually in Democratic papers but sometimes in unhappy Radical publications as well. The mention of the other "usual suspects" besides Mosby—that is, Longstreet and Key—was removed for the purposes of length. Indeed, this article is included only because of the enormity of the crimes charged against Mosby. Usually, such papers were content to call him a guerrilla and/or a bushwhacker, but this one went the extra mile, so to speak.

But as far as engaging such men as the letter writer (if indeed VETERAN was not simply a *deux ex machina* used by the paper to get its point across-vph), he and his fellow "veterans" obviously lacked the needed skills to fill any post of consequence—a fact that should have put an end this kind of claim. The men chosen to fill these positions were capable, whatever their loyalties in a war that had ended over ten years earlier.

The *Atlanta Constitution*, having finished for the moment flaying Mosby, turned its attentions to former president Grant, who was engaged in a round-the-world tour with his family. It is probable that the *Constitution* was encouraged to report on the matter because Grant had reached Hong Kong—that is, *Grant had reached Mosby*:

Atlanta Constitution,- **June 3, 1879**

The Progress of the American Dead-beat

> San Francisco, June 4.—The steamer Oceanic arrived from Hong Kong today bring the following advices: "Hong Kong, May 8.—General Grant's visit everywhere absorbs public attention. He arrived here on the evening of April 30th in the French mail steamship Irrawaddie. The ship was immediately boarded by United States Consul Mosby, of Hong Kong, and Lincoln, of Canton; Charge d'Affaires Holcombe and deputations of citizens of various countries, including Japan. The same evening he and party proceeded to the United States ship Ashuelot, where they were received with a salute of twenty-one guns. They then went ashore in the colonial government launch and were received at the decorated landing pier by Governor Hennessy and staff, members of the legislative council, heads of military and naval services, guard of honor, and multitude of American, European and Chinese spectators. He was escorted to the government house. Many of the streets and houses were adorned with flags and the houses illuminated. Gen. Grant held a public reception at the United States consulate, and on the third attended a state dinner at the government house. On the fifth the party started for Canton in the Ashuelot, escorted by a Chinese gun-boat. They reached Canton on May 6th, and were received with demonstrations similar to those at Hong Kong. The intend leaving for the north on the eleventh, touching al Amor and Fouchow, and reaching Shanghai about the eighteenth; thence they will go to Tientsin, Pekin and Nagusaki.

Grant was not faring any better than Mosby—at least in the newspapers. Here was the Northern "hero" of the Civil War (which, to some extent, excuses the Atlanta paper!) and a former president being presented to the American public and the world as a "dead-beat" even though Grant did not travel on the government dime. This article is included to show that Mosby wasn't the only one who was being badly treated as a result of prior actions however well-intentioned.

Then, for the first time, a hint was forthcoming that not everything was as it should be in the American consulate at Hong Kong. Thus, the press found something far more interesting about which to report than a gaggle of alleged social gaffes as Mosby began to make noises regarding the state of things in the East:

Helena Weekly Herald – June 19, 1879

> Col. John S. Mosby still stirs things at his Hong-Kong consulate. He says in a private letter that when he reached Hong-Kong, he saw at a glance that there had been most discreditable management. He is of the opinion that matters are now in better shape. The editor of the Chinese Mail sued him for subscription due under the former consul, and Mosby won his case in court. The Mail, of recent date, admitted its defeat and complimented Mosby on his reforms.

Mosby had at first picked up what appeared to be bad management and a lack of careful administration at the consulate under Loring, but that soon widened into a much deeper probe regarding the behavior of his predecessors and their cronies in the consular service in China. The second issue in the above article—that is, the suit brought by the Chinese Mail newspaper against the new consul—involved Mosby's refusal to pay for his predecessor's subscription. That worthy had left his post without bothering to "pay up," and the paper simply transferred the bill to the new consul. As Mosby had neither ordered nor received the newspaper, he refused to pay for it and was taken to court. He proved that the subscription was a personal rather than a consulate matter and so was cleared of any obligation to pay. Though the paper lost money, it was decent and honest enough to acknowledge the new consul's attempts at reform.

A small article suggested that Mosby didn't like the city and would return to the United States with Grant. His "dissatisfaction" with his "experience at Hong Kong" had more to do with his attempts to make the Department of State interested in the wholesale theft and corruption going on in China than in his duties as consul. Of course, his treatment by the American colony in Hong Kong upon his arrival did not help matters. Be that as it may, John Mosby was never one to run away from a fight:

Greenville Times – **July 12, 1879**

Kansas City Times.

> Col. Mosby thinks he will come home with the party of Gen. Grant for a short stay, if not for good. He expresses himself as much dissatisfied with his experience at Hong Kong.

However, before the corruption matter was recognized for the immense scandal it was to become, the business of Mosby's alleged "breaches of etiquette" was firmly and finally settled in this article:

New Orleans Democrat – **July 31, 1879**

> Col. Mosby has been vindicated at last. Several weeks ago a silly rumor ran to the effect that he had greatly shocked the European residents at Hong Kong by appearing at the Governor General's reception without the conventional dress suit. When the American newspapers containing this grave charge were received in Hong Kong Mosby was much exercised over it. He at once procured the necessary proof of its falsity and forwarded them to his brother, who has just published them. Col. Mosby says that he refused to go to the reception until the proper habiliments were procured. The only departure from the strictest and highest style he allowed himself was the retention of his slouch hat. This he refused to lay aside, deeming that it was good enough for a reception in Hong Kong, inasmuch as it had done service at the White House. No one can deny that this refusal to go back on the old slouch was eminently patriotic.

> Among the letter published is one from the Governor General himself, in which it is stated that that functionary had "read with astonishment a paragraph from an American newspaper about your costume at Government House, and hasten to assure you that as far as I know the paragraph is without the slightest foundation. You have often done me the honor of being a guest at my table, and I need hardly say there is no one in this country whose social qualities and high character I more fully appreciate. Believe me, my dear colonel, always yours faithfully."

> Thus this very important matter is set at rest forever. With such high indorsements no one will affirm hereafter that the American character and dignity is not fully maintained in Hong Kong, especially in the very essential particulars of full dress, the trifling exception of the slouch hat omitted.

Now that he was no longer being held up as an object of ridicule, the newspapers began to look at what Mosby was uncovering in the Hong Kong consulate. For the new consul had now gone past the questionable practices at the consulate itself and "branched out" to include the entire mosaic of corruption in China, a matter that was almost as large as that country itself. The article below is one of the first that mentioned Mosby's revelations about Frederick Seward, nephew of Lincoln's secretary of state, William Seward, a powerful Republican politician. Apparently, these "revelations" were nothing new as the paper quickly pointed out. However, despite its approval of the probe, Mosby was accused of having "too long a tongue"; yet the insult was somewhat ameliorated by the admission that he also had "too much conscience" and "too many scruples" at least to survive in a Republican administration:

New Orleans Democrat – July 30, 1879

> The general regret that Congress failed to bring Minister Seward to punishment will be revived as a consequence of certain disclosures recently made by Col. Mosby, consul at Hong Kong. Seward, it will be remembered, escaped because of the filibustering tactics of the Republican minority. The administration now seems disposed to come to his further relief. Col. Mosby reports that $40,000 of fees collected before his arrival had never been accounted for, and expresses the opinion that the government has been defrauded of not less than $200,000 in the last seventeen years. Instead of receiving the thanks of the administration for his zeal it is intimated that he is too officious, and will probably be recalled.
>
> It is evident that there is considerable crookedness about this Chinese business. It is also evident that Mosby has not been in the fold long enough to know his duty as a good Republican. He has too much conscience, too many scruples and too long a tongue.

The rest of Mosby's period of service in Hong Kong was centered around this issue, one of the most interesting aspects of which was his defense by the Democratic papers and the attacks against him by the Republican press. This is easily explained because Mosby was "outing" Republican miscreants, and even worse for the Republican administration, it soon became obvious that the Department of State had no intention of moving against those same miscreants. As a result, The Democrats were overjoyed because Hayes had run as a "reformer" given all the corruption in the Grant administration. Yet the situation in Hong Kong demonstrated that there was no interest in bringing Seward and the rest of his accomplices to justice, while Evarts and the Department of State were waging war against Republican Mosby in order to protect Republicans Seward and Bailey. It certainly was a "win-win" for The Democrats. Mosby got hammered in the Republican press—something that they loved—while he continued to embarrass his own party and the Hayes administration with his ongoing exposure of consular corruption and, indirectly, administration malfeasance.

It is also interesting to note that suddenly the Democratic press discovered that John Mosby was honest or, at the very least, that he was honest enough to bring charges against Republicans; and that that party was bound to accept the veracity of those charges because Mosby was himself a Republican. Every once in a while, however, a publication printed a story that lauded Mosby outright and not just "damned him with faint praise" for embarrassing the Republican Party. The following article in a Democratic organ does so but also mentions that his honesty had not made him any friends in his own party, which was true enough:

Daily Globe – July 31, 1879

If we have ever said anything derogatory of the character of Col. Mosby, now consul at Hong Kong, we desire to take it back without reservation. He has been at his post but a short time, yet he has discovered—and told of it too—that forty thousand dollars of fees which belong to the government, collected before his arrival, have not been accounted for, and he reports that, for the last seventeen years, of the fees collected under the law regulating Chinese immigration, in his opinion, at least two hundred thousand dollars have not been reported to the treasury. We feel called upon to praise Col. Mosby's honesty and at the same time commiserate him on his loss of caste and position, for no man who exposes fraud can hope to retain either standing or office in the Republican party.

Sadly, however, the laudatory press reports were not all that many. It was almost a replay of the election of 1873 when the Republican papers were against Mosby, and the Democratic organs could not quite bring themselves to support or praise him. Meanwhile, John Mosby was getting discouraged because the "reformer in the White House" seemed loath to reform anything:

Daily Cairo Bulletin – August 5, 1879

A Washington dispatch reads as follows:

"Colonel John S. Mosby, Consul at Hong Kong, writes his brother-in-law that he is disposed to resign, to see if he cannot arouse the state department to a comprehension of the rottenness of the George F. Seward ring in China. He writes to Secretary Evarts that $40,000 consular fees at that port have been wrongfully retained by his predecessors, and believes that $200,000 has been stolen from the emigration fund."

As the guerrilla Colonel is a good Republican, our Republican friends must accept his testimony.

Rock Island Argus – August 7, 1879

As Mr. Evarts declines to pay any attention to the official statement of Consul Mosby that the government has been cheated out of $200,000 in consul fees at Hong Kong during the past 17 years, Consul Mosby proposes to pass in his resignation. Mr. Evarts seems to be singularly indifferent to irregularities in consular service in China.—*Washington Post.*

Daily National Republican – August 19, 1879

Consul Mosby's Dispatch.

It is ascertained at the State Department that the dispatch of Consul Mosby at Hong Kong, relating to Chinese emigration fees, which was published in yesterday's papers, was acted upon immediately upon its receipt. The Department directed him to comply with its former instructions, which required all fees for emigration certificates to be accounted for and deposited in the Treasury; and that the examination which he was authorized to make should be full and thorough. At the same time a consular officer of long experience in its relation to the consular service, as well as of other matters on which information was desired. The report on these subjects is expected at an early day.

The allusion to Minister Seward is an error, as he was never consul at Hong Kong*

[*Seward had been consul there at one time, a fact that was reported in a prior congressional investigation of his activities before he moved onward and upward in the China service. Seward was never prosecuted because he was the nephew of William Seward and a Republican, and so was Congress.-vph]

Chicago Tribune – **August 22, 1879**
BY MAIL.

Disclosures from China – Swindling Consuls Detected – Col. Mosby.

A noteworthy letter from "Guerrilla" Mosby, our Consul at Hong Kong, has just been published. The letter is dated on the 20th of February last. If it reached the State Department – it is addressed to F. W. Seward, Assistant Secretary – there seems to have been no answer given to it. Another significant circumstance is that the letter is published not from a copy furnished by the State Department, but from a copy presumably furnished by Mr. Mosby. Consul Mosby finds that there are fees attached to the inspection of vessels leaving Hong Kong with Chinese emigrants for the United States. The law making Consular inspection necessary was passed in 1862, and our present Consul estimates that in the period between the passage of that act and the date of his letter fully $30,000 was collected from this source alone. Not a dollar of this sum seems to have been turned into the Treasury of the United States until 1871: no reports of fees from this source were made at all. Since that time reports have been made regularly, the "expenses" balancing the fee with the most scrupulous exactness. Mr. Mosby does not scruple to say that the expenses were outrageous, and to leave the ground for a conclusive presumption that his predecessors made a good thing out of these fees.

Consul Mosby says he would like to retain the fees, and he asks the Department if it can be done legally. The Department should not have hesitated in sending him prompt instructions on the subject. These fees belong to the people of the United States, and those who have converted them to their own use have been guilty of malversation in office. Everywhere the fee system leads to abuse. The State Department owes it to itself to investigate the consular system in China and make an example of those who have brought disgrace upon the service. The policy of silence and suppression will not do. Let no guilty man escape.

It would be better to have all our Consulates full of Rebel Brigadiers than to have them full of the "truly loyal" who make no more distinction between meum and teum than Tammany offenders. Secretary Evarts owes it to himself and the country to promptly answer Consul Mosby's letter, and to examine the charges implied in it. The abuses in our Consular system in China cannot be too soon removed. The persistent smoke in that quarter indicates fire.

Mosby had tried numerous times to provoke the Department of State into action, but when his efforts were unsuccessful (he had been informed that his lengthy reports had been "lost"), he resorted to more "irregular" tactics. First, he sent letters with the evidence he had already sent to both Hayes and the State Department to friends, requesting that they bring the information to the notice of the Secretary personally. If that were unsuccessful, the next step was public exposure of the matter in the press—Mosby knew how to use the press as well as the press knew how to use Mosby! This was far more successful, but it led to the Consul being excoriated by the administration and the Republican press for "failing to follow protocol," which was apparently defined as letting sleeping crooks lie:

Daily Globe – August 25, 1879

CONSUL FEES.

Col. Mosby's Protest Against the Robbery of the Government by Consuls in China and Japan.

John. S. Mosby, the United States Consul-General at Hong Kong, China, has officially notified the state department of the corrupt practices of Minister Seward and others, in the following letter:

Hong Kong, Feb. 20, 1879.

"Hon. F. W. Seward, Assistant, &c.—Sir:

I desire to call the attention of the department to a question of interest both to myself and the government. An act of Congress, passed in 1862, required all vessels carrying Chinese emigrants to the United States to have the certificate of the United States consul residing at the port of departure to the effect of their voluntary emigration. All of the Chinese emigrants go from this port, and, I suppose, have gone with the necessary certificates ever since the enactment of the law.

"On examination of the records of this consulate I can find no credit to the government for any fees collected on this account previous to the forth quarter of 1871, although, as I am informed by those who know, fees have always been charged for this service. Since 1871, in every quarterly statement, there is a credit for the amount of emigration fees collected, and a charge for the expense as per voucher for collecting them. By a strange coincidence the debit for expenses always balances the credit for collection, so that the government gets nothing. The total amount of these fees, as appears by the record since 1871, is $14,345.75.

"The late vice-consul in charge, Mr. Loring, informed me that no record was kept of fees for certificates for Chinese emigrants going to the United States in vessels carrying foreign flags, but that those fees were regarded as unofficial, and remained as the perquisites of the consul. There is a line of steamers, the Oriental and Occidental company, carrying the British flag, that has been running regularly between Hong Kong and San Francisco. As this company runs three large steamers, and the Pacific Mail company only runs two, it may readily be inferred that the Oriental and Occidental line, and other foreign vessels have carried as many emigrants as the other.

"It may be estimated, therefore, that within the last eight years over $30,000 have been collected here in emigration fees, or a sum about equal to the consular fees for that period. I would like, very much to be allowed to retain these fees if it can properly be done; but I do not feel justified in appropriating them in the absence of instructions from the department. No fees from this source have ever, I believe, been turned into the treasury, but all have either been retained by the consul or consumed in the "expense" of examination of emigrants. I do not propose to charge the government anything for the expenses of examination, for I see no good reason why there should be any, and I expect to do this work in person. This duty, I learn, has hitherto been performed by one Peter Smith, whose receipts constituted the vouchers to the 'expense' account.

"The following is a brief history of the ceremony of examination: on the day before a vessel was to leave with the Chinese emigrants, no matter whether American or foreign, the United States Consul was informed that at a certain hour the passengers would be ready for examination. At the appointed time Peter Smith appeared with the Consular seal. The passengers collected on the deck and passed in review before him, each being asked if he was a voluntary emigrant. If he said that he was his ticket was stamped with the Consular seal. It would take on average about one hour to complete the investigation. This is the whole proceeding, the government being charged also with the expense of the boat hire, in addition to the amount for which Peter Smith has receipted.

"From all that I have learned, I have no doubt that Peter Smith has only played the part of John Doe and Richard Roe in the proceeding. The nominal sum covered by his receipts is so absurdly out of proportion to the time he was employed and that value of the services he rendered, or was capable of rendering, as to exclude any other conclusion. He is an illiterate keeper of a sailor's boarding-house, and I have no doubt would contract to-day to do the whole work for $100 a year, and consider himself well paid. As I have already said, I intend personally to inspect the emigrants, no matter whether the department declares the fees received for the service to be official or unofficial."

The "dispatch" printed above demonstrates that Colonel Mosby began the work of exposure without delay. His official testimony shows that Baily, while consul at Hong Kong, deprived the government of over $40,000 in the one item of emigrant fees. Instead of injuring Mr. Bailey in the estimation of the State department and of the administration, this official evidence of his dishonesty seems to have commended him. He was re-nominated for consul-general, and the Senate, not being aware of the Mosby dispatch, confirmed him. It was not the intention of the State department that the contents of this dispatch should ever be made public. It was kept among the "State" secrets of the department, and only reached the public eye by means of a copy mailed from Hong Kong to unofficial quarters.

Mosby's "guerrilla tactics" that had caused such angst in the government when the scandal was made public through the newspapers led to him—and not Bailey or Seward—being punished by the Department of State. But such obviously unjust conduct suddenly caused the Democratic papers to take a more kindly view of their old enemy. He was, after all, making life very uncomfortable not only for the Republican crooks in China but also for their fellow travelers at home, who were undoubtedly protecting them. Whatever appeal Mosby may have had for the Democratic press in the past, a whole new field was opening up for cultivation:

The Republican – August 27, 1879

Mosby Utilized—Little did de facto Hayes expect that when he appointed the "Guerrilla Mosby," Consul to China, that he would expose the crookedness of that Radical scoundrel Seward, who robbed the Treasury of thousands of dollars holding the same position. An exchange says: "Mosby comes to the front from Hong Kong with the startling story that immigration fees to the amount of $40,000 received by his predecessors in the Consulate have never been reported to the Government. As Seward held that office once, and escaped the clutch of Democrats during the last session of Congress on the charges of fraud, the party will be ready to forgive Guerrilla Mosby for going over to Grant, and thus getting a chance to furnish further charges against Seward."

It is quite possible that the paper was correct when it claimed that Hayes did not expect Mosby to be anything but another corrupt—or corruptible—political cypher. But the paper was no better than Hayes, for it praised Mosby for uncovering Seward's misdeeds and, a week later, condemned him in a further article as a murderer and outlaw. And in the middle of this glorious imbroglio, John Mosby was quoted about the "third-term" issue, though why it should have been considered important is not made clear. Perhaps it was because there were others who also considered Grant as the nominee when Hayes stepped down, which was in fact the case:

St. Paul Daily Globe – September 1, 1879

Mosby, one of Grant's chums while the general presided in the White House, advises the American people to insist on his acceptance of a nomination for the Presidency, assuring them that, if urged, Ulysses would accept with thanks. It is just possible that Grant has, like Paul, been sitting at Gamaliel Mosby's feet and imbibing his guerrilla tactics. If so there is not telling where we may find him on his return from his wanderings.

Mosby's fixation with a third term for Grant can be explained only because he didn't consider him a politician, but a soldier. He had made quite clear that he distrusted and despised politicians, but alas, Grant was as much a politician as any of the others. However, Mosby was not wrong regarding the possibility of a third term, for Grant did indeed make himself available to run in 1880, so Mosby cannot be charged with being ignorant or silly as well as naïve. In between scandals, the papers were back to Mosby and Grant or, more accurately, Mosby on Grant:

Millheim Journal – September 4, 1879

Col. Mosby predicts that Grant will run.

Washington, Aug. 29.—Col. Mosby was one of Grant's companions at the White House—one of the convivial old boys who could get more talk out of Grant over a bottle and a cigar than any of his less rough and more diplomatic associates. Mosby has had one of these good old talks with Grant in Hong Kong, the result of which he has communicated to a friend in this city. Mosby says that all the is talk about Grant's not desiring or not accepting a possible Presidential nomination is "poppy cock," to quote exactly from the Mosby vernacular. Grant will run, Mosby predicts, and he thinks he will be elected by an overwhelming majority.

Mosby was right about Grant. He allowed his name to be placed in nomination by Roscoe Conkling while James Garfield did the same for John Sherman. In the end, neither Grant nor Sherman was selected. but Garfield—and he was elected. Could Grant have been elected if nominated? Obviously, if Garfield (a relative unknown and a Federal officer during the war) was elected after the dubious Hayes "victory," it certainly shows that Grant could have been elected.

But soon, the press returned to the scandal in the Chinese consular service—it was better press. They could sense the vultures circling the accused men who had been shielded for so long by the Republicans in Washington. In the Democratic press, there was hope that these aiders and abettors might also fall:

Northern Ohio Journal –September 6, 1879 (Edited)

A Report from Mosby

When Stalwarts clash with Stalwarts we may look to see the fire fly, and the new developments in the case of Minister Seward which are contained in the statements made to the State Department by Consul Mosby will attract wide attention and renew the hope that justice may be done to one who, so far as testimony has been admitted, has been no credit to the country.

The attempted investigation of the doings of the Seward ring in China is fresh in the minds of all. The Republican minority maintained a solid front, and resisted all efforts of the Democratic majority to have this stigma upon the good name of the Government removed... Minister Seward was allowed to go, because the Republicans supported him in every action of contempt of which he was guilty. He escaped by means of the most absurd technicality... His plea was that if these books would criminate him under the Constitution he could not be compelled to produce them, and he did not produce them. But Mosby, in an official report, has come forward with the evidence that was supposed to be derivable from those books. He found the accounts of emigration fees, under Seward's consulate, in a curious state. "By a strange coincidence the debit for expense always balances the credit for the collection, so that the Government gets nothing." He estimates that within the last eight years over $30,000 have collected in emigration fees, yet no fees from this source have been turned into the Treasury, he believes, in all that time. These matters he would like explained for his own satisfaction.

There has not been, in the entire history of Republican maladministration, a more flagrant case of party whitewash than this, which covered up a record that he publicly believed to be so full of corruption that it was a disgrace to the public service. In opposing this very proper investigation that The Democrats are conducting, no Republican was more offensive, unreasonable and vindictive than General Butler... "He not only made a speech against the power of the House to punish Seward for contempt in refusing to produce before the committee the books of the Government, but he was the leader of the Republican side in its efforts to shut off all inquiry into the case. As a member of the Judiciary Committee, he took charge of the contempt case, and reported that Seward's refusal to produce the Government's own books was no contempt holding, in effect, that a Government officer can prevent the use of the official books which are in his custody by some simple trick of writing in them some entries pertaining to his household expenditures... Seward may be a friend of General Butler and a friend of the Republican party, but he can hardly count among his friends any who wish to see the affairs of the Government abroad administered honestly and efficiently. He might have thought it made little difference what he did so far away, but a man's works are very apt to follow him or precede him, even from as great a distance as the antipodes... Meanwhile Mosby's report is fired straight at the State Department, and we wait to see what will be done about it.—*Boston Post*.

Isn't it odd that the same paper—the Boston Post—that published that nasty little poem about Mosby and Grant should report on this subject as it did. Obviously, it was a Democratic organ; for it claimed that that party was the champion of all honesty, while the Republicans were corrupt to the bone. Yet it failed to mention that the man who had exposed this matter—a matter that the Congress itself could not cure even when The Democrats were in the majority—was that much-maligned Mosby, himself a Republican. Where was the mention that Seward's books were now available to Congress because they had been made so by that same Republican guerrilla Mosby? All that was said was that "we"—meaning The Democrats—"will wait to see what will be done about it." Nothing would have been "done about it" if it hadn't been for John Mosby!

The following story was extremely prescient in making note that Mosby also wanted to "pocket" the fees, but he was "too honest [even for a guerrilla!]" to do so without government sanction. This was one of the few stories that brought to the fore Mosby's caution in determining what belonged to him as consul and what did not:

The *Leavenworth Weekly Times* – September 11, 1879

Consul Mosby's Revelations. [San Francisco Bulletin.]

Consul Mosby at Hongkong has let out the "true inwardness" of the Chinese emigration from that port. It has always been noticeable that the people of that coast, in their efforts to stop the "yellow tide" never received much sympathy from our officials in China. But the reason, so far as Hongkong is concerned, is now apparent. It is at that place that all the Chinese embark. In the last few years, according to Mosby, upwards of $30,000 have been collected in fees from emigrants by former Consuls. The fees ought to have been paid into the Treasury. But they have not. The fact is brought out because Consul Mosby wants to pocket them himself, but he is too honest, even if he was a guerilla, to do so without first obtaining the sanction of the Government. The perquisites in question are quite large enough to bias the official mind. What is the use of having a country if one cannot turn it to good account occasionally? A Chinese outpouring on the United States might be bad in the abstract, but there was a great deal of concrete satisfaction in the fees.

So now he was "Consul Mosby" and not "Mosby the guerrilla" or just "Mosby." And there were kudos of a sort given to him in this article, but they do not go far enough. They acknowledged that he had explained the reason why Chinese immigration was not hampered, but in doing so, he also acknowledged that he too could have participated in the spoils but refused before determining if it were lawful for him to do so.

General Julius Stahel, an old Yankee adversary of Mosby's, had been brought from Japan by Secretary Evarts ostensibly to look into the charges. It was suggested by at least one of Mosby's biographers that Stahel was chosen in hopes that his dislike of

Mosby occasioned by the war might lead to something that could excuse the consul's recall or at the very least, blunt his accusations. But Stahel was too honest—or too cautious—to either get the hint or, having done so, to act upon it:

Chicago Tribune – September 24, 1879

Gen. Mosby's Charge of Defalcation Investigated and Reported True— Bailey, the Hong Kong Consul, Shown up—

Something for Secretary Evarts to Explain.

San Francisco, Cal., Sept. 23. – A Los Angeles dispatch says: G. Wiley Wells, of this city, is in receipt of a letter from Col. Mosby, Consul at Hong Kong, by the last China steamer, which will be published in the Journal tomorrow. It is to the effect that before the name of Bailey, late Consul at Hong Kong, was sent to the Senate for confirmation as Consul-General at Shanghai, the Secretary of State was in possession of Consul Mosby's dispatch charging Bailey with being a defaulter to the Government to the amount of $30,000 or $40,000, with a record of evidence sustaining the charge; that not until after Bailey's confirmation, and Mosby's dispatch had in part been published in a Washington paper, did the Secretary of State take notice of the charges. The Department then sent Gen. Stahel, Consul at Hiogo, Japan, and a friend of Seward and Bailey, to investigate the truth of the charges made by Mosby. Gen. Stahel sought to have Bailey explain the charges. Stahel has concluded his investigations, and has been obliged to report to the Department that the charges of Bailey's embezzlement from the Government while Consul at Hong Kong, as made by Mosby, are true; also that Seward's private secretary, Holcomb, has written letters to various officials in China denouncing Mosby; also that Seward is using his influence to shield Bailey and prevent investigation. There is also evidence showing that Bailey was placed at Shanghai to cover Seward's track.

National Republican – September 25, 1879

THE HONG KONG CONSULATE.

A Statement Made by Mr. G. Wiley Wells.

San Francisco, Sept. 23.—A Los Angeles dispatch says: "G. Wiley Wells, of this city, is in receipt of a letter from Colonel Mosby, consul at Hong Kong, by the last steamer from China. The communications, which will be published in the Journal to-morrow, is to the effect that before the name of Bailey, the late consul at Hong Kong, was sent to the Senate for confirmation as consul-general at Shanghai, the Secretary of State was in possession of Consul Mosby's dispatch, charging Bailey with being a defaulter to the Government of $30,000 or $40,000, with a record of evidence sustaining the charge; that not until after Bailey's confirmation and Mosby's dispatch had in part been published in a Washington newspaper did the Secretary of State take notice of the charges. The department then sent General Stahel, of the consulate at Hiago, Japan, a friend of Messrs. Seward and Bailey, to investigate the truth of the charges made by Mr. Mosby. General Stahel sought to have Mr. Bailey explain the charges. General Stahel has concluded his investigations, and has been obliged to report to the department that the charges of Bailey's embezzlement from the Government while consul at Hong Kong, as made by Colonel Mosby, are true.

National Republican – **September 26, 1879**

Evening Star – **September 26, 1879**

The Charges Against Consul General Bailey The Hong Kong Consulate.

The statement reported to have been made by Colonel Mosby, United States Consul at Hong Kong, in communication to G. Wiley Wells at Los Angeles, and which has been telegraphed East from San Francisco, was referred to Secretary Evarts with an inquiry as to the truth of the charges it contained. The Secretary said that Mr. Bailey, against whom the charges are made, was merely promoted by him, he having held office under the previous Administration. His confirmation by the Senate as Consul-General at Shanghai was very tardy, but Secretary Evarts has no theory as to the cause of the delay. During further conversation upon the subject the Secretary said that an investigation has been made into certain Chinese consulates and General Stahel of the consulate at Hiago, Japan, who is considered one of the most competent and upright men in the public service. Until receipt of his report any action by the Department, Mr. Evarts thinks, would be manifestly premature and unjust. With reference to Mosby having been in correspondence with G. Wiley Wells, the Secretary said: "Of course, the Department knows nothing of any correspondence of Consul Mosby with persons not in the public service."

The Sun wrote of "efforts to prevent exposure and punishment," but in the end, the only person actually "punished" was John Mosby:

The Sun – **September 26, 1879**

THE CONSULAR RING IN CHINA.

Efforts to Prevent Exposure and Punishment—Another Consul Accused of Stealing.

Washington, Sept. 25—It is a well understood fact here that the State Department officials are doing all in their power to prevent the exposure and punishment of the Consular Ring in China, of which George F. Seward, United States Minister at Pekin, is the head.

For the last two years, Seward and his dishonest associates have been defending themselves against charges proved before an investigating committee of Congress, and believed by a very great majority of the English-speaking residents of the Chinese Empire. William M. Evarts has been one of Seward's strongest backers in Washington. It may be that the regard Mr. Evarts has for the Seward family induces him to look leniently upon George F. Seward's misconduct. Possibly the influence exerted by Fred Seward, the Assistant Secretary of State, is sufficient to keep Minister Seward in the diplomatic service, notwithstanding a majority of a committee of the House of Representatives found him guilty of stealing and recommended his impeachment.

In a letter which Gen. Mosby, Consul at Hong Kong recently sent to a friend in Los Angeles, Ca., the downfall of another member of the Seward

Ring is predicted. David H. Bailey, Consul at Shanghai is the victim. Several months ago, Mosby ascertained that Bailey, who was promoted to the Shanghai consulate from Hong Kong, had appropriated about $40,000 of Government fees while acting Consul at the last named port. Mosby, in his letter received by the last China steamer, says that before the name of Bailey was sent to the Senate for confirmation as Consul to Shanghai, Mosby's dispatch was sent charging Bailey with being a defaulter to the Government in the amount of $40,000, with a record of the evidence sustaining the charge; that not until after Bailey's confirmation and Mosby's dispatch had in part been published in a Washington newspaper did Mr. Evarts take notice of the charge.

The department then sent Gen. Stahel, Consulate at Hiogo, Japan, a friend of Seward and Bailey, to investigate the charges. Stahel sought to have Bailey explain the charges. Stahel has concluded his investigations and has been obliged to report to the department that the charges of Bailey's embezzlement from the Government while Consul at Hong Kong, as made by Mosby, are true. Seward's private secretary Holcomb has written letters to various officials in China denouncing Mosby. Seward is using his influence to shield Bailey and prevent the investigation. A letter also says that there is evidence showing that Bailey was placed at Shanghai to cover Seward's tracks. When Seward was dragged over the coals before the Committee on Expenditures in the State Department of the Forty-fifth Congress, Bailey was in Washington. He passed much of his time visiting the offices of newspaper correspondents, attempting to create sympathy for Seward. The latter, according to Mosby, is now exerting his good offices to shield Bailey. William M. Evarts to-day declined to say whether or not he had, as Mosby alleges, received information of Bailey's thievery at Hong Kong before Bailey was confirmed Consul at Shanghai. By refusing to either affirm or deny a fact which can easily be ascertained by the Committee on Expenditures of the State Department next winter, Mr. Evarts permits himself to become the subject of suspicion.

Should Bailey be proved guilty of the charges which now appear to be well sustained, the conduct of the defacto Secretary of State in withholding from the Senate information in his possession detrimental to Bailey's character, while Bailey's nomination for an important office was pending, will be severely censured. Mr. Evarts says that the department has not yet received Gen. Stahel's report of his investigation into the Hong Kong Consulate, and until that report is received, he declines to be interviewed.

Mosby had followed all the proper channels and jumped through all the bureaucratic and diplomatic hoops when he discovered the situation in Hong Kong, contrary to those who claimed that he "acted like a guerrilla." Of course, these methods achieved nothing but a continuation of the status quo. On the other hand, his "irregular methods" here complained of, did produce results and the politicians and bureaucrats soon found that they ignored him at their peril.

As noted, one of Mosby's biographers opined that Stahel, a former Federal general who "encountered" Mosby during the war, was chosen for that very reason—even more than for his personal friendship with Seward and Bailey. But Stahel proved to be either honorable or a man who had no desire to challenge John Mosby's dogged persistence and found the Consul's charges to be legitimate, which must have been a shock to Secretary Evarts, who had made it known that he would say nothing until he had Stahel's report.

The chances are, Evarts expected a whitewash as there can be no doubt that the State Department knew all about Bailey before he was confirmed for Shanghai.

Meanwhile, the *National Republican*, a paper that had supported Mosby for the most part, began to realize the enormity of the mess he had uncovered and the probable consequences that would devolve not only on the members of the ring, but also on various other Republicans in government and on the party itself. Therefore, it apparently determined that "it was better for one man to die" for the good of the party than for the whole party to suffer. Of course, that "one man" was John Mosby:

National Republican – **September 27, 1879**

CURRENT CAPITAL TOPICS.

Mosby in His New Role as National Reformer.

Some Explanation in Regard to His Recent Correspondence Mosby Rampaging About the Orient.

It appears from official and unofficial sources that Colonel John S. Mosby, Consul at Hong Kong, China, has organized himself into a widespread smelling committee, so to speak, and since his arrival at his post of duty has done little else than investigate things not only in his own consulate, but in others, near and remote. It also appears that it is his habit to send reports of his investigations official to the Department of State, semi-officially to the President and unofficially to some of his friends in Washington and Virginia. The consequence is that the public is duly informed of the progress he is making in the course of his self-constituted inquiries as promptly as the Government is. This violation of official etiquette is inexcusable; but it is peculiar to Mosby, and undoubtedly serves the purpose he seeks, which it is not evident is to make a National reputation as a Reformer.

Mosby's appointment was one of those peculiarly characteristic things which are always happening to men of his peculiar stripe. He wrote a communication to The *National Republican* and another to the *New York Tribune* about the time of the origin of the Potter committee, defending the validity of President Hayes' title, and urging the Republicans in Congress and the country generally to stand firm in opposition to the Democratic theory that the title was not a valid one. By means of these communications he established friendly and personal relations with the President, and in the natural course of events, after he had declined one or two offices, he was sent to Hong Kong. He always regarded his appointment as one that had been made by the President himself, and when he started for his post of duty he called upon him to bid him good-bye. During the course of this fare-well interview Colonel Mosby incidentally remarked to the President that he might "see some things worth reporting to him (the President) in person." In response to this suggestion the President remarked that he would, of course, be glad to hear from the Colonel at all times, &c., &c. This response was accepted by Mosby as authority express and unqualified from the Chief Magistrate to exercise a vicarious supervision over American affairs throughout the length and breadth of Pagan-land. Hence Mosby's reports to the President.

But it appears that one of these reports, at least, if not more, which reached President Hayes was referred in the routine course of affairs to the Department of State, where it naturally belonged. It contained some complaint or suggestion about the size and profit of the fees of his consulate, as well as allusion to the fact that he had already reported any amount of misdeeds and misdoings by other consuls, dead and alive, to the Secretary of State. When this novel document reached its final destination it created some surprise, but the President, in the interest of official discipline, authorized a reply to be made to it, directing the self-appointed investigator to confine his communications in the future to the proper official channels.

An official letter was accordingly prepared, admonishing Mr. Mosby that his allegiance was first due to the Department of State, that he must obey the orders of the Department of State, and that, in short, he belonged officially to the Department of State. In other words, the letter was expressly designed to impress upon the Colonel the fact that he had a "boss," as it were, and was no longer engaged in the partisan ranger business. Secretary Evarts did not sign the letter, for the reason that he was absent at the time it was written, nor did Assistant Secretary Seward, for the same and other evident reasons, but Assistant Secretary Hunter did, and it was duly sent to Hong-Kong. No direct response has been received to it, so far as known, up to this writing; but information has been received indirectly from Colonel Mosby that he will return to American some time about the reassembling of Congress, and then resign his consulate. There is the same indirect authority for the statement that when he does resign it will be for the purpose of laying all of his alleged information about things in China, Siam and the East generally before Congress, and raising a cloud of fragrant scandal, on the summit of which he hopes to ride into further National notoriety.

Meanwhile, the Department of State, in a quiet, dignified and proper manner, without taking the newspaper public into its confidence or making a splurge in the Opposition press, has taken all the necessary steps to secure reliable and verified information regarding the alleged irregularities Mosby assumes to have unearthed, and will be in readiness when Congress meets to give that body the true inwardness of all of the Mosby scandals.

To begin with, John Mosby's "first allegiance" was to the law and the people of the United States, not to the Department of State or the Federal government much less the Republican party. Second, the "quiet, dignified and proper manner" employed by the State Department for "securing reliable and verified information" sententiously declared in the article was a problem because it also permitted that "information" to be buried so deep that it would never again see the light of day if that were the department's desire; and in this case, that was the department's desire.

Mosby received great assistance when the Honorable G. Wiley Wells, a man of impeccable character and reputation, weighed in on his own interaction with the Seward Ring. The newspapers could no longer abuse Mosby, whose reputation could be called into question, because they had Wells, a man whose reputation nobody questioned. Still, it must have been most galling for Mosby to see himself treated in this way by a paper that had previously defended him.

Mosby's behavior in China echoed his political behavior in Virginia. Knowing that "doing nothing" accomplished nothing, cured nothing, and solved nothing, John Mosby put his neck into the bureaucratic halter and put the Department of State in the position of removing him—and all the publicity that move would evoke!—or cleaning house. He made no friends in government by doing this, but he might have made a few friends among honest Americans willing to overlook his war service or his political apostasy in recognition of his honesty.

A little article in the Brenham Weekly Banner (Texas) succinctly made the point—that is, that those involved were Republicans of "high standing" in that party. Still, it would have been agreeable to have the Banner give a little bit of credit to the fact that Mosby was willing to expose criminality in his own party:

Brenham Weekly Banner – October 3, 1879

Col. Mosby, United States consul at Hong Kong, charges that his predecessors in office, Seward and Bailey, were defaulters; that the fact was known to the government and that Bailey was sent to cover up Seward's short comings. All of these gentlemen are republicans and were in high standing in the party.

Daily Intelligencer – October 5, 1879

A Tribune Washington special says:

Letters received a short time ago at the State Department from Consul Mosby indicate that his resignation may be looked for within the next three months. The Colonel is said to have received a pretty sharp reminder from the Department that communications in regard to official matters should be addressed to the Department and not to the President. A letter addressed to the President, rehearsing some exploding scandals which Col. Mosby had heard after his arrival in China was sent to the Department with an intimation from the President that he did not wish to be troubled with such matters.

Apropos of several communications written by Mosby and published recently in this country, in which he reiterates charges to the effect that Bailey, the present Consul at Shanghai, was a defaulter to the Government to the extent of $30,000 or $40,000, while he was Consul at Hongkong, attention has been called by person s familiar with Consular regulations to the following rule: "Correspondence with newspapers or magazines in the United States by Consular officers is prohibited. This prohibition does not extend to literary articles or subjects disconnected with politics."

Mosby had no intention of retiring, and it might be concluded that this little "expose" of his "intentions to do so" to the newspapers was done by the State Department as a hedge against such time as he would be removed from his position; that is, they could always say that he "retired" of his own accord. Of course, had this been a Democratic paper, a great deal more would have been said about Mosby's situation after his exposure of long-standing corruption in the China consulates. Yet the paper could not forbear putting in the amount of money Mosby had reported stolen! With the Republican papers, this scandal caused them great angst. On the one hand, as usual, Mosby was great copy. On the other, he was exposing far too many skeletons in Republican closets!

Again, there was this unacceptable situation in which the "crime" was exposing corruption rather than committing it. This, of course, was nothing new; neither did it ever end for Mosby during his government service. The secret corruption of Seward and Bailey was more acceptable to the government and its agencies than its open exposure by Mosby. Also, there is the question of whether the exposure of a crime is something that is "connected with politics"? If it is, then it stands to reason that politics per se includes criminality.

The Sun – October 7, 1879 (Edited)
EVART'S CHINESE PETS.

Mr. E. Attempts To Protect Official Thieves.

A Confederate Guerrilla Defending the Treasury of the United States Against the Friends of William Maxwell Evarts.

Washington, Oct. 3.—It has been semi-officially announced that John S. Mosby, United States Consul at Hong Kong, China is to be recalled. The alleged reason for this is that he caused one of his despatches to be printed in the newspapers, and that this, being a violation of the consular regulations, is sufficient to warrant his decapitation.

The real reason, however, is that Mosby has made himself exceedingly active in ferreting out some of the frauds of the Seward Ring in China. He had not been at his post two weeks before he discovered that David H. Bailey, his predecessor, had in one class of fees alone defrauded the United States Government out of $30,000 to $40,000. He instantly reported this fact to the State Department. His dispatch on this subject was sent Feb. 20, 1879, and must have reached Washington long before Bailey, who had been nominated for Consul-General at Shanghai, had been confirmed by the Senate…There was ample time for Mr. Evarts to withdraw Bailey's nomination … Mr. Evarts declared that he knew nothing of these allegations when the nomination was made… But the truth is that formal charges against Bailey had been made at the State Department by Mr. Wells, ex-Consul General at Shanghai, before the nomination of Bailey was sent to the Senate. Wells also tendered this evidence to prove that Bailey was nominated for this position at the special request of Minister Seward… That Mr. Evarts is determined at all hazards to prevent any further exposure of the criminal doings of the Seward Ring in China is shown by his announcement that Mosby is to be recalled. He will not succeed however. He was compelled to order an investigation of Mosby's charges, and the result has been that they are sustained by unimpeachable evidence and the agent directed to make the inquiry has so reported to the department. Mosby will prove an ugly customer to deal with, as the following letters to a personal friend will show:

CONSULATE OF THE United States

Hong Kong, June 3, 1879.

My Dear Sir:

The last time I saw you, you told me that you were opposing the confirmation of Bailey to be Consul-General at Shanghai. I write to inform you that there is enough on the records of this Consulate to damn him forever. On the 20th of February, I sent a dispatch to the State Department showing that Bailey and Loring had in the item of emigration fees alone robbed the Government out of $40,000. I had only been here two weeks then. I have since discovered that this was only a small part of their plundering. I dismissed Loring, the Vice-Consul' he was very anxious to continue here as Vice. In a retaliation for this exposure of their villainy, "the Seward Ring" have published the libel about me you have seen in reference to my refusing to wear a dress suit at an entertainment at the Governor's. The Governor (who is a warm personal friend of mine) when he saw these publications wrote me an indignant letter branding them as libels. I have sent his letter to the United States for publication.

"The Seward Ring" wanted Bailey at Shanghai to cover Seward's tracks and Loring or Lincoln here to cover Bailey's. They have for years dominated China and crushed out everybody that was not subservient to their interests.

I have written Gen. Gordon on the subject. Has Seward prosecution dropped or is it only suspended? Let me hear from you...Jno. S. Mosby.

UNITED STATES CONSULATE,

Hong Kong, Aug. 17, 1879

I wrote to you in June by the Alaska, and gave my letter to the purser to mail in San Francisco. Since then, Gen. Stahel has been sent here by the department to investigate the truth of charges I made against Bailey of malfeasance in office. He is here now—has not written his report, but he cabled to Washington for permission to examine Bailey in person, which convinces me that he will report against him and wishes to give him an opportunity, for if there was no evidence against him there would be no use in asking him to explain it; besides, Stahel on his way here saw Bailey in Shanghai. Bailey then attempted an explanation and also wrote Stahel a long letter here in his defence. But no human ingenuity can explain away the proof I have submitted against him. The records of the Consulate convict him of defalcation of thirty or forty thousand dollars. This does not include his outside rascality. I do not see now how he can escape impeachment. I wrote to Gen. Gordon not to allow him to be confirmed, but he had passed before my letter reached Washington. When he was nominated the last time my dispatch was on file at the State Department, showing Bailey's defalcation by record evidence. Since he was confirmed Stahel was sent to investigate the truth...There is no doubt of the fact that for many years there existed out here a Consular Ring just as corrupt as the old Whiskey Ring that lived and thrived by plundering the Government, shipowners and sailors. Seward and Bailey were the head of the Ring; what is proof of it is the active interest the Seward set is taking in my prosecution of Bailey. Not long after I received a most gushing and flattering private letter from Bailey, evidently written to propitiate me, saying how proud he was to have me for his successor. As I had then discovered his corruption in office, I treated it with contempt.

Very truly, John S. Mosby

P. S.—Stahel has concluded his investigation, and will confirm the truth of my charges against Bailey of a default of thirty or forty thousand dollars. J.S.M.

Los Angeles Herald – October 9, 1879

Mosby on Consular Crookedness in China.

New York, Oct. 8th—A Sun Washington special, on Mosby's alleged exposure of frauds of the Seward ring in China, says: Formal charges against Bailey had been made at the State Department by Wells, ex-Consul-General at Shanghai, before the nomination of Bailey went to the Senate. Wells also tendered evidence to prove that Bailey was nominated for the position at the special request of Seward. He quotes a letter from Mosby, in which he says:

"The Seward ring wanted Bailey at Shanghai to cover up Seward's tracks, and Loring or Lincoln to cover up Bailey's. They have for years dominated China and crushed everybody that was not subservient to their interests. There is no doubt of the fact that for many years there existed out here a Consular ring, just as corrupt as the whiskey ring that lived and thrived by plundering government, ship-owners and sailors. I am in for the war, and intend to either purge the service of these scoundrels or go out if it myself."

Mosby had thrown down the gauntlet. He would not resign. Furthermore, he had made that fact clear in print. Therefore, if Evarts wanted him gone, he would have to remove him; and if he removed him, literally all hell would break loose. By this time, it was probable that Hayes devoutly wished he had kept Mosby in Virginia, where some enraged adherent of the Lost Cause might have relieved him of his problem with a well-placed bullet.

The *Atlanta Constitution*, no friend of Mosby's, was able, in a very few words, to castigate him, the *New York Tribune*, and Secretary Evarts—no mean journalistic feat:

Atlanta Constitution – October 14, 1879

Mr. Evarts contends, we presume, that a man like Mosby, who fought the government, and, in the elevated language of the New York Tribune, threatened the Life of the Nation, has no right to discover that a loyal citizen of the republican party is a thief. Mr. Evarts probably exaggerates Mosby's motives.

John Mosby began his service in China in 1879, accompanied by insulting stories concerning his boorish behavior, stories that were soon proven untrue. But that didn't end his continuing persecution. He was cordially disliked by the American community in the colony to whom he referred as "Yankees!" and had no real friends but the British governor, the Honorable Sir John Pope Hennessy, an Irish Catholic. Hennessy served at that post from 1877 to 1883. He was disliked by both the Americans and the British, first of all because he was an Irish Catholic but also because he was concerned with the rights of the Chinese residents. Hennessy liked Mosby and, he, together with the French consul, Monsieur deJardin, provided the lonely Virginian with such social life as he had, given his frigid reception by the American community. But sadly, even that did not last long; for late in 1879, Hennessy began an investigation into illegal practices carried on in the exceedingly profitable opium trade moving through Hong Kong. As a part of that investigation, the Governor wrote letters to all the foreign consuls "requesting" access to their books. Mosby demurred. Although his position was not reported in detail, he doubtless believed that he had no right to open the consulate's books to anyone without the approval of the State Department:

Daily Globe – November 22, 1879
GUERRILLA MOSBY CREATES A SENSATION.

Shanghai, Nov. 21.—A sensation at Hong Kong has been caused by a quarrel between Gen. Mosby and Gov. Hennessey. The latter official desires to obtain full official information concerning the opium traffic between Hong Kong and Macao in order to check notorious illegal practice, and applied to Mosby for copies of the United States records of shipments, etc. The governor alleges that the request was made for the public good and with perfect courtesy, having been proffered to other foreign consuls, and all of whom willingly responded to it. Mosby alleges that the request implied a claim of right to inspect consular documents that he was bound to resent.

American citizens regret that the United States consul has broken relations with the governor, who had previously shown him great attention and consideration. The actual merits of the question are undetermined, the correspondence being unpublished.

Daily National Republican – November 22, 1879

There is a sensation in Hong Kong, caused by a quarrel between Colonel Mosby and Governor Hennessy. The latter official desiring to obtain full official information concerning the opium traffic between Hong Kong and Macao, in order to check notorious and illegal practices, applied to Colonel Mosby for copies of the U. S. records of shipments, &c. The Governor alleges that the request was made for the public good and with perfect courtesy. The same request has been preferred to the other foreign consuls and all were willingly responded to. Colonel Mosby alleged that the request implicated a claim of the right to inspect consular documents, which he was bound to resent. The American citizens regret that the United States consul has broken friendly relations with the government who had previously shown him great attention and consideration. The actual merits of the question are not yet determined. The correspondence between Colonel Mosby and Governor Hennessy has not been published. There is general curiosity among foreign residents to learn the result of the recent investigation into the alleged irregularities of the Hong Kong consulate by General Stahel, especially appointed by the State Department to conduct the inquiry.

The statement in the article of November 22 "The actual merits of the question are not yet determined" appears to indicate that as the matter died (at least in the American press), Mosby's position could not be assailed. Had it been otherwise, no doubt a great deal more (and negative) press coverage would have resulted.

And so Mosby's situation in Hong Kong continued through 1879 and onward without any resolution. He was not permitted a furlough home to visit his children; and the Department of State punished him with many strokes, both large and small, probably in hopes of forcing him to resign. So much for the rewards bestowed upon honest men and true reformers.

Chapter 19

1880

Gutta cavat lapidem non vi, sed saepe cadendo.
~ Endurance can overcome without force.

"I like not fair terms and a villain's mind." ~ William Shakespeare

THE DAWNING OF the new year saw the consulate corruption scandal still heavily covered in the press:

Salt Lake Herald - January 1, 1880 (Edited)

The House passed a resolution, before recess, calling upon Secretary Evarts, if not incompatible with the public interest, to furnish copies of the correspondence of Col. Mosby, consul at Hong Kong, with the state department, in relation to the consular affairs in China. Secretary Evarts has decided, it is said, that it is incompatible with public interests to make this correspondence public until the reports are received from the department special agents who are now investigating the matters referred to. It seems to be universally understood, however, that official developments on this subject may soon be expected which will lead to important changes.

Considering that Mosby's charges had appeared in the newspapers, their "revelation" by Secretary Evarts could hardly be considered "incompatible with the public interest." Finally, Mosby's full report became public. True, most ordinary readers found the matter confusing and probably mind-numbing in its complexity; but Mosby knew well that there were those who would understand the situation, men of power and civic importance who would not take kindly to unconstrained graft:

Evening Star – January 3, 1880 (Edited)

MOSBY UPON BAILEY

The Charges of Fraud

The letter of Colonel John S. Mosby, United States consul general at Hong Kong, China, detailing charges of official malfeasance on the part of his predecessor at that consulate, is quite a voluminous document. It is dated Hong Kong, October 21st, 1879. This correspondence, it will be remembered, was called for by resolution of the House of Representatives, but has not yet been transmitted to that body by the Secretary of State. In the letter Col. Mosby says:—"In the first place, I will say that while it was notorious here that frauds existed, yet I had not deemed the proof accessible, as almost all the ships that paid extra wages during Mr. Bailey's term here had left this coast, until in the month of August, when investigating the emigration business with General Stahel, my attention was attracted by the internal evidence of fraud furnished by the quarterly returns of Mr. Bailey.

After General Stahel left, I made a careful analysis of these returns, and a comparison of Mr. Bailey's and Mr. Loring's and my own. The result is a most cogent demonstration of their fictitious character."

Colonel Mosby then goes into details concerning the frauds in the matter of seamen's wages and the number of seamen discharged at the consulate. [Here, Mosby's report that appears in other articles is included.-vph]

In conclusion, as Chinese emigration was the original subject of the inquiry, I submit the following extract for a letter just received from the collector of customs at San Francisco, dated August 28, 1879: "I congratulate you on your success in your effort to prevent the shipping of lewd women to this port. The fact that you have succeeded demonstrates the truth of my theory hitherto expressed to your predecessors, that vigilance and activity on the part of the consul at Hong Kong was the proper way to enforce the law."

And still, the press reports went on. The Chinese matter was rather dry and lacked the usual "color" of most Mosby stories, but large amounts of the public monies had been purloined, and that meant that whatever the subject lacked in emotional titillation, it made up for in economic wrath:

Salt Lake Herald – **January 4, 1880 (Edited)**

THE CHINESE CONSULATE.

Colonel Mosby Rises to Explain.

In Doing Which He Says Bad Things of Baily.

Chicago, 3.—*The Times* has the full report of John S. Mosby, United States consul at Hong Kong, on the corruptions of Minister Seward. It bears the date of Hong Kong, October 21, 1879. It begins thus: In my No. 29, dated September 22, 1879, I stated that I would submit to the department a supplementary report on the frauds and abuses practiced here in shipping and discharging seamen, the collection of extra wages and granting relief to destitute seamen. This I now proceed to do. In the first place, I will say that while it was notorious here that those frauds existed, yet I had not deemed the proof accessible, as almost all the ships that paid extra wages during Mr. Bailey's term here, had left this coast, until in the month of August, when investigating the emigration business with General Stahel, my attention was attracted by internal evidence of fraud furnished by the quarterly returns of Mr. Bailey. After General Stahel left, I made a careful analysis of these returns and a comparison of Bailey's and Loring's and my own result is the most cogent demonstration of their fictitious character. I invite attention to the consul. I dated the statement of all returns of extra wages and relief accounts of this consulate from January 1, 1871, to September 30, 1879, prepared by my vice-consul, Mr. Brooks. The most striking feature of this statement is the small number of discharges reported by Mr. Bailey as compared with the number of vessels that he cleared; also the great disparity between the number shipped and discharged. When a vessel enters, it generally discharges a portion of its crew, and when it clears it ships a number of seamen to fill up the vacancies caused by the discharges and desertions at Hong Kong, where desertion is very difficult ...[Here, Mosby quotes several other similar cases, and says there are many more, which, to report in full, would take him six months.]

In conclusion, as this Chinese emigration was the original subject of inquiry, is submitted the following extract from a letter received from the collector of customs, at San Francisco, dated August 28, 1879. 'I congratulate you on your success in your effort to prevent the shipping of lewd women to this port. The fact that you have succeeded demonstrates the truth of my theory hitherto expressed to your predecessor, that vigilance and activity on the part of the consul at Hong Kong was the proper way to enforce the law.'

"I have the honor to be, sir, your obedient servant,

John S. Mosby, United States Consul."

But the Republican press could not just stand by and let John Mosby's "version" of the matter remain uncontested. Their response was to charge him with being, at best, inaccurate and, at worst, a liar:

New York Tribune – **January 5, 1880**

GENERAL MOSBY'S HASTY CHARGES.

His Letter to the State Department Pronounced False – Facts in Regard to Mr. Bailey's Case

[By Telegraph to the Tribune]

Washington, Jan. 4.—The publication of Colonel Mosby's letter to the State Department has caused quite a ripple in that branch of the Government, where it is openly said that he has overstepped the bounds of discretion, as well as given to the public statements in regard to the action of the Department of State which are not true. It is said that he has confused Mr. Bailey with Mr. Bradford, and that there are many other inaccuracies in his letter. The facts in the case are as follows: Mr. Baily was appointed Consul at Hong Kong by General Grant in 1870, and served at that post for eight years without complaint from any quarter whatever. When the troubles at the Consulate-General in Shanghai were brought to light through the inquiries of Consuls-General Myers and Wells, and reflected seriously upon Mr. Seward, Mr. Evarts, in looking for a suitable person for the position, selected Mr. Baily, who at the time was an applicant for promotion, and sent him to Shanghai. This nomination lay in the Senate Committee on Commerce for three sessions, and, through the influence of persons hostile to his confirmation, no action was taken. During this long period of suspended action no accusations were made against Mr. Baily, Senators on the committee admitting that there were no grounds for rejection of his nomination; and he was ultimately confirmed. At a later period Mr. Evarts, coming into possession of information that the affairs of the Consulate at Hong Kong under Mr. Baily had not been satisfactorily administered, directed Consul-General Stahel at Yokohama, and Mr. Mosby, Consul at Hong Kong, to investigate these charges. Mr. Baily was also informed of their character, and the investigation was held. The report submitted by General Stahel sustained the accusations sufficiently to lead to Mr. Baily's displacement and the nomination of Mr. Denny, of Oregon, to succeed him.

It is somewhat surprising to those cognizant of the facts in the case that

Mr. Mosby should have ventured upon such a correspondence, when he was fully aware of the action taken by the Department in regards to the investigation of Mr. Baily's affairs, and which he knew would effectively disprove the assertion that the Department was in any way attempting to shield that gentleman. The statement that the Secretary of State has ignored the resolution of Congress calling for information on this subject is also effectively refuted by the fact that a reply to this resolution ahs been in course of preparation for some time and has only been delayed owing to the necessity of securing further information to go with the reply.

Throughout the whole of Mosby's fight with the Department of State regarding the consular ring, there were those papers that went with that department and against him. The charges against Mosby ranged from his being erroneous—accidentally or deliberately—in his conclusions and/or information to the fact that he did not operate within the prescribed government channels. It is interesting to note that this account was rendered after General Stahel had come from Japan to "investigate" Mosby's charges. Despite the fact that Stahel agreed with the findings, the press continued to present Mosby as both wrong in his facts and questionable in his motives and actions. Sadly, the *Daily Dispatch*, a Virginia paper, took up the cudgels for the government in this article, a reprint from a Washington paper:

Daily Dispatch – January 7, 1880

Consul Mosby.—The publication by Colonel Mosby of his correspondence with the Department of State in regard to the United States consulates at Shanghai and Hong-Kong may lead to the Department's taking into consideration the case of the writer. The statements made by Colonel Mosby are full of errors. The Department has not yet taken action in regard to the matter, but it is pretty certain that somewhere in the near future there will be another Consul at Hong-Kong—Washington Star, yesterday.

Fortunately for John Mosby, however, there were enough newspapers that hated Republicans more than they hated him and therefore worked assiduously to prevent him from being buried by adverse coverage:

Public Ledger – January 8, 1880

A Reform Administration. Courier-Journal.:

About the only man who has done anything toward effecting civil service reform under Hayes' administration is Consul Mosby Hayes' appointee to the United States consulship at Hong Kong, China, and the eminent reformers of Hayes' cabinet and Hayes himself have done all they could to suppress the recital of Mosby's discoveries in his search for official crookedness under the Seward regime. Grant has not hesitated to assert several times since his arrival at San Francisco, that the United States diplomatic service in China and Japan was rotten to its core, and he stated that everything Mosby charged last year is literally true.

Mosby's last report, which Evarts did his best to suppress, was filched by some newspaper correspondents at Washington recently, and it presents still further evidence of fraud. It is devoted to the crookedness of Consul Bailey, who is shown to have made grossly fraudulent reports of the number of seamen shipped discharged; fraudulent and extravagant charges of money disbursed for the relief of distressed American seamen. His defalcation in the matter of fees for the shipping and discharging of seamen amounts to about $40,000. Mosby says that all Bailey's returns to the treasury department were fraudulent, and he furnishes ample evidence to prove it.

Of George Seward's embezzlement there is no doubt. He has during his term of office as minister to China enriched himself by frauds, and he has been persistently screened by the Secretary of State and his cousin Fred, late Assistant Secretary of State. This is a beautiful record for the great "reform" administration. The matter of the administration's failure to even comment, much less act,—upon Mosby's charges, that had been validated by both Generals Stahel and Grant, had become—or at least was becoming—the theme of the matter in most of the newspapers. The fraud and corruption were, in the majority of the press, a "given." What the Democratic papers now reported on was the response of what was supposed to be a "reform" administration to proven corruption well-known for a long time but that now could no longer be ignored thanks to Consul Mosby:

Daily Globe – January 9, 1880

Shortly after Col. Mosby's appointment as consul to China, he discovered that things were not going as they should, and on investigation he discovered that the government was being persistently and systematically swindled by Minister Seward and others. He communicated the facts to the state department, and although Seward was summoned to answer for his misdeeds before a Congressional committee, nothing came of it. Mosby's correspondence with the state department has just been published, however, and reveals a greater degree of corruption that was at first supposed. The announcement has accordingly gone forth that Mosby must walk the plank. The exposure of dishonesty in a public official is regarded as an unpardonable sin by the administration, which has no use for honest men in its employ.

Sadly, this is one of the most truthful comments printed in any paper. But the fact, alas, was that in politics, corruption and cover-up were "equal-opportunity" mind-sets; and Mosby would not have been tolerated under the Democrats any more than he was under the Republicans. That fact was made clear when the first Republican appointee removed upon the election of Democrat Grover Cleveland was John Mosby! Sadly, his "honesty" was tolerated by Democrats as long as he was finding corruption in the Republican Party, but even that was only until a Democrat was elected and he could be removed!

But the press was not finished with the scandal:

Daily Argus – January 10, 1880

There is something very rotten in Shanghai exclaims Moseby, and for this un-partisan expression it has been officially decreed that his scalp must be taken. It is equivalent to losing position to denounce corruption within the ranks of the Republican party—at least that appears to be the invariable outcome. So long as Moseby kept his mouth shut and eyes closed and said nothing concerning crookedness of the Shanghai consulate, he was allowed to retain his position, but when, in the interest of civil service reform he makes an expose of the damnable practices of Seward and his corrupt gang, it is official proclaimed that Moseby must go. The Chicago Tribune a stalwart Republican paper, but which has frequently denounced official corruption, says in referring to this case—

"The rumor goes forth from the state department that Consul General Moseby, at Shanghai, is to be removed, the presumptive cause being, that he has followed the fatal example of two or three predecessors in that consulate by exposing the pilfering practices of the 'Seward ring' in China. Every official agent in China who has heretofore attempted to fight that ring, which appears to exist for the purpose of stealing everything in the Celestial empire, has been removed, and now comes Moseby's turn.

That there is something awfully rotten in the administration of the American mission in China is evident from the mass of proof sufficient to overwhelm any combination of common rogues on earth. What that something is has not been definitely established, but it is high time it should be. The charges against the Seward ring, the chief person in which is the American minister at Pekin, are of the most scandalous character, and the proofs in support of the charges are such, to say the least, as are incompatible with the continuance of Mr. Seward in that position by an administration having a decent respect for the opinion of mankind. Why it is that, instead of determining the truth or untruth of the charges, every witness who ventures to produce new proofs of their truth is straightway officially beheaded, surely ought to be found out."

It is part of the practices of the Washington ring that those on the inside shall remain in there, and any attempt to interrupt the programme of addition, division and silence, is summarily rebuked and the offender against the peace of the "ring" unceremoniously bounced. Thorough reform of the civil service will never come until the Republican party is swept from power. It has grown so corrupt, that its leaders care nothing for public opinion and are strangers to decency. They act on the principle that the Republicans are entitled to all the offices by divine right, and any attempt by the public to dictate the management of public affairs is not only presumptuous but will not be tolerated. To this disgraceful state of affairs has the Republican party brought the country.

The paper was right. This was the state to which the country had been, and continued to be, brought; but this was not just a Republican problem. Mosby found throughout his "service" with the government that honesty, integrity, and the desire to sweep corruption from that service was not only unappreciated, but also actually resisted to the point at which the unwelcome reformer often found himself removed or reassigned. And as the central government—its constitutional restraints removed by the so-called "civil war"—continued to grow in both size and power, the corruption grew with it to the point at which a change of parties simply meant that new criminals with their aiders and abettors were put in place. There was no place for John Mosby among such creatures as he eventually discovered.

But of course, corruption notwithstanding, Mosby continued to be assailed:

Chicago Tribune – **January 10, 1880**
MOSBY'S LETTER

Col. Mosby has been seeking notoriety ever since, in his capacity as a guerrilla chief, he persecuted Union men in the Border States. His letter from China on the Consulates is ascertained to be as crooked in its facts as the means by which it was published were irregular and discourteous. It appears that Col. Mosby has been writing of matters that he ought to know more about than he does, and that he has confounded two very different personages – a Mr. Bailey, who was appointed Consul at Hong Kong by President Grant in 1870, and a Mr. Bradford. There are serious and probably well-founded accusations against Bradford; yet Mosby in his letter has accused Bailey of the wrongdoing which can only properly be attributed to Bradford, if to anybody. Mosby sent his letter here in triplicate; and the persons who boast of having obtained for publication a copy from the State Department mislead the public and libel the State Department. It is pretty well understood that the copy that was published in a New York paper was obtained, either through breach of faith or by purchase, from one of the outside persons not connected with official life, to whom Col. Mosby sent the confused and inaccurate statement. Mosby himself has been guilty of a violation of the regulations of the Department whose honor he seeks to defend, in that he has communicated an official paper to a private person.

Again, it is obvious that the problem with Mosby's exposure of corruption, at least according to the newspapers, was the way that it was done. It seems more than odd that a newspaper should make the claim that if only he could have done it properly—that is, through the "proper channels," dotting all the i's and crossing all the t's. Well, that would have been right way to do it. Never mind that the "proper channels" had permitted that corruption to continue for years with no one, other than the thieves and those protecting them, being the wiser. In fact, neither did a change in administration usually bring such "rings" to an end. It simply peopled them with frauds and crooks of the party coming into power!

Another paper referred to Mosby as a guerrilla—as if he still engaged in that practice! But at least it found more fault with his tormentors than with him:

Free Trader – January 10, 1880

Mosby the guerrilla, who was a great pet with President Grant, and made consul at Shanghai, has never been a favorite with the present administration, and has run against a snag that will probably cost him his political head. The biggest and most shameless thief in our whole diplomatic service is our Chinese minister Seward, but for some reason he is a pet of Evarts and Hayes. Now Mosby, who appears to be an honest man, got an inside view of Seward's operations at Shanghai, and wrote a vigorous letter to Secretary Evarts, exposing his rascalities, and the letter has got into the newspapers. Evarts is in a rage over it, and Mosby is said to be doomed.

As usual, those papers that didn't like the man always began their coverage with "Mosby the guerilla," never giving him his military or even his diplomatic title. But Hayes gave him the office at Grant's request, and as Hayes wanted Mosby as far away from his administration (and Virginia) as possible, he had sent him where he didn't think he could do any harm. This seems to prove that either Hayes was unaware of Seward's depredations, which were well-known in Washington, or he believed that Mosby would simply become part of the ring. Either way, Grant's "favor" cost Hayes dearly:

Stark County Democrat **- January 13, 1880**
CONSUL MOSBY TO BE PUNISHED.

The Hayes administration, Secretary Evarts ordering, is about to remove Consul Mosby from Hong Kong for the reason that he exposed the corruption and thievery of his predecessor, who was David H. Bailey. This seems to be an unpardonable sin in the eyes of Mr. Evart.

When George F. Seward was promoted from the Shanghai Consulate to the mission at Pekin, he was succeeded by John C. Myers of Pennsylvania, who found O. B. Bradford, a confederate of Seward, and Vice Consul, in charge of the office. He soon discovered the fraudulent practices of Seward and Bradford, which were afterward clearly proven before the investigation ordered by the House of Representatives, and reported them to the department.

Evarts, nevertheless, sustained Seward and removed Myers, sending out G. Wiley Wells, a Republican ex-member of Congress from Mississippi, to replace Myers, with very peculiar instructions to let Seward alone. In his examination of Bradford's conduct, he was compelled to convict him as a mail agent of opening letters, and under the power conferred by Congress he convicted and imprisoned him for the felony. Mr. Evarts released Bradford from durance vile by ordering him home as a witness before the investigation at Washington. In the course of his researches, Wells found additional proofs of Seward's guilt, and sent them to the department, and his reward for that service was dismissal.

Bailey was promoted from Hong Kong to Shanghai, and as he has been carrying on the Seward system of stealing he would not likely reveal [the matter]. But Consul Mosby, when he took office, soon found how Bailey had appropriated thirty-five or forty thousand dollars of fees, which should have been returned to the Treasury. Secretary Evarts protected Baily by removal, but Mosby reported the frauds to Evarts, and also made them public. In this way is our commerce plundered. No other commercial nation is thus afflicted, and hence the decline of our commerce. Mosby is too honest to be allowed to remain, and must go.

Quite apart from Evarts's involvement with Seward and Bailey, he also despised Mosby and made clear publicly that had he been aware of the man's nomination to the consulship, he would have put an end to it—always assuming that he could have done so. It is probable that Evarts's opinion of Mosby was, like that of Augur and Alger, based upon his actions during the war in the Shenandoah Valley. It must have been particularly galling for Evarts to realize that his tenure as secretary of state was being ruined by a man whom he despised and would have prevented from being offered the post in the first place.

In another news account, G. Wiley Wells stated that he resigned when he could not force the Department of State to act on the Seward matter. Still, if indeed Wells began his term with instructions to "leave Seward alone," that should have raised red flags even before he arrived. Mosby triumphed where those before him had been ignominiously dismissed or forced to resign and the matter buried. By going "around" the Department of State and arranging for his charges to appear in the press (something that he did not wish to do!), the matter could not be "buried" as it had been for so long. Because

Mosby's charges were now public knowledge and given the situation in the Republican Party both in the national government and in Virginia, the ordinary method of removing "whistle-blowers" (as we call them today) that had been used with Myers and Wells was not available for Mosby. His recall would have been (rightly) blamed upon his attempts to clean up the consular service. It is quite probable that these circumstances allowed Mosby to keep his consulship until the election of Cleveland.

The Cincinnati Daily Star, probably a Republican paper, found quite another reason for Mosby's actions: he missed being a guerrilla. Of course, the paper also acknowledged that the "diplomatic and consular service was a piece of rottenness," but still, and after all, and so forth ... The article was more than a bit "tongue-in-cheek," and Mosby does come out rather better than the government and the "moribund politicians"—but not by much:

> *Cincinnati Daily Star* – **January 15, 1880**
>
> Gen. Mosby made a tolerably lively Confederate cavalry officer during the war, but was thought to be so effectively reconstructed afterward that he secured the appointment of Consul to Shanghai, where his old guerrilla habits broke out from time to time involuntarily, like the Princess who had been formerly a cat that was seized with the old ruling passion when she saw a mouse cross the room. Gen. Mosby has, from time to time during his service abroad, when wearied with the routine of official life, made a brilliant cavalry dash, so to speak into the Tite Barnacles of our Asiatic Ministerial Consular service, and, as is generally thought outside of official circles, bagged game at each charge. Our Minister to China, one Seward, a nephew of the great Secretary of that name, we believe, and hence a cousin of the late Assistant Secretary of State, has, if Gen. Mosby's charges are true, been guilty of participation in practices and peculations by our representatives in Asia disgraceful to the American nation, and which, if proved against a Japanese official, would entitle that functionary to the privilege of a neat but not gaudy hari-kari on the spot.
>
> The fact of the matter is that our diplomatic and consular service is a piece of rottenness that wants overhauling. A swarm of moribund politicians and clamorous party hacks have from time immemorial been pensioned off by sinecures in foreign countries, some of which were mines of wealth to the fortunate incumbent and petty robbers of our own citizens residing or traveling to foreign lands. General Mosby, we understand, is on his way home, where it is semi-officially given out that he will stay. If he will substantiate some of the scandalous stories against our consular agent in Hong Kong and against Minister Seward so as to lead to a general ripping up of things, and either the abolition or purgation of the entire system, we think that loyal people will generally forgive the havoc that General Mosby made in war times with our baggage wagons and commissariat while riding in the neighborhood of the Union army. Sail in, General, and let us have this business well ventilated.

Slowly but surely, much of the dislike of John Mosby by the press was being replaced by a certain, albeit grudging, admiration for his honesty and his pluck—a matter that had gained him nothing while costing him a great deal within his own party. It was obvious that there could no longer be any question of the validity of the charges he had "leaked" to the press, his way of getting around the State Department:

Daily Argus – January 17, 1880

Philadelphia Times

Even yet the administration hasn't quite made up its mind whether it ought not to give Mosby a sound thrashing or expel him from school for telling tales on those bad boys, his consular associates in China. "Gross official discourtesy" is what they call Mosby's downright honesty of speech. The *New York Tribune* reports upon General Stahel's investigation, perhaps the first time this was done despite Evarts' insistence that he was awaiting the General's report before moving on Mosby's claims:

New York Tribune – January 19, 1880 (Edited)

THE CONSULATE AT HONG KONG

The correspondence, papers and documents relative to the Consulate at Hong Kong, transmitted to the House of Representatives is a large mass of manuscript. The most important document is an elaborate report from General Stahel of the results of his investigation into the affairs of the Consulate from December 1, 1870, to January 31, 1879, in compliance with Department orders "I have received a letter from A. R. Mosby [sic], United States Consul at Hong Kong, dated October 4, 1879, in which he says that he has discovered additional wrongs in the Hong Kong Consulate, mostly in the shipping and discharge of seamen. He puts the amount of fees, received and not accounted for, for such serves at no less a figure than $25,000 in substantiation of which statement he informs me that he has the duplicate shipping articles of the Pacific Mail steamers. He further refers to a large amount of extra wages, passport fees, etc., as not being credited, and invites me to return to Hong Kong for the purpose of taking supplemental evidence."

General Stahel refers to the statement of his previous report about the omission of all entries to the ship's journal and seaman's register for a number of years in explanation of his failing to discover the additional frauds indicated by Colonel Mosby.

Consider: Stahel began to defend himself by pointing out that his "previous report" was incorrect because the additional frauds had only been discovered by Mosby after that report had been submitted. Stahel didn't question Mosby's "discoveries" but merely pointed out that the information was not available to him at the time he had submitted his report.

National Republican – January 20, 1880

POLITICAL NOTES.

Between the stalwarts and one side and The Democrats on the other it is probable that a decidedly hot time is in store for Consul Mosby.

Mosby's situation was made clear when a publication like the *National Republican*, which should have been supporting him as a credit to the Republican Party for his honesty and his efforts to fulfill President Hayes promise of "reforms," instead made a joke of his persecution.

Spirit of the Age – January 21, 1880

Col. Mosby is deposed from the consulship at Hong Kong, for uncovering the big stealings illegal fees and corruption of Geo. E. Seward, Minister to China, and his factotum in rottenness, David H. Bailey. Mosby is the third member of the Chinese diplomatic corps who has been reported for dismissal for trying to protect the government from these plunderers. And the worst of it in this case is that Bailey, who is charged with crime is elevated to Mosby's place, and Mr. Evarts and the State Department, persistently refuse to investigate the charge. What possible excuse there can be for these high-handed proceedings it is difficult to conceive.

National Republican – January 23, 1880

Work of the Committee.

The Committee on Expenditures in the State Department has possession of the Mosby correspondence in relation to the alleged corruption in the Consular and Diplomatic service in China, and will to-day determine whether or not to summon Colonel Mosby to testify.

The question never asked by the press was, why wasn't Mosby called to testify? His findings of corruption were not limited to the stealing of fees, but also involved the matter of Chinese immigration into the United States, a very lucrative field that included extortion as well as other crimes as seen here in the Herald:

Salt Lake Herald – January 24, 1880

TELEGRAPHIC MOSBY AGAIN

He Delivers Himself on the Chinese Consulate.

Washington, 23.—Several of Consul Mosby's letters to the state department show that out of Consul Bailey's administration of Hong Kong consulate from 1871 to the latter part of 1878, the inspection of Chinese immigrants to the United States, under acts of Congress requiring consular certificates of their voluntary immigration, was not only a disgrace, but a farce, and merely a means of collecting fees, which Bailey almost wholly pocketed. Mosby, in one letter, writes: The following is a brief history of the ceremony of examination: On the day before a vessel was to leave with the Chinese immigrants, the United States consul was informed. At a certain hour, the passengers would be ready on board for the examination. At the appointed time, Peter Smith, an illiterate keeper of a sailors' boarding house, appeared with the consular seal. The passengers came on deck and passed in review before him, each being asked if he was an voluntary emigrant. If he said that he was, his ticket was stamped with the consul's seal. It would take, on average, about one hour to complete the investigation. This was the whole proceeding.

Mosby also reported that the act of prohibiting the importation of Chinese lewd women, to the United States, was simply made a cover for extortion, it being a general understanding that any woman could procure a consular certificate by paying to the consul a premium of $10 or $15. a letter received by Mosby from the San Francisco collector of customs, dated August 28th, '79, congratulated him on his success in preventing the shipment of lewd women to the United States, this demonstrating that previous failures to enforce the law were attributable to want of proper vigilance and good faith. The general stated in his report of September 20th, of the results of his investigations under orders of the state department, that upon the general question as to the voluntary character of Chinese emigration, I find it difficult to form a satisfactory judgment among foreigners in China.

The prevalent belief is that so far as the Pacific states of the United States are concerned, this immigration is mainly promoted by the Six Chinese companies or guilds of San Francisco, and that immigrants, after arrival, remain in the power of these companies, and are, in fact, controlled by them. I find this belief so strong and so general, even among persons who differ as regards the expediency of the immigration, that I must declare it worthy of serious consideration; but at the same time I have been unable to obtain any direct or clear evidence to support it. This is especially owing to the secrecy which characterizes all such combinations among the Chinese and to the great power and influence they everywhere possess, and as long as the emigrant continues to declare, throughout the several searching examinations to which they are subjected, not only their willingness to go, but that they go freely and voluntarily, it may be impossible to establish any unlawful arrangement between them and said companies.

Every once in a while, Mosby's efforts were rewarded by the acknowledgment of those who benefited from them. Sadly, such tributes were few and far between.

Sacramento Daily Record-Union – **January 24, 1880 (Edited)**

[Special to the Record-Union]

Washington, January 23d.—Several of Consul Mosby's letters to the State Department show that during Consul Bailey's administration of the Hongkong consulate, from 1871 to the later part of 1878, the inspection of Chinese emigrants to the United States, under the Act of Congress requiring Consular certificates of their voluntary emigration, was a disgraceful farce, and merely a means of collecting fees which Bailey almost wholly pocketed.

Mosby in one letter writes: "The following is a brief history of the ceremony of examination: On the day before a vessel was to leave with Chinese emigrants the United States Consul was informed that at a certain hour the passengers would be ready on board for examination. At the appointed time Peter Smith, an illiterate keeper of a sailor's boarding-house, appeared with the Consular seal. The passengers came on deck and passed in review before him, each being asked if he was a voluntary emigrant. If he said he was, his ticket would be stamped with the Consular seal. It would take, on an average, about one hour to complete the investigation. This was the whole proceeding." Mosby also reported that the Act prohibiting the importation of Chinese lewd women into the United States was simply made a cover for extortion, it being a general understanding that any woman could procure a Consular certificate by paying to the Consul a premium of $10 or $15.

A letter received by Mosby from the San Francisco Collector of Customs, dated August 28, 1879, congratulated him on his success in preventing the shipment of lewd women to the United States, thus demonstrating that the previous failures to inforce the law were attributable to a mere want of proper vigilance and good faith.

Evening Star – February 12, 1880

Consul Mosby's Charges.—The committee on expenditures in the State Department to whom the Mosby correspondence covering alleged corruption at the Shanghai and Hong Kong consulates was referred, has not as yet taken any action looking to an investigation of the charges. The general sentiment of the members of the committee is that there is but little doubt of the truth of Consul Mosby's charges, and that it will hence be a needless expenditure of thousands of dollars to summon witnesses from China to testify in relation thereto.

Given that the Department of State continued to do all that it could to stonewall the matter, it would appear that the admission of the truth of Mosby's charges was for no other reason than to prevent his being summoned back to Washington to testify before Congress. The Republicans in both the administration and Virginia considered it infinitely better for them if John Mosby remained half a world away.

Cincinnati Daily Star – February 26, 1880

Indianapolis Sentinel, (Dem.): Mosby is still at work showing up the rottenness of United States officials in China, but Evarts keeps the rascals in office all the same.

But just when it seemed that the newspaper coverage was centered on the corruption in the government and the consulate ring there were always those publications that had to condemn John Mosby even in the process of admitting that he was right:

The Democrat – March 4, 1880

The radicals let Mosby talk in this way: "It is absurd to talk about moral taint attaching itself to men on either side in the war, especially when we see both sides represented in the Cabinet of the 'President.'"

They let him talk in this way because Mosby has turned Republican politician. Any "rebel" who will eat his own principles and turn his coat may walk into the Radical parlor and sit with the elect any time. But Mosby is right.

But Mosby still wasn't finished with the consular scandal. Seeing the matter "stalled," he determined to continue his assault, perhaps fearing that if he did not do so, once again, the scandal would be allowed to sink into bureaucratic and political oblivion:

Sacramento Daily Record-Union – April 8, 1880

Atlanta Constitution – April 11, 1880

States Rights Democrat – April 16, 1880

COLONEL MOSBY WRITES ANOTHER LETTER

He Exposes the Frauds of his Predecessors and Growls at the Administration. [Special to the Oregonian]

Consul Mosby and His Operations at Hongkong.

Chicago, April 7th.—The Inter-Ocean's Washington special says: A private letter just received here from Colonel Mosby contains some additional comments, in his peculiar style, on the peculations and corruptions of Bailey, his predecessor in the Consulate at Hongkong, and of other American Consular officials in the East. Colonel Mosby turned over to the Department, on account of fees, more than $11,000 for the first year of his incumbency, ending in February last, which is several thousand dollars more than was returned by Bailey during the same period. He says that on account of the great expense of living there is not much inducement to an honest man to accept the position of United States Consul. He seems to think that his efforts in behalf of an honest administration of United States Consulates and of the exposure of corrupt officials have not been appreciated, for he says he has received several rebukes from the Department of State, but not one word of encouragement.

He then says: "The reasons why I have not returned are these: I have been threatened with dismissal for uncovering the frauds out here, and I want to give the Administration the opportunity of carrying out their threats, and thereby signalizing their zeal for civil service reform by punishing the only man whom they have appointed to office who has tried to reform it. I continue to hold the fort here because I have not yet completed my investigation, and if I were to resign now and go home, the ring would claim it as a victory for the thieves, and say I resigned under compulsion. I shall show them that I will remain as long as I choose."

The frankness with which Mosby has criticized the President, Secretary Evarts and others of his superior officers has not been at all relished by them, and has been very destructive to discipline; but there is no doubt that he has done much good in uncovering frauds which have been practiced for a long time by American Consuls in China. He has carried on his investigations in the guerrilla fashion, and the good he has done would have been approved had he used somewhat more discretion in his methods.

As noted earlier, there was a certain inevitability in the press coverage of John Mosby, changing only with the issue. It is seen here by the reiteration of the assertion that the problem was not what Mosby charged, but how he brought those charges forward. On the other hand, there was no comment on his claim to have been threatened with dismissal for doing his job properly and honestly. The natural inclination would be for the publication to have been more exercised over the threat of unjust dismissal than by Mosby's supposed lack of "discretion in his methods" even if the latter were "destructive to discipline." Of course, it is interesting to note that wholesale graft was not considered "destructive to discipline" and that the "discipline" practiced by the Department of State was intended to keep the crooks in office and to remove any possible reformers.

In a small article, there suddenly arose reference to Mosby's support of Grant and that he would return to Virginia to function in that capacity. Though little was said about the matter, it might well be that he was kept in China for that very reason:

***Atlanta Constitution* – April 10, 1880**

Mosby, of Virginia, but now consul to China, will be home shortly to help work Virginia in the interest of Grant.

The business of Mosby's return to the United States had been plenteously covered in the press, including the article above, but there was more to that matter than the consular scandal. John Mosby had left the United States for Hong Kong in 1878 and did not return until 1885. During that time, his efforts to secure a furlough in order to see his family—and especially his younger children, whom he had not seen since leaving the country—were denied by the Department of State. An attempt was made by his friends in Virginia to obtain a furlough for him by informing the government that Mosby wished to return home to marry. It was a well-intentioned effort, but the lady mentioned made it very clear that he certainly wasn't returning to Virginia to marry her! Thus, Mosby was made an object of ridicule and humiliation once again. He could have of course simply left Hong Kong and returned home, but to do so was to vacate his consulship, something he had made clear that he would not do under any circumstance. Also, the idea of Mosby returning to the Washington-Virginia area did not sit well with many Republicans, not the least because of his continued support of Ulysses S. Grant. Mosby was very tired indeed of all the old charges that continued to be cast regarding any attempt by Grant to run for president again, and in response, he wrote a long and very detailed article on what he termed "the third-term bugbear":

***National Republican* – May 4, 1880 (Edited)**

THE THIRD-TERM BUGBEAR

A Forcible Letter from John S. Mosby

The following letter was received in this city yesterday:

Hong Kong, China, March 20, 1880

Dear Sir: I have read with interest your last letter in which you discuss the prospects for the next Presidency. Nothing could be more absurd than the objections urged by the third term alarmists against the election of President Grant, who effect to see in it the spectre of monarchy. Such persons, as Dr. Johnson said of the no-Popery men of his day, would have cried fire in the midst of the flood. There is really no sincerity in their clamor. The same men had the same vision when he was a candidate, both for his first and second terms, and Frank Blair predicted that if he once got into the White House he would never come out alive. But time has demonstrated how much reliance can be put in such prophets. Now if anyone will show me when or where Washington ever said or did anything inconsistent with the principles involved in such an election, then I will admit that we have the authority of Washington against it. He gave his reasons for retiring in his farewell address, and at the same time some advice about cherishing the Union, to which another generation paid very little respect. Washington says he declined a re-election for purely personal reasons. But if the example of Washington is to be a sort of bed of Procrustes and furnish for us a standard of conduct in everything, then no one ought now to ride on a railroad, or take a dose of chloroform, because Washington never did it; and as he wore his hair powdered, with short breeches, long stocking and knee-buckles, it might as well be insisted that we ought to do the same.

Mr. Jefferson was in Paris when the Constitution was adopted, and wrote many letters predicting its failure because the President, being eligible to re-election, would use the power and patronage of his office indefinitely to re-elect himself. He said the President of the United States would only be a new edition of a Polish king, but time falsified all of Jefferson's predictions, who not only accepted a second term, but declared his willingness to accept a third. The fact is, that no men ever lived who had less reverence for antiquity than the founders of our Government. Those who imagine they see the phantom of imperialism in the election of General Grant are fond of imputing to him the ambition of Caesar. I confess that I can see nothing in common in the character or action of the man who laid down the power of his high office, in obedience to law and that of the great pro-consul of Gaul, when he crossed the Rubicon and marched on Rome. A comparison suggests more of a contrast than a resemblance; Grant disbanded his soldiers and sent them to their homes. Now, General Grant is the only one spoken of in connection with the nomination, against whom no objection can be urged on this ground. The influence of patronage instead of being in his favor is against him. For years he has been a traveler in foreign lands, without official rank, and mixed up with none of the intrigues for the office. I cannot see how we would violate Republican tradition in electing him any more than any other private citizen, while I believe that his experience both at home and abroad would make him a far better President than he was before. I cannot see how he would have any more power simply because he had once been President, to overthrow the institutions of the country, even if he desired it. In judging General Grant we must always bear in mind the condition of the South as he found it and what it was when he turned it over to his successor. I know it will be said he sustained the carpet-bag governments as he did and while it is true they were bad governments, they were none the less the lawful governments of the States the southern people had acted so unwisely as to allow the rascals to get the advantage of having the law on their side. General Grant simply took the side of the law. He did not send troops to South Carolina or Louisiana on the requisition of their Governors when they were in a state of chaos and revolution for the purpose of setting up or putting down any faction, but to save society from dissolution and anarchy. If they had been sent there in the interests of any party, they would have established it in power... Virginians have glorified President Hayes for taking General Grant's advice and withdrawing the troops from those States when the reasons for keeping them there no longer existed, but have forgotten that General Grant withdrew them from their own soil. I hope that in the next election Virginians will remember this, and also that peace cannot be restored between the sections as long as they beat the Confederate war drums through the South. I said this four years ago, and my words are now prophecy fulfilled. I feel a just pride in their glory and as jealous of the military honor of the Southern people as any man on their side. A generous foe would not ask to deprive us of it. I know that General Grant would not. But I do say that these sentiments are not the proper element to control our political conduct, which must be shaped with reference to the present and the future, and not to the past. A great many forget that we are going to elect a President of the United States, and not of the Southern Confederacy. The late political revolution in Virginia was not so much an expression of popular sentiment on the question nominally at issue as a revolt against the despotism of party rule.

The victors have certainly not made a magnanimous use of their victory, but those who have been preaching a merciless proscription of dissenters hardly have the right to complain when "the poisoned chalice is commended to their own lips." While condemning extremes to which the new party has gone, men will recognize in them the same avenging Nemesis as in the ferocious joy of the mob that howled over the agony of Jeffreys. Such excuses have always been the first effects of the reaction against tyranny. "The blaze of truth and liberty," says Macaulay, "may at first dazzle and bewilder nations which have become half-blind in the house of bondage. But let them gaze on, and they will soon be able to bear it. In a few years men learn to reason. The extreme violence of opinion subsides. Hostile theories correct each other. The scattered elements of truth cease to contend and begin to coalesce, and at length a system of justice and order is educed out of chaos."

I believe a brighter day is dawning when Virginians breaking away from the eternal cycle of tradition and habit, will once more lead the advance of liberty and progress.

"Not in vain the distance beacons,

Forward, forward let us range;

Let the great world spin forever

Down the ringing grooves of change."

Very truly yours, John S. Mosby.

Suddenly, an old enemy from the Vermont press joined the fray responding to both Mosby's situation in China and his letter on a possible Grant presidential run. The paper did not consider its differences on issues to be such that Mosby should be subjected to criticism, much less condemnation; it was willing to "agree to disagree." It would seem that this old enemy was as desirous as Mosby of consigning the past to oblivion:

Burlington Weekly Free Press - May 14, 1880 (Edited)

Col. John S. Mosby on the Third Term Question.

Many of our readers know Col. John S. Mosby of Virginia, as a restless and reckless rebel raider; the capture of Gen. Stoughton, and the hero of the Southern side, of many a skirmish with the Union forces defending the department of Washington in the last war. When the Confederacy collapsed, Mosby was one of the few Southerners, who, like Gen. Longstreet, accepted in good faith the result of the war, and counseled his followers to do the same. For some time Mosby was severely assailed by his old comrades-in-arms for having acquiesced in the verdict of the civil war, but as time wore on, a reaction ensued and he largely regained the confidence of the Virginians while not forfeiting his standing with the powers that be at Washington. He has been an important factor in Virginia politics, and his influence with the Administration during Gen. Grant's occupancy of the executive chair was felt all through that State. He seems to have stood equally well with President Hayes, and a year or so ago he was appointed Consul-General to Hong Kong. Although an officer of the present Administration, Col. Mosby does not hesitate to speak and write his political opinions freely. We find in the Providence Journal a letter from him which puts some points on the third term question, in quite a pithy way… But at any rate his views, as those of an intelligent Southerner, are interesting. His letter is also noticeable for its distinct rebuke to the revengeful spirit and policy at the South which found expression in the ku-klux atrocities, and for its advice to the men of the South to forget the past and look to the present and the future. We copy the larger portion of the letter:[What followed was an edited version of Mosby's letter printed in the May 4 issue of the National Daily Republican.-vph]

Mosby was then quoted on the upcoming election with regard to the Democratic nominee, former General Winfield Hancock in a rather unusual way. It must be remembered that Hancock's statement after Appomattox with regard to the soldiers of the Army of Northern Virginia and Virginia's civilians had also contained notification that Mosby had been declared an outlaw and would not be allowed to surrender for parole. Mosby, knowing that Hancock intended to devastate "Mosby's Confederacy" after Lee's surrender in order to destroy his command, had no love for that general:

National Republican – **September 3, 1880**

Colonel Mosby writes home from Hong Kong that he will vote as he shot—against Hancock.

But with Mosby and the press, there was never a dull moment as this little article carried in at least two papers gleefully mentioned. Nothing more was made of it, so it could not have been all that spectacular, although the idea of Mosby thrusting a spear at some enraged sailor and being arrested as a result had its amusing aspects:

Sacramento Daily Record-Union – **September 8, 1880**

Chicago Tribune – **September 8, 1880**

CHINA.

The latest news from Hongkong is to August 11th

Col. Mosby has got into trouble at Hong Kong, where he is United States Consul. Recently he had an altercation with an American seaman, and assaulted him with a spear. Mosby was arrested and taken before a magistrate, who cautioned him to be more circumspect in his conduct for the future.

This story, on its face, might be discounted as nonsense. But later on, the man who replaced Mosby in Hong Kong, Robert Withers, spoke about violent sailors in the consulate; and he, an older man with health issues, had to call the local constabulary to prevent being injured. So it is quite possible that Mosby went after a drunken sailor with a spear! It is certainly something he would do for his own protection.

Mosby then wrote a letter to a friend who, it is assumed, put it out for publication. In this case, it was carried in, among others, a Vermont paper. The matter of Confederate Republicans had come up, yet again, because of the impending election. For the first time there was a great deal of bitterness in a Mosby letter:

Vermont Watchman and State Journal - **September 8, 1880**

Plain Truth by Mosby.

Colonel Mosby, in a letter to a friend, dated July 20, 1880, says: "As you are no doubt aware, I have differed on questions of public policy with a large majority of the people of the south since the close of the war. Every confederate soldier who has dared to do this has been treated as a deserter in war, deserving to be shot. The south has imitated Saturn in devouring his own children. No amount of service or devotion to its cause during the war is admitted to extenuate the offence of defying the dominant sentiment of the section since the war. But I am not the only soldier of the lost cause whose reputation it has been thought necessary to sacrifice to gratify the rancor of party spirit. General Longstreet—who in the last scene of the great drama might have said with almost as much truth as Ney did on the frozen banks of the Beresina, 'I am the rear guard of the grand army'—has been discovered to have been no soldier at all, and one of his critics who was never distinguished for anything except a habit he had of always keeping where there was no danger of getting hurt, has accused him of treachery at Gettysburg, while he was himself during the battle in the rear with the baggage train. As Longstreet is now a Republican and his great antagonist on that eventful field is the Democratic candidate for the presidency, I have no doubt but that before the close of the campaign the southern people will be persuaded to believe that it was Hancock and not Longstreet who led the Virginians in that immortal charge that will forever rank them on glory's page with those who won the trophies of Marathon and Thermopylae."

Juanita Sentinel and Republican – September 8, 1880

The difference between Mosby and Longstreet, and Wade Hampton, and the general run of leaders of The Democratic party is, that when the rebellion in the field was ended, Mosby and Longstreet said the Lost Cause is indeed a Lost Cause, and we abide by the decision; we accept the situation. The Democracy as a party have never said that; they have not said so since the rebellion. In the first resolution of the platform adopted at Cincinnati—the platform on which Hancock stands—they declared themselves pledged anew to the "Constitutional doctrines and traditions of The Democratic party." Mosby and Longstreet have no such pledges to make; they abandoned such foolishness when they surrendered their swords; and that is the difference between Mosby and Longstreet, and the other Democrats who still pledge themselves to the traditions of Democracy.

More is mentioned about Mosby and Hancock, but this time, it was from a Democratic paper and was hardly complimentary to either Mosby or Longstreet. Indeed, poor Captain Wirz, who was so unjustly executed, was also included for good measure:

The Democrat – September 9, 1880

Hartford Herald – December 1, 1880

Hancock and Mosby. Evansville (Ind.) Courier.

It is a significant evidence of the "mutability of human affairs" that in 1865 Secretary Stanton complimented General Hancock for having captured "nearly all the forces of the rebel guerrilla Mosby, and had offered a reward of $2,000 for the capture of Mosby himself." Now Mosby is a "loil" Republican official while Hancock is denounced as a traitor and rebel, and everything else unpatriotic, by the same party that could not too much praise him for his course in that case.

In the same issue:

"Vote as you shot." Mosby and Longstreet both declare that they intend doing so—against Hancock.

Longstreet, Mosby, Key and Werz, [sic] keeper of the Andersonville prison, will all "vote as they shot"—against Hancock.

Of course, Hancock caught none of Mosby's men. They surrendered. Furthermore, after trying for three months or so, he couldn't catch Mosby either, though the "outlaw" was alone and without protection. Neither did Hancock offer a reward for Mosby; that reward began during the war and was added to by both Grant and Halleck after Appomattox. However, there is proof that before the war, Hancock was far less of an anti-Southern radical than was Garfield, who became the Republican nominee. Garfield was quite desirous of "punishing the South," while Hancock was not. It also appeared that Garfield's feelings toward that South had not changed all that much in the twenty years between the onset of war and the upcoming presidential election. Of course, Mosby did not know that—though he eventually learned about the matter the hard way, it would seem.

Mosby seemed to be the subject—or the victim—of balladeers as can be seen in this little ditty entitled "Mosby in China." Had he seen it, he might have found a certain satisfaction in the admission that he, "guerilla and thief Mosby," was catching thieves among the "hundred thousand strong" who fed at the public crib—and that therefore the "poet" saw him as a "white sheep" amid the flock of what we must assume are of the sable variety.

The Columbian - **September 10, 1880**

"ELECTION BALLADS

Mosby in China

Guerilla Mosby in the war
 Was famous at his trade—
Stampeding trains and gobbling men
And plotting ambuscade.
Soldiers and sutlers then declared,
With most sincere belief,
And would have sworn on Bibles big,
That Mosby was a thief.

Bushwhacking Mosby, friend of Grant,
Who fought the flag so long,
Takes office now beneath that flag,
As Consul at Hong Kong.

And now a wonder comes to light,
Almost beyond belief,
(Although all tongues proclaim it loud,)
That Mosby's not a thief.

A white sheep he amid the flock The office-holding throng
Who fatten at the public crib, An hundred thousand strong.
Though he among vile sinner was
Esteemed in crime the chief, Purged from all foul assailment he
No longer is a thief.

On ancient Asia's fertile soil, Kong foot-pad pupils dwell,
Accustomed long to rule corrupt, As all their annals tell;
But now, behold, from western lands Sails one to their relief
Who'll teach them how to manage war
And how to catch a thief

C. BECKLAW

It had to be election time again, and as a result, all the old horror stories about John Mosby were being trotted out and displayed by Democratic papers as if the man were running for office:

Free Trader – October 30, 1880

A PICTURE FOR THE BOYS IN BLUE TO LOOK AT.—

Near Berryville, Clark county, Virginia, stands an ancient oak on a hillside fronting the village. Upon a single limb of that oak, one lovely spring morning in 1863, hung at one time seven young men, Union soldiers of Custer's command, whom the fortunes of war had made prisoners, but to whom their brigand captor not only denied the treatment due among all civilized nations to prisoners of war, but to whom he denied even a soldier's death by the bullet, but whom he hanged, like the basest malefactors, upon a tree. Who was this field, guilty of this outrage so disgraceful to the civilization of the age? The rebel guerilla chief Mosby, a particular pet of the Republican party and now hold a foreign appointment made by Grant and renewed by Hayes. Hancock, who gave the rebellion its death-blow at Gettysburg, is a traitor and Mosby a loyal patriot! No matter how deep any scoundrel may have dipped his hands in the blood of brave Union soldiers, let him but wash the foul stains in the pool of Republicanism and to that party they become as white as snow.

Sacramento Daily Record-Union – November 15, 1880

The Forthcoming Administration.

Chicago, November 14th.—*The Times*' Mentor special says: Neither the Grant nor Blaine elements have stated their claims. Garfield only remarks that the new administration will have neither the piques to equalize nor the prejudices to combat. The South may be certain of just treatment but no special favors. His intimate friends predict the early recall of Mosby and Longstreet

Chapter 20

1881

Ductus exemplo ~ Leadership by example

"For it is in giving that we receive." ~ Francis of Assisi

FOR A CHANGE, the first notice of John Mosby in the newspapers was a gossipy little piece about presents Mosby had sent from Hong Kong to his dear friend Fountain Beattie, one of his Rangers and his oldest comrade in arms. The presents were to be given to his children, whom he had not seen since he left for China:

National Republican – February 11, 1881

Captain F. Beattie received yesterday from Colonel John S. Mosby, consul at Hong Kong, China, another lot of beautiful presents, to be distributed among the Colonel's several children in this country. Among the collection are a half a dozen Japanese fans, a pair of cats-eye sleeve-buttons, a dozen silk handkerchiefs, a pair of Chinese worked slippers, and a lemon- colored crape shawl.

Then the press reported that Virginia Republicans had determined to make Mosby their candidate for governor at the next election. A Democratic organ responded to that announcement as per usual:

Stark County Democrat – February 17, 1881

According to the report, Colonel John S. Mosby will be the net Republican candidate for Governor of Virginia. —Cleveland Leader.

Well, the "murderous Confederate guerilla" will do for a Republican candidate.

Another Democratic paper carried the story, but instead of calling Mosby names, it acknowledged his skill and the divided condition of The Democrats in the state. However, it also acknowledged Mahone's Readjusters and wondered what that party and its leader would do to keep John Mosby out of Virginia:

Indiana State Sentinel – March 2, 1881

Norfolk (Va.) Landmark: "It is said that Colonel Mosby is to be nominated by the Republicans as their candidate for Governor in this State. If this is so, and we see no reason to doubt it, the necessity for united action among The Democrats becomes more important than ever. Col. Mosby is a man of great energy and fine talents, and, with the Democracy divided into two camps, it does not require a Committee of prophets to foretell the result of such a nomination. Now, then, what are the Readjusters going to do about it?"

It may be that Garfield's demand that the Virginia Republicans form an alliance with Mahone's Readjusters, (which was backed by Northern party members) was done to prevent Mosby from becoming a candidate for governor. But the papers continued to announce the plan to give Mosby the nomination. Not only that, some of them seemed quite pleased at the prospect:

Brenham Weekly Banner – March 3, 1881

Mosby is coming home from China, and it is said he will be the Republican candidate for Governor of Virginia at the next election.

Shenandoah Herald – March 16, 1881

Col. J. S. Mosby is prominently spoken of as the next Republican Candidate for Governor of Virginia. It is thought by many that inasmuch as he has not antagonized either wing of the party on the debt question, the entire strength of the organization could unite on him better than upon any one else that could be run. He is a man of great energy and talent and would make a ringing campaign.—Staunton Vindicator.

This was the second article on the possibility of Mosby returning to Virginia and becoming active in local Republican politics. However, that was not to be. First, he was not permitted to return by the State Department—he was dangerous enough in Hong Kong. Second, with Mosby gone, General William Mahone and his Readjuster Party rose to prominence in Virginia. Mahone was hostile toward Mosby and destroyed any hope of his return to that state. In the little general, Mosby met a man of equal determination and far less honesty and restraint. At the same time, Mahone's "Readjusters," with their strong Negro element, made Virginia Republicans nervously contemplate their party being considered once again in the light of Reconstruction. Mosby, they knew, had strongly rejected that coalition and had worked to make the Republican Party palatable to Virginia whites. Garfield's insistence on the amalgamation of the Republicans and the Readjuster Party should have been a "wake-up call" to John Mosby that not all "sectionalism" was to be found in the South!

Chicago Tribune – April 16, 1881

THE PRESIDENT said the he would give the matter consideration. It is very evident that the Administration is disposed to give Mahone all the encouragement possible, and in the recent appointments in that State, Mahone's wishes have been regarded. Members of the delegation said that the coalition with the Readjusters would be fought by all true Republicans in the State. A Convention of Republicans will be called in ninety days to nominate candidate for State officers independent of the Mahone men. It was their desire to have Gen. Wickham, who was in full-sympathy with the "straight- out" Republicans, head the ticket, but his business interests would prevent it. There was some talk, the said, of putting Col. Mosby, now United States Consul at Hong Kong, at the head of the ticket.

Salt Lake Herald – April 16, 1881

VIRGINIA REPUBLICANS.

They Want No Mahone in Theirs.

Washington, 15.—Virginia republicans, headed by Congressman Jorgensen, called on the President and begged him not to recognize Mahone or to encourage any republican coalition with him. Representative Jorgensen was the principal speaker, and he assured the President the Virginia republicans will not form any coalition with Mahone. He said republicans want a strong republican ticket and any attempt to force an alliance with Mahone will be fatal to the party. A straight republican convention will be held in ninety days to nominate a straight republican ticket for state officers in Virginia. It was intended to nominate General Wickham for governor, but business prevented him from running, and the present purpose was to nominate Colonel Mosby, now consul at Hong Kong. Instead of appointing more Readjusters the delegation urged the President to remove those now holding office. The President said he would thoroughly consider the question, and act for the best good of the republican party. Jorgensen thinks they have stopped any chance of affiliation with Mahone.

The fact is, Garfield despised Southerners, even Republican Southerners—or perhaps especially Republican Southerners. He wanted Mahone's Readjusters to take over the local party in Virginia and place the Negro back in power over the Southern white—a matter that had led to the overwhelming strength of The Democrats in the South. But the fact that such a move would force Virginia back into The Democratic party—probably permanently—seemed not to concern Garfield. Certainly, the president's forced amalgamation of the Virginia Republican Party and the Readjusters kept John Mosby in Hong Kong. Never has a political party been thrown away with such a lack of forethought and restraint—or in the alternative, with so much contempt—as happened with the Virginia Republican Party at the hands of a Republican administration under James Garfield! But Garfield did not live long enough to see the results of his machinations. On July 2, 1881, he was shot by Charles Guiteau as he was about to board a train in Washington and died eleven weeks later on September 19. His death placed Vice President Chester A. Arthur into the White House, but that fact did nothing to change the Mahone situation. As a result, the little General's ascendancy destroyed the state's Republican party and, as well, any hope John Mosby had of a place in Virginia.

But the consular ring scandal was never long out of the press, especially as it seemed that nothing was going to be done about those who had robbed Uncle Sam's coffers of hundreds of thousands of dollars:

Sacramento Daily Record-Union – **November 23, 1881**

Salt Lake Herald – **November 23, 1881**

Severe Charges Against an Ex-Consul to China. Bad Bailey

Chicago, November 22d.—A special from Washington says: Some two years ago Colonel John S. Mosby, United States Consul to Hongkong, preferred charges against his predecessor and then Consul-General at Shanghai, General Bailey. The State Department ordered an investigation, and the charges being sustained, Bailey was removed. It was given out that the Department of Justice would request the Secretary of State to institute proceedings against Bailey in the criminal Courts of this country, but nothing appears, however, to have been done, and, in consequence, Colonel Mosby is now on the warpath, and what he has written here will undoubtedly create a sensation, not only in the State Department but elsewhere.

Colonel Mosby, in his letter says: "I am informed that Bailey, whom I had dismissed for stealing, has now gone home and has got the appointment to some office in Cincinnati. You know that he had been Consul at Hongkong and was promoted to be Consul General at Shanghai, which created a vacancy here, when I was appointed. Well, Judge Denny succeeded him at

Shanghai, and he investigated him there as I had done here, and reported all his robberies while Consul at Shanghai to the State Department, yet no steps have ever been taken to prosecute him or Loring, who was his Vice-Consul, for their crimes out here, and Bailey not only forfeited his bond as Consul at Hongkong, but also at Shanghai." The last act of his rascality was robbing the Bank of California with a bogus draft. He also cheated the Pacific Mail Steamship Company, by a bogus draft, out of his passage home.

1881 had not been a disaster for John Mosby, but certainly what had appeared to be fine opportunities for him in his native state—including being nominated for governor by the Republican Party—had been quashed by the president of his own party. Indeed, that president, with the assistance of Northern Republicans (the men whom Mosby hoped would join with white Southern Republicans to produce a new political reality in the South) had forced the Virginia party into the power of General William Mahone and his Readjusters, a party that heavily depended upon—and made use of—blacks. In so doing, the Virginia Republican Party took a step back toward the position it occupied during Reconstruction under the Radicals. Mosby feared that this would eventually destroy any hope that his party had in Virginia and the South; as usual, he was right.

Chapter 21

1882

Omnia munda mundis. ~ To the pure, all is pure.

"Some rise by sin, and some by virtue fall." ~ William Shakespeare

1882 SAW A few odd little stories about John Mosby that were hardly newsworthy. Indeed, they appeared to be an effort by the press to keep his name in the papers. Some of them were "new," and some were reprints of earlier stories:

The Columbian – January 5, 1882

Mosby writes that there is an opening for a good American dentist in Hong Kong. Mosby has not been minister to China in vain.

Spirit of the Age – January 11, 1882

The guerilla Mosby, now consul at Hong Kong, talks of resigning his office for the purpose of returning to America to practice law.

John Mosby doubtless was homesick—a condition from which he suffered at the start of the war—however, once he began moving against the consular ring in China, he would not have left his position lest it was believed he had been driven out by the Department of State. But it was never really "safe" for Mosby as this article proves. A new tack was taken whether by the consular crooks and their aiders and abettors among the shippers or by some of those Chinese concerns that wanted to be able to send their minions into the United States as they had once done under former consuls. But there can be no doubt that it was an attempt to blacken Mosby's name and hence render his efforts against the Seward ring null and void:

Daily Globe – March 19, 1882

Rock Island Argus – March 18, 1882

Crooked Work in China

Consular Carelessness as to Chinese Immigration.

San Francisco, March 18.—Several Chinese women, supposed to be courtesans, who arrived on the British steamer Anjear, and who were held by the authorities to be sent back to China, were brought into the Superior Court yesterday on a writ of habeas corpus.

Capt. Rohrer of the Anjear, has testified to the great laxity on the part of American Consul Mosby at Hong Kong in relation to Chinese immigrants. In proof he presented blank printed forms, signed by Mosby and bearing his consular seal, the same being certificates required to be produced by immigrants, which, Rohrer stated, could himself fill in as he chose.

As noted, this story hinted strongly at an attempt to compromise Mosby. He had received the thanks of the manager of the port of San Francisco for stopping the prostitution traffic, which suggested that exactly the opposite of the above charge was the case. Then he refused to sign such "consular certificates" despite every effort to force him to do so. Furthermore, no mention was made of how the captain managed to obtain blank signed certificates with the consular seal or what was purported to be the signature and seal of the consul.

Meanwhile, the late president Garfield had forced the Virginia Republican Party into a coalition with General Mahone's Readjusters. The party had pleaded with the president not to force such an amalgamation. Indeed, they asked him to remove those Readjusters who had been given patronage, but at the behest of *Northern* Republicans, the thing was done. The Virginia Republican Party never recovered. John Mosby was aware of what was going on, and he was aware of who and what Mahone was and that he was anathema to all that Mosby had worked so hard to procure for Republicans in the South—that is, the trust and support of whites. All of this was gone, and in 1883, it was going to be destroyed beyond repair during Mosby's lifetime. His letter to a friend regarding his nemesis was printed in a Virginia publication. Sadly, he could do nothing for the party from China, especially given the position of the present Republican administration—and he knew it:

***Staunton Spectator* - December 5, 1882**

WHAT COL. MOSBY THINKS OF MAHONE.—

It seems that Col. Mosby has no feeling but that of the utmost contempt for Gen. Mahone. In writing to a friend, he says:

"I regard Mahone the most vindictive, unscrupulous and meanest tyrant that ever figured in American politics."

To another friend he says:

"I have too great regard for my reputation and good name to have either connected with Mahone in any manner, and I have written to Gen. Grant telling him I would rather be buried beneath the waves of the Chinese ocean than to hold any office by or through such a creature as Mahone."

Col. Mosby has the greatest contempt for Mahone, and he wishes him to know it.

General William Mahone rose to great prominence in Virginia first as a Conservative, then as the leader of a Republican-type party, which worked very closely with the Negroes in that state. Those who spoke of Mosby and Mahone—even when they disliked both men—accounted Mahone as having "more brains" than Mosby, but that Mosby was a "straight-shooter," while Mahone was decidedly treacherous. However, in believing that Mahone was "smarter" than Mosby, the press confused the former's devious mind with intellect. Mosby, of course, was limited in his responses by honesty, while Mahone could do whatever was necessary to "triumph" in any situation. Such a state of affairs tends to make the honest man appear less intelligent than the deceitful one.

Chicago Tribune – December 26, 1882

Salt Lake Herald – December 27, 1882

Atlanta Constitution – December 29, 1882

MOSBY, THE EX-GUERRILLA.

Special Dispatch to the *Chicago Tribune*

Washington, D.C., Dec. 25.—Mosby, Consul in China, is said to have written a letter here in which he says that Mahone is the most arbitrary and vindictive of tyrants. Mosby's friends say that Mahone cannot remove Mosby for the reason that he fears him and considers China a better place for him, and that Mosby has so strong a friend in Gen. Grant that he cannot be removed.

Atlanta Constitution – December 29, 1882 (Edited)

THE BITTER FEELING BETWEEN THE TWO LEADERS.

How the General Got His Appointment and Still Holds on to it—Big Rival in Virginia Politics and their Relations to One Another—What Mosby Thinks of Mahone.

Washington, December 28—The Post says when President Grant and his friends succeeded in winning over to their side and way of thinking the noted guerrilla, Colonel John Singleton Mosby, they flattered themselves that they had drawn a capital prize in the political lottery, and so they had. For did not the famous guerrilla chieftain carry the "mother of presidents" and statesmen for Grant—the first time that the old dominion ever broke from her democratic moorings?

When the fraudulent Hayes anticipated trouble in being seated or inaugurated into the office to which he knew he was not elected, Mosby wrote him a letter offering "his services and a thousand men to see him through." Mr. Hayes "made a note of it." He consulted his cabinet as to appointing the colonel to some office, but every member of it voted solid against Mosby. Secretary Evarts entertained a bitter aversion to him, and in turn the colonel hated the secretary of state… When, however, Mr. Evarts slipped over to New York after his legal fees, upon a certain occasion, Mr. Hayes nominated Colonel Mosby to the senate to be consul at Hong-Kong on his own responsibility, and had him confirmed as such before the secretary of state returned. Mr. Evarts declared that "had he been here Mosby would never have been appointed." [Here the paper presents a long and inaccurate recitation of the consular ring scandal. -vph]

About this time Senator Mahone came before the public. A receiver was appointed for the Atlantic, Mississippi and Ohio railroad and he, by judicial process, was turned out of the presidency. Othello's occupation was gone, and the idler the man the busier the devil. So the latter was not long in finding work for William the First's willing hands to do. Mosby being out of the state, Mahone saw his opportunity and organized the readjuster party as an adjunct to the republican, and with its aid intended to pay off old scores with the Dutch bondholder's of Virginia's securities for turning him out of the presidency of the Atlantic, Mississippi and Ohio railroad. That he has squared accounts with a vengeance is too fresh in the public mind to need recapitulation.

MAHONE'S TACTICS.

Now, whatever can be said against General Mahone politically, in the "grim [illegible] war" he had no superior during the late pleasantness as a hard successful fighter never losing a battle. Mosby was a guerrilla (during the) war, but in politics, a square hitter, [illegible] from the shoulder" or "a Grant [illegible] calls himself. Mahone ... fears Colonel Mosby, and considers China a better place for him, than to be cavorting around Washington and Virginia. In the second place, he could not get him ousted if he wished to, Grant, Conkling and company, being his steadfast friends. Had President Garfield lived the colonel would doubtless have been made to "walk the plank." Mosby is forward in his actions, while Mahone is Machiavellian in his tactics. Mosby is a good catholic and will quarrel with his best friends; Mahone doesn't believe in religion, God or the devil and never forgives an enemy.

MOSBY AGAINST MAHONE.

At the next presidential contest Mosby is sure to resign and try conclusions with Mahone. In the last election Mosby had a club of republicans called the Grant club in Fauquier county, and hearing that the chairman was going to vote the coalition ticket, he wrote him if they did they would have to change their name. He was a straightout [illegible]. They did not vote the coalition ticket.

In writing to a friend from Hong Kong, Colonel Mosby speaks his mind of Senator Mahone as few consuls dare to do. here is his indorsement of the "boss": "I regard Mahone the most vindictive, unscrupulous and meanest tyrant that ever figured in American politics."

Will Mahone dare remove Mosby "for cause?" Nous verrons. [Translation: "Time will tell"-vph]

This is obviously a Democratic publication; and therefore, neither Mosby nor Mahone was going to be treated with much sympathy, though Mosby did seem to get the best in the character-assessment department. However, much of the story is fueled more by partisan politics than by fact. Yet it is probable that the writer believed the truth of what he wrote simply because so much of it was "accepted lore."

Indeed, Mahone's advantage over Mosby in the Virginia Republican Party would not be long lived—but then neither would the Virginia Republican Party.

Chapter 22

1883

Quod differtur, non aufertur. ~ The inevitable is yet to happen.

"Let me embrace sour adversity, wise men say it is the wisest course." ~ William Shakespeare

AS 1883 OPENED, Mosby was still in China and Mahone in was still in Virginia; but the latter was not finding in President Arthur quite the same response as he had found in President Garfield, though it was later noted that he was "thick" with the new chief executive:

***Daily Dispatch* – January 4, 1883 (Edited)**

MAHONE SNUBBED.

In Opposing the Nomination of Mosby He Presumes Too Far—The President Gives Him to Understand That "He Would Do Well Not to Uncork His Advice."

A Washington special to the New York World says: There has been a rupture between the President and Mahone. The trouble grew out of Mahone's opposition to General Mosby, who has been urged for the District Judgeship, vacated in July by Judge Rives, the author of the notorious letter, a year ago, upon the Lynchburg postmastership which disclosed a bargain between the Administration and the Readjusters…

Mosby has tired of the consulship at Hong Kong and wants to be provided for at home. He aims high for a man whose legal experience mainly antedated the war, his practice then barely keeping him alive. But he turned out well as a soldier, was prompt at repentance when the war ended, and since then the party has dealt kindly by him. Among other friends he counts General Grant, by whom the President's attention to Mosby was directed after Judge Rive's resignation. The President thought well of General Grant's suggestion, and Mahone heard of the proceeding. Mosby, in a letter made public not long before, had characterized Mahone as a scapegrace and renegade, and as a person unfit for public trust. Mahone thought his time had come to pay off that score; so he waited upon the President for an explanation. So long had he been accustomed to having his wishes furthered by executive authority that he had grown offensively expectant that he was to be consulted in everything bearing in every way upon Virginia appointments. This time his words were civil enough; but the President was in no humor to put up with his sneering manner, and he was given to understand that his demands transgressed propriety, and that he would do well not to uncork his advice. Mahone persisted in hearing what the prospects were, and expressed himself strongly against Mosby. The President bore with him not altogether patiently, and Mahone was left to infer that he had not influenced the President's mind in any degree. Since then it has dawned upon Mahone that he may have reached the end of his rope as a dictator at the White House. Curiosity is alert to know how he will go about getting even with the President. Mosby's nomination would hardly afford him full opportunity, because he could not unite the Republicans against Mosby, and with The Democrats, he is not on terms of official courtesy, much less of companionship. Besides he must be careful of himself with the Republicans, for upon their caucus action will hang Gorham's chances for nomination to the secretaryship of the Senate at the spring session. Mahone can now afford to seem independent of the President, because there is no Virginia patronage to be dispensed except that named, but it is a safe prediction that he will attempt to place himself on a good footing again whenever he may see anything to be gained by it. Meanwhile he will probably know enough to bear his wrongs in silence. He declares with regard to the Senate offices that unless the Republicans agree to elect Gorham he and Riddleberger will vote against a change in the existing roll, thus preventing the Republicans from getting anything more at present.

The idea that somehow Mosby was a poor lawyer seemed to depend upon whether the writer liked him or not. Certainly, he was more than "good" after the war, so there is no reason to believe that his lack of legal skills counted against him in procuring any government position requiring that profession. Yet every time the matter came up, even those papers not immediately "anti-Mosby" cast aspersions on his legal expertise. However, it is also interesting to note that *every* lawyer's expertise "antedated the war" by virtue of the changes brought about in government and law by the war.

Mosby was a much less abrasive person for all of his prickly temper. Every report of his intercourse with others is of a well-bred, quiet, and pleasant man. Obviously, Mahone was somewhat lacking in social skills. Certainly, he was not very popular among the men in his command during the war, which is diametric to Mosby's situation. On the other hand, Mosby tended to be blunt, especially when exasperated; and he did not suffer fools gladly no matter how "elevated" their position. And so the matter continued:

Rock Island Argus – January 5, 1883
MAHONE VS. GRANT.

New York, Jan. 5.—A Washington special says there is no doubt that a rupture has occurred between the administration and Senator Mahone, growing out of the United States judgeship of Virginia, made vacant by the resignation of Judge Rives. Gen. Grant is pressing the appointment of Col. Mosby, now Consul General at Hong Kong, who is a bitter enemy of Senator Mahone, while the appointment of Congressman Paul is demanded by the latter.

One of the principle objects of Grant's visit to Washington at this time is to back Mosby, and failing to come to an agreement with Mahone, both visited the president yesterday to settle the matter. What occurred at the interview is kept very close, but the result may be inferred from the fact that Mahone declared he would never enter the White House again.

This was an odd matter. Why were Grant's wishes not given preference? Who was actually placed in Judge Rives' office is not mentioned, but certainly, Mahone received no satisfaction if the report of his tirade at the end of his session with Arthur is to be believed. Again, it would seem that Mosby's name was anathema with every Republican administration between Grant and the time that Roosevelt entered the White House. It is still odd, however, that he was not offered the position. It would have kept him out of day-to-day political machinations, and he certainly had the right qualifications—that is, if they included honesty and ethics.

The position causing the ruckus was the result of the resignation of Judge Rives, an old friend of Mosby's dating back before the war; he was an older man, so his retirement was not unexpected. The two worked closely in Virginia to throw out the Reconstruction government of that state, and it is probable that he would have preferred that Mosby replace him. So the question becomes, why did Grant not prevail in getting Mosby appointed if, in fact, he tried to do so? In the end, the office went to Paul, Mahone's candidate, thus validating Mosby's belief that there was no place for him in Virginia's Republican Party.

Again, the Mahone-Mosby contretemps is brought up in a paper that wished a swift end to both men:

Evening Bulletin – January 12, 1883

It is said that Colonel Mosby, consult to Hong-Kong, will challenge Mahone to fight a duel as soon as he gets time to come home. He should be brought home at once. It'll be a blessing, whichever is slain.

In the same paper:

Senator Mahone is reported to have visited the president and informed him that he did not want Col. Mosby appointed United States district judge for Virginia, to succeed Rives. It is also reported that the senator was not pleased with the reception accorded his declaration.

Once again, Mosby found himself a target both of Mahone and the *Evening Bulletin*. However, the administration's response to the little general was not sympathetic either. Could it be that the disease of "sectionalism" so despised by Mosby had raised its ugly head—but this time in the North? Neither man was loved in the North, Mosby for his "guerrilla ways" and Mahone for his part in the Battle of the Crater in which he killed a number of black Union soldiers who had surrendered." But whatever the case, by the time Mosby left Hong Kong, he knew that he had no future in Virginia or the South and so had asked Grant to help him obtain a position elsewhere.

The Statesman – January 18, 1883 (Edited)

The late elections have been a great blow to the Readjusters in the Old Dominion, and already we can hear the mutterings of the approaching violent

WAR IN VIRGINIA

Between the rival of that short lived and disreputable party. Many of the Readjuster leaders have expressed themselves as thoroughly disgusted with the petty tyrannical bossism of Billy Mahone, and have expressed their intention to vote with The Democratic party in congress. Col. Abe Fulkerson of the Ninth district, which is considered a Readjuster stronghold, has said several times lately that the party has fulfilled its mission and either the leaders of it would recede into either of the two great federal parties It is rumored in Washington that Mahone and Arthur are at variance with each other. The president has recklessly appointed several officials in Virginia in direct opposition to the wishes of the little boss, and it is now expected that Mosby will be made United States judge in that state through the influence of Gen. Grant. Mosby and Mahone are bitter personal enemies, and the latter has been at the White House almost every day for a week to oppose his appointment.

The Bee – **January 20, 1883 (Edited)**
THE VIRGINIA SITUATION.

Two years ago the newspapers, many of them, as well as readers in general, proclaimed for a rest from the interminable Virginia question. To a very great extent the political situation in Virginia to-day is a thing as much read about as any subject that is up for public discussion; because something has turned up from Virginia, the only Southern State about which there is now a question of doubt as to how the next electoral vote for President will be counted, or rather which party will get the majority of her votes.

Now and then one reads that, there is a difference of opinion, a coldness, a misdeal, or a rupture between the President and General Mahone; then that Gen. Jno. S. Mosby is coming home to take charge of the Republican ante-readjuster forces opposed to General Mahone, that Jno. B. Seuer is General Grant's choice—for the vacant judgeship—one day and Mosby his choice the next.

There is no rupture between General Mahone and the President, nor between General Mahone and leading Republicans, either in Virginia or out of the State. Very truly there is the same antagonism on the part of the straight-out Republicans and the Senator that existed last season, but beyond this there is none.

Anther thing—speaking now of Democratic politics in Virginia—should General Mosby come home especially to dispute Gen. Mahone's leadership, who of the Republican party, those that are now not Mahone men, will answer the colonel's bugle blast. One thing certain that Col. John S. Mosby has a very small following of Republicans in Virginia, and if he and Mr. Seuer should join forces, they would count for hosts among the colored voters without hope. For when Col. Mosby was a Republican, he voted against the Civil-Rights bill, while he was in Congress, and that settles it, neither of them have a loyal following of colored voters in the State.

John Mosby was never in Congress and therefore did not vote on the Civil Rights Bill, though he certainly rejected it. And though Mosby had nothing against the "colored vote," he believed that the Republicans were destroying themselves in the South if they continued to use the "negro" as a means to power. However, he would certainly have protected the rights of blacks in Virginia. He had no hatred for the race, though he did not believe that they should be given power over whites, whom he considered superior. There is no doubt that whatever political position John Mosby might have obtained in Virginia, the black man would not have suffered as a result. Indeed, Mosby's care for what was both legal and right would have assured Virginia's blacks that they would have been protected against illegal assaults and intimidation but Mosby would have worked to assure that they were not placed into positions of power for which he believed them unsuitable. Of course, Mosby had the entire period of Reconstruction as an example of the consequences of "black rule."

A small article about the "great Chinese Ring scandal" suddenly made its appearance in the press, leading one to believe that, by virtue of the dearth of coverage, the matter was no longer of great concern in either the government or the press:

National Republican – January 25, 1883

A private letter was received from Consul John S. Mosby at Hong Kong yesterday, in which he briefly summarizes the financial transactions of his consulate during the four years ended the thirtieth of June last, as follows: Total amount covered into the treasury, after payment of all expenses, $42,824.70, as against $26,565.73 during his predecessor's incumbency of seven years; amount expended for sick and disabled seamen, $190, as against $8,403.52 in the seven years preceding.

Mosby was still fighting the "good fight" with regard to the corruption in China, but perhaps by this time, he was also getting heartily tired of it. Nothing had happened, nor did there seem to be anything in Congress to suggest that that body was going to act. All that he had accomplished was to make his own life in Hong Kong miserable. Indeed, the matter had so disappeared from public consciousness that the following erroneous report of Mosby's arrival in the United States made the papers:

National Republican – February 3, 1883

Consul Mosby is expected to arrive from Hong Kong by the next steamer reaching San Francisco from that port.

But the Mosby-Mahone controversy had replaced the consulate ring in the minds, and pages, of the press:

Evening Star – February 16, 1883

Col. Mosby and Gen. Mahone They Do Not Sleep Together.

To the Editor of the *Evening Star*.

Washington, Feb. 16, 1883

Please inform the public that if, from any rumor or recent event, unnecessary to enlarge upon here, the impression has gone abroad that Col. Jno. S. Mosby is friendly to Gen. Mahone, the impression carries a falsehood. As the brother-in-law of Col. Mosby, I know and desire to say that for two or three years he has been writing from Hong Kong invective such as might be expected from one whose native state has been made the scene of a bacchanal and her honor bartered away. I went Wednesday evening with his young son to say to Gen. Mahone that whatever was done that looked like compromise was done without Col. Mosby's knowledge and against his wishes. Hoping other things, he was mad. While this is not my controversy, I dislike, as Sir Lucius O'Trigger said, to see "it spoiled by trying to explain it," for it seems to me "the quarrel is a very pretty quarrel as it stands." Charles Wells Russell.

Russell, Mosby's brother-in-law, wasn't very happy with either combatant, save only that they were combatants, and he was enjoying the spectacle because he had no dog in the hunt. It seems that Mosby was not the only one given to literary allusions in his correspondence as Russell used author Sheridan's humorous character in his missal. Of course, brothers-in-law or not, Mosby and Russell were not exactly close friends.

Weekly Citizen – March 4, 1883

The report has been circulated in Virginia that Colonel Mosby and Senator Mahone had come to a friendly understanding; but Charles W. Russell, the brother-in-law of Mosby, writes a letter in which he says: "I know Colonel Mosby has for two or three years been writing from Hong Kong invectives such as might be expected from one whose native State has [been] made the scene of a bacchanal and her honor bartered away."

The Carbon Advocate – March 31, 1883

People are talking a good deal about the fight between Senator Mahone and Colonel Mosby when the latter gets back from China. It will be what Horace Greeley called mighty interesting reading, whenever it does come off. To one who knows the two men there could not possibly be two antagonists better qualified to cope with each other. Mahone is a man of more brains than Mosby, but Mosby has enough to make him dangerous, and he has besides, a dogged and ferocious vindictiveness, so that Mr. Mahone had better be on the lookout, for some letters have been received here from Mosby, promising a circus when he gets back. The two men are alike in a great many particulars. Both of them prefer using their knives to their forks at dinner. Colonel Mosby says little, but what he says is short, plain and to the point. He has the whole history of Mahone's railroad transactions at his fingers' ends, and knows a good many other things which Senator Mahone would prefer to rest in forgetfulness. Mosby's hard fierce determined face is enough to make most people to fear and dislike him.

John Mosby had as good a brain as any man who ever lived as his actions during his life attest. Now he had shortcomings with regard to dealing with politicians, but they were more a matter of morality—he was both honest and naïve—than of brain. No doubt Mahone was smart as well, but not smarter than John Mosby. With regard to the columnist's point about Mosby's appearance, photographs of the man show no such "hard fierce determined face" as alluded to in the paper and neither did "most people … fear and dislike him." He had his enemies, but they hardly amounted to "most people."

An old allegation then appeared—that is, Mosby the boor:

Salt Lake Herald – May 19, 1883

A disgusted traveler, who called on Consul Mosby at Hong Kong, sent up his card and got it back again with the request to bring it up himself. Complying with the request he found the ex-guerrilla with his heels on the tale and his thumbs in his armpits, and was further made unhappy by being interrogated as to who in gehenna* he was, and where in gehenna he came from. [* Hell-vph]

This is another one of those stories like the clothing controversy, the use of a napkin as a handkerchief, and the "feet on the desk" business that attempted to blacken Mosby's name before the public. Throughout all of the accounts of his intercourse with people,

John Mosby was shown to be polite, pleasant and rather reserved, which tends to make this story unbelievable. Mosby was more than aware of his position as United States Consul and would not have done anything to bring the nation he represented into disrepute by his behavior. Sadly, he appeared to be in the minority among his fellow "diplomats" in that regard.

And still, the Mosby-Mahone debate went on even though the combatants were separated by half a world:

Greenville Times – August 18, 1883

Swapping Compliments

Gen. Mosby in a recent letter to a former member of his command, says: "What a beautiful spectacle we now have in Virginia—Mahone teaching the people how to steal, and Dick Farr teaching them how to spell. * * * If anyone asks you what I think of Mahone, just say that I regard him as a common freebooter—a regular Dick Turpin."

It is now in order for Mahone to classify Mosby.

Mosby knew well about all of Mahone's shady dealings with the railroad, and that is one reason why Mahone did not want his nemesis to return to Virginia. Even Mosby's worst enemies—other than disgruntled Union soldiers and the *National Tribune*— usually admitted he was a "straight shooter." Of course, the Mosby-Mahone contretemps was a boon to most of the press in that both men were hated and therefore, both could be castigated with impunity.

Mosby continued to make himself heard about matters in Virginia as he probably believed that the situation did not bode well for the Republican Party in that state. As usual, he was correct:

Salt Lake Herald – October 6, 1883

Gen. Mosby is writing from Japan in reprobation of the methods of Mahone in Virginia. If Consul Mosby is anxious to avoid a recall he will sing low about Mahone and his methods. The Readjuster Senator has a contract with the administration that has not yet expired. Office holders who are opposed to the performance of the government part of that contract are in danger of being turned out to grass.

Mosby was little troubled regarding the consequences of any statement he felt strongly enough to express. If his comments about Mahone got him recalled, his opinion would have been "so be it." Indeed, it is odd that the newspaper did not understand that fact by this point in Mosby's "press career."

Millheim Journal – October 11, 1883

"General Mosby writes all the way from Japan to reprobate the methods of Mahone," says Ex-Chairman Bogert's Wilksbarre Union-Leader. "Everyone seems to be well posted on that matter except Mahone's friend Arthur."

This was the first article that mentioned Mahone had a friend in Chester A. Arthur, Garfield's successor. Arthur had been a friend of Roscoe Conkling; but apparently, when Garfield made him an unlikely choice as vice president, Arthur abandoned his former friend and the stalwart position in the party. Of course, at the time, nobody could know how important Garfield's choice would become. If Arthur was indeed a confidant and friend of Mahone's, that answers many questions regarding Mahone's continuing power in Virginia. On the other hand, it makes Arthur's later treatment of Mahone difficult to understand unless the little general treated his friend, who was now president, as he treated so many men—with contempt. It is possible to push any man too far.

But time was almost up for William Mahone. The election of 1883 was almost at hand, and his "bi-racial" arrangement in the Readjuster Party was about to come home to roost. The problem was that Mahone and his party had swallowed the Republican Party in Virginia, much as the Populists under William Jennings Bryan would swallow the national Democratic Party in 1896. But Mahone used the blacks in Virginia for his own purposes and, as a result, did them little good. The matter came to a head in the town of Danville, Virginia, a hint of that trouble being found in the article below:

Shenandoah Herald – October 31, 1883

More Desertions from Mahone

Duval Porter, a well-known journalist, of Danville, and a speaker of considerable power, has renounced Mahoneism and taken the stump for the democratic ticket. Joseph H. Jewett, the temperance coalition nominee for the House of Delegates in Loudoun county, has withdrawn from the canvass, having learned that the "party ties are more binding on the part of many to whom he had looked for support than temperance convictions." S. T. Nicholas has announced himself as a "coalition-republican candidate" in Mr. Jewett's place. Col. John S. Mosby has written a letter to J. Thos. Seelock, a political worker in upper Fauquier county, chiding him for his affiliation with the Mahone party, and he has replied that he will hereafter act in accordance with Mosby's well known opposition to Mahone's ascendancy. Twenty-eight of the leading mercantile houses of Danville, Va., have issued an address showing "the horrors of coalition rule" in that city, and appealing to the white people of the Southwest in the Valley of Virginia to elect a democratic Legislature which will give them relief.

On November 3, just before the election, rising tensions in Danville, a rapidly growing majority-black city, came to a head in what was called the Danville Riot. The "biracial" Readjusters had taken control of the city council in 1882, though not all party members in the council were black. In October of 1883, a number of white citizens who felt socially, economically, but especially politically threatened signed their names to what became known as the Danville Circular. The circular attacked the Readjusters in general and blacks in their ranks in particular. On November 2nd, two days after the above article, the chairman of the Pittsylvania County Readjusters denounced the circular in a public speech, which roused the passions of his black audience. On the next day, these heightened tensions led to an altercation between a white man and two blacks, which escalated into violence leading to the deaths of at least five people. This riot was the death knell of the Readjuster Party and consequently the Republican Party in Virginia, as Mosby knew it would be. Not another Republican would be elected to high state office for many years thereafter. This sorry incident can be laid directly at the door of President Garfield's insistence that the Virginia Republican Party join with Mahone's Readjusters, a matter that led to John Mosby's continued exile even after he was removed from his position as consul at Hong Kong in 1885.

Chapter 23

1884

"Saepe ne utile quidem est scire quid futurum sit." ~ "Often, it is not advantageous to know what will be." ~ Cicero

"Brave men rejoice in adversity, just as brave soldiers triumph in war." ~ Seneca

ANOTHER YEAR DAWNED, and John Mosby was still in China. Of course, he could have just come home, but to do so was to abandon his efforts to clear up the corruption in the US diplomatic service in that country and give the impression that either he had surrendered to the inevitable or had been forcibly removed, neither of which was he willing to own. But no doubt, Mosby must have been considering the upcoming presidential election and the probability of a Democratic victory. The Republicans had been in office since 1860, and the man now occupying the White House was certainly not the choice of the American people but like Andrew Johnson, he was in the right place at the right time. Who knows had Garfield lived, the Republicans might have had a better chance. But by the beginning of 1884, the party's outlook for winning the presidency was dim.

As noted, Mosby's efforts on the consular ring scandal were still drawing blood. Apparently, his letter of 1881 was included in a "lengthy pamphlet" on the decline of American shipping that had been put on the desk of every member of Congress:

> *Daily Dispatch* – **February 26, 1884**
>
> WHAT COLONEL JOHN S. MOSBY SAYS.
>
> This morning there was placed on the desk of every member of the House a lengthy pamphlet on the decline of American shipping, which contains a letter from Colonel John S. Mosby, consul at Hong Kong, to the Treasury Department, dated October 22, 1881. Colonel Mosby says that during the two years of his consulate he had collected in extra wages and turned into the Treasury $4,723, and expended of the relief of seamen $190. He said his predecessor in eight years expended, or rather furnished vouchers signed by his stool pigeon, for $8,493.

But Mosby's correspondence by 1884 was less concerned with China and more with Virginia. After all, he had done all he could about China. Now he felt obligated to try to do something for his party in his home state:

> *Staunton Spectator* – **March 4, 1884**
>
> Mosby on Mahone—A letter received in Washington by a prominent Virginia Republican from Col. John S. Mosby, under date of January 26, says:' "As Mahone's light has been snuffed out, I do hope that the Virginia Republicans will consign him now to everlasting oblivion. To do that, two things are necessary: 1] Have a Straightout convention and send delegates to Chicago—ignore Mahone and his gang altogether. 2] Put out a straight electoral ticket and don't combine in any way with Mahone.

If he wants to come into the Republican party, let him come as a high private in the rear rank, and then let him serve in that capacity until he is purged of all his sins."

After the debacle of the election of 1883, Mahone had lost his stranglehold on the Virginia Republican Party; and though he was still active, it appeared that his enemies had enough strength to fight back. However, all that accomplished was a further weakening of the Virginia party as a whole. Still, it is interesting to note that Mosby did not immediately return to Virginia or at least make noises about doing so. Perhaps Mahone was still too powerful, or at least he remained strong enough when his relationship with the Arthur administration was factored in.

But the situation in Virginia, once so promising, had turned against Mosby before the election of Cleveland and his anticipated removal from Hong Kong. In recognition of his situation, Mosby wrote asking Grant to find him a position as he believed that he had no future in the East. But the Democratic press now seemed to have the wind up and it may be that the probability of a Democratic victory in November had initiated the process of once again "demonizing" John Mosby in that party's press. Certainly, it wasn't anything that Mosby was doing. Indeed, he was rather quiet:

***Butler Weekly Times* - March 5, 1884**

Unwelcome History

From the La Platte Home Press.

There is a great ado made about Frank James and his mad, reckless career. True it has been bad and bold, but cease your censure until you hear of other men and their crimes and subsequent elevation.

There is Jack Mosby, the famous guerilla chief of Virginia and of the Potomac valley—the man who ordered his men to take no prisoners—and when they did accidentally secure a prisoner he was disarmed and shot down like a dog—Mosby, the worst of American bandits, is to-day a minister to a foreign country, appointed by Grant, a Republican President, and re-appointed by Returning Board Hayes. Mosby, for policy, became a Republican and received his laurels. So does every other influential policy adherent. If Frank James should become a policy man, and so declare himself, he would find sweet repose and welcome in leading Republican circles.

We are not posted in regard to Frank James' politics, but let it be what it may, if he desires to be an office-holder—without repenting of his past bad conduct—let him follow the foot-prints of Mosby, and he'll get there, provided "the part of great moral ideas" continues to exist. We have no apology from Mr. James, neither have we for Mosby or the Republican party or its vasicating [sic] policy.

Obviously, any positive vignettes describing Mosby's war career were immediately repudiated by those who despised the man or the Republican Party—or both. Meanwhile, the consular scandal made another brief newspaper appearance in this small article, which at least had its villains, if not its heroes, straight:

Fort Wayne Gazette – **March 26, 1884**

An Alleged Crooked Ex-Consul

Cincinnati, March 26—In 1870 Hon. David H. Bailey was appointed United States Consul to Hong Kong, China. In 1879 he was appointed consul general to Shanghai. His successor at Hong Kong was Gen. Mosby, who discovered that Bailey was short in his accounts and reported the same to the government. Channing Richards, representing the United States government has entered suit against Bailey for $38,411.89. He is charged with receiving money for disabled United States seamen, with reshipping discharged seamen, and receiving and keeping fees for examining emigrants to the United States.

It would not have hurt the Gazette to make more than a passing reference to Mosby's part in exposing this long existing corruption—or at least get his former military rank correct. But then, as it was "Mosby Season" once more, perhaps even such small courtesies were out of fashion:

National Republican – **April 30, 1884**

VIRGINIA

Richmond, Va.—The straightout republican convention called by Dezendorf will meet here at Mozart hall to-morrow. Among those who it is expected will be in attendance are Judge Rives, Gen. Wickham, Franklin Stearns, Otis H. Russell, James M. Donnan, Judge Willoughby, O. E. Hine, John Underwood, Col. Robert Bolling, Geo. Rhye, Alexander Cochran, and John M. Dawson. A stirring letter from Col. John S. Mosby, consul to China, will, it is said, be read to the convention.

It is asserted that the platform will arraign Gen. Mahone and his following on the two grounds—of a repudiation of the state debt and a prostitution of federal patronage to that end.

Mosby still had some influence in the Republican Party in Virginia as can be seen by this story. However, by the time he was turned out as consul upon the election of Democrat Grover Cleveland that year, the situation had apparently changed considerably as his plea to Grant for help clearly demonstrated. Unfortunately, Mosby did not know that Grant was dying; but true to their friendship, the dying man obtained a position for his faithful friend with the Southern Pacific Railroad through California Senator Leland Stanford.

A newspaper article appeared in a San Francisco paper about the sinking of an American ship, the *Rainier*. In it, Mosby received praise for his prompt action on behalf of the stranded crew. There were other stories about other shipwrecks claiming that Mosby had paid no attention to nor directed any help for the stranded American seamen, but this one was far more positive:

San Francisco Chronicle – **June 6, 1884 (Edited)**

THE LOSS OF THE "RAINIER."

Statement of her Captain — Misleading Charts

Captain Morrison, late master of the American ship Rainier, lost while on the voyage from Philadelphia to China and Japan, arrived here on the City of Rio de Janeiro on …

"General Mosby, the United States Consul, made timely exertion in procuring a Government steamer for our rescue, which proved so successful. On board the Essex we were received and entertained with most cordial and generous hospitality by all the officers and crew… On May 16th went on board the American steamship City of Rio de Janeiro, bound to San Francisco, w(h)ere we arrived June 4th in the afternoon."

This was one of the few "sailors' stories" where Mosby received any praise for his action on their behalf. Almost every article involving sailors and ships made a villain of Consul Mosby and then his replacement at Hong Kong, Democrat Withers. And whereas the Rainier matter was to Mosby's benefit, the good ship Reindeer was something else again:

San Francisco Chronicle – November 17, 1884 (Edited) [Special Dispatches to the Chronicle]

A STORY OF THE SEA.

Adventures of a Party of Shipwrecked Men.

New York, November 17. — The Tribune says: The American ship Pactolus, which arrived at this port yesterday from Yokohama, brought as second and third mates H. W. Drohan and H. C. Percy, who formerly filled the same berths on the ship Reindeer, wrecked on the Marshall islands. The story of the wreck and subsequent adventures of the officers and crew, as told by the mates to a reporter, is as follows: The ship Reindeer, an American vessel of 1900 tons, sailed from Philadelphia August 1, 1883, bound for Japan with a cargo of oil. She was commanded by Captain Morrison. There were three mates and a steward in the cabin and twenty men before the mast. She had fair winds around the Horn and on entering the South Pacific laid her course for Japan. The night of January 2, 1884, was a dark and stormy one and the ship being out of her course, struck on a reef near one of the Marshall islands. Taking to the boats, the officers and crew escaped to an island, upon which they landed. …

The wanderers of the sea, with their boat, were taken on board and well cared for until their arrival at Saigon. There the French Consul, discharging the duties of American Consul, the United States having no representative in the port, was afraid to send the men to Hongkong, whither they wished to go to get shipped to this country. Mr. Tranlett, the British Consul, however, believing that "blood is thicker than water," took the men in charge and forwarded them to Hongkong, with a letter to Colonel Mosby. Mosby, the mates both declare, refused to assist them…

Evening Bulletin – November 19, 1884 (Edited)

[Part of a page-long article on the loss of the steamship Reindeer and the rescue and fate of her crew—and their treatment at Mosby's hands at Hong Kong.-vph]

...On the twenty-fifth day after the rescue the Catalina reached Sigon. There was no American consul there. The French Consular Agent was supposed to look out for Americans who strayed into Sigon, but he refused to give any assistance to the Reindeer's men. C. F. Tumlett, the British Consul, took the responsibility of paying the passage of the men to Hong Kong, where he said, they would find the American man-of-war Essex. He also gave them a letter to Colonel Mosby, the American Consul at the latter port. The steamship Benvue was the vessel which took Mr. Drohan and his three men to Hong Kong. Colonel Mosby communicated with Commodore Davis, who ordered Captain McCormick, of the Essex, to proceed to the Marshall Islands for the remainder of the Reindeer's crew.

Col. Mosby, Mr. Drohan asserts, allowed the four American seamen to shift for themselves in Hong Kong, where they spent thirty-six hours before they reached the Essex. In the meantime they had neither food nor shelter. The Reindeer's boat which had been picked up by the Catalina was placed under the care of Colonel Mosby. The latter sold this for $90, but none of this money went toward feeding or clothing the four men who risked their lives to obtain aid for their comrades. Mr. Drohan has letters proving the sale of the boat for the sum mentioned. Colonel Mosby was the Confederate guerrilla leader whose sudden conversion to loyal principles after the war caused some comment. The men were treated very kindly aboard the Essex, which at once set sail for the Marshall Island.

Mosby was not able to respond immediately, but respond he did! If anyone believes that John Mosby didn't care what people thought of him, his quick response to any slander should prove that he cared very much indeed, if not about the opinion of the person making the charge then about the opinions of those reading that charge.

Democrat Grover Cleveland had been elected, and for the first time in eight years, John Mosby knew that he must leave Hong Kong. Doubtless, like Napoleon on Elba, he had tired greatly of his island prison. However, it was one thing to return to a place in Virginia with the Republican Party and his family and friends, but quite another to simply be cast adrift with no home or position waiting for him. He had already written to Ulysses Grant at his home at Mt. McGregor in New York but had heard nothing. But whether Grant would be able to assist him or not, John Mosby could not have looked forward to the coming year with any real enthusiasm or hope. Once again, he was an outcast and an exile, though in fact, he was going home.

Chapter 24

1885

Quo vadis? ~ Where are you going?

"Now is the winter of our discontent …" ~ **William Shakespeare**

EARLY IN 1885 nothing yet had been said about replacing Republican John Mosby at Hong Kong, and the consular scandal was still making the press, especially in California. Mosby wrote a letter to the Department of State addressing what he called "the absurdity of Consular regulations." A local paper was interested and acted accordingly:

> ***San Francisco Chronicle* – January 23, 1885 (Edited)**
>
> [Special Dispatches to the Chronicle]
>
> THE CONSULAR SERVICE
>
> > Colonel Mosby, United States Consul at Hongkong, has written a letter to the State Department with reference to the Consular service. … Consular Crookedness in China. - How Officials Connive at Frauds on the Government.
> >
> > Washington, January 22.—Colonel Mosby, United States Consul at Hongkong, has written a very interesting letter to the State Department, in which he calls attention to the absurdity of the Consular regulations in many respects. Colonel Mosby makes some valuable suggestions, which, if followed, would undoubtedly have a beneficial effect upon this important branch of the Government service. Referring to this letter, a naval officer who recently returned from China station said to-day to your correspondent: "During my last cruise I ran across American Consuls who occupied all sorts of positions, from that of a Hebrew second-hand clothing dealer to a clerk in a house engaged in exporting goods to this country. The latter was a clerk for the firm of Peel, Hubbell & Co., at Manila. The firm sends hundreds of thousands of dollars worth of goods to the United States annually and their clerk swears to their invoice." It may be legitimate, but it looks bad.

It seems that the corruption in the China service was as much a matter of the indifference of the State Department as it was the venality of those who carried on the corruption, as the above article appeared to indicate.

For the first time, mention was made of the possibility of Mosby's friends at home trying to have him kept on in Hong Kong. Perhaps they knew that there was no place for him in Virginia and were doing all that they could to prevent him facing the same social ostracism and financial ruin as he had in the 1870s:

> ***Clifton Clarion* – February 4, 1885**
>
> General Mosby, our Consul at Hong Kong, is showing some sense just now. His friends are anxious that he should retain his present post under

the new Administration, but he apparently is opposed to any begging in his behalf. Following is an extract written by Mosby to a Virginia friend:

"I wish it to be understood that I have no apologies or recantations to make and no favors to ask of the next administration. I accept the result of the election as the fate of war, to which I have not been altogether unaccustomed. I have survived one lost cause, and may survive another. I have no repinings or complaints to make. Some indiscreet friends of mine, I fear, may ask of Mr. Barbour, or some other Virginia Democrat, to save me in the "massacre of the innocents," which will soon begin. Now, I wish you to understand that nothing could be more offensive to me."

We hope a few of the Federal office-holders who are now whining over a possibility of removal, will try to copy Gen. Mosby's dignified resignation.

Mosby did not resign his position upon the election of Cleveland, something that was claimed at the time, but he knew that he would be replaced as that was the way of the foreign service then—and now. His probable concern was that in trying to "beg" his position, his well-intentioned friends would humiliate him as they had done when they tried to procure for him a furlough with the marriage claim. But Mosby did not make known his dignified demand so the idea that he kept his personal business "public" through the newspapers is wrong and, frankly, would have been as "offensive" to him as a plea for his retention at Hong Kong.

By March of 1885, the calumny against Mosby regarding shipwrecked American sailors had come to his notice—and he had responded accordingly. However, in this article, the ship is identified as the Rainier when, in fact, it was the Reindeer:

Richmond Dispatch – **March 6, 1885**

Colonel Mosby in His Own Defence.

To the Editor of the *New York Times*:

Your issue of November 14th last has a notice of the arrival in New York of the Backtolus, having on board the second mate of the American ship Rainier, of Bath, which was wrecked on the Marshall group of islands in January, 1884. In the report of his adventures, as related by the second mate, Drohan, there is this allusion to myself:

"C. F. Tumlett, the British Consul, took the responsibility of paying the passage of the men to Hong Kong, where, he said, they would find the American man-of-war Essex. He also gave them a letter to Colonel Mosby, the American Consul at the latter port. The steamship Benvenue was the vessel which took Mr. Drohan and his three men to Hong Kong. Colonel Mosby communicated with Commodore Davis, who ordered Captain McCormick, of the Essex, to proceed to the Marshall islands for the remainder of the Rainier's crew. Colonel Mosby, Mr. Drohan asserts, allowed the four American seamen to shift for themselves in Hong Kong, where they spent thirty-six hours before they reached the Essex. In the mean time they had neither food nor shelter. The Rainier's boat, which had been picked up by the Catalina, was placed under the care of Colonel Mosby. The latter sold this for ninety dollars, but none of this money went toward feeding or clothing the four men who risked their lives to obtain aid for their comrades. Mr. Drohan has letters proving the sale of the boat for the sum mentioned. Colonel Mosby was the notorious Confederate guerrilla leader who sudden conversion to loyal principles after the war caused some comment."

The second mate and three seamen were forwarded to Hong Kong from Saigon by the steamship Benvenue. So far from wandering about like disembodied spirits on the Stygian shore, as Drohan asserts, they were within twenty minutes after they reported to the consulate placed on board the Essex. As Drohan volunteered to return to the islands with the Essex, Captain McCormick gave him a berth, rations, and a full suit of clothing on Government account. The three seamen were put at a sailors' boarding-house on the same day they arrived, and in a day or so afterward reshipped on an American vessel. About two months after their departure from here, the British bark Catalina, that had picked them up in the longboat at sea and brought them into Saigon, came to Hong Kong and delivered the long-boat of the Rainier over to me. On my recommendation, the President presented to Captain Williams, master of the Catalina, a gold watch and chain in acknowledgement of his humane services to the crew of the Rainier. If Drohan had said that, after the manner of the Cyclops, I had killed and eaten him and his companions, there would have been as much probability in the story as in that related to your reporter by this "ancient mariner."

The inclosed correspondence [letters to and from the United States Department of State and the owners of the wrecked vessel, including an acknowledgment of the receipt of a draft for $95, less expenses, being the proceeds of the sale of the Rainier's boat] shows what care I took of the shipwrecked seamen who came here, what efforts I made for the rescue of those left on the island, and also what disposition was made of the proceeds of the sale of the boat. Rear-Admiral Davis, commanding our Asiatic squadron, and Captain McCormick, are witnesses to the truth of my statement.

John Mosby, United States Consul

United States Consulate, Hong Kong,

January 13, 1885.

More small stories were coming out about Mosby's soon-to-be recall:

St. Paul Daily Globe – March 7, 1885

Col. Mosby, consul at Hong Kong, bows to the inevitable and says that he is willing to come home.

Hickman Courier – March 13, 1885

Col. John S. Mosby, now United States Consul at Hong Kong, China, says he has no favors to ask of the new Administration, but accepts the result of the Presidential election as the fate of war. Guess John knows it is no use to ask.

Democratic Northwest – **April 2, 1885**

Bring Him Home. [New York Herald]

By the way, can't some Democratic soldier be sent out to Hong Kong to relieve that Confederate Brigadier, General Mosby, who has been holding the office of Consul since receiving his appointment at the hands of Grant? Mosby should be brought home and Americanized.

Even as John Mosby was relieved of his position at Hong Kong, his friend, mentor and fellow outcast Ulysses S. Grant died. *Immediately, everything changed!* No longer the great "American deadbeat," most of the nation rushed forward to pay homage to a man who had almost died in the poorhouse until the American government determined that such an end for the "hero" of the Civil War and a former president did not reflect well on the country. Instantly, newspapers of both parties began their coverage with the Republican organs lauding Grant. Even Democratic papers found a few good things to say about him while, possibly in consequence thereof, both sides began to print a few nice sentiments about his "pet guerrilla," John Mosby. Indeed, there was a sudden resurgence of interest in Mosby's wartime career, but this was a two-edged sword! For every Republican paper that lauded his courage and skill, there was at least one Democratic publication reciting his alleged atrocities! One of the first of these positive Grant-Mosby articles was printed in—naturally!—the *National Republican*:

National Republican, – **April 4, 1885 (Edited)**

THE HERO'S RESTING PLACE.

A Probability that Washington May be Honored as the Repository of His Remains.

The fast approaching dissolution of the nation's hero has naturally suggested to those near and dear to him reluctantly entertained thoughts of the eventual disposal of the remains, and while their fond hearts still cling to the faintest spark of hope for the noble life that is fast ebbing away, they are also determined that its close shall be characterized by all outward evidences of the universal love and esteem for the honored chief. It is understood that Gen. Grant's wishes have been ascertained in the matter, and it is said that some correspondence in reference to the subject has passed between Col. Fred Grant, Gen. Sheridan, Maj. Lydecker, and other friends of the family. Maj. Lydecker, however, in conversation with a Republican reporter last night discredited those reports, so far as his own knowledge of the subject was concerned.

It was stated upon authority that internment at Arlington has been suggested, while other sources of information lead to the inference that Gen. Grant himself expressed a desire to be laid to rest in this city, which he had always loved as his home. Those who know Gen. Grant best, know that he bore no vindictive spirit toward the southern portion of our now reunited country. What military fame he achieved what genius the war permitted him to display, he was ever conscious that duty alone impelled him to do all that arms could accomplish to serve his country, and his well-known friendship for Gen. Joe Johnston, whom he at one time desired to appoint as District commissioner, his treatment of Gen. Longstreet and Col. Mosby showed that his great heart was free from any small vindictiveness of spirit. It would seem more in harmony with his personal feelings, therefore, if he were laid at rest in a place which is now again the capital of our common country, and as dear to the people of the southern states as it is to those of any northern state, than to bury him in Virginia, whose soil was the scene of the late conflict, though the expressions of grief coming from that state are unquestionably as sincere and creditable to its people as those coming from any other source."

In this paper, there was also a lengthy article on Mosby's capture of General Stoughton in 1863. Somehow, one doubts that this was coincidental. The article below combines coverage of the two men, another scenario that would continue as long as there was press coverage of John Mosby:

National Republican – **April 6, 1885**
GRANT AND MOSBY.

An Interesting Reminiscence of the End of the Rebellion.

Editor of The Republican: The severe affliction with which the illustrious soldier is now suffering, and the anxiety of all nations watching the approaching end, and the numerous testimonials of his noble traits of character recalls to my mind an incident which took place on the morning of the 20th of April, 1865, the date of the removal of the remains of President Lincoln from the east room of the executive mansion to the rotunda of the capitol. The writer hereof was appointed by Secretary of War Stanton as assistant to Frank Sands, the undertaker in charge of the funeral ceremonies. I was assigned the duty of adjusting the white silk sashes to the honorary pall-bearers, Gen. Grant being one of them.

While awaiting an opportunity to get the general's attention, he being engaged in conversation with Green Clay Smith of Kentucky, and two or three other gentlemen in relation to the surrender of Gen. Lee, and the extending of parole to the subordinate officers and men, one of the gentlemen asked Gen. Grant if Moseby had surrendered. His reply was, "No, not yet;" whereupon one of the other gentlemen remarked, "Why, general, you certainly do not intend to parole Moseby." "Why not," said Gen. Grant. "Because he is an outlaw," said the gentleman in reply. Gen Grant then spoke out in an emphatic manner, and said that he could not see how that Moseby was any more outlaw than any of the others who were engaged in the rebellion, and that as an officer he was assigned to a specific duty, and performed it satisfactorily to his commanding general, and that he would not only accept his surrender and parole him, but that he had sent a special messenger to notify Moseby of his intentions. I am not cognizant of the facts, but no doubt this one special act of Gen. Grant led to the high esteem thereafter reposed in Col. John Singleton Moseby.

And thus began the interest in Mosby's wartime operations. In fact, those newspaper articles covering his operations are not included here simply because to have printed even a relatively small percentage of them would have required more than one volume or possibly even two. But these accounts did appear in the press frequently. Yet, so much news coverage was given to Mosby's wartime activities (quite without his involvement), it is clear that the claim that John Mosby created his own legend, talking and writing constantly about the war, is erroneous. Yes, he augmented his income by writing and lecturing on the subject, but he was able to do so only because he was already a legend!

However, the fact is that many interviews with Mosby declared his reticence to speak on the subject and that unless he was directly asked about the war, he did not bring the matter up until his old age. Naturally, ruminations on the past is a weakness of age for all men and John Mosby was no exception. On the other hand, Mosby did speak extensively on the affairs of the day, often for publication. But the idea that he harped on the war for the purpose of self-aggrandizement was diametric to his desire that the evils of the conflict should be "consigned to oblivion."

The *National Republican* announced Mosby's removal from Hong Kong and the appointment of Robert Withers in his place while commenting upon the excellence of Mosby's service to the nation as consul:

National Republican – **April 30, 1885**

A DOZEN APPOINTMENTS.

Col. Mosby Relieved.

Hon. Robert E. Withers, appointed to Hong Kong to succeed Col. John S.

Mosby as consul general was graduated as an attorney from the university of Virginia, and practiced his profession until the outbreak of the rebellion. He was an advocate of the Union until his native state passed the ordinance of secession. He entered the confederate army as major in April, 1861, and served in the field until disabled by numerous wounds. In 1866 he established a daily paper at Lynchburg, Va. In the campaign of 1868-69 he was nominated by the conservatives for governor, but withdrew in favor of Gilbert C. Walker, the nominee of the liberal Republicans. Dr. Withers was a Greeley elector in 1872, and in 1873 was elected lieutenant governor of the state. He was elected to the United States Senate as a conservative, and served from March 1875, to 1881, when Gen. Mahone succeeded him. Mr. Withers is a thorough Virginian, and has many warm friends in Washington, though remembered by workingmen as the senator who once killed the eight hour law.

In the same paper:

No man in the foreign employment of the United States has served the interests of his government with greater fidelity and success than Consul General Mosby who is about to be relieved by ex-Senator Withers.

As the year went on, formerly anti-Mosby papers—Democrat and Republican—started to find a few good things to say about the man. The article below is one example and contains a comparison between Republican Mosby and Democrat Withers, his replacement at Hong Kong, which ends with Mosby getting the higher marks. However, this is hardly surprising as the paper was Republican:

The Daily Bee – **May 1, 1885 (Edited)**

DISTINGUISHED "REBELS".

"Mosby," an Eye and Ear of Lee's Army—

"Bob" Withers, A Chevalier Bayard of His Infantry.

A Comrade's Reminiscences.

Rutherford B. Hayes, a republican American president, appointed as United States consul at Hong Kong, the ignorantly-called guerilla, John Singleton Mosby, whose home in childhood and youth was the pretty village of Warrenton in Virginia. The office has from that hour till day before yesterday been filled by this "guerilla Mosby."

The telegraph informs the world that Grover Cleveland, a democratic American president, on Wednesday last appointed "to be consul" at Hong Kong, Robert E. Withers, of Virginia whose life has been passed in his native "city of the hills," Lynchburg, except while a soldier and governor of that state some ten or twelve years ago.

These appointees of two radically differing political presidents, bring back to the writer's memory a long train of reminiscences and recollections of facts and happenings that were almost forgotten, and are now almost covered and obscured by the dust and cobwebs of time. For both these gentlemen were friends of his youth, attending the same schools and institutions, following later the same flag, yielding their sword as he did his, to the silent suffering soldier yonder in New York, whose greatness of brain and heart has a monument of admiring love deep down in the hearts of those who fought him very terribly in war. Mosby and Withers, the one the returning, the other the outgoing consul to a Chinese city."

Who is Mosby? In a short, truthful sentence, he is one of the least and most wrongly understood and estimated men of the United States today.

Mosby is a native of the Piedmont section of Virginia; of gentle birth and lineage, of the best social associations and opportunities of education, which were improved to the fullest extent at home and in institutions to whose curriculum he added travel and reading, all resulting in the more than ordinary accomplishment of a man, who possesses a clear, quick, grasping, wide, bold and logical mind, whose power is proven by its works, and beautified by elegancies and ornamentations that always mark his writings and utterances.

John S. Moby is a giant. Cautious as the Sphinx, his is the reticence of the tomb. Safe and sure as the needle to its bridal star, he possesses a nerve like that of the Nemean lion. With a heart that melts at misery or need, his is a hand always reaching wide open to the true, the honorable and the brave. Dreadful in the charge, his is a woman's tenderness in the truce. Stern in the action, his is mercy's gentleness in the hour after battle. As a subordinate no man is more obedient—as a commander, always appreciative of the truth that is one of the chief blessings of power that it may show mercy to the weak, and the crown-jewel of courage is magnanimity to the helpless. In this trait of character Uysses S. Grant and John S. Mosby will go hand in hand down the dim paths of the historic future.

These are his personal traits. In politics his youth was barren of active opinions, because while adhering in a general way to the commonly entertained doctrines of his section, that is the "union" was a compact depending for existence upon the provisions of the constitution, which was interpreted as are what lawyers call "Articles of limited partnership," permitting and anticipating the dissolution of the partnership upon payment of all dues, at the will of a dissatisfied party thereto, Mr. Mosby was engaged in the pursuit of literature and law, and only cast aside his work to buckle on his sword, when he lifted his eyes from those books to see his state tremble beneath the tread of armed men, coming to shoot down the sons and destroy the homes of the daughters of her, who had been one of the first to create the very government in whose name these soldiers were there. It was then that he, for the first time realized the dignity of the occasion, and said in his quiet, quaint way, "We must send these people back home." And it is safe to say that this sentence contains the entire platform of political principles, on which was based that spontaneity of enlistment into the military service that marked the course of the young men of Virginia in 1861.

How he conducted himself in war, let the commanders of the opposite army answer. He and his friends have no explanation to make, nothing to offer excuses for. Honorable as friend or foe, his place as a soldier is at the top, in the estimation of all who know what they speak of. [The ignorant can have no opinion.] But he is among the herd and masses more misunderstood than any man surviving the American war, while no man stands higher in the respect of those men of the opposite side, who were high in place and power during that period.

Mosby fought for a principle, and lost. He pledged his word and life to accept and maintain the interpretation given by the highest tribunal— war— to the form of American government. He will keep that pledge in the future as he has during the twenty years of the recent past. And he is coming back to the land of his nativity no more to draw his sword, unless its flash be in defence of the banner of this grand land.[*] Mosby yielded his sword, and listening to the voice and teachings of his magnificent manhood and courage, accepted fully the result of a revolution, and bent his great energies to mend the broken homes, to rebuild the waste places, and add glory to the nation's fame.

Withers, his equal in all the manly and admirable traits that constitute and adorn the jewels of a commonwealth, too counsel of his temper and weaker characteristic, and let circumstances and sour surrounding of prejudice shape his course, instead of consulting his higher and nobler attributes both of head and heart. Comment is unnecessary. The one, who has stood in China, the trusted representative of that political party which, as a party, made it possible to-day for the United States flag to fly in token of sovereignty over all this broad land comes home again. The other goes forth to that same Oriental city, in the same capacity, but as the representative of that political party which did not, as a party, make it possible for that flag to fly.[*At this point, the article contains a lengthy comment on Withers that is omitted; however, it ended with a final comparison between the two men in which Mosby came out the best.-vph]

But Cleveland's removal of Mosby is seen as very good indeed in this article in the *Hocking Sentinel*:

Hocking Sentinel – May 7, 1885

President Cleveland is not moving very fast, but he is going straight. Last week he turned out of office the Guerilla Mosby appointed by the saintly, loyal, Republican administration. That alone will afford subject for a month's republican giggle.

On the other hand, the *National Republican* continued to speak well of Mosby and noted that he deserved the highest commendation for his service. But what was "deserved" and what was "received" were two entirely different things:

National Republican – May 30, 1885

Since the death of Anson Burlingame American ministers, charges d'affaires, secretaries of legation, and consuls in China have generally taken the humble back seat, for the reason that they were not the right men in the right places, and this to an immense detriment to the prestige and interests of America in that quarter of the world. As marked exceptions to this rule mention should be made of Minister John Russell Young and Consul John S. Mosby, at Hong Kong, both of whom have deserved the highest commendation.

Then a most unusual story came to light for the first time—making the press in later years as well. When the Chinese government discovered that John Mosby had lost his position and would be returning to the United States, he was approached to lead a "guerrilla army"—not the Chinese army—that would make war on the French supply lines into Vietnam during the Sino-French War. This offer was made by the man who was called the Bismarck of China, Li Hung Chang. Mosby was flattered but refused. However, he remained silent about the offer during the war lest the Chinese be compromised. After the war ended in June, 1885, Mosby told the matter to a friend, the French consul in Hong Kong. Of course, the account was of great interest to the press because it had that "aura of mystical romance" that surrounded Mosby even as he was condemned as a guerrilla:

Richmond Dispatch – June 24, 1885

Colonel Mosby and the Chinese

The following copies of letters relating to the offer of a command in the Chinese army to Colonel John S. Mosby were forwarded by him to his friends in Virginia, by whom they were received a few days ago:

Letter from Colonel Mosby to the French Minister. Propositions of Li Hung Chang to Colonel Mosby:

Hong Kong, April 13,1885

"M. le Ministre: My United States colleague at Hong Kong informed me yesterday that the war seemed to have been brought to a close. Whilst it lasted he told me that I ought to keep secret the offer that the Chinese Government had made me to conduct the war against France. The fact is that Li Hun Chang proposed to me in December last that I should raise and organize 3,000 Europeans for the Chinese army, of which I should have the command."

Another letter from Colonel Mosby:

"To His Excellency the Minister of Foreign Affairs, Paris: The Democratic party, which reproaches me for renouncing its cause in the United States, having returned to power under Cleveland, it appeared probable that I would lose my consulate, when the Chinese offered me an other employment, more conformable to my aptitudes and more lucrative. But I do not comprehend that one should fight for money, and it did not please me to be the champion of China in a conflict with a western Power—above all against France."

From the French Consul at Hong Kong to his Government:

"Colonel John S. Mosby has the traditional sympathy of Virginians for the country of Lafayette, and I do not doubt the sincerity of his final compliment. The propositions made to him by the Chinese will soon be heard abroad without doubt, now that Colonel Mosby ceased to keep them secret, and they will probably inspire some adventurers with the idea of offering their services on the next occasion. As for Colonel Mosby, the terror which his name inspired in the Grand Army of the Potomac during the war of secession, and the reputation for honor and disinterestedness he has acquired here during the past six years, would have caused me greatly to regret his passing over to the Chinese camp.

Leon Dejardin.

The Chinese knew not only of Mosby's military skills, but of his honor and decency and therefore had no qualms about offering him a sensitive and lucrative position with their armed forces. It would seem that the people of China had more sense than Mosby's fellow countrymen. It is too bad that Mosby did not consent. Had he been successful, he would never have wanted for money for the rest of his life; neither would he have been subject to the defamations and harassments that followed him to the day of his death—and beyond. Wealthy men are seldom ill-used.

In the next article, one must wonder why the Sentinel saw fit to mix Mosby in with Mahone! The former's contempt for the latter and his ways—about which the Sentinel complained—were well-known. But somehow, the Democratic papers could not resist taking a shot at Mosby even when they knew it was not deserved:

The Sentinel – July 2, 1885

Gen. John Beatty and Don Quixote McClintock, of the Republican Gazette, are beating the atmosphere with terrible blasts of sound, because the South, they say, is not represented.

There is probably grounds for complaint. The South has not been properly represented. When the infamous guerilla, Mosby, was made a consular agent of our government, the south nor the heroic north, neither were represented. When the Rebel Mahone plays traitor to the Christian West, and through his treachery places the U. S. Senate into the hands of the Republicans, he denies to men of the South their proper representation.

It is not the poor darky who is denied his legitimate representation in our government affairs. It is the heroic men north and south who are betrayed by such men as Mahone, and misrepresented by such guerillas as Mosby, provoking the honest resentment of the country. Yes gentlemen, take care of our debauched Mahone and his kind.—The Democrats will take care that justice is done the honest and inoffensive colored men.

When the mountain would not come to Mahomat, he went to the mountain. In as much as the colored men are not coming to the call of Beatty or the Republican-Gazette, the good sense of Mahomet might inspire a proper proceeding on their part.

Mosby had taken up his pen—as he did his pistols—while still in Hong Kong on a matter that dealt with affairs of the consulate. He once again proved himself a formidable opponent with either weapon:

Daily Bulletin – July 15, 1885
EDITORIAL NOTES

A rather spicy letter from General Mosby, U. S. Consul at Hongkong, on a matter of hospital dues in Boston, is published in this issue by request. A LETTER FROM GENERAL MOSBY

Hospital Tax on Sailors.

A copy of the following letter from General Mosby, late United States Consul at Hongkong, addressed to Messrs. Charles Brewer & Co., Boston, has been forwarded from the Consulate, with a request for its publication in the Boston Journal.—Ed. B. J.

United States CONSULATE, HONGKONG, April 29, 1885.

Messrs. C. Brewer & Co., Boston:

I have the honor to acknowledge the receipt of your letter of March 2 informing me that the Collector of Customs at Boston had exacted $10.55 as hospital dues from the bark Amy Turner on her arrival there; and you now ask me to refund you this sum because I decided when the crew were discharged here in August last that, as the hospital tax had been abolished by the Shipping Act of June 26, it was not a proper charge for the Master to retain against them. You further say that the Secretary of State (Mr. Frelinghaysen) informs you that my action was contrary to law. I have no doubt that he instigated you to make this claim on me.

I have also received from the Department of State a despatch transmitting a letter from you on the subject, and inclose for your information my replay, which you can use as you choose. I am not aware that I ever had in my possession any of your money; therefore I have nothing to refund to you. The wages due the sailors were paid to them and not to me, and they went away happy. I have never seen them since. I am no more responsible for the action of the Collector than I would have been for the Master if he had hoisted the black flag or scuttled your vessel. The Collector's having made the Master pay hospital dues is no proof of his right but only of the fact that he got them. If you will consult General Butler, or any one else who knows the law, he will tell you that your remedy is against the man who took your money. I would be glad if you would make this a test case. Several months ago I wrote to Mr. Donald Kelly urging him to get some ship owner to bring the question into court. There was a time when the people of Massachusetts did not quietly submit to illegal taxation. I commend to you for imitation the example of the men who, on a memorable occasion, threw some chests of tea into Boston Harbor; and the New England farmers (guerillas so called), who on the 19th of April, 1775, carrying resistance still further, as Emerson says, at Concord and Lexington "fired the shot heard round the world." You now hear is echoes from the coast of China. I think it rather hard, after my earnest but unsuccessful effort to relieve you of a burden, that you should now seek to transfer it to me. There would have been as much propriety in the people of Boston asking Prescott and Putnam to pay for the powder burnt at Bunker Hill because they lost the battle. And now in sorrow I must say, that I have met the fate of the benevolent stork who pulled out a bone that was stuck in the throat of a fox.

Very respectfully, (Signed) John S. Mosby, U. S. Consul.

When John Mosby left Hong Kong, he left it "in style." He had not been forced out or thrown out, at least by a Republican administration. He took with him the good wishes and respect of those whom he had served and with whom he had spent his years in exile. Those writing not about Mosby but about the Asian consular service were unanimous in their praise of his efforts to clean out that Augean Stable that had been his country's consular service in China. Did he leave in triumph? In the worldly sense, perhaps not, but in matters of ethics, morals and true "patriotism," his was as pure and excellent a service to his country as any man could have rendered. A very short account of his departure is given in the local paper:

Hong Kong China Mail* – July 29, 1885

Colonel John S. Mosby, late Consul of the United States at this port, left the Colony this afternoon by the Pacific Mail S. S. Company's Steamer, City of New York. Colonel Mosby has for nearly seven years occupied the post of American Consul, and has during that period earned for himself a high reputation by the honorable and straightforward manner in which he has discharged the duties of his office; his conduct in this respect forming a striking contrast to that of many of his predecessors. His sterling and manly character displayed both in his official dealings and in his private relations have naturally gained for Col. Mosby the highest esteem of a very large number of the residents of the Colony of all classes and nationalities.

The popularity of the Colonel was fully demonstrated this afternoon by the large number of members of the community who assembled at Government wharf to wish him farewell and give him a last hearty handshake. After dining with his Excellency General Cameron a little before 2 P.M. the Colonel, as accompanied by His Excellency, went down to Government wharf, where the Government House steam launch was waiting, and after wishing good-bye to a large number of his friends and acquaintances there, amongst who were several government officers, members of the Councils, foreign Consuls, etc., he proceeded, accompanied by His Excellency

General Cameron and a few friends on board the steamer. There they found a large circle of friends, who had gone off by Messrs. Russell and Company's launches awaiting him to take their farewells.

The Colonel was deeply affected at the leave taking and openly showed his deep regret of having to leave the scene of his past labours. We understand that he proposes remaining in San Francisco where he will resume his old profession as a Barrister.

We heartily wish Col. Mosby all the success which he so richly deserves. [*This article was discovered in a two-paged typed message probably designed to submit to the newspaper rather than a copy of the newspaper article itself. No name of the reporter is obtained, but the date and the name of the paper are included in the manuscript.-vph]

By the time Mosby left Hong Kong, the cast of characters had changed. John Pope Hennessy, who had been governor-general when Mosby arrived had been replaced in March of 1883 by George Ferguson Bowen. However, Lieutenant General Sir William Gordon Cameron, commander of the British troops in the colony, accompanied Mosby and not Governor Bowen who left Hong Kong in December of 1885. But whatever the situation with the British government, it is obvious that by the time John Mosby left his position, he was exceptionally well respected, possibly even by the "American community" that had given him such grief in the beginning of his service. Certainly, the Chinese of Hong Kong greatly respected him—as he did them.

Meanwhile, Mosby did not know that Grant had secured for him a position with the Southern Pacific Railroad until he landed at San Francisco. But once he knew, he was ready to again take up the threads of the life that he had left behind years earlier. Before doing so, however, he came East to see his estranged family as this small article relates:

Sunday Herald – August 9, 1885

Col. John S. Mosby and his daughter, Miss Stuart Mosby, passed through Washington last week on their way to visit friends in Fauquier county, Va. It is said that Col. Mosby intends to establish his future residence in California.

Mosby was of particular interest in California because of his service in China. While the rest of the nation—and especially the South—had a "Negro" problem, California and the West had a "Chinese" problem as immigration from China was a matter of great concern. As a result, his opinions on that subject were widely sought.

San Francisco Chronicle – August 25, 1885

Ex-Consul Mosby,

His Opinion of the Inoperative Restriction Act.

J. S. Mosby, ex-Consul to Shanghai, arrived from China yesterday on the steamship City of New York and registered at the Palace. To a CHRONICLE reporter, who last evening asked Mr. Mosby about the character of the present emigration from China to the United States, he said:

"As United States Consul, I had nothing to do with Chinese emigration. I never saw the emigrants and know nothing of their present character—or past, for that matter."

"But you must have formed some ideas, officially or unofficially, as to whether the present emigrants from China are probably men who have lived in this country before or entire strangers."

"No, I did not," stoutly maintained the ex-Consul. "I saw nothing of them and had nothing to do with them. When McCulloch made his order of December 2, 1884, that United States consular certificates should entitle Chinese to land here, I refused to issue such certificates. There was nothing in the Restriction Act providing for such certificates. The CHRONICLE'S correspondent in China interviewed me on the subject, and I said to him then what I say to you now, that McCulloch could order collectors of ports to accept such certificates if he wanted to, but could not order consuls to issue them. I saw in the CHRONICLE subsequently an interview with Consul Bee, in which he said there was a warrant in law for my issuing such certificates, and quoted McCulloch's order, the very thing I had referred to as not law."

"What do you think of the effect of the Restriction Act?"

"From all I hear there is a growing emigration from China to the United States. My impression is that there are a great many Chinese coming here who are not entitled to land. We brought over 600 to-day. I do not speak from personal knowledge as to those who land illegally. It is from all that I hear." Mr. Mosby returns after seven years' residence as Consul at Shanghai, during which times he had no "furlough," and was away from his post but six days. He expressed his intention to make his home on the Pacific coast, probably in San Francisco.

With regard to the consul fees, Mosby had been somewhat confused about this matter early on and approached his superiors in the China service. In a letter printed in the *Daily Globe* of August 25, 1879, before he knew of the "Consular Ring," Mosby had written to Frederick Seward, head of the American consul service in China, the following:

***Daily Globe* – August 25, 1879 (Edited).**
CONSUL FEES.

"Hon. F. W. Seward, Assistant, &c.—Sir:

I desire to call the attention of the department to a question of interest both to myself and the government. ...

"On examination of the records of this consulate I can find no credit to the government for any fees collected on this account previous to the forth quarter of 1871, although, as I am informed by those who know, fees have always been charged for this service. Since 1871, in every quarterly statement, there is a credit for the amount of emigration fees collected, and a charge for the expense as per voucher for collecting them. By a strange coincidence the debit for expenses always balances the credit for collection, so that the government gets nothing. The total amount of these fees, as appears by the record since 1871, is $14,345.75.

"The late vice-consul in charge, Mr. Loring, informed me that no record was kept of fees for certificates for Chinese emigrants going to the United States in vessels carrying foreign flags, but that those fees were regarded as unofficial, and remained as the perquisites of the consul I would like,very much to be allowed to retain these fees if it can properly be done; but I do not feel justified in appropriating them in the absence of instructions from the department. No fees from this source have ever, I believe, been turned into the treasury, but all have either been retained by the consul or consumed in the "expense" of examination of emigrants "

Once Mosby's serious investigation of the ring began, he realized that he could not keep even those fees legally owed to him without "muddying the waters." So he turned into the government all the fees he collected in the belief that when he left the service, those that belonged to him would be returned by the Department of the Treasury. Once again, he proved to be naïve in his trust of the government, a matter he soon learned when he began the necessary arrangements to retrieve his money:

A Democratic paper then weighed in, not on the situation extant, but, as usual, on Mosby's evil war career:

Democratic Northwest – September 3, 1885

John S. Mosby, ex-Confederate partisan ranger and Virginia bushwhacker, has come home from China, at one of those ports of which he has been consul for a dozen years. Mosby, during the war, operated between the lines with a company of young fellows whose patriotism was defined in the love of plunder. Like freebooters, whatever they captured and carried off belonged to them. Mosby hung two or three Union prisoners whom he caught, in fancied retaliation for wrongs done to members of his plundering gang. And on one occasion he threatened to shoot one of his own men, who was a mason, because he permitted a prisoner, also a mason, to escape, who had been condemned to death by Mosby. This man Mosby was outlawed for his brigandage, and officers of the Union army were authorized to hang him if they captured him.

But he is a Republican and a hero. He has been lionized and rewarded for joining the Republican party. He will take a prominent part in the Virginia campaign in behalf of John S. Wise for Governor, another ex-Rebel, and the son of the man who signed John Brown's death warrant. These are the sort of recruits the Republicans gather from the South. If Mosby had not turned Republican, he would probably have met the fate of Wurtz, [sic] a fate he deserved fully as much. But being a Republican, he was honored with office before the grass had grown over the graves of captured Union soldiers he hanged.—Bee.

The same claim that Mosby escaped the gallows because he was or had become a Republican was trotted out again. But Mosby did not support a Republican until 1872 and did not become one until 1876 by which time, the grass had grown over all who had died in the war.

National Republican – September 9, 1885

Virginia is to be bereaved of John S. Mosby, who has written to his friends at Warrenton that he shall settle down to the practice of law in San Francisco.

With regard to the article in the Republican, there seemed to be little complaint on the part of Virginia about the matter. Soon, however, some members of the press made mention of the honors Mosby had received from the Chinese people as he was leaving Hong Kong. It was a gracious tribute to him, and its coverage was warranted:

Richmond Dispatch – September 10, 1885

Colonel Mosby's Silver Cup.

A Warrenton (Va.) letter to the Baltimore Sun says: On the eve of Colonel John S. Mosby's departure from Hong Kong a deputation of Chinese merchants, through Mr. Lee Tuk Cheong, waited on the Colonel in the parlor of the Hong Kong Hotel and presented Colonel Mosby with a handsome silver cup and two magnificent Chinese screens, and at the same time read an address in Chinese, of which the following is a translation:

"To John S. Mosby, Esq., late Consul at Hong Kong for the United States of America:

"Sir,—Since your appointment to the consulship you have benefited the merchants, and have kindness shown to the people, both of whom have felt deeply grateful. As you are now recalled on a sudden we cannot let you depart from us without showing our deep feeling and respect by writing a few ordinary expressions as tokens of affection and remembrance. With sincerity we beg to present you the following address:

"You are both pure and clear;

An example instructive and

Worthy of imitation;

Just and impartial,

Merciful and compassionate,

Accomplished and graceful,

Genial and kind,

Incorruptible and courteous to the people;

Thus should an official be."

"Presented by the Chinese merchants of Hong Kong,

in the middle of the sixth moon,

in the eleventh year of Kwong Sui."

[Here, follow the signatures and seals of the Chinese merchants.-vph]

In reply, Colonel Mosby said he was much gratified at receiving this testimonial from the Chinese merchants of Hong Kong. While he represented the United States as Consul there he endeavored to do justice to all without distinction of race or creed. If he succeeded in doing this, and at the same time gave satisfaction to them, the chief object of his ambition had been fulfilled. He parted from them with deep regret, and hoped they might met again in his own country, where he would be happy to welcome all his old friends.

The silver cup bears upon it the following inscription: "Presented to John S. Mosby, U. S. Consul at Hong Kong, by the Chinese Merchants, July, 1885."

The above sentiments were more gracious—and more accurate—than almost anything written as a tribute to Mosby by his own people during his life or afterward, for that matter.

Peninsula Enterprise – September 12, 1885

On the eve of Col. John S. Mosby's departure from Hong Kong, a deputation of Chinese merchants, through Mr. Lee Tuk Cheong, waited on the Colonel in the parlor of the Hong Kong Hotel and presented Col. Mosby with a handsome silver cup and two magnificent Chinese screens, and at the same time read an address in Chinese.

Daily National Republican, – September 14, 1885 (Edited)

When Col. John S. Mosby, lately United States consul at Hong Kong, was leaving that station to return to his own country, the Chinese merchants there presented him with the following address, in Chinese: [Here, follows the tribute printed in the September 10th Richmond Dispatch.-vph]

There was no better official in the consular service than John S. Mosby. He was honest, capable, and zealous, an example of fidelity.

Though nothing was said in any comments upon it at the time, it is more than possible that this gesture was unusual, if not unique. Of course, the Chinese might have done the same for any foreign consul departing their city, but there were enough newspapers unfriendly to Mosby to point out that such an honor was "routine" and that he was nothing special because of it. If, however, this was not "business as usual," then John Mosby again proved his uniqueness in a totally different situation.

The *National Republican* addressed the claim that Mosby was not removed but resigned his position when Cleveland was inaugurated. Mosby denied doing so. He wanted the new administration to remove him for political reasons and wasn't going to give them the opportunity to claim that he left of his own volition:

National Republican – September 21, 1885

Cleveland's Suspension of Col. Mosby. [Hong Kong (China) Mail.]

Some time ago we cited the case of Col. Mosby as one of the many suspension from office, on the score of political opinions only, which have demonstrated the regard which President Cleveland has shown for civil service reform of the true and genuine type. We have also noted that the President has been credited with an expression of regret at his alleged unwitting suspension of Col. Mosby as consul for the United States in Hong Kong—not so much because of the injustice thus done to the man who has faithfully discharged his public duty, but because Col. Mosby is looked upon as a dangerous political power in his native state of Virginia.

In the *Alexandria Gazette* and Virginia Advertiser of the 29th of May we find the following, dated from Washington on that day:

"Col. Withers, the recently appointed consul to Hong Kong, is in the city to-day, probably to qualify before the Secretary of State. The colonel says his predecessor was not removed and was not asked to resign, but did tender his resignation as soon as President Cleveland was inaugurated to take effect whenever his successor might choose to relieve him."

We have the very best authority for saying that the above statement is not correct. Col. Mosby never intimated a purpose of resigning, either in any private or official communication. Indeed, he has always advised his friends against resigning. He was not disposed to relieve a Democratic President of the odium, which would be inevitably incurred by a wholesale removal of officeholders solely on account of their political opinions. The only official allusion ever made by Col. Mosby to a change of administration was in a dispatch to Mr. Secretary Bayard, acknowledging the receipt of a circular letter from him informing consuls of his appointment as Secretary of State. The following letters will show the precise form of Col. Mosby's removal from the consulship at Hong Kong, the duties of which he has so honorably filled:

DEPARTMENT OF STATE, Washington, May 1, 1885—John S. Mosby, esq., Consul of the United States, Hongkong—Sir: I send you inclosed a communication from the office of consul at Hong Kong. You may continue in charge of the office until the arrival of your successor.

James D. Porter, Assistant Secretary

EXECUTIVE MANSION, Washington, D. C. April 28, 1885—

Sir:

You are hereby suspended from the office of consul of the United States at Hong Kong in accordance with the terms of section 1768, Revised Statutes of the United States, and subject to all provisions of law applicable thereto.

GROVER CLEVELAND

To John S. Mosby, Esq., Hong Kong.

On April 29, Col. Mosby's successor was appointed. An extract from a private letter written by the colonel was published in January last, and very much complimented for its tone of manly independence by the Democratic press. In that letter the colonel said:

"I wish it to be understood that I have no apologies or recantations to make, and no favors to ask of the next administration. I accept the result of the election as the fate of war, to which I have not been altogether unaccustomed. I have survived one lost cause, and may survive another. I have no repinings or complaints to make. Some indiscreet friends of mine, I fear, may ask of Mr. Barbour of some other Virginia Democrat to save me in the 'massacre of the innocents,' which will soon begin. Now, I wish you to understand that nothing could be done more offensive to me."

There is no reference here to resigning. It merely forbids his friends in the states from attempting to secure his retention in office as a favor granted through personal or political influence. What it evidently means is that his record at the State Department could speak for itself, and by that only he was willing to stand or fall. So that, independently of the official documents which prove Consul Mosby's suspension from office, the colonel's whole career has been consistent, manly, and highly creditable to himself.

Mosby was removed and it seemed as if very few, except for his friends and a few newspapers like the Republican, regretted his situation. But it is obvious that Mahone still held sway in Virginia because Mosby did not consider returning East:

Fort Worth Daily Gazette - October 4t, 1885

Col. Mosby, as if doubtful of a good Eastern reception, lingers in San Francisco.

Mosby had every reason to be "doubtful of a good Eastern reception" and lingered in San Francisco in order to earn a living, something that was very doubtful in Virginia. And yet Mosby still had friends as can be seen here:

Daily Alta - November 1885

Hon. John S. Mosby was admitted to practice in the Supreme Court yesterday on motion of Hon. John F. Swift, and on filing a permit from the Supreme Court of Virginia.

Suddenly, another war story appeared—in this case, a very dangerous one. Much had been made at the time by Stanton and others regarding Mosby's alleged involvement in the Lincoln assassination. Stories such as the one that appeared in *The Sun* were not innocuous. Mosby was still well hated and there is no statute of limitations on murder, especially on what had been declared "the crime of the century." If he could have been brought to trial as at least an accomplice of Booth's, it would have destroyed him even had he survived the ordeal:

The Sun - November 22, 1885

A LAST VIEW OF THE CONFEDERACY.

[Halfway through the article, the following is found:]

At last, a train was ordered south, and as many as could squeeze into the wretched box-cars got a ride as far as Charlottesville. Just before we left a rumor was current that Mosby had shot President Lincoln; this was the first news of the assassination.

And then, the matter of "consular Certificates" made a reappearance in the press. Mosby had been chastised by the Department of State for refusing to sign such certificates as ordered by the Treasury Department. Now, it appeared that the new consul, Withers, was signing these spurious certificates on the order of the new secretary of state, a Democrat:

San Francisco Chronicle – December 6, 1885
CONSULAR CERTIFICATES

A Conflict of Department Regulations

A new phase of the Chinese certificate question has just been brought to light by the arrival of a couple of Chinese on the steamer City of Peking direct from China, and claiming the right to land on the strength of papers issued to them by Consul Withers at Hongkong. This claim was at once denied, and immediately communication was had with Washington on the subject, resulting in the following dispatch to Collector Hager:

Washington (D.C.), December 2, 1885

To Collector of Customs San Francisco, Cal.:

Report objections to landing of Young Ah Nee and Tsung Sih Yan per City of Peking from Hongkong.

C. S. FAIRCHIND, Assistant Secretary.

To this dispatch Collector Hagar replied that the Chinese in question had nothing but certificates issued by the Consul at Hongkong, which was not evidence of right to land under the amended Treasury Department circular of January 14, 1884. Chinese Consul Bee says that these certificates were issued according to the instructions of the Department of State; that this department had furnished blanks to the United States Consuls, to be filled out for the benefit of Chinese desiring to come to this country. The certificates presented by the two Chinese both contain a statement by Consul Withers that he is acting in accordance with the instructions received from the Department of State bearing date of August 10, 1885. Ex-Consul Mosby, refused to obey these instructions, giving as his reasons that he considered the order of the Secretary of the Treasury unauthorized by law and a piece of pure department legislation. Following is a copy of one of the certificates:

United States CONSULATE, HONGKONG,

November 2, 1885.

No. 1.: I, Robert E. Withers, Consul of the United States for the port of Hongkong, hereby certify that, in accordance with the instructions from the State Department, bearing date of the 10th day of August, 1885, construing Circular 174 of the Treasury Department, as it applies to merchants and others and the exempt and non-laboring classes of China who desire to visit the United States, I have carefully investigated the evidence and proof offered by (Chinese signature) Young Ah Nee, the person to whom this certificate is given, and am satisfied that he belongs to the exempt and non-laboring class and is entitled under the laws of the United States to land at any port thereof.

Appended is a detailed description of the individual in whose name it is made.

Both these Chinese claim to be students, are young and have never been to the United States before, and it is presumed that they have come to "study English and enter into business," as did so many found in the certificate frauds of two years ago.

As yet, Collector Hagar has received no reply to his dispatch, and it is not clear what the outgrowth of this matter will be.

As his war stories were of interest to the public, Mosby decided that he would accept an invitation to write lengthy articles in several publications regarding his "adventures." For him, this was a good bargain. First, it would increase his income; and second, it would assure the accuracy of the narrative. The first of such articles appeared in *The Sunday Herald* on Mosby's fifty-second birthday, December 6, 1885.

As the halfway point of the decade passed, John Mosby still found himself thousands of miles away from his home and all that he loved. But at least he had a position. His future offered little hope that he could rebuild his life in his native state or be close once more with his family and friends. Indeed, he seemed as isolated and remote as he had been across the broad Pacific in Hong Kong. But he could do nothing but deal with life as he found it and hope for better days.

Chapter 25

1886

Verba movent, exempla trahunt.
~ Words move people, deeds compel them.

"Letter writing is the only device for combining solitude with good company." ~ Lord Byron

JOHN MOSBY'S "NEW life," begun the year before, continued to have its ups and downs. He would soon initiate efforts to recover the fees he had earned as consul but had turned over to the Treasury to protect his name and allow him to proceed with his investigation into consular corruption. This would be the first year he would make such an effort, but alas, it was to prove unproductive. Mosby soon realized that he could not "go through channels" to recover what was his any more than he could "go through channels" to address the corruption in China. At least in the current situation, however, he eventually did have recourse to the courts.

January saw a very nice article on Grant and Mosby in, of all publications, the *National Tribune!* Although it was somewhat inaccurate in stating that it was Grant who sent Mosby to China, the rest of the article was not only gracious, but even spoke well of Mosby's service during the war. The only sad thing was that, compared with the paper's lengthy articles vilifying him, this positive account of Mosby was brief:

National Tribune – **January 14, 1886**

GRANT AND MOSBY

> The strong friendship between Gen. Grant and Col. John Mosby, one of the most daring and troublesome of the hard-riders among the Confederate cavalry leaders, was one of those seemingly anomalous things that cannot easily be explained. It was a marked characteristic of Grant that his friendships were lasting. They were only broken for the best of reasons. While Grant was President he sent Mosby to China, as Consul at Hong Kong, the duties of which office he discharged in a very satisfactory manner. He was removed by the present administration, and has opened a law office in San Francisco. It is said that but a few days before his death, Gen. Grant wrote to Senator Stanford, of California, asking that he would, as a favor to himself, look after and assist his friend Mosby when he should return from China.

The *National Republican* then reported on the Chinese consular certificates Mosby had refused to issue, but that Democratic Consul Robert Withers was now issuing at the State Department's order:

The National Republican – **February 12, 1886 (Edited)**

WITHERS' CERTIFICATES

> The Large Income They Afford a Consul at Hong Kong. [*San Francisco Call*:]

Col. John S. Mosby, the predecessor of Robert E. Withers, as United States consul at Hong Kong, called on Collector Hager yesterday afternoon and had a talk with him in reference to the certificates which Withers has been issuing to Chinamen, and which so far have been accepted at this port. When Col. Mosby was consul at Hong Kong he received the circular instructions of Secretary McCulloch, directing American consuls to issue certificates to Chinese merchants and others of the exempt class, which certificates were to be passports for admission into this country. Col. Mosby declined to do so, and in a letter which he wrote to the department at Washington, pointed out that such certificates were illegal, as the restriction act did not authorize their issuance. He repeated his views on the subject to Collector Hager yesterday.

When seen by a Call reporter Col. Mosby said that the granting of these certificates is very profitable, and that a consul at such a port as Hong Kong can make $100,000 a year by issuing them. "A Chinese merchant," he remarked, "would think nothing of paying $500 or more for such a certificate if he knew that with it he could land here."

When asked as to what method should be pursued in having them rejected altogether, he suggested that the collector refuse to accept the next one that is brought here, and let the bearer of it take the matter into court. Col. Mosby thought that Judge Hoffman would declare them illegal, as he has heretofore agreed with the ex-consul in his opinion of them.

This was just one more instance in which Mosby was obedient to a law to which the government turned a blind eye. Of course, the party that suffered was the man who obeyed the law! Throughout his career in government, this was Mosby's fate. Even when he was directed to enforce the law, if that law interfered with some scheme desired by politicians and their cronies, Mosby suffered from his efforts to follow both the law and the directions of his superiors. Obviously, the law was what the important and powerful people in and out of government wanted it to be rather than what was contained in the statute.

And then there was this example of a newspaper whose dislike of Mosby outweighed the need to discover the facts:

Semi-Weekly Interior Journal – February 12, 1886

—Comptroller Durhan has found it necessary to give a lesson in manners to ex-Minister to China Mosby, in whose accounts he ventured to find an error. The ex-guerilla was taught that the days when his peculiar bushwhacking tactics were desirable had long since passed.

Most of the Mosby "quotes" in the papers came from letters he had written to friends and not from any direct communication between himself and the publication in which those quotes appeared. The only time that such matters were "direct" was when he was interviewed or sent a letter to the paper(s). But how did these "personal" letters get into the hands of papers such as the Staunton Spectator? Were they forwarded by the receiver? There seems to be no other answer. But was Mosby of such interest that his personal letters to friends were desired by the press? The obvious answer to that question is also yes. Until this interaction is understood, it is possible to misjudge the situation as many have done, claiming that Mosby was constantly sending his opinions to the newspapers as a means of keeping his name in print:

Staunton Spectator – **March 10, 1886**

Col. John S. Mosby, late consul to Hong Kong, China, is now engaged in the practice of law in San Francisco. In a letter to a friend in Nelson county, Virginia, Col. Mosby writes: "I was glad that John W. Daniel was elected to the United States Senate, not for any special personal reason, but because his brilliant talents will be a credit to the State and an ornament to the Senate."

Senator Daniel was a Democrat. So much for Mosby being totally partisan in his politics. John Mosby made judgments based upon his knowledge and his understanding of the value of the individual. He never made judgments based solely upon party.

Suddenly, a Washington paper "discovered" that the government owed John Mosby money from his time as consul. It was suggested that he had "inadvertently" turned the money into the Treasury, but of course, that was not the case:

Washington Critic – **April 28, 1886**

Col. Mosby's Fees.—Col. Mosby was recently officially informed that on auditing his accounts as United States Consul at Hong Kong, China, at the Treasury Department, a considerable balance was placed to his credit, he having inadvertently turned over consular fees to the Government that under the law he was entitled to retain himself. The amount to be returned to him is several thousand dollars.

Indian Chieftain – **May 6, 1886**

A very remarkable discovery, it is stated at Washington, has been made by the accounting officers of the Treasury Department. They find that Colonel Mosby, recently Consul General at Hong Kong, has been turning over to the Government fees that under the law he was entitled to retain himself, and he has been notified that several thousand dollars are in the Treasury subject to his disposal. It is said that there never was a case of this kind known, the officers of the Government abroad being generally cute enough to determine what fees they were entitled to and put them in their own pockets.

Seems hopelessly enraptured.

The Iola Register, – **May 7, 1886**

The treasury officials have just found that Colonel Mosby, lately returned from Hong Kong where he has served for several years as Consul- General, has been turning over to the government fees that, under the law, he was entitled to keep himself, and he has been notified that several thousand dollars are in the treasury subject to his disposal. Col. Mosby should be put in a glass case and placed on exhibition.

These articles reveal the belief that Americans expected corruption in their government and that an honest "official" was a matter of considerable astonishment.

Mosby found himself once more in the news regarding a well-paid lecture tour. Because he needed to send money to his children, he was willing to engage in such efforts despite working full-time for the Southern Pacific Railroad:

Spirit of Jefferson – May 11, 1886

It is reported that Col. Mosby has accepted an engagement for a lecturing tour with a Boston manager at compensation of $7,500 per week. The subject of his lecture will be General Grant, and will be first delivered in Boston.

Mosby made several lecture tours in New England; and doubtless, Grant was mentioned as he was mentioned in many of Mosby's reminiscences, especially regarding the events of 1864.

Articles about the war continued to be of great interest as can be seen here:

Bismarck Weekly Tribune – June 4, 1886 (Edited)

The June Magazine of American History is a strong and intensely interesting number. Six articles of antiquarian and historic prominence precede three of current war literature—nine in all, and each a treasure in itself. Mr. Waller gives a vivid account of the capture of Mosby, "The Last of the Confederates." Publication office 30 Lafayette Place, New York City.

New Ulm Review – July 14, 1886 (Edited)

Wahpeton Times – July 22, 1886

The Last Confederate

Magazine of American History for June

It was verging on the summer of 1865. Gen. Lee had surrendered. The southern people had accepted the fiat of Appomattox, and the southern armies had disbanded. Only one prominent in the military history of the late Confederate states was unparoled. This was Col. John S. Mosby, the famous partisan leader, who was under the ban of the war department, and whose capture, if possible, and trial by court martial on the charge of having been guilty of acts not recognized by civilized warfare had been ordered by Secretary Stanton. It was well that his capture had been ordered "if possible." His foot was on his native heath in the mountainous region about Lynchburg, Virginia and he was at home amid its most difficult recesses, being thoroughly conversant with every foot-path and pass in that section of the state. Besides this, he was surrounded by friends, many of whom had been in his old command, and all of whom were on the alert in his interest, ready to warn him at the first approach of danger. He had also many relatives, and several comrades in the city of Lynchburg, the military headquarters of that district, who carefully watched the movements of the United States troops, and had demonstration been made toward his place of refuge they would have been quick to apprise him of it. Thus it may be easily understood that his capture was by no means easy of accomplishment.

At length, however, Stanton reconsidered his decision, and sent orders to Gen. Gregg, the commandant of the district, to parole Mosby if he would yield himself up. This information was imparted to one of "Mosby's men," then in Lynchburg, who, as if by magic, conveyed the news promptly to his former commander. In consequence, the very day after the order had been issued, Col. Mosby came into the city to formally surrender and receive his parole. He was dressed in full confederate uniform and was armed with two army-sized Colt's revolvers fastened in a belt around his waist—the very model of the typical scout. He appeared as cool as an iceberg as he drove up to the law office of his cousin, Charles L. Mosby, one of the firm of Mosby & Speed, then among the leading members of the Virginia bar. Here, as he alighted from his buggy, he was surrounded by a crowd of friends and acquaintances, anxious to greet and tender him congratulations, while United States soldiers crowded the street to catch sight of the famous soldier of whom they had heard so much. To the remark of a gentleman who shook hands with him, "Well, Colonel, so you are to surrender at last," he replied: "Yes, I believe I am ultimus Romanorum," and with that he made his way to the office of Mosby & Speed, where divesting himself of his pistols, he entered into conversation before going to the provost marshal's office to take the amnesty oath and receive his parole.

While he was thus engaged, however, orders came by telegraph to Gen. Gregg from Secretary Stanton, countermanding the former order and instructing him to forward Mosby to Washington as a prisoner of war. The news of this change of programme on the part of the secretary was conveyed to the partisan leader just as he was preparing to leave for the office of the provost marshal. He did not seem in the least moved by it, beyond that his blue eyes dilated and assumed an expression of fixed determination. He arose, coolly buckled on his pistols again and started for the office. When he arrived there he inquired for the provost marshal, and being shown that officer, he asked if it was true what he had been told. On receiving an affirmative reply, he charged the Secretary of War with having acted with treachery and bad faith toward him in having inveigled him into the city on the promise of a parole, and then ordering his capture. "But," he said, "I will never be taken alive. I have in these pistols twelve shots, and I warn you that twelve of you will bite the dust before I am arrested." To this, the provost marshal replied that he would inform Gen. Gregg of the case, and await further orders from him before acting. The general was a chivalrous soldier and a gentleman. He sent word to the marshal that Col. Mosby had come into the city upon assurances from himself that a parole would be granted him. This could not be done in face of the order of the Secretary of War but one thing he would do. He would permit Col. Mosby to return from whence he came unmolested, and would make no effort to effect his capture until the following day. Upon being informed of this Mosby walked out of the provost marshal's office, went direct to his buggy and speedily found himself once more safe in his friendly mountain retreats. The next day squads of cavalry scoured the country to find and arrest him, but to no avail. All pursuit was ineffectual, and after a vain search of several days, report was brought in that Mosby's whereabouts could not be discovered.

More and more articles about Mosby based upon the testimony of his former comrades in arms began to find their way into print. The article below, however, had already done so in the Daily Bee on May 1, 1885. Here, it appeared again virtually verbatim. Why these stories were reprinted is not known unless the press of the time felt that they would be of interest to their readership:

Wood River Times – June 18, 1886 (Edited)

TWO "CONFEDERATES."

The "Eye and Ear" of Lee's Army, and the "Chevalier Bayard" of his Infantry.—

A comrade's Tribute.

[By Request]

The *National Republican* again came to the defense of "Mosby the guerrilla," if not Mosby the Republican:

National Republican – August 9, 1886

John S. Mosby, the noted guerrilla during the war, threatens to lecture next season. If he comes north our only salvation will be to send Private Dalzell or Murat Halstead, south. Revenge is sweet, and we'll have it.— *Cincinnati Enquirer.*

"The noted guerrilla" was he? Then was every cavalry officer in the confederate army a guerrilla, and all the men of their respective commands should be designated by the same terms. Col. Mosby's troops were a part of the army of northern Virginia. Many of the men who served under him are still living in Virginia, and some of them in this city, respected citizens, most of them belonging to The Democratic party. There are few men who can point to a better record since the war than that of John S. Mosby. He won the sincere respect and warm friendship of President Grant, and his conduct has been such as to vindicate Grant's confidence in him. His services in the Chinese consular office, to which he was appointed, were of inestimable value, showing him to be a true reformer, honest, capable, and brave—brave enough to move against and destroy intrenched corruption. Because he is a Republican and the Democratic Enquirer dubs him "the noted guerrilla." Ex-confederate soldiers will note this appellation with peculiar interest.

In the article below, the Republican speaks of Mosby's "recent illness," though nothing is said of the matter either in that paper or elsewhere. But in this article, it picks up where it left off in the article of August 9—that is, that if Mosby were a Democrat, his service to the South would not be used against him, a claim that was true in a limited circumstance. His service would not have been used against him in Democratic papers but certainly would have in Republican organs:

Daily National Republican – September 1, 1886

It is announced that Guerilla Mosby, having recovered from his recent illness, will speedily complete his war papers and give them to the public. The noble guerilla being a Republican in good standing, it is not impossible that we shall have in his book a record of commensurate interest with the efforts of Messrs. Blaine and Logan.—*New York Graphic.*

Because Col. Mosby is a Republican he is "Guerilla" Mosby. If he were a Democrat he would be referred to in Democratic papers as "the brave Gen. Mosby." The simple truth about this gentleman's war record is that he was a regular cavalry officer of Lee's army—just as much of a "guerilla" as Stuart, and no more. Since the war Mr. Mosby has incurred Bourbon hatred by daring to cut loose from The Democratic party. As an official in the consular service Mr. Mosby has won the respect of all who are capable of appreciating conspicuous ability, large capacity, and rare moral courage, but this does not imply that he is respected by the Bourbons of the south or their lick-spittles in New York.

While serving as consul, Democrat Withers discovered the conditions in the Hong Kong consulate with regard to American sailors who had now became his hair shirt instead of Mosby's. Indeed, from the article below, it would seem that Withers was worse than Mosby, if that were possible—at least according to various American mariners:

Washington Critic – **September 10, 1886 (Edited)**

"WORSE THAN MOSBY."

Serious Charges Against the American Consul at Hong Kong.

A BAD STATE OF AFFAIRS.

Yankee Sailors Seeking the Protection of English Officials.

It is likely that charges will shortly be preferred at the State Department against the successor of Consul Mosby at Hong Kong, China, in connection with certain abuses growing out of the discharge and shipment of American seamen at that place. Substantially the allegations are that when a sailor receives his papers he is turned over to a boarding-house master, the consul received $5 as a fee for this service and $5 more when he reships … A sharp American sailor exposed the scheme, for, upon being paid off and discharged from his ship, instead of going to the American Consul, he went to the British Consul and placed himself under the latter's protection, by which he not only saved all fees, but when he was ready to ship again he had a supply of ready money of his own and did not have to go in debt to a boarding-house master There was recently, a great scandal in Hong Kong over the case of a man who had been turned over to a negro boarding-house master by Consul Mosby. The boarder wanted to obtain work in Hong Kong, and tried to get his money out of the hands of his host, but the latter hung on to it and the consul declined to interfere, claiming that he was acting under the laws of the United States. When the case came into court the Chief Justice administered a severe rebuke to Mosby for his action, and did not forget to condemn a country which passed laws the object of which appeared especially to oppress its own sailors and depress its commerce under the new order of affairs at Hong Kong Consul-General Withers is declared to be worse than Mosby, for he not only declines to see and hear complaints from sailors of the United States, but if they persist in making their demands he has them locked up for contempt. Besides, the new Consul has been reported for drunkenness, indecent and immoral practices, and abuse of his position in making prisoners work for the amusement of his friends. One of the principal complaints is a prominent officer of the Asiatic squadron, who will push the matter to the utmost. To quote his own language: "It is a burning shame, for a sailor is the most helpless being in the world, to place him in the power of men like these, whose sole object seems to be a desire to get as much out of him as they can by fair or foul means."

San Francisco Chronicle – September 11, 1886 (Edited)

[Special Dispatches to the Chronicle].

CHARGES AGAINST WITHERS.

Accused of Sharp Practice on American Sailors at Hongkong.

Washington, September 10.—It is reported that serious charges are to be presented to the Secretary of State against Consul General Withers, the successor of Colonel Mosby at Hongkong. It is said that one of the principle complaints against General Withers is a prominent officer of the Asiatic squadron, and the charge is that American sailors are improperly treated and are compelled to place themselves under the protection of the British Consul at that port in order to escape being robbed of their hard-earned wages ... A United States naval officer, speaking of such occurrences said: "It is an outrage that our laws should be so framed that our sailors should be compelled to seek protection from a British Consul, and this case is only a sample one that occurs every day in some foreign port."

The friends of Consul Withers plead in extenuation of the charges that Consul Mosby was guilty of the same practice during his occupancy of that position. Consul General Withers is an ex-United States Senator from Virginia, being superseded by Mahone, and is said to be harder on sailors than Mosby was, refusing to hear their complaints, and if they persist locking them up for contempt. In addition, charges are made against his personal character.

But as was usual with Mosby, no such libel was allowed to stand unanswered; and Consul Withers, who defended himself, was probably very happy to have his capable predecessor weigh in on the charges against them both:

San Francisco Chronicle – September 12, 1886 (Edited)

Charges Denied by Mr. Withers and Colonel Mosby.

A special dispatch from Washington published in yesterday's Chronicle stated that there were rumors current in that city of very serious charges being made against Mr. Withers, United States Consul General at Hongkong, both in his official and private capacity. As Mr. Withers is at present in the city, the guest of Marsden Manson at 2007 Gough street, a Chronicle reported asked and obtained an interview with him on the subject. Mr. Withers has all the appearance of a very sick man, and it was quite easy to see that the slight exertion required of him in descending the stairs to see the reporter was almost more than he could stand. On the reporter's stating his errand Mr. Withers said: [The article presents a lengthy defense by Consul Withers.-vph]

The reporter next interviewed John S Mosby, who is practicing law in this city, regarding the charge said to be made by friends of Withers in Washington that Mosby had been guilty, when Consul General at Hongkong, of the same conduct alleged against Withers. Mr. Mosby vigorously disclaimed having ever made any profit off the shipment of sailors, or by sending them to boarding-houses with the proprietors of which he was in collusion. He said: "I know nothing about the practices of my successor in Hongkong.

The telegram is ridiculous on its face in its frequent allusions to the British Consul at Hongkong, to whom it is charged American sailors are forced to apply for protection. Hongkong is a British port, and therefore there is no such thing as a British Consul there. One might as rationally talk about the American Consul in San Francisco. The present Consul General there may have accepted a fee from boarding masters for throwing custom in their way, or he may not. I know nothing about that. I turned the office over to may successor on July 21, 1885, having assumed charge on February 4, 1879. During those six years and more I never handled one cent of money belonging to sailors, nor did I ever permit my subordinates in the consulate to do it. When sailors were discharged and paid off at the consulate the wages belonging to them left the consulate with them, and I never saw them afterward.

"I once received a letter from the First Controller of the Treasuring instructing me to take possession of the wages of sailors when they were paid off at the consulate and keep them till the sailors reshipped. The object was that the Consul should take care of the sailors' wages—in other words, to convert the consulate into a sailors' bank. I wrote to the Comptroller refusing to do this and then wrote to the State Department saying that I declined to carry out the instructions of the First Comptroller, because any man who handles the sailors' money will be accused of robbing them. The State Department approved my course.

There are two things of interest here: The first is that Withers, who had only recently taken up his office, was in San Francisco and not Hong Kong. Poor Mosby couldn't get a furlough during his just over six years of service, yet Withers came home—probably for health reasons—with no difficulty at all! The second is that Mosby was very careful to declare that he was not in a position to answer for any charges directed at Withers as he did not know what the man had done. This care in a newspaper interview flies in the face of those who declare that Mosby was rather a "loose cannon" and not at all careful regarding what he said to the press!

Mosby's and Withers' responses to the accusations against them were addressed in the Critic based upon a legal gentleman whose apparent knowledge of both men and their statements had proven the matter "a tissue of misinformation"—a polite way of saying that they were "a pack of lies." Again, however, given all that Mosby had suffered during his years in Hong Kong, would such a quick response have been forthcoming if Consul Withers had not also been condemned?

Washington Critic – October 23, 1886

It will be seen by the communication of A. A. Warfield, esq., of Alexandria in this evening's Critic, that the alleged official misconduct of Colonel John S. Mosby, ex-Consul to Hong Kong, has no foundation in fact. The article which appeared in The Critic some weeks ago, reflecting upon him and Consul Withers, proves to have been a tissue of misinformation, by which the author of the article was probably imposed upon, as its publishers certainly were. It is impossible that either the Consul or the ex-Consul could be involved in any scandalous transaction without its coming to the knowledge of the State Department, and upon this point the note of Assistant Secretary Porter should be entirely satisfactory. The whole story, in fact, seems to have originated in the fancied or fabricated grievance of some party, too ignorant or irresponsible to appreciate the injuries that might thus be done to officials, whom the records show to have been diligent and honest in the discharge of their duties.

The Critic blamed some individual who had falsified the charges against both men and supported and held both blameless, which was a far cry from those papers who would have cleared Withers but suggested that Mosby really did do what had been charged simply because of who he was and what he had been.

Mosby's lecture tour once again made the papers with notice of the money he was receiving. It must have galled a lot of people who thought his visit to New England should have been as a resident of a federal penitentiary and not a paid lecturer:

Sacramento Daily Record Union – November 19, 1886

Colonel John S. Mosby has signed a contract to deliver fifty lectures on his experiences during the war, receiving $300 per night and actual expenses. Colonel Mosby will first lecture in Boston.

Mosby's efforts to recover the fees that he had voluntarily turned into the Treasury appeared in the press. He naturally believed that the government would return what was legally his. An unpleasant surprise would soon be forthcoming:

San Francisco Chronicle – November 28, 1886 (Edited)

MOSBY'S ACCOUNTS.

Colonel John Mosby was at the Treasury Department to-day engaged in setting up his accounts with the Government as Consul at Hong Kong. It was found that the department owed him quite a nice little balance. He will go to Boston in a short time to deliver, in accordance with an invitation of the Grand Army of the Republic organization of that city, his lecture on Stuart's Cavalry. He will probably repeat this lecture many times during the winter, and will have it copyrighted before he leaves Washington.

Sacramento Daily Record-Union – November 29, 1886

Colonel Mosby.

New York, November 28th—Colonel Mosby, now here, says he has made his home in San Francisco and will return there. Mosby has in his possession the last letter written by General Grant. It was dictated the day before Grant died, and was addressed to Senator Stanford, asking his influence to secure Mosby a position in California which would help him to enter on the practice of law. This letter was the means of obtaining an appointment as counsel for the Southern Pacific Railroad Company, which Mosby still holds. General Grant had a very strong attachment for Colonel Mosby, which was fully reciprocated by the latter.

Daily Times – November 30, 1886

Colonel John S. Mosby has made an argument before First Controller Durham in support of a claim of $5,140 against the Government. When Colonel Mosby was consul at Hong Kong he paid into the Treasury examination fees collected from Chinese emigrants coming to this country, and now claims that these fees were properly due him for the extra service performed.

The "fees" issue, including the Badeau case was good for Mosby for several reasons. First, it demonstrated that he cared for his name more than for money in that he willingly turned fees legally owed to him into the Treasury to avoid the appearance of the corruption rife in the China service. Second, his treatment by the government in denying funds that were legally—and openly—owed to him, made of him an object of sympathy, at least among objective Americans. Those who hated him, of course, were not interested in finding anything to his good. And finally, as most of the articles on the subject were inherently positive, it helped to at least counter such negative publicity as continued to appear in some of the newspapers:

Daily Times – November 30, 1886

Colonel John S. Mosby has made an argument before First Controller Durham in support of a claim of $5,140 against the Government. When Colonel Mosby was consul at Hong Kong he paid into the Treasury examination fees collected from Chinese emigrants coming to this country, and now claims that these fees were properly due him for the extra service performed.

Fort Worth Daily Gazette – December 3, 1886 (Edited)

READY FOR HIS MISSION.

Washington, Dec.2.—Mr. Benjamin Folsom, lately appointed consul to Sheffield … There are a number of consular agencies attached to this consulate, the notarial fees of which are very considerable, and all of which, it would seem, under the recent decision in the Badeau case in New York, will belong to the consul. Mosby's claim is similar to that of Gen. Badeau. First Comptroller Durham has as yet no opportunity to fully examine the merits of the claim of Colonel Mosby. He asks for the return of monies received for examination fees, under the act of 1862, on foreign vessels leaving China The case is almost parallel with that of Gen. Badeau, ex-consul general to London. The view of the law officer of the treasury in that case was shown in the direction of the treasury for the commencement of a suit in New York.

Mosby spoke of the Badeau matter but said that he preferred to be the plaintiff in a case with the government than the defendant, as Badeau had been.

The article below was a first-person description of Mosby, but the name of the writer was not given, which is rather unusual. Most often, such intimate "reminiscences" bear the name of the person presenting them. Why this one does not is unknown. There is a good deal that is accurate, some that is definitely inaccurate, and some—like the war story—that might simply be a matter of interpretation:

The Daily Gazette - December 8, 1886

MOSBY, THE GUERILLA.

I am told that John S. Mosby, the guerrilla general and ex-consul to Hong Kong, has agreed to deliver fifty lectures for which he gets $300 a night. This will make $15,000 for fifty lectures, or for fifty utterances of one lecture, and it is by no means bad pay. "John Mosby," said one old Confederate friend of his to me, 'is as poor as a church mouse and he will give these lectures because he wants the money. He came out of the war without dollar and I don't think he saved anything abroad. His son graduated with high honors from the Virginia university this year and I think he has other children. His beautiful and talented wife is dead, and I doubt whether be has a home he can call his own. "John S. Mosby is a slight, bent, blonde man, with a cold gray eye containing no more expression than a boy's marble. He talks slowly, never gets exited, and does not know what fear is. He loves his friends and hates his enemies, and he carries his fight to the death. I lately heard a story from a captain in the Union army of a scene in which Mosby took part during the war. A Union regiment had driven him with a small body of his men into a ten acre field about which was a high fence. They could see him plainly within it, and they surrounded the field and began to close in upon Mosby. They wanted to capture him, as he had already killed nearly half their regiment. They closed in upon him slowly, his handful of troops still firing. They backed him up close to a fence, and they apparently had him in their grasp, when he drove his spurs into his horse and went over the fence like in a flash, and as he did so, turned in the air upon his saddle and shot a soldier through the head with his revolver. There are few such shots as Mosby, and during the war he shot to kill.

At the close of the war Horace Greeley wanted Mosby hung. He denounced him as a guerilla and a murderer, and published article after article calling upon the president to hang him. Mosby fled to the mountains, and he told me he intended to fight to the last. Gen. Grant was in Washington at the time. Mrs. Mosby came here with a sucking baby on one arm and these papers of Horace Greeley under the other. She called upon Grant and laid the papers before him. Grant told her to go to her husband and to tell him that he would protect him if he would surrender; that he should go to the nearest (illegible) and give himself up and he would protect his parole as much as he would that of Gen. Lee. Mrs. Mosby carried this news to John S. Mosby in the mountains. He surrendered and Grant protected him. Mosby never forgot it and when the campaign of 1872 came around, in which Greeley was pitted against Grant, Mosby stumped the state of Virginia for Grant. He carried Greeley's papers around and told the people how Grant had treated him. The result was he carried Virginia for the Republicans for the first time in history.

Sometimes the papers that agreed on Mosby—for well or ill—were in entirely different areas of the country! Here is a rather nasty little article coming from the Chicago Herald, which then finds its way into the *Fort Worth Daily Gazette*:

Fort Worth Daily Gazette – December 13, 1886

He is "Loil," You Know. Chicago Herald.

In the Boston newspapers the presence of Mosby, the ex-Guerilla, now a Republican, is spoken of as an ushering in the era of good feeling. As Mosby is making money out of his visit, besides getting good victuals and drink, it also resembles one of his old-time raids in some respects.

But while some papers poked fun at Mosby's lecture tour, the *National Republican*—the paper that had determined that the prickly little Virginian was worth defending—rose to the fore. In this article, it brought out the fact that Mosby was being defended by "seafaring gentlemen" who had met him as consul in Hong Kong and testified to his service at that place, a matter that received no other coverage in the press:

Daily National Republican, – December 15, 1886

A Banquet to Col. John S. Mosby.

Portsmouth, N. H., Dec. 14.—Col. John S. Mosby, the celebrated "rebel guerilla chief," delivered a lecture here last Saturday evening on "Stuart's Cavalry," and on Monday night a banquet was tendered to him by the Union veterans of Portsmouth. Many seafaring gentlemen, who made the acquaintance of the genial southerner in Hong Kong, renewed a friendship which recalls so many pleasant memories. These gentlemen declared that Col. Mosby's administration of American affairs at the port of Hong Kong was much as to compel the respect and regard of men of all nationalities, it being markedly in advance of that of any of his predecessors.

But the Republican was not the only newspaper that found good things to say about John Mosby. A paper from the Wild West reported upon a very pleasant reunion between Mosby and a former Union officer, a man called by the paper a "once captive enemy." The most telling matter in the article was the obvious lack of any sectional hostility on the part of either man, although it is to be noted that the paper still made reference to "Guerrilla Mosby":

Arizona Silver Belt – December 18, 1886

Honoring Guerilla Mosby. [From the Boston Post.]

One of the cozy private banquet halls of the Parker House was occupied last evening by a small gathering of ex-military gentlemen who met to commemorate in a social way their war experiences of twenty years and more ago. The foremost guest about the table was the far-famed "guerilla chief," Col. John S. Mosby. As Col. Mosby was passing through Washington on his way to this city to deliver his war lecture it was with mingled surprise and gratification that he received a telegram from a gentleman whom in the course of many other unpleasant events which fell to the Colonel's lot during the war, he considered it his duty to make a captive.

It was the outcome of his tussle with the Second Massachusetts, which Col. Mosby has always alluded to as one of the severest of his struggles. The Confederates were finally successful, and the gallant Union officer, Major J. M. Forbes, became Col. Mosby's prisoner. The Colonel thought no more about the matter until it was recalled to his memory a few days since by an invitation to dine and spend the evening with his once captive enemy.

Last evening's gathering at Parker's was the result. About sixteen gallant old veterans did justice to an excellent menu, and then, in the elaborate and comfortable seclusion of the banquet hall, after the fragrant Havanas had been lighted, were fought again the old fights, and stirring reminiscences of the old campaigns were told.

Mosby and Forbes remained friends until Forbes death. Indeed, Mosby mentioned that sad matter in a letter in which he lamented the loss of so many of his friends, writing that "old Forbes has died." The next two articles on his tour, show the diametric response of those papers who personally liked Mosby—or at least did not dislike him—and those publications for whom he was still anathema, such as the Fort Worth Gazette:

National Republican – December 20, 1886

Col. Mosby Among Old Friends.

Col. John S. Mosby, the famous Virginia cavalryman, is in the city and registered at the National. Col. Mosby has just returned from a lecture tour in the New England states. He speaks in the highest terms of the cordiality and kind treatment he everywhere received—in fact, he said that he was never more heartily received in Virginia than he was in New England. After a short rest he will return to Boston and continue his course of lectures. He was the center of attraction last night at the National and was surrounded by a number of old Virginia friends, many of whom he had not seen for years. In speaking of Virginia politics, he said that, although absent from the state for some years, he had still kept posted in all that was going on. Great changes had taken place, but not greater than he had expected.

Fort Worth Gazette – December 22, 1886

If Ben Butler could be induced to make a lecturing tour through Southern cities, now that Mosby has received so warm a reception in Boston, there would be no further fear in respect to our fraternal relations. New Orleans might be selected as the most suitable place for the exhibit of reciprocity of feeling.

And then there were the papers that just wanted to print something, and so they lifted part of another paper's earlier article. Nothing of note was then added, but at least the paper could say that it wasn't left out of the coverage of John Mosby, a matter that was often more important than the substance of that being covered:

Times & Democrat – December 23, 1886

The Noted Confederate.

John S. Mosby is a slight, bent, blonde man, with a cold gray eye containing no more expression than a boy's marble. He talks slowly, never gets excited and does not know what fear is.—Detroit Free Press.

Mosby lectured twice more in the North in 1906 and again after he had been removed from his position in the Department of Justice in 1910. However, when he received an invitation along with twenty-five well-known Confederates to attend a gathering in Faneuil Hall, Boston, in July of 1904, some of the old hatred still burned as can be seen in an article appearing in a regimental publication of the time. Sadly, by 1905, all of these myths should have been long since abandoned. Instead, the behavior of some Union veterans was still guided by lies.

As the year was ending, Mosby learned the answer of the First Comptroller to his claim to recover his fees: "No!" But Durham did not take "the contrary view" as claimed. He agreed that the fees were Mosby's, but he opined that once Mosby turned them over, he had relinquished all rights to them. Naturally, as in the past, John Mosby wasn't going to accept such injustice. In this particular definition of what could be considered a "fight," Mosby's biographers were quite right—he was always prepared to engage:

Washington Critic – December 23, 1886

General Mosby's Claim.—First Comptroller Durham to-day decided adversely upon the claim of General Mosby, for the refunding of the fees turned into the Treasury by him as consul at Hong Kong. Mr. Mosby was of the opinion that he had been entitled to retain these fees, and that they had been improperly turned over to the Government and should be refunded. Comptroller Durham takes the contrary view.

Staunton Spectator – December 29, 1886

Col. Mosby's Claim.—As announced in the Associated Press dispatches this morning, the first comptroller of the treasury has decided against the claim of Col. Mosby for $5,013 fees collected by him as United States consul at Hong Kong. Col. Mosby has other claims against the government of a similar character, which, with the claim just disallowed by the first comptroller, aggregate about $15,000. He was at the Treasury Department this morning, and gave notice that he would bring suit for the entire amount in the Court of Claims. It is said that the same principle is involved in his claim as in the suit brought by the government against Colonel Badeau for fees retained while he was consul-general at London, and which the United States Circuit Court in New York has recently decided in Badeau's favor. Mosby turned into the treasury all his fees of the character referred to, expecting to receiving them back when his accounts were settled, but Badeau and other consuls put them in their own pockets, and thus threw the onus of proof upon the government. It is said that Badeau at London and Packard at Liverpool made at least $100,000 during their terms of office by retaining the class of fees which Mosby handed in.—Wash. Cor. Balt. Sun.

Indian Chieftain – December 30, 1886

Comptroller Durham has disallowed the claim of John S. Mosby for $5,013, collected as fees while consul at Hong Kong.

John Mosby sadly realized that the government—his government—was not going to play by the rules. He then went back and looked at all the money he had turned into the Treasury and, based upon the court's findings in the Badeau case, amended his claim—upward.

CHAPTER 26

1887

Virtus tentamine gaudet. ~ Strength rejoices in the challenge.

"Truth never damages a cause that is just." ~ **Mahatma Gandhi**

EARLY 1887 WAS a busy time for John Mosby. He was involved with literary efforts as well as continuing attempts to recoup his lost consul fees; all of this activity was interspersed with a considerable amount of travel:

Alexandria Gazette - January 26, 1887

Col. Mosby.—Col. John S. Mosby is stopping at the Fifth Avenue Hotel in New York, but is on his way to Boston, where he intends to look after the publication of his war reminiscences. Col. Mosby said that he is preparing an article on the battle of Gettysburg, which will explode all former theories regarding that battle. He claims that the true history of the battle has not yet been given. Col. Mosby will call while in New York on Mrs. U. S. Grant and ex-Senator Conkling. He thinks Gen. Grant was one of the greatest of generals, and ex-Senator Conkling one of the greatest of Statesmen, and wishes he could be elected President.

According to an article at the end of Mosby's career in Hong Kong, Conkling was a friend to him. The New York Republican was an interesting man, not the least because of Mosby's loyalty to him. And as for Gettysburg, it is possible that in hunting about for material to include in his reminiscences, Mosby had come across information that caused him to redirect his efforts toward that campaign.

Meanwhile, the former consul continued to be very much involved in his efforts to recover his lost "fees." The court ruling on the Badeau case led Mosby to believe that he had every chance of doing so, and he even increased the amount sought from the government. Mosby also determined to go through the courts instead of through government "channels," that had proved so unproductive in the past:

Alexandria Gazette - January 3, 1887

In accordance with the decision in the case of ex-Consul Badeau, ex-Consul Mosby, whose claim was recently disallowed for the remarkable reason that, though just, as the Government had possession of the money it could not give it up, has amended his claim, which he has taken, on appeal, to the court of claims, by increasing its amount to nearly thirty thousand dollars.

Daily Herald - February 2, 1887

American Consular Fees.

Col. Mosby, who used to skirmish so effectually in Virginia during the war, as many a captured and robbed Union soldier can testify, has returned from Hong Kong, where he has been United States consul, and has commenced suit in the Court of Claims for $15,000 fees collected by him and turned into the United States Treasury. Finding that he had a right to retain them, he demanded them but the treasury officials refused to give them up. The principle involved is exactly the same as in the suit brought by the Government against Col. Badeau for fees retained while he was Consul-General at London, and which the United States Circuit Court in New York has recently decided in Badeau's favor.

Mosby turned into the treasury all his fees of the character referred to, expecting to receive them back when his accounts were settled, but Badeau and other Consuls put them in their own pockets, and thus threw the onus of proof upon the Government. It is said that Badau and London and Packard at Liverpool made at least $100,000 during their terms of office by retaining the class of fees which Mosby handed in.—Washington Correspondence Boston Budget.

National Republican – March 8, 1887

The Claim of Col. John S. Mosby.

Judge W. Willoughby, attorney for Col. John S. Mosby, late consul to Hong Kong, has entered suit in the court of claims to recover $28,000 on account of unofficial fees which were covered into the United States treasury. Col. Mosby claims that the money belongs to him, and was paid for services rendered private parties. A similar claim was made by Gen. Badeau, and a decision obtained in his favor.

Mosby had also begun to write articles and books about the war to supplement his income, most of which was being sent to his family. In the course of these efforts, a rather amusing review found its way into a San Francisco paper and was then reprinted in a Vermont publication:

Burlington Weekly Free Press – January 7, 1887

The San Francisco News Letter says of Col. John S. Mosby: "In a narrative of his military operations in a local Sunday paper, this veteran of a hundred battles, by what infatuate fatality possessed I know not, relates that on one occasion he did the wrong thing! Of all the commanders in the recent lukewarmness who have recorded in print their military services, Colonel Mosby is the only one who was ever guilty of an error. As he was on the confederate side, the conclusion that his blunder lost the war is irresistible."

In the course of his researches, Mosby discovered something that stunned him—evidence of an attempt to buy his services for the Union. The idea that he had been considered a willing traitor for money enraged the man, and his efforts to discover more about the matter were given considerable press at the time:

Alexandria Gazette – January 14, 1887

General Pleasanton being interviewed last night respecting the Mosby case, said Mosby gave him a great deal of trouble during the war, but that he could have captured him any time he wanted, had he been allowed to do so. He said he, Pleasanton, was in the army of the Potomac, out of the territory of which he could not go, while Mosby's operations were chiefly confined to the territory of the army of Washington, which Secretary Stanton created for his own safety. He said Stanton was the most valuable lieutenant Jefferson Davis had.

Whatever the value of Pleasanton's comment about Stanton, his claim that he could have captured Mosby "any time he wanted" is past ridiculous. Mosby was certainly within Pleasanton's sphere of operations often enough to have been captured by him, had he been able to do so. One of the reasons that so many Federal officers hated John Mosby was that he made them look incompetent and even years after the war, that humiliation still stung many proud soldiers in blue.

Richmond Dispatch – **January 15, 1887**
General Ingalls Exonerates Colonel Mosby.

A New York telegram to the Baltimore Sun says: The statement in *The Sun*'s Washington correspondence that Colonel J. S. Mosby had discovered in the War Department letters which had passed between General Pleasanton and General Rufus Ingalls relative to a plan to bribe Colonel Mosby to desert the Confederate cause was shown to General Ingalls to-day. He said:

"I do not wish to be brought into any prominence in this matter, inasmuch as I see that General Pleasanton has been quoted as characterizing the letters as forgeries, and I do not desire to be made to appear as contradicting him. As a matter of fact, however, I recollect the letters distinctly, but I presume that General Pleasanton has forgotten all about the matter. At the great cavalry engagement at Brandy Station General Pleasanton was no doubt flooded with reports and suggestions from other persons, and among other things it was probably suggested to him that Colonel Mosby could be bribed, and thus, I have no doubt, he came to send his dispatch of June 12, 1863 to me. Now, I did not have then, and have not now, any idea that Colonel Mosby or any other leading Confederate officer could be bribed. I had the highest respect for Colonel Mosby then. Didn't he come very near capturing me two or three times? And since the war my respect for him has not diminished. My reply to General Pleasanton shows that I had very little confidence in the scheme to bribe Colonel Mosby, but I had no objection to his being bribed if it could be done. Bribe him? Why yes, if you can.

Colonel Mosby was very active about that time, and he inflicted much injury on our troops, and might have done more if he had known all that we did. In the retrograde movement made at that time to cover Washington, 5000 quartermasters' wagons were strung out miles in front of the army, and Colonel Mosby might, if he had known, destroyed these supplies. Colonel Mosby ought not to feel hurt by General Pleasanton's letter, which contained a suggestion which, not doubt, had been brought to him by some one who thought that it could be carried into effect."

Anderson Intelligencer – **January 20, 1887**
MOSBY IS MAD.

Because of an Attempt to Bribe Him.

Washington, January 11.—the hottest man in Washington tonight is Colonel John S. Mosby, the famous ex-cavalry commander. Mosby is here adjusting his accounts as consul at Hong Kong, and trying to collect six thousand dollars which he claims the government owes him. He is also engaged in the preparation of a volume of war reminiscences, and has been delving extensively into the archives of the war department. While there this morning a clerk said to him,

"Colonel, did you know there was an effort to buy you off during the war?"

"What do you mean?" asked Mosby.

The clerk then drew out a bundle of papers, from which he produced copies of two dispatches which made Mosby's eyes gleam with their old-time fire. These remarkable dispatches are as follows:

HEADQUARTERS CAVALRY CORPS,

June 12, 1863.—Gen. R. Ingalls, Chief Quartermaster: Your dispatch received. Ask the general how much of a bribe he can stand to get Mosby's services? There is a chance for him, and just now he could do valuable service in the way of information as well as humbugging the enemy. There's no news. The rebels are alike that boy the president tells about, who stumped his toe and was too big to cry. Birney is up.

HEADQUARTERS ARMY OF THE POTOMAC,

A. PLEASANTON, Brigadier General

June 12, 1863.—General Pleasanton: If you think your scheme succeed in regard to Mosby, do not hesitate as to the matter of money. Use your own judgment, and do precisely what you think best for the public interest.

RUFUS INGALLS,

Brigadier General

When Mosby had read them, he said:

"This is infamous!"

He then took copies of the dispatches. In conversation to-night he said he meant to go to the bottom of this business and to expose the slander on his character. He said he never dreamed of the existence of any such papers until today, and that there never was the slightest hint in the nature of negotiation with the northern army made to him during the war. The dispatches were written the day before Pope's disastrous defeat by Stonewall Jackson and Longstreet at the second battle of Bull Run, and it is believed emanated from Pope's headquarters. Pleasanton was then in command of the cavalry in Hooker's division, and Rufus Ingalls was quartermaster general of the Federal army. Only three days before Pleasanton and J. E. B. Stuart had fought the bloodiest cavalry engagement of the war at Brandy Station, in which neither side could claim the victory. Mosby bore a conspicuous part in that engagement, and that, at the time of Pleasanton's dispatch to Ingalls, Mosby was harassing Hooker's rear.

Hooker was on the north bank of the Rappahannock and Lee was moving toward Pennsylvania, making his way toward Gettysburg, where three weeks later the Confederacy received its death blow. Just at the time of this correspondence between Pleasanton and Ingalls, however, Lee's star was in the ascendant, and if Mosby had been willing to betray the Confederate cause, it is not likely that he would have chosen such a time. His friends and comrades in Washington share his indignation at the insinuation that he was ready to become the Benedict Arnold of the Confederacy, and express their absolute confidence in devotion to the lost cause.

Just what course Colonel Mosby will pursue in this matter he does not indicate, further than to declare his intention to show the utter falsity of his imputation on his honor.

General Pleasanton is living in Washington in reduced circumstances. Your correspondent sought him tonight, to get his version of this remarkable story, but was unable to find him. General Rufus Ingalls is on the retired list of the army and resides in New York. There may be some sensation[al] developments in this matter within the next few days.

It is interesting that Mosby was so aggrieved to learn that he was thought capable of selling out his country given that the Federals and even some Confederates believed him to be a "land pirate," a renegade, a bushwhacker, a highwayman, and an outlaw, hardly ethical occupations! So why Mosby was astonished that he was seen as willing to sell himself to the highest bidder is somewhat curious.

A gossipy little item appeared in the *Alexandria Gazette* in which Mosby opined on various subjects obviously at the behest of the correspondent:

Alexandria Gazette – January 29, 1887 (Edited)

Col. Mosby.

Col. John S. Mosby, the famous Confederate raider, was at the Fifth Avenue Hotel one day this week en route to Boston. He wore a black slouch hat, a black frock coat and dark moccasin-striped trousers. His face is round, full and smooth, and ruddy complexioned. His eyes are cold blue and only lighten up when he smiles. The Colonel is growing stout, and the slim cavalry man of twenty years ago lives only in recollection. He has six wounds on his person, five bullets and one sabre cut. One of bullets remains embedded in his flesh. The sabre cut was received during a fierce charge, but the gallant Federal cavalryman who gave it received a bullet in his breast from the pistol of Mosby. The Colonel now resides in San Francisco. When asked, "Do you ever dream about the battles you were in?" he replied, "Oh, yes, frequently, and the dreams are very vivid. I carry a bullet in my groin, and that, you know, is a constant reminder." …

"Did you call on President Cleveland while at the capital?"

"No, I did not call on him nor any of his Cabinet offices. I was very busy anyway. I cannot talk politics. I think the republican party is very strong, and will come into power again. I only wish they would run Roscoe Conkling for the Presidency."

Mosby was almost as devoted to Conkling as he had been to Grant, possibly because Conkling was also devoted to Grant. But Conkling had been his own worst enemy and, in a fit of pique, had resigned his Senate seat believing that the New York Republicans would reinstall him; they did not. Finding himself in "political limbo," he returned to private practice. In March of 1888, during the great blizzard that struck that area, Conkling decided to walk home and on his way collapsed, later dying of the consequences of hypothermia. The Conkling story has to be one of the most odd and, frankly, useless ends to a fine career in public service. But it would seem that the editor of the Epitaph held neither man in particularly high regard:

Daily Epitaph – February 4, 1887

To a New York reporter Colonel Mosby said the other day that he considered Roscoe Conkling the greatest man in the world. In return for this compliment Roscoe might say that as a barn-yard raider and hen roost demolisher Mosby has no superior. He is as great in his line as Roscoe is in his.

The Bee commented on Mosby's apparent sartorial eccentricities. However, the slouch hat was his stock-in-trade, and it never changed—at least until he was an old man, where there are some photos of him sporting a straw boater in the summer and even a homburg in a picture taken in Washington in 1910:

Omaha Daily Bee – February 5, 1887

Colonel John S. Mosby is in Boston bringing out his book of reminiscences. He wears an overcoat lined with scarlet and a large slouch hat.

Mosby continued to lecture, but the following article makes notice of an unfortunate incident that occurred during his travels. Of course, there were doubtless many of his detractors who considered the matter as being well deserved given his own wartime depredations against the railroads:

Alexandria Gazette – February 10, 1887 (Edited)

FROM WASHINGTON

Washington, D. C., Feb. 10, 1887.

Col. Mosby has just arrived here from Milwaukee, where he received distinguished attention, and where a crowded audience listened to his lecture. On his return, when passing through Kentucky, his valise, containing his broad cloth lecture suit, the manuscript copy of his lecture, and everything else he had with him except what was on his person, was stolen from the seat in front of him while he was asleep. He mentioned his loss to Senator Beck here this morning telling him that he had supposed that his baggage at least would be safe in passing through Kentucky; but the Senator on the instant replied that the theft had been committed in the country through which John Morgan made his raid, and that that section had never recovered from the demoralization produced by that raid.

Mosby's determination to look into the Gettysburg campaign resulted in pressure being brought on him to "let sleeping dogs lie." Of course, those attempting to dissuade him would meet the same John Mosby that the Union army, both political parties, several presidents, and many, many bureaucrats and not a few opponents in the press had met—to their despair:

Alexandria Gazette – **February 28, 1887**

Washington, D.C., Feb. 28, 1887.

It is said that a great deal of pressure has been brought to bear on Col. Mosby by interested parties to prevail on him not to publish the documents he has recently discovered among the Confederate archives, relating to Gen. J.E.B. Stuart's use of his cavalry in the Gettysburg campaign. But the truth will be told: the documents will appear in the Century, with an article written by Col. Mosby in vindication of Stuart; and also in his "Reminiscences of the War," to be published in March by Geo. A Jones & Co., of Boston.

Mosby was already cheerfully hated among the "old guard" in the South, but in his efforts to exonerate Stuart with regard to Gettysburg, he fell afoul of the so-called "Lee cult." For that reason, he was not only pressured not to publish what was a matter of public record, but was denied access to other documents surrounding the campaign as these were made public.

Mosby's "consular claim" matter was back in the press as he moved from the government to the courts in an effort to regain his money:

National Republican – **March 8, 1887**

The Claim of Col. John S. Mosby.

Judge W. Willoughby, attorney for Col. John S. Mosby, late consul to Hong Kong, has entered suit in the court of claims to recover $28,000 on account of unofficial fees which were covered into the United States treasury. Col. Mosby claims that the money belongs to him, and was paid for services rendered private parties. A similar claim was made by Gen. Badeau, and a decision obtained in his favor.

The difference between the two cases, as Mosby himself admitted, was that Badeau took the fees and contested government efforts to reclaim them while Mosby turned his fees in and sued the government with the same purpose. Mosby preferred to be the plaintiff in any action against the government, but Badeau had his money, and the court found for him while Mosby did not have his. It took him years—and a considerable amount of money!—to finally obtain judgment in his favor. The press made notice of his appeal in a short announcement:

Alexandria Gazette – **April 27, 1887**

COURT OF APPEALS YESTERDAY.—Mosby against Kendrick, Cause reinstated on docket.

Mosby's book of reminiscences was about to make its appearance. A reviewer made note that "the most interesting feature" was Mosby's defense of Stuart in the Gettysburg campaign. Eventually, Mosby would write a book on the issue itself, a matter that only brought him further disfavor among his fellow former Confederates. The newly released book was mentioned in a lengthy article in the *Richmond Dispatch*:

Richmond Dispatch – **May 8, 1887 (Edited)**

MOSBY'S BOOK

A Contribution to the Literature of the Civil War.

The Confederate Rough Rider Defending the Memory of General "Jeb" Stuart.

A Boston telegram says: A remarkable book will make its appearance next week. Colonel John S. Mosby, the dashing Confederate leader of Northern Virginia during the war, has written a book of reminiscences describing his adventurous career.

From a historical standpoint the most interesting feature of the volume is the defence of General "Jeb" Stuart, the commander of Confederate cavalry in Virginia, as well as General R. E. Lee, against the alleged aspersions of General Longstreet. The only trace of bitterness visible in the pages of Colonel Mosby's reminiscences arises from his zeal to defend Virginia's dashing trooper. Between Mosby and Stuart a strong friendship existed, and a chapter is devoted to an explanation of Stuart's conduct. Letters are adduced which have never seen the light of publicity.

A San Francisco paper printed a review of Mosby's book that was not only positive, but declared that his actions during the war did not involve "atrocities" and that the writer was "bright and vigorous." All in all, the book was well received except among the usual suspects:

San Francisco Chronicle – **June 12, 1887**

Mosby's War Reminiscences.

Of the stories told by the brigadiers on both sides during the Rebellion the public has already had a surfeit; hence, it is the highest compliment that can be paid to "Mosby's War Reminiscences," that the reader will be apt to go through with it if he begins it. Mosby saw hard service in Virginia. He was a guerilla, but it can be said for him that he never indulged in any of the atrocities that made the name in the southwest the synonym for all that was vile and cruel. Mosby is a very bright, vigorous writer and he has told a good story here. [Boston: George A. Jones & Co. For sale by J. A. Hofmann; price, paper, 50 cents.]

The Intelligencer – **October 4, 1887**

New Publications.

During the war time loyal people regarded John S. Mosby as altogether a bad man, the worst sort of mixture of the spy and the guerrilla, who would rather take a mean advantage of a Yankee throat than be turned loose in a sutler's tent. The Mosby of fact was a cultivated gentleman, who left his place at the Virginia bar to batter Uncle Sam all he knew how. In this "War Reminiscences," just published, he tells how he got into the army and what he did after he got there. It is a tale of military adventure of great interest modestly told. It deals in criticism in some extent, but it is mainly a narrative of the cavalry movements in which Mosby's men bore a part, and as such it has value and absorbing interest. Not the least entertaining part of the book is that which is devoted to the brilliant J.E.B. Stuart, for whom Mosby shows a particularly warm side. Nobody who reads these reminiscences will regret the time so spent. George A. Jones & Co., Boston; Stanton & Davenport, Wheeling.

This nice review came considerably later than the first reviews and was absent both the praise and type of criticism based entirely on hearsay and legend. Soon, especially the Virginia papers were singling out various anecdotes that were of interest to the locals. One review mentioned Mosby's "rescue" by the young and beautiful Laura Ratcliffe:

Alexandria Gazette – July 29, 1887 (Edited)

HOW MOSBY WAS SAVED BY A FAIRFAX LADY.—Col. Mosby tells in his "War Reminiscences" how he was saved from capture and perhaps death by a lady of Fairfax county, who is beloved and esteemed by all who know her. After describing the re-capture of Dr. Drake's saddlebags and medicines, he says: [the article goes on to describe the incident noted above.-vph]

And yet again, Mosby's natural humility was revealed by his willingness to confess that he was neither omniscient nor omnipotent and would indeed have been captured or killed in the trap set for him. Many soldiers would have passed over such an admission of personal flaws rather than give credit to a mere civilian—and a woman at that! But John Mosby was willing to acknowledge a debt, and such revelations gave a very human quality to his version of the war. It was this quality that made an ally of Secretary of War James Seddon and helped him keep his command after the Partisan Ranger Act had been revoked.

With the arrival of fall, Mosby was back in the fray with regard to his consul fees:

Alexandria Gazette – October 4, 1887

A private letter received here to-day says that Col. Mosby will be in this city next month to prosecute his suit against the government for the recovery of fees to the amount of $30,000 turned by him into the Treasury, while U.S Consul at Hong Kong, by which, under the law and recent decisions in similar cases, he was entitled to retain.

Again, the paper made known that the information it had about Mosby's movements and his intentions were the result of a private letter—and by private, it meant not sent to the newspaper.

In 1889, the court of claims found in Mosby's favor; but just before the period for appeal ran out, the government did indeed appeal the decision, throwing the matter into the Supreme Court, an action that promised to add years to the litigation. Meanwhile, Mosby was being better treated by old foes than he was by fellow "Southrons":

The Sun – December 19, 1887

The familiar figure of Col. John S. Mosby, or "Guerilla" Mosby, was seen on the avenue today. Col. Mosby has been out West, stopping for awhile in Denver, where his son is practicing law. During his stay he was dined by regular army officers, and is quite enthusiastic over the way the veterans of the Union army lionized him.

Another rather odd story surfaced regarding Mosby's reception in Denver. He was accompanied by his namesake son, John Jr. Mosby and asked to respond to a toast—a social custom of the time—but begged off because of a "severe cold." And while that may have been the truth, Mosby did not like impromptu speaking, a fact that might also have led to his reticence. John Jr.'s response was somewhat ominous and cast a portent on the two men's future relationship:

Alexandria Gazette – **December 12, 1887**

Col. Mosby in Denver—The order of the Loyal Legion held a meeting at the Albany Hotel Tuesday evening and afterwards enjoyed a camp-fire banquet in the dining room of the hotel. A sumptuous repast was served and the speeches were then called for in response to toasts. Among the guests was Colonel John S. Mosby, the famous Confederate guerilla chieftain, whose name was, in the language of one of the speakers, a "household word during the war." When the Commander had called the assemblage to order, after the menu had been thoroughly discussed, the glasses merrily clicked and the response to toasts were in order. With eloquent and humorous remarks, Maj. Platte called for a response to the toast: "Our Guest; our pleasure in now seeing him is only equaled by our desire to not seem him during the late unpleasantness." In response Col. Mosby said, "Gentlemen, as I am suffering from a very severe cold, I beg you to excuse me from speaking. Allow me to express my thanks for the very kind sentiments which the eloquent gentleman who proposed the toast expressed, and for the kindly manner in which they were received by you."

Mr. John S. Mosby, Jr., son of Colonel Mosby, who resides in Denver and is an attorney in the United States Attorney Hobson's office, was called upon. He responded: "Gentlemen, I should be very glad indeed to respond fittingly, but I must beg of you to remember that I labor under the disadvantage of both being young and also of having but a faint recollection of the war." A voice: "What do you know about your father?" Laughter. "Well, gentlemen, as I haven't seen him for eight years up to the last week, I really can't tell you much about him."—Denver Republican.

John Jr. was Mosby's war baby, conceived and born during the conflict. Even though after the war he had his father's presence until Mosby Senior was forced to leave for China, much of that time was unpleasant. First, Mosby was hounded by the victorious Federal army, and then he began his political apostasy. Further, his two younger brothers, George and Alfred, died as did his beloved mother. Mosby's pariah status affected his children greatly, John not the least as he bore his father's then-hated name. It is said somewhere that when asked about his father later in his life, John retorted that if it had not been for the war, he might have made a decent parent—hardly a declaration of filial affection. It also did not help that John, a very intelligent and talented man, was always in his father's shadow. The children of "celebrities" tend to suffer as a result of that relationship, no matter how loving and supportive the famous parent.

And still, the consular business remained in the news. Mosby was obviously moving about the country a great deal for personal reasons. What that meant for his position with the railroad is never said. As he was being paid, he must have been fulfilling his duty to that corporation. Even Collis Huntington, who liked Mosby, would not have paid for an absentee "employee":

Alexandria Gazette – December 23, 1887

Col. Mosby, who is here getting his claim of $15,000 for consular fees to which he was entitled in shape, will spend Christmas in Warrenton. He will spend a day or two in Alexandria next week. His attorney here says there is no doubt that his claim is good.

In the same paper:

Mosby for President

["Kennebecker" in Boston Journal, Oct. 22, 1887]

The only fault Colonel Mosby could find with the Maine men was their want of knowledge of their countryman, S. S. Prentiss. This was the Colonel's hobby. He was an ardent admirer of Mr. Prentiss and had some of his speeches by heart. After he became a little acquainted with me he asked me where I belonged. I told him on the Kennebec. Every one would have thought he would have asked me if I knew Mr. Blaine. [If he had, I should have had to tell him no; for though we live only four miles apart, I never saw him.] "Kennebec?" said he, "how far from Portland?" "About fifty or sixty miles." "Do you know Prentiss?" I told him I had heard of him. "Which Prentiss?" "Why, why Prentiss, Prentiss, the editor of the Louisville Journal, wasn't he?" Well reader, you ought to see the look of disappointment that went over his face. He lent me two editions of S. S. Prentiss's life afterwards, and how ashamed I was to think I could not have known him before.

The next ship that came in he inquired of me who the captain was. I told him he was from Maine. I told the captain when I met him of the preference the Consul had for some men who knew Prentiss, and, said I, do you know about him? "Oh, yes, perfectly well." I told the Consul he was very familiar with the history of Prentiss, for he belonged to Portland. In a few days Col. Mosby went for him. 'Are you familiar with Prentiss's life?" Oh, yes sir." "What Prentiss?" "George D., of course." "There; born in the same city, and don't know S. S. Prentiss! Never knew of his father, one of the best shipmasters. Never heard of his grant oration, in which he pictures the new ship 'born and fledged in the woods of Maine.' Oh, you Maine men, where was the schoolmaster?

I guess I felt well the next time I saw him. He declared his loyalty to Maine ships. He had done more for them in his official capacity than any one else had ever done and ever would do. It was something to work for. "Why," said he, "if I were a Maine man I would leave no stone unturned until the ships had their rights in Congress." And he has with his great knowledge, experience and power done so ever since; and every Maine shipmaster he meets he puts a copy of "The Life of S. S. Prentiss" into their hands, if they will take it, and has put many a one to the blush thereby. Guerrilla? I wish we had such a guerrilla in every consulate in the world. There's my sentiments at least. I mean to write more about him in the next series of letters, if he is willing. I know of no man I would rather see President of the United States than Consul Mosby.

Such vignettes are jewels that reveal the character and life of John Mosby. He was a Virginian raised far from the sea, but whose imagination and spirit were captured by a man born in Maine and who lived and died in the South—a man who loved ships. The writer was correct. John Mosby would have made a great president because he was a truly great soul.

> ### *National Republican* – December 24, 1887
>
> It is understood that an invitation will be extended to Col. S. Mosby, who is now in Washington, to deliver his famous lecture in this city for the benefit of the confederate monument fund. Alexandrians are anxious to hear the great guerilla chieftain.

Now Mosby again was "the great guerilla chieftain" and apparently suitable to speak "for the benefit of the Confederate monument fund," something that only a relatively short time earlier would have been seen as blasphemy.

Chapter 27

1888

Faber est suae quisque. ~ Every man is the artisan of his own fortune.

"'Tis best to weigh the enemy more mighty than he seems."
~ William Shakespeare

JOHN MOSBY'S "PRESS year" began with a nasty little article regarding his alleged victory in the court of claims in the fees matter. Of course, Mosby wasn't a general, and the paper made it clear that it considered him anything but "distinguished." Furthermore, in the matter reported, his war history had nothing whatsoever to do with the rightness of his cause in the courts. It was simply another complaint that he was a former Confederate who had become a Republican, obviously an unforgiveable sin. On the other hand, a Virginia paper simply commented upon the court verdict and a "deficiency bill" in the Congress that included the money owed to Mosby according to the court:

Democratic Northwest – January 3, 1888

That distinguished Rebel Brigadier, Gen. John S. Mosby, has just obtained a U. S. Court judgment against the United States Government for $13,839, being the amount of fees claimed by him for certificates issued to Chinese emigrants to this country. Mosby was U. S. Consul General to China under a Republican administration. As a Confederate guerilla during the war, he was pronounced outside of belligerent rights. But since then, like Mahone and thousands of other Rebel officers, he has become a Republican, and his sins that were scarlet are now white as snow.

Alexandria Gazette – January 12, 1888

From Washington.

[Special Correspondence of the Alexandria. Gazette.]

Washington, D.C., Jan. 12, 1888.

The Deficiency bill sent to Congress by the Secretary of the Treasury includes an item to pay John S. Mosby a balance, admitted to be due to him as U. S. Consul at Hong Kong. When Mosby settled his accounts after his return, a balance was found to be due him which could not then be paid, as the appropriation had been exhausted. This item is not any portion of the sum for which Mosby is now suing the Government in the Court of Claims. That claim is for fees collected while Consul and paid into the Treasury to avoid any controversy that might arise if he retained them, and in reliance on the good faith of the Government to refund whatever belonged to him. The first comptroller, while admitting that the greater part of the fees belonged to Mosby, refused to restore them on the ground that their payment into the Treasury was voluntary.

Of course, this effort via legislation to get Mosby his money did not work, though the reason for that failure is not addressed in any later article. As a result, he had to continue to labor through the courts. But Mosby was both patient and persistent. He never gave up, though it took him many years of effort and expense to get back at least some of what he had paid into the Treasury in anticipation of it being returned to him when he left the diplomatic service.

Alexandria Gazette – **March 1, 1888**

The argument in the case of Colonel Mosby against the United States, in the Court of Claims, for the recovery of a large amount of fees turned into the Treasury by him when Consul to Hong Kong, has been completed, and the Colonel will soon start for California. It is said by those who heard Col. Mosby's argument that it was one of the clearest, most concise and most convincing ever delivered before that court.

This article provided more proof of Mosby's ability as an attorney. Certainly, had his performance in the courtroom been mediocre (never mind poor!), it would have been reported with glee in a great many newspapers. Such unprejudiced testimony puts to rest the claim that Mosby was a poor lawyer, one of the assertions that some who have written about the man use to explain the loss of his position with the Southern Pacific after Huntington's departure and his eventual removal from the Department of Justice. Indeed, as has been the case with Mosby whether in the private sector or in his work for the government, the standard allegation seems to have been that he was "kept on" because he was "liked" whether by Huntington or a Republican administration. Frankly, nothing could have been further from the truth.

More was said of Mosby's character with reference to his dealings with the government:

Sacramento Daily Record-Union, – **March 5, 1888**

Mosby's Claim on the Government

MOSBY'S HONESTY.

The Ex-Confederate Officer Has a Claim Against the Government
[Copyright, 1888, by the California Associated Press.]

Washington, March 4th.—Colonel J. S. Mosby, late Consul at Hong Kong, who has become a resident of San Francisco, has been in Washington for some time past engaged in the preparation and argument of a claim he has against the United States Government before the Court of Claims. Col. Mosby says that the law on the subject of fees did not discriminate with sufficient distinctness between the fees which belonged to the Consul and those which belonged to the Government. He adopted the rule of turning all fees into the Treasury, trusting to the good faith of the Government, and supposing that the officials of the Treasury Department, in the final settlement of his accounts, would credit him with whatever was his share. Instead of doing this they kept the fees which he now claims belonged to him, but said he was a fool for turning them into the treasury. At the same time, he having surrendered them, they could not be recovered.

Mosby has sued the Government in the Court of Claims to recover $16,000. He says: "After paying all the expenses of the Hongkong Consulate, including my own salary, I paid a balance to the United States Treasury, in six years, of $60,000. Previous to my appointment there had been a Consulate at Hongkong for thirty years, and the total amount that the United States received during that time was only $25,000. I want to add, however, that if I fail in my suit I will be no worse off than I am now. I am the plaintiff, not a defendant. I paid this money into the Treasury for the purpose of avoiding any controversy about fees with the Government and for the purpose of protecting my reputation and character. I do not regret my action, even if the Court should decide that I am not entitled to any portion of the money thus voluntarily surrendered. I would rather lose the fees than my character. I would also much rather sue the Government than have the Government sue me, as it did the Consul-General to London."

Here is Mosby's ethics in one short statement. He did not regret what he had done because he would "rather lose fees than [his] character." No wonder so many petty politicians and bureaucrats never understood the man! He flew in the face of their very reason for existence.

Though Mosby was long gone from Hong Kong, the consular certificate matter remained of interest to the press. When considered with his efforts to reclaim the money he had rightfully earned in his splendid service in China, it was obvious that only the corrupt were well compensated:

San Francisco Chronicle – **April 4, 1888 (Edited)**

CIPRICO TALKS BACK.

He Gives Some Very Racy Testimony.

BOYD WILL SQUEAL AGAIN.

An Inspector Who Bought Smuggled Goods –

Big Money to be Crooked.

CROOKED CERTIFICATES

Attorney McPike exhibited a return certificate issued on the date mentioned, and which the witness identified by his registry book as having been issued to a Chinese named Le Ah Wun, aged 16, who sailed by the City of Peking on the date mentioned.

The District Attorney announced that he had in his possession sixty-eight return certificates issued on January 10, 1885, for the City of Peking, which he desired to introduce in evidence ..

William H. Mages, a clerk in the employ of the Pacific Mail Steamship Company, was called for the purpose of proving how many Chinese departed on the City of Peking on January 10, 1885. He testified that the books of the company showed that 230 Chinese passengers sailed on that steamer. There were ninety-two Chinese in the crew, and all of them had certificates except twenty. Fifty-six of the Chinese crew were provided with certificates, the crew being shipped in Hongkong for the round trip. The certificates had been take out before Colonel John M. Mosby, at that time United States Consul at Hongkong.

Colonel Mosby, wearing a bright-red tie, was called to the witness stand and identified the shipping articles of the City of Peking for the voyage mentioned. They were issued in December, 1884, and February, 1885.

The shipping articles were admitted in evidence. ...Court here adjourned until this morning.

Mosby then received an invitation to attend a banquet to celebrate General Grant's birthday, one that he seemed to receive almost yearly:

Sacramento Daily Record-Union – **April 12, 1888**
BLUE AND GRAY.

Ex-Confederate Generals Asked to Commemorate Grant's Virtues.

New York, April 11th.—General William T. Sherman, one of the committee in charge of the banquet on April 27th to celebrate Grant's birthday, has addressed to ex-Confederate Generals Longstreet, Gordon, Buckner, Fitzhugh Lee, Mahone, Mosby and Joseph E. Johnston the following letter: My Dear Sir: It has been determined to celebrate the birthday of General Grant (on the 27th inst.), by a banquet at Delmonico's, in this city. I wrote to ask your company on that occasion. Time has developed an affectionate regard which the people of all sections entertain for the virtues of this illustrious man, and it is fitting that those of us who knew him should set an example, to those who are to follow, of thus annually doing honor to his memory.

W. T. Sherman.

His response was carried in a California paper. There was nothing to suggest that he sent it to the paper; therefore, it must be concluded that it was made available to the press by the recipient as was so much of his correspondence during his life:

Sacramento Daily Record-Union - **April 21, 1888**

In response to an invitation from General Sherman to attend the celebration of the birthday of General Grant, Colonel Mosby, who was on "the other side" in the late "unpleasantness," had the grace and courage to say: "I regret that I cannot be with you on the occasion to add my tribute to the memory of the generous soldier whose victories in peace were no less renowned than in war. With feelings of pride I remember that I honored him in life, and am not one of those who did not discover his virtues until he was dead."

We believe Colonel Mosby and that he is sincere in this declaration. If all others who were of his lot in the war were equally as frank and equally as just, the gulf between the Blue and Gray would be more speedily bridged.

Chicago Tribune – **June 21, 1888**
Sheridan and Mosby

"It was only last winter that I met Gen. Sheridan," said Col. Mosby to me the other day, "and I met him at Senator Stanford's house in Washington.

I had gone there to call upon Mrs. Grant, and the Sheridans were calling upon the Senator that evening. I met Mrs. Sheridan in the drawing-room and when I was introduced to her I laughingly remarked: 'I once tried hard to deprive you of your husband, Mrs. Sheridan.' Mrs. Sheridan replied: 'Now, I do not think I ought to be pleased to meet you then.' 'Well,' I answered, 'you must remember your husband tried hard to deprive my wife of her husband.' The General was not in the room at the time, but was with the Senator in the smoking room. Towards the end of the evening Mrs. Stanford took me into the smoking-room and introduced me to Gen. Sheridan. That is the only time I ever met the General. I found him an agreeable companion and I have always regretted the fact that I had not seen more of him. We were opposed to each other in the war, and Gen. Sheridan had made it his boast that he would drive me out of Virginia and I was equally determined to stay. He was a gallant soldier and gentleman and I feel blue about his illness. He was the foremost soldier of his day and it will be too bad if he is carried off at this early age. He is a young man yet, but it seems to me that there are few of the old veterans being left now. The day is fast approaching for all of us to leave this earth," and Col. Mosby stepped well into the street and took a look at the roof of the army headquarters, which are located in the Phelan Building. "Thank God," he said, "he has not passed away yet." – San Francisco Post.

John Mosby was still earnestly trying to consign all the evils and wrongs of the war to oblivion; but eventually, even he had no choice but to recognize the type of warfare waged in Virginia and also that Sheridan was not the glorious military commander everyone, including Sheridan, thought he was.

Mosby was very seldom wrong, and when he was, the matter was usually reasonably inconsequential, except, of course, for his belief in the objectivity of Northern Republicans. However, in 1888, he was just about as wrong as he ever had been or ever would be—and neither was the matter "inconsequential." Mosby's cousin, Republican Benjamin Harrison, had won his party's nomination for president; and his Southern cousin was overjoyed as seen in this article in the *Alexandria Gazette*:

Alexandria Gazette – July 6, 1888

Col. Mosby.—The San Francisco Examiner of June 26th says: "the happiest man in town over the nomination is Col. Mosby, who is a first cousin to Harrison. 'You know,' said he, 'I have been all along hoping that he will receive the nomination. I don't want to say too much, but Harrison is a good man. A strong man, too. There are no half-way measures about him. I certainly admire the man, and I most certainly am pleased, as he is a relative of mine.'"

This was in fact one instance in which John Mosby's judgment proved woefully wrong. Indeed, cousin Ben with his sanctimonious self-righteousness and sectional partisanship drove him to stay home on election day when Harrison ran for a second term. Prior thereto, Mosby, had voted for every Republican president except Lincoln and was known to have left a sick bed to exercise his franchise. But when Harrison ran for a second term, the little Virginian just stayed home. However, recognition of the anti-Southern bias of Harrison seems one of those few instances in which John Mosby was either not being altogether honest or was exhibiting his unfortunate naïvete. The man cannot have been unaware of the "sectional bigotry" of men like Hayes and Garfield and their cabinets, "bigotry" abundantly demonstrated when Garfield, at the urging of Northern Republicans, forced the Virginia Republican Party to embrace William Mahone and his Readjusters with its heavily-Negro element, so reminiscent of reconstruction!

Mosby was not stupid nor, despite being in China at the time, was he ill-informed. That only Harrison should have seen his trenchant disapproval for his anti-Southern sentiments and actions is more than a little suspicious. It is possible that "Cousin Ben," being a "Harrison" and therefore kinfolk, was held by Mosby to a higher standard than Hayes or Garfield or Arthur—and later McKinley—and their factotums. But whatever the reason, Harrison seems to be the only Northern Republican whom Mosby decried for a bias that was evident in every Republican leader after Grant! But at the time, much was being made in the press of Harrison's familial relationship with Mosby. And as was usually the case, not all such references were positive:

Wichita Daily Eagle – July 7, 1888

We notice that a few Democratic papers are compromising themselves by trying to compromise Gen. Ben Harrison with the statement that he is first cousin to General Mosby, of Confederate fame. These would-be smirchers are bound to admit Mosby was perhaps the dashingest cavalry leader in the rebel army; that there never was any half-heartedness about him, but that after making the best fight he could in a bad cause he surrendered unconditionally and without mental reservation, and has since proven his loyalty by acts as well as words.

General Harrison's kinship to General Mosby, although the result of circumstances over which he had no control, is yet a matter over which he has no cause for regret, however much he may deprecate his course in 1861. If the circumstances of being related to Mosby be a discredit to a person who put his own loyalty to the Union to the test at that time, what must be said of those slack-water critics who found unfeigned delight in the rebel chieftain's temporary success, which imperiled the life of the nation? Bah.

Anderson Intelligencer – July 12, 1888

—The Republican biographers of General Harrison are making the most of his war record, and they are bringing in all of his soldier kinfolk. But they have left out one of the general's cousins who cut a considerable figure in the war. This is the famous General Mosby, of Virginia. Mosby is Harrison's own cousin. He was a terror to the Union army and one of the most dashing cavalry leaders in history. Will the Republican campaign biographers please make a note of the fact that Mosby is their candidate's cousin?

The consular chickens were finally coming home to roost to the discomfort of Secretary Bayard of the Department of State. The *San Francisco Chronicle*'s article was a tribute to Mosby and his suffering at the hands of the government he so ably served. Most of the California papers were sympathetic to him, at least while he remained on the West Coast:

San Francisco Chronicle – July 19, 1888 (Edited)
COLONEL MOSBY'S LETTER.

If Secretary Bayard ever passed an uncomfortable quarter of an hour, it must have been while reading the open letter addressed to him by Colonel

John S. Mosby, late Consul of the United States to Hongkong. Colonel Mosby calls Mr. Bayard's attention to the fact that he (Mosby) was charged with insubordination in refusing to obey orders issued to him by a former Secretary of the Treasury in reference to the issuance of consular certificates to Chinamen desiring to come to this country, and then points out to Mr. Bayard that under his management of the Department of State the Treasury orders, as well as his (Bayard's) instructions to Consuls, were promptly revoked, and that the State Department permitted Chinamen who had crossed the ocean on consular certificates to be sent back to their homes.

Colonel Mosby goes on to say: "In August last you instructed my successor to issue such certificates, and charged me with insubordination for not doing it. You then recalled your instructions and now you ask Congress to amend the law so as to enable a Consul to do what you then said he had a right to do. If the law has already conferred the power, why do you want to amend it?"... The trouble appears to be that Secretary Bayard, as usual, allowed the Department of State to be managed by the foreign representative in Washington, in the interests of his Government instead of ours. He yielded to the demand of the Chinese Minister that Consuls be instructed to issue certificates to Chinamen desiring to come to this country and was not careful to read the law before taking action. Had he done so he would have seen at once that the McCulloch circular came into conflict with the Restriction act, just as Colonel Mosby said it did.

Bayard appears to be the most conspicuous failure as head of the Department of State that this country has had for a great many years. Imagine Seward or Blaine so eager to carry out the wishes of a Chinese Ambassador as to instruct the Consuls of the United States to violate a plain and easily understood act of Congress, like the Restriction act. Such a thing can hardly be conceived of, with anybody but a Bayard in charge of that most important department.

Colonel Mosby says to Secretary Bayard that it is the duty of the latter to make atonement for the injustice done to him. We fear he will have to wait a long time for any confession of error from Mr. Bayard. That gentleman is so strongly fortified by self-conceit and a lofty opinion of himself that he will scarcely be persuaded to descend from the pedestal on which he has placed himself, even to do an act of simply justice: but Colonel Mosby's letter is a complete vindication in itself, without a word from Mr. Bayard.

Yet again, Mosby's position was validated by the law and by objective knowledge. This publication had no particular position with regard to him, and so all that it required of Mosby was an argument that upheld his position vis-à-vis the secretary of state. Obviously, he provided one.

The consular certificate matter still grabbed headlines, especially in the papers on the West Coast, an area that was very much concerned with Chinese "immigration." After all, there were not all that many Chinese in Virginia:

San Francisco Chronicle - **August 7, 1888 (Edited)**

BAYARD AND BEE.

How They Worked for the Chinese.

F.'s Touching Devotion to Cheng.

Story of the Mosby Episode and the Consular Certificate Game.

No more interesting chapter of inside political history has recently come to its legitimate denouement than that which involved the removal of Colonel Mosby from his position as Consul at Hongkong. It is another story of Secretary Bayard's un-Bayardlike truckling to foreign powers, of time's revenges, of grave suspicions and of political faithlessness, which is particular pertinent. It runs as follows:

Colonel John S. Mosby was appointed Consul for the United States at Hongkong, by President Hayes, August 28, 1878. He was an interested observer of the extensive Chinese emigration going on from the British port, but he took no part either in aiding or restricting it, and he felt still further justified in maintaining his neutral position when he found that the Restriction act of 1882 imposed no duties upon Consuls, and in fact said nothing at all about them.

It was with a good deal of surprise, therefore, when on or about the first of March, 1885, his friend Captain Berry of the City of Peking handed him the following letter:

IMPERIAL CHINESE CONSULATE-GENERAL

San Francisco, January 21, 1885

Dear Sir: under the instructions given by the Secretary of the Treasury,

American Consuls can give a certificate to the exempt class in any foreign port where there is no Chinese Consul.

One of the Chinese benevolent societies has elected a President and Vice-President for this year (Wing Yung Society) who are residents of Hongkong, and they desire to come here. There is no one authorized to give them a certificate except the Consul, and you will be requested to do so. There is no question about the status of them; they are not laborers, but coming on alone. The President's name is Lee Kim Wah, over 50 years of age; the Vice-President's being Low Yung Fong, aged about 47. Yours truly, F.A. Bee.

P.S. – the credentials of these men have been sent to Hongkong, which you can see if you desire.

Accompanying this letter, in which the thin end of a great disruptive wedge was artfully introduced, was a copy of the circular of instructions referred to in Bee's letter, issued by the Treasury Department at Washington. It was addressed, as it was but right it should be, "to officers of the customs and others," was signed by H. McCulloch as Secretary, and was issued "to promote uniformity in the admission of Chinese persons of the exempt class under the act of July 5, 1884."

When Mosby had read Bee's letter he was equally amused and disgusted. He was amused at the cunning of the play made, and he was disgusted at the attempt made to draw him into it. As a matter of fact, this was the first he had heard or seen of the Treasury circular; and as a matter of fact too, he was certain that he had no more to do with the Secretary of the Treasury than he had with Mr. Bee. In order to dispose of the Bee portion of the affair he sat down at once and wrote on a slip of paper that the Treasury circular was addressed to customs officers, and not to consuls, and that it was at best but an implied permission for consuls to issue the certificates in question. He added that he had no intention to avail himself of this permission by implication, because he believed it contrary to law, and having finished this "opinion," he handed it to Captain Berry, and begged him to give it to Bee as his answer to that Chinese official's attempt to run the United States consular department.

The matter did not end there, however. Evidently the Chinese officials, both at home and abroad, had imagined that the opening power of the carefully prepared and dexterously inserted wedge would have been felt about this time, for not only did the "benevolent" old gentlemen, Messrs. Lee Kim Wah and Low Yung Fon apply to Mosby for the coveted certificates, but these would-be exiles were followed by other "exempts, who wanted to see the Melliean man's land before they died. The thing got so serious at last that Mosby sat him down and wrote the following letter to Mr. Bayard's assistant Secretary.

United States CONSULATE

Hongkong, April 4, 1885.

Sir: Herewith I inclose a letter from F. A. Bee, Esq., Consul for the empire of China at San Francisco, requesting me to grant a certificate to two Chinese residents of Hongkong, who desire to go to the United States, in accordance with paragraph 2 of the circular of the Treasury Department, dated December 6, 1881. I have declined to issue certificates both to these as well as other Chinese claiming to be merchants who desire to go to California, for the following reasons:

First – I have received no instructions from the State Department requiring me to give such certificates to Chinese, and I do not think the Secretary of the Treasury has legal authority to give validity to them if granted, or to impose any such duty on me. I would violate no law in certifying that a Chinaman was a merchant, student or traveler, just as I might certify to any other fact within my knowledge, but in my opinion the certificate would not be admissible as evidence to prove the fact. The Courts decided that the provision in the original act of May 6, 1882, for certificates to be issued by the Chinese Government to its subjects who were entitled by treaty to go to the United States was only directory: that is, that while it provided one mode of proof it did not exclude other evidences. My understanding is that the law was changed so as to meet this very point; that is, the amended act is mandatory, and makes it a condition precedent to the right of continuing of the exempt class to the United States that they shall have a certificate of their status issued by the Government of which they are subjects, and vised[*] by the United States Minister to the country, or the Consul at their port of departure.

Second – It is clear that the law is imperative requiring such certificates, as it is expressly declared to be "the sole evidence permissible on the part of the person so producing the same to establish a right of entry into the United States." A certificate of identification issued by a Government is, therefore, of no legal value or authority unless the person to whom it is given is a subject of that Government. There is nothing in the original or amended act giving even the color of right to a Consul to issue such certificate; his duty is limited to making an "examination as to the truth of the statements set forth in said certificate," etc., before indorsing it. It is a well known fact that all Chinese emigrants to the United States embark at Hongkong (which is a British colony) and, with very few exceptions, are subjects of the Emperor of China. In my opinion, the circular of the Treasury Department, practically enforced, would operate as a nullification of the Chinese Restriction act, as it could never have been intended by Congress to invest the Consul at Hongkong with the power which the circular undertakes to give him. There is no Consul stationed at Hongkong. As the circular of the Secretary of the Treasury, therefore, is clearly ultra vires [beyond one's legal power or authority-vph], I pay no respect to it. It was clearly the intention of Congress to make it a condition of entry by Chinese, other than laborers into the United States, that they shall have first a certificate identifying them from the Government of which they are subjects; second, said certificates must be indorsed by the United States Minister or by the Consul at the port of departure.

In my opinion the Consul, as well as the Minister who indorses the certificate, must be accredited to the country that issues it; in other words, it is not my duty to vise[*] certificates issued by the Government of China. The American Consul in China, living in the district from which the emigrant departs, must do so, as he alone could ascertain the truth of the statements contained in the certificate. The whole of the Chinese emigration to the United States is from the Kwang-tung province of Southern China, and therefore this work must be done by the United States Consul at Canton. The Hongkong government has never undertaken to issue such certificates to Chinese; if it did, it would then be my duty to examine into the truth of them. I shall certainly not volunteer to do this work. I have, etc.,

John S. Mosby

United States Consul

No reply came to this communication of Mosby's but in its place came the curt notification that his services were no longer required by the Department of State. Now this notification of removal Mosby observed was dated May 1st, while his letter to Mr. Adee given above was written on April 4th, so that he could scarcely believe it could have reached Washington in twenty-six days; that is, he could not believe that the removal was a consequence. As a matter of fact Mosby's letter was not received by the State Department until May 13th, or twelve days after the letter of removal was written. The reader is asked to remember this. Mosby waited at Hongkong until his successor, Consul Robert E. Withers, arrived, which was on July 4th, 1885, and then set sail for home, determined to find out one or two things which had at once puzzled and rankled him.

The first thing he found out was that Withers, who had supplanted him, was a great personal friend of Bayard's that he had indeed been one of the leaders in the boom of Bayard for President. He inferred, therefore, that for some reason or other this Hongkong consulate must be considered a very good thing.

He found in the next place that Withers had made the acquaintance of Bee while waiting in San Francisco for the China steamer to start, that he had in fact been conducted to the steamer by the representative of his Imperial Majesty, and that he had been indorsed by that official as a pleasant fellow who was not of the Mosby stiff-neck order.

He found also that this stiff-necked action had considerably exercised the various departments and offices, and had especially roused the Imperial Chinese Consul at San Francisco. He had, by the by, received a sample of engraved Orientalism before leaving Hongkong. When the discussion on the question of Consular certificates was going on the Chronicle interviewed Consul Bee on the matter (June 8, 1885), and a copy of the paper containing the report was received by Mosby in due time. In the interview he found the most extraordinary statements. The first was Bee's assertion that Mosby was behind the times and had not read the latest decisions of the United States Courts, which had distinctly ruled upon the admissibility of Chinese bearing United States Consular certificates. To the contrary, Mosby had pamphlet copies of both decisions on his table at that very time and he knew their contents well. In the cases of Chen Cheong before the Supreme Court and Ah Ping before the Circuit Court – the cases to which Bee referred – the petitioners did not have certificates from any United States Consul, and therefore, as no such question as the right of a consul to grant a certificate was raised on the facts, the Court had expressed no opinion upon it at all.

The second most extraordinary statement of Bee's was that Mosby was all wrong, as the Chinese Restriction act plainly said that United States Consuls could grant such certificates. To "lend artistic verisimilitude to an otherwise bald and unattractive" statement, Bee, like his Oriental prototype actually went so far as to quote this provision from the act. This staggered Mosby for the moment, and he confessed to the editor of the Hongkong Telegraph, with whom he was conversing on the subject, that if this were so he had made an egregious ass of himself and deserved recall. On searching the Restriction act, however, it was found that there was nothing of the sort in it. Then the quotation became familiar to Mosby, and turning to his copy of Bee's communication of January 21st, he found that the clever Consul had been quoting from the famous Treasury circular.

Remembering all this "diplomacy," Mosby could not help thinking that there was a peculiar nearness in certain dates. He had received Bee's letter about the 1st of March. Bee would have received his rather contemptuous answer about the middle of April, both the Chinese Minister at Washington and Secretary Bayard could have been notified by the end of the same month of Mosby's insubordination, and the order of removal was written on the 1st day of May. All this looked strange, and it looked stranger still when the light of future events came to be cast upon it.

Some time after his return to the United States Mosby learned that the heads of the departments had not been without their share of the fun. When Bayard was handed Mosby's letter, received May 13, 1885, he felt so secure of the right of his position that he sent the Mosby letter to Manning as soon as it had been properly filed, indexed, indorsed, etc. This took until May 27th. Unlike Bayard, Manning saw the force of the Mosby reasoning and at once consulted with the Solicitor of the Treasury upon the subject. On the 6th of July, the Solicitor sent his opinion to Manning, it being that the concluding phrase of the second section of the Treasury circular was in conflict with the laws, and that the words "or if there be no such Chinese officer stationed at such port, or a like certificate to be issued by a United States consular officer," should be stricken out of the orders. Acting Secretary Fairchild informed the Collector of Customs at San Francisco of this change in the filing July 13th, and there it was supposed the matter would rest…

By no means was this the case, however. The Treasury, it is true, had reconsidered its own orders, had communicated its new orders to the Collector at San Francisco and had also, there is small doubt, made Bayard acquainted with the change of front, according to the custom of interdepartmental courtesy; but on August 5th, twenty-three days after, Cheng Tsao Ju complains to Bayard that customs authorities at San Francisco are not attending to their duties. …

Having thus paved the way, Minister Cheng then proceeds to give another tap to the wedge. "The Secretary of State," writes the Chinese Minister, "is respectfully requested to instruct the newly appointed United States Consul to Hongkong to issue to such Chinese merchants certificates in accordance with the law and the Treasury circular. This would greatly facilitate the trade and increase the commercial interests between the United States and China."

This "request" of Chang Tsao Ju's, it must not be forgotten, was made nearly three weeks after the rescindment of the vital section of that very circular which he asks to have enforced, but despite this fact the contemptuous tone of the Chinese official's undated and unsigned memorandum, Bayard duly makes his kowtow and writes with as much low-pitched gratitude as though he had been permitted to kiss the Emperor's big toe. His reply ran as follows:

Department of State

Washington, August 11, 1885

Sir: I had the honor to receive, on the 5th inst., through the secretary of your legation, your unsigned memorandum, in which you refer to the frequent departure of Chinese subjects, not laborers, under the stipulations of existing treaty, from the foreign port of Hongkong * * * and ask that the newly appointed consul there be instructed to issue to such Chinese merchants departing from that port certificates in accordance with the existing statues and with the second rule of the circular of the Secretary of the Treasury, darted December 6, 1884 (but which was rescinded in July, 1885).* * * The circular of the Secretary of the Treasury of December 6, 1884, was in due time communicated to the United States Consul at Hongkong, among others, with instructions to carry out its provisions, especially in respect of the second rule thereof. This department is unaware of any obstacle to the fulfillment of that instruction beyond certain technical objections raised by the late consul, Mr. Mosby. Nevertheless, in pursuance of the request conveyed by the memorandum, and in order that no possible interruption of the prescribed rule of conduct of the consul in the premises may ensue by reason of the recent changes in the incumbency of the office at Hongkong, an instruction will be sent forthwith to Mr. Robert E. Withers, the newly appointed consul at that port. * * * Accept, etc., T. F. Bayard.

According to his promise to the Chinese Minister Mr. Bayard that very same day wrote to Mr. Withers. After the usual preamble the letter reads: The representations of the Chinese Minister are probably due to the course of your predecessor in raising obstacles to the execution of the Treasury circular. You will find Mr. Mosby's objection set forth in terms amounting to a refusal on his part to comply with the orders of the authority intrusted by the statute of July 6, 1884, with its execution in his dispatch, April 4, 1885. As a change in the Hongkong Consulate was then determined, it seemed unnecessary to engage in a discussion of the points involved, and preferable to leave the matter until it should be made the occasion of an instruction to you as Mr. Mosby's successor. Without examining Mr. Mosby's argument in detail – it is to be observed that it is specious and technical merely – it ignores wholly the paramount duty of the Government to so administer the statute, and with it the treaty, which is of equal obligation as the supreme law of the land, that the letter and spirit of both shall be alike observed. * * *

It is probable that, in accordance with the suggestion of the Chinese Minister, a form of certificate will shortly be prescribed for the use of our consuls in countries other than China. * * *

The matter is now under the consideration of the Secretary of the Treasury. I am, etc.,

T. F. BAYARD

Here again there are two remarkable statements to be considered: First, that Bayard says that it was determined to remove Mosby because of his insubordination, expressed in his dispatch of April 4, 1885. That dispatch, as has been shown, was not received by the State Department until May 13th, while Mosby's removal had been "determined" on some weeks previous. ... Second, Bayard writes to Withers on August 10th that the suggestions of the Chinese Minister (those contained in the unsigned memorandum of August 5th, were at that time under the consideration of the Secretary of the Treasury. Here again, Mr. Bayard was more inventive than exact, for it was not until a week after that he submitted the matter to Mr. Manning. The date is to be found in the public documents – it was August 17, 1885. ... Bayard goes on to complain of Mosby's insubordination and ends by saying that "instructions will therefore, be sent to Mr. Withers at an early day directing him to carry out the Treasury instructions," when, as a matter of fact, these instructions had been sent out a week before. This is an example of Bayardesque retroscience which is amusing though by no means unique. This letter opened Manning's eyes to what was going on and he wrote back to Bayard that he must surely have overlooked the fact that the Treasury circular had been seriously amended since July. There must have been considerable worry in the Secretary of State's office when this note was received, and it was not until September 19th that Bayard summoned up courage enough to acquaint the terrible Cheng Tsao Ju with the sad news of the death of section 2 of the Treasury circular, and even then he had to do it through the proxy of James D. Porter as acting Secretary. The public documents are silent as to how Cheng Tsao Ju received this information, but it is known that Bayard accepted the dose, and, after waiting as long as he thought safe, wrote out to Withers in November, 1885, revoking the first orders.

Between whiles, however, Mr. Withers had succeeded in issuing quite a goodly number of Consular certificates which in good time were presented at the Custom-house in San Francisco, and then the fun began. Hager would not accept them, Bee complained to Cheng, Cheng worked on Bayard, Bayard appealed to Manning, Manning telegraphed special instructions to Hager, and Hager let the Chinese in on the certificates. The papers got hold of all this wire-pulling, and spoke right out in meeting about it. Morrow went with the papers to Manning, and by February 1886, the kibosh was put on the matter, so far as the Treasury Department was concerned… This was too much for Bayard and on March 30th he addressed a long reply to the Chinese Minister. It is too long to give entire, but like all of Bayard's communications it contains two remarkable statements. The first is as follows:

The act of Congress of July 5, 1884, while purporting to execute the provisions of the treaty, does not in terms do so with regard to certain of the exempted classes. * * * It is silent as to Chinese persons who, being subjects of China, desire to depart for the United States from some other country than China. This ought to be printed in parallel columns with his instructions to Withers, where he says that Mosby's argument is specious and technical and that the law must be observed in letter and spirit.

The second statement is as follows:

The circular of the Treasury Department * * * was designed to remedy the ambiguity of the statute * * * It soon became clear that the warrant of law for such original certification by the United States consuls was insufficient. It involved the absurdity of a consul certifying by his visa to the truth and sufficiency of his own certificate; and under it the consul purported to give official evidence of a matter not within his representative competency to certify. Hence this part of the Treasury circular was revoked on the 13th of July, 1885. This language in its turn ought to be printed in parallel columns with Mosby's letter to the State Department, written April 4, 1885. This method of comparison would show that the language of insubordination upon which Mosby was officially stated to have been removed was now being used by Secretary Bayard as the highest kind of authority. Bayard feels the strength of the Mosby reasoning so thoroughly that he writes to Mr. Cheng that he is "constrained to reply that the reasons which led to the abandonment" of the section "are conclusive against its removal." … This was nothing more or less than asking for the erection of the Treasury circular into law. Cleveland fell into Bayard's line of thinking, and on April 6, 1886, sent a special message to Congress, recommending the framing and passage of the Consular Certificate bill. The message was referred to the Committee on Foreign Relations, and that committee refused to report it as a bill. They saw what an inundation of Chinese the measure would mean, and it should not be forgotten that among those most active in opposing the contemplated measure was that member of the committee, Senator Benjamin Harrison. [* vise/vised (verb): a legal term meaning "to confirm"-vph]

This long narrative is included with only moderate editing because it illustrates the lies and deceits used by the Department of State first in an attempt to suborn Mosby into doing what was illegal and then to punish him for his refusal to do it. It also shows that Withers, a Democratic appointee, was doing what Mosby had refused to do. However, interesting as all of this was with regard to Mosby's situation in Hong Kong, when it came to making a judgment about him as a man (the reason for this book), there is one quote that helps to define the matter, his admission to the Hong Kong newspaper editor that if he were incorrect in his judgment, he had made an "egregious ass" of himself and deserved recall. This seems relatively unimportant in the grand scheme of things, but it takes a man of character to willingly acknowledge when he is in error and, even more importantly, to admit to that error and accept such chastisement as may follow its commission. How many evils have been perpetuated not by evil men, but by men who could not bring themselves to admit that they were wrong? Of course, Mosby was removed by the election of Cleveland, though doubtless that action delighted those in the Republican administration as well as the rejoicing Democrats.

Mosby testified in the following article that the West was "safe" for Harrison, which made him happy indeed. Besides Harrison being his cousin, undoubtedly, Mosby saw Harrison as a "Grant-like" figure—a fellow soldier and not a politician. But politician, soldier, or both, Harrison proved to be a great disappointment to his Virginia relative; and as many found over the years, it was not prudent to disappoint John Mosby:

Alexandria Gazette – August 27, 1888

Col. Tarpey, the California member of the national democratic committee, who is here says that Harrison's record on the Chinese question will give that State to The Democrats. To the contrary, a letter received here from Col. Mosby, now a resident of San Francisco, says the whole Pacific slope is safe for Harrison.

A Republican newspaper tried to explain to a Democratic organ the difference between former Confederates who became Republicans and those who chose to be Democrats. It made the claim that men like Mosby and Longstreet "repented" of their support of the South, a claim that was erroneous. Mosby never repented or asked pardon of anything he did. On the other hand, the paper was right when it stated that Mosby and the others admitted to the reality of the situation and went on with their lives. But the idea that there was any need for "repentance," especially given the type of war waged by the Union, is patent nonsense. All that was necessary, as Mosby understood it, was to accept reality and go on as best one could within the parameters of ethical soundness:

Sentinel and Republican – September 5, 1888

The Difference

It is a difficult thing to get the Register to understand the difference between Longstreet, Mosby and Mahone, and the unrepentant rebel brigadiers. It classes them all together and because the general government favors such ex-rebel soldiers as Longstreet and Mosby and Mahone, who recognize the fact that the Lost Cause was lost when they were whipped, because they were recognized for their manly submission to the settlement of the trouble as they had proposed to settle—because they are favored the Register claims that all the other unwashed, unregenerated rebel brigadiers should be placed on the same footing as to favors and so forth. The Register forgets that the world all over makes a difference between a repentant man and a man who is not repentant. Every community has its cases in which depraved and besotted men have repented and accepted a better life that conforms to moral precepts, and thus it is with Longstreet, Mosby and Mahone, they have repented politically; they recognize the fact that the Lost Cause—slavery is dead, while the other brigadiers are still glorifying the Lost Cause—slavery—and expressing hope for its resurrection. Does the Register see the difference?

One hopes Mosby never saw this article, even though it supported his course of action. It would have offended him. Also, the contention that the "unregenerate" Southern brigadiers—that is, The Democrats!—were glorifying slavery; and hoping for its resurrection was also ridiculous, though no doubt the race problems in the South were very real. Indeed, many Southerners were working toward an end to the "peculiar institution" prior to the onset of the war. But the idea that those who did not embrace the Republican Party were seeking a reinstitution of slavery is offensive drivel.

The "Chinese question" continued apace with Mosby's objections being dismissed out of hand. From the correspondence exposed by the press, it would seem that the matter involved a great deal more than efforts to smuggle into the United States a few coolies and humble merchants:

San Francisco Chronicle – September 6, 1888 (Edited)

[No. 70]

Memorandum of Chinese Minister.

Memorandum received from the Chinese minister August 5, 1885, referring to the second rule of the circular dated December 6 1884, issued by the Secretary of the Treasury for the admission of Chinese persons of the exempt class under the act of July 5, 1884, that "Chinese subjects, not laborers, desiring to come to the United States from countries other than China, may do so on production of a certificate corresponding to that required by section G of the act of July 5, 1884, to be issued by a Chinese diplomatic or consular officer, of if there be no such Chinese officer stationed at such port, on a like certificate to be issued by a United States consular officer,"… The Secretary of State is respectfully requested to instruct the newly appointed United States Consul to Hongkong to issue such Chinese merchants certificates in accordance with the law and circular mentioned It is stated that certain Chinese merchants coming from the Hawaiian islands to this country with certificates issued by a United States Consul there, were met with objections by the customs authorities at San Francisco on the ground that the certificates were not drawn in the proper form. To avoid such objections by the customs authorities, the Secretary of State is also respectfully requested to cause a fixed form of certificate to be drawn and issued to all the United States consular officers residing in those countries where Chinese merchants have commercial intercourse with the United States.

The circular of the Secretary of the Treasury of December 6, 1884, was in due time communicated to the United States Consul at Hongkong, among others, with instructions to carry out its provisions, especially in respect of the second rule thereof. *This department is unaware of any obstacle to the fulfillment of that instruction beyond certain technical objections raised by the late consul, Mr. Mosby; nevertheless, in pursuance of the request conveyed by the memorandum, and in order that no possible interruption of the prescribed rule of conduct of the Consul in the premises may ensue by reason of the recent change in the incumbency of the office at Hongkong, an instruction will be sent forthwith to Robert E. Withers, the newly appointed Consul at that port* [emphasis vph].

The *Alexandria Gazette* then presented a small article that poked a little fun at Mosby in an incident that took place during a Republican parade in San Francisco:

Alexandria Gazette – October 2, 1888

Mosby and the Flag—Col. John S. Mosby, the dashing confederate guerrilla, was standing in line for the republican parade in front of the palace Hotel last evening, with a small Harrison badge in his bouquet button hole. All the other members of the division to which the Colonel belonged carried a small American flag. An eccentric democratic millionaire rushed up to M. M. Estee, the well-known Napa viticulturist, and exclaimed excitedly, "Say! Estee; make that old rebel Mosby carry the stars and stripes. It will do the old reprobate good." Mr. Estee thought it was a good idea, and Jake Steppacher handed a flag to Col. Mosby, who carried it without blushing.— San Francisco Examiner.

And so cousin Ben was elected as Mosby had predicted. Rumors immediately began to circulate that he would be offered a consular position in Harrison's government if for no other reason than their family connection. This rather clearly indicated that Mosby was not all that happy with the railroad, or perhaps the railroad was not all that happy with Mosby. Of course, nothing was said about why that should be the case:

Alexandria Gazette – November 17, 1888

Col. Mosby.—The San Francisco Post says: "Among the most pleased men in the city over the election of General Harrison to the presidency is Colonel Mosby, who, by the way, is the General's first cousin. It is rumored that Colonel Mosby will go back to Hong Kong as Consul. There has never been a Consul at any port of any nation who made for himself so many friends, and who so completely won the respect of everybody with whom he was brought in contact as Colonel John S. Mosby. He was known there as the most honest Consul that Hong Kong ever had.

Mosby's book had been out for quite a while before it was discovered—and rejected—by the *Chicago Tribune*. The Tribune, not content with disliking its contents, went further to call the work "badly written" and to complain about typographical errors—something that should have been taken up with the publisher, not the author! Of course, it was Mosby's method of warfare that was in fact the problem. And finally, the paper took the usual shot in these matters—even Southerners wouldn't like his book:

Chicago Tribune – **November 17, 1888**

Brief Notices

If the story of the exploits of Marion and Sumter were spun out to great length not even all the glamour of the Revolution would make it interesting, because the same thing would be told over and over again, one guerrilla exploit be pretty nearly the counterpart of every other. Therefore the book in which Col. John S. Mosby, C.S.A., tells of his deeds in cutting off Federal outposts, capturing sutlers, and getting the better of railway trains becomes intensely wearisome after the first few chapters. It is too much of a muchness. Furthermore, it is badly written, and the typographical errors are too frequent and inexcusable. Mosby was a thorn in the side of the Union army, and did more real service for the Confederacy than many of its Generals or army commanders. But the narrative of his dashes and forays can never vie in interest with the tale of honest, legitimate warfare. It is doubtful whether Southern readers, even, will be interested in Mosby's long-drawn out account of his monotonous pillagings and plunderings. (Dodd, Mead & Co., New York.)

But not all Northern critics were negative in their comments. The *Indianapolis Journal* was objective and even defended Mosby from the term "guerrilla," also noting that his book did not indulge in some of the "bravado and braggadocio" of which other military writers—North and South—were guilty. For Mosby, that wasn't necessary. The truth was sufficient to give glory to both himself and his command. Still, considering what so many other "soldiers" wrote about their service in the war, it is comforting to see him defended from such a claim—and by a Northern newspaper.

Indianapolis Journal – **November 19, 1888**

"Mosby's War Reminiscences" is the latest contribution to the historical literature of the war period. It is hardly necessary to say the author is John S. Mosby, late colonel in the confederate army and a noted cavalry officer during the war. Mosby was called a guerrilla, but he shows that he was regularly commissioned and attached to the Southern army, though he had pretty large discretionary powers as to his movements and operations. He was a brave and dashing officer, and did good service in his way. His book describes his operations in a style that shows considerable knowledge of the art of war and a good deal of literary culture. There is no bravado or braggadocio about it. Mosby deserves great credit for having fully and unreservedly accepted the results of the war as soon as it ended. He has written a soldierly and interesting book. Illustrated. Cloth, $1.25. New York: Dodd, Mead & Co. Indianapolis: The Bowen-Merrill Company.

Finally, the court of claims made its determination on Mosby's suit for his consul fees:

San Francisco Chronicle – December 4, 1888

STATE AND NATION

Col. Mosby Wins a Victory

Court of Claims has rendered judgment in favor of Colonel John S. Mosby for $13,830.

MOSBY VICTORIOUS

A Decision in His Favor Rendered by the Court of Claims.

Washington, December 3.—The Court of Claims to-day rendered judgment in favor of Colonel John S. Mosby for $13,839. This amount represented certain fees received by him while Consul-General to China, but which the accounting officers of the treasury withheld as belonging to the Government. The Court held that as they were not designated by the President as official fees, they should be considered as the Consul-General's personal emoluments.

Colonel Mosby explained the nature of his claim to a Chronicle reporter yesterday. When he was appointed Consul to Hongkong the American Consulate there was the subject of such unsavory scandals, in connection with the alleged misappropriation of fees, that, to keep his own reputation untarnished, he determined to handle none of this money until his legal right to it was determined. Accordingly, he turned over to the United States Treasury all the fees he received, amounting to $13,839. As is well known, Colonel Mosby was dismissed by the present Democratic Administration for "offensive partisanship," he being one of the first to suffer for that broad infraction of President Cleveland's code.

When he asked for a restitution of the fees the properly belonged to the Consulate, he was met by the plea that, while the fees had undoubtedly been his in the first place, his act of paying them into the Treasury had been purely a voluntary one and was, in fact, a gift of them to the Government. This the Colonel denied, and brought suit against the Government and argued the case himself before the Court of Claims. In spite of the old adage that an attorney who argues his own case has a fool for a client, the Court has given him a judgment for the full amount of his claim.

Mosby had uncovered monumental corruption in the Asian consular system, corruption that involved Republicans! If exposing corrupt Republicans was "offensive" to Cleveland, then Mosby's dismissal was understandable. Surely, the exposure of Republican crooks benefited Democrats! One would think that Cleveland would have left Mosby where he was at least until the whole ring was exposed, but no, he appointed a man who was unlikely to finish Mosby's job even if the crooks were Republicans. As Lewis Carroll once wrote, "Curioser and curioser."

Another paper reported on Mosby's (short-lived) victory in the courts and saw fit to recap the matter for its readership:

Sacramento Daily Record-Union – December 4, 1888

MOSBY'S FEES.

The Ex-Chinese Consul Gets Judgment for $13,829.

Washington, December 3d.—The Court of Claims to-day gave judgment for $13,839, in favor of Colonel John S. Mosby, late United States Consul-General to China. This represents fees for certificates to Chinese immigrants to the United States, etc., collected in an official capacity, and for which accounting the officers of the Treasury refused to allow him credit. The facts in the case are about as follows: General Mosby, while Consul- General at Hongkong from February 1879, till July, 1885, collected for service fees aggregating $8,985, which he believed belong to him as perquisites of the office. The State Department decided adversely and he, in order to avoid a controversy with superior officers, turned the money into the Treasury. On retiring from the position in 1885 he demanded a return of the money, but the Treasury officials declined, although admitting that at least a portion of the fees belong to him. Comptroller Durham refused to allow Mosby credit for the fees, on the ground that he had voluntarily paid his own money into the Treasury. Mosby then brought suit against the Government in the Court of Claims. Last winter he went to Washington and argued his own case before the Court. The Court holds that General Mosby was entitled to that portion of the amount collected.

And still, the coverage went on, including a mention in the Daily Record Union that the court had "rebuked" the government for keeping fees that it knew belonged to plaintiff Mosby:

Daily Morning Astorian – December 4, 1888
MOSBY'S CLAIM RECOGNIZED.

Washington, Dec. 3.—The court of claims to-day gave judgment for $13,839 in favor of Col. John T. Mosby [sic], late U.S. consul-general to China. This represents fees for issuing certificates to Chinese immigrants to the United States, etc., collected in official capacity for which the accounting officers of the treasury refused to allow him credit.

Fort Worth Daily Gazette – December 4, 1888
CLAIMS ALLOWED.

Washington, Dec. 3—The court of claims to day gave judgment for $13,839 in favor of Colonel John S. Mosby, late United States consul-general to China. These sums represents fees for issuing certificates to Chinese immigrants to the United States, etc., collected in his official capacity and for which the accounting officers of the treasury refused to allow him credit.

Sacramento Daily Record Union – December 5, 1888

The Administration's treatment of ex-Consul Mosby, in refusing to pay back to him fees he had paid in, subject to determination of his legal right to them, has been rebuked by the Court of Claims. The Government officials, while admitting that the fees belong to Colonel Mosby originally claimed that as he had turned them in to the Treasury Department, he had surrendered his right to them. Had an ordinary business house set up such a claim against one of its employees who left his money in its treasury subject to final settlement, the business world would have scorned it.

The Gazette published another election article involving Mosby, who believed that "Cousin Ben" might offer him a consular post, but not, he hoped, back in Hong Kong. Why he would want a position that would take him out of the country again is hard to understand as he had returned only three years earlier. Of course, he had seen his children and others in his family as well as his friends; but apparently, something was not right. He couldn't return to Virginia without having another source of income, and it seems his arrangements with the railroad were either unsatisfactory or more tenuous than were admitted:

Fort Worth Daily Gazette – December 9, 1888

Colonel John S. Mosby announces through a San Francisco paper that he will go to Washington next month and remain till after the inauguration. The colonel thinks it is not unlikely that he may be appointed to some consular position, but says that he would like to be sent elsewhere than Hong Kong, as he has spent already six years on that "rock in the sea."

The *Alexandria Gazette* congratulated Mosby on his "victory" against the State Department. Little did either the press or Mosby know that the government did not intend to take his hard-won victory lying down:

Alexandria Gazette – December 12, 1888

Col. Mosby's Claim—Colonel Mosby is to be congratulated on his long fight with the State Department over the fees of the Consulate at Hong Kong. Mosby was an honest Consul, and by his firm stand prevented the flooding of his coast with coolies on consular certificates. He was removed by Cleveland because he was outspoken in his comment, and when he demanded the $13,800 in fees which he had turned over, pending a decision in regard to the right of the Consul to claim them, he was coolly told that he had made a voluntary gift of them to the Government. Mosby brought suit and was fortunate enough to have his case reached in three years by the Court of Claims and to secure a decision in his favor.—San Francisco Chronicle.

In John Mosby's ledger, 1888 would have been considered a successful year. He had triumphed in the courts in his fees' claim. He had seen the consular certificate matter widely exposed in print, including his open letter to Secretary Bayard. His book had been well received; and perhaps the most satisfactory moment of all, his cousin Benjamin Harrison, a Republican, had been elected president. As a result of Harrison's election, Mosby expected the offer of a choice position—and why not? He had proven himself a man of excellent attributes and splendid ethics and had left Hong Kong and China far better than he had found it. Certainly, 1889 promised to be a banner year for the man who was finally overcoming the hatreds of both North and South. All must have seemed right with the world for John Singleton Mosby—but never is the world more dangerous than at such a time.

Chapter 28

1889

Pacta sunt servanda. ~ Agreements should be obeyed.

"It does not matter how slowly you go as long as you do not stop."
~ Confucius

IN THE LAST year of the decade, the press decided to begin its "Mosby coverage" with a very charming and funny "war story." In this case, Mosby was not the figure of fun; rather, his pursuers in the Federal army were:

***Abilene Weekly Reflector* – January 3, 1889**

***St. Paul Daily Globe* – March 15, 1889**

CAPTURING MOSBY.

A Comical Incident of the Late Sectional Difficulty in Our Beloved Country. Youth's Companion.

The truth of the following comical war story is vouched for by its narrator, John Esten Cooke. A body of Federal cavalry had approached very near the Confederate lines, and two or three of them who had gone out to forage came to a cabin in the woods, and, after careful reconnoitering, rapped at the door. A negro woman answered the knock, and seemed very much disturbed at the sight of the bluecoats.

"We want some supper." "Yes, sir."

"But first, is there anybody here?" "No sir."

"Are you sure?"

"Oh, they ain't anybody here but me—'cept—"

"Except who?"

"Only Col. Mosby, sir."

"Col. Mosby!!!" exclaimed the speaker, with at least three exclamation points to his accent, and getting hastily into his saddle.

"Are you joking?" he added. "You'd better not. Is Col. Mosby here?"

"Yes, sir." Stammered the woman in great terror; and at the same moment, a low noise, like that produced by the footsteps of man, was heard inside.

No sooner did the men hear this than they turned their horses' heads and galloped off to their command, where great excitement at once ensued.

It was necessary to act with caution. Mosby's desperate courage was well-known, and he would make all the stouter resistance because he was sure to be hanged to the first tree if he was captured as a "bushwhacker" and an outlaw. Elaborate preparations were made, the cabin surrounded, and the door suddenly burst open. Men rushed in with cocked pistols. But no rebel was to be found.

"Where is Mosby?" thundered the officer.

"Oh, there he is," was the trembling reply of the woman. "Where?"

"There," and the woman pointed to the cradle. "What do you mean?"

"Oh, sir! I don't mean—I didn't mean nothin'! I call him 'Mosby,' sir—'Col. Mosby,' sir—that's his name, sir."

Awaiting her doom, she stood trembling before the intruders. They, on their part, looked from the woman to the baby, sucking away at his thumb, scowled, growled, took another look, saw that the old woman had told the truth, then they burst out laughing, took to their horses and were soon out of sight.

Mosby paid a visit to Harrison and the papers ate it up with many speculations about familial matters, his consular fees, and the possibility of his returning to China—something he had already rather discouraged as a possible situation. Mosby then, in his capacity as a citizen of California, made mention of the fact that the Republicans on the Pacific Slope would like to "have a Department in the cabinet go to California". Mosby pointed out that there were many good Republicans in California who could serve in Harrison's new government but he was dead set against Mahone, apparently the only Virginian being mentioned as a possible cabinet candidate. It would seem that few Virginia Republicans of any power were left after Mahone's takeover of that party.

A reporter suggested that Mosby might be a possible candidate who could serve both California and Virginia, but he "laughed heartily" at this suggestion, though it was not at all out of place. However, why Mosby did not put himself forward as a possible candidate for some position in Harrison's administration is not known; perhaps he did so quietly as he was likely to do under such circumstances. But whatever the case, it soon became clear as it did under Garfield and later under McKinley that no position would be offered to John Mosby—or any other Southerner, even the hated Mahone:

New York Tribune - February 6, 1889

The most important caller to-day on the President-elect was Colonel John S. Mosby, the famous Confederate guerilla leader, later a diplomat in China, now a citizen of California. Colonel Mosby is a relative of General Harrison's as so many hundred other native Virginians are. His grandmother was a cousin of President William Henry Harrison, and he has kept up the family acquaintance. Colonel Mosby while in China overpaid the Government about $16.000 on some Consular transactions. He afterward got a suit for that amount allowed by the Court of Claims, and the item is to go into the appropriation bills before Congress this session. The Colonel is on his way to Washington to look after this business and stopped over here at General Harrison's invitation. He had a long talk with the President-elect to-night.

Talking about the Cabinet, Colonel Mosby said that all the Pacific Slope Republicans were anxious to have a Department go to California. Mr. Swift and Mr. Estee both had their supporters, and Colonel Mosby was inclined to speak of these two candidates impartially. "There are enough other good men, too," he added "to represent California in the Cabinet." Virginia, too, he thought, ought to have a place in the Cabinet. Still he was strongly opposed to General Mahone, who was the only candidate, apparently, from the Old Dominion.

"When I was in Virginia," said the ex-guerilla leader, "General Mahone was fighting on the other side."

"You could represent both States, Virginia and California, Colonel," was suggested.

At this the Colonel laughed heartily. It is understood that he is willing to go back to China under the next Administration.

The meeting of the two men remained, of course, of interest to the press:

Fort Wayne News – February 6, 1889

Harrison and Mosby

They Hold a Conference at the General's Home

Indianapolis, Feb. 6.—The most noted arrival in this city yesterday was Col. Mosby, the ex-confederate guerrilla chieftain, who came to pay his respects to the president-elect. When asked with reference to the object of his visit, he said that he and the president-elect had been in correspondence since the election, and he was invited to stop here on his way to Washington, where he was going on some private business. "The general and I," he added, "are relatives. My grandmother and old President Harrison were first cousins, and we have always preserved the Harrison name in our family."

Mosby sent a note to Gen. Harrison asking at what hour a visit from him would be agreeable. The messenger returned in a short time to the Denison, saying that the general would see him in the evening. Immediately after supper Mosby called, and the two went into a conference.

For the first time, John Mosby spoke in some detail upon the offer made to him in China. He presented the matter as a kind of Arabian Nights fantasy, and perhaps as things were going, he regretted not having taken advantage of an offer that would have settled his finances for the rest of his life—if he had survived and triumphed, of course:

Alexandria Gazette – February 9, 1889

Mosby's Dream of Power

[From the *San Francisco Chronicle*.]

The world has known few men who have had cast at their feet opportunities to become commanders of great armies, with possibilities in sight of forming empires and ruling over them, and fewer still who having possessed such tempting opportunities have had the moral courage to respond to the dictates of conscience and cast them away. Small as is the list of those who have done this, there is an American citizen who can claim the distinguished honor of being numbered among them.

The citizen referred to is the famous Confederate office, Colonel John S. Mosby, whose deeds of valor are registered in the history of a hundred battles of the civil war. Firm as must have been the courage which swayed him in the many bloody campaigns he has seen, it was as nothing in comparison with the fortitude which he called to his aid when he refused an offer from Li Hung Chang, the Bismarck of China, to take command of the armies of that great empire in its war with France. The circumstance of Colonel Mosby's refusal to guide the destinies of the Flowery Kingdom's army to the field during the conflict of over a decade ago, forms a hitherto unwritten page in the history of the Tonquin war, and goes to show how warm is the feeling in the hearts of Americans for the country which gave birth to Lafayette.

It was not without a great amount of difficulty that a Chronicle reporter succeeded in gaining Colonel Mosby's consent to an interview on the subject, but his scruples against allowing his name to appear were finally overcome, and the story of how he declined an opportunity to become the head of one of the greatest armies on earth is now for the first time given to the world.

"Yes, it is true that I once declined an offer to take command of the Chinese army," said the old warrior as he settled back in his easy chair, "and this is how it happened:

"In the month of December, 1884, while I was Consul for the United States at Hong Kong, war was raging in Tonquin between the Republic of France and the empire of China. I remember I was standing at Peddai's wharf, at the Prage, one day, when a passenger came to me from the American house of Russell & Co., telling me that they wanted to see me on important business. Russell & Co., were at that time the confidential agents of Li Hung Chang, Viceroy of China. Never dreaming for what purpose I was summoned, I proceeded immediately to their office, and was handed a translation of a cipher dispatch of which this is a copy."

From Wheeler, Shanghai December 17, 1884

Sound Consul Mosby if he would enter Chinese Government service against French. Could he go or send to the United States and engage several hundred officers and men of good fighting record for our war? Get them out quietly and from foreign force, cavalry or infantry. Command them himself or get first-class fighting General of war experience to command. He will know many good Southern men. Regular army officers cannot well come. Get his views on what may be done, and whether good work may be expected from such a force. Enjoin secrecy.

"You may well believe that I was stunned by the proposition," continued Colonel Mosby. "Although pressed to do so, I would not give an immediate answer, but told them I would consider the proposition and give them my ultimatum next day. Then I went home and slept on the offer.

"It was a fearful temptation. Cleveland had just been elected President, a fact which indicated my early recall to this country. Visions of barbaric riches, splendor and glory disturbed my slumbers, and I dreamed of playing the roles in China assumed by Hastings and Clive in India. Great imaginings of forming a new empire on the ruins of the old one floated airily through my excited brain, and in my delirium I dreamed that after defeating the French I might overthrow the Tartar dynasty at Peking and raise myself to the exalted position of Dictator of China.

"This great power over the destinies of men, ambition, urged me to accept the offer, but the still, small voice of conscience told me to reject it. I never had any respect for mere military adventurers. I could not be a soldier of fortune. I could not fight for gold. It is true that I had been a soldier in a great war and had gathered some of the Olympic dust in that grand struggle, but then I was not prompted by any feeling of self-elevation. I was sustained by a strong conviction of duty. I do not believe that Stonewall Jackson, who will rank with Hannibal and Napoleon as one of the great captains of the age, would have made any reputation fighting for a foreign people and a cause which he could never think was right. Then there is a traditional tie of sympathy between Virginians and the people of France which forbade me drawing my sword against that country.

"Then I had another reason for declining to raise my arm on the side of an Asiatic nation against Europeans. You may call it selfish if you like, but I loved the record I had made so much that I did not care to cast a blemish on it by affixing to my name the dubious title of adventurer. There is a certain amount of odium always attached to such a reputation You may remember Byron's description of Alp, the Christian renegade, leading an Asiatic horde at the siege of Corinth:

He felt how faint and feebly dim

The fame that could accrue to him

Who cheered the band and waved the sword

A traitor in a turbaned horde.

"These lines seared their way into my brain and danced in letters of fire before my eyes. They capped the climax of my resolve and determined me in the course I was to pursue.

"According to promise, I next day gave Russell & Co. my answer to the Viceroy's offer. I declined the command of the Chinese armies. As they had paid me the high compliment of offering the position to me, however, I did not feel justified in violating their confidence, and so kept the fact of the proposition having been made a secret until peace between the two nations had been restored. If it was known that such an offer had been made to me it would have discredited China and been regarded as a confession of weakness. One afternoon, after peace had been declared, I was walking with the French Consul at Hong Kong, and being very intimate with him, I mentioned the matter in his presence and laughingly added: 'You see, now, in refusing to fight against France I have discharged a portion of the debt that Americans owe to Lafayette.'

"I thought no more about it until the 4th of July, when I was having a reception at the Consulate. The French Consul, M. Leon de Jardin, called and gave me a copy of his correspondence with De Freycinet, the Prime Minister of France. The letter of De Freycinet thanking me in the name of France is now in the possession of my son in Colorado, but this is a translation of De Jardin's letter."

The letter referred to by Colonel Mosby reads as follows:

FRENCH CONSULATE

Hong Kong, JUNE 26, 1885

Col. John S. Mosby, United States Consul, Hongkong:

Dear Sir and Colleague:

The Government of the French Republic has learned through my report of the proposition made to you in the month of December, 1884, by the Viceroy of China. The political changes which have taken place in the United States presage your speedy recall from the Consulship at Hongkong. Nevertheless you refused an offer so flattering that it would have tempted anyone but yourself to be the champion of China in the contest against France. The high sentiments which animated you are fully appreciated by the Minister of Foreign Affairs. I fulfill a most agreeable duty, my dear friend and colleague, in conveying to you in the name of his Excellency, M. de Freycinet, the thanks of the republic. I have the honor to be, my dear sir, and colleague, your obedient servant.

Leon de Jardin.

"My friends," said Colonel Mosby in closing the interview, "generally think that I made a great mistake in declining the command of the Chinese army. Maybe I did. You see, I was authorized to employ several hundred of my old Confederate comrades as subordinate officers. They lost a good thing by my refusal, and I can hardly blame them for blaming me."

The story of Mosby being offered a command in—not over—the Chinese army was exposed after he came home, but the matter was not dwelt upon. Though the entirety of the situation is not really known, it is probable that he was to create a command much as he had had in Virginia to harass the French supply lines as he had done to the Army of the Potomac. Now obviously, he had been coaxed into speaking more in detail about the matter, details that may also have included "memories" that existed after the fact—such as dreams of imperial rule. The idea that Mosby would ever consider attempting to overthrow the emperor and take command of China is highly unlikely. His own innate honesty would have forbidden such a thing. But given all that he had put up with both in China and after his return to the United States, perhaps such thoughts might have been comforting. But the matter that is of most interest after all is that Mosby equated his service with the Chinese in light of a Christian who helped the Turks to conquer Greece. He put it this way in the article:

"Then I had another reason for declining to raise my arm on the side of an Asiatic nation against Europeans. You may call it selfish if you like, but I loved the record I had made so much that I did not care to cast a blemish on it by affixing to my name the dubious title of adventurer. There is a certain amount of odium always attached to such a reputation You may remember Byron's description of Alp, the Christian renegade, leading an Asiatic horde at the siege of Corinth:

'He felt how faint and feebly dim

The fame that could accrue to him

Who cheered the band and waved the sword

A traitor in a turbaned horde.'

"These lines seared their way into my brain and danced in letters of fire before my eyes. They capped the climax of my resolve and determined me in the course I was to pursue."

How very odd that John Mosby, who did not consider himself a Christian, should have felt restrained from taking such a momentous offer because he did not want to be seen as a traitor to his people.

Mosby's arrival at Washington was covered in the California papers under the heading "Prominent Californians," and he spoke of Harrison as he did of Grant—that is, that he was a better listener than talker. This "Grant-like" attribute of Harrison's may have led Mosby to believe that the man would be another Grant at the national level, a matter he devoutly wished. A small mention was then made of his remaining to argue a case before the court of claims, but whether this had anything to do with his consul fees is left unsaid:

Sacramento Daily Record-Union – February 9, 1889

PROMINENT CALIFORNIANS

Colonel Mosby and Jesse D. Carr at the National Capitol.

Washington, February 8th.—Colonel Mosby arrived here last night. He believes that the Pacific Coast will be represented in the Cabinet by either Switt or Estee, but he says—speaking of his interview with General Harrison at Indianapolis—that the President-elect is a much better listener than talker.

Colonel Mosby will remain in Washington until the latter part of March to argue a case before the Court of Claims.

Alexandria Gazette – February 11, 1889

Judge Hughes and the Cabinet.—

A letter from Washington to the Baltimore Sun says: Col. John S. Mosby, who arrived here Friday, was much impressed by his interview with Gen. Harrison on his way East from San Francisco. It is understood that among the names of Southern Republicans brought to the notice of the President elect in connection with cabinet places is that of Judge R. W. Hughes, of Virginia. Colonel Mosby is warmly in favor of Judge Hughes, and says he is a native Southern republican of unquestioned character and ability, and not complicated or affected in any way by affiliation with cliques or factions. Judge Hughes, who has been holding a term of the United States Court at Alexandria, comes up to Washington in the evening and remains at the residence of his relative, Gen. Joseph E. Johnston. Among Virginia politicians of both parties his chances and those of Gen. Mahone are discussed with much interest. Some of the representative Virginia democrats incline to the belief that Gen. Mahone, if in the cabinet, would be more conservative so far as Southern affairs are concerned, than Judge Hughes.

Fort Worth Daily Gazette – February 12, 1889

The Ex-Guerrilla Called. Cleveland (Ohio) Plain Dealer.

An Indianapolis dispatch in the Leader yesterday said that among the visitors to Gen. Harrison on Tuesday was "Col. Mosby." The readers of the dispatch would not be likely to suspect that the "Col. Mosby," who was said to be a relative of Gen. Harrison, was no other than the notorious Col. John S. Mosby of guerrilla fame during the war. It was the fashion on the part of the Leader and other Republican papers at that time to refer to Mosby as a "cutthroat," "bushwhacker" and other things of the kind, but he early became a good Republican and was rewarded with the consulship at Hong Kong. Col. Mosby is a relative and friend of Gen. Harrison and it was at the general's special request that the visit was made. The Southern situation was talked over, so Mosby says, and the ex-guerrilla took occasion to put in a word or two against Mahone. It is the opinion at Indianapolis that Mosby would have no objection to return to Hong Kong as consul and it is not unlikely that his desires in the respect will be gratified. The Mosbys and the Harrisons think a good deal of each other, the colonel having a brother and sister named for the Harrisons.

In the same paper:

Ex-Guerrilla Mosby is an applicant for office under the Harrison administration, and will probably get it. Mosby, the war is over.

It is ironic in the extreme that Mosby should have been told that the war was over. After all, he had been acting as if such were the case since 1865, only to be excoriated by both sides for his position. And it is even more ironic that the same paper criticized publications that had no problem with Mosby's war service but now condemned his access to the new president. But the fact is that those papers who denounced Mosby for having been a Confederate or, in the alternative, having been a Confederate who became a Republican were all of a piece; that is, they condemned a man for lawful and thoughtful actions based upon his understanding of the best thing to do at the time. Nothing Mosby did was for gain or power, much less being illegal or immoral! But alas, it was apparent that his motives mattered not one whit:

Fort Worth Daily Gazette – February 13, 1889

Certain newspapers which are raising a howl about "Guerrilla" Mosby's recent visit to Indianapolis, did not find so much fault with Mosby's Northern raids some twenty-five years ago.—[Minneapolis Journal.

And those certain newspapers are reminded that Lee and Mosby both tried to break into the North "twenty-five years ago," and that certain other papers now call Lee a Rebel while advocating Mosby for Federal office. "Certain newspapers" are not at a loss to understand why certain other newspapers see more "loyalty" in Mosby than in McClellan and more in Chalmers, the hero of the Fort Pillow massacre, than in Hancock, the hero of Gettysburg. With these certain other newspapers, Republicanism covers a multitude of sins, such as Little Rock bonds, whisky rings, navy jobs, cadet- ship sales, treason, bribery, etc., etc.

It is amazing to see that though the war had been over for almost a quarter of a century, papers like the Globe continued to act as if it were only yesterday that Mosby was taking potshots at General Harrison and his command! They suggested in this article that he has been "forgiven" not because the war was over and the country reunited and reconciled, but because he had become a Republican. This claim was the enduring and unending script used by many in the Democratic press against Mosby. Its use, however, required a large amount of willful blindness:

St. Paul Daily Globe – February 14, 1889

Col. Mosby was one of the most honored visitors at Indianapolis, and it is discovered that he is a relative of the president-elect. In fact, his private conference was at the special instance of Gen. Harrison. Some are impertinent enough to recall the time when the Harrison organs classed Col. Mosby with the James and Quantrell gangs. But he is now one of the Christian gentlemen that the new president likes to have about. He became a Republican early, and was thus enabled to serve his country at Hong Kong. It is intimated that he will be likely to return there.

The press interest in Mosby was now twofold. On the one hand, there was his connection with the new president, which garnered all sorts of attention. On the other, there was the matter of his consular fees, which had been settled—everyone believed—by the decision of the circuit court. Sometimes both matters were addressed in the same article:

The Columbian – February 15, 1889

Col. John S. Mosby, the famous Confederate guerrilla leader, later than that a diplomat in China and now a citizen of California, is a relative of General Harrison's, as so many hundred other native Virginians are. His grandmother was a cousin of President William Henry Harrison, and he has kept up the family acquaintance. Col. Mosby while in China overpaid the government about $16,000 on some Consular transactions. He afterwards got a suit for that amount allowed by the Court of Claims, and the item is to go into the appropriation bills before Congress this session.

Ouachita Telegraph – February 16, 1889

Mahone Their Choice.

Washington, Feb. 12.—A large meeting of Southern Republicans is being held here to confer on Cabinet possibilities and the Southern policy. Among those present were Southern Republican members of Congress, ex-U.S. Marshal Pitkin of New Orleans, Gens. Longstreet, Mosby and Mahone and others. Mahone was indorsed for the Cabinet.

One doubts that Mosby, who was admittedly in Alexandria at the time, was at this meeting or, even if he was, gave his blessing to Mahone. It is also hardly likely that Mahone would have allowed Mosby to participate in any Virginia Republican caucus unless, of course, his family connection to the new president lessened the little tyrant's hold on the gathering. But even so, Harrison would prove a tougher "nut" for Southerners to crack than had Garfield—and he was tough enough.

Alexandria Gazette – February 19, 1889

Col. Mosby, who is still in the city says he is in constant receipt of letters from Virginia asking his endorsement and assistance in the matter of obtaining office under the incoming administration, but that the people who write these letters may as well save their postage stamps, as he has left Virginia for good, and does not intend to be ever again connected with Virginia affairs of any sort, especially of a political character.

Mosby had said years earlier that he considered himself exiled from Virginia, and he remained very bitter toward that state for his treatment in and after 1872. Of course, he was soon to learn that even had he attempted to assist his fellow Southerners in the Harrison administration, it would have been useless. Harrison, as Mosby was soon to learn, was a "sectional bigot" and no friend of Southern Republicans no matter where they resided. And of course, Mosby would not return to Virginia as long as Mahone retained his power. Mosby's opinion of Mahone is illustrated in a "tongue-in-cheek" comment that appeared in the Gazette regarding a possible federal office for the little general:

Alexandria Gazette – February 21, 1889

Col. Mosby says Gen. Grant appointed Gov. Orr of South Carolina, U.S. minister to St. Petersburg, and he doesn't see why Mr. Harrison can't do the same with Gen. Mahone.

The usual march of supplicants to the White House seeking office continued. The rather sad little article below shows that General William Sherman had not forgotten his old friend Democrat Joe Johnston. Harrison, however, had no intention of retaining Johnston and, despite his explanation for not doing so, of appointing any of the Republican ex-Confederates either. His "duty," as far as Harrison was concerned, was to remove as many Southerners from the government—whatever their party!—as possible, something that Mosby was shortly to discover:

Chicago Times – March 11, 1889

One of the strange sights at the White House since inauguration has been Gen. Tecumseh Sherman pleading for the retention of the ex-Confederate Gen. Joseph Johnston as Railroad Commissioner. It is the only favor, he said, which he would ask from the Administration, and his heart was set on seeing the man who surrendered to him kept in office in old age. Gen. Johnston is past 70 and has been one of the least offensive of the Southern Brigadiers whom Cleveland brought to Washington. It is doubtful, however, if the President accedes to the request of Gen. Sherman, as there are a number of Confederate Generals, such as Longstreet, Mahone, and Mosby, who have borne a great many rebuffs from the Southern chivalry, so called, because of their adherence to the Republican party, and President Harrison thinks it his duty to provide for these men in preference to a Confederate General such as Gen. Johnston.

Alexandria Gazette – **March 12, 1889**

It may be said that Col. John S. Mosby has made no application whatever for any position under the new administration; but that he will be "taken care of" no one doubts.

Mosby's "situation" with Harrison did not take long to develop. It is true that he had not asked for a position, but the natural assumption—and not just by Mosby—was that Harrison would reach out to the South if for no other reason than to diminish Democratic power in that section.

But Harrison was only one problem for Mosby. Nothing was said of his reaction when, upon going to collect his hard-won fees, the former Consul discovered that eighty-seven days into a ninety-day appeal period, the government had filed an appeal—throwing his case into the Supreme Court. The newspapers reported that he was "surprised" and said nothing further, but it is probable that he was more angry than surprised to discover that the government was going to fight to the last to keep his money. However, Mosby would continue the fight as well; he was nothing if not persistent:

Sacramento Daily Record-Union – **March 14, 1889**

MOSBY'S CLAIM.

The Ex-Chinese Consul Must Go Through Another Suit.

Washington, March 13th.—About two months ago the Court of Claims allowed Colonel John S. Mosby about $14,000 for fees collected by him while Consul to Hongkong, which he had turned into the Treasury instead of retaining. He came here a few days ago to collect the amount, but found to his surprise an appeal had been taken by the State Department. The time allowed for an appeal in this kind of case is ninety days, and the State Department took an appeal just when eighty-seven of the days had expired. His claim now goes on the Supreme Court docket, and it will probably be several years before it can be reached.

San Francisco Chronicle – **March 14, 1889**

How Bayard Kept Ex-Consul Mosby Out of His Just Dues

By the action of ex-Secretary Bayard Colonel Mosby will be deprived for two years of fees to which he is entitled

Petty Spite Against Mosby.

Washington, March 13.—About three months ago the Court of Claims allowed Colonel John S. Mosby about $14,000 for fees collected by him while Consul to Hongkong, which he had turned into the Treasury instead of retaining. He came here a few days ago to collect the amount, but found to his surprise an appeal had been taken by the State Department. The time allowed for an appeal in this kind of case is ninety days, and the State Department took an appeal just when eighty-seven of the days had expired. His claim now goes on the Supreme Court docket, and it will probably be several years before it can be reached.

In a short interview, John Mosby made mention of his disposition of the claims case and plainly stated that he had not visited "Cousin Ben" or any of his cabinet and that he would be returning to San Francisco after what was no doubt a very frustrating and disappointing trip to Washington. As Mosby was attending to the necessary paperwork to submit the findings of the court of claims to the Supreme Court, he was asked by the press if he had requested an office from Harrison; he stated that he had not. Meanwhile, he was being approached by his fellow Virginians to intercede for them with Harrison. In the first of the following articles John Mosby made it clear that he would have nothing to do with Virginia politics. The second article, however, shows that where injustice was involved, he was willing to "interfere":

Alexandria Gazette – March 25, 1889

Col. Mosby is still here, attending to the preparation of the papers necessary for the proper presentation of his case, the Court of Claims' decision in which has been appealed by the government to the U.S. Supreme Court. The Colonel says that though he has not applied for any office, and has distinctly stated that he has nothing to do with Virginia politics, he is constantly approached by people who talk to him on both those subjects, and that one of them, a man from Albemarle county, recently went so far as to propose to recommend him for Minister to China, if he, Mosby, would sign his application for the Hong Kong consulate.

Alexandria Gazette – March 26, 1889

Among the many 4th class postoffices in Virginia for which the republicans of that State are applying is that at the Plains, in Fauquier county, now filled by a lady of that place, who discharges the duties of the office efficiently and to the satisfaction of the people who are served with mail there. She will probably be removed as Mr. Agnew has recommended a man for her place. Col. Mosby, who is an old acquaintance of the lady, says he is as good a republican as any other man, but he thinks it a d—d shame to be making war on women in this way, and that it was not so when he had anything to do with Virginia politics. Continuing, the Colonel said he was a true civil service reformer; that if he had been in Mr. Harrison's place he would have made but seven changes—the cabinet officers, and that when vacancies occurred he would have filled them with good and true and efficient republicans, without, however, any civil service examination.

Several more articles on Mosby appeared before he headed west. It was reported that he was going to argue the case regarding his fees; but he also had taken on some similar cases, and if he prevailed, according to the press, the fees "will be large." However, the paper does not make it clear if the "large fees" would belong to the ex-consuls or to Mosby for successfully prosecuting the case:

Alexandria Gazette – May 8, 1889

Virginians as Seen in Washington.

Two gentlemen are walking up Pennsylvania avenue engaged in close conversation. One is probably five feet ten and weighs nigh unto 180 pounds, a smooth face, gray hair and gray eyes; he wears what might be termed a "brick colored" suit, the coat a Prince Albert, tightly buttoned although the day is warm; in his hand he carries a heavy stick; he must be fully 50 years old, although his step is as sprightly as a man very much younger His companion is as dark and as straight as an Indian, with black hair, eyes, and beard. In his black broadcloth suit and soft felt hat he is the typical southerner. These two men were Col. John S. Mosby and his chief lieutenant, Col. Wm. H. Chapman. Col. Mosby used to divide his forces when on a raid. One section he assumed command of himself, and the other was confided to Col. Chapman. Col. Mosby, as it is well known, is now one of the counsels of the Central Pacific railroad, and lives in San Francisco. Col. Chapman has since the administration of Hayes been in the employ of the Treasury Department as special agent, and has rendered the government valuable services in arresting those engaged in the unlawful distilling of whiskey in North Carolina and Georgia.

A personal story of the man that originated in the *New York Tribune* was carried by a Southern paper. Much was made of his time in Virginia before he left for Hong Kong, especially his various "duels." Again, however, the most interesting aspect of this narrative was the description of Mosby's quiet and retiring nature, a man who, according to the narrator, "has never been talkative" and "seldom talks unless one speaks to him"—hardly the blustery, oafish figure so often portrayed in contemporary descriptions of the man:

Atlanta Constitution – **May 12, 1889 (Edited) COLONEL MOSBY.**

How the Confederate Cavalry Leader Looks Now. From the New York Tribune

A few evenings ago when the lobby of the Riggs House had the usual number of people sitting around and standing about, there entered a man rather above medium height, with cleanly shaven face, ruddy complexion and hair almost snow white. His expression was such that he was bound to attract attention as he unconsciously walked to and fro. A group of gentlemen sat in a corner, and one of them said:

"Do you know that man over there by the cigar stand?"

"I do not," said one of the group. "At the first glance he reminded me of ex-Secretary Bayard. Who is he?"

"That is the famous ex-Confederate guerilla, Colonel John S. Mosby, of Virginia."

Then everybody in that portion of the lobby cast a good square look at the man who took such a prominent part in the late war.

"He doesn't look like a man of nerve and daring," said one.

"I always pictured Mosby as a much larger man," said another, "and imagined that he had a stiff, shaggy beard, looked ferocious, and had a heap to say in a crowd. Why he appears to be quite modest, and I have noticed him around the hotel many times of late, but he has never been talkative. Indeed, he seems to be always in a deep study, and seldom talks unless some one speaks to him." In a few minutes the ex-guerilla left the lobby, and then one of the group wanted to know of a Virginian who happened to come along something of Colonel Mosby's career since the war. His dueling "scrapes" were the most interesting subjects brought up … The wrangle continued for several years, and the personalities became so pointed and bitter one day in Warrenton that Colonel Mosby considered himself insulted, and got his blood warm. He wanted to fight, and the town was startled to learn that a duel was imminent. The judge of the circuit court learned of the trouble, and he had two of the men arrested and put under heavy bonds to keep the peace. It seems that Mosby had challenged General William H. Payne, formerly of the "Black Horse" cavalry, Colonel "Tom" Smith, son of "Extra Billy" Smith, a famous ex-governor of the state, and captain "Aleck" Payne, a cousin of General Payne.

The judge got "Billy" Payne and "Tom" Smith, but they did not mind the bond. They put out to Prince William county, the meeting place. Mosby had challenged them all, and declared he would fight any one of the three, or all of the three if he was not killed or seriously wounded in the first two encounters. "Aleck" Payne evaded the officers and was not under bond. The whole side of Virginia was excited, and all of the leading papers had representative in the Piedmont region to get news of the expected duel. For three or four days the challenged parties were evading the officers and trying to meet the ex-guerilla, but the officers got Colonel Mosby as he was going to the last meeting place arranged, and he was put under heavy bonds also, and the matter ended, as he had not sufficient money to reimburse his friends if he should break the peace. The Paynes had the money, and they were desperate men. In his younger days, Colonel Mosby was considered the best pistol shot in all northern Virginia.

And then came a pleasant surprise. John Mosby was as fond of General Robert E. Lee as that general had been of him. It must have been very gratifying to discover that Lee, a man who believed that duty was its own reward, had praised John Singleton Mosby more than any other officer serving in his army! This, hopefully, made up for much of the defamations heaped upon him by other Southern commanders after and even during the war:

Alexandria Gazette – **June 26, 1889**

General Marcus J. Wright, an ex-Confederate, who has been engaged for nearly eleven years in the War Department here as agent for the collection of Confederate military papers for publication in the "Official Records of the War of the Rebellion," has written a letter to Col. John S. Mosby, in which he says that in all the correspondence he has been struck with the fact that General Lee made more complimentary mention of him, Mosby, than of any other officer serving in his, Lee's, command.

A Democratic paper looked at the Republican situation in Virginia with an astonishing lack of accuracy, even for a newspaper:

Fort Worth Daily Gazette - **August 29, 1889**

Mahone, the Brigadier.

Mahone of Virginia was a slashing Confederate brigadier and the Republicans of that state have named him as their candidate for governor. He will have the cordial support of Mosby, the guerrilla, who infested

Northern Virginia during the war and made cowardly ambushes for straggling parties of Union troops.

In the campaign which will now be prosecuted with vigor and with the hope—for the Democratic majority in the Old Dominion is neither large nor stable—Mahone will have the active assistance of the Harrison administration. All the Federal spoils in the state will be freely his to further his cause. And Mahone is notably a spoilsman. When he came into the senate with his face, as Senator Hoar described it, set toward the morning he was demanding as the price of his vote for Republican organization that the sergeantcy-at-arms be given to his henchman, Riddleberger. The party surrendered at the demand of this Confederate and advertised its folly by protesting to the world is fear of Democracy because old-time rebel soldiers were in its ranks.

Of course, Mosby would never have backed Mahone; they hated each other more than cordially. Obviously, the publication did not realize that Mahone was not Mosby's kind of Republican. It is interesting, however, to note if the paper were accurate—and that is a big "if!"—Mahone was cordial with Harrison! Mosby started out with good feelings toward his cousin but soon abandoned them. Perhaps Harrison's association with Mahone put the nail in the coffin of the Mosby-Harrison relationship—at least for Mosby! It is probable that there never was a "relationship" on Harrison's part.

Mahone was never governor of Virginia. There was only one "Readjuster" governor, and that was William E. Cameron (1882–1886). Actually, there were only two Republican governors in the state: Henry Horatio Wells (1868–1869) and Gilbert Carlton Walker (1869–1874). These were followed by two "Conservatives": Kemper (1874–1878) and Holliday (1878–1882); of course, Holliday was followed by Cameron, but beginning in 1886, all Virginia's governors were Democrats until 1966. So Mosby's "solid south" appears to have remained solid in Virginia despite all of his efforts, and for this, Mahone—with the blessings of Garfield and the Northern Republicans—was greatly responsible.

The last decade of the nineteenth century was almost upon the nation, and it would seem that suddenly, the same spirit arose in the North that had led to Lincoln's war. In other words, politicians in that section were trying to arouse the old passions—the "bloody shirt"—in the North against Southerners. Mosby had fought that particular battle in the South and had been forced to leave the field bloody, if unbowed. But there were now men in the North who spoke out against that spirit being roused in their section. As was the case in both sections, these passions were usually based upon politics and the election of some candidate or party that needed a cause other than simple good government.

This little article in the *Alexandria Gazette* is one of those, albeit small, proofs that anything Mosby made it into the newspapers:

Alexandria Gazette – November 25, 1889

The Cumberland Times says: "Mr. C. B. Wetzell, Sr., of Harper's Ferry, owns the sword used by Mosby, the famous Confederate. It is said that the sword was captured by him from a Union soldier. Mr. Thomas Boerly has the spurs worn by Mosby during the war." This will probably be news to Col. Mosby.

It would seem that Bostonians were particularly anxious to bring the facts about the Southern war effort and the men who fought for that section to their citizens. Mosby lectured several times in New England and was graciously received each time:

Stark County Democrat – December 9, 1889

A Grand Army Post in Boston is conducting a notable series of war lectures this winter, mainly from Southern soldiers and statesmen who were on the other side during the misunderstanding. Some time ago it had a brilliant lecture from an admirer of Stonewall Jackson, on that officer's military genius and career. On Wednesday last, "Mosby, the guerilla," lectured on "Jeb" Stuart, the great cavalry leader of Lee's army, and it was both instructive and amusing, especially in Mosby's personal reminiscences, and the way he riddled accepted history. The next lecture, by Governor Vance, of North Carolina, will be on "Political Feeling and Sentiment in the South During the War." As he is a wit and an orator, it holds out rich promise. There is a hint in this Boston movement how some of our local Grand Army Posts can reap both profit and entertainment.

The "Yankees" would have reaped a good deal more than profit and entertainment if such lectures about the mind of Southerners had been held before the war! Much of the problem between the sections was that ordinary Americans, North and South, knew very little about each other. And given the decades of bad press that especially the South received in the rest of the nation, it is understandable not only how the war came to be, but also why so many Americans had no problem with the atrocities committed against Southerners and their homes and states.

1889 had been a "less than banner" year for John Mosby. His consul fees case had been thrown into the Supreme Court by virtue of a late appeal by the government. This move would supposedly require at least two more years of litigation before the matter was settled. Meanwhile, the promise Mosby believed would arise from the election of his cousin Benjamin Harrison for the nation in general and the South—and himself—in particular had waned. Furthermore, if Harrison were cozying up to Mahone, that would have certainly alienated the two men. But the first year of the last decade of the nineteenth century was soon to be upon John Mosby, and if he had a larger plan for his life other than to continue with the status quo, he had yet to make that known to anyone who might have passed it on to the press.

Chapter 29

1890

In nubibus ~ In the clouds; not yet settled

"Never, never, never give in." ~ Winston Churchill

IN AN ARTICLE in a Virginia paper in late January, 1890, we see the first mention of a Harrison-Mahone connection. Such a relationship would have sat very ill with John Mosby who despised Mahone and blamed him—not altogether correctly!—for the disasters that had befallen Virginia's Republican Party. Whether it was the Harrison-Mahone connection or just Harrison alone is not known, but by the beginning of 1890, John Mosby had soured on "Cousin Ben" and would no longer support him:

Alexandria Gazette – January 24, 1890

Mosby on Harrison.

Col. Mosby, when in New York last Wednesday, was interviewed by a reporter for the New York Star. The following is a portion of the published report of that interview:

"How do they like Harrison?" I asked.

"I voted for Harrison in California," he answered evasively; "but if I had been in Virginia I should have voted against him and Mahone. It was the reputable republicans who defeated Mahone in Virginia. It simply showed that the people of Virginia did not desire to perpetuate Mahone rule, and they ended it."

"Will your people in California be for Harrison in '92?" I asked

"Well, I don't care to express an opinion," he said.

"Will they support Blaine again if he comes up in '92?"

"About that I couldn't express an opinion," he said. Then, after a moment's pause: "Roscoe Conkling was a great man, wasn't he? One of the greatest the country ever produced. It was a pity that he was taken away at the time he was."

The next story about Mosby's consul fees is very confusing. According to the records, his claim of $14,000, awarded in the circuit court, had been appealed by the government to the Supreme Court—a matter that was supposed to have delayed a final judgment for years. Now suddenly, the high court apparently had made a determination in a surprisingly short time:

Sacramento Daily Record-Union – February 4, 1890

GENERAL MOSBY.

He Gets a Judgment, But His Claim Is Cut Down Considerably.

Washington, February 3d.—The Supreme Court to-day decided the Mosby cases by reversing the judgment of the Court of Claims and directing that tribunal to enter judgment for the sum of $11,783.50. Mosby sued for $29,180 and was awarded $13,839.21. Both parties appealed.

The item disallowed was $2,065 for certifying invoices for free goods imported into the United States. The Court insists that it is the duty of Consuls to certify all invoices inasmuch as the law requires invoices to accompany all importations of merchandise.

This reduced the sum to $11,744.21, but the Court allowed an item of $3,129 for recording various instruments, which the Court of Claims disallowed, making the sum for which the judgment was rendered.

Suddenly, a whole new economic "side-line" became available to John Mosby when he accepted an offer to lend his name and presence to a Mexican lottery financed by European banks. It was a nice piece of change for a pleasant trip from California to El Paso and on to Juarez, Mexico, once a month. Furthermore, it had the added advantage of annoying cousin Ben, something that must have appealed to Mosby's roguish temperament. Beginning in February, Mosby, the lottery, "cousin Ben," and Ben's son, Russell, simply filled the newspapers to overflowing:

Sacramento Daily Record-Union – **February 5, 1890**

Colonel Mosby.

Washington, February 4th.—Colonel Mosby will start for home in about a week. He has been employed by a syndicate of Paris and Frankfort bankers to take charge of a Mexican scheme of some importance, which is to be pushed in the West.

The Chronicle then ran a new Mosby war story. As he now lived in that city, the local papers took a certain amount of pride and an inordinate amount of interest in him as a very real "celebrity" in their midst:

San Francisco Chronicle – **February 9, 1890**

The correspondent of the Chronicle at Washington telegraphs a story about a meeting between Colonel Mosby and a former Union soldier. The two had met on a previous occasion, and it is stated that the ex-Confederate, envying the Union soldier's possession of a fine set of clothes, said: "Yank, just shed that; I believe it will fit me;" and then subsequently handed back the coat with the remark: "If I wear that some of my men might shoot me for a —— Yankee." This is a pretty story, but those who know the Colonel well will hardly believe it. They will have no difficulty in accepting the statement that the Colonel took the suit of clothes, for in those days he was taking everything he could lay his hands on, but the manner and form of speech are entirely foreign. What the Colonel would have said, and did say if the event really occurred, was: "My dear sah, I am exceedingly sorry, but I am obliged to relieve you of those garments. Please disrobe at once." The Colonel would under no circumstances have displayed brusqueire, not even when he was a guerrilla.

However, the little story did have a certain value in that it seems Mosby was hardly brusque or rude even in war. Again, there are those who insist that he was a "difficult" man in social situations. Obviously, this newspaper thought otherwise— and said so.

Another testimony to John Mosby's honesty and legal ability came from Justice Blatchford of the US Supreme Court. The justice commented that Mosby was sufficiently proficient as an attorney to perform due diligence informing the government of his claim to the fees at the time he paid them into the Treasury. Therefore, the idea that the Treasury could have considered the monies "voluntarily donated" was patently false:

Alexandria Gazette, – **February 13, 1890**

The decision of the U. S. Supreme Court in the case of Col. Mosby has been printed. In it Justice Blatchford, by whom it was rendered, pays the Colonel the following compliment: "the claimant acted with propriety, and with a high sense of honor, in paying the fees into the Treasury, in order to avoid a controversy with the Department; and he asserted his right to have the fees refunded to him, by making a demand that they should be credited to him in his accounts, before such accounts were finally settled. He did not concede the right of the government to retain the fees; and his action was equivalent to a formal protest made at the time of paying them over."

Again, the idea that Mosby built his own legend is proved wrong when such articles as this appear in the papers. Why would anyone care about some old soldier's "war relic" even if he wrote to the papers about it? There were lots of old soldiers—and even more "war relics." And for that reason, the press wouldn't be bothered, unless the old soldier was important enough to demand their attention! The presence of the following story proves that, obviously, "old soldier" John Mosby was just that important:

San Francisco Chronicle – **February 25, 1890**

MOSBY RETURNS

Brings a Relic of His War Experience.

Colonel John S. Mosby, ex-Consul-General to Hongkong, who has returned from Washington, has been engaged by a London banking firm to look after some large interests in Mexico. He will not go there just yet, however, and will only be there a short time. The ex-Consul-General brought back with him some curious relics of war days. When he started out campaigning he wore a large red sash, and the first engagement was with the First California battalion, commanded by Colonel Thompson, now living in Oakland. The sash attracted attention, and Mosby was shot in the thigh and arm, and his horse which received four bullets, was killed. Colonel Mosby's mother is still living and she finding it, presented it again to him. Besides this he brought back several other curious relics.

In the next article, mention was made of Virginia Senator John W. Daniel. It must be remembered that this same Senator Daniel had been fulsomely praised by Mosby in an article of March 10, 1886, at the time of his election, Democrat that he was. It would seem that Daniel might not have been all that worthy of Mosby's praise:

Sacramento Daily Record-Union – **March 31, 1890**

Longstreet and Mosby

The one was called the "Lion" and the other the "Falcon," of the Army of Northern Virginia. In the recent celebration of General R. E. Lee's birthday in Atlanta, above the speaker's stand were pictures of Lee, Davis and his Cabinet, Gordon, Grady and other lesser lights, both of the living and departed. General Longstreet's portrait was conspicuous by its absence. Senator John W. Daniel has delivered two eloquent orations, one on the second battle of Manassas and the other on Jefferson Davis. In both he seemed studiously to take pains to omit any reference to Longstreet or Mosby, although beslobbering with fulsome flattery other men of much less note. Do these mean, narrow-minded embittered sectionalists suppose for an instant they are making history, or rather destroying or reversing history already made? Is not the "animus of the animal" perfectly patent in this silly and vain attempts to obscure two great men of imperishable military renown—great military chiefs whose fame will live and grow and brighten with posterity, when the little "whipper-snappers" of to-day are dead, buried and forgotten. Is it to "make treason odious" that Longstreet and Mosby are thus given the "cold shoulder?" It is to make them pay the penalty of friendship to General U. S. Grant and fealty to the Republican party.—Atlanta (Ga.) National.

Mosby's position with the Juarez lottery was now revealed in the press. It turned out that in this case, Mosby did sell his name, and he could do it because he was known to be scrupulously honest. If he said that the drawing was fair, it was fair. Even his enemies did not cavil. But John Mosby was not the first Confederate to be involved in what the *San Francisco Call* identified as a "lottery scheme." However throughout Mosby's involvement with the lottery, there was never any question of dishonesty while he rather enjoyed his jaunts to Mexico and, perhaps even more, enjoyed tweaking the nose of saintly cousin Ben, who was "hell bent" against lotteries as later articles made very clear:

Alexandria Gazette – April 14, 1890

Personal.—Col. J. S. Mosby has been appointed commissioner of the Grand Lottery of Juarez under the management of the Mexican International Banking Company.

San Francisco Morning Call – April 15, 1890

Colonel Mosby's New Occupation

Ex-Senator Spencer, who is equally a citizen of Nevada and of the Black Hills country, has arrived here with his wife after a winter in Dakota. Senator Spencer was interested there in urging the lottery bill upon the Legislature of North Dakota, but other influences were stronger and the lottery scheme was rejected by the young State. Colonel John S. Mosby, who has just won a verdict from the Supreme Court and received nearly $20,000 of back consular fees, is the last Confederate leader to lend his name to a lottery scheme. With Beauregard, Jubal Early and John S. Mosby all in the lottery business it rather becomes a Republican Congress to keep legislating against the evil which these four Confederates are fostering.

It was fortunate for the Call that it was located in California. Jubal Early, the "High Poo-Bah of the Lost Cause," would have taken very ill at being called a Republican! Most probably, General Beauregard was also a Democrat. Only Mosby was a Republican. The paper speaks of the efforts by Republicans in Congress to end the "evils" of the lottery. Of course, Mosby was the only Confederate involved who was also a Republican, but there were only three Confederates "fostering that evil"—Beauregard, Early and Mosby—not four as reported by the paper. But John Mosby's new source of income was apparently doing very well, which made him happy and cousin Ben unhappy—something else that probably made John Mosby happy:

Omaha Daily Bee – June 21, 1890

LOUISIANA'S SEDUCERS.

The Juarez People Outbidding the Old Lottery People.

New Orleans, La., June 20.—[Special telegram to the Bee.]—The complications in the lottery fight are daily increasing and the offer made by "New York and English capitalists" to give more for the charter to do business in this state than the Louisiana company proposes has still further mixed things. An investigation was set on foot today to find out who the men are who are rivals for the Louisiana company's business, and the results has set everybody to talking. One thing has been demonstrated and that is that the state will get an enormous revenue if the lottery is permitted to continue.

The syndicate is the Mexican International banking company, which has a concession from the Mexican government for the Grand Lottery of Juarez, with headquarters at the City of Juarez, formerly Paso del Norte, Mexico. The tickets of the Grand Lottery of Juarez are backed by General John S. Mosby and the El Paso National bank of El Paso, Tex. The company has not been organized long, its first drawing having taken place last April, but it is hard after the Louisiana company and will prove that it is a dangerous competitor.

"If it is merely a question of money as to which company shall run the lottery business in Louisiana we will show that we have all the capital needed," said Mr. Wells of Richmond, who made the proposition to the house on behalf of "New York and English capitalists," agreeing to give $1,250,000 per annum to step into the Louisiana lottery company's shoes. "The syndicate I represent means business and we shall get the franchise. Our offer raised the Louisiana company's bid $250,000 per annum. If the Louisiana company makes a bid of equal amount, we will offer $1,500,00 and are prepared in case the Louisiana company comes to our figures, to pay the state $2,000,000 per annum."

A particularly apt matter arose that gave Mosby even greater amusement involving cousin Ben and his son—and Mosby's lottery. This was an instance in which John Mosby found neither the need nor the desire to hold his tongue, and so, naturally, he did not:

The World – July 31, 1890

TURNING GRANDPA'S HAT GRAY

The Harrison's Should Get Together on the Lottery Question.

Lottery people are sorely puzzled by the queer antics of the son and heir of President Harrison as exposed in The World to-day.

One of the chief Mexican lotteries is run by Col. Mosby, of San Francisco, just down the Rio Grande from El Paso, Tex. He was paralyzed by President Harrison's anti-lottery measures on account of his recent experiences with the President's son. He says:

"Three weeks ago Russell Harrison was at El Paso and crossed the Rio Grande to the office of the lottery and began to talk business.

"The result was that he got $1,000 in advertising for Frank Leslie's Illustrated Newspaper, and $300 for his paper in Montana out of the lottery officers. The advertisement tells what a good thing the lottery is.

"Now, what bothers me is this: If there is a family combine, is President Harrison after the saints and Russell after the sinners?"

The name of Russell B. Harrison appears in big type at the head of the editorial columns of the Helena Journal as the President of the Publishing Company, so there can be no possible mistake as to his controlling interest in the newspaper.

One of the lottery puffs referred to, appeared in that paper in the issue of July 25, in the shape of a three column scare-head letter from its "regular correspondent" in the City of Mexico. The inevitable conclusion is that Russell B. Harrison's Montana paper has been doing its best to earn the $300 worth of advertising which its president secured during his recent trip to the Mexican border.

What Frank Leslie's Illustrated Newspaper will do for the Mexican lotteries in return for the $1,000 "ad" promised remains to be seen.

Information from reliable sources, however, is to the effect that the "write up" is already in type, with a series of handsome illustrations, and that it has been ordered for publication in an early September issue of the paper.

Alexandria Gazette – August 1, 1890

Referring to President Harrison's newly developed ultra opposition to the lotteries, Col. Mosby says:

"Three weeks ago Russell Harrison was at El Paso and crossed the Rio Grande to the office of the lottery and began to talk business. The result was that he got $1,000 in advertising for Frank Leslie's Illustrated Newspaper and $300 for his paper in Montana out of the lottery officers. The advertisement tells what a good thing the lottery is. Now what bothers me is this: If there is a family combine, is President Harrison after the saints and Russell after the sinners?"

The World – August 2, 1890

THE PRESIDENT AND SON

Russell B. Continues to Print His Lottery Advertisements. Apparently

No Regard For His Father's Words or Repute. This is Really a National Shame—The Lottery Men Laugh at the President's Message to Congress, While His Own Son Profits by Their Money—Mr. Arkeil's Action. [Special to The World]

Saratoga, Aug. 1.—As noted in The World's article upon the publication in Russell B. Harrison's Montana paper of the lottery advertisements, Gen. John S. Mosby, the ex-Confederate raider and present ardent Republican, charged that Mr. Russell B. Harrison, son of the President, had solicited from him certain advertisements of the Mexican lottery with which the General is connected, and for insertion in Frank Leslie's Illustrated Newspaper and the Morning Journal, of Helena, Mon. of the company publishing which Mr. Russell B. Harrison is the president. Gen. Mosby alleged that Mr. Harrison was at the time on a visit to Texas in the interest of Frank Leslie's Illustrated Newspaper.

Mr. Arkeil was met at the Hotel Balmoral, Mount McGregor, this afternoon, and his attention was called to the article in yesterday's World. Mr. Arkeil said:

"In regard to Frank Leslie's Illustrated Newspaper, the columns of that paper will state it's views on the lottery question. It is an imperative rule in the office that all lottery advertisements are excluded from its advertising columns. At the time of the tour of Texas some lottery advertisements were taken down there, but they were promptly excluded on reaching the home office in New York City.

Evening Times of August 2nd, 1890

San Francisco, Cal. Aug. 1.—Gen. Mosby says that the contracts for advertising his lottery and signed by Russell B. Harrison are now in Mexico, but can be obtained and exhibited. He repeated his now celebrated remark:

"It is more than ever clear that President Harrison is after the saints and Russell is after the sinners."

Daily Critic – **August 5, 1890**

RUSSELL B. AND THE LOTTERY.

Colonel Mosby Reiterates His Original Statement About that Ad.

From the New York World.

San Francisco, Aug. 3—Colonel John S. Mosby like Early and Beauregard, has an interest in a lottery to the extent of seeing that the drawing is fair. His particular lottery is the Juarez, at Pasa del Norte, Mexico, just across the border. Once a month he goes to Paso del Norte and superintends the drawing. Mosby is Harrison's cousin. Mosby's clear cut face and sharp gray eye lit up when asked about Russell's success in getting money for puffing the lottery.

"Well, you know it strikes me as sort of funny. You see, Cousin Ben sits there and tells a good moral Congress what a terrible tag a lottery is and how it is demoralizing the country, while Russell goes out and through his papers tells a small portion of the public how they can be demoralized, according to Cousin Ben's idea. It was just after the burning of the Winter Palace at Fort Worth, Tex. when Russell went to Paso del Norte to see about drumming up business. He went personally to the office of the company and laid his scheme before the managers, who are Mandelbaum and Gonjoles. Well, before he left he had made to contracts: one was for a page in Frank Leslie, which will have pictures of the Juarez buildings, the place where the lottery is drawn, a picture of myself and reading matter to describe what a wonderful thing the Juarez Lottery is. For this he got $1,000. The other was a reading notice for the Helena Morning Journal, and this he got $300 for and carried it away with him.

Now, that was business. Russell himself did the soliciting, and before he had time to carry out the contract his father came out with a message against lotteries. I do not believe Cousin Ben would have known of the Juarez Lottery if Russell had not told him. It is the hypocrisy of the thing that strikes me, and the President should watch a little. Whether Harrison was a party to his son's journalistic ventures, or whether he ever knew of them, is not in evidence, but, being so good a man, and knowing the temptations which surround all eminent journalists of Russell's attainments, it is probable that the young man surreptitiously, and likely with malice aforethought, entered the arena in which he shines so conspicuously without the knowledge of him who would have saved him such a fate. Be that as it may, he got there all the same, and the fact that he lives at the White House with his dear old father, and eats at the same table and shares his salt is evidence that he has been forgiven."

There is a certain delicious hypocrisy when government types decry "nefarious schemes to plunder the people." When Mosby was a "government-type" in Hong Kong, he made known vast thefts and plunder done not by lotteries, but by men who were being paid with the taxpayers' "dime." At least in the lottery, the person taking part did so voluntarily, knowing that he was taking a chance on losing his "dime." However, he also had a possibility, however slight, of actually getting something in return for that dime. On the other hand, that which was stolen from him by the government was lost without any hope of recall. And so "lottery fever" continued to appear in print to the satisfaction of those running the lottery and their employees including one John Singleton Mosby:

The Columbian – August 8, 1890
HOW THEY DIFFER

Harrison and His Son on Lotteries

New York, July 31.—The World of last Thursday morning says:

In Yesterday's papers was printed a message from the President of the United States to Congress asking that body for additional stringent legislation against the use of the United States mails for the transmission of letters addressed to the Louisiana Lottery Company and advertisements of that concern. In the course of his message the President refers to "the baleful effect" of the "establishment of one or more lottery companies at Mexican towns near our border."

Last evening the following dispatch was received from the World's correspondent in San Francisco:

Colonel Mosby, who runs a little lottery just across the Rio Grande from El Paso, is in the city and is very much puzzled by the anti-lottery messages sent out by President Harrison. He said today:

"Three weeks ago Russell Harrison was at El Paso and crossed the Rio Grande to the office of the lottery and began to talk business. The result was that he got $1000 in advertising for Frank Leslie's Illustrated Newspaper and $300 for his paper in Montana out of the lottery officers. The advertisement tells what a good thing the lottery is. Now, what bothers me is this: is there a family combine, is President Harrison after the saints and Russell after the sinners?"

A statement of this importance could not, of course, be printed in the World without the fullest investigation. The recent files of Frank Leslie's Illustrated Newspaper were rigorously examined, disclosing no advertisement—at least up to date—of the character referred to.

The World last night also procured a copy of the Helena Morning Journal of Friday, July 25. At the head of the editorial columns of this number of this paper is the name of Russell B. Harrison as president of the company and this, therefore, makes him the responsible person under the law for whatever appears in its columns. It is an eight-page paper. One the seventh page of the Journal of July 25 is a three column letter dated at the City of Mexico.

The letter describes in the most fervid terms the drawing of the "grand lottery of Juarez." The three columns are interspersed with extremely well executed illustrations of the ornate pagoda in which the lottery is drawn, a copy of the lottery ticket and numerous instances of person successful in the lottery. In the course of the enthusiastic description of the drawing itself and of the good fortune of various ticketholders is this paragraph, which is a same of the entire letter.

Luck! Do I believe in Luck? Assuredly I do, since a friend of mine has once drawn $4000, a year later $10,000 and not long ago bought from a friend of his a ticket which was for that lucky mortal a clean $100,000. Then, too, I know a young man who never fails to get a prize, and his list of winnings through a series of years is something formidable. His method? It is to buy of the first man or woman he meets who offers a ticket. Nothing more simple.

This letter is credited to a correspondent of the Boston Herald and its date is contemporaneous with the time of Mr. Russell B. Harrison's visit to the neighborhood of El Paso.

In the adjoining column to this long "reading notice" is a double-column advertisement of the lottery in question, in which it is stated that the drawings are "under the personal supervision of Gen. John S. Mosby," who, it appears, made the statement above given to the World's correspondent in San Francisco.

The advertisement covers a space of something above half a column of the Helena Journal, of the company publishing which, as said, Mr. Russell B. Harrison, son of Benjamin Harrison, President of the United States, is President.

The attempt to destroy the lotteries was perhaps the government's first effort at social engineering after the war. It was as unsuccessful as was the effort to combat the "evils of drink" occurring in the early twentieth century.

But not every paper understood Mosby's actions in the matter as can be seen in this article in the *Globe*, which actually reported that Mosby was attempting to excuse Russell instead of pointing out the delightful irony of his situation. Whether the correspondent was more than a little dense or whether his dislike of Mosby resulted in his erroneous conclusion is not known:

St. Paul Daily Globe – August 22, 1890
MOSBY EXPLAINS.

Col. John S. Mosby, who has been conspicuous as a rebel guerilla and as a Republican officeholder, has been in retirement for the past ten years, and his name has almost passed from the memory of American people until he turned up the other day in the role of a confidential friend to the Harrison family. The delicate task assigned to Col. Mosby was to extricate Russell, the son and heir apparent, from the ugly lottery scrape into which he had gotten. It was to clear the immaculate Harrison name of the stain of being associated with a lottery brokerage that Mosby's services were called into requisition. He did his work in real guerila, bushwhacking style. He stopped over at El Paso the other day to explain the matter to a press reporter. According to Mosby's statement Russell Harrison did not solicit advertising patronage from the Juarez Lottery company. That would be beneath the dignity of a Harrison. He sent an agent to do the soliciting, and to make sure that there should be no hitch in the proceedings on account of his own absence, Russell dropped into a cigar store and awaited the movements of his agent. When the young man came out with the contract in hand duly signed by the lottery company Russell made him go back and strike the company for another advertisement for an Eastern paper.

It would have been far better for the reputation of the Harrison family if Col. Mosby had kept his mouth shut. His attempted exculpation of Russell has only proved the charge. It was lottery advertising that Russell went gunning for, and he got it.

As noted, the reporter was woefully wrong if he believed that Mosby's comment was an attempt to protect Harrison or his family. Indeed, John Mosby had no use for Harrison and said as much. Furthermore, the idea that the family would prevail upon Mosby to settle this "delicate situation" is ludicrous given that he was directly involved with that very same notorious lottery! Mosby's remarks were a pointed comment on the diametric morals of father and son, and undoubtedly, he greatly enjoyed the elder Harrison's embarrassment resulting from that situation.

The next article was the first to suggest Mosby might vote the Democratic ticket in the next presidential election. Indeed, according to the article, he intended to vote Democrat even in the local elections. Mosby had had it with the Republicans in Washington and mentioned the ill-treatment of a Democratic Southern lady who was removed and from her position for the crime of being a Southern woman! The "Gen. Lee" here mentioned was Democrat Fitzhugh Lee. If John Mosby was pushed to the point of voting for Fitz Lee, whom he despised, Harrison and the Northern Republicans must have really made him angry:

Alexandria Gazette – October 4, 1890

Washington, D. C., Oct. 4, 1890.

Col. Mosby writes to a friend here that he intends to vote the democratic ticket in California this fall, to mark his condemnation of Harrison's and Reed's sectional, anti-Southern policy. He says that when ex-Assistant Postmaster General Clarkson visited the Pacific coast last summer, some republicans of San Francisco gave him a banquet, to which he, Mosby, was invited, but he declined to attend it on account of Clarkson's treatment of the southern people, and especially his war on southern women who held small country postoffices. Col. Mosby also says that if he were in Virginia he would vote for Gen. Lee for Congress.

In his war against the lotteries, Harrison had persuaded Congress to outlaw the use of the US mails for advertising those hellish outrages. The matter was really getting quite complex as this next article made clear:

Omaha Daily Bee – October 5, 1890

LOTTERIES AND THE MAILS.

Judge Tyner, assistant attorney general for the postoffice department, was asked this afternoon whether a strict construction of the regulations issued for the guidance of postmasters under the new lottery law will prohibit the transmission through the mails of all foreign papers which contain the advertisements of any lottery company. He replied that the law is definite and strict and that it provides for refusing admission in the mails to all newspapers which contain the objectionable matter, no matter where they may be published. "I can understand how this construction may work great hardship in many instances," he said. "A great many of the foreign newspapers publish lottery advertisements and it frequently happens that these newspapers have subscribers in this country who are interested in the price lists and other business information published in them, but the law allows no discrimination and for the present at least, it will be enforced against all newspapers which contained the prohibited advertisements." It is probable that there may be some consultation in reference to this phase of the situation and some means may be found for permitting the carriage of foreign newspapers through the mails which contain the announcement of lottery companies which do not attempt to do business in the United States, but unless the present regulations are enforced a concern like that with which General Mosby is connected might readily flood this country with Mexican papers filled with advertisements of his company, and it is clearly the intent of the law to break up the lottery business in this country, no matter where the lottery may be situated.

There had been extensive coverage in the Democratic press of former Union Captain Brewster's version of the "Death Lottery" story, once again making Mosby into a monster; but this time, the effort was unsuccessful as the colonel was being lauded in papers in both the South and the West, probably because it was believed that he would vote the "Democratic ticket" in the next election:

Los Angeles Herald – October 14, 1890 (Edited)
Alexandria Gazette – October 23, 1890*

THE GREAT PARTIZAN LEADER

Colonel John S. Mosby Visits Santa Monica.

He Has an Interesting Encounter—He will Vote the Democratic Ticket

When a man of the celebrity of Colonel John S. Mosby changes his politics, the whole people of the United States are interested in the reasons which have impelled him to such a course. He voted for Grant, because he thought there ought to be a considerable following of the dominant party in the south. He voted for Harrison, because he thought his administration would be a national one, and that a president descended from an illustrious Virginia family would treat the south fairly. On the contrary, the Colonel holds, Harrison has acted as if he hated the men of the south who voted against him and despised those who vote for him. This staunch friend of Grant ascribes the pressure to pass the federal elections or force bill to the personal efforts of Harrison and Reed, and he therefore washes his hands of both, and returns to the bosom of the national Democracy.

Colonel John S. Mosby, who has been sojourning for some days at the Hollenbeck, has had a very agreeable time. He announces it to be his purpose to locate in Los Angeles, with whose climate, social and other attraction, he is greatly charmed. The Colonel is connected with the law department of the Southern Pacific Railway and he officiates at the drawings of a Mexican lottery, which circumstance compels him to go to El Paso, Mexico, once a month. He looks upon a residence here as a great convenience, and will be quite apt to make the change.

Sunday, Col. Mosby went to Santa Monica, and while there he was the center of a small group which was approached by a blue-coated veteran from the soldier's home, who asked if Mosby was one of the party. Upon the colonel being pointed out to the inquirer, the latter, who proved to be Corporal John Hodge, was most effusive in his greetings, and thereby hangs a tale. [The article then goes on to present the story of Mosby's involvement with Corporal Hodge and his postwar political peregrinations.-vph]

Colonel Mosby was appointed consul to Hong Kong by President Hayes, and not, as is generally supposed by Grant. He made an efficient and honorable representative of the United States. The Herald is heartily glad to welcome the colonel back to the Democratic fold. Pond and Del Valle and the rest of the Democratic state ticket will have one staunch vote that was not counted on.

Mosby did indeed bolt from the Republican Party when Harrison ran again, but he did not go with The Democrats.

Indeed, much of Mosby's problems with Harrison and the Northern Republicans had to do with so-called civil rights legislation* (see "Addendum" at the end of the chapter). Mosby was not against blacks voting, but he absolutely rejected blacks having political power over whites. Most of all, the idea of federal troops on Southern soil together with the attitude of his cousin and those congressional Republicans who were as much "anti-Southern" as "pro-black" drove him for the first and only time out of that party.

A family tragedy made its way into print as another of Mosby's sisters died. It is interesting to note that the death of a rather inconsequential individual—albeit not to her own family, of course—was carried as a "news item" and not just a "death notice." Such press exposure can only be attributed to the lady's relationship to John Mosby. Indeed, the paper said as much:

> ***Alexandria Gazette* – October 18, 1890**
>
> Miss Lizzie Mosby died at the residence of her sister, Mrs. Russell, near Bedford City, Tuesday, after a short illness. She was a sister of Col. John S. Mosby.

Another article was forthcoming on Mosby's suit against the government. By this time, it was becoming confusing as to which suit was which or even if there were more than one. Back in February, it was reported that he had won his suit, but for a smaller amount than he had claimed. Perhaps this was an appeal or an attempt to obtain the money originally denied. It is difficult to understand the machinations of the matter save only that, according to the press, another decision by the court had been rendered:

> ***The Morning Call* – October 18, 1890**
>
> COLONEL MOSBY'S CASH.
>
> His Suite Against the Government Decided at Last.
>
> Word was received yesterday at the United States sub-Treasury from the Treasury Department at Washington that a warrant for $11,783.50 had been made out in favor of John S. Mosby. This is the first intimation received here that the long-standing suit of Colonel Mosby against the United States Government had been decided.
>
> During the administration of President U.S. Grant Mosby, the once famous guerilla chieftain, was appointed Minister to China. While there he paid into the United States Treasury certain sums which he afterward claimed. His claim was denied, and he then brought suit in the Court of Claims, and obtain judgment, but the Government then appealed to the Supreme Court, where the case has since been pending. Yesterday's dispatch would seem to show that the Supreme Court has sustained the Court of Claims in its judgment.
>
> Colonel Mosby left Los Angeles last Wednesday for Mexico, where he will stay some time in business. In the meanwhile the money will await his appearance at the sub-Treasury.

And still, the consular fees matter continued. Mosby had determined to be a veritable shylock and get his pound of flesh no matter what was required:

San Francisco Chronicle – December 6, 1890

Mosby's Consular Fees.

Colonel John S. Mosby entered suit in the District Court against the United States yesterday for $400 due him as Consul fees while he was Consul for the United States at Hongkong. Owing to a misconstruction of a certain act he erroneously refunded $400 collected from Russell & Co., an American firm of Hongkong. Mosby's successor, R. E. Withers, recollected the money and placed it in the treasury, and it being decided that consular fees are the perquisites of the Consul, Mosby is now suing for the return of the $400 to him.

As the year drew to a close, John Mosby's situation was considerably better than it had been at its opening. He was finally obtaining his stolen fees as well as making economic hay with the Juarez lottery to the annoyance of cousin Ben, something that must have tickled his sense of the absurd. But he was conflicted politically as might well be imagined. The rise of the Populist movement, that began with William Jennings Bryan's "People's Party" in 1891 and the fact that it proceeded to swallow The Democratic party, ended any thought Mosby might have had about joining that party, even temporarily. As a result, he found himself "homeless" politically for the first time since 1876.

ADDENDUM

The Federal Elections Bill of 1890 was an attempt by some Republicans in Congress to establish Federal supervision of elections to ensure the voting rights of blacks in the South. The bill was the last in a series of unrelated bills in the nineteenth century that bore the descriptive title of "force bill" because they authorized the use of the military in its enforcement. Denounced in the South as an attempt to revive Reconstruction, the bill passed the House of Representatives but failed in the Senate on January 22, 1891.

The election of Benjamin Harrison to the presidency in 1888 meant that Republicans would control both the legislative and executive branches of government for the first time since the end of Reconstruction. During his campaign, Harrison had promised to support legislation empowering the Federal government to enforce voting rights in the South. In 1890, Republican Senator Henry Cabot Lodge of Massachusetts introduced the Federal Elections Bill, which would empower Federal courts to appoint election commissioners to oversee Federal elections and use Federal troops to enforce election laws if necessary.

Republicans in the House, united under the leadership of Speaker Thomas Brackett Reed, passed the Force Bill by a slim margin. But Senate Democrats were united against the bill, and when they attempted to stymie it with a filibuster, eastern pro-business and western "silver" Republicans in the Senate refused to stand with their pro-voting rights colleagues in voting to end the filibuster through cloture. Pro-bill senators reintroduced the legislation following the congressional elections of 1890, but Republican losses in those elections ensured that the bill would be defeated again.

John Mosby at War: 1863 ~ 1865
Captain ~ Major ~ Colonel

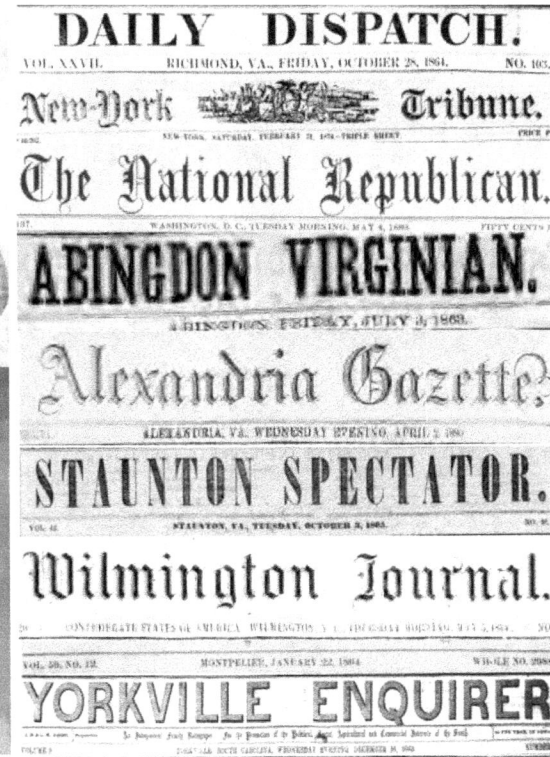

Warrenton

After the War, John Mosby went to live in Warrenton where he remained until he left for his position in China. Below is his physical "transformation" occasioned not just by age, but by suffering. Almost immediately after the war, Mosby had photographs taken in his colonel's uniform alone or with groups of his men as seen here with his Maryland Rangers.

Col. John S. Mosby and His Confederate Raiders

Mosby at the crest of his popularity in his post-war life—a happy and loving husband, father and a successful attorney with an assured future even in a war-ravaged South. There was nothing his fellow Southerners would not have given to him and no limit to what he might have achieved. All that was demanded and required of him was that he "go with his section."

President Ulysses S. Grant		Governor James Kemper

He is a man of courage who does not run away,
but remains at his post and fights against the enemy. ~
Socrates

Col. John S. Mosby, American Consul in Hong Kong 1878 -1885

Silver Cup presented to Consul Mosby by the Chinese Merchants courtesy of John Ward

Hong Kong Harbor circa 1880 by Lai AFong

Colonel John S. Mosby at fifty-five and Collis P. Huntington

Geary Street Wire Rope Rail Road courtesy of cable-car-guy.com
~ Joseph Thompson

~ Colonel John S. Mosby and President Theodore Roosevelt ~

Roosevelt charged Mosby, an agent of the Land Office, with removing fences on public lands erected by stockmen in Nebraska and Colorado contrary to the law. But when Roosevelt was forced to choose between the law and his political ambitions, Mosby was recalled.

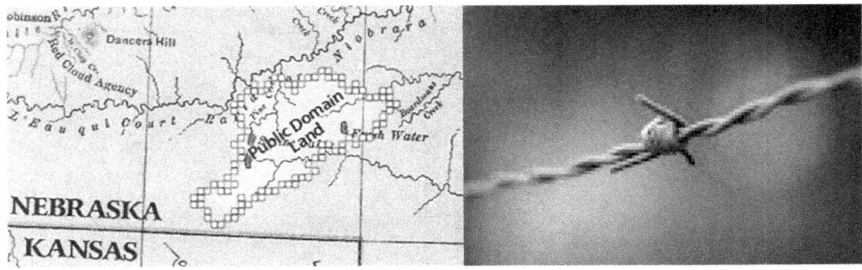

In 1867, Lucien B. Smith of Kent, Ohio obtained the first US patent for barbed wire and is regarded as its inventor. Barbed wire was the first "technology" capable of restraining cattle and a much cheaper alternative to other methods of fencing. When barbed wire became widely available in the late 19th century, it became feasible to fence in muchlarger tracts of land, thus making large-scale livestock ranching economically practical. On the left is a map of public lands in Nebraska. The small "donuts" ranged around that land represent the fences that had been erected on that land.

Colonel John S. Mosby and President William Howard Taft

The Department of Justice building circa 1905

Oklahoma Territory and the lands of the Chickasaw and Choctaw Tribes
courtesy of the Oklahoma Historical Society

As the Sun Sets: Mosby Post-1910
Above left, John Mosby shortly before his death.

The medal given to Mosby by the University of Virginia.

A photo of Mosby during one of his endless perambulations around Washington City. His poverty is made evident in the condition of his clothing.

The letter Mosby wrote to son Beverly in 1914 about the removal of Fountain Beattie from his government office. Mosby was angry and declared himself "down on Woodrow" (Wilson).

Company D, 1st Virginia Infantry marching in Col. John S. Mosby's funeral

Chapter 30

1891

Pueri pueri, pueri puerilia tractant. ~ Children are children (and therefore do childish things).

"It is a wise father that knows his own child." ~ William Shakespeare

IN 1891 THE press began its comments and reports on John Mosby early on. Apparently, the author sent a copy of his book to the *Daily Herald* and was handsomely thanked for doing so:

Daily Herald – January 16, 1891

The Herald is indebted to Col. John S. Mosby for a copy of his war reminiscences. These will be all the more interesting to Angelinos because the distinguished ex-Confederate leader is going to become a citizen of this city. His career has been romantic and sensational in the extreme. We promise ourselves a treat in reading his book, and shall review it in extenso at an early date. It is graced by a well executed cut of the fine and martial face of the author.

This is one of several articles that mentioned Mosby's intention to move from San Francisco to Los Angeles and make that city his abode; it never happened though why is not clear. Of course, as long as he was an employee of the Southern Pacific, he lived in San Francisco. However, when his tenure with the railroad ended, he probably considered that he would obtain an office in a Republican administration. That eventually did happen, but not for another ten years.

A matter then occurred that almost cost Mosby a great deal of money and probably did cause him considerable mortification. A forger attempted to cash a check for $800 at Mosby's bank but was found out because Mosby did not have that much money in his account. The culprit probably assumed that he was wealthy given all the publicity about his consular fees and lottery pay and that the amount he attempted to take was available. The fact that he was wrong, while it prevented loss, did serve to embarrass Mosby when the matter was reported upon in the press:

Record-Union - February 5, 1891

A FORGER FRIGHTENED.

His Want of Nerve Saves a Bank Losing $800

San Francisco, Feb. 4.—The police are searching for a forger who nearly succeeded in robbing the Nevada Bank of $800 to-day. Half an hour after the bank opened a man entered and presented an $800 check for payment, signed as if by Colonel John Mosby.

The signature was perfect, and the teller would have paid it if he had not suddenly remembered that Colonel Mosby did not have quite that amount to his credit. He went to consult with President Hellman, and while he was gone the man took to his heels. Had he waited a few minutes he would have got the money.

Colonel Mosby was at once communicated with, but denied having drawn such a check. As the Colonel expected to leave for Mexico to-morrow, the man would have had a good chance to get away. As the bank's teller can give no description of the man, the police have small hopes in catching him.

Mosby was still busy with the lottery. Perhaps that was why he considered moving to Los Angeles from San Francisco—if indeed he did so. In this article in the Chronicle, he was enthusiastic about the condition of the concern and was more than slightly knowledgeable about the European banking interests involved. It showed that John Mosby was aware that lotteries could be cheats in more ways than by fraudulent drawings:

San Francisco Chronicle – **February 19, 1891**

Colonel Mosby.

Colonel John S. Mosby has just returned from Mexico, where he has been superintending the monthly drawing of the Juarez Lottery, which is in a very flourishing condition, and will soon be one of the greatest financial institutions on this continent. Colonel Mosby states that N. Liepheimer, a millionaire banker of Hamburg, has just been elected manager of the Juarez Company. As is well known, the company is a concession from the Mexican Government, and the stockholders are all wealthy bankers and capitalists of Hamburg, Paris and New York.

Again, Mosby went east, though no speculation was made as to his business there. Given that the lottery still had had monthly drawings, his travel schedule must have been very taxing for a man of fifty seven:

San Francisco Morning Call – **February 25, 1891**

THE SOCIAL WORLD

Colonel John S. Mosby gave an enjoyable breakfast on Monday to a few of his friends prior to his departure for the East. He will leave to-morrow and will remain away until early in April.

Mosby soon found himself at odds with a Midwestern newspaper regarding his connection with the lottery and the law denying the use of the US mails to such enterprises. The paper complained that Mosby was the "patron" of the lottery and that as it was breaking the law, obviously he carried some of the guilt for that offense. Eventually, Mosby became the target of the postmaster general in an effort to shut down the Juarez lottery but needless to say, as he was not personally using the mails on behalf of that concern, he was quite safe:

Indianapolis Journal – **March 18, 1891**

EVADING THE LOTTERY LAW

General John Mosby at the Head of a Mexican Concern That is using Our Mails.

Chicago, March 17.—Postoffice Inspector Fitz has discovered, as the result of several months' investigation, that the Louisiana lottery has succeeded in evading the anti-lottery law by establishing a branch office under the name of the Mexican International Banking Company at Cuidad Juarez, Mexico, under the patronage of General John Mosby. It is flooding the large cities of this country with its circulars openly, and the postal authorities are powerless to prevent it, because they have no authority to tamper with mail from a foreign country, even if they know it contains lottery matter. Captain Fitz has the names of the agents of the concern in most large cities, and the Postoffice Department will prosecute them; but it is not thought that this will affect the business to any considerable extent, as the lottery company has lists of the names and addresses of nearly all who play the lottery.

Mosby was a salaried employee of the Juarez lottery; it was neither financed nor run by him. Furthermore, he was not cowed into submission by the attempt to make him into some sort of moral reprobate. Actually, Mosby found the whole thing rather humorous. This was another example of the government trying to enforce moral codes upon the people, something that never seemed to work. The ultimate stupidity of this type of interference was the Eighteenth Amendment (Prohibition). As a result of this foolish attempt at social engineering, more people drank worse whiskey while organized crime was launched into its heyday.

Mosby then attended General Joseph Johnston's funeral and was not at all pleased with the Southern response as he forcefully stated in an article in the *Alexandria Gazette*:

Alexandria Gazette – March 25, 1891

Col. John S. Mosby, who is still here, is by no means pleased with the manner in which General Johnston's funeral yesterday was conducted. He says the ex-Confederates here, and within reasonable distance, should have made it their business to see that the funeral was as imposing as possible, in order that the people of the whole country might know the respect they entertain for their distinguished leaders. He also thinks that inasmuch as General Johnston lost his life by attending the funeral of General Sherman, in whose army the President was a brigadier, it would have been as little as Mr. Harrison could have well done to have attended the funeral, as Vice-President Morton did. The Colonel is as much of a republican as ever, but he in no wise conceals the low esteem in which he holds the President.

Mosby condemned not just Harrison but all those old Confederates who had made his life so miserable because he wasn't a "good enough" Confederate! As for Harrison, Mosby pointed out that the president could have done much to help "heal the breach" by paying his respects to Johnston, a man who was hardly a fire-eater and who had been a great friend of Union "hero" William Sherman.

The postal authorities had made it known that the only person they wished dearly to apprehend while breaking the lottery mail law was of course John Mosby. Naturally, Mosby—a lawyer—would not have been so stupid as to place himself into their eager hands:

The Times – April 15, 1891

WANAMAKER ON LOTTERY.

Postoffice Officials Are Now After Colonel John S. Mosby.

Washington, D. C.—April 14.—[Special.]—Now the Postoffice Department officials are after Colonel John S. Mosby.

Having seriously crippled the Louisiana lottery, Mr. Wanamaker is reaching out for other fields to conquer. He is even extending his reach in Mexico with the view of squelching the Mexican lottery, which has headquarters at Juarez. Colonel Mosby draws a large salary from this concern for certifying that its drawings are conducted fairly and honestly. It is presumed of course that the Colonel attends each drawing.

Chief Inspector Rathbone, of the Postoffice Department said today that he had received a report that his inspectors had arrested at El Paso, Texas, one Nicholas Leibhamer for mailing matters for the Mexican lottery. The man was represented as a regular employee or agent of the lottery, and he made regular trips across the Rio Grande for the express purpose of depositing the lottery mail. He mailed letters for distribution throughout Mexico as well as the United States. In Mexico the regular letter postage is five cents while a two-cent United States stamp will convey a letter to any office in that Republic if it is mailed this side (of) the Rio Grande.

Chief Inspector Rathbone said that Liebhamer had been caught in the very act of violating the anti-lottery law. He added that there are citizens of this country who are primarily interested in the Mexican lottery and that his Department in on their trail. It is evident that Rathbone feels particularly anxious to catch Colonel Mosby. In fact, he avowed that the distinguished ex-Confederate is the man he most wants. But it is difficult to see how Rathbone can get a point on Mosby, as the letters in connection with the lottery is [sic] confined to the Mexican side. Rathbone says, though, that if Mosby ever writes a letter to the lottery he will have him.

Years later, an article in *The Times* of May 11, 1902, reported that it was Rathbone, not Mosby, who was eventually "convicted" of some shady dealings. Perhaps that gentleman would have been better off doing his own job rather than seeking to "catch" the Gray Ghost. The next article addressed the poor fool who did mail lottery letters and circulars on American soil. Nevertheless, this "coup" could not have been very satisfying. After all, Nicholas Liebhamer was not John Mosby:

State Republican – April 16, 1891
CAUGHT IN THE ACT

The Agent of the Mexican Lottery Concern Caught in the Act of Mailing Interdicted Matter at the Post Office in El Paso, Tex.

Washington, April 15.—The chief post-office inspector has received telegrams from Inspectors Maynard and Clum, whom he dispatched a few days since to El Paso, Tex., that they had just arrested Nicholas Leibheimer, manager of the Mexican International Banking Co., of Juarez, who lives in El Paso. The inspectors caught Leibheimer in the act of mailing a quantity of lottery letters and circulars Monday night from El Paso. A preliminary examination will be held on the 21st.

In disregard of the anti-lottery act this lottery company has been flooding the United States with lottery literature, and in order to save postage, which is five cents on each letter if mailed in Mexico, their practice has been to mail their lottery letters and circulars in El Paso at United States rates, which is two cents. This is the same company of which Gen. John S. Mosby is the commissioner. It is believed at the post office department that the arrest of the United States agent of this lottery will have a tendency to stop the wholesale mailing of interdicted matter at El Paso.

Whether the papers involved in this little story were for or against Mosby is hard to tell. Frankly, whoever was involved, the government had owned that it did not have the authority to interfere with foreign mail:

Southern Standard – June 27, 1891

Col. John S. Mosby, according to the Savannah News, is the manager of a branch of the Louisiana Lottery, established in Mexico, which is literally flooding the country with advertising matter and circulars, which the Government is powerless to suppress, because it has no authority to interfere with the mail coming from a foreign country.

No doubt John Mosby took a certain roguish delight in "sticking it" to the puritanical Harrison, and besides, the lottery game earned him a rather handsome income. It is interesting to note that Mosby made more money from gambling—other people's—than from all the good work he did for the government in Hong Kong and elsewhere. Perhaps "crime"—in this case, the post-office bill—did pay after all.

Mosby had returned to San Francisco in August, and for that usually temperate city, the heat was oppressive. Further, the Mosby family was having a problem with daughter Victoria Stuart and a man called Shoebox Miller who had been introduced to the head-strong and lovely Stuart by "Count" Mitkiewiecz, a mountebank and swindler who was involved with bogus Chinese railroad concessions. The "Count" was married to a woman friend of Mosby's whom he had helped upon the death of her father. The matter was all over the press and involved not only Mosby's daughter, but older son Beverly who had taken a shot at the Count. As a result of this well-covered "romantic scandal," John Mosby was not in the best of humors when he decided to take a ride on the cable cars:

Alexandria Gazette - –August 24, 1891

Col. Mosby on his Muscle.

San Francisco, Aug. 24.—Yesterday Col. John S. Mosby, the old guerilla chieftain, arose from his seat in a cable car in which he was riding to make room for a lady, and seeing vacant seats in the grip asked the gripman if he might cross to the dummy. "You can't and you know it," said that official. Hot words followed, the conductor taking a hand. The Colonel knocked the conductor down and hammered him. The car was stopped and the gripman, a large powerful man attacked Mosby. Three lady passengers assisted by pulling the gripman's hair. The gripman got up and bolted, so did Col. Mosby, so did the battered conductor, the latter to seek the police.

Afterwards Colonel Mosby said: "I generally try to stomach insults from men in that class, for I hate a row, but you see that Mitkiewiecz affair has made me a bit irritable and so I smashed the fellow." Mosby's knees are peeled and his thumb is scratched. The conductor, however, has a face that is unfit for public inspection.

***Princeton Union* – August 27, 1891**

MOSBY ON HIS MUSCLE

The Ex-Guerrilla Chieftain Whips an Insulting Street Car Conductor.

San Francisco, Aug. 25

Fur flew on a Leavenworth street car yesterday. A conductor collided with Col. John S. Mosby, the old guerrilla chieftain, and the Colonel laid the conductor in remnants on the floor. Then the gripman tried to slay the Colonel as he was shaking the prostrate remnants of the conductor. Then the ladies in [the] car came to the old Colonel's rescue and carpeted the dummy with the gripman's hair.

The Colonel started out from his hotel for a quiet ride on the cable cars.

Owing to the crowd Mosby was obliged to take an inside seat. Presently the inside began to fill up. A lady entered and looked around. Every seat was taken. The Colonel gave her his seat. Having performed this courtesy the Colonel looked around and noticed that some of the seats on the grip had become vacant. The afternoon was scorching hot and the Colonel went outside.

"May I come across to the dummy? He asked the gripman. "You can't and you know it." said that official.

Hot words followed. The Colonel knocked the conductor down and hammered him. The car was stopped and the gripman, a large, powerful man attacked Mosby. Three lady passengers assisted by pulling the gripman's hair. Squeals rent the air; the gripman got up and bolted; so did Col. Mosby; so did the battered conductor, and the latter chased out to seek the police.

Afterward Col. Mosby said: Generally I try to stomach insults from men in that class, for I hate a row. But you see that Mitkiewiecz affair has made me a bit irritable, and so I smashed the fellow.

Mosby bears a few marks of the encounter. His knees are peeled and his thumb is scratched. The conductor, however, has a face that is unfit for publication.

At the time, Mosby was fifty-seven years old—hardly an "old man," at least by today's standards. However, the response of the ladies to the assault on Mosby by the gripman seems to indicate that he was in the right in the matter. And finally, it must be assumed that the conductor's refusal to allow Mosby to move to the dummy was anything but courteous. Had it been, the matter would never have degenerated into a brawl. As nothing came of it legally, it is probable that the streetcar company took no action, and neither did Mosby.

The Mosby-Miller-Mitkiewiecz affair was high drama in an era that adored romance, crime, and violence—or at least attempted violence. In the end, Stuart did not marry her convict lover, and perhaps it was for the best; for whatever Miller's guilt regarding the robbery for which he was sent to the penitentiary, it was said that he had three living and undivorced wives running around when he set his cap for Stuart. As for Mitkiewicz's financial matters, he was a known swindler who made a living taking advantage of such men as he called upon to testify to his "good name." Still, many further articles appeared regarding the Mosbys, Shoebox Miller, and Count Mitkiewiecz throughout the rest of the year—an obvious cross for Victoria's and Beverly's not-too-long suffering father.

Every once in a while, Mosby met up with one of those unforgiving Yankees who had run afoul of him in the war but did not recognize him and therefore did not know the identity of their traveling companion. John Mosby had no problem at all making that fact known to them. Below is one such cautionary tale:

Evening World – August 20, 1891
HE WAS COL MOSBY.

A Northern Man Surprised by a Travelling Companion.

Col. Mosby has had many peculiar social experiences. People have met him on the train and have abused him to his face, not knowing he was the famous guerilla chief, says a writer in the St. Louis Globe-Democrat. I heard one story about him on his way to the Del Monte.

Mosby is rather a peculiar man and has no hesitation in asking parties to close windows and do other things which will add to his comfort. He asked a gentleman to close a window, which was done, and they entered into conversation. Mosby gave the stranger his name, whereupon the stranger, with an expletive, said:

"That d—d guerilla of your name once gave me quite a fright. I was with So-and-So, and the report was spread that Mosby and his men were in our immediate neighborhood and we would have a brush with him. Confound the fellow, the fright that news gave me still lingers. I hear he is in California. I would like to meet him and see what the old ruffian looks like."

Mosby's face never moved. He calmly said:

"Yes, I think I gave many of your Northern would-be soldiers chills down the back."

The face of the Northerner was quite picturesque in astonishment.

It must be supposed that Mosby hugely enjoyed such occasions almost as much as he enjoyed meeting men who had fond feelings for him as the result of the treatment they received at his hands. One also has to wonder what the rest of the journey was like after this particular revelation!

A small newspaper prints a small but delightful story of Mosby's kindness and generosity with complete strangers. Such things were one of the more engaging elements of his naïveté:

Tombstone Epitaph – September 6, 1891

John S. Mosby, the ex-guerilla Chief of the Confederate army, went through over the S.P. on his way to El Paso yesterday. He is a fine-looking gray-haired old man. He neither uses tobacco or liquor, but is fond of watermelon. He purchased two immense ones in Los Angeles, and when he cut them he insisted upon each person in the sleeper, eating a huge slice with him.

Part of the article below—in a paper that is well named!—is reminiscent of such diatribes that were far more common immediately after the war. Undoubtedly, the entire article was about those horrible rebels and traitors put into office by the party not favored by the publication. Again, it is based upon partisan politics as can be attested by the contention that Mosby—"this cowardly, cold-blooded human butcher"—was appointed to an office by a "Republican administration." About the only statement of truth in the article was that Mosby was indeed appointed by a Republican administration—however, he did not "displace a Union colonel who had earned leaden memorials of his many battles for the Union!" The man he "displaced" was none other than the crook Bailey, who had left Hong Kong to move further up and further in the ring of corruption in China. The fact that over a quarter of a century has passed since the end of the war apparently made no difference when election season rolled around:

Kansas Agitator - October 6, 1891

[Part of a much longer article.]

One Col. John S. Mosby, who distinguished himself by organizing an independent horde of mountain bandits, who preyed upon isolated camps of Union soldiers, murdering them in their sleep, assassinated single soldiers who lagged behind their regiments, sick and sore with their weary marches. This cowardly, cold-blooded human butcher was appointed by the head of the Republican administration to the United States consulate at Hong Kong, displacing a Union colonel who had earned leaden memorials of his many battles for the Union.

During a dinner party, another war reminiscence was related by a former Federal officer. Mosby was present, and the Captain and doubtless the rest of the guests were astonished to have the narrator's story verified by one of its hitherto unknown participants:

The Morning Call - October 21, 1891

Short Stories Gleaned From Different Sources. The Identity of Captain French's Captor Revealed.

A few evenings ago Colonel E. A. Denicke entertained at dinner Captain French, a Philadelphia banker and an officer of the Signal Corps during the war. Among the other guests were some members of the local corps and Colonel John S. Mosby, the well-known guerrilla chieftain. Captain French has contributed a number of articles to the Century and other magazines relating to his escape from Libby Prison, and at the dinner table he narrated an incident which has not yet been published.

"We were attached to Sherman's army," said Captain French, "and as we were marching towards Gettysburg I was detailed to reconnoiter with another man. We passed a farm-house, but afterward returned to the place to ask for a drink of water. The house was within Union lines and a group of officers was standing in front. Before we had an opportunity of speaking a woman informed us that our dinner was ready, and although we were considerably surprised at this we had no objection in those days to eat a dinner which was obviously designed for some one else.

"As we left the house a man in civilian dress ordered me to throw up my hands and surrender. As I was within Union lines my first thought was that some soldier was playing a practical joke upon me and I carelessly ignored it, but when the man emphasized his order by pointing an ugly looking gun close to my head, I considered it wise to obey. The upshot of that adventure was my confinement in Libby Prison. I don't know who my captor was, but the occurrence was on the 16th of—"

Captain French was interrupted by Colonel Mosby. "You are mistaken as to the date," said the latter, "it was on the 17th, and by the way you probably do not know that you were almost a dead man that day. When I pointed the gun at you I was wiggling the trigger, but somehow it did not work smoothly and your surrender prevented its discharge."

"Were you my captor?" asked Captain French in surprise, "I heard afterward that he was one of Mosby's men."

"I was the man," was Colonel Mosby's grim reply.

The *Alexandria Gazette* published a little "blurb" on Mosby, which, in effect, became a sort of advertisement for the paper. There was no doubt, however, of the paper's accuracy as Mosby had always been an avid reader of the newspapers even during the war:

Alexandria Gazette – **November 20, 1891**

Col. Mosby was on Pennsylvania avenue to-day and, at the request of the "fotografer" over Brentano's had his picture taken. The Colonel says though he lives on the Pacific slope, with occasional visits to Mexico to look after the Juarez Lottery, which is booming, he finds he knows a good deal more about Virginia affairs than many of the people of that State he meets here, and that the reason is he subscribes for the Gazette and reads every line of it.

The Gazette once more used Mosby as a "source" in reporting upon an effort by the newspapers to end the proscription against lottery advertisements. Mosby pointed out that lotteries were as "American" as apple pie—and George Washington:

Alexandria Gazette – **November 21, 1891**

The case argued in the U. S. Supreme Court last week involving the right of the liberty of the press to publish lottery advertisements induces Col. Mosby, who is one of the supervisors of the Mexican lottery, to say that "General Washington himself conducted a lottery and so did Madison; that Congress has at various times authorized dozens of them, and that a number of the public buildings in Washington city were constructed by the proceeds of lotteries."

A Pennsylvania paper reported on Mosby—for absolutely no good reason. It was one of those articles that prove the existence of newspaper interest in the man quite apart from any real "news" in which he was a part:

Pittsburg Dispatch – November 24, 1891

Mosby, the Noted Guerrilla Chief. [Baltimore American.]

The noted Confederate cavalryman, Col. John S. Mosby, is in Washington. People who have pictured the daring raider as a stalwart chieftain, ferocious and grim-visaged, would be disappointed in his appearance. He is not over medium build and weight, though heavier now than when he figured as a combatant. He is in the best of health and vigorous as a youth. His eyes are piercing blue and his hair snow-white. He wears no beard. The Colonel dresses in a neat, business-like costume, but the slouch hat tells of his Southern antecedents. He has been a citizen of San Francisco ever since giving up his consular office at Hong Kong, and is one of the attorneys of the Southern Pacific Railroad.

This story in a Texas paper is much like that above, save that in this case, the reporter had indeed spoken to Mosby. Apparently, nothing of any moment was discussed; but the contact gave the man an opportunity to report, again, on Mosby's physical appearance and his general activities. Such small matters regarding ordinary folk simply do not appear in the newspapers:

Fort Worth Gazette – November 28, 1891

Col. John S. Mosby.

I had an interesting chat the other day with Col. John S. Mosby, the famous old Confederate raider. He is smooth-shaven, white-haired and has a piercing blue eye, but is not of commanding stature. He is doing well in San Francisco, where he is one of the attorneys for the Southern Pacific road, and he supplements his income by going down to Paso del Norte or Juarez, once a month to supervise the drawings of the Mexican lottery located there. He came to Washington to argue a case before the supreme court.

Wheeling Daily Intelligencer – December 4, 1891

Colonel John S. Mosby, the notorious Confederate guerilla, and once the attorney for the Southern Pacific road, is in Washington. His hair is now as white as snow, but his eye is as piercing as a gimlet.

1891 had been reasonably quiet for John Mosby aside from the "ruckus" that had taken place in his family and ended on a San Francisco cable car. As for the family, it was something he was too distant to influence at the time. But there is no doubt that he looked forward to another presidential election. He would not of course vote again for "Cousin Ben," but whether he would vote for the Democrat was a matter of doubt, especially when the Democratic candidate was the man who had removed him from Hong Kong—Grover Cleveland! Cleveland had run against Harrison but had lost and was now back to try again.

Chapter 31

1892

Possunt quia posse videntur.
~ They can because they think they can.

"If we are not ashamed to think it, we should not be ashamed to say it." ~ Cicero

THE INTEREST in war stories continued into the new year, and John Mosby related the incident of his most serious wounding during the war in an article appearing in two newspapers:

Atlanta Constitution – **January 3, 1892**

Los Angeles Herald – **February 4, 1892**

MOSBY, THE GUERRILLA.

He Tells How He Was Captured, Shot and Left for Dead.

Mosby continued to visit Mexico for the lottery and—it would seem if the Call article was correct—took some time to do a little more than just visit:

Los Angeles Herald – **January 5, 1892**

Col. John S. Mosby passed through the city yesterday on his way to El Paso to superintend the drawing of the Mexican lottery. The Colonel is as debonair, handsome and forceful as he was twenty years ago. He has hundreds of friends in this city who are delighted when he drops in once a month.

San Francisco Morning Call – **January 13, 1892**

Colonel John S. Mosby has returned from an extensive tour of Mexico.

Mosby's opinion of the saber as a weapon of war was given mention in a number of articles. Eventually, his view was to become the official assessment of the weapon:

Perrysburg Journal – **April 9, 1892**

The Saber Has Had Its Day.

"The saber," said Col. John S. Mosby, the famous confederate soldier, recently, "is about as useless in actual warfare as the fifth wheel of a coach. It is only a tradition. Gunpowder knocked it out, and it has been retained in the service largely on sentimental grounds. On dress parade and occasions of ceremony the saber does well enough, but no sane man would think of using a sabre in a modern battle. During the Franco-Prussian war only seven men were killed by the saber on both sides, and yet you could count up the men killed in our own war by that weapon on your fingers. We discarded it altogether in my command. In the ancient days when King Arthur was on earth the saber was of some use, but it is entirely out of place in the nineteenth century. The government could save money and at the same time improve the efficiency of the service by abolishing the saber from the army.

Fiction writers will, of course, cling to it, for its loss would deprive them of one of the chief articles of their stock in trade. The paper hero must 'cut his way through the ranks of the enemy' just so often or he is no good. Then, it looks well—on paper—for a regiment or army to 'charge on the enemy with sabers drawn,' etc. All that kind of stuff may 'go' in books, but it is supremely ridiculous to military men."—*Chicago Tribune.*

Mosby's writings involving Stuart's part in the Gettysburg campaign were starting to draw the attention of various former high-ranking Confederates as seen here:

Los Angeles Herald - March 11, 1892

General Beauregard's Letter to Colonel Mosby.

General Beauregard has recently written a letter to Col. John S. Mosby, in which he says he always condemned as dangerous and ill advised the Gettysburg campaign until he read the colonel's late articles on that campaign, but the colonel's explanation of it induces him to withdraw that condemnation. To all familiar with the circumstances of the battle of Gettysburg, it has always been known that it was brought on without General Lee's knowledge; that he was led into it in order to save the division that did bring it on; and that he bore the blame for it, as for that of all his army's other mishaps, patiently and without the slightest attempt to relieve himself.—[*Alexandria Gazette*, Virginia.

In the matter of the consular fees, Mosby had been denied $400; and feeling that it was his by right, he had appealed and won:

San Francisco Chronicle – April 23, 1892

Alexandria Gazette – April 29, 1892

CONSULAR FEES

Suit Against the Government Won by Colonel Mosby.

Judge Morrow yesterday awarded Colonel John S. Mosby judgment of $400 against the Government. While Mosby was United States Consul at Hongkong, he collected $400 in fees for shipping seamen in one of Russell & Co.'s vessels, flying the American flag, but not registered in this country. The Department of State decided that Mosby was not entitled to fees from ships flying the American flag, and the Consul refunded the $400 to Russell & Co. Then the State Department reversed its decision and announced that only vessels registered in the United States were except from the payment of fees. Mosby had retired from the office, and Russell & Co. paid the money to his successor, Consul Withers, who turned it into the treasury. The Government refused to pay the money to Mosby so he brought the action. The Government will appeal.

The article ends with the statement "The Government will appeal." But *the appeal* would cost more than the award, and as it was obvious that Mosby was owed the money that had been paid to his successor, why would there be an appeal? Why indeed! On the answer to that question hangs the whole of the United States government's dealings with John Singleton Mosby.

Another what might be termed "article of description" appeared in the *Alexandria Gazette*. There is nothing of note in the account, just a mention that the person involved was John Mosby, what he looked like, and where he was going—none of which could be considered newsworthy. As such was the case, the only reason for the coverage was the identity of the man being covered:

> *Alexandria Gazette* - **May 12, 1892**
>
> Col. John S. Mosby, of San Francisco, was in the city Monday, visiting friends and his son, Beverley C. Mosby, who is a law student at the university. He has grown stouter, his weight being 183 pounds. He left on the afternoon train for Warrenton.—Charlottesville Jeffersonian.

Never let it be said that any newspaper could be perfect, whether in being right all the time or wrong. The old *National Tribune* proved that point in an article about the obsolescence of the saber. Not only was Mosby mentioned respectfully, but his opinion was presented as correct, only going to show that the Tribune could be accurate rather than vindictive when it chose to be:

> *National Tribune* – **May 12, 1892**
>
> Capt. William Hall, 5th U.S. Cav., advocates the use of the revolver by mounted troops in place of the saber, which, he says, is useless as a weapon in actual warfare. This has long been the theory of Col. John S. Mosby, the rebel guerrilla, who considers the saber a very pretty toy for dress-parade, but really a detriment to a trooper in close combat. Col. Mosby had this belief as far back as the late unpleasantness, when he directed his command to discard their swords and rely on their revolvers.

It was a presidential election year, and as usual, stories appeared with regard to Mosby's relationship with Grant. Mosby never tired of telling the story of his dealings with his dear friend, probably because the relationship had been presented so often as a matter of self-interest. Also, he never missed an opportunity to bring to light General Grant's excellent virtues. One such article was carried in the *Perrysburg Journal*:

> *Perrysburg Journal* – **May 28, 1892**
>
> REMINISCENSES BY MOSBY.
>
> Why the Famous Guerrilla Supported Gen. Grant for President.

A small article about Mosby in Mexico appeared in a Virginia paper. He mentioned Blaine as being the Republican nominee, but of course, he was not for reasons of ill-health. It was obvious that Mosby did not believe Harrison would be renominated, but in that, he was wrong. His percentage of accurate pronouncements regarding Cousin Ben wasn't high:

Alexandria Gazette – June 14, 1892

Col. John S. Mosby, the famous Confederate cavalry officer, arrived yesterday morning from El Paso. He is stopping at the Hotel Iturbide and will remain in the city several days. Col. Mosby visited yesterday morning the American Legation and Consulate General and called at the office of The Two Republics. He is a handsome gentleman of 59 years, tall and straight and well preserved. During Grant's administration he was for several years United States Consul in China and since that time he has made his home in San Francisco. He is in Mexico purely on a pleasure trip, this being his first visit here. Col. Mosby commented on the news of Mr. Blaine's resignation, which appeared in Sunday's paper, and said that he believed Mr. Blaine would be nominated at Minneapolis tomorrow and elected. Being a republican, the Colonel is a protectionist, but he said yesterday laughingly, after his experience in getting his baggage from the depot, that he was only a protectionist in the United States and was in favor of free trade in Mexico.— The Two Republics, City of Mexico, June 7.

Alexandria Gazette – June 16, 1892

Col. Mosby's Views.

City of Mexico, June 16.—Col. John S. Mosby is here from San Francisco. He says: "I am a republican, but will not vote for Harrison. Harrison is a narrow-minded sectional bigot, still believing in hell fire and infant damnation—a man whose illiberal character is now known to the people of the United States, and who can carry neither New York nor Indiana nor any of the southern States whose delegates have renominated him." The Colonel was outspoken in his denunciation of Harrison's connection with the force bill, and said that he would have supported Blaine or McKinley with pleasure.

Mosby was more than just disappointed with Harrison, for whom he had held such high hopes that there might be further moves made toward reconciliation with the South by the national government in a Republican administration. Harrison's support of the Force Bill was probably the last straw for his erstwhile cousin. Earlier, Mosby's comments on Harrison were guarded and evasive; but in this interview, it is obvious that he was downright enraged by the man, perhaps because Harrison was such a disappointment or perhaps Harrison was just the "last straw" in a procession of disappointing Northern Republicans.

The press continued to report on Mosby's lottery movements, perhaps wondering if in an election year, President Harrison might move to make an example of his erring cousin and if it were indeed legally possible for him to do so:

Arizona Republican – August 2, 1892

Gen. Moseby of Confederate fame, spent Sunday in town. He makes a trip monthly from San Francisco to Juarez, Mexico opposite of El Paso, where he superintends the drawings of the Mexican lottery, for doing which he receives $1,000 per trip.—Yuma Times.

Once again, John Mosby's consular fees' litigation made the newspapers. He had won his $400 suit, but whether that was after the government appeal or this was merely a recapitulation of the earlier report is not said. He received interest and costs, so it may be that this was after the government's appeal. It is very difficult to follow press coverage in these stories as different papers often "reported" matters that were months old as if they were current:

The Morning Call – **August 30, 1892**

MOSBY'S LATEST CAPTURE.

He Obtains Judgment Against Uncle Sam for $400.

John S. Mosby, ex-United States Consul at Hong-Kong and more conspicuously in evidence in history as the dashing leader of a troop of Confederate horsemen in Virginia, won another victory over the Government forces yesterday. The contest was a bloodless one. The theater of war was the United States District Court. General Mosby had sued the Government for $400 fees collected by him while acting as consul. The court found judgment in his favor for $400 with interest and costs.

"Articles of interest" continued to appear in the Gazette. It would seem from this type of article, which was appearing more frequently in papers around the country, that Mosby's life had become quite pleasant and prosperous. One story included mention of the kindnesses he continued to perform for his friends and fellow Virginians despite his estranged relations with his home state:

Alexandria Gazette – **December 17, 1892**

Col. John S. Mosby, of California, was in town a few days this week with his children and grandchildren. His face is unseamed and he looks in the full vigor of manhood. His old friends here have this piece of kindness to place to the credit side of his account: he secured lucrative positions in the engineer corps of the Southern Pacific for Ernest Blackwell and Clay Beattie, two Fauquier boys, and both are filling their posts in the most acceptable manner to the company.

Again, Mosby was sought for his opinion on matters having nothing to do with the Civil War, lotteries, or even Benjamin Harrison. Rather, he was acknowledged as "familiar with Mexican affairs" and was questioned about the "revolutionists" in that country. As usual, he did not withhold his assessment:

Alexandria Gazette – **December 27, 1892**

Col. Mosby, who is now as familiar with Mexican affairs as with those of this country, recently told the Gazette's Washington correspondent that the so-called Mexican "revolutionists" were doing all their revolutionizing in this country. What he said was true in every particular. The "revolutionists" are really bandits, who after plundering farm houses and travelers on the south side of the Rio Grande, cross to the north side and by superior numbers set the Texas authorities at defiance. As it is an international affair, and as Mexico is a friendly country, the United States and not Texas, should correct the evil at once, and Mexico has good ground for complaining that this government has not done so long ago.

The election of 1892 was over, and Democrat Grover Cleveland was in the White House—again. Benjamin Harrison was an "ex-President." The man who had been a thorn in John Mosby's side for failing to at least attempt to bind up those wounds that still existed from the war had returned home, defeated. Yet Mosby must have been disappointed with a Democrat in the White House because, though little was being said, there remained a lurking suspicion that he was unsure of his future with the railroad.

Yet despite family problems, John Mosby had had a fairly quiet year. However, his living expenses were as large as his considerable income, mostly the result of the financial support he continued to give to his now-grown children. Yet, Mosby's existence was pleasant enough given his social life among men whom he respected and admired, and not a few of whom he loved. Further, he was now dealing with a fairly friendly press. He may indeed have looked toward 1893 with considerable optimism, even with a Democrat in the White House.

Chapter 32

1893

Dum spiro, spero. ~ As long as I breathe, I hope.

"I am not bound to please thee with my answer."
~ William Shakespeare

THE YEAR BEGAN with another "article of interest," which was embarrassing for two reasons: First, Mosby's rank was wrong as was his middle initial. Worse, his son was not even provided with a name, though it was probably Beverly who lived in Utah, while John Jr. lived in Colorado. The shadow of such a father must have been difficult for Mosby's sons, which is probably why they sought lives far away from Virginia:

> *Salt Lake Herald* – **February 15, 1893**
>
> General Mosby in Town.
>
> General John V. Mosby, the noted ex-Confederate general of cavalry, whose home is now in San Francisco, came down from Ogden yesterday accompanied by his son. They are quartered at the Knutsford.

Mosby complimented the Gazette only to have his good wishes damned with faint praise:

> *Alexandria Gazette* – **March 3, 1893**
>
> "Colonel Mosby congratulates the Gazette on the selection of a third term Grant republican to be the premier or the next administration. The world does move."—Letter from Col. John S. Mosby.
>
> Well, everybody in Virginia, and many outside of it, knows that the Gazette does not think Judge Gresham should have been appointed; but still, few will deny that his is a better appointment that that of his immediate predecessor, who was a professional international lobbyist.

Mosby then responded to that "faint praise" with a follow-up comment:

> *Alexandria Gazette* – **March 29, 1893**
>
> Col. Mosby says he "is willing to admit that what the Gazette says is true: vis: That Gresham is a better man than his predecessor, Foster. But the point is, was it necessary in order to find a better man than Foster, to go outside The Democratic party?" From the Gazette's standpoint it was not, but Mr. Cleveland unquestionably thought otherwise.

The Gazette, a Democratic paper, made a point about Democratic Cleveland going outside of his party to choose a successor to an office holder and admitted that, while the paper thought Cleveland did not have to do so, the President thought otherwise. Perhaps Cleveland believed, as did Mosby, that it was time to put an end to a political system based solely on party rather than ability and ethics.

Another name out of the past and made that one final appearance in the press, an appearance that all men of renown eventually make. Nothing was ever said about whether or not John Mosby and A. D. Payne amicably settled their differences after their abortive attempt at a duel, but it is probable that as Payne remained, as the article stated, both "well known and popular," they did not. When John Mosby heard of the captain's passing, one might legitimately wonder just what went through his mind:

Alexandria Gazette – March 8, 1893

DEATH OF CAPTAIN A. D. PAYNE—The many friends and acquaintances of this well-known and popular gentleman will regret to hear of his death, which occurred at his home in Warrenton last night. Capt. Payne during the war was commander of the famous Black Horse Cavalry, made historic by its almost hand-to-hand conflict with the Ellsworth Zouaves at the first Battle of Bull Run. The deceased followed the fortunes of the Confederacy throughout the four years' struggle, and at the close of hostilities returned to his native heath, where he was honored with positions of public trust, among them Delegate to the Legislature from Fauquier. Of late years he had followed his profession as a lawyer, and was always regarded of a many of ability. The pall-bearers for his funeral will be selected from survivors of his old command.

Many years ago Capt. Payne and Col. John S. Mosby became estranged on account of the attitude taken by the latter in supporting General Grant for the Presidency, and so strained were their relations that a challenge was received by the captain. He was on the field on time, but Colonel Mosby had been arrested in the meantime, and no conflict occurred. The affair was finally adjusted to the satisfaction of both parties.

Payne's life was what Mosby's would have been if he had "gone with his section"— that is, a life of grace and financial well-being together with the respect and affection of his fellow Southerners. Mosby led a life of hostility, contempt, betrayal, and eventual poverty. There is some moral here, but it does not seem to fit standard ethical doctrines. Another article on the late Captain Payne appeared, advising that the man left a large fortune, another clear distinction between his life and John Mosby's:

The Argus – April 11, 1893

CAPTAIN ALEXANDER DIXON PAYNE died the other day in Warrenton, Va., leaving a fortune of $100,000. Payne is the man who, after the war, challenged Colonel John S. Mosby to a duel because Mosby supported General Grant for the presidency. Both colonels had served in the famous Black Horse cavalry of the Confederate army.

As usual, the story was right only in its general thrust—that is, that Captain Payne had died. It was Mosby who challenged Payne after warning him that his personal comments were slanderous and could not, with honor, be ignored. Also, Mosby never served in the Black Horse Cavalry, which was raised in Warrenton. These appear to be small details, but they testify to a lack of a concern for accuracy that mattered very much where more critical matters were being covered by the press.

Perrysburg Journal – April 15, 1893

Capt. Alexander Dixon Payne, who died the other day in Warrenton, Va., enlisted in the famous Black Horse cavalry of the confederate army, and in time came to be captain of the troop. He attracted attention after the war by provoking a challenge to a duel from his old companion in arms, Col. John S. Mosby, whom Capt. Payne assailed because of Mosby's supporting Gen. Grant for the presidency. Capt. Payne went to the dueling ground, but Col. Mosby was kept away by the sheriff.

Suddenly, in the midst of ancient quarrels and sorrows arose a most modern matter, the situation involving the Chinese who had come to America. The "Yellow Peril," as they were seen in the minds of many Americans, found themselves defended by California Senator Leland Stanford and, of course, that champion of the despised and dispossessed, Colonel John S. Mosby:

Alexandria Gazette – May 16, 1893

Every independent government has the right to exclude from its territory any and every body it may deem objectionable. That right is the good old one of might, and can be maintained as long as there is sufficient power to do so. But still, why people from all the other countries of the habitable globe should be allowed free access to the United States, to compete with Americans in every branch of labor, and even to contend with them in the political field, while those from China, whose occupations are limited, and who never even think, let along talk, of politics should be rigidly excluded, is what passes comprehension of many other men besides Senator Stanford and Colonel Mosby.

Mosby had spoken up on the exclusion of the hardworking Chinese from every benefit of American life aside from actual presence in the country. He knew and liked the Chinese people as is shown by the most gracious send-off he received at their hands when he left Hong Kong. He believed that while less industrious people—foreign and domestic—were assiduously courted by American politicians, the Chinese whose presence tended to improve the areas in which they resided and who worked with far more industry than the "emancipated" Negro while causing almost no problems in the way of crime were virtually consigned to internal exile. Interestingly enough, the fear of the "yellow peril" was far more prevalent in places where the Chinese were unknown, while California and the Pacific Slope were far more welcoming to them:

Alexandria Gazette – May 25, 1893

Senator Stanford, whose advice President Cleveland says he will take as soon as that of anybody else, Col. Mosby and many other well-known Californians, democratic and republican alike, say the right-thinking people of the Pacific slope are not in favor of the anti-Chinese law, that in fact the Chinese have made that slope as rich and prosperous as it is, and that save only and except for the Chinese, hundreds of thousands of white people now there would still be on this side of the Rockies. But the demagogues say the negroes shall be clung to with hooks of steel, but that the quiet and industrious Chinese shall be not only driven out of the desert they have made to bloom like the rose, but out of the whole country which, until recently, posed as the refuge of the oppressed of all the nations of the earth.

There followed two more "descriptive articles" void of any newsworthy commentary and thus apparently only intended to keep Mosby's name in the papers:

Omaha Daily Bee – May 19, 1893

Colonel John S. Mosby, the famous ex-confederate guerilla, is nearly 60, and his hair is nearly white, but he stands as straight ass an arrow, walks with a firm step and seems to be full of vigor. He is practicing law in San Francisco.

St. Paul Daily Globe – May 25, 1893

Col. John S. Mosby, the famous ex-Confederate, is practicing law in San Francisco. He is nearly sixty years old, but stands straight as an arrow, and is full of vigor.

A curious article in which John Mosby's reticence about speaking extemporaneously was made manifest. It was also true that he was an extremely modest man. He always presented even his triumphs in war within the context of the help he had received from his men and his superiors. He did admit that he had created the strategic plan that resulted in the famous "Ride around McClellan," but he never placed himself forward as the reason for its success. On the other hand, he was willing to accept full blame when something went awry as with Miskel Farm and the assault on Loudoun Heights. It is also interesting to note that the article spoke of Mosby being "tender," which doubtless referenced his gentleness, kindness and courtesy—a far cry from what is generally put forth and accepted as his personality:

Alexandria Gazette – May 27, 1893

Colonel John S. Mosby was one of the specially invited guests at the recent banquet given to the new United States minister in the city of Mexico. Virginians are always there or there-about when anything is going on. A newspaper printed in that city says the Colonel was called upon to reply to a toast, but was too modest to respond. The bravest are modest as well as tender.

For the first time in any article, John Mosby mentioned a "sweetheart" whom he stated was "the prettiest girl in California." Did Mosby actually have a love interest, or was he referring to the daughter of one of his many friends? The word "girl" seems to suggest a more avuncular relationship than one of a lover. Certainly, Mosby never married again, even though his name was linked with two "heiresses" in the later 1870s. Neither did he ever appear in the press in connection with any romantic (or less socially acceptable) liaison. In any event, the matter was never again mentioned:

Alexandria Gazette – June 10, 1893

Col. Mosby.—Last evening a representative of the Tribune was in Albert's drug store when Colonel Mosby, the famous ex-Confederate cavalry commander walked in and purchased a copy of John Esten Cooke's Hilt to Hilt, with the remark: "I want to send it to my sweetheart—the prettiest girl in California." In his younger days the Colonel was noted for gallantry to the fair, and he is still an excellent judge of feminine beauty and still worships at its shrine. John Esten Cook, who was a member of Gen. J.E.B. Stuart's staff, was a great admirer of the dashing young commander of Mosby's men, and in Hilt to Hilt has this to say of Col. Mosby: "To-day I cannot describe the partisans or their lithe and dangerous commander, with his gray, roving eyes, his smile, revealing the white teeth, his brief words of command and his daring soul. Imagine this king of the rangers, amid the great forest of Fauquier, with his horse saddled near and his gray followers around him. Hear the jest and laughter; see them mount and ride away; hear the crack of their pistols; see the long string of blue prisoners; the "U. S." wagons; the numberless mules captured." Col. Mosby is 29 or 30 years older than he was in those days, but he feels just as young, carries himself just as erect and walks with just as firm and quick step. And though his clean-shaved, pleasant face and bright eyes beam with kindliness, the combative fire of his youth is still there, and unless you want to be stung it were better not to stir him up. Col. Mosby visits El Paso every month and has many personal friends there.—El Paso Tribune.

Mosby had returned to San Francisco as is seen in this, albeit larger, "article of interest" in which his wardrobe was given especial mention. Alas, once he left the private sector and was forced to take a position (job) with the Federal government, his income dropped precipitously while he continued to send what money he could to his children. It is interesting and somewhat melancholy to contemplate what he might have thought had he read of the estate left by the late Captain Payne, the man who had called him a coward and sought to severely punish him for having the temerity to reject the path followed by most of the rest of his fellow Southerners:

Alexandria Gazette – **June 20, 1893**

COLONEL MOSBY.—John S. Mosby, the famous guerilla cavalryman of the Confederacy, arrived here to-day after a six months' trip through the eastern States and Mexico.

Attired in a spick-and-span spring suit of a delicate fawn color, with a flowing necktie of the brightest blue, and a slender cane that he swings with a perfectly "fetching" air, the Colonel made a picturesque figure on the streets to-day.

"I've been 20,000 miles since I left San Francisco," said he when hailed. "I've been all over, but I'm glad to be back."

Colonel Mosby bears his age well; only a slight stoop of the shoulders shows where Father Time's hand has rested. In other ways he is about as active as he was in Virginia in '63.—

San Francisco Bulletin.

In November, the *Edgefield Advertiser*—a South Carolina paper—presented a poem entitled "Mosby at Hamilton," probably the first poem about the Forty-third to appear in print. The occasion was not stated, but it became another mark in Mosby's legend. Poems are not written about nonentities:

Edgefield Advertiser – **November 30, 1893**

MOSBY AT HAMILTON.

Down Loudon Lanes, with swinging reins

And clash of spur and sabre,

And bugling of the battlehorn,
Six score and eight we rode at morn,
Six score and eight of Southern born,
All tried in love and labor.
Full in the sun at Hamilton
We met the South's invaders;
Who, over fifteen hundred strong,
Mid blazing homes had marched along
All night, with Northern shout and song,
To crush the rebel raiders.
Down Loudon lanes with streaming manes,
We spurred in wild March weather;
And all along our war-scarred way
The graves of Southern heroes lay,
Our guide-posts to revenge that day,
As we rode grim together.
Old tales still tell some miracle
Of saints in holy writing—
But who shall say while hundreds fled,
Unless the noblest of our dead
Charged with us then when fighting!
While Yankee cheers still stunned our ears,
Of troops at Harper's Ferry,
While Sheridan led on his Huns,
And Richmond rocked to roaring guns,
We felt the South still had some sons
She would not scorn to bury.

—Fetter's Southern Magazine

    The year had been quiet for John Mosby, both in life and in the press. Perhaps some considered that his long moment in the world's spotlight had passed, and perhaps he would not have minded if he could have gone on with a life of relative ease and contentment. But as any calm before the storm, it was to pass. John Mosby was simply not fated to lie at peace in a calm haven until he reached his final anchorage.

Chapter 33

1894

Amicitias immortales esse opportet.
~ Friendships should be immortal.

"In solitude, where we are least alone." ~ Lord Byron

IT HAD BEEN thirty and three years since the opening salvo of the Civil War, and many had said that the war should be if not forgotten, then certainly put sufficiently into the past so that the nation and its people might move forward. But that was easier said than done as John Mosby had found, often to his dismay and despair. Stories about the war, especially unusual tales of bravery and renown, remained in great demand. These were not so much recitations of great battles, but matters of a more personal, exciting, and romantic nature. Just as there was more interest in the tales of Robin Hood than in the history of King Richard's England, so did the stories of men like Forrest, Quantrill, and especially Mosby find great appeal among the people of the United States, whatever they might think about the struggle. Further, there appeared to be more interest in Southern warriors than in those of the North, and neither did that change much as time went on. Indeed, the gift shop in the Gettysburg national battlefield reported over the years that far more Confederate than Union mementos were purchased!

The following little bit of nonsense was an example of how newspapers tended to be more literal than was often good for them—*or* John Mosby:

Alexandria Gazette – **March 19, 1894**

Personal.—A dispatch from El Paso, Tex., says: "Col. John S. Mosby, the celebrated cavalry leader in the Confederacy, is in the city en route to Washington. In an interview he announced that he will be a candidate for the Presidency next election."

Staunton Tribune – **March 19, 1894**

AN IMPROVEMENT SURELY.

Old Guerilla Mosby Wants to be President of the United States

El Paso, Tex., March 18—Colonel John S. Mosby, the celebrated cavalry leader in the Confederacy, is in the city en route to Washington.

In an interview today he announced the he will be a candidate for the presidency next election.

The above stories demonstrated the literal nature of the press and strongly suggest that Mosby's later problems may often have resulted from his failure to sufficiently acknowledge that situation. Often, any statement he made, especially if it were made in jest, was reported as a serious comment. In this instance, Mosby had said—presumable back in 1892—that his not-well-loved "cousin" Ben's chances of being reelected were on a par with his own prospects. Of course, this was then taken to mean that he, Mosby, was going to run for president! Still, he should have known by this time not to be anything but painfully accurate and, even more important, noncommittal with the press. But that being said, the headline on the Tribune story illustrated that the paper was much wiser than many with regard to Mosby's qualifications for the office, at least vis-à-vis Harrison!

The above small "tempest in a teapot" was followed by a very nice "article of interest" in the *Gazette*:

Alexandria Gazette – March 24, 1894

Personal.—Col. John S. Mosby, in excellent health and dignified avoirdupois, is in town and enjoys his reunion with children, grandchildren and old friends. That reference to his candidacy for President must have been intended as sarcasm on Harrison whose chances he doubtless holds as lightly as his own.—Warrenton Index. Col. Mosby was in this city to-day looking not a day older than he did ten years ago.

More articles on Mosby's "interest in running for president" appeared, as well as a longer article in the Dispatch bringing the first hint of the fact that Mosby was seeking to meet with some of his old comrades:

Shenandoah Herald – March 30, 1894

What John S. Mosby Said.

The Washington correspondent of the *Alexandria Gazette* says:

Among the visitors here today is Colonel John Mosby. The Colonel is here to argue a case before the Court of Claims. He says he supposes the newspaper story about his running for President originated from his telling an acquaintance in San Diego, when on his way here, that Harrison didn't stand as much chance of being elected as he, Mosby, did.

Richmond Dispatch – April 26, 1894

COLONEL JOHN S. MOSBY

The Ranger Commander at Ford's Hotel—A Chat With Him.

Colonel John T. Mosby, [sic] the renowned ranger commander of the Confederacy, arrived in the city yesterday, and is quartered at Ford's Hotel. He will probably be here several days. Colonel Mosby's visit to Richmond is solely for the purpose of seeing some of the members of his old command.

When the Colonel was seen at the hotel yesterday afternoon by a Dispatch reporter he was the picture of health and happiness. Clad in a handsome Prince Albert, with a necktie of crimson, and wearing a soft hat which almost hid from view the tinge of gray that has come over his straight hair, he was a magnificent type of soldiery. His first remark was that he had come down from Washington, where he had been on legal business, with the hope of seeing and talking with some of his boys. Several of those who were members of Mosby's command in its marvelous achievements, called upon their Colonel yesterday, and they were greeted with unfeigned pleasure by the chief of the rangers.

Colonel Mosby is now located in San Francisco being [an] attorney of the Southern Pacific railroad. It has been sixteen years since he was last in Richmond. He had noticed great changes in the old city by the James. The City Hall he considered a beauty and a credit to the energy and noble spirit of any city. Among the Richmonders who were in Colonel Mosby's command, and who paid their respects to him yesterday, were Mr. Joseph Bryan, Lieutenant Benjamin Palmer, and Dr. A. Monteiro. The latter was battalion surgeon, and carried the flag of truce to General Hancock when Colonel Mosby was negotiating for the surrender.

In 1878 Colonel Mosby was appointed as Consul to Hong Kong, China, and served as such for about seven years. His fame as a soldier had preceded him to China, and during his sojourn in Hong Kong, when the Chinese engaged in a war with France, Li Hung Chang, the Prime Minister of China, tendered him the entire command of the Chinese forces.

A few interesting points: First, Mosby was sixty years old; and rather than a "tinge of gray," his hair was snow-white. Second, the approach to Hancock was about establishing a truce, not a surrender. Third, this was the year before Mosby's first battalion reunion. No doubt his reception by the Richmond members was such that when it was determined to hold the reunion, he willingly attended.

Mosby had received yet another invitation to a "local" event that seemed to prove his "reception" in the South was changing. Further, he was beginning to move again in Virginia's social circles, which tended to indicate that he was no longer in exile—at least at that moment and among those particular Virginians:

Alexandria Gazette – **April 27, 1894**

Col. Mosby has officially informed Mr. Isaac Hirsh of his acceptance of an invitation extended to him to be his guest May 10th, on the occasion of the dedication of the Mary Washington monument.—Fredericksburg Lance.

Alexandria Gazette – **April 28, 1894**

Col. Mosby at the Home—Colonel John S. Mosby and daughter, accompanied by Norman Randolph, esq., Mr. Benjamin Palmer, and Mr. Fontaine Beattie, of Alexandria, formerly with Col. Mosby's command, visited the Soldiers' Home Thursday evening. The visitors were cordially received by Superintendent Bigger, and a pleasant time was spent with the veterans. Col. Mosby had a number of callers at the hotel Thursday.—Rich. Dispatch.

Alexandria Gazette – **May 1, 1894**

Entertained Col. Mosby.—There was a happy gathering at Whitby stock-farm yesterday afternoon, when the genial proprietor, Mr. H. Clay Chamblin, entertained his old commander, Colonel John S. Mosby. Mr. Chamblin took his guests over the farm, showing them his fine horses, racecourse, little colts, etc. Refreshments were served, and the party after a very delightful visit, returned to the city about dark greatly pleased with the trip, what they had seen and the hospitable treatment of the host.—Richmond Dispatch.

The Herald – May 3, 1894

The Richmond Times of recent date says: Col. John S. Mosby and his two charming and accomplished daughters, Miss Pauline and Miss Ada, are at Ford's hotel. They arrived yesterday afternoon from Washington, and last evening had many callers. As was stated in The Times' Washington interview with Colonel Mosby in yesterday's issue, he has not visited Richmond for 16 years, and his present visit is entirely in the way of renewing old acquaintances and associations. He will remain in the city only a few days, and will devote the time to sight seeing and looking up old friends. When I saw him at Ford's last evening, he was mailing a copy of The Times containing his interview to a friend, and smilingly remarked that he was glad to have it, as it served as a substitute for a letter, and saved him from writing one. Times has dealt gently with Colonel Mosby. From the slender, wiry figure of the guerrilla chieftain, who 30 years ago struck terror to the hearts of federal troops and pickets, he has grown into a sturdy frame, and presents the appearance of a handsome man in the full vigor of mature years.

It is possible that John Mosby was "testing the waters" for a return to Virginia in the not-too-distant future. His reception had been most gracious, and he was probably very gratified, believing that his period as a pariah might well be in the process of ending. The spate of articles involving his social life in the state continued:

Richmond Times – May 6, 1894 (Edited)

An exceedingly pleasant affair of the past week, which I had the pleasure of sharing, was an informal gathering of ladies and gentlemen at Whitby Farm to meet the noted ex-Confederate Colonel John S. Mosby, who now resides in California.

Alexandria Gazette – May 7, 1894

FROM WASHINGTON.

Among the visitors at the Capitol to-day were Col. John S. Mosby and his daughters. They were received by the two California Senators, and attracted much attention.

Alexandria Gazette – May 11, 1894

One of the most prominent visitors in Fredericksburg yesterday was Col. Jno. S. Mosby, who was accompanied by his three accomplished daughters. Col. Mosby is warmly esteemed by all the men in his command, and has a host of admirers, not alone in his native State, Virginia, but all over the South. He will leave for his adopted home, California, this evening, stopping en route at Bristol for a few days.

Atlanta Constitution – May 18, 1894

MOSBY AT HIS OLD HOME.

He Stops to Look at the House Where He Lived.

Bristol, Tn., May 17.—(Special.)—General John S. Mosley, the famous guerrilla chief, stated here today that he is not a candidate for the presidency. He was en route from Washington to San Francisco. Colonel Mosley stopped here to look at the old house where he lived in war times.

"The hardest fight of the war for me," said he, "was telling my wife and children goodby."

He captured 6,000 federals and mints of property during the war. He came very near capturing Grant at one time. They became great friends after the war. The guerrilla was Grant's minister to China. Three books have been written about Mosby.

The "Mosby for President" matter resurfaced after a hiatus of several months, only going to prove that once a mistake appeared in the press, removing it required persistent denials and corrections, a situation that would plague John Mosby for the rest of his life:

Durham *Daily Globe* – May 19, 1894

Col. John S. Mosby announces that he is a candidate for president. But Hon. Benjamin Harrison is not making his refusals this far in advance.

Richmond Dispatch – May 20, 1894

COLONEL MOSBY NOT A CANDIDATE.

How the Canard Originated

Bedford City, Va., May 19.—(Special.)—Colonel John S. Mosby spent a few days here with his brother, en route to San Francisco. The Colonel was much amused over the newspaper canard that reported him as expressing an intention of becoming a candidate for the presidency of the United States. He was passing through El Paso, Tex., when some one asked him what he thought of ex-President Harrison's chances for re-election. "Why," replied the Colonel jokingly, "I wouldn't swap chances with him." Straightway the news was telegraphed throughout the country that he was a candidate for the presidency, to the great surprise of Colonel Mosby himself.

When speaking of Harrison "running," the paper was referring to the presidential election of 1896 as Cleveland was in the White House, having won in 1892 when he ran against Harrison for the second time. Of course, Harrison could have run again in 1896, but he did not. The Republican candidate in that election was William McKinley.

When Mosby returned to California, he found a very critical situation; that is, the so-called Pullman Strike,* that had begun in May. The strike produced social and political chaos, especially in the West (*see "Addendum" at end of the chapter):

The Times – July 10, 1894

COL. MOSBY HEARD FROM

He Tells of the Serious Strike Situation in California

The strikes and riots in the West and Northwest were the chief topic of conversation at the Capitol today. The consensus of opinion is that the President acted rightly in issuing his proclamation to the rioters at Chicago and the general opinion is that the backbone of the movement has been broken.

MOSBY ON THE STRIKE.

Senators Hunton and Daniel received the following telegram from Col. John S. Mosby to-day:

"The mob reigns in California. State Government paralyzed. Militia useless; general blockade; traffic and passenger service suspended; Federal officers defied and powerless; a conflict between civilization and anarchy.

There are enough Federal troops here to restore order without firing a gun if the President will command them. Prompt action will save us from a bloody revolution. It is our fight to-day. It may be yours to-morrow.

JOHN. S. MOSBY"

The receipt of this telegram from such a source greatly increases the gravity of the situation on the Pacific Slope, as Colonel Mosby's well-known reputation for coolness and courage is a guarantee that the seriousness of the situation is not exaggerated.

In a letter to Samuel Chapman, Mosby noted that the strike was an example of why a strong central government was necessary as California was impotent to do anything to stem the disorder. Mosby forgot, however, that the war in which he fought destroyed the sovereign power of any state, North or South. Prior to the so-called Civil War, the states had exercised far more power than they were able to do afterward. However, Mosby was right about the seriousness of the situation. The civil chaos produced by the strike constituted a very real danger and necessitated the intervention of the Federal authorities as the state had been divested of its ability to deal with such a crisis.

Once again, Mosby proved that he wasn't all "war and poetry" as he opined upon a weighty—and somewhat dull and dry—economic matter then before the nation:

Alexandria Gazette – October 25, 1894
COL. MOSBY ON THE TARIFF BILL

To the Editor of the *Alexandria Gazette*:

I notice that Congressman Wilson says that the English free traders agree with him that the effect of our new tariff will be to make us competitors with them in foreign markets and for the carrying trade of the world. This is a fairy tale which it will be hard to make people of common sense believe. Men are not so generous these days as to give banquets to those who are trying to destroy their business. When they have a good thing they don't hail with delight the appearance of a competitor who is going to take it away.

The London merchants didn't give any bouquet to Blaine when he was there. I am sure they wouldn't give one to Tom Reed or McKinley. The Gazette has always insisted that the McKinley bill was framed so as to give enormous bounties to manufacturers. Be it so. As a bounty to any interest must stimulate its production, the tendency of the McKinley bill must have been to encourage the growth of the manufacturing industries it protected. Its repeal then must have the opposite effect. It gave a bounty on sugar and put it on the free list. The immediate result was a great development of that industry: sugar was never before so cheap. The bounty has been removed and a duty imposed. The consequence is a rise in the price of sugar. Now either Wilson is wrong or the gazette is wrong. I can't see how we are to become successful competitors of the English in foreign markets without something to sell and a great increase in manufactured production. Then if the Wilson- Gorman bill is going to have this effect it must be more favorable to the manufacturers than the McKinley bill; therefore the manufacturers were fools for allowing the republicans "to fry the fat" out of them (as the Gazette said they did) to prevent the repeal of the McKinley law. If Wilson is right the manufacturers ought to be free traders, and it is all a fiction about their being the beneficiaries of a protective tariff. If, as charged, the manufacturing interests were a monopoly, I could understand the meaning of Wilson's phrase, "breaking the fetters of trade." Now, this is all theoretical wind so far as it is intended to apply to American productions. The only fetters imposed by the McKinley act were not on our exports, but imports. I can understand very well why the English should hurrah when these were broken. I don't blame them. A monopoly is a grant of a special and exclusive privilege. The Tudor Princes often made such grants to court favorites. I have never heard of anybody in the United States who enjoyed such a favor. As a protective tariff stimulates manufacturing industries, it at the same time creates competition. If the manufacturers' profits are so enormous (as you say), why don't the Virginia people go into the business? Between the States, at least, there is free trade, and New England has no monopoly. Either the manufacturers' large profits are fabulous or the Virginia people are blind in not getting a share of them. The truth is that more big fortunes have been made by importers than manufacturers. There is just as much proof that the importing interests contributed money to get the Wilson bill as that the so-called protected ones used money to defeat it. The old Whigs always charged that the passage of the Walker tariff act of 1846 was bought with "British gold" (see antebellum files of the *Gazette*).

And now comes Prof. Wilson who says in effect that the manufacturers who were against his bill didn't know it was a Grecian gift to destroy the British, and that he was working for them, and that the London merchants who gave him the feast only did so in the despairing spirit of the gladiator going to die, when he saluted Caesar. Happy are they, says the Roman poet, who know their own good. I see, too, that Gen. Hunton in his speech at Culpeper defends his vote for free wool because, he said, it would make cheap blankets, and then, to appease the farmers, said that the consequence had been a rise in the price of wool.

He did not attempt to explain how removing the duty on wool made it higher in the market, or how an increase in the price of the raw material of which they are made could make blankets cheaper. The free traders have always insisted that the consumer of the goods pays the duty. But, according to General Hunton, free trade makes them higher. Wilson says that free trade will open the markets of the world to American manufactures, and again give us the carrying trade. We suppose it was over this prospect that the London traders smiled when they uncorked their champagne bottles and drank to Wilson's health.

The fallacy of Wilson's idea is in assuming that foreign markets have ever been closed, or that there was any restriction on exports to other countries. Foreign markets are open now as they were before for all our surplus products that foreign nations wanted, and are able to buy. The price of wheat in the London markets is governed by the law of supply and demand, and not by the McKinley or Wilson bill. An English farmer gets no more for his wheat there than an American. The laboring classes are as much interested in cheap bread as cheap clothes. No doubt our friend, Mr. Robert Beverly, would like to get $3 a bushel for his wheat, as he did during the Crimean war: but those who have to buy their bread prefer the present prices.

As a protective tariff is the breath of life to American manufactures, if the manufacturers are destroyed of what use will the foreign markets be, and what benefit would it be to the farmers for the people engaged in manufacturing to go to farming? Now they furnish a home market to the products of agriculture. In exchange for the home market Wilson offers the Virginia farmers the markets of the world (which they always had) where they are brought into competition with Indian wheat produced in a country where the wages of labor are about five cents a day.

It is true that the United States are not the ocean carriers they were fifty years ago; and the reason is that our capital has been diverted to manufactures and railroad enterprises. Instead of ploughing the waves we have turned our attention to internal development and the building up of the West; a seacoast has been practically given to Montana and Dakota. If Americans don't go to sea it is because they can do better at home and can't compete with Norwegian and Italian sailors who live on a tallow candle a day. Ships are simply the vehicle of commerce. Our shipping has decreased but our commerce is now a thousand fold greater than it was when the prows of our vessels vexed every sea, and their sails were woven on an English loom. We were then the poorest nation in the world—now we are the richest. Then we furnished ships and foreigners the cargoes—now we furnish cargoes and hire foreign ships. There is no more reason for our owning the vessels that carry our products abroad than for a Virginia farmer to own the railroad that hauls his corn to Alexandria. There is nothing so deceptive as an index of wealth and commercial power as shipping. At any time in Hong Kong harbor you can see five or six Norwegian vessels to one French or American. The reason is their country is so poor the Norwegians have to go to sea for a living.

The Democrats have just nominated for Governor of New York the only democrat in the Senate who voted against the new tariff act. He will of course be buried out of sight in the coming election; not as a punishment to Hill, but to his party. McKinley is to be the next President of the United States, and now is the time to join the procession.

J. S. M.

San Francisco, Oct. 9th, '94.

Mosby hoped for good things from McKinley—and not only for the nation. He knew that there was nothing that he could depend upon in Virginia despite the good feelings revealed during his last trip east. Certainly, he was greeted warmly by many people, but they were his old friends or at least not his sworn enemies. On the other hand, neither were they the "movers and shakers" of the state. He might have hoped to learn that if he returned, he would be welcome in Virginia's Republican political machine; but apparently, that did not happen. Indeed, it seemed that the number of those who applauded his return was far less than the number who were either disinterested or hostile. Therefore, John Mosby hoped that a McKinley administration would provide him with a position when his time with the railroad ran out.

The first mention was made of a possible reunion of the Forty-third Battalion, which was planned to coincide with Mosby's attendance of daughter Stuart's impending marriage. Stuart was one of only two of Mosby's children to marry; the other was oldest child, May:

Alexandria Gazette – November 27, 1894

Mosby's Men.—Colonel John S. Mosby writes a gentleman in this city that he will leave San Francisco for the East December 1st, to pay a visit to the major of his old regiment, Judge A. E. Richards of Louisville. Some of Mosby's men desire to have a reunion of his command at Alexandria, and it is probable that the visit of Colonel Mosby to the East may be made the occasion of the reunion. Mr. John H. Alexander, of Leesburg, has been corresponding with some of his old comrades on the subject.— Richmond Times.

Washington Times – December 3, 1894

The old soldiers of Col. John S. Mosby's command are taking a deep interest in the reception and banquet which they propose to give him when he comes here from California to attend the wedding of his daughter, Miss Stuart Mosby, to Mr. Coleman, of Washington on the 10th instant. Mr. John H. Alexander would like to hear from all the old veterans of Mosby's rangers who have not been heard from.

Another "war story" appeared in the *Indianapolis Journal*, a publication that was frequently rather "anti-Mosby" in its reporting. Not only was the article effusive in its praise, but it was possibly the first instance in the press in which Mosby was "credited" with prolonging the war:

Indianapolis Journal – December 14, 1894

COL. JOHN S. MOSBY

Reminiscences of the Shenandoah Valley Campaign

By a Man Who Bore a Prominent Part In it, and Whose Efforts Prolonged the Great Rebellion.

Another mention was made of Mosby's Republican proclivities and how it affected his press coverage. Frankly, Mosby's press coverage had as much to do with whether or not the paper "approved" of his war service as it did his political affiliation:

Salt Lake Herald – **December 15, 1894**
Colonel Mosby, the dashing Confederate ranger, arrived in St. Louis Sunday. The Republic ignored him, but the Globe-Democrat gave him a two-column sketch. Thirty years ago or thereabout the conditions would have been reversed. Yea, verily, there is more joy in the Republican party over the one ex-rebel who flops over into the Republican ranks than the ninety and nine Union men who never went astray.—Kansas City Star.

Grover Cleveland had begun his four-year tenure in the White House. His actions had met with the approval of John Mosby, at least with regard to the Pullman Strike. But Mosby believed he saw in William McKinley a "rising star" in the Republican Party who might well be that party's next presidential nominee. As usual, Mosby's political prescience—absent cousin Ben—was "spot on."

And so the year ended without any major personal disasters, but also with a Democrat in the White House—a matter that seldom bode well for Mosby personally. However, as he was not a part of the Republican Party in Virginia, such political matters in which he did become engaged were far away from the seat of power in Washington.

ADDENDUM

The Pullman Strike

The Pullman Strike of 1894 was one of the most influential events in the history of US labor. What began as a walkout by railroad workers in the company town of Pullman, Illinois, escalated into the country's first national strike. The events surrounding the strike catapulted several leaders to prominence and brought national focus to issues concerning labor unrest, socialism, and the need for new efforts to balance the economic interests of labor and capitalism.

In 1859, twenty-eight-year-old George M. Pullman, an ambitious entrepreneur who had moved from New York to Chicago, found success as a building contractor. Pullman quickly became wealthy and continuing his penchant for innovation, Pullman turned in 1867 to the subject of railroad travel, creating a new line of luxury railroad cars. As demand for the "Pullman coaches" grew, Pullman further demonstrated his financial acumen. He did not sell his sleeping cars; instead, he leased them to railroad companies. By 1893, the Pullman Company operated over two thousand cars on almost every major US railroad, and the company was valued at $62 million.

A firm believer in capitalism and moral uplift, Pullman gathered a group of investors and began to build the nation's first model industrial town near Lake Calumet near Chicago. Between 1880 and 1884, the village of Pullman was built on four thousand acres. In addition to the company's manufacturing plants, the town contained a hotel, a school, a library, a church, and office buildings as well as parks and recreational facilities. Houses were well-built brick structures that featured cutting-edge conveniences of the era. However, as an equally firm believer in the necessity of making a profit, Pullman operated his town as he operated his company, leasing the housing to his workers and selling them food, gas, and water at a 10 percent markup.

A significant drop in the country's gold reserves, prodigious spending of US Treasury surpluses, and the passage in 1890 of the Sherman Silver Purchase Act led to the financial panic of 1893. The ensuing corporate failures, mass layoffs of workers, and bank closings plunged the country into a major depression. In response, the

Pullman Company fired more than a third of the workforce and instituted reduced hours and wage cuts of more than 25 percent for the remaining hourly employees. Because Pullman had promised the town's investors a 6 percent return, there was no corresponding reduction in the rents and other charges paid by the workers. Rent was deducted directly from their paychecks, leaving countless workers with no money to feed and clothe their families.

In desperation, many workers joined the newly established American Railway Union (ARU), which claimed a membership of 465 local unions and 150,000 workers. ARU organizer and president Eugene V. Debs had become nationally prominent when he led a short but successful strike against the Great Northern Railway in early 1894. In May, the workers struck the Pullman Company. Debs directed the strike and widened its scope, asking other train workers outside Chicago to refuse to work on trains that included Pullman cars. While the workers did agree to permit trains carrying the US mail to operate as long as they did not contain those cars, the railroads refused to compromise. Instead, they added Pullman cars to all their trains, including the ones that only transported freight.

Despite repeated attempts by the Union to discuss the situation with Pullman, he refused to negotiate. As the strike spread, entire rail lines were shut down. The railroads quickly formed the General Managers Association (GMA) and announced that switchmen who did not move rail cars would be fired immediately. The ARU responded with a Union-wide walkout. By the end of June, fifty thousand railroad workers had walked off their jobs.

The economic threat and sporadic violence led the GMA to call for Federal troops to be brought in. Illinois governor John P. Altgeld, who was sympathetic to the cause of the striking workers, refused the request for troops. In July, United States Attorney General Richard Olney, who supported the GMA, issued a broad injunction called the Omnibus Indictment, which prohibited strikers and Union representatives from attempting to persuade workers to abandon their jobs.

When striking workers were read the indictment and refused to disperse, Olney obtained a Federal court injunction holding the workers in contempt and, in effect, declaring the strike illegal. When the workers still refused to end the strike, Debs and other leaders were arrested; and Olney requested the Federal troops, saying they were needed to move the mail. President Grover Cleveland sent more than two thousand troops to Chicago, and fighting soon broke out between the rioting strikers and soldiers. Soldiers killed more than a dozen workers and wounded many more.

With strike leaders in prison and a growing public backlash over the looting and arson committed by some striking workers, the strike was effectively broken. Most of the workers returned to their jobs in August, although some were blacklisted and never again worked for the railroads. Debs was charged with contempt of court for disobeying the court injunction and conspiracy to obstruct the US mail. Clarence Darrow, an attorney who had quit his job as general counsel of the Chicago & North Western Railway, defended Debs and the other ARU leaders; but they were convicted and spent six months in prison. They were released in November 1895.

The Pullman Strike of 1894 and its aftermath had an indelible effect on the course of the labor movement in the United States. The use of Federal troops and the labor injunction sent a message to US workers that would not change until the new deal of the 1930s. The polarization of management and labor would continue for decades.

Chapter 34

1895

"Arma virumque cano." ~ "I sing of arms and a man." ~ Virgil

"Virtue and genuine graces in themselves speak what no words can utter." ~ William Shakespeare

BY THE BEGINNING of the 1890s, John Mosby was well ensconced in California as an employee in the legal department of the Southern Pacific Railroad, a position obtained for him by the dying Ulysses Grant. Although he traveled east to Virginia, there was apparently still no place for him there. The Republican Party in that state, under the leadership of William Mahone, had been virtually nullified with the election of 1883 and never again achieved true power even after Mahone's death in October of 1895. Mosby's only hope for any position was 'political"—that is, an appointment through the Federal government when that government was in the hands of the Republicans. However, he continued to hold a position with the Southern Pacific because the company's head, Collis P. Huntington, had promised Grant that he would "take care" of the little lawyer. After Huntington's departure from the company followed closely by his death in August of 1900, Mosby was removed.

Many who have covered this period of John Mosby's life, albeit superficially, believe that he was only "kept on" by Huntington for sentimental reasons; and that his removal—the same being claimed for his removal from the Department of Justice in 1910—was the result of incompetence or age or some other failure on Mosby's part to perform the duties of his office. That is false. John Mosby was an *excellent* attorney. Indeed, he was once told by a justice of the Supreme Court that his presentation of a case was so thorough that the man was spared all the usual research involved in making a judgment upon litigation appearing before the high court. Further, with the departure of Huntington, the Southern Pacific underwent a considerable "housecleaning." As a result more employees than John Mosby were "released from service" to that company. It would appear that the matter involved a sort of "changing of the guard" as often happens in large corporations when the original leaders retire and new ones rise to take their place bringing with them their own factotums.

In any event, the middle of the decade saw John Mosby return to Virginia and attend the first—and, for him, the only—reunion of his command. Indeed, the first mention of him in the press was related to that same reunion that had been planned the year before. It had been almost thirty years since the disbanding, but many of Mosby's "boys" still lived in Virginia, Washington and Maryland. Of course, arrangements were immediately begun to greet the man who had been, for them all, a combination of Harry "Hotspur" Percy and King Arthur:

Evening Star – **January 3, 1895**

Arranging a Reception to Col. John Mosby

Meetings of Associations and Officers Elected.

J. H. Alexander of Leesburg was in the city yesterday evening and called to see Mr. John G. Beckham, who is chairman of the committee of arrangements for the reception which is to be tendered Col. John S. Mosby in this city on the 16th instant by members of his old command. Mr. Alexander is chairman of the general committee, and will preside at the reception. He reports encouraging notices from members of Mosby's command from all parts of the United States. Many of his men have been successful in their business affairs since the war, and no means will be spared to make the reception first-class in every particular, and one long to be remembered. Col. Mosby is held in high esteem by his old associates, and has very many bosom friends in the ranks of the southern soldiers everywhere. Arrangements have been made for many prominent Confederate commanders to be present.

Soon, the Virginia and Washington press, and other publications throughout the South and even the rest of the nation, began to speculate on the gathering of this truly unique and famous command. Along with reports on the reunion, the recounting of many of the command's famous operations also began to appear in the press:

Alexandria Gazette – **January 7, 1895 (Edited)**
MOSBY'S MEN

The reunion of the men who fought under Col. John Singleton Mosby of guerilla-warfare fame, which is to be held at Alexandria, Va., next week, will be a notable gathering of the Confederate scouts who played such a daring and picturesque role in the Piedmont region of Virginia during the war and kept the Northern forces which operated in that section of the Old Dominion guessing for about four years. Some personal recollections of the doughty Colonel will therefore be of interest just now to the colony of 35,000 or more Virginians who have settled in Baltimore since those stirring times Mosby aimed to do on land what Admiral Semmes did on the high seas, though on a much smaller scale. His numerous raids upon the enemy's supplies, the way in which he impeded their progress by tearing up railroads and other schemes of strategy, together with the bold captures he effected, sometimes surprising a whole regiment with a mere handful of men, aided the southern army materially in the early stages of the rebellion, and proved him to be a genius in that mode of warfare.

At the close of the war Mosby was an idol in Virginia and could have had any honor within the gift of her people. Neither the prestige of the Governorship nor that of the United States Senate would have hung beyond his reach, probably. But when he repudiated those principles the supremacy of which he had fought so bravely to maintain, and swore allegiance to General Grant, his popularity began to wane. His friends and admirers gave him the cold shoulder and in a few years his name, that had been on some many tongues, lost its magic.

The result was, he abandoned what had been a lucrative law practice at the Warrenton bar, then the ablest in the State, with abundant litigation before it to be settled, sacrificed his beautiful home and accepted a petty consulship at Hong Kong at the hands of a republican administration. This action of Mosby's, like Longstreet's, has never been satisfactorily accounted for, although explanations have been plentiful. It is possible that the true reasons of his sudden and remarkable change of political faith may come out at this gathering of his comrades-in-arms, whose loyalty to their old chieftain never wavered After his term as Consul to China expired he resumed the practice of law at San Francisco and is said to have a large clientele among the Chinese population of that city.

Mosby's wife, who died some years ago, was one of the loveliest characters of her day and, although a woman of exquisite refinement and great gentleness of nature, she gloried in her husband's piratical methods of warfare and is said to have conceived and inspired many of his boldest raids upon the enemy's commissary department.

He has an interesting family of children consisting of two sons and three daughters. One of his sons, John Mosby [Jr.] is a lawyer in Denver, Col. His second daughter, who was recently married is a young woman of literary talent and is as much at home in the saddle as her father was when he chased the federals.

Mosby's personality is a striking one. His clean-shaven face of well-cut features and eagle eyes would attract attention anywhere. He has a preoccupied air and is disposed to be cold and taciturn to strangers, but with his friends he is an affable and entertaining companion, whose conversation reveals scholarly tastes and a close observance of men and affairs.—Baltimore News.

And now all of the newspapers were filled with speculations and reports on the pending reunion intermingled with recounts of all the old campaigns and victories. Among the reports of this festive event, a small blurb appeared in the *Alexandria Gazette* referencing General Hancock's "official report" as it had appeared in that newspaper after Appomattox. It must have been pleasant for Mosby—he, after all, did subscribe to the Gazette!—to see the matter set to rights:

Alexandria Gazette – January 12, 1895

According to an extract from one of General Hancock's official reports, published in the local columns of yesterday's Gazette, it appears that the General, who, it must not be forgotten, supervised the murder of the innocent Mrs. Surratt, had determined to "punish severely those of the inhabitants who had harbored" Col. Mosby, and was only prevented for doing so by the delay caused by the assassination of Mr. Lincoln, during which the Colonel surrendered and was paroled. And yet General Hancock was the democratic candidate for President in 1880 and Virginia cast her vote for him.

After some further "notes" regarding particulars of the reunion, the paper went on to say in that same issue:

A great many ladies and gentlemen who resided here during the war and heard so constantly of the daring deeds of Mosby and his men, are urging the managers of the reunion to have Col. Mosby hold a public reception.

The attendance of the members will be very much larger than was at first expected, many writing that they are coming and are looking forward with pleasure to meeting their famous old chief once more.

These last paragraphs must have given John Mosby considerable consolation. Having been a pariah for so long, aside from those of his men with whom he continued to have contact after the war, it is probable that he wondered what kind of reception he might receive if he returned to meet with his former soldiers and the people of his old "Confederacy." To read that these people, and especially his old men for whom he personally had such affection, still loved him must have been a balm for his soul.

Below are some accounts of the reunion. This was, as mentioned, the one and only such event Mosby attended. He had expected to attend the reunion in 1896 but was suffering so badly from appendicitis—a recurrence of an attack he sustained later in this year—that he was unable to leave his home in San Francisco. The reunion held in 1897 was at the end of that year, but Mosby was in no mood—or physical condition—to attend it.

Alexandria Gazette – January 16, 1895 (Edited)

REUNION OF MOSBY'S COMMAND.

> The long anticipated reunion of the surviving members of Colonel John S. Mosby's command took place to-day in Odd Fellows' Hall. It was a joyous occasion, one of the most pleasant ever witnessed in this city, some meeting face to face who had had probably no social intercourse for a third of a century when as one common band they exercised their vigils over the Army of the Potomac and harassed it day and night. They had met to form an organization and recount their experiences in the four years' war between the States. They are no longer the young and hardy band which caused so many stampedes among the federals, so many panics in army and sutler trains and were such a chronic menace to railroading those days. Their hair and former uniforms are of the same hue and instead of the ardor of youth they bear the beaming countenances indicative of the conservatism which accompanies the period of middle age or the evening of life. Col. Mosby was there with his florid countenance and with the same penetrating eye of yore, but with locks whitened by the snows of many winters, conversing in the pleasant and measured tones of by-gone days, shaking hands heartily with everybody and with traces of the same martial spirit which has rendered him and his famous band immortal.

> What a contrast between Mosby's men as they are and the fanciful description given of them in northern prints during the war! The writer remembers seeing a book at that period purporting to be a "History of Mosby's Command," which emanated from a northern publishing house. The frontispiece represented a band of men who would have compared unfavorably with the forty thieves, around a camp fire playing cards. A jug of whisky stood beside them and a few feet away the mutilated bodies of several Union soldiers lay. The head of one had been cut off, the hands of another hand been amputated and a bayonet had been driven through the body of another. How different the true picture! Assembled to-day was a band of genial souls, the higher types of the soldier and the gentleman, who, like their former commander, exhibited inborn gentleness and good-feeling. The ex-members, now that the dove of peace is hovering o'er a united country, and the sword has been beaten into a plow share and the spear into a pruning hook, are following different avocations—among them being farmers, physicians, lawyers, artisans and ministers of the gospel (one being a presiding elder).

About eleven o'clock those left of the original four hundred—not more than one-fourth—were in Odd Fellows' Hall shaking hands and recounting reminiscences of long ago. Col. Cab. Maddox [sic] entered and temporarily broke up all conversation, all present running to greet him and for a few minutes a regular ovation was tendered him. ... [Henry Cabell (Cab) Maddux was a private in Mosby's command.-vph]

When Col. Mosby and other officers of the command entered the room about 12:15 o'clock, they were greeted by the original rebel yell, which has to be heard to be appreciated, and which is never forgotten. The Colonel was accompanied by Lieut. Col. W. H. Chapman and Major Dolly Richards. After the cheering had ceased the band struck up the inspiring strains of "Auld Lang Syne," followed by "My Maryland," in honor of the distinguished members from that State who were present. "Dixie" was next discoursed, which brought forth another and prolonged yell. It was some time before Colonel Mosby could reach the rostrum, every one pressing forward to greet him, and numbers hugging him It was some time before an organization could be perfected, and cigars were distributed to all present. [What follows is a very lengthy list of attendees and other information that sadly must be edited.-vph]

Richmond Dispatch – January 17, 1895 (Edited)
MOSBY AND HIS MEN

The First Reunion of the Rangers Since They Disbanded in 1865. Veterans' Ovation to the Colonel.

Receives a Rebel Yell and is Cheered and Hugged by Old Soldiers. Speeches of Mosby, Gordon, Daniel, Conrad and Others—Camp Formed— Old Roster—Next Meeting.

Alexandria, Va., January 16th.—(Special.)—Lowering skies did not darken, nor falling rain make damp the reception of Virginia's great partisan officer, Colonel John S. Mosby, by the survivors of his command and scores of others of his friends in this city to-day. The entrance was decorated with American flags and pennants, and two spacious saloons—one filling the first and the other the second story, from wall to wall—were occupied.

GATHERING OF THE CLAN.

The upper hall was dedicated to the reception of Colonel Mosby, and there before noon gathered the remnant of the gallant band, that made each wooded height, each defile, and stream and road and farm-house the fortresses for Virginia's defence and the strong points for the attacks of the invaders…The morning was spent in a renewal of campfire talk, and the registration of names.

MOSBY'S GREETING

Shortly after 12 o'clock, Colonel Mosby, accompanied by Lieutenant Colonel William H. Chapman and Major Dolly Richards, entered the hall. As they came through the door they were greeting with the rebel yell from a hundred throats, and Colonel Mosby and his officers were surrounded by their excited men, each anxious to shake hands with their beloved commander. Some of the old veterans seized the Colonel in their arms and hugged him up to them, while tears coursed down their cheeks. The reception was an ovation. No attempt at permanent organization was made, the men standing about the hall, and chatting their doings during the war and Colonel Mosby left at 3 o'clock to go to the home of Mr. John G. Beckham, where he rested until the hour for the banquet arrived. The old soldiers then dispersed for dinner, to reassemble at 6 o'clock.

Evening Star – January 17, 1895 (Edited)

COLONEL MOSBY'S SPEECH

Reunion Marked by Anti-Sectionalism and Good Feeling.

Permanent Organization Formed—Speeches Made at the Dinner in Response to Toasts.

The banquet of the Mosby men at Odd Fellows' Hall last night in Alexandria was a fitting termination of the day. The banqueting hall was handsomely decorated with the flags of the nation, an the old Confederate flag was conspicuous for its absence, the corners and windows were banked with cut flowers and potted plants, and the scene was one long to be remembered. Covers were laid for one hundred and fifty people, though nearly double that number participated.

At the head of the table sat Col. John S. Mosby, with Senator Daniel, Senator Hunton, Gen. Wm. H. Payne, Gen. Marcus B. Wright, Col. William H. Chapman [Mosby's second-in-command], Maj. Dolly Richards, Capt. Sam Chapman and Dr. A. Monteiro on his right and left. Maj. Dolly Richards of Louisville presided as toastmaster in a becoming manner, and in eloquent language introduced the speakers of the evening. Col. Mosby was the first speaker, and he responded to the toast, "The Forty-third battalion, Virginia cavalry."

Col. Mosby's Speech.

In his remarks Col. Mosby said:

"When on April 21, 1865, I told you that I was no longer your commander, and bade you what we then considered a long, and perhaps an eternal farewell, the most hopeful among us could not reasonably have expected to ever witness a scene like this. Nearly thirty years have passed away, and we meet once more on the banks of the Potomac and in sight of the Capitol; not in hostile array, but as citizens of a great and united country. Gunboats no longer patrol the river; there are no picket guards on its banks to challenge your crossing.

"Your presence here this evening recalls our last parting. I see the line drawn up to hear read the last order I ever gave you; I see the moistened yes and quivering lips; I hear the command to break ranks; I feel the grasp of the hand, and see the tears on the cheeks of men who had dared death so long that it had lost its terror. And I know now, as I knew then, that each heart suffered with mine the agony of the Titan in his resignation to fate:

'The rock, the vulture and the chain, all that the proud can feel of pain.'

"I miss among you the faces of some who were present that day, but have since passed over the great river, and memory brings back the image of many of that glorious band who then slept in the red burial of war.

"I shall make no particular allusion to the part you played in the great tragedy of war. Our personal association was so intimate it would not become me to do so. But standing here as I do amid the wreck of cherished hopes, this much at least I can say, that in all the vicissitudes of fortune and in all the trials of life, I have never ceased to feel as I told you when parting, 'A just pride in the fame of your achievements and [a] grateful recollection of your generous kindness to myself.'"

Salt Lake Herald – **January 17, 1895**

San Francisco Chronicle - **January 18, 1895**

MOSBY'S GUERILLAS.

Alexandria W. Va., Jan. 16—The surviving members of Mosby's command, the Forty-third battalion Virginia cavalry, held a reunion here today. Colonel Mosby, John G. Beckfall, the originator of the reunion and many other distinguished ex-confederates were present.

When Colonel Mosby entered the hall, the walls rang with the old familiar rebel yell. Many of the men who had not seen their old commander since the war, threw their arms around him and tears rolled down their cheeks.

The Times – **January 23, 1895**

COLONEL MOSBY PLEASED

Colonel John S. Mosby was a visitor at the Capitol this morning. He expressed himself as being highly gratified at the reunion of last week in Alexandria, and spoke feelingly of his pleasure in meeting his men again. Colonel Mosby will leave in a few days for California, stopping a day in Lynchburg to visit his old color-bearer Stockton Terry, and a day later he will visit his mother at Bedford City.

John Mosby was reported as having been "pleased" with the reunion; that, perhaps, was an understatement. If all future such events were as this one had been (albeit perhaps not so overwhelming), he might have attended more of them.

During the year, Mosby continued to write about the war, including a review on Sheridan's Shenandoah Valley campaign in which "Little Phil" came off poorly in Mosby's military and ethical judgment. After the war, John Mosby had attempted to "consign all wrongs, real and imagined on both sides to oblivion." But his natural honesty precluded him ignoring what had been done in the Valley of Virginia. However, once again, Mosby showed his peculiar "flaw" with regard to Grant by blaming Sheridan, Hunter, and Custer for acts ordered by Grant. He just could not bring himself to acknowledge that when all was said and done, Grant bore ultimate responsibility for the atrocities committed by the Federal military against noncombatants in Virginia, at least while he was in command of the Army of the Potomac. Grant was not alone, of course! Lincoln and Stanton and generals like Halleck, Augur, and Hancock were also responsible; but there is no doubt that Grant was not blameless.

The Times – January 24, 1895 (Edited)
MOSBY ON SHERIDAN

Thirty years may be considered a fairly good cooling time, even for the fires of the civil war, but there are some embers which keep hot, and underneath whose ashes may yet be found burning coals, and such are the sentiments in the hearts of the people of the Valley of Virginia about General Philip E. Sheridan, who devastated their homes with fire and sword, and whose indiscriminate warfare on men, women and children showed at once his poverty of resource and the desperateness of his character.

If there was any man who had good reason to know Sheridan's method of warfare and the weak spots in his line, it was Colonel John S. Mosby, who with his small force of restless and daring riders assailed Sheridan's flank and rear incessantly.

The story of that border warfare has never been told, and in its entirety doubtless never will be, but little by little it is coming out, and as it does the services of Mosby grow apace.

Colonel Mosby, besides being a great fighter, has for many years been a student of military science, and he has, in the light of the official records of the war—the most complete and impartial compilation of military data ever made—prepared a review of Sheridan's campaign in the Shenandoah Valley. In this he has, from the records and with the most apt and pungent illustration, disclosed Sheridan as he really was.

The giant shrinks to a dwarf, the historian becomes a reckless braggart, the hero a brute. This review containing about 18,000 or 19,000 words, has been secured exclusively by *The Times*, and it will be published in three parts, beginning next Sunday. That it will add to the deep and increasing interest in all matters relating to the war is certain from the importance of the subject and the distinguished character of the reviewer.

An ominous little article appeared with very little fanfare or explanation. Indeed, it could easily have been missed. Mosby accompanied eldest daughter May, who was going for "hospital treatment" in Washington. May—Mosby's firstborn—was very dear to her father, and her condition must have worried him greatly. Sadly, May's husband, Robert, died five years later, leaving his ill wife a widow with two children.

On the twenty-seventh of January, a second and much more detailed and lengthy article appeared by Mosby on Sheridan with a review of the Valley campaign. Despite its length, it was only the first installment of a series of articles on the subject. At that time, Mosby was writing extensively about the war for *The Times*.

January continued to be a momentous month as Mosby resumed his "ovation" in Virginia, visiting Lynchburg for the first time in twenty years. In a rather poetic incident, he was the guest of the man who raised the cavalry troop Mosby reluctantly joined before the beginning of the war:

Alexandria Gazette – **January 28, 1895**

Colonel Mosby in Lynchburg.—Colonel John S. Mosby arrived in Lynchburg on Friday and was tendered quite an ovation. It was the first time the Colonel had been in that city for twenty years. He is on his way to visit his mother, Mrs. Virginia Mosby, in Bedford City. The Colonel was the guest of Capt. C. M. Blackford while in Lynchburg. Capt. Wm. Blackford, brother of his host, commanded the company into which Colonel Mosby enlisted at the commencement of the war. An informal reception in his honor was tendered him at the Piedmont Club during the evening.

Mosby's war account that had begun in the *Times* in January was continued in the next month. For those "moderns" who insist that Mosby was nothing more than an irritant to the Army of the Potomac, the exchange of telegrams among the high command of that "glorious army" included in the article clearly demonstrated their intense concern about the intentions and the dangers posed this "mere irritant."

A Texas paper printed a really amusing story that included a word portrait of Mosby as "a fiery lawyer" in an incident that had occurred while he was consul at Hong Kong:

Fort Worth Gazette – **February 3, 1895 (Edited)**

The War Dog as a Fiery Lawyer.

Gilder Tells the Story of the Lightning-Striker of the Army of Northern Virginia—Is Law in Hong Kong.

By Col. W. H. Gilder.

No command in the entire Confederate army was better known that the Forty-third Virginia cavalry, which held its first reunion since the war in Alexandria, Va., last week, though it was not by that title, but by its nom de guerre, "Mosby's Guerrillas," that it was generally recognized.

Colonel Mosby himself, when I frequently met while he occupied the position of United States consul at Hong Kong, China in 1883 and 1884, despised the name guerrilla, and claimed that his command was regularly enlisted and borne on the rolls of the army and that he was simply allowed to operate independently of the Army of Northern Virginia unless occasion arrived when it was better they should cooperate.

He was a rather unique figure in Hong Kong society and though regarded as a little bit queer in some respects, he was highly esteemed by his fellow citizens. Tall and slender, his features small and almost haggard, with thin lips compressed and a firmly set lower jaw, a slouch hat, perched jauntily upon his rather long iron-gray hair, he was a picturesque and familiar citizen of Victoria, which is the port and principle town on the island of Hong Kong. His legal talents and peculiarly American style of forensic oratory were greatly admired, and I was told that if he would resign his office and commence the practice of law there he could command the best business in town. It only needed one example of his powers to establish his reputation. This occurred when the keeper of a sailor boarding house, a man named Schmitt, brought an action against Colonel Mosby for libel. This man was no better than those in other parts of the world engaged in the same business of robbing poor Jack of his hard-earned wages, and Colonel Mosby had said some severe things about him several times when rescuing poor American sailors from his clutches.

Colonel Mosby conducted his own defense, and when the testimony for the prosecution was all in he arose to address the court. His cross-examination of the witnesses against him had given a foretaste of what was in store, and word had been passed across the street to the British club opposite that something unusual and very interesting was in progress. So by the time he was ready to commence his speech the courtroom was filled with an attentive audience, whose anticipations were fully realized before he got through.

After analyzing the law upon the subject of libel and citing many precedents in his favor, he treated the court to a sample of typical Southern and western oratory such as they had never heard before. My informant, who was an interested spectator on that occasion told me "the air was full of Latin, Greek and Turkey tracks. Metaphors crowded upon poetical quotations and quotations from the holy scriptures and profane Shakespeare."

A Sanguinary Legal Attack.

He drew tears when he described the trusting, guileless sailor in the hands of these rapacious "land sharks," who keep him drunk while they rob him and then ship him aboard some outward bound vessel, grabbing all his advance pay to satisfy some trumped up charges. The he paid his respects to the plaintiff, whose business he had thus described and gave an insight into the character of the man. Then said he, "I am charged with libeling this man; of libeling Schmitt," and he pronounced the name as if it was an opprobrious epithet, and closed saying, "Why, the English language does not contain words vile enough to libel Schmitt."

With this he grabbed his books under his arm and strode out of court, fully expecting to pay damages. A storm of applause followed him, but he paid no heed to it. He had had his way and was satisfied and had established his reputation as an able lawyer and pleader.

The Times then presented a lengthy critique of Mosby's articles on Sheridan in the Valley and came to the same conclusion as did Mosby regarding this great Union "hero":

The Times – February 5, 1895 (Edited)
COL. MOSBY'S REVIEW OF SHERIDAN

The two installments which we have so far published of Colonel Mosby's review of Sheridan's Valley campaign have proved three points very conclusively. The first is that Sheridan was a weak, vacillating, irresolute commander, without genius, without enterprise, and with a greater degree of timidity than any commander of high rank on the Union side of the civil war. Finally, now that intelligent historical criticism has really taken hold of Sheridan and his performances, there will not be enough of him and them to make a striped jacket for a circus clown.

Mosby continued with his narrative. The interesting point he made in the next article involved the use of Southern noncombatants in an attempt to prevent his assaults on the railroad. General Lew Wallace was one of the officers involved in what was a war crime according to the United States' own code of war! Wallace later wrote the Biblical epic Ben-Hur and was seen as a fine Christian man. Wherever his name appeared in Mosby's report, the name of his "Christian" novel was included in brackets. John Mosby missed nothing. As usual, Mosby kept a weather eye out for any publicity that he considered sufficiently inaccurate to require a response—depending, of course, upon the newspaper in which it appeared; he did not waste his time with second-rate publications. Indeed, if Mosby had responded to every inaccurate newspaper report, he would have had no time to live his life:

Alexandria Gazette – August 31, 1895
COL. MOSBY'S DENIAL

Colonel John S. Mosby, the famous Confederate raider, sends the *Richmond Times* the following copy of a correction of an article which appeared in the Confederate Veteran, Nashville, Tenn.: [And the article goes on to print the individual corrections.-vph]

Mosby was back before the court of claims as reported in the *Alexandria Gazette*. Also among the matters covered were the death of Mosby nemesis William Mahone and currency issues in the West:

Alexandria Gazette – October 19, 1895

Colonel Mosby has arranged his business with the court of claims and will leave here tomorrow for Warrenton, and from there will visit his old beat in the upper part of Fauquier county, and then go to Bedford county to see his mother. The Colonel agrees with the Gazette that the death of General Mahone will tend to reunite the Republican party in Virginia. He says the silver feeling is by no means as strong in California as it once was. In alluding to Davies' recent Life of General Sheridan, the Colonel says that "Sheridan's Ride" had just as much foundation as "Barbara Frietchie," and no more, and that hadn't any.

An article of October 19 in the *Evening Times* included much the same miscellaneous matters on which Mosby had opined in the Gazette, the most important of which was the death of General William Mahone. It also carried Mosby's suggestion for the next Republican vice presidential candidate for the election of 1896, a Virginian named James A. Walker, as well as his opinion on the "silver" question that had become a matter of importance at that time:

The *Evening Times*, – October 19, 1895 (Edited)
MOSBY SUGGESTED WALKER

Thinks the Virginian is a Good Man for the Republican Vice.

His Nomination Would, He Says, Go a Long Way Toward Breaking the Solid South.

Colonel John S. Mosby, looking but little older than when he was a conspicuous figure around Washington, arrived here yesterday from

San Francisco. He has come here to attend some law business, and will probably remain in the city a week or two. Discussing the political outlook, Col. Mosby said:

"I am of the opinion that the Republican nominee will either be McKinley or Morton. If Morton were a few years younger, I should say the chances were in his favor, but under existing conditions, I think McKinley is foremost in the race. ...

"The next campaign will show some remarkable changes in the political sentiment of the different sections, and if the Republicans had the courage to nominate for the second place on the ticket an ex-Confederate they would make some inroads into the South which would be surprising.

"I should like to see Gen. James A. Walker, of Virginia, nominated for the Vice Presidency, and I believe if this were done the Republicans would carry Virginia and several other Southern States."

"What effect upon the politics of the South do you think the death of Gen. Mahone will have?"

It will prove a heavy blow to The Democrats in Virginia," replied Col. Mosby. "Without meaning to disparage Gen. Mahone at all, I nevertheless believe for several years past he had been of the utmost service to The Democrats. Their dislike for him served to keep them together. If there were the slightest danger of division in their ranks it was only necessary to raise the cry that Mahone, as the Republican boss, was striving to gain control of the State, in order to drive them all back to their allegiance.

"Mahone's natural successor as the leader of the Republicans in the State is Gen. James A. Walker. He is a strong man, and if he should be nominated for the Vice-Presidency, would add strength to the ticket. A good many people," said the colonel, "think the North would refuse to vote for a Southern man, and especially for one who wore the gray uniform. Now this is all a mistake. The people of the North have dismissed the war from their minds and the only section in which feeling against a man because he fought with the South exists in the West.

"While I am absolutely opposed to the silver movement and feel satisfied that it will be overwhelmingly defeated in the next campaign," continued Col. Mosby, "the agitation has done this much good—it has taken the minds of people off the war and has given them a common cause to fight for, no matter which side of the controversy they take. This may mark, to some extent, the breaking down of the lines between the old parties, but I am not prepare to say that it will do any vast amount of harm."

But Mosby was wrong about Mahone's death helping the Republicans. Virginia Democrats did not need to "unite" against him, or the Republicans. Furthermore, had Mahone lived, Mosby would have "disparaged" him all that he could! But most interesting was the fact that had Walker been the chosen vice-presidential candidate, a Virginian would have been in the White House in 1901.

As the year drew toward its close, John Mosby could look back to a glorious time in Virginia. But as so often happened with Mosby, joy was soon replaced by what almost became an agonizing death. On one of his nostalgic visits, he went to Salem (now Marshall) to the site of the disbanding of his command. While there, he became seriously ill with appendicitis. As in wartime, no sooner had one paper declared him recovering than another paper of the same date or later reported him at death's door:

The Morning Times – October 27, 1895

Col. Mosby Ill. (Special to The Times.)

Richmond, Va., Oct. 26.—It was reported here to-day that Col. John S. Mosby was extremely ill at Marshall, Fauquier county, Va. A private dispatch from Rectortown says it is an attack of an old stomach trouble and though he is worse to-night, that he is not dangerously ill.

Richmond Dispatch – October 29, 1895

COLONEL JOHN S. MOSBY

A Decided Change for the Better in His Condition.

Manassas, Va., October 28—[Special] A message from Marshall, Va., at 6 o'clock this evening says Colonel John S. Mosby's condition is encouraging. Rather a decided change for the better from that of yesterday is noticed. His physician says that with care and ample rest he looks for rapid improvement.

THE NEWS CONFIRMED.

Marshall, Va., October 28.—[Special]—Colonel Mosby is resting easier tonight, and the doctors consider his condition materially improved.

The Times – November 1, 1895

Marshall, Va., Oct. 21.—Special.—Rain commenced falling here about 8 o'clock and has fallen steadily all day. In consequence, Colonel Mosby has had but few visitors, but his spirits have been by no means depressed. His convalescence continues uninterrupted. He had a good night of natural sleep, unaided by narcotics.

Shenandoah Herald – November 1, 1895

Colonel Moseby Seriously Ill.

Richmond, Va., Oct. 27.—Col. John S. Mosby, the famous Confederate guerilla chief, was in a serious condition at Marshall, Fauquier county, last night. He was threatened with appendicitis and his condition was more unfavorable at 6 o'clock last evening than it had been.

In the same paper:

COLONEL MOSBY IMPROVING.

Marshall, Va., October 28.—Special. Colonel John S. Moseby is thought to be better this evening and there are strong hopes of his recovery.

Alexandria Gazette – **November 8, 1895**

A letter from Marshall says: Col. Mosby has continued to improve, and on Wednesday evening went to Warrenton to make a visit to his daughter, Mrs. Campbell. He will go from there to Bedford to spend a few days with his mother and brother, before returning to his home, in San Francisco. He has lost some weight, and is considerably weakened by his recent illness, but hopes to recuperate more rapidly when he can resume his active habits of living.

John Mosby left Bedford City and the home of his brother Willie and his mother Virginia to return to San Francisco. He must have gone with a good heart. He had been royally received, his old men still loved him and an election was in the offing with a good chance of a Republican victory and help in his situation with the railroad. The rest of the century promised to be a new dawn for the man who had forfeited everything for what he considered to be the right thing not for him personally, but for Virginia and the South. It is just as well that men are not able to foresee the future.

Chapter 35

1896

A fronte praceipitium a tergo lupi
~ A precipice in front, wolves behind

"A doubtful friend is worse than a certain enemy."
~ Aesop

JOHN MOSBY HAD been well treated during his return to Virginia in 1895, but 1896 promised to undo much of that goodwill. When General James Longstreet's book on Gettysburg was released, he blamed that defeat on the absence of General Stuart and his cavalry. Naturally, for John Mosby that was akin to waving a red cape in front of a bull and he determined to undertake in great detail and scope the posthumous defense of his friend and mentor. It was not a popular decision in the South for Mosby's defense of Stuart was seen not as an attack on Longstreet, but on General Lee!

The loss of the Battle of Gettysburg had been "explained away" by many in the South even during the war with the claim that Stuart had disobeyed orders to go on a glory-seeking repeat of his "Ride around McClellan" and that without his cavalry (the eyes of his army), Lee was caught flat-footed. John Mosby's research was, as usual, thorough, extensive and meticulous; and as he was never much concerned about "where the chips fell," he was not about to ignore evidence in Stuart's favor to protect anyone—including Lee! But as with everything else, his motives didn't matter anymore than did the painstaking nature of his research. His work on Stuart and Gettysburg raised once again the ire of all those folks in the South who detested him for his "Republican ways." In fact, those who had been involved in the Gettysburg campaign even attempted to keep evidence, then being made public, from him—hardly proof of objectivity *or* honesty! The papers carried Mosby's defense of Stuart, and eventually a book by him on the matter was published. Below is the mention of Mosby's first "report:"

> *The Times* – February 2, 1896
>
> LONGSTREET AND STUART.
>
> Highly Interesting Review by Col. John Singleton Mosby Cause of the Loss of Gettysburg,
>
> Many of Longstreet's Statements in His Book Combatted by Col. Mosby—the Want of Cavalry Had Nothing to Do with the Result of the Battle

Naturally, Mosby's actions created a fierce backlash, starting with fellow Republican James Longstreet. It is probable that as well as "defending Lee," Republican Longstreet wanted to be "on the right side" of this issue in hopes of returning to the good graces of his fellow Southerners. As usual, Mosby responded as quickly as the criticism hit the papers and continued to fire back as more and more of his fellow officers joined Longstreet in his—and Stuart's—condemnation:

***The Times* – March 15, 1896**

COL. MOSBY FIRES BACK.

He Defends Stuart From Longstreet's Criticism

Misleading Extracts Were Given by the General, He Says—"Witnesses are Sworn to Tell the Whole Truth."

And thus, the dogs of at least literary war had been unleashed as John Mosby continued to maintain his defense of Jeb Stuart. Of course, he was dealing with facts, whereas his critics were dealing with opinion or, more properly, passion:

***The Times* – March 22, 1896**

THE CHARGE AGAINST STUART

Col. Mosby Says It Was Invented to Cover up the Errors of Other Men.

A Ringing Reply to Colonel. Marshall.

That Alleged Spy Must Take His Place in Historical Literature with the Ghost of Caesar that Appeared at Brutus' Tent the Night Before Philippi

Many, if not most, of Mosby's biographers cite this and other disputes in the man's life to "prove" that he lived for combat and was therefore happy to initiate the circumstances that led to it. Not so! John Mosby responded because he saw as time went on, history was going to declare that Jeb Stuart had lost Gettysburg and by extension, the war for the Confederacy. Mosby's sense of justice that never deserted him throughout his long life would not permit him to remain mute while a friend and a Southern hero was unjustly blamed for the fall of the South.

If the Stuart matter were not enough, Mosby experienced the first relapse of the appendicitis he had suffered the year before. It was so severe that he was declared "on his deathbed" several times and his hopes of returning to Virginia to attend the second reunion of his command were dashed:

***Chicago Tribune* – May 2, 1896**

COL. J. B. MOSBY [sic] ON HIS DEATHBED

Famous Ex-Confederate General in the Agonies of Appendicitis.

San Francisco, Cal., May 26.—Col. John B. Mosby, the ex-Confederate soldier, and recently Consul to Hongkong, is lying critically ill at his home in this city. He is suffering from appendicitis, and his recovery is a matter of grave doubt.

Last winter Col. Mosby was taken ill in Virginia, whither he went on a visit. His life was despaired of for a time, but he recovered sufficiently to return to this city.

***San Francisco Call* – May 7, 1896 (Edited)**

Colonel John S. Mosby, the noted guerrilla leader during the war, afterward Consul to Hongkong under President Grant, has been quite ill at the Hotel

Imperial, on Sutter street, for two weeks past. Colonel Mosby, while on a visit to Washington over a year ago, was stricken very ill with the grip. He was confined to his bed for several weeks, and as will be remembered by the dispatches was in a dangerous condition. He recovered finally and returned here, looking pale after his long siege. This illness seems to have not been totally eradicated, and was probably the cause of his recent sickness here. He is considerably better now, however, and his friends hope that he will soon be able to be out again and meet his old friends, who have for some time missed him.

Dr. Tirrell has been in attendance on Colonel Mosby. It is stated that the colonel's present ailment is appendicitis. He has been alternately better and worse for several days. Last night the colonel sent out word that he was getting along very slowly. There were many inquiries in regard to his condition yesterday.

His son and two or three daughters have for some years been living in Washington, D.C. A few years ago his son was here, and remained with him for about a year and then went to Washington.

Chicago Times – May 27, 1896

Omaha Daily Bee – May 27, 1896

COL. J. B. MOSBY ON HIS DEATHBED

Noted Confederate Cavalry Leader Believed to be Dying

Famous Ex-Confederate General in the Agonies of Appendicitis

Richmond Times – July 1, 1896

[Part of a much longer article-vph]

Judge A. E. Richards, Louisville, Ky.:

Dear Sir—I write at the request of our mutual friend, Col. Mosby, to thank you for your kind letter and invitation of the 15th inst. The Colonel would love to go to Richmond and stop and see you en route, but he is entirely too weak to undertake the journey He is just now beginning to convalesce from a severe spell of illness, lasting over six weeks. I am glad to write you that I consider him out of danger at this time and I think he will be up and about again as usual in the course of two or three weeks. He has spoken often about the grand reunion to be held in Richmond, and it will be a great disappointment to him that he cannot be with the survivors of his old command on that grand occasion.

With kind regards from the Colonel, I am,

Very truly yours, GEORGE M. TERRILL, Attending Physician

Mosby continued to wrestle with his illness, finally shaking off its last vestiges in mid-September. However, the condition was never truly resolved and contributed to his health problems throughout the rest of his life.

One of the issues that most engaged Mosby in the election of 1896 was that of the challenge to the "gold standard" and the demand for "bimetallism"—that is, the use of both silver and gold as a backing for American currency. Mosby was very much engaged in this matter as it threatened to be a seminal issue in the upcoming election, which saw Democrat-Populist William Jennings Bryan thrill audiences with his famous "Cross of Gold" speech:

Alexandria Gazette – August 20, 1896

The letter written by Colonel Mosby in reply to Judge R. W. Hughes's free silver letter has been published. Col. Mosby holds that bimetallism, or the double standard, is impossible, and says Judge Hughes's plan is a one sided scheme. He thinks the Judge would like to sell by one measure and buy by another. The silver craze, he ways, is one of those periodical epidemics that have visited us.

John Mosby then wrote—at the request of the *Free Lance*—a very lengthy and detailed examination of the "bimetallism" controversy. The following article illustrates two points: first, that Mosby was not just "all about the Civil War," and second, that he knew what he was talking about. Probably as a result of his legal background, John Mosby didn't just have "opinions" in the sense of what today we call "feelings" and (frequently) unfounded political and economic prejudices. Rather, Mosby's views were based upon historical fact filtered through a shrewd intellect. True, he was accused of not having "progressed," but Mosby knew that "progress" was useful only when it was correct. To "progress" into error was counter-productive.

The Times – August 20, 1896 (Edited)

COL. MOSBY FOR SOUND MONEY

Bimetallism, or the So-Called Double Standard Is Impossible, He Says.

Judge Hughes' One-Sided Scheme.

He Would Evidently Like to Sell by One Measure and Buy By Another—

The Silver Craze One of Those Periodical Epidemics That Have Visited Us.

The following letter on the currency question from Colonel John S. Mosby, the famous Confederate soldier will be read with great interest:

San Francisco, August 13, 1896,

Mr. A. P. Rose, Jr., Manager of the "*Free Lance*":

Dear Sir.—I have received your letter asking my views on the political situation, and I infer that you wish to know my position in regard to the presidential candidates and my opinion as to the policies they are supposed to represent. If I had a million votes, I would give them to McKinley. I am opposed to the Populist ticket nominated at Chicago.

The United States was placed on the gold standard by Andrew Jackson over sixty years ago, and we have been there ever since. I am opposed to substituting for it now a depreciated currency, and descending to a commercial level with Siam. I was opposed to the island silver bill in 1878 because I regarded it as repudiation in disguise, and the first financial step in the descent to Avernus, [ancient name for a volcanic crater near Cumae, Italy, in the Region of Campania west of Naples-vph], where Coxey [Jacob Coxey, Ohio businessman-vph] and [William Jennings] Bryan are trying to land us… During a residence of several years in China, and in frequent visits to Mexico, that has free coinage, I never saw a piece of gold in circulation. By natural law, as universal as that of gravitation, the cheaper always drives out the dearer currency.

BIMETTALISM IS IMPOSSIBLE.

Locke, who was an assistant in the recoinage of 1696, announced the theory, which is now accepted as an axiom in finance, that it is impossible to have two standard metals circulating side by side at the same time … The commercial ratio of gold and silver, like all other commodities, must vary according to supply and demand, and the cost of production, and cannot be fixed by legislation Of course, the Government can coin both metals, but only the inferior will circulate On the recognition of this principle the English monetary system is founded. "But," says the Coxey platform, "That is British policy, and we ought not to follow it." And so, I answer, is the habeas corpus and our inheritance of free institutions. To discard a policy merely because a great commercial nation was the first to adopt it would be as absurd as to accept the Reverend John Jasper's theory of the solar system in preference to Newton's.

The question of the so-called double-standard is not a new one; it vexed Europe for about two hundred years, and was finally condemned as impracticably by the greatest statesmen and economists You may ask if I am opposed to that ideal thing that is called bimetallism. I answer, No, neither am I opposed to the discovery of perpetual motion, but I don't think anybody will ever discover it.

DANIEL SHOULD KNOW BETTER.

"But," says Major Daniel, in his speech at the Populist convention, "we have gold and silver dollars circulating together at par to-day by virtue of the Government stamp, which is a refutation of the theory of the economists." If a representative of the Territory of Red Cloud and Sitting Bull had said so, I would have felt no surprise, but a Virginia senator should know better. The reason why silver dollars pass as the equal of gold dollars is the pledge of the Government to maintain their equality with gold; just as the note of a tramp might be recognized in a bank with Astor's or Vanderbilt's endorsement upon it If there is any such magic in a stamp; if by inscribing on an inferior metal "E pluribus unum," and the American eagle, such transformation of value can be effected, then why not try it on copper, and turn the great Anaconda mine into coin? Do you ask if I believe in monometallism? I answer, I do; just as I believe in any other law of nature— the revolution of the earth and the motion of the planets The vain effort to maintain the concurrent circulation of coins of different metallic values is described in one of his most instructive chapters by Macaulay. He says:

"A clipped crown, on English ground, went as far in the payment of a tax or a debt as a milled crown. But the milled crown, as soon as it had been flung into the crucible or carried across the channel, became much more valuable than the clipped crown. The politicians of that age, however, generally overlooked these very obvious considerations. They marveled exceedingly that everybody should be so perverse as to use light money in preference to good money. In other words, they marveled that nobody chose to pay twelve ounces of silver when ten would serve the turn."

OUT OF DATE.

"For the same reason that depreciated greenbacks drove specie out of circulation, depreciated silver with free coinage would drive gold out of circulation These same people now since silver has fallen 50 percent, complain that they are not allowed to coin it on private account at the old ratio.

"When, in 1873, the silver dollar was dropped by law, it had become as obsolete as a Roman coin found in Pompeii. The law simply recognized an existing fact. Theoretically we had a bimetallic standard, practically a monometallic gold standard. There is a combination supporting the Populist ticket with entirely opposite ends in view. The miners, who demonetized silver when it was at a premium by refusing to coin it, now want the government to create for their benefit an artificial value by coining their bullion at the ratio of 16 to 1, when it is worth in the market only 32 to 1. They think that this will lift silver to a par with gold. Coxey and the vagabonds who are following him want silver to go down—the cheaper it is the better for them. The silver kings want it to go up…

JUDGE HUGHES' LETTER.

"I have just read the letter of Judge Hughes in the *Free Lance*. He laments that the Virginia farmers have no metallic money. I was in Virginia some months ago and heard a good deal of complaint about the scarcity but not a word about the quality of the money the people had. All that I saw was as good as gold … "The good old times," says Byron—"all times when old are good." He forgets that this was the price in an inflated currency, and was paid in the ragged notes which he says the people don't want. The exchangeable value of a bushel of wheat for other commodities is as much now as it was then. Judge Hughes is a farmer as well as a judge. He only grieves over the fall in what he has to sell. It is plain that he would like to sell by one measure and buy by another… Judge Hughes censures the Administration for not paying out silver. The Treasury Department would be glad to do so, but people won't have it. Judge Hughes has for over twenty years been drawing a salary from the Government, and I venture to say that he has always drawn it in greenbacks or gold. He teaches by precept, not by example."

A PERIODICAL EPIDEMIC

"There is a widespread alarm in the country, at the remote prospect of the election of the Populist ticket. People are preparing for the deluge by putting their gold in safety deposit boxes or old stockings; every one sees the panic and disorder that must result from a change in the measure of value by which we have lived and contracts have been made for over sixty years.

Wealth cannot be created by blowing bubbles. The silver craze is one of those periodical epidemics that have passed over the country. They always breed demagogues. Men are still living who can remember when people were run mad over the morus multicaulis, and everybody was going to get rich off mulberry-leaves. Mulberry leaves are a surer foundation for a fortune than fiat money ... Associated with this assault on the credit and financial honor of the country is the lawless spirit that animates the Populist party everywhere. Two years ago all railroad transportation was stopped by a mob, and Chicago for several days was under a reign of terror, the same state of things existed in California. San Francisco was as completely blockaded as if it has been under the guns of a hostile fleet. It was doubtful for some time whether Debs or Grover Cleveland was President of the United States. The President ordered his army to disperse the rioters, and the country was saved from a bloody revolution. For this courageous action, every good citizen should applaud him. The Chicago convention could speak no kind word for the President. At the dictation of Altgeld and Debs, it adopted a resolution condemning him. The Virginia people must now decide whether they will stand by Cleveland or follow Coxey and Debs."

Very respectfully, JNO. S. MOSBY

It must be noted here that Mosby called for the people of Virginia to stand with Cleveland, a Democratic president in his actions during the Pullman strike! In other words, party was less than policy, and doing the right thing was more important than mere partisan gain. It was a very telling remark referable to John Mosby as a man and illustrated the hierarchy of his values.

Kansas City Daily Journal – **August 22, 1896**
GENERAL MOSBY IN THE SADDLE.

Many ex-Confederate soldiers have read with deep interest the letter of General John S. Mosby, published in yesterday's journal. General Mosby was one of the brave leaders of the South in the civil war and performed gallant service in behalf of the Lost Cause on many a bloody field. At the close of the struggle he labored heroically and patriotically to bring order out of chaos in the South and to establish peace and prosperity within her borders. He and General Grant were firm friends after the war closed, and the feeling of amity arising from a mutual regard for each other's soldierly qualities. When Lee surrendered to Grant at Appomattox General Mosby accepted the situation like a man, and from that time has been as firm a friend of the Union as any who fought under the stars and stripes.

He is just as patriotic today. In the free silver heresy now being promulgated throughout the land General Mosby recognizes as great a danger to this government as when its existence was threatened in the dark days of '61. He takes strong grounds against the proposition for free silver coinage, holding that gold is the only reliable standard. His opinions are argued with characteristic vigor and clearness, and abound with many keen hits. He has about as little use for a Populist as that deluded individual has for gold, and takes scant pains to conceal his disbelief in Populist honesty or sincerity. The present fiat silver craze General Mosby likes to other deadly epidemics which sweep over the country at intervals. "They always breed demagogues," he says. "Men are still living who can remember when people ran mad over the morus muticaulis, when everybody was going to get rich off mulberry leaves. Mulberry leaves are a surer foundation for a fortune than fiat money."

General Mosby's letter is full of wisdom and shows him to be a student of history and a close watcher of events, as well as a statesman. It is only to be regretted that he hasn't a million votes to give to the cause of sound money.

However, after such glowing praises, Mosby was once again attacked for his position on the gold standard through the use of the usual claims, that is his "notoriety" and the fact that he was a Confederate appointed by Grant to an office although why either should matter is unclear. His main fault here according to the article below was that he had not "progressed." The Populist movement, which included men like Socialist Eugene V. Debs, had pretty much "swallowed" The Democratic party as was illustrated by a political cartoon of the time showing Bryan as the "populist" boa constrictor swallowing the Democratic donkey alive:

Salt Lake Herald – **August 22, 1896**

OUT OF DATE.

Mosby Shows How Little He Has Progressed.

Chicago, Aug. 21.—A special from Washington says: Colonel John S. Mosby, who achieved notoriety during the civil war as one of the most daring rangers on the Confederate side, and who was subsequently appointed consul-general to China by President Grant, has addressed an open letter to a Virginia editor, who asked Mosby's views on the political situation and the policies represented by the two presidential candidates in the country. "Bimetallism," says he, "by which is meant the coinage and circulation of the two metals in private account, with full legal tender value—is a dream that can never be realized To discard a policy merely because a great commercial nation was the first to adopt it, would be as absurd as to accept the Rev. John Jasper's theory of the solar system in preference to Newton's.

"I believe in monometallism, just as I believe in any other law of nature—the revolution of the earth and the motion of the planets. For the same reason that depreciated greenbacks drove specie out of circulation, depreciated silver with free coinage would drive gold out of circulation.

"The silver craze is one of those periodical epidemics that have passed over the county. They always breed demagogues Men are still living who can remember when people were run made over the Morus Multicaulis, and everybody was going to get rich off mulberry leaves. Mulberry leaves are a surer foundation for a fortune than fiat money."

The Norfolk Virginian attributed Mosby's lack of support of the Bryan ticket simply to his being a Republican but no mention was made of his dispute with the policies of that "ticket." This was the natural mind-set of those whose political stance depended solely upon party. And while Mosby chose not to vote at all rather than vote the Democratic ticket when Cousin Ben ran a second time, his mind-set was such that had positions been reversed (that is, if the Republicans were "populist" and The Democrats for sound currency), he probably would have voted the Democratic ticket because of the importance of the issue and his belief that it was the right thing to do.

But John Mosby was once again in his element. Yes, he was in a type of "combat," albeit political and economic rather than martial; and he loved it. But this didn't mean that Mosby loved to fight without purpose—or simply for the sake of fighting. He was a passionate man, but his passions were not those of the mindless brute who seeks combat for its own sake. Rather, he was an educated, opinionated man with a definite viewpoint relative to the important issues of the day. Furthermore, his opinions were sought even by those who disagreed with him! During these controversies, there was nothing asked about the Civil War, and Mosby did not raise the subject.

Finally, Mosby's bout of appendicitis ended leaving him, according to this article, "weak and shaky":

> *San Francisco Call* – **September 13, 1896**
>
> COLONEL MOSBY BETTER
>
> The Ex-Guerrilla Leader Weak and Shaky, but Taking Much Interest in National Politics.
>
> Colonel John S. Mosby, the noted ex-guerrilla leader and United States Consul Hongkong, who has been ill for three months past with appendicitis, part of the time seriously, was up and about yesterday, though he is yet weak. He visited the Palace and met several friends. He says he is nervous from his long confinement.
>
> The colonel has no doubt about the result of the National election, in which he takes much interest. He says he has received a letter from Judge Richards of Louisville, who has been on the Kentucky Supreme bench and who as a boy was major on his staff. The letter says there is no doubt at all about the Republicans carrying Kentucky. There is no doubt either about West Virginia, Maryland or Delaware.
>
> "In fact, Virginia will go for McKinley, as I am assured, and from my own knowledge am certain," said the colonel. "I got a letter from the chairman of the Republican State Central Committee there a few days ago. He says there is no doubt about Virginia going Republican. I am persuaded McKinley will get all the States I have named. They are all interested in protection, the same as people here are."

As the election drew nearer, he was asked for a prediction as seen by this article in the *San Francisco Call*. The length, complexity, and depth of his response to the correspondent's questions must forever put to rest the contention that Mosby was a "one trick pony" whose only interest and expertise was the Civil War—and even then only his part within it

> *San Francisco Call* – **October 5, 1896 (Edited)**
>
> MOSBY SUMS UP BRYAN'S CHANCES
>
> Sees a Sign in the South Portentous of His Defeat.

He Never Can Be Elected With the "Solid South" Broken and Against Him. Advances Irrefutable Logic

The Colonel Hurls Anathemas at the Windy Leader and Calls Him a Revolutionist.

"My opinion is that Delaware, Maryland, West Virginia and Kentucky are just as safe for McKinley as any of the Northern States, and in old Virginia McKinley has an equal show with Bryan of carrying the State."

These were the words used yesterday by Colonel John S. Mosby, who is in close touch with the political situation in the South through the medium of a voluminous correspondence with old-time friends in that section of the country.

"There is the hottest campaign going on in Old Virginia," said the ex-Confederate cavalry leader, "of any State in the Union. A considerable number of leading Democratic papers have come out against Bryan. Then in all the commercial centers, like Richmond, Norfolk, Danville, Lynchburg and Alexandria, great opposition to the free coinage of silver has been developed. The professors in the colleges of the State have declared against free silver. The professors in the University of Virginia have come out against Bryan and free silver.

"At the recent gold convention at Richmond, one of the delegates was a Professor Thornton of the University of Virginia, a nephew of James D. Thornton of San Francisco, formerly one of the Justices of the Supreme Court of California, who by the way is a Democrat but opposed to free silver.

"A great many leading men of Virginia," continued the Colonel, "are now canvassing that State against Bryan and free silver, who have never voted anything but a Democratic ticket in their lives. The president of the Sound Money League in Richmond is William Wirt Henry, a grandson of Patrick Henry. Last week he made a speech in Richmond against Bryan and free silver, and about the same time General Buckner addressed a large meeting there on behalf of the gold standard. The president of the meeting was General Payton Wise, a brother of Collector John Wise of San Francisco. Bruckner was introduced by Governor O'Ferrall, and old-line Democrat, who came out strongly in favor of free silver and against the anarchistic platform adopted at Chicago.

"If McKinley loses Virginia, it will be because he is counted out in the negro counties where they always perpetrate the great frauds. "There was a convention in Richmond last week of Democratic lawyers who opposed Bryan. The object of the meeting was to devise means to prevent McKinley from being counted out. The Republicans hope that the organization of this powerful body will secure a fair election, as their white allies will protect the ballots and see that there is a fair count."

"I see that Bryan is trying to make capital with the Germans out of a pretended letter of Bismarck's a part of which turns out to be a forgery. It is really immaterial whether the whole letter is genuine or not. Of course, Bismarck would like for the United States to adopt free coinage single handed for he knows that we would immediately drop to a silver basis, and all our gold would fly to Europe. Germany would then unload her silver on us and pay our farmers for their grain and pork in our own depreciated silver dollars. His benevolent advice to us is 'Pitch in lemons and get squeezed.' Now Bismarck is the great gold bug of Europe. Germany was under the control of the Iron Chancellor when she demonetized silver.

"I have just examined the report of the monetary conference held at Paris in 1881 by the invitation of the United States . . . .

"Germany was invited to participate in the conference, which was called for the purpose of establishing international bimetallism. Bismarck positively declined to have anything to do with it. All the other European nations sent delegates. Germany alone refused. Bismarck wants to try the experiment of free coinage on the other fellow, both to see how it works as well as to get the other fellow's gold and unload his old silver on him. He wants to use the United States just as a scientist uses a dog for vivisection to test a theory.

"The burden of all of Bryan's speeches is the depression of business, which he pretends to think is due to a contraction of the currency, and with all the art of Mephistopheles, he charges that it is a conspiracy of the rich to oppress the poor. These speeches recall the picture that Milton draws of Satan squatting in Eden in the shape of a toad and whispering damnable suggestions into the ear of Eve. Bryan is not only a quack and a demagogue, but an incendiary. Whoever tries to array one class against another—the rich against the poor—is an enemy of society. We all want to be rich. It is doctrines such as these—the development of the maxim of Rousseau that 'property is robbery,' that set the guillotine to work and drenched Paris in blood. Now Bryan's programme is simply a grand scheme of confiscation and spoliation.

"Those who ascribe the depression in business to a scarcity of money confound cause and effect.

"The prevailing depression is not due to a scarcity of money. There is more money in the country than there ever was before. It is lying idle and is not circulating on account of the alarm created by silver agitation. It is the fear of tampering with the currency, changing the standard of value and dropping to a silver basis that has created distrust, caused a suspension of business and stagnation in trade.

"The silver barons now want the Government to do what the statutes of 1853 said they should not do—i.e. coin a lie and certify that 50 cents is 100 cents. Bryan has a great deal of abuse for corporations and syndicates. He has nothing to say against the silver syndicate that is pouring out its money to elect him

"Bankers are as much depressed as any other class. They don't make money by hoarding it in their vaults, but by exchanging it. Instead of there not being enough money for the requirements of business, there is not enough business to employ the money that is idle. If we had free coinage, those who are rich now would still be rich; those who are poor would be poorer.

"Bryan himself admits that his election will cause a monetary panic, but says such a heroic remedy is necessary to cure the disease from which the country is suffering. I think the remedy he proposes is worse than the disease. Instead of a panic, McKinley's election will restore hope and business confidence to the country and start again the wheels of industry.

"I have just received the Index, published at my old home, Warrenton, Va. It is a Bryan free silver paper. It has a letter giving an account of the organization of sound money club at Marshall, Fauquier county. The platform adopted says: 'The we, members of the upper Fauquier Sound Money League, hereby express our determination to use every legitimate means to advance the cause of sound money by opposing the Chicago platform and the candidates nominated thereon." The letter says: "The league is growing, and the woods are full of gold bugs."

"Mr. Brooke says: 'Believing that the Chicago platform is eminently un-Democratic and fraught with most serious danger to the country in all its interests, and finding myself free and a Democratic platform and candidates ready to my hand, I shall support them (Palmer and Buckner) and let consequences take care of themselves.'"

The election proved to be all that Mosby could have desired. With McKinley's victory, he must have breathed a sigh of relief, knowing—or at least expecting—that the Republicans for whom he had worked so tirelessly and defended so successfully—especially in the press—would and must alleviate his precarious employment situation with the railroad. Furthermore, a combination of Republicans and "sound money" Democrats had, apparently, broken the "Solid South" in the election, but as had happened in the past, Mosby's high expectations for a better year in 1897 proved vain:

San Francisco Call – **November 4, 1896**

NEWS OF VICTORY AT HEADQUARTERS

Republican Leaders Eagerly Awaited Returns From the East.

Scene of Elation When Tidings Came That the Solid South Was Broken. Result Not unexpected.

Magnitude and Sweep of the Triumph Surpassed All Expectations.

As the dispatches came thick and fast announcing the unprecedented Republican gains the enthusiasm at headquarters was intense. When the news came announcing that Virginia had joined the Republican column with 15,000 majority for McKinley, Colonel Mosby was excitedly elated. He remarked: "I said weeks ago that McKinley would carry Virginia and politicians laughed at the idea."

When the tidings flashed over the wires that the "Solid South" no longer existed in fact but only as a memory, the joy of Republicans and sound-money Democrats knew no bounds. The reports that Virginia, Kentucky, Maryland and Tennessee had gone for McKinley caused the greatest rejoicing. As for Nebraska, some regrets were expressed that Bryan had lost his own State.

Chapter 36

1897

Forsan miseros meliora sequentur. ~ For those in misery, perhaps better things will follow.

"The busy have no time for tears." ~ Lord Byron

JOHN MOSBY, WHO had been in Virginia as 1897 dawned, was called to Bedford City and the home of his brother William because of the failing health of his eighty-three-year-old mother. She was suffering at that time from the effects of a fall, and on January 15, Virginia Jackson McLaurine Mosby passed away in the home of her younger son.

Tazewell Republican – **January 21, 1897**

Mrs. Virginia B. Mosby, mother of the celebrated Confederate Chieftain Col. John S. Mosby, died at Bedford City, Va., on last Friday night, from the infirmities of old age, being 83 years old. Col. Mosby came all the way from California to attend the bedside of his aged mother during her last hours.

The *Alexandria Gazette* paid homage to this remarkable woman in this brief recounting of a few of the highlights of her life:

Alexandria Gazette – **January 30, 1897**

Mrs. Virginia Mosby.

Mrs. Virginia Jackson Mosby, mother of Colonel John S. Mosby, who died on Thursday, January 14, at the residence of her son, Mr. William Mosby, in Bedford City, Va. Was born in 1815, and named for General Andrew Jackson, who had just won the great battle of New Orleans in the same year. Her father, James McLaurin, of Powhatan county, was a revolutionary soldier, while her grandfather, one of the first Episcopal clergymen in Virginia, lived at the Glebe in that county, and died in 1772, both he and his wife being buried beneath the chancel of the Petersville Church in that county.

Mr. James McLaurin, Mrs. Mosby's father, lived to a very great age and when an old man, rode on election day into four counties to cast his vote, the law of the State at that time permitting a man to have a ballot in every county in which he held property. His family belonged to the Scotch clan of McLaurin, between which and the clan McGregor there had existed a long feud. The ancient quarrel was peacefully terminated by the inter-marriage of the young people of the respective clans and is referred to in the introduction of Scott's "Rob Roy."

Mrs. Mosby retained the distinguishing characteristics of her race and kept the plaid of her clan in a conspicuous place in her room with a picture of the monument of the McLaurine erected at Edinburgh. Her two sons she gave to the Confederate cause and, during the last winter of the war, when Southerners' hopes were almost gone, she wrote a letter to the Governor of Virginia urging him to never surrender the State to the enemy. Her dauntless spirit was displayed when on one occasion the train on which she was riding to Bedford City was halted at the side of a shaky bridge and the passengers told to walk over after the cars had passed. Mrs. Mosby refused to alight, though all the other passengers did so, and she asserted that, as she had a through ticket, she intended to keep her seat. She did and the train passed over safely, but the very next day the bridge fell to the bottom of the chasm. Such was her remarkable energy that one of her sons often remarked that had she been in command of the army of the South, it would have been fighting now.

Mrs. Mosby was buried at Bedford City. She leaves four children, Mrs. Charles W. Russell, of Washington; Miss Blakely Mosby, of the same city; Col. John S. Mosby and William Mosby. Her last illness was the result of a fall due to the feebleness of old age.

The Gazette reported that Mosby would be remaining in Virginia on legal matters:

Alexandria Gazette – February 17, 1897

The government has taken a appeal in the Van Buren case which Colonel Mosby gained in the Court of claims last December, and for which he will get a large fee. The case has been advanced on the docket and will be argued in the U. S. Supreme Court in April. The Colonel will therefore not return to California before May.

Early in 1897, John Mosby met with newly elected Republican president, William McKinley. The article stated that he was not making any efforts to secure a government office, and that was probably true. However, as with any newly elected chief executive, those who would not turn down such an offer presented themselves with the tacit understanding of their availability:

Evening Star – March 10, 1897

Gen. Mosby's Call

Gen. John S. Mosby, the famous ex-Confederate cavalry leader saw the President. Gen. Mosby is still active and vigorous, clean shaven and with a look of great alertness in his keen blue eyes. He moves and speaks rapidly and looks competent to bestride a horse and lead a dash if necessary. Gen. Mosby has been a Republican for many years.

"Ah, you gave me a lot of trouble in the Shenandoah Valley, general," said the President when Gen. Mosby was presented to him.

"If I did, I have atoned for it," replied the general. "I supported you in the last campaign as ardently as I opposed you in the Shenandoah." General Mosby only came to pay his respects, he said and not to talk about office.

Mosby certainly had no dealings with McKinley, who was only a minor player in the great war. However, McKinley's cabinet was something else again. General Alger was a member of his administration, and Alger despised Mosby for the business in the Shenandoah Valley when Lieutenant Colonel Chapman of his command executed those caught burning civilian dwellings in that area. Alger was complicit, along with

Custer, in that matter. Mosby, though not directly involved, had approved of the action and so informed General Lee. It is interesting to note that Lee did not object either, considering the matter a war crime and the executions justified:

Salt Lake Herald – March 11, 1897

GEN. MOSBY MEETS THE PRESIDENT

Exchange of Complements Between Old-Time Enemies. Had a Pleasant Time

Washington, March 10.—Colonel John S. Mosby, the Confederate cavalry leader, who is now a resident of California, dropped in to pay his respects, and had a pleasant conversation with the president. It was the first time that the two had met.

"You used to give me a great deal of worry in the Shenandoah Valley," said the president.

"I think all the worry was on your side, Mr. President," responded the famous guerilla. "I want to say that I supported you as vigorously in the last campaign as I opposed you then."

"I've heard of it," answered the president with a parting hand shake.

In mid-March, two articles appeared in the *Alexandria Gazette*. The first involved Mosby's possible participation in the upcoming "Grant Day" to be held in New York City upon the dedication of Grant's tomb. This was the first mention of the possibility of not only Mosby, but his command participating in this historic event. The second article likened Mosby's meeting with McKinley as a "raid," which was hardly complimentary or supportive! It also pointed out that all Mosby received from his visit with the new president were meaningless pleasantries voiced mostly by himself, which was true enough:

Alexandria Gazette – March 16, 1897

Washington, March 16.

Col. Mosby has received a letter from New York, suggesting that as many of his old command as possible should come to that city on the 27th proximo, and march as a separate body, under his command, in the procession at the dedicatory ceremonies of the Grant monument there on that day. He has adopted the suggestion, or rather the invitation. He met Colonel Fred Grant here to day, and on mentioning the matter to him, the latter said he would be delighted if the survivors of the Rangers would come to New York on the occasion referred to, and be particularly gratified if they would take part in the ceremonies.

Alexandria Gazette – March 17, 1897

Mosby in Washington.—Colonel Mosby went down to Washington to make a raid on the President, but all that he captured was an expression like this: "Well, Colonel, I am very glad to meet you. I recollect that you gave us a good deal of trouble in the Shenandoah Valley a few years ago." The replay of the famous guerrilla was: "Well, Mr. President, I don't intend to embarrass you during this administration, at any rate."

Colonel Mosby and General Grant were strong friends, and it has been suggested as eminently proper and fitting that the remnant of the band of hardy raiders join the procession on Grant Day, at the dedication of the tomb. Col. John Tyler Dickson, one of the worst of the band and one of the best of the remnant, has written to Mosby on the subject. He thinks that at least fifty can be got together for the occasion. Mosby's guerrillas were of the best blood in Virginia, and what is left of them would be an interesting sight.—N.Y. Press 16th

A few days later, a small article appeared in the *Richmond Dispatch*. It was a purely social item, of little moment or interest except locally, involving Mosby's "namesake" son, John Jr. It is a staple of history that upon such small things evolve great consequences:

Richmond Dispatch, – March 21, 1897

In 1895[*] John S. Mosby, Jr., then a student at the University of Virginia, wrote for the annual (Corks and Curls) a college play, "The Flirt," which attracted favorable attention. The students of the university of Virginia have determined to produce it in such good shape as, they hope, to eclipse the Harvard Greek play. [*The paper has the wrong date; the proper date is probably 1885, at which time John Jr. would have been twenty-one years old.-vph]

Meanwhile, the papers continued to report upon Mosby's activities in the area, some of which hearkened back to less-benign past visits by the old Ranger during the war:

Alexandria Gazette – March 26, 1897

A VISIT FROM COL. MOSBY.

Colonel John S. Mosby, the famous "guerilla chief," raided Fairfax Court House again on Sunday night, and while he did not capture a "Yankee General" this time, he aroused general interest and received a warmer welcome than when he made his celebrated raid here in 1863, and triumphantly carried away Brigadier General Stoughton and a large number of prisoners and horses, without losing a man. He was accompanied by his gallant old comrade and friend, Capt. Fount Beattie, and visited, in company with a number of friends, the house in which the capture of Stoughton was made, explaining, in a most graphic and interesting way, all the details of the daring raid. He went to the room in which the doughty General was sleeping when he was so rudely aroused to a realizing sense of his unfortunate predicament, showed the position of the bed, and related the conversation that ensued after he had given the General a good spank to arouse him from his peaceful slumber. Mosby had with him at the time only 29 men, while several thousand federal cavalry were encamped in the village and vicinity. Contrary to the general belief, he says he did not strike the Fairfax Station road at its intersection with the Braddock road, but approached the town through the fields, passing the Stephenson (now the Canfield) residence.

The Colonel has not visited this place in twenty years, but he readily recognized some of the older inhabitants and was as easily recognized by them. Time had dealt gently with him. His hair is tinged with grey, but he possess the elasticity of step, the bright eye, and the keenness of intellect which were his chief characteristics when in the zenith of his military career. He cordially endorsed the suggestion that a reunion of his old command should be held here, and we think it would be a good idea to have such reunion this summer, in connection with the agricultural fair. It could be made a grand affair and while proving a benefit to Fairfax county, would at the same time be a delightful occasion to the old veterans of the county, both Confederate and Federal.

After taking dinner at the residence of Mr. Thomas Moore, Colonel Mosby and Captain Beattie returned to the home of the latter near Annandale. Now that he has found the way here again, we hope to see [the] Colonel in Fairfax quite often.—[*Fairfax Herald*.

The Mosby-Grant theme was continued in the press, which was understandable. The event itself was widely publicized, and there were many notables who intended to be present at the unveiling of the nation's tribute to General and former president, Ulysses S. Grant:

Alexandria Gazette – March 30, 1897

Lieut. A. C. Dillingham has been named by Secretary Long as the representative of the navy at the Grant memorial in New York, and Colonel Mosby has been invited to be a member of the staff of General Dodge on that occasion.

Chicago Times – March 30, 1897

COL. MOSBY TO BE IN GRANT PARADE.

It Is Probable That the Famous Guerrilla Leader Will Represent the Confederate Soldiers.

New York, March 29.—[Special.]—It is probable that Col. Mosby, the famous guerrilla chieftain of the late war, will ride side by side with Gen. Grenville M. Dodge at the head of the Grant Monument inaugural parade as an aid-de-camp, representing the late Confederacy.

Col. Mosby was a close friend of Gen. Grant after the close of the war, and when he became President Gen. Grant appointed Col. Mosby to a Chinese mission. He became a Republican leader in Virginia. He now lives in California.

Evening Star – March 30, 1897

MOSBY'S MEN

An Appeal to Participate in the Grant Monument Dedication

An appeal has been issued by John Dickson, temporary committeeman, headquarters Confederate Veteran Camp of New York, to the ex-members of Mosby cavalry, otherwise known as the 43d Virginia battalion, to participate in the ceremonies attendant upon the dedication of the Grant monument on April 27, 1897. Mr. Dickson says:

"No greater opportunity has been offered for the expression of the grateful sentiment and appreciation of the magnanimity of Gen. Grant toward our comrades in general, and more particularly the remembrance of his generous protection to our commander, Colonel John S. Mosby, at the close of the late war.

"It is to be hoped that we can gather together a goodly number to swell the ranks of the 'ex-Confederate organizations in the grand parade. Those members desiring to participate are requested to forward their names at once, in order that arrangements may be made for horses, equipments, etc."

Mr. Dickson's effort in this direction is ably seconded by the local Confederate Veterans' Association, which has taken up *The Appeal* and is doing all in its power to have a large representation of the veterans in line from the District of Columbia. Communications to Mr. Dickson are to be addressed to the Windsor Hotel, New York city.

Evening Times – March 30, 1897

Mosby's Cavalry in the Grant Parade To the Editor of The Times:

Sir—The ex-members of Mosby's Cavalry (Forty-third Virginia Battalion) are invited to participate in the ceremonies of the dedication of the Grant monument, on April 27, 1897. No greater opportunity has been offered for the expression of the grateful sentiment and appreciation of the magnanimity of Gen. Grant toward our comrades in general, and more particularly the remembrance of his generous protection to our commander, Col. John S. Mosby, at the close of the late war.

It is to (be) hoped that we can gather together in a goodly number to swell the ranks of other "ex-Confederate" organizations in the grand parade. Those members desiring to participate are requested to forward their names at once, in order that arrangements may be made for horses, equipments, etc., at the small cost of $7.75. This amount includes gauntlets, slouch hat, hat cord and badge.

Address all communications to

JOHN DICKSON,

Windsor Hotel, New York.

March 28, 1897.

But as matters proceeded toward the day of celebration, it seemed that not all were of one mind about the propriety of Mosby's men marching at least as a contingent:

The Times - March 31, 1897

THEY ALL HONOR GRANT

But Mosby's Men Will Not Parade in a Body at New York.

They Think if They Did It Might Revive Feelings Now Nearly Dead.

The ex-members of Mosby's Cavalry are not likely to participate in the ceremonies of the dedication of the Grant Monument in New York, April 27, as a military organization.

Several prominent members of the Confederate Veteran's Union were seen and asked their opinion of the proposition. Some of the were members of Mosby's command. All were agreed on one point; that Gen. Grant was a great soldier and that all ex-Confederates admire and appreciate his magnanimity to the Confederate soldier at the close of the war. This feeling is, if possible, more decided among the followers of Col. Mosby, as they remember the generous protection extended their gallant leader after the surrender at Appomattox.

Only one, however, of the followers of the great cavalry leader, who were seen favored the project of participating in the dedicatory exercises as an organization of ex-Confederates. Even this gentleman, however, would not sanction the participation of Mosby's men if there was even the suspicion of objection from the members of the G.A.R.

A prominent member of the Confederate Veterans' Union, said, while he had the highest regard for Grant as a soldier and would like very much, as an American, to participate in doing him honor, he did not think it proper for the survivors of Mosby's Cavalry, or any other organization of Confederate veterans, to take part as such.

He also spoke of the possibility of some thoughtless boys or women along the line of march shouting "Rebels" or "Traitors" at them. Such an incident as this he said would mar the whole occasion, and possibly revive feelings now nearly dead.

Nearly every one spoken to on the subject, referred to the objections raised last July by the Grand Army of the Republic to the ex-Confederates participating in the parade in New York City.

Mr. W. Ben Palmer of Richmond, Va., in writing to Mr. Robert M. Harrover on the subject ways: "I don't think I will go on the Grant parade. I think Gen. Grant's friendship for Col. Mosby and high esteem he had for Gen. Lee and his men is all right, and we might take part in this parade to do honor to the memory of Gen. Grant, but the G.A.R. men have heretofore so sat down on us rebs when we had to parade with them that I would rather stay at home. Col. Mosby ought to take part, but I have not forgotten last July when they tried to get up a turn-out at New York with the blue and gray" Mr. Harrover was seen and said that he agreed perfectly with Mr. Palmer, but was doing all he could to inform the ex-cavalrymen of the situation as to expenses, railroad fare and other details of the trip.

Apparently, the concerns expressed above were not nearly so irrational as might be believed. The attitude of most of the members of the GAR toward Mosby and the Forty-third—at least outside of New England—was well-known and decidedly negative. The fact that McKinley was loath to grant an office to Mosby, as was discovered to his dismay before the end of the year, made the above concerns more than pertinent. Meanwhile, however, reports of his participation personally and the participation of former Confederates in their official capacity continued:

Richmond Dispatch – March 31, 1897 (Edited)

Colonel John S. Mosby is to be invited, it is said, to be a member of the staff of the grand marshal at the Grant monument unveiling.

In the same paper:

CONFEDERATES WILL TAKE PART.

Several Companies Given Places in Grant Monument Parade.

But while all seemed to be "sweetness and light," as the matter involved John Mosby, one could not expect that it would remain so. At this point, the Staunton Spectator and Vindicator decided to add its discordant voice to the choir of otherwise-harmonious comments:

Staunton Spectator & Vindicator – April 1, 1897

Asking a Little too Much.

There is a call issued by one John T. Dickson, purporting to come from the Headquarters of the Confederate Veterans of New York city, requesting Mosby's men to participated in the Grant Monument parade to take place in New York, April 27. Personally our respect for Gen. Grant is greater than almost any man who commanded on the Union side. We have had an admiration for his genius, and his leniency, which, notwithstanding all that was said of him as a butcher, and in other respects has never wavered. But in the face of the conduct of the G.A.R.'s in this matter, and in the face of the fact that Col. Mosby did not elevate himself in public estimate by changing the colors of his political coat for what seemed to be a reward, we hope the command will not go; although the call states that it will be a fitting way of remembering the generous protection accorded to Mosby at the close of the war by Gen. Grant. Should Gen. James A. Walker be sent as consul to Hong Kong by McKinley we hardly think the Stonewall Brigade would march in a McKinley monument parade to show their appreciation of the act.

Of course, the paper's broadside is against Mosby; but it also included a swipe at Grant, damning him with faint praise with regard to his "genius" and "leniency" but then reminding their readership that Grant was called a "butcher." Now Grant was called a butcher, but that name referred to the casualty rate of his own soldiers! If anyone had the right to excoriate Grant on that issue, it was the people of the North, not the South.

And just as all of this "stew" was simmering on the national fire, a new matter arose to further cause concern among Southern Democrats:

Evening Times – April 1, 1897
The Times – April 2, 1897

Rumor has it that Col. John S. Mosby, the famous Confederate "guerrilla," would like to succeed Fitz Lee as consul general to Cuba. In case the President is adverse to sending him to Havana, it is said that Col. Mosby would be willing to accept the Hawaiian mission, or some other place of equal importance. Mosby's guerrilla warfare give very material aid to Gen. Lee during the civil war.

Mosby is passionately fond of fighting, and delights in all things pertaining to actual warfare. He would like above all other things to represent this country at Cuba at the present critical stage of the contest that is now being waged there between the insurgents and the Spanish foes. Mosby has lived in California since the close of the war, and Senator Perkins of that State called at the White House today to urge his claims. Senator Proctor of Vermont who is also a personal admirer of the Confederate leader, also called to see the President in reference to his appointment.

Mosby was appointed by President Grant to represent this country as consul at Hong Kong, China, which position he held until 1882. His record in China was an enviable one, and this fact may stand much in his favor in enabling him to land the position he now covets.

The Havana consulate was of great interest and importance as the dispute between Spain and the United States proceeded apace. Indeed, the war between the two countries was only a year away, so this was not just a minor diplomatic post! The second problem was the identity of the present consul in Cuba: General (and former Virginia governor) Fitzhugh Lee,* a Democrat and Mosby's enemy since 1862. Now though Mosby did want a position, he had not officially requested one. He did however have many important members of Congress—Republican and Democrat—who were inclined to help him. However, though much was made of the probability of his being offered Cuba and even reports in the newspapers that he wanted that post, Mosby was, as usual, wary.

To begin with, despite all of the speculation (and the papers were full of it!), there had been no intimation by the administration that it was considering removing Lee, much less replacing him with Mosby. (*See "Addendum: Fitzhugh Lee in Cuba" at the end of the chapter.-vph) Second, any open or even covert effort by Mosby to gain the consulship would have been seen as an attack on if not Robert E. Lee, then on a member of his family. Mosby still had not recovered in the South from his defense of Stuart. To be seen as attempting to oust Lee would put another cluster of nails in the coffin of his reputation! No matter how much John Mosby wanted a position to assure against his situation with the railroad, nothing could be worse than being seen as desirous of Lee's post—and then to not even be offered it! It would have been a disaster for him.

And still the speculations and reports continued:

Alexandria Gazette – **April 2, 1897**

The statement in some of the Washington newspapers to the effect that Colonel Mosby, accompanied by Senators Perkins and Proctor, went to the White House yesterday and that the latter had asked the President to appoint the former Consul General to Cuba in place of General Lee, is incorrect. The two Senators referred to did call upon the President yesterday, but not together, and being personal friends of the Colonel, did so voluntarily, and suggested to him that in view of the Colonel's services in California during the last campaign, and of his conceded competence, it would be well to recognize him in some official way, and from the manner in which their suggestion was received, they seem to think the Colonel will not be forgotten. The Colonel himself, however, did not know that such calls were to be made, and did not believe they had been, until he came here this morning and was informed by the Senators referred to that they had been. Cuba was not mentioned during the calls, nor was any particular office, all that being left to the President, who intimated that he had previously conceived the idea that the Colonel should be recognized.

What is very interesting here is the fact that these men were acting without Mosby's approval or even his knowledge. Those who have said that John Mosby "pressed for an office" seem unaware that he himself was also "unaware." And then there was the ongoing strong intimation that the president was in favor of providing "recognition" to Mosby in the form of an office. Finally, some of the papers started to present the Cuban matter as a fait accompli—almost:

Evening Times – April 5, 1897

MOSBY MAY SUCCEED LEE

Famous Confederate Leader Said to Have Been Selected.

PRESIDENT HAS FAITH IN HIM.

It is confidently predicted at the Capitol this afternoon that President McKinley has selected the successor of Gen. Fitzhugh Lee as consul general at Havana. It is stated that he has determined to name the famous ex-guerrilla, Gen. John S. Mosby, of Virginia, for this very important post. Mosby has long been an ardent Republican, and it is the hope of the President that the ex-Confederate will be as much of a success in this office as Gen. Fitzhugh Lee has been.

And while the Havana consulate was receiving wide coverage, the press continued its reports on the upcoming Grant celebration:

Daily Tribune – April 4, 1897

[Part of a very long article on the Grant dedication ceremonies.-vph]

Former Confederates continue to take great interest in the preparations for the dedication, and their appearance in line will doubtless be one of the most significant features of the day. A large number of Confederate societies and organizations have signified their intention of sending delegations, and many of them have applied for places in line, and their applications are being considered with the rest. From their number it is likely that a squadron of cavalry will be formed, and the proposition to use this squadron as an escort for General Bradley Johnson or Colonel John S. Mosby is now receiving consideration. It may be remembered that Colonel Mosby was a warm friend of General Grant, and received from him an appointment as one of the Consuls in China. Thus his appearance, surrounded by an escort of ex-Confederates, would seem to be peculiarly appropriate and striking. The Sons of Veterans will also be largely represented in the parade, posts from all over the country having already applied for places in line.

Leaving Mosby out of the whole matter, it was amazing how Grant went from a "deadbeat" and a "political abortion" to a great hero mainly by the providence of dying, something that Mosby almost had managed to accomplish himself in 1895! It is also interesting to note how Mosby's friendship with Grant was now being presented in the most auspicious light!

New York Tribune – April 4, 1897
THE GRANT DAY EXERCISES

Imposing Demonstration in Memory of the Hero

In the Belief of Many it Will Excel Any Pageant in the Country's History— People Expected from Many States of the Union

Former Confederates continue to take great interest in the preparations for the dedication, and their appearance in line will doubtless be one of the most significant features of the day.

A large number of Confederate societies and organizations have signified their intention of sending delegations, and many of them have applied for places in line, and the applications are being considered along with the rest. From their number it is likely that a squadron of cavalry will be formed, and the proposition to use this squadron as an escort for General Bradley Johnson or Colonel John S. Mosby is now receiving consideration. It may be remembered that Colonel Mosby was a warm friend of General Grant, and received from him an appointment as one of the Consuls in China. Thus his appearance, surrounded by an escort of ex-Confederates, would seem to be peculiarly appropriate and striking. The Sons of Veterans will also be largely represented in the parade, posts from all over the country having already applied for places in line.

Occasionally, a champion appeared out of the blue. This had happened a number of times in the past for John Mosby, and it happened again when the spiteful article that had appeared in the Staunton Spectator and Vindicator of April 1 was answered by one Major Yost, who used the facts of history to make his point—and John Mosby's case:

Staunton Spectator & Vindicator – April 8, 1897
Col. John S. Mosby

Editor of the Spectator-Vindicator:

In your issue of April 1, in noticing an invitation for Col. John S. Mosby to participate in the "Grant Monument Parade" in New York on the 2th of April, you say: "But in the face of the conduct of the G.A.R. in this matter, and in the face of the fact that Col. Mosby did not elevate himself in public estimate by changing the color of his political coat for what seemed to be a reward," &c. I am sure you would not do Col. Mosby an intentional injustice, and that your reference to him was penned without thought of the conditions which surrounded when he refused to support Greeley for President in 1872, and did support Gen. Grant. There was an intimate personal friendship between Gen. Grant and Col. Mosby, growing out of incidents during the war and personal contact afterwards. Grant was a great soldier and exhibited his soldierly qualities at the surrender of Appomattox, and subsequently when he arrested the vindictive policy of President Johnson towards Confederates by announcing that if the terms of the surrender of Gen. Lee were not observed to the letter he would resign his commission in the army.

Mosby was a brave soldier and was drawn close to Gen. Grant by his manly action on the matter cited. Greeley had been a political agitator, and one of the fiercest enemies the South had previous to the war. He was not the timber out of which Presidents should be made, and Mosby took the position, as many other Confederates did, that it was the duty of the South to vote for the brave soldier rather than the political agitator. The people of Virginia agreed with Mosby, as the electoral vote of the State was given to Grant.

Mosby declined the tender of office frequently offered to him by President Grant, and not until some time after the election of 1872 would he consent to accept the consulship at Hong Kong—a position he did not seek and did not accept until many of his Confederate associates urged him to do so.

President Grant entertained a warm friendship for Col. Mosby and consulted him about Federal appointments in Virginia and in the South preferring to gain information from him as to the fitness of applicants rather than from politicians. Had other prominent Confederates pursued a similar course to that taken by Col. Mosby, it would have been infinitely better for the South, and avoided much of the bitter feeling manifested during President Grant's administration. There are very few Confederates at this day who do not consider that the defeat of Greeley and the election of Grant in 1872 was the best result for the South, and who will not now admit that Mosby was right in giving his support to the considerate, humane soldier rather than the political agitator.

Y. [Major S. M. Yost]

Mosby, never a man to overlook a kindness, sent a letter to Major Yost that was printed in the same paper on April 15. And although the Spectator did print Mosby's letter, it was not without a caveat calling into question the credibility of his position:

Staunton Spectator & Vindicator – April 15, 1897

In this issue we print a letter from Col. John S. Mosby, written to his friend, Maj. S. M. Yost, in relation to an editorial which appeared in this paper the week before last. We regret that such men as Col. Mosby and Capt. John S. Wise felt the pressure so great on account of the changed political views, that they perforce must expatriate themselves. The good they might have done had their people followed them must forever remain an unknown quantity, and posterity will always continue to wonder why brave men like these turned away from their old mother and sought the sterile soil of States with whom those traditions and history must be forever out of sympathy. But as Gen. Grant honored Col. Mosby with his confidence, so should Col. Mosby revere the memory of his dead friend, and whatever may be the opinion of many Virginians as to the wisdom of his political course or the motives which prompted it, none will condemn him for his fealty to the memory of his benefactor.

Letter From Col. Jno. S. Mosby.

Alexandria, Va.,

April 10, 1897.

Major S. M. Yost,

Staunton, Va.

Dear Major:—I have just received the copy of the Vindicator and Spectator you sent me in which there is an editorial saying that "Colonel did not elevate himself in public estimate by changing the colors of his political coat for what seemed to be a reward," &c. This refers to my support of General Grant in 1872. No doubt it is true that I not only did not elevate myself in the esteem of the Virginia people by my political course at the time, but that I lost whatever credit I had won by the four years I had served in defense of their cause. But whether that is a reflection on me or on them it is not for me to say. As to the "seeming reward" which it is insinuated that I received for my support of General Grant, all I have to say is that I never saw it except in the favors he did for the Virginia people on account of his friendship for me.

These were the only rewards I asked and all that I received. I did change my politics—because politics changed. Politics, said Burke, is the science of circumstances. I had sense enough to see the new political conditions that had arisen in the South, and the courage to defy popular passions and prejudices. I did not according to the cant of the day—"go with my people"—Judas Iscariot did. If they had followed me I would have led them to victory. The world moves and I had to move with it. My support of Grant was a no wider departure from what I had been than General Robert E. Lee's when he asked Grant to endorse his petition for amnesty and pardon. General Lee simply changed in conformity with circumstances.

The people of Augusta remember when A. H. H. Stuart and John B. Baldwin were bitter foes of The Democratic party; they lived to see them become its leaders. They made as long a leap as I did; they did not realize it, because nearly everybody went with them. A few lunatics criticized them. If my motives were sordid in supporting Grant, I paid dearly for it. This ought to satisfy the Virginia people; especially as I shall never disturb them again. It is true that six years after I announced my support of Grant, Mr. Hayes appointed me Consul at Hong Kong; the only office I ever held. I have no idea now of acting the part of Timon and spending my life in reproaching fortune; but those acquainted with the facts will say that the emoluments of that position were a very inadequate compensation for those I lost "by changing the colors of his (my) political coat."

In a public letter in 1876 advocating the election of Hayes, I said—"I know very well the measure of denunciation which the expression of these sentiments will receive from the people in whose cause I shed my blood and sacrificed the prime of my life. Be it so. I wait on time for my vindication." It has come. The curses that are ringing on Cleveland are a vindication of me. Virginia is no longer my home; if friendship for Grant be treason to her she has at least the consolation of knowing that my name is not heard when the roll of the children she has honored is called,—

"And be the Spartan's epitaph on me—

Sparta hath many a worthier son than he."

Yours truly, JNO. S. MOSBY.

But Mosby's participation in the Grant celebration was not the only topic that was of interest to the press. His obvious desire for an office and speculations about the matter also continued to make the papers:

Butler Weekly Times – April 8, 1897

What Mosby Wants.

Washington, D. C., April 1—Col. Mosby, the noted Confederate guerrilla chief, who turned Republican on the advice of Gen. Grant, wants the Consul Generalship to Cuba first, the Hawaiian mission next or his old place at Hong Kong as a last resort.

Alexandria Gazette – April 12, 1897

Washington, April 12.

Senator Proctor told the Gazette's correspondent to day that he is certain the President intends to appoint Colonel Mosby to as lucrative a position under the government as the one he held before. He added that as the President had no time to be picking out offices for people, it would be well or the Colonel to let him know what particular office he may want. The Colonel's application, he said, would receive the endorsement of many other Senators than that of himself and Senator Perkins, who has spoken to the President about him.

The *Evening Star* picked up on the controversy because Mosby was a very "hot topic" at that time between the Grant celebration, the Cuban consulate, and the reemergence of Southern criticism of Mosby's Republican politics. The Star reproduced the earlier-letter printed in the Vindicator—minus the poetry—but making the same point:

Evening Star – April 15, 1897

COL. MOSBY ON HIS CRITICS

He Says the General Denunciation of Cleveland Vindicates Himself.

Col. John S. Mosby in a letter to Major S. M. Yost of Staunton, Va., replies to the criticism of his course in joining the Republican party in 1872. He denies that is acceptance six years later for President Hayes of the Hong Kong consulship was a bribe for his support.

"As to the seeming reward," says Colonel Mosby, "which it is insinuated that I received for my support of General Grant, all I have to say is that I never saw it except in the favors he did for the Virginia people on account of his friendship for me. These were the only rewards I asked, and all that I received."

In concluding he says: "In a public letter in 1876, advocating the election of Hayes, I said: 'I know very well the measure of denunciation which the expression of these sentiments will receive from the people in whose cause I shed my blood and sacrificed the prime of my life. Be it so. I wait on time for my vindication.' It has come. The curses that are ringing on Cleveland are a vindication of me. Virginia is no longer my home. If friendship for Grant be treason to her, she has at least the consolation of knowing that my name is not heard when the roll of the children she had honored is called."

This was a very despondent letter. John Mosby's frustration, anger, and sorrow are seen in his last sentences: "Virginia is no longer my home. If friendship to Grant be treason to her, she has at least the consolation of knowing that my name is not heard when the roll of the children she had honored is called." This sentiment was first stated at the end of his letter to Major Yost, in a quotation from Mosby's favorite poet, Byron, and his favorite poem, Childe Harold's Pilgrimage: "And be the Spartan's epitaph on me—Sparta hath many a worthier son than he." Consider that all of this must be seen in light of the speech Mosby had given at the glorious reunion of 1895. Only two short years had passed since he spoke to an adoring audience and said of Virginia:

"A great poet of antiquity said, as descriptive of the Romans, that they changed their sky but not their hearts when they crossed over the sea. As long as I lived in far Cathay, my heart untraveled dwelt among the people in whose defence I had shed by blood and given the best years of my life.

In the solitude of exile it was a solace to hear that my name was sometimes mentioned by them with expressions of good will. Nothing that concerns the honor and welfare of Virginia can ever be indifferent to me. I wish that life's descending shadows had fallen upon me in the midst of the friends and the scenes I love best."

But the ills of 1897 were yet to be played out, for almost immediately, it appeared that John Mosby would not be paying his respects to his friend and sometime mentor Ulysses Grant:

Alexandria Gazette – **April 13, 1897**

TO-DAY'S TELEGRAPHIC NEWS

Mosby Won't Go. [Special to the Gazette]

Washington, D. C, April 13.—Col. Mosby received some weeks ago from the Sons of Confederate Veterans in New York an invitation to be their guest and take command of them in the parade at the dedication of the Grant mausoleum. He replied that be could not give a definite answer then. Last week they informed him that they would not take "No" from him, he must come. He then wrote that he had received no invitation from the committee in charge of ceremonies, and that he would not go without an official invitation. There were statements in the New York papers that Gen. Dodge had invited him, but that was all he knew about it. To-day he received another letter from one of the Sons saying that he had seen Gen. Dodge and Mayor Strong. The mayor had invited four Confederate generals to be guests of the city and they had accepted. Gen. Dodge had also invited four Confederate generals to serve on his staff, who had accepted. The line seemed to be drawn on colonels, and Mosby was only a colonel. The letter urged him to come, but Mosby wrote informing his correspondent that he would not appear in the parade as he had not received an official invitation. A few years ago when there was a dinner in New York to celebrate General Grant's birthday General Sherman sent Mosby a special invitation, recognizing him as the personal friend of General Grant. At the request of the New York Herald Mosby has written an article for its Grant edition to appear on the 25th, giving some reminiscences of Grant.

Fort Wayne Gazette – **April 16, 1897**

Wants an Official Invitation.

Alexandria, Va., April 15.—Col. John S. Mosby wrote to a New Yorker that he would not appear in the Grant parade because he had received no official invitation. Considerable surprise is expressed over this here tonight, for a number of Mosby men of this region contemplated attending and marching in the procession with Mosby at their head.

Now it can be deduced by the press coverage that Mosby's refusal to attend arose from the fact he had not been sent an "official invitation." That, of course, was true; but it was also probable that this was—and is, even today—seen as some sort of tantrum on his part to be thus excluded and that he demanded to be "officially recognized" as a participant before he would consent to appear. However, that was neither the point of Mosby's response nor the reason for it. First, anyone could attend the event—it was not limited to invitees by any means! But only those invited officially could participate officially. John Mosby learned that such invitations had indeed been sent, but only to those who held the rank of general; and as a mere colonel, he did not meet the criteria established for "official participation." upon discovering this, Mosby removed himself from the proceedings. This was not a matter of ego or pique. John Mosby was a Virginia gentleman and a former diplomat and, as such, understood the workings of society. He knew that for him to simply "appear" and expect to be accommodated because he had been Grant's personal friend would be seen (and rightly so!) as a violation of the social norms so important in the society of the day. It would make of him a boor—something he was already considered by many people!—and Grant's memorial could be marred by his inappropriate actions. But far too many people knew that if anyone deserved to be recognized for his relationship with the honoree, it was John Mosby. So almost immediately, the movement got under way to correct the problem:

The Times – **April 18, 1897**

Gen. Dodge, general marshal of the Grant Day parade, is trying to clear up the misunderstanding which has arisen over the non-receipt by Col. Mosby of an invitation to participate in the parade. The famous ex-Confederate was yesterday sent the tender of an appointment as aide-de-camp on the staff of the Grand Marshal Dodge.

Alexandria Gazette, – **April 20, 1897**

COL. MOSBY.

Colonel John S. Mosby, who is now in Richmond, has changed his mind and will go to New York. He has received an invitation from General M. Dodge, the grand marshal of the Grant Monument dedication parade, requesting him to act as aide upon the staff of the grand marshal upon that occasion. "I will accept," said Colonel Mosby yesterday, "and have written General Dodge to that effect today."

The second part of the Gazette article of April 20 involved what was pretty much the final word on the speculations regarding Mosby replacing Fitz Lee at Havana. In his statement on the matter, Mosby referred specifically to General Robert E. Lee in declaring his personal desire to see Fitz remain in Cuba. Frankly, given his personal opinion of Fitz Lee, the sentiment must have stuck in his throat:

> When asked regarding the statement that the impression prevailed he would succeed Gen. Fitzhugh Lee in Cuba, Colonel Mosby said: "I have no knowledge whatever of the matter aside from what I have seen in the papers." Continuing, Colonel Mosby said: "If my wishes were to be consulted, I should say that it would be a compliment to Virginia, to the old Confederate soldiers and more especially to the memory of Gen. Robt. E. Lee, for President McKinley to continue Gen. Fitzhugh Lee at that post."

And so it would seem that for John Mosby, two difficult problems were (successfully) behind him: first, the matter of his appearance at the Grant celebration, and second, the Cuban consulate question. He had acquitted himself well in both—or at least he had prevented the wrath of Virginia society from descending upon his head for any perceived "boorishness" or insults to the Lee family. Mosby, however, was still without any offer of a position from the McKinley administration; but he may well have thought that after the Grant event, such an offer probably would be forthcoming. After all, he had managed to avoid all of the pitfalls that appeared as 1897 began; and surely, matters could only get better. Sadly, such was not the case.

Now we return to that small article that appeared earlier in the year, an article that seemed to have no aura of disaster about it:

Richmond Dispatch – March 21, 1897

> In 1895 John S. Mosby, Jr., then a student at the university of Virginia, wrote for the annual (Corks and Curls) a college play, "The Flirt," which attracted favorable attention. The students of the university of Virginia have determined to produce it in such good shape as, they hope, to eclipse the Harvard Greek play.

In anticipation of this visit, Mosby was reported to be spending some time with one of his old command, the wealthy and important Mr. Joseph Bryan, Richmond newspaper mogul:

Alexandria Gazette – April 14, 1897

> Personal.—Col. J. S. Mosby left here to-day for Richmond to spend some days there as the guest of Mr. Joseph Bryan. He, with his two daughters, will leave Richmond in time to attend the performance at Charlottesville on the 21st instant of "The Flirt," a stage satire on society at the university of Virginia and Charlottesville, the production of John S. Mosby, Jr., now a lawyer at Denver. The object of the performance is to raise funds to purchase a bell for the university.

On April 23, Mosby took a buggy ride accompanied by the daughter of an old friend. Why he did so has never been disclosed, and neither are the particulars of the ride known. During the outing, something happened. Again, many different explanations have been presented over the years. But the one that seems most likely is that for some reason, the reins became entangled or Mosby may have dropped them; and as he leaned forward to either untangle or retrieve them, the foot plate of the buggy gave way, pitching him under the horse's feet. Startled, the animal kicked back, its hoof striking Mosby in the face—more particularly, full on his left eye. The blow was horrendous. The eyeball burst, and the bone around the eye socket shattered. The skin was severely lacerated, and blood poured from his head. Mosby was rendered insensible and left lying in the road covered in dust and blood.

The first notice of this disaster appeared in the April 24 issue of *The Times*—among many other newspapers—and continued until almost the middle of May, when the papers were able to report that his recovery was assured. During that interval, his life was frequently despaired of. Below are some of the papers with headlines alone or, when the article is of further interest, either edited or presented in tact:

The Times – April 24, 1897

COL. MOSBY TERRIBLY HURT.

Distressing Accident to the Gallant Soldier at the University

Kicked on the Head by a Horse.

The Outer Plate of His Skull Was Broken and His Left Eye So Badly Injured That It Had to be Removed—Board of Visitors Adopt Resolutions of Sympathy.

University of Virginia, April 23.—Special.—Colonel John S. Mosby received a very severe injury this evening about 5 o'clock near the University of Virginia which has resulted in the loss of his left eye and may be even more serious. The Colonel, who had come to the university last Wednesday to attend the performance of a play written by his son, was driving out in a buggy with Mrs. Dudley Dubose on the road west of Carr's Hill and just within the western limits of the grounds of the University when some part of the harness became broken, and as he leaned over the spatter-board to examine it, he lost his balance and fell headforemost behind the horse's heels. The horse kicked out, struck the prostrate soldier over the left eye, and rendered him insensible. Mrs. Dubose instantly stopped the horse and ran off for help, which was soon gotten from Mr. L. L. McKay, near whose residence the accident occurred.

BORNE OFF INSENSIBLE.

In a few minutes many persons had reached the spot. Among the first being Mr. and Mrs. J. Triplett Haxall, who were driving out. Mr. McKay brought a stretcher, and with the aid of students, Colonel Mosby was borne insensible to the infirmary of the University, where preparation had been made to receive him. His daughters, Misses Pauline and Ada, soon came with friends, but were not permitted to see their father whose appearance, covered with blood and dust, was distressing.

There was no lack of medical attendance. Dr. Hugh T. Nelson, who was given charge of the case, was assisted by Professors Buckmaster,

Barringer, Christian, Davis and Dr. Randolph. After an hour and a half the Colonel began to recover consciousness and the doctors determined to make a thorough examination of his wound, which presented a ghastly appearance. He was put under the influence of chloroform and the examination disclosed the melancholy fact that the left eye was totally destroyed, and was immediately removed. The outer plate of the skull just above the eye was broken. There were symptoms of brain trouble, but at this writing the surgeons have not ascertained the extent. Dr. Nelson telegraphed to Washington, D.C. requesting Dr. N. S. Lincoln, the family physician, to come to the bedside of the Colonel.

RESOLUTIONS OF SYMPATHY.

The Board of Visitors of the university were in session in the infirmary when Colonel Mosby was brought in. Mr. McIllwaine, of Petersburg, offered the following resolution, which was unanimously adopted: "Whereas the Board has just heard with profound regret of the serious accident which has just happened to Colonel John S. Mosby, within the bounds of the University of Virginia. Resolved: That we deplore his misfortune and trust that a kind providence will soon restore him to perfect health and strength, and the use of the infirmary is hereby tendered to Colonel Mosby and daughters so long as they need it. The greatest sympathy is felt and expressed by everyone for the wounded hero, and his grief-stricken daughters.

COL. MOSBY RESTING QUIETLY.

At 1:50 this morning Colonel Mosby was resting quietly, partially under opiates. He answers questions rationally and shows no indications of concussion of the brain. His pulse and breathing are fairly good.

Evening Times – **April 24, 1897**

COL. MOSBY HURT.

Seriously Injured by a Fall From His Carriage.

The Sun – **April 24, 1897**

COL. MOSBY INJURED.

Richmond Dispatch – **April 24, 1897**

COLONEL MOSBY HURT

Thrown from a Buggy near the University

His Wounds both Painful and Dangerous—

Carried to the Infirmary on a Stretcher—His Eye Seriously Endangered.

University of Virginia, April 23.—(Special)—Colonel John S. Mosby, who came here to witness the student presentation of the burlesque operetta, "The Flirt," which was written by his son, John S. Mosby, Jr., was seriously injured this evening in a driving accident, and is being cared for at the infirmary of the university of Virginia. He was driving with Mrs. Emma DuBose a mile west of the university, when the horse shied at a passing train. Colonel Mosby caught at the reins and fell from the buggy. He received a wound over the eye; whether from the horse's foot or otherwise, is not known. The wound is both painful and dangerous, though immediate serious results are not expected. The eye is seriously endangered. He was carried on a stretcher to the infirmary in an unconscious condition where he is attended by Dr. Barringer and Dr. Christian. His daughters are with him. He is too nervous now to stand careful examination.

Richmond Dispatch – April 25, 1897

COL. JOHN S. MOSBY

The Recent Severe Accident to Him in Albemarle. Character of his Wound.

Removal of the Eye Found Necessary—The Misfortune Excites the Deepest Sympathy—Old Soldiers Watching the Bulletins.

Charlottesville, Va., April 24.—(Special.)—Colonel John Singleton Mosby, who was so severely injured last evening by being thrown from a carriage a mile west of the grounds of the University of Virginia, is now comfortable, and shows signs of returning reason.

Colonel John S. Mosby and his daughters—Misses Pauline and Ada— were to take tea at Judge Cochran's last evening. Having an hour before the time fixed for his arrival there, Colonel Mosby went with Mrs. Emma Dubose for a drive along the Ivy road, which follows and often crosses the Chesapeake and Ohio railroad. In spite of the nearness of the highway to the Chesapeake's tracks, it is one of the most popular drives in the county. Colonel Mosby and Mrs. Dubose and proceeded about a mile west of the university of Virginia, and were near a crossing when the accident occurred, which has already resulted in the loss of an eye, and may end in death.

NOT REALLY KNOWN.

Just how it occurred is really not known. Two accounts are given. According to one, the horse shied, and Colonel Mosby, attempting to take the reins from Mrs. Dubose, lost his balance and fell under the animal's heels. Whether the wound he received resulted from a kick or otherwise is uncertain. The other account is to the effect that some part of the harness got loose, and that Colonel Mosby leaned over the splashboard to put it in order, when he was kicked so violently that he fell from the vehicle and lay on the road unconscious.

HELP ARRIVES.

Mrs. Dubose hurried off in search of help, which she was not long in finding. Mr. L. L. McKay, who lives near-by; Mr. J. T. Haxall, who was driving that way at the time, and others lent their aid. A stretcher was provided, upon which the wounded man, covered with dust and stained with blood, was carried to the university infirmary. Dr. H. T. Nelson, of this city, was put in charge of the patient, and Drs. Barringer, Buckmaster, Davis, and Christian were called as consultants. An immediate examination was impossible on account of the nervous shock resulting from the terrible blow, but in the course of an hour and a half the physicians were able to determine that a surgical operation could not be avoided as the eye was ruptured and the lens released. This necessitated the removal of the ball. There is an extensive laceration of the soft parts around the eye. Perhaps the bony structure about the orbit was fractured.

DR. LINCOLN'S OPINION.

Dr. N. T. Lincoln, of Washington, D. C., who had been summoned by Colonel Mosby's daughters, met Dr. Nelson and the constant at 10 o'clock this morning. Dr. Nelson offered to anesthetize the patient and allow Dr. Lincoln a complete investigation. Dr. Lincoln, having heard Dr. Nelson's description of the condition of the wound, did not think further surgical interference advisable. Dr. Nelson, in explaining to Dr. Lincoln, in the presence of the medical staff of the university, the conditions present at the time of the operation, asked Dr. Lincoln if, under such conditions, he would have advised the opening of the skull and further investigation. Dr. Lincoln replied that he was convinced that the investigation was carried far enough to satisfy any surgeon.

Colonel Mosby's misfortune has excited the deepest sympathy, and he is receiving every attention which it is in the power of the citizens and old soldiers to bestow on him. Moreover, his four daughters, and his son, John S. Mosby, Jr., are at his bedside. He has not rallied sufficiently to give any account of the mishap. Still his condition is growing better and his physicians are much more hopeful.

WATCHING THE BULLETINS.

The old soldiers of the late war, in which "Mosby's Confederacy" was a decided factor, are watching the bulletins from his physicians with much solicitude. They say it is a strange fate which brought the chieftain through four years of war, in which he led a daring band into many a fierce fight only to receive his most severe wound, if not his death-blow, during a quiet afternoon drive along a country road in Albemarle, where the acts of peace have long succeeded those of war.

Alexandria Gazette – **April 26, 1897**

Col. Mosby's Condition.—The condition of Colonel John S. Mosby, who was so badly hurt by being kicked by a horse Friday afternoon, near Charlottesville, is much improved. His mind has cleared, and his physician says that while bad turn might come, every indication points to a speedy recovery. While conscious most of the time, he has intervals of apparent wandering, and is very restless. A dispatch received in this city this morning stated that Col. Mosby had not regained his consciousness and that he is critically ill.

Evening Times – April 26, 1897

COL. MOSBY DYING.

Members of the Family Summoned to the Bedside

New York, April 26.—A special dispatch from Richmond, Va., says Col. John S. Mosby who was injured in a runaway accident at Charlottesville last Friday, is said to be dying. All the members of the family have been sent for.

Perhaps the greatest miracle was that Mosby did not develop tetanus. The disease is rampant in stables and barns. Mosby not only suffered the destruction of his eye, but also, as noted above, "extensive lacerations" of the "soft parts' around the eye. Of course, these injuries must have been cleansed thoroughly, and perhaps this was enough to prevent the disease from developing. Still, as there was no vaccination against "lockjaw" at that time, John Mosby was spared a hideous death.

The Sun – April 27, 1897

MOSBY HAS A FIGHTING CHANCE.

A Slight Fracture of the Frontal Bone Near the Nose Has Been Found. Richmond, Va., April 26.—"Col. Mosby has a fighting chance for his life," said Dr. Hunter McGuire who returned to-night from consultation over his case at the university of Virginia.

The veteran was placed under the influence of ether to-day, and a more thorough examination of his eye was made. A slight fracture of the frontal bone near the nose was found. No operation was deemed necessary and no unfavorable development has occurred. His mind is slightly clearer. His health generally is excellent, and he possesses remarkable recuperative powers.

Col. Mosby has passed a comparatively easy day and is resting quietly. During most of the time since the accident, which occurred on Friday afternoon, he has been conscious, but his mind has appeared to wander at intervals. There appeared to be a change last night for the worse, but he has held his own well during the day, and his apparently suffering no pain. His two sons, Beverly C. Mosby of Salt Lake City and John S. Mosby, Jr., of Denver, Col., have been summoned. The other members of his family are here and the entire Infirmary building has been turned over to them for their use.

The Times – April 28, 1897

COL. MOSBY MUCH BETTER.

He Spent a Quiet Night and His Mind is Clear.

Richmond, Va., April 27.—Col. Mosby spent a quiet night and at 1 o'clock this afternoon his mind is perfectly clear, and for the first time he made inquiries about the runaway accident of last Friday in which he was injured. His improved mental condition is taken as a good indication of his physical condition, and it is now confidently believed that he will recover.

Richmond Dispatch – April 28, 1897
COLONEL MOSBY'S CONDITION.

Rational During the Day Yesterday, Not So Well at Night.

University of Virginia, April 27.—(Special)—While the condition of Colonel John S. Mosby seemed to show decided improvement this morning, and he was entirely conscious during the day, there appeared to be rather a falling back as the evening came on, and to-night he is not considered so well by those of his family who are at his bedside. Dr. Hugh T. Nelson, his physician, has not seen him since this morning. But is expected to spend a part of the night at the infirmary with him. Mr. Robert M. Campbell, his son-in-law, stated in an interview to-night that he did not consider the Colonel as well as he had been during the day, and that he was suffering some pain in his head. His temperature is quite high, and he is not as rational as he was during the early part of the day. This morning he discussed several matters of private business with members of the family, and talked with the medical attendants about his accident, asking numerous questions as to where it occurred and where the infirmary he was in was located. He expressed thanks for all the kindness that had been shown him in allowing the use of the infirmary building for his family, and spoke of how much he appreciated the attention that was being given him. His son, Mr. Beverly Mosby, of Salt Lake City, utah, who was wired to Sunday morning to come on, is now on his way here, and upon his arrival the whole family will be with him, with the exception of his daughter, Mrs. Charles W. Russell.

At 1:50 this morning, Dr. Nelson had just left Colonel Mosby's room and gave the following statement to the Dispatch correspondent: "Colonel Mosby's condition is as follows—Pulse registers, 66; temperature 99 ½; mental condition much improved since last evening. His wounds are in as good condition as could be expected. Strong hopes are entertained of permanent recovery and restoration to previous vigor and activity."

Since Dr. Nelson's visit, the family seem much encouraged, and are more hopeful than they were yesterday afternoon and earlier to-night.

A high fever can produce symptoms of irrationality as was seen in Mosby in the latter part of the day. In fact fevers tend to rise through the day, becoming highest in the late afternoon and early evening.

New York Times – April 29, 1897
HIS FIRST THOUGHT OF GRANT

Col. Mosby Has Returned to Consciousness and May Recover.

Richmond, Va., April 28.—Col. John S. Mosby, the famous Confederate ranger commander, who was so terribly hurt at Charlottesville, returned to consciousness to-day.

His first words upon gaining his mental balance was about the dedication of Gen. Grant's monument. He insisted that one of his friends at his bedside read to him the last newspaper accounts of the event. That was done, and upon the conclusion of the reading the old guerrilla chief referred tenderly to Gen. Grant.

Col. Mosby's condition is still very critical, but his medical attendants now think there is little doubt of his recovery. If he recovers, though, it will be with the loss of an eye, and possibly more serious effects still.

Evening Times— April 29, 1897

Col. Mosby's Condition.

Richmond, Va., April 29.—Col. Mosby's pulse was not so strong this morning. There is yet no material change in his condition, which is still the occasion of considerable anxiety.

Richmond Dispatch – April 29, 1897

COLONEL MOSBY'S CONDITION

He Is Much Better—Has a Quiet Day.

University of Virginia, April 28, (Special.)—The condition of Colonel John S. Mosby seemed somewhat better this morning, and has remained practically the same during the day. The Doctor entertains hope of his entire restoration to his former good health, but realizes that under the circumstances he might suffer a relapse at any time.

During the day he rested comparatively quiet, but this afternoon suffered considerably with pain in his head. Only one member of his family has been allowed to see him to-day, in order to avoid the excitement which would more than likely cause his condition to grow less favorable.

Salt Lake Herald – April 29, 1897

Colonel Mosby is Better.

Richmond, Va., April 28.—Colonel John S. Mosby shows a distinct improvement in his condition. He is exhibiting remarkable recuperative power and unless inflammation supervenes where the brain is bruised from the hoof of the animal which destroyed his eye and where the resting of the blood clot is suspected, his recovery will be steady.

Richmond Dispatch – May 1, 1897

Colonel Mosby's Condition.

UNIVERSITY OF VIRGINIA. April 30. (Special.)—Colonel Mosby suffered a slight setback this morning, but his condition this afternoon seems to be about the same as it was previous to to-day. His family have been much encouraged by his holding his own so well. The only fear is that a collapse may occur in such a case at any time. However, no immediate danger is apprehended, and it is hoped that he may be able to withstand the strain that he is being subjected to from time to time. His sons—John S. Mosby, Jr., of Denver, Col. And Beverly S. Mosby, of Salt Lake City, Utah—arrived here this morning, and are expected to remain until their father is well on the road to recovery.

Richmond Dispatch – May 2, 1897
COLONEL MOSBY'S CONDITION

It Continues About the Same—The Fear of Relapse.

University of Virginia, May 1.—(Special.)—The condition of Colonel John S. Mosby seems about the same as for the past few days. However, the physicians are not so much encouraged as might be expected. It is acknowledged that his case is a desperate one, and that the chances of recovery are not as bright as many would have thought. He has been entirely conscious throughout the day, and every precaution has been taken to prevent his becoming excited, for fear of consequences. Not even the members of his family have been permitted to see him during the day. Those in charge at the infirmary consider that he is doing well to-night, and state that he is resting quietly. His pulse, which has fallen considerably below the normal several times, and caused worry as to his condition, is to-night about regular. The fear of his suffering a relapse is a source of constant anxiety. At a late hour his physician had not seen him, and no professional statement could be secured.

The Sun – May 2, 1897
John S. Mosby Still Dangerously Ill.

University of Virginia, May 1.—the condition of John S. Mosby is about as it has been for several days past. While he has been resting quietly to-day and every precaution has been adopted to prevent his becoming excited, his case is acknowledged now to be a desperate one. He appears to have rallied from the sinking spell of Friday, but frequently his pulse drops below the normal and causes much anxiety. He is fully conscious all the time and has apparently suffered no pain to-day.

Soon, the papers were able to report that Mosby had recovered sufficiently to return "home"—that is, to his daughter's home in Warrenton. He was mentioned as being "very little disfigured" and in "exceptionally fine spirits." Perhaps he was. After all, he had once again escaped death, and perhaps he thought that his accident—a matter that had occasioned so much sympathy throughout the country and especially in Virginia—might help him secure a position in the new administration and gain him some consideration and acceptance among his fellow Virginians, Stuart and politics notwithstanding:

Alexandria Gazette – May 15, 1897

To-day Colonel Mosby left Charlottesville for Warrenton, Fauquier county, where he will visit his daughter, Mrs. R. R. Campbell. Among his callers yesterday were Col. W. H. Chapman, of Greensboro, N.C. Colonel Mosby is looking remarkably well. Save the loss of his eye he is very little disfigured, and he is in exceptionally fine spirits.

Newspapers continued to report on Mosby whether in the past or the present. As had happened during the war when he was wounded, there was always a spate of short "biographies" to inform any of the especially younger readers just who was receiving so much printers' ink:

Sacramento Daily Record-Union – May 17, 1897
COLONEL JOHN S. MOSBY.

One of the Most Conspicuous Fighters Of the Confederate Army.

John Singleton Mosby was one of the most conspicuous fighters In the Confederate army. As a dashing raider, he was unapproachable, even among the boldest of the raiders of the Southern semi-guerrillas. He was born in Powhatan County, Va., December 6, 1833. At the beginning of the war he enlisted in the Confederate cavalry and served in the campaign in the Shenandoah, under General Joseph E. Johnston. At the close of the war Mosby went to Warrenton, Va., and took up the practice of law. He was there in 1872 when the Greeley-Grant campaign came, and the incorrigible rebel guerrilla amazed his friends and compatriots of the South by hoisting his standard for Grant instead of the Democrat. He supported Hayes in 1876 and was rewarded with the Consulship at Hongkong. He was a proud man and excessively sensitive in those trying times and twice refused to accept office under President Giant. On his return from China he settled In California, and has done well there as a lawyer. As a soldier he was a terrible disciplinarian and as a lawyer a shrewd reader of statutes, though not a brilliant pleader.

The Sacramento paper took a little "dig" at Mosby's abilities as a lawyer. At least they didn't find him inadequate—or not totally so. However, past reports of Mosby's "pleadings" in court render the last determination somewhat less than accurate, not an unusual matter with newspapers.

John Mosby had been in a terrible accident. His survival was nothing short of miraculous given his age and the nature of the injury. He did not succumb to the trauma itself or subsequent blood clots or infection. His heart didn't give out. He didn't have a stroke or a cerebral hemorrhage after severe cranial trauma. Furthermore, sympathy poured in from all over the country and even the political spectrum—with the usual exceptions, of course. As a result, there seemed to be nothing that could be denied him by the new administration for whom he had worked so loyally and with such dedication. No decent man knowing of the situation extant with Mosby could possibly believe that he would not find succor from the government he had served with such integrity and capability as the press continued to point out:

Alexandria Gazette – May 20, 1897

A special car brought Col. Jno. S. Mosby to this place Monday evening. He stood the trip very well and at this writing is resting quietly at the residence of his son-in-law, Mr. R. R. Campbell. Col. Mosby's recovery is joyfully received by his friends and admirers all over the country.— [Warrenton Virginian.

Richmond Dispatch – May 21, 1897
PLUM FOR MOSBY.

The Colonel, However, Declined to Oust Lee.

Washington, D. C., May 20.—(Special)—Reports from the home of Colonel John S. Mosby are to the effect that he is rapidly recovering from the injuries he received when driving near Charlottesville. Colonel Mosby has pleasing assurances that he will be tendered a good office by the Administration. There is however, senatorial authority for the statement that when Colonel Mosby was asked if he would accept the consul-generalship at Habana, he promptly and almost indignantly replied: "Under no circumstances will I become the executioner of General Fitzhugh Lee." This announcement, coming from the senator to whom the reply was made, is very gratifying to the friends of both General Lee and Colonel Mosby.

There is nothing to suggest, and considerable evidence to the contrary, that John Mosby had changed his long-held opinion of Fitz Lee (and vice versa). However, having defended Stuart and by so doing enraged many who believed that his defense was a criticism of the other General Lee it is probable that Mosby (perhaps in the assumption that he would get some office from the McKinley administration) determined not to be seen as the man who displaced Lee's nephew. But it is also probable (given what was later learned about McKinley, Alger, and the GAR) that had Mosby been willing to say yes to Cuba, he would have found that it wasn't offered to him anyway and that he had forfeited considerable goodwill to no purpose. It is interesting to wonder, however, if there were any mutual friends of "both General Lee and Colonel Mosby." Probably not. And still, the matter of an office for Mosby continued in the press, albeit it may be that some of the old veterans of the fourth estate were beginning to sense quite another story:

Omaha Daily Bee - May 28, 1897

Colonel John S. Mosby has been taken from Charlottesville, Va., to his home in Warrenton, in the same state. He has nearly recovered from the injuries received in the accident that lately befell him, except that he has lost the sight of one eye. It was feared for a while that his injuries would be fatal.

Alexandria Gazette – June 5, 1897

Colonel Mosby is here. He will have a glass eye adjusted to the socket of the natural one he recently lost at Charlottesville, next Monday. He and Mr. Huntington, the great railroad king, who are personal friends, had a talk at the latter's hotel to-day.

Evening Star – June 7, 1897

Col. Mosby Calls.

Col. John S. Mosby, the famous Confederate officer, was at the White House today with Gen. Walker, member of the House from Virginia. Col. Mosby's head is still bandaged from his recent severe accident in Virginia. Col. Mosby will lose his left eye as a result of the accident and will have it replaced with an artificial eye. He had a pleasant chat with the President. It is said that if Col. Mosby wants a consular place of some kind, he can have it.

Of course, Mosby had already lost his left eye in the accident. It was burst in the socket, and its remains had to be removed. As for the "pleasant chat," one cannot but wonder what was going through McKinley's mind as a loyal fellow Republican who had been so grossly injured spoke with him all unknowing that he had no hope at all for a position. At the very least, the president should have been honest enough to disabuse Mosby of any further hope; but apparently, even that courtesy was not provided given the speculations that continued in the press. Mosby, however, was astute enough to know that he was on the outside looking in, a place he had occupied many times before. So as disappointing as that must have been, at least he probably did not hold out any futile hopes regarding McKinley:

The Times – June 8, 1897

Col. John S. Mosby and Gen. Walker, member of Congress from Virginia, called on the President. Col. Mosby is still suffering from his serious accident in Virginia last month, but is recovering rapidly.

The name of Col. Mosby has been suggested for the consul generalship to Cuba. He has had several years of experience in consular work, and his appointment to the position, to succeed Gen. Lee, would give great satisfaction to the South. The name of Mr. Frank Aldrich, of Chicago, for the last few days has been most prominently connected with the position, and it has been semi-officially suggested that he is being considered.

As there was really nothing to report regarding a proffered office to Mosby, the papers kept him in print with various stories, all of which mentioned his recent injury. As usual, when there was nothing else upon which to report, the newspapers went back to the war. For those who believe that it was Mosby who kept his wartime experiences in the papers, it soon becomes obvious with the perusal of any amount of press coverage that the matter was entirely initiated by the press. The article that appeared in the Press and the Kentuckian was a recapitulation of Mosby's career not included because of its length.

Evening Times – June 10, 1897

Gen. Mosby, the ex-Confederate cavalry leader, who has just recently recovered from a severe illness, was at the District building today to see Mr. Ross.

Two Virginia publications presented a small and very complimentary comment upon Mosby's press accounts of his command's activities during the war:

Alexandria Gazette – June 14, 1897

Staunton Spectator & Vindicator – June 17, 1897

That Atlanta Journal says that Col. John S. Mosby is contributing to the press a series of personal experiences during the war which would make the author of "The Three Guardsmen" green with envy, if he were here. The beauty of Mosby's stories is that they are all true and they are written in a vivid style of narration which few of our makers of fiction can equal.

The matter of Mosby's "position" continued to receive coverage. The newspapers "worried" it like a dog with a bone. It is probable that no especially Virginia publication could imagine that McKinley wouldn't offer their wounded hero something—even Hong Kong, an office Mosby had rather discouraged when it was originally raised in speculation:

Alexandria Gazette – June 19, 1897

Among the callers at the White House to-day was Colonel John S. Mosby, who was accompanied by Senator Proctor. The President two months ago informed some of Mosby's friends that he intended giving him a good place, and it is understood to-day that that place may be his old one as consul to Hong Kong, the salary of which is $5,000. There was newspaper talk some time ago about the Colonel in connection with the Havana consulate, but the subject was never mentioned to or by the colonel at the White House or the State Department.

Roanoke Times – June 22, 1897

Pacific coast and Western State politicians have not as yet received much recognition in the way of foreign appointments, but are looking after their interests with wide open eyes. Senator McBride and Representatives Ellis and Tongee, of Oregon, informed the President Saturday that they had some good men wanting consulates, and he promised to help them all he could. Col. John S. Mosby will also get a good position of that character in China or South America. President McKinley seems to have much more regard for the party that elected him than the great Grover did.

It seems, if this newspaper article is true, that the cry of the South against Cleveland, as indicated by Mosby, had to do with him failing to appoint either Democrats or Southerners in his administration. And while McKinley did favor Republicans, Mosby wasn't one of them, at least until he lost his position with the Southern Pacific; and then what he received from McKinley was a pittance not a position.

A very interesting article found its way into the Western press having to do with the looming question of a conflict with Spain and the possibility of a "guerrilla war" if such a conflict should erupt. The Chronicle pointed out that thirty-five thousand men might be far too few in the event of such a struggle and hearkened back to Mosby's war in northern Virginia to speculate upon the results of another such war in Cuba and the Philippines. This article also pointed to something astonishing that eventually occurred—that is, that the United States had a man who was a genius in such warfare but whose services were never utilized because of the "bad feelings" arising from a war that had ended over thirty years earlier! The idea that American soldiers would not be given every strategic advantage because a few old Yankee generals held a grudge seemed incredible, but that was in fact what did happen:

San Francisco Chronicle – June 24, 1897

It is a grave question whether 35,000 more men will serve the President's purpose. The history of all guerrilla wars show that both numbers and genius are wasted in the effort to suppress them. Spanish guerrillas were mainly instrumental in driving Napoleon's veterans from Spain. Irregular warfare won an empire in turn from the Spanish crown, which extended from San Francisco to Buenos Ayres. Had the Southern Confederates fought a guerrilla war they might have saved themselves. At least we judge so from the fact that Colonel Mosby with 500 men neutralized the services of 40,000 Federal troops for three years. An army of 200,000 men under the redoubtable Weyler did nothing to rescue Cuba from the rabble of Gomez. Judging by these examples, the doubling of General Otis' command is in no sense a guarantee of victory, especially if Aguinaldo carries the war into other Islands than Luzon.

And still, the speculation about where John Mosby would go in a consular position was debated. His place, the paper noted, "is assured." It was also noted that McKinley had every intention "for some time" to give Mosby a "good" position; but it never seemed to go beyond intentions or, more likely, expressions of intentions. Mention was made again of McKinley's wartime experience with Mosby, but that should have been no more than an interesting sidelight, especially with a man who had been an intimate friend of Grant's, the great hero who had just been massively celebrated in New York! The paper seemed to think that the problem was where that position would be. In the end, when nothing was forthcoming, it was blamed on Mosby—that is, that he couldn't make up his mind, and when he did, everything he wanted was already taken:

> *United Opinion* – July 2, 1897
>
> Senator Proctor of Vermont and Colonel John S. Mosby, the ex-Confederate general, had an interview with President McKinley the other day. The talks between the president and Colonel Mosby are always of a pleasant character. During the war Senator Proctor was stationed near Washington and was in close proximity to Mosby and his warriors. The Vermont senator told the president that Mosby caused him a good many uneasy moments. Notwithstanding this he was willing that Mosby should have a good place in the consular service. Colonel Mosby wants a good consulate in China or South America, and is going to get it. That much is settled on. It has been the president's intention for some time to provide for Colonel Mosby, and the only question has been the place to be given him.

Finally, the light dawned on at least some in the fourth estate, and the Gazette was one of the first papers to realize that there would be no office for John Mosby:

> *Alexandria Gazette* – July 5, 1897
>
> It is said here that President McKinley not only promised Col. Mosby himself, and Senators Perkins and Proctor, that the Colonel should be well provided for, but that he made a similar promise to Mr. Huntington, the great railroad King. But no more faith can be placed in modern Presidents than in old time princes.

Huntington knew that Mosby's time as an employee of the railroad was ending as was his own, so he had asked the president to help a man whom he admired even if many in his company did not. The Dispatch gave a quick recap of the matter and consigned Mosby once again to the Southern Pacific:

> *Richmond Dispatch*, – July 11, 1897
>
> COLONEL JOHN S. MOSBY
>
> He Is Looking as Well and as Vigorous as Ever.
>
> A Warrenton (Va.) special to the Baltimore Sun: Colonel John S. Mosby, who is visiting his daughter here, is looking as well and vigorous as ever, although he says that the shock he received in the accident at the university of Virginia this spring was so severe that he does not expect to fully recover from its effects for several months. Prior to his mishap he gave a sitting to an Alexandria artist for a portrait, which was completed a few days before he lost his eye. The artificial eye, which was accepted by his oculist, has proven a misfit, and is now being altered. The loss of his eye has happily

not affected the fine contours of his face, and his appearance is but little altered. The Colonel will leave for San Francisco about the 1st of August, where he will resume his duties as counsel for the Southern Pacific railway.

Alexandria Gazette – **July 22, 1897**

The President led Colonel Mosby and Senators Perkins and Proctor to believe that he would appoint the former to a lucrative foreign position, but he has disappointed them, and the colonel, who was here to-day, consulting an oculist about his eye, will go back to San Francisco between the 1st and 15th proximo and resume his business as counsel for the Southern Pacific Railroad.

Alexandria Gazette – **July 29, 1897**

A prominent Virginia republican here to-day, in talking about the treatment Colonel Mosby has received from this administration, says he hears the Colonel's way to a lucrative position was unobstructed until the G.A.R. who are opposed to the recognition of any ex-Confederate, interfered, and that their opposition was effective. There is no doubt of the fact that the President not only informed the Colonel, but other prominent and reliable republicans that he intended to give him a good place.

But of course, not everybody was upset that John Mosby had been bypassed. The *Chicago Tribune*, a newspaper that frequently had little good to say about the man, presented the idea that he was asked to submit the names of five places that would be acceptable to him. There is absolutely nothing to imply—much less prove—that any such suggestion was ever made or that Mosby ever submitted any such list. There really is no proof at all that the Havana consulate, so much in the press earlier in the year, was ever going to be offered to John Mosby—and what's more, he knew it:

Chicago Tribune – **July 30, 1897**

Colonel John S. Mosby has returned to California in a most unhappy frame of mind because of his failure to obtain what he thought merited recognition at the hands of the present administration. It was suggested to the former rebel guerrilla chieftain, who made things so lively in this vicinity during the rebellion, that he should submit the names of five places either one of which would be acceptable to him. This program was carried out, but everything Mosby wanted had been promised to somebody else. Finally it was said he could be Consul General to Cuba, as the successor of Fitzhugh Lee. This met with an emphatic and vigorous declination by Colonel Mosby, who said he would not be Lee's executioner under any circumstances. Negotiations ceased at this point so far as Mosby's diplomatic and consular aspirations are concerned, and he has gone back to the Pacific slope a sadder but wiser man.

The truth finally began to come out about McKinley's treatment of Mosby. The GAR was blamed, but it was former General Alger in the president's own cabinet who had never forgiven Mosby for the execution of the house burners Alger had sent into the Valley; that situation came to be known the following year when the refusal by the McKinley administration to give Mosby a position spilled over into the refusal to allow him to volunteer for service in the Spanish-American War:

Alexandria Gazette – **August 3, 1897**

It is now pretty generally understood here that the reason the President did not fulfill his promise to appoint Col. Mosby to a lucrative position in the foreign service of the government was the opposition of the G.A.R. Indeed one post of that organization in Pennsylvania passed public resolutions protesting against the appointment of any man to a federal position who had "massacred Union soldiers." But people from Richmond here to-day say the G.A.R. has been invited to hold its reunion there.

The Sun – **August 5, 1897**

WILL MOSBY GET AN OFFICE?

Grand Army Men Said to Be Protesting Against Giving Him a Consulate.

Richmond, Va., Aug. 4.—Soon after McKinley's election, it was said on authority of two Senators close to him that the President had Col. John S. Mosby slated for a foreign consulate. Mosby's accident, in which he lost an eye, was supposed to have delayed the appointment, and now the friends of Col. Mosby who felt sure of the President's promise are uneasy because of the reported opposition to Mosby by the G.A.R. Col. James D. Brady, when asked to-day, said the opposition came from an obscure post in Pennsylvania, who passed resolutions opposing his appointment.

Col. Brady declared that he knew it to be a fact that some of the most prominent G.A.R. men in the country were in favor of Col. Mosby's appointment.

The Times – **August 7, 1897**

Some People Object to Mosby.

Richmond, Va., Aug. 6.—President McKinley's intimation that he would give Col. Mosby something has begun considerable criticism throughout Virginia. It is said some Pennsylvania Grand Army post protested against Mosby being given anything. The colonel wants to go back to California, but his friends are desirous of seeing him stay in the East or go back to Hong Kong. * [*see Addendum Ringgold Cavalry vs. John Singleton Mosby at the end of the Chapter-vph]

One newspaper said it all in an article about Mosby's problems in Virginia and especially his response to those who said that they did not want him "credited to Virginia." Mosby, of course, frequently used poetry; and in this instance, it was a mortal riposte to his small-minded and mean-spirited critics:

North Platte Semi-Weekly Tribune – **August 13, 1897**

Colonel Mosby and the Virginians.

Said a Virginia politician recently: "Poetry may be losing its hold on some people, but it is still pretty strong in Virginia. A happy quotation from Byron recently made capital for Colonel John Mosby all over the state. When it was announced that Colonel Mosby was apply to President McKinley for an office, some of his old opponents opened fire on him again for going over to the Republicans after the war and particularly for his always cordially expressed admiration for General Grant. It was rather poor business, and for a time Colonel Mosby paid no attention to it, but finally, when the hope was expressed that if appointed, he would not be credited to Virginia, the colonel prepared a card in reply, and it appeared in the newspapers He reviewed briefly his career as a soldier and citizen, stood by his guns and reminded his opponents that he was no longer a citizen of the state. He would abide by the record, he said. He had done his duty, and if Virginia chose to reject him let her, said he, quoting from 'Childe Harold:'

"Lift the laurels on a loftier brow

And be the Spartan epitaph on me,

Sparta hath many a worthier son than he.'

"Do you know, the Colonel's grit and his poetry caught the popular feeling, and the attacks on him ceased. A short time after that came the accident to Colonel Mosby at Charlottesville, which cost him an eye, and sympathy was expressed for him in every quarter. The Virginians like sentiment, and that bit from Byron, grittily applied, did the work for Mosby's enemies."— *New York Tribune.*

The newspapers were now catching up to the end of the story. After all the hoopla and the dreadfulness, the hope and the disappointment, Mosby was going west, no better off than at his arrival—indeed, far worse off. He had missed his chance to honor Grant, he had suffered a horrendous and painful accident and lost an eye, he had not been succored by a president for whom he had labored long and hard to help elect—in fact, he had not even seen his son's prize-winning play! All he had to show as he went back to San Francisco (besides a glass eye!) were the comments in the newspapers— some sympathetic, others smug, and some even hostile and derisive. But there would be no doubt that east or west or anywhere in between, the press would continue to report on John Mosby:

Alexandria Gazette – August 28, 1897

A Baltimore republican newspaper says: "President McKinley is not only a man who keeps his public promises, but one who keeps his private promises as well." Before that paper says anything more on the subject of the President's private promises, it should interview Senators Perkins and Proctor about the promise he made to them to appoint Col. Mosby to an office. Mr. McKinley is no exception to the rule that promises of modern Presidents cannot be relied upon.

Alexandria Gazette – September 9, 1897

MOSBY RETURNS.

After many months' absence Colonel John S. Mosby returned yesterday from his old home in Virginia, where he came near leaving his bones. When he left this city for Washington early in the spring on legal business he only expected to be away for a few weeks at the most. An accident befell him, however, that not only delayed his return for months, but placed his life in extreme danger. Thanks to his robust condition and to excellent medical care, he comes back to San Francisco as vigorous and alert as ever, but with a memento of his narrow escape from death in the form of a fracture of the left frontal bone and an artificial eye, which replaces the optical organ that was destroyed by the kick of a horse. A resultant change in the Colonel's appearance is the wearing of a pair of spectacles, not so much for the sight of his remaining eye as for the protection which it affords the injured socket.

The accident took place on April 23d last while Colonel Mosby was being driven in a carriage by a lady in the vicinity of the university of Virginia at Charlottesville, near where he was born and in which institution he completed his education. The harness became disarranged, and, as Colonel Mosby leaned over to adjust the breaching, the dashboard gave way. He was precipitated under the hoofs of the frightened animal and kicked into a condition of insensibility, from which he did not entire lyemerge for days, while for some weeks his life hung by a thread. He was conveyed to the university Hospital, and in response to telegrams, Dr. Lincoln, who had been Gen. Grant's physician, came on from Washington, and Dr. McGuire, surgeon of Stonewall Jackson's corps, in whose arms the great Confederate leader expired, hurried from Richmond. Meanwhile, however, Col. Mosby had undergone an operation at the hands of Dr. Hugh Nelson, his left eye having been removed. Of this he was unaware at the time. It was several days after he had regained consciousness that the fact was made known to him. They he showed that grit for which he is famous. Mosby's only remark, if it can be so called, was to quote the following lines from "Childe Harold'"

"Blind old Dandolo, the octogenarian chief,

Byzantium's conquering foe."

Two months were required for Col. Mosby's recovery. Before leaving Washington he was informed by the President that he would be nominated to some position, either a consulate or a mission. He is strongly supported, especially by a number of Vermont men, whose friendship he gained during the war by his treatment of soldiers from that State whom he took prisoners.— [*San Francisco Chronicle*, Sept.1]

Again, the Gazette got it right! It wasn't just Mosby who was unwelcome in the McKinley government, though he was more unwelcome than most! It would seem that John Mosby—a Southerner, a former Confederate—was willing to let the old hostilities die, but the very men he supported for office were apparently of an entirely different mind. Perhaps "Cousin Ben" was not so bad after all and certainly not the only "sectional bigot" in the Republican Party:

Alexandria Gazette – October 2, 1897

Mosby, Lamb, Rives, Lurty, Wise, Walker, nor any of the other Virginia ex-Confederate republicans have the countenance of the administration. All of its favors are bestowed upon the members of its party who have come from the North. One of the latter doesn't hesitate to say that even now, the sight of a Confederate flag is offensive to him. His feelings are those of the man who appointed him, who removed his hat at the graves of John Brown and of the recipient of the stolen Presidency, and, of course, such a man doesn't like to give offices to men who fought under that flag.

This wasn't the first time that John Mosby was mentioned as a gubernatorial candidate for the Republican Party in Virginia. He would have been nominated if Garfield had not forced the Virginia party to join with Mahone's Readjusters. Could Mosby have been elected? Possibly. Between the natural sympathy shown to him at the time of his accident and the knowledge that he was not loved by the McKinley administration, he might have taken the state. Of course, as the candidacy was not offered, that is mere profitless speculation.

> *Alexandria Gazette* – October 5, 1897
>
> The convention determined to elect Col. Wm. F. Wickham, of Hanover, as chairman of the State committee, and James Lyons will be chosen as candidate for attorney general. There is talk of nominating Col. John S. Mosby for Governor.

For the third year, Mosby's men would have a reunion; and as usual, especially the local papers were enchanted. This reunion would be particularly interesting as it was being held in a "Union" state, Maryland. But Mosby had quite a number of Marylanders in his command. However, he did not attend. It is probable even if he were in the East at the time of the reunion, such emotional trauma would have been too much for him in his exhausted state.

John Mosby had reached an age at which he would more frequently learn of the deaths of those with and against whom he had fought in the war. One such death— "Fighting Major" Forbes—particularly touched him as was reported by newspapers on both coasts:

> *San Francisco Chronicle* – October 17, 1897 (Edited)
>
> *Alexandria Gazette* – October 26, 1897
>
> COL. MOSBY AND COL. FORBES
>
> An Incident of the Civil War.
>
> Both had been soldiers, both had met on the battle-field not merely as units in two great opposing military machines, but as foes within a contracted area, each seeking the other's life. Theirs was a friendship formed on the battle-field and cemented during the years of pacific comity. Therefore, when the news was received of the death of Colonel William H. Forbes at Milton, Mass, a few days ago, to no one did the passing away of the Yankee officer cause a deeper pang than to Colonel John S. Mosby, the Confederate guerrilla chieftain. …
>
> "Attached to the Federal troops guarding Washington on the Virginia side of the Potomac," began Colonel Mosby, "was the Second Massachusetts Cavalry It was the best body of mounted fighting men that I encountered during the war; that is, the men fought better in the saddle. As a rule they had seen much of camp life; and were accustomed to privations, habituated to face danger and skilled in the use of arms and in mounting horseback.
>
> "One of the Majors of the regiment was William H. Forbes. He was a member of one of the leading families of Massachusetts. His father was

one of the princes of the China trade residing in Boston, and he himself married the daughter of Ralph Waldo Emerson "It was on July 6, 1864, at Aldie, on the farm where President Monroe lived, that Forbes and I made our acquaintance. I shall never forget the occasion, and I know he never did. It was black gum against thunder. Forbes commanded the Union forces and I was at the head of my men. We were both about equal in number. Forbes acted with great gallantry in the fight... After the war we all met in Washington, and nothing would do but that Chapman and I should dine with him at the Arlington ... Forbes' friendship for me continued ever afterward and was shown on many an occasion. When I lectured in Boston he gave a dinner in my honor at which James Russell Lowell, then just returned from England, and Oliver Wendell Holmes, the 'Autocrat of the Breakfast Table,' were present. When I was made Consul at Hongkong he published a letter defending my appointment, and when twice I had to go to the hospital, Major Forbes rendered me pecuniary assistance. I tell you this to show that we did not all misuse our Yankee prisoners and to explain the noble character of the Massachusetts officer, whose death I have such reason to deplore.

The Gazette continued to point out the anti-Southern bias of the McKinley administration. Not only did the president fail to fulfill promises to former Confederates such as Mosby and Longstreet; but his actions were doing everything to assure, as the paper pointed out, that the South would be "more solidly democratic than it ever was." Considering what John Mosby had relinquished to prevent that very situation, one wonders if he ever considered his efforts a colossal waste:

Alexandria Gazette – October 21, 1897

The G.A.R. estopped President McKinley from fulfilling his promise to appoint Colonel Mosby to a federal position, and now it appears that they have also prevented him from fulfilling his promise to make General Longstreet Commissioner of U. S. Railroads. The G.A.R. don't want any "ex-rebels" in theirs, and they don't hesitate to say so, and their influence with Mr. McKinley, who is one of them, is potential. The appointment of negroes to office in the South and the treatment of ex-Confederates by the present republican administration are making the South more solidly democratic than it ever was.

The *Richmond Dispatch* seemed rather hostile to Mosby in the next article. The paper said nothing about the fact that he had refused the Havana consulate, although, of course, there really was nothing to refuse as it was not offered. Mosby never said anything about being offered any position or asking for one, for that matter. It is interesting that the paper says of the Virginia Republicans that the "present machine's committee takes no interest in him" when in October, Mosby's name was being bandied about as a possible candidate for governor! Be that as it may, however, the Dispatch was correct. There was nothing for John Mosby in McKinley's government—or in Virginia:

Richmond Dispatch – November 9, 1897

MOSBY IN THE COLD.

Colonel John S. Mosby seems to be severely left out in the cold. Months ago he was slated for the consul-generalship at Habana to succeed General Fitzhugh Lee, but the President, finding that it would be neither prudent nor popular to make any change there, the Colonel was side-tracked, and put on the waiting list. The next thing that came up in the way of a foreign plum was the mission to Guatemala and Honduras and it was understood that Colonel Mosby was promised that position. The announcement to-day of the appointment of Dr. W. Godfrey Hunter, of Kentucky, as predicted in these dispatches, to the latter place, blasts the Colonel's hopes of anything in the shape of a good foreign office. There are very few offices left, and the best that Colonel Mosby can now expect is an ordinary consulship, which will pay about $3,500 per annum, and it is doubtful if he will even get one of these. Mosby has not figured in Virginia politics, and, of course, the present machine's committee, which controls the State's patronage takes no interest in him, and consequently he will have to depend on his own personal influence, and that of his friends, with the administration. This influence does not amount to much, and according to present indications, and the statements of leading Virginia Republicans, the Colonel's prospects for Federal pap are exceedingly slim and misty.

As is usual with newspaper coverage, old stories were made new again when another part of the country became involved. In this case, it was a San Francisco paper commenting upon Mosby's attempt to secure a position. The paper, that had formerly been quite friendly, was far less so here. Possibly, its coverage mirrored the belief that Mosby's days with the Southern Pacific, and subsequently in that city, were numbered. Given the change of much of the press from sympathy to hostility, it must sometimes have seemed to John Mosby that he had wandered onto a firing range and was now the most popular target extant:

San Francisco Call - **December 2, 1897**

COLONEL MOSBY'S CLAIMS.

The Ex-Confederate Thinks He Is Entitled to a Consulship.

Washington, Dec. 1.—Colonel John S. Mosby, the famous ex-Confederate, has returned to Washington from his California home and will again press his claims for a consulship. Colonel Mosby was at the White House to-day, but owing to the press of official visitors did not remain to see the President. It will be remembered that he was here early last summer and saw President McKinley on several occasions. He returned to California to await a more favorable opportunity to press his application.

A final effort was made on Mosby's behalf by his California senator, but it was wasted. However, the idea that a US senator of the same party as the president would have to "wait his turn" in a room full of supplicants is nonsense. If Perkins was left to wait, it was because McKinley didn't want to see him. Several other articles also emerged, including an interview with Mosby. It appeared that the positions mentioned were put forth by well-known Republican senators. But Mosby was never considered for any of them—including Havana if Congressman Aldrich was telling the truth about that post being offered to him by the president. Mosby surely would have done very well in Mexico, a country that he knew well and that knew and apparently liked and respected him from his time with the Juarez lottery:

Alexandria Gazette – December 18, 1897

Senator Perkins of California went to the White House to-day to see the President in reference to Colonel Mosby, who will soon return to San Francisco, and find out, if possible, why Mr. McKinley after promising him and Senator Proctor that the Colonel should be well provided for, has failed to fulfill that promise, but there was such a crowd of importunates there that he hadn't time to wait for his turn.

Roanoke Times – December 22, 1897

COL. JOHN S. MOSBY.

Says He Has no Expectation of Getting an Appointment.

Warrenton, Va., Dec. 21.—It was currently reported in Washington last week that Col. John S. Mosby would succeed General Lee as consul at Havana. In an interview with Colonel Mosby this morning he said: "I have never directly or indirectly applied for the Havana consulship. There was a statement last spring in the newspapers that I had done so and I promptly denied it. Not a single word has ever passed between myself and the president or any member of his cabinet about the Havana consulate. Several Senators called on the president last spring and urged my appointment to a first-class consulate. The consulates named were the City of Mexico, Yokahoma, Japan, and Shanghai or Hong Kong, China. These have all been filled and I have no expectations of getting an appointment from the administration. I was in Washington last Saturday and met ex-Congressman Aldrich, of Chicago, on the street, who is an old acquaintance of mine. He told me that last spring the president promised him the Havana consulship, but that the appointment had been indefinitely postponed. I came on to argue a case in the supreme court and will leave for San Francisco to-morrow. I suppose Fitz Lee will remain at Havana.

Alexandria Gazette - December 29, 1897

A republican friend of Colonel Mosby from the far West here to-day, talking about the Colonel, who has returned to San Francisco, says the treatment he received from the President was most remarkable and has only been explained upon the ground of the objection of the G.A.R. to the appointment of a "rebel guerrilla," which objection it had been supposed was too slight for even Mr. McKinley to consider. He said he was assured that the President had not only promised the Colonel, but two influential republican Senators, who are his personal friends, that he would appoint him to a good position, and one that would be agreeable to him, and how he could have broken that promise it was difficult to understand, that is, if he have any regard for his word or have any moral courage.

And so a tempestuous and disappointing year came to an end. On the good side, John Mosby was alive—a matter in considerable doubt at one time! On the debit side, he was still in a very unsettled and unsettling relationship with the Southern Pacific Railroad without any clear indication that when that relationship ended—as it certainly would—he would have anywhere else to go. Physically, he was slowly regaining his strength, but he would never regain his eye. And yet, he was prepared to soldier on as he had done through every dry spell or crisis or tragedy in his life. But John Mosby knew that he wasn't getting any younger and his life was still so very, very unsettled. Perhaps 1898 would be better. Knowing his spirit, he was probably more than willing to believe that such would be the case.

ADDENDUM

Fitzhugh Lee in Cuba

Democratic President Grover Cleveland appointed Democrat Fitzhugh Lee as consul general to Havana in 1896. Lee arrived in June to an island torn by civil war and mass poverty. Three weeks after his arrival, the new consul informed the State Department that Cuban rebels did not have the strength to drive the Spanish out, but that the Spanish were equally unable to subdue the rebellion. In other words, Cuba was in a state of what could only be called "violent stalemate." However, while Lee staunchly opposed the Spanish tactics being used to suppress the rebels, his main focus was protecting the rights of American citizens in Cuba.

Ironically, Lee's strong stance against Spain won the praise of some of Cleveland's staunchest critics, who used his nominee as further fuel against the more altruistic president. Republican critics wrote of Lee's "good sense and firm courage" while lamenting that the consul "was not sustained by the (Cleveland) Administration as he should have been." December 1897 saw increasing unrest in Havana. Actually, much of the violence was caused by the Cuban rebels and often directed toward American-owned sugar plantations! However, as Lee's main concern remained the safety of Americans on the island, he apparently exaggerated the threat he feared from Spanish officials and loyal Cubans, not the revolutionaries. Finally, he became so concerned that he requested a warship be ready in Key West in case violence erupted.

In consequence, the battleship *Maine* was ordered to Florida in January 1898. Shortly after the arrival of the *Maine*, the situation appeared to Lee to have taken a turn for the worse and he sent a preliminary signal to Charles Sigsbee, prompting him to ready his ship. But newly installed Republican President William McKinley ordered the *Maine* to Havana. Lee was unnerved by the ship's sudden arrival as he had specifically advised against an American warship's "visit" to the island at that time. Lee's actions as consul were not without importance. Indeed, his supporters saw him as decisive and pro-American, and they credited his actions as leading nicely to the "splendid little war" with Spain. On the other hand, Lee's critics would charge that his misreading of the Cuban situation, which some believed was intentional, moved both sides closer to war.

When the *Maine* arrived in Havana on January 25, there was an undeniable tension, and the explosion on the ship on February 15 changed everything. As the United States moved closer to war, Lee asked the president to delay his ultimatum until at least Saturday, the ninth, to allow the evacuation of Americans from the island. Under intense pressure, McKinley delayed the message that would lead to war until Monday, April 11, a day after Lee's arrival in Florida. Under the circumstances extant, nobody would have replaced Fitz Lee in Havana. The situation was entirely too unsettled to allow for a change of consuls. There were those who said that Mosby would have been in Cuba what Sickles was in Spain, but that is not so. Despite being a doughty fighter, John Mosby did not consider violence as an answer to anything no matter what his "biographers" and others who have reported on the man have maintained. Could he have *stopped* the war or prevented it? That is not known, but certainly he never believed that Spain was responsible for the sinking of the Maine.

ADDENDUM

The Ringgold Cavalry vs. John Singleton Mosby

After the Hayes administration, John Mosby was denied any position with every Republican administration until McKinley's *second* term after the President learned that Mosby was unemployed! In McKinley's *first* administration, though many people had sought a position for him—including some important Democrats!—he was passed by. Yet, even after Mosby became unemployed, all that McKinley offered was a poorly paid job as an agent in the Department of the Interior.

Though there were some former federal commanders in Republican administrations who were against Mosby, there was another group who despised the man and did all in their power to prevent him from obtaining any position in the government after he returned from China. These were certain groups of the GAR, mainly from Pennsylvania. While the New England GAR had been supportive of Mosby even directly after the war, the Pennsylvania group did all in their power to prevent him from getting help from the very men he had worked to elect! No "forgive and forget" or thoughts of "reconciliation" passed through *their* minds! They held their grudges and "waived the bloody shirt" until death – theirs *and* Mosby's! The most aggressive of these groups was a minor cavalry command from Pennsylvania, the Ringgold Cavalry. Their hatred for Mosby was summed up in a statement that has appeared in many books:

> "Here I will state, as the war is over and no ill feeling to any man who wore the gray, if the Ringgold cavalry had caught John S. Mosby any time after the Snicker's gap affair (July 17, 1864) all he would have been worth to his country or to his people would have been his insurance policy Then and there his doom was for once sealed, the only man by them thus doomed during the Civil war."

What possible "crime" could John Mosby have committed that made him so hated by a cavalry unit with which he had very little interaction? They certainly weren't one of the commands with whom Mosby made war—to their detriment. The truth is contained in an article regarding the Snicker's Gap incident of July 17th, 1864 that appears in *Ellwood's Stories of the Old Ringgold Cavalry* though the name of the narrator is not included:

> "The next morning we were out early hunting up our boys who were with Hunter, and whom we had not seen for nearly two months. We were all glad to meet and exchange experiences. Some of our noble boys had been killed, others had been captured while with Hunter, and others at Lost river. All this and more was hurriedly related. At four o'clock we moved up four miles when we met the Confederates in force in the Louden valley. In this little scrap we captured thirty wagons, if one could call them wagons. We continued our march until two o'clock at night when the command went into camp. We broke camp at eight o'clock on the morning of the 17th, and marched by way of Snicker's gap to the Shenandoah river. We found the enemy holding this ford in force, and had a brisk brush, bringing up the artillery on both sides. Our forces were repulsed, and our loss was reported as fifteen or twenty killed, and some ten or twelve wounded.

> *"The same evening John S. Mosby, who was in sight of our troops during the day, caught some of our men, killing and wounding twelve or fifteen."*
> [emphasis vph]

This was the heinous crime that caused the Ringgold Cavalry to "doom" John Mosby and no other Confederate! It was a skirmish between their command and Mosby's men after they had been "repulsed" at the Shenandoah ford. Before that encounter, they had been universally successful whether riding with Hunter in his depredations among non-combatants in the Valley or capturing thirty wagons, dismissed with contempt as not being worthy to be called "wagons." Thus, when they found the Confederates at the ford, they expected another victory and were surprised and angry when *they* were "repulsed." Mortified and aggrieved at their forced retreat after so many victories, Mosby's unexpected attack was an insult not to be endured.

As was usually the case, Mosby had been watching these operations and as the Ringgold command retreated from their defeat at the river, he attacked the remnant – a legitimate act of war at which these Pennsylvanians took umbrage because he successfully engaged them after they had already been soundly beaten! Not used to being the loser against mere Confederates, this result created an eternal hatred of John Mosby occasioned by nothing more than a valid act of war!

As well, it must also be remembered that at least part of this command was engaged in Hunter's criminal actions against non-combatants in the Shenandoah Valley! Far from Mosby's attack on the Ringgold being morally or legally reprehensible, the "wrong" was all on *their* side. As Mosby himself said when such incidents were used against him, "men go to war to kill and be killed!" There was no atrocity that might have excused such long-held hatred, rather, only a lot of arrogant Yankees who didn't like that their noses had been bloodied and who held on to their resentment in perpetuity. Obviously, John Mosby comes out the better man in this whole matter.

Chapter 37

1898

Aquila non capit muscas.
~ An eagle does not bother with flies.

"The man of knowledge must be able not only to love his enemies but also to hate his friends." ~ Friedrich Nietzsche

1898 ENTERED QUIETLY for John Mosby. What appeared in the papers referable to him were accounts of his command, including two long articles by former Ranger George Baylor. However, the Havana matter had not yet been entirely dismissed as can be seen by this article:

Princeton Union – **January 13, 1898**

Personal Mention.

Col. John S. .Mosby denies the report that he asked to be appointed to the Havana consulate.

The first "whiff" of anything of real interest appeared in the *San Francisco Call* of February 24 and involved the possibility of war with Spain. Naturally, there were former soldiers from the Civil War who were interested in participating if war broke out. Mosby, as can be seen in this article, did not believe that Spain was responsible for the destruction of the Maine and said so. He also made clear, however, that if war came, he would offer his not-inconsiderable services to the nation not because he loved war, but as a gesture of reconciliation and reunion.

San Francisco Call – **February 24, 1898**

In army circles of this department the war talk is largely discounted. The veteran officers who were engaged in the battles of the Civil War reason that a conflict is possible, but not probable. They are content to leave the question of declaring war to Congress and the executive department of the national Government. The younger officers grow indignant at the thought of hostilities between Spain and the United States, and fancy that all the war talk emanates from sensational press correspondents. It passes their comprehension that Congress should think of permitting war without consulting the army.

Colonel John S. Mosby, the noted Confederate leader of cavalry, takes a keen interest in the war news. He does not entertain the thought that the Spanish Government had anything to do with the disaster to the battleship Maine, but holds that Spain has every reason to avoid a conflict with the United States.

"Spain is in a position," said the Colonel, "somewhat similar to that of the North when the Civil War came. The North did not want war with a foreign nation, and so gave up Mason and Sidell after they were taken from a British ship. In the South we hoped that the North would not surrender the prisoners. We wanted to see England get in and blockade Northern ports. The Government in Washington was ready to make any reasonable concession to avoid war with England. Spain is bending her energies to suppress the rebellion in Cuba. She would have everything to lose and nothing to gain in a war with the United States.

"If war comes I shall offer my services," continued Colonel Mosby. "Yes, my health is all right, barring the loss of one eye. I am stronger now than when I went into the army in 1861. I could endure the hardships of a campaign in Cuba. At the time of the Virginius affair, when war with Spain seemed imminent, I called on President Grant and told him that I was ready and willing to go. I assured him that the men of the South were willing to support the Government of the United States in the field. While I was talking to General Grant, Hamilton Fish, of the Cabinet came in and remarked that the affair with Spain, was in a fair way of adjustment without resort to war. I do not believe that Spain was wrong in the Virginius controversy. She did what England or the United States would have done."

And of course, as soon as this first response by the man so many folks loved to hate hit the streets, Mosby found himself rather viciously attacked, especially with regard to his opinions on the Virginius matter. The Virginius was a ship involved in smuggling arms to the Cuban insurrectionists in 1873 during the Ten Years' War. Its fate came near to causing war between Spain and the United States at the time. The ship was considered a pirate ship and fraudulently flew the American flag even though it was owned by Cuban interests. The Virginius was captured by the Spanish off Cuba on October 31, 1873. It might be remembered that John Mosby offered his services and that of many of his men to President Grant should the nation go to war with Spain in Cuba! In any event, the captain, Joseph Fry, and fifty-two of the crew and passengers— among them several Americans—were executed as pirates and gunrunners. More would have been killed, but for the intervention of the British ship Niobe.

After the incident, negotiations were undertaken by Daniel Edgar Sickles, US minister to Spain, former Union general, and moral reprobate. Sickles' intemperate attitude worsened the situation, but Secretary of State Hamilton Fish took negotiations out of his hands, and a settlement was reached. Spain paid the United States an indemnity of $80,000. However, in spite of the settlement, war hysteria briefly flared up when news of the executions arrived. Many American newspapers initially exaggerated the death toll, mistakenly alleging that every captive had been killed. It is no doubt that the Spanish were more brutal in their treatment of the captives and their methods of execution than either the United States or Britain would have been, but after the Virginius was proven not to be an American owned ship, nothing further occurred between the two governments. Yet the treatment by the Spaniards of those on the ship was still considered a heinous "war crime" by many in the United States, and Mosby's dismissal of the affair by saying that Spain did what both England and the United States would have done under the circumstances led to a very nasty response by a *San Francisco Call* columnist, Henry James:

San Francisco Call – February 27, 1898
WITH ENTIRE FRANKNESS

By Henry James

Colonel Mosby is a much older man than he would have been had he been hanged at the time he first merited the distinction. He is entitled now to all the disrespect due a certain sort of old age. When the colonel says that Spain was right in the Virginius affair I take the liberty of saying he talks as if his recent accident had knocked out his brains instead of an eye. He adds that the United States or England would have done the same thing as Spain, wherein he wantonly slanders two nations, neither of which has done anything to deserve it. England may at times have a strange conception of her rights but she does not do more than maintain them as they appear to her. The United States, acting on the principle now advocated by Mosby, would have reduced her population considerably, and I do not see how Mosby's feet could have reached the ground save through the breaking of the rope.

For the Virginius affair, a matter recently exploited anew in the daily press, there was no excuse. It was murder, and the bodies of the victims were treated to indignities such as might have been expected had the captors been Apaches. That the matter was settled on a monetary basis has been a shame to America ever since and accounts in great measure for the Spanish notion that we are an inferior people. Colonel Mosby indicates a willingness to lead an army against the Spanish, but I would rather have it led by somebody else, almost anybody who might be mentioned. But if war come, and he gets into hostile territory and suffers the indignity of capture, the vision of his own head adorning a pole, a jest for the rabble, may not comfort his last moments particularly, but it will work within him a change of heart and dissipate the clouds of senility which seem to have obscured his vision.

Mr. James was of course obviously ignorant of the horrendous treatment of so many Southerners at the hands of his "enlightened" government. Mosby knew better; and besides, he was not speaking of the methods of execution—whatever they were—used by Spain, but of the fact that as pirates, the captain and crew of the Virginius would have suffered the same fate at the hands of both the English and the Americans! For the first time, however, we see the next form that assaults against Mosby would take in the press and elsewhere when he expressed an unpopular opinion—that is, that he was senile or becoming senile. There is nothing to suggest that John Mosby responded to James. Perhaps he didn't see the article, but it is most likely that he couldn't be bothered with a man who merely stated his own opinion and did not pretend to be reporting the news. Mosby was of the belief that people had a right to their opinions however erroneous or stupid.

In another article, Mosby again stated his opposition to the war, but he also reiterated that he would volunteer if war came:

Alexandria Gazette – **March 23, 1898**

COL. MOSBY OPPOSED TO WAR.

Colonel John S. Mosby has written a letter from San Francisco, under date of March 17, in which he gives his views on the Spanish situation:

"I am opposed to going to war with Spain. First, because I see no just reason for war, and second, because if war comes, I shall go to war. I wrote Senator Perkins a few days ago to say to the President I thoroughly approved of the moderation he has shown, and do not believe there will be any developments to justify war; if war comes that the old Confederate soldiers will be the first in the field, and that I should be with them. There is no more proof of the Spanish people or government being responsible for the blowing up of or the explosion on the Maine than there was that the Southern people procured the assassination of Abraham Lincoln."

Salt Lake Herald – April 18, 1898

Colonel Mosby, who carved out several pages of history during the war of the rebellion and who was more feared than any other officer on the other side, because of his wonderful faculty for riding a hundred miles after dark and coming in to take breakfast with the Union forces next morning, without waiting for an invitation, has tendered his services to President McKinley in the event of a war with Spain. The old man is 64 years of age, but doesn't look it, and is as hardy and energetic as some people at 40. He would make a rattling good cavalry commander, and if he should be sent out against the dons some of them would rue his visit. It is only a short time since he was in Salt Lake.

Alexandria Gazette – April 20, 1898

Gen. H. Kyd Douglas, of Hagerstown, Md., yesterday received a letter from Col. John S. Mosby, in which the Colonel says: "I am bitterly opposed to war with Spain, but if it comes, consider it my duty to go, and have written Gen. Miles. I still hope war will be averted."

It is interesting to recall those authors who wrote about Mosby and declared that his "violent streak" made him gleefully anticipate fighting in another war, yet here is evidence that he was opposed to war because he could see no need or reason for it. John Mosby did not believe that Spain had anything to do with the Maine disaster and he was right. However, what Mosby did not consider—because he had yet to believe that "his America" was imperialistic—was the fact that the United States viewed war with Spain as a means of gaining colonies in the Pacific. China and Japan were opening ever more to world trade, and the United States had no colonies in the Pacific to support American shipping and commercial interests. The place to get those colonies was from Spain, hence the perceived "need" for a war with that colonial power.

San Francisco Call – May 3, 1898

Colonel Mosby's Services.

Colonel John S. Mosby is in receipt of a letter from Major-General Nelson A. Miles, U.S.A., wherein the latter says: "I have recommended you for a position in connection with the troops of the South."

In tendering his services to the Government, Colonel Mosby did not signify that he desired any particular work in the service, and neither did he ask for any special command. He simply offered his services to his country.

Colonel Mosby denies most explicitly that he has made an application for the position of brigadier-general of volunteers.

And here the matter stood, all perfectly fine as far as Mosby was concerned. He had made it clear that he was no warmonger, but if war came, he wanted to serve. Therefore, as of that point in time, Mosby's service was considered dependent upon "if" war were declared rather than any problem with his service per se. But that was not to last:

San Francisco Call – **May 5, 1898**

MILES AND MOSBY.

Col. John S. Mosby wants to rally round the old flag and Major-General Miles wants him to rally, but impediment in the form of Congressional influence prevent the colonel's advance upon the Spanish works. The situation is thus concisely explained by two military chieftains:

"WASHINGTON, D.C. May 4.

"Colonel John S. Mosby, San Francisco, Cal.: I would be very glad to have your services, but think it will require some influences. Suggest that you communicate with your Senators.

NELSON A. MILES,

"Major-General commanding." "SAN FRANCISCO, May 4, 1898.

"General Nelson A. Miles, United States Army, Washington, D. C.: Your telegram received. I have no influence except my military record.

"JOHN S. MOSBY."

San Francisco Call – **May 6, 1898**

THE REPLY OF MILES TO MOSBY

Stirs up Something of a Sensation at Washington.

It Has Not Been Supposed That Influence Had Anything To Do With Commands in the Army.

New York, May 5.—The Herald's Washington correspondent says: Despite President McKinley's announcement that "political influence" will have no weight in army appointments, it now seems probable that Colonel John S. Mosby, who has applied for a command, will be compelled to resort to the services of politicians before he gains his wish.

I asked General Miles to-night if the published report were true that he had replied to General Mosby's telegram offering his services to the Government with the suggestion that he "see his Senators" and exert what influence he could.

The general appeared much disturbed by the question, and said to me very determinedly that he had nothing to say in regard to the matter.

"I cannot see, said General Miles, "how these things become public. It certainly looks to me as though some one had been tampering with private telegrams. I have received a message from General Mosby and he has offered his services and asked for a command. Further then this I have nothing to say on the subject.

There has been considerable speculation as to what would be the outcome of the matter since General Miles' reply to Mosby became public. An army officer said to me this evening: "if it is true that General Miles told Mosby that he must get political influence in order to secure command, he has placed himself in a rather embarrassing position. Mosby's reply that he had no influence except his military record was most appropriate. He was a good cavalry commander, as the Union army found to their sorrow, during the war, and if he has applied for a command now he surely deserves one.

COLONEL MOSBY HAS NO POLITICAL PULL.

Colonel John S. Mosby, the famous Confederate raider, said last evening, in regard to the tender of his services to the Government and the reply of General Nelson A. Miles, in which the latter advised him to secure the influence of his Senators:

I wrote to General Miles two weeks ago, just about the time that the resolutions passed, and on the day that President McKinley sent his ultimatum to Congress I telegraphed offering my services to the Government. I did so, not out of vanity or thinking that my services would be of any value, but because I thought, and so wrote, that any Confederate officer who had won prominence in the late war should offer his services and thus show his loyalty to the flag. If I had served in the Union army I would not have done so. "Last Saturday I received a letter from the general, in which he said he recommended me for a position in connection with the troops that were to be raised in the South. When I received the telegram from Miles advising me to secure the influence of my Senators I was greatly surprised. I could not understand why they wanted political influence as a condition of accepting my services as a soldier. They know my war record. I fought against Miles, against McKinley in the Shenandoah and against Alger, and what the devil good can White or Perkins do. Major McKinley knew me before he ever heard of White or Perkins. Another thing, you know the publication of war records, which has been going on during the past ten or twelve years, is superintended by a joint board of Union and Confederate officers. General Marcus Wright, chairman of the Confederate Board, voluntarily wrote me two years ago that he had read every report and dispatch of General Robert E. Lee, and that there were more complimentary notices of me than of any other man in the whole Confederate army."

As the gray-haired officer thought of their forgetfulness he became more heated. "After the war General Grant wrote his memoirs when he was dying at Mount McGregor, and he paid the highest tribute to me both as a man and a soldier. Now, I say, the President, General Miles and Secretary of War Alger know my record perfectly well, and, as it was indorsed by General Lee during the war and by General Grant afterward, for me to ask some Congressman to indorse my fitness as a soldier would be like asking Vanderbilt to indorse a tramp's note and give him credit. If my record as a soldier is not recognized by the Government I can stay at home. I have done my duty.

"General Miles is a friend of mine, and his suggestion was friendly advice. I have not a bit of influence, and I don't think that politics or influence would be necessary. I would not ask a Congressman to indorse me if it was to make me a major-general; I have too much pride. I did not say one word about rank or commission, but offered my services to the Government.

> "My son Beverly, who is a lawyer in Salt Lake City, wrote me that he would leave in an hour for Virginia, where he will fight in the ranks of a Virginia regiment."

As seems usual in government circles, Miles was upset not about the content of his comment, but that his comment had been made public. It may be that Mosby told someone when he received the telegram (he certainly was offended by the suggestion that he needed "influence"), but he obviously did not divulge it directly to the press. Had he done so, he would have admitted to it or someone in the press would have acknowledged that he, Mosby, was the source. However, his failure to secure a position in the administration the year before was proof indeed that he, in fact, had no political "pull" no matter what politician spoke for him—as indeed was discovered later when it became known that various important people in Congress had pressed his case.

Alexandria Gazette – May 6, 1898

> It is currently reported here that when Colonel John S. Mosby offered his services to the Commander-in-Chief of the army General Miles advised him by letter to obtain political backing, and that the Colonel replied that he had no such backing, and that the only sort he did have was his own public military record.

But suddenly, it had become a matter of "political influence," something that was even of more import than the individuals involved including John Mosby. Certainly, Miles had said nothing about such influence in his early response. Yet the rules had changed, probably, because Alger had made it clear that he did not want Mosby's services. His subordinate—Miles—unable to make such a matter public, (for obvious reasons), probably hoped that political influence would get Mosby past Alger. Mosby, either in ignorance, naïveté, or both, saw the matter merely as a political maneuver and was angry. He pointed out that McKinley—and Alger—knew his military capabilities before they knew the California senators, and that was true enough. But what Mosby did not realize was that very knowledge was keeping him out of the army and any other part of McKinley's government.

San Francisco Call – May 7, 1898

> MOSBY'S POSITION.
>
> Services Offered as an Example of a United Country.
>
> Colonel John S. Mosby still maintains his position that Congressional influence cannot add to the value of his services as a soldier. In an interview yesterday he remarked:
>
> "I offered to serve the Government as a soldier, without specifying any rank or position. I was not prompted by ambition, but a desire to set an example that would be evidence of a united country. The offer was made to the War Department through the commander-in-chief of the army. I did not consider that I was asking a political favor of the administration. I was surprised to hear that Congressional influence was required to secure the privilege of fighting the battles of the country. I have no control over any such influence and would not ask it. I cannot imagine what any Congressman could say that would add anything to the indorsements I have received from General Grant and General Robert E. Lee."

"Again, John Mosby mentioned why he had volunteered; that is, he wanted to demonstrate that the country had become "unified" if a former Confederate soldier fought for the flag. It was not, as has been speculated by those who write about the man, a desire to "shoot people and get famous – again." Rather, Mosby hoped to demonstrate that the country had become "unified" if a former Confederate soldier participated in the upcoming conflict. Again, he stated his belief that the "indorsements" he received from men like Lee and Grant should make any other "influence" unnecessary. Of course, the newspapers, not knowing about Alger, picked up the "political influence" issue as being of utmost importance, especially as it would affect the competency of the armed forces quite apart from denying a place in the military to John Mosby. And so the press coverage went on, some of the papers going back to the beginning of the exchange of correspondence between Miles and Mosby, making note of the fact that Miles had recommended Mosby for service with Southern troops and that Mosby had requested no particular place, both being a matter of great moment in the situation extant as it was understood at the time:

Houston Daily Post – May 7, 1898

A MILITARY RECORD

Does Not Count for as Much as a Political "Pull."

Washington, May 6.—Despite President McKinley's announcement that "political influence" will have no weight in army appointments, it now seems probable that General John S. Mosby, who has applied for a command, will be compelled to resort to the services of the politicians before he gains his wish.

I asked General Miles if the published reports were true, that he had replied to General Mosby's telegram offering his services to the government with the suggestion that he see "his senator" and exert what influence he could. The general appeared much disturbed by the question, and said to me very determinedly that he had nothing to say in regard to the matter.

"I can not see," said General Miles, "how these things become public. It certainly looks to me as though some one had been tampering with private telegrams. I have received a message from General Mosby, and he has offered his services and asked for a command. Further than this I have nothing to say on the subject."

An army officer said to me, "If it is true that General Miles told Mosby that he must get political influence in order to secure a command, he has placed himself in a rather embarrassing position. Mosby's reply that he had no influence except his military record, was most appropriate."

Salt Lake Herald – May 10, 1898

MILES AND MOSBY.

In making his appointments of major generals, brigadier generals and colonels the president appears to have considered fitness and merit as the recommendations for preferment, and the result has been good; they are the recommendations that should count and the only ones. But an unfortunate case has arisen, not one that in any way involves the president, but that does involve the major general in command of the army.

It appears that General John S. Mosby, of Confederate guerrilla fame, made application to General Miles for a command, and the story goes that General Miles told him to see "his senator" and exert what influence he could. To this Mosby replied, so it is said, that he had no influence except his military record; a most fitting reply for a soldier to make to a politician's suggestion.

This is not merely a newspaper story, though the papers are taking it up; there is much in it. The Washington correspondent of the New York Herald says he called on Miles and asked him if the published reports to the effect that he had replied to Mosby's telegram offering his services to the government, with the suggestion that he see "his senator." The correspondent says the general appeared very much disturbed by the question, and said determinedly that he had nothing to say in regard to the matter. Then General Miles says, "I do not see how these things become public. It certainly looks to me as though some one had been tampering with private telegrams. I have received a message from General Mosby, and he has offered his services and asked for a command. Further than this I have nothing to say on the subject."

There is little doubt that Miles told Mosby to see "his senator," for the general in command of the army is known to place considerable reliance on political influence, many people think entirely too much for a military man.

At this time above all others one would prefer to think of the general in command of the army as a military man and nothing else. It is General Mosby who cuts the best figure in this story.

There is a certain irony and a not inconsiderable gratification in the discomfort McKinley and his administration were suffering in this matter! The despised Mosby, brushed off by the president and his factotums and sent packing back to California with his tail between his legs had created a hornet's nest for the administration at the worst possible time and in the worst possible way. And as they had no intention of granting Mosby any part in the administration—not even in the army—there wasn't a whole lot they could do about it but try to ride out the storm.

Finally, a newspaper—the *San Francisco Call*, the home of the insulting columnist discovered the crux of the matter and reported it:

San Francisco Call – May 11, 1898

Alger Dislikes Mosby.

It has come to light that one of the reasons that Colonel Mosby has a hard time to get recognition at Washington is that he made himself active by hanging a number of the men under Secretary Alger, who was a captain of Michigan Cavalry during the war. According to a book called "Mosby's Rangers," a number of Union soldiers were engaged in burning houses at Castleman's Ferry on August 14, 1864. They were under Alger. Mosby was sent after them and he killed about twenty-five of the number, for which General Lee commended him. It is said that Alger has never been able to forgive the deed and that he has always done all he could to block Mosby in his ambitions.

But soon, the papers were back at work on the issue of "political influence" and the Alger-Mosby matter was abandoned. It must be remembered that this was not simply a "Mosby matter," but a "military matter." If a man of talent and with a stunning record of military achievement could be denied a command because he did not have political "pull," then it stood to reason that a man without either talent or a stunning record could obtain one if he did have "pull," and that consideration exercised much of the press—and the public:

Evening Times – May 12, 1898

Colonel Mosby.

(From the Hartford Courant.)

For a dozen years past Col. John Singleton Mosby has been peacefully practicing law in San Francisco. His life between the May of '61 and the May of '65 was not so peaceful. In point of fact, it was just about as full of excitement and adventure as a life could well be. The colonel was one of the best three partisan fighters produced by the war of secession. His daring was as the daring of Mad Anthony, and his foxiness was as the foxiness of Francis Marion. The fame of him and his rangers spread through the land. Ubiquitous, elusive, tantalizing, a will-o'-the-wisp and hornet in one, he was the plague, the despair and the admiration of the Federal officers set to catch him. They never caught him.

For more than a quarter-century he has been a peaceful, loyal citizen; a good, country-loving American. The other day he offered his services to the Government for the campaign in Cuba. The general of the army was able to make the pleasant reply that he had already recommended Col. Mosby for a commission.

Colonel Mosby will be sixty-five on his next birthday, but he can ride a horse yet, and if there is to be fighting in Cuba he'll be a handy man to have around. What he doesn't know about the handling of irregular cavalry and about scouting isn't worth knowing. He could give Maximo Gomez lessons in the guerrilla industry and Gomez at present thinks he knows it all.

Butler Weekly Times – May 12, 1898

MILES' REPLY TO MOSBY A FAUX PAS

Political Influence Necessary to Gain Army Appointments.

Washington, May 5—Despite President McKinley's announcement that "political influence" will have no weight in army appointments, it now seems probable that General John S. Mosby, who has applied for a command, will be compelled to resort to the services of the politicians before he gains his wish.

General Miles admitted tonight that he had replied to General Mosby's telegram offering his services to the government with the suggestion that he "see his senator."

"I cannot see," said General Miles "how these things become public. I have received a message from General Mosby and he has offered his services and asked for a command. Further than that I have nothing to say on the subject."

There has been considerable speculation as to what would be the outcome of the matter since General Miles' reply became public. An army officer said this evening: "If it is true that General Miles told Mosby that he must get political influence in order to secure a command he has placed himself in a rather embarrassing position. Mosby's reply that he has no influence except his military record was most appropriate. He was a good cavalry commander, as the Union Army found out to their sorrow during the war, and if he has applied for a command now he surely deserves one. General Mosby is still in his prime and would be a most valuable man in command of cavalry."

Evening Times – May 13, 1898

San Francisco Call – May 13, 1898

MOSBY IN DEFENSE OF MILES.

Satisfied With the Recommendations Given by That Officer. Yesterday Colonel Mosby sent the following explanation to Richmond: San Francisco, May 12, 1898.

The Times, Richmond, Va.: The criticisms of General Miles do him great injustice for his friendly suggestion to get political influence to bear in my behalf on the appointing power to induce the acceptance of the offer of my services as a soldier. He is not the appointing power. He can only recommend me, which he did. I made no condition about rank; in fact, I am as indifferent to rank now as I was in our late war. I cannot go as a private, as I did then, because both my age and the loss of an eye exclude me from enlistment. I would as soon be a lieutenant as a brigadier general, provided I go in front of our army and in rear of the enemy. As my military record was indorsed during the war by General Robert E. Lee, and by General Grant after the war, I do not think a Congressman's indorsement would add to its credit, and shall not ask it. I do not think Grant and Lee need any Congressional indorsement. JOHN S. MOSBY.

It is probable that Mosby felt badly for Miles who was on the "front lines" of the matter. However, as was later learned, Mosby had all the "Congressional indorsement" anyone needed to be appointed if, in fact, such had even been necessary—or, in Mosby's case, useful.

Los Angeles Herald – May 21, 1898

General Mosby was presumptuous in supposing he could break into the new army, with nothing but his war record to commend him. It doesn't appear to be that kind of a war.

The Herald – May 30, 1898

FAVORITISM A CAUSE OF DELAY

When the services of matured and experienced soldiers, such as General John S. Mosby, are spurned because of their political convictions, and a score or more of callow youths, with no other recommendation than that their fathers are rich and influential, are commissioned as officers to lead the volunteer army, we need look no further for the delay in the invasion of Cuba. Raw recruits may not be speedily metamorphosed into well drilled and thoroughly disciplined corps by unskilled and inexperienced officers, and that many such are, with the consent of the senate, being daily clothed with authority, must be apparent to all who scan the lists sent in for confirmation.

Mosby "scholars" tend to make this matter into a rather pathetic and vainglorious attempt by him to return to his "heroic days." But it was no such thing. John Mosby volunteered because he had been a Confederate soldier during the Civil War. He flatly stated that had he fought for the Union in that conflict, he would consider that he had already done his duty by the nation and at his age and with his physical infirmities, no further service was required.

There was another small matter that then arose and has been used to illustrate Mosby's "need" for the war to give his life meaning. The matter involved a squadron of cavalry that he supposedly raised when he could not get into the regular army. In an article in the *Alexandria Gazette*, we discover the *origins* of this group—and it wasn't John Mosby:

Alexandria Gazette – May 30, 1898

The San Francisco Hussars are about completing the organization of their squadron of light cavalry. It is the intention of the organizer to offer the command to Colonel Moseby as soon as the full quota of four troops has been enlisted.

Such units were often raised by a municipality to fight in a war. Indeed, most of the units that fought in the "civil war" were raised by local towns and counties and, as was the case with Mosby's own "Washington Rifles," even individual citizens. So the idea that "Mosby's Hussars," as they were finally called, was a result of Mosby's actions and desires is patently false. The men who raised the squadron offered it and themselves to him, and he graciously accepted. Once again, the vainglorious, the egotistical, and the trivial that have been ascribed to John Mosby by this matter are proven false. Notice, in the Gazette the contingent is called "The San Francisco Hussars."

The press now began to "connect the dots" between Mosby's particular type of warfare and the effect it might have on the present war, especially in Cuba:

Alexandria Gazette – June 14, 1898

THE REASON WHY—A contemporary asks why, if the Cubans in the field have but a few scattered bands, I should be necessary for Spain to support an army of more than 100,000 to look out for them. The reason is that Spain has a great deal of territory to protect and cannot tell at what point the scattered bands may unite and strike. During the civil war Col. Mosby, with 300 men, neutralized a federal army of 40,000, that being the number of federals detailed to guard railways, towns, wagon trains and supply depots which Mosby threatened. Precisely the same conditions, though on a broader scale, exist in Cuba.—[San Francisco Chronicle.

More about "Mosby's Hussars," as they eventually became known, appeared in a local newspaper with the belief that the group would provide the needed impetus to get their new commander into the fray. Again, this situation has been dealt with by contemporary writers as something Mosby created in an attempt to fulfill his need to get into the war in order to regain his former glory and/or give his present life "meaning":

San Francisco Call – **June 24, 1898**

MOSBY'S COMMAND.

The Noted Confederate Raider Will Lead a Company of Cavalry

Colonel John S. Mosby, the famous Confederate raider of the Civil War, may yet have an opportunity to show his devotion to the stars and stripes. The man who telegraphed General Miles some months ago that "he had no influence but only a military record" when told to get the assistance of the Senators from his State when he volunteered his services at the outbreak of the war, is determined to show that he is still capable of leading a charge. As captain of the Light Cavalry Troop that is daily drilling in Kohler's Hall in Oakland, the old soldier is instilling the same vim that he shows when at the head of his "Raiders."

It is the intention of the company to recruit to the limit and present it services to the Government fully equipped and ready to proceed to the front. In this the members have the support of the leading citizens of Oakland and this city. The company is composed of men who are expert with the rifle and on horseback, and many have had experience as cavalrymen in uncle Sam's service.

The men who are learning the first rudiments of cavalry drill are members of the best families in the Athenian City. Colonel Mosby's first lieutenant is Paul S. Luttrell, a son of the ex-Congressman, W. J. Tormey, the second lieutenant, has been in the cavalry service five years, during which time he has been in two engagements. At Wounded Knee he suffered a wound, and in another outbreak he was struck again. Under the able drilling of their officers the men are being rapidly "licked" into shape and will soon be able to offer their services. They appreciate the fact that so far the cavalry has not been called into the field, but they hope to be chosen, as they will be able to offer a fully equipped company.

The "Hussars" appeared once more in print. If they could not go and fight, they could at least help to raise funds for the cause:

San Francisco Call – **July 4, 1898**

(Edited) MOSBY'S HUSSARS.

Entertainment for the Benefit of the Equipment Fund and the Red Cross.

The military concert and ball to-morrow evening in Golden Gate Hall, 625 Sutter street, for the benefit of the equipment fund and the Red Cross Society, promises to be quite an attractive event. It will be given under the auspices of Troops A and B of Mosby's Hussars, who will march from the corner of Van Ness and Golden Gate avenues to the hall. Among the invited guests are

Governor Budd, Mayor Phelan, Major General Otis, Colonel Sullivan and the executive committee of the Red Cross Society. The principle address of the evening will be delivered by Colonel John S. Mosby.

All members of the Hussars are requested to meet at the armory, Tenth and Market streets at 8 o'clock this morning to take part in to-day's parade.

Meanwhile, back in Washington, efforts were still being made to get Mosby into the army. Eventually, he discovered that the political influence he did not deign to seek was being sought for him—and tendered. Naturally upset by what might appear as either going back on his word not to seek such influence or, worse, to have lied about the matter, Mosby wrote to Senator White and received a most gracious response:

Alexandria Gazette – July 5, 1898

COLONEL MOSBY TO SENATOR WHITE.

San Francisco, June 25,

To Hon. Stephen M. White, U. S. Senate, Washington, D. C.:

Dear Sir—I have been informed that a friend of mine, the Rev. S. F. Chapman, of Virginia, who has just been appointed a chaplain in the U. S. army, recently requested Senator Perkins and yourself to call with him on the President in my behalf. As soon as I heard of it I wrote to Chapman requesting him to inform you that he had done so without any authority from me, and without my knowledge or consent. Of course he acted from the best motives of friendship. When war became imminent, I wrote and telegraphed to General Miles, because he was commander-in-chief of the army, offering my services as a soldier, without any conditions as to rank, but expressing a desire to go with the advance of the army under General Miles, as I do not want to be left with the home-guard on the Pacific coast. I received a very friendly answer from him, saying that he wanted my services and had recommended me for a commission. Afterwards I got a telegram from him saying that influence was required, and suggesting that I should communicate with my Senators. To this I replied that I had no influence to rely on except my record as a soldier, with which the President and the Secretary of War ought to be familiar, as they served in the Shenandoah Valley, and especially as the President in the first interview I had with him told me that I had kept him miserable all the time he was there.

By my answer to Gen. Miles I did not mean to intimate an opinion that I had exhibited military capacity that warranted my appointment, but that "in the big wars that made ambition virtue" those who have the appointing power had full opportunity of judging of my fitness to command, and nothing could be said now that ought to have any influence on their judgment. The record was made up, and could not now be amended. I confess that I had a hope that my services would be accepted by the government, as General Grant had paid me a tribute in his memoirs, and President Hayes, who served in the same regiment with President McKinley, had given me a commission to represent the United States in a foreign country.

I hope that you and Governor Perkins will understand this letter as a simple explanation due to myself, and not as a complaint of any one.

Very respectfully,

JOHN S. MOSBY

San Francisco Call – **July 9, 1898**

MOSBY AND WHITE.

Correspondence on the Topic of Political Influence for War Commissions.

It seems likely that Colonel John S. Mosby's desire to serve his country will not be gratified unless political influence is invoked in his behalf. At the first sign of conflict with Spain, Col. Mosby, whose military record is too well known a story to require new telling, wired to his friend General Miles, who had desired his services that he was ready to serve.

Much to his surprise, the gallant Mosby received from Miles a brief response suggesting that he use "influence;" suggesting further that Colonel Mosby enlist in his cause the Congressional representatives of his State.

This the Colonel positively declined to do and allowed matters to remain as they were until two weeks ago when he received word that Rev. S. F. Chapman, of Virginia, an old friend, had approached Senator White on the subject. The colonel, knowing that Mr. Daniels was acting in a spirit of friendship, deemed it best, however, to inform Senator White that the action of Mr. Daniels was taken without his knowledge or consent [*There is an error in this obviously. The confusion is whether it was Chapman who approached White on Mosby's behalf, or Daniels. From White's response to Mosby, it becomes obvious that Chapman approached White, Daniels seemingly having nothing to do with the matter.-vph]

In his letter to Senator White Colonel Mosby, speaking of General Miles' suggestion that political influence be secured, wrote: "To this I replied that I had no influence to rely on except my record as a soldier, with which the President and the Secretary of War ought to be familiar, as they served in the Shenandoah Valley, and especially as the President in the first interview I had with him told me that I had kept him miserable all the time he was there. By my answer to General Miles I did not mean to intimate an opinion that I had exhibited military capacity that warranted my appointment, but that in the 'big wars that made ambition virtue' those who have the appointing power had full opportunity of judging of my fitness to command, and nothing could be said now that ought to have any influence on their judgment. The record was made up and could not now be amended. I confess that I had a hope that my services would be accepted by the Government, as General Grant had paid me a tribute in his Memoirs, and President Hayes, who served in the same regiment with President McKinley, had given me a commission to represent the United States in a foreign country. I hope that you and Governor Perkins will understand this letter as a simple explanation due to myself, and not as a complaint of any one.

In response to Colonel Mosby's letter of explanation, Senator White wrote:

Washington, D. C. July 2, 1898

Colonel John S. Mosby, Attorney, San Francisco, Cal.—

Dear Colonel:

Yours of the 25th ult. Received. Senator Perkins and I indorsed you to the President and urged your appointment, but I took the liberty of stating to the Rev. S. F. Chapman that I thought it absurd to request anybody to indorse you. Your record must be known to every intelligent American, and to assume that anything could be told the President regarding your military qualifications would be to insinuate a lack of ordinary mentality on his part. Nevertheless it seemed to some of our delegation that we ought to show we were in favor of your aspirations, and the matter was therefore placed before Mr. McKinley with our emphatic indorsement.

Yours truly, STEPHEN M. WHITE.

A local newspaper interviewed Mosby on his opinion of the conduct of the war and the Cuban "assistance" given American forces. As usual, he was happy to oblige:

San Francisco Call – July 10, 1898 (Edited)

A FAMOUS SOUTHERN GUERILLA COMMANDER.

What Colonel Mosby Thinks of Garcia's Failure to Stop Pando.

Colonel John S. Mosby thinks that the Cubans are poor soldiers, and that they have hurt rather than helped the United States troops in his opinion. The Cubans should be adapted to guerrilla warfare in their own country. They have had years in which to practice that style of fighting. No man in America is more competent to speak of what guerrillas should accomplish than Mosby. He was the guerrilla leader of the South in the Civil War. By his tactics he was able to offset forces that outnumbered him at least one hundred to one. To-day he has the same keen face and keen mind as then. He is grayer, he has lost one of his unflinching eyes, and fortune has not treated him as well as it promised; but he is still cool, alert and sagacious. When this Confederate officer who won historical fame as a guerrilla strategist speaks of the guerrillas of Cuba his words express scorn.

"The Cubans under Garcia should not have permitted Pando, with his thousands of Spanish troops to enter Santiago," he said "Pando, as I understand it, was 125 miles from Santiago, and to reach that city he had to cross a mountainous country, going through narrow passes. There were a thousand opportunities for Garcia to repeat what Leonidas and his 300 Spartans did at the pass at Thermopylae. A few hundred men could have so checked the march of the Spaniards that they would have needed six months to get to Santiago. That may seem a remarkable assertion, but I know by experience how it is possible for a few men to impede a large body by obstructing the advancing force in front and harassing it in the rear."

"Give an example from your own experience," was suggested. [Here Mosby went into a description of his command's war against Sheridan in the Valley.-vph]

Mosby observed that in Cuba the natural conditions are far more favorable for guerrilla operations than they were where he operated.

"In a hilly region a small force can be more affective than in a pastoral country," he said. "The defiles, rocks and declivities are an advantage. We were in an open country and had to fight on horseback. We had no shelter. Bushwhacking is perfectly legitimate in war, and if the Cubans had availed themselves of the protection afforded by their mountainous country and bushwhacked Pando's army it would have taken him six months to reach Santiago. A bushwhacker should have a long-range gun and shoot from behind cover. My men had nothing but a pair of Colt's revolvers. They fought mounted and campaigned in the blue grass region, and no men in the Confederate army were so little entitled to the name of bushwhackers; but what they accomplished showed how much energetic guerrillas may do.

In the opinion of Mosby, the Cubans are fit for nothing if they are not fit for guerrilla warfare. He mentioned the services rendered by Marion and his men in the swamps of South Carolina in the beginning of this Nation's history in speaking of the help which such fighters can render a cause.

"I do not see where the Cubans gave any sort of assistance at Santiago," he continued. "They should have been useful as scouts and guides, and if they were Roosevelt and his Rough Riders would not have run into that ambuscade, which resulted in the killing of many of our soldiers. The Cuban army is to me as much of a phantom as Cervera's fleet is at the present time. The Cubans seem to look on the United States Army as their big brother, and are willing to let it do all the fighting."

Mosby states that he began operations for the Confederacy with only fifteen men in February, 1863; and his command gradually increased to about 300. He hovered around Washington, and on account of his jumping from place to place, thus making it uncertain as to how many men he had for attack, from 20,000 to 30,000 troops were kept at the capital.

Mosby this year offered to raise a battalion or regiment of cavalry for operations like that which he carried on in the Civil War, but the suggestion made by General Miles regarding the procedure to be followed to obtain a commission was not in accord with his views, and the matter fell through. He says that John A. Edmunds, who while a small boy joined his command and was wounded in a fight with the California Cavalry Battalion in Virginia on February 23, 1864, has been appointed a Colonel of one of the Texas regiments by the Governor of that State. A few lessons in the art of war might have been of value to the Cubans, Mosby thinks, and his men would have been able to afford them such instruction as they seem to have required.

Finally, in late July, as the war was ending, the *Alexandria Gazette* brought the matter into sharper focus. Mosby had been pointed out to Secretary Alger while that gentleman was staying in a San Francisco hotel. His response at learning Mosby's identity made all that had happened perfectly clear:

Alexandria Gazette – July 20, 1898

A Virginia ex-Confederate here to-day says the reason Colonel Mosby was not offered a commission in the volunteer army, though hundreds of less conspicuous ex-Confederates have been, is the objection of Secretary Alger, who once in a San Francisco hotel when the Colonel was pointed out to him, remarked that he didn't like to look upon a man who had treated some Union prisoners as the Colonel had, and that that remark having been subsequently reported to the Colonel, he sent his respects to Mr. Alger with the expressed regret that he, Alger, had not been one of the prisoners referred to.

John Mosby's response to Alger was typical Mosby! Alger sent his men to rob, pillage, and burn; so Mosby would have preferred seeing the man who ordered these crimes pay the price his men paid. Meanwhile, other newspapers around the country weighed in on Mosby's offer of service and the benefit that such service might have provided to a nation that engaged in a particular type of war—Mosby's type of war. And once again, Mosby was quoted on his opinion of the Cuban soldiers, an opinion with which the Gazette obviously agreed:

Alexandria Gazette – August 2, 1898

Col. Mosby.—Col. John S. Mosby, the noted Confederate guerrilla leader, has a poor opinion of the fighting qualities of the Cubans, and thinks that they have hurt rather than helped the American arms. He says Garcia should not have permitted Pando to effect a juncture with Linares' forces in Santiago, and claims that a few hundred men, if they were good guerilla fighters, could have so checked the march of the Spaniards that they would have needed six months to get to Santiago. When we judge of the effective work accomplished by Mosby and his band of 300 men in checking the advance of Sheridan's army of 50,000 in the Shenandoah valley in 1864, we are forced to the conclusion that his estimate of the Cuban soldiers is about correct.—[Downieville, Cal., Messenger.

In August, as the war ended, a singular article appeared in the *San Francisco Call*. John Mosby had made his desire to serve known to Collis Huntington, his employer and friend, president of the Southern Pacific Railroad. After all, as an employee of the road, Mosby felt the need to advise his employer that he might have to absent himself for the duration. The Call reported with some pride, Huntington's gracious response:

San Francisco Call – August 30, 1898

An Act of Colossal Generosity.

When the war with Spain was in its incipiency and the fervor of patriotism was performing triple somersaults in the breasts of old and young, Colonel Mosby, of the Southern Pacific law department, determined to offer his services to his country. The native hue of his resolution paled somewhat when he thought of his chief and master, Collis P. Would he sanction the action was the question the fighter of another generation plied himself with to his complete confusion of mind. Collis listened attentively to his interlocutor, and when he was told that Mosby wanted to buckle on the armor of his youth and fight for the stars and stripes the venerable and charitable president of an impoverished road rose up from his seat, his eyes ablaze with charity and benevolence to all the world. In the loftiness of self-sacrifice, he said: *"Tell Mosby I will place an official sanction on his act. I have been pondering for some time how I could assist the Government in its present trouble. This will be my gift to my country. Others of vast wealth may give batteries and ships, but I give a man* [emphasis vph]*."*

It had been many a long year since someone had said such a gracious thing to or about John Mosby. He certainly had deserved that and much more from those for whom he had done better service! Nonetheless, it must have been some consolation, deprived as he had been from serving.

But Mosby was not finished "fighting" with his pen. He sent another missal to the *Alexandria Gazette* regarding what had begun to "shake out" after the armistice. In his comments, Mosby proved to be no advocate of the emerging American empire:

Alexandria Gazette – **September 9, 1898**

COLONEL MOSBY ON THE WAR

To the Editor of the *Alexandria Gazette*:

In the declaration of war against Spain, Congress stultified itself by declaring that "Cuba is, and of right ought to be free and independent," but refusing to admit the existence of any government in the island that was hostile to Spain. When Louis XVI became the ally of the colonials in the war of the revolution he recognized the American Congress as the government of the country, and George Washington as commander in chief of its armies. Could anybody imagine such a correspondence between Washington and Lafayette as that between Garcia and Shafter? Now, by independence I meant a community or body politic, that exercises the functions of government over a territory to the exclusion of any other sovereignty. How people can be independent without being united under some from of government is as hard to conceive as the existence of a human being without any vital organs. If there was ever such an organization in Cuba the U. S. army has dispersed it and made war on a people they professedly went on a crusade to liberate. Outside the American line there is not the phantom of a government, while on the inside the Spanish officials by permission continue to discharge their duty to society. The insurgents are simply allowed to draw rations. On such an adventure and in behalf of such a race a great army has been raised and taxes imposed. In every pot of tea we pour a libation to Gomez and Garcia. The close of the 19th century has witnessed the renaissance of the institution of chivalry, but not a Richard or a Saladin. Don Quixote is no longer the representative of an absolute idea, the type of a pre-historic age. The imagination that created national heroes out of Cuban banditti could also see Mambrinos' helmet in a barber's basin and a self-sacrificing patriot in Jesse James. In his description of the Knight of La Mancha, Cervantes says: "In time, his judgment being completely obscured, he was seized with one of the strangest fancies that ever entered the head of a madman; this was a persuasion that it behooved him, as well for the advancement of his glory as the service of his country, to become a knight-errant and traverse the world, armed and mounted in quest of adventure, and to practice all that had been performed by the knights-errant of whom he had read, redressing every species of grievance and exposing himself to dangers to which, being so mounted, might secure to him eternal glory and renown." Which means that Don Quixote is no longer a Spaniard, but a naturalized American.

In the protocol already signed Spain has surrendered her West Indian possessions, where her flag has floated ever since Columbus caught sight of land from the deck of the Pinta, but she has really sacrificed nothing but pride. The same casuistry that persuaded Congressmen that the cause of banditti was the cause of humanity, will enable them to see their way clear to disregard their pledge not to annex the gem of the Antilles.

The annexation of the Philippines is the next problem to be solved. The archipelago is inhabited by some eight million Malays and half-caste Spaniards. Piracy is the natural occupation of the race. They live in a chronic state of rebellion, and it would require a large army and navy to enforce the national authority among them. The islands lie in the tropics and the white race can never flourish among them. The industries are largely controlled by Chinese; sugar is one of the principal products of the islands; a great deal of raw sugar and hemp are exported to the United States. The wealth is largely in the hands of the Catholic church, but a large portion of the population is Mohammedan. The constitution requires "all duties, imports and excises shall be uniform throughout the United States." We now derive a large revenue from imports from the Philippines. If they are annexed we will have to stand the loss of this revenue as well as the cost of governing a distant dependency that will always keep us in danger of war. We could no more levy customs duties on imports from the Philippines than Virginia could tax the fruit she imports from California. In other words, we will have free trade with the Philippines. Then what say the advocates of a protective tariff and Chinese restriction laws that were designed to encourage home production and a home market, and as a defense of American against cheap Asiatic labor? Can the beet sugar industry thrive here in competition with the Philippines? If we hold the Philippines, a conflict with the Catholic Church is inevitable. Congress deprived the Mormon church of its holding, making polygamy a felony. But the wealth and power of the Church of Mormon were insignificant compared with that of the monasteries and Spanish friars in the Philippines. It may devolve on President McKinley to act the part for the Church of Henry the Eighth. This may bring upon us a religious war and a papal bull of excommunication. A large portion of the population is Mohammadens and the Malay has as many wives as the Koran allows a Mussulman, But the statutes of the United States make polygamy a felony. Are we going to punish the Mormons and grant a plenary indulgence to the Malays? In holding such distant territory we assume a burden without compensating benefit. It is said that American capital would develop them, and pour into our lap the wealth of Ormus and of Ind. Even if it did develop them the world at large would get the benefit; we would have no monopoly. There never was a greater fallacy than the idea that trade follows the flag. Commerce is not governed by sentiment, but by the markets. The day has passed when colonies could be governed for the benefit of the mother country. In the English colonies foreigners enjoy every privilege in trade that an Englishman has. In annexing the Philippines we would simply play the part of universal philanthropists. Adventurers like Clive and Hastings are no longer sent out to plunder them.

But the truth is we are borrowers and have no surplus capital to send to foreign lands; we need it for our own internal development. Instead of dissipating the United States should concentrate its power and its wealth. We can find employment at home for all our capital in building railroads and canals, and irrigating the arid lands of Colorado and Arizona. Water will make our deserts more fruitful than the Asiatic jungles. To every suggestion of a departure from the traditions under which we have let the answer be "Procul, O procul este, porfani!"**

J. S. M. San Francisco, Cal. Sept. 2, 1898

[**"Keep away, oh keep away, you profane ones!" (Virgil)-vph]

Denouncing his country's thrust into empire building, Mosby stated that the old "days of empire" were over and that any such efforts would produce waste and war without any of the economic returns politicians believed justified their actions. He brought to light the religious problems as well as the imposition of American social laws and customs upon these conquered people. And he further noted that if attempts were made to enforce American values in the Philippines, the result would be unknown and unintended consequences. Most Americans, even those who were Catholic, had no idea of the very different understanding of that Church in those areas of the world formerly under Spain and therefore could not understand what might happen when a clash not only of race and culture, but of politics and religion arose.

The reunion of Mosby's Men again took place in the fall and, as usual, began to attract press coverage:

Evening Star, – **October 25, 1898**

IN ANNUAL REUNION

Survivors of Mosby's Battalion Meet and Elect Officers Sketch of the Commander of the Celebrated Rangers
HIS WORK DURING THE WAR

Evening Star, – **October 26, 1898**

MOSBY SENT HIS REGRETS

Unable to Attend the Banquet at the Reunion of His Veterans.

As the last year of this most turbulent century began, John Mosby still found himself in the thick of national, international, and personal tumult. His situation with the Southern Pacific was still in flux, and he still had little hope of a position with the government under the present Republican administration! The consequences of his efforts to serve during the short-lived war with Spain were still resonating badly in the halls of government and across the nation's fourth estate, while the coming new year, 1899, did not promise any quick or favorable end to his many woes.

Chapter 38

1899

"Pede poena claudo." ~ "Retribution comes slowly, but surely."
~ Horace

"Oh Time! the beautifier of the dead, adorer of the ruin, comforter
and only healer when the heart hath bled ... Time, the avenger!"
~ Lord Byron

EARLY IN 1899, a little article appeared illustrating Mosby's natural generosity of spirit:

Richmond Dispatch – January 19, 1899

A Tribute to Mr. Jordan

Mr. H. M. Smith, Jr., has received from Mr. H. Colie Jordan a copy of Williamson's "Mosby's Rangers." It was intended as a Christmas present, but arrived a little late, because the donor sent it to his old colonel, John S. Mosby, for his autograph. Colonel Mosby has written the following inscription on the flyleaf:

"This book was a present to H. M. Smith, Jr., from H. Colie Jordan, one of the best and bravest men of my command.

JOHN S. MOSBY.

"January 11, 1899."

It was a small and seemingly unimportant piece filled with good cheer appropriate to the season. But it was also far more than that. It showed Mosby's greatness of heart, of which Mr. Jordan was obviously aware when he sent the book to his commander to be "autographed." Notice, Mosby did not just sign his name but took the time and trouble to acknowledge the value of the giver. One of Mosby's most endearing qualities was his willingness—indeed, eagerness—to recognize the worth and heroism of his men and others with whom he had campaigned. One of his Rangers pointed out that of all the treasures Mosby's men gained in the war, nothing was more coveted by them than to hear him say, "He is one of my best men!"

The press never tired of the tales of Mosby's Men. Their recounting no longer required some reason such as a reunion or anniversary, and certainly few press recitals could be directly linked to Mosby himself; those that were, carried his byline. Indeed, these narratives had taken on the aspect of lore and legend, especially in the South. One such appeared in the *Edgefield Advertiser* on February 22, a recounting of the capture of General Stoughton—one of the most popular of the tales.

Meanwhile, Mosby kept up his objections to what was becoming ever more clear after the Treaty of Paris ending the Spanish War; that is, American "expansionism." When it was obvious that the "liberation" of the Philippines had become simply the exchange of one foreign rule (Spain) for another (the United States), Mosby sent a letter to *The Times* which that paper termed as a "bold plea" for Filipino independence:

The Times – **March 11, 1899**

BOLD PLEA FOR THE FILIPINOS.

Col. Mosby Says They Should Be Given Their Independence.

THE CRY OF "ANARCHY" A RUSE.

References to Striking Incidents of History to Support of the Contention—Commercial Gains the Real Motive for Expansion.

San Francisco, March 2, 1899 Editor of *The Times*:

Sir:—It is urged that if we withdraw from the Philippines we abandon the islands to anarchy and chaos. This is a pure assumption; reason and experience are against it. The inhabitants of the Philippines are superior as a race and have shown far more capacity for political organization than the Cubans, to whom, we have promised independence. We owe a duty to ourselves as well as to the Filipinos to let them work out the problems of government as our fathers did in the American forests. If the rule of the Spaniard was cruel and despotic, then anarchy would at least be a relief. Disorder has always been the first fruit of revolution; but revolution is the parent of progress. Change is better than a stagnant despotism; even anarchy in Asia would be a sign of improvement. But the dread of anarchy did not deter the lovers of liberty from giving their aid and sympathy to Bolivar and Marco Bozzaris. When Byron drew his sword for the Greeks he advised them to trust in themselves.

"In native swords and native ranks The only hope of courage dwells."

NO DANGER OF ANARCHY

The Filipinos have certainly attained as high a degree of civilization as the Turks, Persians, Corsicans, Siamese and Chinese, whose right to self-government we recognize by receiving their ambassadors and sending ambassadors to their courts. A larger portion of the people of the Philippines profess Christianity than of any other country in Asia. Why should they not be at least on an equality with the Mahommodans and Buddhists whose flags fly over the legations at Washington? Why is the Crescent preferred to the Cross? A small part of the force that has been applied to extinguish national life in the Philippines might have aided the people to restore peace and establish order, and might thus have saved us the bloody tragedies of Manila and Hoilo. Instead of commanding them to disperse, a friendly offer of cooperation would have been more in harmony with American traditions. When negotiations first began all that was asked was a coaling station. This was only tentative to feel the public pulse.

A SPECIOUS COVER

In an article in "The Nation," of August 18th last, the writer said: "The plea of a necessity for having coaling stations is made a pretext for demanding the permanent occupation of ports in the Ladrones and Philippines. It is a specious cover to justify the extension of our dominion over the area and is Beucufield's policy* (in spirit) of extending the boundaries of the empire to secure a scientific frontier that always recedes before the advance of the British army. [*British general of the era – vph] The argument is as plausible as that which persuaded the Donna Julia to permit 'a Platonic squeeze'— the first step that led to her fall. The claim of the annexationalists soon included the whole archipelago, and as we could not need 1,200 islands for coaling stations, the mask of anarchy was dragged on the stage as a substitution. If the Philippines were left alone order would soon be evolved from chaos. Such is the law of nature. Under the rule of a foreign dictator, they would learn no more about self-government than the Hindoo in a century has from his English masters. Macaulay, in his essay on Milton, has answered the objections of those who are not willing to trust men to govern themselves until they have learned the art of government. "There is only one cure for the evils which newly acquired freedom produces, and that is freedom. Many politicians of our time are in the habit of laying it down as a self-evident proposition that no people ought to be free till they are fit to use freedom. The maxim is worthy of the fool in the old story who resolved not to go into the water till he had learnt to swim. If men are to wait for liberty till they become wise and good in slavery they may indeed, wait forever.

FOR COMMERCIAL GAIN

Those who have carried the torch of liberty in the van of progress have not been frightened by the spectre of anarchy. Commercial gain, not philanthropy is the real motive for territorial extension. That is the phantom that lured us to the Orient. When the islands are annexed they will still be as far away as they are now, their population and climate will still be the same. The political connection will not increase their capacity to consume; the United States would not have a monopoly of their trader colonies can no longer be exploited as a plantation. There has been an enormous growth of our commerce with China in the last few years but that is due primarily to the railroads that have developed the Pacific coast. As soon as the United States acquires possessions in Asia we become involved with European nations in the question of the balance of power. One hemisphere is enough for us.

DO NOT ENSLAVE THEM

In his famous figure of the Indian Chief, Erskine portrayed the feelings of men of every race and every clime who are compelled to bow to a foreign yoke. "I know what they feel," said the great advocate, "and how such feelings can alone be repressed. I have heard them in my youth from a naked savage in the indignant character of a prince surrounded by his subjects, addressing the Governor of a British colony, holding a bundle of sticks in his hand as the notes of his unuttered eloquence. 'Who is it,' said the jealous ruler over the desert encroached upon by the restless foot of English adventure. 'Who is it that causes this river to rise in the high mountains and to empty itself into the Ocean? Who is it that causes to blow the cold winds of the winter and then calms them again in the summer? Who is sit that rears up the shades of the lofty forests and blasts them with the quick lightning at His pleasure? The same being that gave to you a country on the other side of the water and gave ours to us, and by this title we defend it,' said the warrior, throwing down his tomahawk upon the ground and raising the war sound of his nation. These are the feelings of subjugated men all around the globe and, depend upon it, nothing but fear will control where it is vain to look for affection.

The Bengal princes would have hailed anarchy as a benediction when Englishmen were plundering the [illegible] of Oude. That the Filipino is not in the torpid state of other Asiatics is shown by his active resistance to foreign rule and proves his superiority and capacity for self-government. And now it is proposed that we imitate the English in India and repeat our own folly by shipping a lot of vultures to the Philippines. That the Filipino is not fit to govern the Anglo-Saxon is admitted; that the Anglo-Saxon should not enslave the Filipino should not be disputed, at least by those who enfranchised the negro and made the South the footstool of the African.

THE PROMISE BROKEN

On the trial of Warren Hastings, Sheridan gave voice to sentiments that find an echo in every heart not callous to human suffering. Alluding to the despairing cry of the Hindoo, the great orator said:

"What motive, then could have such influence on their bosom? What motive! That which nature—the common parent plants in the bosom of men—and which, though it may be less active in the Indian than in the Englishman, is still congenial with and makes a part of his being. That feeling which tells him that man was never made to be the property of man; but that when, in the pride and insolence of power, one human creature dares to tyrannize over another it is a power usurped and resistance is a duty."

The Filipinos, as an ally of the United States, was fighting for independence. As soon as the treaty was signed, and long before it was ratified, they were commanded by proclamation to disperse. Instead of an offer to co-operate with them in forming a government, they were told that "the military government heretofore maintained by the United States in the city, harbor and bay of manila is to be extended with all possible dispatch to the whole of the ceded territory." The word of promise was thus broken to the hopes. The proclamation was a declaration of war. It converted friends into enemies. Yet, Mr. Foraker declared in the Senate that he knew nobody who wanted to deny independence to the Filipinos "except temporarily." But why temporarily? When the proclamation was issued there was far more semblance of local government in the Philippines than there was in Mexico when the treaty of Guadalupe-Hidalgo was concluded. In his history of the Mexican war, Ripley says that after the flight of Santa Ana, all the elements of Mexican national authority was dissipated and dispersed over the whole extent of the country. Scott had first to create a government with which to negotiate peace How many revolutions were there in Mexico before it had a stable government?

I DENY THE FACT

At a meeting of the Academy of Sciences of France the question was opened for discussion, "Why is it that a pail of water will weigh no more with five fish in it than out of it? Each member gave his response, a priori in support of the theory that nobody opposed, when it came to Dr. Franklin's turn, who then answered, "I deny the fact" and then, according to the Baconian method, he illustrated the falsehood by experiment. So, when in demonstration of the teaching of history, it is assumed that anarchy and chaos must result from the withdrawal of the American troops from the Philippines, I say with Ben Franklin—I deny the facts.

In their feverish exultations,

In their triumph and their yearning,

In their passionate pulsations,

In their words among the nations,

The Promethean fire is burning.

John S. Mosby

But Mosby wasn't finished quite yet with McKinley. The Republican Party in Massachusetts was kicking up a fuss, and with tongue set firmly in cheek, Mosby wrote to the president offering his services to "suppress the rebellion in Boston." The matter was carried with considerable glee in the newspapers, especially the Southern Democratic organs:

Alexandria Gazette – **May 10, 1899**

The *Free Lance* – **May 18, 1899**

Mosby and McKinley.

The *Alexandria Gazette* says: "Col. Mosby is a keen satirist. Remembering that McKinley, after assuring him and his friends that he intended to appoint him to a "good position" abroad, broke that promise because the G.A.R. protested against the appointment of a 'rebel,' has telegraphed the President, tendering his services to suppress the 'rebellion' of Hoar and Atkinson in Boston. The Col. can fight with the pen as well as with the sword."

In a way, however, the "rebellion" was one with which Mosby agreed as the Bostonians were also against the colonization of the Philippines. Still, the idea that opposing government policies was "treason"—the belief of both Abraham Lincoln and Daniel Webster!—gave Mosby the opportunity to tweak the nose of the strongly Northern administration. McKinley had proven himself no friend of Mosby's or the South. By noting that such rebellious sentiments could be found in the North as well as the South (and offering to represent the government in any stand against it), Mosby made his point with McKinley and his administration in a way that they undoubtedly understood, if not appreciated.

Meanwhile, the GAR continued to cause grief for any former Confederates in McKinley's government as can be seen by this article in the *Alexandria Gazette*. It was becoming more and more clear that as the new century approached, *Northern* rather than Southern prejudices continued the passions of a war that had been over for almost half a century:

Alexandria Gazette – May 19, 1899

The opposition of the G.A.R. to Mr. Evans, the Commissioner of Pensions, who wants to conduct his office honestly, is causing the administration no little anxiety. The influence of that organization is not to be disregarded, as was shown by the effect of its opposition to Col. Mosby. The leaders of it have no love for Southern men, no matter how pronounced their republicanism may be.

However, events were catching up at least with Secretary Alger, as events always do; and his mismanagement of the military was being widely reported with Mosby's situation being a prominent, but by no means only example of Alger's incompetence:

Anaconda Standard – June 5, 1899

Another Case of Algerism.

Besides being incompetent, Secretary Alger is a pretty small man in every way. Colonel Mosby, the famous Confederate guerilla raider, tells a story that illustrates the fact Mosby says he was unable to serve in the war with Spain because he would not ask for political backing to get an army appointment. He says when war broke out he offered his services to General Miles, who replied that he would be very glad to recommend him for a position, but suggested that, inasmuch as political influence was important in securing command, he write to the senators from California and ask them to recommend him to the president. Colonel Mosby thought that his fighting record needed no political endorsements when it had the endorsements of both Generals Grant and Lee as to efficacy, and he declined to ask the senators. By way of adorning the take of his failure to get a fighting chance he tells of meeting President McKinley after the inauguration, when the president said: "Well, colonel, you made me more miserable during the war than any other man I know of." "I trust I have atoned for it now, Mr. President," replied the Colonel, "for I both voted and worked for your election." "I did not think it necessary," he continued, referring to the incident, "to ask a couple of senators to try to get me a commission, when McKinley knew me before he ever heard of them. I have learned since that the fact that I was recommended by General Miles antagonized Alger. I did not then know of the enmity between them."

In this small piece in the Bee, John Mosby declared that time had vindicated him and that his Southern enemies of the past "see it now." Yet given the still "solid South," the less-than-welcoming nature of Republican administrations to Southerners taken with his own ambiguous situation in Virginia, Mosby's confident determination seemed somewhat premature:

Omaha Daily Bee – June 6, 1899

Col. J. S. Mosby, once famous as a confederate guerrilla, said recently in a Spokane interview: "I won the animosity of the south by turning republican in the reconstruction days and it has taken all these years to make my enemies begin to see I was right, but I'm sure they see it now."

John Mosby had often been damned by Union veterans, but he had also been praised. One such letter appeared in *The Times*. The odd thing about these tributes is that they never seemed to make the GAR publications:

The Times – September 9, 1899 (Edited)

HE PRAISES MOSBY.

A Union Veteran's Tribute to the Famous Confederate Raider.

The following is taken from the Madison (Indiana) Courier, and will be read with interest by many of the friends of Colonel John S. Mosby in Virginia. It is from the pen of Thomas G. Day, who was a member of Company E, Third Indiana Cavalry, during the Civil War.

Correct, Ind. August 21, 1899

Editor Courier:

Dear Sir.—

We scarcely ever do a good turn but we receive a reward. I see in your weekly issue of August 16th a letter from Professor H. W. Wiley, chief chemist of the United States Department of Agriculture, of an interview with Colonel J. S. Mosby, the great Confederate guerila. Prof. Wiley was one of the lecturers at our Farmers' Institute at Osgood last winter; he told me Salon Tilford and John Gassaway of Company E. were cousins of his, and he was well acquainted with Justice Hall and Velmore Prentice, who were in Andersonville prison with me. The latter died there. He was one of our best soldiers. I told Mr. Wiley I was captured by Mosby and how kindly he treated me, and that I would be very glad to see him. He said he met Colonel Mosby at his home in Washington, and I asked him if he could get me his address, and since seeing your valuable paper I shall write to him I have always had a kindly feeling for Colonel Mosby from that time and hoped some time to hear from him or to see him, and if he ever gets in this part of the country and will visit us, we will give him the best we have.

I can't see to write well, but some time if the spirit moves and it is acceptable to you, I will write a full account of the capture, (and, as Colonel Mosby said to an Indianapolis paper some years ago), "one of the most romantic episodes of the war," taken in connection with the character we than had of Mosby (the) Guerrilla, the man that hung Yanks at Berryville and on the Aldie pike. The reason for this he explained to me, Mosby's Guerillas were more dreaded by us than all Stuart's cavalry and damaged our army more than any other Confederate corps.

The reunion of Mosby's men was scheduled for the twenty-third of September. But this was a very different year. It wouldn't just be feasting and singing and happy reminiscences. A very serious and mournful matter was to be accomplished, the dedication of the Front Royal Monument. Because of the nature of the reunion (and possibly the belief that Mosby would attend the dedication), there was a great deal of press coverage:

The Times – September 10, 1899 (Edited)

IN MEMORY OF THEIR COMRADES

Mosby's Men to Dedicate a Monument at Front Royal. Occasion Tinged With Pain. Still Feel Indignation at Cruel Action. The Programme Arranged for the Event, Which Occurs on September 23rd.

The reunion of Mosby's gallant men at Front Royal on the 23rd of this month is to them an occasion pleasant but not unmixed with sadness. They meet to dedicate a monument to seven of their comrades who were hung on September 23, 1864 by order of General Custer.

Though the blood of the veterans has been cooled by the flight of years, they still feel indignation at the cruel and unusual practice in civilized warfare, although their comrades were avenged by the subsequent hanging of an equal number of Custer's soldiers who fell into the hands of Mosby's men.

THE MONUMENT.

The monument is a handsome one. It is of granite and twenty-five feet in height. On one side appears a Confederate flag and the motto: "Dulce et Decorum est pro patria mori." On another side is the following inscription:

In Everlasting Honor Of

Thomas E. Anderson,

— Carter,

Duval L. Jones,

Lucian Love,

William Thomas Overby,

Henry C. Rhodes,

Albert C. Willis,

Forty-third Battalion, Virginia Cavalry,

Mosby's Command, C. S. A.

On the third side can be found the following:

Erected 1899

By the Survivors of Mosby's Command.

In Memory of Seven Comrades Executed While Prisoners of War,

Near this Spot.

September 23, 1864.

Mosby's Men.

All of these gallant men, who gave their lives for their country, were natives of Virginia, except Overby, who came from Georgia.

The full name of Carter cannot be ascertained.

Although all the war records have been searched,

no mention is made of the "gallant" deed near Front Royal.

Though it was seldom mentioned (however, Mosby mentioned it!), the treatment of Mosby's men at Front Royal made no "official report," which seems strange given that Grant had ordered any of the command, including Mosby himself, hanged without trial if captured. Ergo, none could claim that the murders went unreported for fear of official reprisal! Yet they were not reported, at least officially for the record. The reason why was also not reported.

As the war in the Philippines went on, there was a great deal of complaint about the "competency" of the American military leaders, but some newspapers pointed out that the regular US forces had never been very successful in the type of war that was being waged in that island nation:

Commercial Advertiser – November 18, 1899 (Edited)
Hawaiian Gazette – **November 21, 1899**
COMPETENCY OF OTIS

We print elsewhere some interesting Commentary upon the state of affairs in the Philippines in which the author, Mr. Albert P. Taylor, criticizes General Otis' management of the war. The points made reduce themselves to the postulate that if Otis were a strong commander he could, without much delay, bring the fighting to an end. For ourselves we confess a doubt as to the justice of this conclusion. General Otis has a small army in a large country. With from 20,000 to 50,000 men—the former figure standing for his active force during the first year's campaign—he has operated amidst an unfriendly population of several millions and against a guerrilla army aggregating 30,000 men and capable of indefinite and instant reinforcement. A guerrilla war is the most difficult of any for a General engaged in legitimate operations, to contend with. During the American Civil war Colonel Mosby with 500 mounted farmers, lineal descendants of the stout swashbucklers of Sumter and Marion, terrorized the Union border for two years and kept 40,000 Federal troops idly guarding points which he might possibly attack. Mosby was too much for Custer, Sheridan and Grant and his little command held its ground until after Appomattox. In the light of these examples of partisan warfare we cannot justly blame General Otis for his failure, in a year and a half, to capture or destroy the elusive native riflemen who haunt the wide swamps and jungles of Luzon. Were dashing Phil Sheridan in his place we do not believe the showing would be better.

This article was a faint echo of what might have happened at the end of the so-called Civil War. Some of Lee's subordinates wanted him to order his men to the hills and fight the kind of war noted here. Of course, he already had the "Prince of Partisans" in his own theater. Indeed, Mosby sent a scout to Lee in Richmond after his surrender to ask if he should fight on. Had Lee said yes, there is no doubt that Mosby and most of his stalwarts would have done so. Of course, as the Union troops occupied more of the South, others would have joined them. As a result, the situation in the South would soon have deteriorated into a deadly game of death and retaliation. As the total war already waged by the North had made their government and armies hated, it is quite probable that many Southerners would have acquiesced to and joined in such a war. And with the Federal capital virtually within the upper borders of the former Confederacy, the matter could have become far more ugly than it did even under Reconstruction.

Mosby's last newspaper appearance of the nineteenth century was a lengthy article in the *Alexandria Gazette* printed on December 28 recounting the Berryville Wagon Train Raid of August 13, 1864. The article was introduced by a letter dated December 16 from Mosby to his favorite scout, John Russell, in which he spoke of paintings of the raid created in Paris from photographs of his men. It was a fine letter, rather "gossipy" and filled with gentle reminiscences of both the tragic (the death of young Ranger Lewis Adie) and the absurd (the attack of the yellow jackets). Mosby then went on to speak of other incidents of the war, his writings being accompanied by his usual classical references. Whatever lay ahead in the new century, it is clear from this letter that John Mosby was prepared to "soldier on".

Chapter 39

1900

Pro opportunitate ~ As circumstances allow

"A wise man will make more opportunities than he finds." ~ Francis Bacon

THE TWENTIETH CENTURY had finally dawned, and it was an election year with the same opponents as had skirmished four years earlier. It proved to be a brief "hiatus" for Mosby, absent the controversies, conflicts, and tumults that had attended the second half decade of the previous century. At his last birthday (December 6, 1899), John Singleton Mosby had reached the venerable age of sixty-six, a respectable achievement for a man destined never to survive to reach manhood (according to the physicians of his youth), who had fought in a bloody war and been seriously wounded several times, as well as being ordered hanged without trial if captured and who, for the last five years, had suffered a horrendous injury coupled with intermittent, debilitating bouts of appendicitis. Indeed, John Mosby was proving to be far hardier than anyone could have anticipated, a further annoyance to his enemies.

But the old century had ended on an uncertain note as Mosby's employment situation remained in limbo. The election, and eventual reelection, of Republican William McKinley—far from solving his problem—seemed to suggest that there was little hope of succor in that direction. And still, Mosby's financial obligations to members of his family caused him anxiety, especially after the departure of his friend Collis P. Huntington from the Southern Pacific, followed shortly thereafter by the great man's death. However, it soon became obvious that Mosby had the support not only of important Republicans, but even of many Democrats at the federal level; and at the end of his employment with the railroad after Huntington's departure, McKinley, grudgingly perhaps, provided his challenging supporter with an office—or more precisely, a *job*—in his second term. Mosby was not offered a consulate, something for which a man of his age and experience as a lawyer and former consul was eminently suited, but a "job" as an investigator in the Office of Land Management, part of the Department of the Interior. In fact, he was glad enough to get it! Further, Mosby as an agent of the Land Bureau sent willy-nilly about the country on various relatively unimportant assignments appeared harmless enough to the Washington politicians and bureaucrats. Yet employing John Mosby in *any* capacity was seldom harmless. But that situation was still a year away as Mosby was not released from the road until January of 1901.

In other matters, the "war" in the Philippines continued. The death of American General Henry Ware Lawton at the hands of Filipino guerrillas close to the capital city caused a stir, but the *Daily Tribune* pointed out that "guerrilla activities" ceased once the side on which such contingents fought had been defeated. As part of a much longer article, the *Tribune* pointed this out using Mosby's command as an example:

New York Daily Tribune **– January 2, 1900 (Edited)**
THE MARAQUINA VALLEY CAMPAIGN

The killing of General Lawton within fifteen miles of the capital city of the Philippines has been clamorously seized upon by the anti-imperialist organs to enforce their plea that they insurgents are no nearer subjugation than they were at the outbreak of Aguinaldo's rebellion. They make an object less of Lawton's death in an engagement within hearing of the American military headquarters in proof that a bloody war is waging, notwithstanding recent official assurances that the war was about over. Of course, the killing of an American general in actual combat is evidence that hostilities are still maintained, which has not been denied, but its occurrence so near to Manila is of no consequence. It is far from signifying that our arms have made no progress, or that the rebels are not even now in straits, or that they are unconquerable. The fact that a small force of Aguinaldo's irregulars had continued to hold this advanced post cannot be set down to their invincibility; it simply means that in the strategy of the campaign no decisive attention has been paid to them and their whereabouts, the valley, it should be remembered also, has been penetrated several times by General Otis's detachments, though evidently without any intention of holding it permanently. Upon their withdrawal the enemy resumed his former position. But having scattered Aguinaldo's forces on the north, it appears that General Otis finally turned his attention to cleaning out this valley and holding it securely.

It was with this purpose in view that General Lawton attacked San Mateo on the 18th. It seems to have been of no advantage to Aguinaldo's cause. He was elsewhere. It has no more menaced American success than the unchecked roaming of Colonel John S. Mosby's guerilas through Loudon, Fairfax and Fauquier counties in Virginia during the Civil War endangered the cause of the Union. Mosby committed depredations almost within cannon shot of Washington, in the rear of the great Union Army, up to the very close of the war. His command consisted of only a few hundred irregulars, perfectly familiar with every cow-path in three counties. They were occasionally chased and some were captured and hanged, but as a body they could not be run down and finally dispersed, because, like Aguinaldo's rebels, they simply scattered when too closely pressed, each man hiding out himself. Soon after the General Lee surrendered, on guarantee of immunity, Mosby and his men also surrendered and became afterward law-abiding citizens. In other words, when the main body fell, all the branches fell with it. So it will be in the Philippines In this aspect, perhaps, a Mosby's guerilla operations had something of a moral effect favorable to his cause, but their influence upon crucial events or the final result was almost nil."

The author was correct. Mosby's efforts were never intended to win the war, merely to help in that effort. He could not affect large strategies, nor could he influence either Confederate military failures or the endless supply of men and materials open to the Union. Once it became a war of attrition, the smaller, weaker South could not hope to prevail. It is interesting to note that many of Mosby's detractors, then and now, harp upon the fact that his successes as a guerrilla did not lead to a Confederate victory. That is true! But the same thing can be said for the operations of every Confederate military leader, including Robert E. Lee and Stonewall Jackson! The mere fact that the war was lost reduces the successes of those on the losing side to irrelevancy. Had the Confederacy won, however, Mosby's actions would have been lauded as a crucial part of that success!

The earlier rather dismissive report by the press of Mosby's style of warfare was given a much more discerning and accurate view in this small article in the *Hawaiian Gazette*:

Hawaiian Gazette – May 22, 1900

The plain truth about the Filipinos is that they have hit upon a method of fighting which it is next to impossible to meet in "squadron and right form of war." Great commanders have often been balked by it. General Grant had to set apart 40,000 men to look out for places which Colonel Mosby was likely to attack with 500 men, and with all his skill, and with the overwhelming numbers at his command, he was never able to lay hands on the rebel chief. It is admitted by military men that if the Southern soldiery had dropped their organization and gone in for guerrilla fighting they might have broken up the Union.

The gist of the article was true. Despite overwhelming numbers, the Federals could not stop John Mosby. However, if the South had fought a guerrilla war, eventually, those states would have been overwhelmed and left with nothing on which to build. Lee knew as much, which is why he refused to continue the war as a partisan effort despite being urged to do so by aide Porter Alexander. As it was, fighting a "civilized war," the South was devastated by an enemy that fought what came later to be known as "total war." Given the Federal response to the limited campaigns of John Mosby, it is obvious that the final result of such a partisan war would have been a Union victory accompanied by the virtual extinction of the people of the South, much as was the fate of the American Indian.

International events also found their way into the American press. Coverage of the Boer War even included the occasional complimentary reference to Mosby and the efficacy of his method of warfare:

San Francisco Call – June 17, 1900

[Part of an article on cavalry tactics in various wars-vph]

The Boers have had no military training except of actual practice and their methods correspond very closely to ours.

There is no doubt that when the war is ended and their true stories come out, there will be some of the most wonderful tales of endurance and execution that have ever been given the world, with the exception perhaps of the feats performed by the band under Colonel Mosby.

As often happens, past matters were finally being addressed, albeit many long years after the fact. In a lengthy article about the American consulate service, there was reference to a report on that service that included a rather blunt quote from John Mosby on the issue of consular fees.

Evening Times, – June 27, 1900

[Part of a long article about the United States consular service.]

Secretary Frelinghuysen, in his report of 1884 on the Consular Service said:

"In the opinion of the department, the present system of compensation by fees, either official or unofficial, should be abolished. Whatever money comes into the consul's hands should be turned into the Treasury of the United States, and he should depend for his support entirely upon the salary allowed by Congress." In 1885, writing on the same subject to the department, Gen. John S. Mosby, consul at Hongkong, expressed himself even more emphatically. He said:

"Consular fees should, in my opinion, be altogether abolished. The best way to secure honesty in the public service is to make it impossible for officers to be dishonest. I can see no sound reason for sending consuls abroad to collect revenue for the Government. You might as well send the Navy to do it."

Meanwhile, Mosby was again "quoted" in the papers as having been ahead of his time militarily when he discarded the saber as a weapon of war. The fact is Mosby was able to make that determination based not only upon experience, but also owing to the fact that he was not "hampered" by formal military training. He didn't have to overcome that which professional soldiers had acquired from such grand temples of knowledge as West Point and VMI. To Mosby, it was just common sense. However, his lack of a "ring" also made him rather despised among professional soldiers such as Rosser and Fitzhugh Lee while men like Stuart, Jones, and Robert E. Lee were not so closed-minded with regard to the man's natural talents despite his lack of validation by one of those venerable institutions:

St. Louis Republic – **July 8, 1900**

THE PASSING OF THE SWORD.

America First Discarded the useless Weapon.

America was nearly forty years ahead of England in discovering the uselessness of the sword in war, even by mounted troops. Colonel John S. Mosby of the Confederate army claims the distinction of having been the first man to do away with the cavalry saber; and his example was soon followed by other commanders in both armies.

Soon after his command was organized, Mosby ordered his men to strap their swords to their saddles and let them hang there, except when needed on dress parade, or for cutting fire wood. In their stead, he gave each man a pair of heavy Colt pistols and taught them how to shoot straight.

The effectiveness of Mosby's cavalry was soon recognized; and that his ideas were approved is evidenced in the fact that today the United States cavalryman wears his sword on his saddle, instead of at his waist and uses it only when he isn't fighting.

Mosby's domestic matters appeared from time to time at least in the local press, from the reinstatement of brother Willie as postmaster of Bedford City to other happy family events. However, tragedy was never far away. On August 7, the *Alexandria Gazette* reported the death of Robert Campbell, the husband of Mosby's oldest daughter, May, at the young age of forty-eight. The couple had two children, Mosby's much-beloved grandsons, Alexander Spottswood and John Mosby Campbell:

Alexandria Gazette – **August 7, 1900**

Death of R. R. Campbell—Mr. Robert R. Campbell died at his home in Warrenton at 8 o'clock this morning, after an illness of ten days. Mr.

Campbell was the son of the late R. A. Campbell, who some years ago moved from Spottsylvania to Faucuier. He was about 48 years old and married a daughter of Col. J. S. Mosby. His wife, who is now the postmaster at Warrenton, and two children survive him. He was a lawyer of recognized ability and for some time had been prominent in republican politics in this district. He was the supervisor of census for this, the Eighth district. Mr. Campbell some years ago lived in this city, where he made many friends.

It must be remembered that Mosby daughter, now a widow, also had health problems as a news article of January 1895 indicated.

With the approach of the reunion of Mosby's men, the ritual accounts naturally began to appear in the press. One of the more interesting matters was a poem about the command, printed in two Virginia papers:

Alexandria Gazette – **September 12, 1900**

Staunton Spectator – **September 21, 1900**

MOSBY'S MEN

The following poem written by Mr. A. C. Gordon, of this city, was read at the Mosby reunion at Fairfax last week. It will be read with interest by our readers:

Mosby's Men ~ Armistead Churchill Gordon

They tell the tale, with magic word
    The spirit's depths to stir,
Of him who fought with Sidney's sword,
    Or rode with Percy's spur;
For Honor bourgeons from the mould
    And blossoms from the dust,
Though Percy's shining spur be cold,
    And Sidney's sword be rust.

In a yet unforgotten day,
    When hearts and hopes were high,
A little band rode down this way
    Whose fame will never die.
Their cause was right, their blades were bright,
    And Honor shone again,
A cloud by day, a fire by night,
    To beckon Mosby's Men.

The bravest days of all that shine
    Through immemorial years;
Days of life' sacrificial wine
    Of Love's divinest tears;
When Valor guarded all the land,—
    When hears and hopes were high,—
And Love and Death went hand in hand
    With Faith, that could not die.

—But Harry Percy's spur is cold,
    And Sidney's sword is rust;
And many a lad, who rode of old
    With that gay band, is dust.
While those, bereft, who linger yet,
    Are wearier now than then: —
—What matter? They cannot forget
    That they were Mosby's Men-

The wilderness their secret kept,
    They bivouacked 'neath the blue;
The tents they spread - the sleep they slept
    The foeman never knew.
No bugle blast nor tuck of drum
    Proclaimed their headlong fight;
—The startled picket saw them come,
    And perished with the sight.

They came as lightnings come; they went
    As swift the west-wind blow;
And blood ran red and life was spent
    Where'er they met the foe.
They buckled to the deadly fray
    Where they were one to ten.
— He spurred and drew to die or slay,
    Who rode with Mosby's Men.

They carried on their sabers there
    The fortunes of the Truth;
The breath they breathed was Freedom's air,
    In their immortal youth.
It boots not if the unequal fight
    Was lot, though fierce and long:
— 'Tis written that eternal right
    Can never be made wrong.

Down the dim years, long gone, once more
    Appears that phantom band;
I hear the clanging charge of yore,—
    I see a war — rent land.
The vision of the desperate strife
    Returns through mists again.
— Those were the bravest days of life,
    The days of Mosby's Men.

—That they were Mosby's Men, and rode,
    As soldiers love to ride,
Where the red stream of battle flowed
    With its most swelling tide.
—No other stream may run so red-
    No higher tide may flow,-
Till God shall wake the dreamless dead,
    When the last trumpets blow.

—The circling seasons come and go,
    Springs dawn, and autumns set;
And winter with its drifted snow
    Repays the summer's debt;
And song of bird and tint of bloom
    Are gay and bright, as when
Those gallant lads rode to their doom
    Long since, with Mosby's Men.

But winter wears a sadder guise,
    And ghastlier for its snow,
To him who looks with time-worn eyes
    On scenes of long ago;
And neither autumn's glow, nor spring,
    Nor summer's emerald sod
To hearts grown old again may bring
    The dead who sleep with God.

It is His will. The sword may rust
    That battles for the right;—
The banner may be trailed in dust
    That leads the holiest fight;—
And Wrong may wear the victor's name,
    Where one shall strive with ten;—
But fate can never take from fame
    The deeds of Mosby's Men.

What Mosby, a lover of poetry, thought of the work is not known; but he would have taken some comfort, at least, in the last lines of the last verse as it echoed his own sentiments:

"But fate can never take from fame The deeds of Mosby's Men."

Once again, John Mosby followed the course that he had begun in 1897; that is, he did not attend the reunion, although doubtless he sent his regards to his much-loved "boys." In a letter dated July 28, Mosby wrote to his son Beverly that he had received an invitation from his old command to attend its annual reunion. The men, he said, begged him to return; and he sadly wrote:"All the wealth I have saved is in the affection of my old men."

It was just as well that Mosby did not attend. He would not have appreciated the trend that the reunions had taken—from the first reunion, where only American flags were displayed and not one Confederate banner hung (as noted at the time in the reports), to what the *Evening Star* reported as Confederate banners floating over the streets of Fairfax Courthouse and the "Lost Cause extolled." John Mosby would not have appreciated either. It is not that he rejected his former flag, but he did not think that it was useful or proper to continue the discords of the past.

Of course, what Mosby either did not recognize or, more likely, refused to admit, was the fact that those same "discords" had kept him and other Southerners out of three Republican administrations and that they were still very much "alive" in the North as well as the South. The presence of Fitzhugh Lee, who never had anything good to say about Mosby, would have made the day "complete," so to speak—in the negative sense. In fact, it is odd to the extreme that Fitz Lee who despised John Mosby and his command, took every opportunity to "participate" in the reunions of the Forty-third. It may well be that it was the only opportunity Lee had to bask in his own former "glory." But whatever the case, the participation of men like Lee, Rosser, A. D. Payne and others who never had a good word to say about John Mosby and his men during the war, never mind afterward, is another example of the fact that "Mosby's Legend" was real enough for his scoffers and critics to use for their own aggrandizement.

Mosby continued to be in rather poor financial straits as a result of the generous gifts he continued to send to his family, even though, in some instances, such assistance had become unnecessary. It is more than probable that he felt obligated to succor his children even as adults because of the necessity of "abandoning" them when he could no longer earn a living—or even live—in Virginia, a result of his political course of action at that time. Certainly, there can be no doubt that Mosby's political and ethical convictions had greatly burdened his family. Pauline had died during the worst of it, though her death cannot necessarily be attributed to the matter, and his children were bullied and persecuted by people who had not the courage to assail him personally. The suffering caused by Mosby's path of political martyrdom was not limited to himself—and he knew it.

As the year drew to its close, John Mosby was still very much exercised by the promise of Democrat-Populist William Jennings Bryan to remove the nation from the gold standard. In regard to this concern, the Colonel wrote a letter to the secretary of the Treasury asking what results might ensue if Bryan were elected and his intentions made a reality. With the contest mere months away, the *San Francisco Call* printed the secretary's response, doubtless forwarded to that publication by Mosby. Notice that he did not include his original letter but only Vanderlip's reply:

> *San Francisco Call* – **September 19, 1900**
>
> HOW NATIONAL CREDIT MIGHT BE DISHONORED
>
> A short time ago Colonel John S. Mosby of this city wrote to the Secretary of the Treasury asking if, in his opinion—and in the event Bryan was elected—it would be in his power to make use of standard silver dollars in the payment of the Government's obligation. Yesterday he received the following letter in reply:
>
> Treasury Department, Office of the Secretary, Washington, Sept. 13, 1900
>
> Mr. John S. Mosby, San Francisco, Cal.—
>
> Sir:
>
> In reply to your letter of the 6th, inst. I have to say that the Secretary has recently stated publicly that, in his opinion, a President, unfriendly to the existing standard of value, would have it in his power to seriously injure the business interests of the country by paying in the standard silver dollars such obligations of the United States as are not specifically payable in gold. The amount of standard silver dollars available for this purpose at present is comparatively small, but it is believed that upon indication of a purpose on the part of the Government to disburse them in preference to gold the amount of payments into the treasury in silver would be largely augmented, this providing the Government with the additional silver with which to make further payments. It is also believed that in the event of such action unfriendly to the existing standard of the commercial and

industrial interests of the country would be injuriously affected, not only by the actual occurrence, but by apprehension as to the final results. Respectfully yours,

F. A. VANDERLIP Assistant Secretary.

And thus, the curtain fell on the first year of the new century with the reelection of Republican William McKinley. And it cannot be doubted that despite his treatment at the hands of the administration, Mosby was very relieved to see the Populists defeated and McKinley returned to the White House. But what John Mosby could not have known—or anyone else, for that matter!—was that it was not McKinley who was of infinite importance as 1901 dawned. When the Republicans were sorting out the ticket that they would field in 1896, John Mosby suggested a Virginian by the name of James Walker for the vice presidency. But he could not have known that the party's standard bearer, William McKinley, was every bit as much of a "sectional bigot" as had been his unlamented cousin, Benjamin Harrison, and the refusal to consider Walker had only presaged the new administration's refusal to consider any other Southerner—including Mosby—for a government office. In looking around for a running mate for McKinley, the eventual, if not altogether popular, choice was a young man of only forty-two years, who was often referred to by his detractors as "that damned cowboy." The candidate, a former New York City chief of police, assemblyman and governor was Theodore Roosevelt. Such are the vagaries of history.

ADDENDUM

The repeat of the two candidates for president in 1896 and 1900 was most unusual. The nation was going through a period of financial disruption, and the Populists under Bryan had done pretty much what Horace Greeley and his "liberal Republicans" had done to The Democratic party in 1872—that is, they had overwhelmed and virtually "gobbled up" that party. Below are the electoral votes for both candidates in both elections. Bryan ran—and lost—again in 1908:

1896

William McKinley (271 Electoral Votes) William Jennings Bryan (176 Electoral Votes)

1900

William McKinley (292 Electoral Votes) William Jennings Bryan (155 Electoral Votes)

In both elections, the South went "solidly" for The Democrats, although the issues had changed from one of "populism" and financial issues—bimetallism and the gold standard in 1896—to American expansionism in 1900.

Chapter 40

1901

Ignis aurum probat, miseria fortes viros.
~ Fire tests gold; adversity tests strong men.

"Real courage is when you know you're licked before you begin, but you begin anyway and see it through no matter what." ~
Harper Lee

LATE IN DECEMBER 1900, Mosby had written to a friend in Richmond, taking some joy in the fact that he had not died of his terrible wound in December of 1864. The same sentiment was expressed in the new year in the *Alexandria Gazette*, possibly taken from the same letter:

> ***Clarke Courier* - January 9, 1901**
>
> In a letter to a friend received in Richmond, Col. John L. Mosby, writing from San Francisco, says: "I will visit Virginia some time next year and hope to see you. My health is better than it ever was. Yesterday 36 years ago Sheridan telegraphed from Winchester: 'Mosby died of his wound a few days ago at Charlottesville.' Not much!"

Mosby frequently mentioned his health in his correspondence with friends and family, a matter that was probably a "throwback" to his sickly youth. Given his bouts of appendicitis and his terrible accident three years earlier, he undoubtedly was concerned with health issues, especially as they affected his ability to earn a living. At the same time, this spate of elation was probably the result of the reelection of President McKinley and the belief that he had a hope of an office now that, with the departure of Huntington, he would soon be released by the railroad. (Mosby was "let go" on January 29, 1901). Certainly, the president's treatment of the South in general and Mosby in particular had kept that section solidly in the Democratic column, so it was not impossible that the administration might reach out the hand of "friendship" to some well-known Southern Republicans. If that were the case, John Mosby might well benefit.

But the major press coverage devoted to Mosby and his men—and it was in fact, *major*—involved a report that Prussian nobleman and former Mosby's Ranger, Baron Robert von Massow, now a general in the kaiser's army, had left a bequest of some $2,000,000 to the survivors of the command! Beginning in late January 1901 and continuing into May, reports of the bequest sandwiched between articles on von Massow and his time with the Forty-third were disseminated throughout the nation and read with great interest, especially by the potential benefactors. Eventually, the matter, as Mosby had always opined, was found to be a fraud.

In February, the *Free Lance* printed an article from the *Denver Times*. It is possible that Mosby began to notice the problems that "Johnnie" was having, problems that became life-threatening in late 1902:

Alexandria Gazette, – **February 20, 1901**

The *Free Lance* – **February 23, 1901**

Colonel Mosby.—Colonel John S. Mosby, the distinguished Confederate ranger, is in this city as the guest of his son, Attorney John S. Mosby, Jr.

In spite of his 68 years and the fact that he has led a strenuous life, Colonel Mosby is hale and his step is as elastic as it was in the '60s. His mind is as robust and as active as ever, and when he can be induced to talk on things affecting his stirring past the listener is charmed. He is now one of the general counsel of the Southern Pacific Railway at San Francisco, having left Virginia for good at the expiration of his term as consul general to Hong Kong (to which office his warm friend President Grant appointed him during his first term). Immediately after the war a close friendship between Grant and Mosby began, which ended only with the latter's death. Colonel Mosby is on his way to Virginia, where he will visit his daughters, still residing at the old home at Warrenton, in Fauquier county. Reports from Virginia say that his men, many of whom still reside in the State, are preparing a warm reception, as this is his first visit to the State in about four years.—[Denver Times.

In between the remarkable news coverage of the von Massow story, *The Times* printed a small article noting that Mosby had been invited to deliver an address before a Southern organization, something that only a few years earlier would probably have been an impossibility:

The Times – **March 13, 1901**

Colonel Mosby Invited to Speak

Winchester, Va., March 12.—Colonel John S. Mosby will be invited to deliver an address before General Turner Ashby Camp of Confederate Veterans.

Mosby was also feted by some friends in New York at a banquet given for him by the son of Confederate General John C. Pemberton. It is to be assumed that Pemberton the younger was unconcerned about being drummed out of his family for associating with the Great Pariah:

Alexandria Gazette – **March 13, 1901 (Edited)**

Richmond Dispatch – **March 13, 1901**

DINNER TO COL. JOHN S. MOSBY.

Confederate Chieftain Honored by Friends in New York City

(*New York Times*—12th.)

Colonel John S. Mosby was the principal guest at a banquet given in his honor by F. R. Pemberton, son of the Confederate General, John C. Pemberton, at the Waldorf-Astoria, last night. Colonel Mosby comes from Virginia, but he is at present stationed at California, where he looks after the legal interests of the Southern Pacific railroad. Colonel Mosby is in the city on business connected with the railroad, and is the guest of Mr. Pemberton. A number of other entertainments in his honor have been arranged by his friends in New York.

After Huntington retired in August of 1900, John Mosby was removed from the railroad. According to a letter to son Beverly, he had received notice of his termination on January 29, 1901. But as he did not mention the matter, the newspapers continued to report that he was an employee of the road. But Mosby was not the only head to fall after Huntington's departure. There had been a general "housecleaning," and many of the old guard were cast adrift, Mosby being but one. So again, it was not a matter of inferior legal skills that ended his association with the company, but simply the inevitability of change, whether in the private or the public sector.

For whatever reason, John Mosby began to opine in print about the South, past and future, including the matter of race. He saw no problem with blacks in the United States because he believed that they would "disperse" among the population rather than remaining in large groups contained in small areas, as had been the case under both slavery and Reconstruction. Mosby believed that the "race problem" was the result of Negroes being "hedged into" small geographical areas, a fact creating many problems, not the least of which were areas of strong black political power—something that never bode well for either race. And he also, once again, stated his belief that there was no longer a "solid south." Now if by that Mosby meant "politically," he was wrong because the South remained almost uniformly Democratic in its politics. If, however, he meant socially and culturally, that might have been closer to the truth because of immigration into the section. Whatever John Mosby believed when he made these pronouncements, he was always optimistic about the future of Virginia and the South:

Minneapolis Journal – April 1, 1901

WAR A BENEFIT

Colonel Mosby Says it Helped the South—Slavery as Incubus.

New York, April 1.—Colonel John S. Mosby, the famous Confederate raider, writes a letter on "The Dawn of the Real South," in which he says:

"Without the war of secession the south could never have hoped to attain the future that is now certain. Slavery was a great incubus, paralyzing natural energy. By abolishing this wrong our war benefited every state south of the Mason and Dixon line. The negroes are producing more as free men than they ever did as slaves and the great mass of the people are vastly better off to-day than they were under the old ante-bellum system.

"There are the soundest reasons for asserting that the negroes' status is bound to improve. While they are not as near to equality with white people as they were under the system of slavery, they are certain to be absorbed by immigration, and in this engulfment they will disappear. This is the natural and wisest solution of what we now call the race problem.

"It is well nigh folly to-day to speak of the "solid south.""

St. Louis Republic – April 1, 1901 (Edited)

COLONEL MOSBY ON THE SOUTH'S FUTURE.

Predicts That It Will Eventually Be Far Richer and More Powerful Than the North.

BETTER OFF WITH NO SLAVERY.

Richmond, He Says, Will Become the Commercial Headquarters of the World.

New York, March 31.—In its forthcoming issue, Leslie's Weekly, will print a paper by Colonel John S. Mosby, the famous Confederate raider, on "The Dawn of the Real South," in which he says:

"The real South is just at its birth. The growth of this child of the Nation may be gradual, but in the end the South will be far richer and more powerful than the North. In days to come the South will become the dominant section of the country.

"Without the War of Secession the South could never have hoped to attain the future that is now certain. Slavery was a great incubus, paralyzing natural energy. By abolishing this wrong our war benefited every State south of the Mason and Dixon line. The negroes are producing more as free men than they ever did as slaves, and the great mass of the people are vastly better off to-day than they were under the old antebellum system.

Solution of Race Problem.

"Socially, as well as industrially, the abolition of slavery was highly beneficial in its results to the masses, for slavery was a great wrong and no community can exist in the highest state of happiness when its system is based on a wrong.

"There are the soundest reasons for asserting that the negro's status is bound to improve. While they are not as near to equality with white people as they were under the system of slavery, they are certain to be absorbed by immigration, and in this engulfment they will disappear. This is the natural and wisest solution of what we now call the race problem."

"Richmond is the city most likely to become in time the banking center and commercial headquarters of this country and therefore the world. The days of that famous old city as a political capital are past; but its career as the central point of manufactures for the whole South, and from there for the world at large, is just beginning.

As noted, much of Mosby's belief was based upon the understanding that slavery protected blacks—it did!—and allowed their numbers to artificially increase. Once such protection disappeared, their numbers would be reduced to the point at which this projected scenario—dispersion among the rest of the nonblack population—would occur. This same thing was stated in a news article (not by Mosby) during Reconstruction—that is, that the Negroes were not surviving as they had under slavery because they were not being "cared for." But of course, such dispersion of blacks did not occur, and neither did the Negro "disappear." Indeed, the "race problem" outlived Colonel Mosby.

As noted, Mosby always maintained a very hopeful and optimistic attitude regarding the future of the South. He believed that the Republican Party could help that future come to pass. The problem was that that party, run by its Northern adherents, had no desire for it to come to pass. The Democrats were no help because they kept power in the South by supporting the Lost Cause, something that Mosby saw as restricting the section's forward momentum. The movement of blacks into the rest of the country—something Mosby saw as necessary to prevent racial strife—did not come about in any great numbers until the manpower shortage occasioned by the First World War. But even that didn't help because as the nation was becoming "industrialized," people were leaving the land and going into the cities. Southern blacks did the same. So there were still population concentrations, albeit in different places. Mosby was not looking for the extinction of blacks, merely for a political situation in which whites would always be in the majority in government because he did not believe that blacks should rule over whites or that they were capable of maintaining good government. But not everyone agreed with the colonel's viewpoint on the racial issue as this letter to the *Times* reveals:

The Times – April 3, 1901

WAR OF SECESSION.

Colonel John S. Mosby, in his recent comments on the South, said that without the war of secession the South could never have hoped to obtain the future that is now certain. "Slavery," said he, "was a great incubus, paralyzing natural energy. By abolishing this wrong our war benefited every State south of the Mason and Dixon line. The negroes are producing more as freemen than they ever did as slaves, and the great mass of the people are vastly better off to-day than they were under the old ante-bellum system. Socially, as well as industrially, the abolition of slavery was highly beneficial in its results to the masses, for slavery was a great wrong and no community can exist in the highest state of happiness when its system is based on a wrong."

We agree with Colonel Mosby as to the general result, but if he means top say that the war of secession was necessary to free the slaves, or that the South is better off and the negro is better off and conditions generally are better than they would have been had their been no war of secession, then we respectfully dissent. The war of secession ought not to have been, and would not have been but for the meddling of the northern fanatics. The Southern people were driven into it because the Northern people insisted upon invading our rights. The slavery agitation was begun by the rank abolitionists of New England and kept up until there was a bloody war. After the war was ended these same people again undertook to meddle with the negro question in the South and sorry mess of it they made. No man can say for a certainty what would have been, but we are firm in the belief that if these fanatics at the North had not meddled with things that did not concern them, if they had left the Southern people alone to settle their own problems in their own way, in the course of time slavery would have been abolished without any bloody conflict and without the iniquity of reconstruction.

Slavery as in institution could not have continued. Civilization was opposed to it and there was a strong sentiment in the South, especially in the State of Virginia, in opposition to slavery. Many men had already set their slaves free and others had provided in their wills that their slaves would be freed at the death of the testator. And so by degrees, if not by concurrent action on the part of all slave-holders, the negroes would in time have been emancipated and the friendly relationship between the blacks and whites which had for so long existed would have continued.

Can any fair-minded man say that the method employed by the Northern people to free the slaves was successful? First of all a cruel and bloody and devastating war was waged, which killed off large numbers of the most promising men of both sections, and especially of the South. The fields of the South were laid waste and her cities destroyed, and at the close of the war poverty stalked like a lean monster from one end of the land to the other. Then came the surrender and the day of military rule in the South and the damnable days of reconstruction and carpet-bag rule. The negroes were arrayed by their Northern leaders against the whites and there was clash here and clash there, the negroes always getting the worst of it. And then came the days of ballot-box stuffing and all sorts of devices to keep the negro from ruling. Oh it was one wretched piece of business from beginning to end. The South passed through the ordeal with her proverbial heroism, and thanks to the courage and energy of her people, she has built up her waste places and put her farming lands in order and restored her cities and erected factories here and there all over the land. She is in a prosperous condition and bids fair, as Colonel Mosby says, to be the most prosperous of all sections, and Richmond, the capital of the Confederacy, which a little while ago was burned to the ground by the enemy, is destined to be the South's leading city, if not, as Colonel Mosby predicts, the nation's leading city. But we do not owe all this to the war of secession. We have prospered in spite of it.

This response to Mosby's claim about the war was true, but it didn't address Mosby's point. He never said that the war was necessary to end slavery; he merely said that it did end it, which was true. Mosby believed that his viewpoint on the Negro had been mistakenly represented, so he moved to correct the matter—more proof that he did care what people thought of him and his views:

The Times – April 6, 1901

Colonel Mosby on the Negro.

The *Washington Post* of yesterday printed the following letter from Colonel John S. Mosby:

I have just read in The Post Dr. Martin Scott's criticism of what he calls my forthcoming paper. I know nothing of such paper. A few days ago in New York a reporter for Leslie's Weekly asked my opinion about the South, and I replied that the South was a new and undeveloped country and that I thought the race problem there would be solved by immigration. I said nothing about amalgamation. That is a spectre created by Dr. Scott's imagination. He affirms and I deny that process of amalgamation of the races is now going on. With no desire to raise an issue with Dr. Scott on an ethnical point, I must say that the descendants of Pocahontas will never admit the correctness of his theory of degeneracy that results from a mixture of races. While I am something of an optimist, he takes a pessimistic view of the situation, but proposes no remedy for the evil. It does a patient no good for a doctor to tell him how sick he is if he has no medicine to cure him. Diogenes may have been happy in his tub, but he suggested nothing for the happiness of mankind. There are many negroes in California, Ohio, and all the Northern States; but they have no race problem, although there is no amalgamation, simply because the negro population is an insignificant minority in the North, and soon will be in the South.

In the same paper:

CURRENT TOPICS.

COL. MOSBY ON THE NEGRO.

Colonel John S. Mosby says in a letter to the *Washington Post*:

"I have just read in The Post Dr. Martin Scott's criticism of what he calls my forthcoming paper. A few days ago in New York a reporter for Leslie's Weekly asked my opinion about the prospects and industrial condition of the South, and I replied that the South was a new and undeveloped country, and that I thought the race problem there would be solved by immigration. I said nothing about amalgamation."

Certainly not. Every sensible man like Col. Mosby knows that the white race will not mix with the black race. Americans have absorbed the blood of Europeans of every nation. But they will not absorb the blood of negroes and Chinese.

John Mosby visited the University of Virginia, but as the guest of a friend, a professor of Latin. He had been most bitter against that institution from the time of his incarceration in the Turpin matter, and it was said that when an invitation from the University was sent to him a few years earlier, he had replied that he was no better a man than he had been when he shot Turpin—and refused to go. Of course, Mosby and his family had been treated by the school with all courtesy and every amenity after his terrible accident, so it is to be supposed that his former anger had been ameliorated:

Times-Dispatch – **May 29, 1901**

WARM RECEPTION

Col. John S. Mosby a Visitor at the University of Virginia.

UNIVERSITY OF VIRGINIA, May 28.—Colonel John S. Mosby, the well known hero of '65, arrived at the university yesterday, as the guest of Colonel Peters, professor of Latin.

The scenes which greeted Colonel Mosby as he entered the university campus were familiar ones, recalling his college days here, when he and Colonel Peters were classmates.

Notwithstanding the rain of last night, a stirring reception and surprise for the Colonel had been planned among the students, and about 8 P.M., the Citizens' Band, which had been secured met a large number at the end of the east range. The band and students marched up the east range, the ranks becoming large and larger until they had reached the lawn, where a very large crowd had gathered. Proceeding up the lawn, singing "Glory be to Colonel Mosby" and "John Brown's Body," &c., they reached Colonel Peters' house, where all the college yells were given in honor of Colonel Mosby.

The students yelled for the war veteran until he, accompanied by Colonel Peters, made his appearance. At the sight of the old Confederate officer, the students bared their heads and yells for a speech rent the air. But here the Colonel's modesty again interceded, and notwithstanding the repeated cries for a speech, the Colonel could not be forced to enter upon the field of oratory, and take the prominent position he had formerly occupied on the field of battle. But the Colonel greatly appreciated the enthusiastic welcome and big surprise accorded him, and as the large crowd lined up, he shook hands with every one. Amid college yells the crowd dispersed, all feeling better for having had the opportunity of seeing the brave warrior and the great military genius.

Mosby's interaction with the students is another example of his natural modesty, which is a far cry from the accusation of "publicity hound" by some who have written about the man. Although he refused to speak extemporaneously (as was usual with him), he did something more personal and probably more appreciated by his young devotees. He shook the hand of each student who had come to welcome him and spoke with them individually. Certainly, that took more time and effort than a five-minute "pep talk."

Richmond Times – **June 1, 1901 (Edited)**

Clarke Courier – **June 12, 1901**

COL. J. S. MOSBY AT UNIVERSITY

Found by a Reporter in a Reminiscent Mood. An Interesting Talker.

His Early Life in Albemarle When There Was Bitterness Between Town and Gown.

Spent Eleven Months in Charlottesville Jail. (Special to *The Times*.)

Charlottesville, Va., May 31.—Colonel John S. Mosby, the famous "partisan ranger" of old Confederate times, is spending a few days with Colonel Peters on West Lawn, at the university. When seen by a Times reporter this morning, he gave many interesting reminiscences of his early manhood, spent in Charlottesville and Albemarle county.

The Colonel is now in his sixty-eighth year. He is of medium height, of strong and compact figure, and carries his shoulders as erect as a West Pointer. His hair is almost snow white, his features are irregular, though strong, and his quiet gray eye flashes with old-time fire at the recollection of stirring events. His face is an interesting study—rugged, strong and intellectual. In fact, it reminds one of an old portrait, and it requires but a slight trick of the imagination to see it hung in a prominent place among the "high-stock," silver-snuff-box gentry of a half-century ago.

Colonel Mosby is an interesting talker. He is especially strong on incidents and localities, and can describe an event of fifty years ago with perfect ease and readiness. In fact, his ability in this direction is remarkable, and lends added charm and interest to his many exciting experiences. [The article then goes on to recap Mosby's life.-vph]

By this point, Mosby's state of unemployment must have become known, and President McKinley probably decided he could hardly leave a bone fide hero—and staunch Republican—without a position. As that was the case, he finally offered Mosby a government job. The announcement was made first in the Midwestern press:

Minneapolis Journal – July 10, 1901

Bismarck Daily Tribune – July 11, 1901

ASSIGNED TO MINNESOTA

Colonel Mosby of Civil War Fame, Gets a Government Job

MOSBY COMING HERE

Confederate Raider Special Agent of the Land Office

Washington, July 10.—Colonel John S. Mosby, who was so well known in the Virginia civil war campaign because of his daring raids, has been appointed special agent of the general land office and assigned to duty in Minnesota and Nebraska. Colonel Mosby has for many years been connected with the law offices of the Southern Pacific railway, but upon the readjustment of the affairs of that company was left without a position. His present appointment was made at the special request of President McKinley, who is said to entertain a high regard for the colonel because of his bravery. His new position pays $2,250 a year.

And so once again, John Mosby was working for the government. Of course, he had been promised a far more lucrative and exalted situation than one earning less than $2,500 a year! Perhaps when he was given this "handout," he remembered that in the famous Greenbawck Raid, his men earned only slightly less than his annual salary for a few hours' work! In fact, Mosby had hoped for a position in the Department of Justice, where his experience and talents could be put to better use. But this is what he was offered, and in his situation, he had no choice but to accept. Very soon, however, government "job" or not, Mosby's financial situation started to deteriorate and there were no more dinners in New York, fashionable clothing, and all of the material things that he had enjoyed between his return from China and his departure from California.

Economically restricted or not, John Mosby could not help reaching out to someone whom he admired—in this case, a little boy who had been elected a page at large from Prince William County. Again, it was not Mosby who made this little gift known to the press. His letter with the check was sent to Albert Fletcher and not the *Dispatch* or the *Gazette*:

Alexandria Gazette – July 11, 1901

COL. MOSBY'S GIFT TO A PAGE.—An interesting incident of yesterday's session of the constitutional convention in Richmond was a letter from Col. John S. Mosby, now in Washington, to Delegate Albert Fletcher, of Warrenton, inclosing a check on (a) Washington bank for $10 for the benefit of Walter Moncure, the little boy who was elected as a page last week. After telling how he read of the hardships endured by the lad, Col. Mosby goes on to say: "I wish you to give this money to the boy as a mark of my appreciation of his filial conduct in remembrance of his grandfather. I argued a good many cases before Judge Moncure, and always had the highest respect as well as great affection for him. While I have no expectations that this bread cast upon the waters will ever return, yet it gives me great satisfaction to contribute my mite to a boy who has proved himself so worthy a grandson and who has certainly done something that everybody will approve."

In the same paper:

FROM WASHINGTON

[Correspondence of the *Alexandria Gazette*.] Washington, July 11

Col. J. S. Mosby, who has been quite sick at the residence of his daughter here, has gone to Fairfax county, Virginia to spend a few days with his old friend, Capt. Fountain Beattie. While sick the colonel lost his voice, which, however, he has entirely recovered. He will leave for his home in California in about two weeks.

Another article appeared about Mosby's new position with the claim that he would have little to do outside of Nebraska, a claim that was true in a way, but not a good way:

Minneapolis Journal – **July 15, 1901**

What Mosby Will Do.

Colonel John S. Mosby, the noted confederate guerrilla leader, who has been appointed a general agent of the land office, will have his headquarters at Valentine, Neb. Colonel Mosby will also make trips into nearby states when the exigencies of his work require, but his duties will be mainly in looking out for land frauds in the state in which his headquarters are located. The duties of the office consist mainly in investigating fraudulent entries of public lands. A most lucrative practice has arisen in nearly all the public land states in connection with what are known as soldiers' additional homestead entries. Under the law any soldier of the civil war is entitled to make an entry for from eighty to 160 acres of land in addition to that for which he has made a regular entry as a homesteader. In some cases the soldier does not want to take the land personally, but he transfers it to someone for a consideration, which he is allowed to do under the law. From time to time discoveries are made that fraudulent entries of this class are made and they are investigated and the entries canceled and those concerned in the fraud are prosecuted by the land office. There are enough of these attempts to secure government land by unlawful means to keep a special agent busy in addition to other duties he might have to perform and it is probable that Colonel Mosby will have little to do outside of Nebraska.

— W. W. Jermane.

More articles appeared on Mosby's new "position" with the Department of the Interior:

Alexandria Gazette – **July 17, 1901**

FROM WASHINGTON

[Correspondence of the *Alexandria Gazette*.] Washington, July 17.

The many friends here of Col. J. S. Mosby, who is now visiting friends in Fairfax county, are much pleased that he has been appointed a special agent of the general land office, though they say he deserves a much better position and should have been given an appointment years ago. They say he made a most excellent record as U. S. Consul at Hong Kong, but that members of the G. A. R. have prevented him from being "recognized" by republican presidents since Grant's death. Some of the colonel's democratic friends say that when he goes to Nebraska, where he has been assigned to duty, and becomes acquainted with that "great and good man," William Jennings Bryan, he will forget the political oblivion he has endured in recent years.

There are two things in the Gazette article: First, Mosby's friends declared that he deserved a much better position—he did. Second, that he should have received a position years ago—again, they were correct. With regard to the opinion voiced by Mosby's "democratic friends" (apparently, he had them!), Mosby was well acquainted with Bryan and rejected him utterly. It was not Bryan's kind feelings for his fellow man that Mosby rejected, but his idea of what constituted the best for humanity, at least economically.

Mosby's new "position" initiated further press coverage of his past, especially in publications located in those states in which he would now be working. True, such papers had carried other stories of the man no doubt, but now he was moving among them, and the people in those areas wished to know more. It wouldn't be too long, however, before the "instructions" he received from the Department of the Interior turned him from an interesting historical figure into, once again, "Mosby the Monster":

Omaha Daily Bee – July 18, 1901 (Edited)
CAREER OF COLONEL MOSBY

Coming of Old Warrior to Nebraska Recalls Many Thrilling Incidents His Connection With The Civil War

Life Story of This Virginian Reads Like Fiction, But It is a Part of Verified History—What Senator Millard Says.

The assignment of Colonel John S. Mosby as special land agent of the United States to Nebraska will bring to the state the second distinguished Virginian to visit it in an official capacity within a year.

Forty years ago the name of Mosby was on the tongue of every man and woman in the United States. In the south he was looked upon as a rather capable but unruly man, with whom the officers of the confederate army would rather treat as an independent partisan than as a subordinate. A man of infinite daring, of personal bravery, who could not be held down to the strict rules of camps, but who could get more fight out of a small personally conducted party of men than any other man in the confederate service, regular or irregular.

In the north, Mosby was considered a little worse if anything than Henry Morgan, the buccaneer, or Captain Kidd. He was looked upon as a red-handed murderer, a spy and guerrilla in whose favor the rules of war did not apply, but who was to be shot upon sight. [The article presents another recapitulation of Mosby's career in the war.-vph] Colonel Mosby is an author of no mean repute, his "Recollections of the War" being considered an interesting and trustworthy account of the scenes through which he passed.

Speaking in regard to the assignment of Colonel Mosby to Nebraska, Senator Millard said that he had known nothing of it until he saw the announcement in the newspapers. "I have nothing against Colonel Mosby," he said. "He has proved his ability as a man and his devotion to the Republican party, but if the government wanted an agent to work in Nebraska, I do not see why it did not come to Nebraska for the man."

Consider the seemingly benign contention by Nebraska Senator Millard that "if the government wanted an agent to work in Nebraska, I do not see why it did not come to Nebraska for the man." Mosby soon learned the reason when he began his investigation. Had the government followed the good senator's advice, the fox would have continued to be in charge of the henhouse.

More papers began to report on Mosby's new position. It is interesting to note that the same stories tended to appear in more than one newspaper. It is also interesting to note that few (if any) low-paid agents of a government bureaucracy would rate such extensive press coverage for a job that was, or should have been, of little interest to the public at large. As the task itself was of interest only to the relatively few people it impacted, it stands to reason that the interest was occasioned by the man performing the task:

Washington Times – **July 18, 1901**

Goodland Republic – **July 19, 1901**

Norfolk Weekly News-Journal – **July 19, 1901**

Col. J. S. Mosby Gets an Appointment.

COLONEL MOSBY'S MISSION.

The Ex-Confederate Soldier on the Land Office Force.

Col. John S. Mosby, the well known ex-Confederate soldier, has been appointed a special agent in the General Land Office.

Colonel Mosby now resides in California and has been assigned to duty in Nebraska.

Small items now appeared as Mosby prepared to go west, not to his old home in San Francisco, but to the wilds of Nebraska and thereabouts:

Alexandria Gazette – **August 3, 1901**

FROM WASHINGTON

[Correspondence of the *Alexandria Gazette*.] Washington, August 3.

Colonel J. S. Mosby will leave here on Monday for the west, and will soon enter upon the discharge of his duties in Nebraska as special agent of the United States land office. He went over to Alexandria yesterday to see his portrait that Miss Katherine Critcher of that city is painting for the university of Virginia.

Alexandria Gazette – **August 6, 1901**

FROM WASHINGTON

[Correspondence of the *Alexandria Gazette*.] Washington, August 6.

Col. J. S. Mosby spent Sunday with his relatives and friends in Warrenton, Va., and returned to this city yesterday morning. In the evening he left for the west and will soon enter upon the discharge of his duties in Nebraska as special agent for the government land office. Col Mosby severed his connection in San Francisco with the Northern Pacific Railway Company soon after the death of the late C. P. Huntington.

It would have been more accurate to say that Mosby was removed from his position with the railroad once the man who had protected him was gone. Contrary to the contentions of many modern writers, Mosby was not removed because of incompetence or any failure on his part to serve the road. He was removed for the same reason he was not able to get an office in any Republican administration after Hayes until McKinley's second term—the hatred of former Federal officers and the GAR, taken together with the natural antagonism of "new management" with regard to those whom they considered as having served in "old management." With regard to former Union soldiers employed in executive positions in the railroad, an interesting story came to light and was carried in the *San Francisco Call* of February 16, 1910, involving Mosby's first interaction with his new employers:

> The first time Colonel Mosby presented to Assistant Treasurer Charles H. Redington of the South Pacific a pay voucher he remarked that he supposed that he would have to be identified, whereupon Redington (who had belonged to the Eighth Illinois cavalry) replied: "No, that is not necessary. I have chased you and been chased by you too many times down in Virginia to need any identification for you."

Mosby saw the above incident as humorous, but the Eighth Illinois was heavily involved in the Shenandoah Valley in 1864, the same "venue" as the home burners. If Alger had retained his hatred of Mosby from that period, it is entirely possible that Mr. Redington did so as well. That would have made Mosby a target for removal almost before he began his tenure with the railroad.

North Platte Semi-Weekly Tribune – August 16, 1901 (Edited)

Col. Mosby Reappears.

The recent appointment, to please President McKinley, of Col. John S. Mosby as special agent of the General Land Office, with headquarters in the west, has brought into prominence one of the picturesque figures of the civil war—a man admired by the south for his dash and brilliancy and reviled by northern soldiers because his warfare was of the guerrilla type. A Virginian by birth, he is now approaching his 69th birthday.

Many papers chose to look more deeply into the nature of the man in an attempt to get past his oft-repeated "war history." Such an attempt appeared in the two papers below:

Sunday Morning Globe – August 25, 1901 (Edited)

Richmond Dispatch – September 8, 1901

COL. JOHN MOSEBY.

Another Chapter on This Famous Man. A Classical Scholar

And a Soldier of the School of Napoleon and Caesar and One of the Greatest

Generals of Modern Times—His Exploits in the Field and His Charming Personality—The President His Admirer and Firm Friend.

Col. John S. Mosby, who was recently appointed special agent of the General Land Office—at the request of President McKinley himself, it is said—will be assigned to a Western district which will include Minnesota and Nebraska.

Perhaps there was never a better illustration of the typical young American than John S. Mosby was in 1861 when, in his 28th year, he enlisted as a private under Gen. Joseph E. Johnston. It is impossible for anyone who knows the type and knows Mosby from his record and his writing to mistake him. He was full of Byron and Scott, Campbell, Shakespeare and the writers whose genius perpetuates the romance of the middle ages to our own times—to our lasting detriment as Mark Twain insists, though he has no great following in his view that if all Scott's novels had been burned in ten years after they were written we might have got over the nineteenth century in America with little or no expenditure of gunpowder. ...

And still, John Mosby in his new if insignificant position continued to make the papers:

Salt Lake Herald – August 28, 1901 (Edited)

COLONEL JOHN S. MOSBY

Famous Guerrilla Who Now Holds a Government Position (Cincinnati Enquirer)

The United States, young as it is in the history of the great nations of the earth, has had the distinction of producing more than its share of the picturesque characters of the last century, but never was the time so prolific of this production as that period covering the war, which has been described by historians the bloodiest conflict ever waged between two opposing armies— the civil war. It was a time when such forceful characters as Lincoln, Grant, Lee, Greeley, Davis and a host of others first gave the country a test of their power; it was a time when such soldiers as Thomas, Meade, Sherman, Sheridan, Stewart [sic], Johnson [sic], Hooker and Mosby were made, and it is of the latter that this story has to deal. Nearly forty years ago after the close of those scenes of carnage the name of Mosby occasions as much enthusiasm in the land of Dixie as it did in the strenuous times of the sixties, and his recent appointment to be commissioner of the general land office for the state of Nebraska has more strongly than ever marked the fact that the rupture between two great peoples has been cemented and that they are now once and indivisible. The man who once created terror by the mention of his name is an official of the government he fought so hard to overthrow. [The article then goes on to recite Mosby's history—again.-vph]

Another reunion of Mosby's command was approaching and with it all the attendant publicity. However, this reunion was deeply affected by the death of President William McKinley at the hands of an assassin on September 14, 1901:

Richmond Dispatch – August 31, 1901

MOSBY'S OLD COMMAND

Invitations Sent Out for the Eighth Annual Reunion and Warrenton

The eighth annual reunion of the survivors of the Forty-third Battalion, Virginia Cavalry (Mosby's Men) will be held at Warrenton on Saturday, the 14th instant, under most flattering auspices. Warrenton is in the heart of the region on which Mosby's daring sabreuers* ranged in the days of the war. [*sabreuer(s): one who wields a sabre-vph]

The Times – September 15, 1901

THE REUNION OF MOSBY'S MEN

Great Crowd Attends the Annual Meeting. A SHADOW OF SADNESS

President's Death Turns Joyous Meeting to Solemn Aspect

There is a certain irony in the fact that Mosby only attended one of his command's gatherings while men who despised him were many times guests of Mosby's men.

But John Mosby was not yet out of certain newspaper crosshairs as this article in the *Sunday Morning Globe* demonstrated. The writer went to the "official records" to illustrate his wicked ways—and proving, one supposes, that he was unworthy of even the lowly position given by a government that he had, supposedly "tried so hard to destroy." Again, the year was 1901. Over thirty-five years had passed since Appomattox. Mosby and others, including former Federal officers, had written many times proving that he had done nothing contrary to the existing rules of war. But none of that apparently mattered as all the old charges were dragged out again. The sort of reasoning used by his enemies proved, in fact, that it was not his method of warfare that was problematic, but his success in its use and the side on which it was waged:

Sunday Morning Globe – September 29, 1901 (Edited)

THE OTHER SIDE

Gen. John S. Mosby's War Record as Partisan From the Official Records

But Federal and Regular Ex-Confederates Repudiated Him in War— his Recognition by Secretary Hitchcock Over Gallant Ex-Federal and Confederate Soldiers—Globe Critics Fairly Answered.

The Globe has heretofore published in these columns several chapters on the famous Confederate partisan leader, Gen. John S. Mosby. From both Federal and Confederate correspondents we have been receiving criticism, from time to time, touching the tenor and sentiment of the articles published and we have been challenged to publish the official war record of this recent appointee of Secretary Hitchcock. The Globe, having no other interest in the matter than that of an ex-loyal soldier of the Union who has been raised with the conviction that everything else being equal, the ex-Federal should be preferred to the ex-Confederate soldier, by that Government the one helped to save and the other endeavored to destroy, for official positions in the gift of President, Cabinet officers and heads of Departments, lays the following before its readers. It will be seen even General Mosby does not come under the appellation of a recognized ex-Confederate regular soldier and that his own side repudiated him equally with the government he did so much to destroy. And for the benefit of the A.A.P.A. (Anarchist American Protective Association) we desire to state that Gen. John S. Mosby is neither an Irishman nor Roman Catholic.

Here is the record: [And of course, the article goes on to find the worst it can find, especially those in the Confederate armies who didn't like irregulars like Mosby.-vph]

An unusual and, frankly, tender story on Mosby reached print regarding an incident that had occurred in Denver while he was visiting son John Jr. on the way to his new post. Of course, as with almost every other article, his new position was mentioned in passing:

St. Louis Republic – October 16, 1901

MOSBY MOVED TO TEARS.

Confederate Rider Discovers One of His Old Battle Flags.

Denver, Colo., Oct. 15—Colonel John S. Mosby, the famous Confederate raider, stood to-day in front of a Denver book store with tears streaming down his cheeks.

A tattered battle flag displayed in the window had caught his eye. Once it had been a banner of splendid silk, an uncommon luxury among the Confederates at that time, and it floated proudly in several engagements in which Colonel Mosby took a conspicuous part.

The design on the flag was a cross of blue in a field of pink. The cross was dotted with eleven stars. Now it is all faded into a pale brown with age. At Colonel Mosby's suggestion the flag will be sent to the Confederate Museum at Richmond, Va.

Colonel Mosby is employed by the Government at the Federal Land Office in Akron, Colo., and is visiting his son, John S. Mosby, Jr., an attorney in Denver.

Mosby didn't obtain a "battle flag" for his command until the middle of 1864; and the first time he carried it into battle, if the account is correct, was in the Berryville Wagon Train Raid in August of that year. However, that flag was a first national—that is, the "Stars and Bars—and not the St. Andrew's Cross or what is known as the Confederate battle flag. Of course, Mosby may have had more than one flag; but aside from Berryville, nothing much has been said about the matter.

Mosby's amiable new relationship with the University of Virginia continued as noted in this article about a presentation of his portrait to that institution. There had been several previous attempts to have a portrait of the man donated in other venues, but Mosby had always eschewed such endeavors. First, he believed that such "memorials" should occur after the death of the person being "memorialized." Second, he did not want the people's money used to pay for a tribute to himself; and finally, he was simply too modest to entertain such attempts, however well meaning. It is interesting to note that this particular portrait was "received" by former General Fitzhugh Lee. On

November 24, 1901, Mosby wrote to his son Beverly, "It is one of the revenges of time to have Fitz Lee receive my portrait to hang at the university of Virginia. Fitz Lee who did all he could to prevent me from rising above the rank of a private."

Mosby's first "stop" in his new position was not Nebraska, but Colorado. The Colorado papers were not at all hostile to their new visitor as can be seen in a reprint by two Virginia papers of an article from the *Sterling Advertiser*:

Alexandria Gazette – December 4, 1901

Clarke Courier – December 11, 1901

Col. Mosby in Colorado

Our town has had a gentleman doing business with some of its citizens today who made a whole lot of history some thirty years ago. He was then without doubt one of the leading cavalry officers of the world. He had the dash of a Murat and the skill and cunning of a Marion. Sheridan, for at least two years, found him an unconquerable, tireless antagonist. He faced and fought the gallant Custer, Kilpatrick, Averill, Torbert and Merritt, and never acknowledged a superior among them. We allude to Colonel John S. Mosby, whose name must be familiar to everyone who has read the history of the Civil War. At present he is a special agent of the general land office and is here in that capacity. Personally he is a quiet, smooth-shaven, medium-sized, elderly gentleman, a typical American in every particular, and a fine representative of the southland in ante-bellum days. He will probably remain in town until tomorrow.—Sterling (Col.) Advertiser.

Mosby had been kept out of the McKinley administration until that president gave him a position shortly before his assassination. Now members of the cabinet were to learn what happened to the secretaries of the departments to which John Mosby was appointed. Generally, the matter was not at all pleasant for the official, who suddenly found himself in the anti-Mosby spotlight as wielded by the anti-Mosby press:

The Leader – December 21, 1901 (Edited)
BURNER FOR HITCHCOCK

Some Few Things the People Ought to Know The Washington Globe says: Some things the people have a right to know—the antecedents of public officials and the manner in which they administer the public business.

Some one tell us something about the public and private life of Ethan Allen Hitchcock, prior to his appointment as secretary of the interior.

By referring to "Official Register of United States, page 893," we find the name Ethan Allen Hitchcock, secretary of the interior, born in Alabama, appointed from St. Louis, Mo., salary $8,000 per year...

Is this all of the official acts and deeds of Ethan Allen Hitchcock, secretary of the interior? By no means.

Holding the official position he does, he has many smaller offices under his immediate supervision to be filled by good, responsible and reliable men, who will work in harmony with Ethan Allen & Co. So on July 5,

1901, he looks the whole United States over for some good man to fill the responsible position of special agent for the interior department. He did not have to go to Wyoming to find such a person, neither did he have to go to "old Missouri" and get Frank James, Cole or Bob Younger. He found a good man in Col. John S. Mosby, whose war records the Globe published September 29. No doubt Colonel Mosby will do his bidding. If not, he deceives his previous record.

What other official acts has this man Ethan Allen Hitchcock done? Many we could mention, but forbear for want of space in your valuable religious weekly, but will mention the fact that the much abused Henry Clay Evans, from Tennessee, not Wyoming or Missouri, is under the immediate control and direction of this man, born in Alabama and hailing from Missouri. Ethan Allen Hitchcock who could find no better man south of Mason and Dixon's line than Col. John S. Mosby to fill the responsible position of special agent (to himself) for the interior.

John S. Miller

Whether or not the corruption "revealed" in the unedited article was true (it probably was), Mr. Miller forgot that Colonel Mosby had already dealt with rampant corruption in the China service and could not be dissuaded from exposing all involved.

A most busy and important year had ended on a perceived high note. John Mosby was employed! However, there were serious family problems lurking in the shadows, especially with icon child, John Jr. Further, Mosby was soon to find that the "public land" issue, especially in Nebraska, had been investigated before without any appreciable results—a matter that was somewhat ominous. The coming year promised to present both problems and possibilities, the length, breadth, and scope of which could not be determined. But as had happened in the past, John Mosby showed no trepidation regarding the future.

Chapter 41

1902

Durum hoc est sed ita lex scripta est.
~ This is harsh, but the law is written.

"Where the battle rages, there the loyalty of the soldier is proved." ~ Martin Luther

THE FIRST FULL year in his new position found John Mosby going west to look into the encroachment onto the public lands by private individuals and corporations. However, this in no way detracted from the interest of the press in his historical activities as noted in this article commenting upon the actions that took place in the Boar War as they pertained to Mosby's strategies in the Civil War. It is also interesting to note that a whole new section of the nation's press began to take an interest in John Mosby. Gone was coverage limited to the two coasts or large cities such as Chicago. New publications now began to carry stories on this mythic man who had been in the crucible of the nation's struggles for over forty years:

> *Arizona Republican* – **January 8, 1902**
>
> Many an old soldier has doubtless read with peculiar interest the story of DeWet's raid on Firman's camp, says the Providence Journal. Mosby used to "strike" federal posts in almost precisely the same way and with equally successful results. In the dim light of breaking day his force would rush the pickets and tear through the camp, shooting and slashing at the Federals who ran out of their tents. In a very short time the raiders would be out of sight, before any effective resistance could be made or pursuit planned. Recalling Mosby's remarkable successes in thus annoying the Federal troops, any person who fails to understand why the British cannot end the Boer war may learn what difficulties they meet with.
>
> Mosby was on the border, often between large bodies of Federal troops, during four years, and he could not be captured or his band broken up. When diligently pursued his men would separate until the trail was lost. He captured his supplies from Federal camps. DeWet is equally dashing and resourceful though a much older man, and perhaps he cannot be taken in any less time than Mosby could. The latter was never captured.

There is one point that is seldom, if ever, made when writing about Mosby and his command's success in the war; that is, they were never destroyed. Many of them were captured and killed, but those lost were always replaced. And they all could be replaced—except John Mosby! Now it is said that William Chapman was "almost Mosby" and "as good as Mosby," but that is only because Chapman had Mosby behind him. Had Mosby been killed or incapacitated or captured, would Chapman have simply "replaced" Mosby? I think not. Chapman was certainly a fine officer, or Mosby would not have made him his second-in-command. But without John Mosby, it is doubtful that the Forty-third Battalion would have maintained its strength or its success. We see that fact during those periods Mosby was absent due to wounds. Indeed, in one case, he had to return prematurely because two of his commanders were having a "tiff" and affecting the efficiency of the command.

One of Mosby's old "bills" for money owed to him from the immediate postwar period was finally paid—or was it? Of course, this was disputed because of who Mosby was, how he fought, and on what side; but the facts were the facts:

Alexandria Gazette – February 23, 1902

Colonel Mosby Gets Pay.

The Washington correspondent of the Richmond News-Leader says: "Colonel John S. Mosby is one of the happiest men in Washington today. In 1865 he had some 7,000 pounds of tobacco in Richmond warehouses. The United States troops then stationed there made use of it. It was after the close of the war, and Colonel Mosby had been paroled, and thereby became entitled to all the protection of life and property than an American citizen enjoys. He therefore had a claim against the government for his tobacco. For years he has been trying to get Congress to pay for his "weed," but without success. This year, however, his claim went into the omnibus claims bill, and as a result, after forty years, Colonel Mosby will get paid for the smokes and chews the northern men had at his expense. The amount allowed him on the claim is $3,950.

It would seem that Mosby's "claim" was not paid after all but referred to the court of claims, where his attempt to recoup his consul fees had been found in his favor only to have the government appeal the verdict to the Supreme Court. Obviously, this matter was going on the same long, drawn-out rigmarole as Mosby's earlier efforts. A lesser man would have cut his losses and given up—but not John Mosby:

Richmond Dispatch – May 2, 1902

TOBACCO CLAIM OF MOSBY'S.

Senator Martin to-day reported, without amendment, Senator Daniel's bill, referring the claim of John S. Mosby against the United States, for the value of certain tobacco, to the Court of Claims.

The bill provides that the claim of John S. Mosby for the value of 7,900 pounds more or less, of tobacco, mentioned in an official paper dated at Rockettes landing, Richmond, Va., July 27, 1865, signed "W. H. D. Cochran, major, depot quartermaster," purporting to give "a list of captured tobacco, marked in the name of Colonel John S. Mosby, transferred to Colonel J. S. Loomis, Treasury agent, June 7, 1865," be referred to the Court of Claims, with full jurisdiction to try and adjudicate said claim, and render judgment against the United States in such sum as may be found just, without the interposition in behalf of the government of any bar arising from the existing statutes of limitation.

Right of appeal to the Supreme Court of the United States is expressly reserved to the government and to the claimant, but it is provided that any portions of such sum, representing tobacco beneficially belonging to the father, sister or other relatives of said Mosby, shall be held in trust by him accordingly.

Evening Times – **May 6, 1902**

COLONEL MOSBY WINS RIGHT TO NEW TRIAL

Senate Gives Permission to Further Press His Claim.

The Senate today passed a bill to refer the claim of John S. Mosby vs. the United States for the value of certain tobacco to the Court of Claims. This is to settle the action instituted by Colonel Mosby to secure payment for the tobacco taken when he was in the Confederate service in the civil war. The case is a long-pending one, judicial decision depending upon technical points of the law relating to the rights of those then in arms against the Federal government.

But when the tobacco was stolen, Mosby was not "in arms against the Federal government," and that is why he had a case in the first place. Another attempt was made to have the bill paid, but it was objected to as establishing a precedent "for those in arms against the Federal government"—again:

Times-Dispatch – **May 7, 1902**

MOSBY BILL PASSES

If Claim is Allowed It Will Establish a Precedent.

OMNIBUS CLAIMS MEASURE.

Sometimes the proof of the fascination of the press with John Mosby—absent any attempt or effort by him to provoke that interest—could be found in little items such as this. The article began as a mere mention of Mosby's "location" and ended with a sentence consigning the man to immortality. Anyone who knows or understands the newspaper business would see in such an item a matter beyond traditional reporting:

Free Lance – **March 2, 1902**

The Warrenton Virginian says: "Col. John S. Mosby is in Warrenton visiting his daughter on his way from San Francisco to New York. When the deeds of Col. Mosby have received the glamour of a more distant past, his name will be mentioned with Prince Rupert and Henry of Navarre."

Now for the first time, news stories begin to appear that specifically referenced Mosby's new position as an agent with the General Land Office. These became more numerous and more complex as time went on:

Arizona Silver Belt – **March 13, 1902**

Colonel John S. Mosby, the famous cavalry leader of the civil war, is in Denver as a special agent of the interior department. Colonel Mosby insists that fences erected unlawfully on the public range will have to come down. He says that many cattle kings have fenced in and appropriated to their own use tracts of land larger than that governed by many a German prince. He cites a case of one man near Sterling in which 25,000 acres has been enclosed. The law forbidding the practice was passed in 1885, but there is no evidence that it was ever enforced. He is trying to enforce it now, and it is raising an awful storm among the big cattlemen who have grabbed the land.—Drovers Telegram

The bloodshed and range wars that had erupted were not taking place in Nebraska, but they certainly were in Colorado and Wyoming. As these were reported in the newspapers, Mosby—by virtue of his reputation as a "warrior"—found himself being presented as a participant in these events rather than as a government agent looking into illegal fences, a matter that eventually proved fatal to his efforts:

Atlanta Constitution – **March 23, 1902 (Edited)**

*St. Louis Republic*an – **March 23, 1902**

MOSBY LEADS GOVERNMENT FORCES IN RANGE FIGHT

Famous Confederate Cavalryman Becomes a Spectacular Figure in Western Cattle War—His Duty to Clear Public Land of Private Fences—Work Requires Courage of a High Order.

Colonel John Mosby Famous Cavalry Leader Who Is Conspicuous in Range War

Denver, March 23—Colonel John S. Mosby, the famous Confederate cavalry leader, who is now special agent of the Government in charge of United States lands, has become a prominent and spectacular figure in the bitter fight for the range that is being waged by conflicting interests in the cattle and sheep country of the West.

Colonel Mosby's special duty is to clear the Government land of private fences—work that requires courage of a high order, for the annual sacrifice of lives in the West's great range fight is estimated at 500 victims, and death by assassination is the common lot of those who dare oppose one faction or another.

Colonel Mosby, whose headquarters are at Sterling, Colo., the center of a great cattle country, declares that some of the cattle kings have fenced in and appropriated to their own use tracts of land larger than many German principalities. In defiance of the law, they have seized upon Government land, fenced it in, forbidden settlers to touch it, and have made themselves wealthy from this illegal use of Uncle Sam's property.

COLONEL MOSBY'S STAND

Colonel Mosby's determined stand against the fencing in of public lands will do much to simplify matters if the example of the famous Confederate leader is followed by other United States officials. the next step will be to bring peace between the three conflicting interests of the range country—the cattle owners, the sheep men and the small ranchers. Until some sort of a truce is brought about, the yearly record of violent deaths on the range will more than equal the mortality of the American army in the Philippines.

To say that Mosby "stirred up" the cattlemen is nonsense. John Mosby was an agent of the Department of the Interior. He undoubtedly cared nothing about the matter until he addressed it in that capacity. Had he been a nonentity, no one would have made him personally responsible for the cattlemen's reaction to his investigation. It was Mosby's notoriety that made his involvement a personal matter especially in the press.

However, Mosby's greatest problems did not arise in Colorado and other areas where actual bloodshed had broken out, but in Nebraska, where huge cattle interests had virtually purchased that state lock, stock, and "ballot," making the great cattle kings secure in their belief that their fences would not be coming down, law or no law.

But the news coverage of Mosby's efforts "out west" made little out of *where* he was but created an entire "mystique" regarding *who* he was in the grand scheme of things. The investigative agent whose job it was to find and report illegal fences was being turned into a stern soldier whose job it was to fight for the right and to remove the fences and punish the lawbreakers. And while it is true that Mosby's information eventually secured grand jury indictments against those cattlemen who refused to adhere to the law, he had nothing at all to do with removing the fences; that was the job of the Department of Justice. But things in the land business seemed all astir, a situation adored by the press. It was the best of all possible worlds, a story of greed, corruption, and the rape of public lands—topped by the presence of a man who had been making headlines since 1862. As a result, the press dove right in, and the devil take the hindmost:

The Times - May 11, 1902 (Edited)

Richmond Times - May 11, 1902

COLONEL MOSBY IN THE SADDLE AGAIN

Colonel John Mosby, whose raids made him one of the greatest terrors of the Civil War, is in the saddle again, says the Philadelphia North American.

The famous Confederate cavalry leader is causing consternation among the Western cattle kings who have calmly fenced in Uncle Sam's land and grown rich by using it for grazing purposes. Colonel Mosby, armed with governmental authority, has just precipitated himself into the cattle country with characteristic vigor and has ordered that the fences be removed and the small ranchman given an equal chance with the rich companies to graze his cattle on the free lands.

It is not likely that the old Confederate raider, Colonel Mosby, will quail before the threats of the cattle kings, and with his advent on the scene will begin a new chapter in the struggle. He has ordered the companies to take down their fences, and has allowed them a stated time to do the work. The cattle kings are defying Mosby. They assert that the law forbidding the fencing of grazing land is a dead letter. One company which has fenced in 25,000 acres near Sterling, Col., Colonel Mosby's headquarters, declares that there fence is not a fence within the law's meaning because it encloses only one side of a triangle. The other two sides are formed by the fences of the Union Pacific and Burlington railroads. Colonel Mosby declares the company is trying to evade the law, and threatens to pull down the fence unless it is removed in the given time.

Alexandria Gazette - May 16, 1902 (Edited)

After Illegal Fences.—The famous old Confederate Colonel John S. Mosby, leader of the most desperate cavalry commands of the civil war, is again in the saddle, but on this occasion as United States special agent to protect the government domain. Col. Mosby, the same intrepid man as of old, when mounted on his swift charger, at the head of his dauntless dragoons, he dashed fearlessly into the ranks of the enemy, is creating the same confusion among the big cattle companies who have illegally fenced in millions of acres of government land, not only forcing out the small stockmen but preventing homeseekers from locating thereon. In one section of Nebraska more than 6,000,000 acres valued at more than $9,000,000, has been illegally fenced. It is understood that the big cattle interests have offered every inducement to call him off, but he turns a deaf ear to their most alluring offers. He goes after a law breaker with the same spirit of enthusiasm with which he used to go after the Yankee cavalry, and in three months has created more trouble than the grabbers of government land had seen before in fifteen years. The cattlemen are beginning to realize that the old guerrilla still loves a merry fight, and can fight hard.—[Ranche and Range.

Suddenly, what had been a "local story" had become a matter of national interest as can be seen from the sheer number of newspapers all over the country carrying it! Why? The matter certainly had little "news interest" before John Mosby was sent West! Indeed, he was not the first man to investigate the matter—nor was he the last! The fact is however that he was the most interesting and, in the public mind, the most important man to do so! Again, the matter was reiterated in a long article carried by at least nine newspapers and probably more. It is interesting to note that the newspapers started to call for Federal action against the lawbreakers, indicating that the collusion of local and state officials in these illegalities was no secret. Below is a list of the very diverse publications carrying the now well-known story:

New Enterprise - **June 12, 1902* (Edited)**

Atlanta Constitution – **March 22, 1902**

St. Louis Republic – **March 23, 1902**

The Sun – **March 30, 1902**

Florida Star – **April 11, 1902**

Washington Bee – **April 12, 1902**

Beaver Herald – **April 24, 1902**

San Juan Islander – **April 24, 1902**

Camden Chronicle – **June 13, 1902**
MURDER ON THE RANGES

War Over Western Ranges

Bloody Strife Between the Cattle Companies and Others

Colonel John Mosby, the ex-Confederate Cavalry Leader is Acting For the Government in Clearing Its Land of Squatters—Annual Sacrifices of Life.

John Mosby was not alone in this matter. There were other government agents and officials, some of whom had been there before Mosby and remained after he was gone. Among these were Commissioner Hermann, District Attorney Summers, and Agent Lesser. Also, according to stories published in the summer of 1902, illegal fences found by Mosby and others were in fact being removed! In a scenario not unlike the newspaper coverage of Mosby's wounds during the war, all through this matter (and while the fences continued to stand!), there were countless reports of fences being removed, about to be removed, or having been removed. Below is one such:

Salt Lake Herald – July 10, 1902
FENCES ON PUBLIC RANGES BEING REMOVED

(Special to the Herald)

Washington, D. C., July 9.—Special agents of the general land office in various parts of the west are reporting general success in their efforts to secure the removal of fences from the public rangers.

Colonel Mosby of civil war fame, now special agent in Colorado and Nebraska, in a conference with Land Commissioner Hermann today, said the removal of fences in his district is proceeding rapidly, and in only two or three cases has it been necessary to institute suit against the owners. The land office officials have been aided in the work by the trespassers themselves. Those who have been forced to remove fences have, in turn, given information of other fences erected illegally. Commissioner Hermann says the work of fence removal will be continued, either by the owners or by the aid of United States marshals, whose aid will be invoked where resistance is offered.

At this point, Mosby came east to be with his spinster daughter, Pauline, who was being operated on for appendicitis. While in Washington, he met with Secretary Hitchcock while Commissioner Hermann, in the meantime, publicly noted the complaints arising in Nebraska, not against Mosby but against "the cattle barons," who were said to be usurping land not their own:

Ranche and Range – July 24, 1902 (Edited)
FENCES MUST COME DOWN.

Col. John S. Moseby, of ex-confederate fame, and who is a special agent of the land department detailed for work in Colorado, Wyoming and the extreme western portion of Nebraska, is in Washington. Col. Moseby had an interview with Secretary Hitchcock a few days ago, and in the course of the conversation stated that the fences on the public domain in the western part of Nebraska were being taken down without any great trouble.

Commissioner Hermann, of the general land office, speaking of the work of removing the fences by cattle barons and large corporations on the public lands in Nebraska, stated that from Col. Moseby's district he had heard little or no complaint, but that from other sections of Nebraska he had heard many complaints as to the high-handed manner in which the cattle barons were usurping lands not their own.

This article in the *Alliance Herald* was more than a little odd. Eventually, the paper became Mosby's implacable foe and attacked him mercilessly. But here, it stated that the stockmen knew that the fences had to come down, and Mosby was simply "here" to see that the law "is complied with." Had the newspaper retained that position, there would have been no problem—but it did not. Whether it changed its position or whether the position put forth here was a façade in hopes that Mosby would leave as did all the other General Land Office agents (that is, with the fences still intact), it is impossible to say:

Alliance Herald – **August 8, 1902**

A special dispatch from this city to the Lincoln Journal states that the presence here of Col. John S. Mosby has occasioned considerable uneasiness among the stockmen of this section. There is no occasion for uneasiness. Those who have fences around government land were long since apprised of the fact that those fences must come down, and Col. Mosby is here in accordance with the wishes of the interior department to see that the law is complied with. His mode of procedure will be, as the Herald understands it, to notify parties who have fenced in any part of the public domain to remove said fencing within sixty days after notification. The immediate cause of Col. Mosby's presence in Alliance is a speech delivered at the cattlemen's convention held in this city last February, but President S. P. Delatour, in which the statement was made that in the Alliance and Sidney districts there were over 6,000,000 acres of government land under fence. But be that as it may, there is nothing to be made by protesting against the inevitable and growling about the hardships and inconvenience that will accrue, Uncle Sam says these fences must come down, and that settles it.

On August 8, a reporter from the *Alliance Herald* described his interaction with the newly appointed General Land Office agent thusly:

"There is present in the little city of Alliance today a man who, during the four long, memorable and cruel years of carnage and bloodshed between the sections from 1861 to 1865 played as prominent a part and did as much toward making history as any other one man, save, perhaps, U.S. Grant or Robert E. Lee. This man is none other than the redoubtable Col. John S. Mosby, of Confederate guerilla fame."

The reporter interviewed Mosby and stated that he "enjoyed immensely an hour's visit with the gray-haired old veteran. The Mosby of today doesn't impress one as the Mosby of history. About the battle-scarred old trooper there is nothing that smacks of ferocity, nothing to indicate the daring, dashing cavalry commander, who, with never more than three hundred men, neutralized and held at bay for two years from forty to fifty thousand splendidly armed and equipped federal soldiers. *But instead there is every indication of the plain, unostentatious, intelligent old gentleman with a mind as vivid and active as in the years of long ago, and a bearing as pleasing and manner as courteous as a diplomat.*"

Again, here is firsthand testimony of the real John Mosby and not the blunt, abrasive, and difficult individual presented to the public in so many books and articles. If any of Mosby's biographers have referred to him as having "a bearing as pleasing and a manner as courteous as a diplomat," apparently, that particular observation was unfortunately edited out of their books to the detriment of the work. However, just as the Herald appeared to be at least objective in the matter, a week later, it presented a very different viewpoint with regard to the fence business:

Alliance Herald – **August 15, 1902**

Col. Mosby has received a number of complaints about fences on government land and is sending out orders for their removal. One complaint from Newport was addressed to the "U.S. government fence destroyer."

Commissioner Hermann had reiterated something that the newspapers never seemed to understand or, more to the point, wanted to understand: The land department notified offending ranchers of their illegal fences and gave them a period of time in which to remove them voluntarily. If they did not, the department informed the US district attorney of their failure to comply. The removal of the fences was then in the hands of the district attorney and federal marshals. So the drumbeat of claims that Mosby was there "to take down the fences" is legal and factual nonsense. But what Mosby did provide was a well-known face and a better-known name to be used by those who rejected the government's effort to implement an unpopular law. He became the focus of all the negative response to that law and its enforcement as can be seen in the following:

Richmond Dispatch, – **August 20, 1902 (Edited)**

MOSBY NOW RAIDING FENCES

He is in Montana, Defying the Cattle Barons. [Baltimore American.]

The many friends of Colonel John S. Mosby will enjoy the following glimpses of the present day life of the noted ex-Confederate given in a special dispatch from Omaha, Neb.:

"Colonel Mosby," says the dispatch, "is about to invade Wyoming. He will not ride into the state on a wild charger at the head of a troop of daring Confederates, like those who followed him in the sixties, but his coming will cause much excitement, especially among the large cattle owners, who have millions of acres of government land fenced illegally.

"Colonel Mosby is now special Agent of the United States General Land Office, and for several months he has been detailed in Colorado to see that the fences in that State come down.

VIOLATIONS PLENTIFUL.

"Never in the history of the western ranges has such a daring, uncompromising and absolutely fearless official been sent against the power of the millions of wealth commanded by the cattle barons. Heretofore special agents have made attempts against the illegal fencing of land, but intimidation, threats of death or money manipulated in various ways have served to cause a vigorous prosecution of the work to become abandoned, and the consequence was at the time Colonel Mosby went to Colorado there were 6,146,200 acres of government land illegally fenced in, worth $9,219,300. So long as these fences are allowed to remain the settler is barred from securing land upon which to build a home; indeed, one of the chief objects in erecting these fences is to keep out settlers, thus reserving the land for ranges upon which cattle may roam and feed. The cowboy has become practically unknown, for his services are but little needed when owners know that their stock cannot mix. This also is a saving of hundreds of thousands of dollars to cattle companies, while it deprives thousands of men of following their chosen vocations.

Colonel Mosby was sent to get the barriers down. At first he was coaxed and made much of by the wealthy classes, but this scheme didn't make an impression. Later he was approached with financial offerings, but he refused to wink, and went on about his business with such a startling chain of surprises that he was finally threatened. What Colonel Mosby can do against the powers remains to be seen 'I am satisfied that I could clean up a fortune if I would only wink at what I see,' said Colonel Mosby, 'and allow those fences to stand as they have for ten years, but I am ordering them down, just same; and if the department stands by me I'll carry out my present instructions, even if I have to get soldiers to back me.'"

We now begin to see Mosby being "quoted" in the press, and while he did occasionally speak to those organs, a great deal was reported said that was never said. However, that fact didn't mean anything when the political collusion purchased with cattle money made Mosby's removal desirous. At this point, however, the matter had not gotten that far, albeit it was more than probable that bribery—and perhaps even threats—had already been attempted. And for the second time, the name of one of the Nebraska senators appeared, Senator Millard, claiming that Mosby was being "too active" in enforcing the law:

Omaha Daily Bee – **October 14, 1902**

CATTLEMEN ARE OBJECTING

Complain Colonel Mosby is Too Active Tearing Down the Fences
SENATOR MILLARD BACKING THEM UP

Washington, Oct. 13.—(Special Telegram.)—Colonel John S. Mosby, special agent of the land office, is in Washington to give President Roosevelt and Secretary of the Interior Hitchcock his views regarding conditions affecting the reduction of fences in western Nebraska. Colonel Mosby was authorized by the land department of the government to see that the fences the cattlemen have unlawfully erected upon public lands be taken down and Mosby has seen to it that the fences of the cattlemen had run on the public domain were removed. This action of Mosby in carrying out the regulations of the Secretary of the Interior has created such a feeling of indignation on the part of the cattlemen that Senator Millard has taken a hand in the fence war. He protests against Mosby's activity and has asked for an investigation of his acts. Accordingly, Colonel Mosby has reported to Washington to explain what he has done in the way of carrying out the regulations of the Interior Department.

Colonel Mosby is obdurate. He says the fences are down in his district, a region comprising six or seven counties bordering on Wyoming, and that so far as he is concerned they will stay down. If, however, the Secretary of the Interior decides that the aggressive work now going on looking to the removal of the fences be curtailed, Colonel Mosby will execute the wishes of his superior officer. Charges are made against him of undue severity in carrying out the regulations of the Interior Department. It is asserted cattlemen who have rights in the premises are being deprived of the inclosures by reason of the manner of which Colonel Mosby interpreted his orders from the land office. It was stated today at the Interior Department that in view of the president's illness and the interest in which he is taking in the anthracite coal strike, the conference with Colonel Mosby will not take place until the end of the week. The fact remains, however, that Senator Millard is active in bringing about the conference as soon as possible and that he appears as the spokesman of the cattlemen. Meanwhile the fences were, but are not.

Mosby had supposedly been recalled to Washington for "upsetting" the Nebraska cattle barons, but that was not so. However, to call Mosby "obdurate" is senseless. He was sent to do a job, but he had also made clear that if his superiors changed his orders, he would obey. In other words, that the scope and strictness of the interpretation of the law were not in his purview to alter.

Reference to the charge that Mosby was guilty of "undue severity" in carrying out the regulations of the Interior Department were reiterated ever more loudly and frequently; and in a later article, Mosby published in great detail exactly what his "instructions" were, probably in hopes of deflecting those charges:

Omaha Daily Bee – **October 22, 1902**
MOSBY REPORTS ON FENCES.

Has Conference with Secretary of the Interior Over Complaint of Cattle Men Washington, Oct. 21.—(Special Telegram)—Colonel John S. Mosby, special agent of the land office, is in Washington and has had a conference with secretary of the interior regarding the removal of fences in western Nebraska. Colonel Mosby has taken a very strong position in administering the law regarding these fences and cattlemen have protested with the result that Colonel Mosby is called upon by the secretary to explain. It could not be learned what had occurred at the conference between the secretary and Colonel Mosby, but the latter is requested to make a report covering the controversy from his viewpoint. It was said at the interior department today that Colonel Mosby, it is supposed is writing his report and will doubtless submit it in a few days.

Meanwhile, papers all over the nation had joined in to report the matter. These reports usually depended upon the location of the publication and ranged from defense of the stockmen to charges that they were illegally preventing the authorized use of public lands. The treatment of Mosby usually depended upon the newspaper's "side" on the issue. Pro-stockman, anti-Mosby; anti-illegal fencing, pro- or "almost" pro-Mosby:

The Times – **October 23, 1902**

St. Paul Globe – **October 23, 1902**

San Francisco Call – **October 23, 1902**

Bisbee Daily Review – **October 23, 1902**
WESTERN LANDS OCCUPIED ILLEGALLY BY STOCK RAISERS SAYS HOME-SEEKERS ARE DEPRIVED OF LAND

Colonel Mosby Reports to Roosevelt That Stockraisers Should Be Ousted. Interior Department Will Take Measures to Oust Them

Washington, D. C., Oct. 22.—

Col. John S. Mosby, special agent of the interior department, called upon the president today and laid before him the result of his investigation into the alleged illegal occupation of public lands in Colorado and other Western states by stock raisers.

Col. Mosby told the president that millions of acres of public land that ought rightfully to be opened to the homestead settler were occupied by stock raisers. The interior department, it is expected, will take measures to oust such stock raisers as are not occupying the public lands lawfully.

As usual, the matter was made to appear as if it were Mosby who was ruling against the cattlemen and not the law he was sent to enforce. At this point, it appeared that he had presented his report to the president, and it was Roosevelt who had chosen to enforce a law that had been a virtual dead letter since its passage. But whatever Mosby's situation, there seemed no question that his findings were correct; and if Roosevelt wanted the fences down, Mosby's presence or absence made absolutely no difference in the matter as noted in this article:

Omaha Daily Bee – October 24, 1902 (Edited)

Columbus Journal – October 29, 1902

MOSBY FILES HIS REPORT

Indications Interior Department Will Stand By Inspector Hermann to Protect Homesteaders

Department Held to Have No Discretion in the Matter, but Must Enforce the Law Which is Held to be Clear.

Washington, Oct. 23—[Special Telegram.]—Colonel John S. Mosby, special agent of the Interior department, today called upon Secretary Hitchcock and laid before him the results of his investigations of the illegal occupancy of public lands in Nebraska and other states by stock raisers. … It is said at the land office that it has been estimated that millions of acres of public land that ought rightfully to be open to homestead settlers is now occupied by cattlemen. Land Commissioner Hermann is most emphatic in his statement that he will make very effort to enforce the law and remove the fencing and give every assistance to the homesteader to enter peacefully upon the lands now fenced and rightfully a part of the public domain. …

The law is clear and it will be most rigidly enforced against such cattlemen as are found to be illegally upon public domain. Colonel Mosby will remain in Washington to be at hand to aid the Secretary of the interior in solving the present contention between the fenced-in cattle raisers, small cattlemen and homesteaders.

Commissioner Hermann reiterated what Mosby had said in press interviews—the ones he actually gave, that is—that he, Hermann, was not in a position to abridge the law and that if the cattlemen and their congressional representatives were unhappy, they had to prevail upon Congress to amend or repeal the statute. Finally, however, there was an example of actual journalism. Whatever the opinion of the papers' editors, the report pointed out that the Department of the Interior—and Mosby as its agent—had no options in their endeavors. A lot of the press in the West would have been far more help to their readers if they had been similarly accurate in their reporting rather than creating straw men to attack in print.

Aberdeen Herald – October 27, 1902

Chanute Times – October 31, 1902

To Oust Stock Raisers.

Interior Department Will Remove Them From Public Lands

Washington, Oct. 27.—Colonel John S. Mosby, special agent of the interior department, laid before the president the result of his investigation of the illegal occupation of public lands in western states by stock raisers. Colonel Mosby told the president that millions of acres of public land, that ought rightfully to be open to the homestead settler, were occupied by stock raisers. After concluding the investigation it is making, the interior department will undertake to oust such stock holders as are not occupying the public lands lawfully.

Alliance Herald – October 31, 1902

Concerning Col. John S. Mosby's Return.

A special dispatch from Washing to the Denver News says:

Washington, Oct. 22.—Colonel John S. Mosby, special agent of the interior department, called upon the president to-day and laid before him the result of his investigation of the illegal occupation of public lands in Colorado and other western states by stock raisers. Colonel Mosby told the president that millions of acres of public land that ought rightfully to be open to the homestead settlers were occupied by stock raisers. After concluding the investigation it is thought the Interior will oust such stock raisers as are not occupying the public lands lawfully.

A ranchman living about fifteen miles from Alliance wrote Congressman McClellan in regard to removal of fences and received the following reply:

Washington, D. C., Oct. 21, 1902.

Dear Sir:—I beg to acknowledge the receipt of your letter of October 15th. I am informed at the United States General Land office that Colonel John S. Mosby has been neither removed nor transferred. He is now in Washington, D. C., having been called here by the president on business, upon the transaction of which he will return to Nebraska. I am, Yours very truly,

George B. McClellan.

That little bit of news must have stuck in the craw of a lot of newspapers and not just the *Alliance Herald*. So Mosby wasn't "recalled" after all. Then suddenly, a new and important matter came to light:

New York Tribune – **November 6, 1902**

St. Paul Globe – **November 6, 1902**

LAND ENTRY FRAUDS

SOLDIERS' WIDOWS SAID TO BE GUILTY OF THEM

IN NEBRASKA GOVERNMENT SUSPENDS LARGE NUMBER OF ENTRIES

Special Agent, an Iowa Man, Is Put Out of Business in This Connection Result of Investigation by Special Agent Mosby, Who Led Guerrilla Bands in the Civil War.

Washington, Nov. 5.—The interior department has suspended with a view to cancellation a large number of alleged fraudulent land entries in Nebraska made by soldiers' widows, who, it is charged, have entered into an agreement for the transfer of the lands to cattlemen. W. N. Lesser, of Iowa, a special agent, whose headquarters have been for several years at North Platte, Neb., has been suspended in connection with these proceedings.

The action follows an investigation that had been conducted in Nebraska by Col. John S. Mosby, the former guerrilla leader, who is now a special agent of the general land office. The exact extent of these operations is not disclosed, but so far as known there are about 45 or 50 of them, each entry being for 160 acres. The government recently has been enforcing its regulations for the removal of fences erected by cattlemen on public lands and an effort to validate as far as possible the land now occupied by the cattlemen. Under the law soldiers' widows have a right to make entries of public lands without any residence requirements, but they are required to make improvements and cultivate the lands.

It is understood that the women who made the entries are mostly Chicago people who were influenced to take theses steps by the agents of cattlemen, with the agreement to transfer the land to the latter by leases with the right to purchase.

The Times – **November 6, 1902**

MOSBY'S INVESTIGATION LEADS TO SUSPENSION

(by Associated Press.)

Washington, Nov. 5.—The Interior Department has suspended with a view to cancellation, a large number of alleged fraudulent land entries in Nebraska made by soldiers' widows, who, it is charged, have entered into an agreement for the transfer of the lands to cattlemen.

W. N. Lesser, of Iowa, a special agent, whose headquarters for several years have been at North Platte, Neb. Has been suspended in connection with these proceedings.

The action follows an investigation that has been quietly conducted in Nebraska by Colonel John S. Mosby, the former guerrilla leader, who is now a special agent of the general land office.

Perhaps the most enlightening comment in the above article, short as it was, was the first part of the last sentence: "The action follows an investigation that had been quietly conducted in Nebraska by Col. John S. Mosby ..." Where now was the "bull in the china shop"? Where the boisterous, loud, thoughtless, bumbling old man who made a fool of himself, his government, and his party? Throughout Mosby's years in the Department of the Interior and later in the Department of Justice, he consistently rendered good and useful service involving many matters that were of great political and diplomatic delicacy and did so without fail while gaining the trust and respect of those with whom he was engaged. Just as "Mosby the guerrilla" could not have been cruel to prisoners and noncombatants on one day and noble and generous the next, the idea that he was a bumbling lout sometimes and a paragon of diplomacy at others is—to use John Mosby's own words—poppycock!

Stark County Democrat – **November 11, 1902**

LAND FRAUDS Widows of Soldiers Take Claims to Help the Cattlemen.

McCook Tribune – **November 14, 1902**

Valentine Democrat – **November 13, 1902**

Salt Lake Herald - **November 6, 1902**

Alliance Herald – **November 7, 1902**

IT LOOKS MUCH LIKE FRAUD. LAND ENTRIES SUSPENDED.

Colonel Mosby Finds Chicago Women Holding Lands for Cattle Companies Land Entries in Nebraska May Be Cancelled.

[A long story about the land frauds followed, and the paragraph below was added in the *Valentine Democrat* and the *Alliance Herald*.-vph]

It is reported that Colonel Mosby will return to Alliance in the near future and it is predicted that the Alliance editors who lambasted him after his departure will be seeking shelter when Mosby lands in Alliance.

The main thrust against Mosby was his supposed "high profile" involvement with the press during his investigation. But certainly, his early efforts—here described as "quiet"—seem to counter claims that he was a disruptive figure from the beginning of the investigation. However, John Mosby was, perforce, "high profile" within the press establishment. It didn't matter what he did or where he did it. This condition was simply the situation extant, and to blame him for something over which he had no control is both unjust and unreasonable.

Wichita Daily Eagle – **November 16, 1902**

Yorkville Enquirer – **December 3, 1902**

Anderson Intelligencer – **December 1, 1902**

MOSBY'S LAST RAID.

Colonel Mosby of civil war guerrilla war fame has made another raid, this time rounding up a band of men and women who have been systematically defrauding Uncle Sam out of western grazing lands. Colonel Mosby is a special agent of the land office of the interior department, and lately has been engaged in clearing certain public lands in Nebraska and other western states of the fences that had been illegally erected by cattle men in their efforts to control grazing fields. Mosby was located in a small Nebraska town, in which there is a land office, when about thirty women got off the train in charge of a slick looking individual. All the women marched to the land office and filed claims for grazing plots, on the ground that they were the widows of Union soldiers. In each case the soldier's service was given as just sufficient to cover the claim.

Colonel Mosby was suspicious of the outfit, and engaged one of the women to conversation, with the result that he found that the whole scheme was a fraud and none of the women were widows of Union soldiers. After getting their warrants they proposed to turn the land over to a big syndicate that is monopolizing grazing lands. Wholesale arrests were made at Colonel Mosby's recommendation.—Brooklyn Eagle.

Omaha Sunday Bee – **November 16, 1902 (Edited)**
WORK FOR THE COURT

Government Sustains Colonel Mosby in Fence Removal Matters

RETURNS TO NEBRASKA TO RESUME WORK

Civil Suits to Be Brought to Compel Removal of the Fences

Grand Jury Also Has Grist to Grind

District Attorney Summers Instructed to Act on the Complaints

TO GO INTO MATTER OF WIDOWS' CLAIMS

Peculiar Methods Adopted by Special Agent Lesser Are Also to Be Brought to Attention of Grand Jury.

[This very lengthy article recapping most of the situation becomes of interest because of Special Agent Lesser. The narrative is picked up when he appears:-vph]

In connection with the fraudulent entries, Special Agent W. R. Lesser has been suspended by the land office and it is stated he will be dismissed and his irregularities laid before the grand jury. The grand jury will be asked to indict him for the use of fraudulent vouchers uttered to obtain money from the government. Mr. Lesser was appointed special agent of the department about six years ago from Iowa. He was assigned to work in the state of Nebraska with headquarters at North Platte. Mr. Lesser was suspended November 1 and since that time his actions have been undergoing rigid investigation. At least one false voucher has been discovered. It appears that while the department believed him in Nebraska he has really spent much of the time during the last year at his home in Tama, Ia., mailing all official mail aboard railway trains so the postmark would not give away his exact whereabouts.

Every agent of the department is compelled to make weekly reports, showing just where he has been from day to day and what he has been doing. It is asserted that of the eighty-two days from March to August 1, which his weekly reports shows he spent at North Platte, Lesser in reality was only at headquarters nine days during that time. The register of the land office at that place states that Lesser was really only at headquarters nine days and has not been there since July. Mr. Lesser's reply to this is that he was traveling about Nebraska on official business, but the postmaster at Tama says he was at his home in Tama during the time alleged to have been at North Platte or traveling. Another account against Lesser is that he has sent in an expense account averaging $100 a month, incurred in railroad travel. It is asserted at the Interior department that investigation shows that even when he did travel he rode on passes. During all the six years Mr. Lesser has been assigned to Nebraska he has never even hinted to a cattleman that his fence should be removed, according to the Interior Department officials. Mr. Lesser is credited with asserting that Senator Allison, who secured his appointment, will come to his rescue and obtain his reinstatement. As yet, however, Senator Allison has not written or spoken a word in behalf of Lesser.

Implicates Lesser.

Colonel Mosby in a letter to Agent Lesser, suggested that A. B. Todd of Plattsmouth, Neb., should be indicted for complicity with fraudulent widows' entries. "Mr. Lesser," said Colonel Mosby, "refused to act. I have seen Todd several times at the Alliance land office in company with alleged widows and was told he came several hundred miles as their escort. It is not thought that he was actuated by a sentiment of mere gallantry, or charitable motives."

Lesser defended himself by blaming all of his woes on Mosby. Yet this article suggested that a lot more people in the Department of the Interior than John Mosby were after Lesser's scalp. Still, it was just one more piece of the fabric of lies that finally allowed Mosby to be dismissed when his continuing honesty started to get in the way of political ambitions and economic expectations. But Lesser wasn't the only problem. District Attorney Summers was also less than anxious to proceed against the cattlemen:

Omaha Daily Bee – November 17, 1902 (Edited)

WILL FOLLOW INSTRUCTIONS

United States District Attorney Refers to Charges of Colonel Mosby

United States Attorney W. S. Summers denies that he has been apathetic in the matter of compelling those who have fenced in government land in western Nebraska to remove such structures as charged by Colonel John S. Mosby, special agent of the general land office. Commenting on the dispatch from Washington, printed in *The Sun*day Bee, Attorney Summers said:

"While Special Agent Mosby was in Nebraska on duty he sent to me some five or six affidavits relative to fences on government land, and in each instance he notified me that he had given the parties named in the affidavits sixty days in which to remove the fences. The sixty days' time given by Mosby as special agent has not yet expired, except in one case. In that case the sixty days expired on the 8th of this month, at which time I was engaged in arranged for the examination of, in all, perhaps 150 or 200 witnesses before the grand jury, and since then I have been engaged in work before the grand jury. There is no disposition on my part to neglect any duty, and should any instruments be received by me from the Department of Justice they certainly will be followed to the letter. As to the questions submitted to or being investigated by the grand jury, I have nothing to say.

In a later article, Agent Lesser testified that he was aware of what was going on with the cattlemen including their obtaining property through various (and nefarious) means and that he had made all of this information known to the Department of the Interior. However, according to Lesser, it had been ignored. It was obvious that "official" collusion in the matter was not limited to Nebraska.

Omaha Daily Bee, November 21, 1902
MOSBY IS COMING TO OMAHA

Later He Will Go to North Platte on Special Mission for Land Department Washington, Nov. 20.—[Special Telegram.]—

Colonel John S. Mosby will leave Washington Saturday for Omaha. Colonel Mosby is not certain how long he will remain in Omaha, as he is under orders to precede to North Platte, Neb., to do a little investigating for the general land office into the conduct of Special Agent Lesser, who is under suspension pending an investigation into charges preferred against him. After concluding his investigation at North Platte Colonel Mosby will proceed to his former post in Alliance.

Minneapolis Journal – November 21, 1902 (Edited)
LAND FRAUDS IN NEB.

United States Grand Jury at Omaha Is Probing an Alleged Monumental Scandal Filings by Hundreds of Soldiers' Widows in Behalf of the State's Cattle Barons

Omaha, Neb., Nov. 21.—Nebraska is on the eve of the greatest scandal so wide-spreading and far-reaching that thousands of people from twenty or more states are concerned in its different ramifications.

The Times – November 23, 1902
COLONEL MOSBY'S PLAN

After Visiting in and About Washington, He Returns to Nebraska.

Washington, November 22.—Colonel John S. Mosby, who has been here or hereabouts since the early portion of last month on business relative to some large domains of public land out in Nebraska, received his final instructions this morning, and after spending a few hours with friends and old comrades in arms over in Alexandria this afternoon, left tonight for the West.

The Colonel looks spry, and says he feels quite spry, yet he is getting well along in life, and the past several years have not been his best. His hair is white as driven snow and the wrinkles of his face are growing somewhat more marked, yet the Colonel trips along little bent, and like unto a music teacher or dancing master who has music ever ringing in his ears, will spring in his very soul. Colonel Mosby wears good clothes now too. Not store clothes exactly, but tailor-made garments—cut, as an old comrade says, for a dudey dude, and carries a silk umbrella and sometimes wears patent leather shoes. There is a noticeable nervousness about the Colonel just now, however, that several have spoken of, yet some that are more intimate with him say it is but his natural way when he gets bent on doing something thoroughly and going into it in earnest

Mosby made an attempt to counter the charges that he was personally motivated to attack the cattlemen, and in a lengthy and detailed article provided the complete text of his instructions from the Department of the Interior. He also cited what he had already done, and provided the "legal precedent" bolstering the "law" he had come to enforce including the common law origins of the right to graze animals upon "public lands". As usual with Mosby, it didn't help:

Omaha Daily Bee – November 24, 1902 (Edited)

REPORTS ON FENCES

Colonel Mosby Deals at Length with the Troublesome Question

CITES THE LAW IN REGARD TO SAME

Has No Discretion Except to Compel Cattlemen to Remove Them

TAKES UP ALLEGED FRAUDULENT ENTRIES

Men Holding under Them Not Protected by a Color of Title

MANY THOUSANDS OF ACRES ARE INVOLVED

Parties Who Erect Fences Pay No Attention to Notices to Pull Them Down unless Backed up by Suit.

Quotes His Instructions.

"The instructions of February 6, 1902, say:

You will, therefore, give notice verbally or by letter to all persons maintaining inclosures or drift fences on public lands without color of title, calling attention to their violation of the law and advising them that in the event of their failure to remove the fences within sixty days institution of suit b e recommended.

You are directed to use utmost vigilance and activity in examining and reporting upon unlawful inclosures or drift fences in your districts.

"The instructions of October 3, 1902, say:

While, judging from the numerous complaints received at this office, unlawful fencing of public land by stockmen is still carried on to a great extent in the western section of the country, comparatively few cases are reported by special agents, notwithstanding existing instructions issued by the land department with the aim of breaking up the practice of controlling public lands by fencing in violation of the act of February 25, 1885 (23 Stat. 321).

You will push the fencing matter vigorously hereafter in order that all the public land unlawfully occupied may be opened to the general public as soon as possible, being strictly governed by the circular order of February 6, 1902, and so much of the instructions to special agents attached to blank form (4-495), etc.

"I have endeavored to execute the law and to conform to the instructions of the general land office."

"Very respectfully, "JOHN S. MOSBY, Special Agent."

Those who have written about this period in John Mosby's life have either not read his "report," or they have chosen to ignore the fact that everything he did was completely validated by those instructions and the law. Further, Mosby had no desire to "punish" or bring criminal proceedings against the stock raisers. All he wanted to do was what he had been ordered to do—that is, have the fences removed! The idea that he somehow had a personal vendetta against those involved is absurd. He was given very specific, and somewhat forceful instructions; and he followed them to the best of his considerable ability—more's the pity. And still, the reports continued:

The Sun – **November 24, 1902**

Woodville Republican – **November 29, 1902**

WIDOWS SECURED IN DROVES—HOMESTEAD ENTRY FRAUDS

Big Land-Stealing Scheme by the Cattlemen

A Great Scandal in Western Land Entries is About to Be Made Public. WIDOWS OF UNION SOLDIERS INVOLVED.

Scheme to Prevent the Government From Taking Down Fences on Grazing Lands—One Man Planned to Form a Cordon of Widows 100 Miles Long— Grand Jury After Conspirators.

San Francisco Examiner – **November 24, 1902**

San Francisco Call – **November 24, 1902**

BIG CONSPIRACY OF CATTLE KINGS

Soldiers' Widows Lured Into Entanglements With Government.

No matter what the situation with the "widows" and the homestead law, even if the land on which the fences stood had been legally owned or leased by the ranchers, the land enclosed by those fences belonged to the people of the United States and once enclosed by barbed wire that land was no longer available to anyone but the cattlemen who owned the fences. That is the crux of the entire "fencing" matter.

The Times – **November 25, 1902**

COL. MOSBY TO GIVE GRAND JURY INFORMATION

(Special Dispatch to *The Times*.)

Omaha. Neb., November 24.—Colonel John S. Mosby will go before the grand jury to give information concerning the land frauds. In the future when a widow of a Union soldier presents herself at a land office and attempts to obtain a homestead she will be rigidly examined to see that she isn't in league with some cattle "baron" before her application is accepted.

Minneapolis Journal – November 27, 1902

MOSBY IS ON THE TRAIL

He Has Instructions From the President to Enforce Land Laws in Nebraska

Chicago, Nov. 27.

—Wholesale land frauds, involving some of the wealthiest cattlemen in western Nebraska, are being investigated by the federal grand jury in Omaha.

Colonel John S. Mosby, the special agent of the land department, who was sent to Alliance to inquire into alleged frauds, passed through the city yesterday bearing instructions from President Roosevelt to enforce the law and compel the removal of all fences on government lands. Colonel Mosby criticizes severely the attitude taken in the matter by Senators Millard and Dietrich of that state.

The inquiry of Colonel Mosby already has resulted in the removal of Special Agent W. R. Lesser, who failed to enforce the law.

Mosby never "severely criticized" the Nebraska senators, although it was reported that he did so. It may be assumed that the Journal merely repeated the allegation, though there was no basis for it. Interestingly enough, Dietrich was impeached for accepting bribes, but not as the result of anything allegedly said by John Mosby.

Custer County Republican – November 27, 1902

Gen. Mosby seems to have lost none of his old time vigor, as is shown by his report to the secretary of the interior on his efforts to have the fences of the cattle kings removed from the public domains.

Hickman Courier – November 28, 1902

[*Some damage to the paper at the bottom of the article-vph]

EVICTING THE CATTLE KINGS.

President Roosevelt and Secretary of the Interior Hitchcock have decided to go after the cattle kings who have been fencing in and using the public domain for cattle grazing in several Western States. Several months ago the gallant old Confederate soldier, Col. John S. Mosby, now an Inspector for the Land Department, was sent to Nebraska to see what these cattle men were doing. He soon found that thousands of acres of public lands had been confiscated and fenced in by the cattle men; that the most unblushing corruption in order to attain their ends had been resorted to by these men; that the United States officials were guilty of collusion with them, and that colonies of bogus settlers had been employed by the cattle companies to file homestead entries on the land under fence, with the ultimate intention of turning the property over to the cattle companies. As soon as Col. Mosby began work, a terrific howl went up, and influences were brought to bear upon Senators and Representatives and others to have him called off, but Mosby won, and now the order has gone forth to evict the cattle men in Nebraska, and in every other State and Territory where they are unlawfully occupying the public domain. Uncle Sam is sometimes a trifle slow, but when he does put on his armor, something [*is bound?] to drop.

McCook Tribune - **November 28, 1902**

Columbus Journal – **November 26, 1902**

Butte Inter-Mountain – **November 28, 1902**

Alliance Herald – **November 28, 1902**

GOVERNMENT LAND IS FENCED ABOUT

And Uncle Sam is Going to Take Measures to See That the Barriers Are Removed

AS TO ILLEGAL FENCING

Mosby Takes Issue Regarding an Interview.

Washington.—Colonel Mosby, special agent of the general land office charged with the duty of reporting illegal fences on the public domain in Nebraska, is not at all satisfied with the interview which was published, with District Attorney Summers. Colonel Mosby stated he had made no agreement with District Attorney Summers that proceedings in court against the fence men should be withheld until after sixty days expired. He stated that he had no lawful right to make such an agreement, nor had the district attorney.

"My letters to Colonel Summers," said Colonel Mosby, "will show that I complained against the violation of the fencing law in Nebraska long since and that I stated that the statutes regarding illegal fencing were a dead letter so far as Nebraska was concerned. The general land office, in its instructions, directs special agents to give to cattlemen sixty days' notice within which to remove a fence as soon as an affidavit is filed complaining of it. I had no right to repeal the statute. I was appointed to enforce the law by calling the attention of the district attorney to illegal fences and it was his business to bring suit to remove the same.

If Mr. Summers has not been apathetic then why has he not resented my letters complaining of his apathy? The letters which I have written to him regarding this matter, covering a period of several months, are made a part of my report. Complaints were filed a year ago with Mr. Summers against Miller & Leith for the notorious negro entries which appear in the Alliance land office and later complaint was filed with this same officer of the government calling attention to the illegal fences which they maintained, yet nothing was done by Mr. Summers to correct these gross violations of the statutes."

Omaha Daily Bee – November 28, 1902

Columbus Journal,– December 3, 1902

McCook Tribune – December 5, 1902

MOSBY BRINGS HIS BROOM.

Bears from Washington Instructions to Sweep Away Illegal Fences.

Omaha—Col. Mosby, who is in the city, says: "I have come out here with instructions from President Roosevelt down to the land office, to clean out all the fences on government land and incidentally to clean out all the fraudulent homestead entries, particularly those of subsidized soldiers' widows. If District Attorney Summers is indifferent in the matter I shall report so to the attorney general, as I have once before reported. As for the interview recently given out by Special Agent A. M. Lesser, concerning the charges against him, it is simply an evasion of the real charge, which is obtaining money from the government by the use of false and fraudulent vouchers. Senator Allison at whose instance he was originally appointed, has not yet spoken in his behalf. Senator Millard has requested his reinstatement, but that is because those cattlemen up there want Lesser kept. I haven't heard anything from Senator Dietrich."

Mosby's interaction with the Nebraska senators was complex. He mentioned speaking to Millard for a few moments in Chicago while on his way West and, in doing so, went to great pains to mention that their conversation was on minor matters that could not be misconstrued as pertaining to the investigation. He did this because it was probable that he was seen speaking with Millard and did not wish their conversation to be misinterpreted. The claim that Mosby severely criticized either or both senators was vigorously denied by him; and though Mosby was given to a certain amount of naïveté in his dealings with the press, under the circumstances extant he would have been most circumspect. There was more than ample evidence that the press in that area did all that it could to sabotage both the man and his mission.

Alexandria Gazette – November 29, 1902

It is said at the Interior Department that Col. John S. Mosby will shortly be asked to explain some of his criticisms of Senators Millard and Dietrich, of Nebraska, in a recent interview with a newspaper correspondent. The colonel is made to imply that the Nebraska Senators are endeavoring to place obstacles in the way of a rigid investigation of the efforts of the land barons to secure large tracts of government lands by means of illegal entries and transfers from "war widows." The officials of the department say Colonel Mosby talked too freely and that his utterances, considering the position he occupies as an official of the government, were not in good taste. It is believed Colonel Mosby is in a position to prove all the charges he has made and if there are any hindrances to an investigation of the acts of these land barons, it is hoped that the people may be made to know the individuals who are placing obstacles in the way. At the same time the position in which the colonel finds himself should be more than a hint to all public men who place themselves at the disposal of the interviewer. The system is comparatively modern, and was denounced by the more sagacious statesmen as soon as it was inaugurated. Colonel Mosby, pleasant and approachable as he generally is, has ever since the close of the civil war been easy prey for the aggressive interviewer. While a private citizen, his utterances were as permissible as those of any other American; but a government official is expected to be extremely cautious in talking for print. Besides, if should such an one have anything in the way of a charge to urge against representative men or those in official position, the newspaper is not considered to be the medium in which to exploit them.

The *Gazette* admitted that Mosby had "been easy prey for the aggressive interviewer." Why? Because he was "pleasant and approachable… since the end of the civil war." Considering that Mosby has often been portrayed—both then and now—as anything but "pleasant" (at least in his later years), the question then must be just what was he? Later articles revealed that Mosby often spoke "off the record," which never seemed to stop the publication of what he said. But in this matter, his relationship with the press which was by no means as egregious as reported!—became a means of silencing him altogether.

Minneapolis Journal – **November 29, 1902**

A BRIDLE ON MOSBY

Old Confederate Raider Displeases Washington by His Criticisms of Nebraska Senators.

He Discusses the Attitude of Millard and Dietrich and Promises a Great Sensation.

Washington, Nov. 28.—The offices of the Interior Department are not pleased with the very free utterances of Col. John S. Mosby, the special agent of the General Land Office, regarding the wholesale land frauds which are now being investigated by the Federal Grand Jury in Omaha and in which some of the wealthiest cattlemen in western Nebraska are involved.

In the newspaper dispatches from Chicago, containing this interview with Colonel Mosby he was made to criticize severely the attitude taken by Senators Millard and Dietrich of Nebraska with regard to the alleged frauds. The department has no information as to the attitude of the Nebraska senators, but does not believe that they would endeavor to place any obstacles in the way of a rigid investigation or in any other way countenance the efforts of the "land barons" to secure large tracts of government lands by means of illegal entries and transfers from "war widows."

In any event the department considers that Colonel Mosby talked too freely and that his utterances, considering the position he occupies as an official of the government, were not in good taste. It is probable he will receive an intimation to this effect and will be asked for an explanation of his criticisms of the Nebraska senators.

STILL TALKING

Mosby Quotes the President and Speaks out on His Own Account.

Special to the *Journal*.

Omaha, Neb., Nov. 29.—"There will be bloodshed in Nebraska over that fence matter before it is done with, but I propose to have the fences torn down if I have to send a regiment of cavalry there to do it," is the remark Colonel John S. Mosby says President Roosevelt made to him as he was leaving the capital for Omaha to take up again the work of tearing down the illegal fences which the cattle kings have erected on government lands.

Colonel Mosby arrived yesterday and was immediately served with a summons to appear before the grand jury and tell what he knows of the fraudulent land entries which have been made by the widows of Union soldiers for the benefit of the cattle barons.

"I accomplished a great deal while in Washington," said Colonel Mosby. "While out west I could not get my reports on the condition to the right people. They were pigeon-holed in the office before reaching the heads. I was compelled to write a private letter to a friend before it reached the commissioners. Then I was called to Washington immediately. The president was up in arms and promised me the necessary assistance to enforce the laws.

"Senator Millard wished me to hold off and not pull down the fences for the present. He said he would attempt to get a new law passed which would permit the fences to remain. But I said no. Senator Millard also wanted an agent who was suspended last week to be reinstated, but that was because that agent stood in with the cattle kings.

"I will go before the grand jury Monday and tell them something which will create a sensation. There will probably be some big Nebraskans in the penitentiary over this and there will also be some blood spilled before the fences are removed."

As for Mosby's denial of the reported criticism of the Nebraska senators: it appears that the "interview" involved never took place. Several years later, a similar incident occurred, and Mosby was excoriated by Senator Dietrich. However, he denied ever having given the interview in question and verified that denial. Dietrich—who had been impeached and removed from the Senate by that time!—had no choice but to believe Mosby.

However, Mosby was right about several "big Nebraskans" going to jail—that is, of course, if he ever said it. Bartlett Richards and his partner William Comstock were sent to the penitentiary, albeit for a relatively short time, but Richards sickened and died before he was released.

As far as the fence matter was concerned, Mosby was safe as long as Roosevelt was on his side, but when Teddy had to choose between enforcing the law and the political support of the cattle states in the next presidential election, Mosby was removed.

St. Louis Republic – **November 29, 1902**
ROOSEVELT ORDERS FENCES TORN DOWN

Declares Fraudulent Land Entry Stakes Must Tumble if it Requires Bloodshed.

Sends Mosby to Nebraska.

Washington Land Agent Has Been Subpoenaed to Testify Before the Grand Jury at Omaha.

As with Hong Kong, Mosby was raked over the coals for "unprofessional" behavior and failing to follow protocol. It seemed that those who exposed corruption were punished, while those who indulged in it were ignored or rewarded. No further mention was ever made of the request by the senator from Montana for Mosby to come to that state and expose the same type of corruption. And the only danger that the "widows" faced was a matter of fraud if they were not, in fact, soldiers' widows.

St. Paul Globe – **November 29, 1902**

Salt Lake Herald – **November 29, 1902**

San Francisco Call – **November 29, 1902**

Bismarck Daily Tribune [*] – **November 29, 1902**

Houston Daily Post – **November 29, 1902**

MOSBY TEARING DOWN FENCES.

Former Guerrilla Leader Moves Against Cattlemen.

Omaha, Neb., Nov. 28.—John S. Mosby, special inspector of the United States land office of Washington, has arrived in Omaha and will at once begin proceedings for the removal of fences from government land in Nebraska. Col. Mosby said that tracts containing thousands of acres have been illegally fenced in by cattlemen, and that his purpose was to have these fences torn down. After conferring with United States District Attorney Summers, he will go to North Platte and Alliance, where notices will be served upon the alleged violators, giving them sixty days to remove the fences. [* Bismarck Tribune story ends here.-vph]

Col. Moby, who has been called here to testify before the federal grand jury now in session, said tonight:

"There will be blood shed in Nebraska over that fence matter before it is done, but I propose to have the fences down if I have to send a cavalry force there to do it. President Roosevelt has assured me that the fences must be removed. He said 'This thing must stop or there will be blood shed over it.' And President Roosevelt knows just as much about this Western land question as anyone in the country does, for he lived in the West a number of years. Just as soon as I get through with this grand jury work I will go on to Alliance and look after the Standard Cattle company. That firm probably has more land fenced in Nebraska than any other concern.

Again, Mosby didn't "move against the cattlemen." The claim that he was involved in a less-than-professional way with the investigation was without foundation. If John Mosby spoke of "bloodshed," he was quoting Roosevelt, who had made such a prediction given what had happened in the past.

Omaha Daily Bee – November 29, 1902

If Colonel Mosby follows the program he has mapped out he will be busy for some months and he will at the same time keep a lot of other people busy.

It would seem that this "interview" had a lot in common with other such "interviews" in which Mosby was quoted as saying things that caused him great problems in Washington, even though he denied having ever said them.

More articles were forthcoming about the "soldiers' widows," but it had already been stated that this matter was well-known in Washington. If Mosby did "discover it" (as he believed), then the matter had been very well hidden to that point in time. And as the narrative suggested, his "discovery" was not all that gratefully received. Meanwhile, the newspapers—aside from the local press—went back and forth, making first Mosby, then the cattlemen the villains of the piece. The law seems to have been of no interest to anyone in the matter.

Salt Lake Herald – November 30, 1902

FENCES MUST BE REMOVED

Government Seems Disposed to Push Matters [Special to the Herald.]

Washington, Nov. 29.—Colonel John S. Mosby, former Confederate guerrilla, who has been leading in the movement to compel western stockmen to remove fences enclosing government lands, has been ordered by the general land office to North Platte, Neb., to investigate charges made there against Special Agent V. R. Lesser, who is now under suspension from duty pending an investigation. At the conclusion of this duty Colonel Mosby is ordered to Wyoming to investigate supposed fencing of government lands by stockmen in that state.

Editor Rosewater of Omaha, who has sustained Colonel Mosby in his controversy with Nebraska Senators Dietrich and Millard in the matter of fence removals, called upon President Roosevelt today and talked with him about the trouble encountered by the government in its efforts to compel Nebraska stockmen to take down illegal fencing and the possible remedy for existing complications in western stock raising districts in his message.

St. Paul Globe – December 1, 1902

COLONEL MOSBY DENIES THAT HE EVER SAID IT

Special Land Agent In Trouble Because of an Inference.

Omaha, Neb., November 30.—Col. Mosby, special land agent for the government, who is to testify before the federal grand jury here tomorrow with regard to illegal fencing of public lands in Western Nebraska, denies having severely criticized the Nebraska senators, as stated in dispatches from Chicago to Eastern papers. On the day after his arrival a local paper contradicted the report, on Mosby's authority. He also denies saying the president would use cavalry to tear down fences. He was asked what would be done if the cattlemen refused to remove their fences. He replied that Grover Cleveland sent a company of cavalry to pull down fences in

California, and he supposed the same thing might happen in Nebraska.

***Omaha Daily Bee* – December 1, 1902**

MOSBY IS IN EARNEST

Taking Down of Fences by Cattlemen Not a Passing Fancy

GETS AFTER LARGE OFFENDERS FIRST

Letter to District Attorney Indicates How He Feels on Question

WIDOW TELLS HOW SCHEME WAS WORKED

Becomes Suspicious that She Was Not Getting a Square Deal.

WRITES A LETTER TO THE DEPARTMENT.

Indications that Someone Was Making a Good Thing in Fixing the Filings up to Suit the Cattle Barons.

Once again, Mosby refuted what he had allegedly said; but apparently, no amount of denial was going to help:

***New York Tribune* – December 1, 1902**

***San Francisco Call* – December 1, 1902**

DENIES CRITICISING SENATORS.

COLONEL MOSBY ALSO SAYS HE DID NOT ASSERT PRESIDENT WOULD USE CAVALRY TO TEAR DOWN FENCES.

Omaha, Neb., Nov. 30.—Colonel Mosby, special land agent for the government, who is to testify before the federal grand jury here to-morrow with regard to illegal fencing of public lands in Western Nebraska, denies having severely criticized the Nebraska Senators, as stated in dispatches to Eastern papers. On the day after his arrival here a local paper contradicted the report on Mr. Mosby's authority.

He also denies saying that the President would use cavalry to tear down fences. He was asked what would be done if the cattlemen should refuse to remove their fences. He replied that President Cleveland had sent a company of cavalry to pull down fences in California, and he supposed the same thing might happen in Nebraska.

A small article in the *St. Paul Globe* puts Mosby's supposed "verbosity" into perspective with regard to the actual problem that existed while the *Alexandria Gazette*, a Virginia paper, kept up the drumbeat of the charge that Mosby had "criticized" the Nebraska senators despite his repeated denials:

***St. Paul Globe* – December 1, 1902**

It is evidently quite true from the politician's point of view, no doubt, that Mosby does talk too much about those land frauds; but, as all the politicians have disappeared, and the statesmen and philanthropists have taken their places since Roosevelt took hold of things, there ought really to be little fault found with the very plain talk of the Southern brigadier about the robberies of the public lands.

Alexandria Gazette – December 1, 1902

Senator Dietrich has made a most vigorous denial of Colonel Mosby's charges and a protest against insinuations by an officer of the government reflecting upon members of the United States Senate. Senator Millard will probably add his protest to that of Senator Dietrich. It is a rule of the government that its officers shall not criticize members of the Senate, and it is probable that Colonel Mosby will be called upon to prove all his charges or be subjected to a reprimand by the President.

The idea that there might actually be bloodshed now that the matter had gone to the grand jury was still being trumpeted in the press, especially as it was evident that Mosby did not intend to back off, even in his present situation. Of course, he could not; that option had not been given him by the Department of the Interior:

Minneapolis Journal – December 2, 1902 (Edited)

The Professional World – December 5, 1902

MOSBY HITS HARD

Brave old General Gives Some Sensational Evidence Before the Grand Jury

He Starts on a Hazardous Trip to Alliance and Blood May Yet Flow

Omaha, Neb., Dec. 2.—Colonel John S. Mosby appeared on the stand before the grand jury yesterday in the land fraud cases. His testimony was something of a sensation, although not all unexpected.

He testified both in regard to the illegal fencing and the widow scheme of the cattle companies. He added several new names to his list of cattle companies violating the law. He reiterated the statements he made while in Chicago. A letter was introduced which Colonel Mosby had written to United States Attorney Summers here from Washington, in which the former says that while the widows are technically guilty the real criminals to be punished are the men who hired them to commit perjury and fraud... This widow says that they were all required to sign at the time when they filed their applications, leases or contracts to sell their lands to somebody.

"She does not give the name of the person who hired them. As Bartlett Richard's fence is located on their claims no doubt he expected to be the chief beneficiary in the transaction, and is liable to a criminal prosecution. I gave Richards notice to pull down his fence."

Colonel Mosby displayed the widow's letter in which she told him how she, with fifty other widows, were cheated out of their lands with nothing to show for it. This letter was written by Mrs. Carrie L. Carrigan from her home in Clarindan, Iowa, and was addressed to Binger Hermann, commissioner of the general land office.

Colonel Mosby leaves for Alliance, Neb., to-day. It is generally admitted that he is going into a country that will be particularly dangerous for him, and bloodshed is predicted.

It is probable that John Mosby would have relished a bloody confrontation. He certainly would have preferred being shot to being slowly impaled by the crooked bureaucrats and time servers in the government he so honorably served. At least it would have been quicker and cleaner than the fate he eventually did suffer.

The *Salt Lake Herald*, a paper formerly friendly to Mosby when he lived in California, now sensed blood in the water and joined in the feeding frenzy, savaging him personally in a short article:

> ### *Salt Lake Herald* – December 2, 1902
>
> Colonel Mosby now denies that he criticised the senators from Nebraska adversely. Of course, the reporter who interviewed him was to blame. That is always the case with the man who has a hair-trigger mouth.

The matter of Mosby's alleged criticism was taken up with the tongue of its pen firmly ensconced in its cheek by the *St. Paul Globe*, a paper that had not previously been pro-Mosby. It is possible that given the choice between Mosby and hack politicians, the Globe considered the latter a more worthy target than the beleaguered government agent whose only crime was that he was doing his job:

> ### *St. Paul Globe* – December 2, 1902
>
> Considering the amount of fuss which was created over a statement of Col. Moseby which he declares he never made, it is quite evident that the two senators from Nebraska are tender and sensitive souls, who, beyond all others, cannot endure any imputation arising out of land transactions. And, yet, even men as high on the moral calendar as Western senators have been known in the past not to have been ignorant on the ways in which the people have been robbed of their lands by the syndicates.

This publication had put its finger on the pulse of the issue: the two Nebraska senators were "tender and sensitive" because they were corrupt! Those in the wrong frequently engage in a campaign of "blame" against whoever exposes those wrongs. Something now had become obvious. For almost the entire period that this matter was covered in the press, virtually the same issues, quotes, misquotes, statements, and disclaimers constantly appeared. Even when a new charge was forthcoming (such as the spurious widows' claims), if the article was of any length, these same matters appeared within it. For instance, almost always, Mosby's alleged quotes on the use of the cavalry to pull down the fences or the claim of his "criticism" of the Nebraska senators or the "bloodshed" contention continued to appear over and over and over again, even after they had been refuted and refuted—and refuted again. Why this happened is not known. Perhaps the scenario had become "set in stone," so to speak, and could not be rewritten or reassessed without a loss of the people's faith in the press. But whatever the reason, it was soon obvious that the genie could not be put back into the bottle.

> ### *Richmond Dispatch* – December 3, 1902
>
> [This article is part of an article of the Clarke Courier dated December 10, 1902.] Washington, D. C. December 2.—(Special)

Colonel John S. Mosby, who is in the West investigating the refusal of cattlemen to take down the fences they have put up on government property, is likely to have trouble by reason of the fact that he has been talking. The old cavalry chieftain feels somewhat elated over what he has accomplished in the way of fighting the cattlemen in the East. In giving vent to his satisfaction he has criticized in an indirect way both of the Nebraska Senators, and especially Senator Millard, who has come to town. Senator Millard proposes to make an investigation of what Colonel Mosby has been saying, and the chances are decidedly strong that he will go after the scalp of the famous Confederate warrior, if he finds that the latter has said anything that ought to have remained unsaid.

Colonel Mosby is an employee of the Interior Department and to criticize a Senator, even by insinuation is something horrible. So Senator Millard is going to see what can be done. He would probably demand the official scalp of Colonel Mosby if he thought the President would accede to such a request, if he cannot make a successful fight in that direction, he will probably ask that Colonel Mosby be requested to cease his comments, on fear of future punishment. Senator Millard was at the White House to-day, but did not take the matter up with the President then, owing to the fact that the chief executive was exceedingly busy.

As happened with Mosby every time he dealt with corruption, those whom he exposed and those who protected them found little to say about the facts and a great deal to say about the man who revealed the facts. And as Mosby remained more than a little unpopular in both sections, very few indeed were those who would take his part. In the plight of John Mosby is found the truth of Mark Twain's cynical motto "Be good and you will be lonely."

Butler Weekly Times – **December 4, 1902**
BLOODSHED IN NEBRASKA?

President Roosevelt Threatens to Send Troops There.

Sadly, Mosby's naïveté came to the fore once again. He believed in Roosevelt as he had believed in Hayes and Garfield and Arthur and Harrison (in the beginning) and McKinley! As a result, he would suffer the same dismaying blow when he discovered that Roosevelt's passion for the law—and thus his support for that faithful servant of the law, John Mosby—became of less worth than the political price he would pay in the next election. But rather than admitting that matters had "changed" and advising Mosby to "back off," Roosevelt stepped nimbly aside and permitted his agent to be ridiculed, humiliated, and made to appear a fool so that he could be got rid of with no one hurt but the honorable old warrior. Sad to say, this was not the last time that this scenario played out in Mosby's life; but the next time it came to pass, John Mosby would lose his position with the government and be cast into poverty in his old age.

Fate sometimes throws a bone to the starving, and Mosby received what must have been a most welcome invitation for a man who found himself, yet again, a pariah for acting with honor:

Alexandria Gazette – December 5, 1902

Omaha Daily Bee - December 2, 1902

Middlesex Club and Mosby.—Colonel J. S. Mosby, who is in Omaha on business of the general land office, of which he is a special agent, has just received from Senator Henry Cabot Lodge, of Massachusetts, a letter enclosing an invitation to be present on "Great night," next April. The Middlesex is one of the most exclusive of all the New England clubs, and its "nights" are events of more than ordinary import. President Champlin, of the club, writes to Colonel Mosby: "We would like to add your name to the roll of our distinguished guests. The members of the club, the republicans of Massachusetts, and the people of Boston would be glad to see and welcome you. I beg to assure you that this invitation is not perfunctory or formal. We earnestly desire that you may be able to accept it." Colonel Mosby is at present of the opinion that communications may safely be addressed to him in care of the Middlesex club, Boston, Mass., on the night of April 27, 1903, for he certainly expects to be present on that night.—[Omaha Bee, Dec. 2.

Still, the press was of the belief that Roosevelt would continue to push the fence matter and reported accordingly:

Alliance Herald – December 5, 1902

Senator Millard intimates that Colonel Mosby has seen a mountain in a molehill in the fencing of public lands by the cattle barons, but the colonel insists that his eyesight is as good now as it ever was.—Omaha Bee.

Chicago Tribune – December 5, 1902

CATTLEMEN FACE JURY.

Nebraskans Gather to Explain Illegal Fences.

Representatives of Large and Small Interests Pour into Omaha at Court's Call—Soldiers' Widows Attend to Defend Rights—Hints That High Officials Are Back of Land Grab by Big Combines—Congress Will Be urged to Act.

More articles appeared regarding land frauds, and the Globe saw the right of it—that is, "no reasonable prospect of anything … being done":

St. Paul Daily Globe – December 5, 1902

A NEEDED MEASURE

The frauds recently revealed in Nebraska in connection with the entry of land under the homestead law by widows of deceased soldiers helps to show what ingenuity has been displayed in the robberies that have been achieved by cattle-grazing corporations through the agency of the desert land law. They give point to the recognition in the president's message, that the provision of the homestead law which confines the land to be entered by the actual settler to an area of 160 acres should be amended with reference to public land adapted chiefly for the purposes of extending the available area very materially.

If the officials of the interior department had any serious thought of pushing the investigations into the frauds which have been perpetrated by those operating under the homestead law even during the last five years there would be an immense area of valuable land, especially in Minnesota, South and North Dakota, restored to the public domain. But as there is no reasonable prospect of anything of this kind being done, notwithstanding the discoveries of Col. Mosby, it is earnestly to be hoped that some such measure as that introduced by Senator Quaries will be as speedily as possible enacted into law.

By this time, all the fences should have been taken down given the repeated reports in the press that they were being, had been, would be, etc. Another article in the *Richmond Dispatch* exonerated Mosby and pronounced him "safe" from the attack by the Nebraska senators. However, the Dispatch still believed that Mosby had criticized those senators in the newspapers despite his repeated denials:

Richmond Dispatch – December 6, 1902

MOSBY IS UNHARMED

Efforts of Senators Dietrich and Millard Fail of Effect

Will Not Lose His Position.

His Recent Talking Was Not for Publication

He Is Doing Good Work

To "Transfer Him," as Was Advised by the Nebraska Senators Would Be to Do Just What the Cattle Barons Wish Done—

"Once a Guerilla, Always a Guerilla." One of the Thing Said by Dietrich of Mosby

Washington, D. C., December 5.—(Special.)—Despite efforts of Senators Dietrich and Millard, of Nebraska, to have Colonel John S. Mosby, the famous Confederate guerila chief, removed from the government service because he had been talking about the attempt of the two Senators to pull him away from prosecution of Western cattlemen who are using government lands for pasture purposes the Virginian will hold his position. He is doing good work, and his only trouble has been a disposition to talk. For this he has received an intimation from the Secretary of the Interior that it is improper for him to talk too much, and this intimation has had its effect. Immediately after the appearance in newspapers of interviews with Colonel Mosby, who is operating against cattle barons in Oklahoma and territory adjacent to Nebraska, the Interior Department in a personal letter from Secretary Hitchcock, it is learned suggest to Colonel Mosby the impropriety of talking, and especially of saying anything that appeared to be a criticism of the two Nebraska Senators. In response to this, it is learned, Colonel Mosby telegraphed the Interior Department that the interviews with him were unauthorized. He has followed this with a letter, in which he reiterates this assertion. He says that he met a man in Nebraska who appeared to know all about the cattle business, and talked with him on some phases of the use of government lands by the cattle barons. He did not intend any of this for publication, however.

Pending the receipt by the Interior Department of the letters from Colonel Mosby, the Nebraska Senators, especially Senator Dietrich, tried to make trouble for Colonel Mosby, and wanted to have him transferred. This was refused. "To transfer him," said an office of the Interior Department to a Dispatch correspondent to-day, "would be just what the cattle men want.

Colonel Mosby is executing the orders of the Interior Department in a fearless manner [missing] letting any one influence [missing] reason he will [missing] though it will be [missing] talk any more."

Charges Against Dietrich.

In one of the interviews with Colonel Mosby, he said that when on his way to his post out West, he received a letter from Senator Dietrich asking him to go by and see the Senator. To have done so would have been to go nearly 200 miles out of his way, and he declined to do this. He also intimated that Senator Dietrich was interested in some Nebraska banks that had loaned heavily to cattle men, who might be severely hurt financially should the government's orders about taking down fences be complied with. The understanding is that Colonel Mosby did do the talking all right, and said the things attributed to him, but he says they were not given out for publication.

Senator Dietrich, in a hot interview published in Lincoln, Neb. Denied the charges of Colonel Mosby, and says that "once a guerilla, always a guerrilla." Senator Dietrich has been at boiling heat, but if Colonel Mosby says no more he will remain where he is. It is known that Senator Dietrich did write Colonel Mosby asking the latter to call at Senator Dietrich's home.

Embattled Agent Lesser made note of the charges against Mosby for speaking with the press and decided to use it as part of his own defense while warning that the removal of the fences would result in chaos:

Omaha Daily Bee – December 7, 1902

LESSER TALKS ABOUT MOSBY

Deposed Land Agent Says the Colonel is Garrulous and Fussy.

DOES NOTHING BUT TALK TO REPORTERS

As to the Fences, Lesser Believes They Ought Not to Be Disturbed until Congress Acts on Leasing Bill.

"It is not my part to be conspicuous with newspaper interviews," said Land Agent Lesser yesterday when asked to state his side of the trouble between himself and Colonel Mosby, which resulted in the former's suspension from office. Lesser, after being closeted with the grand jury here for a few days, returned to his Iowa home yesterday. It was his love of home life, according to Colonel Mosby, that caused the land agent's downfall, the veteran alleging that Lesser spent the time for which the government paid him to be in Nebraska at his home in Tama City, Ia.

"I do not believe Colonel Mosby's idea of pushing his way into print is good for any cause," went on Lesser. "And that to my mind is very beautifully illustrated in the Colonel's own case. They is about all that I can see that Mosby has succeeded in accomplishing. All that he has reported to the government on the fencing and land-leasing questions was reported by me before Mosby ever went into office.

"Why hasn't it been acted upon? That is not for me to say. My duty did not lay in calling out troops of cavalry and causing bloodshed. I could not have done that if I had wanted to, and neither can Mosby. The duty of my position was simply to examine into the conditions and make my report to Washington, and these things I did and kept still about it. I reported as soon as I went into office that the government land was illegally fenced in and I reported the conditions in regard to the widow question.

Anticipates "Awful Mess."

"As far as my personal opinion goes, I hardly see how they can take down the fences all at once without causing an enormous disaster. The fences are not all one or two men's doing. Practically every cattleman in the vicinity of government lands is involved. One may will fence in a piece of property and the next man that comes along will use one stretch of his fence and a stretch of some other fence, so that a fence erected years ago by several parties may serve the purpose of separating two or three properties. The sudden removal of these fences would make an awful mess.

"The use of this land ought certainly to be allowed. Now the government has allowed this law to be a dead letter for so long a time, it certainly ought to continue the delay of its enforcement until the present congress could enact a land leasing measure or else give a good long notice to enable the parties involved an opportunity to adjust themselves to the new conditions.

"The differences between Colonel Mosby and myself were started by my objecting to the large number of garrulous communications which he insisted on writing me and because I asked him to confine himself to matters connected with our official business. He took a personal affront to this and the war he has waged against me has been a personal matter with him all through."

Lesser also decided that he would add himself as another of Mosby's personal targets in order to take advantage of such sympathy as redounded to those poor stockmen and noble politicians who were being brutally persecuted by "Mosby the guerrilla." There is nothing to show that Mosby communicated with Lesser on anything but "official business," unless, of course, Mosby asked questions as to why Lesser did not act on matters that he knew to be contrary to the law. Perhaps Lesser did not consider such questions related to "official business."

Minneapolis Journal - December 8, 1902

THE NEBRASKA WAR

Both Senators Ask That Col. John Mosby Be Sent Somewhere Else. The President Says "No." and the Cattle Barons Will Be "Against It."

Mosby did have his defenders, however, as can be seen here:

Omaha Daily Bee **– December 8, 1902 (Edited)**
EX-OFFICIAL DEFENDS MOSBY

Cites Some Law in Regard to the Entry of Land in Public Domain.

Alliance, Neb., Dec. 7.—To the Editor of The Bee: I received a marked copy of a paper a day or two ago, the marked article therein containing severe strictures on Colonel Mosby, special agent of the government, in his efforts to carry out his instructions from the general land office in the matter of having fences removed from the public lands. The writer of the article in question seems to take particular umbrage at Colonel Mosby for his exposures in regard to the homestead entries of the widows of soldiers, and it said widows were the real target. I would say men to his article, as I am on old soldier myself, and my sympathies naturally favor the veterans and their widows, but the soldiers' widows are not the persons who built the fences, and are "in it" incidentally to show the fraudulent manner in which the cattlemen sought to obtain color of title, or right to possession, of many tracts of public lands to the exclusion of bona fide homesteaders. The evidence of Mrs. Carrigan as to the affairs at Gordon, is strong proof of the allegations made.

FRANKLIN SWEET.

The *Alexandria Gazette* saw that the fences weren't coming down and that Mosby was still being harassed in Nebraska, with very little support from the government that had sent him there:

Alexandria Gazette **– December 11, 1902**
COLONEL MOSBY.

Colonel John S. Mosby arrived in the city yesterday from Omaha and has taken up his abode at the Hila Grand. Mr. Mosby is not inclined to talk of his business here or elsewhere, and when asked by a Herald representative as to how long he expected to remain in Alliance, replied, "You'll have to ask President Roosevelt about that." It seems that the President should take the Colonel with him on some bear hunting expeditions instead of sending him out here to annoy our stockmen and injure one of the state's greatest industries, or better yet, let Mr. Roosevelt forego the pleasure of a bear hunt and take the time to come out here and investigate the "outrages" those "cattle barons" are committing. It's up to you, Mr. Roosevelt.

Col. W. H. McCann, former register of the United States land office at Chadron, was in the city yesterday on his return from a trip to the sand hills. While at one of the small towns east of Alliance, Mr. McCann met an acquaintance who greeted him as "Colonel." Bystanders mistook the Chadron man for Colonel Mosby and the news spread quickly that the distinguished "government fence destroyer" was there. The citizens became excited and were eager to get sight of the supposed Mosby while the ranchmen who had government land fenced shrugged their shoulders and volunteered to take down their fences. Things were becoming pretty warm about the time McCann established his identity. Col. McCann and Colonel Mosby resemble each other somewhat in appearance.—[Alliance (Neb.) Herald.

A dispatch from Omaha dated December 9 says: President Roosevelt's agent, Col. John S. Mosby, is strangely missing. Several days ago he left Omaha after giving his testimony before the grand jury, ostensibly to go to Alliance, Neb., to begin the destruction of the fences raised illegally on Government land. The grand jury was not through with him and he was only temporarily excused. The jury is again ready to receive testimony from him and he cannot be found. There is as yet no suspicion of foul play, although the tales of intended armed resistance have floated down from the Northwest, and some persons at the federal building think Mosby has read a sensational story emanating from Cheyenne, in which it was alleged there is a plot to assassinate him and that he has disappeared for a few days.

The tenor of the above stories printed in the *Alexandria Gazette* and emanating from the local press in Nebraska illustrated the situation that Mosby faced. However, if Mosby believed that someone was "gunning" for him, he would have armed himself. John Mosby liked nothing better than an open fight.

The Times – December 11, 1902

MOSBY KEEPS 'EM GUESSING AS HE DID YEARS AGO

(Special Dispatch to *The Times*.)

OMAHA, NEB., December 10.—Colonel John S. Mosby, President Roosevelt's land agent here, has got some people guessing as to his whereabouts, just as he used to have them guessing from 1861 to 1865. Several days ago he left Omaha after giving his testimony before the grand jury, ostensibly to go to Alliance, Neb., to begin the destruction of fences raised illegally on government land.

Minneapolis Journal – December 11, 1902

Colonel Mosby is Tearing Down the Fences and Was Alive at Last Accounts. Special to The Journal.

Omaha, Neb., Dec. 11.—Colonel John S. Mosby, the special agent of the land department, whose whereabouts have been unknown here for several days and concerning whom some anxiety had been felt, is now near Alliance, Neb. Tearing down fences around range lands belonging to the government despite the threats of violence made by some ranchmen.

He is also looking into the fraudulent homestead entries made by soldiers' widows. It is expected he will return to Omaha in a few days to give further testimony before the federal grand jury.

The state of Mosby's situation appeared still in flux, though it was being strongly hinted that he had been recalled:

Alexandria Gazette – December 15, 1902

President Recalls Col. Mosby.

Omaha, Neb., Dec. 15.—Though he has not completed his work, Colonel Mosby, who was sent to Nebraska by President Roosevelt to investigate the fencing of public lands by the cattle millionaires, has been recalled. When Colonel Mosby found how boldly the cattle kings had appropriated the public domain he declared they would be promptly ousted, even if the President had to send troops to tear down the fences. This remark and others caused ill-feeling, and the Washington Government has found it necessary to find another place for Colonel Mosby.

Atlanta Constitution – December 15, 1902

MOSBY BEATEN BY THE BARONS

Colonel's Fight Against Cattle Kings Causes His Recall to Washington. Omaha, Nebr., December 14.—(Special.)

According to the men in close touch with the situation, the case of the government against the cattle barons on the charge of illegal land entries has been considerably weakened, if not entirely destroyed, by the lack of judgment on the part of Colonel Mosby in the discharge of his duties.

It is the general opinion here that it is for this reason that Colonel Mosby has been recalled to Washington and will, according to reports, be sent to the lower part of California.

It is conceded that Colonel Mosby has been a sincere and honest official in the discharge of his duties, but he was sadly in lack of necessary diplomacy. The sensational disclosures which the veteran made, in the ordinary since, he knew to be the truth, but in the legal sense he did not. It is thought that the officials are aware that a prosecution on the strength of what evidence Colonel Mosby could now furnish would fail in its intent, and in place of convicting the large cattle owners would catch, if anybody, but a few small men used by the large ranchers as catspaws. This condition of affairs, it is asserted, is the result of Colonel Mosby's indiscretion in tipping off his hand. The custom of heralding his official actions and intents through the newspapers gave the real culprits a chance to cover up their guilt before any evidence was collected.

Of course, all the evidence had already been collected, so no "infraction" could have weakened or ruined the government's case against the ranchers. The "diplomacy" demanded of Mosby was silence about a matter that was already known by the government. Of course, confusion remained as this article in *The Times* demonstrated:

Washington Times – December 16, 1902

COLONEL MOSBY HERE FOR A SHORT STAY

Will Return to Nebraska in Short Time to Prosecute Land Cases.

Col. John S. Mosby, special agent of the Interior Department, who has been investigating land frauds in Nebraska, arrived in Washington last night and will remain here several days attending to matters in the office of the land claims office.

He has not been recalled, but completed his work before the grand juries and will return to Nebraska the latter part of the week. It is announced at the Interior Department this morning that violations regarding fences on public lands will be vigorously prosecuted, and Colonel Mosby will continue the work of securing evidence and pushing prosecutions.

Omaha Daily Bee – December 18, 1902
MOSBY IS NOT OUT OF FAVOR

Secretary Hitchcock Takes Occasion to Compliment Him on His Work Washington, Dec. 15.—[Special Telegram.]

Colonel John S. Mosby is again in Washington, and today reported at the general land office. The sudden appearance of Colonel Mosby in Washington has given rise to the story that Mr. Mosby, because of some rather breezy interviews printed while the Colonel was en route to Omaha, has been recalled by Secretary Hitchcock, in order that censure might be administered. Secretary Hitchcock, however, today said that this was not true. "Colonel Mosby was sent to Omaha upon a special mission with instructions to report to the general land office upon its completion," said Mr. Hitchcock. "the fact that he returns at this time is only an indication that he has accomplished his mission and returns to report. Colonel Mosby has accomplished a good work, and the story that he is in bad odor with this department I wish to deny most emphatically."

Colonel Mosby will have a conference with Secretary Hitchcock tomorrow on several questions growing out of the illegal fencing.

Mosby's situation with the Department of the Interior was in constant flux. But in reality, he did not "lose favor" until Roosevelt had to choose between the fence law and the support of Western Republicans in his election bid in 1904. When that situation arose, Mosby's removal was the easiest way to indicate the president's choice.

Alexandria Gazette – December 18, 1902 (Edited)
COLONEL MOSBY.

As heretofore stated, Col. John S. Mosby, special agent of the general land office in the matter of the illegal erection of fences on government land on the ranges in Nebraska, Wyoming, Montana, Idaho and utah, has arrived in Washington for a short visit. The statement has been made the Col. Mosby has been recalled from his post of duty on account of the trouble in which he became involved with some of the cattlemen who insisted on maintaining fences on government property. The Secretary of the Interior, Mr. Hitchcock, denies that this is so, and states that so far as he knows the President is fully satisfied with the manner in which Col. Mosby has conducted himself. His visit at this time has no significance whatsoever.

And suddenly, the charge against Mosby relative to the "criticism" of Nebraska's senators was back in the news while he was charged here with waging a "campaign against land-grabbing cattlemen." Apparently, at least the paper understood that Mosby would be punished for doing his job:

Richmond Dispatch – December 18, 1902 (Edited)
DISCIPLINE FOR MOSBY.

The Colonel's Campaign Against Land Grabbing Cattlemen. (Chicago Chronicle.)

Of course, "it is highly probable that Colonel Mosby will receive an intimation that his remarks were improper and will be asked for an explanation of his criticisms of the Nebraska Senators."

Colonel Mosby declares—and most people will believe him—that he has had intimations from these statesmen that he might do well to be less active in his proceedings against the cattle barons. He has very properly refused to be swerved from his duty, and he has made public the facts.

It will be interesting to see how far Colonel Mosby's superiors will dare to go in reproof of his refusal to wink at scoundrelism, even though it is tacitly defended by United States Senators. If it be true—and it probably is—that President Roosevelt is back of Mosby in the matter, there may be some slight difficulties in having the ex-guerrilla disciplined for his characterization of rascality as rascality no matter by whom committed.

Minneapolis Journal – December 18, 1902
St. Paul Globe – December 19, 1902
NEBRASKA CATTLEMEN PROTEST AGAINST MOSBY'S ACTS

Nebraskan Senators and Cattle Men Call on the President

They See the President About Encroachment upon Public Lands.

Washington, D. C., Dec. 18—Senators Dietrich and Millard, of Nebraska, called upon the president today, accompanied by a of prominent cattle raisers of their state, to discuss the alleged encroachment upon government lands by the big cattle interests of Nebraska and other Western states. They entered a vigorous protest against the action and words of Col. John S. Mosby, who has been investigating the matter as an agent of the interior department. Many of the Western cattlemen are here not to appear before the interior department and their members of congress with a view of protecting their interests. The subject is being carefully considered by the president and interior department. The president has let it be known that he will permit no improper or illegal encroachment upon government lands, and the interior department is acting along that line.

As had happened before, the focus of the matter was moved from the illegalities of the cattlemen and those who supported them in and out of office and the alleged behavior of the investigator. The only accusations against Mosby were of being "undiplomatic" and "severe." So on one side, there was a crime and efforts to support and continue that crime; and on the other side, the claim of a lack of diplomacy. These are hardly equitable matters in law.

And finally, it was over. No muffled drums, no cigarette and blindfold before a shot-scarred wall, but John Mosby knew that he was beaten as he told a Dispatch correspondent that his stay in Washington was "indefinite" and that he, the correspondent, would have to ask "the gentleman in the White House" if he would return West. But as usual, the correspondent was not really paying attention; for in the very next sentence, he reports that Mosby would "visit Richmond before he returns West." No wonder John Mosby couldn't make himself understood—nobody was listening:

> *Richmond Dispatch* - December 19, 1902 (Edited)
>
> Col. Mosby's Ideas.
>
> Col. John S. Mosby has returned from the West is now awaiting the orders of President Roosevelt.
>
> When seen in Senator Daniel's committee-room this morning by the Dispatch correspondent, Colonel Mosby said: "My stay here is indefinite.
>
> When will I return West? You will have to go up and see the gentleman in the White House to learn that."
>
> Colonel Mosby expects to visit Richmond before he returns West. He will probably do so Sunday week.

Alas, there was another melancholy moment in John Mosby's life as he waited to be officially removed as the result of political pressure brought upon the man who sent him to do a job—a job that he did all too well. Not content with his humiliation in being relieved, the *McCook Tribune* fired off one more nasty little shot at a man who was punished for being "too good at his job and too honest":

> *McCook Tribune* - December 19, 1902
>
> They breathe more freely at Alliance since Colonel Mosby returned to Washington. Prolixity is the colonel's greatest fault in his dotage.

Again, insults and falsehoods replaced journalism. Mosby was not in his dotage. In fact, he never reached that life stage. And while it is true that he occasionally was far too candid for his own good, everything he said was true, which was a far cry from those who either "reported" what he didn't say or falsified what he did. Yet as much as Mosby was reviled, the truth could not forever be concealed. In an article sympathetic to the cattlemen, in the third subheadline was the short statement "Mosby's Report [Is] Fair Enough":

> *St. Louis Republic* – December 19, 1902
>
> CATTLEMEN APPEAL TO THE PRESIDENT
>
> Are Prepared to Make Bitter Fight to Retain Their Grazing Lands. Senators on Their Side.
>
> No Claim Is Made of Any Right to Maintain Fences Around Government Land—Mosby's Report Fair Enough.

Alliance Herald – December 19, 1902

Somehow or other the strenuous talk put up by Colonel Mosby concerning the fences reminds us of the equally strenuous vociferation indulged in against the trusts by one Theodore Roosevelt a few months ago.

In a way, the Herald was right; it had just named the wrong man. Mosby's "strenuous talk" was far more than talk. He was prepared to do what the law demanded. It was Roosevelt whose talk was just that—talk. Mosby was gone, but the *Alliance Herald* didn't miss the chance to further humiliate him in absentia:

Alliance Herald – December 26, 1902

The Vanished Mosby

Somehow or other, every time The Herald recalls the erudite and strenuous gentleman named Mosby, it is reminded of an old verse that was wont to travel about the country. The Herald can not recall the exact words of this beautiful and touching verse, but it went something like this:

If we were General Mosby now,

We'd tell you what we'd do,

We'd crawl into an augur hole,

A gimlet hole,

Or a knot hole,

And pull the hole in, too.

We do not know where the gallant and dashing Mosby may be, whether in Washington or in Seattle; in Philadelphia or Tacoma. But wherever he is we wish him a happy New Year. And may the gallant and dashing ex-Confederate's shadow never grow less, nor his strenuity less strenuous.

With the dastardly Mosby gone from the scene, the allies of the noble stockmen stepped forward to "help" by passing legislation that would permit them to keep the lands they had stolen:

McCook Tribune – December 26, 1902

HELP CATTLEMEN

Mr. Richards Confident of a Leasing Bill

A Conference With President

Senators Millard and Dietrich Presented the Delegation of Cattle Growers to the President—Mosby Like to be Relieved of Duty in Nebraska.

Most of the press and the courts in the area were in the pocket of the cattle barons. When Mosby brought the government's case to court, the fix was in, and he found himself dismissed as a crank. Thus, he was relieved of his duties in the West and sent away to what was probably believed to be personal and professional obscurity. Mosby's recall made obvious the fact that Theodore Roosevelt, in the antithesis of his own oft-repeated maxim, preferred being president to being right.

And so 1902 made its mortifying exit, metaphorical tail between its equally metaphorical legs; yet when 1903 dawned, John Mosby was still an employee of the Department of the Interior. As he had once said, time would be his vindicator, but such vindication—at least at the end of 1902—was nowhere to be seen.

Chapter 42

1903

"Vitam regit fortuna, non sapientia."
~ "Fortune, not wisdom, rules lives." ~ Cicero

"As flies to wanton boys, are we to the gods; they kill us for their sport." ~ William Shakespeare

THE FIRST OF January 1903 found the land controversy still very much alive. An article in a rather small Western publication recapitulated the range wars that had been of such lively interest in that part of the country. The paper opined upon the fate of Indian fighter, government scout, and cattleman "hired gun" Tom Horn,[*] who had been found guilty of murdering the fourteen-year-old son of a small rancher. Horn had obtained a stay of execution, and the paper made the (erroneous) prediction that he would not pay the ultimate price for his crime. (See "Addendum" at the end of the chapter.) John Mosby was mentioned, especially with regard to threats upon his life for his efforts to thwart the power of the cattlemen for whom Horn had worked at the time of the death of Willie Nickell.

Mosby was also defended with regard to the "widows' claims":

Omaha Daily Bee **– January 1, 1903 (Edited)**
OLD SOLDIER ON LEASING

Takes Decided Stand Against the Cattlemen's View of the Proposition Omaha, Jan. 2.—To the Editor of The Bee: While I understand there is a grand jury of the United States in session in the federal building (having a recess for a few days at present) which is generally understood in taking evidence in these alleged fraudulent homestead entries by certain negroes and soldiers' widows, also the cattlemen's fencing in of government lands, with a view to say whether in its judgment infringements of the law have been made, and if so bring in "true bills" of indictment against them, the very interested parties—the fence builders—have not had the patience to wait and see what the grand jury had to say on the subject, but are doing everything possible to make the world believe they are being very much maligned, and that in compelling them to pull down their fences, fencing in large tracts of land which do not belong to them, a very unjust thing will be done. I guess the bulk of us know their little game.

From newspaper reports and otherwise it is well known the grand jury has, with the assistance of the district attorney, called for evidence from the cattlemen, the soldiers' widows, the local land officials, Colonel Mosby and Mr. Lesser (the special and ex-special land office agents from Washington), and I think the public interest is safe in the hands of twenty-three good men and true forming the grand jury, which is probing the matter to the bottom.

AN OLD SOLDIER.

A day later, the *Alliance Herald*—an old foe of Mosby's or rather of government efforts to take down the fences—happily reported that cooler heads had prevailed and the "fence matter" had been settled, at least for the winter:

Alliance Herald – January 2, 1903

United States Senator Millard returned from Washington Tuesday. He says: "The fence question is settled for this winter at least, and, in a way, for the future as well. It is understood that the matter will be allowed to rest until a land-leasing law can be passed, which will very likely be in the near future. Such a law will restrict the cattlemen to a certain extent while not imposing any unnecessary hardships, such as tearing down their fences would do. Besides, this is a bad time of the year to begin tearing down fences, anyway. "Colonel Mosby is in Washington now and Senator Millard thinks that he will be eliminated from the question by an appointment elsewhere.

According to the reports, the cattlemen had given their word that the fences would be removed depending upon the outcome of proposed leasing legislation before Congress; and for that reason, a period of time was given them, during which the fences could remain, though in violation of the law. However, it was later learned that these wealthy men had no intention of keeping their word if the legislation were defeated; that fact redounded badly for them when the matter was eventually discovered.

Rock Island Argus – January 3, 1903 (Edited)

CATTLE RANGE WAR

What the Confession of Tom Horn May Lead To

The Western Desperado Implicates Cattle Kings In an Alleged Plot to Murder Small Ranchers—Colonel Mosby's Part In the Fight

Few persons appreciate the strenuous efforts that the cattle kings have for years been making for the possession of the ranges on the government lands of the west. But the recent conviction of Tom Horn for murder and his confession that he had been paid $2,100 for the assassination of Willie Nickell, son of a small rancher in Wyoming, and had been paid similar sums for killing other men who threatened to invade the broad range which the cattlemen have looked upon as their own serve to bring the subject sharply before the public.

Colonel John S. Mosby, the veteran Confederate cavalry leader, has been concerned in this great fight during the last few years. Colonel Mosby holds a government inspection office, and it is his duty to see that the public land is not fenced in for private use. He has incurred the enmity of many western cattle kings by ordering down hundreds of miles of barbed wire fence which has been illegally erected and which has been inclosing the public domain in defiance of Uncle Sam's orders. Mosby's life has been threatened, but he has been undaunted in his war on the cattlemen, and now the startling features of the Tom Horn case have around public sentiment in the cattle states to such an extent that it is probable that the deathknell of the open cattle range has been sounded...

Colonel Mosby's determined stand against the fencing in of public lands will do much to simplify matters if the example of the famous Confederate leader is followed by other United States officials. The next step will be to bring peace between the three conflicting interests of the range county—the cattle owners, the sheep men and the small ranchers.

Since Horn's conviction desperate efforts have been made to get a new trial for the prisoner, but public feeling is so high that it is probable his doom is sealed. It is openly asserted in Cheyenne that if any indication is shown of granting Horn a new trial the jail will be stormed and the man lynched. Horn is a typical western desperado.

And as public sentiment turned against the "cattle kings," it turned for John Mosby! The garrulous old man who couldn't hold his tongue and made a fool of himself and the Department of the Interior was suddenly a knight in shining armor again! If nothing else, this should put to rest forever the contention by "Mosby scholars" that the problems and persecutions he suffered so often during his government employment were the result of his lack of ordinary common sense and his unfailing loquacity, especially as it related to the press. To suggest that John Mosby—and only John Mosby—spoke "out of turn" is false. Of course, the reason that this is important is that it arose one more time during Mosby's tenure with the Department of Justice in the Indian frauds, leading to his ultimate dismissal from that agency seven years later.

But the final "nail" in the coffin of the contention that Mosby "waged war" against the cattlemen in a "personal vendetta" that far exceeded his instructions as a government agent appeared in an article carried in the Omaha Bee, which is self-explanatory and, hopefully, puts to rest forever the claim that Mosby's behavior was governed by personal animosity toward the stockmen:

Omaha Daily Bee – **January 12, 1903 (Edited)**

RELIEF FOR THE STOCKMEN

Colonel Mosby Suggest Plan to Soften Fence-Destroying Blow.

WOULD SUSPEND LAW FOR SIX MONTHS.

Writes to Senator Daniel Recommending Action by Congress to Prevent Loss from Execution of Department's Orders.

Washington, Jan. 11.—(Special)—Colonel John S. Mosby has taken steps to advocate some softening of the blow which will strike the cattlemen of Nebraska, if the fence-destroying order is pushed. He advocates the passage of a law by congress which will suspend the anti-fence law for at least six months. On this matter the following letter, written by Colonel Mosby to Senator Daniel of Virginia, will be of interest to Nebraskans concerned:

Alliance, NEB., DEC. 8, 1902.—

Hon. John W. Daniel, United States Senator:

Dear Major—No doubt you have seen notices of the excitement in western Nebraska produced by the orders of the land office to remove fences from public lands The act prohibiting it was passed February 25, 1885, but has been a dead letter here until I came last August. A very large portion of the public domain has been inclosed by big cattlemen to the exclusion of those who have small herds or want homesteads. The practice has gone on so long, with the connivance of officials, that the trespassers claim a sort of vested interest in the lands for grazing their cattle, and set up a sort of equitable estoppel against the government. Then *The Appeal* is made to let the fencing stand, even if wrong in the beginning, as it would be injurious now to the public interest to remove it.

How to Help Stockmen

As those fences have stood a long time by sufferance I think some indulgence should be shown to those who own them. But as an official I have no discretion, but must obey instructions and execute the law. They are certainly an obstruction to settlement and should be removed; but as they were erected by an implied license and have stood so long by the acquiescence of the government, good faith requires that they should be removed with as little damage to individuals as possible. Time should be given cattlemen to adjust themselves to new conditions, just as Mr. Lincoln favored the gradual emancipation of slaves. I am opposed to harsh measures and would be glad if congress, by a joint resolution, would suspend the fence law for at least six months, or even a year. This would put a stop to fencing public lands, as nobody would build a fence that would have to come down in a few months, and the cattlemen would then pull down their fences.

Last spring I wrote a letter to the general land office recommending that the homestead law be so amended as to permit a person in the semi-arid region to enter at least one full section. I think two would be better. In an agricultural country a homestead of 160 acres may support a family, but it will not where land is not worth much for anything but grazing. I think such a policy would promote the settlement of the country. The president in his message recommends it. Such a amendment of the homestead law might be embraced in a joint resolution suspending the fence law. I suggest that you confer with Senator Millard of Nebraska and Senator Gibson of Montana about it.

I hope to see you soon. I am out on the prairie enjoying the Arctic weather.

Very Truly,

JOHN S. MOSBY.

This "letter" by Mosby sent to various government functionaries was sufficiently detailed in nature and scope to make the points he wished to make in all the particulars of the land matter as it had developed to that time. No matter how incorrect and inaccurate all of the news stories were to some degree or another, there can be no doubt that what Mosby "said" in the newspapers, if he was reported accurately, was the essence of the truth regarding whatever matter under consideration.

Soon, the grand jury results began to appear; and wonder of wonders, John Mosby was credited with the discovery of wrongdoing—at least in a Virginia newspaper:

Alexandria Gazette – January 14, 1903

MOSBY FOUND THEM OUT.—A dispatch from Omaha, Neb., says

W. R. Lesser, formerly a United States land agent, appointed to investigate alleged fraudulent land entries, was indicted yesterday by the federal grand jury on a charge of presenting false claims to the government in the shape of expense accounts. The indictment, however, is in connection with the recent investigation by Colonel Mosby of land entries by soldiers' widows on government lands, which were at once leased to cattle owners and fenced in by them. It is alleged that soldiers' widows from several States were brought into Nebraska by interested parties, where they made homestead entries, being told that it was not necessary for them actually to reside on them. These lands were at once leased to or purchased by cattlemen.

Meanwhile, Agent Lesser, who had had such nasty things to say about Mosby, found himself on the wrong end of the law and without John Mosby as an excuse:

St. Paul Globe – January 14, 1903

HUNTER OF FRAUDS IS HIMSELF ACCUSED OF FRAUDS

Agent of Government Investigating Alleged Rascality in Connection with Nebraska Lands, Said to Have Turned in Bogus Expense Accounts.

Omaha, Neb., Jan. 13.—W. R. Lesser, formerly a United States land agent, appointed to investigate alleged fraudulent land entries, was today indicted by the federal grand jury on a charge of presenting false claims to the government in the shape of expense accounts. The indictment, however, is in connection with the recent investigation by Col. Mosby of land entries by soldiers' widows on government lands, which were at once least to cattle owners and fenced in by them. It is alleged that soldiers' widows from several states were brought by interested persons into Nebraska, where they made homestead entries, being told that it was not necessary for them to actually reside on them. These lands were at once leased to or purchased by cattlemen.

Norfolk Weekly News-Journal – January 16, 1903

GRAND JURY INDICTS LESSER.

Former Special Agent of the Land Office Charged with Fraud.

Omaha Jan. 14.—Among the indictments returned by the federal grand jury yesterday was one against W. R. Lesser, former special agent of the interior department, living at Tama, Ia. Lesser is charged with defrauding the government in the matter of expense accounts.

Colonel Mosby, who was chiefly responsible for Lesser's losing his government position, charged that Lesser, while his duties should have kept him in Nebraska examining into suspicious land entries, was remaining quietly at home and making regular reports from there.

It is true that Mosby accused Lesser of failing to follow up on his reports of wrongdoing by the cattlemen, but Lesser was indicted not for failing to do his job, but for charging the government for having done it! His failure to do his duty was not the basis of the indictment against him. The problem was that he billed the government for doing what it was proved he did not do and from areas in which it was known he had not been! And still, the reports on the land issue continued—absent any criticism of John Mosby. But now the Nebraska cattlemen were "Greedy Land Robber Barons" and no longer put-upon, long-suffering, badly misused stockmen. Here is also mentioned for the first time a government act that will soon take John Mosby to Alabama in his position as an agent of the General Land Office, the "Stone and Timber Act":

Bisbee Daily Review – January 30, 1903 (Edited)
GREEDY LAND ROBBER BARONS

Under the above caption the Daily Picayune of New Orleans gives some information which, to the people of this portion of the great west may be classified as "important if true." It is true that Colonel Mosby of confederate army fame was sent out somewhere in Nebraska or Wyoming to look after some parties who were engaged in some crooked work in connection with the public lands, by which the federal government suffered loss.

Among the charges made by the Picayune is that the "land robbers were not pitiful thieves or petty intruders who had squatted on small patches of land without permission, but they were rich and powerful corporations. It appears that in one case parties mined and carried from the public domain 200,000 tons of coal. In Nebraska, New Mexico and elsewhere enormous tracts of public land were seized, a single land company having fenced in unlawfully 1,077,000 acres. During the year the department learned of the theft of 3,952,844 acres One man was found to have fenced in over 60,000 acres belonging to the government."

And while the land matter remained in the news, Mosby was not idle. He was still trying to reclaim the funds owed to him by the government for the theft of almost eight thousand pounds of tobacco immediately after the war. This claim and Mosby's untiring efforts to retrieve the fees owed to him during his time as consul at Hong Kong must be seen as a testimony to the man's perseverance! In two more years, the tobacco claim would be forty years old!

Alexandria Gazette – January 31, 1903

Col. Mosby's Claim.—Colonel John S. Mosby is trying to secure the passage by the House of a bill to refer his claim against the United States for the value of 7,900 pounds of tobacco, seized by the Union army July, 1865, after the cessation of hostilities, with full jurisdiction to try to adjudicate the claim and render judgment against the government for the amount they may deem due him. Both sides reserve the right in the bill to carry the matter to the Supreme Court. It passed the Senate unanimously last June.

But just when it seemed that the "land issue" was being sorted out and justice *might actually prevail*, it appeared that, in fact, the Nebraska cattlemen had triumphed, at least according to the *Minneapolis Journal* and the *Mt. Sterling Advocate*:

Minneapolis Journal – **February 3, 1903 (Edited)**
CATTLE KINGS ON TOP

They Now Have the Nebraska Matter Carefully Shelved in the Interior Office.

New York Sun Special Service.

Washington, Feb. 3.—The fight being made by the cattle kings to prevent destruction of their fences on the public lands in Nebraska, Wyoming and other western states is attracting considerable attention in Washington. President Roosevelt sent Colonel John S. Mosby, the famous Confederate guerrilla chieftain, to investigate the conditions on the plains. After some time spent in looking into the matter Colonel Mosby became convinced that the cattlemen were trespassing seriously upon the public domain and ordered that the fences be torn down. The cattlemen appealed to Washington and several western senators interceded for them with the president. Colonel Mosby finally was recalled to give the cattlemen the opportunity to present their case. They have forwarded to the secretary of the interior a lengthy protest against tearing down the fences and petitioned that no further steps be taken against them. The matter is now in the hands of Secretary Hitchcock.

Almost every account of this time in John Mosby's life places at least some blame for the problems with the fence matter at his door. He was too boorish, he couldn't keep his mouth shut, he spoke without thinking, etc. But it is obvious not only from this article but also from many others in reasonably objective publications that Mosby's behavior was not the problem. Rather, when it came to choosing between the law and the support of the Western states in a presidential bid, Roosevelt chose the latter. Of course, the results of that choice redounded badly to John Mosby whose only crime was doing the job Roosevelt had sent him to do.

Mt. Sterling Advocate – **February 11, 1903 (Edited)**
CATTLE BARONS

To Lease Government Land—Settlers Deprived of Rights

The cattle barons appear to have friends at court who are helping them to perpetuate their monopoly of Government lands in the Western States. A special dispatch from Omaha to the *Washington Post* says:

"The land-leasing bill, as now constructed was introduced into the Senate and House at last session of Congress. Its advent created a furor of indignation in the Western States, and its effect on the approaching elections was the cause of laying aside of the measure. Opponents of the measure denounce it as a glaring attempt to create a land monopoly in the Western States.

"It is proposed to lease for a period not exceeding 20 years any Government land remaining unapplied for, at the rate of from one to six cents an acre per annum. The proposition on its face means the acquiring of a revenue by the government from lands now unoccupied and seemingly worthless.

The reality, it is claimed, will be an increasing annual draft on the Federal Treasury for cost of collection, the establishment of large numbers of new fat offices, the control of immense acres of Western land, and the consequent prevention of settlement by industrious individuals, by a few great cattle and sheep-raising corporations, and the consequent absolute and unrestricted control of prices of meats by the land monopoly."

The dispatch further says: "Col. Mosby was rapidly informing the public of the actual facts when he was recalled."

As Col. Mosby was the special agent of the land department at Washington, and had been given orders to remove the wire fences the cattle barons had erected, his recall must mean that the administration has given up its fight against the cattle men.

The policy of the Government from the first has been to reserve the public lands for those who wish to make homes upon them, and its reversal by the present administration, in the interest of the cattle barons, should be denounced by all. Senators and Congressmen should be written to, demanding that the honest settler be protected and the cattle barons' fences be removed so that all can have free access to the public domain. B.W.H.

And so what did Washington do next? *Why, it sent another investigator to "take down the fences!*

Omaha Daily Bee – March 27, 1903 (Edited)

MOVE AGAINST THE FENCES

Special Agent of Land Department Detailed to Western Nebraska.

ORDERS ISSUED TO HIM ARE EXPLICIT

In Addition to Seeing that Fences are Removed He is Ordered to Investigate Charges of Fraudulent Entry.

Washington, March 26.—(Special.)—W. A. Richards, commissioner general of the land office, today ordered Special Agent W. D. Defrees to proceed from Crookston, Minn., to assume charge in the Alliance land district in Nebraska. Special Agent Defrees is to take up the work inaugurated by Colonel John S. Mosby in the matter of illegal fencing of the public domain and kindred subjects in the Alliance and North Platte land districts. This designation of Special Agent Defrees is significant in that it is the initial step looking to the ultimate overthrow of all fences which may have been erected by cattlemen contrary to law.

It will be recalled that Colonel Mosby made a rather complete and exhaustive examination of the condition the, and rendered a report which startled the department regarding the practices of cattlemen and their agents, who endeavored to gain possessions of vast tracts of public land and fence the in for grazing purposes. Colonel Mosby's report created quite a furor at the time.

As the most flagrant violations are said to have occurred in Nebraska, the eyes of the department naturally turn in that direction. Special Agent Defrees is to take up the investigation heretofore prosecuted by Colonel Mosby, and his directions are said to be of such an explicit character that abuses complained of will be overturned root and branch.

Instructions Are Positive

Mr. Defrees' instructions embrace a rigid examination of all allegations of fraud regarding entries upon public lands and a through investigation of alleged illegal fencing. Special Agent Defrees is a man of experience and mature judgment and has the confidence of the commissioner of the general land office. It is believed at the general land office he will proceed upon his new duties in an intelligent manner and with the utmost firmness carry out the instructions of the department, which is simply that the law regarding illegal fences be enforced. Special Agent Defrees was appointed from Indiana and has been three years in the service.

This, then, was how the matter was handled. As soon as all the work was done, save for the removal of the illegal fences, the former agent was removed and replaced by a new agent, who began the whole rigmarole all over again. Such a plan of action guaranteed that the fences remained in perpetuity. The article then stated, "This designation of Special Agent Defrees is significant in that it is the initial step looking to the ultimate overthrow of all fences which may have been erected by cattlemen contrary to law." "Initial step?" "May have been erected?" The reality of these fences could not be denied by anyone. The fences had been found, recorded, and acknowledged—several times in fact!

And yes, John Mosby's report was "exhaustive," so why the need for another one? Why was his "exhaustive report" not acted upon? Probably because it did "create a furor" that Washington did not wish to deal with. Furthermore, the leasing bill was not passed because it became known that upon obtaining leasing rights, the cattlemen would press for ownership of the land that they had occupied for many years without a leasing agreement. Like a common-law marriage, their hold on the land would became legal over time by virtue of the passage of that time.

Nobody's "directions" were more explicit than John Mosby's! And no one fulfilled and followed those directions better and more faithfully than he did, only to be removed, and the "investigation" turned over to another man—more local in his origins (Indiana)—to begin the process all over again.

Finally—and most offensively—the article assured readers of Agent Defrees's "experience" and "mature judgment as well as his "intelligent manner," which "has the confidence of the commissioner." How this is presented more than strongly suggested that his predecessor lacked all of those marvelous qualities and, as a result, did not have "the confidence of the commissioner." What an official slap in the face to John Mosby! He had labored so long, so hard, and so productively and brought the matter almost to fruition only to be cast aside and replaced by—one is led to believe—a better official who was sure to "fix" everything always assuming he would be permitted to do so.

Meanwhile, in an article appearing in the *Alexandria Gazette*, the first mention was made of Mosby's new field of activity: Alabama. Given all that had gone before, it must have been pleasing for him to be so graciously received there:

Alexandria Gazette – **April 13, 1903**

Col. Mosby.—General John S. Mosby, the famous Confederate cavalry officer, is a distinguished visitor to Montgomery. While in the city General Mosby is the guest of Mr. and Mrs. R. D. Browder. General Mosby is in excellent health apparently, with many years of activity before him. He was one of the picturesque and daring leaders of the Confederacy. The independent command of cavalrymen led by General Mosby achieved a fame second to none in the great struggle. In daring, in rapidity of action, in deeds accomplished "Mosby's Men" have but few equals in history. No true history of the war has failed to pay tribute to their gallantry and activity. Confederate soldiers throughout Alabama will rejoice to know that his years sit lightly upon their former comrade in arms. General Mosby is the agent of the Interior Department, looking after timber lands of the United States, and may remain in Montgomery several days. – [Montgomery Ala., Advertiser.

It would seem that some newspapers, finally, were beginning to see past "partisanship" and to understand Mosby's relationship with Grant as a mark of an exalted character and a genuine nobility of spirit:

Alexandria Gazette – **April 25, 1903**

COL. J. S. MOSBY.

Colonel John S. Mosby has received from Senator Henry Cabot Lodge, of Massachusetts, a letter enclosing an invitation to be present on "Grant night" with the Middlesex Club. The Middlesex is one of the most exclusive of all the New England clubs, and its "nights" are events of more than ordinary import. President Chamblin of the club writes to Colonel Mosby: "We would like to add your name to the roll of distinguished guests. The members of the club, the republicans of Massachusetts, and the people of Boston would be glad to see and welcome you. I beg to assure you that this invitation is not perfunctory and formal. We earnestly desire that you may be able to accept it."

Never before was friendship bought at the price Colonel Mosby paid for Grant's. At the time of which we speak Colonel Mosby was yet a very young man. He owned a beautiful home in Warrenton, where lived his devoted wife and interesting children. He was enjoying a law practice of perhaps $10,000 a year. He was the idol of the people of this county and of the State—young, handsome, brilliant and famous, there was no office in the State he might not have aspired to and won. His friendship for Grant cost him all these things. He was too far in advance of the times to escape the partisan hatred which burned nowhere so bitterly against the North as it did in Warrenton. Colonel Mosby's good reasons for preferring Grant to Greeley made no more impression than a human breath against a tornado. He lost his practice, his home, his certain advancement in politics because of his friendship for Grant, but his courageous spirit never yielded. He would not have turned his back on Grant for all that friendship cost him, though his old age finds him as poor as when he surrendered his arms after the war. —[Warrenton Virginian].

This article is correct to a certain extent, but it did not go nearly far enough. Mosby did not sacrifice everything for his friendship with Grant, though at first blush, that would seem to be the case. Indeed, in 1872, when he backed Grant instead of Greeley, it was not a matter of friendship—that had yet to develop between the two men—or even of gratitude, though Mosby certainly was grateful to Grant! Rather, it was a matter of principle and conscience on Mosby's part. Indeed, the little Virginian made it clear to Grant that if the Democrats ran a true member of that party, he would back that candidate even though he knew that in a national election, the man didn't have a prayer of victory. Mosby's position was made even more clear in 1873, when he refused to back the local Republican nominees and went with the Conservatives (Democrats). For this, he received little support from the Democrats while being rebuked by the Republicans—but not Grant, who, by that time, was beginning to have fond feelings for this strange little maverick who followed his principles into hell itself if it became necessary. Unfortunately, for a reason not given, Mosby was denied a few moments of honest tribute when he could not attend the function whose honored guest he would have been:

Times-Dispatch – **April 28, 1903**

Colonel Mosby Was Unable To Be Present

Boston Mass., April 27.—Grant night was celebrated by the Middlesex Club to-night without the principal speaker, Colonel John S. Mosby, of Virginia. Word was received at the last moment that he could not be present, but no reason was assigned. The members and guests were much disappointed, for they had counted much on hearing the "Marion of the Confederacy" present General Grant from the standpoint of a man who fought him for four years. The South was represented by Hon. Joseph C. Manning, of Alabama.

In May, Mosby suffered another bout of illness, no doubt the result of the physical and mental stress he had been under and the weakness resulting from his numerous bouts of intestinal ills. At his age, any surgery was problematic, but, as usual, John Mosby soldiered on without complaint:

Free Lance – **May 16, 1903**
COL. MOSBY AT HOSPITAL

Col. John S. Mosby is at Garfield Hospital, Washington, where he will probably undergo an operation. He holds a position in the Department of Justice, Washington.

From time to time, another reference was made to the land issue, but even the papers were getting heartily tired of the matter, albeit they were coming around to the belief (at last!) that the problem in resolving the issue had not been John Mosby:

Hocking Sentinel – **May 21, 1903**

The Land Department at Washington was intent a few months ago on wiping out the monopoly of the public lands in the West by the cattle barons. Col. Mosby was sent out there to cut the barbed wire fences and allow the settlers a chance. But suddenly Col. Mosby was ordered to Washington and the cattle barons are holding the fort. Another scandal will be uncovered when the matter is investigated.

What the Sentinel conveniently forgot was that the matter had been investigated—and investigated and investigated—but nothing had ever come from those efforts pursued at taxpayer expense. Indeed the man who had last done such a thorough job as to bring the matter before a grand jury had been railroaded out of Nebraska and sent on to Alabama, where it was devoutly hoped by the politicians and bureaucrats that he would sink into oblivion.

Meanwhile, May continued to see some sniping from the papers on the land issue, most of which were now decidedly "pro-Mosby" and against the cattlemen and their hired political hacks:

Hocking Sentinel – May 28, 1903

The Powerful Cattle Barons.

The administration has a kindly heart for the cattle barons, so has ordered the strenuous Colonel Mosby to other pastures than the public domain in Nebraska, where his presence caused so much annoyance to the cattle men in removing their fences several months ago.

The Republican Senators from Nebraska made it plain to the Secretary of the Interior that the cattle barons would defeat the Republican ticket in the State, unless the raid on them was discontinued. It is stated that the cattle barons appealed to the President, who, having been a cattle man himself, was induced to aid them. The settlers are indignant that their rights have thus been trampled on, but as they are but few their opposition counts but little against the power and wealth of the cattle men.

The Sentinel was not exactly a Mosby supporter, but it appeared that after the dust cleared and Mosby was removed on false and insulting grounds, the paper began to see the facts of the issue and reported accordingly.

At this point, preparations for another reunion of the Forty-third were well under way; and in response to that, the *Times-Dispatch* printed a series of articles and notifications:

Times-Dispatch – June 3, 1903
ARRANGING REUNION OF MOSBY'S MEN

Followers of Intrepid Leader to Gather in Culpeper on August 5 for Reunion

Times-Dispatch – June 14, 1903 (Edited) NUGGETS OF THE WAR

Mosby and His Brave Men

Erroneous Impressions Concerning Them MOSBY AND HIS MEN

I was often thrown in company with Mosby's men and knew many of them personally. They were not a set of ruffians, as was pictured by many Northern writers during the exciting times in "Mosby's Confederacy." A large majority of them were college-bred young men, sons of Southern planters, and men of influence in the State. A more chivalrous, daring, patriotic set of men never fought for the cause we loved so dearly. They endured hardships and many sacrificed their lives while fighting against superior numbers and resources.

And just when it seemed that the land issue was passé, as with the proverbial "bad penny," it appeared once again—this time declaring that the cattle barons had lost and that the fences would come down. Once again, however, the charge was made that Mosby had been relieved for talking too much or for speaking "inappropriately"—take your choice:

Washington Times – August 21, 1903

Minneapolis Journal – August 21, 1903

Government Land Will Be Thrown Into Ranges.

Omaha, Neb., Aug. 21.—Nebraska cattlemen who have fenced thousands of acres of Government land for ranch purposes have abandoned the fight to maintain boundaries and the land will be thrown into ranges.

The Cattlemen's Association informed the district attorney in this city that by September 1 the barriers will be down. These are the famous fences which Colonel Mosby was sent from Washington to tear down. Colonel Mosby was recalled for inflammatory talk at Omaha regarding the cattlemen.

In November, some "big guns" began to fire in the fence matter, especially against the Nebraska senators, one of whom, Dietrich, had been indicted for bribery and conspiracy. The *Alexandria Gazette*, a Democratic organ, took the occasion to pummel the Republican administration, although the fences had stood and the law been ignored through Democratic administrations as well:

Alexandria Gazette – November 9, 1903

The theory among republican officials that a public trust is a private snap is becoming more prevalent and it seems that those occupying the highest positions share this belief. The latest instance brought to light is that of U. S. Senator Dietrich, of Nebraska, who is openly charged with putting the postmastership at his home town of Hastings up at auction and disposing of it to Jacob Fisher for $1,500, the highest bid made. So open are the charges that the federal grand jury at Omaha will investigate the matter. When United States Senators engage in such unsavory grafting transactions, it invites the inquiry as to who can be trusted. Senator Dietrich, it will be remembered, had sufficient influence with the administration last spring to have Colonel Mosby transferred from Nebraska, where he was honestly and effectively performing his duties concerning the public lands, to an unimportant post in Alabama, where he could not be in the way of the Nebraska cattle kings, who were being taught by the colonel the difference between their own and the government's lands.

Alexandria Gazette – November 18, 1903

Senator Dietrich, of Nebraska, who has just been indicted for bribery and conspiracy, is said to be furious with U. S. District Attorney Summers, of Omaha, who drew the indictment, and has demanded the latter's removal' and his demand will probably be complied with, as the Senator has a "pull" in Nebraska and that State is wanted by Mr. Roosevelt next year. That he has a "pull" was clearly shown last spring when he had Colonel Mosby removed from Nebraska where he had been sent by the President to protect the public lands and assigned to an unimportant position in Alabama. Colonel Mosby was performing his duty so well in Nebraska that he interfered with the cattle kings of that State, who had fenced in and were using the public lands free of rent. This did not suit Mr. Dietrich, the friend of the cattle kings, and on his demand Colonel Mosby was transferred.

Perhaps John Mosby began to believe that there was such a thing as justice after all. The chickens had come home to roost, at least for Senator Dietrich. Meanwhile, the resurgence of interest in the fence matter was now in full cry as the eventual, if somewhat tardy, triumph of justice was being reported all round. All that Mosby had uncovered, all that he had said and written about the issues, and all that he had claimed had proven true. It must have given him at least some consolation even though the Republican only mentions him in the context of the phrase ". . Colonel Mosby made his grand stand play. . " which was not only unexplained, but decidedly uncomplimentary as well:

Custer County Republican – December 10, 1903 (Edited)
WATCH GRAND JURY

Special Agent Defrees Has a Mass of Testimony

CATTLE FENCES MUST GO

Washington Interest in Work at Omaha Testimony Being Taken

Charges Against District Attorney Summers Said To Be In Connection With Violations of Cattlemen

Washington, Dec. 3—Newspaper reports of the progress of the federal grand jury at Omaha in fence cases are attracting considerable attention here. At the general land office it was stated yesterday that Special Agent J. B. Defrees had been at work upon the cattle ranches of Nebraska ever since Colonel Mosby made his grand stand play, and that Defrees has served the required sixty days' notice upon a number of ranchmen who had unlawfully fenced in public lands. When Governor Richards, commissioner of the general land office, was in Nebraska two months ago he spent more than a week reviewing the work of Special Agent Defrees, whose duty it is to work in conjunction with District Attorney Summers, and the commissioner expressed himself entirely satisfied with the work those two officials had done.

The commissioner is not here now but one of the subordinate officials of the general land office said that its special agents had collected a vast amount of important testimony against violators of the federal statutes relating to the illegal fencing of the public domain in Nebraska, and it is the policy of the officers of the president to compel obedience to the law.

Incidentally it may be stated that one of the charges preferred against Summers was collusion with the Nebraska cattle kings, the charge having been made personally to the president when he visited Nebraska in the early fall, and the president, in conversation with Governor Mickey, is said to have indicated that he believed the charges well founded.

It is said that this charge was reiterated recently in Washington, and it is supposed that the affidavits were filed, hence the action of the grand jury is being watched with unusual interest.

St. Louis Republic – December 11, 1903 (Edited)
RICHEST RANCHMEN IN NEBRASKA ARE UNDER INDICTMENT

One is Bartlett Richards, Whose Range of 200,000 Acres Consists Largely of Public Land

Now in California Home

Cases pending Involve 700 Cattlemen and About 6,000,000 Acres of Land Report in Bribery Case

Former State Senator Formally Accused of Conspiracy to Bribe United States Senator Charles H. Dietrich.

Omaha, Neb., Dec. 10.—The United States Grand Jury, which has been investigating Post-Office bribery cases and the alleged illegal fencing of Government lands in Western Nebraska, to-day made a partial report to the court, returning twenty-two indictments. One is against former State Senator Elliott Lowe, charging bribery in connection with the appointment of a Post-master at Alma, Neb.; ten are against ranchmen charging illegal fencing, and the others were Indian cases, mostly of a minor character.

Those against ranchmen include true bills against Bartlett Richards, president of the Nebraska Land and Feeding Company; W. G. Comstock, vice-president of the same company, and Secretary Charles C. Jameson, all of Ellsworth, Neb. and former State Senator Frank M. Currie, a large individual cattle owner of Broken Bow, Neb. The other seven indictments are against extensive ranchmen of Cherry and Custer counties.

MORE TO COME.

The foreman of the Grand Jury stated to the court that it will later give a supplementary report, and it is stated that this action will include several more indictments of prominent ranchmen and also one against a former State official who was charged with disposing of a considerable amount of Government military supplies without making a report of the disposition of the money.

The indictment against former State Senator Lowe contained two counts and charges conspiracy to violate section 17891 of the Revised Statutes, by conspiring to bribe Senator Charles H. Dietrich by acting as intermediary in the payment of $400 in consideration of which J. B. Billings, who at the time of the alleged action was Postmaster at Alma, Neb., was to receive the recommendation of the Senator for reappointment.

IMMENSELY RICH

Richards, it is said, is the largest individual cattle breeder and owner in the world, and is rated as a man of immense wealth. In the summer he has resided on his ranch near Ellsworth, Neb., and in the winter at Santa Barbara, Cal., where he is now living

The land-fencing cases have excited intense interest because of the large number of wealthy men and influential ranchmen concerned, and because of charges, some of which have been filed in Washington, that certain public officials were in collusion with the ranchmen to prevent an indictment.

MOSBY'S WORK

Colonel Mosby's visit to the range country was the occasion for considerable comment, and it was he who first gave peremptory orders for the removal of the fences. In several instances his instructions were obeyed, but in the majority of cases they were ignored and many ranchmen, it is said, threatened to maintain by force what they considered their rights.

And so the matter was finally being set to rights despite the article labeling Mosby's actions "preemptory." The true situation had been determined and published—at least in a Virginia newspaper! Further, Mosby's "exile" to Alabama was put in its proper perspective and no longer attributed to his alleged "prolixity."

Something now was being added, at least in the Virginia papers; and that was the recognition of John Mosby's birthday, a matter that continued for the rest of his life:

Free Lance – **December 12, 1903**
COLONEL MOSBY NOW SEVENTY YEARS OLD.

Late as it was, the land issue was still not settled as the press continued to cover what was in fact an immense matter not only economically, but socially and politically as well. Mosby was "out of it" at this point, save for what he had done during his tenure as an agent for the Department of the Interior, efforts that received universal—if tardy— admiration by not only various political leaders, but the press as well. Seemingly, complaints about his personal failings had given way to a genuine appreciation of his actions on behalf of a most ungracious and ungrateful government:

Alexandria Gazette – **December 15, 1903**

Strenuous efforts to minimize the reports of huge land frauds are made by Secretary Hitchcock in his annual report on the Department of the Interior just made public. Emphatic denial is made that the frauds involve from $15,000,000 to $20,000,000 in land values, and that five United States Senators and many representatives are implicated therein. Evidently fearing that the department may have been thought to be implicated in disseminating the reports of the frauds, Secretary Hitchcock adds: "It can be positively stated that they did not originate in this department."

The details and results of the investigations into the frauds, it is further stated, are known but to a few, and "at the proper time a full statement will be made covering the results of the entire investigation and the whole matter will be given to the public." There is a strong suspicion entertained by many that by "proper time," after the presidential election is meant, and that no investigation into the affairs of any of the departments will be made until after the election. In his report Secretary Hitchcock makes no mention of the recall of Col. Mosby from Nebraska, where the President had sent him to prevent land grabbing by the cattle kings. The Colonel, it will be remembered, was performing his duties so honestly and effectively that he was interfering with these kings, so Senator Dietrich forced the President to recall him and send him to Alabama!

As 1903 was ending, John Mosby must have had some sense of validation for his efforts in Nebraska and elsewhere in the West. Certainly, the majority of public opinion, as evidenced in the press, was now against the cattlemen and their political servants. And while most of the applause was bestowed upon the new "investigator," there was no doubt that Mosby's contribution had not been entirely overlooked. Perhaps he believed that 1904 might carry on what 1903 had begun to his benefit.

ADDENDUM

Tom Horn

Tom Horn is a legendary figure who concerns this book in only one way. Horn was said to have "outlived his era." He was brought to "justice" for doing what he had been hired to do by his cattlemen employers, something that he had done for years and was the natural way of things in the "wild west." Sadly, Horn had not retired before "business as usual" was found to be unacceptable by the increasingly "civilized" region. Many say that John Mosby also "outlived his era" and that he could not adjust to life in the new century. But that is false. Mosby moved very quickly with the times as his behavior at the end of the Civil War proved. Far from attempting to live in the past, Mosby adjusted to the present and the future even in his old age—unless one wishes to suggest that rampant corruption, that he would not tolerate, was the "wave of the future." That may be (is?) true, but if Mosby would not adjust to corruption, that was a matter of moral standards, that are supposed to be eternal.

It is true that at the end of his life, John Mosby was not interested in a world he knew that he would never live to see, but he had opined about the automobile and the airplane. Indeed, in an article in the *Times-Dispatch* of November 4, 1910, Mosby said that aircraft would become a "big addition to armament." He had already said the same about the automobile, and just as he was willing to consign the saber to obsolescence, he would have done so with the horse. John Mosby was no Tom Horn, captured by an era that had passed and destroyed by an era he could neither understand nor accept. Mosby was "modern" as long as he participated in the world around him, even though, as his life closed, he preferred to remember the past. Indeed, the final proof that John Mosby never lost his presence of mind is to be found in the report of his physicians at the time of his passing: "he was conscious and interested in what was going on about him until an hour before his death."

Chapter 43

1904

Curae leves loquuntur ingentes stupent. ~ Minor griefs can be talked away; profound ones strike us dumb.

"Adversity is the first path to truth." ~ Lord Byron

1903 HAD ENDED on a somewhat triumphant note for John Mosby. If the land matter was still in legal limbo, he at least was no longer being blamed for that situation. Of even more significance, the death of James Longstreet brought to public attention the fact that Mosby was one of a very few surviving Confederates of note. As a result of this "discovery", articles on him began to appear in even greater numbers in the press:

> *Hawaiian Gazette* – **January 5, 1904**
>
> Since General Longstreet's death, General Gordon and Col. Mosby are the most distinguished survivors of the Confederate Army. For years Col. Mosby lived in San Francisco as one of the law-staff of the Southern Pacific Railroad. He was put there by C. P. Huntington at the request of the dying ex-President Grant but when Huntington died the old soldier lost his place. Within a year or two Col Mosby has been in Wyoming looking after some people who were defrauding the Government.

Mosby had been hired through the influence of Leland Stanford, California senator and former president of the road. Stanford did so at the dying request of his good friend Ulysses Grant. Collis P. Huntington liked and admired Mosby and protected him from those in the company who had no love for the former Confederate guerrilla—or probably for Huntington, one of the "old guard." Unfortunately, articles such as the one in the Gazette made it appear that Mosby was "kept on" for sentimental reasons and not because he was a fine lawyer and an able employee. That mind-set has since found its way into later works about the man, indicating that his service to both the railroad and the government—after Hong Kong—required that he be "protected" in order for him to remain employed. Nothing could be further from the truth. Indeed, the only reason John Mosby asked for Grant's assistance in obtaining a position after Hong Kong was his "pariah" status in the country in general and the South in particular! Had John Mosby been welcome in Virginia, he would not have sought Grant's help. But for some inexplicable reason there is a "divide" between Mosby's able service in China and everything that he did as an attorney after he left Hong Kong. Whether overt or covert, most people reading "histories" of the man come away with the idea that he was "kept employed" out of the goodness of someone's heart and not because of his own abilities.

An article in the *Times-Dispatch* revealed Mosby's personal "trail of tears" after the war:

> *Times-Dispatch* – **January 31, 1904 (Edited)**
>
> COL. MOSBY AND GRANT
>
> Interesting Reminiscences of Their Relations Recalled by the Death of Longstreet.

Why He Was Republican

Letters that Bear upon Mosby's Political Career and Reveal His True Character.

The recent death of General James Longstreet brought to the minds of many persons his political attitude after the war, and the fact that he had gone to the Republican party recalled the action of other distinguished Confederates who took the same course. Among others, Colonel John S. Mosby was cited as one who separated himself from his Democrat friends and aligned himself with the Republicans. The innuendo that the men who took this action were all actuated by a desire to get office, and that there was a sacrifice of principle for profit, has always been resented by Colonel Mosby's friends who knew that his action was controlled by a sense of what he sincerely believed to be for the best interest of his State, and that so far from seeking gain, he knew it would be at the expense of his personal interest ...

What Colonel Mosby suffered immediately after the war by reason of his extraordinary efficiency as a Confederate soldier is not generally known, but it is a fact that he was saved from constant and harassing interference by malevolent Federals through the influence and protection of General Grant. This was the first step towards a close personal friendship between Grant and Mosby, and in the Greeley and Grant campaign of 1876, Colonel Mosby, with many other Virginia Democrats supported Grant and carried the State for him. In the Kemper and Hughes campaign for Governor which followed the next year, Colonel Mosby refused to support the Republican ticket because of its alliance with the negroes and he informed General Grant in a letter that he "repelled the idea that he intended to identify himself with the negro party of Virginia." Though he obtained many offices for his friends, he would never take any office for himself from General Grant; but when Mr. Hayes became president and commenced the policy of practical reconstruction, and took the Confederate and conservative Democrat, D. M. Key, into his cabinet as Postmaster-General, Colonel Mosby accepted the consulate to Hong Kong.

In conversation recently with Judge Keith, he told the writer that he remembered well the circumstances under which Colonel Mosby was placed after the war, and his connection with the Republican party and he has set them forth in a letter printed below.

No more loyal son of Virginia ever braved death in defense of her soil than John S. Mosby, and it is well now that the mists of ignorance and unreasoning prejudice have dissolved away that this heroic soldier can stand in the clear light of truth, his high character untarnished, and his unswerving loyalty to his people unshaken.

Judge Keith's Reminiscences

Richmond, Va., Jan. 27, 1904

And still, the land issue had not entirely disappeared whatever the court findings. However, this was understandable as noted in an article in the *Hocking Sentinel*—it was, after all, an election year:

Hocking Sentinel - April 14, 1904

The fencing of the public domain in Nebraska and other States by the great cattle barons, which Colonel Mosby was sent to investigate, has been dropped at the urgent request, it is stated of the Republican delegation in Congress from that State, who fear its effect on the coming elections. Many settlers are anxious to go on these public lands and acquire homesteads, but are unable to do so from fear of the armed partisans of the cattle barons.

The recounting of Mosby's Civil War career continued apace. There were several reasons for this: First, he was still alive, a matter that always tended to increase the interest of the readership. Second, he had been perhaps the most successful of the independent Confederate commanders—and not a few regular commanders as well. Even the great Wizard of the Saddle, Nathan Bedford Forrest, was not only dead but his reputation had been somewhat tarnished by the claim that he was involved with the Klan. John Hunt Morgan, another heroic cavalier, had been shot down and killed while being taken prisoner. Of course, Mosby nearly died as the result of being shot while at dinner, but in truth, there had been none—North or South—like John Mosby. He hadn't even surrendered, and for those looking back on the war, whatever apostasy he had committed afterward did not negate his prodigious heroics, at least by this point in time. The article below involved Mosby both during and after the war and tried to explain what many found to be, under the circumstances, inexplicable:

Fairfax Herald - April 29, 1904 (Edit) Col. John S. Mosby,

Striking Incidents in the Career of a Great Historic Character.

The career of Col. Jno. S. Mosby, in both military and civil life, has been a remarkable one. In war he was idolized by his people and feared by his enemies. But peace resulted in placing the Southern people in a most deplorable condition, the hardship and injustice of which they strove in every way to ameliorate or avert. It so happened that Col. Mosby took a radically different view of the requirements of the situation from that entertained by the great majority of his former comrades and friends, and thus incurred the better enmity of those who had previously regarded him with admiration and affection, while those who had denounced him as a guerilla and an outlaw, became his staunch political associates and admirers. It has been thirty-nine years since the war closed, and the people of the present generation can hardly realize the horrible condition that obtained at that time and during the Reconstruction period that followed. The bitterness of feeling that was engendered by the Reconstruction Acts of Congress was intense. Those who had never heard the whistling of a bullet or met brave men in combat, at once became the South's most violent oppressors. They sought to disfranchise the white people and to blight one of the fairest lands on earth by placing it under the domination and control of ignorant negroes and unscrupulous carpet-baggers. In Col. Mosby's opinion, the only escape from such a fate was in securing the friendship and intercession of Gen. Grant, who had so often manifested the qualities of a humane and magnanimous conqueror. Col. Mosby wrote Gen. Wade Hampton about this time, "You and I have not differed about the end, but the means of restoring white ascendancy in the South," and however much people may have differed then as to the wisdom of his course, no one now doubts the absolute sincerity of his motives, or believes that he intended for one moment to add to the bitterness and woe of the people for whom he had risked his life on countless battlefields. But these feelings have long since subsided, and the people of Virginia will yet bestow upon Col. Mosby substantial evidence of their appreciation of his brilliant military services.

Before giving some interesting correspondence, with Col. Mosby's notes thereon, we take the liberty of saying that in a letter dated April 20, 1904, to the editor of the *Fairfax Herald*, Col. Mosby says: "As I write the date of this I am reminded that on this day 39 years ago, the truce I had negotiated with Hancock expired, and he informed me that unless I surrendered he would devastate the country. I refused to surrender, as nothing had been heard from Joe Johnston, but disbanded my men to save the country." [This lengthy article goes into Mosby's postwar career and especially his dealings with Conservative Governor Kemper and President Grant.-vph]

It was in consequence of Grant's well-known friendship for Mosby that the latter's aid and influence were frequently invoked to secure Grant's interference to prevent the perpetration of gross wrongs and oppressions, and it was the knowledge of that friendship that inspired the following correspondence, which we now give, with Col. Mosby's notes, or comments thereon:

Culpeper, Monday Morning (December—1873)

Dear Sir:

At Kemper's request I went to Gordonsville yesterday and spent the night with him.

We went through the message and his policy. Keep what I say strictly to yourself. But it is of great consequence for you to come here tomorrow and if you concur with me go from here to Washington at once.

For the present, however, say nothing of our purpose, even to your friends. I write in great haste—just off the cars.

Yours truly,(Signed) JAMES BARBOUR

Note: The above letter read between the lines implies a great deal more than it expresses. After supporting Grant for President in 1872, I supported Kemper, the Conservative candidate for Governor in 1873. The Conservatives denied being Democrats and claimed they were a local party to keep the white people in control of the State. Kemper repeated this in his inaugural message in January 1874, in which he foreshadowed a coalition with the party in power. The platform on which he was elected disclaimed any hostility to Grant's administration. I was invited to the conference at Gordonsville; to read Kemper's forthcoming Inaugural and then go to Washington to inform Grant of its contents and that Kemper and the Virginia Conservative were marching to join him. For some reason I did not go to Gordonsville but did go to Culpeper, and afterwards saw Grant and arranged for an interview with Kemper. Kemper got frightened and took the back track. I held my position. It was a perfect understanding that Kemper and the Barbours were to go over to Grant and carry the Conservatives with them. I had already announced myself in favor of a third term for Grant. I stood my ground although they deserted me.

I read Kemper's inaugural in his room at the Ballard before it was published and by agreement with him went to Washington to get Grant's influence against the Civil Rights bill which was then under discussion in the House It—the amnesty bill—slept there over a year. I returned to Richmond and reported to Kemper. He was delighted. I had arranged for him to visit Grant. the prospect for an alliance between Grant's administration and the Virginia people looked bright; if consummated it meant the death knell of negro government and carpet-baggery. It failed, through Kemper's weakness. On the day after my return to Richmond, Kemper came to the hotel to see me. He was all broken up. The secret of my mission to Washington had got out and a lot of politicians had called on him and frightened him. I was very mad at the way I had been duped and never spoke to him again. Having since seen so much of human weakness, I feel more charity for him than I did then.

See Kemper's inaugural; also his lame letter to the Whig of July 1874 trying to explain; also my interview in the Enquirer about the last day of June 1874, maybe July 1st.

I failed in this attempt to restore the South to power and had to pay the penalty of failure.

"Such a fate as this was Dante's fate, By defeat and exile maddened;
Thus were Milton and Cervantes,
By affliction touched and saddened."*

(Signed) Jno. S. Mosby

(copy of Gen. Wade Hampton's telegram to Col. John S. Mosby*) Dated Columbia, S. C. Personal July 1876 Received at Washington:

To Col. Jno S. Mosby

Present our case as it stands, and help us. Supreme Court recognizes our House, which has 63 members holding certificates. We only ask that the Constitution be obeyed. Peace and quiet will follow my inauguration, and this only will secure these. See Bradley Johnson and consult him.

(Signed) Wade Hampton

Note: As soon as I received the above telegram (during the Hayes-Tilden contest) I left for Washington and called at the White House that night to see Gen. Grant. He was at dinner; he made me come in and dine with him. I showed him Hampton's telegram. Grant assured me that he would only use military force to preserve peace and save the State from anarchy. [Here, the article recounts Mosby's informing Hampton and how Hampton's approach to him became known, leading to the matter becoming public.-vph] This provoked severe criticism by Southern politicians on Hampton for appealing to me to help him through my influence with Grant. They preferred to see South Carolina damned under negro rule to her getting relief through me.

Soon afterward a letter of Hampton's was published in which he said that he would not have asked me to aid him if he had known how odious I was to the Virginia people. The truth was that Hampton appealed to me because he knew I was odious to the Virginia people—Grant's friendship for me had made me odious to them. Hampton used and then abused me. He did not appeal to any of the so called true Virginians to help him.

On the evening of the day of my first visit to the White House I took the Aquia Creek boat for Alexandria. Gen. Hampton was aboard going to Richmond. I told him all about my interview with Grant and what I thought the opportunity was offered the Southern people by supporting Grant to get relief from many evils they were suffering. Hampton certainly did not dissent from anything I said. I was so intense in my feelings and so absorbed in the subject that I was unconscious of the boat's stopping at Alexandria, and did not discover it until the bell tolled when we were passing Mt. Vernon. A year afterward I got a letter from Hampton asking me to see Grant and get him to pardon some of his friends who had been convicted as kuklux. I wrote him that I would go with pleasure to see Grant, if he would go with me. Hampton declined. My political experience suggests the fable of "Belling the cat"—one man to incur all the danger and risk while others keep under cover and enjoy the benefit.

(Signed) JNO. S. MOSBY

This was a very important article that was sadly damaged in the only copy of the paper available for transcription. Mosby explained in it many things during and after the war, things of which he had said very little at the time, although most did become somewhat known much later when his biographers began to write about him.

Parenthetically, it is interesting to see all of the homage paid to Wade Hampton, a man who did not have the grace or the guts to defend his use of Mosby to save his state from Federal occupation. Indeed, Mosby pointed out that those who abused Hampton for using him in that circumstance "preferred to see South Carolina damned under negro rule to her getting relief through me [Mosby]."

Then there was a very important point regarding Hampton's request that Mosby help some of his friends when they were indicted under the ku klux laws. Mosby had asked Hampton to go with him to Grant to plead for his friends, but Hampton refused. What man would abandon his friends because he didn't want to be criticized? Perhaps Hampton didn't want to be seen with Mosby. Yet he certainly had no problem asking for Mosby's help for his friends—*or* for his state. Many speak of the "greatness" of Wade Hampton, but his treatment of John Mosby indicates very little "greatness" in the man.

At this point, Mosby was "transferred" from the Department of the Interior to the Department of Justice. He had wished to enter the latter from the beginning, but with the understanding that "beggars can't be choosers," he had accepted the former position. Now it was reported that he had "resigned" from the Department of the Interior to take up a position in the Justice Department:

Times-Dispatch – May 24, 1904 (Edited)
MOSBY AS ASSISTANT ATTORNEY-GENERAL

The Gallant Confederate and Able Lawyer is Honored by the President The Work of His Friends

Senator Daniel and Others Interceded with Mr. Roosevelt and Secure Appointment.

Washington, D. C., May 23.—Colonel John S. Mosby was to-day appointed as assistant attorney general of the United States and immediately took the oath of office. His future home will be in this city, and his office will be in the Department of Justice.

This prodigal has returned home," said Colonel Mosby this afternoon. "I was appointed from Virginia, and I gave my place of residence as Warrenton, Fauquier county. I have lived all around.

Colonel Mosby's hair is as white as snow, but his clean shaven face is ruddy as a school boy's and his gait is not that of an old man. He is as active as ever he was, apparently, and fair to see much of life yet, though in his adventurous career, there is not much he can hope to see that will impress him as distinctly new. He is an able lawyer, and his long experience in the practice of his profession, which he gave up for four years to follow the fortunes of Lee, coupled with his native ability, and thorough legal training, have made of him an antagonist to be feared. ... .

Alexandria Gazette – May 24, 1904

The many friends and acquaintances of Colonel John S. Mosby will be glad to hear of his appointment as assistant attorney in the Department of Justice in Washington, and they will be more glad to learn that after he shall have entered upon the discharge of the duties of his new position that he contemplates making Alexandria his permanent home. The colonel since 1865 has virtually been an Alexandrian, his frequent visits and often prolonged stays here having been the means of extending his acquaintance with most of our citizens. He has been welcomed and his society enjoyed, especially by his fraters who learned to esteem him during the four years civil war when his fame became world wide.

Mosby's promotion, if one could call it that, to the Department of Justice was not explained at the time. However, it may have been that his position in Alabama was an obvious result of his efforts in Nebraska and that those "in charge" considered it was better to move him out of the Department of the Interior altogether for the sake of appearance as his presence tended to reopen all the old charges of corruption arising from the Nebraska land issue. In the Department of Justice, Mosby no longer could be connected to the Interior's business and so the press could not use him as such.

But the land issue was still in the press. The times they were a'changin' as both the cattle industry and John Mosby were about to learn, albeit, for a change, Mosby's lesson was less painful when all was said and done

Herald and News – June 21, 1904 (Edited)

CATTLE RANCHES FREE.

Large Tracts of Land in Nebraska for Homesteaders.

"A Nebraska cattle ranch one mile square absolutely free" is the offer which the government is preparing to make to every man or head of a family of the United States, says a special dispatch from Omaha, Neb. To the New York Herald. As there are 8,884,757 of these acres from which a selection may be made any one desiring to become the possessor of 640 acres of fine grazing land will have no trouble finding a tract which is suited to his taste. Great tracts of this land have been fenced by cattle barons of Nebraska and it was to have these illegally constructed fences removed that the government last year sent Colonel Mosby, the former Confederate cavalry leader in the state to enforce the law regarding these fences. It is said that one ranch, with headquarters at Ellsworth, Neb., had under such fencing nearly 2,000,000 acres of government land. There were dozens of other great ranches which also included hundreds of thousands of acres of government land within their fences.

But the Kincaid bill sounds the deathknell of the cattle barons, whose herds of thousands roamed over the ranges, more effectually than any fence removal order which the president might promulgate. With settlers from all parts of the United States flocking in and taking homesteads of 640 acres each the public domain in Nebraska is a thing of only a few months more, and then, without the necessary lands upon which to graze their herds, the cattle barons must go out of business.

And so the great land debacle ended. Whatever the outcome, it was the end of the problem of the use of "the public domain."

At this time, a very interesting matter appeared—that is, another invitation to Mosby by the Massachusetts GAR to attend a reunion at Faneuil Hall in Boston. Mosby had long said that New England was not the problem for Southerners, but rather the bulk of the remnant of "the bloody shirt" crowd was to be found in the Midwest and even the West. The almost constant invitations he received from the Massachusetts GAR rather proved his point:

Free Lance – July 21, 1904

National Tribune – July 21, 1904

Union Veterans Invite Col. Mosby.

Col. John S. Mosby has been invited to attend a Grand Army reunion at Faneuil Hall, Boston, August 25. The invitation came from Commander Graves, of Edward Kingsley post, G.A.R., with a personal letter urging Col. Mosby to accept it. The Boston veterans hope to have at least twenty five former Confederate officers at the reunion, and plans have been made to give them a hearty welcome among the men whom they fought. Col. Mosby probably will accept.

Alexandria Gazette – July 23, 1904

Fairmont West Virginian – July 25, 1904

Col. Mosby Hears from His Prisoner.

And then an article appeared in two publications regarding Mosby's view of the Fourteenth and Fifteenth Amendments. Again, this illustrates that press interest in Mosby's viewpoint was not limited to matters of the "late unpleasantness" or even the land issue:

Times-Dispatch – September 13, 1904

Wilmington Messenger – September 20, 1904

The Fourteenth Amendment.

Colonel John S. Mosby has addressed a communication to the *Washington Post*, in which he discusses the Fourteenth and Fifteenth Amendments in their relation to each other. He points out that the Fourteenth Amendment, adopted in 1868, declares that "when the right of any citizen in any State to vote is denied or abridged, the basis of representation therein shall be reduced in the proportion to the number of such male citizens shall bear to the whole number of male citizens twenty-one years of age in such States." But he goes on to say, the Fifteenth Amendment adopted in 1870, restored the original constitutional basis of national representation, and made it unlawful to deny or abridge the right of any citizen to vote on account of race, color or previous condition of servitude. This provision of the Fifteenth Amendment on the same subject, and, adopted subsequent to it, annuls it, as the Thirteenth Amendment annuls the clause for surrendering fugitive slaves; and hence no State has a constitutional right to abridge suffrage on account of race or color, nor has Congress a constitutional right to reduce a State's representation for having done it. The question was ably discussed a year or so ago by Mr. Charles A. Gardiner, a prominent lawyer of New York, who took the same view as that now presented by Colonel Mosby. Mr. Gardiner's argument seems to be unanswerable, but the doctrine as expounded by him and Colonel Mosby is not generally accepted, and the question should be taken to the court. A test case should be made up, if practicable, and the Supreme Court of the United States should be asked to decide and dispose of the question definitely and forever.

John Mosby's interpretation was valid, no doubt, but he failed to make note that the Fourteenth Amendment was never legally ratified. Further, Mosby had been very much against the Fifteenth Amendment. In a letter to son Beverly of January 30, 1900, Mosby wrote that he had written to William Stewart, author of the Fifteenth Amendment, protesting his bill; for "if Negro votes were counted, they would control several Southern states. I don't think Negroes are fit to govern white people. Where they occupy the same soil, the white superior race, although a minority, will and must govern." Here it must be noted that a comment placed at the end of the letter by the archivist holding Mosby's correspondence stated: "Colonel Mosby, the lawyer, stated a view held by many Southerners in 1900." The archivist is wrong. Colonel Mosby stated a view that was held by almost every white man or woman, in the United States and other Western countries. The only reason that the amendment passed is that the North—having few Negroes at that time—was spared the problem that would arise in many states in the South. To suggest that Mosby's viewpoint was limited to other

Southern whites is false. Had there been the same percentage of blacks in the North as in the South, the Fifteenth Amendment would never have passed. Indeed, it probably never would have been offered.

The *Alliance Herald*, Mosby's old foe from Nebraska, finally printed the story of his "promotion" to the Department of Justice. But the paper could not help putting in just a bit of "sour grapes" in its conclusion:

Alliance Herald – September 16, 1904

Colonel John S. Mosby who led the famous "Mosby Guerrillas" during the civil war has recently been promoted to an assistant attorneyship in the department of justice at Washington. Colonel Mosby is well known in Alliance having spent several months here sometime ago ordering stockmen to take down their fences. The colonel is in his seventy-first year. He did not need the endorsement of western cattlemen to secure his new job.

The election being over, Mosby sent to the press correspondence between himself and reelected president Theodore Roosevelt. It was a rather interesting matter in which Roosevelt declared that he was sympathetic toward the South. However, several of the articles following were written by Southerners who questioned the president's veracity regarding that claim. The matter received quite a bit of press at the time, including the suggestion that Mosby might have been gulled by Roosevelt, but that his natural sense of honor had defeated the president's machinations:

Times-Dispatch – November 19, 1904

SOUTH VERY DEAR, SAYS ROOSEVELT

The President Saddened, Rather Than Angered, at Attacks on Him

WRITES LETTER TO COL. JOHN S. MOSBY

Declares The He guards the Interests of This Section as Jealously as He Does those of the North. Half a Southerner Himself.

Washington, D.C., November 18.—President Roosevelt says that attacks which have been made upon him by Southern people and by the press of the section have saddened rather than angered him, as he is of Southern extraction and has the interests of the Southern States as much at heart as those States of the North.

Some time ago, Colonel Thomas R. Roulhac, a Democrat, who the President appointed to the office of district attorney for the Northern District of Alabama, wrote a letter to Colonel John S. Mosby, of the Department of Justice in this city, in which he expressed regret that Southern people criticized Mr. Roosevelt so severely, and said he thought it was due to misapprehension of the President's views. Colonel Roulhac is a native of North Carolina, and was a Confederate soldier.

Letter to Mosby.

Colonel Mosby sent the letter to President Roosevelt, who was then at Oyster Bay, but he did not give out the reply during the campaign, as he thought the President's motives in writing as he did, might be misconstrued. The following is the President's reply, permission to use which was obtained from the White House to-day:

"My Dear Colonel Mosby:

"Oyster Bay, N. Y., September 10, 1904.

That is a fine letter of Roulhac's, and I appreciate it. I have always been saddened rather than angered by the attacks upon me in the south. I am half a southerner myself, and I can say with all possible sincerity that the interests of the south are exactly as dear to me as the interests of the north.

"Sincerely yours,

"THEODORE ROOSEVELT."

Although there has come no word from the White House to indicate it, there is most general belief that the President will pursue what the people of the South will look upon as more acceptable policy toward that section than he has followed in the past. Every Southern men interviewed in Washington since the election has urged that the press of the South and the people give Mr. Roosevelt full credit for good intentions toward them until there is some positive act of his to justify the contrary opinions. In short, to wipe off the slate, and begin all over again with the new administration.

Cairo Bulletin – **November 21, 1904**

THE PRESIDENT AND THE SOUTH.

Col. John S. Mosby, the noted Confederate cavalry leader, who turned Republican and is now holding a position in the Department of Justice at Washington through the appointment of President Roosevelt, gave to the press a very interesting communication a few days ago.

It was a letter from President Roosevelt to Mosby concerning a letter written to the latter by Judge Thomas R. Roulhac, of Alabama, in which the latter commented on the attitude for the southern people toward the president personally. Colonel Mosby sent the letter to Oyster Bay, so the dispatch said, as he thought the sentiments expressed in it by a Confederate veteran would be gratifying to the president. He received a reply which he did not publish during the campaign as he felt "that the president's motives in writing the letter would be misconstrued." The letter is as follows: [Here the paper prints Roosevelt's letter to Mosby.-vph]

This letter, it is observed, was written during the presidential campaign, and before the remarkable victory its writer achieved at the ballot box two weeks ago.

There would be no room for questioning the sincerity of the president's letter if his record on the southern question was not so contradictory. A year or so ago President Roosevelt went on a visit to the city of Charleston, S.C., and while there made a broad, patriotic speech, full of kindness and friendly feeling for the south. He paid a high tribute to the southern people and their past. The city of Charleston received him with open arms for they thought they had found a new-found friend. A few months later Mr. Roosevelt delivered a speech in the north in which he denounced the southern people as anarchists. And a few months later on he was found trying to force down the throats of the very people who had received him with such generous enthusiasm a negro politician, whom he appointed to one of the highest positions in the city, over the earnest and emphatic protest of the entire white population of Charleston.

In Alabama he started out by appointing a white Democrat to a United States district judgeship, and at the same time letting it be known that he was going to lend his influence to a movement to build up a "white man's Republican party" in the south. His Republican officeholders in that state, taking the appointment of Judge Thomas G. Jones as their cue, began a movement to eliminate the negro from Republican conventions. Then there went up a howl from Africa and suddenly the wind listed. The president, with head set on capturing the Republican nomination for the presidency, suddenly switched. The negroes are very powerful in Republican politics in the south. The constitute a large part of the delegates to Republican national conventions from that section—or they did, and they are to be reckoned with. To grab the nomination, Mr. Roosevelt had, he thought, made a mistake and he lost no time in changing, With a somersault that has hardly been equaled in politics, he completely reversed himself. The "white man's Republican party in the south" was scuttled. The very men who had led the movement which, they thought, had come inspired from Mr. Roosevelt, were removed from their federal positions. Then, to prove he was a friend of the negro, he entertained one at dinner at the White House. Then followed the Indianola, Miss. incident, the Crum appointment and a dozen others.

In view of this record, might not Col. Mosby, who did not publish Mr. Roosevelt's letter during the campaign for fear "that the president's motives would be misconstrued," have misconstrued them himself? Isn't it possible that the president intended for the letter to be published, as a campaign contribution in the southern states?

A wise young statesman once remarked that "words are good when backed up by deeds." Mr. Roosevelt now has the opportunity to prove his own words. His conduct the next four years toward the people of the south will show just how "dear" to him are the interests of the south.

The Bulletin just after the election expressed the opinion that Mr. Roosevelt's second administration would be marked by a spirit of conciliation and sympathy toward every section of the country—including the south, basing this belief on what it thought was the president's ambition to give to his country in the next four years one of the most splendid and one of the most glorious administrations in history. The same day, however, the press dispatches announced that the president had just appointed, over the protest of almost every citizen of the town, a negro postmaster in Arkansas. What his policy is to be we don't know. Nobody knows. A few smart Washington correspondents have recently sent out glowing dispatches to their papers about the president's "new policy of friendship" toward the south. It was the next day officially denied.

But this much we do know: and that is that "words are good when backed up by deeds." If the interests of the south are as "dear" to the president as are the interests of the north, let him prove it. Not only the south, but the north, east and west will be glad to see him do it.

The second response to the Mosby-Roosevelt correspondence was a great deal more nuanced and, probably, more correct. Ever naïve with regard to the men he respected, Mosby believed that the president's motives "would be misconstrued" if he sent the letter to the newspapers before the election. But the journalist offers a much more cogent deduction: might not Mosby have "misconstrued" Roosevelt's motives in that the president wished to see his letter printed in the Southern press prior to the election? The Federal government's insistence on appointing Negroes to Federal positions only in the South was of long standing. Indeed, Mosby once suggested that a Republican administration might prove its lack of sectional bigotry by appointing a black candidate to a Northern office—at the time, he suggested the postmaster of Boston, but without success.

But even while the racial issue was in the news, something a great deal more important and considerably more ugly raised its head. While Mosby was in Alabama, a Democratic politician, Thomas Heflin, made some joking remarks about Roosevelt and Booker T. Washington after the president invited Dr. Washington to a luncheon at the White House—something unheard of at the time. Mosby's response to Heflin was instant, severe and censorious:

***Evening Star* – October 7, 1904 COL.**

MOSBY IS ANGRY

Incensed at Representative Heflin's Violent Remarks

AN INTERESTING TALK

The Ex-Confederate Believes Parker Will Lose Votes.

His Recollection of Peonage Trials and Heflin's Position Then—Not a Subject for Joking.

Col. John S. Mosby of Confederate guerrilla fame is mad all the way through because of the violent remarks of Representative J. Thomas Heflin of the fifth Alabama district who, in speaking of the luncheon to Booker Washington by President Roosevelt, said:

"If Czolgosz or some other anarchist had thrown a bomb under the table no great harm would have been done the country."

Colonel Mosby is satisfied that this remark will lose The Democrats many votes in the north, despite the fact that Heflin has since declared that the remark was made as a joke. This is what Col. Mosby says:

"Until my appointment last May in the Department of Justice I had been a year in Alabama investigating fraudulent homestead entries and timber trespassing on public lands. I was transferred there from Nebraska, where I had been engaged mostly in having the fences of the great cattle kings inclosing large acreages of public lands and preventing settlement, removed. I arrived at Montgomery about the time the peonage trials began before Judge Jones in the United States court. The court room is in the same building with the land office, and so I was a witness of the proceedings.

Peonage in Georgia.

"Under cover of state law on fictitious charges of breach of labor contract or of vagrancy negroes were arrested and conclusive judgment given against them. Under pretext of satisfying these judgments negroes were imprisoned and sold to parties who held them in the worst form of slavery. Judge Jones, notwithstanding the clamor it raised, had several of the offenders convicted and heavily fined. Some were sent to the penitentiary. Judge Jones deserves great honor for breaking up the peonage business in Alabama. It was simply a new from of slavery, but much worse than the old form, when the master had a property in the slave, and of course, there was a motive of self-interest, but these peons were in as bad a condition as the galley slaves of the Barbary corsairs.

"A Mr. Heflin, then a state officer, and now a democratic member of Congress, published a letter severely condemning Judge Jones on account of the punishment of these criminals, because Jones had sentenced them to punishment. Heflin compared him to Jeffries, the infamous tyrant of the English judges. After these criminals had suffered a short imprisonment, on the recommendation of Judge Jones, the President pardoned them and sent them out in the world admonished to go and sin no more.

"Representative Thompson, the representative from Tuskegee district, died, and The Democrats rewarded Heflin for abusing Jones and defending peonage by electing him to fill out Thompson's unexpired term. Heflin is now a candidate for re-election.

Heflin's Whole Speech.

"I have received a copy of a Montgomery paper, which prints the entire speech of Heflin delivered at Tuskegee on October 3, in which Heflin discusses the negro problem and the alleged dinner to Booker Washington by President Roosevelt. The paper authoritatively says that Heflin stated that if Czolgosz or some other anarchist 'had thrown a bomb under the table no great harm would have been done to the country.' A dispatch in this morning's papers says that Heflin declares he was merely joking when he made this remark. I notice that Heflin adheres to what he said about having Booker Washington lynched if he took any part against him in the congressional election. Now, there is no doubt that pressure from northern democrats, on account of the injury that Heflin's speech is doing to Parker, has forced Heflin to publish his card of denial. Yesterday I met an Alabama representative who had just been to New York making speeches, and he referred with great regret to Heflin's ill-advised speech. He said that it would do The Democratic party a great deal of harm. But, really, I cannot see that Heflin's talk of a joke puts the matter in any better position that it was before. Heflin must have expected his audience to enjoy the joke about the assassination of a President of the United States, but people who would laugh at such an awful crime could have no real horror if the crime were actually committed. But to lynch Booker Washington for taking part as a citizen in a congressional canvass, I think in every moral sense would be as bad as the assassination of a President.

Ex-Gov. Oates' Advice.

"I am glad to see that ex-Governor Oates, a one-armed Confederate soldier, and former colleague in Congress with Mr. McKinley, has come out in a card advising the democratic committee to muzzle Heflin. I do not think the people who heard Heflin saw the point if he intended his remarks about assassination as only a joke. As for the talk about forcing the social equality of the races, that is nonsense. Nobody wants to do such a thing, and nobody can do it. Social intercourse rests on sympathy in taste and mutual consent. That law of nature is the foundation of society, and regulates not only the conduct of men, but of all animals. There is just as marked a line of division between different classes of white people as between white people and negroes. You never see a Jew in a church or a Christian in a synagogue, yet all live harmoniously together."

New York Tribune – October 14, 1904

SOUTHERNERS REPUDIATE HEFLIN.

Hope His Incendiary Speech Will Cost Him His Seat in the House

[FROM THE TRIBUNE BUREAU.]

Washington, Oct. 13.—A prominent citizen of Alabama has written to Colonel John S. Mosby regarding the Heflin outburst against the President, expressing the hope that the House of Representatives will refuse to seat the Alabama Congressman because of his seditious speech. He says in part: All of the thoughtful men in this community are outspoken in their condemnation of Heflin. However, there is a large element, especially in this district, of the vicious and ignorant, who are for anything that is "agin the nigger," and he was playing to this element when he made the infamous speech which has recoiled on him, and The Democratic party, with great injury to both. I hope in case he should be elected that the Republicans will refuse to seat him, on the ground of his incendiary and seditious speech against the President. I believe that the greater part of the white people in Alabama would be pleased to see this come to pass. Commenting on this letter, Colonel Mosby said:

"The writer of this letter is a prominent citizen of Alabama, who has always voted the Democratic ticket. As a Congressman is supposed to represent the sentiment of his constituents, the result of the election in Heflin's district will show whether the Alabama people indorse or repudiate Heflin's sentiments in favor of assassination and anarchy."

Mosby was no egalitarian. He was strongly against any racial mixing, and he did not believe in "the equality of the races" except under the law. However, he did believe that to threaten a man of any color with "lynching" because he was participating— as was his right as a citizen—in the electoral process was worse than to joke about the assassination of a president. Most people of the day would have found a greater moral sin in the assassination of a president than in the murder of a simple citizen (and especially a black citizen), but John Mosby found the greater moral fault in the sanctioned murder of a man for claiming his rights as a citizen granted him under the law. This is a very revealing look at Mosby's moral purity; that is, such extraneous matters as personal importance, political affiliation, and even race were of no concern to him. All that mattered was the moral right.

The Department of the Interior was back in the news with Secretary Hitchcock reviewing the investigation of various land frauds in the past eighteen months. The *Gazette* noted that Hitchcock had nothing at all to say about John Mosby:

> *Alexandria Gazette* – **October 10, 1904**
>
> Secretary of the Interior Hitchcock, in a statement for the press, reviews the investigation of land frauds during the last eighteen months, and says that the leading spirits in the fraudulent transactions have been indicted on the charge of conspiracy, and that the cases against Hyde and Benson, the principal conspirators, are being contested in the higher courts. The Secretary makes no allusions however, to the recall from Nebraska of Col. Mosby who was sent there by President Roosevelt to protect the government's interest in the public lands and who was faithfully and strenuously performing his duty when he was suddenly transferred to Alabama!

Mosby's opinion on "racial mixing" was picked up by *The Appeal*, a Minnesota publication. It is interesting to see that as early as 1904, blacks were starting to be called "Afro-Americans" and that "political correctness" was in vogue, apparently because Mosby's belief that people—like animals—sought their own kind was something that Southerners were "afraid to voice." That fear probably went back to Reconstruction and efforts by Radical Republicans to force social amalgamation of Southern whites and blacks in an effort to prevent Southern whites from returning to power.

> *The Appeal* – **October 15, 1904**
>
> Col. John S. Mosby of Confederate guerrilla fame says that talk of forcing social equality of the races is all nonsense. "Nobody wants to do such a thing and nobody can do it. Social intercourse rests on sympathy in taste and mutual consent. That law of nature is the foundation of society, and regulates not only the conduct of men but of all animals. There is just as marked a division between different classes of white people as between white people and Afro-Americans." There are other Southerners who see this thing as Col. Mosby sees it, but they are afraid to talk out.

However, just as Mosby's life seemed to be changing for the better, long shadows appeared within his own family as beloved firstborn May Virginia's illness became ever more serious. Perhaps it was his concern for his child or the questions asked by the interviewer, but the idea that "… [h]e looks back on those days smilingly" was hardly the case:

> *Alexandria Gazette* – **November 11, 1904**
>
> Col. Mosby.
>
> Col. John S. Mosby is in Warrenton on account of the health of his daughter, Mrs. R. R. Campbell, who we are glad to say is much improved. While standing in the vicinity of the polls on election day the colonel said, "I remember this day in Warrenton, thirty-two years ago, when Grant was elected over Greeley," and as he spoke we saw or thought we saw the shadow

on his face of many memories passing in a ghostly parade before his mental vision. If they did not, they might have done it, for those were stormy days in politics and Col. Mosby was in the thickest of it. It was a very bold position that he took. He gave up home and affluence for what "sudden death" would have been a merciful dispensation. But he has lived through it all and has overcome the prejudice that existed against him. He looks back on those days smilingly and with regret perhaps.—(Warrenton Virginian.)

But sadly, the Leslie's Weekly and the Oregonian articles back in October were more optimistic than realistic. The "rancors" of the Civil War had not been, as John Mosby had so devoutly wished, "consigned to oblivion"; and if there was any Confederate who had proof of that unhappy fact, it was Mosby. Here, he was forced, once again, to defend himself against the charge of cruelty and murder; but as usual, he picked up his mighty pen and weighed into the fight in a lengthy (unedited) article. Notice that Mosby responded to two "mainstream" publications and not "yellow journals" like the *National Tribune*:

Washington Post – **November 21, 1904**

Fairfax Herald – **November 25, 1904**

MOSBY'S DEEDS IN WAR

Guerrilla Chief Denies He Was Cruel to Prisoners. Replies to Hustead Charges

Never Shot Union Soldiers Captured by His Men During the Civil War— Warm Friends To-day Among Men Who Were His Prisoners Forty Years Ago—Never unkind in Word or Deed.

Col. John S. Mosby, the noted Confederate guerrilla chieftain, has made public a letter which contributes an interesting chapter to civil war history, as particularly relating to Mosby's command, its operations and general conduct, and is designed to defend that body against charges of inhuman treatment toward Mosby's prisoners among the Federal forces.

The letter is written to Frank P. Moss, of Boston, Mass., a Union veteran who was captured by Mosby in Fairfax County, Va., on October 13, 1863. During the Grand Army Encampment in Boston last summer, Col. Mosby received an invitation from Mr. Moss and Capt. Barton, of Brookline, Mass., both of whom are his warm personal friends, inviting him to attend a Union Veterans' banquet to be held there. When this invitation was made public, Mr. Edward Campbell, of Uniontown, Pa., another Union veteran wrote a letter to Mr. Moss inclosing another attacking Col. Mosby's conduct during the civil war. Mr. Moss transmitted this letter to Col. Mosby, who has replied as follows:

"My Dear Sir: Your letter of the 4th instant was forwarded to me at Warrenton, Va., where I was spending a few days. With it was inclosed a letter from Mr. Edward Campbell, of Uniontown, Pa., who says 'that I have a very excellent friend here who served in West Virginia during the war who holds an opinion of Mosby which I do not share. My friend, Capt. Hustead, declares that Gen. Mosby (I never was a general) deliberately shot one of his, Hustead's men, after Mosby's men had captured him.'

"Capt. Hustead no doubt believes what he says, but he is speaking from hearsay—if he had been a prisoner and saw the shooting, I can see no reason why he would not have been shot too. The rules of judicial procedure require a criminal charge to be sufficiently definite to give reasonable notice to a party of the time and place where the alleged offense was committed.

No Witness Against Him.

"You observe that I am not informed of either; but I can plead in general terms that I never myself, nor did I ever know any one of my men, having been guilty of any such atrocity. If I had been guilty of this cold-blooded murder, then I could just as easily have murdered several thousand prisoners that I took in the war. There are many of these men now living and not one had ever appeared as a witness against me. Some of the best friends I have had since the war were my prisoners during the war. I had a great many collisions with the Second Massachusetts and the First Vermont Cavalry. In one affair with the Second Massachusetts we captured Maj. Forbes, of Boston, and sixty-nine of his men. The Forbes family are my warm friends; they gave me a dinner at Parker's a few years ago. Among the guests were Dr. Oliver Wendell Holmes, James Russell Lowell, and Mr. Justice Holmes. Gov. Grout, of Vermont, was an officer of the First Vermont Cavalry. He was wounded and captured by me. I met him a few years ago in Washington. If any one wants to know how I treated my prisoners let him ask Gov. Grout. Gen. Wells—now dead—belonged to the same regiment; he was my prisoner and my friend. I have received cards of invitation to the weddings of two of his children.

"When I was appointed by President Hayes consul at Hongkong, Gen. Wells wrote a letter to Senator Edmunds asking him to vote for my confirmation. Senator Proctor, whose general (Stoughton) I captured at Fairfax Court House, called on President Roosevelt to urge my appointment to the Department of Justice. In the campaign of 1864 in the Shenandoah Valley, the war records show the activity of my command against Sheridan; but in all the reports and correspondence you cannot find a complaint from any officer of the violation by me of any of the usages of war. Gen. Sheridan knew all about my character as a soldier. He published his memoirs, and while he has a good deal to say about the annoyance we gave him, he makes no complaint against me or my men.

"You observe that Mr. Campbell says that Capt. Hustead served in West Virginia. If I would condescend to rest my defense on a alibi, I could easily prove it, as my command did not operate in West Virginia, except in a small strip of the counties of Berkely and Jefferson bordering on the Shenandoah River. The valley pike runs south from Martinsburg about twenty miles west of Harper's Ferry to Staunton, Va., in a parallel line to the Blue Ridge. Our operations in the Shenandoah Valley were in the country lined east of the valley pike, and never extended into West Virginia.

Murder a Moral Impossibility.

"But I do not rely on the plea of the physical impossibility of my having done such a deed, but on the moral impossibility of it. No man can truthfully say that I ever did an unkind act or spoke an unkind word to a prisoner. This is not the first time that such a crime has been imputed to me and located in West Virginia. A few years ago I was introduced in Washington to a man from West Virginia by a friend who told me that the man had once been my prisoner. I asked him when and where I captured him; he said in 1861 or 1862 at a certain place in West Virginia. I told him that at that time I was a private in the First Virginia Cavalry, with my regiment in Eastern Virginia, and that I had never been within a hundred miles in my life of the place where he said he was captured. The fellow was a Methodist preacher, who had called to get my friend to take him to the Pension Office—he wanted to be put on the pension rolls. He had told my friend that I had treated him with great cruelty, and that he would thrash me on sight. When I exposed the fraud, he went off at a double-quick.

"Captain Hustead's report is simply an echo of the mythical stories that were told about me in the war that will someday be published as an appendix to the 'Arabian Nights.'"

1904 was almost over, and it had been a relatively good year for Mosby. The land issue was being settled, albeit slowly, and he was no longer being pilloried as the reason for the "failure" to remove the fences. He had labored in Alabama for the Department of the Interior and been successful. He had gotten a new position in the Department of Justice and was able to continue to contribute financially to his family. His health appeared stable, and his friends were once again around him as he now lived in Washington. But fate would not permit John Mosby to escape the year without heartbreak. On November 24, his beloved May Virginia—his firstborn child, one of his dear "tilluns"—passed away. John Mosby was devastated:

Times-Dispatch – **November 25, 1904**

Mrs. May Mosby Campbell (Special to The Times-Dispatch.)

Warrenton, Va., Nov. 24.—Mrs. May Mosby Campbell, postmaster at this place, died this morning at 4 o'clock, after a lingering illness of several weeks. She was the oldest daughter of Colonel John S. Mosby, and is survived by two sons—Mosby and Spotswood Campbell.

Mrs. Campbell was appointed postmaster of this office in June, 1897, by President McKinley, and has held the office continuously.

Her funeral will take place Friday afternoon. She was the widow of Robert R. Campbell, a well known lawyer of the Warrenton bar.

Late in the year, the Roosevelt and the South matter, begun by Mosby's sending the newly elected president's personal letter to the press, was back in the news. It seemed that the South had not found much friendship from any "Northern establishment" Republican administration. Of course, some Northern Democrats were not all that friendly either! Mosby had tried to show that Grant would respond, but Grant's presidency was unique; and once he was gone from office, Mosby had no friends in the White House until Roosevelt—or at least he had believed that Roosevelt was his friend:

Bisbee Daily Review – **November 27, 1904 (Edited)**

MOST AFFECTING SADNESS

Now that the campaign is over we are arriving at many truths which were impossible to come at during the term of heated politics. One of these truths just now coming to light is the real inwardness of Mr. Roosevelt's feelings toward the south. Some months ago, one Judge Roulhac, of Birmingham, Ala., wrote to one Colonel Mosby of the department of justice at Washington, D. C., commenting on the attitude of the southern people toward Mr. Roosevelt; whereupon Colonel Mosby sent the letter to the president, and the president in due course wrote a letter to the aforesaid Colonel Mosby, excellent politician that he is, did not publish during the campaign, conceiving the possibility that some persons might misconstrue the president's motives in writing the same.

Now, however, there being no votes to be won or lost, Colonel Mosby makes public the letter, which is as follows: [Roosevelt's letter to Mosby-vph]

Ninety millions of people, more or less, honor Mr. Roosevelt as president of the United States, and many of those millions respect him as Mr. Theodore Roosevelt. All of the millions will be deeply touched by his epistolary exhibition of sadness, though it may be that some of the whites south of Mason and Dixon's old line will find it difficult to be as thoroughly sympathetic as some of the people further north. Even these, nevertheless will rejoice to learn, if somewhat tardily perhaps, that Mr. Theodore Roosevelt's feeling toward them is not one of anger but sadness. They will be glad to know that, indeed, he has never been angry at them, but has always regarded them with that tender melancholy, that profound solicitude wounded with disappointment with which the parent regards the refractory infant; that he looks upon them with the painful regret of the fond father who contemplates the well spanked darling.

Spanking is always an unfortunate business for both parties. Ordinarily it hurts the parent worse than it hurts the child, and Mr. Roosevelt's sadness is no exception to the rule. And like all the other fathers he feels it incumbent to say so. And since he has said so, the child may perhaps be pardoned for indulging the inevitable observation that it didn't hurt him in the same place, though. That is the fact—it may be a sad affair for Mr. Roosevelt, but the sadness is far more poignant in the case of the southern whites who have rebelled in spirit at what they cannot help but regard as threatened negro domination as a result of Mr. Roosevelt's forcing methods.

That Mr. Roosevelt feels sad, however is some consolation—if he really does feel sad … If he is really sad he will not force the issue of the Crum appointment[*]. His expression of sadness will possibly not be received as a positive unguent upon southern wounds until such matters as the question of representation and his federal appointments have been disposed of. Meanwhile, there is a disposition to "wait and see." [*See "Addendum" at the end of the chapter.-vph]

John Mosby had reached the middle of the first decade of a new century. Though he still had to deal with tragedy, as with the death of his firstborn child and with other family grief yet to come, he continued in his usually optimistic attitude about life, an attitude that had sustained him thus far through joy and sorrow, triumph and failure.

ADDENDUM

Those who questioned President Roosevelt's desire to raise his popularity in the South seemed to be vindicated by his appointment of William Crum, a Negro, to be collector of customs at Charleston Harbor in the face of vehement objections from the citizens of that State. Crum had been nominated during the special session of the Senate immediately following the president's inauguration, but nothing came of it and Roosevelt thereupon gave Crum a recess appointment on March 20.

Roosevelt's action was roundly denounced by Democratic Senator Tillman, who took the lead in opposing "the new gloss on the Constitution." At the close of the debate, the Senate directed the Judiciary Committee to report upon the powers and limitations of the Executive in making recess appointments. The matter was soon forgotten however, and when the nomination was again forwarded to the Senate on December 6, 1904, it was confirmed within a month.

Chapter 44

1905

Cave quid dicis, quando, et cui.
~ Beware of what you say, when, and to whom.

"There's a punishment for [truth], and it's usually crucifixion." ~ John Steinbeck

IN AN ARTICLE early in 1905 about the relative strength of the two sides in the so-called Civil War, John Mosby's name was mentioned in excellent company. If he saw the story, he would have been very pleased to see his contribution to the glories of the South, even in defeat, being recognized for their value:

Times-Dispatch – **January 8, 1905**

[Part of a much longer letter published in the paper.-vph]

> While it is a historical fact that we fought as a whole about five men to our one, and that it took four years to conquer us, and while the Northern men were better equipped, better armed, better clothed and fed, still it does not prove that they were less brave, for they came from the same race of people, but it does prove they were without a great cause and without leaders. A great leader will incite men to brave action even in a bad cause but a noble cause will incite them to brave action without a leader. The attempt was made to convince the North that they fought for the Union, and some think so even now, but the truth is, if the Northern leaders had loved the Union as devotedly as did Davis, Stephens, Lee and the Johnstons war would have been impossible. What the North did fight for was the fanatical frenzy on the part of its leaders to free the negroes, in which nine-tenths of the men felt no interest, and on the part of the politicians and contractors to feather their nests.
>
> On the other hand, the cause of the South could not be better stated than in general order No. 16, to the Army of Northern Virginia, which says: "Let every soldier remember that on his courage and fidelity depends all that makes life worth living, the freedom of his country, the honor of his people and the security of his home."
>
> Could they fight for a better cause, and has not such a cause made men superhumanly brave in all ages?
>
> Did the North produce in their respective sphere men of such extraordinary military genius as Lee, Jackson, A.S. Johnston, Stuart, Forest [sic] and Mosby? No intelligent, candid Northern man of today claims that it did. When I look at the snap judgments on posterity, statues to Northern generals (though most of them are Southern men) in Washington. I wonder how posterity will treat those outrages on justice. They will not find an impartial competent military historian that will give to one of them, except, perhaps, McClellan, one particle of military genius. These I

believe to be the true reasons for the long-delayed success of the Northern armies, notwithstanding their overpowering numbers and resources.

CAZENOVE G. LEE.

Washington, D. C.

An extremely odd matter appeared in the *Alexandria Gazette* at this time. Frankly, it made no sense. It reported upon Mosby as an employee of the General Land Office, though he had left the Department of the Interior in 1904 and moved to the Department of Justice. Whatever the circumstances, Mosby was apparently sent to Alabama—again or still—to investigate a very "sensitive" and "delicate" issue at that time:

Alexandria Gazette – **February 6, 1905**

Col. Mosby to Investigate.

Col. John S. Mosby, now employed by the General Land Office, at Montgomery Ala., has been detailed to fathom a political quarrel at Mobile. His report will probably have great weight with the President in determining who shall be collector of customs at the port.

Collector William Frye Tibbetts, a near kinsmen of Senator Frye, of Maine, is a candidate for another term. A vigorous fight over the appointment has been in progress for several weeks; in fact, it began long before Mr. Tibbetts' four-year commission expired last December. Senator Frye has been insisting that his namesake shall have, at least, a square deal. Some Alabama republicans, among them several negroes, are relentless in opposition to him. Two decidedly different stories are brought to Washington about young Tibbetts. Many, including good democrats and representative citizens, say he is a fine young man; that he has conducted his office efficiently, and that he has been decent in politics. Others say that he is a fresh young man, having a deal to say about his distinguished relative, and that he entertains ideas about the negroes too much like the ideas of Southern democrats generally. It is also alleged that he has treated negroes contemptuously.

With such conflicting narratives, urged for and against the candidate, it seemed wiser to send Col. Mosby over to Mobile in the hope that he might ascertain the exact situation and report impartially. Further action accordingly awaits his report. The office pays a salary of about $3,500.

The thing of great interest about this matter is that the issue was considered to be one of the utmost delicacy, requiring very careful handling. Yet, for years, the supreme criticism of Mosby was—and continues to be to this day—his lack of those very qualities. Despite that contention, he was sent down to deal with, if we are to believe the claims herein made, an exceptionally subtle and delicate situation requiring the most diplomatic handling. Frankly, either Mosby was a bull in a china shop or he was not. The above article suggests that the latter was the situation extant.

Mosby was also in Alabama looking into the conduct of "prominent Government officials" regarding chicanery with campaign funds—obviously another very delicate matter. In this case, the newspaper acknowledged that Mosby was an agent of the Department of Justice:

Washington Times – February 10, 1905

SPOILS REFEREES TO GO ON THE RACK

Colonel Mosby, Now a Federal Sleuth, Probing Activity of Alabama Officials.

Birmingham, Ala., Feb. 10.—Col. John S. Mosby, famous in the civil war as a Confederate scout and now special agent of the Department of Justice, is here investigating the conduct of certain prominent Government officials, especially with reference to their activity in partisan politics.

The investigation centers around J. O. Thompson, collector of internal revenue for Alabama and chief of President Roosevelt's patronage referees in Alabama.

Colonel Mosby will endeavor to ascertain whether or not Thompson violated civil service regulations during the last campaign in collecting or disbursing campaign funds.

The attention of the United States court has been called to the activity of certain Government officials in collecting campaign funds from Government employees. Federal Judge Thomas G. Jones is behind the inquiry which Colonel Mosby is prosecuting. There are rumors that the present referee system in the distribution of Federal official patronage will be changed by the President.

Mosby's postwar "tobacco claim" was finally determined and paid. If he could have collected interest after forty years, he could have retired in comfort:

Alexandria Gazette – February 23, 1905

Colonel Mosby Gets Pay.

The Washington correspondent of the Richmond News-Leader says: "Colonel John S. Mosby is one of the happiest men in Washington today. In 1865 he had some 7,000 pounds of tobacco in Richmond warehouses. The troops then stationed there made use of it. It was after the close of the war, and Colonel Mosby had been paroled, and thereby became entitled to all the protection of life and property that an American citizen enjoys. He therefore had a claim against the government for his tobacco. For years he has been trying to get Congress to pay him for his "weed," but without success. This year, however, his claim went into the omnibus claims bill, and as a result, after forty years, Colonel Mosby will get paid for the smokes and chews the northern men had at his expense. The amount allowed him on the claim is $3,950.

Now the scene changed, and John Mosby was caught up in the case, or more accurately, cases, that eventually drove him from government service. Mosby had no better luck with the Indians than did George Custer—albeit, Mosby managed to survive his encounter. The following article contains the first hint of the dark path ahead:

Guthrie Leader - March 22, 1905 (Edited)

EMBRY CASE BEING HEARD

Inspector Husted is Busy Hearing Evidence at Chandler

Chandler, Okla. March 22.—The Publicist says: In view of the fact that Inspector Husted of the Interior Department is now here investigating the charges upon which John Embry's appointment as prosecuting attorney from Oklahoma is being held up, the following facts concerning these charges taken from a Kansas City paper.

Secretary Hitchcock transmitted Allen's report to the president and informed him of the report made by Mosby. Mr. Roosevelt at once communicated with Attorney General Moody, who looked up Mosby's report and informed the president of its contents. The president then withdrew Embry's nomination and directed that his connection with the alleged irregularities be further investigated.

At the interior department it said that Secretary Hitchcock had called the attention of the Oklahoma officials to the evidence presented by the inspectors and had recommended prosecutions and that they had replied that the prosecutions would be very expensive and that the territory had no funds with which to bear this expense.

Mosby was not the original attorney in the matter—Inspector Allen was. Mosby merely investigated Allen's charges and found them factually correct. The prosecution by Oklahoma of the fraud was dismissed as "too expensive." Sadly, as with Hong Kong and Nebraska, money, pull, and politics were more important than what was decent, right, and legal.

And of course, personal stories about Mosby continued to make their various appearances in a press that never seemed to tire of the subject:

Free Lance - **March 30, 1905**

Col. John S. Mosby has been to Richmond on a visit and received interested attention from his friends and the old members of his command. His eye is yet undimmed and he walks with strength and courage surprising for his age.

And as the year progressed, once again, Nebraska made the headlines as the final facts were being placed upon the scales of justice. This was just another example of Mosby being vindicated by his old (but tardy) friend, "Time":

Evening Star - **April 10, 1905 (Edited)**

TRIAL OF CATTLEMEN

Charged With Fencing Government Land

Result of the Work of Col. John S. Mosby in the West.

OMAHA, Neb., April 10.—After nearly two years of waiting and postponing, the great cattle barons of Nebraska are to be placed on trial for fencing up large bodies of government lands and preventing homesteading thereon. Every device which their great influence could bring to bear on the national government has been exhausted and the edict has gone forth that they must now appear before the United States court in Omaha and plead to the indictments which were returned against them nearly two years ago. The cases have been set for hearing in the early days of the May term of court, and there will be no more postponements. The charge against them is for "maintaining a fence on public lands," and the penalty is $1,000 fine and six months' imprisonment.

Because of the prominence and wealth of the parties concerned, as well as the far-reaching effect of the result of the trial, the cases have attracted more attention in the west than anything in recent years. Even the investigation of the beef trust is of no more importance to the west than the trial of the cattle barons, is the prevailing opinion of both cattlemen and farmers in Nebraska, Wyoming and the Dakotas.

Indictments Against Nineteen

Indictments have been returned against nineteen of the most prominent stock raisers in Nebraska, and these will be placed on trial first. Afterward, if the government is successful in its prosecutions, more indictments will be returned.

Col. Mosby's Work.

It required strenuous work on the part of the government agents to secure the information necessary to return these indictments, and picturesque Col. Mosby, the old rebel raider and cavalry leader, spent several months on the Nebraska ranges in an attempt to remove the fences. But the "pull" of the cattle raisers was too much for the doughty Colonel, and he was called off before he finished his work. But partially from the information gathered by Mosby and partially from other sources, enough evidence was secured to have these nineteen leaders indicted.

The government cases are all prepared and the witnesses have already been summoned. It is given out that there will be no more delays and that all the cases will be brought to trial immediately.

Omaha Daily Bee – **June 2, 1905 (Edited)**

CATTLEMEN FACE THE JURY

Land Fencers Case Begin with Trial of Kraus Brothers

PROCEDINGS ARE ACTUALLY IN MOTION

District Attorney Baxter, in Outlining Case, Tells of Alleged Attempt of Defendants to Oust Homesteaders.

The trial of the land fencing cases began before Judge Munger in the United States district court Thursday morning, with the court room filled with interested spectators, among whom was Bartlett Richards, the well known cattleman of northwestern Nebraska, and who is also under indictment for the illegal fencing of portions of the public domain.

In the edited portion of the above article, there was still considerable hostility directed at Mosby by the defense despite the fact that Mosby's replacement, DeFrees, testified that he did exactly as Mosby did—demand the removal of the fences— and with the same negative results. And while Mosby was still being assaulted in Nebraska, quite another grand jury matter involving the Chickasaw Indians was proceeding in Oklahoma, indictments having been found by that grand jury based upon an investigation conducted by Attorney Mosby for the Department of Justice. According to the headlines, the matter promised "serious trouble" for some "Men in High Position." Usually, such "promises" tended to redound to the detriment of the investigator rather than the "men in high position":

Fairmont West Virginian – June 24, 1905

FEDERAL GRAND JURY FINDS INDICTMENTS

Investigation of Million Dollar Fraud Case Among Chickasaw Indians Results in Serious Trouble for a Number of Men in High Position.

Ardmore, I.T., June 24.—The Federal grand jury which has been investigating the alleged $1,000,000 frauds in connection with the government of the Chickasaw Nation has returned indictments against the following persons:

W. T. Ward, deputy district clerk and treasurer of the Chickasaws.

D. S. Johnston, Governor of the Chickasaws.

B.H. Colbert, United States Marshall

Kirby Purdom, banker, who is alleged to have absconded.

Mansfield, McMurray and Cornish, the law firm acting as attorneys for the Chickasaws.

The indictments are based on the charge of re-issuing school and general fund warrants of the Chickasaw nation and it is said that $1,000,000 was obtained in this manner. The fraudulent warrants are held by bankers of Joplin, Kansas City and St. Louis.

The investigation was conducted by Attorney Mosby for the Department of Justice.

Daily Ardmore – July 3, 1905

MANY HEADS TO FALL

As a Result of Warrant Scandal, Says Hitchcock.

Inspector Jenkins Has Orders to Keep His Mouth Shut—Mosby Has Not Yet Reached Washington—No Action until His Arrival

Guthrie Daily Leader – July 24, 1905

INSERTING THE PROBE.

Col. J. S. Mosby, Government Inspector, Arrives in Guthrie.

Colonel John S. Mosby, special government inspector, as announced in the Leader dispatches last week, arrived in Guthrie yesterday and is staying at the Royal Hotel. Colonel Mosby is the special agent that unearthed the alleged warrant frauds in the Chickasaw nation recently and who was responsible for the indictment of several prominent Indian officials, including United States Marshal Colbert. Colonel Mosby is the noted guerrilla chieftain who kept the federal forces so uncomfortably busy in Virginia during the Civil War days and nothing apparently gives the genial veteran as much pleasure as in talking of episodes of that stirring and exciting period. But he will not talk of his present mission to Oklahoma except to state in vague terms that he may remain for some time. It is known, however, that Colonel Mosby is here to conduct an investigation of some sort on behalf of the government and it is believed that a certain land office located on the west side is under fire. About two months ago a government land office inspector was in Oklahoma and made searching inquiry into certain matters pertaining to this particular land office and it is inferred that the charges assumed sufficient gravity to justify the following up of the investigation.

Here is an article that seems to contradict all of the stories that Mosby "talked too much" about the matters he was investigating. Of course, a great deal could be "construed" and "deduced" by the talk and actions of other agents and their investigations. The idea that the press could learn nothing without John Mosby—that is, that Mosby was the only source of press reports—was untrue. Meanwhile, the Indian matters went forward:

Guthrie Daily Leader – July 19, 1905
MOSBY'S SILENT MISSION

Government Special Attorney Coming to Oklahoma for Long Visit.

Washington, D.C., July 19.—Col. John S. Mosby left Washington today for Guthrie, Okla. Colonel Mosby is a special attorney for the department of justice, and was before the grand jury in Muskogee recently, during the time the investigation of alleged school warrant frauds in the Chickasaw nation was in progress. A number of federal officials, the governor and a former governor of the Chickasaw nation, some bankers and a law firm, were indicted by this grand jury. Col. Mosby would not state what the nature of his business was in Oklahoma, but said he would probably be there some time, and would visit other towns besides Guthrie. He had an interview with Judge Ryan, acting secretary of the interior, yesterday afternoon in regard to his mission to Oklahoma.

According to this small story, indictments were in fact returned by the grand jury; but what further matters were still to be taken up by that jury was not mentioned, an indication that Mosby was closemouthed in these situations:

Daily Ardmore – July 25, 1905
THE WARRANT FRAUDS

Investigation May Involve Senator Burton[*] of Kansas [*See "Addendum I" at the end of the chapter.-vph]

His Name on Back of Many of Them. He is Said to Have Cashed $15,000 Worth in St. Louis—Inspectors in Guthrie Investigating.

Guthrie, Ok. July 24.—The investigation of the school warrant frauds of the Indian Territory may involve Senator J. Ralph Burton of Kansas. It became known here tonight, indirectly through Inspector Jenkins who assisted in the investigation of the alleged school warrant fraud at Ardmore for which United States Marshal Ben Colbert has been indicted, that Senator Burton came into possession of $15,000 worth of these warrants. The Department of the Interior at Washington has been unable to find out how he came in possession of these warrants and does not care to know particularly, but the department has been informed that Senator Burton received $15,000 cash from a St. Louis bank, for the Ben Colbert school warrants.

It is charged in the indictment that about $100,000 worth of school warrants were turned into a bank at St. Louis and there sold again. Ben Colbert was connected with the bank and it was because of the charges that his position as United States marshal has been endangered

Colonel John S. Mosby, assistant attorney for the Department of Justice at Washington arrived here tonight. He said he had arrived here to assist United States Attorney Horace Speed but would say nothing further of his mission. "I came here to help investigate something, all right," he added, "you can say that much. This is a great country and is going to come into statehood this winter. It needs to be cleaned up first, though. It needs a bath, politically."

Col. Mosby's business is in connection with interior department affairs. Before starting for Guthrie he had a conference with Acting Secretary of the Interior, Ryan.

According to the press reports, the person passing information "indirectly" was not Mosby, but Inspector Jenkins. The newspaper makes a judgment call in "supposing" that the Department of the Interior wished to remain ignorant of Senator Burton's actions even though those actions involved his obtaining some $15,000 through fraudulent warrants that had previously disturbed that department! It would seem that the involvement of a US senator changed the rules of the game as Mosby had discovered in Nebraska.

The convoluted and complex nature of the Indian matter slowly came to light with every passing report:

Chickasha Daily Express – July 27, 1905 (Edited)

MOSBY WILL INVESTIGATE

Dead Indian Claims in Chickasaw Nation Sold Without Order of Court
LAND DEALERS ARE UNEASY

In Some Sections, Judge Dickerson Ordered a Sale.

It is contended that Colonel Mosby will come here with full instructions to investigate all such sales, and if he finds the heirs have not been paid a fair and reasonable price the matter will be turned over to the United States courts and a legal sale will be ordered.

Guthrie Daily Leader – July 27, 1905
COL. MOSBY IS BUSY

Sent Here to Clean up Federal Rottenness.

It develops that Colonel Mosby, special federal inspector, has been given special carte blanche by the Department of Justice to investigate and make immediate report on every phase of federal rottenness existing in Oklahoma territory.

It was first thought that Colonel Mosby was here on a special mission relative to warrant frauds, but evidence is now patent that he is merely taking up the work left off recently by other inspectors.

"There must be a whole lot of cleaning up before Oklahoma is ready for statehood," said Colonel Mosby this morning as he hurriedly ran through a huge pile of documents. "These documents are copies of every charge filed within the past four years against federal officials in Oklahoma with the President and the Department of Justice." [*] The judiciary and the district clerks will command the major portion of Colonel Mosby's time. Inspector Harris who has been here several months, checking up the affairs of former district clerk Neal, has orders, it is understood, to co-operate with Colonel Mosby. "One or two heads have dropped," said an official, who is in the know, today, "but I look for some more sensational denouements. If the signs read right and I think they do, the east part of the territory will not do all the suffering. There will be some hurrying and scurrying on the west side of the territory. The fixers here in Guthrie have already been trying to get next to Mosby, Jenkins and Harris, but they are getting the "frozen face." A big fire is being built under our district clerk, and I shall not be surprised to hear of him decamping very shortly. His resignation will not be accepted, and he will not only be removed on point blank evidence, but prosecuted criminality as well. This clerk has suddenly grown rich. His assurance has led him into ventures which when exposed will surprise the people. He is an ignorant fellow and not content with grafting, has gone out of his way to knock others. The special inspector has a mass of evidence bearing on shady deals in which this clerk holds stock. With his removal there will be confiscation of some ill-gotten property.

In the same paper: (Edited)
WILL BEGIN AT PAWNEE

Indian Guardian Situation Will Be Dug up MANY SIGNS OF GRAFT

Colonel Mosby to Begin Investigation Monday.

Colonel Mosby, who is in the city as a special inspector from Washington will probably go to Pawnee Monday where he will institute a careful and thorough investigation of the Indian guardian situation. From there he will go to Alva and [illegible].

It is believed that Col Mosby's investigation will result in the discovery of some of the blackest work ever known in the history of either of the territories. Only a few days since it is said that a man deposited $25,000 in a Ponca City bank. The man had in trust $20,000 of Indian money.

[* To begin with, Mosby was dealing with what were apparently large numbers of charges that had been sent to the president and the Department of Justice "in the last four years," long before John Mosby was involved or even a member of the Department.] Now that Mosby had come to investigate, apparently the local press was highly enthusiastic. A great deal was being said about the matter—but not by Mosby! The article in the *Guthrie Daily Leader* of July 27, stated that those attempting to "get close" to Mosby to learn what is going on were "getting the frozen face ..." Also, Mosby's mission had been called "silent." Those opining were local people and even "Inspector Jenkins," but not John Mosby! Oklahoma was a far cry from Nebraska, but it ended no better for Mosby—or the Indians.

However, those who had been defrauding the tribes probably for years, now knew that John Mosby was coming. They probably already determined that the same result would soon obtain; that is, the matter would become more about Mosby, what he said, and what he did than about the topic under investigation—especially if they helped it along on that path. Mosby had been destroyed in Nebraska by a combination of crooked politicians and a complicit press. It is probable that the same type of people saw the possibility of repeating the success of the Nebraska conspirators in Oklahoma:

Daily Ardmore – **July 28, 1905**

COL. MOSBY COMING.

Will Investigate it is Rumored, Dead Indian Claims—in Oklahoma

Again, the inquiry seemed to focus not on the situation or its antecedents, but on the investigator—John Mosby. This is what had happened in Hong Kong and then in Nebraska. The problem, the charge, the investigation—nothing mattered but the man involved. Of course, the major problem was indeed the man, as Mosby could not be frightened or bought off. Prior to his coming on the scene, these illegalities had been quietly buried or helped along by the involvement of all concerned in and out of government. Mosby was a bright light in a dark place, and as was always the case with all vermin, human or otherwise, they didn't like it. Soon, in response to the developing situation, the language began to change. In the next article in the Journal, the headlines stated that Mosby was "going after Burton." Of course, John Mosby didn't "go after" Senator Burton any more than he "went after" Bartlett Richards:

Topeka State Journal – **August 2, 1905**

GOING AFTER BURTON

Colonel Mosby Is Expected to Investigate His Chickasaw Dealings.

Guthrie, Okla., Aug. 2.—Colonel John S. Mosby, assistant attorney in the department of justice in Washington, now in Oklahoma investigation alleged frauds in the management of estates of Indian minors by guardians, will go shortly to Ardmore, I. T., where it is expected he will inquire into the connection of Senator J. Ralph Burton of Kansas with the Chickasaw tribal government. Burton was tribal attorney of the Chickasaws at one time.

H. A. Allen, a special United States Indian agent, has arrived here to assist Colonel Mosby.

Obviously, Mosby did not "target" individuals or organizations unless ordered to do so by the Justice Department. As with the land issue, he studied the law and then investigated the situation extant. If he found actions contrary to the law, he reported them. That was his job! The idea that he had the option to pursue or not to pursue a line of inquiry was specious. However, in that Mosby always seemed to find wrongdoing at high levels that other investigators had sense enough to leave alone, the response to his findings were seldom appreciated by the government agency he served.

Daily Ardmoreite – **August 14, 1905**
COULD NOT BE MUCH WORSE.

Colonel Mosby Comments on Indian Affairs in Oklahoma.

Guthrie, O. T., Aug. 12.—After an investigation of the management of the Indian affairs in Oklahoma, Col. John Moby has come to the conclusion that they could not be much worse and as soon as he returns to Washington will take up the matter of Indian guardians with Secretary Hitchcock. He will recommend that the estates of Indian minors be taken out of the hands of the guardians and placed in the hands of the Indian agents.

"There are men in Oklahoma who have become rich grafting from Indian children," said Colonel Mosby. "It is a matter which should be taken out of the hands of private individuals, and regulated by the Indian department. I shall recommend to secretary Hitchcock that a bill be introduced in congress taking away from private citizens the right of guardianships, and placing the estates of Indians in the hands of an Indian agent."

Colonel Mosby is at work this week in Pawnee and Ponca City securing evidence of fraud. The cases will be prosecuted by Horace Speed, United States attorney. Charles Wrightsman, who filed the original charges, will probably be employed to assist him.

In the next article, Mosby was specifically mentioned as "refusing to discuss the case:"

Guthrie Daily Leader – **August 17, 1905**
MOSBY NOW IN MUSKOGEE

Federal Inspector Will Investigate New Charges Against Raymond

Special to Daily Leader.

Colonel Mosby refused to discuss the case. He has been at South McAlester for several days making an investigation at that point, and will remain here several days taking testimony. It is said the charges were made against Judge Raymond by a prominent attorney, but what they are, or the name of the complainant, are maintained in secrecy. The charges were filed through Senator Berry of Arkansas, about two weeks ago.

Two things were made clear in this short article. The first was that Mosby was anything but "garrulous" in his contact with the public through the press. He said nothing, and the investigation was described as being "maintained in secrecy." But unfortunately, Mosby then made a fatal mistake, and not for the first time: he spoke without truly considering the consequences of what he said. For though he mentioned no case or individual, and his general statements were not problematic, per se, what he did not consider was that in making the connection between local and federal corruption, he had become a danger to men in the very agency in which he served:

Chickasha Daily Express – **August 18, 1905**

COL. MOSBY IS A FRIEND OF OKLAHOMA

Will urge Statehood at the Next Session

Guthrie, O.T. [Oklahoma Territory]; Aug. 17.—Colonel John Mosby left for Muskogee, I.T. this morning where he will carry on the Indian investigations in that territory. He said a number of persons would be arrested in the Indian districts of Oklahoma and prosecuted by the courts. One agent is here now assisting him and he expects two more will be sent before the investigation is completed. The work will be carried on throughout the two territories. Oklahoma has gained a friend in Colonel Mosby since he has been here on official business and he says if he is in Washington next winter, he will do everything he can to help the two territories get statehood.

"I shall have a talk with Senator Daniel and Martin of Virginia, as soon as I go back," he said. "I may have some little influence with them. I didn't know much about Oklahoma when I came here, but I have seen some things that have opened my eyes. It is easy to see there some people in Indian territory who are talking about double statehood. The fact of the matter is they don't want statehood at all. They want to keep Indian territory in its infancy. There are a lot of men making a good thing out of the Indians and Indian lands and it is too good a thing for them to let go. The federal officeholders who hold the smaller jobs are also doing everything they can [to] prevent statehood.

Guthrie Daily Leader – **August 25, 1905**

[Only the first part of a much longer article is included here.-vph]

MOSBY TO ALVA NEXT

Special Agent to Return to Oklahoma Soon

PROTECTING INDIANS NOW

Col. Mosby Says There is Much Cleaning up to be Done

Special to Daily Leader

Washington, D.C., August 25.—Col. John Mosby, special agent, is in the city having just returned from the Indian Territory. Col. Mosby has a "little raiding to do," as he expresses it. "That finished, he will go to Alva, Okla. To investigate some things in connection with the new court house and other matters. "I am on a trail," said Col. Mosby, "and some heads will drop unless my reports drop off the department table, which," he winked one eye, "I don't think they will."

A Unique Character

Col. Mosby is a unique character. Since coming to Oklahoma he has become a staunch single stater. "I am trying to protect the Indians, now," said Col. Mosby, "and ripen 'em up for statehood. The work will take time, but all good work requires time."

Gave Soldiers Trouble

Colonel Mosby is the person who gave the Union soldiers more trouble than any other one person in Virginia during the civil war. He is literally battle scarred. During different skirmishes he was wounded in battle six different times. One bullet penetrated the right side of his abdomen, just above the hip. This makes it necessary for him to walk with a cane. Another shot went through the left side of his abdomen. He was shot through the right leg, the same bullet killing the horse he rode. Another shot struck his back and followed a ring around to the right side, leaving a scar eighteen inches long. A bullet has left a bald streak through his scanty gray hair. He came near having his right arm severed with a saber.

His left eye is also missing, but the accident which caused this defect came about while he was on a mission of peace. After the civil war was over he was one of the first to come to the support of the Union. While on his way driving overland to the ceremonies at the unveiling of Grant's monument, his horse ran away. He did not remember what happened, but he came to senses in a hospital. When he asked if had time to attend the ceremonies at the monument, he was told that event had happened several days ago. He discovered then that he had been in the hospital for several days and that his eye was gone.

Is a Genuine Virginian

Colonel Mosby was in Ardmore and took an active part in the work of the federal grand jury that indicted B. H. Colbert, United States marshal; Governor Johnstone, ex-Governor Palmer Mosley, the members of the law firm of Mansfield, Cornish and McMurray, and other persons for offenses against the federal government and the Chickasaw nation.

Col. Mosby, from an ancestral standpoint, is a genuine Virginian. True to his Virginia instincts, he tells of Virginia and things Virginian. He recalls vividly the stirring events which he helped mold into the permanent history of his land. He has strongly cut features, the jaw and nose of a fighter, and small, dark eyes, deeply set, that peer quizzingly and ask questions without the use of words. Colonel Mosby may have been a dandy in his younger days, but he is no longer fastidious in his dress.

Left the Confederacy

Probably the most remarkable action in Col. Mosby's life was when he left the Confederacy and joined the Republican party. The scorn and contempt shown by his fellow Virginians when he broke Southern traditions became practically a social and political tragedy for Colonel Mosby. He was a flourishing lawyer in Warrenton, Va., when he changed. Life-long friends turned their backs upon him and denounced him as a traitor to his people and his family. To speak of Mosby in Virginia was to execrate him. Colonel Mosby talked about this unhappy experience. Tapping his cane on the floor, he said: "My old friends are now ashamed of what they did and said. They agree with me that it would have been better had all of us in the South begun early to heal the scars left by the strife that had devastated our land."

Consul at Hong Kong

President Hayes appointed Col. Mosby American consul in Hong Kong, where he remained seven years. He was offered a place by President Grant, who declared that he owed the electoral votes of Virginia to Mosby. Mosby, however did not accept. Mosby afterward was for sixteen years an assistant attorney of the Southern Pacific Railroad company in San Francisco. President McKinley remembered Mosby and gave him a place as special agent in the general land office. President Roosevelt transferred him to the Department of Justice.

Entertained General Grant.

When General Grant was on his trip around the world and reached Hong Kong, Colonel Mosby as official representative of the United States, boarded the steamer to welcome President Grant and his party.

Despite his many wounds and the fact that he is 75 years of age. Colonel Mosby has the activity of a young man and is a tireless worker. His principal article of diet is buttermilk. He likes buttermilk before, and after meals and keeps a pitcher of buttermilk in his room all the time. He does not use tobacco.

This was a charming personal story. It is a shame that it was so difficult to decipher because of the quality of the copy. As for Mosby's clothing, he was not financially well off any more and used most of what money he had for his family, now including his orphaned grandsons. But he was always clean and neat although railway travel tended to render one's clothing somewhat less than spotless and well pressed.

Suddenly, a report appeared that Mosby had "spoken out of turn" on Senator Burton. Having already had this problem in Nebraska, it seems odd that Mosby should openly discuss much less criticize the senator:

Alexandria Gazette – **August 26, 1905**
Col. Mosby Criticized.

Col. John S. Mosby is being criticized by government attorneys. He is alleged to have given out to the press the information concerning the latest charges against Senator Burton, of Kansas, of which he was the official investigator, before he had made his report to acting Attorney-General Robb. Prosecuting officers habitually desire the conviction of offenders before they talk much about it, but some of Colonel Mosby's friends evidently persuaded him that public policy required some dissemination of the latest information as a check to the rising tide of sentiment in Burton's favor among Kansas politicians.

Colonel Mosby is employed by the department as a special attorney, and in that capacity went to the Indian Territory to investigate the case. When in Kansas and Nebraska investigating the land and cattle frauds some months ago his work was strikingly effective and resulted in many prosecutions. He was next sent to Alabama to follow the peonage cases.

The Department has issued a stringent order against further public statements regarding pending cases, supposed to be aimed at Colonel Mosby, and with this, it is thought, the matter will be dropped although it has been predicted that an effort would be made to dislodge him from office.

Colonel Mosby has been a great favorite of republican Presidents. He espoused the republican cause at the close of the civil war, and Grant gave him the Hongkong consulate. McKinley placed him in the Department of Justice, where he has been promoted by President Roosevelt. He is 72 years old and in full physical and mental vigor.

Mosby's so-called popularity with Republican presidents was a fallacy. Only two of them—Grant and Roosevelt—ever liked him personally. He was ignored and dismissed by Hayes and disregarded by Garfield, Arthur, Harrison, and McKinley, albeit the latter did finally give him a position, if grudgingly, when he could hardly refuse to do so any longer. The idea that John Mosby was "kept on" in government service because the Republicans had a "soft spot" for him began to be widely circulated as a means of explaining why he wasn't just removed and, eventually, why he wasn't given anything to do while still drawing a salary. Meanwhile the Burton matter quietly disappeared, at least for a time.

The Indian affair(s) then returned to the news with Mosby as the lead figure, naturally. If the press were to be believed, Mosby was just about the only government investigator involved, a matter that tended to make all that happened devolve upon him whether he was responsible for it or not. Meanwhile, there seemed to be no reaction about the Burton incident; but a month later, Mosby was again accused of speaking to the press about Senator Burton, the man involved in the warrant scandal. Though he apparently said nothing in response to the charge, the papers "defended" him by saying that his friends—no doubt his *political* friends—advised him to say *something* as Burton was successfully defending himself in the press and with no official voice countering his claims. Be that as it may, the story surfaced once again; and Mosby found himself, once again, being crucified for "talking out of turn" to the press:

Evening Bulletin – **September 28, 1905**

MOSBY TALKED FREELY OF BURTON'S AFFAIRS

Washington, August 25,—Colonel John Mosby, the noted Confederate guerrilla chieftain, the head of Mosby's Partisan Rangers, "is the center of a tempest which has broken forth in the Department of Justice. He is charged with having given out to the press the information concerning the latest charges against Senator Burton of Kansas, of which he was the official investigator, before he had even made his report to Acting Attorney General Robb.

Mosby's friends persuaded him that public policy required some dissemination of the latest information as a check to the rising tide of sentiment in Burton's favor among Kansas politicians.

Colonel Mosby is employed by the Department as a special attorney and in that capacity went to the Indian Territory to investigate the case. When Kansas and Nebraska were investigating the land and cattle frauds some months ago, his work was strikingly effected and resulted in many prosecutions. He was next sent to Alabama to follow up the peonage cases. He has been under suspicion at headquarters for "talking too much" in all these affairs, although his friends show that the information could have become public through other channels, and that his offense is less serious than it seems. The Department has, however, issued a stringent order against further communication regarding pending cases, supposed to be aimed directly at him, and with this it is thought the matter will be dropped.

Mosby has been a great favorite of Republican presidents. He espoused the Republican cause at the close of the war, and Grant gave him the Hong Kong consulate. McKinley placed him in the Department of Justice, where he has been promoted by President Roosevelt. He is 72 years old and in full physical and mental vigor. It is intimated that Colonel Mosby gave out the information to check the turn of sentiment in favor of Burton."

This inclusion in the first story was left out of the later: *"Mosby's friends persuaded him that public policy required some dissemination of the latest information as a check to the rising tide of sentiment in Burton's favor among Kansas politicians."* It's strange that it was left out for while Mosby may not have been prudent to act upon the advice of his friends, if Burton had been able to prevent the matter from being properly adjudicated, then Mosby might well have been tempted to try to offset his fallacious contentions as they appeared in the press. Mosby certainly had sufficient experience in Nebraska to know what crooked politicians were capable of doing if there was no counter to their claims.

Meanwhile, away to the West, the fence matter was still treading judicial water as noted by the *Bee*, a paper that had not always been supportive of Mosby's efforts on behalf of the fencing law:

Omaha Daily Bee – October 10, 1905

Defiance of Land Grabbers

Illustration of the Wrath of People "Caught with the Goods." Pittsburgh Dispatch

An example of the persistent way in which those who get hold of property that doesn't to belong to them fight for their plunder seems to be presented in Nebraska, where cowboys in the employment of the leading ranchers have begun the work of intimidating and driving away witnesses as to the grabbing and fencing in of public lands. The process in a certain class of minds is very simple. Land, or other property, is recognized as a very nice thing to have; the grabbers lay hold of it, and when the tardy law comes along and calls for restitution they indignantly proceed to fight for their "rights."

Some two years ago Colonel John S. Mosby, investigating this subject as a government agent reported that the cattle ranchers had fenced in millions of acres of public lands and proposed to institute measures of ejection. The cattlemen at once proceeded to threaten civil war and horrified senators from Nebraska hastened to Washington to protest against the rash proceedings. It has to be confessed that a discreditable retrograde was made and Colonel Mosby was silenced.

Secretary Hitchcock has been proceeding quietly but surely to the same end. In response to his measures and in the defense of millions of plunder the land-grabbing interest is reported to be driving witnesses out of the country and threatening worse things to come. Since this amounts to a clear defiance of justice it is to be hoped that the administration will show no swerving from its support of the secretary's measures.

Those infamous chickens were about to "come home" to wealthy stockman Bartlett Richards[*] as seen by this article in the Bee (*see "Addendum II"-vph):

Omaha Daily Bee – **November 21, 1905**

RICHARDS CASE CAUSE OF MUCH TALK

Notice Served on Him By Mosby in 1902 Cited to Show Violation of Fencing Law Was Deliberately Persisted In.

Sore over Richards Case.

Officers of the Interior department and of the Department of Justice are still very much worked up over the extreme leniency shown in the case of Bartlett Richards and W. G. Comstock, who pleaded guilty to violating the fencing law. According to an item in the New York Sun, District Attorney Baxter some time ago advised the Department of Justice to *nolle prossequi* the case against Richards, but the reply was a rebuke from the attorney general. Subsequently the district attorney proposed a compromise with the law breakers, but he was instructed to go ahead and prosecute the case vigorously. Now the department officers understand that the district attorney himself represented to the judge that there was no evidence of bad faith and that it was on this representation that Judge Munger declared the defendants to be without moral turpitude. The department people here insist that there is plenty of evidence to show that the defendants willfully and persistently defied the laws in spite of repeated notifications calling on them to cease doing so. One of these notices was served on Bartlett Richards as early as 1902 by Special Agent Mosby, a copy of which has been dug up as follows:

ALLIANCE, Neb. Oct. 2, 1902.—Mr. Bartlett Richards, Ellsworth, Neb.— Sir: I have been instructed by the commissioner of the general land office to notify you that certain fencing of public lands, erected and maintained by you in violation of law in Sheridan and Cherry counties, Nebraska, must be removed within sixty days; otherwise the civil and military authority of the government will be employed to do it.

The notoriously fraudulent homestead filings of so-called soldiers' widows within the territory enclosed by your fence are no protection to it as they do not constitute, in the language of the statue, "a claim of title made or acquired in good faith." Said fence is located between the Burlington road on the south and the Elkhorn on the north, in Alliance and Valentine, Neb, land districts from township 25 to township 35, ranges 40, 41, 42 and 43.

Respectfully,

JOHN S. MOSBY, Special Agent.

As Mosby so often declared, he would be vindicated by time. The Richards prosecution is an example of the accuracy of that prophecy. This particular account makes note of the fact that District Attorney Baxter had advised the Department of Justice to file a formal notice of abandonment of the action; that is, the prosecutor for the government wanted the government to cease its prosecution. As noted in the story, this "suggestion" was rebuked by the attorney general. Baxter then tried to soften the charge by informing the judge that he saw no "bad faith" on Richards's part with regard to removing the fences. However, the documents filed by Mosby clearly showed that Richards had plenty of notice to do as the law demanded but that he chose otherwise. A year later, the final act was played out:

Omaha Daily Bee – November 21, 1905

LAST WORK FOR HITCHCOCK

Secretary Will Devote Energies to Finishing up Land Fencing Cases Nebraska Suits Are Most Prominent

Washington, Nov. 20—(Special Telegram.)—Secretary of the Interior Hitchcock will devote the remainder of his time as a cabinet official to the prosecution of the cases which he has worked up against the cattlemen of Nebraska, charged with illegal fencing of the public domain.

Colonel John Mosby procured the greatest amount of evidence against the cattle barons while acting as special agent of the Interior department several years ago. Recently a number of other cases in Nebraska of alleged illegal fencing have been investigated and these are to be prosecuted before Secretary Hitchcock leaves the position of Secretary of the Interior. Further than this he has prepared and will print in his report to congress as an appendix a full list of the names of cattlemen who are charged with illegally occupying the public domain, with a description of the lands which they are alleged to have illegally fenced, and, in fact, all the details upon which the Department of Justice, through the evidence furnished by the Interior department, has entered upon legal proceedings against the cattle growers.

Thus in a single sentence in a short article in a small town newspaper—"*Colonel John Mosby procured the greatest amount of evidence against the cattle barons while acting as special agent of the Interior department several years ago*"—was Mosby vindicated for his work against the cattle barons and crooked officials in Nebraska. It wasn't much, but it was more than his own government was willing to provide.

ADDENDUM I

Joseph Ralph Burton (November 16, 1852–February 27, 1923) was a lawyer and the Republican US senator from Kansas. On January 23, 1904, Burton was indicted by a Federal grand jury at St. Louis, Missouri, on the charge of having accepted $2,500 from the Rialto Grain and Securities Company (a "get-rich-quick" concern) to represent Rialto before the post office. He was to have prevented issuance of a fraud order against the company, thus denying it the use of the US mails. Burton was tried before Judge Adams of the US District Court for the Eastern District of Missouri in St. Louis, found guilty in March, and sentenced to pay a fine of $2,500 and serve six months in the jail at Ironton, Missouri.

He appealed the case to the US Supreme Court, which in January 1905 reversed the decision of the district court on the grounds that the venue was improper since the money was paid to Burton in Washington DC and remanded the case for a new trial there. The second trial was before Judge Van Devanter of the US Circuit Court. In November 1905, he was found guilty and given the same sentence. A second appeal to the Supreme Court followed, and this time, the decision of the lower court was sustained.

On June 4, 1906, Burton resigned from the Senate to avoid impeachment.

ADDENDUM II

Bartlett Richards was born in Weathersfield, Vermont, in 1862. After arriving in Cheyenne, Wyoming, in 1879, he became involved in the cattle business and elected to remain in Wyoming rather than return East. Discouraged by the blizzard of 1886, Richards sought adequate rangelands for his cattle in the Nebraska sand hills. In the late 1880s, he and J. J. Cairnes established the Spade Ranch, headquartered in Ellsworth, Sheridan County, Nebraska. That company later became the Nebraska Land and Feed Company operated by Richards, his brother Jarvis, and a new partner, Will Comstock. Richards and Comstock were faced with a problem common to the cattle industry: the need to obtain sufficiently large tracts of land to support their livestock. As at least a partial solution to their problem, they encouraged soldiers and soldiers' widows to file for land under the Homestead Act and then quietly deed these "buried claims" to their holdings. Of course, the problem with the fences was not the title to the land upon which they stood, *but the public land that they enclosed*! As a result, efforts to claim the land on which the fences stood did not affect the fact that they were enclosing public lands and therefore in violation of the law.

In April of 1902, at the insistence of President Theodore Roosevelt, Secretary of the Interior Hitchcock announced that the formerly dormant law would be enforced; and therefore, all fences on the public domain had to be removed. This ruling was opposed and often ignored by the cattle interests, and as these interests were very wealthy, they wielded a great deal of power at both the state and federal levels. John Mosby went West as an agent of the Department of the Interior to look into the matter and to work toward having any such fences removed. Mosby was not the first agent involved nor the last, but he was the best and for that reason, incurred the wrath of the cattle barons and their political allies. Even after being relieved of his duties when Roosevelt bowed to pressure by the Republican politicians, his work held up and eventually led in 1905 to Bartlett Richards and Will Comstock being charged in federal court with illegally fencing public lands.

In June of 1905, they testified that they had not fenced surveyed government land; but government agents entered the area of the Spade Ranch and, by extending the lines of the original government surveys, demonstrated that the Nebraska Land and Feed Company had illegally enclosed 212,000 acres of government land, just as John Mosby had shown earlier in the investigation. Before the November trial, Richards and Comstock pled guilty and were sentenced to pay a small fine of $300 each and to remain in the custody of the US marshal for six hours. However, the leniency of the sentences and the manner in which the convicted men spent their "imprisonment" (six hours at the Omaha Club) aroused the ire of President Theodore Roosevelt and the attorney general. Roosevelt removed the district attorney and the federal marshal, and Richards and Comstock soon realized that they would have been better off quietly paying their fine and going home!

In 1906, Richards and Comstock were again indicted and convicted, but on the more serious charge of conspiracy to defraud the government of the use of public lands. For this, both men were ordered to pay a fine of $1,500 each and serve one year in jail. After three years of unsuccessful appeals, the two men were incarcerated in Hastings rather than in Omaha to prevent their social and commercial positions from interfering with the dispensing of justice. But Richards was not a well man; and one month before the end of his sentence, on September 5, 1911, at the age of forty-nine, he died in a Hastings hospital. His friend Comstock was given a short leave to attend his funeral and then returned to prison to serve out his sentence.

The truly sad thing is that not long after the entire "illegal fencing" matter was made into a crusade by Roosevelt, Congress moved to ease restrictions on homesteaders, allowing them to take a claim and then, if they could not survive on it, to sell that claim to the cattlemen. If Richards and Comstock had obeyed the law and removed their fences, they soon could have recouped all that they had lost in doing so. As it was, Bartlett Richards no longer needed tens of thousands of acres of range, only a plot of range eight by four by six feet deep.

Chapter 45

1906

Corruptisima re publica plurimae leges.
~ In the most corrupt state are the most laws.

"If an offense come out of the truth, better is it that the offense come than that the truth be concealed."
~ Thomas Hardy

1906 WAS A relatively quiet press year for Mosby, but while a great deal of importance was taking place, little that involved him made the headlines. However, the usual small personal matters were chattily presented for all of those, especially local folks, who were interested in the colonel's "doings":

Alexandria Gazette – February 1, 1906

Col. John S. Mosby, of Confederate fame, called at the White House this morning to hand the President a letter which General Joseph Wheeler wrote a week before his death, recommending an Alabama man for office. The President was considerably touched by this message from the grave and promised to do what he could for General Wheeler's friend. While at the White House Col. Mosby was asked why he did not try to get his young grandson into the Military Academy. "Because I don't want him to shoot anybody," replied the old warrior. "If he went to either one of these schools and was hazed he'd surely shoot the fellows that tried to do it. As everybody seems to be hazed when they get there, I don't want my grandson to go."

Reports started to appear once more regarding affairs in Oklahoma:

Guthrie Daily Leader – March 17, 1906

CHARGES PERSONAL

Charges Against Embry Made by Inspector Mosby

Washington, D. C., March 17.—It is understood the charge against Embry is that he collected a fee of four thousand dollars in an estate of a minor Indian without rendering any service. The charge against Embry was made by Indian Inspector Mosby, who was in Oklahoma some months ago investigating conditions.

Guthrie Daily Leader – March 22, 1906

EMBRY CASE BEING HEARD

Inspector Husted is Busy Hearing Evidence at Chandler

Chandler, Okla., March 22.—The Publicist says: In view of the fact that Inspector Husted of the Interior Department is now here investigating the charges upon which John Embry's appointment as prosecuting attorney for

Oklahoma is being held up, the following facts concerning these charges taken from a Kansas City paper:

This morning Secretary Hitchcock sent to the White House a report from J. C. Allen, an inspector in the Indian bureau, made to the Interior department last fall, in which Embry's name is mentioned. Allen was sent by Secretary Hitchcock to Oklahoma to investigate charges that some of the guardians appointed by the Oklahoma probate courts to administer the property of Indian children had defrauded the children and that as their bondsmen could not be found, the children would have no redress.

In his report, Allen criticized the law firm of Hoffman & Embry of Chandler, which he alleged was involved in some of the charges he had investigated. When Allen submitted his report Secretary Hitchcock transmitted it to the Department of Justice and recommended prosecutions. Before taking action the attorney general sent Colonel John S. Mosby, special agent of the Department of Justice to Oklahoma to make an investigation. In his report Mosby also criticized Hoffman & Embry.

Secretary Hitchcock transmitted Allen's report to the president and informed him of the report made by Mosby. Mr. Roosevelt at once communicated with Attorney General Moody, who looked up Mosby's report and informed the president of its contents. The president then withdrew Embry's nomination and directed that his connection with the alleged irregularities be further investigated.

Delegate McGuire this afternoon said that Embry would satisfactorily explain any reference on him in relation to the frauds referred to. He added that Embry's enemies made the charges against him which the inspectors had not fully investigated. McGuire said he had not heard that Embry's name appeared in the reports of Mosby and Allen until today.

At the interior department it was said that Secretary Hitchcock had called the attention of the Oklahoma officials to the evidence presented by the inspectors and had recommended prosecutions and that they had replied that prosecutions would be very expensive and that the territory had no funds with which to bear this expense.

Hoffman and Embry was one of the two major law firms involved in the Oklahoma scandals. The other firm—the one that led to John Mosby's being given no work in the Department of Justice and eventually to his dismissal—was the firm of Mansfield, McMurray and Cornish. This was the firm mentioned in the infamous telegram from Attorney Russell, in which it was strongly indicated that the firm was to receive "a square deal" at Mosby's hands. To this, Mosby waspishly replied that if such were the case, the attorneys involved would go to the penitentiary.

With regard to Hoffman and Embry, the article makes known that Mosby was not the first to bring charges against this firm. The first of such charges were brought by Inspector Allen of the Indian Bureau. Mosby was then sent to check on Allen's report and agreed with his findings. Roosevelt, upon seeing both reports, withdrew the nomination of Embry for a government position and ordered a further investigation of the alleged irregularities.

Articles then appeared about the invitation to Mosby by the Massachusetts GAR and the circumstances surrounding his response:

Times-Dispatch – April 23, 1906

Colonel Mosby Captured by Former Prisoners (From Our Regular Correspondent.)

WASHINGTON, D.C., April 22.—Colonel John S. Mosby will leave tomorrow for Boston, where he will remain as the guest of some members of the Middlesex Club of that city. Colonel Mosby will be the special guest of certain members of the club who were his prisoners during the war between the States. They intend that their former captor shall be their prisoner for a week or so, and sent Mr. Stillings, of Boston, father of the public printer, to escort the old soldier to the Hub. Colonel Mosby will be present at the celebration Friday night of the anniversary of the birth of General Grant.

Times-Dispatch – April 27, 1906

COL. MOSBY CAPTURED BY FORMER CAPTIVES

The Famous Confederate Guerilla Royally Entertained By G.A.R. Men. (Special to The *Times-Dispatch*.)

Alexandria Gazette – May 4, 1906 (Edited)

COL. MOSBY IN BOSTON.

We publish Col. John S. Mosby's speech in Boston, at the banquet in celebration of Grant's birthday. The Colonel was royally received in Boston, and he has had a fine time. He says that two men whom he captured during the war, and between whom he sat at the banquet, were so kind to him that he felt sorry he had ever captured them and almost wished they had captured him. He visited "Marshfield," the home of Daniel Webster, of whom he is a great admirer, and in a letter to a friend here telling of his emotions quoted Milton's words on Shakespeare's tomb.

"And so sepulchred in such pomp doth lie, That Kings for such a tomb might wish to die."

He also went to Plymouth and got a piece of the mortal rock and saw Miles Standish's monument. Those who know him need not be told that Col. Mosby is not by practice or profession a subscriber to Puritan theology, but in common with all thinkers he knows they were a noble band and did their duty as they understood it. He called on Mrs. Webster at Harvard whose father, Major Forbes, he captured during the war. She is a granddaughter of Emerson whose home, at concord, Col. Mosby visited. There is no state in the Union with such memories as Massachusetts, and by imagining yourself in his place, you can understand Col. Mosby's pleasure better than when described in words.—[Warrenton Virginian.]

Col. Wm. H. Dyer, presided. The guests were Gov. Guild, the Hon. James M. Beck, of New York, ex-assistant attorney general of the United States; Col. John S. Mosby, of Virginia, and William H. Elroy, journalist, of New York.

Col. Mosby was appropriately seated between the two Massachusetts men whom he captured during the war, Frank P. Morse and Fred Broughton. Col. Mosby said:

"I desire to express my thanks to this company for the kind sentiments that have been spoken and for the hospitable reception they have given me. I was in Boston 20 years ago; when I went home I reported that the Boston people were more like the Virginia people than any I had ever seen. I was perfectly sincere, of course, I intended the comparison as a compliment to the Bostonians. I am here this evening as the guest of the Middlesex Club to pay my tribute of respect to the memory of Gen. Grant, and to testify that my affection for him has not changed. No man ever had a better friend than he was to me.

"No soldier clung longer to the Southern Confederacy than I did; and I can apply to myself the words which the Roman poet put into the mouth of the champion of a lost cause: 'If Troy could have been saved by this right hand, even by the same it would have been saved.' But the southern people were not lost with their cause, for in their ashes lived their wonted fires. From the wreck and ruin of war they have risen, and today there is a stronger sentiment of nationality among them than ever existed before the conflict of arms.

"The credit of this is largely due to Gen. Grant in keeping the faith that he pledged at Appomattox. He allowed no pomp of war to humiliate the vanquished; he did not compel them to go through the form of passing under the yoke, like the Roman legions in the Caudine Forks. His first order after the articles were signed was to issue rations to the starving Confederates; his next was to silence a battery that was firing a salute. His great soul would not add one pang to defeat or join in a paean of triumph on the field of victory. "It is for this reason that if the news of Appomattox brought sorrow, the memory of it brings no sense of humiliation to southern hearts. In the last scene of the great tragedy the two great actors appear at their best. One rose to the summit of power; the other went to the shades of the academy—but not with the despair of Caius Marius, sitting among the ruin of Carthage. "And lived and died—as none can live or die."

After the vociferous applause had died away, William H. Elroy brought the meeting to a close with stories and praise to the republicanism of the Middlesex Club.

Events such as this should—again—have forever put to rest the charges of atrocities, but it seems that far too many members of the GAR harbored their old grudges in preference to the truth. Also of interest were the kisses exchanged between the old warrior and the maiden of Boston. Such gentle affection must be contrasted with Mosby's reception in his old home of Bristol, Virginia, several years later.

Mosby's rather kindly claim that he had wished his captives had captured him was meant to testify to the end of any antagonistic sentiments between the former enemies. Unfortunately, it also indicated that he had forgotten—or chose not to remember!—that had he actually been captured, he would not have survived to be so sumptuously feted. This was the occasion which produced the castigation of Mosby in a regimental publication published the year before and mentioned in an earlier chapter:

13th Regimental Association [Massachusetts Volunteers] Circular, – December, 1905

WHY WE WOULDN'T MEET MOSBY

Captain Charles F. Morse

Some years ago we received an invitation to meet Col. John S. Mosby, at Young's Hotel, Boston, where some misguided but well-intentioned men, having little acquaintance with his career, sought to show him attentions which, in our opinion, were unmerited. We didn't accept it. We didn't want to see him then, and we never wanted to when he was a bushwhacking guerila down in Virginia, and was murdering Union soldiers. The war is over, and all its strifes, animosities, bitternesses and hates ought to be laid forever at rest. We have met a large number of men, both officers and privates, who were engaged in the war on the wrong side, and have been only too glad to fraternize with them, and talk about the old unpleasantness, but they were soldiers, who bravely fought and nobly suffered in a wrong cause, which now they see was wrong. They were brave soldiers and honorable enemies.

Col. John S. Mosby was neither a brave soldier nor an honorable enemy. All through the war he led a gang of bushwhacking outlaws, who through preying only on the Union army and its supplies, were none the less a gang of execrable thieves, robbers and murders, and John S. Mosby was as villainous a scamp as any of the detestable gang with which he was connected.

It is all very well for him to glibly talk about what he and General Stuart did in the way of raids on our supplies, but we have faith enough in J.E.B. Stuart's manliness and soldierly qualities to believe that if he were where he could hear this blustering braggart boast of his achievements, he would promptly disown him, and deny that he ever availed himself of the dastardly cut-throat's help. Stuart was a fighter as well as a raider. Mosby was an assassin as well as a thief. All through the war he hung on the rear of the army, seeking chances to pillage and murder, and many a noble officer and soldier has been murdered and robbed by him and his outlaw gang.

In the fall of 1863, while the army under General Meade was advancing toward the Rapidan, after falling back to Manassas Junction, when Lee's feint on Washington made that move prudent, a staff officer of our army had occasion to go from the vicinity of Warrenton to Bealton Station. His business was urgent, and it not being convenient to take an orderly along with him, he rode alone. Near Fayetteville he was joined by another person wearing a staff officer's uniform but without anything to indicate the corps he belonged to. Thinking, of course, that it was one of our own officers he rode along unsuspectingly, until a piece of woods was reached, when the stranger suddenly drew a revolver and shot the officer, and leaving him lying on the ground, apparently dead, hastily rode away with his horse and equipment, probably not daring to stop long enough to strip him of his uniform. That stranger was one of Mosby's men, if not Mosby himself.

On the occasion of that falling back of Meade's, one of the guards of the Third Corps supply train, a young man from Malone, N.Y., belonging to the One Hundred and Sixth N.Y. Volunteers, was shot down in the road, near Wolf Run Shoals, by a bushwhacker concealed in the bushes by the side of the road. That is the kind of work Mosby's men were continually doing, and of which Mosby boastingly claimed the credit.

After the Sixth Corps had repulsed the attack on Washington, in 1864, it moved up the Potomac to Harper's Ferry, where it crossed into the Shenandoah Valley. As the corps pushed on up the valley, the supply train followed, taking the route via Charlestown, where John Brown was hung five years before. Capt. Evan M. Buchanan, of Lochiel, Penn., a relative of the Camerons, was commissary of subsistence of the third division. When near Charlestown, some of the officers with the train rode a little distance away from the road, to visit a substantial looking residence—a not infrequent custom—and stayed chatting with the ladies of the household until the rear of the train had passed, when they started to catch up with it. Captain Buchanan, always rather moderate in his movements, was lingering behind, when one of the party advised him to hurry up or he would be gobbled by Mosby's men. But he didn't hurry, and the rest of the party started off, leaving him behind with his orderly. Scarcely was the party out of sight when a squad of Mosby's men swooped down on the house. The orderly escaped, but Captain Buchanan was captured, and was never seen again.

James Harris, Captain Buchanan's clerk, was a cousin of Don Cameron's also, and with the Cameronian influence at Washington, was able to make a diligent search for his chief, it was found that he had been taken to the vicinity of White Plains, on the other side of the mountains, and there killed and buried. After long search the place of his burial was found, and the body exhumed, when it was discovered that his body had been shockingly mutilated, and that in all probability the mutilation had been done before the death of the victim of the diabolic cruelty!

This was the work of Col. John S. Mosby and his gang.

All of the so-called atrocities Morse mentioned were either matters of the ordinary consequences of war—soldiers did get killed, and Mosby was not obligated to fight as the enemy desired—or pure fiction as was probably the fate of Captain Buchanan. Furthermore, if Captain Morse had paid attention to the names of the men who invited John Mosby in 1886 or 1904 or 1906 or 1910, he would have realized that many were his former captives and therefore hardly "ignorant of his career"!

Mosby's late wife, Pauline, received a short but gracious tribute in an article about Southern women. If Mosby saw it, he would have been grateful for the honor paid to his beloved wife now thirty years in her grave:

Times-Dispatch – **June 3, 1906**

[Part of a larger article about Southern women.-vph]

One of the loveliest characters of those anxious times, whose memory is still fresh in the hearts of the Warrentonians, was the wife of Col. Mosby, who died about 1880. Although a woman of deep religious fervor and exquisite gentleness of nature, Mrs. Mosby gloried in her husband's daredeviltry, and is reputed to have inspired many of his most hazardous and successful exploits.

Mosby was now publishing articles again as he had done earlier to supplement his income. The "Sunday Magazine" features were a wonderful venue as they permitted illustrations and a large amount of text space that provided all Mosby needed to spin a good "yarn." The fact that the "yarn" was true was a bonus. And as everyone was so interested in the story of his unique command, Mosby undoubtedly believed that he might as well provide all the color that the public demanded.

Soon, what had become an annual event—the "celebration" of Mosby's birthday—appeared in quite a number of papers, probably far more than are listed here:

Evening Times – December 6, 1906

Palestine Daily Herald – December 6, 1905

Lewiston Evening Teller – December 6, 1906
THIS IS MY 73RD BIRTHDAY.

Another year had come to an end. Books on the command by John Alexander and John Munson had been published and were very well received. But the matter in Oklahoma still lingered. However, that was hardly unusual given its complexity and scope when taken together with the move by Oklahoma toward statehood. Mosby would continue to work diligently—as he always did—toward unraveling what was essentially a "Gordian knot" of corruption and incompetence. Yes, he would work, and he would persevere, and he would triumph as he had persevered and triumphed in Hong Kong and Nebraska. Unfortunately, Oklahoma, as had the others, would prove a Pyrrhic victory.

Chapter 46

1907

Deficiente pecunia deficit omnia.
~ It's all over when money is gone.

"The simple step of a courageous individual is not to take part
in the lie. One word of truth outweighs the world."
~ Aleksandr Solzhenitsyn

1907 SAW A return of the illegal fence issue as directives had been received from the General Land Office that the destruction of all such fences as had not already been removed would commence after April 1st of that year. The article below in the *Alexandria Gazette* points out the odd business of Mosby's involvement in that issue and identified his recall as being politically motivated:

Alexandria Gazette – January 5, 1907

By direction of the President, Secretary Hitchcock yesterday issued an order to Commissioner Richards of the general land office to at once notify all special agents and receivers and registers of local land offices that the act of February 25, 1885, for the summary destruction of illegal enclosures and obstructions existing on public lands will be rigidly enforced after April 1, 1907. The order means that all the fences inclosing public lands in violation of law must be removed before April 1. If they are not taken down by that time they will be torn down by representatives of the government. Two or three years ago President Roosevelt sent Col. J. S. Mosby, of this State, out to the northwest to enforce the self same law, but when the Colonel commenced to carry out the President's instruction he was suddenly recalled and sent to Alabama. The reason was that the land grabbers of the northwest threatened the President that if he did not recall Col. Mosby the northwestern States would go against him at the next election. Col. Mosby was at once recalled. If it is really intended that the law shall be enforced Col. Mosby is the man to enforce it.

Then suddenly, there was another interesting development. One of the Nebraska senators who had claimed that Mosby had publicly criticized him in the press during his investigation took issue with another such vilification that had appeared in the Lincoln Journal of January 3, 1907. This was a very serious charge given that the senator was addressing a recent interview with Mosby, who was still under a cloud about the Burton matter; and if it could be shown that he continued to publicly denounce senators (or more precisely, in this case, former senators!), the consequences could be very severe for him. Apparently, Dietrich was very much exercised by this attack on his character and made a rather loud public outcry against Mosby in a Nebraska news organ:

Omaha Daily Bee – January 5, 1907
DIETRICH IN HIS DEFENSE

Former Senator Denies Allegations Made by John S. Mosby

Did Not Defend or Aid Cattlemen

Attack in State Journal Inspired by Friends of Joe Bartley and Enemies of D. E. Thompson.

A second article then surfaced, and it was apparent that the matter was getting more serious, for it now appeared in the *New York Tribune*, hardly a local outlet. It is rather pointless to make much comment upon former Senator Dietrich's "defense" (he was a former senator because he had been impeached for bribery and corruption) because Mosby never gave the interview of which the senator complained. In subsequent articles, when asked about the matter, Mosby flatly denied having even mentioned Dietrich's name for several years; and he certainly pointed out that he would never say that he wasn't "afraid of any man" simply because it was unnecessary.

However, one thing should be noted regarding Dietrich's "off the record" efforts to speak with Mosby during the investigation of the land issue. The senator said he merely wanted to inform Mosby of the accord reached by the parties who met at the White House, but that makes no sense. Surely, if that meeting was to influence Mosby's actions, Secretary Hitchcock would have passed that information along and advised him to monitor the matter to be sure that the cattlemen were keeping their part of the bargain. For Mosby to meet with an official of a state that had proven itself in collusion with the objects of his investigations would have been more than unwise; it could have been considered dereliction of duty and possibly a matter of illegal activity on his part. Like Caesar's wife, John Mosby had to keep himself above suspicion lest he be thought a part of what was a huge ring of corruption. As it was, the newspapers printing the purported "interview" were able to destroy his reputation as a credible agent of the Department of the Interior simply by making him appear if not dishonest, then indiscreet and "vigorous." Apparently "political correctness" is not all that new a means by which to silence unwelcome viewpoints.

New York Tribune – January 6, 1907 (Edited)
DENIES MOSBY CHARGES.

Ex-Senator Dietrich Says He Never Aided in Illegal Fencing.

(By Telegraph to The Tribune.)

Hasting, Neb. Jan. 5.—Ex-Senator Charles Dietrich to-day denounced Colonel John S. Mosby, the famous Confederate raider, and calls on Mosby to produce the proofs that the Senator assisted the great cattle owners of the West to fence the government range while he was a member of the United States Senate. Mr. Dietrich's statement is in answer to an interview with Mosby printed in Washington Thursday. It is in part: [And here, the ex- senator's charges are reprinted.]

Neither Dietrich nor the newspapers were about to allow the matter to die, and so follow-up stories appeared in the Bee and two Virginia papers, the *Alexandria Gazette* and the *Times-Dispatch*. The papers, even the Bee, were not all that supportive of the former senator; and the Virginia publications decided that it was time to get John Mosby on the record:

Omaha Daily Bee – **January 7, 1907**

Senator Dietrich pays his compliments to Colonel Mosby in characteristic style and incidentally at the same time to Senator Millard, Embezzler Bartley and former District Attorney W. S. Summers, all in a bunch. Some people will be inclined to view the Mosby interview as simply a good foil for Senator Dietrich to hit the other fellows over his shoulder.

Alexandria Gazette – **January 7, 1907 (Edited)**

Times-Dispatch – **January 7, 1907**

"INFAMOUS LIAR" SAYS DIETRICH

Ex-Senator Charles Dietrich Denounces Famous Col. Mosby.

Sneers at His Fine War Record

Calls on Cavalry Leader for Either Proof of Charges or Apology—Regrets That He Cannot Boast of Past Record for Bravery.

[Dietrich's charges are again reiterated.-vph]

Mr. Dietrich is as brash as is President Roosevelt in calling people "liars" but it is dollars to buttons that what Col. Mosby said about him is true. At any rate Mr. Dietrich's connection with the land grabbers lost him his seat in the Senate. It would be well to make President Roosevelt a witness in the case as he might tell why he recalled Col. Mosby from Nebraska and sent him to Alabama.

Col. Mosby Has Not Seen Statement

Colonel John S. Mosby is confined to his bed at his room, No. 1406 I street, northwest, Washington.

"I have not read the interview with Dietrich, in which it is alleged he said I was an infamous liar," said Colonel Mosby last night. "I do not care to make any statement until I have read the interview."

It is believed he could disclose facts which came under his observation while acting for the government in the fight against land grabbers in Nebraska several years ago which would be very embarrassing to Senator Dietrich.

In his response, Mosby was cautious regarding "quotes" that he had supposedly made. He refused to comment until he has seen just exactly what Dietrich had said. Indeed, for a "loquacious" man, Mosby's response was the essence of brevity: "I do not care to make any statement until I have read the interview." But of course, the matter was not permitted to rest:

Alexandria Gazette, – **January 8, 1907**

Times-Dispatch – **January 8, 1907**

COL. MOSBY HITS BACK AT DIETRICH

Says His Opinion of Ex-Senator Long Been in Land Office Declined to Meet Him in Conference.

Refused Invitation of Dietrich to Visit Him and Discuss Matters "He Did Not Wish to Commit to Writing"—Further Exposures.

The Washington correspondent of the Richmond *Times-Dispatch* says: Col. John S. Mosby, who has been confined to his room for several days with a severe cold, was well enough yesterday to take very sharp notice of the statement attributed to ex-Senator Dietrich, of Nebraska in which the ex-Senator denounced as false the statement alleged to have been made by the colonel that the ex-Senator had endeavored to have any firm or corporation fraudulently acquire the title to or inclose any part of the public domain.

Regarding the alleged interview with him as painted in the Lincoln (Neb.) Journal, Colonel Mosby says such interview never took place. The Washington bureau of the Journal, whence the interview purported to have emanated, disavows all knowledge of the alleged interview. Colonel Mosby said he had not used the name of Mr. Dietrich in a year. "The brash language imputed to me," said Colonel Mosby, "stamps the whole thing as spurious. I have never felt it necessary to say I was not afraid of anybody."

"As for my opinion of Dietrich and his efforts to prevent the removal of illegal fences on the public domain, all these are matters of public record in the General Land Office," said the colonel (and) smiled sardonically.

"Enough to say," he continued, "that Dietrich's statement that he was actuated by the humane motive of protecting poor cattle from starvation is of a piece with his conduct throughout the matter. How pulling down fences and thus temporarily given cattle more range would result in starvation is beyond the ken of mortals and the General Land Office, as the result shows. About all the fences came down, and those that haven't will shortly be pulled down by United States soldiers.

"In September, 1902, while I was at Alliance, Neb., Dietrich wrote me to come to Hastings, 200 miles away. He wrote that he wished to confer with me 'about matters he didn't wish to commit to writing.' I have his letter now. There was but one inference to be drawn and I declined the invitation. "Now, Dietrich says he only wished to inform me confidentially of a conference which had been held between the President, Secretary Hitchcock, the cattlemen and myself.

"Dietrich knew that a Senator is not used as a channel for confidential instructions to a special land agent, as I was. They could only come through the land office."

Col. Mosby, as the special agent of the land office, was the first man to unearth even a small portion of the enormous amount of rottenness which subsequent investigation and developments have shown to exist in connection with the wholesale theft of public lands in the west. The present controversy may be regarded as only surface indications of that old exposure, and of exposures that will be made in the course of the next few months, involving men in high official positions, unless Secretary Garfield, who succeeds Secretary Hitchcock on the 4th of March, calls off the dogs of war.

Omaha Daily Bee - January 15, 1907
DENIAL BY COLONEL MOSBY

Official Says He Did Not Make Alleged Charges Against Dietrich

MATTER REFERRED TO THE PRESIDENT

Former Senator Publishes Letter from Mosby, Who Thinks Interview Was Manufactured In Nebraska.

HASTINGS, Neb. Jan. 14.—(Special.)—

About a week ago a Lincoln newspaper published what purported to be an interview with Colonel Mosby of the Department of Justice, in which that official was quoted as having said that former Senator Dietrich had aided the cattlemen in fencing and holding public lands in this state. Mr. Dietrich denied all of the charges and took the matter up with the president.

This morning Mr. Dietrich made public the correspondence which he had had with the president, and which has brought about a denial by Colonel Mosby to the alleged interview which appeared in the State Journal of January 3. Mr. Dietrich's first letter follows:

HASTINGS, Neb., Jan 5, 1907—My Dear Mr. President: I ask as a personal favor that you read the within clipping and give me a personal answer. This is the second time that Mosby has been quoted as making false statements as to myself. I am sincerely yours,

C. H. DIETRICH

To this the president replied:

THE WHITE HOUSE, WASHINGTON, Jan. 6, 1907.—

My Dear Senator: until I received you letter I had no knowledge of the matter to which you refer. I have at once sent it for report to the Department of Justice. Wishing you and yours many happy New Years, believe me, Sincerely yours,

THEODORE ROOSEVELT.

This morning Mr. Dietrich received the following letter with correspondence from the Department of Justice:

THE WHITE HOUSE, WASHINGTON, Jan. 11, 1907.—

My Dear Senator:

Referring to your note of the 5th instant, with enclosed clipping, the president directs me to send to you for your perusal and return the enclosed correspondence from Attorney General Bonaparte, which will explain itself. Very truly yours,

WILLIAM LOEB, JR.

Secretary to the President.

The following is that portion of the letter received from Colonel Mosby by the Department of Justice, which refers directly to the alleged interview which appeared in the State Journal:

The correspondent of the Richmond *Times-Dispatch* came to my room and informed me he had a telegram from his paper saying that Mr. Dietrich had denounced an interview of mine published in the Lincoln State Journal as a lie. The reporter wanted to know what I had to say about it. I replied that I had not mentioned Mr. Dietrich's name for some years and had no interview with any newspaperman on any subject and had nothing to say. I advised him to call on Mr. Scott Smith, which he did. The correspondent also went to the office of the Lincoln Journal to find out about the author of the dispatch in that paper purporting to come from Washington. He was told there that it was not sent from or through the local office here. My own opinion is that the alleged interview was written up in Nebraska and falsely represented as a dispatch from Washington.

In making public the above correspondence, Mr. Dietrich said today: "Having so often been the victim of false charges by vicious and reprehensible newspapers and certain of their allies, I feel that an apology is due Colonel Mosby for having paid any attention to the purported interview which appeared in the State Journal of January 3, 1907, which Colonel Mosby in very strong language brands as false. Were I guilty of the charges made against me by such papers and persons, they would not be as wicked and as unpardonable as the malicious, cowardly and wicked assassination of character, which they have been guilty of in order to gain political power and prestige. The conspiracy against myself, like that against Alfred Dreyfus of France, has been most cruel, inhuman and wicked, and some day will be righted."

So the contretemps seems to have been "settled" as Dietrich accepted Mosby's denial of the purported interview. In this matter, it would seem that both men were pawns of those who wished ill to John Mosby. Dietrich was no longer in a position to be harmed except for his "reputation," which was already in shambles, but Mosby most definitely was. This was another "interview" that never took place. While Mosby was involved in the Nebraska investigations, nobody in the Department of the Interior believed that he had not criticized the Nebraska senators in the press. In this instance, as Mosby had sufficient validation for his claim, whatever the intention of those involved it was apparently forestalled—at least for the moment.

Meanwhile, Mosby never allowed criticism of his political path or of his command to pass unanswered. And although the editorials mentioned in the following article are, sadly, no longer available, their contents are easily deduced by his response:

Times-Dispatch – January 23, 1907

Clarke Courier – January 23, 1907

COLONEL MOSBY WRITES A LETTER.

The Staunton Leader recently accused Col. John S. Mosby of being a "turncoat for political preferment," and the gauntlet was at once taken up by the Old Dominion Sun, which espoused the cause of Colonel Mosby and expressed approval of his entire political course.

The Colonel has now stepped into the arena with a letter to Capt. S. F. Chapman, the genial "Sam," who is so well liked by all the old members of the famous Mosby's Men.

The letter, which Colonel Mosby writes from Washington, under date of January 12, 1907, and which is printed in full, presents an extremely interesting and readable document. The letter follows:

Dear Sam,—I have received the Staunton Leader with the editorial calling me a "turncoat for political preferment," and the Old Dominion Sun with an editorial reply to it. Yes, I did change my jacket, after I was paroled, for a civilian suit, just as all other Confederate soldiers did but I didn't hide my gray jacket for I was then and now am, proud of it. You can see it, with my hat and bust in Confederate uniform preserved in a glass case in the National Museum in Washington. So far as party management is concerned, I have never been a politician. I have, however, always taken an interest in public questions. I never in my life took part in a political caucus or convention except in 1869, in a meeting at Warrenton, in which I took an active interest to get Jimmie (now Judge) Keith nominated for the Legislature as a stepping-stone to his promotion to the bench. I was then one of the few Confederates of any prominence who was not under political disability. Then was my opportunity if I had wanted political preferment. I did seek it for others. The election was on July 6th. Walker, the Confederate candidate for Governor, was announced to speak in Warrenton on a certain day in June. It happened to be the day on which Dougless Taylor was married at the home of his bride (Miss Harrison) near upperville, in Loudoun. Walker came that morning on the train from Alexandria. Before it arrived all the gentlemen at Warrenton, who have since won political honors, left for the wedding. I was invited to it, but stayed there. I regarded the election as a contest between civilization and barbarism, and as Walker, a Northern man, was distasteful to our people, I hoped that my example might have some influence to gain votes for him in spite of their prejudices. I remember saying then that I would as soon have thought of riding to the rear when I ordered a charge, as to leave Warrenton that day. I introduced Walker and made a speech, which was reported in the Richmond papers. You know the victory we won. I got no benefit from it except in common with all Virginia people. As Virgil says, "Sic vos non vobis."
* ["Thus do ye, but not for yourselves."-vph]

Some years afterward, when General Grant had become a private citizen, the late A. H. H. Stuart published a letter giving General Grant great credit for the aid he gave Virginia people in getting rid of military government. When Grant was a candidate in 1872, and I was supporting him, just as I had supported Walker, Mr. Stuart did not seem to remember what Grant had done for us. When it became convenient, he refreshed his memory. I have no criticism to make of the Southern people who did not approve my political course in 1872; but I say this much, that if they had followed me then, I would have led them to victory and the carpet bag government would have fallen by natural process, just as a rotten apple falls from a tree. You know that there was no man in Virginia whom the carpet baggers hated as they hated me, as I was the only man who had the power to harm them. The last appointment I got General Grant to make a few days before he left the White House was a Confederate soldier, Braxton, to be collector of the port of Norfolk. His opponent was a Union soldier, who had been wounded and had all the carpet-bag influence behind him. I stood alone for Braxton, and had no sympathy from the Democratic politicians in Virginia.

If General Grant were living, there is no act which he did through my advice which he would regret. If I had chosen to swim on the popular tide, I think that I had as fair a prospect as many of the favorite sons whom the State has honored.

All that Virginia ever did for me was to lock me up in the Albemarle jail. If I have changed my coat, I have not, like Fitz Lee, put on the blue. Some years ago, a Spanish girl in San Francisco told me that she heard Southern people say that I had deserted from the Confederate army, and she asked if it were true. I replied that just the reverse was true; that the Confederate army deserted me—that General Lee surrendered on April 9, 1865, and that I did not surrender until June 17th of the same year. And just here I will tell you something which you may never have heard. I received a message from General Gregg, who was in command at Lynchburg, that if I would come in, he would give me a parole. My brother and I drove to town in a buggy and we went to the law office of my relative, Charles L. Mosby. Soon we were informed that General Gregg had received an order not to parole but to arrest me. I had brought my pistols in my holsters with me; they were lying on the floor; I took the pistols from the holsters and laid them on the table by me and remarked: "I am ultimus Romanorum. I will not submit to arrest. I will kill the first man who attempts it." John Speed ran downstairs, mounted his horse and galloped off to General Gregg's headquarters. I threw my holsters with my pistols, across my shoulder, and with my brother, walked down the street. A great crowd of citizens and soldiers had collected, but there was no hostile demonstration. Just then Captain Charles Blackford came up and told me that several gentlemen of Lynchburg had authorized him to say to me if I wished to leave the country, they would furnish all the money I needed. I declined the offer. I preferred to stay in the fiery furnace and share the lot of the Virginia people; nor was I willing by flight to confess that I had been guilty of any act that should make me an exception from other Confederate soldiers. I would not seek the reputation of a Cato by running off to Canada. We drove home. Two days afterward General Gregg sent me another message, I came and was paroled. I no longer feel the romantic enthusiasm I did then.

"So sleeps the pride of other days—so glory's thrill is o'er."

Yours truly, JOHN S. MOSBY

This is a surprisingly bitter letter from Mosby this late in his life, especially in his comments about Virginia and, one would assume, the treatment he received at the hands of her people. For a man who had called Virginia "my mother" and who at the reunion of 1895 had spoken so lovingly of that state and her people to now say, "All that Virginia ever did for me was to lock me up in the Albemarle jail," appears to be at least a repudiation of his former feelings for his state. It certainly seemed that Mosby had become heartily sick of being called a "turncoat" for self-interest over and over again, no matter how many times it was acknowledged that he received nothing in return for acting in accordance with his conscience—quite the opposite, in fact.

This letter was also a cry of pain—emotional and, undoubtedly, physical. John Mosby was in constant physical discomfort as a result of years' long intestinal troubles stemming from repeated bouts of appendicitis—a condition that probably eventually killed him. This condition was physically obvious in photographs in his old age showing his distended abdomen. Also, he had not entirely recovered from the accident that cost him his eye. But even more to the point, it is possible that he had perhaps begun to think that with all the affection and honor that had been showered upon him both North and South, his pariah status was over. Now it appeared that such was *not* the case as the resurrected fence matter and the Staunton editorial made clear. It must have been a great sorrow for him to see it all dug up again and spread about like a vile stain. Virginia— *his* Virginia, the Virginia for which he had spilt his blood and spent his youth—still harbored many who believed him to be a Judas.

However, for once, John Mosby was not being entirely honest. If his offer to volunteer in the Spanish-American War had been accepted, he too would have, like Fitz Lee, "put on the blue." But it must have galled him to realize that while Lee's actions were overlooked, poor Longstreet was condemned as was he—and in his case, without even having donned a Federal uniform."So sleeps the pride of other days—so glory's thrill is o'er." This was as near to an epitaph as John Mosby ever wrote for himself.

But not all stories about Mosby were serious and important. As with ordinary people, he was involved in a number of humorous incidents, the result of which were stories such as this:

Evening Statesman – **February 5, 1907**

Los Angeles Herald – **February 27, 1907**

Demoralizes the Bankers

COL. JNO. S. MOSBY A TERROR TO YANKS

Creates Wild Confusion in Washington Bank when Bottle of Madeira Falls—Officers Thought It Was a Deadly Bomb.

Washington, D.C., January 22.—Colonel John S. Mosby, the Southern cavalry leader, had a recent reminder of the stirring days in the '60's, when, amid bursting shells, he crashed into Sheridan's trains, destroying army supplies and spilling costly wines destined for the mess of the general's staff. This time, however, the colonel was the loser, but he scared them all badly in the Riggs National Bank. On his recent birthday, Mr. Joseph Bryan, of Richmond, an old rough rider of the colonel's and his intimate friend, sent him as a present some Madeira wine that for forty years had lain in the casks of London Dock, longing to touch the lips of man. Colonel

Mosby felt special pride in the gift because each bottle was handsomely labeled with the legend, "Birthday Madeira," together with the date of his birth. He determined to present one to an old friend.

On his way down town he stopped in the Riggs National Bank, carrying the intended present carefully wrapped in concealing paper. Suddenly, while the Colonel was bending over a glass counter inscribing his name on a check, the bottle slipped from its covering and struck the floor with an explosion like a 5-inch shell that threw customers and bankers into consternation. Vice-President Milton Alles, who was reading a harrowing account of the late Philadelphia bank dynamiter, according to sworn statements, shot up ten feet in the air and lit with hair standing. Even President Glover almost looked up from his desk. As the rich aroma floated through the brass-barred cages of the clerks, they grew restless as the Zoo animals when the smell of fresh meat heralds the long expected dinner. But there was nothing coming to these live ones, save the disgusted explanations of the colonel, who said he'd rather have missed a wagon train than lost that Madeira.

And sure enough, the fence business was back in the news, this time during the trial of Commissioner Binger Hermann for destroying public records. Mosby testified on Hermann's behalf, confirming his honesty:

Arizona Silver Belt – **April 17, 1907 (Edited)**

Yakima Herald – **April 17, 1907**

HERMANN GIVEN GOOD REPUTATION

Justice McKenna and Colonel Mosby Tell of Congressman's Good Qualities
By Associated Press

Washington, April 16.—The defense in the case of Binger Hermann for destroying public records ended this afternoon and the prosecution began evidence in rebuttal. Testimony is expected to be brief, after which arguments will be made and the case given to the jury.

That Hermann's reputation for honesty and integrity was good was testified to today by Justice McKenna of the supreme court of the United States, Justice Lowery of the United States court of claims, Justice Gould of the supreme court of the District of Columbia, and Chief Clerk H H. Gilroy of the United States senate.

John C. Mosby [sic], leader of Mosby's guerrillas during the Civil War, produced two letters from the defendant commending his work in running down land frauds in Nebraska in 1902, when Mosby was special agent of the land office. These letters are regarded important, as showing that not all of Hermann's correspondence was copied in letter books.

Many who have written about John Mosby tend to point out his behavior as indicative of a combative nature. But actually, Mosby did not like "rows," as he put it; but he did like—nay, he demanded, justice. As a result, when he made up his mind to defend his friend and mentor General James Ewell Brown "Jeb" Stuart against the charge that it was Stuart's actions that led to the loss of the Battle of Gettysburg, Mosby knew that he would be stirring up trouble. Indeed, he had already done so when he had delved into that subject in 1896. Now his findings had been released in book form, but the new venue did not make the results any more palatable to former Confederates and devotees of the Lee cult:

Times-Dispatch – June 21, 1907
COL. MOSBY SMASHED IDOLS

Monograph on Stuart Will Be Rather Severe on Some Officers. By Walter Edward Harris.

Washington, D.C., June 20.—Colonel John S. Mosby, who has for a considerable time been engaged in writing a monograph on General Stuart in the Gettysburg campaign, completed the last chapter of the work to-day. He will revise the manuscript at once and send it to the publishers. The MacMillans will probably bring out the volume in the early fall.

"I smash some idols," said Colonel Mosby to-day, "but the book will contain nothing but the truth. Incidentally, I have had to be rather severe upon certain officers. This was from no animus towards them. In writing the book I was moved solely by a desire to tell the truth, and defend the memory of General Stuart."

New York Tribune – November 17, 1907
MOSBY AS A WORD FIGHTER.

Colonel John S. Mosby, the famous cavalry leader of the Southern army, is as keen with his tongue as he was with his sword when it spread panic through the Federal outposts in the 60's.

He has always maintained that the South went to war over slavery, not secession, as claimed by later apologists of that section. One evening, while sitting in the Occidental Hotel in San Francisco, a fire eating ex-Confederate from Alabama approached him and entered into a lengthy dissertation to prove that the South had never fought to perpetuate slavery, but only in defense of "States' Rights."

Colonel Mosby bore it in silence for a time, but finally, growing impatient, "Look here," he interrupted, "what were we quarreling with the North about from the time of the Missouri Compromise in 1820 to the day Sumter was fired on? Slavery, wasn't it?"

"Ye-e-es," reluctantly admitted the other.

"Well," continued Colonel Mosby dryly, "during the four years I was in the Southern army I was always under the impression we were fighting about the same thing we had been quarreling about."

His course in voting from Grant in 1872 was bitterly resented by many of his old comrades of the Virginia army, and in the heat of politics, it was charged that he had deserted the Southern cause; and this, though in actual war he had kept his battle front for three weeks after Lee had surrendered.

"Colonel Mosby," said an Englishwoman who had heard these charges, "is it true that you deserted Lee's army?"

"No, madam," replied the Colonel. "Lee's army deserted me."

After the war a soldier said to him, "General Blank says that he's tired of all this talk about your men having done all the fighting that was done on the Southern side," to the Colonel. "What shall I tell him you say about it."

Colonel Mosby read the man's malicious intention. "You tell General Blank that I say I am too." Was the Delphinian response.

A Southern General who was invited to address Mosby's men at one of the reunions drew a contrast between "the poor regulars sleeping in wet trenches and living on hard-tack" and Mosby's men, "sleeping in feather beds and living on the fat of the land."

Colonel Mosby was not present, but the remark came to his ears. "In war," was his comment, "the paramount duties of a commander are two: To take the best possible care of his own troops and to inflict the greatest possible damage upon the enemy. Now, if I kept my troops in such comfort and even luxury as General Blank maintains I did, and if I inflicted on the enemy as much damage as the official reports of the Northern officers admit I did, then instead of criticizing me, General Blank ought to rank me as a greater military leader than Napoleon."

Mosby always believed that the war was about slavery; that is why his service to Virginia was so amazing as he despised the institution and therefore proved himself willing to succor his "mother" state without stipulations. However, Mosby was wrong if he believed that slavery was the only cause of the war. As Jefferson Davis had said, slavery was an occasion of the war, but certainly not its root cause. But occasion or cause, that is a topic that is still under discussion a hundred years after John Mosby's death.

Mosby's book on Stuart and Gettysburg had a specific audience: military men and historians. He wasn't interested in the general public, though, of course, he didn't mind if they bought his book. This book was a legal tome designed to "prove" that Stuart had acted according to orders and that the blame for the defeat at Gettysburg lay with others and not the bold Cavalier. Of course, this very intention was what ruffled the feathers of many of his old comrades in arms:

Alexandria Gazette – **November 29, 1907**

COL. MOSBY'S BOOK ON STUART'S CAVALRY

The reader for the publishing house of Moffat, Yard and Company, of New York, gives the following opinion about Colonel Mosby's book which they will publish in January.

"I have read with much interest, the manuscript of Colonel Mosby's book, "Stuart's Cavalry in the Gettysburg Campaign." Let me frankly say at the start that this is not a book of the so-called popular type. There is no doubt of its value as a contribution to the literature of the civil war, and as such it will make a strong appeal to all survivors on both sides, of the great struggle. It will be of interest, too, to critical students of the period. It is an able presentation of the case, much as counsel would make for his client. For my own part, I could wish that there were more incidents, some sketches of character, and sidelights on the personalities of the distinguished and gallant men with whom the book deals. But that has evidently not been the author's intention. Colonel Mosby must have material in his own experience for a dozen thrilling romances, abounding in incident, where mirth and pathos, gallant deeds and hairbreadth escapes were dialing occurrences. I hope that some day we may have from his pen such a book, accurate of course, in its statement, but free from the great array of documentary evidence of which the present book is full. Such a book from such an author would be of great popular value and have a sale much larger than 'Stuart's Cavalry,' etc."

The reviewer was correct. Mosby's book was a legal defense. He was not interested in a "romance," even an "accurate romance." He knew if he delved into personalities, he would be accused of allowing his friendship with Stuart to influence his findings—something he could not afford to do. Neither would the sort of homey personal vignettes desired by the reader have furthered Mosby's defense of Stuart. This definitely was a book for the historian, the military expert, and students of war.

And so 1907 ended with very little newspaper coverage of John Mosby's involvement in Oklahoma, which itself was odd given how much attention he had received when he first went to that territory. Indeed, the only newspaper coverage of Mosby's government activities dated back to the fencing issue in Nebraska while no speculations appeared in the press as to Mosby's investigations of corruption and malfeasance among the Indians—something that in itself was decidedly peculiar and should have raised warning signals to the fourth estate.

Chapter 47

1908

"Sine amicitia, vita esse nullam."
~ Life is nothing without friends. ~ Cicero

"To live in the hearts we leave behind is not to die."
~ Thomas Campbell

1908 BEGAN WITH more coverage on the Stuart book, with the reviewer making note of the fact that the book presented the Gettysburg campaign "in a new light," which was, of course, Mosby's intent:

Washington Herald – March 8, 1908

STUART DEFENDED

Famous Guerrilla Leader Writes of His Chief The Battle of Gettysburg

A Contribution of History of Civil War Which is Designed to Clear the Name of a Famous Cavalry Leader. The Evidence on Both Sides Impartially Presented.

Times-Dispatch – March 22, 1908

STUART'S CAVALRY IN THE GETTYSBURG CAMPAIGN,

By John S. Mosby,

Moffat, Yard & Company, of New York, publishers. $2.00

This volume written by a famous Virginian and Confederate leader during the War Between the States, is inscribed by its author: "As a tribute of devotion to the memory of General J. E. B. Stuart, the champion of a cause more interesting than prosperous—one of those causes which please noble spirits, but do not please destiny—which have Cato's adherence, but not heaven's."

Because John Mosby refused to accept a handsome bribe in the Oklahoma matter, he had been removed from his duties in Oklahoma and denied any work in the Department of Justice. As a result, he spent long, weary, painfully useless days ignored and humiliated while the Indian affairs were making their way back into the news in a very big way. Little was said about him, but a very long article in the *Guthrie Daily Leader* did bring his name to the fore once more. It had also mentioned brother-in-law Russell's demand that the indictments against Mansfield, McMurray, and Cornish obtained by Mosby be quashed and that the firm be offered a public apology. The last time John Mosby's name appeared in any reference to the Department was a justification, however brief, of everything he had attempted to do:

Guthrie Daily Leader – **April 13, 1908 (Edited)**
ANOTHER CHAPTER REVEALED

High Personages Are Dragged Into More Scandal

MOODY'S REMARKABLE LETTER TO STEPHENS

W. B. Johnston Sheds Some Light on Grand Jury Transactions

Washington D. C., April 13—High personages are involved in the latest chapter to the book of scandal—high enough to make the average reader feel dizzy. For when former Attorney General Moody, until recently a member of the president's official family, is quoted as having used the following language at the Department of Justice on a certain and well known occasion it is time for the country to open its ears and listen: "Gentlemen, It was the duty of the district attorney to advise the grand jury to return an indictment on the evidence they had before them. He has conscientiously performed his duty and should be commended by everybody. I will further say to you I do not approve of this way of disposing criminal cases and have so advised, but have been overruled. This is not the first instance when similar actions have been taken against my judgment and my conclusion is that however innocent a man may be, he will never be able to convince the people of the fact of being discharged in this kind of a hearing."

The above words are taken from a remarkable letter just received by Representative John H. Stephens, of Texas, who openly charged in the house that there was something "rotten in Denmark," as far as the department of justice's relations with conspiracy indictments against Governor D. H. Johnston, of the Chickasaw nation, former Gov. P. S. Mosely, of the same nation, and the law firm of Mansfield, McMurray and Cornish was concerned. The letter is from the pen of W. B. Johnson of Ardmore, and former United States district attorney for the Southern district of Indian Territory.

General Moody's words are all the more significant because Special Assistant Attorney General Charles W. Russell, who had been detailed to make an investigation had previously recommended that the indictments be dismissed because the evidence did not warrant their existence and that an apology be offered the defendants publicly. Throughout Mr. Johnson's letter there may be found an air of pessimism. Evidently his confidence in human nature has been destroyed by the so-called investigations into the now famous conspiracy charges. ...

The fact that Col. John S. Mosby, who represented the department of justice before the grand jury that brought the indictments was never called upon by the department to make a report in the matter, is made clear. It is true that Mr. Mosby was directly interested in the Chickasaw warrant fraud which was gone into by the grand jury but it was the evidence produced before the grand jury in that fraud that threw suspicion on others higher up including the governors of the nation and the law firm already mentioned. It is said that the testimony of one Taylor, an expert accountant who had gone over the books of the Chickasaw treasurer in looking for the warrant frauds discovered other irregularities and these were brought out by him before the grand jury during the warrant investigation and subsequently led on to the indictment of the alleged conspirators.

In his book Rebel: The Life and Times of John S. Mosby, author Kevin Siepel wrote about the matter that concluded with the infamous exchange of telegrams between Mosby and brother-in-law Russell. According to Siepel

> "In June the seventy-one-year-old investigator was sent by Russell to Indian Territory [present-day Oklahoma] to look into charges being brought against U. S. Marshal Benjamin H. Colbert—a former Rough Rider—and others, allegedly involved in land frauds against the Chickasaws. While there he turned up information which, it was widely reported, led to the indictment not only of Colbert, whom Roosevelt refused to rescue, but of several other territorial personages, among them a firm of lawyers from McAlester.
>
> These attorneys, representing the Chickasaw and Chocktaw nations in a potentially lucrative suite against the government, had, Mosby alleged, actually been misappropriating tribal funds. When the firm's three partners— George Mansfield, John F. McMurray, and Melvin Cornish— were indicted, he triumphantly wired the results to Russell. Russell's lack of enthusiasm for the proceedings stunned him. Pointing out that the evidence against the three was skimpy, and that there was the further question of bias among members of the grand jury, Russell cautioned his exuberant brother-in-law, warning that the men must get a square deal.
>
> 'Dear Mr. Russell," Mosby fired back,
>
> 'I received your telegram asking for "a square deal" for Mansfield, McMurray and Cornish. I think every man is entitled to a square deal; there has been no discrimination between Mansfield, McMurray, and Cornish and other criminals; they have the same kind of reputation among lawyers that Captain Kidd had among sailors... I feel very sure that if there is a square deal they will land in the penitentiary."

The indictments against Mansfield and the others were in fact quashed, but in a very suspicious and incredibly unusual way. When District Attorney W. B. Johnson was instructed to quash the indictments, knowing the guilt of those involved, he refused. As a result, he was removed from his position for a period of fifteen minutes! During that time, his "replacement" quashed the indictments. When that was done, the district attorney was reinstated. Of course, once the indictments were quashed, he could do nothing about the matter, except speak to the press—which he did. Of course, this happened two years later, after John Mosby had been "let go" from the Department of Justice because he was "superannuated:"

Spokane Press – August 15, 1910

East Oregonian – August 15, 1910

FORMER DISTRICT ATTORNEY ON STAND

Tells Committee of Quashing of Indictments

W. B. Johnson, Who Was Dismissed From Office and Reinstated in 15

Minutes, Tells How Indictments Against McMurray Were Dismissed

Sulphur, Okla., Aug. 15.—Former District Attorney W. B. Johnson, who entered a protest when the indictments against Mansfield, McMurray and Cornish were quashed, and who was dismissed from office for this action and reinstated 15 minutes later, was called before the investigating committee today. He said, "During the eight years I was United States district attorney 5,000 indictments were returned in my court, and only one was investigated. That one was against McMurray, Mansfield and Cornish. I was called to Washington in August, 1905, and Assistant Attorney General Russell was kept busy writing for nine days for McMurray to appear. There were three hearings. Cecil Lyon of Texas, was present at all of them." Johnson stated after he had protested and returned home he received a telegram dismissing him and fifteen minutes later came another telegram reinstating him, but his successor had had time to dismiss the indictments.

Johnson testified that Lyon explained his presence in Washington at that time by saying, "they kept wiring me to come."

C. D. Ledbetter, an attorney showed a check for ten thousand dollars signed by McMurray, Johnson testified. He said he remarked to Ledbetter that ten thousand was a nice fee. "That isn't all; I have some good contracts," Ledbetter replied, according to Johnson.

Palestine Daily Herald - **August 15, 1910**

Chickasha Daily Express - **August 15, 1910**

ATTORNEY JOHNSON TALKS.

Testifies to What He Knows About the McMurray Contracts

Sulphur, Okla., Aug. 15—W. B. Johnson, a former United States attorney, was on the witness stand this morning before the congressional committee investigating the Gore charges. He told of a trip he made to Washington and a conference concerning the Mansfield, McMurray and Cornish indictments. He said that Cecil Lyon of Texas attended the conference, having come from Colorado to Washington. Lyon told him that he was not interested in the deal. He said W. A. Ledbetter of Oklahoma City, an attorney, showed him a check for $10,000 from McMurray for representing him in an injunction case.

In most of the books on Mosby covering this period, the authors lead the reader to believe that Mosby was "over-enthusiastic" and brought indictments where either no guilt obtained or the matter was lacking any serious wrongdoing. It would seem that there was nothing wrong with John Mosby's legal instincts, his abilities or the indictments he obtained from the grand jury. What was wrong was a culture of corruption in which he refused to engage. It is easy to see, after Mosby's brother-in-law was sent off to Persia, how simple it was to remove him from the Department of Justice without either anything redounding to Russell's detriment or his being available to answer any embarassing questions.

Once again, Mosby's health became an issue as he underwent surgery for another intestinal problem. As usual, he appeared unconcerned; but naturally, his friends and family were anxious on his behalf.

Evening Star – May 13, 1908

COL. J. S. MOSBY ILL.

Veteran Soldier is Taken to Garfield Hospital for Operation.

Col. John S. Mosby, who gained fame in the civil war as the commander and leader of a force of partisan cavalry in the Confederate army known as "Mosby's Rangers," has been removed to Garfield Hospital, suffering from an ailment with which he has been troubled for several years. The statement was made today that the condition of Col. Mosby is not serious, but that he was taken to the hospital pending a decision as to whether an operation will be necessary. Dr. Francis R. Hagner is the surgeon in charge of the case. Col. Mosby is assistant attorney of the Department of Justice, and his home is at 1400 K street. Owing to his otherwise rugged constitution, his friends are not apprehensive of any serious results.

The decision was reached after a consultation of surgeons this afternoon to perform an operation on Col. Mosby to-morrow.

Times-Dispatch – May 16, 1908

[From Our Regular Correspondent.]

Washington, D. C., May 15.—Colonel John S. Mosby rallied finely from he effects of operation which he underwent at Garfield Hospital yesterday. The sattending physician said to-night that the patient was doing well, and would probably leave the hospital, cured, in ten days or so.

Clarke Courier – May 27, 1908

Colonel Mosby Rapidly Recovering

The many friends and admirers of Col. John S. Mosby will be glad to hear that the operation performed on him recently at the Garfield Hospital, Washington, was successful, and he is now getting along as well as could be desired. A letter from one of his daughters gives this good report, and adds that he is expected to be out again in due time.

The article below is included because it acknowledged a friendly attitude toward Mosby by Secretary Taft, who would become president after Roosevelt. Taft certainly had no problems with Mosby as is evident by their short conversation, and yet it was Taft who allowed Mosby to be dismissed without even looking into the matter:

Washington Times – June 5, 1908

(part of an article on White House visitors-vph)

Probably equal in age, but with a hand as steady as that of his grandson, who accompanied him, was Colonel Mosby, the famous guerrilla leader of the Confederate forces. As the veteran was waiting to see the President, Secretary Taft came along.

Gets Unconscious Promotion.

"Good morning general," he said genially, shaking hands with the old soldier.

"General!" exclaimed Colonel Mosby. "Jeff Davis thought the rank of colonel was good enough for me. Do you intend to give me a promotion, Mr. Secretary?"

"I think one is due you," replied the Presidential candidate as he walked away.

Slowly, the Grim Reaper was cutting down the remaining veterans on both sides of the old conflict. Two Western papers acknowledged Mosby's value, noting that not only did he have the chance to win "national fame," but that he had done so:

Pacific Commercial Advertiser – June 12, 1908

Hawaiian Gazette – June 12, 1908

The death of General Stephen D. Lee leaves Colonel John S. Mosby almost the only living Confederate officer of national distinction. Colonel Mosby is now employed in the Attorney General's department at Washington. During C. P. Huntington's lifetime he had a similar billet in the Southern Pacific law department at San Francisco, Mr. Huntington having promised General Grant to look after the Confederate officer, for whom Grant had a strong admiration. Although never commanding more than five hundred men at a time, Colonel Mosby, by his constant cavalry raids in the border country, neutralized the services of 40,000 Union troops by compelling them to guard exposed lines of communication. But for that they would have been free to operate against the Confederate Army of Northern Virginia. No other Confederate colonel had such a chance or was able to win such national fame.

Finally, Mosby began to hear from those for whom he had written the book on Stuart and Gettysburg. Perhaps he forwarded this letter to the Gazette in order to make his point about the book's value and its reception in the military community:

Alexandria Gazette – July 28, 1908

COL. MOSBY'S BOOK.

Col. J. S. Mosby has received the following complimentary letter concerning his book, which will explain itself:

Army War College Washington, July 24, 1908

Col. J. S. Mosby:

My dear sir: I have just finished reading your book on Stuart's Cavalry in the Gettysburg campaign and I cannot refrain from thanking you for the contribution you have made to military history. I have been a student of military history for some years but your book has been a revelation to me in many ways.

Hoping to have the pleasure of meeting you some day and of talking over these great events in which you have taken such an active part, I am, dear sir, Very respectfully,

EBON SWIFT,

Major, General Staff Director Army War College.

Thus the year ended on a quiet if ominous note. Press coverage of the investigation by the Department of Justice in Oklahoma did not mention John Mosby even in passing.

It had not been a "bad" year, though more friends like Johnny Munson and James Bryan were no more. But his book on Stuart and Gettysburg had been released and had not only been well received, but also well covered in the press, which was odd for a rather dry legalistic work. But of course, the book had one overwhelmingly important ingredient in its favor "press-wise"; it was written by Colonel John Singleton Mosby.

Chapter 48

1909

Cineri gloria sera est. ~ Glory paid to ashes comes too late.

"Proclaim the truth and do not be silent through fear."
~ Catherine of Siena

1909 BEGAN WITH a newspaper "expose" of President Roosevelt's expenditure on "detective work." Apparently, during 1908, some $20 million had been paid out by the government for such work. Among the issues mentioned was the old Nebraska land case. Mr. Clark, looking into the matter for the House, had called upon the attorney general to report the number of special agents employed by the Department of Justice as well as their salaries, duties, and by the authority of what law they were appointed. During the proceedings, the Nebraska matter was raised, and Mosby's situation cited:

> *Alexandria Gazette* – **January 14, 1909**
>
> It is reported that during the past year twenty million dollars was spent under the direction of the president in every species of detective work. If the truth be anything approaching this a congressional investigation of the matter is imperative, and the resolution offered in the House yesterday by Mr. Clark calling on the attorney general to report to the House the number of special agents employed by the Department of Justice, their duties, salaries and authority of what law they were appointed, should at once be adopted The employment of detectives is excessive. But much of the employment of detectives is evidently improper. For example, in the president's secret service message he said: "In Nebraska it was necessary to remove a United States attorney and a United States marshal before satisfactory progress could be made" in the punishment of men guilty of public land frauds.
>
> Now, if Mr. Roosevelt was so eager to punish those who were stealing public lands in the west, why did he recall Col. Mosby who was sent there for the very purpose of preventing such robbery? The answer is that Senator Dietrich (who was subsequently turned out of the Senate) and others interested in the land grabbing threatened Mr. Roosevelt that if he did not recall Mosby the northwest would vote the democratic ticket at the next election. If this is questioned let the investigators put Col. Mosby on the stand. Mr. Roosevelt is the king four flusher of his time and every word that has been said of him this week by Senators Tillman and Foraker is absolutely true.

The dawning year saw Mosby suffer from another, albeit seemingly minor, health issue; and the usual coverage went on for some time. The abdominal problems that afflicted him were normal for a man of his age, but these had been severely exacerbated by recurring bouts of appendicitis beginning in 1895. His condition was further worsened by the results of the natural wear and tear to that sensitive area of the body affected by years of hard riding in the era of the horse:

Evening Star – January 22, 1909

Col. Mosby Improving

Reports this morning of the condition of Col. John S. Mosby, who is suffering from a severe cold, which it was feared had affects parts of the abdominal region which have been extremely weak since an operation performed last spring, are that he will in all probability recover. Dr. J. H. Holland, the attending physician, gives the family every hope.

On the other hand, the diagnosis here was one of a "cold" or possibly, as had been the case at the time of the Blazer fight, influenza. It is really hard to know exactly what the problem was, but Mosby recovered without the need of surgery, though one article did claim that he had undergone a surgical procedure:

Alexandria Gazette – January 23, 1909

Washington Herald – January 23, 1909

Col. John S. Mosby is quite ill in Washington.

COL. MOSBY RECOVERING

Was Ill with Cold Taken During Recent Storm.

Col. John S. Mosby, the Confederate rough rider, who has been seriously ill, is now pronounced out of danger by his physician, and his early recovery is practically assured. His illness was due more to a cold, contracted during the recent storm, than any organic trouble, and the passing of the cold wave has brought him the needed relief.

As became the case with Mosby's advancing age, every illness was treated with a sort of "review" of his life in preparation, it is supposed, for an eventual obituary. As that was the case, the following question then arises: how did this particular paper manage to spell his name wrong?

Marion Daily Mirror – January 25, 1909

MOSELY [sic] IS HARD TO KILL

Veteran Warrior, Has unique Career—Refused Chinese Command.

Salt Lake Herald – February 2, 1909

DEATH PUT TO ROUT.

Mosby lamented the deaths of his men, mentioning Thomas Sealock, who had been one of his "best friends," according to this article in the Gazette. However, he did not limit his remarks to Sealock alone. Indeed, though he did not mention them all, their passing affected him deeply:

Alexandria Gazette – February 27, 1909

DEATH OF MOSBY'S MEN

Col. John S. Mosby has written the following for the Warrenton Virginian"

"I have just heard of the death of one of my old men and best friends, Tom Sealock, at his home in Fauquier on a peak of the Blue Ridge. I always addressed him as Roderick Dhue, for he had many of the characteristics of the great Highland Chief. In fact I do not think Tom would have come out worsted if Fitz James had encountered him in the duel which Scott describes in the Lady of the Lake. I don't know any soldier who had more scars than Tom; he always pointed to them as badges of honor. Even when I was in far Cathay I kept up correspondence with him, and a few years ago our friend, Willie Thompson, drove me up to his home on the mountain which commands a view of three counties. Here we spent several days listening to Tom's wit and humor. If Tom had had the advantage of education he would have risen to distinction; for he was naturally one of the smartest men I ever knew. In the month of February two of my best men, Johnnie Alexander and Tom Sealock, passed over the great river and left me to mourn for them. I am beginning to feel very lonely in this world now; nearly all of my old friends are gone and I have made no new ones. Col. Mosby has also written the following letter to the *Fairfax Herald*: Herewith is a letter just received from Missouri informing me of the death of one of my best men, "Joe" Richards, who was a Fairfax boy when he joined me in July, 1863. I was then raising a command with Joe and French Dulany and several others from the neighborhood of Falls Church came through the enemy's lines to join me. He was a member of my first company; I never had under me a truer man, or a braver soldier. Three years ago he was on a visit to see his family in Virginia and came here to see me. Of course, I was delighted to meet him once more and talk over the old days. This is the kind of reunion I enjoy. He was one of the most absolutely fearless beings I ever saw. Whenever I gave an order to charge Joe went through the enemy's ranks like a solid shot. Today is the anniversary of that day—February 22, 1864—45 years ago—when he acted with conspicuous bravery in a fight. The California Cavalry battalion had left their camp in Vienna to go on an expedition through Loudoun and upper Fauquier in search of me. One Charles Binns, also from Fairfax, who had deserted from my command to prevent being arrested for misconduct, was their guide.

I went in pursuit of the Californians and intercepted them returning to their camp on the Leesburg pike near Dranesville. When the fight began about 10 o'clock in the morning we could hear the roar of the guns in the forts celebrating Washington's birthday. The result of the affair is pretty well known. One of the wounded on our side was Baron von Massow, a Prussian. He is or was, a few years ago, in command of a German army corps. We were particularly anxious to catch Binns, and I detailed some men who knew him well with orders not to let him escape. Joe Richards was one of the men. If Joe had caught him I doubt it he would have brought him alive to me. But Binns got away and crossed the Potomac a lone fugitive about Seneca. Colonel Thompson, who was in command there, told he me that he met Binns when he reached Maryland shore and that he was a perfect picture of fright and despair. When he got back to Washington he was treated ungratefully—accused of treachery in leading the Californians into a trap, was arrested and locked up in prison. He got his reward—was never trusted as a guide any more.

During February three of my best men and best friends—Joe Richards Johnnie Alexander and Tom Sealock passed over the great river. So "Leaf by leaf the roses fall—drop by drop the springs run dry."

Mosby's rather untrammelled life apparently continued with no mention of his duties at the Department of Justice most probably because, by that time, he had none:

Evening Star – June 19, 1909

Washington Times – June 19, 1909

Col. John S. Mosby, accompanied by his niece, Miss Lucy Virginia Russell, daughter of the Assistant Attorney General and Mrs. Charles W. Russell, has returned from a most enjoyable visit to friends in Charlottesville, Va., where they have been attending the commencement exercises of the University of Virginia, of which institution Colonel Mosby is an alumnus.

Meanwhile, responses to the Stuart book continued to be received and forwarded to the newspapers or at least to the Gazette. It was obviously important to Mosby that the true value of his work be "officially" recognized in the press. Again, this was a result of the subject involved, that is, Mosby's defense of Stuart. No other of his works were so relentlessly defended by the author in the press. This was the last service that John Mosby could render his dead friend and he wanted its acceptance in the military and historical communities publicly recognized and acknowledged:

Alexandria Gazette – July 13, 1909

STUART'S CAVALRY IN THE GETTYSBURG CAMPAIGN.

Col. John S. Mosby has received the following letters from an English officer in Canada, which explain themselves:

Department of Militia and Defense,

Ottawa, June 28, 1909 Dear Sir—I have recently read your book on "Stuart's Cavalry in the Gettysburg Campaign" and feel that I should like to let you know how much pleasure and instruction your work has given to one who always felt a keen interest in the true account of the actions of the war of 1861-65.

Some years ago, as a British officer, I was studying for our promotion examinations for the rank of major, and our military history subject dealt almost entirely with the operations in the Shenandoah Valley—1861-62—and on the Chickahominy—1862. Our textbook was Colonel Henderson's "Stonewall Jackson." Your book throws a great deal of light upon what I, as a British student, thought obscure about Chancellorsville and Gettysburg. I am so pleased to know the real reason of the meeting at Gettysburg. It never was clear to me why General Lee fought the battle there. I think you have done good service in throwing light on these hitherto obscure points. You have certainly championed your old friend Stuart as a real Knight Errant, with all the enthusiasm of earnest belief and conviction. In Canada here we have always admired Stuart immensely, though probably Robt. E. Lee and "Stonewall" Jackson were our chief heroes of the war. I hope you will pardon my troubling you in this way, but I admired so much the manner in which you advanced your cause, and the arguments brought forward seemed so irresistible, that I wanted as a Canadian soldier, to let you know of the satisfaction your book has given, at least to me.

Yours truly,

Charles F. Winter, Major D.A.A.G.

Colonel John S. Mosby,

Care of Messrs, Moffat, Yard & Company, New York,

U.S.A. Department of Militia and Defense,

Ottawa, July 10th, 1909 My dear sir, I much appreciated your letter of 1st, instant, and can well understand how painful it must have been for you to speak so plainly about many of your old comrades in the war, but I agree with you that it was a duty that should be performed by somebody in fairness to the memories of both General Lee and General Stuart, and, being yourself in possession of exceptional information owing to the peculiar circumstances under which you served at the time, I feel that you were perfectly right in bringing out the points you did.

Personally I feel grateful to you, because I never really understood the Gettysburg campaign before, but your descriptions have made it very plain and simple.

With kind regards, and trusting you will long to vindicate Stuart's memory,

I am respectfully yours, Charles F. Winter, Major, D.A.A.G.

Lt. Col. John S. Mosby,

Department of Justice, Washington D.C.

Mosby's still rather odd situation in Virginia—loved and hated, admired and despised, welcomed and rejected—continued apace. Apparently, at least in Mosby's Confederacy, he was still very much welcome:

Washington Herald – August 12, 1909

PLAN RECEPTION TO MOSBY.

Confederate Commander Will Attend Berryville Horse Show. Special to the *Washington Herald*.

Berryville, Va., Aug. 11.—Col. John S. Mosby, the noted Confederate commander, now of Washington, will be one of the distinguished guests of the Clarke County Horse and Colt Show Association at the annual exhibition of the society here next week, and will have his headquarters at the Battletown Inn. Many of Col. Mosby's faithful followers were from Clarke County, and some of his most daring exploits took place in this section. It is certain that the brave old soldier will be accorded a hearty reception upon his arrival here. All of the local "Mosby men" are making arrangements to meet their old commander.

An article appeared in the Gazette in which Mosby was mentioned in passing to illustrate the change of attitude that had taken place since he had been arrested at a racetrack in New York City soon after the war. The Gazette declared that he was taken into custody "for no other reason ... but the fact that he was an ex-Confederate." Well, not quite! He was both recognized and arrested because he was not just any "ex-

Confederate"—he was "John Singleton Mosby. There was a difference; there had always been—and there always would be—a difference:

Alexandria Gazette – September 9, 1909

The truth of the saying, "times change and men change with them," is often manifest. At the close of the civil war Col. John S. Mosby visited New York state and while on his travels went to a racetrack. He was recognized and taken into custody for no other reason, it seemed, but the fact that he was an ex-Confederate. He was, of course, soon released. Another spirit seems to be animating the residents of the Empire State in this day. A dispatch from Utica says about 50 ex-Confederate soldiers from the vicinity of Wilmington, N. C., arrived there yesterday for a reunion of the survivors of the fight at Fort Fisher, January 15, 1865. According to the dispatch the men from the south are getting a pleasant reception. Not only are the grand army men present from all of central and northern New York, but the city has been decorated. Yesterday was spent in sight-seeing and yesterday evening a formal welcome was extended. This evening Governor Hughes and Vice-President Sherman are to speak at a meeting to be held in the armory. In the forenoon there was a parade, with 10,000 school children in line. Thursday will be given up to an excursion to Cooperstown and Otsego Lake. Several receptions and regimental reunions have been planned.

Mosby would have applauded such fraternal celebrations and perhaps seen it as, to a small extent at least, the result of his own tireless efforts toward that end.

The annual "birthday" press notices then appeared. There was nothing much to say, but still, the event "made the papers":

Alexandria Gazette – December 7, 1909

PERSONAL

Looking hale, feeling hearty, and still active Col. John Singleton Mosby passed the seventy-sixth mile-stone of his eventful career yesterday. Col. Mosby, who is now an attorney in the United States Department of Justice, resides in Washington.

Free Lance – December 11, 1909

Col. Mosby

Looking hearty and still active Col. John S. Mosby passed the seventy-sixth mile stone of his eventful career Wednesday. Col. Mosby who is now an attorney in the U.S. Department of Justice, resides in Washington.

And so 1909 came to a rather ominous end. As he had been given nothing to do despite constantly requesting at least some duties, Mosby knew—as he had known with the railroad—that his days with the Department of Justice were numbered. The end of the first decade of the new century would see the matter finally play out as he had doubtless anticipated.

Chapter 49

1910

Ave, Caesar! Nos morituri te salutamus!
~ Hail, Caesar! We who are about to die salute you!

"The powerful hate truth that puts them in bad light."
~ **Bangambiki Habyarimana**

1910 BEGAN WITH a rather gentle, sympathetic, and altogether false article appearing in the *San Francisco Chronicle* making the point that Mosby had a "position" with the government which served as a sort pension. This belief helped bolster the claim that he was let go from the Department of Justice because he was no longer able to perform his duties. Of course, few knew that he was repeatedly refused such duties by that department for the very purpose of excusing his dismissal. The article's reference to Mosby's association with Grant also furthered what was to become an "accepted fact," that is, that Mosby was kept employed in the government because of the support of Republican administrations. Of course, the facts prove the opposite was true:

> *San Francisco Chronicle* – **January 16, 1910**
>
> A friend of mine met Colonel Mosby the other day in the New Willard at Washington and found him looking about the same as he did in the days long before the fire when his soldierly figured walked the streets of San Francisco. He has an office in one of the departments which serves him in lieu of a pension. While here the famous guerrilla leader was in the law department of the Southern Pacific railroad where C. P. Huntington had put him in the fulfillment of a death-bed promise made to General Grant. The latter was fond of Mosby. He remembered that the Confederate raider with scarce five hundred men, had done such damage to outposts, railroad, scouting parties and camps that it finally neutralized the campaign services of forty thousand men who had to guard the threatened points. This was fine soldiering and Grant knew it.
>
> Afterward, Mosby had shown the moral courage to accept the results of the war and cast in his lot with the Republicans. Grant took his former enemy into full confidence; and while President he kept Mosby in office, part of the time as Consul-General at Shanghai. His influence aided him under Hayes and Arthur administrations; but Cleveland let Mosby out and then Grant turned to his friend Huntington. It was at Mount McGregor, where the great commander died. "I wish you would do something for Colonel Mosby," the General whispered for the cancer in his throat had nearly deprived him of the power of speech. "Give him a position and keep him as long as he lives." Huntington promised and kept his word. Every now and then the law department found some excuse for letting the old Confederate out, but as soon as Huntington heard of it, Mosby was put back. However, one morning the railroad king went over to the great majority and within a week the law department had Mosby's scalp. But the old man had not lost his pull at Washington and he will probably die in harness.

Some years ago the guerrilla chief was looking over old Virginia scenes when the horse he was driving leaped and ran away, throwing Mosby over the dashboard of the buggy, under the animal's heels. One of Mosby's eyes was kicked out. As his senses came back and he realized his hurt, the first words that sprang from his lips were:

… blind old Dandolo! Th' octogenarian chief, Byzantium's conquering foe.

It was just like the white-haired partisan ranger that the soldier spirit and the martial phrase should arise to meet each crisis of his life.

W. G. S.

The end of January saw the announcement of the departure of newly appointed minister to Persia, Charles W. Russell for his new post. And thus, the stage was set:

Sunday Star – **January 30, 1910**

Charles W. Russell, the newly appointed minister to Persia, will leave Washington Tuesday afternoon and sail February 5 for Naples. He will be accompanied by Mrs. Russell and their daughter, Miss Lucy Russell, who was a debutante of last year. Miss Russell is a graceful and accomplished girl, whose knowledge of French and other languages will be of signal service to her in the diplomatic post to which her father has been assigned. Mrs. Russell is a sister of Col. John S. Mosby, the rebel ranger of the civil war. Minister Russell and his family will visit Rome and Constantinople on their way to Teheran.

A further mention of the old land scandal next appeared. Former Land Commissioner Hermann had been acquitted of the charges made against him; Mosby had been one of those who testified on his behalf at trial:

The Sun – **February 15, 1910**

HERMANN JURY DISAGREES

Fails to Convict Former Land Commissioner

Was Charged with Frauds in Securing Possession of Large Slices of the Public Domain—Has Been in Public Life a Long Time and Often Accused.

In February, a very unusual matter came to light involving one of "Mosby's men," former Ranger John H. Core. Core had died a very wealthy man and left $100,000 out of his $750,000 estate for the building of a mausoleum to house his remains and those of his wife upon her death. Mosby was asked about the matter and made a very telling comment in response:

San Francisco Call – **February 16, 1910**

Los Angeles Herald – **February 17, 1910**

Evening Star – **February 17, 1910**

MOSBY GUERILLA LEAVES $100,000 FOR MAUSOLEUM

Remarkable Will Disposes of $750,000 Estate

The *Evening Star* article contains the additional text:

When shown the dispatch from Norfolk this morning at his residence, 1333 L Street, Col. John S. Mosby stated he recollected Core as being a member of his command and a soldier who had been always worthy of his superior's confidence. He was in the ranks of the Mosby command throughout practically the entire four years of the war. [Mosby's command existed for only two and a half years, beginning in January of 1863.-vph]

"I remember him best for an incident after the war," remarked the former Confederate ranger, "as the only one of my old men who censured me for advocating the election of Gen. Grant to the presidency. He wrote me a bitter letter."

If Mosby recalled Core's "bitter letter" thirty years after the fact, it must have hurt him deeply. On the other hand, such a retentive memory precludes any diagnosis of mental deterioration.

Washington Times – February 18, 1910
MOSBY CRITICIZES WILL OF RANGER

Col. John S. Mosby is showing considerable interest in the terms of the will made by John R. Core, one of Mosby's Rangers, who died in Norfolk. Leaving an estate estimated at $750,000, Core directed that $100,00 be used for the erection of a mausoleum.

"I think he would have done better," said Colonel Mosby, "if he had left the $100,000 for the erection of a hospital. That would have been a gift for which he would have been blessed by his fellow-men."

Also in February, Mosby picked up the Stuart gauntlet once again with very detailed accounts of the fiasco that led to the Battle of Gettysburg. Of course, he had a lot of time on his hands as he was being given no work in the Department of Justice and did not even have Russell as a means to attempt redress for his situation. Doubtless, by that time, he probably knew that Russell, the sender of the infamous telegram, was as much his enemy as anyone else.

In the following article, Mosby provided a name upon which to place blame for the unfortunate conclusion to Gettysburg, what was believed to be the seminal campaign of the war:

Times-Dispatch – February 27, 1910
HETH INTENDED TO COVER HIS ERROR

Colonel John S. Mosby Gives His Version of New Chapter in Lee-Stuart Controversy.

But with the departure of "Mr. Russell" for *The Sunny Middle East*, the axe was about to fall on John Mosby in the Department of Justice. Countless articles were written about the matter. In the beginning, most simply accepted the explanation of age and the lack of ability to "do the job." But that too soon changed. The first article was carried in the *Evening Star* in early July. Interestingly enough, this article mentioned that Mosby told no one of his situation, which, of course, meant he had been released much earlier in the year. Indeed, he never complained about it, though he did wonder why he was released by a man who no longer worked for the department and that no one—even President Taft—ever bothered to find out if he was as "useless" as was claimed. As happened whenever there were reports of his imminent death, these articles tended to recap his history:

Evening Star – July 8, 1910

COL. MOSBY OUT OF GOVERNMENT JOB

Old Age Supposed Cause of Dismissal from Department of Justice.

Col. John S. Mosby, the famous Confederate guerrilla of civil war days, has lost his position as a special attorney in the Department of Justice, after eight years there.

In the absence of Attorney General Wickersham no explanation is made at the department. Old age, that nightmare of superannuated government employees, it is understood, was the main reason for his dismissal.

Col. Mosby is, about seventy-three years of age. To his old friends he appears active and energetic. He has been blind in one eye since he was a young man, and lately has been getting deaf.

Mosby Told No One.

Comparatively few know of his loss of position, which dates from July 1. He has made no appeals to anyone to aid him in being restored. Whether such appeals will be made to the Attorney General and the President is not known today. It is considered probable.

Attorney General Wickersham, the most active head of the department within its history, on the hustle physically and mentally at all times, has kept his department on the go for months. He has been reorganizing his forces so as to get the best results from them.

Other changes have been made, it is said, but Col. Mosby's dismissal is the most conspicuous that has taken place. His history as a fighting man, his achievements with a small band of guerrillas during the great war between the states, has given him a place in history that has marked him for distinction.

Appointed under Roosevelt

He was appointed a special attorney of the department early in the first part of the Roosevelt administration, and was assigned to break up the cattlemen's operations against government lands in the middle west. His fearlessness in this work, in spite of numerous threats, won him the approbation of President Roosevelt.

He did other work of the same kind, showing neither fear nor favor. In the last few years, he has been given little work on account of his advancing age, although asking that he be assigned to active duty.

Col. Mosby became a Republican some time after the civil war, believing that to be the best method for securing concessions to the south. He was a special favorite of Gen. Grant, who kept him in the best Federal positions to be had and consulted him often as to important government matters.

It is probable that Col. Mosby will now devote his time to writing a book of the civil war, in which he took such a conspicuous part.

As with every other "milestone" in Mosby's life, the press coverage was both momentous and relentless:

Times-Dispatch – July 9, 1910 (Edited)
COL. JOHN S. MOSBY LOSES POSITION

Famous Southerner Asked to Resign From Federal Service

ACTION IS TAKEN BY WICKERSHAM

Virginia Colony in Washington Is Stirred by Dismissal of Aged Confederate Veteran From Department of Justice—Cause of Enforced Retirement Not Known.

Favorite of Grant. The Probable Cause.

It is understood that one of the reasons that prompted Attorney-General Wickersham to ask for Colonel Mosby's resignation was the fact that the latter had recently been assigned to some very important work in securing evidence against prominent business men soon to figure before the public. He received a telegram, it is said, from friends of these parties asking him to see that they received justice, to which he replied: "If the parties you name receive justice, they will go to the penitentiary."

This may or may not have been the direct cause of Colonel Mosby's forced retirement, but it is characteristic of the man, as the persons in whose behalf leniency was asked are prominent in the public eye and have vast business interests. This probably brought about his detachment from the government service.

Mr. Wickersham is expected back in Washington in a few days, and then an official statement regarding the matter will no doubt be made.

P. H. McH.

The above article began to make the connection between Mosby's refusal to turn a blind eye to the same type of chicanery in Oklahoma as in Nebraska and his loss of position. Mosby's son John Jr. also commented that this outcome was not unexpected. He mentioned "personal reasons" that the family did not believe "it would be wise to make public just now."

Unfortunately, the matter never became public at least in its entirety, and many who have written about Mosby have simply accepted the claim that he was "superannuated." Below are a number of articles, all of which brought up various subjects referable to the matter. But even as early as July 9, there began to appear reports doubting the "official version" of his dismissal:

Washington Herald – **July 9, 1910**
COL. J.S. MOSBY LOSES OFFICE

Famous Confederate Guerilla Dismissed July 1.

As Special Attorney of Department of Justice He Had Been Administration Favorite.

Evening Times – **July 9, 1910**

New York Tribune – **July 9, 1910**

Rock Island Argus – **July 9, 1910**
COLONEL MOSBY DISMISSED

Age Costs Noted Ex-Confederate His Place.

Washington Times – **July 9, 1910**
COLONEL MOSBY LOSES POSITION

Col. John S. Mosby, an appointee of Colonel Roosevelt eight years ago, has been dismissed …

St. Mathews Journal – **July 9, 1910 (Edited)**
Washington, D. C., July 9.

Colonel John S. Mosby, who distinguished himself in the Confederate cause during the civil war as a daring guerrilla fighting, and who in the early part of President Roosevelt's administration was appointed a special attorney in the Department of Justice, has lost his Government position. The reason therefor has not been made known, but it is understood old age was the main cause of the dismissal.

Colonel Mosby is seventy-three years of age although his friends say he is still active and energetic. He has made no appeal to be restored, although this is deemed probable, and the President and the Attorney General may be asked to intervene. The Colonel, it is said, may now devote his time to writing a book on the civil war, in which he took an active and picturesque part.

When appointed a special attorney about eight years ago, he was assigned to break up the cattlemen's operations against Government lands in the Middle West, and he did other work of a similar sort. His fearlessness is said to have won the approval of President Roosevelt.

Something Behind It

Friends of Colonel Mosby in Richmond have an idea that there is some other reason than old age for the dismissal of Colonel Mosby. While they will not say so, it is plain that they are not altogether satisfied with the reputed reason. Colonel Mosby is seventy-three years of age, but his friends here and in Washington claim that he is still hale and hearty. It has not been very long, they point out, since he gained the approbation of President Roosevelt for his activity in certain cattlemen's operations in the West, and he had suffered nothing since that time.

But the order of dismissal was not unexpected by some of the closest of his friends here.

"I have not heard from Colonel Mosby for some time now," said Colonel Chapman, one of the boy members of Mosby's famous guerrillas, "but I knew that action taken yesterday was contemplated as long ago as last May. No; I do not know what was the cause of his dismissal."

When told that old age was assigned by some as the reason, the colonel looked dubious, but would not say that was not the real reason.

The *Times-Dispatch* wrote an article that was highly critical of Mosby's dismissal. The major problem with the story was that it tended to take for granted that Mosby actually was unable to fulfil his duties at the Department which, of course, was untrue. However, John Mosby never approved of those who sought to assist him by invoking sympathy and claims of "gratitude" for past services:

Times-Dispatch – July 9, 1910 (Edited)

TURNING MOSBY OUT.

Colonel John S. Mosby, the famous Confederate cavalry leader, has been dismissed from his service of the Government at Washington as special attorney in the Department of Justice. This is nothing short of an outrage and a specimen of the ingratitude of politics. We do not believe that Mr. Taft would stand for it a minute if he were fully informed of the facts in the case of this hard old fighter. Such a statement should be made to him directly for his consideration…

It was early in Roosevelt's administration that Colonel Mosby was appointed special attorney to break up the operation of the cattlemen on the Government lands in the West, and so vigorous was his pursuit of the trespassers that he commanded the admiration of the authorities at Washington. Now, that he is old and full of years, the services he has rendered to the country and to the Republican party with which he has been identified are forgotten, and he has been turned out to grass. It is an outrage. It shows how little Wickersham knows or cares for the past and the men who were a large part of the past. The Republican who would not be moved by the story of Mosby's fidelity to Grant, against the protests of his own people, against all his training and traditions must indeed be devoid of any sentiment of gratitude or high political responsibility. Half an hour's study of this case would impress Mr. Taft with the claim that this old Confederate has upon the good offices of the party in power.

Ah, but it was the *Chicago Tribune*, strange as that may seem—a past foe of Mosby's—that took the lead in clearing away the sentimentality and fictions in order to set the record straight:

Chicago Tribune – July 10, 1910

KNOWLEDGE OF INDIAN GRAFT COSTS COL. MOSBY HIS U.S. JOB.

Confederate Veteran Ousted by Department of Justice,

Possibly as Aftermath of Gore Corruption Charges.*

Washington, D.C., July 9 – (Special) – The friends of Col. John S. Mosby, the famous confederate guerrilla, find in his dismissal from the department of justice an echo of the Gore charges of corruption and bribery in connection with the Choctaw and Chickasaw Indians.

While it is asserted that the reason for Col. Mosby's dismissal was old age and general incompetency, it is stated on high authority that the bug under the chip is too much knowledge on the part of the colonel of the inside working of things with reference to Mansfield, McMurray and Cornish, the firm which formerly represented the Chocktaw and Chickasaw Indian nations.

This firm recently dissolved, but McMurray has continued its relations with the Indians and it was to prevent him from getting an enormous fee, approximately $3,000,000 that Senator Gore made public charges in the senate of corruption in the Indian affairs.

In May, 1905, Col. Mosby was ordered by the department of justice to proceed to Ardmore and assist the district attorney in the investigation and prosecution of certain persons charged with criminal irregularities in the office of the United States marshal for that district.

In the grand jury investigation certain statements were made reflecting on McMurray and his partners. It became evident that the grand jury would indict them on charges of defrauding the Indians.

At once the partners began using every influence within their power to prevent an indictment. It has since been learned that they had friends at Washington interceding for them so strenuously that Col. Mosby received a telegram from the department to "see that Mansfield, McMurray and Cornish get a square deal."

To this telegram Col. Mosby replied by wire, it is asserted, that if Mansfield, McMurray and Cornish got a square deal they would go to the penitentiary.

[*] The idea that Mosby had been released because he was unable to perform his duties were pretty much accepted publicly until there was an attempt to bribe a blind Senator from Oklahoma named Thomas P. Gore as they had tried to bribe Mosby. Senator Gore made the matter public and thereafter, Gore's name is mentioned in conjunction with Mosby's on this issue. Whether Mosby began to "hint" at attempts at bribery before the Gore matter came to light is not said at least in any press release available, but prior to Gore's expose, he had said nothing about the matter publicly. It should be remembered that Mosby had also made no claim regarding bribery attempts in Nebraska though at least the press was of the opinion that such efforts had been made – along with threats of bodily harm – when he first took up his efforts against illegal fencing.

Times-Dispatch – July 22, 1910

MAY HAVE OFFERED BRIBE TO MOSBY

Cavalry Leader Says he Could Have Retired Rich Had He Sided "With Them."

It is the belief of Richmond friends of Colonel John S. Mosby, the famous Confederate cavalry leader, recently dismissed by the United States

Department of Justice, that he may be a star witness in the congressional investigation of the charges made by United States Senator Gore, of Oklahoma, that a bribe of $50,000 had been offered him to vote for certain bills pending in Congress relative to the sale of Indian lands.

After the blind Senator's startling statements on the floor of the Senate, a committee was appointed in the dying hours of the last session of Congress to investigate the charges to bribe Senator Gore. The committee has been called to meet in Muskogee, Okla. On August 4. It was contended by Senator Gore that if the bills before Congress were passed hundreds of Indians would be defrauded of about $1,000,000 worth of lands.

Colonel Mosby was dismissed by the Department of Justice a short time ago. The reason given for his dismissal was that he had outlived his usefulness. Colonel Mosby and his friends take a different view of the matter.

Gives Real Reason.

In writing to a friend in Richmond yesterday Colonel Mosby said the "real reason" for his dismissal is because he "secured indictments against those trying to rob the Indians of their lands." He also said that he is surprised that some newspapers should claim that he lost his official position because of probing he did into the crookedness of cattle barons in the West eight years ago.

It seems probable that the old Confederate leader, as well as Senator Gore, was offered a bribe. In the letter to his friend he wrote this significant paragraph: "I have no doubt that I could have retired rich had I taken sides with them."

Colonel Mosby explains that he investigated the Indian land scandal and procured the evidence that resulted in several prominent persons in Oklahoma being indicted by the United States Grand Jury. It was while this case was pending that he received letters and telegrams from friends of the men under fire asking that they get justice. His reply was that if they got justice they would be in the penitentiary. His official head was whacked off in a very short time.

It appears inasmuch as Colonel Mosby played such an active part in obtaining the evidence that brought about the indictments of those who will figure in the investigation at Muskogee next month, he will be summoned by Senator Gore or members of the committee to substantiate the charges of fraud and attempted bribery.

Daily Ardmoreite – July 11, 1910 (Edited)

MOSBY WAS TOO ACTIVE IN PROBE

Famous Confederate Fell In Disfavor When Roosevelt Left Office.

Washington, July 10.—the intimate friends of Colonel John S. Mosby, the famous Confederate guerrilla, who was dismissed from the Department of Justice apparently because he did not stand with the present administration, are claiming that his summary dismissal is the outgrowth of the investigation of certain Indian contracts in Oklahoma which congress ordered to be prosecuted following the sensational charges made by Senator Gore of that state.

In fact, Colonel Mosby himself is encouraging this view of his retirement from the department of justice. Several years ago Colonel Mosby was detailed to investigate land frauds in the west, particularly in Nebraska. His report implicated in fraudulent acquisition of government land men of great prominence in public and business life.

It is a matter of common knowledge that Colonel Mosby never has been assigned to work of any character by his superiors since he made that report. President Roosevelt is understood to have backed Colonel Mosby in his investigation.

Colonel Mosby uncovered more evil-scented facts which would tend to cast suspicion on government officials. He has remained mum as concern these, but now that he has left the service he may feel free to tell what he knows.

The president has also fired Major John Carson, the veteran head of the bureau of manufacturers, department of commerce and labor. Carson, like Mosby, is a warm admirer of Roosevelt. The two were the last Roosevelt appointees left in positions of any importance. If that of Director Newell of the reclamation service is excepted, and Secretary Ballinger and the president have taken from Newell's hands almost the last vestige of power he possessed and ledged in the hands of army engineers and others.

Neither Carson nor Mosby were partisans when it came to the discharge of official duties.

Mosby by making reports showing up the connection of certain "big" men with land frauds, and Carson by publishing certain consular reports which unset the dearest theories of the "stand-patters," made them shining marks for the headman's ax.

Shenandoah Herald – July 15, 1910

Col. John Mosby's Dismissal Arouses ire of Virginians.

The Attorney General insists that Col. Mosby was requested to resign because he is too old. The people, however, believe that it was because he is too honest.

Dispatches from Washington state that the dismissal of Colonel John S. Mosby, of the Department of Justice, because of "age and inefficiency," has aroused the ire of Virginians at the national capital as nothing else in recent years has done.

A few days ago, Colonel Mosby, who has rendered valuable service in the Attorney General's department since President Roosevelt's first administration, was asked to resign, and his resignation went in at once. It was no surprise to him, for he knew that forces were at work to oust him from his office. All of Colonel Mosby's old civil war comrades and many other friends were astounded, however, when they read in the papers that he had been put out of office by scheming politicians.

Friends of Colonel Mosby in Washington say that the real causes of his dismissal was his attitude toward certain dealings between Government officials and the firm of attorneys, Mansfield, McMurray and Cornish, who formerly represented the Chocktaw and Chickasaw Indian nations. It is this firm that figured to the charges recently made in the Senate by Senator Gore, of Oklahoma, in which he charged an attempt at bribery.

Colonel Mosby made a full investigation of the Indian troubles and the efforts to take away their lands, and it is said that his report was held up for five years. After Senator Gore made his charges in the Senate recently, that attempts had been made to bribe him, the matter was reopened, and Col. Mosby is said to have received a telegram from friends of the lawyers involved in the Indian matter asked to see that they received justice, to which he replied: "If the parties you name receive justice, they will go to the penitentiary."

In a day or to the wires became hot between the lawyers and the politicians, with the result that Colonel Mosby was asked to resign for "the good of the service."

The Herald brought to light the infamous telegram that came not just from "friends of the lawyers," but from those friends serving within the Department of Justice; indeed, it came from Mosby's brother-in-law Russell who was conveniently in Persia and therefore could not answer embarrassing questions about the matter! Several of Mosby's biographers use his rather blunt response to Russell to prove that Mosby lacked "diplomacy" and that his behavior in Oklahoma was much as it had been in Nebraska, excusing his removal on that basis. But we know from the facts that much of Mosby's "prolixity" in Nebraska was bogus; that is, it was the result of press interviews that never took place! We also know that Mosby's removal from Nebraska had nothing to do with Mosby and everything to do with the upcoming presidential election of 1904. From Hong Kong to Nebraska to Oklahoma, John Mosby was persecuted by the very government he so ably and honestly served and, indeed, for that very reason.

Staunton Spectator & Vindicator – **July 15, 1910**

COL. MOSBY DISMISSED.

The dismissal of Col. John S. Mosby by the Taft administration, will not be a strengthening movement with it in the South. It is possible that Col. Mosby is old, that his efficiency is not as great as it once was, but the republican party got all that the prestige of such appointment gives, out of him, and now, like the old horse, he is turned on the commons to die. This is gratitude.

Col. Mosby is informed that he can now "write a book on the civil war." He will possibly say something about the civil service as he goes along, and may also not be very civil toward some persons now in high places. There is a little fight left in the Colonel yet, even though, at present he is only a civilian.

Many wonder whether Col. Mosby will surrender, or die fighting.

It was not in Mosby's nature to fight to retain a position if he were removed or about to be removed. He had refused to fight to keep the consulship at Hong Kong and forbade his friends to attempt to do so on his behalf. Perhaps, after all, Mosby was tired of trying to work for a government that seemed to reject an honest man's labors and that all he was doing was "kicking against the goads," the very thing his biographers assure us was his life's blood. Had that been so, each and every instance in which he was removed would have resulted in a ferocious fight on his part to retain or at least defend his situation. That never happened.

Mathews Journal – July 28, 1910

COL. J. S. MOSBY TALKS OF BRIBERY

The Real Cause Explained in a Letter of Old Confederate Leader to His Friends

Richmond, Va.—Special—On the day the dismissal of Colonel John S. Mosby from the Department of Justice, ostensibly on account of old age, The Journal printed a story to the effect that the friends of Colonel Mosby in Washington and in Richmond strongly suspected that ulterior motives were the real causes of his summary dismissal. Since that time stories that the charges of bribery brought by Senator Gore, of Oklahoma, in the matter of certain Indian lands, had something to do with the dismissal of the man who had secured indictments against parties in that State. In a letter to a friend in Richmond, Colonel Mosby states that he has no doubt he could have retired rich had he consented to take sides with "them." The "them referred to being those whom, as he said, he had secured indictments, "for trying to rob the Indians of their land."

Colonel Mosby will probably be summoned to Muskogee to testify against these same men, who will be investigated as the result of the charge brought against them by Senator Gore.

A Democratic paper summed the matter up nicely. Indeed, it was a shame that the Herald did not go back through Mosby's career in Republican administrations to discover that this was not the first time he was punished for being honest. It would have made a fine story as well as serving the paper's partisan interests, but alas, it turned out to be just another lost opportunity:

Shenandoah Herald – July 29, 1910

Colonel Mosby is deservedly unpopular with the Republican administration. He refused to accept a bribe of $50,000 to help defraud some poor Indians. There was, of course, under the circumstances nothing for Attorney-General Wickersham to do but remove him. He was manifestly out of sympathy with Wickersham's administration of the Department of Justice and, indeed, his offense bordered closely on insubordination.

A man like Mosby at large in the Department of Justice is as dangerous as a package of dynamite. The danger is that somebody might get justice, and this the Republican party is organized to prevent, unless the culprit is some poor, friendless sort of a thief.

We congratulate Wickersham upon the dismissal of Mosby. He and the Indian thieves can sleep soundly.—Winchester Star.

However, no coverage of anything "Mosby" would be complete without the usual comments by the *National Tribune*:

National Tribune– July 21, 1910 (Edited)
REMOVAL OF COLONEL MOSBY

While the newspapers pass without comment the separation from the public service of worthy Union soldiers who served their country well in the field and in civil employment, the press bureau, which has always been at the service of the ex-guerrilla Mosby, is filling the papers with complaints over his removal. This is exceedingly impolitic, as there are too many Union veterans alive who remember with horror and execration the deeds of the band of guerrillas Mosby led Col. Mosby's attempts to glorify himself and his men have gone beyond the point of all endurance, and the true history will come out which will be ruinous to their reputation.

Then began a spurt of stories about Mosby's situation after having been dismissed. Some were such as to make many believe that he was slowly starving to death while attempting to live on the pittance he earned from writing about the war. A particularly wretched description of the man and his circumstances was found in a *Washington Herald* story of June 24. This story was followed by one in which Mosby responded with humor and amazement to the Herald article:

Washington Herald – July 24, 1910
DISMISSED HERO WILL WRITE LIFE

Col. John Mosby Working on Memoirs of Civil War Lives in Poor Home

Famous Warrior Waxes Indignant Over Discharge

"I'm Not Superannuated," He Shouts, as Fire of Old Ranger Days Gleams in His Eyes—Guerrilla Leader is Tearful When He Recites the Story of His Service in Government Department.

Times-Dispatch – July 25, 1910
WARTIME HERO NOT LIVING IN PENURY

Colonel Mosby Indignant and Amused Over Absurd Story.

Declares It All A Fabrication

Jocularly Admits The He Makes His Own Coffee and Sleeps In One Bed, but He Is Not Reduced to Stage Where Copious Tears Are In Order.

(Special to The *Times-Dispatch*)

Several other stories carrying Mosby's denial of his state of poverty followed the *Times-Dispatch* article. But denial notwithstanding, Mosby was very hard up financially. In one of the articles, he made a small reference to his financial state: "My present condition is a part of the game—it's war, and I take it as such. I have been up against it during the war, and did not take it seriously to heart. I shall endeavor not to do so now."

Once again, the late Joseph Bryan's newspaper printed an article that, while not "newsworthy," was the type of tribute that Mosby having seen so much of his life's work criticized, condemned and rejected would have taken comfort in reading:

Times-Dispatch - July 26, 1910

Just what a high opinion Alabamians have of Col. John S. Mosby— and they know him—is shown in the following editorial article from the Montgomery Advertiser:

"Although Colonel John S. Mosby, of Virginia, became a Republican soon after the war closed, his motives have never been questioned, and his high personal and social standing never affected. He was of immense benefit to Virginia and Virginians because of his intimate relations with General Grant. He has held several important positions under the Government, and met every requirement with ability and fidelity. His duties at one time brought him to Montgomery, and all our people hold him in most affectionate regard. He has recently been deprived of the position he held, we believe in the Department of Justice, and while age is ostensibly given as the cause, there is very general belief that his fearless exposures of men caught in criminal acts had most to do with the desire to get rid of him. He knew too much for the personal comfort of some people high up in financial and other circles. We trust his lines for the future may fall in pleasant places."

That was a very nice thing to say, and it must be gratifying to Colonel Mosby to feel that the Alabama folk hold him in such regard.

But another article appeared at that time, a story that perhaps more than any other before or after seemed to understand John Mosby and what he had done and attempted to do. Interestingly enough, it appeared in a "Democratic" organ; but after finding the requisite fault with Republicans for their lack of understanding of the South, it condemned the present administration for its (mis)treatment of Mosby and acknowledged that his actions were based not on politics and still less on self-interest. In that acknowledgment, the writer used a word that is seldom used for any but the great saints and martyrs, the latter of which John Mosby can be considered in his efforts to help Virginia and the South; that word was sublime:

Clarke Courier – July 27, 1910

MOSBY'S DISMISSAL

Scattered here and there throughout the country we observe newspaper correspondents who from time to time announce with all solemnity that the one great aim, hope and ambition of the Republican President is to "break the Solid South," and the aforesaid correspondents tell, with great minuteness of detail, how the President's heart bleeds and his eyes weep brine when he sees the South clinging to its Democratic traditions in the face of all that he can do to lead it out of the darkness into the light— Republican light.

But there is no great mystery about the Solid South.

The South has been, is now, and will continue to be, solidly Democratic, so long as Republican Presidents from New York, Ohio and elsewhere inflict upon us such degradation as a black collector of customs at Charleston, a yellow postmistress in Mississippi, "imported" officeholders elsewhere, and lastly, the dismissal of Mosby.

The Republican party and the Republican President have done nothing to alley the fear and suspicion of the South; but they have done much to keep alive the spirit which insists that local people should have the greatest "say" in the choice of their office-holders.

Colonel Mosby's war record needs no praise from our pen; it stands upon the records of the very "History of the Rebellion" which Republican office-holders have compiled and Republican promoted warriors passed as true.

The years since '65 have not dimmed it; but it has grown brighter with each passing year, as the true facts and history of "the other side" became available.

But all of his soldierly bravery and dash were as nothing compared with the moral courage which was required of him to forsake the associations of youth and enlist beneath the Republican banner. He believed that was the best way to help the South, *but it took courage of a sublime kind to take the step.*[emphasis-vph]

After a record in the Department of Justice which is eclipsed by none, he is "set down and out."

Breaking the Solid South under such circumstances as these is the talk of fools.

"Wherever the body lies, there the eagles gather." John Mosby, though not dead was certainly stricken, and he now found that there were still "Yankees" out there who couldn't wait to defame his already-wounded reputation. The article below is printed in its entirety because such articles as appeared in earlier years—and after—have not been included in this book for space considerations. Yet this web of fable and falsehood was the standard "Northern" account of John Mosby's war service as reproduced countless times during and after the war:

Washington Herald – July 31, 1910

FLAYS COL. MOSBY

War Record of the "Dismissed Hero" Subject of Sarcasm Editor of the *Washington Herald*:

After reading the account of the "Dismissed Hero," as printed recently, I am led to suggest another article on this threadbare, overworked subject in the Washington press.

Take up the account of Mosby's murder of defenseless wounded and unarmed prisoners found in "Partisan Life with Mosby," by Scott. Give the real facts about the capture of the pay train which had one lone, unarmed soldier on it. Tell the truth about how Mosby's gang of robbers and murderers robbed citizens, and even women, on the train—a species of heroism equal to the highwaymen of Hounslow Heath, with this difference—those robbers of old never robbed women. Tell of the brutal hanging and shooting of the companions of Bennett, whose affidavit you will find uncontradicted in the Pension Office.

See if your reporter can get a flood of tears from the "dismissed hero," who has never found an apologist or defender among the real soldiers of the Confederacy, by the recollection of these crimes, rather than his failure to continue drawing a salary that he never earned.

A few real facts about this man, who has worked a press bureau for forty years to keep him on the payroll of the government would be more interesting than a lot of falsehoods that are known to be so by hundreds of your readers. You might also ask him why he and his gang of freebooters did not turn over the pay chest to the Confederate government as captured property.

The monotonous drivel about a "dismissed hero" is as ridiculous to the ex-Confederates as to the Union veterans. All knew his record. The ex-Confederates feel keenly the imposition. They know it will be exposed in time. Just ask for a subscription for the old "dismissed hero" and see how many dollars you will get from the soldiers of the Army of Northern Virginia who gave him his proper name, "Old Chicken Thief."

Washington, July 2

H.T. DURYEA

In one article about Mosby's dismissal, the writer's tongue was so far into his cheek as to make it somewhat difficult to discern exactly what he intended to convey. But after several attempts, it can be seen that he too believed that Mosby was removed because he wasn't "quick enough" to accept a good bribe and shut up:

Marble Hill Press – **August 4, 1910**

Fair Play – **August 6, 1910**

Makes Way for a Younger Man.

Col. John S. Mosby once the brilliant and daring leader of Mosby's Partisan Rangers, which played havoc with the wagon trains of the Army of the Potomac and had an unpleasant habit of going right into the Union camps at dead of night and carrying off the officers has lost his government job. Colonel Mosby makes no complaint. In fact, he has no foundation for one, although he has been a patriotic supporter of the Union ever since he laid own his command in the Confederate army, and a Republican in politics ever since he became an intimate friend of General Grant. He was consul at Hong Kong from 1878 to 1885, special agent of the general land office for Colorado from 1891 [1901!] to 1904 and assistant attorney of the Department of Justice since 1904. At the age of 73, although still hale and hearty, he is considered a little too old and perhaps a little too conservative for his job. With various knotty questions concerning the rights of land grabbers, and opposition of the conservationists, with the friar lands scandal [*], resulting from the sale, contrary to law, of the best lands to agents of the sugar trust in 50,000 acre lots, and at about one tenth the price the government paid for them, the Department of Justice needs younger men who are lively of foot, nimble of wit and a good punch in either hand. We could not expect Colonel Mosby to execute all the quick shifts, sidesteps and ducks that the pending cases would seem to require. [* See "Addendum" at the end of the chapter.]

And still, the articles about Mosby's removal for being "too honest" continued. It was probably for the best that brother-in-law Russell was basking in the brilliant sun of "Persia," or he might not have taken kindly to so many of both political parties taking up the cudgels for his wife's obnoxious brother:

Tacoma Times – **August 1, 1910 (Edited)**
IN THE PUBLIC EYE

The recent dismissal of Col. John S. Mosby, the famous southern cavalry leader of the civil war, for his position of attorney in the department of justice at Washington, removes from public life one of the most picturesque figures of that war.

Col. Mosby made many powerful enemies in the employ of the government. Among them were wealthy cattle barons of the west who were defrauding both the government and the settlers out of millions of acres of land. Secretary Wickersham, now on his way to Alaska, denies that this had anything to do with Col. Mosby's dismissal.

Wickersham was right. It was not the Nebraska and Wyoming land frauds that caused John Mosby to be dismissed from the Department of Justice, but the Oklahoma Indian frauds and Mosby's move to indict those responsible—a politically powerful law firm.

Another paper then took up the cudgels for John Mosby. Sadly for the Department of Justice, the connection between the chicanery in Oklahoma and Mosby's rock-solid integrity made the true reason for his removal too obvious for all but the willfully blind to see:

Clinch Valley News – **August 5, 1910**
COL. MOSBY "TOO STRAIGHT"

The merciless treatment of Col. Jno. S. Mosby, the famous old Confederate Guerrilla, by the Department of Justice in Washington when he was recently kicked out of the public service for prosecuting land thieves in Oklahoma, is one of the crying shames of the present administration, and is receiving just condemnation of fair-minded men everywhere.

The story of the sudden dismissal of Col. Mosby from the position he had filled so ably for a number of years, is almost harrowing in its details, for it betrays not only the "yellow streak" of base ingratitude down the back of the Republican party, but it reveals as well, the protection, under the very dome of the national capitol, of land pirates, vampires and human leeches, who are merciless robbing the poor, unsuspecting Indians on the western plains of the little property they have been able to accumulate.

According to reports sent out from Washington, Col. Mosby was assigned to look after some of these cases, and after going into them he found a firm of influential land attorneys criminally involved.

He had these lawyers indicted, but they at once started to work on the Department of Justice, by the "underground system," invoking political "influence" and "pull" to keep them from behind bars.

"See that Mansfield, McMurray and Cornish get a square deal," was the language of a telegram sent Col. Mosby from the Department, after the "leaven had worked," to which the old Confederate hero promptly replied that if the members of the firm got a "square deal," they would go to the penitentiary. This was the "straw that broke the camel's back." Col. Mosby was too willing to do his duty, and to require thieves and grafters to answer for their crimes before the Bar of Justice, and so this grand old man, known and loved for his honesty and matchless courage throughout the country, was cruelly beheaded and kicked out of office in order to protect men who had been adjudged guilty by a grand jury of the Federal courts.

Col. Mosby has been a prominent and consistent Republican leader ever since the story days when he was engaged in electrifying the civilized world with his dash and brilliancy as a Confederate leader, and yet his head "went into the basket" with as little ceremony as though he had been a $50 clerk, disobeying orders from a Bureau chief, when he showed a dogged determination to do his duty as he saw it.

In a letter to a friend in Richmond, Col. Mosby says: "I have no doubt I could have retired rich had I taken sides with them," which clearly indicates that a move was on foot to offer him a bribe to stand with the crooks he was seeking to convict.

But this is one of the Republican ways of doing things, and as that party is defiantly "standing pat" with reference to all its deeds and misdeeds, the matter will probably end where it is, shameful as it may appear in all its details to the public.

But Mosby's distressing situation after his dismissal was not yet a matter of disinterest in the nation. Indeed, concern for him actually found expression outside of the South as this article in the *Times-Dispatch* indicated:

Times-Dispatch – **August 11, 1910 (Edited)**
TAKE CARE OF MOSBY

Sympathy for Colonel Mosby in his deposition from the Department of Justice has leaped over sectional boundaries to find expression all over the nation. No words of commendation for the action of Attorney General Wickersham in releasing the famous cavalry leader and able lawyer from the service of the Government has been heard. With poor grace came from the lips of Mr. Wickersham his fulsome praise of General Lee and the South in the Lee Statue decision, when but a month before he ordered out of his own Department a man who is said to have received from General Lee "more compliments and commendations than any other officer in the Confederate army." Not only that, but Colonel Mosby has long been a Republican, was the friend of Grant and of Hayes, and has served the Government well and faithfully...

"The removal from office of Colonel Mosby on account of age by the Government, although he is still vigorous, was a cruel enactment. Any man with a war record such as Colonel Mosby's is deserving of admiration and all the assistance a great Government can afford. Now is the time for some man of wealth who admires grit, bravery, daring and loftiness of purpose to show his appreciation of these qualities by providing a home in which perhaps the bravest veteran of the Rebellion may spend the few remaining years of his life in plenty, peace and comfort."

There is a breadth of view in this letter that we like, but we do not think that Colonel Mosby is to be considered for one moment as an object for private charity...

The truth of the matter is that the Government that he has served with the vigor and the fidelity that is in him—and who can measure the greatness of those qualities in Mosby?—ought to provide for him in some way. There are plenty of offices vacant which he could fill with ability. He is along in years, that is true, but we venture to say that there is more of fire and earnestness and strength in him now than there is in many men twenty years young who are in the Government service. There are many Union veterans older than he still in positions of trust and responsibility under the Government. Mosby is as able as any of them, far abler we believe than most of them, and we respectfully submit that he is just as much entitled to consideration as any one of them. ...

Mosby deserves well at the hands of the Government to which he has given faithful service. North, South, East and West, his dismissal has been deplored, and we feel sure that his reinstatement in the Federal service would meet with national approval.

The writer identified as "J.A.K" in the New York Herald wrote of granting some sort of financial relief to Mosby unless the "bloody shirt" were still being waived:

"unless we are still waving the bloody shirt after forty-five years it appears to me that something ought to be done to relieve the necessities of perhaps the most picturesque figure of the Civil War—Colonel Mosby, of guerrilla fame."

J.A.K. was proper in his concern for what was a sort of "national treasure," though, of course, not everyone saw John Mosby in that light, but Mosby would not have permitted such efforts though he would have appreciated the sentiments expressed.

Suddenly, reports appeared from the British press or, more correctly, reports on reports from the British press:

Times-Dispatch - **September 2, 1910**

The English papers have lately been full of complimentary references to Colonel John S. Mosby, who was recently removed from office by Wickersham. The English people do these things better than we. Contrast the reconstruction of South Africa with the reconstruction of the Southern States of this country. Mosby is honored everywhere by brave men.

Alexandria Gazette – September 2, 1910
WANTS DATA FROM COL. MOSBY.

The following communication from a London publishing house has been received by Col. John S. Mosby. Col. Mosby is now with his brother at Bedford City and will return to Washington about the 15th:

To Colonel John S. Mosby, Washington, D.C.

My Dear Sir: I am writing for a leading publishing house (Messrs Nelson & Sons) a book on famous guerilla leaders, and I am writing this letter to ask if you will be so kind as to favor me with a signed photograph of yourself and some facts of your career as a leader in the southern states army. I am aware that I shall find the facts about yourself in the history books, but you can if you will, send me some personal facts of great interest. If it is in the form of printed matter, this, of course, will be all the better for my purpose. Any way, if you are so kind as to oblige me, I shall feel very grateful. I am dear sir,

Yours faithfully,

Percy Cross Standing.

P.S. The English papers have lately been full of complimentary references to yourself.

In September, a letter from Mosby was published in the *Times-Dispatch* and also commented upon in other publications, giving some detail regarding the matter that had precipitated his dismissal:

Times-Dispatch - September 8, 1910
WHY MOSBY WAS DISMISSED

There is nothing "superannuated" in Colonel John S. Mosby's use of the English language in his letter to Leroy Sweetser, of Boston, in which he writes of his dismissal from the Department of Justice. He was dismissed on the ground that he is superannuated, or, at least, he has heard that was the excuse made for his removal. He thinks, however, that this was a mere pretext, that "the real reason was to punish me for having three scoundrels indicted for robbing the Indians, and my opposing their application, which was finally successful, to get the prosecution dismissed. They had arranged another $3,000,000 steal, and wanted me out of the Department. Senator Gore near the close of the session exposed it in a speech in the Senate."

The only fault Colonel Mosby has to find with Mr. Taft and Mr. Wickersham is "that they condemn me without a hearing on the word of an Assistant Attorney-General who is not now in the Department; who represented that I was superannuated. He had to do that to justify himself for giving me no work. The true reason was that he was an active partisan of those criminals who wanted to punish me as well as to get me out of the way for another steal."

Colonel Mosby claims that all his faculties, mental and physical, are in as good condition now as they were thirty years ago, and there is certainly nothing that indicates decrepitude in the way he writes about the cause of his dismissal. His case should have the immediate attention of the President. He is a just man and would doubtless, upon a careful review of this case that Colonel Mosby, who was the friend of Grant at the sacrifice of the friendship of many of his own people, has been outrageously treated, to the disadvantage of the public service and the injury of one of the bravest of the brave.

But for all of his apparent acceptance of the situation, John Mosby could not quite let it go. It is probable that the injustice of the whole thing, that is, that the minor crooks he had pursued in Nebraska, and the major criminals he had set his sights upon in Oklahoma were all going to get away with their wrongdoings. Such a conclusion to all of his good work must have frustrated and angered him. Of course, the stockmen were eventually brought to justice, but they were insignificant compared with the lawyers and power brokers in Oklahoma! However, there was no doubt that John Mosby was feeling a little bit sorry for himself. But he was an old man; and despite his excellent mental facilities, the "pitiless storm" to which he referred was only the last of many he had endured in his long, hard life, so perhaps he should not be scolded for this momentary act of self-indulgence:

Mt. Sterling Advocate – September 14, 1910

Col. Mosby Writes on His Dismissal.

"Turned out like Lear to bide the pelting of the pitiless storm," is the way Col. John S. Mosby, the famous Confederate cavalry leader, describes his dismissal by President Taft's Attorney General. Col. Mosby was appointed to a position in the Department of Justice by Col. Roosevelt and thrown out last month by the Taft administration. Col. Mosby has written to a friend in Baltimore about the matter. He says he was fired because a report made to the department by him prevented the robbery of Indians in the West, all of which was exposed by Senator Gore in his speech near the close of the session.

Los Angeles Herald – September 19, 1910
COL. MOSBY'S CASE

In a letter to a Boston friend explaining why he is no longer connected with the department of justice at Washington, Colonel John S. Mosby, whose free-lance cavalry was one of the most picturesque and thrilling incidents of the Confederate side of the civil war, says:

"The real reason was to punish me for having three scoundrels indicted for robbing the Indians, my opposing their application, which was finally successful, to get their prosecution dismissed. They had arranged for another $3,000,000 steal and wanted me out of the department."

Colonel Mosby says that his only complaint is that he was dismissed as superannuated without a hearing, on the word of an assistant attorney general no longer in the department, who had to justify himself in giving Colonel Mosby no work, and this he did by representing the Virginian as superannuated.

There is abundant reason to be found in recent revelations in Oklahoma for believing that the lawyers who were gouging the Indians had strong influence in Washington. There is therefore that much circumstantial probability that the story told by Colonel Mosby is partly, if not wholly true. It is a case, anyway, that calls for the attention of President Taft and for reparation if it is found true that the old soldier's dismissal was due to the fact that he opposed the Indian graft.

In October, Mosby received an invitation to lecture at Yale. It was the sort of thing that he loved doing because he saw it as a means of healing the old wounds of the war that still persisted. Yet, despite his financial situation, one paper reported: "At New Haven ... he lectured ... for the benefit of Rev. J. C. Collins' "Friend for Boys Work" ..." Below are a few of the many, many stories about the lecture tour, the last such tour that John Mosby ever gave:

Times-Dispatch – October 17, 1910 (Edited)

COL. MOSBY WILL LECTURE AT YALE

Noted Confederate Cavalry Officer to Tell War-Time Experiences.

(Special to the *Times-Dispatch*.)

Washington, D. C., October 16.—Col. John S. Mosby has accepted an invitation to lecturing during the month of December at Yale university. The subject, it is understood, will be "Recollections of the Civil War." Colonel Mosby, in speaking of the lecture, said:

"I think my visit will do something toward healing the wounds of the war." In speaking of Colonel Mosby, the Morning Courier, of New Haven, says: "He has fought a corrupt gang of officials in the American consular service in far-off Asia and purged the consulates of their corruption from Vladivostok to Aden. And in later years he has warred so fiercely upon the cattle barons of the West that even his superior officers at Washington had to repeatedly caution him about needlessly exposing his life to their vengeance. Between whiles he has written military works, read Byron, Tom Moore and the Greek tragedies and played with his grandchildren."

Shenandoah Herald – October 21, 1910

Col. John S. Mosby, will deliver a series of twelve lectures in the principal cities of New England, telling his experiences in the civil war. Except for one or two lectures delivered twenty years ago, Col. Mosby has never appeared upon the lecture platform. It is learned that he will receive $200 for each of his lectures, and that after the course is completed in New England it maybe extended to the middle and middle western states.

Mosby was presented in the article below as an object lesson to officials who promise decent government and honesty. It appeared that the word was being quickly and widely spread that John Mosby had not been dismissed for "superannuation" after all:

Lexington Gazette – October 26, 1910

Alexandria Gazette: Collector Loeb, of New York, says he is going after the millionaires who buy smuggled works of art; but will he? Anyway, he'd better be careful, or "business interests" may soon discover that he is a "public enemy," as was Col. Mosby when he interfered with the cattle barons in the west who were grabbing public lands. Then he was removed at the insistence of the "interests".

In November, Mosby reached his Northern destination, and the press took great interest in this reverse invasion:

Norwich Bulletin – November 11, 1910

To Welcome Mosby

The Southern club of Yale university, whose members are from all parts of the south, have extended to Col. John S. Mosby, the famous Confederate cavalry leader, an invitation to meet the members of the club informally at the time of his visit to New Haven and lecture on December 6th. Colonel Mosby has written the club, accepting the invitation. The committee to receive Colonel Mosby are Catesby L. Jones, 1911, S., H. S. Irons, 1911 academic, C. R. Wood, 1911 law. The reception by the southern men in Yale to their distinguished fellow-southerner will be given at the university club on the evening of December 5. It is looked forward to as one of the most events in the history of the club.—New England Palladium.

It would seem that younger Southerners were not necessarily against the apostate Mosby for his actions after the war. Time perhaps did heal some wounds at least. Grant's son General Frederick Grant had been invited to attend when Mosby was feted in New Haven, but his duties prevented. The *Times-Dispatch* printed his gracious response:

Times-Dispatch – November 21, 1910

GRANT'S COMPLIMENT TO COLONEL MOSBY

(Special to the *Times-Dispatch*.)

Washington, D. C., November 20.—Colonel John S. Mosby, who is soon to go North on a lecturing trip, is meeting with many kind words from the men of that section who were his foes in the bitter days of the Civil War. Discussing this matter the Army and Navy Register says to-day:

"A dispatch from New Haven, Conn. says: 'In declining an invitation to attend the reception to be given in this city to Colonel Mosby on December 6, General Frederick D. Grant wrote to the local committee as follows: "I send my greatest thanks to you and your committee for your kind invitation, which I fully hoped and expected to accept, but because of pressing duties I find, unexpectedly, that it will be impossible for me to do so, much as I would have enjoyed being with you on December 6 during that pleasant occasion of your reception. I should also have considered it an especial pleasure to honor and meet Colonel Mosby, and to have paid my respects to him, whom I have always so much admired. Colonel Mosby was one of the most distinguished and gallant officers who was on the side opposed to my own dear father, General U. S. Grant, during the great Civil War; but he was a brave and splendid opponent, and after the terrible strife was over Colonel Mosby accepted the situation and was one of the first to help bring about that harmony between the North and the South which now so happily exists. I feel for Colonel Mosby as did my father, warmest friendship and admiration. With my highest regards to Colonel Mosby and yourself, and my repeated regrets to you and your committee that it is impossible for me to be with you December 6, believe me. Sincerely yours, Frederick D. Grant."

The local press was reporting upon Mosby's coming and reminding its readers that, at one time, his name "struck terror" in the people of the North; but apparently, they expected more amicable relations this time around:

Bridgeport Evening Farmer – **November 30, 1910**

CONFEDERATE LEADER COMING

Colonel John S. Mosby, whose name struck terror to the North during the Civil War, will come to Bridgeport at Jackson's Theatre on December 7 for the purpose of lecturing. Mosby was the leader of the Confederate cavalry which made such daring and successful raids on the Union territory. A committee comprising F. W. Bolande, Frank Miller, Dr. G. L. Porter, Judge A. B. Beers and G. C. Waldo is arranging for his reception here.

Washington Herald – **December 2, 1910 (Edited)**

Alexandria Gazette, – **December 3, 1910**

COL. MOSBY THE HERO.

Famous Confederate Leader to Be Given Reception in New Haven. From the New Haven Journal-Courier

Connecticut's reception to Col. John S. Mosby bids fair to be one of the most memorable events in the remarkable career of this most distinguished of living Confederate leaders. Some of the most prominent citizens in the State are making active preparations to receive him with great cordiality and are making every effort to impress him with a sense of northern hospitality. In New Haven, Col. Mosby will also be greeted Monday evening, December 5, the night before his reception and lecture in the grand Opera House, by the 150 Southern students in Yale, who will tender him a reception at the University Club.[New Haven Journal-Courier.

Mosby gave an interview in which he was far more gracious than President Taft had any right to expect from a man to whom Taft paid no attention after he had been summarily—and humiliatingly—dismissed. This was typical of Mosby. He was too big a man to be petty.

And while he was "up North," Mosby's birthday was yet again remembered—and not just in the South:

Topeka State Journal – **December 5, 1910 (Edited)**

Deseret Evening News – **December 5, 1910**

Evening Standard – **December 5, 1910**

ARE PROUD OF TAFT

Colonel Mosby says the Southerners Admire the President

"Just look at the reception of the people at Richmond gave Taft when he visited them. No other Republican president ever got such a fine send off in the South. The people below Mason and Dixon's line are very proud of him. Of course, that may not mean that they will vote for him in 1912. You never can tell how a Southerner will vote by the way he talks. The South has never got over its dislike for Republicanism. It votes for Democracy by force of habit but generally prays for a Republican president.

Now the local coverage of Mosby in New England began in earnest. This "love fest" with the Yankee press must finally put to rest any claim that John Mosby created his own legend using the newspapers. Whatever can be said for the fourth estate, those in it were not stupid. If Mosby was a self-creation and he had used the press for that purpose, that fact could not have been unknown to its members. Certainly, after having been so "used," their treatment of the man would have reflected that situation. Nothing in the press coverage of John Mosby, with the exception of those publications that despised him for his "guerrilla" tactics, indicated that such a great fraud had taken place under their auspices and with their assistance:

Calumet News – December 6, 1910

Palestine Daily Herald – December 6, 1910

Wenatchee Daily World – December 6, 1910

Vermont Watchman – December 8, 1910

Tribute to Colonel Mosby (Herald Special.)

New Haven, Conn. Dec. 6.—Colonel John S. Mosby, the famous Confederate scout and cavalry leader, received an enthusiastic welcome upon his arrival in New Haven today to attend a public reception arranged in his honor. The occasion is the seventy-seventh birthday anniversary of Colonel Mosby, who was born in Virginia, December 6, 1833.

The Farmer – December 6, 1910 (Edited)

Bridgeport Evening Farmer – December 6, 1910

Cordial Reception Planned for Mosby

Connecticut's reception to Col. John S. Mosby bids fair to be one of the most memorable events in the remarkable career of this most distinguished of living Confederate officers. Col. Mosby will lecture tomorrow evening at Jackson theatre. Active preparations are being made by some of the most prominent residents of the city to receive him with cordiality and to impress him with the sincerity of Northern hospitality. Among this number are many members of the Grand Army, who were pitted against Col. Mosby in the four years' battles.

Mosby's "speech" would state his belief that the loss of the opportunity to destroy Pope's army and possibly end the war in 1862 was the result of the disobedience of then Colonel Fitzhugh Lee and General Robert Toombs, a "political" officer. Mosby was right. General Robert E. Lee never had such a chance again:

Times-Dispatch – December 7, 1910
CAUSE OF SURRENDER

Colonel Mosby Attributes It to Disobeying of Orders.

New Haven, Conn., December 6.—In an address here to-night, Colonel John S. Mosby, the Confederate cavalry leader, gave many reminiscences of the Civil War, and stated that in his opinion the downfall of General Lee was due to the disobeying of orders by Generals Fitzhugh Lee and Toombs. Their disobedience, he said, caused the surrender of Lee and the Confederate army. During Colonel Mosby's stay here he has been entertained by the students of Yale university, whose homes are in the South.

Alexandria Gazette – December 7, 1910
COL. MOSBY ACCUSES LEADERS.

In his address, which followed a reception at the Grand Opera House in New Haven, Conn., last night, Col. John S. Mosby, the former Confederate cavalry leader, made the statement that the disobedience of Gens. Robert Toombs, of Georgia and Fitzhugh Lee, a nephew of General Lee, saved the Union army under General Pope not only from defeat, but destruction.

Colonel Mosby was discussing the strategy of Gen. Robert E. Lee in his campaign against General Pope.

The fact that these generals disobeyed orders Colonel Mosby said, had never been made public, and it caused comment among the military men present. Other interesting facts not published in the histories regarding incidents of the war were told—how it was that McClellan was forced to abandon his position on the James River and start another campaign on the Potomac, and how, by accident, the plan of raising a partisan corps to operate on General Pope's rear was defeated and postponed for eight months.

Yesterday was Colonel Mosby's seventy-seventh birthday.

Mosby's lecture was hampered by a severe snowstorm that kept the numbers, but not the enthusiasm, of his audience down:

The Farmer – December 8, 1910 (Edited)
CHEERS FOR COL. MOSBY, FAMOUS REBEL LEADER

But Audience That Heard His Lecture Was Much Smaller Than He and the Occasion Deserved

Greeted by an audience which numbered less than 100 souls, Colonel John Singleton Mosby, the last of the distinguished leaders of the Southern troops, delivered a highly interesting and enlightening lecture at Jackson's Theatre, last evening. Evidently those who regard history and the men who made it were not warmly enthused over the presence of Col. Mosby, whose name was on every tongue during the four years' war. But what the house lacked in numbers it made up in appreciation. The old soldier was warmly greeted and his remarks often applauded. One would never believe that Col. Mosby had celebrated his 77th birthday Tuesday, Dec. 6. He is firm and erect, though he suffered many hardships.

Seated on the flag-bedecked stage with Col. Mosby were Dr. G. L. Porter, who introduced him; David F. Read, A. M. Cooper and Judge A. Beers.

The lecture was replete with anecdotes and historical allusions, and showed the historical and as well the military genius of the speaker. "My old school reader," he said, "taught me that a rebel is the noblest of men. In those days I read Gen. Israel Putnam and his men escape from the redcoats. I've had more and narrower escapes than Putnam." He said, "I've had everything from negro babies to Southern dogs named after me."

The lecture closed with three rousing cheers given to the veteran leader.

Gold Leaf – December 15, 1910 (Edited)
COLONEL JOHN S. MOSBY

Famous Confederate Cavalry Fighter on Lecture Tour in Connecticut—

Is Paid High Honors by Former Foes in War Time and Other Citizens Who Greet Him as Friend and Brother.

Col. John S. Mosby the Confederate cavalry fighter whose daring exploits and dashing deeds made him famous during the Civil War, has been on a lecture tour in Connecticut speaking at several points. At New Haven, where he lectured on the 5th inst. for the benefit of Rev. J. C. Collins' "Friend for Boys Work," the old warrior met with a warm reception and was accorded many courtesies. Among those who heard Col. Mosby's lecture and had the pleasure of meeting and shaking hands with him afterward was our young friend Mr. Clifton Bullock. In a personal letter enclosing a couple of newspaper clippings Mr. Bullock says: "I heard the grand old man speak and afterwards had the honor of shaking hands with him. I told him I was from North Carolina and had always read about him and had always wanted to shake his hand. This seemed to please him—whether the statement that I was from North Carolina, or that I was delighted to meet him, I don't know." Preceding the lecture Col. Mosby was interviewed by a reporter of the New Haven Times-Register, from which the following is taken:

A true Southern gentleman of the old school is Col. John S. Mosby of Virginia, who is visiting New Haven today for the first time. And in fact, it is the Colonel's first visit to Connecticut. One would almost know he was a Southerner at the first glance, the atmosphere of the South is in his appearance, and nobody but a Southerner was ever known to enter a room with the bearing such as is Col. Mosby's.

And the broad brimmed black felt hat which he carried in his hand was of the style as is always worn by a gentleman of the South, and worn by them in a manner, which in spite of imitation, has never been and never will be accurately acquired by the Northerners.

Col. Mosby is a most interesting old gentleman, and while his greatest interest is perhaps in the affairs of the South, where he lived and fought, and where he still has his home, he is nevertheless interested in the places and people of the North. It is like reading in history of the Civil War to listen to Colonel Mosby. His reminiscences are as accurate as a historian's records, and every detail of a number of engagements, which were referred to, were given by the Colonel without hesitation. When asked if he was going to speak entirely of his experiences during the war this evening, he smiled as he replied, "Yes, that is all I am supposed to know anything about." [*]

Col. Mosby holds the interest of his hearers for any length of time he is willing to talk. He is interested in all matters of public importance and is well posted. His career has been a varied one and he has traveled extensively.

An interesting feature of this evening's meeting will be the presence of Captain Carey of Hartford, who nearly captured Col. Mosby during the war. "It was in Virginia," as Col. Mosby tells it, "and Captain Carey got my knapsack he came so near capturing me. In that knapsack there was a letter from General James Stuart recommending me for promotion. Carey kept the letter but let me go. Later he gave the letter to the National Museum in Washington, where it is at the present time. I have a photograph of that letter and I am going to ask Captain Carey to read it to the audience this evening at the theatre. Captain Carey never saw me but once in his life and at that time he was trying to shoot my head off. I suppose I saw him but all I was thinking of was getting away, is it might be said that I never saw him. I am looking forward with considerable pleasure to meeting him to-night as a friend."

The New Haven Register of the 6th in speaking of Col. Mosby's lecture said this:

The worst stage of the snowstorm did not prevent a large audience well representative of the people of New Haven who regard history and highly honor the men who made it from gathering at the Grand Opera House last evening to hear Col. John S. Mosby, the famous Southern cavalry leader whose name was on every mouth in the four years of the Civil War, give a most interesting chapter out of his experience. They saw a man whom his 77 years-his 77th birthday was yesterday—have not bowed. Whose strenuous life has not abated its fire, whose real Virginia heartiness is as rich as ever, give a lecture live with interest, replete with humor and beautiful in literary charm. It covered only one chapter of the great cavalry leader's great book of experience, only one summer of his four years of war activity, bit it was an excellent choice… and at the close of the lecture Judge Studley thanked Colonel Mosby and proposed a rising vote of thanks. This was followed by three rousing cheers, and singing by Mr. Harry Treat Beers closed the program.

[*] Nothing more demonstrates Mosby's mental acuity than this remark; that is, that the sum of his knowledge was limited to the Civil War. Apparently, that belief was contemporary to his time as well as having been carried forward down to today. How many of today's Mosby "biographers" and "experts" have declared that the man knew little or nothing, (aside from his repository of classical and literary knowledge), but

the war. Obviously, Mosby was well aware that he was so defined in his own time and he probably would not have been very surprised to see the matter continued into the modern era.

Alexandria Gazette – December 17, 1910
COLONEL MOSBY'S VISIT.

Col. John S. Mosby's visit to Waterbury is an event of more than ordinary interest and importance. It is probably the last time the people of this city will have of hearing and seeing this famous Confederate cavalry leader as this was his first trip into Connecticut and he is not planning another tour of the state in the near future.

Col. Mosby is one of the last of the really great fighters of the civil war. There are still many men with splendid war records but the brilliant leaders of the rebellion have nearly all passed on and Col. Mosby is probably more widely known than any other living leader of the Union or Confederate forces. He has been accorded an ovation in every city he has visited in Connecticut. While he is most loyal to the south yet he delights in the fact that he has lived to see a united people.

While in Hartford a few days ago he was presented with an American flag. The presentation took place after one of his lectures while he was still on the platform and being greeted by many from the audience. The flag was wrapped around him and it was one of the proud moments of his life as he stood there, a true and loyal American citizen, beneath the folds of the stars and stripes. One country and one flag is his motto now and always will be. And this grand old man is spending the last day of his brilliant career in a most useful manner. He has turned his talents from warfare to working to aid friendless boys. Certainly no man of his age could turn part of his attention to many more worthy causes. His war reminiscences are so interesting that it is a pleasure to hear him speak. Waterbury was glad to see Col. Mosby and hopes that his life may be prolonged so that he may yet come here again.—

[Waterbury, Connecticut Republican, December 15.]

One can only hope that the demonstration in the hall as they wrapped him in the American flag gave John Mosby some consolation for his lengthy travails.

Below is the best and most fitting story ending a year of rejection and rebuff and illustrating the true nature of a man who even today, after years of scrutiny and analysis, remains seriously misjudged. This short article by an unnamed journalist captured not just the events of that moment in Mosby's life, but also the nature and meaning of that life. Oddly enough, the newspaper was neither of the North nor the South—but the West:

Arizona Republican - December 27, 1910
Mosby's Northern Greeting.

"I hope," said Col. Mosby in conversation in the afternoon before his lecture, "not to say anything that will offend anybody." He did not say anything which offended the most sensitive of hearers, says the New Haven Register. His lecture was keyed accurately to the southern view point, yet it did not jar on northern ears. And therein is the value of his visit. It has demonstrated anew that we are getting together at last.

Those who attended the lecture at the grand opera house last evening saw a grand knight of the south, retaining still, with all his 77 years, no little of the fire and spirit of the days when he was a dashing cavalry leader in gray, whom every northern soldier feared for what he might do and respected for what he had done. He is a man well worth seeing and well worth hearing, and New Haven is the better for the touch. The heartiness with which the audience swarmed to the stage last night for opportunity to grasp the hand of the man who did all that angels could do to smash the northern cause in the days of '61 shows how the bitterness of those days has been buried and how eager all are to get together now. Among the hearers were not a few of the men who wore the blue in those early days of the war when Mosby was at his worst. They honored him then, little as they might have loved him. They both honor and love him now. Still more do they honor and love that south whose splendid spirit he represents, and to whose understanding his visit to the north is contributing.

We do begin to understand each other, north and south. Every day and every year increases the light and softens whatever hardness may remain. Many thanks to Col. Mosby, best of soldiers and trust of patriots, for so ably fulfilling a mission in which he may rejoice.

John Mosby—the "bull in the china shop," the man who talked too much and lacked diplomacy and discretion and who insulted young men and old—was concerned about "offending" his audience! Although he represented the "southern viewpoint" (which was understandable!), he still offended no one. Yet Mosby's biographers state to a man that he became more abrasive, bad-tempered, and difficult as he became older! Really? Could it be that it wasn't Mosby's age that was the problem, but his audience? Could it be that John Mosby, who never suffered fools and knaves gladly, found himself surrounded while he worked for the government with people who brought out the very qualities complained of? On the other hand, when he moved among decent, honest people, he was sensitive, gentle and inoffensive? These commentaries seem to provide a contemporary view of Mosby that many who wrote—and write—about him have apparently overlooked.

And so it was that John Mosby, now without position or income, went forth from what had been a momentous year. He was down, but not out; castigated, but sustained; destitute, yet optimistic. And it could be that he finally understood the reality regarding the ethics of those who inhabited the corridors of power in government *whatever* their party labels. In it, he may have recalled the Greek philosopher Aesop who wrote in his cautionary tale *The Woodsman and the Serpent*, "Expect no gratitude from the wicked."

Chapter 50

1911

Ad augusta per angusta ~ To high places by narrow roads

"For in itself a thought, a slumbering thought, is capable of years, and curdles a long life into one hour." ~ Lord Byron

AS 1911 OPENED, press coverage of Mosby's "Northern conquest" remained robust which is interesting given the nature of the matter being covered. Mosby was no longer what should have been considered a "high profile" subject for the press. He wasn't a politician nor was he associated with the government any more. His "doings" were personal and hardly of monumental importance, yet he continued to receive, as in the past, heavy press coverage:

Times-Dispatch – January 8, 1911 (Edited)

COL. MOSBY AS LECTURER LIKED IN CONNECTICUT

Introduced by the President's Brother—Modest as to His Own Achievements—How He and Stuart Were Almost Captured

[From the *Waterbury American*.]

Colonel John S. Mosby, one of the last surviving conspicuous figures of the Civil War, delivered his lecture on certain phases of that conflict before an audience of moderate proportions in the Buckingham last evening. Colonel Mosby was introduced by Principal Horace W. Taft, of the Taft School, and was escorted to the platform by a body of representative citizens, including several members of the G.A.R.

The Colonel, who is now 77, read his lecture from typewritten manuscript. His style of address was something like that of the old-time lawyer, and his voice was full and strong. Particularly was this noticeable when at the close of his formal remarks he abandoned his manuscript to declare that he was not here to say *"Morituri saluramus,"* and that he hoped to visit New England again.

Colonel Mosby described at great length Lee's attempt to crush Pope, which was spoiled by Fitz Lee and Toombs, and he related some dashing exploits of Stuart, but he didn't tell much—certainly not enough—of those thrilling times when he and his Hellions were raiding rough shod over Virginia, bagging Yankee paymasters, capturing the First Rhode Island Cavalry, which was engaged in the task of capturing them, and driving Phil Sheridan into raging profanity. He didn't tell of the time when he rode up to Long Bridge, handed a lock of his hair to a woman who was crossing and requested that she give it to Abe Lincoln and "tell him I'll be in after some of his about day after tomorrow." *Perhaps no living American has had a more adventurous past. It is to be regretted that the Colonel modesty keeps him from its full relation.*[emphasis vph]

But it was interesting to see Colonel Mosby and to hear of great flights from the lips of a famous fighting man. He was warmly welcomed, warmly applauded, when he concluded, and he will be warmly received if he again visits this city.

This article demonstrates, in my opinion, why there is a need for this book. Many who have written about Mosby declare that he was "a legend" only because he had created that legend. But any man who engages in such an undertaking is, of necessity, an egotist who cannot resist trumpeting his own achievements. There are many such men—and women— throughout history down to today. These people will not allow the hearer (or the reader) to miss their greatness and they will make that greatness known at every opportunity. It is obvious from this account of Mosby's lecture that the audience would have reveled in such a man—that they wanted to hear him recount all of his splendid victories, his hairbreadth escapes and the results of his genius. Indeed, they had come for that very purpose. But John Mosby had not come to talk about himself save with a few minor accounts necessary to make the point for which he had come. And though what he said about the great opportunity for victory that had been squandered, for his audience, that truth was far less interesting than would have been an evening's recital of the great deeds of Mosby's men—and of John Mosby himself.

For a man who had just been thrown out of office for the most insulting of reasons and cast into poverty, the opportunity to regain the luster of his reputation must have been hard to resist—or was it? It is not that John Mosby was immune from either shame or pride. Indeed, he had said that he preferred service in the West, where his poverty was less galling than it was when he served in the South. As for the opposite, at one time Mosby had written that any man who did not need praise "was either too good or too bad for this world." Yet when the opportunity came for him in his old age to glory in his well-deserved reputation, he foreswore doing so in order to bring out the facts of history he considered more important than enhancing his own prestige and image. How different the *real* John Mosby from the man often presented to us today.

Evening Standard – **January 16, 1911 (Edited)**

COL. MOSBY TO LECTURE.

Col. John S. Mosby, the famous Confederate cavalry leader, now 77 years old, is about to deliver a course of lectures in various northern cities, telling about his experiences in the civil war. Notwithstanding "Mosby's men" were the terror of Yankee soldiers, Col. Mosby has come to be much honored in the north.

Mosby never missed an opportunity to praise General Grant, a custom that he followed in *The Times* on Valentine's Day:

Washington Times – **February 14, 1911**

Wartime Foe Pays Tribute To the Courtesy of Grant

"In spite of the parole that I had taken, after I had settled down to practice law," says Col. John S. Mosby in Munsey's Magazine, "I was several times arrested by provost marshals stationed at the courthouses where I went on the circuit. This was both annoying and unfair. My parole was a contract with the Government that was binding on both parties. To arrest me before I had violated it was a breach of it.

"As my wife passed through Washington on her way to Baltimore, she determined to go to the White House, not to ask for a pardon, but to make a complaint. She had not intimated her purpose to me. Her father and President Johnson had served in Congress together, and had been friends; so she told Johnson whose daughter and whose wife she was. Instead of responding kindly, he was rude to her.

"She left him and went to see General Grant at the War Department. He treated her as courteously as if she had been the wife of a Union soldier, and then wrote a letter, which he gave to her. He did not dictate the letter to a clerk; the whole is in his handwriting. It gave me liberty to travel anywhere unmolested as long as I observed my parole. I preserve that letter, framed, among my most precious possessions."

Marion Daily Mirror – **March 4, 1911**

GEN. MOSBY'S HIGH REGARD

For General Grant Founded on the Humane Spirit Manifested By That Great Warrior

Gave Mosby The Same Terms He Did General R. E. Lee

On Account of Frequent Arrests Mosby Was Given a Letter Protecting Him. Grant Always Spoke in the Friendliest Terms of His Old Army Comrade Who Went With the South Firm in Hayes—Tilden Controversy.

Despite being out of a job, anything "Mosby" remained of interest to the press, and so this little item appeared. It was of especial interest for at least two reasons: First, it involved a Union, not a Confederate soldier. Second, the soldier was both poor and black. No financial gain would obtain from any action Mosby took, and neither would he obtain the good report of most Southerners. Indeed, he probably could not expect any such good report from many in the GAR either!

Washington Herald – **March 17, 1911**

COL. MOSBY AIDS IN GETTING PENSION

Gets Back Pay for Destitute Colored Veteran.

New Haven, March 16.—By the aid of Col. John S. Mosby, the Confederate cavalry officer, William A. Porter, negro of this city, has just received back pension amounting to about $600. Porter was in very destitute circumstances.

He went to the war in a Connecticut regiment. He had been drawing a small pension for a number of years, when, without any apparent cause, his name was dropped from the rolls. Efforts had been made to get him restored to the pension list after that, but all record of his enlistment seemed to have been lost. Affidavits were sent to the Pension Office in Washington showing Porter's war record. Finally Col. Mosby was appealed to, and he started an investigation. It was discovered that by a clerical error Porter's name in the regimental roster had been changed to Parker, the "o" in Porter being made an "a" and the "t" altered so that it looked like "k."

Col. Mosby showed to the pension officials in Washington the error, and had Porter's name placed back on the pension list.

Washington Times – March 17, 1911

Colonel Mosby Helps Negro to Get Pension

New Haven, Conn., March 17.—A small fortune of $600, in back pension allowances, has been received by William A. Porter, a negro, through the aid of Col. John S. Mosby, Confederate cavalry officer. Porter's name had been dropped from the pension rolls through a clerical error, changing his name to Parker. He was unable to obtain reinstatement until Colonel Mosby took an interest in his case, and discovered the cause of his trouble.

Evening Star – March 17, 1911

MOSBY WINS CONTEST

Succeeds in Establishing Pension Claim for Colored Union Veteran.

New Haven, Conn., March 17.—Col. John S. Mosby, the Confederate cavalry officer, has won his fight to secure the restoration to the honor rolls of the Union Army and the pension rights of William Porter, a colored civil war veteran.

Several years ago Porter's application for a pension was refused because the regimental records registered him as William Parker, although several of his comrades testified that he was the man who performed the military service.

When Col. Mosby lectured here two months ago, he learned of Porter's case and was interested in it. He immediately took it up with the pension department, and Porter has just received word that his application has been granted through Col. Mosby's efforts. He is very infirm from age and disease and his arrears of pension will insure comfort for his remaining years.

This small matter testifies to the greatness of the man's spirit. After all, why should John Mosby care about any Union soldier, much less a black man who fought against the South? Furthermore, it was not his business to correct the errors committed by government. He had worked at doing so when he was actually employed in that capacity, and the thanks he received for those efforts should have dampened any enthusiasm he might have felt in that regard. But for Mosby, it was a matter of justice. The man had served. Testimony had been given that he was the man who had served. He had received a pension that had suddenly been terminated without explanation. There was a problem, and Mosby had both the ability and the time to investigate the matter. He did, and it was corrected. A small matter no doubt, but of such are the proofs of a man's character.

By now, Mosby had indeed begun to speak mainly about the war because as one of the last surviving "celebrities" on either side, that was what people wanted to hear from him. No doubt, he opined to his friends and others on the affairs of the day, but the interest shown him in general was of a historical nature. This little article is indicative of the situation extant:

Clinch Valley News – June 2, 1911
TALKED WITH COL. MOSBY.

Geo. W. Doak returned last Saturday from his recreation trip feeling much benefitted

Mr. Doak had the pleasure of his life in meeting Col. John S. Mosby, the distinguished Confederate soldier, in a Washington hotel, and enjoyed a long conversation with him, hearing from his own lips many stirring incidents of the war. Upon the whole Mr. Doak had a great time.

Stories about Mosby continued to appear in the press whether or not they might be considered "newsworthy." The following is an excellent example of this sort of gentle personal coverage:

The Sun – August 19, 1911
THRILLS FOR COL. MOSBY.

Famous Confederate Leader Rides in an Auto and Visits a Battleship.

Norfolk, Va., August 18—Col. John S. Mosby to-day had his first automobile ride and walked the decks of a battleship for the first time.

He got a big reception from the sailors on the Louisiana. When he left the ship he was saluted by 500 blue jackets.

"My, I am glad I'm off that boat," said Col. Mosby, "because while I was on her I couldn't help thinking of the Maine, and that if an explosion occurred while I was on the Louisiana they would say right away, 'Mosby did it.'"

After paying his respects to Admiral Reynolds, commanding the naval station, Col. Mosby and party found an automobile waiting to take them to Norfolk.

"I won't go in that thing." Col. Mosby told his friends. "I have always been afraid and I don't want to ride in one.' Despite the persuasion of those in his party Col. Mosby refused to ride in the automobile. They were taken to Garretts Winery, where the Colonel rested for an hour. When he was ready to start again another automobile was waiting. Again the Colonel refused to ride, but after much persuasion he decided to take a chance.

"If you fellows can stand it, I can," he shouted and jumped into the machine. He took a five mile ride in the country and when he returned said automobiles were not as bad as he thought they were.

He left this afternoon for Ocean City, Md., to visit his daughter.

Mosby's movements continued to be reported in the press for no other reason, of course, than that he was John Mosby:

Washington Times – August 20, 1911
MOSBY AT THE GRAVES OF LEE AND JACKSON

There was a touching reunion the other day in the Valley of the Shenandoah, when Col. John S. Mosby made a pious pilgrimage to the graves of Jackson and Lee. The three had met many times in life, in the course of that stirring struggle which has lent an enduring fame to so many names. This was a reunion of the living with the dead. Each had played, indeed, a conspicuous part in the great conflict. The beau sabre, the knight without fear or reproach, who was commander in chief of the Confederate forces has bequeathed to posterity a character which even his foes admire. The great strategist who left the academic shades of the Virginia Military Institute to become the daring Rupert of many a desperate charge, and the "Stonewall" against which the Federal forces beat in vain at Manassas has won the unqualified praise of the world's military authorities.

And the man who made this pilgrimage in his declining years to the consecrated spot on which they both are buried was himself the thunderbolt of war. The very name of Mosby and his Rangers spread terror through the ranks of the enemy riding through the night and penetrating the impenetrable places, striking when and where he was least expected, and away before the dawn, eluding and perusing, he made the enemy all but superstitious of his uncanny skill.

Those were trying years they spent together, those three. The tragic day when Jackson fell, mortally wounded from the fire of his own men, and "passed over the river to rest under the shade of the trees." In the fullness of time the quiet career to which Lee had dedicated the remnant of his days at the great Virginia University which now links his own name with that of Washington, came to an end peacefully as became a Christian soldier.

Many years have passed, but during all that time the great guerrilla leader had not until recently stood at the graves of those he had known so well in life. His affairs had taken him around the world. He had served his country in China and on the Pacific coast. The chances and changes of time have brought him back to the scenes of those earlier struggles in which he and his comrades found distinction, and at last he seeks out the final resting place of the brightest ornaments of the Confederacy. It was a tender and touching tribute from one who is himself worthy of the highest praise.

This article was a very fine tribute to all three men and it must have pleased Mosby to see himself included with men of the caliber of heroes like Lee and Jackson. But the praise afforded by the newspapers to Mosby demonstrated the fact that to most of them, he was worthy of that praise. Had Mosby used the press to create his "legend" somebody in the fourth estate would have reported the matter especially any of those publications for whom he was still anathema.

Mosby's birthday again appeared in print, an event that continued until there were no more birthdays:

Washington Herald – December 7, 1911 (Edited)

COL. MOSBY AT 78 STILL FEELS YOUNG.

Veteran Eats Turkey Dinner at Daughter's Home.

A large turkey, the gift of one of his men, "Bob" Shacklett, of Fauquier

County, Va., provided a birthday dinner last night for Colonel John Singleton Mosby, who was seventy-eight years old yesterday, and his daughter, Mr. Stuart Coleman, and her two children, at their home, 1212 Twelfth street northwest.

"I don't feel any older to-day," said Col. Mosby, when seen last night, "than thirty years ago. This day forty-seven years ago I took dinner with Gen. Robert E. Lee at his headquarters, near Petersburg, Va., only about three months before the close of the war."

After the war, Col. Mosby opened a law office at Warrenton, Va., and became a member of the Republican party, which he thought could most satisfactorily settle the reconstruction question. He has since occupied a number of important offices in the government service and is now engaged in writing his memoirs.

Never let it be said that newspapers don't, can't, or won't say something of seminal importance and interest. In this very short piece aimed only at the recognition of one of the few remaining "heroes" of the great war, in less than twenty words, it summed up not only the "what" of John Mosby's postwar politics, but, more importantly, the "why," which was something that despite all of Mosby's efforts to explain, just never seemed to be understood or if understood, accepted. The writer stated that after the war, "Mosby ... became a member of the Republican party, which he thought could most satisfactorily settle the reconstruction question." And that was the whole thing in a nutshell. Amazing!

Evening Star – **December 7, 1911**

COL. MOSBY'S BIRTHDAY

Noted Confederate Raider Is "Seventy-Eight Years Young."

1911 had been a fairly easy year for the old soldier. There were family matters that were brewing well hidden from the press, but his public persona was, on the whole, no longer being subjected to a drumbeat of negative reports. He continued to be as active as a man his age had any right to expect given all of his underlying physical problems and those natural afflictions that strike all people who have reached nearly four score years. But John Mosby knew that time was passing him, and his era, by. The world was changing at a rate unheard of in all of the eras of the past. Indeed, it had changed more during his lifetime than it had changed for his father's father and his father's father before him. Many of those who write of him in this period tend to dismiss him as an old man who refused to "move on." Of course, this is absurd. To begin with, Mosby knew and understood the changing times, but he also knew that at his age he had no need to "move on" to keep up with them. He had assessed the military value of the airplane and the automobile in the press and had abandoned the saber as antiquated long before many trained soldiers. In the same way, he would have abandoned the horse. But given his age and situation, he did not have to dwell on those matters, and so he did not.

Several years ago, there was an article on Mosby's relationship with his closest friend, Fountain Beattie when both were old men. The author's source was Beattie's son. According to the son, his father was interested in the airplane, but "Colonel Mosby was not." Neither was this a simple recitation of fact. Rather, the author used this comparison to disparage Mosby. Beattie was still "engaged" in the matters of the day while Mosby had retreated into the past, and one must assume, his dotage. But, of course, the comparison—as with so many such comparisons made about John Mosby and others—was false. It is true that Mosby had no interest in the airplane or the automobile for that matter, but that did not mean that he was senile. The two men's divergent interests were not an "age" issue or an "intellect" issue, but an "interest" issue. The archeologist and paleontologist concern themselves with the distant—and even very distant—past. The historian may have no interest in an era in which such inventions obtain but prefers the Middle Ages or even Antiquity. Does that mean that such scholars are feeble-minded? Of course not. It simply means that their interests lie elsewhere. John Mosby never reached a time in his life at which he had no interest in anything but the past as testified to by the physicians at his bedside when he died. That he chose in his old age to dwell more on the things he enjoyed at eighty-two is both understandable and pardonable. He should not be adjudged inferior for what was his right as a rational man; that is, to give his remaining attentions and affections to those matters that were important to him.

But it must be remembered that John Mosby had "moved on" when and where it counted most: at the end of the Civil War. He did not, as did so many in the South, continue to reside in the world as it existed in the 1850s and 1860s. He accepted "the arbitrament of the sword" and worked, to great personal disadvantage, to move beyond the war and to bring his state and his people into the postbellum era. His success, or lack thereof, cannot be attributed to any lack of zeal or effort, much less interest on his part.

Chapter 51

1912

Fac fortia et patere. ~ Do brave deeds and endure.

"Sweet are the uses of adversity." ~ William Shakespeare

1912 BEGAN POORLY. Another attack of his ongoing abdominal problems put Mosby under the knife once again. This article, carried in several newspapers, made rather clear that there was still a great deal of dislike for the man despite all the positive press that had come his way in the previous few years. However, such "bad press" now was usually limited to nasty innuendos and comic insults. But for a man of Mosby's age, there was nothing "comic" about going under the knife. However, for every negative report, there were others more benign in their coverage of the old warrior's trials:

Dakota Farmers' Leader – **January 26, 1912 (Edited)**

Celina Democrat – **February 2, 1912**

Alamagordo News – **February 29, 1912**

NOTED GUERRILLA SURVIVES THE KNIFE

Washington.—Col. John S. Mosby, known some years ago to the good people of the north as a guerrilla, and occasionally as something worse, a men who, it is said, went about his raiding with a price on his head, lives in Washington today and goes about its streets sturdily, with his head up, his eye bright and his falcon nose as warlike in expression—for noses have expression—as it was in the days of civil strife.

Two years ago Colonel Mosby was taken to a hospital to be operated on for appendicitis. The surgeons told him that he probably could not pull through. "I'll pull through," he said, and he did. Recently he has been writing stories about his civil war career, taking up the pen just after stepping off the lecture platform.

Last winter the old ranger went into Connecticut to speak in a village which, during the Civil war days, had been the scene of a meeting called to execrate Mosby's method of warfare. The Union veterans turned out to meet the former Confederate, and gave him a somewhat warmer reception than their comrades had been able to give him at any time during his raiding career.

At this point, Mosby responded in print with a lengthy story of his own on the Valley campaign. Such articles added to his miniscule income:

Washington Post – **February 18, 1912**

Evening Times – **February 22, 1912**

With Mosby in Sheridan's Rear

Col. John S. Mosby in the New York Evening Post.

More and more publications sought "history" from the man who had actually lived it, and on May 30, a lengthy article by Mosby appeared in the Leslie's Weekly:

Leslie's Weekly – May 30, 1912

A Famous Confederate's Thrilling Adventure

By Colonel John S. Mosby, One of the Most Noted Surviving Figures of the American Civil War.

In July, Mosby returned to Bristol, the town in which he and Pauline lived after their marriage and from which he went into the Confederate cavalry. Apparently, as he was marching off to war (a not–very-impressive soldier by all accounts!), a young woman of prominent family in the town swore to bestow upon him a kiss when he returned if he "distinguished himself." Very few men on either side of that or any other war "distinguished" themselves as did John Singleton Mosby! Upon his return to Bristol, he found the lady and gently attempted to collect his prize. The event received some little press coverage:

Washington Times – July 31, 1912

PROMISED KISS TO COLONEL MOSBY IS DENIED WHEN ASKED.

Gallant Confederate Cavalryman Lingered Too Long From Home.

Bristol, Va., July 31.—Col. John S. Mosby, the noted Confederate guerrilla warrior, is a visitor in Bristol this week for the first time since he left here to enter the civil war. Colonel Mosby, incidentally, came back to hold a prominent Bristol woman to a promise she made him when he entered the civil war.

Colonel Mosby lived in Bristol and practiced law here until the outbreak of the civil war. This is the first visit here in fifty-one years.

Colonel Mosby called upon Mrs. Wirt-Johnson Carrington to remind her of a promise she made him when he left Bristol to enter the war in behalf of the South. She was then a beautiful young girl and she told the young recruit that if he should distinguish himself in the army that upon his return she would give him a kiss.

After the war he did not return to Bristol. This week he met Mrs. Carrington for the first time since before the war and reminded her of the promise. She remembered it, too.

He Came Too Late.

"You told me that if I should distinguish myself that when I returned you would give me a kiss," said Colonel Mosby. "Now, I don't exactly ask for the kiss, unless you feel that I did distinguish myself in the army, and am, therefore entitled to it."

Mrs. Carrington readily agreed that the Colonel distinguished himself, but she maintained that he had slept on his right, and that the statute of limitations barred his claim to a kiss.

"Hello, Bill," was the way the grizzled guerrilla warrior greeted Mayor William L. Rice, the veteran chief executive of Bristol, Va., whom he had not seen since he left Bristol for the war.

Finds Same Mayor.

"Bristol has not changed in one respect. It has the same mayor it had when I left here."

Sure enough, it has. Mayor Rice was the first mayor of the city, and was in office when Colonel Mosby left to enter the Confederate army as a private.

Colonel Mosby is here to meet his comrades and most of them he has recognized instantly. He is the guest of Col. Sam L. King, a wealthy Bristolian, whose father was his personal friend and neighbor.

The Star – August 6, 1912

Fort Wayne Sentinel – September 3, 1912

Waits 50 Years for a Kiss

Colonel Mosby, of Civil War, Reminds Woman of Promise.

Bristol, Va., Sept. 3. – Col. John S. Mosby, the noted confederate guerrilla, came here just to hold Mrs. Wirt J. Carrington to a promise she made him fifty years ago, that if he distinguished himself in the war she would kiss him when he returned. Mosby had never returned to Bristol until this visit. Mrs. Carrington told him that statute of limitations barred the promised kiss.

Alas, here was another example of sectional pettiness. This woman promised a mere kiss if Mosby "distinguished himself" in the war, but his postwar "apostasy" prevented even this small kindness truly owed him. Yet when he was in the North, young girls—not old ladies—were happy to bestow upon him affectionate kisses. It also proved that Mosby was hardly in his dotage as he recognized people he had not seen since 1861!

Several other stories appeared in October, one in which Mosby claimed that he didn't need a barometer by virtue of the bullets that he still carried in his body. Actually, he only carried one, but that was in his left groin and so was sure to be felt under changing meteorological conditions. Another interview was carried in the *Washington Herald* and involved Mosby being, in the paper's words, "retrospective":

Washington Times – October 15, 1912

Col. Mosby's Barometer

"I don't need a barometer to tell me when there's going to be a change in the weather; the Yankees turned me into one for the rest of my life, some fifty years ago," remarked Col. John S. Mosby, the Confederate cavalry leader, with a smile, the other day when the gathering clouds portended a rainy spell. "How? Why they landed several bullets in me during the parlous days of the '60s, and, while most of them were cut out, a couple lodged where the surgeons of that time declared it would be fatal to disturb them.

So there they've remained for half a century. They never bother me in good weather, but, when there's going to be a change to a rainy spell, they commence to ache—generally about twenty-four hours before the change.

"So, you see, I made something out of it, anyhow—saved me the expense of a barometer," concluded the colonel, with a chuckle over his little joke.

Washington Herald - October 27, 1912 (Edited)

Colonel Mosby Talks Of War Time Days Hale and Erect at Seventy-nine Years of Age, Old Confederate, Styled a Guerrilla, Becomes Retrospective.

Bristol, Tenn., Oct. 26. Marching In triumphant old age back across the scenes of strife and carnage which laid waste many of Virginia's fair possessions of nearly half a century ago, silencing forever many of the heroes of the Northern and Southern armies. Col. John Singleton Mosby, persistently and erroneously styled a guerrilla, told to old comrades and neighbors in this city what, to his mind, was the hardest battle he ever fought. With his head and shoulders erect, carrying still that poise of the distinguished warrior that he was, this striking figure of the Virginia campaign related to ante-bellum friends and neighbors here many of the thrilling incidents of his life from 1861 until the surrender at Appomattox in 1865.

"Of the many conflicts," he said with a show of feeling, "in which I was engaged in that great war which tried men's souls, none, to my mind and heart, was so hard as that on the day in 1861 when I kissed my devoted wife and my darling little baby good-by and marched away to fight for the Southland. The rest of my experiences, covering four years of service and sacrifice, were easy compared with that of the taking leave of my family. I never expected to live to get back home. I was not afraid of death, but the thought that I might never again see my family or be of direct service to them was the one crushing sentiment which raged in my heart. I was overpowered for the time, but blindly marched on in response to the call to arms."

Now, in his seventy-ninth year, naturally his great mind is clear upon incidents and events of half a century ago, and it was somewhat confusing to many of the residents here, being almost entirely of a new generation, when he made inquiry of this or that man or woman, whom he knew here prior to the civil war.

While here Col. Mosby visited the old home on North Moore Street, in which he and his family lived prior to the Civil War. He was much gratified to find that the family now occupying the house was posted as to his war achievements and took special pride in the fact that they were living in the house that was once occupied by this famous warrior.

Col. Mosby is undoubtedly one of the most unique figures of the civil war, and when finally the impartial history of that world-renowned struggle is written, this man will stand out as one of the most distinguished men of the times – to the civil war what Francis Marlon was to the Revolution.

However, 1912 went out as inauspiciously as it had begun with yet another bout of illness necessitating surgery. This was the second surgery of the year and the third in the last five years. Mosby's general health was good, but such physical strains to the body were problematic even for a much younger man:

San Francisco Call – October 27, 1912
GENERAL MOSBY MUST UNDERGO AN OPERATION

Confederate Veteran Sufferer from Kidney Trouble

Pensacola Journal – October 28, 1912
*Daily Ardmore*ite – October 28, 1912
COL. JOHN MOSBY CRITICALLY ILL

Friends Fear Advanced Age Will Militate Against the Famous Veteran.

Times-Dispatch – October 29, 1912
COLONEL MOSBY BETTER

Condition Improves Slightly, but Friends Fear Outcome.

Washington, October 23.—The condition of Colonel John S. Mosby, who is in a hospital here suffering from kidney trouble, was slightly improved to-night. Colonel Mosby is said to be in no immediate danger from the disease, but his friends are alarmed on account of his advanced age.

Washington Times – November 3, 1912
Col. John S. Mosby Is Out of Danger.

Col. John S. Mosby, who has been ill for the past three weeks in Garfield Hospital, is now pronounced out of danger. Dr. Hagner, who has attended him, stated last night that all necessity for the operation that was contemplated has passed, and that within a short while Colonel Mosby would be out.

Although Colonel Mosby is no longer a young man, his constitution is such that his physicians and his friends have no fear that he will not regain strength. He is seventy-nine years old.

Washington Times – November 6, 1912
Col. Mosby Quits Sick Bed to Cast His Vote

Rising from a sick bed in Garfield Hospital, Col. John S. Mosby, with a spirit as indomitable as when he headed Mosby's guerrillas in the civil war, went to Virginia to cast his ballot yesterday.

His trip seemed to improve his condition after his ten days' siege in the hospital. Colonel Mosby went against the wishes of his physicians, but the old soldier could not be denied the satisfaction of exercising his suffrage.

The *Washington Herald* had a laudatory article including a very lengthy recounting of Mosby's service during and after the war (omitted here). But the headline tells it all:

Washington Herald – November 24, 1912

Col. John S. Mosby Again Victorious in Hard Battle with the Great Enemy. Survives Operation.

Noted Confederate Leader Who Defied Death for Four Years During Civil War Recovers from Illness

Guerrilla Chieftain undergoes Operation Successfully and Will Be Able to Leave Hospital in Near Future.

An article in the *Washington Times* combined mention of Mosby's birthday with news of his recovery:

Washington Times – December 6, 1912

Colonel Mosby spent today at Garfield Hospital, Tenth street and Florida avenue, where he was taken about five weeks ago for an operation. Yesterday afternoon he was taken for a short automobile ride and had dinner with his daughter here, the event thus providing a celebration for his birthday anniversary. At the hospital, it is reported that the colonel, in spite of his advanced years, is feeling well and is recovering rapidly from the effects of the operation.

He has received many inquiries concerning his condition and is being well attended by his friends and members of his family.

Many times the colonel faced a ruthless death in naked violence, and he showed another mark of his remarkable versatility in recovering from the most insidious attack of slowly advancing disease. It is believed that he will fully recover from an operation that removed the cause of the sickness.

Often Near Death.

Colonel Mosby not only escaped with his life after the surrender, but was appointed to office by the Government he sought so valiantly to destroy. In peace he became almost as great a character as in war, and won a place in the nation and in the minds of his countrymen that wiped out the horrible tales told of him in war-time.

Bismarck Daily Tribune – December 6, 1912

79th BIRTHDAY OF COL. MOSBY

Washington, Dec. 6.—Slowly recovering from a severe illness, Col. John S. Mosby, the famous Southern cavalry leader of the Civil war, today quietly celebrated the birthday anniversary which leaves him only one year short of the mark of fourscore years. Born at Edgemont, Va., Dec. 6, 1833, coll. Mosby was practicing law at Bristol when the war began. He was one of the first to enlist in the Confederate army, and with the exception of a short time when he was disabled by a wound, he served continuously until Lee's surrender, when he disbanded his famous troop and gave himself up and upon the recommendation of General Grant was released on parole.

As if with his last serious illness, the press felt the chill of the approaching separation that would remove Mosby the guerrilla, Mosby the raider, Mosby the famous Confederate cavalry leader—John Singleton Mosby—forever from their presence, for any reason or none, stories suddenly appeared in the press:

Times-Dispatch – **December 15, 1912 (Edited)**

THE FAMOUS HEAD OF A FAMOUS BAND

John Singleton Mosby, Cavalry Leader, Confederate States Army

By. P. H. McGowan

Washington, November 3.—Walking down Pennsylvania Avenue or elsewhere in Washington, should you have chanced to observe a tall, keen-eyed, gray-haired man, wearing a typical Southern wool hat with a red handkerchief around his neck and a rough mountain cane grasped firmly in his hand, you needed not to stop to ask of a nearby policeman or handy newsboy who he was, though should you have asked you would have been told: "That's Colonel Mosby, sir, the man who fought the Yankees in the war—lives right around the corner on Twelfth Street. Pretty straight for an old man, eh?"

That's who Colonel Mosby—John Singleton Mosby—the famous cavalry leader and all-round dare-devil in the War Between the Sections, now lying ill in a Washington hospital.

Almost as straight as an Indian, despite his seventy-eight years, with a single eye that could look through you at a glance, and a fund of ready information marking him as a man well versed in the game of life, John Singleton Mosby is indeed, an interesting, if eccentric character long after he has passed the threescore year and ten milestone.

Interesting Career.

There are few careers which in intensity of interest can equal that of the game old fighter, now traveling toward the land of perpetual peace.

While his life has been full and his career well rounded in every particular, it is with the stirring days of the war that he is most intimately known. Mosby's command—or Mosby's men—were the dread of all the Federal forces in Northern Virginia and Maryland. His an independent cavalry command, played mighty havoc with the opposing lines during the days from 61- to 65, when the green Virginia fields ran red with the blood of the best Southern and Northern manhood. Many was the Federal cavalry outpost and supply train which this band of fearless daredevils captured while Lee, Grant and the other great generals of the War Between the Sections were planning and maneuvering here and there to strike a blow to the opposing forces.

Let Records Speak.

In recent years Col. Mosby has become very reticent and only with his most intimate friends will he discuss the issues of the "lost cause" or the daring escapes from the enemy's lines or his own capture of Federal troops. He prefers to let the records of history speak for themselves and he is satisfied with what he has done. Until a year or two ago he would not consent to discuss publicly any of the incidents of his career but he received a flattering offer to go North and tell of his exploits. Such a proposition could hardly be rejected and he went into the enemy's country and related some of the scenes and incidents of the days of the war.

Stories that Col. Mosby has been in a starving condition are untrue. He has a son and a daughter in this city—John S. Mosby, Jr., a well known newspaper writer, and Mrs. Stuart Coleman—the latter named for "Jeb" Stuart—who are ministering to his wants and rendering every known attention.—Columbia State.

Washington Times – **December 21, 1912**

Col. John S. Mosby has recovered sufficiently from his recent illness to leave the hospital, and he is now at his home at the Alamo apartment.

And so another year had come to an end. It had been a physically trying time of illness and pain, but as usual, Mosby had gotten through it and prepared himself for the coming new year. His life had formed a pattern of social gatherings and involvement with a still very much interested press corps. But his health was becoming ever more fragile, and he was keenly aware that more and more of his friends were crossing that Great River. And although he seldom spoke of death, he could not have been unmindful of its inevitability—and its proximity.

Chapter 52

1913

Faber est suae quisque fortunae.
~ Every man is the artisan of his own fortune.

"The only real battle in life is between hanging on and letting go." ~ Shannon Alder

1913 AGAIN SAW another of Mosby's reports on the genius of his friend and mentor "Jeb" Stuart, whom he never ceased to defend and magnify at every opportunity:

Times-Dispatch – **March 24, 1913**

STUART CHANGED USES OF CAVALRY.

Colonel Mosby Tells His Personal Recollections of Confederate Leader.

General J. E. B. Stuart brought about a revolution in the use of cavalry and adapted it to modern conditions of war, according to Colonel John S. Mosby, who writes his personal recollection of Stuart in the April Munsey's. "He was the first," writes Colonel Mosby, "to see that in modern warfare the chief function of the cavalry should be preliminary to the battle, and that mounted charges of cavalry against infantry are, or should be, ancient history."

Many reminiscences of the famous cavalry leader are given by Colonel Mosby. He tells of his first personal meeting on the Rapidan with Stuart, who said: "General Jackson wants to know if this is McClellan's army, or only a detachment." Colonel Mosby' replied that he would find out if he could get a guide. "Here is one," replied General Stuart. The man's name, adds Colonel Mosby, was Mort Weaver, who died recently in the Soldier's Home in Richmond.

Colonel Mosby was practicing law in Bristol, Va., when the war began. He had been there two years. The town was brand new, and he was its first lawyer. "I have always," he says, "claimed the credit of discovering it."

Missed Great Chance.

He thinks that the premature movement of A. P. Hill's Corps to the Potomac on June 24, 1863, defeated a plan of Stuart's to break up Hooker's communications and isolate Washington. "This," says Colonel Mosby, "would have been the most brilliant achievement in war since Bonaparte came down on the rear of the Austrians in the valley of the Po." No event of the war, he adds, has been so much misrepresented as this.

His article concludes with a part of a letter written by John Esten Cooke, the author:

"On a summer morning a solitary man was seen beside the grave of Stuart, in Hollywood Cemetery, in Richmond. The dew was on the grass; the birds sang overhead The green hillock at the man's feet was all that remained of the daring leader of the Southern cavalry, who, after all his toils, his battles and the shock of desperate encounters, had come here to rest in peace. Beside this unmarked grave the solitary mourner remained long, pondering and remembering. Finally, he plucked a wild flower, dropped it upon the grave, and, with tears in his eyes, left the spot. This lonely mourner at the grave of Stuart was Mosby."

As was usual with most of Mosby's articles, his thrust was always the accomplishments of others, whether of Stuart or his men. Indeed, his mention of himself—when such mention did appear—was usually rather dismissive as with his claim that his runaway horse had made him a hero in Middleburg when he and his few "conglomerates" brought about the release of the old men taken from that town by Federal Major Gilmer early in 1863.

In 1913, stories began to appear across the nation under the heading of "The War Day by Day" or "Fifty Years Ago." This always brought Mosby's famous skirmishes into print, depending upon the date. In many instances, these were the first stories of Mosby that many people had read by the second decade of the new century, especially if they lived in the West. The Reno Gazette published one such incident, including within it, definitions of Mosby and his command unnecessary for older readers. It was difficult to imagine for those of Mosby's age, but the war had actually become "history" to younger Americans.

Reno Evening Gazette – **August 11, 1913**

The War Day By Day Fifty Years Ago

Aug. 11, 1863—Mosby's Guerrillas, Operating In the Rear of the Army of the Potomac. Captured a Federal Wagon Train Near Annandale, Va.— Methods of a Celebrated Band of Partisan Rangers.

One of the words that had been used over the years to describe Mosby's command— and Mosby himself, for that matter—was "picturesque." Of course, this was at least a relatively positive description and, as a result, was never found in those papers that despised the man and his command! The word can be used as a noun, an adjective, or an adverb; but the meaning remains pretty much the same: "visually attractive, vivid and/or distinctive." There can be no doubt that both Mosby and his men were "picturesque" in appearance and even in their mode of warfare. The word, however, is neutral in its moral implications as pirates were also considered "picturesque" while being morally reprehensible.

Small stories about Mosby's "doings" in his forced retirement still reached the papers as shown by this gentle offering in the *Times-Dispatch*:

Times-Dispatch – **August 20, 1913**

IN HONOR OF COLONEL MOSBY.

H. A. Thomlinson Entertains at Liangollen, His Country Home. Upperville, Va., August 19.—Colonel John S. Mosby, who is visiting Edward Shacklett, one of his soldier boys, at Delaplane, was entertained yesterday by H. A. Tomlinson, at Liangollen, his country home, where the Colonel so often stopped during the war. From the elevated position of this country mansion, at the foot of the Blue Ridge, there is a splendid view of a large part of that section formerly known as "Mosby's Confederacy," and with his field glasses the famous soldier and scout could locate many of the points where his hard-fought conflicts were won. The Colonel, of course, shows that the years are rapidly piling on his shoulders, and yet a time his eye flashes as brightly as it did at the midnight hour of March 15, 1863, when in the very heart of the great Yankee camps in Fairfax, he quietly told General Stoughton, "My name is Mosby."

But the years were not "rapidly piling on [the] shoulders" of John Mosby alone. Yet another family tragedy was in the offing as younger brother, Willie, suddenly died at his home in Bedford City. Willie was Mosby's only brother; he had already lost two younger sisters. Time was performing quite another service as well as vindicating John Mosby—a very sad service indeed:

Times-Dispatch **– August 28, 1913 (Edited)**

WILLIAM H. MOSBY DIES SUDDENLY

Brother of Col. John S. Mosby and Postmaster at Bedford City Passes Away.

Bedford City, Va., August 27.—The announcement this morning of the sudden death of William H. Mosby, which occurred at his home, on Longwood Avenue, at 2 o'clock this morning, caused a great shock throughout the community, and was a crushing blow to the members of his family and friends. He had been very well and cheerful of late, except for attacks of neuralgia and toothache. He had seemed to receive much pleasure from a new automobile he had recently purchased, and had made several extensive trips in it, the first of which as to the recent reunion of the blue and gray at Gettysburg. Only yesterday, he had, in company with his wife, made a trip in his car to Salem to attend a wedding of a relative, returning last night about 8 o'clock in fine spirits.

After reaching home he had quite a severe attack of pain, and took a dose of a patent medicine, which did not afford relief, and a physician was summoned, who administered morphine hypodermically, but he still suffered; and after the physician left, took another dose of patent medicine and almost at once fell into a sleep from which there was no awakening.

The funeral will take place from the residence on Longwood Avenue at 4:30 o'clock Thursday afternoon, and the internment will be at Longwood Cemetery.

Washington Herald **– August 28, 1913**

COL. MOSBY'S BROTHER DIES.

Was Postmaster at Bedford City, Va., for Twenty-Five Years.

Evening Star **– August 28, 1913**

COL. MOSBY'S BROTHER DEAD.

Virginia Postmaster Also Was Ranger During Civil War.

The *Times-Dispatch* was both courteous and empathetic to recognize Willie Mosby as himself and not merely as an appendage of his famous brother as did the *Washington*

Herald. Doubtless his family appreciated their beloved husband and father recognized as an individual in his own right at the time of his death.

And finally, as had been the custom for a number of years, John Mosby's birthday was "celebrated" in newsprint:

Washington Times – December 6, 1913 (Edited)
COLONEL JOHN S. MOSBY CELEBRATING HIS 80TH BIRTHDAY

This (is) the eightieth birthday of Col. John Singleton Mosby, the guerrilla chieftain in the civil war, and the most feared cavalry leader in the ranks of the Confederacy.

Eighty years ago he was born in Powhatan county, Va., where he was raised. Later Colonel Mosby went to the university of Virginia, and he was practicing law at Bristol when the war broke out.

Colonel Mosby appears to be in excellent health, despite his years. He lives at 1223 Twelfth street northwest, this city.

Washington Herald – December 7, 1913
Col. Mosby has 80th Birthday.

Col. John Singleton Mosby, dear to the hearts of all Confederates for his remarkable work during the civil war, yesterday celebrated his eightieth birthday. He lives as 1223 Twelfth street northwest.

Evening Star – December 7, 1913
"I will be eighty years old tomorrow and I feel like I am only twenty- five," Col. John S. Mosby wrote to an old friend in this city. The card being received today, the anniversary of his birth. Many friends of Col. Mosby in this city sent congratulations to him.

And so 1913 passed into history. It had been a quiet year for John Mosby except for the death of his beloved brother William. But with each death, whether of friend or family, doubtless Mosby was cognizant of the fact that the end of his own long struggle could not be all that far off. But as was usual with the man, John Mosby did not live to die.

Chapter 53

1914

Fortis in arduis ~ Strong in difficulties

"One day, in retrospect, the years of struggle will strike you as the most beautiful." ~ Sigmund Freud

1914 BEGAN WITH an excellent article in the ever-redoubtable *Times-Dispatch* on the lessons learned from the "late unpleasantness" and especially as those lessons pertained to John Mosby. It is produced unedited as a summation of the matter:

Times-Dispatch - January 4, 1914

LESSONS FROM THE CONFEDERACY

Perhaps the greatest specific benefit the world received from our Confederate service was the establishing of a new branch of the old cavalry service called Partisan Raiders. This innovation was as soundly abused as was the one made about the then Secretary of War, Jefferson Davis, when he formed the Second Regiment of Cavalry in order to try out new methods and theories. The Partisan Ranges were regular organized bands of Southern sympathizers under commissioned leaders; these bands were on the same footing, and served under the same rules of war, as did all regular enlisted troops, but instead of being under the direct control of the general commanding a certain division, the Raiders were under the authority of an independent leader. This leader, while acting upon his own initiative, always did so in the interest of the general commanding the division of which the Raiders or Rangers formed a part. During the Spanish-American War the Rough Riders were a Partisan Ranger company.

The Northern press in the sixties constantly abused and called these Rangers guerrillas, but the South never used that term until during the bitter days of reconstruction, when it became a matter of indifference whether the guerrilla or rebel term was used, for in either case, it was a synonym for patriot, gentleman, honest, law-abiding citizen.

The Partisan Rangers were a wizard branch developed under the protection of General Stuart, by John Mosby, of Virginia, and to these Raiders is due the change to-day found in the equipment of the cavalry. The sword which before the Constitutional War was the necessary weapon of attack for cavalrymen, has been abandoned, and in its place the Colt's revolver has been substituted, but up to that time the cavalry general fought with and always carried the sabre. Mosby appreciated the handicap, and as soon as he had the opportunity, proved that sabres were as useless against skillfully handled revolvers as would be the wooden swords of the harlequins. Revolvers in Partisans' hands were as effective in surprise engagements as were a whole line of light ordinance during a skirmish with the enemy. And all Partisan attacks were surprises, and all Raiders were daring men of unusual, accurate and rapid marksmanship. It was not unusual for a Raider to gallop by a tree at full tilt, and in succession put three bullets into its trunk. Southern youths almost leaped into the saddle from birth. The habits and education of the Northern youth had not been such as to adapt them equally to the cavalry service without going through a process of drilling. Naturally the Yankee complained that the Raiders did not fight fair Just to an old Austrian general complained that Bonaparte violated all military maxims by flying about from point to point in Italy "breaking up cantonments and fighting battles in the winter time." The Raiders fought at any time, and all times, whenever the found a weak point in the enemy's lines. They fought for success, and never declined the advantage of the first fire; and believed the only way to secure peace was to destroy the resources of the enemy with as small loss as possible to their own members. This rule of their conduct was then, and is to-day, approved in all military usages. This also was the policy of Jackson and Grant, Forrest and Sherman, Semmes and Farragut.

It is a great mistake to speak of these Rangers as guerrillas or bushwhackers; unjust to them and the country which authorized their organization. I cannot speak of the Northern rangers as a whole, knowing but little of their life.

But of those in the South, the greater percentage of them were well- bred, refined gentlemen, many of whom had widely traveled. There were among them few adventurers, but even they compare most favorably with the adventurers in the armies of the North. I do know that fair-minded people well versed in these records of actions, must ever acknowledge the true courage, the chivalry, the high sense of honor with which was blended less vice, selfishness and meanness of those men who wore the gray. The standard uniform was "something gray," and always worn. No Southern raider was ever willing to fight under false colors. They fought in the open as true men of war, under orders and in uniform, and followed the teachings of the plantation life, enlarged, but to meet the necessities of war. They obeyed the mandate, "to ride, to shoot and to speak the truth, and to make no woman or child fear them." The Raiders were fastidious in dress. Justly they were called the "dandies of the army." However this be, they at all times were blithe in the face of danger, full of song and story, indifferent as to the events of the morrow, keyed to a high pitch of anticipation, and unconsciously full of that pride which is but the result of repeated victories and much spoils. But to his glory be it, the Ranger or Raider never went disguised, he always wore the gray and honored it. The Raiders could not hide their colors even at night, when all colors looked alike, they didn't have to deceive the Yankee to get at him. A Union man said: "We knew them just after they hit us, and then, if we were not running from their Colts, we sure had to look out for their fool horses." There was, however, a Northern partisan company of cavalry in the command of the Army of the Potomac, in correctly called "Jesse's Scouts," which always wore Confederate gray, but they fully realized the danger of their disguise, and should never be confused with the Partisan Rangers of the South, for there is a great gulf dividing the work of a scout from that of a spy, a difference applicable to the place in history occupied by the guerrillas and Raiders. The latter being the duplicated, rather multiplicited scout. Among the Northern Partisan Rangers can be found Dahlgren, Blazer, Stoneman and Kilpatrick's commands, which in the Northern army were designated by a company letter, band regiment number. In the South the company bore its leader's name. Our Raiders reflected the effulgent glory of Morgan, Roddy and Mosby.

About the name of John Mosby is woven the organization of partisan ranger. At the breaking out of the Constitutional War, Mosby joined the First Virginia Regiment of Cavalry. Though he petitioned the Governor of Virginia for permission to join an infantry company which numbered many of his friends, his request was refused. So Mosby was mustered in at Abingdon, Va., his company becoming a part of the First Cavalry. And though he was in the command of Stuart, which was stationed at Manassas, Mosby, beginning in the cavalry, lost the chance of being, as were his special infantry friends, a "Stonewall Brigade" man. For a short period Mosby enjoyed being an adjutant, though only commissioned a Lieutenant, but lost his commission where Cornwallis lost his sword, resigning at Yorktown. The army, through gaps made by war, was being reorganized in 1862, and many late commissioned officers were thrown out, Mosby among the number It was while again a private under Stuart, that he was called upon to serve as a scout for that general. Mosby had found his opportunity; it was like throwing a rabbit into a briar patch; and Mosby recognized and seized his chance.

Very soon the world became aware of a new war power. Mosby's first notable scouting expedition, at that time unparalleled in history, was to successfully, and unaided, make a scout to the rear of McClellan's army, which was then lying in front of Richmond. This was in June of 1862. This feat was soon followed by one of the great and most marvelous marches of all history; the passing of Stuart's cavalry around McClellan's army, and a partisan ranger scout led Stuarts magnificent body of cavalry.

This exploit made possible for the young Virginian to carry out a perfectly conceived plan of warfare, gain the consent of his general to that plan, who detailed a certain number cf the First Virginia Cavalry, fifteen suitable men, with whom Mosby worked out most brilliantly and with glorious results, the problem of the effectiveness of an independent command harassing an enemy's rear.

Very soon his exploits began to be heard of in the North and South. Each day the newspapers recorded the "deeds of this dare-devil Southerner." Sutlers' trains and wagons were raided; bridges were burned; ammunition, arms and supplies were taken; pickets disappeared as if swallowed up by the earth. Scouts and stragglers from the Northern army were captured by seemingly invisible hands and camps were raided and broken up. Mosby and his Raiders seemed to be in a dozen places at the same time, which was often true, for sixty miles a day was not an unusual ride, for each Ranger kept from eight to ten horses. Mosby followed early the idea which became Grant's policy. Mosby kept a large detail of the enemy busy guarding the Federal lines, while Grant forced the South to look after the Federal sick and prisoners whom he refused to take North or exchange. Every man from the firing line is that much loss; and Mosby introduced the measure of "fighting the enemy's rear," which was just as honorable as fighting his front.

The Partisan Ranger organization became regular early in February of 1863 when the Confederate Congress passed an act framed by a Major Scott, of Virginia known as the Partisan Ranger Act." There were many organizations formed under this measure, but "Mosby's Conglomerates" and "Morgan's Raiders" are the only two command of either army which survived during the entire war. And John Morgan was an Alabamian by birth.

The Rangers were not outlaws, as so often conceived by the ignorant; to the contrary they were of the best blood of the Confederacy; men whose sires had made glorious records in Colonial times, and during the days of the revolution. These, their sons, were courageous men of firm conviction, who found in Mosby's tactics a natural outlet for feelings which made action necessary. To be a Partisan Raider was a badge of honor, and every man who so desired did not always measure up to the requirements. Marauders, unprincipled men were never tolerated in one of the organizations. Quickly and quietly they were weeded out; deserters from the regular army were never accepted; the discipline of the regular army was always observed. The Partisan recruits, however, enlisted from all the ranks of life. The poor man, the rich man, the planter's heir and the overseer's son, the young man, the old man, the cripple, the strong, rode side by side.

Obedience, nerve, cleanliness, daring, endurance, honesty [sic], loyalty, alertness, a thinking man who in an emergency was capable of independent action, was what was demanded of the man who offered his life upon the altar of this country as a Raider, a man who operated within the enemy's lines.

"Fight as your fathers fought,
Fall as your fathers fell
Thy task is taught—they shroud is wrought,
So—forward and farewell."

This was the Partisan call to arms, the Partisan's requiem. The principle aim of all raids was first, to secure information of the enemy's movements and to report same as soon as possible to the commanding general. Secondly, to annoy the enemy by destroying wagon trains, supply trains, by burning bridges, intercepting dispatches, and capturing scouting parties. In fact, to neutralize a larger command of the enemy through the demonstration of a smaller and friendly force, and to destroy all material things that you cannot appropriate whenever you capture the sutlers' "flesh pots." Many men of the North bitterly criticized these "innovations" called "thefts." They seemed to forget the "tes quoque" argument*. The Raiders simply enforced the exercise of belligerent rights, and those following Mars must accept all the risks of war. Jomini says that the irregular warfare of the Cossacks from the Steppes, did more to destroy the French army on their expedition to Moscow than the sum total of all the elite regiments of the Russian guard. These "hordes" were condemned by all nations as "brutes, beasts!" Yet when peace was declared, all Europe hailed the Cossack Lieman Platoff as the hero of the war; even the Conservative Corporation of London voting him a sword.

True, men who follow the fortunes of border warfare are not quite of the saintly character, nor are they excited by only pious aspirations. They are far from being "Canterbury pilgrims." Patriotism plus adventure always impels the Ranger, though it is to be doubted whether any of them ever find fighting a lucrative or healthful recreation. Killing men at any time is a painful business, and to contemplate it coolly is somewhat a fearsome ordeal; still, when the first pistol crack sounds there follows an involuntary bracing up, while the smell of smoke and powder the sight of blood results in a reaction which will cause the gentlest spirit to perform the most desperate deeds.

David Harun's Golden Rule among the Partisans was literally followed: They knew "everything depended upon getting the bulge on" the enemy. The raiders in the march did not preserve the same order as did the regulars. They broke lines, sang, swapped yarns, played jokes, officers and men mingling freely and upon an equal footing. Men reported for duty all along the line of march. In fact, there were but five commands: "Fall in and count off by fours; march; close up; charge' skedaddle." After one of the last orders the company seemed to melt away before the eyes of the enemy. Each man looked out for himself, and departed in his own sweet way toward that house where he boarded. The Partisan had no camp life, but each man knew the homes of the Raiders, and when a call for duty came Paul Revere's ride was reproduced. Much of their recklessness was the knowledge "that the boldest front oft wins the battle," and that it was the best policy to be the aggressor, and, like Scipio, carry the war into the enemy's country. Many of the Rangers were boys whom Mosby said made the best soldiers. "They are the best fighters I have, for they haven't sense enough to know danger when they see it, and will fight anything I tell them to." Ranger companies held usually, therefore, many young fellows just coming into manhood; retired army officers anxious to return to the field; an occasion soldier of fortune; here and there a titled adventurer, a hot-headed patriot turning the shady-side of life.

True, the Raiders reaped the spoils of war, but they were unlike Sherman and his men, for the Rangers never plundered, nor warred upon non-combatants and women. This policy of appropriating and dividing the spoils of war was no new innovation, for though the Raiders stood upon the same footing with all cavalry companies in respect to ranks and pay, they had the additional prerogative and benefit of the "maritime prize." And if they won rewards in shape of good horses and arms, these, like the Rangers' lives, were devoted to them by the cause for which they were fighting. England believed in the divisions of spoils, and her East Indian service brought wealth to many an impoverished noble and to the proverbially "poor, younger sons. "The spoils of Waterloo were divided among the captors; even the great Wellington claimed his share; while the booty of Delhi was the subject of litigation in the English Chancery Court for years. Campbell, Outram and Havelock returned from the East loaded with barbaric spoils.

The excitement of adventure, the wealth captured upon these raids, the ambuscades spread far and wide. In the North consternation was the result, while in the South recruits gathered like iron filings to a magnet. At Montgomery for may years lived a Mosby man, the only Mosby man in Alabama, Renalder Elwood Hunt. Though he "passed over the river and rests beneath the shade" with many an old army comrade, he is survived by his wife, a son R. E. Hunt, Jr., and three daughters, Mrs. J. L. Harris, Mrs. Otto F. Flinn and Miss Geraldine Bibb Hunt, all residents of Montgomery.

In February of 1863, Mosby was given a commission and fifteen men were detailed from his old company, the First Virginia Cavalry, and instructed to "operate inside the enemy's lines." This meant almost a cutting off of all communications with lines that were friendly. It meant to be in closer touch with Washington than Richmond. The men would only have the earth for a couch; their only equipment, that which each man brought with him at the start; but they had the right to fight the enemy and to wrest from him, by sheer force, that which was necessary to maintain the command. Out of this command of fifteen grew the Forty-third Virginia Battalion of Cavalry, comprising eight companies and numbering 600 men. These raiders demonstrated to the world the great results that may be accomplished by a small band of cavalry moving rapidly from place to place. Sixty miles a day was not an uncommon occurrence. Of course, one horse was not required to make this record, for each raider possessed from three to six mounts, which he boarded in various places in that section where he operated. The rule of the border warfare was never to let the enemy attack you, always strike first; and do it with a rush. Above all, carry the warfare, and make the skirmishes always in the enemy's country. Thereby you will force them to guard their own lines and not advance into your territory.

It is most interesting to study this rather unknown miniature replica of our own Confederacy, which is known to the world as "Mosby's Confederacy," which occupied the Virginia counties of Loudoun, Fauquier and Fairfax. This Confederacy was established within the lines of the enemy, being only fifty miles from Washington. The young people will enjoy reading of these Rangers in John Eston Cook's "Surrey of Eagles Nest." The father of this author was a professor in the old Transylvania Medical College, at Lexington, in the blue grass country, and as one of the faculty signed the diploma of Dr. Thomas Burwell Grigg, the father of the present recording secretary of the Alabama division, U.D.C.

The record of our Roddy, who began his career as a partisan ranger in North Alabama, should prove an interesting as well as an absorbing study for those chapters of our division which are in the territory Roddy patrolled. Morgan the Raider, the name Morgan figuring in the poem, "Kentucky Belle," was born an Alabamian. It will be of some interest to know that the present commander-in-chief of the Confederate Veterans, Bennett H. Young, is one of Morgan's Raiders. He was captured with Morgan on that famous Ohio raid, and was imprisoned with him, escaping at the same time from the Ohio State prison. General Young fled over the border to Canada and thence made his way to England. Going to the Bermudas, he ran the blockade into the Confederacy. Morgan reached his own lines, and was soon brutally betrayed and killed at Greenville, Tenn.; but Bennett H. Young and many a Raider has lived to prove a "Partisan Ranger" to be a good soldier, a good Christian, a good and useful American citizen.— Montgomery Advertiser.[*tes quoque argument: A very common fallacy in which one attempts to defend oneself or another from criticism by turning the critique back against the accuser. This is a classic "red herring" since whether the accuser is guilty of the same or a similar wrong is irrelevant to the truth of the original charge. However, as a diversionary tactic, tu quoque can be very effective since the accuser is put on the defensive and frequently feels compelled to defend against the accusation thus weakening the original charge.-vph]

In April, Mosby traveled to Canada to give a lecture on Stuart's movements during the Gettysburg campaign. As continued to be manifest to all who were in any way interested, Mosby's "dotage" had yet to be reached—and, in fact, it never was:

Times-Dispatch – April 16, 1914

MOSBY GOES TO CANADA

Will Deliver Address on Movements of Stuart's Cavalry at Gettysburg. [Special to The *Times-Dispatch*.]

Washington, April 15.—Colonel John S. Mosby, the famous ex-guerrilla chief of the Confederate Army of Northern Virginia, left Washington today for Toronto, Canada, where he was invited by the Canadian War College to deliver an address on the movements of Stuart's Cavalry in the Gettysburg campaign. Colonel Mosby recently passed his eightieth birthday but is well preserved in mind and body.

G.H.M.

Washington Times – May 4, 1914

Col. John S. Mosby, the famous Confederate officer, spoke at a dinner given him last night in Toronto, Canada by the Cavalry Officers of the Military Institute.

But John Mosby's opinions regarding the events of the day were still of interest to the press. In this article, he was interviewed by the *New York Times* on the situation in Mexico—to which his responses were anything but confused and "superannuated." It would seem that his removal from the Department of Justice was not a matter of age after all as can be deduced by the fact that a paper of the prestige of the *New York Times* saw fit to interview him on such a complex matter:

Times Republican – May 8, 1914

MOSBY WOULD DIVIDE MEXICO

Huerta No Worse Than Average Mexican

Col. John S. Mosby, the famous guerrilla leader of the Confederate army, did not exactly say that his voice was for war when he arrived from Toronto, but it was that way a week ago when he wrote down to a friend in Washington to tell the president that he (Colonel Mosby) was 80 years old, quite old enough not to go to war, but offering his services. The Colonel went to Toronto by invitation of the Canadian militia officers to deliver an address on Stuart's cavalry in the Gettysburg campaign.

"Do you believe there will be a war?" Colonel Mosby was asked.

"There is practically war now," he replied.

"You have no hope of the A-B-C mediation proving successful?"

"On the contrary, I believe that there is great probability of its being so. But it is my opinion," went on Colonel Mosby, "that the Mexican people in their present condition are not fit to be given their country to govern. Personally, I have a great contempt for the Monroe doctrine as a practical instrument in these times. I think the United States ought to combine with England and France and take over Mexico and split into three zones, each under control of one of those powers. They would then engage to take care of the Mexicans, and give them life, liberty and the protection of property, and, above all things, good government.

"I do not recall any situation like the present in the course of my whole 80 years. But let me tell you, in spite of the fact that I have passed fourscore, I don't feel today a bit over 30. I have always said that this country ought to recognize Huerta, or send an army down into Mexico and ask England and France to come in and help straighten out things, there being no prejudice down there against them. Let me tell you, I would rather have the English for neighbors than Indians. As I said before, I have a great contempt for the Monroe doctrines, and I believe Huereta is just as good as any other Mexican—no worse, no better.

"As a matter of fact, there is no question of favoritism involved. American shipping has a monopoly of coastwise trade, even without a subsidy of free tolls proposed by the objectionable clause in the canal bill. A little more reasoning instead of a blind following of prejudices and agitators that have no place in American life would make not only for better patriotism but a broader and saner view of public affairs.

"I lived for seven years among Englishmen when I was United States consul at Hong Kong and they make pretty good friends, after all.—*New York Times*.

John Mosby spoke over the years of the little vindications that time brought his way and the satisfaction that they afforded him. The following story is one such example. Finding that his portrait would hang in a GAR post in New York, and given the grief Mosby suffered at the hands of that organization, must have been comforting to say the least:

Times-Dispatch - May 23, 1914 (Edited)
MOSBY'S PORTRAIT TO HANG IN GRAND ARMY POST HALL

Veteran Confederate Cavalry Chieftain Writes of His Reception in Canada. Arthur B. Clarke, of this city, is in receipt of a private letter from Colonel John S. Mosby, who has recently returned from a trip to Canada and New York. In this letter Colonel Mosby says:

"Yesterday I received a copy of The *Times-Dispatch* of last Sunday that had a notice from a Toronto paper of my address there on Stuart's Cavalry in the Gettysburg campaign. It was not a popular address, but before the military institute, I think it was very well received. I had the advantage of an impartial audience. I was royally treated in Canada, and also during my two weeks' stay in New York. I was never in better health, and am quite as vigorous as I was forty years ago. You may be surprised to hear that the LaFayette G.A.R. Post in New York got me to sit to an artist for my portrait to hang in their hall; which really looks like we are in a new era. There was a banquet given to Forbes Robertson, the English actor, while I was in New York. Spottswood [his grandson] and I went as invited guests."

Mosby's claim that the address "was not popular" arose from the belief by many in the South that his defense of Stuart was a criticism of General Lee and why he mentioned that the Canadian military was an "impartial audience," and thus did not have the need to "mentally defend" Lee against perceived criticisms during his lecture.

The last paragraph of the article (edited out) mentioned that Mosby's two sons "live in the Far West." While Mosby's older son, Beverly, lived in Spokane, Washington, younger son, John Jr., had moved back to Virginia and lived with his sister, Stuart. John had severe health and personal problems and had suffered from them for a lengthy period of time. It was said that he left Denver because the altitude had affected his health. That is possible, but a lot more was involved, and the matter weighed heavily upon his father's mind. Mosby wrote to Beverly in a letter dated September 15, 1902, twelve years earlier:

> "I have just returned from Denver, broken down and heart-broken. Johnny is a wreck, mentally, physically and financially. I want to quietly get him out of Colorado and into a sanitarium. He is a victim of cocaine. I told Irby to look up the checks, and if they do not exceed my ability to pay, I shall pay them for him. I shall also pay his typewriter, a very nice girl, $50. I left Alliance, Neb., Saturday evening on a freight train for Denver. I hear Johnny has conceived a bitter antipathy for me. Of course, that does not change my love for him."

And still it went on. In another letter to Beverly of September 16 of the same year, Mosby wrote that Johnny had requested $300 transferred to him from his father's St. Louis bank and that he had signed the request "J. S. Mosby." The bank had assumed the signature to be his and had forwarded the money as requested. Mosby was distraught to learn that his son would steal from him to support his drug habit. Shortly thereafter, Mosby took John Jr. to Virginia, where he underwent an agonizing "cure" for his addiction that was partially successful. It was at that time that Johnny began to write—and have published—articles in, among other papers, the *Washington Post*. However, in a letter to Beverly dated January 21, 1910, Mosby wrote that Johnny was again out of work because of his drug problem; but this time, his addiction was to alcohol and patent medicines containing morphine.

It must be remembered that these problems with his namesake son—or at least letters regarding the matter—first appeared in 1902! When one considers what Mosby put up with during that year and all the rest of the time in which he labored in the sour vineyard of "government service," the fact that he was able to soldier on must be seen in a very different light than that in which it is presently viewed!

December had come again, and once more, John Mosby received the kudos of a now sympathetic and supportive press—well, for the most part, anyway:

Times-Dispatch – December 3, 1914

Mosby Is Eighty-One.

Colonel John S. Mosby expects to celebrate his eighty-first birthday on Sunday. Hale and hearty, the aged Confederate cavalryman will spend the day in his apartments, 1223 Twelfth Street, Northwest, Washington, receiving such of his comrades as are able to greet him and his numerous friends.

Colonel Mosby, according to letters received here recently, still feels the fire of a warrior coursing through his veins. He says he feels as young as he did forty years ago, and would like nothing better than to from a regiment of English suffragettes to lead against the forces of the Kaiser in France. Colonel Mosby, who until a year ago, was a government employee in Washington, now resides with his daughter, Mrs. Stuart Mosby Coleman.

Times-Dispatch – December 6, 1914 (Edited)

MOSBY CELEBRATES HIS EIGHTY-FIRST BIRTHDAY

Confederate Cavalryman Admits Ambition to Join in European Conflict
WOULD LEAD SUFFRAGETTES

Unique Career of One of Most Noted Men Produced by War Between the States—Has Held Several Government Positions.

The *Times-Dispatch* included the requisite "biography," with all the usual inaccuracies, but of more interest was its mention in both articles of Mosby's humorous offer to lead a squadron of British suffragettes against the kaiser. Given that daughter Stuart was a leading light in that movement, it might have been seen as a bit of a "gibe" at his daughter. But Mosby had always credited women for their strength, from his mother and his wife to the ladies of Northern Virginia who supported him during the war, so perhaps it wasn't a jest after all.

But the press was still interested in Mosby's views on current events, especially the war in Europe, views that he, as usual, was more than happy to provide:

Washington Times – December 6, 1914

COL. MOSBY'S STRATEGY

Col. John S. Mosby, who knows more about fighting with cavalry than any other man in the world, says he could take 10,000 Cossacks and cut the communication between Belgium and Berlin. We haven't much doubt that he could. He has done a lot of things to communications, supply trains, and the like, that were rather more startling than would be a raid on the communications of the German army at this time.

The Europeans don't know much about cavalry operations that they didn't learn from the study of our civil war; and those European soldiers who know most about American cavalry have for many years been lecturing other European soldiers on the necessity of adopting more of the American models in cavalry management. Some day the American Indian, whose fighting methods were largely responsible for developing the high efficiency of our cavalry, will come into the recognition he deserves as one of the world's great military inventors and instructors. The men like Mosby, Forrest, Sheridan, Stonewall Jackson, and other civil war specialists in the business of harassing an enemy, have been studied all over the world, and are studied today; but the European armies somehow refuse to take the lesson to heart and apply it. Colonel Mosby admits that he doesn't understand why; nobody else seems to understand.

North Platte Semi-Weekly Tribune – December 11, 1914

MOSBY ON THE WAR

"If I was there with 10,000 Cossacks and some of my old officers who served under me in our war, I'd break up all communication between the German army and Berlin, and I would run William back to his capital in a hurry."

This was the statement made by Col. John S. Mosby, late of the Confederate army and leader of Mosby's men, who caused so much trouble for the Union army during the Civil war. The venerable warrior lives in Washington, and is eighty-one years of age. Although his hair is white and snow and he is a little deaf, he is by no means feeble. He is now engaged in writing his memoirs and hopes to complete the volume in about six months.

"The communication of an army is its vulnerable point," he continued. "If I was over there in Europe I would do on a large scale what I accomplished on a smaller scale in the Shenandoah Valley, when I cut off General Sheridan's communication. I had only three hundred men with me at that time.

"I don't look to see the war last more than six months. It is such a tremendous affair that it will break down of its own weight."

"What do you think of the war as compared with our Civil war?" Colonel Mosby was asked.

"They are making no progress in Europe. We made progress every day on one side or the other. As near as I can determine they are simply killing. The tide does not ebb and flow a single bit. We advanced or retreated and were not in the struggle simply to kill. And with how much humanity on both sides our war was conducted! It presents the greatest contrast."

Mosby was off on the length of time left in the war, but if the United States had not become engaged, he probably would have been correct. The combatants were as tired of useless slaughter as was Mosby and, in fact, considered declaring an armistice and then everyone just going home. But the entrance of the United States into the conflict changed everything—and not for the better.

The next year marked the middle of the second decade of the twentieth century, and John Mosby was as mentally prepared for what was to come as he had been in the past. Sadly, however, as had happened before, events became more than even he could have anticipated.

Chapter 54

1915

Tempus, edax rerum ~ Time, devourer of all things

"My Life is My Message." ~ Mahatma Gandhi

THE DAWN OF 1915 did not see John Mosby consigned to oblivion quite yet. A story about his confrontation with George Turpin that had led to his imprisonment—and eventually to his law career—was carried in the *Times-Dispatch* of January 3, narrated by someone who claimed to have been there. Alas, however, this "eye-witness's" memory was no more accurate than is the case with so many "eye-witnesses." In February, Mosby was interviewed by the *Washington Times* in a nice little article that suggested that he had passed through the storm of sectional animosity and arrived at the calm of national affection, an assumption that was without question devoutly wished by the man:

Washington Times – February 8, 1915 (Edited)

Col. Mosby Insists He Will Finish Memoirs

Nearing Seventy-Eighth Year, Guerrilla Leader Cares Not Who Reads His Book.

"Past Memories to Remain"

Hated by North and South, He is Now Regarded as One of Nation's Grand Old Men.

Alternately hated by both North and South, Colonel Mosby, in recent years has come into his own, and is regarded as one of the nation's grand old men by both sections.

Fought Corrupt Officials.

All idea that his action was dictated by a desire for an easy berth in Government service was dispelled when, as an attorney in the Department of Justice during the Grant Administration, he fought, almost singlehandedly, a corrupt gang of officials in the American consular service in far-off Asia.

Later he warred so fiercely upon the robber cattle-barons of the West that even his official superiors in Washington repeatedly cautioned him against needlessly exposing his life to their vengeance.

Not only North and South alike now unite in their admiration for the heroism and courage of the daring guerrilla captain, who recalled the days of Robin Hood, and other heroes of past ages, but he has friends in all parts of the globe. His correspondence, alone, would make an interesting volume.

Just the other day, following the appearance of his letter in the London Times, he received a letter from Col. Herbert Hughes of the British cavalry, who said, in part:

"You and your people look to the war over and over again, and it must please you to see your young successors turning their hand to your game (referring to the sniping matter). Your letter delighted me when I read it in the paper.

The University of Virginia presented Mosby with a medal, which was well received. Mosby's antagonism toward the institution had been overcome by the gracious care and treatment given to himself and his family after his dreadful accident in 1897. Mosby could hold a grudge, but it required that the other party continue to do the same. In this case, it was obvious that the University regretted the treatment of its young scapegrace so many years earlier:

Washington Times – **February 15, 1915**

University of Virginia Gives Col. Mosby Medal

Col. John S. Mosby has been presented a bronze medal by Dr. Charles W. Kent on behalf of the faculty of the university of Virginia.

This medal was to have been presented on January 28, when Colonel Mosby was invited to go to the university during the visit of former President Taft. Colonel Mosby was unable to attend so Dr. Kent was designated by President Alderman to deliver the medal in person.

The medal sets forth that Colonel Mosby, a son of the university of Virginia, served with distinction in the Confederate army.

Mosby was then asked about the ongoing war in Europe. He stated unequivocally that he was against American involvement, praising the man who had kept the country out of war by defeating the Ship Purchase Bill, Elihu Root. No mention was made by him of Mr. Root's party affiliation, though he was a Republican. However, Mosby was not Root's only admirer. Indeed, the gentleman was awarded the Nobel Peace Prize one assumes for the action here mentioned. It is also interesting to note that this was yet another war rejected by a man frequently accused of being addicted to war's violence:

Harrisburg Star-Independent – **March 27, 1915**

COLONEL JOHN S. MOSBY

"England's blockade of Germany is just and, I believe, will end the war within two or three months at the outside. I predict the Dardanelles will be opened and the Turk driven from Europe, as he should be. And to Mr. Elihu Root, the ablest man in the country, the United States owes a great debt, for he defeated the Ship Purchase bill, and thereby kept America from becoming involved in the present conflict." Such was the opinion expressed by the famous cavalryman Colonel John Singleton Mosby, of Warrenton, Va., civil war veteran, lawyer, author and story teller, who is more than eighty years old, but is still active and as military in mien as he was when he led the famous Mosby Partisan Rangers in the days of '61, causing great damage upon the rear ranks of the Federal army and giving no little amount of worry to the Union commanders.

Once again, Mosby was called upon to defend his command—this time from a letter that appeared in, of all places, the London Times:

Washington Herald **– April 19, 1915**

Evening Star **– April 19, 1915**

The Farmer **– April 20, 1915**

MOSBY DENIES SNIPING CHARGE

American Wrote the London Times Confederate Were Snipers at Night Refuted by Aged Raider

Mosby Says Baron von Massow, Now German Corps Commander, Was with Him in 1864

The famous Confederate raider, Col. John Singleton Mosby, who is now in his 82nd year, wrote to the London Times from Washington, under date of December 19, a remarkable letter on alleged sniping in the American civil war.

The Times on November 14 had printed a letter from George Haven Putnam, of New York, in regard to the question of sniping in Belgium. In the course of this letter Mr. Putnam said:

"In the Shenandoah Valley, in 1864, the crippled old farmers whom we saw hobbling around their fields because at night active raiders with Mosby, and rarely troubled themselves to change their garments. I do not believe, however, that any attempt was made either in the Shenandoah Valley or elsewhere (except in the case of a man shown to be a spy) to make the absence of uniform a ground for the execution of the citizen who was using his rifle to defend his home."

Mosby Denies This.

In reply to this letter, Col. Mosby wrote:

"The homes of a large portion of my command were not in the region where we operated; many of my men were from Maryland. There were some Canadians who joined us for love of adventure. I was never in the Shenandoah Valley before the war; my home was more than 100 miles away. The Union cavalry knew the country as well as I did. When my men were captured they were sent to Fort Warren, near Boston; all who saw them know that they wore gray uniforms."

"His statement shows that the writer was never in the Shenandoah Valley as a soldier; or, if he was, that he was prudent enough to keep out of sight of us. My own uniform can be seen in the National Museum."

Confederates used Pistols.

"A sniper, I believe, shoots under cover with a long-range gun. The foes we often met by daylight in open combat know that my men always fought with pistols in a mounted charge; and I am sure that our antagonists would not admit that they had ever met defeat from a band of cripples. The published of our war show the relations of my command to the main Confederate army; and refute the implications of your correspondent's letter."

"An English officer, Capt. Hoskins, who had the Crimean medal, served with us. He had passed through the fire of the Redan and the Malakoff and fell by my side in a skirmish. A German officer, Baron von Massow, was also in my command until he was disabled by a wound and returned home. A few years ago he wrote me that he then commanded the Ninth German Army Corps. If you were to ask Massow if he was ever a sniper in the Shenandoah Valley he would answer from the mouth of a Krupp gun."

Of course, the entire debate was spurious. Both sides had "sharp-shooters" who used long-range rifles to fire on the enemy: so there was nothing illegal, immoral, or militarily problematic with the use of such weapons. As for being in civilian clothing, that and wearing the uniform of the enemy would get the individual involved executed as a spy. Mosby was sentenced to be hanged anyway, so his use of "mufti" in his scouting operations did not concern him on that account. But on the whole, he and his men fought in Confederate uniform, albeit as the war drew on, sometimes they did use captured outer clothing from the enemy for the purpose of warmth rather than stealth.

Mosby returned once more to the university, where he spoke about his command's history during a gathering at Charlottesville. This was not a reunion per se; but twenty of Mosby's men, along with their commander, were present:

Washington Times – May 21, 1915
VIRGINIA STUDENTS HEAR COL. MOSBY

Confederate Veteran Tells of Experiences at Reunion of His Command.

Charges and Captures.

Taking up next his life as a commander and a partisan leader, Colonel Mosby had the absorbed interest of the audience as he told of scouting trips and fights, of charges and captures and all that goes to make up the life of an active military organization. Nearly all the episodes were of a comic character, and one of his old veterans remarked at the close of the meeting: "He did not tell about killing a single Yankee."

In conclusion Colonel Mosby said: "I have only related events all of which I saw and part of which I was. No man clung longer to the Confederacy than I did. If Troy could have been saved by this right hand, it would have been saved."

The conclusion of Mosby's speech had been used before and would be used again. He had used it in New England in his lecture tour in 1906 and he used it again to end his posthumously published memoirs. There is, I most firmly believe, a very cogent and seminal reason for its usage that far exceeds the graceful ending it lent to any lecture or book by John Mosby. That matter will be covered in the last chapter.

At the end of August, yet another blow fell on the elderly soldier. His namesake son, John Jr., died after what was called a "long illness." John Singleton Mosby Jr. had been a brilliant but star-crossed man. He bore his father's name and as a child had suffered for his father's perceived "sins." When asked about his father, Jack was quoted as saying that if it hadn't been for the war, he might have made a decent parent. Certainly, Mosby knew that Johnny had formed a loathing for him. He had mentioned it to Beverly in a letter in 1902. Whether John ever was able to make peace with his father, much less form any real affectionate attachment for him, is not known. Certainly, Mosby loved all his children. But his "icon" children, May and Johnny, were taken from him; and he could do nothing to save either of them. It is unnatural for a parent to bury a child, but John Mosby had already done so four times:

Washington Times – August 27, 1915

JACK MOSBY IS DEAD AFTER LONG ILLNESS

Son of Famous Confederate Cavalry Leader Succumbs to Throat Affection.

John S. Mosby, Jr., for many years a writer for Washington newspapers and periodicals of this and other cities, died yesterday at Emergency Hospital, where he had been confined for nearly a month following an operation for an affection of the throat.

He was in his fifty-second year and a son of the famous Confederate cavalry leader, Col. John S. Mosby. He was born in Warrenton, Va. In 1883 he was graduated from the law department of the university of Virginia with the degree of LL.D.

Later he went to Colorado, where he practiced law in Denver. Here he held a lecture chair in the Colorado School of Mines. The high altitude having affected his health he returned to Washington ten years ago and continued his literary work.

Besides his father, Mr. Mosby is survived by a brother, Beverly Mosby, of Spokane, Wash., two sisters, Mrs. Stuart M. Coleman, of this city, and Miss Pauline A. Mosby, of Baltimore. Funeral services will be held tomorrow at Warrenton, the old home of the Mosbys where internment will also be made.

Evening Star – August 27, 1915

JOHN S. MOSBY, JR. DIES IN A LOCAL HOSPITAL

Son of Noted Confederate Cavalry Leader of the Civil War Succumbs.

John S. Mosby, Jr., fifty-one years old, son of Col. Mosby, the famous Confederate Cavalry leader, and veteran journalist and writer, died yesterday afternoon at the Emergency Hospital. He had been at the hospital for nearly a month, following an operation for an affection of the throat.

The body will be taken tomorrow morning to Warrenton, Va., the old home of the Mosbys, where funeral services will be held in the afternoon. Internment will be at that place.

Native of Virginia.

Mr. Mosby was born at Warrenton in December, 1863. He was the son of John S. and Pauline Clark Mosby. He was graduated from the law department of the university of Virginia in 1883 and following his graduation he engaged in newspaper work in this city.

Mr. Mosby practiced law in Denver, Col., in the nineties, with much success, and also lectured in the Colorado School of Mines. Ten years ago he returned to Washington, where he had lived since making his home with his sister, Mrs. Stuart Mosby Coleman, 1223 12th street northwest, where his father, Col. Mosby also resides.

Engaged in Newspaper Work.

Since his return to Washington Mr. Mosby wrote extensively for local papers. He contributed columns of chess and poker stories and took keen interest in his work to the last. Mr. Mosby had a wide acquaintance among newspaper and other professional and business men in this and other cities throughout the country.

Besides his father and the sister named, two other sisters, Miss Pauline Mosby and Miss Ada Mosby of Baltimore, and a brother, Beverly Mosby of Spokane, Wash. survive him.

Herald and News – September 7, 1915

MOSBY DIES GAME

Only Son of Colonel Mosby of Confederate Fame.

Washington, Sept. 1.—"With one foot in the grave, I'll die game," wrote John S. Mosby, Jr., on his last page of copy as the editor of a chess and poker column, half an hour before he died.

Mr. Mosby was the only son of Col. John S. Mosby, of Confederate fame, and was the biographer and literary adviser of his distinguished father. He died of cancer of the tongue.

Alas, these stories were riddled with inaccuracies, but probably Mosby cared nothing about the vagaries of press coverage in this matter. Johnny wasn't born in Warrenton, and there was no "old Mosby home" in that lovely town. Mosby had moved there after the war and taken up residence, but there was nothing familial about the area or the town. However, infant sons George Prentiss and Alfred were buried there, as was his daughter May and his beloved Pauline.

Was Mosby with Johnny when he died? Nothing is said of the matter, and perhaps Johnny preferred not to have his father at his bedside. We do not know. But grief was now John Mosby's constant companion, and when his own death came, it may well have been a release for him.

The oddest matter in Johnny's death was its cause. One story said it was cancer of the tongue. Certainly, he could not speak when he wrote his epitaph—"I'll die game"—on the last page of his column on chess and poker. But other reports say that he died of an "affection of the throat," which probably meant throat cancer—the same malignant affliction that killed Mosby's great friend Ulysses Grant. Suffice it to say, after the death of Mosby's firstborn, May Virginia, the death of John Jr. was a blow from which he never truly recovered—dying less than a year after his namesake son.

Finally, the newspapers once again announced Mosby's birthday. Some effort was made to show that there was still a celebration and that Mosby was surrounded by friends and family, but there were no interviews, though the papers continued to state that he was "still in the full vigor of health."

Times-Dispatch – December 4, 1915

COLONEL MOSBY IS 82

Will Celebrate Birthday on Monday With Friends and Family in Washington.

Washington Times – December 6, 1915

COL. MOSBY IS 82 YEARS "YOUNG" TODAY

Noted Confederate Guerilla Chieftain Congratulated by Men He Captured. Col. John Singleton Mosby, guerilla chieftain and the most feared cavalry leader in the Confederate army during the civil war, is eighty-two years "young" today. The grizzled warrior is still in the full vigor of health, and was today the recipient of many congratulations in person by letter and by wire, on passing the four-score and two mile post. Among the letters were some from prominent men whom he captured during the war.

The last article appearing on John Mosby in 1915 spoke volumes about the passage of time and what it meant in the scope of an individual's life, even a very famous and well-known individual. The *Evening Ledger* found it necessary—even in this small inclusion—to explain to its readers just whose birthday was being reported upon. "You know, he was that Mosby, the fellow who had those guerrillas during the old war!" John Mosby understood this. He had seen great heroes rise, fall, and then, upon falling, cease to be any more a part of the mortal world. Stuart was a great hero, and then Stuart was dead and buried, and Mosby visited the grassy place where he lay hidden forever and absent from those who loved him. John Mosby knew that he was already being forgotten if not by those closest to him, then by the world at large as that world moved on and left him behind even while he still lived. Mosby often fell back upon the classics, especially upon his Latin, to define the course of his life. In this case, he probably would have chosen to declare, "O quam cito transit gloria mundi! (O how quickly passes the glory of the world!)"

Chapter 55

1916

Consummatum est. ~ It is finished.

**"For the sword outwears its sheath, and the soul
wears out the breast." ~ Lord Byron**

1916 IN WASHINGTON was ushered in with moderate temperatures and little or no rain. While there were days here and there of cold, by the time spring arrived, the year was proving mild and dry. Unlike so many other years, however, John Mosby did not appear in any newspaper article until early in May—and then it was the beginning of the end. He was reported ill once again in Garfield Hospital as the month began; but these accounts regarding the seriousness of his condition, as usual, contradicted one another. However, it was soon understood that the old soldier would not win this battle and so the deathwatch began:

Washington Times – May 3, 1916

Col. Mosby Lies Ill At Garfield Hospital

Col. John S. Mosby, famous guerilla leader of the Confederacy is seriously ill in Garfield Hospital.

He was taken in the hospital yesterday. It was said this afternoon that his condition was slightly improved and that he seemed stronger than he did yesterday.

Washington Times, – May 3, 1916

Col. Mosby Lies Ill At Garfield Hospital

Col. John S. Mosby, famous guerilla leader of the Confederacy is seriously ill in Garfield Hospital.

He was taken in the hospital yesterday. It was said this afternoon that his condition was slightly improved and that he seemed stronger than he did yesterday.

Washington Post – May 5, 1916

COL. MOSBY SERIOUSLY ILL.

Confederate Chieftain Suffering From Infirmities of Advanced Age.

Col. John S. Mosby, the famous Guerrilla Chieftain of the Confederacy, is dangerously ill at Garfield Hospital, and his friends are very much alarmed and fear he will not recover. His condition is due to advanced age, he being now 82.

Col. Mosby went to the hospital Tuesday night. Physicians, while holding out little hope said he seemed slightly stronger yesterday. Until his illness he has been one of the most picturesque figures in the streets of Washington.

Day Book – **May 8, 1916 (Edited)**

Seattle Star – **May 10, 1916**

Col. Mosby, Near Death, Was Terror to Union Troops as Guerrilla Leader. Washington, May 9.—Col. John S. Mosby, ill in a hospital here, is known as the intrepid leader of "Mosby's Guerrillas," which terrorized the South during and immediately after the civil war.

"Just old age," doctors give as the cause of his illness.

Colonel Mosby has been failing since he was dismissed, on account of age, from his office as attorney in the Department of Justice, five or six years ago

Ogden Standard – **May 16, 1916**

Bisbee Daily Review – **May 19, 1916**

Col. John S. Mosby

Col. John S. Mosby, a picturesque figure in Washington and widely known as a Confederate guerilla chief during the Civil war, is seriously ill in a Washington hospital. He is eighty-two years old.

Evening Herald – **May 19, 1916**

Aged Guerilla Chief Is Ill

Mahoning Dispatch – **May 19, 1916**

> Col. John S. Mosby, who gained fame as a leader of irregular Confederate cavalry during the Civil War, is ill in a Washington hospital. He is 82 years old.

Washington Post – **May 21, 1916**

MOST FAMOUS GUERRILLA CHIEFTAIN

ALTHOUGH PRICE WAS SET ON JOHN MOSBY'S HEAD,

HE AFTERWARD BECAME GREAT FRIEND OF GENERAL GRANT.

Washington Times – **May 22, 1916**

Col. Mosby Is Improving.

Col. John S. Mosby, who has been critically ill at Garfield Hospital for several weeks past, is reported as improving. Physicians at the hospital today said that his condition was better than it has been for some time, and that chances for his recovery are good.

Times-Dispatch – **May 29, 1916 (Edited)**

COL. JOHN S. MOSBY SINKING

In Critical Condition at Garfield Hospital in Washington, and His Family Gives up Hope.

Washington, May 28.—Colonel John S. Mosby, famous as a Confederate cavalry officer, who is critically ill at the Garfield Hospital here, was reported to-night in a sinking condition. His family has abandoned hope for his recovery. Colonel Mosby has been ill for the past few weeks with the infirmities of old age. To-day his condition became worse.

Washington Times – May 29, 1916

Colonel Mosby Suffers Relapse at Hospital

Col. John S. Mosby, famous Confederate guerrilla chieftain, who has been ill in Garfield Hospital for several weeks, is reported to be in a critical condition today. The general suffered a relapse late yesterday, and has been sinking steadily.

Times-Dispatch - May 30, 1916

MOSBY'S END IS NEAR

Condition Becomes Alarming, and Physicians Tell Family That Death Is Not Far Off.

[Special to the *Times-Dispatch*.]

Washington, May 29.—The condition of Colonel John S. Mosby, the famous Confederate cavalry officer, who is critically ill at a local hospital, became alarming to-night, when he was seized with a severe sinking spell, from which he later rallied. His physicians have informed Colonel Mosby's family that the end is not far off. Colonel Mosby's illness followed a short visit to Norfolk about a month ago.

On Tuesday, May 30, 1916—Memorial Day—shortly after 5:30, the sun rose on the city of Washington. As was fitting, Nature seemed to make an especial note of the day as a blazing sun alternated with lowering clouds—a fitting tribute to a waning life filled with glorious triumphs and dark defeats. At or around 9:00 o'clock, some three and a half hours after the rising of the sun, the man who had lived that life of triumph and defeat, John Singleton Mosby, crossed the Great River to join those of his friends and loved ones who had preceded him on that final journey. With him went the last of the great heroes of America's bloodiest war and an era rich in song and story.

Of course, his passing initiated a veritable orgy of news coverage. Everything that had ever been said about him so often in the past was recalled, reconstructed, reiterated, and reprinted replete with the inaccuracies and inconsistencies with which they had been adorned while the man lived. The coverage was from coast to coast and even across the great oceans. Below are but a few of the tributes paid to him and the life he had lived among those who now paid those last tributes.

The stories presented are an example of the very small amount of press coverage given to a man who had never been of great importance in the accepted understanding of that word. He was not exceptionally wellborn or wealthy or a man of high military rank or political position. His cause in war had failed; his attempt to deliver his state and his people from the grip of Reconstruction had been if not a complete failure, then certainly not recognized for what it was and had led to his condemnation by the very people he strived to serve. His efforts to overcome corruption and criminality as he served the government he embraced had redounded to his ignominy and privation, and his beloved son despised and hated him as a result. And yet at his death, the United States, represented by its fourth estate, paid him homage as it had done few others before—or since.

Oakland Tribune – May 30, 1916 (Edited)
COL. MOSBY, FAMED CONFEDERATE, DEAD

Washington, May 30 – Colonel John Mosby, 83, daring Confederate leader in the Civil War, died today at Garfield hospital. He had been critically ill since Sunday. As leader of Mosby's guerrillas, the colonel made a place for himself in history during the conflict between north and south. [And hereafter was a lengthy description of Mosby's life and service.-vph]

Colonel Mosby's death, his physicians said, was due solely to old age. Until six months ago, when he went into a sudden decline, he was a familiar sight about the streets of the capitol.

He will be buried at his ancestral home at Warrenton, Va., probably Thursday, and such survivors of his noted command will be the pallbearers.

Washington Times – May 30, 1916 (Edited)
Col. John S. Mosby, Famed Confederate Chief, Is Dead Here

Commander of Dread Guerrilla Band in Civil War Succumbs at Hospital

Ill For Several Months Aged Warrior Had Picturesque Career, Romantic in Both Peace and Battle.

Col. John S. Mosby, leader of Mosby's Rangers during the Civil War, and one of the most picturesque and noted figures of the sixties, died at Garfield Hospital at 9 o'clock this morning.

Death was directly due to complications of age. Colonel Mosby was in his eighty-second year.

The aged guerrilla fighter had been in failing health for more than six months. His condition became so serious about a month ago that he was taken to Georgetown University Hospital and subsequently moved to Garfield Hospital.

The patient's years caused apprehension when he was first stricken. Present at his deathbed were his sister, Miss Blakely Mosby; his brother-in- law, Charles W. Russell, and his three daughters, Miss Ada Mosby, Miss Pauline Mosby, and Mrs. Stuart Mosby Coleman of this city.

Arrangement for the funeral will be completed late this afternoon. Interment will be at Warrenton, Va., the former home of the aged warrior.

Last Picturesque Figure.

The death of Col. John S. Mosby means the passing of probably the last of the really picturesque figures of the old-time Southern Confederacy. His was a life of daring, of adventure, of oft-tried bravery, conjuring visions of romance in war and peace. In the great civil conflict between the States, he was much of what General Marion was in the Revolutionary times, and a paraphrase of Bryant's poem, "The Song of Marion's Men," would apply to Mosby and his little band of partisan rangers:

Woe to the Union soldiery
That little dread us near!
On them small light at midnight
A strange and sudden fear
When, waking to their tents on fire,
They grasp their arms in vain,
And they who stand to face us
Are beat to earth again;
And they who fly in terror deem
A mighty host behind
And hear the tramp of thousands
Upon the hollow wind.

Equally true of Mosby and his guerrilla band are Bryant's words on Marion here paraphrased*:

Our band is few, but true and tried.
Our leader frank and bold:
The Union soldier trembles
When Mosby's name is told.

There was little in the early life of John S. Mosby to indicate that he would become one of the most famous and feared warriors of the long struggle between North and South. As a young Virginia lawyer he enlisted in the Southern cause as a volunteer cavalryman. He was attached to the command of Col. later General "Jeb" Stuart.

Destinies are shaped on little things and a rainstorm played its part in making the name of Mosby something to be dreaded later in Union camps. One day General Stuart ordered Mosby, then a private trooper, to escort two young women to a place of safety. In person Mosby reported that he had conducted the general's friends beyond the danger zone.

Ocala Evening Star – May 30, 1916 (Edited)
JOHN S. MOSBY

Famous Confederate Raider Died in Washington After a Long Illness at the Age of Eighty-two

Washington, May 30.—Col. John S. Mosby, the famous Confederate raider in the war between the states, died here this morning after a long illness. He was a native of Virginia, aged 82. The funeral will be held at Warrenton, Va., but no time has been announced. Mosby, who had been employed in the Department of Justice for many years, resigned several years ago.

Physicians in attendance said that Col. Mosby's death was due solely to old age. He was conscious and interested in what was going on about him until an hour before his death. The funeral will probably be held Thursday. Members of Mosby's old command will be pall bearers.

Chickasha Daily Express – May 30, 1916

Topeka State Journal – May 30, 1916

TAPS FOR FAMOUS VETERAN

Col. Mosby, Confederate Cavalry Leader, Passes Away at Age 83 After Brief Illness In Capital Hospital

WAS DASHING FIGURE DURING CIVIL WAR

Ogden Standard – May 30, 1916

Norwich Bulletin – May 31, 1916

Evening Banner – June 2, 1916

Hartford Republican - June 2, 1916

COLONEL MOSBY DIES AT CAPITAL –

FAMOUS RAIDER'S CAREER

Most Famous Confederate Raider of Civil War Succumbs to Long Illness in Washington

New York Times - May 30, 1916

COL. JOHN S. MOSBY, WAR GUERRILLA, DIES

Famous Confederate Raider, Who Was Terror to the North,

Expires in Washington at 82.

He Was Never Captured

Kidnapped General Stoughton on One of His Daring Exploits—His Services After the Civil War.

Evening Times-Republican, – May 30, 1916

Rock Island Argus, – May 30, 1916

Col. J. Mosby, Noted Raider Passes Away

Evening Herald – May 30, 1916

Evening Ledger – May 30, 1916

Tacoma Times – May 30, 1916

Mosby, Romantic Raider, Answers Final Summons

Man Who Shared With "Jeb" Stuart the Credit for Confederacy's Brilliant and Daring Cavalry Achievements, Dies Today At the Home of His Daughter in Washington

Harrisburg Telegraph – May 30, 1916

Evening World – May 30, 1916

Daily Ardmoreite – May 30, 1916

Manchester Democrat – May 31, 1916

COLONEL MOSBY DIES

Confederate Raider Performing Daring Feats in War.

Captured General Stoughton With Handful of Men—Saved From Death by General Grant.

Washington, May 30.—Colonel John S. Mosby, the most famous Confederate raider of the Civil War, died here to-day after a long illness in his eighty-second year.

Colonel Mosby's death, his physicians said, was due solely to old age, and he was conscious and interested in what was going on about him until an hour before he passed away.

Honolulu Star Bulletin – May 30, 1916 (Edited)

Bennington Evening Banner – May 30, 1916

COL. MOSBY DIES OF OLD AGE IN WASHINGTON

Famous Confederate Raider was 82 Years Old Close Friend of Grant

Federal General Once Saved Guerilla Leader from Hanging During Civil War Washington, May 30.—Col. John S. Mosby, the famous Confederate raider in the war between the states, died here this morning after a long illness. He was a native of Virginia, aged 82.

Physicians in attendance said that Col. Mosby's death was due solely to old age. He was conscious and interested in what was going on about him until an hour before his death.

Colonel Mosby's death, his physicians said, was due solely to old age, and he was conscious and interested in what was going on about him until an hour before he passed away.

Until six months ago, when he went into a sudden decline, he was a familiar sight about the streets of the capital, apparently vigorous despite his age.

He will be buried at his ancestral home at Warrenton, Va., probably Thursday, and some survivors of his noted command will be his pallbearers. Some sisters, a son and daughters survive him.

Bryan Daily Eagle – May 30, 1916

GREAT CONFEDERATE LEADER IS DEAD

Col. John S. Mosby, Most Daring of All Confederates, Died in Washington.

Washington, May 30.—Colonel John S. Mosby, the most famous raider of the civil war, died here today after a long illness. He was a native of Virginia, and was 82 years of age.

Bemidji Daily Pioneer – May 31, 1916
COL. JOHN S. MOSBY DIES AT WASHINGTON

Honolulu Star Bulletin – May 30, 1916
Bennington Evening Banner – May 30, 1916
COL. MOSBY DIES OF OLD AGE IN WASHINGTON

Famous Confederate Raider was 82 Years Old Close Friend of Grant

Federal General Once Saved Guerilla Leader from Hanging During Civil War

Times-Dispatch – May 31, 1916 (Edited)
John S. Mosby

John S. Mosby, who died in a Washington hospital yesterday, won more deserved renown in the War Between the States than any subordinate cavalry leader on either side. The chief element in his equipment, that made him the beloved of his friends and the terror of his enemies, was a daring that had no qualification whatever, but with it he possessed and displayed military skill of a high order.

How much damage Mosby and his few hundred men inflicted on the Federal forces perhaps would be impossible even to estimate. On the money basis it ran into many millions of dollars, but his chief value to the Confederacy was in the uncertainty and demoralization he inspired in the enemy.

He was a gallant soldier, the recital of whose deeds will thrill Virginians through many generations. There was something appropriate in his soul's passage from earth on the day his native State dedicates to honoring the memory of the Confederate dead. In that brave company of his comrades, with the Lee he served so loyally and the Stuart he loved more than a brother, he will receive a soldier's welcome home.

The Intelligencer – May 31, 1916 (Edited)
Washington, May 30—John S. Mosby, the most famous Confederate raider of the war between the states died here after a long illness. He was a native of Virginia and aged eighty-two.

In spite of his advanced age, Col. Mosby, until a few weeks ago took many walks through the down town section of the city. His age had not bent his figure or dimmed the keenness of his eye. He seldom passed through a crowd without being recognized. Mosby was for many years in the service of the justice department, but quit several years ago. He became ill a few weeks ago and was taken to Garfield hospital. The funeral will be at Warrenton, Virginia. The time is not announced.

From Old Age

Washington, May 30.—Mosby's death was due entirely to old age, the doctors said. He was conscious and interested in what was going on about him until an hour before his death.

He will be buried in Warrenton probably Thursday. Some survivors of his noted command will be pallbearers. It was said of Mosby that he never took part in veterans' reunions because he was so overcome he was unable to speak. Some sisters, a son and a daughter survive.

Evening Star – May 31, 1916

COL. MOSBY TO BE BURIED AT OLD VIRGINIA HOME

Funeral Services at Warrenton, Va., With Honorary Pallbearers from His Former Command.

New York Tribune – May 31, 1916

Interior Journal – June 2, 1916

COL. J. S. MOSBY DIES IN CAPITAL

Most Famous Confederate Raider Succumbs in 82d Year.

Pledged Allegiance to U. S. After War

"Last of Partisans" Gained Fame Through Capture of Gen. Stoughton.

Evening Public Ledger – May 31, 1916

Mosby, famous Confederate cavalryman, whose passing fell by odd chance on Memorial Day, invented a style of warfare which "made each man equivalent to a hundred." Oh, for a Mosby now for our border work!

Bridgeport Evening Farmer – May 31, 1916 (Edited)

COLONEL MOSBY, GUERILLA CHIEF, DIES AT CAPITAL

Daring Leader of Confederate Band in Civil War, 82, Succumbs.

Mosby accepted the result of the war philosophically, even patriotically. He became a Republican in politics and took the stump for Grant. He was United States Consul at Hong Kong from 1878 to 1885 and filled other Federal positions with ability and honor.

Richmond Dispatch – May 31, 1916 (Edited)

Picturesque Leader of Southern Cavalry Dead in Washington.

Col. John S. Mosby, Famed in Annals of War Between States, Falls Before Burden of Years.

Washington, May 30.—Colonel John S. Mosby, famous Confederate cavalry leader of the Civil War, died here to-day, after a long illness. He was a native of Virginia, and was eighty-two years old.

Colonel Mosby was one of the most picturesque figures in the capital, where he had lived for many years after the war. In spite of his advanced age, until a few weeks ago it was his custom to take many walks through part of the downtown section of the city. Age had not bent his figure nor dimmed the keenness of eye that commanded the hand that made vivid history in the war, and it was seldom he passed through a crowded street that he was not recognized.

For many years, the Confederate leader was employed at the Department of Justice, but he left the service several years ago. A few weeks ago he became ill, and was taken to Garfield Hospital, where he lingered until he died today. Colonel Mosby's surviving children are: Mrs. Stuart Mosby Coleman, of 1440 Rhode Island Avenue, Northwest, who made her home with her father during his declining years, Miss Ada Mosby and Miss Pauline Mosby, of Baltimore, and Beverly C. Mosby, of Spokane, Wash. Two sisters also survive. They are Miss Blakely Mosby and Mrs. Charles W. Russell, of Washington.

Washington Post – May 31, 1916 (Edited)
COL. JOHN MOSBY DEAD

Noted Confederate Cavalryman Expires at Age 82. Was Terror to Union Forces. Held Back Sheridan in the Shenandoah and Harassed Others in Trying Days of Civil War—Grant's Friend Later—Funeral at Warrenton Tomorrow. Col. John Singleton Mosby, famous Confederate cavalry leader, died yesterday morning at Garfield Hospital after an illness of about three weeks. He was in possession of all his mental faculties to the end. With him at the time of his death were his three daughters, Misses Ada and Pauline Mosby, of Baltimore and Mrs. Stuart Mosby Coleman of this city, with whom he had lived latterly.

The body will be taken to his former home, Warrenton, Va. It is expected special honor will be accorded his memory at the celebration of Memorial day by the Confederate veterans at Arlington next Sunday. Internment will be tomorrow at 9 o'clock in the family plot near the home occupied for generations by his forbears. Four of his six pallbearers have been chosen, all white haired men who served with the daring raider.

Coincidence in His Death.

The coincidence of Col. Mosby's death occurring on Memorial Day, when the graves of blue and gray alike are being decorated at Arlington and other cemeteries, lent a touch of additional sadness to his demise.

The other survivors of Col. Mosby's family are a son, Beverly C. Mosby, of the State of Washington, and two sisters, Miss Blakely Mosby and Mrs. Charles W. Russell, wife of the former United States Minister to Persia, the latter two of this city.

Daily Capital Journal – May 31, 1916
COLONEL JOHN MOSBY FAMOUS RAIDER DEAD

Commanded Mosby's Guerillas

Washington, May 30.—Colonel John Mosby, age 83, daring Confederate leader in the civil war, died today at Garfield hospital. He had been critically ill since Sunday. As leader of Mosby's guerillas, the Colonel made a place for himself in history during the conflict between the North and South.

Mosby suffered from complications of diseases, partly incurred through exposures suffered in his picturesque raids upon the Union army and later, when he was a federal prisoner. He received a government pardon.

***Washington Herald* – May 31, 1916**
MOSBY FUNERAL HELD TOMORROW

Veteran Rangers Will Escort Body to Warrenton, Va., For Last Rites.

It is rather amazing to consider that the above often exceptionally lengthy articles (edited) are only a few of those printed about Mosby's death and that these only date to May 31, the day after he died! Coverage of his passing continued well into the rest of the year. Below is a particularly gracious "obituary" carried in the West Virginian on the first of June:

***West Virginian* – June 1, 1916**
JOHN SINGLETON MOSBY

That Col. Mosby should strike his colors before the all-conquering presence on Memorial Day of all days seems after all, but natural. It was to be expected that there would be an element of the dramatic in his death, for there was scarcely an episode that was ordinary in his whole long life. He was a nature keyed high and he played the game of life at full pitch. America, the home of the picturesque, has seen few characters of such varied and striking personal traits as were possessed by this famous cavalry leader and guerilla chieftain, and it is a significant commentary upon the American spirit that death should find him full of years and honors whom it had once sought with such relentless bitterness.

Perhaps no man in the history of this country was hated by so many people with such an intensity of passion as was once evoked by John Mosby.

His name during the Civil War became a byword and an anathema in the North and he was the bogey with which mothers threatened dire punishment to their children. But though the warfare he waged against the Union troops was ruthless to a degree, it has come to be known in later years that he was quite guiltless of much of the frightfulness attributed to him and his men.

Of his deeds of daring volumes might be written and several have. He was one of those bold and impetuous spirits who know not the meaning of fear and his useful career in civil life following the Rebellion was characterized by no less ardent service of his reunited country than had been his espousal and prosecution of the activities of the "lost cause." May his sleep be as tranquil as his life was turbulent, will be the wish of thousands who once derided his name without measure.—*Gazette Times.*

Whoever wrote this piece "knew" more about John Mosby than many of those who considered—and consider—themselves "experts" on the man and his life. It would have pleased him to see such a tribute at the hands of an anonymous admirer.

Times-Dispatch – **June 1, 1916**
MOSBY FUNERAL TO-DAY

Services and Internment at Warrenton, Old Home of Confederate Cavalry Leader.

Washington, May 31.—Funeral services for Colonel John S. Mosby, famous Confederate cavalry leader, who died here yesterday, will be held tomorrow at Warrenton, Va., his old home. The body will leave here for Warrenton to-morrow morning, and services will be held at the cemetery in Warrenton after the body arrives.

Honorary pallbearers will be members of Mosby's troop, and will include Captain Fount Beattie, Alexandria, Va.; Captain Samuel Chapman, Covington, Va., and D. Mason, of Warrenton.

It is expected that most of the surviving members of Mosby's troop will attend the services.

Telegrams of sympathy and condolence poured into the Mosby home to-day. They came from all sections of the country, the North as well as the South.

One, received from Governor Henry C. Stuart, of Virginia, was as follows:

"I am greatly bereft by the sad announcement that comes from Washington. I prized the friendship and affectionate regard of Colonel Mosby as that of a few men in the world. I cherished for him the highest admiration, both as a man and as a soldier, and considered it a privilege and honor to have known him in life, and I shall ever honor him in memory.

President E. A. Alderman, of the University of Virginia sent the following:

"The University of Virginia lost one of her bravest and noblest sons. The president and the faculty send expressions of the most profound sympathy and affection."

Press coverage continued with regard to Mosby's funeral in Warrenton and, as with Stuart before him, Mosby's passing was acknowledged by the London Times of June 1st in which is mentioned his letter to *The Times* defending the men of his command, itself a noble testimony to what John Mosby considered of supreme importance:

The London Times – **June 1, 1916 (Edited)**
DEATH OF COL. JOHN MOSBY.

A Famous Confederate Cavalry Leader.

The death is announced in his 83rd year of Colonel Mosby, a famous partisan leader on the Confederate side of the American Civil War.

John S. Mosby was, perhaps, the most celebrated of the guerilla leaders produced by the war. At the outbreak of hostilities in 1861 he enlisted in the 1st Virginia Cavalry of the Confederate Army. Taken prisoner by

Northern troops he was exchanged in the summer of 1862. General Lee quickly recognized Mosby's fine qualities and promotion came rapidly. At the close of 1862 he became colonel of Mosby's Partisan Rangers, a little force which under his dashing leadership soon grew famous. In a recent private letter he said, "My command never consisted of more than two or three hundred men." Some of his most brilliant exploits were achieved with a much smaller force.

In *The Times* of December 30, 1914, there appeared a spirited letter from Colonel Mosby, in reply to Mr. George Haven Putnam, in which he denied that his men in 1864 were crippled old farmers, who at night became active raiders, and declared they were in uniform and mounted and fought by daylight with pistols.

Washington Herald – June 1, 1916

VETERANS AT MOSBY FUNERAL

Former Comrades Will Bury Confederate Leader Today

Military organizations from Alexandria and Charlottesville will act as escort of honor at the funeral in Warrenton, Va., today of Col. John S. Mosby. Veterans of the civil war and allied organizations of young members from so many towns surrounding Warrenton also will attend.

The body of the noted warrior will leave Union Station at 9 o'clock this morning and arrive at Warrenton at 11 o'clock. Accompanying it will be Charles W. Russell, brother-in-law of Col. Mosby; the three daughters, Miss Ada Mosby, Miss Pauline Mosby and Mrs. Stuart Mosby Coleman and nieces and nephews. Among the friends who will go from here are Dr. Murray Russell, Miss Nona Thompson, Richard Brooke and Lawrence Washington.

Farmington Times – June 2, 1916

Col. John Mosby, the dashing cavalry leader of the Confederacy, died in Washington City last Tuesday (Memorial Day,) aged 82 years. There was no more daring man that Col. Mosby on either side of the civil war, and though in command of but a few daring rangers like himself, there was no undertaking too venturesome for him.

One of his most brilliant exploits occurred, according to historical records, on "a night in March, 1863, when with thirty followers, he rode through the Federal army to Fairfax Court House, only 15 miles from Washington, where Gen. Stoughton was asleep. Although surrounded by an army said to have been 17,000 strong, the rangers calmly kidnapped the general, his staff and many sentries, and turned them over to the Confederate authorities at Culpeper without having lost a man."

Mosby's funeral was carried in many newspapers, and he undoubtedly would have appreciated the military tribute as he was laid to rest:

Times-Dispatch – June 2, 1916

COL. MOSBY IS BURIED WITH MILITARY HONORS

Four Companies of Virginia National Guard Act as Escort—Funeral at Warrenton

Warrenton, Va., June 1.—With four companies of Virginia National Guard acting as an escort of honor, the body of John S. Mosby was borne to its last resting place in the cemetery here to-day.

Many of the daring Confederate raider's comrades and other veterans of the Civil War attended the funeral.

The body was brought from Washington this morning, accompanied by Charles W. Russell, brother-in-law of Colonel Mosby; the three daughters, Misses Ada and Pauline Mosby and Mrs. Stuart Mosby Coleman.

Colonel Mosby rests beside his wife in the Mosby plot in Warrenton cemetery. The services were conducted by Father S. R. Gill, of the Catholic Church.

When the funeral train arrived at 11 o'clock, the Alexandria, Culpeper and Charlottesville military companies were aboard. The Warrenton Rifles joined them at the station, and the body was escorted to the town hall, where it lay in state for four hours, before it was taken to the cemetery.

The honorary and active pallbearers were all members of Colonel Mosby's old command. Governor Stuart was represented at the funeral by John Stewart Bryan, publisher of the Richmond News Leader.

All the business houses of Warrenton were closed for four hours, as a mark of respect to the Confederate chieftain.

Washington Times – June 2, 1916

JOHN SINGLETON MOSBY

In his beloved foothills of Virginia they laid at rest yesterday the last great figure of the Rebellion. Ardently loved by those for whom and with whom he fought; feared if not hated by those whom he opposed; a warrior of Roman cast and Spartan courage, Colonel Mosby was no less brave in peace than in war and no less loyal a citizen than as a soldier. He craved no pomp in life nor panoply in death. Had he in his last hours but had the strength to make request his words would have taken the spirit if not the from of the too little known sonnet, "Resurgam."

When I return to earth again—build though
No stately mausoleum for my grave,
(No polished slab of marble do I crave
With richly chiseled letters) or allow
Aspiring shafts of granite to arise.
Stew not fresh flowers on a holiday,
Nor cut the riotous weeds and grass away;
But let me rest unnoticed 'neath the skies

For flowers fade, and granite falls away.
White marble crumbles into dust, the wind
Will tear the flags to tatters, and the rain
And moss will blur my name—while yet my clay
Shall revel in the grasses unconfined,
And, flushed with sun and rain, find Life again.

Perhaps *The Times* remembered John Mosby's response to the testament of a former Ranger who had spent a very large sum of money on a mausoleum to house his mortal remains. If so, the newspaper was more accurate than most because Mosby despised the trumpery of funerary displays and would indeed have preferred to be laid quietly in the soil of his native state. However, he probably would not have despised a stone to mark his resting place as he had already provided five such for those he loved who had gone on before him.

The Sun – June 4, 1916 (Edited)

LAST OF THE SOUTH'S DARING CAVALRYMEN

Gen. Mosby's Death Recalls Stories of the Exploits of the Famous Guerrilla Leader

The death of John Singleton Mosby removes from the thinning ranks of civil war veterans one of the most picturesque figures of them all. He was the last of the brilliant quintet of Confederate swift riders—Stuart, Mosby, Morgan, Forrest and Wheeler—whose daring achievements crowned the Southern cavalry with glory even in defeat and made them the wonder and envy of their foes.

The popular Northern conception of the famous guerrilla was that of a dark browed brigand, heavy and ferocious in feature as he was ruthless in deeds. Those who met the real Mosby of that stirring period experienced a shock at the sight of the fair haired, smooth faced young commander, his delicate, sensitive mouth parting over his white teeth in a constant satirical smile, and only the well-defined chin carried proudly forward and the steel blue eyes roving restlessly from side to side indicating the potentiality of his slender, wiry frame.[Here, there appeared a very long recounting of Mosby's military and civilian careers.-vph]

Mosby ever expressed great contempt for his Confederate colleagues who made the "constitutional right of secession" the pretext for rebellion. "I was a rebel," he would declare, "and I am proud of it. I never indorsed secession and I fought on that side only because Virginia did. Men don't fight from principle, but from sentiment; I was going to fight with my own people no matter whether they were right or wrong!"

He was blunt to the point of brusqueness, impatient of interruption or contradiction with the intolerance that belongs to an imperious nature. The habitual expression of his face in repose was one of sadness, but in recital of stirring reminiscences became the ready reflector of his imperious will and his tones took on the clarion note which once sounded in the furious charge.

The following incident related by himself gives a fleeting glimpse of a proud humility at odds with his usual imperiousness:

"I never knew Joe Wheeler during the war, but when they brought him to Washington for internment at Arlington I thought I would attend his funeral. So I went around to St. John's Church where the service was to be held, and arriving there just as the Confederate veterans were filing in the door, I fell into line with them.

"As I didn't have on the badge nor any Confederate insignia the sentinel at the door challenged my right in the line and turned me back. I turned without a word and was making my way out to the street when some one in charge who recognized me and had witnessed my rejection at the door said to the doorkeeper, Why that's John Mosby,' and sent him running after me. I went back and took my place among the old soldiers next to the bier."

As he finished this unaffected narrative, apparently unconscious of its pathos, the pensive, far away look settled on the thin features of the aged chieftain while the eyes of his listener filled with unshed tears.

This article from the New York Sun was one of the more moving of the tributes to Mosby. Certainly, for all his "imperiousness" and lack of patience exhibited in his old age (undoubtedly exacerbated by constant physical discomfort and the shocks of fortune), Mosby's response to being turned away from Wheeler's funeral is a far better gauge of his character and natural modesty than his querulous episodes. He didn't complain; he never did. He didn't demand; he didn't do that either. He simply left. Had he not been recognized, he would have gone his way without a word of complaint.

Iowa City Citizen - **June 5, 1916**

When John S. Mosby, a young Virginia lawyer, at outbreak of the civil war enlisted as a private, he had absolutely no military training. By his audacity, resourcefulness and tireless love of adventure, he became one of the South's most effective cavalrymen. He and Fitz Lee were "Jeb" Stuart's two favorites. As a scout and a raider, operating in the northern tier of Virginia, Mosby made his name hated and feared by northern generals.

Whether at the head of his picked body of horsemen, the "Partisan Rangers," or a battalion of Virginia cavalry, be was always on the move, always preparing surprises. If he was hard pressed or in serious danger he disbanded his men, to meet them again at a given place. It was Mosby's boast that he held receipts for over 6,000 federals taken by himself and his troopers. He destroyed and captured millions of dollars' worth of supplies. In one raid he captured two federal paymasters with $168,000 in money, cut Sheridan's railroad communications, burned a large quantity of rolling stock and bagged a northern brigadier general. In the north, Mosby was branded as a lawless and barbarous guerrilla and accused of robbery and murder. Custer threatened to hang him and all his men if captured. From the nature of his methods as a leader of irregulars, it was inevitable that he should be denounced as little better than a bandit, but severe retaliation was the order on both sides, and cavalry raiders, north and south, were not overnice in their regard for property. Even at their worst, Mosby's war methods were mild compared with what Europe has experienced in the last twenty-two months.

When John Mosby was a sickly child confined to bed for weeks at a time, he comforted himself with books, many about great military heroes of the past. In his memoirs, he wrote:

"In my books were two pictures that made a lasting impression on me. One was of Wolfe dying on the field in the arms of a soldier; the other was of Putnam riding down the stone steps with the British close behind him."

Much of the reading done by this frail child, whose physical restrictions prevented more strenuous activities, involved great soldier heroes such as Francis Marion, the famous Swamp Fox of the Revolutionary War. And although Mosby said little about it, he probably dreamed of being a soldier and at the end of his life receiving a funeral fitting for a hero forged in war. However, it is also probable that given his health, young Jack Mosby knew that such a glorious fate would never be his. If one believes that death is not the end, then one must wonder what this man thought of his funeral. Were the dreams of the child fulfilled in the man? As his was the life of a hero, it is comforting to know that he received a hero's tribute in death.

And still there were publications that did not let Mosby's accomplishments as a soldier fade away at his death, believing that what he was and what he did still had value even with all the new technologies. It is probable that John Mosby would have been pleased to see that his method of warfare was not considered obsolete and that he still had something to contribute, albeit posthumously, even in the new century:

Daily East Oregonian – June 5, 1916
MOSBY, AVIATOR OF THE SADDLE

Col. John S. Mosby was a military aviator of the Civil War period. That is, he was as close to an approximation to the fighters of the air was possible at the time of the warfare in which he participated. From the lower plane of a saddle he performed prodigies in scouting and in other independent services scarcely surpassed by those who patrol or give battle in the marvelous devices from the plane of the clouds.

A cultured man of engaging qualities, he found some of his most sincere admirers among the enemy, who once held him in such detestation that they designed hanging him when captured. The South's wonderful mobilization of its military resources drew to its defense many men of whom he was a type. Until nearly 28 years of age, he had been a lawyer and scholar to whom the practical problems of soldiers were almost unknown.

How was the South able to transform him and many other men of like peaceful careers into men of prompt decision, quick action, resourcefulness in adopting means to ends, and an almost unerring capacity for doing the right thing at the right time—in short into men with almost ideal qualities for command? How also was she able to transform men of peaceful pursuits into peerless rank and file? For this transformation of men at the call of patriotism was even more remarkable in the South, which fought against great odds, than in the North.

When we have learned the South's secret of discovering and utilizing Mosbys among its unprepared masses, we shall have learned a valuable lesson in preparedness.—St. Louis Post Dispatch.

Ogden Standard – June 5, 1916
WHEN THE CAVALRY LEADER GAINED GLORY

The Northern papers give Col. John S. Mosby his fitting place in history, which is added evidence that the sting of the great war is entirely forgotten. Frank Knox in his paper says:

"The death on Memorial day of Col. John S. Mosby ends a striking and remarkable career. Famous half a century ago as one of the most dashing raiders of the Confederacy; famous too, for the ban of outlawry at one time resting upon him; not less marked in the public eye because of his complete acceptance of the new order when the war was over, this Rebel who never formally surrendered yet who bowed to the verdict of Appomattox, came to hold a unique place in the history of his time. With our minds full of the present great war, we find the record of Mosby's exploits in the '60's curiously unlike those which now fill the press. The dashing cavalryman is out of place and out of date on the long western front, and indeed, on most of the stretches where German and Austrian face the Russian. Trench warfare, and lines running from sea to mountains have ended flanking movements. There is no chance for such cavalry achievement as that which made Mosby and eye-filling figure in the Civil War by his ride around McClellan's army.

Even in the East there has been of late nothing to appeal to the lover of the brilliant dash unless it is the ride of the Russians to join the British on the Tigris. Possibly it may be said that the swifter air-craft have displaced the hard-riding squadrons, and that a Mosby today would win distinction as an aerial scout, but the fact remains that the branch of the service in which he attained high reputation seems to have seen its best days of promise and of performance.

And still, the little news stories that had accompanied him through his life continued after his death, though they did not address any great and momentous matters. Rather, they tended to be gentle and somewhat intimate in nature:

Daily East Oregonian – June 13, 1916

Late Colonel Particular

Washington, June 13.—"The late Colonel John S. Mosby differed from many military men in that instead of being pleased at being given a higher designation than he was properly entitled to, the conferring of the higher title was extremely obnoxious to him," remarked Henry D. Rose of Norfolk, Va., as the Raleigh. "People who thought to please him by calling him general instead of finding favor, invoked upon themselves the resentment of the old partisan chief. "I never was a general, sir," I heard him once say with great warmth to a young Virginian who thus addressed him. 'I am Colonel Mosby, and I never attained any higher rank than colonel, so please don't call me general.'

"As brave a spirit as ever lived, the old warrior was full of eccentricities. One of his peculiarities was his persistent declination to attend any of the reunions of Mosby's men. He probably gloried in the fact that these reunions were held, but no amount of persuasion could get him to be present. He used occasionally to indulge in a little grim humor regarding the number of those who attended the reunions. As the years went by, naturally many of his old followers would cross to the great beyond, but curiously enough, according to the Colonel's own statement there seemed to be just as many of Mosby's men at these annual gatherings a generation after the civil war as ever he had enlisted in his command at the height of its numerical strength."

Anderson Intelligencer **– June 16, 1916**

MOSBY A GOOD SOLDIER

Kept Northern Forces in Virginia and Maryland in Dread.

Washington, May 30.—Col. John S. Mosby, the most famous Confederate raider of the civil war, died here today after a long illness. He was a native of Virginia and 82 years old.

Colonel Mosby's death, his physicians said, was due solely to old age. He was conscious and interested in what was going on about him until an hour before his death.

There are few career which in intensity of interest can equal that of Colonel Mosby. Mosby's command, or "Mosby's Men," as they came to be known, were the dread of all the Federal forces in northern Virginia and Maryland during the civil war.

His cavalry command played havoc with the opposing lines. Many were the Federal cavalry outposts and supply trains which this band of fearless men captured.

Hairbreadth escapes were as common to them as the incidents of ordinary life today. Many were the times when Mosby and his men saw hope of life vanish, for they knew no quarter would be given them.

But in spite of all Federal efforts, the great leader never was taken. In his books, "Mosby's War Reminiscences" and "Stuart's Cavalry Campaign," much is told of warfare in Virginia.

In recent years, Colonel Mosby became reticent. Only with his most intimate friends would he discuss the issues of the "lost cause" or his many daring escapes from the enemy's lines and his capture of Federal troops. He preferred to let the records of history speak for themselves.

As the year went on, so did the publicity—most of it involving the telling, retelling, and further retelling of all the old Mosby stories and a few new ones that may or may not have been the result of fond, if not accurate, memories. In August, a movement began to erect a monument to a man who had refused all attempts to do so while he lived:

Evening Star **– August 2, 1916**

Times-Dispatch **– August 3, 1916**

Washington Herald **– August 3, 1916**

ALEXANDRIA AFFAIRS

Movement Started to Erect Monument to John S. Mosby Brigade Survivors to Aid

Proposed Shaft Likely to be Put up in Fauquier County, Probably at Warrenton

Times-Dispatch – **August 20, 1916 (Edited)**
SAYS COLONEL MOSBY WAS NOT A GUERRILLA

His Command Was Strictly Cavalry, Fully Officered, Declares Confederate Veteran

SOME EXPLOITS RECALLED

Took Federal General Out of Bed at Fairfax Court House and Carried Him Off—Followers Were Picked Young Men.

To the Editor of the *Times-Dispatch*:

For historical accuracy, as well as to remove a delusion which long ago seized the minds of many persons regarding the late Colonel John S. Mosby and "Mosby's men" of Confederate fame, I beg to submit what follows. The Baltimore Catholic Review, on June 24, 1916, published the following item: "Colonel John S. Mosby, the famous Confederate guerrilla, died in Washington May 30, and was interred at Warrenton., Va, his old home. In his late days he became a convert and was received into the Catholic Church."

I may say here the Colonel Mosby's wife was a Catholic and his daughters are of that faith.

There is irrefutable evidence that Colonel Mosby was not a "Confederate guerrilla" The Confederate army had no guerrillas. So far from being "guerrillas," Colonel Mosby's command was strictly cavalry. He commanded his Forty-third Battalion, Virginia Cavalry, Partisan Rangers, formed according to Confederate army regulations by companies, fully officered.

The Confederate Congress enacted a law creating mounted troops, thus designated, independent of other cavalry commands serving with the cavalry corps of respective armies. Partisan Rangers, when not engaged in open combat, operated upon the flanks, in the rear and within the lines of the enemy, also acting as scouts, Colonel Mosby was himself a born scout. Alone he would enter the enemy's lines, acquire information and bring out prisoners he had captured. With Mosby present, there was always something doing or planning but with Mosby absent (wounded), affairs lagged. Upon his return he would chide his officers. Once, severely wounded, lying prostrate and in the enemy's hands, he told them he was Lieutenant Johnson, Sixth Virginia Cavalry, mortally wounded, whereupon they rode off. One of Mosby's dashing exploits was taking a Yankee general out of his bed, at Fairfax Court House, and carrying him off.

After the war, Colonel Mosby's intercourse with Gen. Grant now historical, was alike grateful, wise and creditable. General Grant certified to Colonel Mosby and his command the paroles and terms generously accorded to General Lee and his army at Appomattox. Mosby, without compromising his convictions, or career, buried his resentment. Grant knowing Mosby's rare worth, met him on equal terms wherefore the conclusion seems inevitable that, had General Grant likewise been approached, he would have treated Confederate leaders with the justice accorded to General Lee at Appomattox. Moreover, General Grant protected General Lee when threatened with prosecution. Grant, once a Democrat—the "coign of vantage"[*] ignored—was let drift among radical Republican leaders and agitators and the result was the "reconstruction" period with its horrors and infamies.

WINFIELD PETERS

[*A favorable position for observation or action: "coign" being an earlier spelling of "coin" or "corner"; this saying was first used in the English language in 1605.-vph]

The last article of any length about Mosby in 1916 appeared in the *Times-Dispatch* in the nature of a "letter to the Editor" (see above) and contained most of the usual matters with one exception—that is, the claim by the article's author that, according to the Baltimore Catholic Review of June 24th, 1916, "in his late days he became a convert and was received into the Catholic Church." The writer of the article was a Mr. Winfield Peters. No mention was made as to his connection to Mosby, whether it was personal or more in the nature of a historian but the matter is of interest because it has been claimed that as Mosby lay unconscious shortly before his death, his devout daughters baptized him into their faith, the claim being made afterward by some Mosby critics that such an attempt "didn't take" with the old sinner. Yet, Mr. Peters' testimony cannot be denied for the proof is contained in the report that the graveside services "were conducted by Father S. R. Gill, of the Catholic Church." No such religious services could have been conducted had John Mosby *not* been received into that Church.

And so 1916 ended without the usual stories in the press about Mosby's birthday celebration. There would be no more birthdays. He had been allotted eighty-two such, far more than even the most optimistic of his family believed possible in his sickly youth or his comrades in arms anticipated when the red tide of war raged around him. It was supposed to have been said of Abraham Lincoln at his death, "Now he belongs to the ages." But as with Lincoln, death did not end John Mosby's romance with the press—it only ended his ability to influence it.

Chapter 56

JOHN S. MOSBY THE MAN: FACT VS. FICTION

Ecce homo. ~ Behold the man.

"Sincerity may be humble, but she cannot be servile."
~ Lord Byron

THE NEWSPAPER ARTICLES, or parts thereof, appearing in this chapter are at least some of those that specifically describe John Mosby's general character and behavior in his relationship with other people. Indeed, this matter has already been addressed numerous times, but given that Mosby's personality has been so badly represented, especially in modern accounts of the man, these gentle "reminders" may, hopefully, be of use for those who still fault the Colonel:

Abingdon Virginian – **December 11, 1863**

In his address and demeanor he is a perfect gentleman, and in his relations with ourselves was highly courteous.

Ouachita Telegraph – **November 27, 1869**

Those who know Col. Mosby personally, will bear testimony to the fact that he is one of the most quiet, unobtrusive gentlemen they ever met. The soul of honor, and a very pink of chivalry.

Yorkville Enquirer – **June 9, 1870**

We first met him on the train coming from Washington to Lynchburg—have met him here several times—find him always a quiet, unassuming, modest, perfect gentleman.

His face is smooth, wearing, except when lit up with a smile, a calm, kind, earnest, studious, thoughtful expression... he was the man of uncontrollable action, yet with perfect control over himself and others.

Donaldsonville Chief – **April 19, 1873**

The Colonel is a quiet and unassuming individual .

New Ulm Weekly Review – **August 14, 1878**

Mosby, the ex-guerilla, is described as a quiet-looking, medium sized man of pleasing manners ...He is very reserved in speaking of his own exploits ...

Leavenworth Weekly Times – **January 2, 1879**

This quiet, middle aged and grey-headed celebrity was on his way to Hong ... Col. Mosby is a man of fine bearing, and is quite reserved in his manners.

Holt County Sentinel – **January 17, 1879**

In manners he is pictured as a most refined gentleman; his voice they say, is as tender as that of a woman, and his bravery, morals and ability are untarnished. A man of the greatest judgment, whom I heard speak of him last night, said "John S. Mosby is the sweetest man I ever knew."

Burlington Weekly Free Press – **March 21, 1879**

He is at all times inclined to retirement.

Atlanta Constitution - **May 12, 1889**

"Why he appears to be quite modest, and I have noticed him ... many times of late, but he has never been talkative. Indeed, he seems to be always in a deep study, and seldom talks unless some one speaks to him."

Daily Herald – **March 27, 1891**

Los Angeles Herald – **March 27, 1891**

... a young man of medium size, with a quiet, taciturn disposition ...

Alexandria Gazette – **January 7, 1895**

He has a preoccupied air and is disposed to be cold and taciturn to strangers, but with his friends he is an affable and entertaining companion, whose conversation reveals scholarly tastes and a close observance of men and affairs.

Alexandria Gazette – **December 4, 1901**

Clarke Courier – **December 11, 1901**

Personally he is a quiet, smooth-shaven, medium-sized, elderly gentleman ...

Alliance Herald – **August 8, 1902**

About the battle-scarred old trooper there is nothing that smacks of ferocity, nothing to indicate the daring, dashing cavalry commander ...But instead there is every indication of the plain, unostentatious, intelligent old gentleman with a mind as vivid and active as in the years of long ago, and a bearing as pleasing and manner as courteous as a diplomat."

Washington Post – **September 28, 1904**

Washington Times – **September 28, 1904**

... Today he is a reticent as ever concerning his heroic exploits.

Times-Dispatch – **July 9, 1910**

Colonel Mosby is opposed to appearing in the press, and has declined to talk for publication following his invariable rule to remain silent.

Times-Dispatch – **December 15, 1912**

In recent years Col. Mosby has become very reticent and only with his most intimate friends will he discuss the issues of the "lost cause" or the daring escapes from the enemy's lines or his own capture of Federal troops. He prefers to let the records of history speak for themselves and he is satisfied with what he has done.

Below is the only article, aside from those written by his implacable foes and motivated by hostility, that depart from the above description of Mosby's personality. However, it is a description of him as an old man, a time when the passage of years tends to cause such "foibles" in even the best of humanity. Yet his comrade at the time was able to understand and accept these small failings arising from the burden of age and the tragedies of life:

The Sun – **June 4, 1916**

He was blunt to the point of brusqueness, impatient of interruption or contradiction with the intolerance that belongs to an imperious nature. The habitual expression of his face in repose was one of sadness, but in recital of stirring reminiscences became the ready reflector of his imperious will and his tones took on the clarion note which once sounded in the furious charge.

The Sun article is the only one that reports Mosby being "imperious and impatient of interruption or contradiction". John Mosby had been personally humiliated a great many times during his life, especially in his old age, and so it is no wonder he could be said to be "proudly humble!" But in the end, the real man appeared when he was turned away from General Wheeler's funeral. His response to what must have been yet another insult was pure John Mosby: he didn't complain or argue or demand—he simply left. And had he not been noticed, he would not have objected to being dismissed like a beggar or a servant. That is true humility and gentleness of spirit.

However, the article that said the most about Mosby's persona appeared as a reprint in the *Wood River Times* on June 18, 1886. It was written by well-known journalist D. C. Russell in the *Omaha Bee* in May of 1885. Russell was not stinting in his praise of Mosby, which went far beyond mere partisan support (the *Bee* was, after all, a Republican paper):

Wood River Times – **June 18, 1886**

John S. Mosby is a giant. Cautious as the Sphinx, his is the reticence of the tomb. Safe and sure as the needle to its bridal star, he possesses a nerve like that of the Nemean lion. With a heart that melts at misery or need, his is a hand always reaching wide open to the true, the honorable and the brave. Dreadful in the charge, his is a woman's tenderness in the truce. Stern in the action, his is mercy's gentleness in the hour after the battle. As a subordinate no man is more obedient—as a commander, he is always appreciative of the truth that it is one of the chief blessings of power that it may show mercy to the weak, and the crown jewel of courage is magnanimity to the helpless. In this trait of character Ulysses S. Grant and John S. Mosby will go hand and hand down the path of the historic future

The above newspaper articles testify that the bad-tempered, ill-natured, waspish little man given to profanity and peevishness is a caricature that far too many "Mosby scholars" simply accept. It didn't exist—or rather, it existed only under certain definite— and limited—circumstances. Certainly, there is no doubt that John Mosby could, and would, respond with hostility and more than a bit of profanity under duress! But he was no "blowhard," no habitual growler and complainer, and certainly no overweening self-centered egotist. Indeed, in his treatment of his fellow man, with very few exceptions, John Mosby was every inch a Virginia gentleman.

Of course, Mosby was a passionate man and, as such, had a temper. But his ire was never raised by the ordinary vicissitudes of life. Even when true injustice was involved, as in his constant arrests after the war, his intelligence and self-restraint precluded actions that would have exacerbated the situation, making it into something infinitely more dangerous. He remained polite and calm as was reported by his persecutors. In point of fact, though Mosby's "prickly" nature made him difficult—one of his friends said that when his ire was aroused, it was like holding a wasp in your hands!—he never lost control. The idea that he was what one biographer declared, "an aginner," is altogether wrong; the facts disprove this claim. Nowhere is this particular error of judgment better identified than in biographer Kenneth Siepel's version of Mosby's first interaction with prosecutor William Robertson after he had been sent to jail as a result Robertson's prosecution in the Turpin case. Years earlier, Mosby himself had written on the subject shortly after Robertson's death in 1898:

> "As you may know, the circumstances under which we first met were not calculated to awaken a feeling of friendship between us. He was the prosecuting attorney for Albemarle County; I was just nineteen years old, and on trial in court on a criminal charge for shooting ... He prosecuted me, as it was thought, not only with great ability but with a great deal of zeal; but in neither of the powerful speeches he delivered in opening and concluding the case did he utter a word to wound the sensibilities of me or of my father, or that rankled in my memory after the trial was over. He discharged a public duty with so much fidelity, but at the same time with so much delicacy, that no other sentiment was inspired by one of respect. I very well remember his saying to the jury that it was a cup which he wished might have passed from him.
>
> You may remember that I was sentenced to pay a fine, and to imprisonment in the county jail ... A few days after the trial he had business with the jailer. I heard them talking at the front door. No doubt he thought it would be natural for me to feel some resentment at the vigor of his prosecution. I went to the door, spoke to him pleasantly, and extended my hand laughing. He responded promptly, and came into the room. I had a book in my hand' he asked me what I was reading. I told him it was Milton's 'Paradise Lost,' but that I hoped soon to enjoy 'Paradise Regained.' ... He made a playful allusion to John Bunyan's writing 'The Pilgrim's Progress' in a prison cell. I remarked that I had determined to study law, and jocularly said, 'The law has made a good deal out of me; I am now going to make something out of the law.' He offered me the use of his library ... I remember borrowing Greenleaf on evidence from him. Our acquaintance began at this meeting; it ripened into a friendship over which, in the vicissitudes of fortune through which I have since passed, not a shadow was ever cast." (the text then goes on-vph)

Lest anyone believe that Mosby's memory some forty-five years after the fact was faulty, Robertson took the youth upon his release from jail into his law office, tutored him in the law and within a year saw him pass his entrance into the Virginia bar and become an attorney. As Mosby mentioned, the two remained close friends for the rest of Robertson's life. Surely, had the matter transpired as Siepel claimed, that would never have been the case, for, according to Siepel, the matter went something like this:

> "He (Mosby) asked his jailer for a law book, but not surprisingly, got nowhere. As he sat brooding in the hot cell, breathing air that was ripening with the advancing season, he could think of only one other person to ask: an attorney he had seen frequently at the jail that spring, William J. Robertson, prosecutor for the Commonwealth, and the man who had put him behind bars. He resolved to speak to Robertson, distasteful though this might be. The older man listened dubiously, one imagines, as Mosby spoke—*probably in the haughty manner of one needing a favor from an enemy, and not wanting to act as though it were being asked* [emphasis vph]. He described his interest in the law, his lack of success in finding appropriate reading material, and wondered if Robertson could see his way toward loaning him a book." (Rebel: The Life and Times of John Singleton Mosby, Kevin H. Siepel, pg. 29)

Why Siepel should have written such a fictional account is not known since the facts of the matter had been presented by, among others, Pat Jones almost forty years earlier. However, it is probable that Jones' account (see the following) did not "fit" Sieple's image of Mosby as an ill-tempered, rebellious and belligerent youth and therefore, to present him as affable and accepting of his fate was akin to pounding a square peg into a round hole. In other words, what Kenneth Siepel thought he knew about John Mosby would have resulted in his description of the incident, not Jones'—even though the latter's version was fact and was undoubtedly taken from Mosby's own account as described in his letter:

> "As ready as Albemarle residents had been to punish Mosby, equally as ready were they after his quiet demeanor in court to help him gain his freedom… And as unexpected to this drive came the sudden news that the prisoner and the Commonwealth's attorney who had prosecuted him had struck up a friendship.
>
> *This had come about surprisingly through the defendant's affability* [emphasis vph]. The attorney, William J. Robertson … stopped by the jail one day to discuss business with the jailor. While they talked a voice sounded behind them. They turned to find Mosby, smiling through the bars, a book under one arm and the other extended toward Robertson.
>
> The attorney was dumbfounded. He had expected only animosity from this youth to whom his vigorous prosecution had brought punishment… Later that day a package was handed through the bars. It contained a copy of Blackstone's 'Commentaries' and a volume of Greenleaf on evidence." (Ranger Mosby, Virgil C. Jones, pgs. 24, 25)

In speaking of the origins of his relationship with Robertson, Mosby stated that nothing said or done by his prosecutor during the trial wounded (the) sensibilities of himself or his family and therefore he had no reason to hold a grudge against the man! John Mosby could hold grudges but they were well earned and easily terminated when the cause that had occasioned them was settled to his satisfaction.

With regard to another matter, some who have written on Mosby make the charge that as an old man he displayed an attitude of entitlement; that he borrowed money he felt no need to repay and that he expected his friends to support him when he was in need. Yet everything that is actually known about the man reveals exactly the opposite. When daughter Pauline was ill and required surgery, Mosby, then an agent with the Land Office, came east to be with her. Upon her recovery, Mosby was to return West but he had to contact his superiors and beg leave to remain because after paying for his daughter's medical bills he did not have the money for the train fare—under $20!—and he did not wish to borrow it. Surely, as Mosby was in the East, he had many friends who would have provided such a small sum to him, but he preferred to humiliate himself by admitting his poverty rather than seek their financial assistance. In the same vein, at least three times in his old age there were efforts to purchase him a home. Those who wanted to subscribe to such an effort were not only Mosby's friends but also Americans who realized the worth of the man. But John Mosby would not hear of it. It is true that upon the death of his daughter May, Mosby was greatly relieved to know that his wealthy friend Joseph Bryan would help with his grandsons' education, but that is hardly an equivalent situation. His grandsons were orphaned and Mosby simply did not have the financial resources to assure their future; Bryan did.

Even in the poverty of his old age, John Mosby was a "giver" not a "taker." He gave of his time and effort to secure the pension of an old black Union veteran; of his limited money to reward a youngster whose behavior he deemed worthy; and of his lecture fees to support a charity for homeless boys. There are doubtless many other examples of selfless behavior that are either unknown or little known but taken together—like the dots of the half-tone process—they prove that the grasping, sour old man of legend does not survive the narrative of history.

From Another Perspective: The Testimony of Alexander Hunter

No argument is proven by presenting only one side. Alexander Hunter knew John Mosby—and didn't like him. Hunter was both an intelligent man and a Southerner and is presented here as a witness for the other side of the question of "who was John Mosby?" Ten years younger than Mosby, Hunter joined the Seventeenth Virginia Infantry, later transferring to the famous Fourth Virginia or Black Horse Cavalry. He authored a number of books on the Civil War. In his book *The Women of the Debatable Land*, Hunter wrote at some length about Mosby; and although he had nothing but praise for his military genius, he did not like Mosby the man. It would seem from Hunter's description of his interactions with Mosby that the feeling was mutual:

> "Mosby, unlike most leaders of men, had no magnetism; he was as cold as an iceberg, and to shake hands with him was like having the first symptoms of a congestive chill. He was positive, evidence of a self-centered man; and he did not know what human sympathy was. He would have been a Stoic had he lived in Athens in the days of Pericles. *The general impression of Mosby is that he was a rough-and-ready, fighting Cracker-Jack, while on the contrary he was a literatus, a classical scholar and a thorough student; but he reminded one strongly of Goldsmith's* lines:*

> "Who wrote like an angel, But talked like poor Poll."

> Mosby was fond of reading the old English literature, and was familiar with Lord Chesterfield's letters; yet, withal, he had the manners of an Indian. His was a fascinating character to study; he was a "stormy petrel," [one who brings discord or appears at the onset of trouble; a rebel] a born soldier, a light cavalryman by instinct, and a partisan who, under no

orders, could accomplish wonders, but in the regular army he would, in all probability never have been heard of. In the piping days of peace he was as a fifth wheel, and steady, plodding work was his abomination. He was of the meteoric type.

Though cold, indifferent and utterly self-centered, yet he was the greatest leader of irregular warfare that history or tradition gives to us."

[*The lines were not by Goldsmith, but about him. David Garrick wrote this-vph:]

"Here lies Nolly Goldsmith, for shortness called Noll,

Who wrote like an angel, but talked like poor Poll."

That Hunter should liken Mosby in any way to Goldsmith is no compliment, for although it was said that Goldsmith "was a very great man," according to J. H. Plumb: "[n]one of them (Goldsmith's contemporaries) knew quite why (he was very great)." Again, according to Plumb:

"He baffled Dr. Johnson with his absurdities; Horace Walpole dismissed him as "an inspired idiot"; David Garrick immortalized him in the biting lines: 'And even Sir Joshua Reynolds, who saw further and deeper into Goldsmith's character than anyone else, realized that no man could get such a reputation for absurdity without there being reason for it.' All agreed that the most absurd thing about Goldsmith, more absurd even than his asinine and inappropriate remarks, was his transparent envy. *He could not bear praise of any man* [emphasis vph]. The adulation rendered to Samuel Johnson gave him acute pain. Sometimes he tried to discharge his envy by making a joke of it and a mock of himself, as when he leaped onto a chair to show that he could deliver a better speech than Edmund Burke and dried up after two sentences. Yet the envy was there; as unmistakable as it was painful. And naturally his friends rubbed salt and acid on the raw aching heart. Solace he found for his strange nature in jokes, in absurdity, and in writing. He was driven by the deep urges of his personality as much as Dr. Johnson or James Boswell, but their urges were powerful, sensual, religious, locked in a massive, virile framework of passion. Oliver Goldsmith was blown about like a butterfly: his character seemed to lack core or mass. He longed for applause, love, affection, to be known to be good, to be wholesome, to be wanted. And the effect became ludicrous. The urgency of his desires, the immediacy of his responses, the unawareness of their excess, made him foolish; his features and his manner rendered him ludicrous. People laughed at him but wanted to be with him, so what began as an absurdity became a practise in folly. Notoriety and laughter, even against himself, were better than isolation and neglect."

It is clear that Hunter saw Mosby in this description of Goldsmith, and so while he was honest enough to admit to the man's military genius, even that was limited to his own particular brand of warfare. In the regular army, according to Hunter, "he would, in all probability, never have been heard of." Yet we know that is untrue. Mosby's name made the papers even before he "went independent" as General "Jeb" Stuart's scout in the "Ride around McClellan." True, had he stayed with Stuart, he never would have reached the fame that he achieved as the leader of an independent command; but given his courage and genius, John Mosby would not have remained "obscure."

But it is not Hunter's evaluation of Mosby as a soldier, but as a man that was so devastating—and so provably false. It is true that Mosby did not try to govern his command through affection. That was the judgment of many including those who were in that command. Yet affection was there and remained through the long years. Neither was it the sort of soldierly "camaraderie" that is found in any army, but a deep abiding love between Mosby and his men. Ranger John Munson began his book, *Reminiscences of a Mosby Guerrilla*, thusly:

> "Our little body of men was called Mosby's Men, and Mosby's Command, and this was largely due to Mosby himself. He took great pride in speaking of us as "my men" and "my Command," but never as "my battalion," or "my troops," or "my soldiers."

John Alexander in his book Mosby's Men makes the most complete statement regarding the bond between commander and command:

> "He knew each man personally, and seemed to read him at a glance ... He mingled with his men, rode with them, slept with them and fought side by side with them. Few members of the command had a longer list of wounds and captures than himself, and fewer still perhaps were more responsible for more personal execution. His care against needlessly exposing them; his great skill in securing them every possible advantage; his cool, quiet courage and the almost unvarying success of every enterprise which he personally conducted secured the perfect confidence of his men. His ready sympathy with them ... revealed his big and tender heart and inspired them with an affection for him which has survived the ... years...

> "At the same time he was absolutely imperious, and no one cared to provoke the second time his trenchant disapproval..."

How different is this testimony of those who served with John Mosby from the report of author Hunter when he stated:

> "Mosby, unlike most leaders of men, had no magnetism; he was as cold as an iceberg, and to shake hands with him was like having the first symptoms of a congestive chill. He was positive, evidence of a self-centered man; and he did not know what human sympathy was... Though cold, indifferent and utterly self-centered, yet he was the greatest leader of irregular warfare that history or tradition gives to us."

But how could Hunter have seen his John Mosby and Munson and Alexander theirs? The two Rangers saw the man who wept at the bedside of a dying Tom Turner and who used himself as a decoy to lure Federal troops into an ambush or away from any of his men who were unable to convey themselves from the scene of a skirmish. Munson saw a man whom he "loved" and who loved him. Hunter never met that man. Munson's description of his first meeting with Mosby is legendary, but the act by Mosby that he most appreciated was the silencing of another Ranger who had begun to laugh at the awkward boy. Munson stated, "Of all the favors for which I am indebted to Colonel Mosby, none was ever more appreciated than this." Such is not the act of a "self-centered man."

The reason for Hunter's dislike of Mosby is not known except that it may have been, as they say, "just one of those things." Those who wrote on the matter did say that when men came into his command whom Mosby could not "engage" as he did men like Munson, they were sent back to the regular army. Mosby knew that they would never follow him as he needed to be followed in order to accomplish his ends, and so he did not burden his command with such men. However talented he was as a soldier, Alexander Hunter would have been one of those Mosby returned to the ranks of the regulars.

Perhaps one of the best descriptions of John Mosby's personality came from the pen of his friend from his university days and his command's second surgeon, Dr. Aristedes Monteiro, who joined the Forty-third late in the war:

> "He seemed to possess two distinct and separate natures. When in a state of repose and not in the presence of the foe, he was quiet, gentle and sociable, fond of jest and raillery, would laugh with boyish glee over a good joke and enjoy with acute zest a witty anecdote or a lively narrative. I had never seen him when his true genius was ignited by the active excitement of the fray. He was not the same individual. He looked like a different man."

But neither the quiet, gentle, sociable man nor the man whose "true genius was ignited by the active excitement of the fray" was seen by Hunter. What he did see was a cold, taciturn man who isolated himself emotionally from Hunter to the point at which the author could not engage that John Mosby experienced by Monteiro or Munson or any of the rest of the men of Mosby's command. The question then becomes why? What made him warm and affectionate, caring and concerned with some, and the cold, unfeeling stoic described by Hunter? There cannot have been two John Mosbys; therefore, the only answer is that there was one John Mosby with two responses to those with whom he interacted. The one response is written about many times by his friends and his comrades in arms and, yes, even some newspaper reporters. The other was the John Mosby known to Alexander Hunter, William Mahone, Jubal Early, and Fitzhugh Lee.

But Hunter was not the only such person known to Mosby. Many who wrote about him stated that with strangers and those for whom he felt no personal warmth, he was "taciturn" and silent. In recognition of this trait, one of his biographers declared him to be "an uncomfortable companion." But the men who served with him and those who knew him after the war maintain the very opposite. When he was among friends, Mosby was genial and "fun loving," enjoying a jest like any schoolboy, as Dr. Monteiro testified. Both were John Mosby, but under different circumstances. Years later, the relationship of Mosby's men with their commander was put into a sort of "motto:"

> *Anywhere with Mosby—gladly, joyously, in darkness, in light, in safety or in peril, with no good reason or bad or no reason at all—anywhere with Mosby!*

However, no examination of John Mosby would be complete without an acknowledgement of two behavioral traits that were a very real part of his character. To leave these unexamined would be detrimental to the credibility of this work and make of it not an apologia, but an exercise in excusing his less comprehensible or satisfactory qualities. One of these problematic conditions was not amenable to change or correction; it was "hard-wired" as they say, into the man's nature. The other carried some onus of blame; in other words, if desired it could have been if not entirely overcome, then at least ameliorated—with effort.

We shall consider first that innate character trait. To begin with, there was nothing intrinsically *wrong* or negative in this trait. Indeed, it was the catalyst of Mosby's genius! However, it also influenced his behavior over his life and not always in a positive way. This trait was most clearly elucidated again by Mosby's friend, Monteiro who wrote:

> "Our leader was, in the fullest acceptation of the term, a man of character. Conventional laws, or the established rules of society, and the ordinary modes of thought were habitually ignored in his conduct and action alike. With uncommon quickness of conception and promptness of execution he followed alone the dictates of his own original and decided reason. *What appeared irrational to other men he would assume as the perfection of wisdom.* [emphasis vph]"

Of course, such a trait meant that everything John Mosby experienced over his life was "filtered," as it were, through a lens most uncommon and, therefore, out of the experience of ordinary people. It also made it difficult for him to understand the more prosaic mental processes of the rest of humanity. When he moaned feelingly to a friend about the inability of so many Southerners to let go of the ills of the war and get on with their lives, his friend told him simply, "They cannot, John!" Mosby did not understand their inability; his own thought processes did not permit it. Eventually, of course, he simply had to accept even if he could not understand. But the real tragedy, of course, was that Mosby's "mental processes were as impossible for most of his fellow Southerners to understand, resulting in a post-war life of censure and strife.

However, while the first trait was a matter over which he had no control, the second was a very real failing at least with regard to social intercourse. This was not a matter of Mosby's *judgment* regarding the worth of his fellow men, but his response to or use of that judgment. If John Mosby didn't like someone, he made little effort to hide that fact—and that *was* a failing, at least as it affected his relationship with those around him. When to this rather disruptive response was added the fact that, like God, John Mosby was no "respecter of persons," the matter could be very problematic—*especially* given the social milieu in which he moved in both his public and private life. For Mosby did not make judgments based upon worldly standards such as fame or wealth or position or family name but upon integrity, courage and talent. Of course, this mindset was ideal when it came to filling the roster of officers for his command, but it caused him considerable grief in his relationship with those who believed that by virtue of those very same worldly standards they should have had at least his respect and probably even his deference.

One such example of this situation was his "relationship" with Fitzhugh Lee. Lee was intuitive enough to know that Mosby did not have—and even more importantly, *demonstrate*—the proper deference to his rank or his name and he responded accordingly. In the military, Mosby had learned the cost of this lack of deference from his first commander, mentor and friend, Col. William Jones. Jones was affectionate and careful with his men, but had no compunction whatsoever in "butting heads" with his superiors, a matter that seriously affected his usefulness as an officer, good as he was. Mosby wrote that his own somewhat caustic temperament was curbed by the consequences of Jones' belligerency.

Also, Mosby was naturally modest. He idolized Stuart and when he found himself in the company of *other* Confederate generals at Stuart's headquarters, he was too overwhelmed by their presence to eat, hungry as he was. Personal modesty precluded this aspect of Mosby's personality negatively affecting him during his military service, though there were still problems in his interactions with Fitz Lee, illustrating that even in uniform he refused to bow to a man whose only gifts were ego, an honored name and a West Point ring. But once Mosby returned to civilian life, he was probably no longer concerned about this particular matter and therefore it is quite possible—as reported in the *Salt Lake Herald* and *Atlanta Constitution* in late 1882—that in private correspondence he characterized his superior, Secretary of State Evarts, as "a d—d spavined, spareboned old fossil!"

I don't think that an argument can be made against the contention that at least some of the grief Mosby suffered at the hands of others during his life was a direct result of his failure to show what was deemed "proper respect" to those who believed that they were *owed* such respect for whatever reason. This doesn't mean that John Mosby was wrong necessarily, but the charge made against him of a "lack of diplomacy," while it did not obtain in most of his *professional* actions was probably true enough in his personal life.

"Let Loose the Dogs of War"

Many of those who have written about John Mosby maintain that he had "a violent streak." They say that he lived for the excitement generated in war and spent the rest of his life attempting to recapture the "glory" of that period of his life. Now it is true that Mosby spoke of being "intensely exhilarated" going into battle:

> *Richmond Climax* – **May 11, 1898**
>
> … Col. Mosby was asked by one of his men if he ever became excited when in battle? "No," said he, "that's hardly the word to express (it); I don't become excited, but I do become intensely exhilarated."

Of course, it is hard to make a distinction between "excited" and "exhilarated" when all is said and done; and doubtless, John Mosby was a man who "enjoyed" war; that is, he responded as a warrior to the realities of battle. The quote above makes that quite clear. However, it is a very different thing to be emotionally and psychologically suited to be a soldier engaging in combat and to have "a violent streak." Many is the coward who displays a penchant for violence, but only against those whom he can easily overcome! But to charge John Mosby with this character flaw—and it cannot be considered anything but a flaw—because he did a lot of fighting in his childhood ignores the situation extant at that time. If Mosby had initiated his youthful physical encounters, then he would have lacked intelligence and rationality, which is demonstrably false. With the exception of the time he pummeled a town constable in Charlottesville with his own nightstick (and no, he did not club him with a gunstock!), all of Mosby's encounters were responses to attacks upon his person. Even the incident with the constable was a response to a very large—and one assumes none too bright—oaf clubbing a small fellow student with that same nightstick, a matter that inflamed young John Mosby's rather sensitive precept of "justice"!

The "violence" John Mosby exhibited during his youth was in response to the fact that he was the constant target of bullies. Mosby wrote in later years about the cruelty of boys—that is, that the largest always picked upon the smallest among them, and Jack Mosby was *always* the smallest among them. But Mosby always fought back even though, admittedly, he lost all of his battles. Certainly, he had a naturally *combative* nature (most small men do); but not to fight back would, in the South of that time, have branded him a coward, and that would have been fatal to his future.

Even Mosby's fight with George Turpin was not of his doing. Now Turpin *was* by nature violent, beating weaker smaller boys insensible while a coterie of hangers-on watched. The frail delicate classics scholar may have already caught his eye, but there is nothing to suggest that Mosby responded openly to Turpin's attentions. However, once the die was cast, had Mosby attempted to ignore Turpin, it would have been perceived that he did so out of fear and he would have been socially ruined. Yet Mosby attempted to *defuse* the situation with a respectful note asking for an explanation of Turpin's insult. But Turpin made it known that he would "eat him (Mosby) up blood raw!" upon their next meeting and then went looking for his chosen victim. Perhaps Mosby took the pistol to use as a deterrent to his opponent's obvious intentions because when the two met, Mosby tried to forestall matters by initiating a conversation: "I hear you have been making assertions …" But Turpin was not interested in conversation; rather, he put his head down and charged. Mosby pulled out the pistol and fired from mere feet away.

In the Turpin affair, Mosby adopted several characteristics seen during the war. First, he stood up against a notorious bully—and was there *ever* a bigger bully than the Army of the Potomac and its master, the Federal government? He was prepared to take a beating, but when a better option presented itself (that of being armed), he was willing to choose it despite its obvious dangers. Mosby later stated that the war had given smaller men an advantage that they usually lacked in such confrontations—*that of being armed!* And when he was convicted at trial, he suffered a severe blow to his naïve concept of justice, yet—*and this is the most important point!*—he did not become angry or bitter or petulant but used adversity to his advantage. Indeed, his behavior toward prosecutor William Robertson resulted in the older man becoming his mentor and tutoring him in the law. Mosby's amiability astonished Robertson, probably demonstrating to the older man that the youth was of a higher character and greater maturity than Robertson had supposed. Perhaps he too believed the claim that John Mosby had a "violent streak."

In his book *The Gray Ghost*, author James Ramage "diagnosed" Mosby as "bi-polar"—a psychological disorder producing extreme mood swings from depression to mania (a disorder which includes obsession and unnatural euphoria). Bipolar disorder is very serious and can result in severe bouts of both depression and unnatural euphoria. Certainly, if any man ever had a right to periods of "severe depression," it was John Mosby; and doubtless, he had moments of despair as well as exhilaration, but there is no evidence that Mosby was "bi-polar" or a manic-depressive.

Ramage also wrote that "Pat" Jones interviewed Mosby's children and others who had known him personally and that, according to those interviewed, Mosby's dominant trait was his tendency to fight. But Jones' "diagnosis" is as dangerous and unproven as Ramage's. To begin with, people's memories are very fragile—as those reading the newspaper accounts in this book will soon discover! Mosby's children may well have remembered most strongly those instances in which their father was *required* to "fight" rather than those periods in which he was a quiet, contented father and husband. Actually, Mosby's postwar life became one long battle, which most of the time, was not of his own making! Of course, John Mosby was not a *passive* man and neither did he seek to avoid difficult and controversial positions, but there is no reason to believe that he created conflicts for the joy of fighting. Indeed, there is a great deal of evidence to the contrary as can be seen in his constant rejection of war throughout his life, *including* the war that made him famous! Then too, as previously noted, small men tend to be more "belligerent" than larger ones usually because they have something to prove, especially in a society in which height is considered evidence of superiority.

John Mosby was a fighter—of that there can be no doubt! But there is a vast difference between a man who responds to aggression by fighting back and a man who generates acts of violence for the sake of conflict. It is said that when a cadet at West

Point, Philip Sheridan—another little man—often picked fights with Southern cadets (Sheridan despised Southerners). If that claim is accurate, then Philip Sheridan *did* possess "a violent streak." But there is nothing in the life of John Mosby that suggests he was by nature violent. After all, men like Robert E. Lee, Thomas "Stonewall" Jackson, and "Jeb" Stuart also felt "the exhilaration of battle", but no one dares suggest that these noble soldiers were possessed of a "violent streak"!

Chapter 57

CONCLUSION

Determinatio ~ In conclusion

"The heart will break, but broken live on." ~ Lord Byron

IN THIS BOOK, I have attempted to address claims made about John Mosby by various persons over time and present evidence to contest those claims as I have discovered it in the vast newspaper coverage of Mosby's life. Below are what I consider to be the most important of the claims and my response to each based upon the information here presented:

1. Claim: That the "legend" of Colonel John Singleton Mosby, the "Gray Ghost," was created by Mosby himself through postwar writings, lectures, and the testimonies of friends and sycophants.

2. Claim: That "today's" John Mosby is the creation of Virgil Carrington Jones, and had Jones written about partisan Elijah White, White would be famous and Mosby obscure.

3. Claim: That John Mosby deserted the South and the Democratic Party of which he had been a member and embraced the hated Republicans to further his fortunes after the war.

4. Claim: That John Mosby was "over-rated" both during and after the war; that he made little difference in the war itself, and that his postwar "career" consisted of being hired, kept, and protected by various Republican administrations and/or important and powerful men in the private sector.

5. Claim: That John Mosby was at best, a mediocre attorney unable to maintain a decent private practice after the war and, as a result, forced to seek government office, something that he continued to do throughout his life.

6. Claim: That John Mosby's method of warfare was not only ineffective and unproductive, but resulted in criminal acts that, had he been appropriately prosecuted after the war, would have led to disgrace, imprisonment or execution.

7. Claim: That John Mosby was bad-tempered, profane and unpleasant; possessed of a "violent streak" and whose personality and behavior left him with few friends and even fewer defenders by the end of his life.

Response to Claim 1: The idea that John Mosby the man created John Mosby the legend is disproved by the reputation he gained *in the war*, a reputation that followed him *after* the war for the rest of his life! The strength of public interest in the man, as evidenced by the wealth of news coverage over the years, attests to his undying fame—or infamy—both during his life and after his death. According to the press reports alone, John Singleton Mosby was *never* obscure after 1863. Mosby did indeed write and lecture about his experiences after the war, but he also wrote about contemporary issues and other figures involved in the war. Furthermore, Mosby wrote and lectured about his wartime experiences because people wanted to read and hear about them. His efforts were not a means of enhancing his reputation, but of using an already-celebrated reputation for the purpose of enhancing his income; and his efforts were successful because his reputation preceded the books, articles, essays, and lectures based thereon. Obscure people are not sought out for their opinions or their narratives, and John Mosby was sought out for both by the public and the press.

Response to Claim 2: When Virgil Carrington Jones wrote the book *Gray Ghosts and Rebel Raiders*, he encountered John Mosby and determined to write a book about the man individually. Now I don't mean to denigrate Jones. *Ranger Mosby* was certainly well written and interesting enough to bring John Mosby back before the American public—but the operative word here is "back"! For doing that, Jones deserves the praise that he has received.

It is also probable that had Mosby lived his life after the war as a "lost cause" defender, the narrative Jones provided would have been pleasant enough to both write and read. Most of the people in the South, then and now, would have considered such a conclusion to be the best of all narrations. Sadly for them and sadly for Jones and, most of all, sadly for John Mosby, it didn't happen that way; and Mr. Jones had to "ruin" his wonderful story with the unpalatable facts contained in the long years between April 21, 1865, and May 30, 1916. It was undoubtedly a trial for him—but not nearly so much a trial as it was for John Mosby.

In his book *Mosby's Rangers*, Jeffry Wert saved himself that lengthy penance by ending the story with the war while authors like James Ramage and Kevin Siepel attempted the whole story but spent most of their books on the war, finishing up as quickly as possible with what they probably saw as a somewhat embarrassing—for Mosby at least—messy and disorderly anticlimax between the disbanding at Salem and Mosby's death in Washington.

To the claim that Pat Jones "made John Mosby famous," the overwhelming preponderance of evidence proves otherwise. Indeed, it is probable that it was *Mosby* who made *Jones* famous for which of Jones' books is better known than *Ranger Mosby* even after seventy years?

Response to Claim 3: John Mosby was never a Democrat! Indeed, his support of the Conservative (Democratic) party in Virginia after the war was a total change of political allegiance for him. He identified himself and his family as Henry Clay Whigs, and as such, Mosby had more in common politically with Abraham Lincoln than he did with Jefferson Davis! Anyone who questions Mosby's family's political persuasion has forgotten Alfred Mosby choice of a lady abolitionist from New England as a tutor for his daughters! That was not an accident.

Mosby's pre-war unionist sentiments are well known but forgiven because he followed Virginia out of the Union and fought magnificently for a cause he eventually embraced wholeheartedly. Indeed, he called the Confederacy "the most noble cause ever defended by the sword." It seems strange to some, therefore, that he appeared to be willing to abandon that cause so quickly after the war. But among John Mosby's strongest character traits was a streak of pragmatism. Although he was game to attempt what seemed impossible if reason told him that there was a chance of success (however slight)—that willingness did not extend to the *truly* impossible. *The war had been lost.* There was nothing he could do to change that; and therefore, having sworn an oath never again to take up arms against the United States, he turned his mind to doing all he could to succor his family and the people of a ruined South. And thus arose Mosby's peculiar political position.

As noted, during Reconstruction he rejected the Radical Republican "government" of Virginia filled with carpetbaggers, freedmen, and scalawags, which he (rightly) believed was pledged to rob and plunder. But at the same time, he knew that the Democrats, whom he blamed for the election of Lincoln when they split that party in 1860, could not be elected nationally—at least in 1872. Therefore, if Virginia and the rest of the South continued to vote Democratic *nationally*, they gave the more powerful Republicans no reason to bestow upon them any favors. As far as Mosby was concerned, continued mindless support of the *national* Democratic Party was political suicide for the South as it made the war the main issue of any election—an issue that the South could not win in politics any more than it could with arms.

The motives of Mosby's support of Grant are well covered in this book, but they were certainly not a matter of self-interest—quite the opposite in fact. However, all of this was known in the South then and now. But to many, both then *and* now, it matters not. All they saw was the deed and not the motives behind the deed, motives that included Mosby's desire to aid and rescue the people of Virginia and the South from post-war tyranny. In his great poetic play *The Countess Cathleen*, W. B. Yeats addressed just such a situation: After the saintly Cathleen sells her soul in order to rescue her people from their pact with the devil, a grieving friend asks the angel that appears at the time of her death as to her ultimate fate. The angel defines the matter of *motive vs. deed* thusly:

"ANGEL... the Light of Lights looks always on the motive, not the deed,
The Shadow of Shadows on the deed alone."

Very few who opposed John Mosby's postwar actions looked upon his motives. First, of course, as noted earlier, *they could not understand them!* Thus they saw only his deeds and made of them what they wished. Some hated the man anyway, so his "apostasy" was a welcome opportunity to ignore his wartime heroism and success. Others, however, were glad enough to embrace him as another glorious member of the Southern chivalry after the war but were unwilling, or unable, to understand those actions with which they so vehemently disagreed. Interestingly enough, most—but not all—of Mosby's men disagreed with his politics, *but they loved him anyway*! So it was possible to do both as was made obvious—by the press, of course.

But it wasn't only poets who claimed that John Mosby spoke and acted in a way far beyond the capacity of many men of his time to understand, much less to accept. In the "silver" controversy that arose during the election of 1896, the *Kansas City Daily Journal*, in commenting upon a letter of Mosby's on that complex issue, stated:

General Mosby's letter is full of wisdom and shows him to be a student of history and a close watcher of events, as well as a statesman.

Response to Claim 4: First, before this matter can be intelligently considered, it is necessary to acknowledge that *no* leader in a losing cause can be considered "effectual" however many victories he may have won. Once a cause is lost, nothing achieved by *anyone* who fought for that cause was "effectual" within the meaning of that word. Therefore, to say that John Mosby was "over-rated" because he didn't "help win the war" is senseless! In looking at the war itself, however, Mosby certainly contributed mightily to the Southern cause in Virginia. Gen. Robert E. Lee said he did; and that, frankly, should end the controversy.

But even before Mosby's efforts against Sheridan in 1864 saved Richmond for six months, there was an event that testified to his effectiveness in the Battle of Brandy Station, the largest cavalry battle ever fought in North America. As Mosby and his very few men—well under fifty—were ranging and raiding around Washington, the authorities in the capital would not permit the cavalry troops of General Stahel to leave the area. Testimony on this matter is given below:

The Count of Paris, a staff officer in the Union army testified:

"In Washington ... General Heintzelman was in command, who ... had under his control ... Stahel's division of cavalry, numbering 6000 horses, whose only task was to pursue Mosby and the few hundred partisans led by this daring chief."

Regarding this matter, Mosby noted in his War Reminiscences:

"If Pleasanton had had those 6000 sabres with him ... in his great cavalry combat with Stuart at Brandy Station, the result might have been different. Hooker had asked for them, but had been refused, on the ground that they could not be spared from the defense of Washington."

Mosby also included General Hooker's testimony before the committee on the conduct of the war:

"I may here state that while at Fairfax Court House my cavalry was reinforced by that of Major-Gen. Stahel. The latter numbered 6100 sabres, and had been engaged in picketing a line from Occoquan River to Goose Creek... The force opposed to them was Mosby's guerrillas, numbering about 200 [Mosby puts in the phrase: "not over thirty men"];... From the time I took command of the Army of the Potomac there was no evidence that any force of the enemy, other than that above named, was within 100 miles of Washington City; and yet, the planks on the chain bridge were taken up at night during the greater part of the winter and spring."

Neither is this matter raised only in the testimony of the time. In his book *Ghost, Thunderbolt, and Wizard: Mosby, Morgan, and Forrest in the Civil War*, author Robert W. Black also makes reference of the possible consequences to Stuart's cavalry had Mosby *not* kept over six thousand Federal sabers out of the battle. Black wrote:

"... at the time the 6,000 man Union cavalry division under Major General Stahel was tied down trying to guard against the Rangers and to find and destroy Mosby. On Tuesday, June 9, 1863, the great cavalry battle between Stuart and Pleasanton was fought at Brandy Station. Then thousands of cavalrymen went into action on each side and both sides had reason to claim victory. One additional Union cavalry division may well have made it a decisive victory for the North."

For those familiar with such things, a decisive Union victory at Brandy Station might have seen the decimation of Lee's cavalry and the wounding, death, or capture of General Stuart—serious, if not fatal blows to the Army of Northern Virginia. So for those who state that John Mosby never "influenced" a major battle—as did historian James McPherson—that claim has been disproved; or in the alternative, Brandy Station, the largest cavalry engagement fought on American soil, cannot be considered a "major battle".

With regard to Mosby's postwar life, there is irresistible and irrefutable proof that he was not "kept in office" by anyone. Indeed, every position Mosby held (public or private), he held precariously; and the only position in which there was any "protection" from a "higher-up" was his place with the Southern Pacific Railroad. However, when he lost that position with the departure of his "protector," Huntington, there is no evidence that he was removed because his skills as an attorney were inadequate or that he was kept on simply as a matter of kindness. And as for Mosby's "government offices," all such were fulfilled with the *highest* legal, moral and intellectual standards, a matter that did nothing to save him from persecution by politicians—Republican and Democrat—and toadying bureaucrats.

Response to Claim 5: Throughout this book, articles testifying to Mosby's skill as an attorney have been included as well as reference to the testimony of, among others, a Justice of the Supreme Court on that skill. It is not necessary to repeat them here. The claim is clearly repudiated.

Response to Claim 6: The same can be said with even more overwhelming testimony to the legal nature of Mosby's method of warfare. It is only necessary to consider the North's hatred of the man. If any case at all could have been brought against him during or after the war, such would have been acted upon. Even Grant's "pass" only protected him from harassment. It did not prevent him from having to answer to charges brought against him by "competent authorities." At the end of the war, guerrillas like Jerome Clarke and Champ Ferguson had been hanged as had Andersonville commandant Captain Henry Wirz, while many others who fought in the Western Theater such as the James and Younger brothers were outlawed—the fate that awaited Mosby had Grant not intervened. So there was no paucity of precedence in the matter. The newspaper stories in the latter part of 1865 and well into 1866 show that such efforts were being made to bring John Mosby "to justice." The fact that nothing came of those efforts strongly repudiates the claim that his warfare was in any way criminal.

Response to Claim 7: As with claims 4, 5, and 6, the overwhelming proof is carried in the wealth of the articles in this book, and does not require reiteration. John Mosby was a human being with his own array of personal foibles. But it is obvious that those who adjudged Mosby anything other than a true Virginia gentleman were either his personal enemies or those who repeated what the loudest of those enemies had to say. When the matter is justly considered, so, too, must the response of his old companions who shouted out to him in 1895 as he stood before them for the first time in thirty years, *"We love you!"* as well as those of his former enemies who embraced him after the war. And these examples do not even take into consideration the evidence of the kindnesses he did for others, quietly and without public acclaim, throughout his life. When taken altogether, the bad-tempered, irascible, profane Mosby of "fable" is just that—fable.

John Mosby and The Lost Cause

After the war, John Mosby decried those who continued to espouse what came to be called "the Lost Cause." He had no patience with efforts to continue a war that was lost. And indeed, he had no choice under the circumstances as endless recitations of wrongs prevented the South from regaining any political or economic power and validated the enmity against it in the North. However, during his postwar life, Mosby eventually learned that "the bloody shirt" was not raised alone in the South; neither were sectional hatreds limited to below the Mason-Dickson line. Sadly, another of his failings was his tardy recognition of this fact, something that also contributed to his fellow Southerners' rage against him.

Even more destructive to Mosby's attempt to "consign the evils of the war to oblivion," was that, as he later learned, the government he served so ably and honestly proved neither able nor honest and finally, even the naive, well intentioned John Mosby could no longer entertain the belief—as he had, at one point—that the United States had no desire for foreign conquest or imperialist designs upon other lands and peoples. Thus, by the time Mosby was an old man, certain circumstances appeared—circumstances to which he personally testified if, in the beginning, albeit rather obliquely.

In 1906, he gave a speech at the Middlesex Club in Boston. In it, he repeated what he had said many times before—that is, that he had "clung to the Confederacy longer than anyone else." Mosby told the audience that he applied to himself "the words which the Roman poet put into the mouth of the champion of a lost cause: 'If Troy could have been saved by *this* right hand, even by the same *it would have been saved*.'" Now at that time, he also declared that "the Southern people were not lost with their cause" and that they had risen from the ashes of defeat with "a stronger sentiment of nationality among them than ever existed before the conflict of arms." But might not John Mosby have been voicing a personal hope rather than describing the circumstances as they actually existed at that time? After all, he was still a pariah in the South for his alliance with the hated Republicans, and that same "lost cause" was still very much alive, else he would not have avoided his battalion's reunions for that very reason by his own admission!

But whatever John Mosby believed in 1906, he believed very differently in 1865! On learning of Lee's surrender, he spoke with great feeling of the cause for which he had so gloriously fought:

> "The noblest cause ever defended by the sword is lost. This is the bitterest hour of my life."

The "noblest cause ever defended by the sword" is a very long way from Mosby's claim that the war was a struggle to preserve slavery! Of course, Mosby had often claimed that a man "fights for his country, right or wrong." But it is one thing to fight for Virginia because that state was, as he put it at the time, "my mother" and to declare that the cause for which Virginia seceded and fought was "noble;" these are two different if not totally incompatible sentiments! Thus, it appears that either John Mosby changed his mind about that "lost cause" and embraced the idea that the South fought for slavery, or he was being dishonest in 1865—which seems unlikely. Mosby's later assertion that slavery was the reason for the war is contradicted by his heartfelt cry upon learning of Appomattox, a cry further reiterated in his farewell address upon the disbanding of his command:

> *"Soldiers: ... The vision we cherished of a free and independent country has vanished, and that country is now the spoil of a conqueror."*

Mosby's declaration of a "vision of a free and independent country" does not invalidate his postwar efforts to foster reunion and reconciliation as the original vision had been lost, but it certainly does confirm that he did not reject that vision *before* it was lost. The former statement was from his heart, the latter from the very practical concern of preserving what was left of Virginia and the South from obliteration. But as his life changed and the end drew nearer, it is possible that his state of mind *also* changed. For that same avowed fidelity to the defense of a "lost cause" spoken of in 1906 was repeated not only in his last lectures given in 1910, but at the conclusion of his posthumously published *Memoirs*.

Few realize how *extraordinary* is John Mosby's reiteration of this singular sentiment when considered in light of his long years working to achieve ultimate reconciliation and reunion between the North and the South. It is far more logical to assume that his final words to posterity would affirm the rectitude of the *Union* cause with an admission that the South's defeat was for the good of the nation and the Southern people. After all, he had reiterated that latter sentiment many times after the war.

Yet in his final testament, John Mosby reaffirmed his fidelity to that "lost cause": *"If Troy could have been saved by this right hand,* **even by the same it would have been saved.**" The significance of those nineteen words can be neither misunderstood nor misconstrued but should and must be considered an affirmation of his fidelity to that "free and independent nation" created by the people of the South in 1861—a nation that now existed only in memory. And while John Mosby did not reject the nation that had prevailed in that struggle, his final witness leaves little doubt that at the conclusion of a long and tempestuous life filled with honorable service to *both* nations, Colonel John Singleton Mosby truly wished that "The Cause" had *not* been lost.

Final Thoughts

In his youth, it was believed John Mosby would die young and be remembered only by his kin for a generation or two. But young Jack dreamed of military glory, though he was probably astute enough as he grew older to realize that such would remain for him just a dream. In the end, however, he did live a warrior's life both in war and in peace—and his struggle in peace was more manly and glorious than in war, great as that was. Although he ended his course sans worldly riches, he took from this world a wealth that few men have gained: the love and respect of the *worthy—* friend *and* foe—and a life of heroic courage without moral spot or blemish. And yet, like the Emperor in Goethe's *Faust*, John Mosby also endured **"lawlessness by law itself maintaining, a world of error evermore obtaining"** and in the end, his *true* greatness—a greatness seemingly overlooked by those who have studied and written about the man—was that he faced and fought that "world of error" and emerged in glorious triumph!

Johann Wolfgang von Goethe

Faust, part 2, act 1

The highest virtue like an aureole

Circles the Emperor's head; alone and sole,

He validly can exercise it:

''Tis justice!—All men love and prize it; '

'Tis what all wish, scarce do without and ask'

To grant it to his people is his task.

But ah! What good to mortal mind is sense,

What good to hear is

Kindness, hands benevolence,

When through the state a fever runs and revels,

And evil hatches more and more of evils?

Who views the wide realm for this height supreme,

To him all seems like an oppressive dream,

Where in confusion is confusion reigning

And lawlessness by law itself maintaining.

A world of error evermore obtaining.

About the Author

VALERIE PROTOPAPAS (née Hughes) was born on May 30th, 1941 in New York City. Throughout her long life, she has been an avid reader and diligent researcher of history using as her particular approach to the discipline, the choice of a central figure and studying the time period relative to that person. Among her "studies" were the great Scottish hero, Sir William Wallace, Sir William Marshal, eulogized as "the best knight that ever lived," Sir Henry Percy, known to history as "Hotspur" and John Churchill, 1st Duke of Marlborough, who in war, defeated the ambitions of King Louis XIV. But her first field of research was the American Civil War and though a native New Yorker, she chose sympathy for and allegiance to the South. A television program in 1957, *The Gray Ghost*, provided as her "person of interest," Colonel John Singleton Mosby, one of the most unique and interesting figures of any historical era. In a twist of fate, she learned that Mosby had died twenty-five years to the day and (almost) the hour of her own birth, thus making him of continued personal interest long after her research moved to other historical persons and periods.

In the late 1990s, she returned to the study of John Mosby and began to collect magazine and internet articles, period newspapers and microfilmed documents, spending hours sifting through and printing out all things of interest. Of course, every article had to be transcribed, edited and properly placed into the historical timeline together with all relevant information and the comments referable to it. In so doing, she soon discovered that most of what is "known" – and therefore written – about John Mosby, and especially his post-war life, consisted of lies, myths and misconceptions created and disseminated by those who detested the man, North *and* South and that this defamatory "history" was incorporated into the first "modern" account, Virgil Carrington Jones: *Ranger Mosby*. And while Jones was favorable to Mosby the soldier, he despised the man for his post-war political apostasy, declaring that it would have been better for Mosby had he not survived the conflict. But Jones' opinions were frequently based upon those very lies and falsehoods discovered in her research! Worse, they formed the foundation of all later "biographies!" In other words, *not one contemporary account* of "the life and times" of John Singleton Mosby is altogether accurate! Even reports of his wartime operations are frequently tainted by these errors as well as the prejudice of Northern historians and today's rejection of all things Southern.

It was at this point that, using her maiden name, she authored a book to reveal to modern readers, the truth by use of the contemporary testimony found in the massive newspaper coverage of the man from 1862 through 1916. For the sake of objectivity, she also included the negative accounts that were previously just about the *only contemporary source* available to earlier biographers! Simply put, there is no book other than *Col. John Singleton Mosby In The News 1862-1916* can lay claim to all the facts regarding the life of this damaged hero! The response from those for whom the book was written was all that she could have hoped, there being fulsome praise from her readers including at least one fellow author.

As John Mosby was being universally crucified for his efforts to deliver his people, his State and the South from political subjugation and cultural eradication, he patiently endured all the calumny and condemnation his actions brought upon him with the stated belief that he would *be vindicated by time. Col. John Singleton Mosby In The News 1862-1916* was released one hundred years after Mosby's death with the hope that, through the book, Time has fulfilled its obligation to a great and noble man.

Available From Shotwell Publishing

If you enjoyed this book, perhaps some of our other titles will pique your interest. The following titles are now available for your reading pleasure... Enjoy!

MARK C. ATKINS
WOMEN IN COMBAT
Feminism Goes to War

JOYCE BENNETT
MARYLAND, MY MARYLAND
The Cultural Cleansing of a Small Southern State

GARRY BOWERS
SLAVERY AND THE CIVIL WAR
What Your History Teacher Didn't Tell You

DIXIE DAYS
Reminiscences Of A Southern Boyhood

JERRY BREWER
DISMANTLING THE REPUBLIC

ANDREW P. CALHOUN, JR.
MY OWN DARLING WIFE
Letters from a Confederate Volunteer

JOHN CHODES
SEGREGATION
Federal Policy or Racism?

WASHINGTON'S KKK
The Union League during Southern Reconstruction

WALTER BRIAN CISCO
WAR CRIMES AGAINST SOUTHERN CIVILIANS

JAMES C. EDWARDS
WHAT REALLY HAPPENED?
Quantrill's Raid on Lawrence, Kansas: Revisiting The Evidence

TED EHMANN
BOOM & BUST IN BONE VALLEY
Florida's Phosphate Mining History 1886-2021 and the Looming Ecological Crisis

DON GORDON
SNOWBALL'S CHANCE
My Kidneys Failed, My Wife Left Me & My Dog Died (I Still Miss That Dog!)

PAUL C. GRAHAM
CONFEDERAPHOBIA
An American Epidemic

WHEN THE YANKEES COME
Former Carolina Slaves Remember Sherman's March FROM the Sea

CHARLES HAYES
THE REAL FIRST THANKSGIVING

T.L. HULSEY
25 TEXAS HEROES

JOSEPH JAY
SACRED CONVICTION
The South's Stand for Biblical Authority

SUZANNE PARFITT JOHNSON
MAXCY GREGG'S SPORTING JOURNALS 1842 - 1858

JAMES RONALD KENNEDY
DIXIE RISING: Rules for Rebels

WHEN REBEL WAS COOL
Growing Up in Dixie, 1950-1965

NULLIFYING FEDERAL AND STATE GUN CONTROL:
A How-To Guide for Gun Owners

JAMES R. & WALTER D. KENNEDY
PUNISHED WITH POVERTY
The Suffering South – Prosperity to Poverty and the Continuing Struggle

THE SOUTH WAS RIGHT!

YANKEE EMPIRE
Aggressive Abroad and Despotic at Home

PHILIP LEIGH
CAUSES OF THE CIVIL WAR

THE DEVIL'S TOWN
Hot Springs During the Gangster Era
U.S. GRANT'S FAILED PRESIDENCY

THE DREADFUL FRAUDS:
Critical Race Theory and Identity Politics

LEWIS LIBERMAN
SNOWFLAKE BUDDIES
ABC Leftism for Kids!

JACK MARQUARDT
AROUND THE WORLD IN EIGHTY YEARS
Confessions of a Connecticut Confederate

MICHAEL MARTIN
SOUTHERN GRIT
Sensing the Siege at Petersburg

SAMUEL W. MITCHAM
THE GREATEST LYNCHING IN AMERICAN HISTORY: New York, 1863

CHARLES T. PACE
LINCOLN AS HE REALLY WAS

SOUTHERN INDEPENDENCE. WHY WAR?
The War to Prevent Southern Independence

JAMES RUTLEDGE ROESCH
FROM FOUNDING FATHERS TO FIRE EATERS
The Constitutional Doctrine of States' Rights in the Old South

ANNE WILSON SMITH
CHARLOTTESVILLE UNTOLD
Inside Unite the Right

ROBERT E. LEE:
A History Book for Kids

KIRKPATRICK SALE
EMANCIPATION HELL
The Tragedy Wrought by Lincoln's Emancipation Proclamation

KAREN STOKES
A LEGION OF DEVILS
Sherman in South Carolina

CAROLINA LOVE LETTERS

JACK TROTTER
LAST TRAIN TO DIXIE

LESLIE R. TUCKER
OLD TIMES THERE SHOULD NOT BE FORGOTTEN
Cultural Genocide in Dixie

JOHN VINSON
SOUTHERNER, TAKE YOUR STAND!
Reclaim Your Identity. Reclaim your Life.

HOWARD RAY WHITE
HOW SOUTHERN FAMILIES MADE AMERICA:
Colonization, Revolution, and Expansion From Virginia Colony to the Republic of Texas 1607 to 1836

UNDERSTANDING CREATION AND EVOLUTION

DR. CLYDE N. WILSON
LIES MY TEACHER TOLD ME
The True History of the War for Southern Independence & Other Essays

THE OLD SOUTH
50 Essential Books (Southern Reader's Guide 1)

THE WAR BETWEEN THE STATES
60 Essential Books (Southern Reader's Guide 2)

RECONSTRUCTION AND THE NEW SOUTH, 1865-1913
50 Essential Books (Southern Reader's Guide 3)

THE SOUTH 20TH CENTURY AND BEYOND
50 Essential Books (Southern Reader's Guide 4)

THE YANKEE PROBLEM
An American Dilemma (The Wilson Files I)

NULLIFICATION
Reclaiming the Consent of the Governed
(The Wilson Files II)

ANNALS OF THE STUPID PARTY
Republicans Before Trump
(The Wilson Files III)

JOE A. WOLVERTON, II
"WHAT DEGREE OF MADNESS?"
Madison's Method to Make American STATES Again

WALTER KIRK WOOD
BEYOND SLAVERY
The Northern Romantic Nationalist Origins of America's Civil War

(Literary Imprint)

CATHARINE SAVAGE BROSMAN
AN AESTHETIC EDUCATION
and Other Stories

CHAINED TREE, CHAINED OWLS: Poems

RANDALL IVEY
A NEW ENGLAND ROMANCE
and Other SOUTHERN Stories

JAMES EVERETT KIBLER
TILLER

THOMAS MOORE
A FATAL MERCY
The Man Who Lost The Civil War

KAREN STOKES
BELLES
A Carolina Love Story

CAROLINA TWILIGHT

HONOR IN THE DUST

THE IMMORTALS

THE SOLDIER'S GHOST
A Tale of Charleston

WILLIAM A. THOMAS, JR.
RUNAWAY HALEY
An Imagined Family Saga

GOLD-BUG
(Mystery & Suspense Imprint)

MICHAEL ANDREW GRISSOM
BILLIE JO

BRANDI PERRY
SPLINTERED
A New Orleans Tale

MARTIN L. WILSON
TO JEKYLL AND HIDE

Free Book Offer

Visit **FreeLiesBook.com**
Sign-up for new release notifications and receive a **FREE** downloadable edition of:

*Lies My Teacher Told Me:
The True History of the War for
Southern Independence*
by Dr. Clyde N. Wilson

and

*Confederaphobia:
An American Epidemic*
by Paul C. Graham

You can always unsubscribe and keep the book, so you've got nothing to lose!

www.ingramcontent.com/pod-product-compliance
Lightning Source LLC
Chambersburg PA
CBHW051530230426
43669CB00015B/2558